# For Reference

**Not to be taken from this room**

# Ottemiller's Index to Plays in Collections

An Author and Title Index to Plays Appearing in Collections Published since 1900

*Eighth Edition, Revised and Enlarged*

Denise L. Montgomery

The Scarecrow Press, Inc.
Lanham • Toronto • Plymouth, UK
2011

Published by Scarecrow Press, Inc.
A wholly owned subsidiary of The Rowman & Littlefield Publishing Group, Inc.
4501 Forbes Boulevard, Suite 200, Lanham, Maryland 20706
http://www.scarecrowpress.com

Estover Road, Plymouth PL6 7PY, United Kingdom

British Library Cataloguing in Publication Information Available

**Library of Congress Cataloging-in-Publication Data**

Ottemiller, John H. (John Henry), 1916–1968.
  [Index to plays in collections]
  Ottemiller's index to plays in collections : an author and title index to plays appearing
in collections published since 1900. — 8th ed. / revised  and enlarged [by] Denise L. Montgomery.
     p. cm.
  ISBN 978-0-8108-7720-7 (hardcover : alk. paper) — ISBN 978-0-8108-7721-4 (ebook)
  1. Drama—Indexes. I. Montgomery, Denise L., 1953– II. Title.
  Z5781.O8 2011
  [PN1655]
  016.80882—dc22                                        2010053010

∞™ The paper used in this publication meets the minimum requirements of
American National Standard for Information Sciences—Permanence of Paper
for Printed Library Materials, ANSI/NISO Z39.48-1992.

Printed in the United States of America

To Fred Shapiro,
editor of *The Yale Book of Quotations*,
and
William Smart,
editor of *Eight Modern Essayists*
and *Women & Men, Men & Women*

Without the experience, discipline, and organizational skills which I learned while assisting on editing their books, I never would have had the confidence to undertake this book.

"In the dark of the theatre we remember ourselves."

—Sidney Michaels, "Preface," *Dylan: A Play in Two Acts*, 1964

# Contents

# Acknowledgments

No one is ever entirely alone in undertaking a project of this magnitude, so at the risk of sounding like an old-fashioned Academy Awards speech, I will begin by expressing my deepest gratitude to my ILL staff, Lina Wallace and Meghan Donathan, and our student assistants who processed the flood of books I got through interlibrary loan; as well as thanking Meghan's mother, Ramona Ice, who processed many others I obtained through our state patron-initiated borrowing system, GIL Express. I also thank my colleagues of the past four years in the reference department for putting up with me, and the book, and our Director and Assistant Director, Dr. George Gaumond and Dr. Betty Paulk, for giving me time to work on it and for paying the few ILL charges that occurred very rarely. I must also express my sincere gratitude to my ILL colleagues at the 192 libraries in thirty-seven states and the District of Columbia, two Canadian provinces, and Australia which supplied the books, especially those in the state of Georgia, which supplied 68.1% of all the books via ILL and GIL Express. The University of Georgia deserves special commendation for having provided 184 books, which represents 26.1% of the total books I obtained from outside my library.

I want to thank my editors, Jayme Bartles Reed of Rowman and Littlefield, for taking my manuscript and fine-tuning it to give it the beautiful appearance on the page, rather like the fairy godmother transforming Cinderella for the ball; and Stephen Ryan of Scarecrow Press, who was very helpful throughout all steps of the process of writing the book and who gave me time enough to complete the job. I wish all writers could be fortunate enough to work with such complete professionals who are also a delight.

I received excellent assistance entirely through e-mail on individual queries from the following individuals: playwright Marc Estrin, who supplied his year of birth, editor Myra S. Gann, who confirmed that one anthology attributed to her in Worldcat was never published, Nanci S. Young, Smith College Archivist who provided extensive background on Rosamond Kimball, and Håkon M.E. Sundaune, librarian at the National Library of Norway, who not only corrected my birth date for Trygve von Tangen Kielland, but also tracked down his grandson to provide the missing date of death that the National Library did not even have. Also, my old friends at Project Wombat, formerly the Stumpers listserv, attempted to provide an obituary for John Wilson (b. 1921), author of *Hamp*, but were as unsuccessful as I had been. And finally, thank you to Mark Carson and Dennis Lien, also at Project Wombat, for helping with some last-minute queries.

Living playwrights were a source of great help to me not only because their own individual web sites and Facebook pages were extremely important resources for background information, but because I also drew strength, inspiration, and joy from their works that I read and delighted in while compiling this edition.

Finally, I wish to thank my father for his love and support on this project, and Gerald Smith, who listens and is always there for me, and provided an online source for foreign alphabets when I needed it for this book.

# Introduction

*Ottemiller's Index to Plays in Collections* was originally compiled by Dr. John Henry Ottemiller of Yale University in order to provide access to plays published in anthologies or literature textbooks. He completed four editions before his death in 1968, when the title was taken over at the urging of the publisher by John Michael Connor. Assisted by his wife, Billie M. Connor, he edited the fifth and sixth editions, and was working on the seventh edition at the time of his death in 1978. Ms. Connor was then joined by Helene G. Mochedlover, a colleague from Los Angeles Public Library, to help her complete the seventh edition, which was published in 1988.

My association with *Ottemiller's Index* began shortly after the seventh edition was published, when I ordered it after reading a favorable review. It turned out to be as useful as the review had promised, so the book soon found a permanent home on our ready reference shelves for many years. Still, I wondered if some day the publisher might bring out a new edition, so in all innocence I wrote to them after seeing the seventh edition still advertised in a 2005 Scarecrow Press catalog and asked if they would be issuing a new edition in the next year or two, because I wanted to order one.

What happened next is too long a story to go into here, but the edition you are looking at now is the result of that initial e-mail. It further embraces technology because I am an interlibrary loan librarian, so I used my ILL background to go deep into the farthest recesses of Worldcat to uncover collections of plays in English from around the world, from 103 countries in all. And instead of relying upon a few physical collections in my region or traveling to view other collections, every book that was not in my own library's collection came to me for examination via interlibrary loan. The extended amount of time that I could keep each volume meant that I could be more careful in compiling this edition.

The eighth edition of *Ottemiller's Index to Plays in Collections* includes books published throughout the English-speaking world from 1900 through 2000, though a few multi-volume sets whose final volumes were published after 2000 have been included in their entirety.

Plays indexed are full-length with the following exceptions: 1) the *Best Plays* . . . series, which includes excerpts and synopses only. This exception is made because of the historical significance of this series, and sometimes because it is the only place where some plays can be found in an anthology. 2) When an anthology or collection includes full-length plays along with short plays, monologues, or excerpts, the latter are indexed as well. 3) Two Canadian collections that contain leading minority and women playwrights are also included.

Seven hundred forty-four collections were analyzed for this edition, which is a 55% increase to the previous edition's 1,350 titles. More than 2,300 new authors, co-authors, and composers were added, which is almost as many as the 2,555 which was in the previous edition. And 3,593 new plays were added to the 6,548 titles that were in the previous edition's title index.

New features to this edition include the following: First, three appendixes—appendix A lists authors by country, racial, and ethnic group; appendix B provides a list of female authors; and appendix C lists authors by sexual orientation. Second, this volume contains an Anthology Title Index. Among the changes which have been made are the following: 1) all errors that have been identified in the seventh edition have been corrected; 2) a number of collections have been assigned new mnemonics in order to fit in the additional collections; 3) efforts have been made to bring Chinese and Japanese names up to date in regards to current transliteration of the names of older literary figures; 4) exhaustive research has been done to add yet more birth dates, close more death dates, and find more first performance dates for 625 authors from the seventh edition. When in doubt, a question mark is assigned.

Every collection that is new to this edition has been personally examined by me, so the contents should be accurate. If any errors are found by users of this index, please contact me at dmontgom@valdosta.edu so they can be corrected in a future edition.

# How to Use This Book

Since more than two decades have passed since the last edition of *Ottemiller's Index*, it is likely that many younger librarians who have become employed in recent years are unfamiliar with it. Therefore, an explanation of the reason for its original compilation and how to use it is in order.

When Dr. Ottemiller first compiled this book, the tables of contents of anthologies or literature textbooks were rarely included on cataloging records, so there was a great need for a reference book like this one, since otherwise the plays were inaccessible. Though widespread acceptance of Worldcat as a standard reference tool and an increasing tendency to include tables of contents has somewhat lessened usage of this book, I have found in compiling this edition that there are still many anthologies and literature textbooks that do not have their contents listed in Worldcat. So there is still a vital need for this book.

This edition of *Ottemiller's Index* covers plays published in English by authors in 103 countries from 1900 to 2000. There are significant increases in the number of works by women, Hispanic-American, and Asian-American playwrights, and by playwrights from Canada, Ireland, Australia, the Caribbean and South America, Africa, Singapore, China, and other parts of Asia. Appendix A allows for searching by places that are not independent nations, such as Scotland, Wales, Northern Ireland, and Puerto Rico, and linguistic regions, such as Catalan and French Canadian.

The Index is useful for the following purposes: 1) to locate plays not available as a separate edition or in the collected works of an individual author; 2) to provide additional copies needed for class assignments, reading groups, amateur theatricals, and plays newly popular due to a recently released movie, a local production or television broadcast, or auditions for college productions; 3) verifying and identifying authors, dates, titles (English and other languages), and first performance dates; 4) all three appendixes can be useful to college professors constructing a course in or theater directors who are looking for playwrights from a particular continent or country, racial or ethnic group, or women or LGBT playwrights, and are looking for different possibilities than the persons they have usually taught or presented; 5) the Anthology Title Index can prove useful for collection development librarians, or for persons who would like to see what anthologies are available on a particular type of playwright.

To be included in the Index, a play anthology is defined as having plays by at least three or more authors within the book. This definition can also be applied to literature textbooks, though there are exceptions. Plays in languages other than English are included if they are published in any English-speaking country. Full-length plays only are included with the exceptions mentioned in the introduction. Children's plays, one-act plays, radio and television plays, holiday and anniversary plays are all excluded unless they happen to appear among the anthologies as defined above. Collections which contain plays by only one author are excluded.

The five parts of this Index are: 1) Author Index, 2) List of Collections Analyzed and Key to Symbols, 3) Title Index, 4) Anthology Title Index, and 5) the appendixes.

Most users will consult the Author Index first. Under each name will be listed all the plays by the author contained in the collections analyzed and will give the mnemonic symbol(s) for each one. The user then turns to the second part, List of Collections, to get to the mnemonic symbol in order to locate the bibliographic citation for the book. (Holders of previous editions of the book, including my own library, usually annotated this section to include call numbers of the collections owned by the library, for the convenience of the librarian and the patron.)

In cases where only the title of the play is known, the search starts in the Title section, which retrieves the author's name, and the search proceeds onward as described above.

Aside from where to find a play, the Author Index provides the following information: the author's full name, variations, or pseudonyms, birth and death dates when these can be found; title of play, year of first production (or publication if production date is unknown or it was never performed); cross-references from original, variant, or foreign titles; and references from joint authors, composers, or adapters. Translators are given credit for plays translated into English. Plays with no attributed author are listed under Anonymous Plays. If uncertainty exists in regards to dates, the most widely accepted date is used with a question mark beside it.

The Title Index contains the original titles followed by the author's names, as well as cross-references from all forms of the titles including variants and subtitles.

The List of Collections is arranged alphabetically by the mnemonic symbols. Each symbol is followed by a full bibliographic citation, then a contents list of the plays in the collection arranged alphabetically by the author's last name (or by title, if the work is an Anonymous play). If there is more than one volume in a set, or it is published annually, individual volumes are identified by attaching a number or year to the mnemonic symbol; i.e., WES17, HUMANA95.

The Anthology Title Index is arranged alphabetically by the title of each index.

The appendixes are alphabetical by the name of each country, group, sexual orientation, and gender. Countries with a number of playwrights and diverse cultures, such as the United States, the United Kingdom, and Canada will have a variety of *See also* references such as Hispanic-American, African-Canadian, Asian-British, and French-Canadian. Playwrights who belong to linguistic groups such as French-Canadian and Catalan can be looked up under those headings. Playwrights who reside in Greenland, Northern Ireland, Puerto Rico, Scotland, and Wales are listed under those countries even though they are not independent nations.

The editor welcomes suggestions for improvements to this work. Please e-mail me at dmontgom@valdosta.edu.

# Anthology Codes and Titles

| | |
|---|---|
| **ABCA** | Literature: The Human Experience. 1973. |
| **ABCB** | Literature: The Human Experience. 2nd ed. 1978. |
| **ABCC** | Literature: The Human Experience. 3rd ed. 1982. |
| **ABCD** | Literature: The Human Experience. 4th ed. 1986. |
| **ABCE** | Literature: The Human Experience. 5th ed. 1990. |
| **ABCF** | Literature: The Human Experience. 6th ed. 1994. |
| **ABCG** | Literature: Reading and Writing, the Human Experience. 7th ed. 1998. |
| **ABCH** | Literature: Reading and Writing, the Human Experience. Shorter 7th ed. 2000. |
| **ABL** | Modern Egyptian Drama: An Anthology. 1974. |
| **ABRA** | Norton Anthology of English Literature: Major Authors Edition, The. 1962. |
| **ABRB** | Norton Anthology of English Literature, The. 1962. |
| **ABRE** | Norton Anthology of English Literature. Rev. ed. 1968. |
| **ABRF** | Norton Anthology of English Literature, The. Rev. ed. 1968. 2v |
| **ABRH** | Norton Anthology of English Literature, The. 3rd ed. 1974. 2v |
| **ABRJ** | Norton Anthology of English Literature, The. 4th ed. 1979. 2v |
| **ABRK** | Norton Anthology of English Literature, The. 5th ed. 1986. 2v |
| **ABRL** | Norton Anthology of English Literature, The. 6th ed. 1993. 2v |
| **ABRM** | Norton Anthology of English Literature, The. 7th ed. 2000. 2v |
| **ACE** | Access to Literature: Understanding Fiction, Drama, and Poetry. 1981. |
| **ACTOR** | Actor's Book of Gay and Lesbian Plays. 1995. |
| **ADA** | Chief pre-Shakespearean Dramas. 1924. |
| **ADAP** | Adaptations of Shakespeare: A Critical Anthology of Plays from the Seventeenth Century to the Present. 2000. |
| **ADV** | Adventures in World Literature. 1970. |
| **AFR** | African Plays for Playing. 1975–1976. 2v |
| **AFRUBU** | Afrique: New Plays. 1987–1991. 2v |
| **AFTAP** | After Apocalypse: Four Japanese Plays of Hiroshima and Nagasaki. 1986. |
| **AGOR** | Generous Donors: A Dramatic Expose on AIDS and other Plays. 1997. |
| **ALD** | French Comedies of the XVIIIth Century. 1923. |
| **ALG** | Action: The Nuyorican Poets Café Theater Festival. 1997. |
| **ALI** | Dialogue and Dialectic: A Canadian Anthology of Short Plays. 1972. |
| **ALL** | Four Continental Plays. 1964. |
| **ALLE** | Three Medieval Plays. 1953. |
| **ALLI** | Masterpieces of the Drama. 1957. |
| **ALLJ** | Masterpieces of the Drama. 2nd cd. 1966. |
| **ALLK** | Masterpieces of the Drama. 3rd ed. 1974. |
| **ALLM** | Masterpieces of the Drama. 4th ed. 1979. |
| **ALLN** | Masterpieces of the Drama. 5th ed. 1986. |
| **ALLO** | Masterpieces of the Drama. 6th ed. 1991. |
| **ALONG** | Along Human Lines: Dramas from Refugee Lives. 2000. |
| **ALP** | Diez Comedies del siglo de oro. 1939. |

| | |
|---|---|
| **ALPE** | Teatro hispanoamericano. 1956. |
| **ALPF** | Three Classic Spanish Plays. 1963. |
| **ALPJ** | Anthology of Indian Literature, An. 1971. |
| **ALPJR** | Anthology of Indian Literature, An. Second Revised Edition. 1987. |
| **ALS** | Exploring Literature: Fiction, Poetry, Drama, Criticism. 1970. |
| **ALT** | Introduction to Literature: Plays. 1963. |
| **ALTE** | Introduction to Literature: Plays. 2nd ed. 1969. |
| **ALTJD** | Alternative Japanese Drama: Ten Plays. 1992. |
| **AMB** | America on Stage: 10 Great Plays of American History. 1976. |
| **AME** | American Caravan: A Yearbook of American Literature. 1927–1929, 1931, 1936. 5v |
| **AMEM** | American Melodrama. 1983. |
| **AMENW** | American Plays of the New Woman. 2000. |
| **AMP** | America's Lost Plays. 1940–1941. 20v |
| **AMPA** | America's Lost Plays. v21. Satiric Comedies. 1969. |
| **AND** | This Generation. 1939. |
| **ANDE** | This Generation. Revised Edition. 1949. |
| **ANDF** | Genius of the Oriental Theatre, The. 1966. |
| **ANDI** | Masterpieces of the Orient. Enlarged Edition. 1977. |
| **ANG** | Three Elizabethan Plays. 1929. |
| **ANT** | Anthology: An Introduction to Literature: Fiction, Poetry, Drama. 1977. |
| **ANTH** | Anthology of Austrian Drama, An. 1982. |
| **ANTHC** | Anthology of Contemporary Austrian Folk Drama. 1993. |
| **ANTL** | Anthology of Living Theater. 1998. |
| **ANTM** | Anthology of Modern Belgian Theatre: Maurice Maeterlinck, Fernand Crommelynck, and Michel de Ghelderode, An. 1981. |
| **ANTN** | Anti-naturalism: Six Full-length Contemporary American Plays. 1989. |
| **ANTU** | Nuestro New York: An Anthology of Puerto Rican Plays. 1994. |
| **ANTUR** | Recent Puerto Rican Theater: Five Plays from New York. 1991. |
| **ARGJT** | Argentine Jewish Theatre: A Critical Anthology. 1996. |
| **ARM** | Armenian Literature Comprising Poetry, Drama, Folklore and Classic Traditions. 1901. |
| **ARMS** | Elizabethan History Plays. 1965. |
| **AROUN** | Around the Edge: Women's Plays. 1992. |
| **ARRIZ** | Latinas on Stage. 2000. |
| **ASF** | Mirrors for Man: 26 Plays of World Drama. 1974. |
| **ASG** | Nineteenth-Century British Drama. 1967. |
| **ASH** | Types of English Drama. 1940. |
| **ASIAM** | Asian American Drama: 9 Plays from the Multiethnic Landscape. 1997. |
| **ATT** | Attic Tragedies. 1927. 3v |
| **AUB** | Drama through Performance. 1977. |
| **AUDE** | Portable Greek Reader, The. 1948. |
| **AUG** | Landmarks in Modern Drama, from Ibsen to Ionesco. 1963. |
| **AUS** | Australia Plays: New Australian Drama. 1989. |
| **AUSG** | Australian Gay and Lesbian Plays. 1996. |
| **AXT** | Medieval French Plays. 1971. |
| **BAC** | Drama for Composition. 1973. |
| **BAI** | British Plays of the Nineteenth Century. 1966. |
| **BAIC** | Drama. 1973. |
| **BAIE** | Norton Introduction to Literature, The. 1973. |
| **BAIG** | Norton Introduction to Literature, The. 2nd ed. 1977. |
| **BAIH** | Norton Introduction to Literature, The. 3rd ed. 1981. |
| **BAIK** | Norton Introduction to Literature, The. 4th ed. 1986. |
| **BAIL** | Norton Introduction to Literature, The. 5th ed. 1991. |
| **BAIM** | Norton Introduction to Literature, The. 6th ed. 1995. |
| **BAK** | Modern American Plays. 1920. |
| **BAKS** | Soviet Scene: Six Plays of Russian Life. 1946. |
| **BALD** | Six Elizabethan Plays. 1963. |
| **BALL** | From Beowulf to Modern British Writers. 1959. |

| | |
|---|---|
| **BALLE** | Playwrights for Tomorrow: A Collection of Plays. 1966–1975. 13v |
| **BANH** | Contemporary African Plays. 1999. |
| **BARA** | Echoes of Israel: Contemporary Drama. 1999. |
| **BARAM** | Plays by Mediterranean Women. 1994. |
| **BARB** | Eight Great Comedies. 1958. |
| **BARC** | Eight Great Tragedies. 1957. |
| **BARD** | Genius of the Early English Theatre, The. 1962. |
| **BARF** | Genius of the Irish Theatre, The. 1960. |
| **BARG** | Genius of the Later English Theater, The. 1962. |
| **BARH** | Introduction to Literature, An. 1961. |
| **BARI** | Introduction to Literature, An. 4th ed. 1971. |
| **BARIA** | Introduction to Literature: Fiction, Poetry, Drama, An. 5th ed. 1973. |
| **BARIC** | Introduction to Literature Fiction, Poetry, Drama, An. 6th ed. 1977. |
| **BARID** | Introduction to Literature Fiction, Poetry, Drama, An. 7th ed. 1981. |
| **BARIE** | Introduction to Literature Fiction, Poetry, Drama, An. 8th ed. 1985. |
| **BARIF** | Introduction to Literature Fiction, Poetry, Drama, An. 9th ed. 1989. |
| **BARIG** | Introduction to Literature Fiction, Poetry, Drama, An. 10th ed. 1993. |
| **BARIH** | Introduction to Literature Fiction, Poetry, Drama, An. 11th ed. 1997. |
| **BARJ** | Tragedy and Comedy. 1967. |
| **BARK** | Types of Drama: Plays and Essays. 1972. |
| **BARKA** | Types of Drama: Plays and Essays. 2nd ed. 1977. |
| **BARKB** | Types of Drama: Plays and Essays. 3rd ed. 1981. |
| **BARKC** | Types of Drama: Plays and Essays. 4th ed. 1985. |
| **BARKD** | Types of Drama: Plays and Essays. 5th ed. 1989. |
| **BARKE** | Types of Drama: Plays and Essays. 6th ed. 1993. |
| **BARKF** | Types of Drama: Plays and Essays. 7th ed. 1997. |
| **BARN** | Understanding Plays. 1990. |
| **BARNA** | Understanding Plays. 2nd ed. 1994. |
| **BARO** | Generations: An Introduction to Drama. 1971. |
| **BARR** | Introduction to Literature, An. 1959. |
| **BARS** | American Experience: Drama, The. 1968. |
| **BART** | Currents in Drama. Rev. ed. 1968. |
| **BARU** | English Tradition: Drama, The. 1968. |
| **BARV** | Modern English Drama. 1964. |
| **BAS** | Elizabethan and Stuart Plays. 1934. |
| **BAT** | Drama: Its History, Literature and Influence on Civilization, The. 1903–1904. 22v |
| **BAUG** | English Literature. 1954. |
| **BAUL** | Tradition of the Theatre, The. 1971. |
| **BAYM** | In the Presence of This Continent: American Themes and Ideas. 1971. |
| **BEAC** | Beacon Lights of Literature. 1940. 7v |
| **BEAD** | York Mystery Plays: A Selection in Modern Spelling. 1984. |
| **BEAL** | Complete Reader, The. 1961. |
| **BEAM** | Complete Reader, The. 2d ed. 1967. |
| **BEAN** | SourceBook of African-American Performance: Plays, People, Movements, A. 1999. |
| **BEAR** | Theme and Form. 1956. |
| **BEAS** | Theme and Form: An Introduction to Literature. 4th ed. 1975. |
| **BEATA** | Norton Introduction to Literature, The. 7th ed. 1998. |
| **BECK** | Five Plays of the English Renaissance. 1993. |
| **BEFOB** | Before Brecht: Four German Plays. 1985. |
| **BELC** | Bell's British Theatre, Farces—1784. 1977. 4v |
| **BELG** | Bell's British Theatre: Selected Plays, 1791–1802, 1797: 49 Plays Unrepresented in eds. of 1776–1781 and 1784. 1977. 16v |
| **BELK** | Bell's British Theatre, 1776–1781. 1977. 21v |
| **BELLN** | Five from the Fringe. 1986. |
| **BELLW** | Contours: Plays from across Canada. 1993. |
| **BEN** | Modern French Theatre: The Avant-Garde, Dada, and Surrealism: An Anthology of Plays. 1964. |
| **BENA** | Modern Spanish Theatre: An Anthology of Plays. 1968. |

| | |
|---|---|
| **BENB** | Postwar German Theatre: An Anthology of Plays. 1967. |
| **BENN** | English Literature. 1935. |
| **BENP** | On the High Road. 1935. |
| **BENPB** | Facing Some Problems. 1970. |
| **BENQ** | Idea of Tragedy, The. 1966. |
| **BENR** | Classic Theatre, The. 1958–1961. 4v |
| **BENS** | From the Modern Repertoire. 1949–1956. 3v |
| **BENSA** | Genius of the Italian Theater, The. 1964. |
| **BENSB** | Great Playwrights: 25 Plays, The. 1972. 2v |
| **BENSC** | Let's Get a Divorce! and other Plays. 1958. |
| **BENSD** | Misanthrope and other French Classics, The. 1986. |
| **BENT** | Modern Theatre, The. 1955–1960. 6v |
| **BENU** | Play: A Critical Anthology, The. 1951. |
| **BENV** | Servant of Two Masters: And other Italian Classics, The. 1986. |
| **BENY** | Development of English Drama, The. 1950. |
| **BENZ** | Easy French Plays. 1901. |
| **BER** | French Plays. 1941. |
| **BERMD** | Dozen French Farces: Medieval to Modern, A. 1997. |
| **BERMG** | Genius of the French Theater, The. 1961. |
| **BERN** | Anthology of Romanticism. 1948. |
| **BERP** | Theatre Alive! An Introductory Anthology of World Drama. 1991. |
| **BERPA** | Theatre Alive! An Introductory Anthology of World Drama. 1995. |
| **BERR** | NeWest Plays by Women. 1987. |
| **BERS** | Best American Plays: Eighth Series, 1974–1982. 1983. |
| **BERT** | Best American Plays: Ninth Series, 1983–1992. 1993. |
| **BES** | Applause/Best Plays Theater Yearbook of 1990–1991: Featuring the Ten Best Plays of the Season, The. *See* Best Plays of 1894/1899–1999/2000 |
| **BES** | Best Plays of 1894/1899–1999/2000. 1894/95–1999/2000. 86v |
| **BES** | Burns Mantle Theater Yearbook of 1989–1990 Featuring the Ten Best Plays of the Season. *See* Best Plays of 1894/1899–1999/2000 |
| **BEST** | Best Plays of the Seventies. 1980. |
| **BETW** | Between Worlds: Contemporary Asian-American Plays. 1990. |
| **BEV** | Macro: The Castle of Perseverance, Wisdom, Mankind, The. 1972. |
| **BEVD** | Medieval Drama. 1975. |
| **BEVI** | Eighteenth Century Drama: Afterpieces. 1970. |
| **BEYO** | Beyond the Pale: Dramatic Writing from First Nations Writers & Writers of Colour. 1996. |
| **BIER** | Dramatic Experience, The. 1958. |
| **BIES** | Three Plays of the Argentine. 1920. |
| **BIG** | Big-time Women from way back when. 1993. |
| **BIN** | Gemme della letteratura italiane. 1904. |
| **BIR** | Anthology of Chinese Literature. 1972. 2v |
| **BLAAP** | Black and Asian Plays Anthology. 2000. |
| **BLAC** | Black Comedy: Nine Plays: A Critical Anthology. 1997. |
| **BLACQ** | Black Quartet: 4 New Black Plays by Ben Caldwell, and others, A. 1970. |
| **BLACTH** | Black thunder: An Anthology of Contemporary African-American Drama. 1992. |
| **BLAG** | Literature. 1949. |
| **BLAH** | Repertory. 1960. |
| **BLAI** | Literature of the United States, The. 1946–47. 2v |
| **BLAJ** | Literature of the United States, The. Single Volume ed. 1949. |
| **BLOC** | Masters of Modern Drama. 1962. |
| **BLOD** | Readings for Our Times. 1942. 2v |
| **BLON** | Great Plays, Sophocles to Brecht. 1965. |
| **BLOND** | Great Plays, Sophocles to Albee. 3d ed. 1975. |
| **BLOO** | Ten Plays. 1951. |
| **BOA** | Five pre-Shakespearean Comedies (Early Tudor period). 1934. |
| **BODY** | Body Blows: Women, Violence, and Survival: Three Plays. 2000. |
| **BOGA** | Legacies: Fiction, Poetry, Drama, Nonfiction. 1995. |

| | |
|---|---|
| **BOGO** | College Miscellany, The. 1952. |
| **BOH** | Grove Plays of the Bohemian Club, The. 1918. 3v |
| **BOHV** | Bohemian Verses: An Anthology of Contemporary English language Writings from Prague. 1993. |
| **BONA** | Studies in Drama. 1963. |
| **BONB** | Studies in Drama. 1964. |
| **BONC** | Studies in Drama. 2nd ed. 1968. |
| **BOND** | Early Plays from the Italian. 1911. |
| **BOO** | Eighteenth Century Tragedy. 1965. |
| **BOOA** | English Plays of the Nineteenth Century. 1969–1976. 5v |
| **BOOB** | Hiss the Villain: Six English and American Melodramas. 1964. |
| **BOOK** | Book of Plays, A. 2000. |
| **BOOL** | Inchape bell, The. *See* The Lights o' London and other Victorian Plays. |
| **BOOL** | Lights o' London and other Victorian Plays, The. 1995. |
| **BOOM** | Magistrate, and other Nineteenth-Century Plays, The. 1974. |
| **BOR** | Nineteenth Century French Plays. 1931. |
| **BOUC** | Six Medieval French Farces. 1999. |
| **BOUR** | Rough Magic: First Plays. 1999. |
| **BOV** | Promenades littéraires et historiques. 1940. |
| **BOVE** | Promenades littéraires et historiques . . . Nouvelle édition. 1948. |
| **BOVI** | Five Roman Comedies: in Modern English Verse. 1970. |
| **BOW** | Drama. 1971. |
| **BOWL** | friendly Fire: An Anthology of Plays by Queer Street Youth. 1997. |
| **BOWY** | Victorian Age, The . . . 2nd ed. 1954. |
| **BOY** | Introduction to the Play. 1969. |
| **BOYN** | Introduction to the Play: in the Theater of the Mind. Rev. 2nd ed. 1976. |
| **BPD** | American Tradition in Literature, The. 4th ed. 1974. 2v |
| **BPE** | American Tradition in Literature, The. 4th ed. Shorter ed. in One Volume. 1974. |
| **BPW** | Crosswinds: An Anthology of Black Dramatists in the Diaspora. 1993. |
| **BQA** | On Thrones of gold: Three Javanese Shadow Plays. 1970. |
| **BRA** | Traditional Asian Plays. 1972. |
| **BRAK** | DramaContemporary Scandinavia. *See* Scandinavia: Plays |
| **BRAK** | Scandinavia: Plays. 1989. |
| **BRAKA** | Aboriginal Voices: Amerindian, Inuit, and Sami Theater. 1992. |
| **BRAS** | Black Drama: An Anthology. 1970. |
| **BRAZ** | Traditional Japanese Theater: An Anthology of Plays. 1998. |
| **BRAZT** | Twelve Plays of the Noh and Kyōgen Theaters. 1988. |
| **BREK** | Going it Alone: Plays by Women for Solo Performers. 1997. |
| **BREN** | Eighteenth Century French Plays. 1927. |
| **BRET** | Nineteenth Century Spanish Plays. 1935. |
| **BREW** | Black Plays. 1987–1995. 3v |
| **BRIDGE** | Bridge across the Sea: Seven Baltic Plays. 1983. |
| **BRIG** | English Literature. 1934. |
| **BRIK** | Romance. 1932. |
| **BRIM** | Plays of the 70s. 1998. 3v |
| **BRIMA** | Plays of the 60s. 1998. 3v |
| **BRIN** | Factory Lab Anthology, The. 1974. |
| **BRIP** | Now in Paperback: Six Canadian Plays of the 1970's. 1973. |
| **BRIQ** | West Coast Plays. 1975. |
| **BRIT** | Literature as Art. 1972. |
| **BRIU** | Reading Apprenticeship Literature, A. 1971. |
| **BRW** | Wines in the Wilderness: Plays by African-American Women from the Harlem Renaissance to the Present. 1990. |
| **BRIX** | Plays for the Theatre: An Anthology of World Drama. 1967. |
| **BRIY** | Plays for the Theatre: An Anthology of World Drama. 2nd ed. 1974. |
| **BRIZ** | Plays for the Theatre: An Anthology of World Drama. 3rd ed. 1979. |
| **BRJ** | Plays for the Theatre: An Anthology of World Drama. 4th ed. 1984. |
| **BRJA** | Plays for the Theatre: A Drama Anthology. 5th ed. 1988. |
| **BRJB** | Plays for the Theatre: A Drama Anthology. 6th ed. 1996. |

| | |
|---|---|
| **BRJC** | Plays for the Theatre: A Drama Anthology. 7th ed. 2000. |
| **BRN** | En scène: Trois comédies avec musique. 1942. |
| **BRNB** | Close-up: A Collection of Short Plays. 1970. |
| **BRNS** | Seven Plays of Mystery and Suspense with Writing Manual. 1982. |
| **BRO** | Shakespeare Apocrypha, The. 1918. |
| **BROC** | English Drama, 1580–1642. 1933. |
| **BROE** | American Literature: The Makers and the Making. 1974. 2v |
| **BROF** | Approach to Literature, An. 1936. |
| **BROG** | Approach to Literature, An. Rev. ed. 1939. |
| **BROH** | Approach to Literature, An. 3rd ed. 1952. |
| **BROI** | Approach to Literature, An. 5th ed. 1975. |
| **BROJ** | Understanding Drama. 1945. |
| **BROK** | Understanding Drama: Twelve Plays. 1948. |
| **BROTA** | Tragedy. 1968. |
| **BROV** | Made in Scotland: An Anthology of New Scottish Plays. 1995. |
| **BROWLD** | Liberty Deferred and other Living Newspapers of the 1930s Federal Theatre Project. 1989. |
| **BROX** | Quarto of Modern Literature . . . , A. 3rd ed. 1950. |
| **BROY** | Quarto of Modern Literature, A. 5th ed. 1964. |
| **BROZ** | Literature for Our Time. 1947. |
| **BRP** | Quarto of Modern Literature, A. 1935. |
| **BRR** | Present Tense. 1941. 3v |
| **BRS** | Present Tense. Rev. ed. 1945. |
| **BRW** | Wines in the Wilderness. 1990. |
| **BRZ** | Four Modern Verse Plays. 1957. |
| **BRZA** | Three European Plays. 1958. |
| **BRZE** | Three Irish Plays. 1959. |
| **BUCK** | Anthology of World Literature, An. 1934. |
| **BUCL** | Anthology of World Literature, An. Rev. ed. 1940. |
| **BUCM** | Anthology of World Literature, An. 3rd ed. 1951. |
| **BUFF** | Reichard Collection of Early Pennsylvania German Plays, The. 1962. |
| **BUL** | Collection of Old English Plays, A. 1964. 7v in 4v |
| **BURB** | Playing with Fire: Five StagePlays from Riding Lights Theatre Co. 1987. |
| **BURG** | Drama: Literature on Stage. 1969. |
| **BURN** | Burning the Curtain: Four Revolutionary Spanish Plays. 1995. |
| **BURNS** | Chester Mystery Cycle: A New staging Text, The. 1987. |
| **BURR** | Myth and Motifs in Literature. 1973. |
| **BUSHB** | Bush Theatre Book, The. 1997. |
| **BUSHT** | Bush Theatre Plays. 1996. |
| **CADY** | Literature of the Early Republic. 1950. |
| **CAIR** | Ariosto's The Supposes, Machiavelli's The Mandrake, Intronati's The Deceived: Three Renaissance Comedies. 1996. |
| **CAIRT** | Three Renaissance Comedies. 1991. |
| **CAL** | Calamus: Male Homosexuality in Twentieth Century Literature, An International Anthology. 1982. |
| **CALD** | Forms of Drama. 1969. |
| **CALE** | Scot-free: New Scottish Plays. 1990. |
| **CALG** | Reading American Literature. 1944. |
| **CALM** | Patterns for Living. 1940. |
| **CALN** | Patterns for Living. Alternate Edition. 1943, 1947. 2v |
| **CALP** | Patterns for Living. 3rd ed. 1949. |
| **CALQ** | Patterns for Living. 4th ed. 1955. |
| **CAM** | German Plays of the Nineteenth Century. 1930. |
| **CAN** | Plays of Changing Ireland. 1936. |
| **CAP** | Plays of the Irish Renaissance, 1880–1930. 1929. |
| **CAPU** | Modern Drama: Authoritative Texts . . . Backgrounds, and Criticism. 1966. |
| **CARL** | American Literature: Themes and Writers. 1967. |
| **CARLE** | American Literature: Themes and Writers. 3rd ed. 1978. |
| **CARLG** | British and Western Literature. 3rd ed. 1979. |

| | |
|---|---|
| **CARM** | Encounters: Themes in Literature. 1967. |
| **CARME** | Encounters: Themes in Literature. 3rd ed. 1979. |
| **CARMI** | Insights: Themes in Literature. 3rd ed. 1979. |
| **CARN** | Western Literature: Themes and Writers. 1967. |
| **CARP** | Book of Dramas, an Anthology of Nineteen Plays, A. 1929. |
| **CARPA** | Book of Dramas, A. Rev. ed. 1949. |
| **CARR** | Kuntu Drama: Plays of the African Continuum. 1974. |
| **CART** | Famous Plays of Crime and Detection. 1946. |
| **CAS** | Divided Home/Land: Contemporary German Women's Plays, The. 1992. |
| **CASB** | Split Britches: Lesbian Practice/Feminist Performance. 1996. |
| **CASH** | Introduction to Theatre and Drama, An. 1975. |
| **CASK** | What Is the Play? 1967. |
| **CASS** | Modern American Plays. 1949. |
| **CASU** | Masters of Ancient Comedy. 1960. |
| **CATH** | American Profile. 1944. |
| **CAWL** | Everyman and Medieval Miracle Plays. 1959. |
| **CAWM** | Wakefield Pageants in the Towneley Cycle, The. 1958. |
| **CEN** | Center Stage: An Anthology of 21 Contemporary Black-American Plays. 1981. |
| **CEQ** | Four Contemporary American Plays. 1961. |
| **CEQA** | Plays of Our Time. 1967. |
| **CER** | Pocket Book of Modern American Plays, The. 1942. |
| **CES** | Six American Plays for Today. 1961. |
| **CET** | Sixteen Famous American Plays. 1941. |
| **CEU** | Sixteen Famous British Plays. 1942. |
| **CEW** | Sixteen Famous European Plays. 1943. |
| **CEY** | S.R.O.: The Most Successful Plays in the History of the American Stage. 1944. |
| **CHA** | Twentieth Century Plays. 1934. |
| **CHAN** | Twentieth Century Plays . . . Rev. ed. 1939. |
| **CHAP** | Twentieth Century Plays, American . . . Rev. 1939. |
| **CHAR** | Twentieth Century Plays, British . . . Rev. and enl. 1941. |
| **CHARN** | Classic Comedies. 1995. |
| **CHEL** | Chester Mystery Cycle, The. 1974. |
| **CHELM** | Chester Mystery Cycle: A New Edition with Modernized spelling, The. 1992. |
| **CHES** | Chester Mystery Plays . . . Adapted into Modern English, The. 1957. |
| **CHESE** | Chester Mystery Plays: Seventeen Pageant Plays from the Chester Craft Cycle, The. 2nd ed. 1975. |
| **CHEU** | Oxford Anthology of Contemporary Chinese Drama, An. 1997. |
| **CHG** | Chicano Voices. 1975. |
| **CHI** | Second Shepherds' Play, Everyman, and other Early Plays, The. 1910. |
| **CHIN** | Chinese other 1850–1925: An Anthology of Plays, The. 1997. |
| **CHOT** | New Woman and other Emancipated Woman Plays, The. 1998. |
| **CHR** | World Literature. Reprint. 1971. |
| **CHU** | Curtain! A Book of Modern Plays. 1932. |
| **CLA** | Favorite American Plays of the Nineteenth Century. 1943. |
| **CLD** | Four Plays of the Free Theater. 1915. |
| **CLDM** | Masterpieces of Modern Spanish Drama. 1917. |
| **CLF** | World Drama. 1933. 2v |
| **CLH** | Nine Modern Plays. 1951. |
| **CLK** | Voices of English and America, The. 1939. 2v |
| **CLKJ** | Dimensions in Drama: Six Plays of Crime and Punishment. 1964. |
| **CLKW** | Chief patterns of World Drama. 1946. |
| **CLKWI** | Classic Irish Drama. 1964 (1979 [printing]). |
| **CLKX** | Classic Soviet Plays. 1979. |
| **CLKY** | Classic Theatre: The Humanities in Drama. 1975. |
| **CLL** | Drama and Discussion. 1967. |
| **CLLC** | Drama and Discussion. 2nd ed. 1978. |
| **CLM** | Contemporary Drama. 1962. |
| **CLN** | Contemporary Drama: 13 Plays. 2nd ed. 1970. |

| | |
|---|---|
| **CLOU** | Anthologie de la litterature française. 1960. 2v |
| **CLOUD** | Anthologie de la litterature française. 1975. 2nd ed. 2v |
| **CLOUDS** | Anthologie de la litterature française. 1990. 3rd ed. 2v |
| **CLUM** | Asking and telling: A Collection of Gay Drama for the 21st Century. 2000. |
| **CLUMS** | Staging Gay Lives: An Anthology of Contemporary Gay Theater. 1996. |
| **CLUR** | Famous American Plays of the 1930s. 1959. |
| **COD** | Book of Modern Plays, A. 1925. |
| **COF** | Five Significant English Plays. 1930. |
| **COH** | Longer Plays by Modern Authors (American). 1922. |
| **COHM** | Milestones of the Drama. 1940. |
| **COI** | Twelve Plays for Theatre. 1994. |
| **COJ** | Making a Scene: The Contemporary Drama of Jewish-American Women. 1997. |
| **COK** | Twentieth Century Drama: England, Ireland [and] The United States. 1966. |
| **COLD** | Drama: Classical to Contemporary. 1998. |
| **COLDE** | Early English Drama: An Anthology. 1993. |
| **COLEL** | College Survey of English Literature. 1942. 2v |
| **COLI** | Theater Wagon Plays of Place and Any Place. 1973. |
| **COLR** | Comedy Restored or Ten English Plays of Manners. 1986. |
| **COLT** | Comedy Tonight! Broadway Picks Its Favorite Plays. 1977. |
| **COM** | French Romantic Plays. 1933. |
| **COMS** | Coming on Strong: New Writing from the Royal Court Theatre. 1995. |
| **COMV** | Coming to Terms: American Plays and the Vietnam War. 1985. |
| **CONB** | Conflict in Social Drama: Plays for education. 1972. 2v |
| **CONF** | Confrontations with Tyranny: Six Baltic Plays . . . 1977. |
| **CONG** | Drama Reader, The. 1962. |
| **CONN** | Literature: The Channel of Culture. 1948. |
| **CONO** | Man and His Measure. 1964. |
| **CONP** | The Types of Literature. 1955. |
| **CONR** | Contemporary Chicano Theatre. 1976. |
| **CONT** | Contemporary Danish Plays. 1955. |
| **CONTG** | Contemporary Greek Theatre. 1999. |
| **CONTNZ** | Contemporary New Zealand Plays. 1974. |
| **CONTSL** | Contemporary Slovak Drama. 1999–2004. 5v |
| **CONTSO** | Contemporary South African Plays. 1977. |
| **COOA** | Anthology of Greek Tragedy, An. 1972. |
| **COOF** | Small Town in American Literature, The. 1969. |
| **COOJ** | America through Literature. 1948. |
| **COOK** | Hidden Treasures in Literature. 1934. 3v |
| **COOP** | Preface to Drama. 1955. |
| **COOPA** | Four Russian Plays. 1972. |
| **COP** | Copeland Reader, The. 1926. |
| **COPB** | Copeland Translations, The. 1934. |
| **COPC** | Copeland's Treasury for Booklovers. 1927. 5v |
| **COQJW** | Three Jacobean Witchcraft Plays. 1986. |
| **CORB** | Twelve American Plays, 1920–1960. 1969. |
| **CORBA** | Twelve American Plays. 1973. |
| **CORD** | Pulitzer Prize Plays, 1918–1934, The. 1935. |
| **CORE** | Pulitzer Prize Plays . . . , The. New ed. 1938. |
| **CORF** | New Edition of the Pulitzer Prize Plays, A. 1940. |
| **COT** | Representative Modern Plays. 1929. |
| **COTE** | Twentieth Century Plays, American . . . 3rd ed. 1947. |
| **COTH** | Twentieth Century Plays, British, American, Continental . . . 3rd ed. 1947. |
| **COTK** | Off-Broadway Theatre, The. 1959. |
| **COTKA** | Four Restoration Marriage Plays. 1995. |
| **COTKB** | Landmarks of Modern British Drama: The Plays of the Sixties, vol. 1: The Plays of the Seventies, vol 2. 1986. 2v |
| **COTKB1** | Plays of the Sixties, The. 1986. *See* Landmarks of Modern British Drama, v. 1 |
| **COTKB2** | Plays of the Seventies, The. 1986. *See* Landmarks of Modern British Drama, v. 2 |

| | |
|---|---|
| **COTKICC** | Classical Comedy Greek and Roman. 1987. |
| **COTKICG** | Classical Tragedy Greek and Roman: Eight Plays in Authoritative Modern Translations. 1990. |
| **COTKICO** | Comedy: A Critical Anthology. 1971. |
| **COTKIR** | Forms of Drama, The. 1972. |
| **COTKIS** | Laurel British Drama: The Nineteenth Century. 1967. |
| **COTKIT** | Laurel British Drama: The Twentieth Century. 1965. |
| **COTKJ** | Masterpieces of the Modern Central European Theatre: Five Plays. 1967. |
| **COTKR** | Masterpieces of the Modern English Theatre. 1967. |
| **COTKW** | Masterpieces of the Modern French Theatre: Six Plays. 1967. |
| **COTL** | Masterpieces of the Modern German Theatre: Five Plays. 1967. |
| **COTM** | Masterpieces of the Modern Irish Theatre: Five Plays. 1967. |
| **COTN** | Masterpieces of the Modern Italian Theatre: Six Plays. 1967. |
| **COTO** | Masterpieces of the Modern Russian Theatre: Five Plays. 1967. |
| **COTP** | Masterpieces of the Modern Spanish Theatre. 1967. |
| **COTQ** | Modern Theatre, The. 1964. |
| **COTR** | New Theatre of Europe, The. 1962. |
| **COTS** | New Theatre of Europe, 2, The. 1964. |
| **COTT** | New Theatre of Europe, 3, The. 1968. |
| **COTU** | Roman Drama, in Modern Translations. 1966. |
| **COTX** | Tragedy: A Critical Anthology. 1971. |
| **COTY** | Art of the Theatre, a Critical Anthology of Drama, The. 1964. |
| **COUL** | Dutch and Flemish Plays. 1997. |
| **COUR** | Treasury of Classic Russian Literature, A. 1961. |
| **COUS** | Treasury of Russian Life and Humor, A. 1943. |
| **COV** | The Coventry Corpus Christi Plays. 2000. |
| **COXJ** | Seven Gothic Dramas, 1789–1825. 1992. |
| **COXM** | Image and Value: An Invitation to Literature. 1966. |
| **COY** | Six Early American Plays, 1798–1890. 1968. |
| **CRACK** | Crack in the Emerald: New Irish Plays, The. 1990. |
| **CRAF** | Logic, Style and Arrangement. 1971. |
| **CRAN** | Twelve Hundred Years: The Literature of England. 1949. 2v |
| **CRE** | Tudor Plays: An Anthology of Early English Drama. 1966. |
| **CRIT** | Critics' Prize Plays, The. 1945. |
| **CROS** | World Literature. 1935. |
| **CROV** | Heath Readings in the Literature of Europe. 1933. |
| **CROX** | American Writers. Rev. ed. 1955. |
| **CROZ** | Cross-section. 1944–1948. 4v |
| **CRU** | Chinese Theater in the Days of Kublai Khan. 1980. |
| **CRY** | Cry of Kings: Six Greek Dramas in Modern English, A. 1999. |
| **CTR** | CTR Anthology: Fifteen Plays from Canadian Theatre Review, The. 1993. |
| **CUB** | Cuban American Theater. 1991. |
| **CUBE** | Modern Drama for Analysis. 1950. |
| **CUBG** | Modern Drama for Analysis. Rev. ed. 1955. |
| **CUBH** | Modern Drama for Analysis. 3rd ed. 1962. |
| **CUN** | Early English Classical Tragedies. 1912. |
| **CURB** | Amazon All Stars: 13 Lesbian Plays. 1996. |
| **DAI** | English Literature. 1968. |
| **DANI** | Written Word, The. 1960. |
| **DAPO** | Seventh Generation: An Anthology of Native American Plays. 1999. |
| **DAU** | 9 Dramaturgos hispanoamericanos: Antología del teatro hispanoamericano del siglo XX. 2nd ed. 1983. 3v |
| **DAUR** | 3 Dramaturgos rioplatenses: Antología del teatro hispanoamericano del siglo XX. 1983. |
| **DAV** | Dominant Types in British and American Literature. 1949. 2v |
| **DAVI** | Modern American Drama. 1961. |
| **DAVJ** | Corpus Christi Play of the English Middle Ages, The. 1972. |
| **DAVK** | Readings for Enjoyment. 1959. |
| **DAVM** | Inscape: Stories, Plays, Poems. 1971. |
| **DAVN** | NonCycle Plays and Fragments. 1970. |
| **DAVR** | Restoration Comedies. 1970. |

| | |
|---|---|
| **DAY** | Czech Plays: Modern Czech Drama. 1994. |
| **DAZZ** | Dazzling Dark: New Irish Plays, The. 1996. |
| **DEAD** | Dead Proud: From Second Wave Young Women Playwrights. 1987. |
| **DEAN** | Elizabethan Drama. 1950. |
| **DEAO** | Elizabethan Drama. 2nd ed. 1961. |
| **DEAP** | Nine Great Plays from Aeschylus to Eliot. 1950. |
| **DEAR** | Nine Great Plays, from Aeschylus to Eliot. Rev. ed. 1956. |
| **DEAS** | Twelve Great Plays. 1970. |
| **DEAT** | Intimate Acts: Eight Contemporary Lesbian Plays. 1997. |
| **DEC** | Decade's Drama: Six Scottish Plays, A. 1980. |
| **DEM** | Three English Comedies. 1924. |
| **DEN** | Alternate Roots: Plays from the Southern Theater. 1994. |
| **DENT** | Plays and Playwrights for the New Millennium. 2000. |
| **DESH** | Modern Indian Drama: An Anthology. 2000. |
| **DICD** | Chief Contemporary Dramatists. 1915. |
| **DICDS** | Chief Contemporary Dramatists, Second Series. 1921. |
| **DICDT** | Chief Contemporary Dramatists, Third Series. 1930. |
| **DICEM** | Contemporary Plays. 1925. |
| **DICIN** | Continental Plays. 1935. 2v |
| **DIEA** | Art of Drama, The. 1969. |
| **DIEB** | Art of Drama, The. 2nd ed. 1976. |
| **DIER** | Realities of Literature, The. 1971. |
| **DIGBY** | Digby Plays, Rendered into Modern English, The. 1973. |
| **DIRTY** | Dirty Laundry, Mergers & Undercover: Plays from TheatreWorks' Writers' Lab. 1995. |
| **DIS** | Killing Time: A Guide to Life in the Happy Valley. 1972. |
| **DIX** | By Southern Playwrights: Plays from Actors Theatre of Louisville. 1996. |
| **DIXD** | Decade of New Comedy: Plays from the Humana Festival, A. 1996. 2v. |
| **DIXP** | Plays from Actors Theatre of Louisville. 1989. |
| **DIYL** | Literature: Reading Fiction, Poetry, and Drama. Compact ed. 2000. |
| **DIYLA** | Literature: Reading Fiction, Poetry, Drama, and the Essay. 1986. |
| **DIYLB** | Literature: Reading Fiction, Poetry, Drama, and the Essay. 2nd ed. 1990. |
| **DIYLC** | Literature: Reading Fiction, Poetry, Drama, and the Essay. 3rd ed. 1994. |
| **DIYLD** | Literature: Reading Fiction, Poetry, Drama, and the Essay. 4th ed. 1998. |
| **DIYRD** | Reading Drama: An Anthology of Plays. 1990. |
| **DOA** | Five Heroic Plays. 1960. |
| **DOB** | Five Restoration Tragedies. 1928. |
| **DODGE** | Of time and Experience: Literary Themes. 1972. |
| **DODGS** | First Lines: Young Writers at the Royal Court. 1990. |
| **DODGSG** | German Plays: New Drama from a Changing Country. 1997. |
| **DODGSP** | German Plays 2. 1999. |
| **DODGSS** | Spanish Plays: New Spanish and Catalan Drama. 1999. |
| **DODS** | Twelve Modern Plays. 1970. |
| **DOLAN** | Introduction to Drama. 1974. |
| **DOOL** | Heroines: Three Plays. 1992. |
| **DOUC** | Drama of Our Past: Major Plays from Nineteenth-Century Quebec, The. 1997. |
| **DOWM** | American Drama. 1960. |
| **DOWN** | Art of the Play, The. 1955. |
| **DOWS** | Great World Theatre: An Introduction to Drama. 1964. |
| **DPR** | Drama of the English Renaissance. 1976. 2v |
| **DRAC** | DramaContemporary Czechoslovakia: Plays. 1985. |
| **DRAD** | Dramatic Masterpieces by Greek, Spanish, French, German and English Dramatists. Rev. ed. 1900. 2v |
| **DRAF** | Dramatic Representations of filial piety: Five Noh in Translation. 1998. |
| **DRON** | Nine Medieval Latin Plays. 1994. |
| **DRU** | Lake guns of Seneca and Cayuga and Eight other Plays of Upstate New York, The. (Reprint) 1972. |
| **DRUR** | Three Team Plays. 1988. |
| **DUC** | Complete Roman Drama, The. 1942. 2v |
| **DUH** | Literature: Form and Function. 1965. |

| | |
|---|---|
| **DUK** | Avant Garde Drama: A Casebook, (1918–1939). 1976. |
| **DUN** | Eight Famous Elizabethan Plays. 1932. |
| **DUP** | Plays of Old Japan. (Reprint) 1973. |
| **DUR** | British and American Plays. 1830–1945. 1947. |
| **EAG** | Women in Literature: Life Stages through Stories, Poems, and Plays. 1988. |
| **EAVE** | Informal Reader, The. 1955. |
| **EDAD** | Drama of the East and West. 1956. |
| **EDMON** | Quiché Dramas and Divinatory Calendars. 1997. |
| **EIG** | Eight Chinese Plays: From the 13th Century to the Present. 1978. |
| **EIGH** | Eighteenth-Century Plays. 1952. |
| **EIGHT** | Eight Plays for Theatre. 1988. |
| **EIGHTRP** | Eight Twentieth-Century Russian Plays. 2000. |
| **ELAM** | Colored Contradictions: An Anthology of African-American Plays. 1996. |
| **ELK** | Literary Reflections. 1967. |
| **ELKE** | Literary Reflections. 3rd ed. 1976. |
| **ELLI** | College Book of American Literature, A. 1939. 2v |
| **ELLK** | College Book of American Literature, A. 2nd ed. 1949. |
| **ELLM** | Multicultural Theatre II: Contemporary Hispanic, Asian and African-American Plays. 1998. |
| **EMB** | Embassy Successes. 1946–1948. 3v |
| **ENC** | Enclosure: A Collection of Plays. 1975. |
| **ENG** | Two Ages of Man. 1971. |
| **ENGE** | English Mystery Plays: A Selection. 1975. |
| **ENGL** | English romantic Drama: An Anthology, the Major Romantics. 1976. |
| **ENGLMI** | English romantic Drama: An Anthology, the Minor Romantics. 1978. |
| **ERN** | Three Japanese Plays from the Traditional Theatre. 1976. |
| **ESA** | Essential Self: An Introduction to Literature, The. 1976. |
| **ESS** | Genius of the German Theater, The. 1968. |
| **ETO** | English Masques. 1976. |
| **EUP** | Eastern Promise: Seven Plays from Central and Eastern Europe. 1999. |
| **EVA** | Masterworks of World Literature. 1947. 2v |
| **EVB** | Masterworks of World Literature . . . Rev. ed. 1955. 2v |
| **EVC** | Masterworks of World Literature. 3rd ed. 1970. 2v |
| **EVEM** | Everyman and other Miracle and Morality Plays. 1995. |
| **EVEP** | Everyman and other Plays. 1925. |
| **EVER** | "Everyman," with other Interludes, Including Eight Miracle Plays. 1928. |
| **EXP** | Expressionist Texts. 1986. |
| **FACES** | Faces of African Independence: Three Plays. 1988. |
| **FACO** | Chloe plus Olivia: An Anthology of Lesbian Literature from the Seventeenth Century to the Present. 1994. |
| **FAD** | Speaking for Ourselves: American Ethnic Writing. 2nd ed. 1975. |
| **FAIR** | Far from the land: New Irish Plays. 1998. |
| **FAL** | Three Restoration Comedies. 1964. |
| **FALE** | Fallen Crown: Three French Mary Stuart Plays of the Seventeenth Century, The. 1980. |
| **FAM** | Famous American Plays of the 1950's. 1962. |
| **FAMAB** | Famous American Plays of the 1980s. 1988. |
| **FAMAD** | Famous American Plays of the 1970s. 1981. |
| **FAMAF** | Famous American Plays of the 1940s and 1950s. 1988. |
| **FAMAH** | Famous American Plays of the 1960s. 1972. |
| **FAMAL** | Famous American Plays of the 1930's. 1959. |
| **FAMAN** | Famous Plays of 1931. 1931. |
| **FAMB** | Famous Plays of 1932. 1932. |
| **FAMC** | Famous Plays of 1932 33. 1933. |
| **FAMD** | Famous Plays of 1933. 1933. |
| **FAME** | Famous Plays of 1933–34. 1934. |
| **FAMF** | Famous Plays of 1934. 1934. |
| **FAMG** | Famous Plays of 1934–35. 1935. |
| **FAMH** | Famous Plays of 1935. 1935. |
| **FAMI** | Famous Plays of 1935–36. 1936. |

| | |
|---|---|
| **FAMJ** | Famous Plays of 1936. 1936. |
| **FAMK** | Famous Plays of 1937. 1937. |
| **FAML** | Famous Plays of 1938–39. 1939. |
| **FAMO** | Famous Plays of 1954. 1954. |
| **FAO** | Famous Plays of to–day. 1929. |
| **FAOS** | Famous Plays of Today. 1953. |
| **FAR** | Anonymous Plays. 3rd Series. 1906. |
| **FARM** | Five Anonymous Plays. 4th Series. 1908. |
| **FARN** | Recently Recovered "Lost" Tudor Plays with Some Others. 1907. |
| **FARO** | Six Anonymous Plays. 1st Series. 1905. |
| **FARP** | Six Anonymous Plays. 2nd Series. 1906. |
| **FAT** | Fat Virgins, Fast Cars, and Asian values: A Collection of Plays from Theatreworks Writers' Lab. 1993. |
| **FAV** | Voicings: Ten Plays from the Documentary Theater. 1995. |
| **FED** | Religious Dramas, 1924–25. 1923–26. 2v |
| **FEE** | Federal Theatre Plays. 1938. |
| **FEF** | Federal Theatre Plays. 1938. |
| **FEFG** | Grove New American Theater. 1993. |
| **FEFH** | German Literature since Goethe. 1958. 2v |
| **FEFL** | Comedy: Plays, Theory, and Criticism. 1962. |
| **FEFM** | Dramatic Romance. 1973. |
| **FEFNC** | Female Playwrights of the Nineteenth Century. 1996. |
| **FEFNV** | Female Voices. 1987. |
| **FEFO** | Female wits: Women Playwrights on the London Stage, 1660–1720, The. 1981. |
| **FEY** | Shattering the Myth: Plays by Hispanic Women. 1992. |
| **FFLD** | Fickle Finger of Lady Death and other Plays, The. 1996. |
| **FGP** | Fifteen Greek Plays Translated into English. 1943. |
| **FIF** | Fifteenth Century Prose and Verse. 1903. |
| **FIFFN** | Fire and Night: Five Baltic Plays. 1986. |
| **FIFHL** | First Run: New Plays by New Writers. 1989–1991. 3v |
| **FIFR** | Four Greek Plays. 1960. |
| **FIFT** | Greek Plays in Modern Translation. 1947. |
| **FIFV** | Six Greek Plays in Modern Translation. 1955. |
| **FIFVE** | Five Canadian Plays. 1978. |
| **FIFW** | Five Chinese Communist Plays. 1975. |
| **FIG** | Five Great Modern Irish Plays. 1941. |
| **FIJ** | Five Italian Renaissance Comedies. 1978. |
| **FIL** | Five Modern Scandinavian Plays. 1971. |
| **FIN** | Five New Full-length Plays for all-Women Casts. 1935. |
| **FINBN** | 5 Plays: British Council/Association of Nigerian Authors (1989 Drama Prize). 1990. |
| **FIO** | Five Plays for Stage, Radio, and Television. 1977. |
| **FIP** | Five Plays of 1937. 1937. |
| **FIR** | Five Plays of 1940. 1940. |
| **FIS** | Five Restoration Comedies. 1984. |
| **FIT** | Five Three-act Plays. 1933. |
| **FLAN** | Folklore in American Literature. 1958. |
| **FLEA** | Flea in Her Rear: or, Ants in Her Pants and other Vintage French Farces, A. 1994. |
| **FLET** | Lorraine Hansberry PlayWriting Award: An Anthology of Prize-winning Plays, The. 1996. |
| **FLOR** | Masterpieces of the Spanish Golden Age. 1957. |
| **FLOS** | Spanish Drama. 1962. |
| **FOL** | By Women: An Anthology of Literature. 1976. |
| **FOR** | Orestes and Electra: Myth and Dramatic Form. 1968. |
| **FORD** | Black Insights: Significant Literature by Black Americans 1760 to the Present. 1971. |
| **FOS** | Anatomy of Literature, An. 1972. |
| **FOT** | Foundations of Drama. 1975. |
| **FOUA** | Four Australian Plays. 1977. |
| **FOUAC** | Four Contemporary French Plays. 1967. |
| **FOUAD** | Four French Plays. 1985. |

| | |
|---|---|
| FOUAF | Four French Renaissance Plays. 1978. |
| FOUB | Four Great Comedies of the Restoration and 18th Century. 1958. |
| FOUD | Four Great Elizabethan Plays. 1960. |
| FOUF | Four Modern French Comedies. 1960. |
| FOUK | Four Modern Plays: First Series. Rev. ed. 1963. |
| FOUM | Four Modern Verse Plays. First [and] Second Series. 1957, 1961. 2v |
| FOUN | Four Morality Plays. 1979. |
| FOUNC | Four New Comedies. 1987. |
| FOUPAP | 4 Plays by Young Australian Playwrights. 1999. |
| FOUPL | Four Plays of 1936. 1936. |
| FOUR | Four Renaissance Tragedies. 1966. |
| FOUS | Four . . . Soviet . . . Plays. 1937. |
| FOUT | Four Soviet War Plays. 1944. |
| FOUX | Fourteen Great Plays. 1977. |
| FOWL | Classical French Drama. 1962. |
| FRA | German Classics of the Nineteenth and Twentieth Centuries, The. 1913–14. 20v |
| FRAN | Seven Miracle Plays. 1963. |
| FREE | Three Plays about Crime And Criminals. 1962. |
| FREG | Tragedy: Texts and Commentary. 1969. |
| FREH | Controversy in Literature: Fiction, Drama and Poetry with Related Criticism. 1968. |
| FREI | Adventures in Modern Literature. 4th ed. 1956. |
| FRIED | On to Victory: Propaganda Plays of the Woman Suffrage Movement. 1987. |
| FRO | From Classroom to Stage. Three New Plays. 1966. |
| FROLIN | Frontline Intelligence: New Plays for the Nineties. 1993–1995. 3v |
| FRY | Adapting Classics. 1996. |
| FRYE | Practical imagination: Stories, Poems, Plays, The. 1980. |
| FRYEA | Practical Imagination: Stories, Poems, Plays, The. Revised Compact Edition. 1987. |
| FUCHS | Plays of the Holocaust: An International Anthology. 1987. |
| FUL | New College Omnibus, The. 1938. |
| FULT | Drama and Theatre. 1946. |
| GALB | Plays without Footlights. 1945. |
| GALL | Mothertongue: Four Plays of the Women's Action Theatre. 1999. |
| GANN | Contemporary Mexican Drama in Translation. 1994–1995. 2v |
| GARR | He reo hou: 5 Plays by Maori Playwrights. 1991. |
| GARSA | Best American Plays: Fifth Series, 1957–1963. 1963. |
| GART | Best American Plays: Fourth Series, 1951–57. 1958. |
| GARTL | Best American Plays: Seventh Series, 1967–1973. 1975. |
| GARU | Best American Plays: Supplementary vol., 1918–58. 1961. |
| GARW | Best American Plays: Third Series, 1945–51. 1952. |
| GARX | Best Plays of the Early American Theatre: from the beginning to 1916. 1967. |
| GARZ | Best Plays of the Modern American Theatre: Second Series. 1947. |
| GARZAL | Four New Yale Playwrights. 1965. |
| GARZB | Medieval and Tudor Drama. 1963. |
| GARZE | 19th Century Russian Drama. 1963. |
| GARZG | 20th Century Russian Drama. 1963. |
| GARZH | Twenty Best European Plays on the American Stage. 1957. |
| GAS | Twenty Best Plays of the Modern American Theatre. 1939. |
| GASB | Twenty-Five Best Plays of the Modern American Theatre: Early Series. 1949. |
| GASY | Yale School of Drama Presents . . . , The. 1964. |
| GAT | Best American Plays, Sixth Series, 1963–1967. 1971. |
| GATB | 50 Best Plays of the American Theater. 1969. 4v |
| GATG | Elizabethan Drama. 1967. |
| GATS | Introducing the Drama, an Anthology. 1963. |
| GATT | Tragedy, History and Romance. 1968. |
| GAUB | Four Classic French Plays. 1961. |
| GAVE | Critics' Choice: New York Drama Critics' Circle Prize Plays 1935–55. 1955. |
| GAY | Gay Plays. 1984–1994. 5v |

| | |
|---|---|
| **GAYIA** | Gay Plays: An International Anthology. 1989. |
| **GAYLE** | Representative English Comedies. 1903–36. 4v |
| **GEIO** | Stories of Our Way: An Anthology of American Indian Plays. 1999. |
| **GEMM** | Law in Literature: Legal Themes in Drama. 1995. |
| **GEOR** | Six Plays by Black and Asian Women Writers. 1993. |
| **GERLC** | German-language Comedy: A Critical Anthology. 1992. |
| **GERO** | Doubles, Demons, and Dreamers: An International Collection of Symbolist Drama. 1985. |
| **GETH** | Lunatic Lover and other Plays by French Women of the 17th and 18th Centuries, The. 1994. |
| **GHAN** | Iranian Drama: An Anthology. 1989. |
| **GIA** | Introduction to Modern Greek Literature: An Anthology of Fiction, Drama, and Poetry. 1969. |
| **GIBS** | Six Renaissance Tragedies. 1997. |
| **GILB** | Modern and Contemporary Drama. 1994. |
| **GILL** | German Theater before 1750. 1992. |
| **GLASH** | Key to Our Aborted Dreams: Five Plays by Contemporary Belgian Women Writers, The. 1998. |
| **GLE** | Three Soviet Plays. 1966. |
| **GLI** | Munching on Existence: Contemporary American Society through Literature. 1971. |
| **GLO** | Plays by Four Tragedians. 1968. |
| **GOL** | Plays of the Italian Theatre. 1921. |
| **GOLB** | Golden Steed: Seven Baltic Plays, The. 1979. |
| **GOLD** | Drama: Traditional and Modern, The. 1968. |
| **GOLH** | Contexts of the Drama. 1968. |
| **GOLK** | Mentor Masterworks of Modern Drama: Five Plays. 1969. |
| **GOM** | Jacobean Tragedies. 1969. |
| **GONZ** | Cuban Theater in the United States: A Critical Anthology. 1992. |
| **GOO** | From Script to Stage: Eight Modern Plays. 1971. |
| **GOOD** | Drama on Stage. 1961. |
| **GOODE** | Drama on Stage. 2nd ed. 1978. |
| **GOON** | Modern Sri Lankan Drama: An Anthology. 1991. |
| **GOOR** | Agit-prop to Theatre Workshop: Political Playscripts 1930–1950. 1986. |
| **GORDP** | Introduction to Tragedy. 1973. |
| **GORE** | Literature in Critical Perspectives: An Anthology. 1968. |
| **GOS** | Restoration Plays from Dryden to Farquhar. 1929. |
| **GOSA** | Restoration Plays from Dryden to Farquhar. 1932. |
| **GOSS** | Jacobean Academic Plays. 1988. |
| **GOU** | Western Humanities, The. 1971. 2v |
| **GOW** | Five Broadway Plays. 1948. |
| **GOWA** | Five Broadway Plays. 2nd ed. 1968. |
| **GPA** | Freshman English Program. 1960. |
| **GRA** | Chief French Plays of the Nineteenth Century. 1934. |
| **GRAF** | Four French Plays of the Twentieth Century. 1949. |
| **GRAV** | Drama for a New South Africa: Seven Plays. 1999. |
| **GRAW** | Second Wave Plays: Women at the Albany Empire. 1990. |
| **GRAY** | Market Plays. 1986. |
| **GRAYS** | South Africa Plays. 1993. |
| **GRAYTO** | Theatre One, New South African Drama. 1978. |
| **GRAYTT** | Theatre two: New South African Drama. 1981. |
| **GRD** | Great American Parade. 1935. |
| **GRDB** | Great Books of the Western World. 1952. 54v |
| **GRDBA** | Great Books of the Western World. 2nd ed. 1990. 61v |
| **GRDG** | Greek Drama. 1965 (1982 printing). |
| **GRE** | Great Plays (English). 1900. |
| **GREA** | Great Plays (French and German). 1901. |
| **GREAAI** | Great Irish Plays. 1995. |
| **GREAAR** | Great Rock Musicals. 1979. |
| **GREAB** | Introduction to Imaginative Literature. 1960. |
| **GREB** | English Literature and Its Backgrounds. 1939–40. 2v |
| **GREC** | English Literature and Its Backgrounds. Rev. ed. 1949. 2v |

| | |
|---|---|
| **GREE** | Greek Dramas. 1900. |
| **GREEN** | Russian Symbolist Theatre: An Anthology of Plays and Critical Texts, The. 1986. |
| **GREENU** | Unknown Russian Theater: An Anthology, The. 1991. |
| **GREG** | Temper of the Times. 1969. |
| **GREJ** | All those Voices: The Minority Experience. 1971. |
| **GREN** | Three Greek Tragedies in Translation. 1942. |
| **GREP** | Complete Greek Tragedies, The. 1959. 4v |
| **GREPA** | Complete Greek Tragedies, The. Centennial Edition. 1992. 4v |
| **GRER** | Greek Tragedies. 1960. 3v |
| **GRERA** | Greek Tragedies. 2nd ed. 1991. 3v |
| **GRIF** | Living Theatre. 1953. |
| **GRIFG** | Herstory: Plays by Women for Women. 1991. 2v |
| **GRIH** | Eight American Ethnic Plays. 1974. |
| **GROS** | Literature of American Jews, The. 1973. |
| **GROV** | Grove Press Modern Drama. 1975. |
| **GUE** | Treasury of Russian Literature, A. 1943. |
| **GUI** | Latin Literature in Translation. 1942. |
| **GUIN** | Latin Literature in Translation. 2nd ed. 1952. |
| **GUTDF** | Discovering Literature: Fiction, Poetry, and Drama. 1993. |
| **GUTDS** | Discovering Literature: Fiction, Poetry, and Drama. 2nd ed. 1996. |
| **GUTH** | Idea and Image. 1962. |
| **GUTL** | Literature. 2nd ed. 1968. |
| **GUTR** | Guthrie New Theater. Volume I. 1976. |
| **GWYN** | Drama: A HarperCollins Pocket Anthology. 1993. |
| **GYOR** | Mirror to the Cage: Three Contemporary Hungarian Plays, A. 1993. |
| **HACJT** | Half a Century of Japanese Theater. 1999–2006. 8v |
| **HAE** | To Read Literature: Fiction, Poetry, Drama. 1981. |
| **HAEA** | To Read Literature: Fiction, Poetry, Drama. 2nd ed. 1987. |
| **HAEB** | To Read Literature: Fiction, Poetry, Drama. 3rd ed. 1992. |
| **HAH** | Legend of the Rood, The. 1955. |
| **HAL** | American Plays. 1935. |
| **HALM** | Modern Turkish Drama, an Anthology of Plays in Translation. 1976. |
| **HALU** | Pulitzer Prize Reader. 1961. |
| **HAM** | Three Greek Plays. 1937. |
| **HAMI** | London Majority: 1931–52. 1952. |
| **HAN** | Eighteenth Century Plays. 1928. |
| **HANG** | Three Australian Plays. 1968. |
| **HANNA** | Monstrous Regiment: Four Plays and a Collective Celebration. 1991. |
| **HAO** | Tudor Interludes. 1972. |
| **HAP** | Harbrace Omnibus. 1942. |
| **HAPD** | Tragedies Old and New. 1939. |
| **HAPO** | Forms of Imagination, The. 1972. |
| **HAPRA** | Anchor Anthology of Jacobean Drama, The. 1963. 2v |
| **HAPRB** | Jacobean Drama: An Anthology. 1968. 2v |
| **HAPRL** | Humanist Tradition in World Literature: An Anthology of Masterpieces from Gilgamesh to the Divine Comedy, The. 1970. |
| **HAPS** | Major British Writers. 1954. 2v |
| **HAPT** | Major British Writers. Enl. ed. 1959. 2v |
| **HAPU** | Totem Voices: Plays from the Black World Repertory. 1998. |
| **HAPUE** | Classic Plays from the Negro Ensemble Company. 1995. |
| **HAPV** | Anthology of Roman Drama, An. 1960. |
| **HARA** | America's Literature. 1955. |
| **HARB** | Patterns in Modern Drama. 1948. |
| **HARC** | Harvard Classics. 1909–10. 50v |
| **HART** | Representative Plays from the French Theatre of Today. 1940. |
| **HARV** | Promenade littéraire au vintième siècle. 1949. |
| **HARW** | Christmas Plays from Oberufer. 1944. |

| | |
|---|---|
| **HARY** | Black Theatre, U.S.A.: 45 Plays by Black Americans, 1847–1974. 1974. |
| **HARYB** | Black Theatre, USA: Plays by African Americans, 1847 to Today. Revised and Expanded Edition. 1996. |
| **HARYL** | Lost Plays of the Harlem Renaissance, 1920–1940. 1996. |
| **HAT** | Modern American Dramas. 1941. |
| **HATA** | Modern American Dramas. New ed. 1949. |
| **HAU** | Modern British Dramas. 1941. |
| **HAV** | Modern Continental Dramas. 1941. |
| **HAVD** | Modern Dramas. Shorter ed. 1944. |
| **HAVE** | Modern Dramas. New Shorter ed. 1948. |
| **HAVG** | Modern Repertory, A. 1953. |
| **HAVH** | Drama: Principles and Plays. 1967. |
| **HAVHA** | Drama: Principles and Plays. 2nd ed. 1975. |
| **HAVHN** | Fire and Ice: 3 Icelandic Plays. 1967. |
| **HAVI** | Selection: A Reader for College Writing. 1955. |
| **HAVL** | Contact with Drama. 1974. |
| **HAY** | Portable Elizabethan Reader, The. 1946. |
| **HAYD** | Renaissance Treasury, A. 1953. |
| **HAYE** | Port-Royal and other Plays. 1962. |
| **HEA** | Heath Introduction to Drama, The. 1976. |
| **HEAA** | Heath Introduction to Drama, The. 2nd ed. 1983. |
| **HEAB** | Heath Introduction to Drama, The. 3rd ed. 1988. |
| **HEAC** | Heath Introduction to Drama, The. 4th ed. 1992. |
| **HEAD** | Heath Introduction to Drama, The. 5th ed. 1996. |
| **HEAL** | Heath Introduction to Literature, The. 1980. |
| **HEALA** | Heath Introduction to Literature, The. 2nd ed. 1984. |
| **HEALB** | Heath Introduction to Literature, The. 3rd ed. 1988. |
| **HEALC** | Heath Introduction to Literature, The. 4th ed. 1992. |
| **HEALD** | Heath Introduction to Literature, The. 5th ed. 1996. |
| **HEALE** | Heath Introduction to Literature, The. 6th ed. 2000. |
| **HEID** | Maritime Lines: An Anthology of Contemporary Plays. 1988. |
| **HEIL** | Anthology of English Drama before Shakespeare, An. 1952. |
| **HEIS** | Discovery and Recollection: An Anthology of Literary Types. 1970. |
| **HELB** | Gay and Lesbian Plays Today. 1993. |
| **HERZ** | Early 20th-Century German Plays. 1998. |
| **HEWE** | Famous American Plays of the 1940's. 1960. |
| **HIB** | Writers of the Western World. 1942. |
| **HIBA** | Writers of the Western World. Rev. ed. 1946. |
| **HIBB** | Writers of the Western World. 2nd ed. 1954. |
| **HIBH** | Contemporary Japanese Literature: An Anthology of Fiction, Film, and other Writing since 1945. 1977. |
| **HIG** | Five World Plays. 1964. |
| **HIJ** | High Energy Musicals from the Omaha Magic Theatre. 1983. |
| **HIL** | Five Contemporary American Plays. 1939. |
| **HILEB** | Black Heroes: Seven Plays. 1989. |
| **HILEP** | Plays for Today. 1985. |
| **HILET** | Time . . . and a Season: 8 Caribbean Plays, A. 1996. |
| **HILL** | Cuatro Comedies. 1941. |
| **HILP** | Living Art: An Introduction to Theatre and Drama, The. 1971. |
| **HILPDH** | Our Dramatic Heritage. 1983–1992. 6v |
| **HOEP** | Drama. 1994. |
| **HOF** | Gay Plays: The First Collection. 1979. |
| **HOGE** | Seven Irish Plays, 1946–1964. 1967. |
| **HOGF** | Drama: The Major Genres. 1962. |
| **HOGI** | Literature: A Collection of Mythology and Folklore, Short stories, Poetry, Drama. 1973. |
| **HOGN** | Literature: A Collection of Mythology and Folklore, Short stories, Poetry, Drama. 2nd ed. 1977. |
| **HOLM** | Complete College Reader, A. 1950. |
| **HOLP** | Keys to Understanding: Receiving and Sending: Drama. 1970. |
| **HOLTM** | Modern Spanish Stage: Four Plays, The. 1970. |

| | |
|---|---|
| **HOLTS** | DramaContemporary Spain. *See* Spain: Plays |
| **HOLTS** | Spain: Plays. 1985. |
| **HOM** | Homosexual Acts: Five Short Plays from The Gay Season at The Almost Free T Theatre. 1975. |
| **HOPP** | Medieval Mystery Plays. 1962. |
| **HORN** | Cavalcade of World Writing, A. 1961. |
| **HOUE** | Golden Age, The. 1963. |
| **HOUG** | Great Russian Plays. 1960. |
| **HOUK** | Romantic Influence, The. 1963. |
| **HOUP** | Seeds of Modern Drama. 1963. |
| **HOUR** | Hour of One: Six Gothic Melodramas, The. 1975. |
| **HOUS** | Types of World Literature. 1930. |
| **HOUST** | But still, like air, I'll rise: New Asian American Plays. 1997. |
| **HOUSTP** | Politics of Life: Four Plays by Asian-American Women, The. 1993. |
| **HOW** | Ten Elizabethan Plays. 1931. |
| **HOWA** | Scotland Plays: New Scottish Drama. 1998. |
| **HOWE** | Greek Literature in Translation. 1924. |
| **HOWF** | Greek Literature in Translation. 1948. |
| **HOWJ** | Roman Literature in Translation. 1924. |
| **HOWK** | Roman Literature in Translation. 1959. |
| **HOWM** | McGraw-Hill Book of Drama, The. 1995. |
| **HOWP** | Literature of America, The. 1971. 2v |
| **HUB** | American life in Literature. 1936. |
| **HUBA** | American life in Literature. 1949. 2v |
| **HUD** | Introduction to Drama, An. 1927. |
| **HUDE** | Angels of Vision. 1962. |
| **HUDS** | Nelson's College Caravan. 1936. 4v |
| **HUDT** | Nelson's College Caravan. 3rd ed. 1942. 4v in 1. |
| **HUDV** | Victorian Theatricals: From Menageries to Melodramas. 2000. |
| **HUER** | Necessary Theater: Six Plays about the Chicano Experience. 1989. |
| **HUGH** | O Solo Homo: The New queer Performance. 1998. |
| **HUGL** | Ten English Farces. 1948. |
| **HUMANA** | Humana Festival: The Complete Plays 1993–2000. 1993–2000. 8v |
| **HUNG** | Classical Chinese Plays. 2nd ed. 1972. |
| **HUNGDC** | DramaContemporary Hungary. *See* Hungary: Plays |
| **HUNGDC** | Hungary: Plays. 1991. |
| **HUNT** | Our Living Language. 1961. |
| **HUST** | Classics of the Renaissance Theater: English Plays. 1969. |
| **HUTC** | American Twenties, The. 1952. |
| **HUTCH** | Open Space: Six Contemporary Plays from Africa. 1995. |
| **IFKO** | American Letter: Immigrant and Ethnic Writing. 1975. |
| **INCA** | Modern Theatre: A Collection of Plays, The. 1968. 10v in 5 |
| **INCI** | Incisions. 2000. |
| **INDI** | Indiana Experience: An Anthology, The. 1977. |
| **ING** | Adventures in American Literature. 3rd ed. 1941. |
| **INGA** | Adventures in American Literature. 4th ed. 1947. |
| **INGB** | Adventures in American Literature. 5th ed. 1952. |
| **INGE** | Adventures in English Literature. Rev. ed. 1938. |
| **INGG** | Adventures in English Literature. 4th ed. 1946. |
| **INGH** | Adventures in English Literature. Mercury Edition. 1952. |
| **INGW** | Adventures in World Literature. 1936. |
| **INSI** | Inside 2000. 2000. |
| **INTE** | International Modern Plays. 1950. |
| **IRW** | Four Classical Asian Plays in Modern Translation. 1972. |
| **JACOB** | Bedford Introduction to Drama, The. 1989. |
| **JACOBA** | Bedford Introduction to Drama, The. 2nd ed. 1993. |
| **JACOBD** | Bedford Introduction to Drama, The. 3rd ed. 1997. |
| **JACOBE** | Compact Bedford Introduction to Drama. 2nd ed. 1996. |

| | |
|---|---|
| **JAFF** | Laureate Fraternity, The. 1960. |
| **JAPDC** | Japanese Drama and Culture in the 1960s: The return of the gods. 1988. |
| **JAY** | Modern Arabic Drama: An Anthology. 1995. |
| **JEFF** | Restoration Comedy. 1974. 4v |
| **JENN** | Slant Six: New Theater from Minnesota's Playwrights' Center. 1990. |
| **JENS** | Sensational Restoration, The. 1996. |
| **JOH** | Anthology of Italian Authors from Cavalcanti to Fogazzaro (1270–1907), An. 1907. |
| **JOHN** | Play and the Reader, The. 1966. |
| **JOHO** | Play and the Reader, The. 1971. |
| **JOND** | New Mexico Plays. 1989. |
| **JONE** | Black Fire: An Anthology of Afro-American Writing. 1969. |
| **JONI** | La Mama Collection: 6 Plays for the 1990s, The. 1997. |
| **JONT** | Sharing the Delirium: Second Generation AIDS Plays and Performances. 1994. |
| **JONW** | Men and Angels: Three South American Comedies. 1970. |
| **JORG** | College Treasury, A. 1956. |
| **JORH** | College Treasury, A. 2nd ed. 1967. |
| **JUAN** | Likhaan Book of Philippine Drama, 1991–1996: From Page to Stage, The. 2000. |
| **KAB** | Kabuki: 5 Classic Plays. 1975. |
| **KAL** | Collection of Canadian Plays, A. 1972–1978. 5v |
| **KAM** | Modern Indian Plays. 2000–2007. 3v |
| **KANEL** | Nuevos pasos: Chicano and Puerto Rican Drama. 1989, 1979. |
| **KANI** | More Market Plays. 1994. |
| **KAT** | Eight European Plays. 1927. |
| **KAU** | Nineteenth Century English Verse Drama. 1973. |
| **KAYD** | Devils & Demons: A Treasury of Fiendish Tales Old & New. 1987. |
| **KAYF** | Frantic Comedy: Eight Plays of Knockabout Fun. 1993. |
| **KAYS** | Sweet Revenge: 10 Plays of Bloody Murder. 1992. |
| **KAYT** | 13 Plays of Ghosts and the Supernatural. 1990. |
| **KEE** | Twenty Plays of the Nō Theatre. 1970. |
| **KEEP** | Keeping on: Four Plays about Senior Citizens. 1990. |
| **KEL** | Modern Drama by Women 1880s–1930s. 1996. |
| **KER** | Anthology of English Literature, The. 1973. 2v |
| **KERN** | Character and Conflict: An Introduction to Drama. 1963. |
| **KERO** | Character and Conflict: An Introduction to Drama. 2nd ed. 1969. |
| **KERP** | Classics of the Modern Theater, Realism and after. 1965. |
| **KET** | Three Masters of English Drama. 1934. |
| **KEY** | Comparative Comedies Present and Past. 1935. |
| **KIAN** | Anthology of Non-Western Drama, An. 1993. |
| **KILG** | Golden Age of Melodrama: twelve 19th Century Melodramas, The. 1974. |
| **KILGC** | Contemporary Plays by Women: Outstanding Winners and Runners-Up for the Susan Smith Blackburn Prize (1978–1990). 1991. |
| **KIN** | Adventures in Values. 1969. |
| **KINH** | Black Drama Anthology. 1971. |
| **KINHB** | Black Drama Anthology. 1986. |
| **KINHN** | National Black Drama Anthology: Eleven Plays from America's Leading African-American Theaters, The. 1995. |
| **KINHP** | New Plays for the Black Theatre. 1989. |
| **KINNR** | Renaissance Drama: An Anthology of Plays and entertainments. 1999. |
| **KINNS** | Symposium on love. 1970. |
| **KIRLA** | Literature: Reading, Reacting, Writing. 1991. |
| **KIRLB** | Literature: Reading, Reacting, Writing. 2nd ed. 1994. |
| **KIRLC** | Literature: Reading, Reacting, Writing. 3rd ed. 1997. |
| **KIRLD** | Literature: Reading, Reacting, Writing. Compact 4th ed. 2000. |
| **KLEIN** | Playbook. 1986. |
| **KLIS** | Anthology of American Drama, An. 1993. 2v |
| **KNIC** | Interpreting Literature. 1955. |
| **KNID** | Interpreting Literature, Rev. ed. 1960. |
| **KNIE** | Interpreting Literature. 3rd ed. 1965. |

| | |
|---|---|
| **KNIF** | Interpreting Literature. 4th ed. 1969. |
| **KNIG** | Interpreting Literature. 5th ed. 1974. |
| **KNIH** | Interpreting Literature. 6th ed. 1978. |
| **KNIJ** | Interpreting Literature. 7th ed. 1985. |
| **KNIRH** | Robin Hood and Other Outlaw Tales. 1997. |
| **KNO** | Mirrors: An Introduction to Literature. 1972. |
| **KNOJ** | Mirrors: An Introduction to Literature. 2nd ed. 1975. |
| **KNOK** | Mirrors: An Introduction to Literature. 3rd ed. 1988. |
| **KNOW** | Six Caroline Plays. 1962. |
| **KOH** | Hebrew Anthology, A. 1913. 2v |
| **KON** | Six Complete World Plays and a History of the Drama. 1963. |
| **KOU** | Ta matou mangai: Our Own Voice. 1999. |
| **KOZ** | Best Short Plays of the Social Theatre, The. 1939. |
| **KRE** | Poetic Drama. 1941. |
| **KRIT** | Plays by Early American Women, 1775–1850. 1995. |
| **KRM** | Cavalcade of Comedy. 1953. |
| **KRO** | Eighteenth Century Miscellany, An. 1936. |
| **KRON** | Pleasure of Their Company, The. 1946. |
| **KUMU** | Kumu Kahua Plays. 1983. |
| **LAB** | Three French Farces. 1973. |
| **LABO** | Balkan Blues: Writing out of Yugoslavia. 1995. |
| **LAH** | Showcase 1: Plays from Eugene O'Neill Foundation. 1970. |
| **LAL** | Great Sanscrit Plays. 1964. |
| **LAM** | Range of Literature: Drama, The. 1969. |
| **LAMO** | Women on the Verge: 7 Avant-Garde American Plays. 1993. |
| **LAMP** | Five German Tragedies. 1969. |
| **LANC** | Five French Farces, 1655–1694? 1937. |
| **LAND** | Land Called Morning: Three Plays, The. 1986. |
| **LAO** | Dybbuk, and Other Great Yiddish Plays, The. 1966. |
| **LAOG** | Great Jewish Plays, The. 1972. |
| **LAP** | Four Famous Greek Plays. 1929. |
| **LAQCF** | Landmarks of Classical French Drama. 1991. |
| **LAQCW** | Landmarks of Contemporary Women's Drama. 1992. |
| **LAQID** | Landmarks of Irish Drama. 1988. |
| **LAR** | New Dramatists, 2000: Best Plays by the Graduating Class. 2001. |
| **LAS** | Art from the Ashes: A Holocaust Anthology. 1995. |
| **LAT** | Late Medieval Religious Play of Bodleian MSS Digby 133 and e Museo 160, The. 1982. |
| **LATIN** | Latin American Plays: New Drama from Argentina, Cuba, Mexico, and Peru. 1996. |
| **LATTH** | Latin American Theatre in Translation: An Anthology of Works from Mexico, the Caribbean and the Southern Cone: Plays. 2000. |
| **LAV** | Unity of English, The. 1971. |
| **LAW** | Modern Plays, Short and long. 1924. |
| **LAWR** | Early Seventeenth Century Drama. 1963. |
| **LAWS** | Jacobean and Caroline Comedies. 1973. |
| **LAWT** | Jacobean and Caroline Tragedies. 1975. |
| **LAX** | New Anthology of Contemporary Austrian Folk Plays. 1996. |
| **LAXC** | Seven Contemporary Austrian Plays. 1995. |
| **LEAK** | Special Occasion: Three Plays by Clive Jermain, Alma Cullen, Bill Naughton, A. 1988. |
| **LEG** | Eva Le Gallienne's Civic Repertory Plays. 1928. |
| **LEIS** | Three Parnassus Plays (1598–1601), The. 1949. |
| **LES** | Lesbian Plays. 1987–1989. 2v |
| **LET** | Trissino's Sophonisba and Aretino's Horatia: Two Italian Renaissance Tragedies. 1997. |
| **LEV** | Plays for the College Theater. 1932. |
| **LEVE** | Plays for the College Theater. 1934. |
| **LEVG** | America in Literature. 1978. |
| **LEVI** | Tragedy: Plays, Theory, Criticism. 1960. |
| **LEVJ** | Tragedy: Plays, Theory and Criticism. Alternate ed. 1965. |
| **LEVY** | Modern Drama: Selected Plays from 1879 to the Present. 1999. |

| | |
|---|---|
| **LEWI** | Among the Nations. 1948. |
| **LIBR** | Library of Universal Literature. 1906. |
| **LID** | Plays, Classic and Contemporary. 1967. |
| **LIDE** | Roman Drama. 1964. |
| **LIE** | British Drama. 1929. |
| **LIED** | British Prose and Poetry. Rev. ed. 1938. 2v |
| **LIEE** | British Poetry and Prose. 3rd ed. 1950. 2v |
| **LIEF** | Modern Age, Literature, The. 2nd ed. 1972. |
| **LIEG** | Modern Age, Literature, The. 3rd ed. 1976. |
| **LIFE** | Life is a Dream, and other Spanish Classics. 1985. |
| **LIFS** | Epic and Folk Plays of the Yiddish Theatre. 1975. |
| **LIND** | Ten Greek Plays in Contemporary Translations. 1957. |
| **LINDB** | Bottled Notes from Underground: Contemporary Plays by Jewish Writers. 1998. |
| **LINDC** | Court Masques: Jacobean and Caroline Entertainments. 1605–1640. 1995. |
| **LITC** | Literature: A College Anthology. 1977. |
| **LITI** | Literature: An Introduction to Fiction, Poetry and Drama. 1976. |
| **LITIA** | Literature: An Introduction to Fiction, Poetry and Drama. 2nd ed. 1979. |
| **LITIB** | Literature: An Introduction to Fiction, Poetry and Drama. 3rd ed. 1983. |
| **LITIC** | Literature: An Introduction to Fiction, Poetry and Drama. 4th ed. 1987. |
| **LITID** | Literature: An Introduction to Fiction, Poetry and Drama. 5th ed. 1991. |
| **LITIE** | Literature: An Introduction to Fiction, Poetry and Drama. 6th ed. 1995. |
| **LITIF** | Literature: An Introduction to Fiction, Poetry and Drama. 7th ed. 1999. |
| **LITJ** | Literature: An Introduction to Fiction, Poetry and Drama. Compact ed. 1995. |
| **LITJA** | Literature: An Introduction to Fiction, Poetry and Drama. 2nd Compact ed. 2000. |
| **LITP** | Literature: Fiction, Poetry, Drama. 1977. |
| **LITQ** | Literature as Experience: An Anthology. 1979. |
| **LITR** | Literature for Composition: Essays, Fiction, Poetry, and Drama. 1984. |
| **LITRA** | Literature for Composition: Essays, Fiction, Poetry, and Drama. 2nd ed. 1988. |
| **LITRB** | Literature for Composition: Essays, Fiction, Poetry, and Drama. 3rd ed. 1991. |
| **LITRC** | Literature for Composition: Essays, Fiction, Poetry, and Drama. 4th ed. 1996. |
| **LITRD** | Literature for Composition: Essays, Fiction, Poetry, and Drama. 5th ed. 2000. |
| **LITT** | Plays from Black Africa. 1968. |
| **LIU** | Six Yuan Plays. 1972. |
| **LOC** | Plays of Negro Life. 1927. |
| **LOCK** | Introduction to Literature. 1948. |
| **LOCL** | Introduction to Literature. Rev. ed. 1952. |
| **LOCLA** | Introduction to Literature. 3rd ed. 1957. |
| **LOCLB** | Introduction to Literature. 4th ed. 1962. |
| **LOCM** | Literature of Western Civilization. 1952. 2v |
| **LOCR** | Chief rivals of Corneille and Racine, The. 1956. |
| **LOCU** | More Plays by Rivals of Corneille and Racine. 1968. |
| **LOGG** | Three Great French Plays. 1961. |
| **LOND** | World of law: A Treasury of Great Writing about and in the Law, Short Stories, Plays, The. 1960. 2v |
| **LONG** | Modern Catalan Plays. 2000. |
| **LONO** | London Omnibus. 1932. |
| **LOO** | Modern English Readings. 1934. |
| **LOOA** | Modern English Readings. Rev. ed. 1936. |
| **LOOB** | Modern English Readings. 3rd ed. 1939. |
| **LOOC** | Modern English Readings. 4th ed. 1942. |
| **LOOD** | Modern English Readings. 5th ed. 1946. |
| **LOOE** | Modern English Readings. 6th ed. 1950. |
| **LOOF** | Modern English Readings. 7th ed. 1956. |
| **LOOM** | Representative Medieval and Tudor Plays. 1942. |
| **LOQA** | Love and Thunder: Plays by Women in the Age of Queen Anne. 1988. |
| **LOR** | Modern Drama: An Anthology of Nine Plays. 1963. |
| **LOV** | College Reader, The. 1936. |
| **LOVR** | Adventures in Living. 1955. |

| | |
|---|---|
| **LOW** | Our Land and Its Literature. 1936. |
| **LOWE** | Peace Plays. 1985. |
| **LOWE2** | Peace Plays: Two. 1990. |
| **LUCA** | Greek Drama for Everyman. 1954. |
| **LUCAB** | Greek Drama for the Common Reader. 1967. |
| **LUCAF** | Greek Tragedy and Comedy. 1968. |
| **LUP** | Arthurian Drama: An Anthology. 1991. |
| **LUPW** | Arthurian Literature by Women. 1999. |
| **LUST** | Classical German Drama. 1963. |
| **LUZ** | Ten Modern Macedonian Plays. 2000. |
| **LYK** | Six Soviet Plays. 1934. |
| **LYN** | Voices from the Landwash: 11 Newfoundland Playwrights. 1997. |
| **LYO** | Eight French Classic Plays. 1932. |
| **LYON** | Female Playwrights of the Restoration: Five Comedies. 1991. |
| **MAB** | 19th Century Russian Drama. 1963. |
| **MABA** | 20th Century Russian Drama. 1963. |
| **MABC** | Dramatic Tragedy. 1971. |
| **MAC** | College Omnibus, The. 1933. |
| **MACB** | College Omnibus, The. 1934. |
| **MACC** | 1936 College Omnibus, The. 1936. |
| **MACE** | Revised College Omnibus, The. 1939. |
| **MACF** | College Omnibus, The. 6th ed. 1947. |
| **MACL** | Century Types of English Literature Chronologically Arranged. 1925. |
| **MACN** | Nobel Prize Treasury, The. 1948. |
| **MACU** | Spanish Drama of the Golden Age: Twelve Plays. 1979. |
| **MAD** | Modern Plays. 1932. |
| **MADB** | Four Stages. 1967, c1966. |
| **MADG** | America in Literature. 1944. |
| **MADI** | Romantic Triumph: American Literature from 1830 to 1860, The. 1933. |
| **MAE** | Forms in English Literature. 1972. |
| **MAEC** | Perceptions in Literature. 1972. |
| **MAF** | Famous American Plays of the 1920s. 1959. |
| **MAFC** | Famous American Plays of the 1920s and the 1930s. 1988. |
| **MAH** | Artists' Theatre: Four Plays. 1960. |
| **MAK** | Five Elizabethan Comedies. 1934. |
| **MAKG** | Five Elizabethan Tragedies. 1938. |
| **MAKJ** | Five Stuart Tragedies. 1953. |
| **MAL** | Augustans, The. 1950. |
| **MALC** | Continental Edition of World Masterpieces, The. 1962. |
| **MALG** | World Masterpieces. 1956. 2v |
| **MALI** | World Masterpieces. Rev. ed. 1965. 2v |
| **MALN** | World Masterpieces. 3rd ed. 1973. 2v |
| **MALR** | Classics in Translation. 1952. 2v |
| **MALY** | Festival Plays. 1986. |
| **MAM** | Year of Protest, 1956: An Anthology of Soviet Literary Materials, The. 1961. |
| **MAMB** | Frogs and other Greek Plays, The. 1970. |
| **MAME** | Plays on Women. 1999. |
| **MANA** | Explorations in French Literature. 1939. |
| **MANCA** | Anthology of American Literature. 1974. 2v |
| **MANCB** | Anthology of American Literature. 2nd ed. 1980. 2v |
| **MANCD** | Anthology of Amcrican Litcrature. 3rd ed. 1985. 2v |
| **MANCE** | Anthology of American Literature. 4th ed. 1989. 2v |
| **MANCF** | Anthology of American Literature. 5th ed. 1993. 2v |
| **MANCG** | Anthology of American Literature. 6th ed. 1997. 2v |
| **MANCH** | Anthology of American Literature. 7th ed. 2000. 2v |
| **MANCI** | Concise Anthology of American Literature. 1974. |
| **MANCIA** | Concise Anthology of American Literature. 2nd ed. 1985. |

| | |
|---|---|
| **MANCIO** | Concise Anthology of American Literature. 3rd ed. 1993. |
| **MANCIU** | Concise Anthology of American Literature. 4th ed. 1998. |
| **MAND** | Plays of the Restoration and Eighteenth Century. 1931. |
| **MANF** | Plays of the Restoration and Eighteenth Century. 1938. |
| **MANH** | Restoration and Eighteenth Century Comedy. 1973. |
| **MANK** | Literary Types and Themes. 1960. |
| **MANL** | Literary Types and Themes. 2nd ed. 1971. |
| **MANM** | Chinese Literature: An Anthology from the Earliest Times to the Present Day. 1974. |
| **MANN** | Beginnings of English Literature, The. 1961. |
| **MAO** | Pocketful of Plays: Vintage Drama, A. 1996. |
| **MAP** | Storm, and other Russian Plays, The. 1960. |
| **MAQ** | Moon marked and Touched by Sun: Plays by African-American Women. 1994. |
| **MAR** | Miracle Plays: Seven Medieval Plays for Modern Players. 1956, 1959. |
| **MARG** | Malvern Festival Plays MCMXXXIII. 1933. |
| **MARH** | Five Comedies of Medieval France. 1970. |
| **MARJ** | Theatre of Don Juan: A Collection of Plays and Views, 1630–1963, The. 1963. |
| **MARK** | Stage in Action: An Introduction to Theatre and Drama, The. 1989. |
| **MARL** | Stage in Action: An Introduction to Theatre and Drama, The. 2nd ed. 1998. |
| **MARLC** | Threads and other Sheffield Plays. 1990. |
| **MARLG** | Introduction to Ghanaian Literature, An. 1999. |
| **MARLI** | Literatura Española: Selección. 1968. |
| **MARO** | New American Drama. 1966. |
| **MARP** | Open Space Plays. 1974. |
| **MARR** | Plays for the End of the Century. 1996. |
| **MARRA** | Theatre of the Ridiculous. Revised & Expanded Edition. 1998. |
| **MART** | Great Modern British Plays. 1932. |
| **MAS** | Canadian Plays from Hart House Theatre. 1926–27. 2v |
| **MAST** | Masterpieces of Greek Literature. 1902. |
| **MASW** | Black Crook, and other Nineteenth Century American Plays, The. 1967. |
| **MASX** | Nineteenth-Century American Plays. 1985. |
| **MATT** | Chief European Dramatists, The. 1916. |
| **MATTL** | Chief British Dramatists Excluding Shakespeare, The. 1924. |
| **MAUS** | Four Revenge Tragedies. 1995. |
| **MAYER** | Playing out the Empire: Ben-Hur and other Toga Plays and Films, 1883–1908: A Critical Anthology. 1994. |
| **MED** | Medieval Drama: An Anthology. 2000. |
| **MEDN** | Best of the West: An Anthology of Plays from the 1989 & 1990 Padua Hills Playwrights Festival. 1991. |
| **MELB** | Melbourne Stories: Three Plays. 2000. |
| **MELO** | Melodrama Classics: Six Plays and How to Stage Them. 1982. |
| **MEN** | English Literature, 1650–1800. 1940. |
| **MERC** | 1000 Years of Irish Prose. Part 1. The Literary revival. 1952. |
| **MERS** | Three Comedies of American Family Life. 1961. |
| **MERT** | Three Dramas of American Individualism. 1961. |
| **MERU** | Three Dramas of American realism. 1961. |
| **MERV** | Three Plays about Doctors. 1961. |
| **MERW** | Three Plays about Marriage. 1962. |
| **MES** | On Stage, America! a Selection of Distinctly American Plays. 1996. |
| **MESC** | Fateful Lightning: America's Civil War Plays. 2000. |
| **MESCO** | When Conscience Trod the Stage: American Plays of Social Awareness. 1998. |
| **MESE** | Modern Drama from Communist China. 1970. |
| **MESH** | Modern Literature from China. 1974. |
| **MESSE** | From the other Side of the Century II: A New American Drama 1960–1995. 1998. |
| **MESSN** | Collection: Literature for the Seventies. 1972. |
| **METR** | Metropol: Literary Almanac. 1982. |
| **MEY** | The Bedford Introduction to Literature. 1987. |
| **MEYB** | The Bedford Introduction to Literature. 2nd ed. 1990. |
| **MEYC** | Compact Bedford Introduction to Literature, The. 3rd ed. 1993. |
| **MEYCA** | Compact Bedford Introduction to Literature, The. 4th ed. 1997. |

| | |
|---|---|
| **MEYCB** | Compact Bedford Introduction to Literature, The. 5th ed. 2000. |
| **MEYD** | Bedford Introduction to Literature, The. 3rd ed. 1993. |
| **MEYE** | Bedford Introduction to Literature, The. 4th ed. 1996. |
| **MEYF** | Bedford Introduction to Literature, The. 5th ed. 1999. |
| **MID** | Middle Age, Old Age: Short Stories, Poems, Plays, and Essays on Aging. 1980. |
| **MIG** | Five Modern Yugoslav Plays. 1977. |
| **MIH** | Here to Stay: Five Plays from the Women's Project. 1997. |
| **MIHPW** | PlayWriting Women: 7 Plays from the Women's Project. 1993. |
| **MIHWW** | WomensWork: Five New Plays from the Women's Project. 1989. |
| **MIJ** | Explorations in Literature. 1933–34. 2v |
| **MIJA** | Explorations in Literature. Rev. ed. 1937–38. 2v |
| **MIJB** | Dimensions of Literature, The. 1967. |
| **MIJH** | Heritage of American Literature. 1991. 2v |
| **MIJT** | Translations from the French. 1971. |
| **MIJY** | American Dramatic Literature. 1961. |
| **MIK** | Classics, Greek & Latin, The. 1909–10. 15v |
| **MIKE** | Major Writers of America. 1962. 2v |
| **MIKL** | Reading Drama. 1950. |
| **MIL** | Play's the Thing, The. 1936. |
| **MIMN** | Minnesota Showcase: Four Plays. 1975. |
| **MIN** | Minor Elizabethan Drama. 1913. 2v |
| **MIO** | Minor Elizabethan Drama. 1939. 2v |
| **MIR** | Minor Elizabethan Tragedies. 1974. |
| **MISC** | Miscellaneous Plays. 2000. |
| **MIT** | Red Pear Garden: 3 Great Dramas of Revolutionary China, The. 1974. |
| **MLAB** | Modern ASEAN Plays. Brunei Darussalam. 1994. |
| **MLAM** | Modern ASEAN Plays. Malaysia. 1993. |
| **MLAP** | Modern ASEAN Plays. Philippines. 1992. |
| **MLAS** | Modern ASEAN Plays. Singapore. 1991. |
| **MLAT** | Modern ASEAN Plays. Thailand. 1994. |
| **MNOD** | Modern Nordic Plays: Denmark. 1974. |
| **MNOF** | Modern Nordic Plays: Finland. 1973. |
| **MNOI** | Modern Nordic Plays: Iceland. 1973. |
| **MNON** | Modern Nordic Plays: Norway. 1974. |
| **MNOS** | Modern Nordic Plays: Sweden. 1973. |
| **MOAD** | Modern Drama in America, Volume 1. 1982. |
| **MOADE** | Modern Israeli Drama: An Anthology. 1983. |
| **MOCPD** | Modern Persian Drama: An Anthology. 1987. |
| **MOD** | Modern Plays. 1937. |
| **MODS** | Modern Scandinavian Plays. 1954. |
| **MOE** | Mondala: Literature for Critical Analysis. 1970. |
| **MOGS** | Monologues: Plays from Martinique, France, Algeria, Quebec. 1995. |
| **MON** | Experience of Literature, The. 1966. |
| **MONA** | Experience of Literature, The. 2nd ed. 1970. |
| **MONB** | Theatrical Landmarks. 1983–1987. 4v |
| **MONCC** | Culture Clash: Life, Death, and Revolutionary Comedy. 1998. |
| **MONR** | Dramas from the American Theatre, 1762–1909. 1966. |
| **MONV** | Elizabethan Age. 1965. |
| **MOO** | Representative English Dramas. 1929. |
| **MOR** | English Plays, 1660–1820. 1935. |
| **MORR** | Four English Comedies of the 17th and 18th centuries. 1950, 1962. |
| **MORT** | College English: The First Year. 4th ed. 1964. |
| **MORV** | College English: The First Year. 5th ed. 1968. |
| **MORW** | College English: The First Year. 6th ed. 1973. |
| **MORWA** | College English: The First Year. 7th ed. 1978. |
| **MORWB** | College English: The First Year. 8th ed. 1983. |
| **MORX** | Imaginative Literature: Fiction, Drama, Poetry. 1968. |

| | |
|---|---|
| **MORXB** | Imaginative Literature: Fiction, Drama, Poetry. 2nd ed. 1973. |
| **MORXD** | Imaginative Literature: Fiction, Drama, Poetry. 3rd ed. 1978. |
| **MORXE** | Imaginative Literature: Fiction, Drama, Poetry. 4th ed. 1983. |
| **MOS** | Moscow Art Theatre Series of Russian Plays. 1923. |
| **MOSA** | Moscow Art Theatre Series of Russian Plays, Direction of Morris Gest. 2nd Series. 1923. |
| **MOSE** | British Plays from the Restoration to 1820. 1929. 2v |
| **MOSG** | Dramas of Modernism and Their Forerunners. 1931. |
| **MOSH** | Dramas of Modernism and Their Forerunners. Rev. ed. 1941. |
| **MOSJ** | Representative American Dramas, National and Local. 1926. |
| **MOSK** | Representative American Dramas, National and Local. Rev. ed. 1933. |
| **MOSL** | Representative American Dramas, National and Local. Rev. and Brought up-to-date. 1941. |
| **MOSN** | Representative British Dramas, Victorian and Modern. 1918. |
| **MOSO** | Representative British Dramas, Victorian and Modern. New rev. ed. 1931. |
| **MOSQ** | Representative Continental Dramas, Revolutionary and Transitional. 1924. |
| **MOSS** | Representative Plays by American Dramatists. 1918–25. 3v |
| **MOST** | Most Popular Plays of the American Theatre: Ten of Broadway's Longest-running Plays, The. 1979. |
| **MURD** | Exploring Relationships through Drama: Three Plays for Performance and Discussion. 1990. |
| **MURP** | Greek and Roman Classics in Translation. 1947. |
| **MYB** | My Best Play. 1934. |
| **MYSCC** | Mysteries at Canterbury Cathedral, The. 1986. |
| **MYTH** | Mythic Women/Real Women: Plays and Performance Pieces by Women. 2000. |
| **N-TOW** | The N-town Play: Cotton MS Vespasian D.8. Vol. 1: Introduction and Text, The. 1991. |
| **NAGE** | Drama in Our Time. 1948. |
| **NEI** | Chief Elizabethan Dramatists, Excluding Shakespeare, The. 1911. |
| **NELS** | Contemporary Trends: American Literature since 1900. 1949. |
| **NELSDI** | Strictly Dishonorable and other Lost American Plays. 1986. |
| **NER** | Nero & other Plays. 1904. |
| **NES** | Elizabethan Plays. 1971. |
| **NET** | British Dramatists from Dryden to Sheridan. 1939. |
| **NEVI** | This England. 1956. |
| **NEWA** | New American Plays. 1965–71. 4v |
| **NEWAMP** | New American Plays. 1992. 2v |
| **NEWCAD1** | New Canadian Drama. 1980. |
| **NEWCAD2** | New Canadian Drama 2. 1981. |
| **NEWCAD3** | New Canadian Drama 3: Alberta Dramatists. 1984. |
| **NEWCAD4** | New Canadian Drama 4: Manitoba Dramatists. 1986. |
| **NEWCAD5** | New Canadian Drama 5: Political Drama. 1991. |
| **NEWCAD6** | New Canadian Drama 6: Feminist Drama. 1993. |
| **NEWCAD7** | New Canadian Drama 7: West Coast Comedies. 1999. |
| **NEWCAD8** | New Canadian Drama 8: Speculative Drama. 2002. |
| **NEWDAN** | New Danish Plays. 1996. |
| **NEWDI** | New Directions in Prose and Poetry. 1936–1955. 15v |
| **NEWDR1** | New Drama One. 1972. |
| **NEWDR2** | New Drama Two. 1972. |
| **NEWE** | New English Dramatists. 1958–1971. 14v |
| **NEWFPA** | New French Plays. 1989. |
| **NEWFPB** | New French Plays. 2000. |
| **NEWFPL** | New French-language Plays: Martinique, Quebec, Ivory Coast, Belgium. 1993. |
| **NEWJV** | New Jewish Voices: Plays Produced by the Jewish Repertory Theatre. 1985. |
| **NEWL** | New Lafayette Theatre Presents: Plays with Aesthetic Comments by 6 Black Playwrights. 1974. |
| **NEWNOR** | New Norwegian Plays. 1989. |
| **NEWP** | New Plays by Women. 1979. |
| **NEWPAB** | New Plays from the Abbey Theatre. 1996–2001. 3v |
| **NEWQ** | New Plays USA: 1. 1982. |
| **NEWQA** | New Plays USA: 2. 1984. |
| **NEWQB** | New Plays USA: 3. 1986. |
| **NEWQC** | New Plays USA: 4. 1988. |

| | |
|---|---|
| **NEWR** | New Playwrights: The Best Plays of . . . (1998–2000). |
| **NEWS** | New Road. 1943–47. 5v |
| **NEWT** | New Swedish Plays. 1992. |
| **NEWV** | New Voices in the American Theatre. 1955. |
| **NEWWD** | New Welsh Drama. 1998–2006. 3v |
| **NEWWP** | New Woman Plays. 1991. |
| **NEWWT** | New Women's Theatre: 10 Plays by Contemporary American Women, The. 1977. |
| **NEWWUX** | New Works 1. 1987. |
| **NEWWW** | New World Writing. 1952–1956. 10v |
| **NIC** | Lesser English Comedies of the Eighteenth Century. 1927. |
| **NIL** | Nine Plays of the Modern Theater. 1981. |
| **NIN** | Nineteenth-Century Shakespeare Burlesques. 1977. 5v |
| **NOEL** | Caribbean Plays for Playing, 1985. |
| **NOH** | 'Noh', or Accomplishment: A Study of the Classical Stage of Japan. 1999. (originally published in 1916) |
| **NOR** | Ten Spanish Farces of the 16th, 17th, and 18th Centuries. 1974. |
| **NORALW** | Norton Anthology of Literature by Women, The. 1985. |
| **NORALWA** | Norton Anthology of Literature by Women: The Traditions in English, The. 2nd ed. 1996. |
| **NORG** | The Norton Anthology of World Masterpieces. 4th Continental ed. 1980. |
| **NORGA** | Norton Anthology of World Masterpieces, The. 5th Continental ed. 1987. |
| **NORI** | Norton Anthology of World Masterpieces, The. 4th ed. 1979. 2v |
| **NORIA** | Norton Anthology of World Masterpieces, The. 5th ed. 1985. 2v |
| **NORIB** | Norton Anthology of World Masterpieces, The. 6th ed. 1992. 2v |
| **NORIC** | Norton Anthology of World Masterpieces, The. 7th ed. 1997. 2v |
| **NORJ** | Norton Anthology of World Masterpieces, The. Expanded ed. 1995. 2v. |
| **NORJA** | Norton Anthology of World Masterpieces, The. Expanded ed. in One Volume. |
| **NOTH** | Ethnicities: Plays from the New West. 1999. |
| **NOY** | Masterpieces of the Russian Drama. 1933. |
| **NTIR** | Roots and Blossoms: African American Plays for Today. 1991. |
| **OAM** | Greek Literature in Translation. 1944. |
| **OAT** | Complete Greek Drama, The. 1938. 2v |
| **OATH** | Seven Famous Greek Plays. 1950. |
| **OBG** | Obie Winners: The Best of Off-Broadway, The. 1980. |
| **OBI** | Onitsha Market Literature. 1972. |
| **OBSE** | Observer Plays, The. 1958. |
| **OCONNC** | Contemporary Spanish Theater: The Social Comedies of the Sixties. 1983. |
| **OCONNF** | Plays of Protest from the Franco Era. 1981. |
| **OCONNP** | Plays of the New Democratic Spain (1975–1990). 1992. |
| **OFF** | Off Broadway Plays. 1971–72. 2v |
| **OHL** | Frames of Reference: An Introduction to Literature. 1974. |
| **OLH** | Elizabethan Dramatists other than Shakespeare. 1931. |
| **OLI** | Shakespeare and His fellow Dramatists. 1929. 2v |
| **OLIV** | Contemporary Black Drama. 1970. |
| **OLIW** | Voices of Change in the Spanish American Theater. 1971. |
| **ONE** | One Woman, One Voice: Plays by Sharon Morgan, Christine Watkins, Lucy Gough, Lucinda Coxon, Gwenno Dafydd. 2000. |
| **OPE** | Three Works by the Open Theater. 1974. |
| **ORI** | Oriental Literature. Rev. ed. 1960. 4v |
| **ORK** | At the Junction: Four Plays by the Junction Avenue Theatre Company. 1995. |
| **ORNC** | Elizabethan and Jacobean Comedy. 1964. |
| **ORNT** | Elizabethan and Jacobean Tragedy. 1964. |
| **ORT** | We Are Chicanos. 1973. |
| **ORZ** | Eight Plays from Off-Broadway. 1966. |
| **OSB** | On New Ground: Contemporary Hispanic-American Plays. 1987. |
| **OSBW** | The Way we Live Now: American Plays & the AIDS Crisis. 1990. |
| **OSME** | Gay Sweatshop: Four Plays and a Company. 1989. |
| **OULD** | Book of the P.E.N., The. 1950. |
| **OUT** | Out from Under: Texts by Women Performance Artists. 1990. |

| | |
|---|---|
| **OWEC** | Irish Drama, 1900–1980. 1990. |
| **OWER** | Spontaneous Combustion: 8 New American Plays. 1972. |
| **OXF** | Oxford Anthology of American Literature. 1938. |
| **OXFC** | Oxford Anthology of Canadian Literature, The. 1973. |
| **PAIS** | Paris Stage: Recent Plays, The. 1988. |
| **PAJ** | Adventures in Playmaking: 4 Plays by Carolina Playmakers. 1968. |
| **PAR** | English Drama: An Anthology, 900–1642, The. 1935. |
| **PARR** | Old Plays for Modern Players. 1930. |
| **PARRI** | Parricidio a la utopia: El teatro argentine actual en 4 claves mayors, Del. 1993. |
| **PARRY** | Three Renaissance Travel Plays. 1995. |
| **PARV** | Generation of 1898 and after, The. 1961. |
| **PASS** | Passions and Poisons: New Canadian Prose, Poetry, and Plays. 1987. |
| **PATM** | Patterns of Literature. 1967. 4v |
| **PATP** | Patterns of Literature. 1969. |
| **PATR** | Black Theatre: A 20th Century Collection of the Best Playwrights. 1971. |
| **PATT** | Representative Spanish Authors. 1942. 2v in 1 |
| **PEN** | Dramas by Present-Day Writers. 1927. |
| **PENG** | Penguin Book of Modern Canadian Drama. 1984. |
| **PER** | Black Female Playwrights: An Anthology of Plays before 1950. 1989. |
| **PERA** | Black South African Women: An Anthology of Plays. 1998. |
| **PERC** | Contemporary Plays by Women of Color: An Anthology. 1996. |
| **PERF** | Strange Fruit: Plays on Lynching by American Women. 1998. |
| **PERKY** | Major Plays of the Canadian Theatre, 1934–1984. 1984. |
| **PERR** | Plays for Stage and Screen. 1989–1998. 3v |
| **PERS** | Dimensions of Drama. 1973. |
| **PERT** | Literature: Structure, Sound and Sense. 1970. |
| **PERU** | Literature: Structure, Sound and Sense. 2nd ed. 1974. |
| **PERV** | Literature: Structure, Sound and Sense. 3rd ed. 1978. |
| **PERW** | Literature: Structure, Sound and Sense. 4th ed. 1983. |
| **PERX** | Literature: Structure, Sound and Sense. 5th ed. 1988. |
| **PERY** | Literature: Structure, Sound and Sense. 6th ed. 1993. |
| **PERZ** | Perrine's Literature: Structure, Sound and Sense. 7th ed. 1998. |
| **PES** | Perspectives: An Anthology. 1976. |
| **PETER** | The Plays of CODCO. 1992. |
| **PETERS** | Stars in the Sky Morning: Collective Plays of Newfoundland and Labrador. 1996. |
| **PFIS** | Tremendous Worlds: Australia Women's Drama 1890–1960. 1999. |
| **PHI** | Trumpets Sounding: Propaganda Plays of the American Revolution. 1972. |
| **PHIL** | Philippine Drama: Twelve Plays in Six Philippine Languages. 1987. |
| **PIC** | Treasury of Drama: Classical through Modern, A. 1975. |
| **PIE** | Fiction and Fantasy of German Romance. 1927. |
| **PIET** | Five African Plays. 1972. |
| **PING** | Playful Phoenix: Women Write for the Singapore Stage. 1996. |
| **PLA** | Places, Please!: The First Anthology of Lesbian Plays. 1985. |
| **PLAA** | Playbook: Five Plays for a New Theatre. 1956. |
| **PLAAB** | Playboy of the Western World and Two other Irish Plays, The. 1987. |
| **PLAAC** | Playmakers, The. 1976. 2v |
| **PLAAD** | Plays by American Women: The Early Years. 1981. |
| **PLAAE** | Plays by American Women: 1900–1930. 1985. |
| **PLAAF** | Plays by American Women: 1930–1960. 1994. |
| **PLAAG** | Plays by French and Francophone Women: A Critical Anthology. 1994. |
| **PLAB** | Plays by Greek, Spanish, French, German and English Dramatists. Rev. ed. 1900. 2v |
| **PLABE** | Plays by Women. 1983–1994. 10v |
| **PLABI** | Plays by Women: An International Anthology. 1988–1996. 3v |
| **PLAC** | Plays for a New Theater: Play Book 2. 1966. |
| **PLACA** | Plays for Actresses. 1997. |
| **PLACB** | Plays for the Nuclear Age. 1989. |
| **PLACC** | Plays from Black Australia. 1989. |

| | |
|---|---|
| **PLACD** | Plays from the Circle Repertory Company. 1986. |
| **PLACE** | Plays from Padua Hills 1982. 1983. |
| **PLACF** | Plays from Playwrights Horizon. 1987. |
| **PLACG** | Plays from South Coast Repertory. 1993–1998. 2v |
| **PLACGH** | Plays from South Coast Repertory: Hispanic Playwrights Project Anthology. 2000. |
| **PLACHA** | Plays from the Contemporary American Theater. 1988. |
| **PLACHB** | Plays from the Contemporary British Theater. 1992. |
| **PLACI** | Plays from the New York Shakespeare Festival. 1986. |
| **PLACJ** | Plays from Woolly Mammoth. 1999. |
| **PLACK** | Plays Introduction: Plays by New Writers. 1984. |
| **PLAD** | Plays of a Half-Decade. 1933. |
| **PLAG** | Plays of the Greek Dramatists. 1946. |
| **PLAH** | Plays of the Moscow Art Theatre Musical Studio. 1925. |
| **PLAJ** | Plays of the Sixties. 1966–1967. 2v |
| **PLAL** | Plays of the Thirties. 1966–1967. 2v |
| **PLAN** | Plays of the Year. 1949–1980. 48v |
| **PLAP** | Plays of To-day. 1925–1930. 3v |
| **PLAU** | Plays on a Human Theme. 1979. |
| **PLAWE** | Playwrights of Exile: An International Anthology: France, Romania, Quebec, Algeria, Lebanon, Cuba. 1997. |
| **POB** | Polish Romantic Drama: Three Plays in English Translation. 1977. |
| **POCH** | Masters of American Literature. 1949. 2v |
| **POLK** | Sampler of Plays by Women, A. 1990. |
| **POLL** | English Miracle Plays, Moralities and Interludes. 8th ed. rev. 1927. |
| **POOL** | England in Literature. 1953. |
| **POP** | New British Drama, The. 1964. |
| **POQ** | After Censorship: New Romanian Plays of the '90s. 2000. |
| **POR** | Portable Roman Reader, The. 1977. |
| **PRAT** | Masters of British Literature. 2nd ed. 1958, 1962. 2v |
| **PRED** | Contemporary Slovenian Drama. 1997. |
| **PRER** | Prerogatives: Contemporary Plays by Women. 1998. |
| **PRIMA** | PrimaFacie . . . : An Anthology of New American Plays. 1985–1991. 6v |
| **PRIN** | Medieval Dutch Drama: Four Secular Plays and Four Farces from the Van Hulthem Manuscript. 1999. |
| **PRO** | Reading & Writing about Literature: Fiction, Poetry, Drama, and the Essay. 1990. |
| **PROA** | Three Modern French Plays of the Imagination. 1966. |
| **PROB** | Prose and Poetry for Appreciation. 1934. |
| **PROC** | Prose and Poetry for Appreciation. 1942. |
| **PROD** | Prose and Poetry for Appreciation. 4th ed. 1950. |
| **PROF** | Prose and Poetry of America. 1934. |
| **PROG** | Prose and Poetry of America. South-Western ed. 1934. |
| **PROH** | Prose and Poetry of America. Catholic ed. 1940. |
| **PROI** | Prose and Poetry of America. 1949. |
| **PROM** | Prose and Poetry of England. 1934. |
| **PRON** | Prose and Poetry of England. Catholic ed. 1940. |
| **PROW** | Prose and Poetry of the World. 1941. |
| **PROX** | Prose and Poetry of the World. 1954. |
| **PUCC** | French Theater since 1930, The. 1954. |
| **PURK** | Three Tragedies by Renaissance Women. 1998. |
| **PURO** | Puro Teatro: A Latina Anthology. 2000. |
| **QUI** | Contemporary American Plays. 1923. |
| **QUIJ** | Representative American Plays. 1917. |
| **QUIJR** | Representative American Plays from 1880 to the Present Day. 1928. |
| **QUIK** | Representative American Plays, 1767–1923. 3rd ed. rev. and enl. 1925. |
| **QUIL** | Representative American Plays from 1767 to the Present Day. 5th ed. rev. and enl. 1930. |
| **QUIM** | Representative Plays from 1767 to the Present Day. 6th ed. rev. and enl. 1938. |
| **QUIN** | Representative American Plays from 1767 to the Present Day. 7th ed. rev. and enl. 1953. |
| **QUIO** | Literature of America, The. 1929. 2v |
| **RAI** | Modern Drama and Social Change. 1972. |

| | |
|---|---|
| **RALPH** | Boneman: An Anthology of Canadian Plays. 1995. |
| **RAP** | Sugbuanon Theatre from Sotto to Rodriguez and Kabahar: An Introduction to Pre-war Sugbuanon Drama. 1982. |
| **RAVE** | Rave: Young Adult Drama. 2000. |
| **RAVEL** | Canadian Mosaic: 6 Plays. 1995. |
| **RAVELII** | Canadian Mosaic II: 6 Plays. 1996. |
| **RAVIC** | Early Colonial Religious Drama in Mexico: From Tzompantli to Golgotha. 1970. |
| **RAVIT** | Disinherited: Plays, The. 1974. |
| **RAY** | Masters of American Literature. 1959. 2v |
| **READ** | Reading and Understanding Plays, Level I and Level II. 1989. 2v |
| **REAL** | Reality in Conflict: Literature of Values in Opposition. 1976. |
| **REAR** | Black Teacher and the Dramatic arts: A Dialogue, Bibliography, and Anthology, The. 1970. |
| **RED** | Designs in Drama. 1968. |
| **REDM** | Drama II. 1962. |
| **REEV** | Anthology of Russian Plays, An. c1961, 1963. 2v |
| **REF** | Reflections in Literature. 1975. |
| **REIL** | Classic through Modern Drama. 1970. |
| **REIN** | Drama: An Introductory Anthology. 1961. |
| **REIO** | Drama: An Introductory Anthology. Alternate ed. 1964. |
| **REIP** | Modern Drama: Nine Plays. 1961. |
| **REIT** | Modern Drama. Alternate ed. 1966. |
| **REIV** | Six Plays, an Introductory Anthology. 1973. |
| **REIW** | Thirteen Plays: An Introductory Anthology. 1978. |
| **REIWE** | Twenty-Three Plays: An Introductory Anthology. 1978. |
| **RENDW** | Renaissance Drama by Women: Texts and Documents. 1996. |
| **RES** | Restoration Plays. 1974. |
| **RESL** | Restoration Plays. 1992. |
| **REST** | Restoration Plays. 1955. |
| **RET** | Restoration Tragedies. 1977. |
| **REV** | Revolution: A Collection of Plays. 1975. |
| **RHE** | Novelists' Theatre. 1966. |
| **RHO** | Contemporary French Theatre, The. 1942. |
| **RICH** | A Study of the Types of Literature. 1921. |
| **RICHE** | Early American Drama. 1997. |
| **RICI** | Best Mystery and Suspense Plays of the Modern Theatre. 1971. |
| **RICIS** | Best Plays of the Sixties. 1970. |
| **RICJ** | Best Short Plays of the World Theatre 1958–1967. 1968. |
| **RICK** | Best Short Plays of the World Theatre, 1968–1973. 1973. |
| **RICM** | Great Musicals of the American Theatre. 1976. |
| **RICN** | Ten Classic Mystery and Suspense Plays of the Modern Theatre. 1973. |
| **RICO** | Ten Great Musicals of the American Theatre. 1973. |
| **RICT** | Tony Winners: A Collection of Ten exceptional Plays, Winner of the Tony Award for the Most Distinguished Play of the Year, The. 1977. |
| **RIL** | Heritage of American Literature, The. 1951. 2v |
| **RIR** | Plays and Pageants from the Life of the Negro. 1979. |
| **RIRA** | Plays and Pageants from the Life of the Negro. 1994. |
| **RIS** | Plays of Provocation. 1999. |
| **RITS** | Seven Expressionist Plays: Kokoschka to Barlach. 1968. |
| **RITV** | Vision and Aftermath: Four Expressionist War Plays. 1969. |
| **ROB** | Western World Literature. 1938. |
| **ROBE** | Literature of Medieval England, The. 1970. |
| **ROBI** | Anthology of Greek Drama, First Series, An. 1949. |
| **ROBJ** | Anthology of Greek Drama, Second Series, An. 1954. |
| **ROBJA** | Spring of Civilization, Periclean Athens, The. 1954. |
| **ROBK** | Genius of the Greek Drama, The. 1921. |
| **ROBM** | Harvard Dramatic Club Miracle Plays: Ten Plays, The. 1928. |
| **ROBR** | They Said You Were Too Young. 1989. |
| **ROE** | Five Russian Plays, with One from the Ukrainian. 1916. |

| | |
|---|---|
| ROEB | Balkan Plots: New Plays from Central and Eastern Europe. 2000. |
| ROES | Seven Plays by Women: Female Voices, Fighting Lives. 1991. |
| ROET | Touch of the Dutch: Plays by Women, A. 1997. |
| ROF | Introduction to Drama. 1962. |
| ROGEBD | Meridian Anthology of 18th- and 19th-Century British Drama, The. 1996. |
| ROGEW | Meridian Anthology of Restoration and Eighteenth-Century Plays by Women, The. 1994. |
| ROGEX | Explorations in Living. 1941. |
| ROHR | Introduction to Literature, An. 1968. |
| ROLF | Modern Omnibus, The. 1946. |
| ROM | Roman Drama. 1965. |
| ROMA | El espejo—The Mirror: Selected Chicano Literature. 1972. |
| ROOTS | Roots of African American Drama: An Anthology of Early Plays, The. 1991. |
| ROSENB | World Literature: An Anthology of Great Short Stories, Drama, and Poetry. 1992. |
| ROSS | Arts of Reading, The. 1960. |
| ROWC | Late Victorian Plays, 1890–1914. 1968. |
| ROWE | Nineteenth Century Plays. 1953. |
| ROY | Literary Spectrum. 1974. |
| ROYE | Literature I. 1976. |
| RUA | Four Jewish Plays. 1948. |
| RUB | Great English Plays. 1928. |
| RUDAK | Dangerous Traditions: A Passe Muraille Anthology. 1992. |
| RUN | Map of the Senses: Twenty Years of Manitoba Plays, A. 2000. |
| RUSS | Literature in English. 1948. |
| RUSSCO | Russian Comedy of the Nikolaian era. 1997. |
| RUSV | Satire, 1967. |
| RVI | Russian Satiric Comedy: Six Plays. 1983. |
| RYL | Elizabethan Tragedy. 1933. |
| RZH | Anthology of Russian Literature from Earliest Writings to Modern Fiction: Introduction to a Culture, An. 1996. |
| SACL | Saclit Drama: Plays by South Asian Canadians. 1996. |
| SACR | Sacred Earth Dramas: An Anthology of Winning Plays from the 1990 Competition of the Sacred Earth Drama Trust. 1993. |
| SAFF | Great Farces. 1966. |
| SAFM | Great Melodramas. 1966. |
| SALA | Women Writing Women: An Anthology of Spanish-American Theater of the 1980s. 1997. |
| SALE | English Drama in Transition 1880–1920. 1968. |
| SALF | Four Jacobean City Comedies. 1975. |
| SALG | Three Jacobean Tragedies. 1965. |
| SALR | Three Restoration Comedies. 1968. |
| SALS | One Step in the Clouds: An Omnibus of Mountaineering Novels and Short Stories. 1990, 1991. |
| SAN | By popular demand: Plays and other works. 1980. |
| SAND | College Reading. 1953. |
| SANE | Synthesis: Responses to Literature. 1971. |
| SANK | Discovery of Drama, The. 1968. |
| SANL | Phaedra and Hippolytus: Myth and Dramatic Form. 1966. |
| SANM | Medea: Myth and Dramatic Form. 1967. |
| SANO | Oedipus: Myth and Dramatic Form. 1968. |
| SANR | God, Man, and Devil: Yiddish Plays in Translation. 1999. |
| SATA | Satan, Socialities, and Solly Gold: Three New Plays from England. 1961. |
| SATI | Reading Literature. 1964. |
| SATJ | Reading Literature: Stories, Plays and Poems. 1968. |
| SAY | Eleonora Duse Series of Plays, The. 1923. |
| SCAN | Scandinavian Plays of the Twentieth Century. 1944–1951. 3v |
| SCAR | 5 Comedies. 1971. |
| SCAT | English Morality Plays and Moral interludes. 1969. |
| SCH | Typical Elizabethan Plays. 1926. |
| SCI | Typical Elizabethan Plays. Rev. and enl. ed. 1931. |

| | |
|---|---|
| **SCJ** | Typical Elizabethan Plays. 3rd ed., rev. and enl. 1949. |
| **SCL** | Awake and Singing: 7 Classic Plays from the American Jewish Repertoire. 1995. |
| **SCM** | Fruitful and Multiplying: 9 Contemporary Plays from the American Jewish Repertoire. 1996. |
| **SCN** | Nouvelle anthologie française. 1936. |
| **SCNN** | Range of Literature, The. 1960. |
| **SCNO** | Range of Literature, The. 2nd ed. 1967. |
| **SCNP** | Range of Literature, The. 3rd ed. 1973. |
| **SCNPL** | Elements of Literature: Essay, Fiction, Poetry, Drama, Film. 1978. |
| **SCNQ** | Elements of Literature Five: Fiction, Poetry, Drama, Essay, Film. Rev. ed. 1982. |
| **SCNQCA** | Elements of Literature. Canadian ed. 1987. |
| **SCNQCB** | Elements of Literature. 2nd Canadian ed. 1990. |
| **SCNR** | Galaxy: Literary Modes and Genres. 1961. |
| **SCNT** | Literature of America: Twentieth Century, The. 1970. |
| **SCV** | American Place Theatre, The. 1973. |
| **SCVDO** | Drama for Reading & Performance. Collection One: Seventeen Full-length Plays for Students. 2000. 2v |
| **SCVDT** | Drama for Reading & Performance. Collection Two: Nineteen Full-length Plays for Students. 2000. 2v |
| **SCVG** | German Expressionist Plays. 1997. |
| **SCVN** | Nineteenth Century German Plays. 1990. |
| **SCW** | Early English Plays. 1928. |
| **SCWE** | Adventures in American Literature. 1930. |
| **SCWG** | Adventures in American Literature. Rev. ed. 1936. |
| **SCWI** | Adventures in Appreciation. 1935. |
| **SCX** | Reading and Writing from Literature. 1997. |
| **SCY** | Traditional Chinese Plays. 1967–75. 3v |
| **SDQ** | Scribner Quarto of Modern Literature, The. 1978. |
| **SEA** | Seven French Plays (1730–1897). 1935. |
| **SEARS** | Testifyin': Contemporary African Canadian Drama. 2000–2003. 2v |
| **SEBO** | Readings in European Literature. 1928. |
| **SEBP** | Readings in European Literature. 2nd ed. 1946. |
| **SECK** | Eighteen-nineties, The. 1948. |
| **SECO** | 2nd Conference for Asian Women and Theater: A Compilation of Plays, The. 2000. |
| **SEIS** | 6 Dramaturgos españoles del siglo XX: Teatro de liberación, vol. 1: Teatro en democracia, vol. 2. 1988. 2v |
| **SEIS** | Teatro de liberación. *See* 6 Dramaturgos españoles del siglo XX, v. 1. 1988. |
| **SEIS** | Teatro en democracia. *See* 6 Dramaturgos españoles del siglo XX, v. 2. |
| **SELF** | Classic Drama. 1998. |
| **SELOV** | Lovesick: Modernist Plays of Same-Sex Love, 1894–1925. 1999. |
| **SEN** | Plays: Wadsworth Handbook and Anthology. 1970. |
| **SER** | Nine Classic French Plays. 1936. |
| **SERD** | Three Classic French Plays. 1935. |
| **SET** | Five French Comedies. 1925. |
| **SETR** | Best of the Fest: A Collection of New Plays Celebrating 10 Years of London New Play Festival. 1998. |
| **SEUC** | Seven Cannons: Plays. 2000. |
| **SEV** | Seven Plays. 1935. |
| **SEVD** | Seven Plays of the Modern Theatre. 1962. |
| **SEVE** | Seven Sacred Plays. 1934. |
| **SEVP** | Seven Soviet Plays. 1946. |
| **SEVT** | Seventeen Plays: Sophocles to Baraka. 1976. |
| **SHA** | American Literature. 1926. 2v |
| **SHAH** | From Beowulf to Thomas Hardy. 1924. 2v |
| **SHAI** | From Beowulf to Thomas Hardy. Rev. ed. 1931. 2v |
| **SHAJ** | From Beowulf to Thomas Hardy. New ed. 1939. 2v |
| **SHAK** | Shakespeare the Sadist. 1977. |
| **SHAR** | English and Continental Literature. 1950. |
| **SHAT** | Contemporary Canadian Drama. 1974. |
| **SHAV** | Collection of Readings for Writers: Book Three of A Complete Course in Freshman English, A. 6th ed. 1967. |
| **SHAW** | Complete Course in Freshman English, A. 5th ed. 1959. |
| **SHAX** | Complete Course in Freshman English, A. 7th ed. 1973. |

| | |
|---|---|
| **SHAY** | Treasury of Plays for Women, A. 1922. |
| **SHER** | Lively Arts: 4 Representative Types, The. 1964. |
| **SHEW** | Out Front: Contemporary Gay and Lesbian Plays. 1988. |
| **SHIM** | Noh, The. 1972–1998. 8v |
| **SHIM** | Restless Spirits from the Japanese Noh Plays of the Fourth Group. 1995. *See* The Noh, v. 4, bk. 1 |
| **SHIM** | Troubled Souls from Japanese Noh Plays of the Fourth Group. 1998. *See* The Noh, v. 4, bk. 2 |
| **SHIM** | Warrior Ghost Plays from the Japanese Theater. 1993. *See* The Noh, v. 2, bk. 2 |
| **SHOW** | Showing West: Three Prairie Docu-Dramas. 1982. |
| **SHR** | Reading for Understanding: Fiction, Drama, Poetry. 1968. |
| **SHRCD** | Conscious Reader, The. 4th ed. 1988. |
| **SHRCE** | Conscious Reader, The. 5th ed. 1992. |
| **SHRCF** | Conscious Reader, The. 6th ed. 1995. |
| **SHRCG** | Conscious Reader, The. 7th ed. 1998. |
| **SHRO** | Types of Drama. 1970. |
| **SIG** | Signet Classic Book of 18th- and 19th-Century British Drama, The. 1979. |
| **SILK** | Quartet: A Book of Stories, Plays, Poems and Critical Essays. 1970. |
| **SILKI** | Quartet: A Book of Stories, Plays, Poems and Critical Essays. 2nd ed. 1973. |
| **SILM** | Trio: A Book of stories, Plays, and Poems. 1962. |
| **SILN** | Trio: A Book of stories, Plays and Poems. 3rd ed. 1970. |
| **SILO** | Trio: A Book of stories, Plays and Poems. 4th ed. 1975. |
| **SILP** | Trio: A Book of stories, Plays and Poems. 5th ed. 1980. |
| **SILS** | Trio: A Book of stories, Plays and Poems. 6th ed. 1987. |
| **SIM** | American Reader, The. 1941. |
| **SIN** | Introduction to Literature, An. 1966. |
| **SIXA** | Six Canadian Plays. 1992. |
| **SIXB** | Six Great Modern Plays. 1956. |
| **SIXC** | Six Modern American Plays. 1951. |
| **SIXD** | Six Plays. 1930. |
| **SIXH** | Six Plays. 1934. |
| **SIXL** | Six Plays of 1939. 1939. |
| **SIXN** | Six Nuevomexicano Folk Dramas for Advent Season. 1999. |
| **SIXP** | Six Plays of Today. 1939. |
| **SLAT** | Three Pre-Surrealist Plays. 1997. |
| **SMA** | Making of Drama, The. 1972. |
| **SMB** | Russian Mirror: Three Plays by Russian Women. 1998. |
| **SMC** | Best off off-Broadway, The. 1969. |
| **SME** | More Plays from off off-Broadway. 1972. |
| **SMI** | Types of Domestic Tragedy. 1928. |
| **SMK** | Types of Historical Drama. 1928. |
| **SML** | Types of Philosophic Drama. 1928. |
| **SMN** | Types of Romantic Drama. 1928. |
| **SMO** | Types of Social Comedy. 1928. |
| **SMP** | Types of World Tragedy. 1928. |
| **SMR** | Types of Farce Comedy. 1928. |
| **SNO** | China on Stage: An American Actress in the People's Republic. 1972. |
| **SNYD** | Book of English Literature, A. 4th ed. 1942–43. 2v |
| **SOK** | Anthology of German Expressionist Drama: A Prelude to the Absurd. 1963. |
| **SOM** | Dramatic Experience: The Public Voice. 1970. |
| **SOMA** | Literary Experience: Public and Private Voices. 1971. |
| **SOME** | Four Tudor interludes. 1974. |
| **SOSGA** | Women's Acts: Plays by Women Dramatists of Spain's Golden Age. 1997. |
| **SOUL** | Theatre of the Mind, The. 1974. |
| **SOUT** | South African People's Plays: ons phola hi. 1981. |
| **SPC** | Spearhead: 10 Years' Experimental Writing in America. 1947. |
| **SPD** | British Literature. 1951. 2v |
| **SPDB** | British Literature. 2nd ed. 1963. 2v |
| **SPE** | Elizabethan Plays. 1933. |

| | |
|---|---|
| **SPEF** | British Literature. 1951, 1952. 2v |
| **SPER** | Favorite Modern Plays. 1953. |
| **SPES** | Living American Plays. 1954. |
| **SPI** | Roots of National Culture: American Literature to 1830, The. 1933. |
| **SPR** | Genius of the Scandinavian Theater, The. 1964. |
| **SRY** | High Lights in English Literature and other Selections. 1940. |
| **SRYG** | High Lights in English Literature. 1940. |
| **SSSF** | Twentieth Century American Writing. 1965. |
| **SSSI** | Stages of Drama: Classical to Contemporary Theater. 1981. |
| **SSSIA** | Stages of Drama: Classical to Contemporary Theater. 2nd ed. 1991. |
| **SSSIB** | Stages of Drama: Classical to Contemporary Theater. 3rd ed. 1995. |
| **SSSIC** | Stages of Drama: Classical to Contemporary Theater. 4th ed. 1999. |
| **SSSN** | Staging the North: Twelve Canadian Plays. 1999. |
| **SSST** | Creative Reader, The. 1954. |
| **SSSU** | Creative Reader, The. 2nd ed. 1962. |
| **SSTA** | Three Anglo-Irish Plays. 1943. |
| **SSTE** | Plays of the Southern Americas. 1942. |
| **SSTF** | Treehouse: An Introduction to Literature, The. 1974. |
| **SSTG** | Camille and other Plays. 1957. |
| **SSTW** | Eight Spanish Plays of the Golden Age. 1964. |
| **SSTX** | Stars in the morning sky: Five New Plays from the Soviet Union. 1989. |
| **SSTY** | Broadway's Beautiful Losers. 1972. |
| **STA** | Progress of Drama through the Centuries, The. 1927. |
| **STAT** | Adventures in Modern Literature. 1939. |
| **STAU** | Adventures in Modern Literature. 2nd ed. 1944. |
| **STAV** | Adventures in Modern Literature. 3rd ed. |
| **STE** | Plays from the Modern Theatre. 1931. |
| **STEI** | Aspects of Modern Drama. 1960. |
| **STI** | Das Deutsche Drama, 1880–1933. 1938. 2v |
| **STJ** | Omnibus of French Literature. 1941. 2v |
| **STJM** | Literature for Writing. 1962. |
| **STJN** | Literature for Writing. 2nd ed. 1967. |
| **STL** | American Literature Survey. 1962. 4v |
| **STM** | Types of English Drama, 1660–1780. 1923. |
| **STN** | NeXtFest Anthology: Plays from the Syncrude NeXt Generation Arts Festival, 1996–2000. 2000. |
| **STOC** | Recueil de lectures. 1950. |
| **STORJ** | Story of Joseph in Spanish Golden Age Drama, The. 1998. |
| **STOTD** | Harbrace Anthology of Drama, The. 1994. |
| **STOTLA** | HBJ Anthology of Literature, The. 1993. |
| **STOTLB** | Harbrace Anthology of Literature, The. 2nd ed. 1998. |
| **STRA** | Strawberries, Potatoes, and Other Fantasies: Plays from Trinity College. 1988. |
| **STRI** | Strike while the Iron Is Hot: Three Plays on Sexual Politics. 1980. |
| **STRO** | Literature of Comedy: An Anthology, The. 1968. |
| **STS** | Structure and Meaning: An Introduction to Literature. 1976. |
| **STUA** | Stuart Academic Drama: An Edition of Three University Plays. 1987. |
| **STUR** | Three Elizabethan Domestic Tragedies. 1985. |
| **STURM** | Sturm und drang. 1992. |
| **STY** | Challenge of the Theatre, The. 1972. |
| **SUB** | Plays by and about Women. 1973. |
| **SUL** | Literature: An Introduction. 1960. |
| **SUM** | Restoration Comedies. 1921. |
| **SUMB** | Shakespeare Adaptations. 1922. |
| **SUT** | Ideas and Patterns in Literature. 1970. 4v |
| **SUTL** | Journeys: An Introduction to Literature. 1971. |
| **SVICH** | Out of the Fringe: Contemporary Latina/Latino Theatre and Performance. 2000. |
| **SWA** | Man and the Gods: Three Tragedies. 1964. |
| **SWANS** | Playwrights of Color. 1999. |

| | |
|---|---|
| **SWI** | Three Distinctive Plays about Abraham Lincoln. 1961. |
| **SWIT** | Great Christian Plays. 1956. |
| **SWO** | Twelve Plays of Christmas: Traditional and Modern Plays for the Holidays, The. 2000. |
| **SYM** | Two Voices: Writing about Literature. 1976. |
| **SZO** | 3 Contemporary Brazilian Plays in Bilingual Edition. 1988. |
| **TAFT** | Minor Knickerbockers. 1947. |
| **TAK** | Modern Japanese Drama, an Anthology. 1979. |
| **TAT** | Representative English Plays. 1916. |
| **TAU** | Representative English Plays. 2nd ed. rev. and enl. 1938. |
| **TAUB** | Israeli Holocaust Drama. 1996. |
| **TAUJ** | Ritual, Realism, and Revolt: Major Traditions in the Drama. 1972. |
| **TAV** | European and Asiatic Plays. 1936. |
| **TAY** | Eighteenth Century Comedy. 1929. |
| **TEN** | Ten Greek Plays. 1930. |
| **TENN** | Tenth Muse: Classical Drama in Translation. 1980. |
| **TEX** | Texas Plays. 1990. |
| **TEZ** | Three Contemporary Hungarian Plays. 1992. |
| **THA** | Best Elizabethan Plays, The. 1890. |
| **THB** | Theater and Politics: An International Anthology. 1990. |
| **THC** | Theater and Society: An Anthology of Contemporary Chinese Drama. 1998. |
| **THEA** | Theatre. 1953–56. 1953–56. 4v |
| **THEC** | Theatre for Tomorrow. 1940. |
| **THF** | Theatre Guild Anthology, The. 1936. |
| **THG** | Theatre of Images, The. 1977. |
| **THGA** | Theatre of Images, The. 1996. |
| **THH** | Theatre Omnibus. 1938. |
| **THL** | Theatre of the Holocaust: Four Plays, The. 1982. |
| **THLA** | Theatre of the Holocaust, Volume 2: Six Plays, The. 1999. |
| **THMD** | Four Georgian and Pre-Revolutionary Plays. 1998. |
| **THMF** | Six Restoration and French Neoclassic Plays. 1998. |
| **THO** | Plays and the Theatre. 1937. |
| **THOD** | Theatre Today. 1965. |
| **THOM** | Our Heritage of World Literature. 1938. |
| **THON** | Our Heritage of World Literature. Rev. ed. 1942. |
| **THOP** | Three Australian Plays. 1963. |
| **THOQ** | Three Danish Comedies. 1999. |
| **THOR** | Three East European Plays. 1970. |
| **THOS** | Three French Comedies. 1996. |
| **THP** | Three Great Greek Plays. 1960. |
| **THQ** | Three Great Jewish Plays. 1986. |
| **THR** | Three Late Medieval Morality Plays. 1981. |
| **THRCD** | Three Masterpieces of Cuban Drama. 2000. |
| **THRIN** | Three Modern Indian Plays. 1989. |
| **THS** | Three Modern Plays from the French. 1914. |
| **THT** | Three Negro Plays. 1969. |
| **THTN** | Three Nigerian Plays. 1967. |
| **THU** | Three Plays. 1926. |
| **THUAA** | Three Plays by Asian Australians. 2000. |
| **THUG** | Three Political Plays. 1980. |
| **THV** | Three Popular French Comedies. 1975. |
| **THW** | Three Rastell Plays: Four Elements, Cafisto and Melebea, Gentleness and Nobility. 1979. |
| **THWI** | Three Sanskrit Plays. 1981. |
| **THWO** | Three Sixteenth-Century Comedies. 1984. |
| **THX** | Three Southwest Plays. 1942. |
| **THY** | Three Soviet Plays. 1961. |
| **THZ** | Three Tudor Classical Interludes: Thersites, Jacke Jugeler, Horestes. 1982. |
| **TICK** | Restoration Dramatists. 1930. |

| | |
|---|---|
| **TICO** | Shakespeare's Predecessors. 1929. |
| **TIME** | Time to Go: Three Plays on Death and Dying, with Commentary on End-of-Life Issues. 1995. |
| **TOB** | To Be: Identity in Literature. 1976. |
| **TOBI** | College Book of English Literature. 1949. |
| **TOD** | Today's Literature. 1935. |
| **TOR** | Torch to the Heart: Anthology of Lesbian Art and Drama. 1994. |
| **TOU** | Touchstones: Classic Texts in the Humanities. 1991. |
| **TOV** | Towneley Plays, The. Volume One: Introduction and Text. 1994. |
| **TOWN** | Towneley Plays. The Wakefield Mystery Plays. 1961. |
| **TOWN** | Wakefield Mystery Plays, The. 1961. |
| **TRAD** | Traditional Korean Theatre. 1988. |
| **TRAN** | Transformation, Miracles, and Mischief: The Mountain Priest Plays of Kyōgen. 1993. |
| **TRE** | Treasury of the Theatre . . . from Aeschylus to Eugene O'Neill, A. 1935. |
| **TREA** | Treasury of the Theatre . . . rev. and adapted for Colleges, A. 1940. 2v |
| **TREB** | Treasury of the Theatre . . . from Aeschylus to Ostrovsky, A. 3rd ed. 1967. |
| **TREBA** | Treasury of the Theatre: from Henrik Ibsen to Eugene Ionesco, A. 3rd College ed. 1960. |
| **TREBJ** | Treasury of the Theatre, A. 4th ed. 1970. |
| **TREC** | Treasury of the Theatre . . . A. Rev. ed. for Colleges. 1950–51. 2v |
| **TREE** | Treasury of the Theatre . . . A. Rev. ed. 1951. 3v |
| **TREI** | Treasury of the Theatre, A. Rev. ed. 1963. 3v |
| **TRES** | Tres Dramas romanticos. 1962. |
| **TRI** | Experience of Literature, The. 1967. |
| **TRIA** | Experience of Literature, The. 1967. |
| **TRUE** | True Misteries and a Chronicle Play of Peterborough Cathedral. 1997. |
| **TRUS** | Burlesque Plays of the Eighteenth Century. 1969. |
| **TUCD** | Modern American and British Plays. 1931. |
| **TUCG** | Modern Continental Plays. 1929. |
| **TUCJ** | Modern Plays. 1932. |
| **TUCM** | Twenty-Five Modern Plays. 1931. |
| **TUCN** | Twenty-Five Modern Plays . . . Rev. ed. 1948. |
| **TUCO** | Twenty-Five Modern Plays. 3rd ed. 1953. |
| **TUP** | Representative English Dramas from Dryden to Sheridan. 1914. |
| **TUQ** | Representative English Dramas from Dryden to Sheridan. New and enl. ed. 1934. |
| **TUQH** | Turkish Literature. Rev. ed. 1901. |
| **TUQT** | Black Drama in America: An Anthology. 1971. |
| **TUQTR** | Black Drama in America: An Anthology. 2nd ed. 1994. |
| **TUR** | Contemporary Spanish Dramatists. 1919. |
| **TWE** | Twelve Famous Plays of the Restoration and Eighteenth Century. 1933. |
| **TWEH** | Twentieth-Century Chinese Drama: An Anthology. 1983. |
| **TWEI** | Twentieth Century Italian Drama: An Anthology: The First Fifty Years. 1995. |
| **TWEN** | Twentieth-Century Polish Avant-Garde Drama: Plays, Scenarios, Critical Documents. 1977. |
| **TYDE** | Four Tudor Comedies. 1984. |
| **TYEW** | War Plays by Women: An International Anthology. 1999. |
| **TYLG** | Granny Mountains: A Cycle of Nō Plays. 1992. (Vol. 2 of 2v set. *See* TYLP for v.1) |
| **TYLJ** | Japanese Nō Dramas. 1992. |
| **TYLP** | Pining wind: A Cycle of Nō Plays. 1992. (Vol. 1 of 2v set. *See* TYLG for v.2) |
| **UHL** | Best Eighteenth Century Comedies, The. 1929. |
| **ULAN** | Makers of the Modern Theater. 1961. |
| **UNO** | Unbroken thread: An Anthology of Plays by Asian American Women. 1993. |
| **UNTE** | Britannica Library of Great American Writing, The. 1960. 2v |
| **UPOR** | Hungarian Plays: New Drama from Hungary. 1996. |
| **VAN** | Borzoi Reader, The. 1936. |
| **VANM** | Modern American Prose. 1934. |
| **VANV** | Continental Literature: An Anthology. 1968. 2v |
| **VENA** | Drama and Performance: An Anthology. 1996. |
| **VER** | Verity Bargate Award: New Plays 1986. 1987. |
| **VERI** | Verity Bargate: The 1988 Award-Winning New Plays. 1989. |

| | |
|---|---|
| **VICK** | From Valley Playwrights Theatre. 1986–1989. 2v |
| **VICT** | Victorian Melodramas: Seven English, French, and American Melodramas. 1976. |
| **VIET** | Vietnam, Perspectives & Performance: Two Plays about Real People Affected by the Legacy of the Vietnam Conflict, Told in Their Own Words from Their Own Experiences. 1996. |
| **VIT** | Three Turk Plays from Early Modern England: Selimus, A Christian Turned Turk, and The Renegado. 2000. |
| **VOAD** | Four Good Plays to Read and Act. 1941. |
| **VOI** | Voices: Plays for Studying the Holocaust. 1999. |
| **VOLI** | Introduction to Literature: Drama, An. 1967. |
| **VOLP** | Poetry, Drama, Fiction. 1967. |
| **VONG** | Mass Culture in Soviet Russia: Tales, Poems, Songs, Movies, Plays, and Folklore, 1917–1953. 1995. |
| **VONS** | Western Literature. 1971. 3v |
| **VORE** | New Plays for Mature Actors: An Anthology. 1987. |
| **VOTE** | How the Vote Was Won, and other Suffragette Plays. 1985. |
| **WAGC** | Our Reading Heritage. 1956. 4v |
| **WAGE** | Read up on Life. 1952. |
| **WAGN** | Canada's Lost Plays. 1978–80. 3v |
| **WAGNOX** | Oxford Book of Women's Writing in the United States, The. 1995. |
| **WAIT** | Literature for Our Time. Rev. ed. 1953. |
| **WAIU** | Literature for Our Time. 3rd ed. 1958. |
| **WAIW** | Dramatic Moment, The. 1967. |
| **WAJ** | Noh Plays of Japan, The. 1957. |
| **WAK** | Seven Plays of the Modern Theater. 1950. |
| **WALAG** | Making, Out: Plays by Gay men. 1992. |
| **WALAQ** | Quebec Voices Three Plays. 1986. |
| **WALJ** | Book of the Play, The. [195n] |
| **WALL** | Early Seventeenth Century Plays, 1600–1642. 1930. |
| **WARF** | American mind, The. 1937. |
| **WARH** | Representative Modern Plays, American. 1952. |
| **WARI** | Representative Modern Plays, British. 1953. |
| **WARL** | Representative Modern Plays: Ibsen to Tennessee Williams. 1964. |
| **WARN** | World in Literature, The. 1950. 2v in 1. |
| **WASCP** | Modern Canadian Plays. 1985. |
| **WASCPA** | Modern Canadian Plays. 3rd ed. 1993–1994. 2v |
| **WASCPB** | Modern Canadian Plays. 4th ed. 2000. 2v |
| **WASCT** | Twenty Years at Play: A New Play Centre Anthology. 1990. |
| **WASD** | Five Plays of the Sturm und Drang. 1986. |
| **WAT** | Elizabethan Dramatists. 1903. |
| **WATA** | Contemporary Drama: American, English and Irish, European. 1959. |
| **WATC** | Contemporary Drama: American Plays. 1931–38. 2v |
| **WATE** | Contemporary Drama: Eleven Plays: American, English, European. 1956. |
| **WATF** | Contemporary Drama: English and Irish Plays. 1931. 2v |
| **WATI** | Contemporary Drama: European, English and Irish, American Plays. 1941. |
| **WATL** | Contemporary Drama: European Plays. 1931–34. 4v |
| **WATO** | Contemporary Drama: Nine Plays: American, English, European. 1941. |
| **WATR** | Five Modern Plays. 1933. |
| **WATS** | College Reader. 1948. |
| **WATT** | Ideas and Forms in English and American Literature. 1932. 2v |
| **WATTAD** | American Drama: Colonial to Contemporary. 1995. |
| **WEAL** | Edwardian Plays. 1962. |
| **WEAN** | Eleven Plays. 1964. |
| **WEAT** | English Heritage, The. 1945. 2v |
| **WEAV** | Heritage of European Literature, The. 1948–49. 2v |
| **WEB** | Typical Plays for Secondary Schools. 1929. |
| **WEBER** | DramaContemporary Germany. 1996. |
| **WED** | Classics of Greek Literature. 1963. |
| **WEE** | Week-end Library. 3rd issue. 1930. |
| **WEHL** | DramaContemporary: France. 1986. |

| | |
|---|---|
| **WEIM** | Drama in the Modern World. 1964. |
| **WEIP** | Drama in the Modern World: Plays and Essays. Alternate ed. 1974. |
| **WEIS** | Drama in the Western World: 15 Plays with Essays. 1968. |
| **WEIW** | Drama in the Western World: 9 Plays with Essays. 1968. |
| **WEJ** | Seven Different Plays. 1988. |
| **WEK** | Theatre of Wonders: Six Contemporary American Plays. 1985. |
| **WEL** | Six Sanskrit Plays, in English Translation. 1964. |
| **WELG** | German Drama between the Wars. 1972. |
| **WELK** | New Generation Spanish Drama: An Anthology. 1976. |
| **WELL** | New Wave of Spanish Drama, The. 1970. |
| **WELT** | Themes of Drama: An Anthology. 1973. |
| **WELV** | Three Catalan Dramatists. 1976. |
| **WES** | West Coast Plays. 1977–1987. 22v |
| **WETZ** | The Best of Off-Broadway: Eight Contemporary Obie-Winning Plays, 1994. |
| **WHE** | Six Plays by Contemporaries of Shakespeare. 1928. |
| **WHF** | Understanding Literature. 1967. |
| **WHFA** | Understanding Literature. New ed. 1970. |
| **WHFM** | PlayReader's Repertory: An Anthology for Introduction to Theatre. 1970. |
| **WHI** | Representative Modern Dramas. 1936. |
| **WHK** | Seven Contemporary Plays. 1931. |
| **WHT** | Youth and the World. 1955. |
| **WIEG** | Literature and Gender: Thinking Critically through Fiction, Poetry, and Drama. 1999. |
| **WIGG** | Four Jacobean Sex Tragedies. 1998. |
| **WILK** | 9 Plays by Black Women. 1986. |
| **WILL** | Three Fin-de-siècle Farces. 1996. |
| **WILLG** | Theatre Anthology: Plays and Documents, A. 1990. |
| **WILM** | Portraits of Courage: Plays by Finnish Women. 1997. |
| **WILMET** | Staging the Nation: Plays from the American Theater, 1787–1909. 1998. |
| **WILSP** | Six Eighteenth Century Plays. 1963. |
| **WILSR** | Six Restoration Plays. 1959. |
| **WIM** | Popular Performance Plays of Canada. Vol. 1. 1976. |
| **WINE** | Drama of the English Renaissance. 1969. |
| **WINN** | Three Elizabethan Plays. 1959. |
| **WISD** | College English: The First Year. 1952. |
| **WISE** | College English: The First Year. Rev. ed. 1956. |
| **WISF** | College English: The First Year. 3rd ed. 1960. |
| **WOLC** | Contemporary Realistic Plays. 1988. |
| **WOLCS** | Staging Diversity: Plays and Practice in American Theater. 1992. |
| **WOMA** | Woman That I am: The Literature and Culture of Contemporary Women of Color, The. 1994. |
| **WOMD** | Women in Drama: An Anthology. 1975. |
| **WOMP** | Women Playwrights: The Best Plays of 1992–2000. 1992–2000. 9v |
| **WOMQ** | Women with Guns: Six New American Plays. 1985. |
| **WOMR** | Women Writers in Russian Modernism: An Anthology. 1978. |
| **WOMS** | Women's Project: Seven New Plays by Women, The. 1980. |
| **WOMS2** | Women's Project 2, The. 1984. |
| **WONR** | Restoration Drama: An Anthology. 2000. |
| **WOO** | Literature of England, The. 1936. 2v |
| **WOOD** | Literature of England, The. Rev. ed. 1941. 2v |
| **WOOE** | Literature of England, The. 3rd ed. 1947. 2v |
| **WOOG** | Modern Stage in Latin America: Six Plays, The. 1971. |
| **WOOGLA** | Latin America: Plays. 1986. |
| **WOQ** | WordPlays: An Anthology of New American Drama. 1981–1986. 5v |
| **WORL** | World in Literature, The. 1949. 4v |
| **WORM** | World of Tragedy, The. 1981. |
| **WORN** | World Turned upside down: Prose and Poetry of the American Revolution, The. 1975. |
| **WORP** | World's Great Plays. 1944. |
| **WORY** | African American Literature: An Anthology of Nonfiction, Fiction, Poetry, and Drama. 1993. |

| | |
|---|---|
| **WOTHA** | HBJ Anthology of Drama, The. 1993. |
| **WOTHB** | Harcourt Brace Anthology of Drama, The. 2nd ed. 1996. |
| **WOTHC** | Harcourt Brace Anthology of Drama, The. 3rd ed. 2000. |
| **WOTHM** | Modern Drama: Plays, Criticism, Theory. 1995. |
| **WOZA** | Woza Africa: An Anthology of South African Plays. 1986. |
| **WRIH** | Four Famous Tudor and Stuart Plays. 1963. |
| **WRIR** | Four Great Restoration Plays. 1964. |
| **WRIT** | Writing north: An Anthology of Contemporary Yukon Writers. 1992. |
| **YASU** | Masterworks of the Nō Theater. 1989. |
| **YEAR** | Years between: Plays by Women on the London Stage, 1900–1950, The. 1994. |
| **YOHA** | Treasury of Asian Literature, A. 1956. |
| **YOHB** | Treasury of Asian Literature, A. 1994. |
| **YORU** | Yoruba Popular Theatre: Three Plays by the Oyin Adejobi Company. 1994. |
| **YOUP** | Young Playwrights Festival Collection, The. 1983. |
| **YUCHD** | Chinese Drama after the Cultural Revolution, 1979–1989: An Anthology. 1996. |
| **ZDA** | Four French Comedies of the Eighteenth Century. 1933. |
| **ZEE** | New Namibian Plays. 2000. 2v |
| **ZIM** | Four European Plays. 1965. |
| **ZIMM** | Taking the Stage: Selections from Plays by Canadian Women. 1994. |

# Author Index

A, JIA, 1907–1994. *See* Weng, Ou-hung, joint author.

AARON, JOYCE, and TARLO, LUNA
  *Acrobatics.* 1980. WOMS

ABA, NOUREDDINE, 1921–1996
  *Une si grande espérance. See* Such Great Hope
  *Such Great Hope.* 1994.
    Miller, R., translator PLAWE
    Variant title: *Une si grande espérance*

ABBOTT, GEORGE, 1887–1995, and BISSELL,
    RICHARD
  *The Pajama Game* (lyrics and music by Richard Adler
    and Jerry Ross; based on the novel, *7-1/2 Cents*, by
    Richard Bissell). 1954. THEA54

—— and BRIDGERS, ANN PRESTON
  *Coquette.* 1927. BES27

—— and GLEASON, JAMES
  *The Fall Guy.* 1925. BES24

——. *See* DUNNING, PHILIP; HOLM, JOHN CECIL;
    WEIDMAN, JEROME, joint authors

ABBOTT, JEAN
  *Forced Out.* 1988. ROES

`ABD al-SABUR, SALAH, 1931–1981
  *Night Traveler.* 1969.
    Inani, M., and Hollo, A., translators JAY
    Variant title: *Musafir layl*
  *Musafir layl. See* Night Traveler

ABDOH, REZA, 1963–1995
  *The Law of Remains.* 1991. MARR

ABE, KOBO (KIMIFUSA), 1924–1993
  *Friends.* 1967
    Keene, D., translator HIBH
    Variant title: *Tomodachi*
  *Omae Nimo Tsumi Ga Aru. See* You, Too, Are Guilty
  *Tomodachi. See* Friends
  *You, Too, Are Guilty.* 1965.
    Takaya, T. T., translator TAK
    Variant title: *Omae Nimo Tsumi Ga Aru*

À BECKETT, GILBERT ABBOTT, 1811–1856
  *King John, with the Benefit of the Act.* 1837. NIN2

ABEL, LIONEL, 1910–2001
  *Absalom.* 1956. MAH
  *The Death of Odysseus.* 1953. PLAA

ABELL, KJELD, 1901–1961
  *Anna Sophie Hedvig.* 1939.
    Larsen, H., translator SCAN2
  *Days on a Cloud.* 1947.
    Roughton, A., and Bredsdorf, E., translators SPR
  *Dronning gear igen. See* The Queen on Tour
  *The Queen on Tour.* 1943.
    Pearce, J., translator CONT
    Variant title: *Dronning gear igen*

ABEYSINGHE, RASIKA
  *Family Bonds.* 1989. GOON

ABLEMAN, PAUL, 1927–2006
  *Green Julia.* 1972. BES72

ABOAB, ISAAC DE MATATIA, 1631–1707
  *Harassed but Happy.* 1685–1686?
    McGaha, M., translator STORJ
    Variant title: *El perseguido dichoso*
  *El perseguido dichoso. See* Harassed but Happy

ABSE, DANNIE, 1923–
*House of Cowards*. 1960. DEAS, PLAN23

ABUN, YASUDA. *See* Yasuda, Abun

ACCADEMIA DEGLI INTRONATI, c.1527–1947
*The Deceived*. 1532.
   Newbingin, N., translator CAIR
   Variant title: *Gli ingannati*
*Gli ingannati*. *See* The Deceived

ACEVEDO HERNANDEZ, ANTONIO, 1886–1962
*Cabrerita*. 1927.
   Bailey, W., translator SSTE

ACHARD, MARCEL, 1889–1974
*Auprès de ma blonde*. *See* Behrman, Samuel Nathaniel
*I Know My Love* (adapted from) *Patate*. *See* Rollo
*Rollo* (adapted by Felicity Douglas). 1956. PLAN20
   Variant title: *Patate*

ACHESON, SAM HANNA, 1900–1972
*We Are Besieged*. 1941. THX

ACKER, KATHY, 1948–1997
*The Birth of the Poet*. 1985. WOQ5

ACKERLEY, J.R., 1897–1967
*The Prisoners of War*. 1925. GAY3

ACKERMAN, MARIANNE
*Meanwhile, Goodbye*. 1996. BREK

ACKERMANN, JOAN
   Ackermann, J., et al. *Back Story: A Dramatic Anthology* (based on characters created by Joan Ackermann). HUMANA2000 (Consists of the following nineteen brief plays: Ackermann, J. *Norman Rockwell's Thanksgiving in the Year 2000*; Ackermann, J. *Time to Think*; Baron, C. *Blackfish*; Beber, N. *The Reluctant Instrument*; Congdon, C. *Moby Ethan at the Sculptor's Museum*; Klein, J. *Something to Do with Bolivia*; Lauro, S. *Turn Down*; Lucas, C. *Good Morning to the Horse*; Machado, E. *Trying to Get There*; Margulies, D. *Misadventure*; Martin, J. *The Deal*; Miller, S. *Introducing Dad*; Olive, J. *Star Skating*; Palmer, T. *Barbra Live at Canyon Ranch*; Rambo, D. *Maid of Athens*; Sanchez, E. *Ethan's Got Get*; Shank, A. *Or Maybe Not*; Simon, M. *What Became of the Polar Bear?*; Smith, V. *Dead Men Make No Dollars*)
*The Batting Cage*. 1996. HUMANA96
*Norman Rockwell's Thanksgiving in the Year 2000*. 2000.
   *See* Ackermann, J. *Back Story: A Dramatic Anthology*. HUMANA2000

*Off the Map*. 1994. WOMP94
*Stanton's Garage*. 1993. HUMANA93
*Time to Think*. 2000. *See* Ackermann, J. *Back Story: A Dramatic Anthology*. HUMANA2000
*Zara Spook and other Lures*. 1990. DIXD1

ACKLAND, RODNEY, 1908–1991
*After October*. 1936. FAMI
*Before the Party* (based on a short story by W. Somerset Maugham). 1949. PLAN2
*A Dead Secret*. 1957. PLAN16
*The Diary of a Scoundrel*. *See* Ostrovsky, Alexander. *The Diary of a Scoundrel* (translated and adapted by)
*The Old Ladies*. 1935. FAMG
*Strange Orchestra*. 1932. FAMC

ADAM DE LA HALLE (Adam Le Boçus; Adam Le Bossu, pseudonyms), ca.1250–ca. 1306
*Le jeu de la feuillée*. 1275?
   Axton, R., and Stevens, J., translators AXT
   Variant title: *The Play of the Greensward*
*Le jeu de Robin et Marion*. 1285?
   Axton, R., and Stevens, J., translators AXT
   Mandel, O., translator MARH
   Variant title: *The Play of Robin and Marion*
*The Play of Robin and Marion*. *See* Le jeu de Robin et Marion
*The Play of the Greensward*. *See* Le jeu de la feuillée

ADAM LE BOÇUS. *See* Adam de la Halle

ADAM LE BOSSU. *See* Adam de la Halle

ADAMOV, ARTHUR, 1908–1970
*All against All*. 1952.
   Gildea, D., translator WELT
   Variant title: *Tous contre tous*
*Professor Taranne*. 1953.
   Bermel, A., translator BERMD, FOUF, TAUJ
   Variant title: *Le Professeur Taranne*
*Le Professeur Taranne*. *See* Professor Taranne
*Tous contre tous*. *See* All against All

ADAMS, LEE, 1924–
*Applause* (lyrics by). *See* Comden, Betty and Green, Adolph. Applause
"It's a Bird, It's a Plane, It's Superman" (lyrics by). *See* Newman, David and Benton, Robert. "It's a Bird, It's a Plane. It's Superman"

ADAMS, PHILIP
*Free's Point*. 1996. SSSN
*Tears, Mama*. 1991. WRIT

ADAMSON, SAMUEL, 1969–
*Clocks and Whistles*. 1996. CLUM

ADDISON, JOSEPH, 1672–1719
  *Cato.* 1713. BELK3, DOB, EIGH, HAN, LIBR, MAND,
    MANF, MOR, NET, STM, TAT, TAU, TUP, TUQ
  *The Drummer.* 1716. BELK11

ADE, GEORGE, 1866–1944
  *The College Widow.* 1904. COT
  *The County Chairman.* 1903. BES99

ADESINA, FOLUKE
  *A Nest in a Cage.* 1997. AGOR

ADLER, HANS, 1880–1957. *See* Vulpius, Paul,
    pseudonym

ADLER, RICHARD, 1921–
  *The Pajama Game* (lyrics and music by). *See* Abbott,
    George and Bissell, Richard. *The Pajama Game*

ADSHEAD, KAY, 1954–
  *Thatcher's Women.* 1987. PLABE7
    A. E., pseudonym. *See* Russell, George William

AERENSON, BENJIE
  *Lighting Up the Two-year Old.* 1997. HUMANA97

AESCHYLUS, 525–56 B.C.
  *Agamemnon.* 458 B.C.
    Anonymous translator CHR, EVB1
    Blackie, J., translator BUCK, BUCL, BUCM
    Campbell, L., translator LAP
    Cookson, G., translator GRDB5
    Fagles, R., translator NORGA, NORIA1, NORIB1,
      NORIC1, NORJ1, NORJA, WOTHA, WOTHB,
      WOTHC
    Grene, D., and O'Flaherty, W., translators JACOBD
    Hamilton, E., translator EVC1, HAM, KRE, TREB,
      TREC1, TREE1, TREI1
    Harrison, T., translator COTKICG
    Lattimore, R., translator FIFT, GRDBA4, GREP1,
      GREPA1, GRER1, GRERA1
    Lloyd-Jones, H., translator COLD
    Lucas, F., translator LUCA, LUCAB, LUCAF
    MacNeice, L., translator ALLK, ALLM, ALLN,
      ALLO, DEAP, DEAR, DEAS, FIFR, FREG,
      LIND, MALC, MALG1, MALI1, MALN1,
      MALR1, NORG, NORI1, SSSI, SSSIA, SSSIB,
      SSSIC, SWA, VANV1, VONS1
    Morshead, E., translator GEMM, HARC8, IIOWE,
      HOWF, LOCM1, MATT, OAM, OAT1, OATH,
      ROBJA, THP, WARN1
    Murray, G., translator CARP, CARPA, FGP, TEN,
      TRE, TREA2
    Plumpe, E., translator HIB, HIBA, HIBB, HOUS,
      ROB, THOM, THON

    Potter, R., translator GREE
    Robinson, C, translator ROBK
    Sylvester, W., translator COOA
    Thomson, G., translator AUDE, DIS, FIFV, HAPRL,
      HILPDH1, ROBI, WEAV1
    Vellacourt, P., translator BENQ, SOUL, STY
    Verrall, A., translator GRDG
    Way, A., translator PLAG
    Young, D., translator HOEP
  *The Choephori. See* Choephoroe
  *Choephoroe.* 458 B.C.
    Arnott, D., translator CLL, CLLC, FOR
    Cookson, G., translator GRDB5
    Fagles, R., translator NORIA1, NORIB1, WOTHC
    Grene, D., and O'Flaherty, W., translators JACOBD
    Harrison, T., translator COTKICG
    Lattimore, R., translator GRDBA4, GREP1,
      GREPA1, GRER2, GRERA1
    Morshead, E., translator HARC8, OAT1
    Murray, G., translator FGP, TEN
    Thomson, G., translator AUDE, FIFV, HILPDH1,
      ROBJ
    Way, A., translator PLAG
    Variant titles: *The Chosphori; The Libation-Bearers;
      The Mourners*
  *Eumenides.* 458 B.C.
    Cookson, G., translator GRDB5
    Fagles, R., translator NORIA1, NORIB1, NORIC1,
      NORJ1
    Grene, D., and O'Flaherty, W., translators JACOBD
    Harrison, T., translator COTKICG
    Lattimore, R., translator GRDBA4, GREP1,
      GREPA1, GRER3, GRERA3, WOTHC
    Morshead, E., translator HARC8, OAM, OAT1
    Murray, G., translator FGP, TEN
    Paley, F. GRDG
    Plumptre, E., translator BAT1
    Thomson, G., translator AUDE, FIFT, FIFV,
      HILPDH1, ROBJ
    Way, A., translator PLAG
    Variant titles: *The Furies; The Gracious Ones*
  *The Furies. See* Eumenides
  *The Gracious Ones. See* Eumenides
  *Hepta epi Thebas. See* The Seven against Thebes
  *Hiketides. See* The Suppliants
  *The House of Atreus* (trilogy: Agamemnon,
    Choephoroe, and Eumenides). *See* Agamemnon;
    Choephoroe; Eumenides; Oresteia
  *The Libation Bearers. See* Choephoroe
  *The Mourners. See* Choephoroe
  *Oresteia* (trilogy: Agamemnon, Choephoroe, and
    Eumenides).
      458 B.C. Arranged for the stage by A. V. Griffin.
      GRIF
    *See also* Agamemnon, Choephoroe, Eumenides

*The Persians.* 472 B.C.
  Anonymous translator WED
  Bernadete, S., translator GRDBA4, GREP1,
    GREPA1, GRERA2
  Cookson, G., translator GRDB5
  Potter, R., translator OAT1
*Prometheus Bound.* 478? B.C.
  Anon. translator ATT3, LLC, CLL
  Blackie, J., translator BUCK, BUCL, BUCM, CLF1,
    SEBO, SEBP
  Browning, E., translator CROS, DRAD1, GREB2,
    GREE, MAST, MIK7, PLAB1
  Cookson, G., translator GRDB5
  Dolin, E., and Sugg, A., translators COOA
  Grene, D., translator COI, GRDBA4, GREN, GREP1,
    GREPA1, GRER1, GRERA2
  Hamilton, E., translator BURR, DOWN, FIFT, HAM,
    HAPRL, MALI1, NORI1
  Harrison, T., translator COTKICG
  Havelock, E., translator BARC
  Hilburn, E., translator TENN
  Lucas, F., translator LUCA, LUCAB, LUCAF
  McLeish, K., translator MAMB
  Mendell, C., translator CLKW, ROBJ
  More, P., translator MURP, OAM, OAT1, OATH
  Plumptre, E., translator CROV, HARC8, SML
  Walker, C., translator BENSB1
  Warner, R., translator LIND
  Whitelaw, R., translator FGP
  Variant titles: *Prometheus Desmotes*; *Prometheus
    Vinctus*
*Prometheus Desmotes.* See Prometheus Bound
*Prometheus Vinctus.* See Prometheus Bound
*Septem contra Thebas.* See The Seven against Thebes
*The Seven against Thebes.* 467 B.C.
  Cookson, G., translator GRDB5
  Grene, D., translator GRDBA4, GREP1, GREPA1,
    GRERA2
  Variant titles: *Hepta epi Thebas*; *Septem contra
    Thebas*
*The Suppliant Maidens.* See The Suppliants
*The Suppliants.* 492? B.C.
  Bernadete, S., translator GRDBA4, GREP1,
    GREPA1, GRERA2
  Caldwell, R., translator TENN
  Cookson, G., translator GRDB5
  Morshead, E., translator OAT1
  Variant titles: *Hiketides*; *The Suppliant Maidens*

THE AFANASJEFF FAMILY CIRCUS, 1958–1964? *See*
  Afanasjew, Jerzy, joint author

AFANASJEW, JERZY, 1932–
  *The World Is Not Such a Bad Place . . .* (selections from)
  Gerould, D., and Gerould, E., translators TWEN

——— and the AFANASJEFF FAMILY CIRCUS
*Good Evening, Clown* (selection from). 1962.
  Gerould, D., and Gerould, E., translators TWEN
——— and the BIM-BOM TROUPE
*Faust* (part of *Joy in Earnest*). 1956.
  Gerould, D., and Gerould, E., translators TWEN
*Snouts* (part of *Joy in Earnest*). 1956.
  Gerould, D., and Gerould, E., translators TWEN
*Joy in Earnest* (includes *Faust*, *Snouts*, and *The
    Professor* by Mrozek, S.)

AFINOGENOV, ALEXANDER. *See* Afinogenyev,
  Aleksandr Nikolaevich

AFINOGENYEV, ALEKSANDR NIKOLAEVICH,
    1904–1941
*Distant Point.* See Far taiga
*Far taiga.* 1935.
  Bakshy, A., translator BAKS
  Variant titles: *Distant Point*; *Remote*
*Fear.* 1931.
  Malamuth, C., translator LYK
*On the Eve.* 1942.
  Affnogenova, E., translator SEVP
*Remote.* See Far taiga

AFINOGENYOV, ALEKSANDR NIKOLAEVICH. *See*
  Afinogenyev, Aleksandr Nikolaevich

AGEE, JAMES, 1909–1955
*Abraham Lincoln, The Early Years.* SHER
*The Bride Comes to Yellow Sky* (screen play; based on
    the story by Stephen Crane). 1971? SUT3
*A Death in the Family.*
  See Mosel, Tad. *All the Way home* (based on)

AGENOUX, SOREN
  Charles Dickens' *Christmas Carol.* 1966. SMC

AGORO, S.N.A.
  *Co-tenants.* 1997. AGOR

AGUIRRE, CARMEN
  *Chile con carne.* 1995. RAVE
——— and THE LATINO THEATRE GROUP
  *¿Que pasa with La Raza, eh?* 1999. ALONG

AGUIRRE, ISABEL, 1919–
  *Altarpiece of Yumbel.* 1986.
    Salas, T., and Vargas, M., translators SALA
    Variant title: *El retablo de Yumbel*
  *El retablo de Yumbel.* See Altarpiece of Yumbel

AH, CHIA. *See* A, Jia

AHMAD, RUKHSANA
*Song for a Sanctuary.* 1990. GEOR

AHRENS, LYNN, 1948–
*Once on This Island* (lyrics by Lynn Ahrens, music by
Stephen Flaherty; based on a novel by Rosa Guy).
1989. BES89
*Ragtime* (lyrics by). *See* McNally, Terrence. Ragtime

AIDOO, AMA ATA, 1942– (b. Christina Ama Ata Aidoo)
*Anowa.* 1970. BANH

AIKEN, GEORGE L., 1820–1876
*Life among the Lowly. See* Uncle Tom's Cabin
*Uncle Tom's Cabin; or, Life among the Lowly* (based on
the novel by Harriet Beecher Stowe). 1852. AMEM,
BERP, BERPA, BLAI2, CEY, GARX, GATB1,
MESC, MONR, MOSS2, RICHE, WILMET

AIKINS, CARROLL, 1888–1967
*The God of Gods.* 1919. MAS2

AJIBADE, SEGUN
*Rakinyo.* 1975. AFR1

AKALAITIS, JOANNE, 1937–
*Dressed like an Egg*; taken from the writings of Colette.
1977. WOQ4
*Ti Jean Blues*; adapted from the works of Jack Kerouac.
1998. HUMANA98

AKERMAN, ANTHONY, 1949–
*Somewhere on the Border.* 1982. GRAYS

AKIHAMA SATOSHI, 1934–
*Comedy Duo in Hibernation.* 1965.
Boyd, M., translator HACJT7
Variant title: *Tōmin manzai*
*Tōmin manzai. See* Comedy Duo in Hibernation

AKIMOTO MATSUYO, 1911–2001
*Hitachibō Kaison. See* Kaison the Priest of Hitachi
*Kaison the Priest of Hitachi.*
Goodman, D., translator JAPDC
Variant title: *Hitachibō Kaison*
*Kasubuta shikibukō. See* Our Lady of the Scabs
*Our Lady of the Scabs.* 1969.
Kaiser, S., and Henry, S., translators HACJT7
Variant title: *Kasubuta shikibukō*

AKINS, ZOE, 1886–1958
*Declassee.* 1919. BES19
*The Old Maid.* 1935. BES34

AKIP, MASRI HAJI
*Guests.* 1994.
Kumanireng, A., translator MLAB

AKRITAS, LOUKIS, 1909–1965
*Hostages.* 1956.
Gianos, M., translator GIA
Variant title: *Omiroi*
*Omiroi. See* Hostages

AKSENOV, VASILII, 1932–2009
*The Four Temperaments: A Comedy in Ten Tableaux.*
(1967?)
Jakim, B., translator METR

AKSYONOV, VASILY. *See* Aksenov, Vasilii

ALAM, JUAN SHAMSUL, 1946–
*Midnight Blues.* 1987. ANTUR
*Zookeeper.* 1989. ANTU

AL-`ANI, YUSUF. *See* `Ani, Yusuf, al-

ALARCON Y MENDOZA, JUAN RUIZ DE. *See* Ruiz de
Alarcon y Mendoza Juan

ALBANESE, ELEANOR
*The Body Image Project.* 1992. ZIMM (excerpt)

ALBEE, EDWARD, 1928–
*All Over.* 1971. GARTL
*The American Dream.* 1961.BLOND, FRYE, LEVG,
LITC, MANL, MARO, REIO, RIS
*A Delicate Balance.* 1966. BES66
*The Lady from Dubuque.* 1980. BES79
*The Sandbox.* 1960. BARIF, BARKE, BARKF, BARS,
CORB, CUBH, KIRLA, KIRLB, KIRLC, LITIE,
LITIF, LITRA, LITRB, LITRC, PERT, PERU,
PERV, PERW, PERX, PERY, PERZ, SATI,
SATJ, THOD
*Seascape.* 1975. BES74
*Three Tall Women.* 1991. BES93, COLD, PLACA,
SSSIC
*Tiny Alice.* 1964. BES64, GAT
*Who's Afraid of Virginia Woolf?* 1962. ABCE, BES62,
FOUX, GARSA, GATB4, MANCIO, REIL,
REIW, REIWE, TREBJ
*The Zoo Story.* 1959. COK, FAM, FAMAF, GILB,
GOLII, HAE, HOWP2, KERP, KLIS,
LEVY, LITI, LITIA, LITIB, LITIC, MANCA2,
MANCB2, MANCD2, MANCE2, MANCF2,
MANCG2, MANCH2, MANCI, MANCIA,
MANCIU, MESSE, MIJH, REIT, SCNQCB,
SCNT, SDQ, SHR, SSSIB, WAIW,
WATTAD

ALBERT, LYLE VICTOR, 1960–
    *Cut!* 1985. BELLN
    *The Prairie Church of Buster Galloway.* 1983.
       NEWWUX

ALBERTI, RAFAEL, 1902–1999
    *El hombre deshabitado.* 1931. SEIS1
    *Night and War in the Prado Museum.* 1956.
       Johnson, L., translator BENA
         Variant title: *Noche de guerra en el Museo del Prado*
    *Noche de guerra en el Museo del Prado. See* Night and
       War in the Prado Museum

ALBERY, JAMES, 1838–1889
    *Two Roses.* 1870. ROWE

ALBERY, PETER, 1912–1979
    *Anne Boleyn.* 1956. PLAN14

ALCORN, JOHN
    *Capote at Yaddo: A Very Gay Little Musical* (music by).
       *See* Gilbert, Sky. *Capote at Yaddo: A Very Gay
       Little Musical*

ALDRIDGE, IRA, 1807–1867
    *The Black Doctor.* 1847. HARY, HARYB

ALEKAR, SATISH, 1949–
    *Begum Barve.* 1979.
       Gokhale, S., translator KAM2
    *Mahapoor.* 1975.
       Bhirdikar, U., translator DESH
         Variant title: *The Deluge*
    *The Deluge. See* Mahapoor

ALEXANDER, ROBERT
    *Factwino vs. Armageddonman* (script by). *See*
       San Francisco Mime Troupe. *Factwino vs.
       Armageddonman*
    *Home Free.* 1981. WES11/12
    *The Hourglass.* (1978) CEN
    *I Ain't Yo' Uncle.* 1992. ELAM
    *The Last Orbit of Billy Mars.* 1999. PLACJ

ALFARO, LUIS, 1961–
    *Bitter Homes and Gardens.* 2000. PLACGH
    *Downtown.* 1998. HUGH
    *Straight as a Line.* 1998. SVICH

ALFIERI, VITTORIO, 1749–1803
    *Myrrha.* 1788?
       Bowring, E., translator BAT5
    *Saul.* 1784. BIN
       Bowring, E., translator CLF2

ALFRED, WILLIAM, 1922–1999
    *Hogan's Goat.* 1965. BES65, FAMAH, GAT, GRIM

ALFRIEND, EDWARD M., 1843–1901, and WHEELER,
    ANDREW CARPENTER
    *The Great Diamond Robbery.* 1885. AMP8, CLA

ALGARIN, MIGUEL, 1941– , and LAVIERA, TATO
    *Olú Clemente.* 1973. KANEL

AL-HAKIM, TAWFIG, 1898–1987
    *The Donkey Market.* 1981.
       Johnson, Davies, D., translator HUTCH
    *The Sultan's Dilemma.* 1959.
       Johnson, Davies, D., translator NORJ2
       Wahab, F., translator ABL, KIAN

ALI, AKHUND-ZATH FATH'. *See* Fath'Ali,
    Akhundzadah

ALIANAK, HRANT, 1950–
    *Mathematics.* 1972. BRIP
    *Passion and Sin.* 1976. CTR
    *Western.* 1972. BRIP

ALLAIS, ALPHONSE, 1854–1905
    *Le pauvre bougre et le bon genie. See* The Poor Beggar
       and the Fairy Godmother
    *The Poor Beggar and the Fairy Godmother.* 1899.
       Shapiro, N., translator FLEA
         Variant title: *Le pauvre bougre et le bon genie*

ALLARD, JANET
    *Painted Rain.* 1989. SCVDO1

ALLEN, JAY PRESSON, 1922–2006 (b. Jacqueline
    Presson)
    *Forty Carats.* 1968. BES68

ALLEN, RALPH G., 1934–2004
    *Sugar Babies.* 1979. BES79

ALLEN, WOODY, 1935–
    *Death Knocks.* 1971. ABCC, ABCD, ABCE, ABCF,
       ABCG, LITIC, SCVDT1, SCX
    *The Floating Light Bulb.* 1981. BES80
    *God.* 1975. STOTD, STOTLA
    *Play It Again, Sam.* 1969. GARTL

ALLERS, ROGER, 1949– , and MECCHI, IRENE
    *The Lion King* (book by Roger Allers and Irene Mecchi;
       music and lyrics by Elton John and Tim Rice;
       additional music and lyrics by Lebo M, Mark
       Mancina, Jay Rifkin, Julie Taymor, and Hans
       Zimmer). 1997. BES97

ALLIKSAAR, ARTUR, 1923–1966
*The Nameless Island.* 1966.
  Kurman, G., translator FIFFN
  Variant title: *Nemetu saar*
*Nemetu saar. See* The Nameless Island

AL-MADANI, `IZZ AL-DIN. *See* Madani,`Izz al-Din al-

ALOMA, RENE R., 1947–1986
*A Little Something to Ease the Pain.* 1986. CUB

ALONSO DE SANTOS, JOSE LUIS, 1942–
*Bajarse al moro.* 1985. SEIS2
  — *See also* Going Down to Marrakesh
*Going Down to Marrakesh.* 1985.
  Zatlin, P., translator OCONNP
  Variant title: *Bajarse al moro*

ALPERT, HOLLIS (Robert Carroll, pseudonym), 1916–
  2007
*Heat Lightning.* 1949. BRNB, BRNS

ALRAWI, KARIM, 1952–
*Fire in the Lake.* 1985. PLACB

ALSINA, ARTURO, 1897–1984
*La marca de fuego.* 1926. ALPE

ALURISTA, pseudonym. *See* Urista, Alberto H.

ALVAREZ, LYNNE, 1947–
*Analiese.* 1997. WOMP97
*The guitarron.* 1983. OSB
*The Reincarnation of Jaimie Brown.* 1994. MESSE,
  WOMP94

ÁLVAREZ QUINTERO, JOAQUIN, 1873–1944. *See*
  Álvarez Quintero, Serafín, joint author

ÁLVAREZ QUINTERO, SERAFIN, 1871–1938, and
  ÁLVAREZ QUINTERO, JOAQUIN
*An Autumn Morning. See* A Bright Morning
*A Bright Morning.* 1905.
  Castillo, C., and Overman, E., translators DIK1
  Floyd, L., translator EDAD, WHF
  Variant titles: *An Autumn Morning; Mañana de sol; A
    Sunny Morning*
*The Centenarian. See* A Hundred Years Old
*Doña Clarines.* 1909.
  Granville-Barker, H., and H., translators CHA,
    CHAN
*A Hundred Years Old.* 1909.
  Granville-Barker, H., and H., translators PLAP3
  Variant titles: *The Centenarian; Papá Juan:
    centenario*

*Malvaloca.* 1912.
  Fassett, J., translator DICDT
*Mañana de sol. See* A Bright Morning
*Papá Juan: centenario. See* A Hundred Years Old
*Pueblo de las mujeres. See* The Women's Town
*A Sunny Morning. See* A Bright Morning
*The Women Have Their Way. See* The Women's Town
*The Women's Town.* 1912.
  Turrell, C., translator TUR
  Variant titles: *Pueblo de las mujeres; The Women
    Have Their Way*

ALVARO, CORRADO, 1895–1956.
*The Long Night of Medea.* 1949.
  Friedman, E., translator PLAC

ALWORTH, REBECCA. *See* Larson, Larry, joint author

ALYOSHIN, SAMUIL, 1913– (b. Samuil Iosifovich
  Kotlyar)
*Alone.* 1956.
  McLean, H., and Vickery, W., translators MAM
  Variant title: *Odna*
*Odna. See* Alone

AMAKALI, MARIA, 1973–
*Checkmate.* 2000. ZEE1

AMANO, LYNETTE, 1949–
*Ashes.* 1972. KUMU

AMEND, HOWARD T.
*All the Comforts of Home.* 1987. VORE

AMES, WINTHROP, 1871–1937
*A Kiss in Xanadu.* 1932? LEV, LEVE

AMESCUA, ANTONIO MIRA DE. *See* Mira de
  Amescua, Antonio

ANAGNOSTAKI, LOULA, 1940–
*The Parade.* 1965.
  Revi, A., and Glastras, Y., translators CONTG1

ANAYA, RUDOLFO A., 1937–
*Who Killed Don José?* 1987. JOND

ANCEY, GEORGES, pseudonym. *See* Curnieu,
  Georges de

ANDERSON, GARLAND, 1886–1939
*Appearances.* 1925. HARY, HARYB

ANDERSON, JANE, 1946–
*Defying Gravity.* 1997. WOMP97
*The Last Time We Saw Her.* 1994. HUMANA94

*The Reprimand.* 2000. HUMANA2000
*Tough Choices for the New Century.* 1995.
    HUMANA95

ANDERSON, LAURIE, 1947–
*United States* (excerpt). 1983. OUT

ANDERSON, MAXWELL, 1888–1959.
*Anne of the Thousand Days.* 1948. BES48, GARW,
    OHL
*The Bad Seed* (based on the novel by William March).
    1954. BES54, RICI, THEA55
*Barefoot in Athens.* 1951. BARS, BES51
*Both Your Houses.* 1933. BES32, CORD, CORE,
    CORF, LOOA, LOOB
*Candle in the Wind.* 1941. BES41
*Elizabeth the Queen.* 1930. BES30, STEI, THO, TRE,
    TREA1,TREBA, TREBJ, TREC2, TREE3, TREI3,
    WATC2, WATI, WHI
*The Eve of St. Mark.* 1942. BES42
*The Feast of Ortolana.* 1938. KIN, STAT
*A Girl from Lorraine. See* Joan of Lorraine
*Gypsy.* 1929. BES28
*High Tor.* 1937. BES36, CLH, CRIT, GAS, GATB2,
    GAVE, GOW, GOWA, HAP, MERT
*Joan of Lorraine.* 1946. BES46
    Variant title: *A Girl from Lorraine*
*Journey to Jerusalem.* 1940. GALB
*Key Largo.* 1940. BES39, ROLF
*Mary of Scotland.* 1933. BES33, CLKW, THF
*The Masque of Kings.* 1936. MOSL
*Saturday's Children.* 1927. BES26, GASB, TUCD
*The Star-wagon.* 1937. BES37
*Storm Operation.* 1944. BES43
*Valley Forge.* 1934. AMB, BES34, WARH
*The Wingless Victory.* 1936. LOR, SANM
*Winterset.* 1935. BES35, BROZ, CALM, CALN2,
    CASS, CHAN, CHAP, COTE, COTH, CRIT,
    DAV1, DUR, GAS, GAVE, GRIF, HAT, HATA,
    HAVD, HAVE, HIL, HOLM, MOSH, NELS,
    QUIM, QUIN, RAVIT, SIXC, WAIT, WAK

——— and HICKERSON, HAROLD
*Gods of the Lightning.* 1928. GASB

——— and STALLINGS, LAWRENCE
*What Price Glory?* 1924. BES24, CHA, GASB, MAF,
    MAFC, TRE, TREA1, TREBA, TREC2, TREE3,
    TREI3, VANM

——— and WEILL, KURT
*Lost in the Stars* (based on the novel *Cry, the Beloved
    Country* by Alan Paton). 1949. BES49, FAMAF,
    HEWE, RICM

ANDERSON, ROBERT WOODRUFF, 1917–2009
*I Never Sang for My Father.* 1968. BES67, MID
*I'm Herbert.* 1967. PERR3
*Silent Night, Lonely Night.* 1959. GARSA
*Tea and Sympathy.* 1953. BES53, FAM, FAMAF,
    GART, GATB4, NEWV, STS, THEA54
*You Know I Can't Hear You When the Water's Running.*
    1967. BES66, GAT

ANDERSON, SHERWOOD, 1876–1941
*Textiles.* 1938. ING

ANDONOVSKI, VENKO, 1964–
*The Slavic Chest.* 1998.
    Ančevski, Z., and Gaughran, R., translators LUZ

ANDREEV, LEONID NIKOLAEVICH, 1871–1919
*He Who Gets Slapped.* 1915.
    Guthrie, J., adapter HOUG
    MacAndrew, A., translator GARZG, MABA
    Reeve, F. D., translator REEV2
    Zilboorg, G., translator BES21, DICDT, MOSG,
    MOSH, THF, TUCG, TUCM, TUCN, TUCO,
    WATI, WATL4
    Variant titles: *The Knock About; The Painted Laugh*
*An Incident.*
    Anonymous translator CHR, ROY
*The Knock About. See* He Who Gets Slapped
*The Life of Man.* 1906.
    Meader, C., and Scott, F., translators SML
    Seltzer, T., translator DICIN2, MOSQ
*The Painted Laugh. See* He Who Gets Slapped
*Professor Storitsyn.* 1912.
    Minkoff, I., Noyes, G., and Kaun, A., translators
    NOY
*Requiem.* 1916.
    Gerould, D., translator GERO

ANDREWS, REGINA M. ANDERSON, 1900–1993
*Climbing Jacob's Ladder: A Tragedy of Negro Life.*
    1931. PERF

ANDREYEFF, LEONID NIKOLAEVICH. *See* Andreev,
    Leonid Nikolaevich

ANDREYEV, LEONID NIKOLAEVICH. *See* Andreev,
    Leonid Nikolaevich

ANDRIEU DE LA VIGNE. *See* La Vigne, Andrieu de

ANDRIEV, LEONID NIKOLAEVICH. *See* Andreev,
    Leonid Nikolaevich

ANGEL, LEONARD, 1945–
*Forthcoming Wedding.* 1972. BRIQ

ANGEL PEREZ DE SAAVEDRA, RIVAS. *See* Rivas, Angel Pérez de Saavedra

`ANI, YUSUF, AL-, 1927–
*The Key*. 1967–1968.
Jabsheh, S., and Brownjohn, A., translators JAY
Variant title: *al-Miftah al-Miftah*

THE ANNA PROJECT
*This Is for You, Anna*. 1985. CTR

ANNE, CATHERINE
*Agnès*. 1994.
Gearing, N., translator NEWFPB

ANNENSKY, INNOKENTY, 1856–1909
*Thamyris Kitharodos*. 1916.
Green, M., translator GREEN

ANNUNZIO, GABRIELE D', 1863–1938
*La città morta*. *See* The Dead City
*The Daughter of Jorio*. 1904.
Porter, C., Isola, P., and Henry, A., translators MOSQ
Variant title: *La figlia di Jorio*
*The Dead City*. 1898.
Mantellini, G., translator SAY
Variant title: *La città morta*
*La figlia di Jorio*. *See* The Daughter of Jorio
*Francesca da Rimini*. 1902.
Symons, A., translator DICIN1, TUCG, TUCM, WATL3
*Gioconda*. 1898.
Symons, A., translator DICDS, SMI
*Sogno d'un mattino di primavera*. *See* A Spring Morning's Dream
*A Spring Morning's Dream*. 1897.
Oldcorn, A., translator TWEI
Variant title: *Sogno d'un mattino di primavera*

ANONYMOUS PLAYS
*Abraham* (Wakefield). 15th century DAVJ, TOV, TOWN
*Abraham* (York). 15th century DAVJ
*Abraham and Isaac* (Brome). 15th century ABRH, ADA, ANTL, BARD, BENY, CAWL, CHI, COLDE, DAVJ, DAVN, ENGE, FRAN, FREH, GARZB, GREC1, HOPP, IIUD, KINNS, LIE, MAR, MATTL, PAR, PARRY, POLL, SCW, SNYD1, SWIT, TAT, TAU, TREA2, TREB, TRECl, TREE1, TREI1
Variant titles: *The Brome Abraham* and *Isaac: The Sacrifice of Isaac*
*Abraham and Isaac*. *See* Abraham, Melchisedec and Isaac

*Abraham and Isaac* (adapted from four major cyles by Kenneth Pickering, Kevin Wood and Philip Dart). 15th century MYSCC
*Abraham and Isaac* (Dublin). 15th century DAVJ
*Abraham and Isaac* (Ludus Coventriae). 15th century DAVJ
*Abraham and Isaac* (N Town). 15th century DAVJ, N-TOW
*Abraham and Isaac* (Northampton). DAVN
*Abraham, Lot, and Melchysedeck*. *See* Abraham, Melchisedec and Isaac
*Abraham, Melchisedec and Isaac* (Chester). 15th century ASH, BURNS, CHEL, CHELM, CHES, CHESE, COLDE, DAVJ, ENGE, EVER, KRE, POLL
Variant titles: *Abraham and Isaac*; *Abraham, Lot, and Melchysedeck*; *Abraham, Melchizedek and Lot, with the Sacrifice of Isaac*; *The Histories of Lot and Abraham*; *Lot and Abraham*; *The Sacrifice of Isaac*
*Abraham, Melchizedek and Lot, with the Sacrifice of Isaac*. *See* Abraham, Melchisedec and Isaac
*Abstraction*. 14th century?
Chamberlin, B., translator CLF1, ORI2
*Ad Dominican missam*. *See* For the Mass of Our Lord (from Limoges)
*Ad faciendam similtudinem Dominici sepulcri*. *See* For Representing the Scene at the Lord's Sepulchre (from Fleury)
*Ad interfectionem puerorum*. *See* The Slaughter of the Innocents (from Fleury)
*Ad repraesentandum conversionem Beati Pauli Apostoli*. *See* For Representing the Conversion of the Blessed Apostle Paul (from Fleury)
*Ad repraesentandum quomodo Sanctus Nich(o)laus Getranslatoron(is) filium Iiberavit*. *See* For Representing How Saint Nicholas Freed the Son of Getranslatoron (from Fleury)
*Adam*. 1150?
Axton, R., and Stevens, J., translators AXT
Barrow, S., and Hulme, W., translators CROV
Stone, E., translator CLF1, KRE
Variant titles: *Le jeu d'Adam*; *Le mystère d'Adam*; *The Mystery of Adam*; *The Play of Adam*
*Adam and Eve* (Chester). 15th century CHEL, CHELM, MED
*Adam and Eve* (Norwich, Text B, non-cycle mystery play). 12th century? FRAN
*The Adoration* (York). 15th century ENGE
*The Adoration of the Kings*. Anonymous. translator RAVIC
*The Adoration of the Kings* (Chester). *See* The Adoration of the Magi (Chester)
*The Adoration of the Magi* (Chester). 15th century CHES, CHESE
Variant title: *The Adoration of the Kings*

*The Adoration of the Shepherds* (Chester). 15th century
   CHES, CHESE
*The AIDS Show (Artists Involved with Death and
   Survival).* 1984. WES17/18 (Consists of the
   following twenty-six brief plays: Attinello, P.
   *Hospital*; Attinello, P. *Party 1981*; Attinello, P.
   *Party 1982*; Attinello, P. *Party 1983*; Attinello, P.
   *Party 1984*; Attinello, P. *Party 1985*; Barksdale,
   W. *Land's End*; Brown, K., and McQueen, M.
   *Rimmin' at the Baths*; Brown, K., and McQueen,
   M. *Safe Livin' in Dangerous Times*; Curzon, D.
   *Reverend What's His Name*; Davis, E. *The Nurse*;
   Holsclaw, D. *It's My Party*; Holsclaw, D. *Spice
   Queen*; Morris, M. Alice; Morris, M. *Nobody's
   Fool*; Moss, L. *Murray 1981*; Moss, L. *Murray
   1982*; Moss, L. *Murray 1983*; Moss, L. *Murray
   Now*; Prandini, A. *Mama's Boy*; Real, P. *Stronger
   and Stronger*; Stone, R. *The Bar*; Stone, R. *To
   Tell the Truth*; Turner, D. *Invitation (Part One)*;
   Turner, D. *Invitation (Part Two)*; Weigand, R.
   *Ricky*)
*Albion, Knight. See* A Moral Play of Albion, Knight
*All's One, or One of the Foure Plates in One, called A
   Yorkshire Tragedy. See* A Yorkshire Tragedy
*The Anchor Draping. See* Ikarikazuki
*The Announcement to the Three Marys; Peter and
   John at the Sepulchre. See* Three Marys at the
   Tomb (N Town)
*The Annunciation* (adapted from four major cyles by
   Kenneth Pickering, Kevin Wood and Philip Dart).
   15th century MYSCC
*The Annunciation* (N Town) 15th century CAWL
*The Annunciation* (Wakefield). 15th century BEVD,
   LOOM, TOV, TOWN
*The Annunciation and the Nativity* (Chester). 15th
   century CHEL, CHELM
*Antichrist* (Chester). 15th century CHEL, CHELM,
   CHES, CHESE
*Apius and Virginia* (sometimes attributed to Richard
   Bower). 1563? FARM, HAO
   Variant title: *Appius and Virginia*
*The Apostles at the Tomb* (N Town). 15th century DAVJ
*Appearance to Cleopas and Luke* (N Town). 15th
   century DAVJ, N-TOW
   Variant title: *Cleophas and Luke; The Appearance to
   Thomas*
*Appearance to Mary Magdalen* (N Town). 15th century
   DAVJ, N-TOW
*Appearance to Thomas* (N Town). 15th century DAVJ,
   N-TOW
   Variant titles: *Cleophas and Luke; The Appearance
   to Thomas Appius and Virginia. See* Apius and
   Virginia
*Archibald Cameron of Locheill, or an Episode in the
   Seven Year's War in Canada.* 1759.
   Doucette, L. E., translator DOUC

   Variant title: *Archibald Cameron, ou un episode de la
   guerre de Sept ans en Canada.*
*Archibald Cameron, ou un episode de la guerre de Sept
   ans en Canada. See* Archibald Cameron of Locheill,
   or an Episode in the Seven Year's War in Canada
*Arden of Faversham. See* Arden of Feversham
*Arden of Feversham* (sometimes attributed to Thomas
   Arden; Thomas Kyd; William Shakespeare). 1586?
   BAS, BRO, DPR1, GATG, KINNR, MAKG,
   MAME, MIN1, MIO1, MIR, MONV, OLH, OLI1,
   SCH, STUR
   Variant titles: *Arden of Faversham; The Lamentable
   and True Tragedy of Master Arden of Feversham
   in Kent*
*Asaina.*
   Tyler, R., translator TYLG
*The Ascension* (Chester). 15th century BURNS, CHEL,
   CHELM, ENG
*Ascension* (N Town). 15th century DAVJ, N-TOW
   Variant titles: *The Ascension; The Selection of
   Matthias*
*Ascension* (Wakefield). *See* The Ascension of the Lord
   (Wakefield)
*The Ascension of the Lord* (Wakefield). 15th century
   TOV, TOWN
   Variant title: *Ascension*
*The Ascension; The Selection of Matthias. See*
   Ascension (N Town); Matthias (N Town)
*The Ashmole Fragment.* DAVN
*Assumption* (N Town). 15th century DAVJ, N-TOW
   Variant title: *The Assumption of Mary*
*The Assumption and the Coronation of the Virgin*
   (York). 15th century ENGE
*The Assumption of Mary. See* Assumption (N Town)
*Atia yaw.* MARLG
*Attowell's Jig (Francis' New Jig)* (sometimes attributed
   to George Attowell). 1595? BAS, NES
   Variant titles: *Francis' New Jig; Mr. Attowell's Jig*
*Azalea Mountain.* 1973.
   Anon. translator FIFW
*Balaack and Balaam* (Chester). 15th century CHEL,
   CHELM, ENGE
   Variant title: *Balaam, Balak and the Prophets*
*Balaam, Balak, and the Prophets. See also* Balaack and
   Balaam
*Balaam, Balak and the Prophets* (adapted from four
   major cyles by Kenneth Pickering, Kevin Wood
   and Philip Dart). 15th century MYSCC
*Banns* (adapted from four major cyles by Kenneth
   Pickering, Kevin Wood and Philip Dart). 15th
   century MYSCC
*Banns* (Chester). 15th century CHELM, ENGE
*Banns* (N Town). 15th century ADA, BEVD, SCW,
   N-TOW
   Variant title: *The Marriage of Mary and Joseph*
*The Baptism* (N Town). 15th century N-TOW

*The Battle of Brooklyn* (published Anonymously by James Rivington). (1776) AMPA, PHI, WORN

*Ba-wang bie-ji. See* Hegemon King Says Farewell to His Queen

*The Beauty and Good Properties of Women* (commonly called *Calisto and Melibaea*). 1530? FARO

*The Benediktbeuren Play.* 13th century
 Robinson, D., and Francke, K., translators and adapters ROBM

*The Betrayal* (adapted from four major cyles by Kenneth Pickering, Kevin Wood and Philip Dart). 15th century MYSCC

*The Betrayal. See* The Betraying of Christ (N Town)

*The Betrayal* (Wakefield). 15th century HEIL

*The Betrayal of Christ* (Chester). 15th century CHEL, CHELM, CHES, CHESE, GARZB

*The Betraying of Christ* (N Town). 15th century ADA, N-TOW
 Variant title: *The Betrayal*

*The Bilker Bilk'd.* 1742? HUGL

*Bilsen Play. See* The star

*The Bird Catcher in Hell. See* Esachi Juo

*The Birth of Jesus* (York). 15th century ADA, BEVD

*The Birth of Merlin; or, The Child Hath Found His Father* (sometimes attributed to William Rowley; William Shakespeare). 1597? BRO, LUP

*Birth of the Son* (N Town). 15th century DAVJ

*The Blind Chelidonian* (Chester). 15th century BURNS, CHEL, CHELM
 Variant titles: *The Healing of the Blind Man; The Healing: The Blind Man and Lazarus*

*The Blockheads; or, The Affrighted Officers* (attributed to Mercy Otis Warren). 1776. PHI

*Blow-in-the-box.* 15th century
 Prins, J., translator PRIN

*The Blue Blouse Skit.* 1924.
 Anon., translator VONG
 Variant title: *Siniaia bluza*

*Boketey larweh.* MARLG

*The Book of Job. See* Job

*Boot and Spurre.* 1611? GOSS

*Bōshibari.*
 Katō, E., translator BRAZT
 Variant title: *Tied to a Stick*

*The Bridegroom* (from Limoges). 11th century
 Dronke, P., translator DRON
 Variant title: *Sponsus*

*The Brome Abraham and Isaac. See* Abraham and Isaac (Brome)

*Brome Plays. See* Abraham and Isaac (Brome)

*Buffeting* (Wakefield). *See* The Buffeting (Wakefield)

*The Buffeting* (Wakefield). 15th century BEVD, ENGE, TOV, TOWN
 Variant title: *Buffeting*

*The Buggbears. See* Jeffere, John (supposed author)

*The Building of the Ark* (York). 15th century BEAD

*The Bull Dance.* early 20th century
 Edmonson, M., translator EDMON

*Los buñuelos.* NOR

*The Burial; The Guarding of the Sepulchre. See* Passion II (N Town)

*Busu. See* The Delicious Poison

*Butterfly.*
 Shimazaki, C., translator SHIM 3, bk. 1
 Variant title: *Kocho*

*The Butterfly Dream.* 1368?
 Scott, A., translator KIAN, SCY1
 Variant title: *Hu tieh meng*

*Buying Rouge.* 18th century
 Dolby, W., translator EIG
 Variant title: *Mai yanzhi*

*Caesar Augustus* (Wakefield). 15th century TOV, TOWN

*Cain and Abel* (adapted from four major cyles by Kenneth Pickering, Kevin Wood and Philip Dart). 15th century MYSCC

*Cain and Abel* (Chester). 15th century BURNS, CHEL, CHELM

*Cain and Abel* (N Town). 15th century CAWL, DAVJ, FRAN, N-TOW

*Calisto and Melibaea. See* The Beauty and Good Properties of Women

*The Cambridge Prologue.* 13th century? CHEL

*Candlemes Day and the Kyllung of pe Children of Israelle. See* Killing of the Children

*The Castle of Perseverance.* ca. 1405–25. ADA, BEV, BEVD, FOUN, HOPP, POLL, SCAT

*Celestina. See* Rojas, Fernando de. Celestina

*The Chalk Circle.* 13th century?
 Van Der Meer, E., translator CLF1, KRE

*The Chantilly Play. See* Bourlet, Katherine. The Nativity Chester Play of the Deluge; The Deluge

*Chapayev Anecdotes.* 1930s.
 Sahonee, R., translator RZH

*The Chester Play of Noah's Flood. See* The Deluge (Chester)

*Chester Plays. See* Abraham and Isaac; Abraham, Melchisedec and Isaac; Adam and Eve; The Adoration of the Magi; The Adoration of the Shepherds; The Annunciation and the Nativity; Antichrist; The Ascension; Balaack and Balaam; Banns; The Betrayal of Christ; The Blind Chelidonian; Cain and Abel; Christ and the Doctors; Christ and the Moneylenders; Christ Appears to the Disciples; Christ at the House of Simon the Leper; Christ at the Road to Emmaus; Christ's Ascension; Christ's Ministry; Christ's Passion; Christ's Resurrection; The Creation of Man; The Death of Herod; The Deluge; Doubting Thomas; Epilogue; The Fall of Lucifer; The Harrowing of Hell; Interlude; Judas' Plot; The Last Judgment; The Last Supper; The Magi's

Oblation; Moses and the Law; The Nativity;
The Passion; The Pentecost; The Prophets; The
Prophets of Antichrist; The Purification; The
Raising of Lazarus; The Resurrection, Harrowing
of Hell, and The Last Judgment; The Sacrifice
of Isaac; The Shepherds; Simon the Leper; The
Slaying of the Innocents; The Temptation; The
Three Kings; The Trial and Flagellation; The
Woman Taken in Adultery

*The Chicken Pie and the Chocolate Cake.* 15th century
  Mandel, O., translator MARH
  Variant title: *Le pâté et de la torte*

*Chief Kaku Ackah of Nzima.* MARLG

*Chikubu-shima.*
  Tyler, R., translator TYLJ

*Chiu keng t'ien. See* One Missing Head

*Christ and the Doctors* (Chester). 15th century CHEL,
  CHELM

*Christ and the Doctors* (N Town). *See* Jesus and the
  Doctors (N Town)

*Christ and the Doctors* (Wakefield). *See* The Play of the
  Doctors (Wakefield)

*Christ and the Moneylenders* (Chester). 15th century
  CHEL, CHELM

*Christ Appears to the Disciples* (Chester). 15th century
  BEVD

*Christ at the House of Simon the Leper* (Chester). 15th
  century CHEL, CHELM

*Christ before Annas and Caiaphas* (York). 15th century
  BEAD, MED

*Christ before Herod* (York). 15th century BEAD, MED

*Christ before Pilate* (1) (I): *The Dream of Pilate's Wife*
  (York).
    *See* The Dream of Pilate's Wife (York)

*Christ before Pilate* (2) (II): *The Judgment* (York). 15th
  century BEAD, MED

*Christ on the Road to Emmaus* (Chester). 15th century
  CHEL, CHELM
    Variant title: *Emmaus*

*The Christians and the Moors. See* Los moros y los
  cristianos

*A Christmas Messe.* 1619. GOSS, STUA

*A Christmas Mumming: The Play of Saint* [Prince]
  *George.* 15th century GARZB
    Variant titles: *Christmas Play of St. George; The Play
    of St. George*

*A Christmas Pageant.* 1981. SWO

*The Christmas Play* (from Benediktbeuern). 12th
  century BEVD
    Variant title: *Ludus de nativitate*

*Christmas Play of St. George. See* A Christmas
    Mumming: The Play of Saint [Prince] George

*Christ's Appearance before the Doctors. See* Christ and
    the Doctors (Chester)

*Christ's Appearances to the Disciples* (N Town). 15th
  century ENGE

*Christ's Ascension* (Chester). 15th century CHES

*Christ's Burial and Resurrection* (Digby). 15th century
  DIGBY, LAT
    Variant titles: *Christ's Burial; The Prologe of this
    Treyte or Meditation off the Buryalle of Christe and
    Mowrnying Perat*

*Christ's Death and Burial* (York). 15th century BEVD

*Christ's Ministry* (Chester). 15th century ADA

*Christ's Passion* (Chester). 15th century BURNS,
  CHEL, CHELM, CHES
    Variant title: *The Crucifixion, The Passion*

*Christ's Resurrection* (Chester). 15th century BURNS,
  CHES
    Variant title: *Resurrection*

*Christ's Resurrection* (Digby). 15th century LAT
    Variant title: *Her Begynnes His Resurrection on
    Pas(c)he Daye at Morn*

*The Cicada.*
  Haynes, C., translator BRAZ, BRAZT
    Variant title: *Semi*

*Cleophas and Luke; The Appearance to Thomas. See*
    Appearance to Cleophas and Luke (N Town);
    Appearance to Thomas (N Town)

*The Coleorton Masque.* 1618. LINDC

*Coliphizacio* (Wakefield). 15th century CAWM

*A Comedy Called Misogonus. See* Misogonus

*The Coming of Antichrist. See* Antichrist (Chester)

*Common Conditions.* 1570? FARM

*The Conspiracy* (Wakefield). 15th century TOV, TOWN
    Variant title: *The Conspiracy and Capture*

*The Conspiracy* (York). 15th century BEAD, MED

*The Conspiracy and Capture* (Wakefield). *See* The
    Conspiracy (Wakefield)

*The Contract of Marriage between Wit and Wisdom.*
  1519? FARM
    Variant titles: *The Marriage of Wit and Wisdom; Wit
    and Wisdom*

*The Conversion of St. Paul* (Digby). ADA, BEVD,
  COLDE, DIGBY, LAT, MARG, SWIT
    Variant title: *The Digby Conversion of St. Paul*

*The Cornish Mystery Play of the Three Maries. See*
    The Three Maries Cornish plays. *See* The Death of
    Pilate; The Legend of the Rood; The Three Maries

*Courtois d'Arras.*
  Axton R., and Stevens, J., translators AXT

*Coventry plays. See* Ludus Coventriae plays

*The Crab. See* Crab Bites Yamabushi

*Crab Bites Yamabushi.*
  Morley, C., translator TRAN
  Tyler, R., translator TYLP
    Variant titles: *The Crab; Kani Yamabushi;
    Kaniyamabushi*

*The Creation* (Wakefield). 15th century TOV, TOWN

*The Creation, and Adam and Eve. See* The Creation of Man: Adam and Eve

*Creation and Fall* (Chester). *See* The Creation of Man: Adam and Eve (Chester); The Fall of Lucifer (Chester)

*Creation and Fall of Lucifer* (N Town). *See* The Fall of Lucifer (N Town)

*The Creation and Fall of Lucifer* (York). 15th century BEAD, CAWL, GARZB, MED, POLL
  Variant title: *The Fall of the Angels*

*Creation and Fall of Man* (N Town). 15th century DAVJ, N-TOW
  Variant title: *The Creation of the World; The Fall of Man*

*The Creation and the Fall of the Angels* (Wakefield). 15th century BEVD

*The Creation of Adam and Eve* (adapted from four major cyles by Kenneth Pickering, Kevin Wood and Philip Dart). 15th century MYSCC

*The Creation of Adam and Eve* (York). 15th century CAWL

*The Creation of Eve, with the Expelling of Adam and Eve Out of Paradise.* 15th century ADA

*The Creation of Heaven; The Fall of Lucifer. See* The Fall of Lucifer (N Town)

*The Creation of Man: Adam and Eve* (Chester). 15th century BURNS, CHES, CHESE, ENGE Variant titles: *The Creation, and Adam and Eve, Creation and Fall*

*The Creation of the World; The Fall of Man. See* Creation and Fall of Man (N Town)

*The Croxton Play of the Sacrament. See* The Play of the Sacrament (Croxtun)

*Crucifixion* (Wakefield). *See* The Crucifixion (Wakefield)

*The Crucifixion* (adapted from four major cyles by Kenneth Pickering, Kevin Wood and Philip Dart). 15th century MYSCC

*The Crucifixion* (Chester). *See* Christ's Passion (Chester)

*The Crucifixion* (Wakefield). 15th century EVER, GARZB, TOV, TOWN
  Variant title*: Crucifixion*

*The Crucifixion* (York). 15th century ABRK1, BEAD, BEVD, CAWL, COLDE, HEIL, MED, WOTHB
  Variant titles: *The Crucifixion of Christ; The York Crucifixion*

*The Crucifixion of Christ. See* The Crucifixion (York)

*Las cuatro apariciones de Guadalupe/The Four Apparitions of Guadalupe.* 16th century
  Torres, L., translator SIXN
  Variant title: *The Four Apparitions of Guadalupe*

*Le cuvier. See* The Washtub

*The Daimyo.*

Duran, L., translator DUP

*Dallot.* PHIL
  Tupas, F., translator PHIL

*Dampu.*
  Smethurst, M., translator DRAF

*The Dance of Death. See* Totentanz

*Daniel Ludus. See* The Play of Daniel (from Beauvais)

*Danielis ludus. See* The Play of Daniel (from Beauvais)

*The Dead Stone's Banquet. See* Don Juan and Don Pietro

*The Death and Burial* (York). 15th century BEAD, ENGE
  Variant title: *The Death of Christ* (York)

*The Death of Christ* (York). *See* The Death and Burial (York)

*The Death of Herod* (Chester). 15th century GARZB

*The Death of Herod* (N Town). 15th century BEVD, ENGE

*The Death of Judas; The Trials before Pilate and Herod. See* The Trial of Christ (N-Town)

*The Death of Karna.*
  Siswoharsojo, P., translator; Brandon, J., and Alkire, S., adapters BQA
  Variant title: *Karna tanding*

*The Death of Pilate* (Cornish). 15th century CAWL, GARZB, HAH, TREB

*The Death Stone.*
  Aston, W., translator BAT3

*Debate of Winter and Summer.* 15th century
  Prins, J., translator PRIN

*The Deceived.* 1531.
  Peacock, T., translator BENSA
  Variant title: *Gl'ingannati*

*The Delicious Poison.*
  Kenny, D., translator BRAZ
  Variant title: *Busu*

*The Deliverance of Souls* (Wakefield). 15th century TOWN

*The Deluge* (Chester). 15th century ABRL1, ABRM1, ADA, BURNS, BENY, CAWL, CHEL, CHELM, CHES, CHESE, ENGE, EVEM, EVER, FRAN, HOPP, MAR, MARK, MARL, MIL, PARRY, POLL, SNYD1, TAT, TAU, WEAT1
  Variant titles: *The Chester Play of Noah's Flood; Chester Play of the Deluge; Noah; Noah's Deluge; Noah's Flood*

*The Deluge* (Wakefield). 15th century BRJB, BRJC, GARZB, TOV
  Variant title: *Noah and His Sons*

*Depositio cornuti typographici. See* The Printer's Apprentice

*Los desposorios de Joseph. See* Joseph's Wedding

*The Destruction of Jerusalem.*
  Anon., translator RAVIC

Variant title: *Ad faciendam similtudinem Dominici sepulcri*

*For the Mass of our Lord* (from Limoges). 11th century BEVD
   Variant title: *Ad Dominicam missam*

*Forsaken Love.*
   Duran, L., translator DUP

*The Four Apparitions of Guadalupe. See* Las cuatro apariciones de Guadalupe

*The Four Elements. See* The Nature of the Four Elements

*Francis' New Jig. See* Attowell's Jig

*Fukurō yamabushi. See* Owls

*Futari daimyō. See* Two daimyō

*Gammer Gurton's Needle. See* Stevenson, William (supposed author)

*Le garçon et l'aveugle.*
   Axton, R., and Stevens, J., translators AXT

*Gargoyle.*
   Tyler, R., translator TYLP
   Variant title: Oni-gawara

*Genji kuyō.*
   Goff, J., translator BRAZT
   Variant title: *A Memorial Service for Genji*

*George a Greene, the Pinner of Wakefield. See* Greene, Robert (supposed author)

*Gigantomachia, or Worke for Jupiter.* 1613–1619? GOSS, STUA
   Variant title: *Worke for Jupiter*

*Gl'ingannati. See* The Deceived

*Gloriant.* 15th century
   Prins, J., translator PRIN

*Godley Queen Hester.* 1525? FARP, MED
   Variant titles: *The Enterlude of Godly Queene Hester; An Interlude of Godley Queen Hester*

*Gowne, Hood, and Capp.* GOSS

*Grandee's Son Takes the Wrong Career.* Late 13th or early 14th century
   Dolby, W., translator EIG
   Variant title: *Huan-men zidi cuo li-shen*

*Grim the Collier of Croydon; or, The Devil and His Dame* (sometimes attributed to John Tatham). 1600? FARM

*Hagoromo. See* The Feather Mantle

*Hahoe Pyŏsin-kut.*
   Cho, O., translator TRAD

*Hajitomi. See* The Push-up Shutter

*El Hambriento.* NOR

*Hamlet! The Ravin' Prince of Denmark!!, or, The Baltic Swell!!! and the Diving Belle!!!* NIN4

*Hanago.*
   Tyler, R., translator TYLG

*The Hands in the Box.*
   Duran, L., translator DUP

*Hanging of Judas* (Wakefield). *See* The Hanging of Judas (Wakefield)

*The Hanging of Judas* (Wakefield). 15th century TOV, TOWN
   Variant title: *Hanging of Judas*

*The Harrowing of Hell* (Chester). 15th century ADA, BURNS, CAWL, CHEL, CHELM, POLL

*The Harrowing of Hell, Part 1.* (N Town). 15th century N-TOWN

*The Harrowing of Hell, Part 2; Christ's Appearance to Mary; Pilate and the Soldiers. See* Harrowing of Hell II (N Town); Resurrection and Appearance to Mother (N Town)

*Harrowing of Hell II* (N Town). 15th century DAVJ, N-TOW
   Variant title: The Harrowing of Hell (Part 2); Christ's Appearance to Mary; Pilate and the Soldiers

*Harrowing of Hell* (Wakefield). *See* The Harrowing of Hell; or, The Extraction of Souls from Hell (Wakefield)

*The Harrowing of Hell* (York). 15th century BEAD, ENGE, MED

*The Harrowing of Hell; or, The Extraction of Souls from Hell* (Wakefield). 15th century BEVD, EVER, TOV

*The Healing of the Blind Man. See* The Blind Chelidonian (Chester)

*The Healing: The Blind Man and Lazarus. See* The Blind Chelidonian (Chester); The Raising of Lazarus (Chester)

*Hegemon King Says Farewell to His Queen.* Late 13th or early 14th century
   Dolby, W., translator EIG
   Variant title: *Ba-wang bie-ji*

*Hegge plays. See* N Town plays

*Henry the Fifth. See* The Famous Victories of Henry the Fifth

*Her Begynnes His Resurrection on Pas[c]ke Daye at Morn. See* Christ's Resurrection (Digby)

*Herod* (N Town). *See* The Magi, Herod, and the Slaughter of the Innocents

*Herod and the Magi* (N Town). *See* The Magi, Herod, and the Slaughter of the Innocents

*Herod and the Magi* (York). *See* The Three Kings (York)

*Herod and the Slaying of the Innocents* (adapted from four major cyles by Kenneth Pickering, Kevin Wood and Philip Dart). 15th century MYSCC

*Herod and the Three Kings* (N Town). *See* The Magi, Herod, and the Slaughter of the Innocents

*Herod the Great* (Wakefield). 15th century BEVD, CAWL, TOV, TOWN

*Herod; The Trial before Annas and Cayphas. See* The Trial of Christ (N Town)

*Herod's Killing of the Children* (Digby). 15th century
COLDE, DIGBY
    Variant title: *The Digby Killing of the Children*
*Herodum. See* The Service for Representing Herod
    (from Fleury)
*He's Much to Blame.* 1798. INCA4
*The Hessian Christmas Play.* 15th century
    Robinson, D., translator and adapter ROBM
*Heteroclitanomalonomia.* 1613? GOSS, STUA
*Hickscorner.* 1534? EVEM, FARO
*The Histories of Lot and Abraham. See* Abraham,
    Melchisedec and Isaac
*The History of Jacob and Esau. See* Jacob and Esau
*The Holy Resurrection. See* La seinte resureccion
*The Honor of Danzo.*
    Duran, L., translator DUP
*The Honorable Entertainment Given to the Queen's*
    *Majesty in Progress, at Elvetham in Hampshire.*
    1591. KINNR
*The Horns.*
    Duran, L., translator DUP
*How the Blessed Saint Helen Found the Holy Cross.*
    McAfee, B., translator RAVIC
*Hu tieh meng. See* The Butterfly Dream
*Huan-men zi-di cuo li-shen. See* Grandee's Son Takes
    the Wrong Career
*Hung luan hsi. See* Twice a Bride
*Hung teng chi. See* The Red Lantern
*Identifying Footprints in the Snow.* (mid-1950s version)
    Dolby, W., translator EIG
    Variant title: *Ping-xue bianzong*
*Ikarikazuki.*
    Gabriel, J., translator BRAZT
    Variant title: *The Anchor Draping*
*Impatient Poverty.* 1560? FARN
    Variant title: *An Interlude of Impatient Poverty*
*In an Oval Office* (from the Watergate Transcripts).
    1973. ESA
*[I]ncipit ordo ad repraesentandum*
*Interlude* (Chester). 15th century BURNS
*An Interlude of Godley Queen Hester. See* Godley
    Queen Hester
*An Interlude of Impatient Poverty. See* Impatient
    Poverty
*The Interlude of John the Evangelist. See* John the
    Evangelist
*An Interlude of Wealth and Health. See* Wealth and
    Health
*The Interlude of Youth. See* Youth
*Irawan Rabi. See* Irawan's Wedding
*Irawan's Wedding.*
    Alkire, S., and Siswoharsojo, P., translators; Brandon,
    J., adapter BQA
    Variant title: *Irawan Rabi*

*The Iron Crown.*
    Kato, E., translator KEE
    Shimazaki, C., translator SHIM4, bk. 2
    Variant title: *Kanawa*
*Isaac* (Wakefield). 15th century TOV, TOWN
*Item de resurrectione Domini. See* Of the Resurrection
    of the Lord (from St. Gall)
*Jack Juggler* (attributed to Nicholas Udall). 1553? FAR,
    THZ, TYDE
    Variant titles: *Jacke Jugeler; A New Enterlued for*
    *Children to Playe Named Jacke Jugeler: Both*
    *Wytte, Very Playsent, and Merye*
*Jacke Jugeler. See* Jack Juggler
*Jacob* (Wakefield). 15th century TOV, TOWN
*Jacob and Esau.* 1558? FARP
    Variant title: *The History of Jacob and Esau*
*Jesse* (N Town). 15th century DAVJ, N-TOW
    Variant title: *Jesse Root*
*Jesse Root. See* Jesse (N Town)
*Jesus and the Doctors* (N Town). 15th century DAVJ,
    N-TOW
    Variant title: Christ and the Doctors
*Le jeu d'Adam. See* Adam
*The Jizō Dance. See* Jizō-mai
*Jizō-mai.*
    Tyler, R., translator TYLG
    Variant title: *The Jizō Dance*
*Joachim and Anna* (N Town). 15th century N-TOW
*Job.* 400? B.C. BUCL, BUCM, DAVK, SML, TRE,
    TREA2
    Variant title: *The Book of Job*
*John the Baptist* (adapted from four major cyles by
    Kenneth Pickering, Kevin Wood and Philip Dart).
    15th century MYSCC
*John the Baptist* (Wakefield). 15th century TOV,
    TOWN
*John the Baptist* (York). 15th century ENGE
*John the Evangelist.* 1557? FARN
    Variant titles: *The Interlude of John the Evangelist;*
    *Saint John the Evangelist*
*Joseph* (N Town). 15th century ENGE, N-TOW
    Variant title: *Joseph's Doubt*
*Joseph's Doubt. See* Joseph (N Town)
*Joseph's Trouble about Mary* (York). 15th century
    BEAD, MED
*Joseph's Wedding.* 16th century
    McGaha, M., translator STORJ
    Variant title: *Los desposorios de Joseph*
*The Joyful Hall of Jade. See* The Faithful Harlot
*Juan Rana Comilón.* NOR
*Judas. See* Judas' Plot (Chester)
*Judas' Plot* (Chester). 15th century BURNS, CHEL,
    CHELM
    Variant title: *Judas*

*The Judgement* (Chester). *See* The Last Judgment
    (Chester)
*Judgment* (Wakefield). *See* The Judgment (Wakefield)
*The Judgment* (Wakefield). 15th century TOV,
    TOWN
*The Judgment* (York). *See* The Judgment Day
*Judgement Day. See* Doomsday (N Town)
*The Judgment Day* (York). 15th century ADA, BEAD,
    CAWL, ENGE, MED, SCW
    Variant titles: *The Judgment; The Last Judgement*
*Julius Caesar Travestie.* (1861) NIN4
*Kaga-Sodo. See* The Fatal Error
*Kagekiyo.*
    Shimazaki, C., translator SHIM4, bk. 2
*Kagyū. See* The Snail
*Kakiyamabushi. See* Persimmons
*Kaminari. See* Thunderbolt
*Kanaoka.*
    Haynes, C., translator BRAZ
*Kanawa. See* The Iron Crown
*Kani Yamabushi. See* Crab Bites Yamabushi
*Kaniyamabushi. See* Crab Bites Yamabushi
*Kantan.* 15th century
    Tyler, R., translator TYLJ
    Waley, A., translator WAJ
*Karna tanding. See* The Death of Karna
*Kazuraki.*
    Shimazaki, C., translator SHIM4, bk. 1
*The Kept Mistress.* 1756. BEVI
*The Killing of Abel* (Wakefield). 15th century ADA,
    BEVD, ENGE, TOWN
*Killing of the Children.* 1512. LAT
    Variant title: *Candlemes Day and the Kyllung of pe
        Children of Israelle*
*King Darius.* 1565? FAR
*King Edward the Third. See* The Reign of King Edward
    the Third
*King Herod* (Chester). 12th century? FRAN
*King Richard III Travestie.* (1823) NIN1
*Kkoktu Kaksi*: Puppet Play.
    Cho, O., translator TRAD
*Kocho. See* Butterfly
*Kuruwa Banshō. See* Love Letter from the Licensed
    Quarter
*Kusabira. See* Mushrooms
*Kuzu.*
    Yasuda, K., translator YASU
*The Lamentable and True Tragedy of Master Arden of
    Feversham in Kent. See* Arden of Feversham
*The Lamentable Tragedy of Locrine* (sometimes
    attributed to George Peele; William Shakespeare).
    1586? BRO
    Variant title: *Locrine*
*Lancelot of Denmark.* 15th century
    Prins, J., translator PRIN

*The Last Judgement* (York). *See* The Judgment Day
    (York)
*The Last Judgment* (Chester). 15th century BURNS,
    CHEL, CHELM, CHES, CHESE
    Variant title: *The Judgement*
*The Last Judgment* (Wakefield). 15th century BEVD
*The Last Supper* (adapted from four major cyles by
    Kenneth Pickering, Kevin Wood and Philip Dart).
    15th century MYSCC
*The Last Supper* (Chester). 15th century BURNS,
    CHEL, CHELM
*The Last Supper; The Conspiracy with Judas. See*
    Passion I (N Town)
*The Law* (adapted from four major cyles by Kenneth
    Pickering, Kevin Wood and Philip Dart). 15th
    century MYSCC
*Lazarus* (Wakefield). 15th century ENGE, TOV, TOWN
*The Legend of the Rood* (Cornish). 15th century HAH
*Leicestershire St. George Play.* 1863. ADA
*The Life and Death of Lord Cromwell. See* Thomas,
    Lord Cromwell
*Lippin.* 15th century
    Prins, J., translator PRIN
*The Little Clay Cart. See* Shudraka, King (supposed
    author)
*Locrine. See* The Lamentable Tragedy of Locrine
*London by Night* (sometimes attributed to Charles
    Selby). 1844. VICT
*The London Prodigal* (sometimes attributed to William
    Shakespeare). 1603? BRO
*Longing for Worldly Pleasures.* 1368? SCY2
    Variant title: Ssu fan
*Lot and Abraham. See* Abraham, Melchisedec and Isaac
*Love Letter from the Licensed Quarter.* 1780.
    Brandon, J., translator KAB, WOTHB
    Variant title: *Kuruwa Bunshō*
*Ludus Coventriae plays. See* N Town plays
*Ludus de nativitate. See* The Christmas Play (from
    Benediktbeuern)
*Ludus de passione. See* The Passion Play (from
    Benediktbeuern)
*Ludus de passione. See* The Passion Play (from the
    Carmina Burana [Bressanone?])
*Ludus super iconia Sancti Nicolai.* 15th century POLL
*The Lunchbox Thief.*
    Morley, C., translator TRAN
    Variant title: *Tsuto yamabushi*
*The Maastricht Play* (adapted from Paachapel). 14th
    century
    Robinson, D., translator and adapter ROBM
*Macro Morals. See* The Castle of Perseverance;
    Mankynd; and, Mind, Will, and Understanding
*Mactacio Abel* (Wakefield). 15th century CAWM,
    GARZB, ROBE, TOV
    Variant title: *The Murder of Abel*

*The Magi. See* The Magi, Herod, and the Slaughter of the Innocents (N Town)

*Magi and Innocents* (Chester). *See* The Magi's Oblation (Chester); The Slaying of the Innocents (Chester)

*The Magi, Herod, and the Slaughter of the Innocents* (N Town). 15th century ADA, DAVJ, MAR, N-TOW
  Variant titles: *Herod; Herod and the Magi; Herod and the Three Kings; The Massacre of the Innocents; The Slaughter of the Innocents; The Magi*

*The Magi's Oblation* (Chester). 15th century CHEL, CHELM, CHES, CHESE
  Variant titles: *Magi and Innocents, The Offerings of the Three Kings*

*Magnus Herodes* (Wakefield). 15th century CAWM

*Mai yan-zhi. See* Buying rouge

*A Maiden at Dōjōji.*
  Oshima, M., translator BRAZ
  Variant title: *Musume Dōjōji*

*Manju. See* Nakamitsu

*Mankind. See* Mankynd

*Mankynd.* ca. 1465–1471. ADA, BEV, BEVD, COLDE, FARN, MED, SOME, THR
  Variant title: *Mankind*

*Manohra.*
  Bhukkanasut, U., translator BRA

*Man's Disobedience and the Fall of Man* (York). 15th century GARZB

*Mari.*
  Waley, A., translator WAJ
  Variant title: *The Football*

*Maria Marten. See* Maria Martin; or, The Murder in the Red Barn

*Maria Martin; or, The Murder in the Red Barn.* 1840. KILG
  Variant titles: *Maria Marten; The Murder in the Red Barn; The Red Barn*

*The Marriage of Mary and Joseph. See* Banns (N Town)

*The Marriage of Wit and Science.* 1569? FARM
  Variant titles: *Wit and Science; Wyt and Science*

*The Marriage of Wit and Wisdom. See* The Contract of Marriage between Wit and Wisdom

*The Martyr'd Souldier.* BUL1

*The Martyrdom of Ali.*
  Pelly, L., translator BAT3
  Variant title: *Ta'ziya*

*The Martyrdom of Samuel Otu.* MARLG

*The Martyrs of Karbala.* 19th century KIAN

*Mary Magdalene* (Digby). 15th century ADA, BEVD, COLDE, DIGBY, LAT, POLL
  Variant titles: *The Digby Mary Magdalene; Saint Mary Magdalen*

*Mary Magdalene and the Apostles. See* The Mystery of Mary Magdalene and the Apostles

*The Mary Play* (N Town). 15th century MED

*Mary's Salutation of Elizabeth. See* The Salutation of Elizabeth

*The Masque of Flowers.* 1614. ETO

*The Massacre of the Innocents. See* The Magi, Herod, and the Slaughter of the Innocents

*The Massacre of the Innocents. See* The Slaying of the Innocents

*Master Peter Patelan. See* La farce de Maître Pierre Pathelin

*Master Pierre Patelin. See* La farce de Maître Pierre Pathelin

*Los matachines desenmascarados/Los Matachines unmasked.* 16th century Torres, L., SIXN
  Variant title: *Los Matachines unmasked*

*Los Matachines unmasked. See* Los matachines desenmascarados

*Matsuyani. See* Pinegum

*Matthias* (N Town). 15th century DAVJ, N-TOW
  Variant title: *The Ascension; The Selection of Matthias*

*The Mayde's Metamorphosis.* BUL2

*Mei lung chen. See* The Price of Wine

*A Memorial Service for Genji. See* Genji kuyō

*The Merchant.*
  McAfee, B., translator RAVIC

*The Merry Devil of Edmonton* (sometimes attributed to Michael Drayton). 1600? BRO, GAYLE2, MAK, OLH, OLI1

*Miidera.* 15th century
  Katō, E., translator BRAZ

*The Miller's Daughter of Manchester with the Love of William the Conqueror. See* Fair Em

*Mind, Will, and Understanding.* ca.1460–1463. BEV, COLDE, LAT, MED
  Variant titles: *Wisdom; or, Mind, Will, and Understanding; Wysdom*

*The Ministry: Healing, Teaching and Plotting* (adapted from four major cyles by Kenneth Pickering, Kevin Wood and Philip Dart). 15th century MYSCC

*The Ministry: Temptation and Teaching* (adapted from four major cyles by Kenneth Pickering, Kevin Wood and Philip Dart). 15th century MYSCC

*Minstrel Show.* ca.1850–ca.1870. MONR

*The Miracle of Saint Nicholas and the School-boys.* 15th century LOOM

*The Miracle of Saint Nicholas and the Virgins.* 15th century LOOM

*Misogonus.* 1560? BOND, FARP
  Variant title: *A Comedy Called Misogonus*

*Mr. Attowell's Jig. See* Attowell's Jig

*Moonflower.*
  Shimazaki, C., translator SHIM 3, bk. 1
  Variant title: *Yugao*

*A Moral Play of Albion, Knight.* 1566? FARP
  Variant title: *Albion, Knight*

*A Morality of Wisdom, Who Is Christ* (Digby). 15th
century DIGBY
*Los moros y los cristianos/The Christians and the
Moors.* 16th century Torres, L. SIXN
    Variant title: *The Christians and the Moors*
*Moses* (adapted from four major cyles by Kenneth
Pickering, Kevin Wood and Philip Dart). 15th
century MYSCC
*Moses* (N Town). 15th century DAVJ, N-TOW
*Moses* (York). 15th century BEAD, ENGE
    Variant title: *Moses and Pharoah*
*Moses and Pharoah* (York). *See* Moses (York)
*Moses and the Law* (Chester). 15th century CHEL,
    CHELM
*A Most Pleasant Comedic of Mucedorus the King's
Sonne of Valentia and Amadine, the King's
Daughter of Arragon. See* Mucedorus
*Mother of Mercy* (N Town). 15th century (Mother of
Mercy: Conception; Parliament of Heaven and
Annunciation; Joseph; Salutation). DAVJ
*The Motley Assembly* (attributed to Mercy Otis Warren).
1779. PHI
*Mucedorus* (sometimes attributed to Thomas Lodge;
William Shakespeare). (1598) BAS, BRO, DPR1,
NES, WINN
    Variant title: *A Most Pleasant Comedie of Mucedorus
    the King's Sonne of Valentia and Amadine, the
    King's Daughter of Arragon*
*Mundus et infans. See* The World and the Child
*The Murder in the Red Barn.* 1828. *See* Maria Martin;
or, The Murder in the Red Barn
*The Murder of Abel* (Wakefield). *See* Mactacio Abel
(Wakefield)
*Mushrooms.*
    Morley, C., translator BRAZ, TRAN
    Variant title: *Kusabira*
*Musume Dōjōji. See* A Maiden at Dōjōji
*Le mystère d'Adam. See* Adam
*Le mystère de Robert le diable. See* Robert the Devil.
14th century FOUAD
*Mysterium resurrectionis D. N. Jhesu Christi.* 15th
century POLL
*The Mystery of Adam. See* Adam
*The Mystery of Mary Magdalene and the Apostles.* 15th
century EVER
    Variant title: *Mary Magdalene and the Apostles*
*The Mystery of the Delayed Dawn* (a Ming Dynasty
story). *See* One Missing Head (adapted from)
*The Mystery of the Redemption* (N Town). 15th century
LOOM
    Variant title: *The Redemption*
*The Mystery Play of Elche.* 13th century
    Starkie, W., translator SSTW
    Variant title: *The Elche Mystery Play; Festa de Elche*

*N Town plays. See* Abraham and Isaac; The
Annunciation; The Apostles at the Tomb;
Appearance to Cleopas and Luke; Appearance
to Mary Magdalen; Appearance to Thomas;
Ascension; Assumption; Banns; The Betraying of
Christ; Cain and Abel; Christ's Appearances to the
Disciples; The Creation and Fall of Man; The Death
of Herod; Doomsday; The Fall of Lucifer; The
Harrowing of Hell, Part 1; The Harrowing of Hell
II; Jesse; Jesus and the Doctors; Joseph; The Magi,
Herod, and the Slaughter of the Innocents; Matthias;
Moses; Mother of Mercy; The Mystery of the
Redemption; The Nativity Plays; Noah; The Pageant
of the Shearmen and Tailors; Passion Play I;
Passion Play II; Passion III; Pentecost; Presentation
and Purification; Raising of Lazarus; Resurrection
and Appearance to Mother; The Salutation and
Conception; The Shepherds' Play; Story of the
Watch; Three Marys at the Tomb; The Trial of
Christ; Trial of Joseph and Mary; The Woman
Taken in Adultery; Variant cycle titles: Coventry
plays; Hegge plays; Ludus Coventriae plays
*Nakamitsu.*
    Smethurst, M., translator DRAF
    Variant title: *Manju*
*The Nativity* (The Chantilly Play). *See* Bourlet,
Katherine. The Nativity
*The Nativity* (Chester). 15th century BURNS, CHES
*The Nativity Play* (N Town plays). *See* The Pageant of
the Shearmen and Tailors
*The Nativity* (Wakefield). *See* The Second Shepherds'
Play
*The Nativity* (York). *See* The York Nativity
*The Nature of the Four Elements* (sometimes attributed
to John Rastell). 1520. FARO, POLL, THW
    Variant titles: *The Four Elements; A New Interlude
    and a Mery of the Nature of the Four Elementis*
*Negi yamabushi. See* The Shinto Priest and the
Mountain Priest
*Nero.* 1623? NERO
*New and Very Merry Farce of a Chimney Sweep. See* La
farce du ramoneur
*New and Very Merry Farce of a Cobbler Called
Calbain. See* The Farce of Calbain
*New Custom.* 1573? FAR
*A New Enterlued for Chyldren to Playe Named Jacke
Jugeler: Both Wytte, Very Playsent, and Merye. See*
Jack Juggler
*A New Interlude and a Mery of the Nature of the Four
Elementis.*
    *See* The Nature of the Four Elements
*The Newcastle Play.* 15th century? DAVN
    Variant titles: *Noah's Ark; The Shipwrights Ancient
    Play, or Dirge*

or, The Scourge of Simony, pt. I (1601?). LEIS
pt. II (1602?) LEIS, SCH, SCI, SCJ
Variant titles: *The First Part of the Return from
Parnassus; The Second Part of the Return from
Parnassus*

*The Reversby Sword Play.* 1779. ADA

*The Reynes Extracts.* 15th century? COLDE, DAVN

*The Rickinghall* (Bury St. Edmunds) fragment. 14th
century DAVN

*Rip Van Winkle* (as played by Joseph Jefferson;
adapted by Dion Boucicault). 1865. CEY, LAW,
MASW, MASX, MES, QUIJ, QUIK, QUIL,
QUIM, QUIN
— *See also* Burke, Charles. Rip Van Winkle

*Robert the Devil.* 14th century
Merwin, W.S., translator FOUAD
Variant title: *Le mystère de Robert le diable*

*Robin Hood and His Crew of Soldiers.* 1661. KNIRH

*Robin Hood and the Friar.* 15th century ADA, CHI,
KNIRH, PAR, SCW

*Robin Hood and the Knight.* 15th century CHI

*Robin Hood and the Potter.* 15th century CHI, KNIRH

*Robin Hood and the Sheriff of Nottingham.* 15th century
ADA, KNIRH

*Robyn Hod and the Shryff of Notyngham. See* Robin
Hood and the Sheriff of Nottingham

*Ruben.* 15th century
Prins, J., translator PRIN

*Ruff, Band, and Cuff.* 17th century GOSS

*The Sacrifice of Isaac.*
Adams, J., ed. VENA
McAfee, B., and Cornyn, J., translators RAVIC

*The Sacrifice of Isaac* (Brome). BAIG, BAIH, BAIK,
BEVD

*The Sacrifice of Isaac. See* also Abraham and Isaac;
Abraham, Melchisedec and Isaac

*St. George and the Dragon.* 19th century EVER, SCW

*St. George* plays. *See* Leicestershire St. George Play;
The Oxfordshire St. George Play; The Play of St.
George, version reconstructed from memory by
Thomas Hardy; St. George and the Dragon

*Saint John the Evangelist. See* John the Evangelist

*St. John's Gospel,* adapted for the stage by Murray
Watts. 1984. BURB

*Saint Mary Magdalen. See* Mary Magdalene (Digby)

*Saint Nicholas and the Three Scholars.* 12th century
MAR
Variant title: *Tres cleric*

*Saint Nicholas* plays. *See* The Miracle of Saint Nicholas
and the School-boys; The Miracle of Saint Nicholas
and the Virgins; Saint Nicholas and the Three
Scholars

*The Salutation and Conception* (N Town). 15th century
ADA, ENGE, N-TOW, POLL

Variant titles: *The Parliament of Heaven; The
Parliament of Heaven, The Salutation and
Conception*

*The Salutation of Elizabeth* (Wakefield). 15th century
BEVD, TOV, TOWN
Variant title: *Mary's Salutation of Elizabeth*

*Sambaso jiutai. See* The Song of Sambasō

*Satan and Pilate's Wife; The Second Trrial before
Pilate. See* Passion II (N Town)

*Schachiapang.* SNO

*Le savetier calbain.* 1500? BRN

*The School Act* (vaudeville skit). RAVIT

*The Scourge of Simony. See* The Return from Parnassus

*Scourging* (Wakefield). *See* The Scourging (Wakefield)

*The Scourging* (Wakefield). 15th century BEVD, ENGE,
TOV, TOWN

*The Second Part of the Return from Parnassus. See* The
Return from Parnassus; or, The Scourge of Simony

*The Second Play of the Shepherds. See* The Second
Shepherds' Play

*Second Shepherds' Play* (Wakefield). *See* The Second
Shepherds' Play (Wakefield)

*The Second Shepherd's Play* (Spanish). *See* Los
pastores

*The Second Shepherds' Pageant. See* The Second
Shepherds' Play

*The Second Shepherds' Play* (Wakefield). 15th century
ABRB1, ABRF1, ABRH1, ABRJ1, ABRK1,
ABRL1, ABRM1, ADA, ALLK, ALLM, ALLN,
ALLO, AUB, BARD, BARKE, BARKF, BAWL,
BENY, BEVD, BRIX, BRIY, BRIZ, BRJ,
BRJA, CALD, CAWL, CAWM, CHI, CLF1,
CLK1, CLKW, COLD, COLDE, COLEL2,
DAV1, DOLAN, ENGE, EVEM, EVEP, EVER,
FRAN, GARZB, HARW, HEA, HEAA, HEAD,
HEAL, HEIL, HILPDH1, HOEP, HOPP, HUD,
KER, KRE, LIE, LIED1, LIEE1, LOOM, MAR,
MATTL, MED, PAR, POLL, ROBE, RUB, SCW,
SEN, SEVT, SHAJ1, SPD, SPDB, SPEF1, SSSI,
SSSIA, SSSIB, SSSIC, STA, TAT, TAU, TAV,
TOBI, TOV, TOWN, TREB, TREC1, TREE1,
TREI1, WOO1, WOOD1, WOOE1, WOTHC
Variant titles: *Second Shepherds' Play; The Nativity;
The Second play of the Shepherds; The Second
Shepherds' Pageant; Secunda pastorum; The
Shepherds; The Wakefield Nativity; The Wakefield
Second Nativity Play; The Wakefield Second
Shepherds'Pageant; The Wakefield Second
Shepherds' Play*

*Secunda pastorum. See* The Second Shepherds' Play

*La seinte resureccion.* 12th century BEVD
Axton, R., and Stevens, J., translators AXT
Variant title: *The Holy Resurrection*

*Semi. See* The Cicada

*Taking the Bandits' Stronghold. See* Taking Tiger
    Mountain by Strategy
*Taking Tiger Mountain by Strategy* (1969). SNO
    Ebon, M., translator FIFW
    Strassberg, E., translator MIT
    Variant title: *Taking the Bandits' Stronghold*
*The Talents* (Wakefield). 15th century TOWN
*Tamura.*
    Pound, E., translator NOH
*Tanikō. See* The Valley Rite
*Ta'ziya. See* The Martyrdom of Ali
*The Tempation, and the Woman Taken into Adultery.*
    *See* The Temptation (Chester); The Woman Taken
    in Adultery (Chester)
*The Temptation* (Chester). 15th century BURNS, CHEL,
    CHELM, CHESE, ENGE
    Variant titles: *The Temptation, and the Woman Taken*
    *into Adultery; The Temptation of Christ*
*The Temptation* (York). 15th century BEAD
*The Temptation of Christ. See* The Temptation
*The Ten Commandments, Balaam and Balak, and the*
    *Prophets* (Chester). BEVD
*Tenko.*
    Shimazaki, C., translator SHIM4, bk. 1
*Thersites* (attributed to Nicholas Udall). 1537? FARO,
    POLL, THZ
    Variant title: *A New Enterlude Called Thersytes: Thys*
    *Enterlude Folowynge Doth Declare Howe that the*
    *Greatest Boesters Are Not the Greatest Doers*
*A Thin Slice of ham let!* (1863) NIN4
*Thomas, Lord Cromwell.* 1592? BRO
    Variant titles: *The Life and Death of Lord Cromwell;*
    *The True Chronical History of the Whole Life and*
    *Death of Thomas Lord Cromwell*
*Thomas of India* (Wakefield). 15th century TOV, TOWN
*Thomas of Woodstock. See* Woodstock
*The Three Cuckolds.* 16th century
    Katz, L., adapter BENR1
    Variant title: *Li trc becchi*
*The Three Daughters* (from Hildesheim). 11th century
    Dronke., P., translator DRON
    Variant title: *Tres filie*
*The Three Kings* (Chester). 15th century CHEL,
    CHELM
*The Three Kings* (Spanish). *See* Los tres reyes magos
*The Three Kings* (York). 15th century BEAD, ENGE
    (introduction to, only), FRAN
    Variant title: *Herod and the Magi*
*The Three Kings' Play* (Oberufer). 16th century HARW
*The Three Maries* (Cornish). 15th century EVER
    Variant title: *The Cornish Mystery Play of the Three*
    *Maries*
*Three Marys at the Tomb* (N Town). 15th century
    DAVJ, N-TOW

    Variant title: *The Announcement to the Three Marys;*
    *Peter and John at the Sepulchre*
*The Three Students* (from Hildesheim). 11th century
    Dronke, P., translator DRON
    Variant title: *Tres clerici*
*Thunderbolt.*
    Tyler, R., translator BRAZ, TYLP
    Variant title: *Kaminari*
*Tied to a Stick. See* Bōshibari
*Tom Tyler and His Wife.* 1550? FARP
*Tomoe.*
    Shimazaki, C., translator SHIM2, bk. 2
*T'ongyŏng Ogwangdae.*
    Cho, O., translator TRAD
*Totentanz* (translated by Margaret Trinklein from the
    German text of Martin F. Schloss). 15th century
    SWIT
    Variant title: *The Dance of Death*
*The Towneley Play.* 15th century
    Burrell, R., adapter ROBM
*Towneley* plays. *See* Wakefield plays
*Tragedy of Nero.* BUL1
*The Traveling Dragon Teases a Phoenix. See* The Price
    of Wine
*Li tre becchi. See* The Three Cuckolds
*Tres clerici. See* Saint Nicholas and the Three Scholars
*Tres clerici. See* The Three Students (from Hildesheim)
*Tres filie. See* The Three Daughters (from Hildesheim)
*Los tres reyes magos/The Three Kings.* 16th century
    Torres, L. SIXN
    Variant title: *The Three Kings*
*The Trial. See* The Trial and Flagellation (Chester)
*The Trial of Atticus before Judge Beau, for a Rape.*
    1771? AMPA
*The Trial and Flagellation* (Chester). 15th century
    BURNS, CHEL, CHELM
    Variant title: *The Trial*
*The Trial of Christ* (N Town). 15th century ADA,
    N-TOW
    Variant titles: *The Death of Judas; The Trials before*
    *Pilate and Herod; Herod; The Trial before Annas*
    *and Cayphas*
*The Trial of Jesus* (adapted from four major cyles by
    Kenneth Pickering, Kevin Wood and Philip Dart).
    15th century MYSCC
*Trial of Joseph and Mary* (N Town). 15th century
    DAVJ, N-TOW
    Variant title: *The Trial of Mary and Joseph*
*The Trial of Mary and Joseph. See* Trial of Joseph and
    Mary (N Town)
*Trial of Treasure.* 1565? FAR
*Trope for Easter.* ca. 923–934. BEVD
    Variant title: *Trophi in Pasche. See* Trope for
    Easter

*The True and Honorable Historie of the Life of Sir John Oldcastle, the Good Lord Cobham. See* Sir John Oldcastle, pt. I

*The True Chronicle History of the Whole Life and Death of Thomas Lord Cromwell. See* Thomas, Lord Cromwell

*The Tryall of Chevalry.* BUL2

*Tsuen* (a parody of Yorimasa).
 Tyler, R., translator TYLG

*Tsunemasa.*
 Pound, E., translator NOH

*Tsuto yamabushi. See* The Lunchbox Thief

*Twenty-four Hours: A.M.* 1982. WES17/18 (Consists of the following twelve brief plays: Brown, D. *Four in the Morning*; Chais, P. *Sunny Side Up*; Kingsley-Smith, T. *I Want to Hold Your Hand*; Leeson, M. *Love Sonnet*; Levy, J. *Shotgun Willis*; Link, D. *Sleeping Together*; Mayer, J. *The Underachiever*; Miller, A. *Faro Rides Again*; Rimmer, C. *Pelicans*; Silver, S. *The Five Minute Romance*; Thomas, L. *Joe's Not Home*; Zindel, B., and Zindel, P. *Lemons in the Morning*)

*Twenty-four Hours: P.M.* WES 17/18 (Consists of the following twelve brief plays: Bobrick, S. *An Eastern Fable*; Bobrick, S. *Opening Night*; Cooper, D. *Rules of the House*; Hailey, O. *About Time*; Henley, B. *Hymn in the Attic*; Lenz, R. *So Long, Mr. Broadway*; Lewis, M. *Sunrise on Earth*; McGinn, J. *The Termination*; Matcha, J. *Aerobics*; Raymond, A. *Lifeline*; Rodd, M. *Conversation 2001*; Towbin, F. *Love in a Pub*)

*Twice a Bride.*
 Hung, J., translator HUNG
 Variant title: *Hung luan his*

*Two daimyō.*
 McKinnon, R., translator BRAZ
 Variant title: *Futari daimyō*

*Two men on a String.*
 Hung, J., translator HUNG
 Variant titles: *Feng yi T'ing; Phoenix Pavilion*

*The Two Noble Kinsmen. See* Fletcher, J., and Shakespeare, W.

*The Umbrian Play.* 14th century
 Robinson, D., translator and adapter ROBM

*The Unrin Temple. See* Unrin'in

*Unrin'in.*
 Jackson, E., translator BRAZT
 Variant title: *The Unrin Temple*

*The Valley Rite.*
 Tyler, R., translator KEE
 Variant title: *Tanikō.*

*Verses about the Stranger* (from Vic). 12th century
 Dronke, P., translator DRON
 Variant title: *Versus de pelegrino*

*Verses pascales de tres Maries. See* Easter Verses of the Three Maries

*Versus de pelegrino. See* Verses about the Stranger (from Vic)

*The Visit to Elizabeth* (N Town). 15th century N-TOW

*The Visit to the Sepulchre* (from Aquileia?). BEVD
 Variant title: Visitatio sepulchre

*The Visit to the Sepulchre* (from *The Regularis Concordia of St. Ethelwold*). 965–975. BEVD
 Variant title: *Visitatio sepulchri*

*The Visit to the Sepulchre* (from St. Lambrecht). BEVD

*The Visit to the Sepulchre* (from the tenth-century trope of Winchester). 978–980. BEVD

*Visitatio sepulchre. See* The Visit to the Sepulchre (from Aquileia?)

*Visitatio sepulchri. See* The Visit to the Sepulchre (from *The Regularis Concordia of St. Ethelwold*)

*The Votive Tablets. See* Ema

*Wahju Purba Sedjati. See* The Reincarnation of Rama

*The Wakefield Nativity. See* The Second Shepherds' Play (Wakefield)

*The Wakefield Noah. See* Noah (Wakefield)

*Wakefield* plays. *See* Abraham; The Annunciation; The Ascension of the Lord; The Betrayal; The Buffeting; Caesar Augustus; Coliphizacio; The Conspiracy; The Creation; The Crucifixion; The Deliverance of Souls; The Deluge; The First Shepherds' Play; The Flight into Egypt; The Hanging of Judas; The Harrowing of Hell; Herod the Great; Isaac; Jacob; John the Baptist; The Judgment; The Killing of Abel; Lazarus; Magnus Herodes; Noah; The Offering of the Magi; Pharaoh; The Pilgrims; The Play of the Doctors; The Procession of the Prophets; Processus noe cum filiis; The Purification of Mary; The Resurrection of Christ; The Salutation of Elizabeth; The Scourging; The Second Shepherds' Play; The Talents; Thomas of India

*The Wakefield Second Shepherds' Pageant. See* The Second Shepherds' Play

*The Wakefield Second Nativity Play. See* The Second Shepherds' Play

*The Wakefield Second Shepherds' Play. See* The Second Shepherds' Play

*The Washtub.* 15th century
 Bermel, A., translator BERMD
 Mandel, O., translator MARH
 Variant title: *Le cuvier*

*Wealth and Health.* 1557? FARN
 Variant title: *An Interlude of Wealth and Health*

*The Weavers' Pageant* (Coventry). 16th century COV

*The Wept of the Wish-ton-wish* (based on the novel by James Fenimore Cooper). 1834 BAT19

*The Whisker Tweezers.* 1717? *See* Tsuuchi, Hanjurō;
    Yasuda, Abun; and Nakada, Mansuke. *Saint
    Narukami and the God Fudō* (based on)
*The White-haired Girl.* 1945.
    Ebon, M., translator EIGH
*The Widow of Watling Street. See* The Puritan
*The Wisdom of Dr. Dodypoll.* 1600. BUL2
*Wisdom; or, Mind, Will, and Understanding. See* Mind,
    Will, and Understanding
*The Wise Virgins and the Foolish Virgins.* 1150?
    Hughes, B., and G., translators CLF1
*The Wisemen* (The Spanish play). 12th century
    Robinson, D., translator and adapter ROBM
*Wit and Science. See* The Marriage of Wit and Science;
    Redford, John. The Play of Wit and Science
*Wit and Wisdom. See* The Contract of Marriage between
    Wit and wisdom
*The Witch.* 15th century
    Prins, J., R. PRIN
*Woman Taken in Adultery. See* The Woman Taken in
    Adultery (N Town)
*The Woman Taken in Adultery* (Chester). 15th century
    BURNS, CHEL, CHELM
    Variant title: *The Temptation, and the Woman Taken
    into Adultery*
*The Woman Taken in Adultery* (N Town). 15th century
    BEVD, CAWL, DAVJ, N-TOW
*Woodstock,* ca. 1591–ca. 1595. ARMS
    Variant titles: *The First Part of the Reign of King
    Richard the Second; or, Thomas of Woodstock;
    Thomas of Woodstock*
*Worke for Jupiter. See* Gigantomachia, or Worke for
    Jupiter
*The World and the Child.* 1522? FARO, SCAT, THR
    Variant title: *Mundus et infans*
*Wysdom. See* Mind, Will and Understanding
*Wyt and Science. See* The Marriage of Wit and Science;
    Redford, John. The Play of Wit and Science
*Yangju Pyŏlsandae.*
    Cho, O., translator TRA
*The York Crucifixion. See* The Crucifixion (York)
*The York Nativity.* 15th century MED
    Baird, J., translator LEV, LEVE, MAK
    Bead, R., and King., P. BEAD
    Variant title: *The Nativity*
*The York Play of the Crucifixion. See* The Crucifixion
    (York) York plays. *See* The Adoration; The
    Assumption and the Coronation of the Virgin; The
    Birth of Jesus; The Building of the Ark; Christ
    before Annas and Caiaphas; Christ before Herod;
    Christ before Pilate (2): The Judgement; The
    Conspiracy; The Creation and the Fall of Lucifer;
    The Creation of Adam and Eve; The Crucifixion;
    The Death and Burial; The Dream of Pilate's

Wife; The Entry into Jerusalem; The Fall of Man;
    Flight into Egypt; The Flood; The Harrowing of
    Hell; John the Baptist; Joseph's Trouble about
    Mary; The Judgment Day; Moses; Pentecost;
    Resurrection; The Slaughtering of the Innocents;
    The Temptation; The Three Kings; The York
    Nativity
*A Yorkshire Tragedy* (sometimes attributed to William
    Shakespeare). 1605? BRO, OLH, OLI1, RUB,
    STUR
    Variant title: *All's One, or One of the Four Plates in
    One, called a York-Shire Tragedy*
*Youth.* 1555? FARP, HAO, SCAT
    Variant title: *The Interlude of Youth*
*Yu lung hsi fen. See* The Price of Wine
*Yü t'ung ch'un. See* The Faithful Harlot
*Yugao. See* Moonflower
*Yuya* (a woman play).
    Tyler, R., translator TYLG
*Zaqi Q'oxol and Cortés: The Conquest of Mexico.*
    Adapted and translated by M. Edmonson from
    six manuscript versions dating from 1726–1954
    EDMON

ANOUILH, JEAN, 1910–1987
    *L'alouette. See* The Lark
    *L'amour puni. See* The Rehearsal
    *Antigone.* 1944. GRAF
        Anon. translator FOUAC, PATP, SUT2
        Galantière, L., translator and adapter ASF, BES45,
        BLOC, CASK, DODS, ELKE, GORDP, JOHO,
        MANK, MIJT, SSSU, ULAN, WATE, WISF
        Variant titles: *Antigone and the Tyrant; Antigone et le
        tyrant*
    *Antigone and the Tyrant. See* Antigone
    *Antigone et le tyrant. See* Antigone
    *Ardèle.* 1950 CLOUD2, CLOUDS2
        Hill, L., translator COTK
        Variant titles: *Ardèle; ou, la Marguerite; The Cry of
        the Peacock*
    *Ardèle; ou, la Marguerite. See* Ardèle
    *Le bal des voleurs. See* Thieves' Carnival
    *Becket; or, The Honor of God.* 1959.
        Hill, L., translator ALT, ALTE, BES60, CUBH,
        GOLH, MORV, MORX, RICIS
        Variant title: *Becket; ou, L'honneur de Dieu*
    *Becket; ou, L'honneur de Dieu. See* Becket; or, The
        Honor of God
    *Cecile; or, The School for Fathers.* 1953.
        Klein, L., and A., translators BENS3
        Variant title: *Cécile; ou, L'école de pères*
    *Cécile; ou, L'école des peres. See* Cecile; or, The School
        for Fathers
    *The Cry of the Peacock. See* Ardèle

*Le dîner deg têtes. See* Poor Bitos
*Episode de la vie d'un auteur. See* Episode in the Life of
    an Author
*Episode in the Life of an Author.* 1948.
    John, M., translator RICK
    Variant title: *Episode de la vie d'un auteur*
*The ermine.* 1932.
    John, M., translator PLAN13
    Variant title: *L'hermine*
*Euridice. See* Eurydice
*Eurydice.* 1941.
    Black, K., translator COTKW, COTQ
    Variant titles: *Euridice; Legend of Lovers; Point of*
      *Departure*
*L'hermine. See* The ermine
*L'invitation au chateau. See* Ring Round the Moon
*The Lark.* 1955.
    Fry, C., translator BERMG, CLL, WEAN
    Hellman, L., adapter BES55, GARZH, THEA56,
      TREB, TREBA, TREBJ, TREI3
    Variant title: *L'alouette*
*Legend of Lovers. See* Eurydice
*Léocadia. See* Time Remembered
*Madame de . . .*
    Whiting, J., translator RICJ
*Medea.* 1948.
    Klein, L., and A., translators BENT5, SANM
    Small, L., translator PLAN15
    Variant title: *Médéé*
*Médéé. See* Medea
*The Orchestra.* 1962.
    John, M., translator RICJ
    Variant title: *L'orchestre*
*L'orchestre. See* The Orchestra
*Pauvre Bitos. See* Poor Bitos
*Point of Departure. See* Eurydice
*Poor Bitos.* 1956.
    Hill, L., translator BES64
    Variant titles: *Le dîner des têtes; Pauvre Bitos*
*The Rehearsal.* 1950.
    Johnson, P., and Black, K., adapters BES63
    Variant titles: *L'amour punt; La répétition; ou,*
      *L'amour punt*
*La répétition; ou, L'amour punt. See* The Rehearsal
*Ring Round the Moon.* 1947.
    Fry, C., translator BRZA
    Variant title: *L'invitation au chateau*
*Thieves' Carnival.* 1932.
    Anon. translator ZIM
    Hill, L., translator BENT3, BLOC, HILPDH6
    Variant title: *Le bal des voleurs*
*Time Remembered.* 1954.
    Moyes, P., translator and adapter BES57
    Variant title: *Léocadia*

*La valse de toréadors. See* The Waltz of the Toreadors
*The Waltz of the Toreadors.* 1952.
    Hill, L., translator and adapter, BES56, PLAN8
    Variant title: *La valse de toréadors*

—— and AURENCHE, JEAN
*Augustus. See* Humulus the mute
*Humulus le muet. See* Humulus the mute
*Humulus the mute.* 1948.
    Benedikt, M., translator BEN
    Hanger, G., translator TOB
    Variant titles: *Augustus; Humulus le muet*

ANSKI, S. A., pseudonym. *See* Rappoport, Shloyme Zanvl

ANSKY, S. A., pseudonym. *See* Rappoport, Shloyme Zanvl

ANSPACHER, LOUIS KAUFMAN, 1878–1947
*The Unchastened Woman.* 1915 BAK, BES09, DICEM

ANTHONY, C. L., pseudonym. *See* Smith, Dorothy
    Gladys

ANTHONY, TREY, 1974–
*'da kink in my hair: voices of black womyn.* 2001
    SEARS2

ANZENGRUBER, LUDWIG, 1839–1889
*The Farmer Forsworn.* 1872.
    Busse, A., translator FRA16
    Variant title: *Meineidbauer*
*The Fourth Commandment. See* Das vierte gebot
*Meineidbauer. See* The Farmer Forsworn
*Das vierte gebot.* 1877 CAM
    Variant title: *The Fourth Commandment*

AOKI, BRENDA WONG, 1953–
*The Queen's Garden.* 1992 PERC

APOLINAR, DANNY, 1934–1995
*Your Own Thing* (music and lyrics by). *See* Driver,
    Donald. *Your Own Thing*

APOLLINAIRE, GUILLAUME, pseudonym *See*
    Kostrowisky, Guillaume Apollinaire de

APPELL, GLENN
*Factwino vs. Armageddonman* (music and lyrics by,
    excerpt "Blow This Mother Up" by Shabaka).
    *See* San Francisco Mime Troupe. Factwino vs.
    Armageddonman

APPLEGATE, JAMES EARL *See* ADV Adventures in
    World Literature

APSTEIN, THEODORE, 1918–1998
*Wetback Run.* 1956. GRIH

ARAGON, LOUIS, 1897–1982
*L'armoire a glace un beau soir. See* The Mirror-
    wardrobe One Fine Evening
*The Mirror-wardrobe One Fine Evening.* 1923.
    Benedikt, M., translator BEN
    Variant title: *L'armoire à glace un beau soir*

ARAI, ANUAR NOR, 1943–2010
*Vacuum.* 1993.
    Ishak, S., translator MLAM

ARAKARA, JEREMY
*Body Leaks* (music by). *See* Terry, Megan. *Body Leaks*

ARBATOVA, MARIA, 1957–
*On the Road to Ourselves* (1998)
    Smith, M., translator SMB

ARBUTHNOT, JOHN, 1667–1735. *See* Gay, John, joint
    author

ARBUZOV, ALEXEI, 1908–1986
*It Happened in Irkutsk.* 1959?
    Prokofieva, R., translator THY, WEIM
*Tanya.* 1939.
    Miller, A., translator CLKX

ARCE, ELIA, 1961–
*My Grandmother Never Past Away: A Stream of
    Consciousness and Unconsciousness* (excerpt
    from *Stretching My Skin Till It Rips Whole*). 1995.
    ARRIZ
*Stretching My Skin Till It Rips Whole. See* My
    Grandmother Never Past Away: A Stream of
    Consciousness and Unconsciousness

ARCE, GASPAR NUNEZ DE. *See* Núñez de Arce,
    Gaspar

ARCHER, WILLIAM, 1856–1924
*The Green Goddess.* 1921 BES20, CARP, CEU, LAW,
    LOV

ARCHIBALD, WILLIAM, 1917–1970
*The Innocents* (based on the novel *The Turn of the
    Screw* by Henry James). 1950. BES49, RICN

ARCIPRESTE DE HITA. *See* Ruiz, Juan

ARDEN, JANE, 1927–1982
*The Party.* 1958. PLAN18

ARDEN, JOHN, 1930–
*Death of a Cowboy.* PLAAC1
*Live like Pigs.* 1958. NEWE3
*Serjeant Musgrave's Dance.* 1959. COTKB1, POP
*Soldier, Soldier.* 1960. CONB2
*When Is a Door Not a Door?* 1958. PLAAC2

—— and D'ARCY, MARGRETTA
*The Happy Haven.* 1960. NEWE4

ARDEN, THOMAS, d. 1551
*Arden of Feversham* (sometimes attributed to). *See*
    Anonymous Plays. *Arden of Feversham*

ARDOV, VICTOR, 1900–1976
*The Case of the Entry Room.* 1929.
    Langen, T., and Weir, J., translators EIGHTRP

ARDREY, ROBERT, 1908–1980
*The Murderers. See* Stone and Star
*Shadow of Heroes. See* Stone and Star
*Stone and Star.* 1958. BES61
    Variant titles: *The Murderers; Shadow of Heroes*
*Thunder Rock.* 1939. FIR

ARENAS, REINALDO, 1943–1990
*Traitor.* 1986.
    Gonzalez-Cruz, L., and Colecchia, F., translators
    GONZ

ARENT, ARTHUR, 1904–1972
*Ethiopia.* 1936. FAV
*One-third of a Nation* (edited by). 1938. FEE, NAGE
*Power, a Living Newspaper.* 1937. FEF

ARETINO, PIETRO, 1492–1556
*Horatia.* 1546.
    Ukas, M., translator LET
*Il Marescalco. See* The Stablemaster
*The Stablemaster.* (1533).
    Bull, G., translator FIJ
    Variant title: *Il Marescalco*
*Talanta.* 1542.
    Cairns, C., translator CAIRT

ARIADNE (a young lady), fl. 1696
*She Ventures and He Wins.* 1695. LYON, MISC

ARIAS, RON, 1941–
*The Interview.* 1979. KANEL

ARIOSTO, LUDOVICO, 1474–1533
*I suppositi. See* The Supposes
    *See also* Gascoigne, George. *Supposes* (adapted from)

*Lena.* 1528.

 Cairns, C., translator CAIRT

 Williams, G., translator FIJ

 Variant title*: La Lena*

*La Lena. See* Lena

*The Supposes.* 1509.

 Lorch, J., translator CAIR

 Variant title: *I suppositi*

ARISTOPHANES, 446?–385? B.C.

*The Acharnians.* 425 B.C.

 Anonymous translator OAT2

 Casson, L., translator CASU

 Frere, J., translator KRE

 Rogers, B., translator GRDB5

 Sommerstein, A., translator GRDBA4

*The Assemblywomen. See* The Ecclesiazusae

*Aves. See* The Birds

*The Birds.* 414 B.C.

 Anonymous translator FIFV, OAT2, WED

 Barrett, D., translator GRDBA4

 Fitts, D., translator BARJ, BARK, FEFL, FIFR

 Frere, J., translator CROV, HOUS

 Kerr, W., translator COTKICC, VENA, WHFM

 MacGregor, M., translator CLKW

 McLeish, K., translator MAMB

 Rogers, B., translator FGP, GRDB5

 Variant title: *Aves*

*The Clouds.* 423 B.C.

 Anonymous translator BAT2, MURP, OAT2, PLAG

 Cumberlund, R., translator HOWE, HOWF

 Hickie, W., translator GREE

 Lucas, F., translator LUCA, LUCAB, LUCAF

 Mitchell, T., translator CLF1

 Rogers, B., translator BARB, FGP, GRDB5, MIK7, ROBJ, WARN1

 Sommerstein, A., translator GRDBA4

 Variant title: *Nubes*

*The Council of Women. See* The Ecclesiazusae

*The Ecclesiazusae.* 392 B.C.

 Anonymous translator BAT21, OAT2

 Barrett, D., translator GRDBA4

 Rogers, B., translator GRDB5

 Variant titles: *The Assemblywomen, The Council of Women*

*Equites. See* The Knights

*The Frogs.* 405 B.C.

 Anonymous translator PLAG

 Barrett, D., translator GRDBA4

 Fitts, D., translator SHRO

 Frere, J., translator BUCK, BUCL, BUCM, HIB, HIBA, HIRE, LAP, MATT, SEBO, SEBP, SMR, TAV, TEN, THOM, THON

 Hawthorne, J., translator MALR1

 McLeish, K., translator MAMB

 Murray, G., translator HOWF, OAT2 OATH

 Rogers, B., translator FGP, GRDB5, HARC8, ROB, ROBJ, TREB, TREC1, TREE1, TREI1

 Webb, R., translator GRDG

 Variant title: *Ranae*

*The God of Riches. See* Plutus

*The Knights.* 424 B.C.

 Anonymous translator OAT2

 Frere, J., translator DRAD1, PLAB1

 Rogers, B., translator GRDB5

 Sommerstein, A., translator GRDBA4

 Variant title: *Equites*

*Lysistrata.* 411 B.C.

 Anonymous translator DAVM, GOU1, OAT2, PLAG, SCNPL, WORP

 Fitts, D., translator BARKA, BARKB, BARKC, BARKD, BARKE, BARKF, COLD, HEA, HEAA, HEAB, HEAC, HEAD, JACOB, JACOBA, JACOBD, JACOBE, SAFF, VANV1, WELT

 Murphy, C., translator ALLK, ALLM, ALLN, ALLO, BAIL, BOW, HOLP, JOHN, LIND, LOCM1, MALI1, NORG1, NORGA, NORI1, NORIA1, NORIB1, NORJ1, NORJA, OAM, ROBI, SCNQ, SCNQCA, SOUL, SSSI, VONS1, WOMD

 Oates, W., and Murphy, C., translators EVC1, MALN1, SSSIA, SSSIB, SSSIC

 Parker, D., translator CHARN, HILPDH1, HOEP, HOWM, NORIC1

 Roby, D., translator MESSN

 Rogers, B., translator GRDB5

 Seldes, G., translator TRE, TREA2

 Smolin, D., translator and adapter PLAH

 Sommerstein, A., translator GRDBA4, WOTHA, WOTHB

 Sutherland, D., translator COTKICC, COTKICO, COTY, FRYE, FRYEA, HAPRL, SEVT, WOTHC

 Wilbur, R., translator WEIS, WEIW

*Nubes. See* The Clouds

*Pax. See* Peace

*Peace.* 421 B.C.

 Anonymous translator OAT2

 Reynolds, T., translator TENN

 Rogers, B., translator GRDB5

 Sommerstein, A., translator GRDBA4

 Variant title: *Pax*

*Plutus, the God of Riches.* 388 B.C.

 Anonymous translator OAT2

 Hickie, W., translator GREE

 Rogers, B., translator GRDB5

 Sanford, D., translator TEN

 Sommerstein, A., translator GRDBA4

 Variant title: *Wealth*

*The Poet and the Women. See* Thesmophoriazusae
*Ranae. See* The Frogs
*Thesmophoriazusae.* 411 B.C.
    Anonymous translator OAT2
    Barrett, D., translator GRDBA4
    Rogers, R., translator GRDB5
    Variant titles: *The Poet and the Women; The Women
        Celebrating the Thesmophoria*
*Vespae. See* The Wasps
*The Wasps.* 422 B.C.
    Anonymous translator OAT2
    Barrett, D., translator GRDBA4
    Rogers, B., translator GRDB5
    Variant title: *Vespae*
*Wealth. See* Plutus
*The Women Celebrating the Thesmophoria. See*
    Thesmophoriazusae

ARIZA, RENE, 1940–1994
    *Declaration of Principles.* 1979. *See* Four Minidramas
    *Doll's Play.* 1971. *See* Four Minidramas
    *A Flower Vendor for These Times.* 1980. *See* Four
        Minidramas
    *Four Minidramas* (*The Meeting, Doll's Play,
        Declaration of Principles*, and *A Flower Vendor for
        These Times*). 1971–1980. GONZ
    *The Meeting.* 1971. *See* Four Minidramas

ARIZMENDI, YARELI
    *Nostalgia maldita: 1–900–Mexico, a stairmaster piece.*
        2000. PURO

ARKEKETA, ANNETTE, 1958–
    *Hokti.* 1997. GEIO

ARLEN, MICHAEL, 1895–1956 (b. Dikran
        Kouyoumdjian)
    *The Green Hat.* 1925. BES25

ARLT, ROBERTO, 1900–1942
    *Savierio el cruel.* 1936. DAUR

ARMORY (pseudonym of CARLE DAURIAC), 1877–
    *The Gentleman of the Chrysanthemums.* 1908.
        Senelick, L., translator SELOV
        Variant title: *Le monsieur aux chrysanthèmes, pièce
            en trois actes*
    *Le monsieur aux chrysanthèmes, pièce en trois actes.
        See* The Gentleman of the Chrysanthemums

ARMSTRONG, ANTHONY, pseudonym *See* Willis,
        Anthony Armstrong

ARNO, OWEN G., 1934–1969
    *The Other Player.* 1964. BRNB

ARNOLD, DANIEL, and HAHN, MEDINA
    *Tuesdays and Sundays.* 2000. STN

ARNOLD, MATTHEW, 1822–1888
    *Empedocles on Etna.* 1852. KAU, PRAT2
    *The Strayed Reveler.* 1849. PRAT2

ARON, GERALDINE, 1941–
    *Mickey Kannis Caught My Eye.* 1978. GRAYTT

ARONSON, BILLY
    *The Art Room.* 1999. PLACJ

AROUT, GABRIEL, 1909–1982
    *Beware of the Dog* (adapted from short stories of
        Chekhov). 1967.
        Mitchell, Y., translator PLAN33

ARRABAL, FERNANDO, 1932–
    *First Communion.* 1962.
        Benedikt, M., translator BENA
    *Picnic on the Battlefield.* 1959.
        Anon. translator ANT, HOGI, HOGN, OHL
        Hewitt, J., translator COXM, KERO
        Wright, B., translator BARO
        Variant title: *Pique-nique en campagne*
    *Pique-nique en campagne. See* Picnic on the Battlefield

ARRIVI, FRANCISCO, 1915–2007
    *Masquerade.* 1958.
        Coulthard, G., translator HILET
        Variant title: *Vejigantes*
    *Vejigantes. See* Masquerade

ARSKY, PAVEL, 1886–1967
    *For the Cause of the Red Soviets.* 1919.
        Anon. translator VONG
        Variant title: *Za krasnye sovety. P'esa v odnom
            deistvii*
    *Za krasnye sovety. P'esa v odnom deistvii. See* For the
        Cause of the Red Soviets

ARTAUD, ANTONIN, 1896–1948
    *Le jet de sang. See* The Jet of Blood
    *The Jet of Blood.* 1925.
        Cohn, R., translator TREBJ
        Wellwarth, G., translator BEN, MARK, MARL,
            WILLG
        Variant titles: *Le jet de sang; The Spurt of Blood*
    *The Spurt of Blood. See* The Jet of Blood

ASADA, ITCHO. *See* Namiki, Sōsuke, joint author

ASCH, SHOLEM, 1880–1957
    *God of Vengeance.*
        Landis, J., translator LAO, LAOG, THQ

ASHBERY, JOHN, 1927–
*The Heroes.* 1953. MAH

ASHTON, GREG. *See* Ross, Lesley, pseudonym

ASHTON, WINIFRED (CLEMENCE DANE,
    pseudonym), 1888–1965
*A Bill of Divorcement.* 1921. BES21, COT, MART,
    MOSO
*Granite.* 1926. MYB, TUCD
*Moonlight Is Silver.* 1934. SEV
*Wild Decembers.* 1932. BARV, SIXH
*Will Shakespeare—An Invention.* 1921. YEAR

ASPENSTROM, WERNER, 1918–1997
*The Apes Shall Inherit the Earth.* 1959.
    Sjöberg, L., and Goodman, R., translators GOO
    Variant title: *Det eviga*
*Det eviga. See* The Apes Shall Inherit the Earth

ASSUNCAO, LEILAH, 1943– (b. Maria de Lourdes
    Torres de Assunção)
*Boca molhada de paixão.* 1980. SZO
*Moist Lips, Quiet Passion.* 1980.
    Gouveia Marques, L., translator SZO
    Variant title: *Boca molhada de paixão*

ASTOR DEL VALLE, JANIS, 1963–
*Fuchsia.* 1996. DEAT, PURO
*I'll Be Home para la Navidad.* 1993. CURB, TOR
*Transplantations: Straight and other Jackets para mi.*
    1996. ALG
*Where the Señoritas Are.* 1992. TOR (excerpt)

ATAI, UKO
*SAP Rites.* 1990. FINBN

ATHAS, DAPHNE SPENCER, 1923– *See* Campbell,
    Marion Gurney, joint author

ATLAN, LILIANE, 1932–
*Mister Fugue or Earth Sick.* 1967.
    Feitlowitz, M., translator FUCHS
    Variant title: *Monsieur Fugue ou la mal de terre*
*Monsieur Fugue ou la mal de terre. See* Mister Fugue or
    Earth Sick

ATLAS, LEOPOLD LAWRENCE, 1907–1954
*"L."* 1928. LEV, LEVE
*Wednesday's Child.* 1934. BES33

ATTINELLO, PAUL
*Hospital.* 1984. *See* Anonymous Plays. *The AIDS
    Show . . .*

*Party 1985.* 1984. *See* Anonymous Plays. *The AIDS
    Show . . .*
*Party 1984.* 1984. *See* Anonymous Plays. *The AIDS
    Show . . .*
*Party 1981.* 1984. *See* Anonymous Plays. *The AIDS
    Show . . .*
*Party 1983.* 1984. *See* Anonymous Plays. *The AIDS
    Show . . .*
*Party 1982.* 1984. *See* Anonymous Plays. *The AIDS
    Show . . .*

ATTOWELL, GEORGE, fl. 1599
*Attowell's Jig* (sometimes attributed to). *See* Anonymous
    Plays. *Attowell's Jig*

AUBIGNY, D', pseudonym *See* Bauflouin, Jean Marie
    Théodore

AUDEN, WYSTAN HUGH, 1907–1973, and
    ISHERWOOD, CHRISTOPHER
*The Ascent of F6.* 1937. TUCN
*The Dog beneath the Skin.* 1935. KOZ, KRE

AUGIER, EMILE, 1820–1889
*Le mariage d'Olympe.* 1855. BOR
    Clark, B., translator SSTG
    Variant title: *Olympe's Marriage*
*Olympe's Marriage. See* Le mariage d'Olympe

—— and SANDEAU, JULES
*Le gendre de M. Poirier.* 1854. BOR, GRA, SEA
    Clark, B., translator CLF2, MATT
    Variant titles: *M. Poirier's Son-in-law; The Son-in-
    law of M. Poirier*
*M. Poirier's Son-in-law. See* Le gendre de M. Poirier
*The Son-in-law of M. Poirier. See* Le gendre de M.
    Poirier

AULETTA, ROBERT, 1940–
*Stops.* 1972. BALLE10

AURENCHE, JEAN, 1904–1992. *See* Anouilh, Jean, joint
    author

AURTHUR, ROBERT ALAN, 1922–1978
*A Very Special Baby.* 1956. BES56

AUSTEN, JANE, 1775–1817
*Emma. See* Fry, Michael. Emma (based on the novel by)
*Pride and Prejudice. See* Jerome, Mrs. Helen (Burton).
    *Pride and Prejudice* (based on the novel by)

AVEDON, BARBARA, 1930–1994, and CORDAY,
    BARBARA, and ROSENZWEIG, BARNEY

*You Call this Plainclothes?* (a *Cagney & Lacey*
    episode). 1982. MEYB

AVERILL, RIC. *See* Willmott, Kevin, joint author

AVI, 1937–
    *Nothing but the Truth. See* Smith, Ronn. Nothing but the
        Truth (adapted from the novel by)

AVRAAMIDOU, MARIA, 1939–
    *Harsh Angel.* 1986.
        Frangofinou, R., translator BARAM

AW, ARTHUR
    *All Brand New Classical Chinese Theatre.* 1978. KUMU

AXELROD, GEORGE, 1922–2003
    *The Seven Year Itch.* 1952. GART, GATB4, NEWV,
        THEA53

AXENFELD, ISRAEL, 1787–1866, and REZNIK, LIPE
    *Recruits; or, That's How It Was.* 1935 (U.S.).
        Lifson, D., translator LIFS

AYALA, ADELARDO LOPEZ DE. *See* López de Ayala,
    Adelardo

AYCKBOURN, ALAN, 1939–
    *Absurd Person Singular.* 1973. BEST
    *Bedroom Farce.* 1975. BES78
    *Just between Ourselves.* 1976. COTKB2
    *Living Together. See* The Norman Conquests
    *The Norman Conquests.* 1974. BES75 (Three
        interlocking plays, each in two acts: *Table
        Manners; Living Together;* and *Round and Round
        the Garden*)
    *Round and Round the Garden. See* The Norman
        Conquests
    *Season's Greetings.* 1984. BES85
    *Table Manners. See* The Norman Conquests

AYKROYD, JULIET
    *The Clean-up.* 1986. FEFNV

AYME, MARCEL, 1902–1967
    *Clérambard.* 1950.
        Denny, N., translator FOUF
        Variant title: *The Count of Clerambard*
    *The Count of Clerambard. See* Clérambard

AYVAZIAN, LESLIE
    *Nine Armenians.* 1996. WOMP96

AZAMA, MICHEL, 1947–
    *Le sas. See* The Sifter

*The Sifter.* 1986.
    Miller, J., translator MOGS
    Variant title: *Le sas*

AZCARATE, LEONOR, 1955–
    *Margarita Came Back to Life.* 1994.
        Gann, M., translator GANN1
        Variant title: *Margarita resucitó*
    *Margarita resucitó. See* Margarita Came Back to Life

AZEVEDO, ANGELA DE
    *Dicha y desdicha del juego y devoción de la Virgen.*
        17th century SOSGA
    *La margarita del Tajo que dio nombre a Santarén.* 17th
        century SOSGA
    *El muerto disimulado.* 17th century SOSGA

BABE, THOMAS, 1941–2000
    *Junk Bonds.* 1990. PRIMA91
    *Kid Champion.* 1975. WOQ4
    *A Prayer for My Daughter.* 1977. BERS, BES77
    *Rebel Women.* 1976. BES75

BABEL, ISAAC, 1894–1941
    *Marya.* 1967.
        Glenny, M., translator GLE
        Glenny, M., and Shukman, H., translators PLAN35
    *Sundown.* (1928)
        Senelick, L., translator RVI
        Variant title: *Zakat*
    *Zakat. See* Sundown

BABO, JOSEPH MARIUS VON, 1756–1822
    *Dagobert, der franker König. See* Dagobert, King of the
        Franks
    *Dagobert, King of the Franks.* 1779.
        Thompson, B., translator BAT12
        Variant title: *Dagobert, der franker König*

BACHER, WILLIAM A., 1900–1965
    *The Snow Goose. See* Gallico, Paul. The Snow Goose
        (adapted by)

BACON, FRANK, 1864–1922. *See* Smith, Winehell, joint
    author

BADIAN, SEYDOU, 1928–
    *The Death of Chaka.* 1962.
        Wake, C., translator FACES
        Variant title: *La mort de Chaka*
    *La mort de Chaka. See* The Death of Chaka

BADLAM, ROBB, 1970–
    *Slop-ulture.* 1999. HUMANA99

BAGNOLD, ENID, 1889–1981
*Call Me Jacky*. 1968. PLAN34
*The Chalk Garden*. 1955. BES55, COTKIT, THEA56
*National Velvet*. 1946. EMB2

BAHR, HERMANN, 1863–1934
*The Concert*. 1909.
   Morgan, B., translator DICDS
   Variant title: *Das konzert*
*Das konzert. See* The Concert

BAILEY, BRETT, 1967–
*Ipi Zombi?* 1998. GRAV

BAILEY, MAXINE, 1959– , and LEWIS, SHARON M.
*Sistahs*. 1994. SEARS1

BAILLIE, JOANNA, 1762–1851
*De Monfort*. 1800. COXJ, ENGLMI
*The Family Legend*. 1810. FEFNC

BAITZ, JON ROBIN, 1961–
*A Fair Country*. 1996. BES95
*The Film Society*. 1987. BES86, NEWQC
*The Substance of Fire*. 1991. BES90, SCM

BAIZLEY, DORIS, 1948?–
*Catholic Girls*. 1979. WES11/12
*Daniel in Babylon*. 1982. WES19/20

BAKER, BENJAMIN A., 1818–1896
*Glance at New York*. 1848. MES

BAKER, DON, and COCKE, DUDLEY
*Red Fox/Second Hangin'*. 1976. DEN

BAKER, E. IRENE, 1905– , and DRUMMOND,
   ALEXANDER MAGNUS
*A Day in the Vineyard*. DRU

BAKER, ELIZABETH, 1879–1962
*Chains*. 1909. DICEM, NEWWP, PLAP1

BAKER, GEORGE M., 1832–1890
*New Brooms Sweep Clean*. 1871. CHIN

BAKER, SUSAN
*Respectfully Yours*. 1988. STRA (excerpt)

BAKYR, MAHMUD HAJI
*The Chaffed Sky the Cracked Earth*. 1994.
   Abdullah, K., translator MLAB

BALALIN COMPANY OF JERUSALEM, THE, 1971–
   1974

*al-`Atma. See* Darkness
*Darkness*. 1972.
   Bamia, A., and Ezzy, T., translators JAY
   Variant title: *al-`Atma*

BALDERSTON, JOHN LLOYD, 1889–1954
*Berkeley Square*. 1926. BES29, GASB
   — *See also* Deane, Hamilton, joint author

BALDRIDGE, MARY HUMPHREY, 1937–
*The Photographic Moment*. 1987. ZIMM

BALDWIN, JAMES, 1924–1987
*The Amen Corner*. 1964. HARY, HARYB, PATR
*Blues for Mister Charlie*. 1964. GAT, HOWM, OLIV

——— and HUMPHREY, HUBERT H.
*My Childhood*. 1964. BAYM

BALE, JOHN, 1495–1563
*God's Promises*. 1538? EVER
   Variant title: *A Tragedy or Interlude Manifesting the*
      *Chief Promises of God unto Man*
*Johan Baptystes preachynge*. 1538. MED
*King Johan. See* King John
*King John*. 1539? ARMS, CRE, FOUN, POLL
   Variant titles: *King Johan; Kynge Johan*
*Kynge Johan. See* King John
*The Three Laws*. 1548. MED
*A Tragedy or Interlude Manifesting the Chief Promises*
   *of God unto Man. See* God's Promises

BALL, ALAN EGERTON, 1944– , and BRADBURY,
   PAUL
*Professor Fuddle's Fantastic Fairy-tale Machine*. 1974.
   KAL4

BALL, DAVID, 1942–
*Assassin*. 1968? BALLE7
*Woyzeck* (adapted by). *See* Büchner, Georg

BALLESTEROS, ANTONIO. *See* Martinez Ballesteros,
   Antonio

BALZAC, HONORE DE, 1799–1850
*Mercadet*. 1851. BOR

BANCIL, PARV
*Made in England*. 1998. BLAAP

BANDELE, 'BIYI, 1967–
*Two Horsemen*. 1994. SETR

BANGS, JOHN KENDRICK, 1862–1922
*Katharine: A Travesty*. 1888. NIN5

BANKS, JOHN, 1650?–1706
*The Albion Queens.* 1704. BELK14
*Anna Bullen, or Virtue Betray'd.* 1682. BELK14
Variant titles: *Anne Bullen; Virtue Betray'd*
*Anne Bullen. See* Anna Bullen, or, Virtue Betray'd
*Virtue Betray'd. See* Anna Bullen, or, Virtue Betray'd

BAPTISTE, ROSELIA JOHN, 1962– (early pseudonym of Trish Cooke)
*Back Street Mammy* (extracts). 1987. DEAD
*No Place like Home* (extracts). 1987. DEAD

BARAITSER, MARION
*LOUIS/lui.* 1998. LINDB

BARAKA, IMAMU AMIRI, pseudonym. *See* Jones, LeRoi

BARBA, PRESTON ALBERT, 1883–1971
*Au der lumpa part.* 1933. BUFF
*Dié verrechelte rechler* (adapted from the novel by Charles C. More). 1933. BUFF

BARBER, PHILIP WILLSON, 1903–1981
*I, Elizabeth Otis, being of Sound Mind.* 1964. BALLE3

BARBIER, MARIE-ANNE, c.1670–1745
*Arrie et Petus. See* Arria and Paetus
*Arria and Paetus.* 1702.
Gethner, P., translator GETH
Variant title: *Arrie et Petus*

BARBU, PETRE, 1962–
*On the Left Hand of the Father.* 1998?
Voiculescu, M., translator POQ

BARCA, PEDRO CALDERON DE LA. *See* Calderón de la Barca, Pedro

BARFIELD, TANYA
*Without Skin or Breathlessness.* 1998. HUGH

BARING, MAURICE, 1874–1945
*The Rehearsal.* 1911? WEB

BARKENTIN, MARJORIE, 1891–1974
*Ulysses in Nighttown* (adapted from the novel *Ulysses* by James Joyce). 1958. COTK

BARKER, HARLEY GRANVILLE. *See* Granville-Barker, Harley

BARKER, HOWARD, 1946–
*Hated Nightfall.* 1994. COLD

BARKER, JAMES NELSON, 1784–1858
*The Indian Princess; or, La belle Sauvage.* 1808. MOSS1, RICHE
*Superstition,* 1824. GARX, HAL, MESCO, QUIJ, QUIK, QUIL, QUIM, QUIN

BARKSDALE, WILLIAM
*Land's End.* 1984. *See* Anonymous Plays. *The AIDS Show . . .*

BARKSTED, WILLIAM, fl. 1607–1630, and MACHIN, LEWIS
*The Insatiate Countess* (from a draft by John Marston). c.1610. WIGG

BARLACH, ERNST, 1870–1938
*Squire Blue Boll.* 1926?
Ritchie, J., and Gsrten, H., translators RITS

BARLOW, ANNA MARIE
*Mr. Biggs.* 1965. NEWA1

BARNARD, CHARLES, 1838–1920. *See* De Mille, Henry Churchill, joint author

BARNES, CHARLOTTE MARY SANFORD, 1818–1863
*The Forest Princess, or Two Centuries Ago.* 1844. KRIT
Variant title: *Two Centuries Ago*
*Two Centuries Ago. See* The Forest Princess

BARNES, DEREK
*The Strange Passenger* (music by). *See* Linden, Sonja. *The Strange Passenger*

BARNES, DJUNA, 1892–1982
*The Dove.* 1923. KEL

BARNES, PETER, 1931–2004
*Auschwitz* (*Part II of Laughter*). 1978. FUCHS
*The Ruling Class.* 1968. COTKB1

BARON, COURTNEY, 1972–
*Blackfish.* 2000. *See* Ackermann, J. *Back Story: A Dramatic Anthology* HUMANA2000
*The Blue Room.* 1999. HUMANA99

BARRAS, CHARLES M., 1826–1873
*The Black Crook.* 1866. MASW

BARRETT, WILSON, 1846–1904
*The Sign of the Cross.* 1895. MAYER

BARRIE, SIR JAMES MATTHEW, 1860–1937
*The Admirable Crichton.* 1903. CHAR, CLKW, COTH,
    DUR, RED, REDM, SALE, SPER, TREBA,
    TREC2, TREE3, TREI3, WARI
*Dear Brutus.* 1917. BROW, COTKR, WATF2, WATI
*The Little Minister.* 1897. BES94
*Mary Rose.* 1920. BES20
*The Old Lady Shows Her Medals.* 1921. INGG, INGH
*Shall We Join the Ladies?* 1928. WORL4
*The Twelve Pound Look.* 1910. BARKE, BOGO, CONP,
    DAV1, MANK, WEAT2
*A Well-remembered Voice.* 1918. FULT
*What Every Woman Knows.* 1908. CEU, WATF1,
    WATI, WATO
*When Wendy Grew Up: An Afterthought to Peter Pan.*
    1908. KAYT
*The Will.* 1914. MIKL

BARRIE, SHIRLEY
*Straight Stitching.* 1989. NEWCAD5
*Transition* (one of three monologues from *A Witch's
    Brew*). 1997. BREK

BARROGA, JEANNIE, 1949–
*Talk-story.* 1992. HOUST
*Walls.* 1989. UNO

BARRY, LYNDA, 1956–
*The Good Times Are Killing Me.* 1991. BES90

BARRY, PHILIP, 1896–1949
*The Animal Kingdom.* 1932. BES31, GAS
*Foolish Notion.* 1945. BES44
*God Bless Our Home. See* The Youngest
*Here Come the Clowns.* 1938. BES38, GARU
*Holiday.* 1928. BES28, KEY, MAF, MAFC, MERW,
    MOSK, MOSL, WATTAD
*Hotel Universe.* 1930. LEV, LEVE, THF, WATC2,
    WATI, WHI
*In a Garden.* 1925. TUCD, TUCM
*The Joyous Season.* 1934. CATH, DAVI
*Paris Bound.* 1927. BES27, GASB, QUIL, QUIM,
    QUIN
    Variant title: *The Wedding*
*The Philadelphia Story.* 1939. BES38, BROZ, GARZ,
    GATB2, WAIT, WAIU
*Second Threshold* (revised by Rohert E. Sherwood).
    1951. BES50
*Tomorrow and Tomorrow.* 1931. BES30
*The Wedding. See* Paris Bound
*You and I.* 1923. BES22, HAL
*The Youngest.* 1924. BES24
    Variant title: *God Bless Our Home*

BARTA, BERRY L.
*Journey into that Good Night.* 1995. TIME

BARTEVE, REINE
*The Orphanage.* 1984.
    Mac Dougall, J., translator PLABI2
    Variant title: *L'orphelinat*
*L'orphelinat. See* The Orphanage

BARTHOL, BRUCE, 1949–
*Factperson* (script and songs by). *See* San Francisco
    Mime Troupe. Factperson
*Factwino Meets the Moral Majority* (songs by). *See* San
    Francisco Mime Troupe. Factwino Meets the Moral
    Majority
*Factwino vs. Armageddonman* (music and lyrics by,
    excerpt for "Blow this Mother Up" by Shabaka).
    *See* San Francisco Mime Troupe. Factwino vs.
    Armageddonman

BARTLETT, NEIL, 1958–
*A Vision of Love Revealed in Sleep* (Part Three). 1989.
    GAY4

BARTON, BRUCE, 1958–
*Roswell.* 1999. NEWCAD8

BARTRAM, G.W., 1944– . *See* Brown, Alex, pseudonym

BART-WILLIAMS, GASTON N.O., 1938–1990
*The Drug* (radio play). 1972. PIET

BAR-YOSEF, YOSEF, 1933–
*Difficult People.* 1972.
    Bernard, H., Oklans, D., and Silk, D., translators
    MOADE

BARYLLI, GABRIEL, 1957–
*Buttered Bread.* 1987.
    Cervania, M., translator LAXC
    Variant title: *Butterbrot*
*Butterbrot. See* Buttered Bread
*Honeymoon.* 1992.
    Cervania, M., translator LAXC
    Variant title: *Honigmond*
*Honigmond. See* Honeymoon

BASS, GEORGE HOUSTON, 1938–1990
*Black Masque: The Passion of Darkie's Bones.* 1971.
    TUQTR

BASS, KINGSLEY B. (pseudonym of Ed Bullins)
*We Righteous Bombers.* 1968. TUQT

BASSART, CLIVE
*A Myth Is Good for a Smile.* 1986. MONB3

BASSHE, EMANUEL JO, 1900–1939
*Doomsday Circus. See* The Dream of the Dollar
*The Dream of the Dollar.* 1933. AME5
    Variant title: *Doomsday Circus*

BATE, HENRY. *See* Dudley, Sir Henry Bate

BATEMAN, MRS. SIDNEY FRANCES (COWELL),
    1823–1881
*Self.* 1857. MOSS2

BATES, ESTHER WILLARD, 1884–
*The Two Thieves.* 1925? FED2

BAUDOIN, JEAN MARIE THEODORE (D'AUBIGNY,
    pseudonym). *See* Caigniez, Louis Charles, joint
    author

BAUER, IRVIN S. *See* Gordon, Richard, joint author

BAUER, WOLFGANG, 1941–2005
*Insalata mista.* 1995.
    Nielsen, C., translator LAXC
*Shakespeare the Sadist.* 1970. SHAK

BAUM, L. FRANK (Lyman Frank), 1856–1919
*The Wonderful Wizard of Oz. See* Brown, William F.,
    *The Wiz* (adapted from)

BAUM, TERRY, 1946–
*Death's Angel. See* Immediate Family
*Immediate Family.* 1983. PLA
    Variant title: *Death's Angel*
*Two Fools.* 1996. DEAT

——— and MYERS, CAROLYN
*Dos Lesbos.* 1981. PLA

BAUM, THOMAS
*Cold Hands.* 1990.
    Ritchie, D., Ingeborg, G., and Borgert, U., translators
    LAX
    Variant title: *Kalte hände*
*Kalte hände. See* Cold Hands

BAUM, VICKI, 1888–1960
*Grand Hotel. See* Davis, L. *Grand Hotel: The Musical*
    (based on the play by) 1930.
    Drake, W., translator BES30, CEW
    Variant title: *Menschen im hotel*
*Menschen im hotel. See* Grand Hotel

BAUS, MANUEL TAMAYO Y. *See* Tamayo y Baus,
    Manuel

BAX, CLIFFORD, 1886–1962
*The Rose without a Thorn.* 1932. FAMB, PLAD
*Socrates.* 1929. SIXD
*The Venetian.* 1930. MYB

BAXTER, JAMES K., 1926–1972
*The Wide Open Cage.* 1959. CONTNZ

BAYARD, JEAN FRANCOIS ALFRED, 1796–1853
    — *See* Scribe, Augustin Eugène, joint author
    — *See also* Théaulon, Marie-Emmanuel-Guillaume-
      Marguerite, joint author

BAYON HERRERA, LUIS, 1889–1956
*Santos Vega.* 1913.
    Fassett, J., translator BIES

BAYZA'I, BAHRAM. *See* Beyza'i, Bahram

BEACH, EMMETT LEWIS, 1891–1947
*The Clod.* 1914. BURG, GASB
*The Goose Hangs High.* 1924. BES23, KEY

BEACH, LEWIS. *See* Beach, Emmett Lewis

BEARD, JOCELYN A.
*The Ornamental Hermit.* 1998. WOMP98
*Vladivostok Blues.* 1996. WOMP95

BEASLEY, ELOIS
*The Fallen Angel.* 1989. KINHP

BEAUMARCHAIS, PIERRE AUGUSTIN CARON DE,
    1732–1799
*The Barber of Seville. See* Le barbier de Seville
*Le barbier de Seville: ou, La préeaution inutile.* 1775.
    BOV, BOVE, BRN, STJ1, ZDA
    Bermel, A., translator BERMD, BERMG, THV
    Fowlie, W., translator FOWL
    Myrick, A., translator MATT
    Taylor, W., translator CLF2
    Variant title: *The Barber of Seville*
*Figaro's Marriage; or, One Mad Day. See* Le mariage
    de Figaro
*Le mariage de Figaro.* 1784. BREN, CHN, SEA
    Barzun, J., translator BENR4, BENSD, HILPDH3
    Gaskill, W., translator LAQCF
    Holcroft, T., translator THMD
    Variant titles: *Figaro's Marriage; or, One Mad Day;*
      *The Marriage of Figaro; The Marriage of Figaro,*
      *or, The Follies of a Day*

*The Marriage of Figaro. See* Le mariage de Figaro
*The Marriage of Figaro, or, The Follies of a Day. See*
Le mariage de Figaro

BEAUMONT, FRANCIS, 1584–1616, and FLETCHER,
JOHN
*Jovial Crew. See* Brome, Richard
*A King or No King.* 1611. DPR2, WALL
*The Knight of the Burning Pestle.* 1610. ANG, BALD,
BAS, BAT14, BENY, BROC, DPR2, HILPDH2,
HOW, KINNR, NEI, OLH, OLI2, ORNC, SCI,
SCJ, SPE, WHE, WINE
*The Maid's Tragedy.* 1611. BAS, BROC, CLF1, CLKW,
DUN, MACJ, NEI, OLH, OLI2, RUB, SCH, SCI,
SCJ, SPE, WIGG
*Masque of the Inner Temple and Gray's Inn.* 1613. ETO
*Philaster; or, Love Lies A-bleeding.* 1609. BAS,
BELK18, BROC, HARC47, HOW, HUD, LIE,
MATTL, NEI, OLH, OLI2, PAR, SCH, SCI, SCJ,
SPE, TAT, TAU, THA, WAT, WHE, WINE
— *See* also Fletcher, John, joint author

BEAUVOIR, SIMONE DE, 1908–1986
*The Woman Destroyed.* 1994.
Quick, D., translator and adapter PLABE10

BEBER, NEENA
*Misreadings.* 1997. HUMANA97
*The Reluctant Instrument.* 2000. *See* Ackermann, J.
*Back Story: A Dramatic Anthology* HUMANA2000

BECHER, ULRICH, 1910–1990. *See* Preses, Peter, joint
author

BECKETT, SAMUEL, 1906–1989
*Act without Words.* 1957. ALLJ, ALLK, ALLM, BROI,
HAVH, HAVHA, MARK, MARL, REIW, REIWE
*Act without Words II.* 1960. DIEB
*All that Fall.* 1957. ALLJ, ALLK, ALLM, ALLN,
ALLO, CALD, CLL, CLLC, HOEP, JACOBA,
LAQID, OWEC, SCNO, WEIM, WEIP, WEIS
*Les beaux jours. See* Happy Days
*Catastrophe* (Programmed with *Ohio Impromptu* and
*What Where*). 1983. BES83 (synopsis only),
WOTHM
*La dernière bande. See* Krapp's Last Tape
*Embers.* 1959. COK
*En attendant Godot. See* Waiting for Godot
*Endgame.* 1957. ABRM2, COLD, GILB, LEVY,
JACOBA, JACOBD, JACOBE, NORGA,
NORIC2, NORJ2, SSSI, SSSIA, SSSIB, SSSIC,
WOTHB, WOTHC, WOTHM
Beckett, S., translator BLOC, COTQ, NORIA2,
NORIB2, NORJ2
Variant title: *Fin de partie*

*Enough* (Short story programmed with *Footfalls* and
*Rockaby*). 1984. BES83 (synopsis only).
*Fin de partie. See* Endgame
*Footfalls* (Programmed with *Enough* and *Rockaby*).
1984. BARNA, BES83 (synopsis only).
*Fragment de théâtre I. See* Rough for Theatre I
*Happy Days; ou, Les beaux jours.* 1961. ABRK2,
ABRL2, BARKB, BARKC, BARKD, BARKE,
BARKF, BRJ, BRJA, BRJB, BRJC, EIGHT,
GOLD, JACOB, WOTHA
Variant titles: *Les beaux jours; Ou les beaux jours*
*Krapp's Last Tape.* 1958. ANTL, BAIK, BAIL,
GOODE, HAEA, HAEB, JACOB, MEY, MEYB,
MEYC, MEYD, MEYE, MEYF, OBG, PERY,
SCNQ, SCNQCA, SCNQCB, WILLG
Variant title: *La dernière bande*
*Not I.* 1972. FRYE, FRYEA
Variant title: *Pas moi*
*Ohio Impromptu* (Programmed with *Catastrophe* and
*What Where*). 1981. BES83 (synopsis only),
WETZ
*Ou les beaux jours. See* Happy Days
*Pas moi. See* Not I
*Play: A Stage Play.* 1963. VENA
*Rockaby* (Programmed with *Enough* and *Footfalls*).
1981. BES83 (synopsis only)
*Rough for Theatre I.* 1978.
Beckett, S., translator HOWM
Variant title: *Fragment de théâtre I*
*Waiting for Godot.* 1952. BES55
Beckett, S., translator GRDBA60, NIL, SEVD
Variant title: *En attendant Godot*
*What Where* (Programmed with *Ohio Impromptu* and
*Catastrophe*). 1983. BES83 (synopsis only)

BECKINGTON, CHARLES
*Hamlet the Dane, a Burlesque Burletta.* 1847. NIN2

BECQUE, HENRI, 1837–1899
*Les corbeaux.* 1882. BOR, GRA, SEA, STJ2
Tilden, F., translator MOSQ, TREBA, TREBJ,
TREC2, TREE2, TREI2, WATL1
Variant titles: *The Crows; The Ravens; The
Vultures*
*The Crows. See* Les corbeaux
*The Parisian Woman. See* La Parisienne
*La Parisienne.* 1882.
Barzun, J., translator BENS1, BENT1
Vaughn, F., translator COTKW
Variant titles: *The Parisian Woman; The Woman of
Paris*
*The Ravens. See* Les corbeaux
*The Vultures. See* Les corbeaux
*The Woman of Paris. See* La Parisienne

BEDDOES, THOMAS LOVELL, 1803–1849
  *Death's Jest Book, or, The Fool's Tragedy.* 1826.
    ENGLMI
    Variant title: *The Fool's Tragedy*
  *The Fool's Tragedy. See* Death's Jest Book, or, The
    Fool's Tragedy

BEECHER, CLARK. *See* Kummer, Mrs. Clare (Beecher)

BEECHER, HARRIET ELIZABETH. *See* Stowe, Mrs.
    Harriet (Beecher)

BEERBOHM, MAX, 1872–1956
  *A Social Success.* 1913. BENT6

BEHAN, BRENDAN, 1923–1964
  *The Hostage.* 1958. BES60, POP
  *The New House.* 1958. RICJ
  *The Quare Fellow.* 1954. LAQID, OWEC, SEVD
    — *See also* McMahon, Frank.
  *Borstal Boy* (adapted by)

BEHN, MRS. APHRA (AMIS), 1640–1689
  *An Alderman's Bargain. See* The Lucky Chance, or, An
    Alderman's Bargain
  *The Banished Cavaliers. See* The Rover, or, The
    Banished Cavaliers
  *The Emperor of the Moon.* 1687. HUGL
  *The Feigned Courtesans, or, A Night's Intrigue.* 1679.
    LYON
    Variant title: *A Night's Intrigue*
  *The Lucky Chance, or An Alderman's Bargain.* 1687.
    FEFO, JEFF3
    Variant title: *An Alderman's Bargain*
  *A Night's Intrigue. See* The Feigned Courtesans, or, A
    Night's Intrigue
  *The Rover, or The Banished Cavaliers.* 1677. BARKF,
    HOWM, JACOBA, JACOBD, JEFF2, WONR,
    WOTHA, WOTHB, WOTHC
    Variant title: *The Banished Cavaliers*
  *Sir Patient Fancy.* 1678. ROGEW

BEHRMAN, SAMUEL NATHANIEL, 1893–1973
  *Amphitryon 38* (adapted from *Amphityron 38,* by Jean
    Giraudoux). 1937. BES37, CEW, THH
  *Biography.* 1932. BES32, BROZ, CET, GARU, MIJY,
    WAIT, WARM, WARL, WHI
  *Brief Moment.* 1931. BES31
  *The Cold Wind and the Warm.* 1958. BES58, SCL
  *End of Summer.* 1936. BES35, CLUR, FAMAL, GAS,
    MAFC, WATS
  *I Know My Love* (adapted from *Auprès de ma blonde* by
    Marcel Achard). 1949. BES49
  *Jacobowsky and the Colonel* (adapted from the play by
    Franz Werfel). 1944. BES43, GARZH

*Jane* (from the story by W. Somerset Maugham). 1952.
    BES51
  *No Time for Comedy.* 1939. BES38, CER, SIXL
  *Rain from Heaven.* 1934. CHAN, CHAP, THF
  *The Second Man.* 1927. CARP, CARPA, GASB,
    MOSK, MOSL

—— and LOGAN, JOSHUA
  *Fanny* (based on the trilogy *Marius, Fanny, and César*
    by Marcel Pagnol) (music and lyrics by Harold
    Rome). 1954. THEA55

BEIR, ULLI, 1922– . *See* Ijimere, Obotunde (pseudonym
    of)

BEISSEL, HENRY, 1929–
  *Inuk and the Sun.* 1973. SSSN

BEITH, JOHN HAY, 1876–1952. *See* Hay, Ian,
    pseudonym

BELASCO, DAVID, 1859–1931
  *La belle Russe.* 1881. AMP18
  *The Girl of the Golden West.* 1905. AMEM, MES,
    MOSJ, MOSK, MOSL
  *The Heart of Maryland.* 1895. AMP18, BES94, CLA,
    MESC
  *Naughty Anthony.* 1899. AMP18
  *The Return of Peter Grimm.* 1911. BAK, MIL, MOSS3
  *The Stranglers of Paris.* 1881. AMP18

—— and DE MILLE, HENRY CHURCHILL
  *The Charity Ball.* 1889. AMP17
  *Lord Chumley.* 1888. AMP17
  *Men and Women.* 1890. AMP17
  *The Wife.* 1887. AMP17

—— and FYLES, FRANKLIN
  *The Girl Left behind Me.* 1893. AMP18

—— and LONG, JOHN LUTHER
  *The Darling of the Gods.* 1902. BES99
  *Madame Butterfly.* 1900. QUIJ, QUIJR, QUIK, QUIL,
    QUIM, QUIN, QUIO2

BELBEL, SERGI, 1963–
  *Caresses.* 1991.
    London, J., translator DODGSS
    Variant title: *Carícies*
  *Carícies. See* Caresses
  *Fourplay.* 1989.
    Feldman, S., translator LONG
    Variant title: *Tàlem*
  *Tàlem. See* Fourplay

BELBER, STEPHEN, 1967–
*Tape.* 2000. HUMANA2000

BELL, FLORENCE, 1851–1930, and ROBINS,
ELIZABETH
*Alan's Wife.* 1893. FEFNC, NEWWP

BELL, NEAL
*Ready for the River.* 1989. PRIMA89-90
*Somewhere in the Pacific.* 1999. CLUM
*Will You Accept the Charges?* 1999. HUMANA99

BELL, ROBERT, 1800–1867
*Macbeth Modernised* (attributed to). (1838) NIN2

BELLIDO, JOSE-MARIA, 1922–1992
*Bread and Rice or Geometry in Yellow.*
Lima, R., translator WELL
Variant title: *El pan y el arroz o geometría en
amarillo*
*Football.* 1963.
Turner, D., translator BENA
*El pan y el arroz o geometría en amarillo. See* Bread
and Rice or Geometry in Yellow
*Train to H . . .* 1968?
Flores, R., translator WELL
Variant title: *Tren a F . . . Tren a F . . . See* Train to
H . . .

BELLON, LOLEH, 1925–1999 (b. Marie-Laure Bellon)
*Bonds of Affection.* 1996.
Bray, B., translator PLABI3
Variant title: *De si tendres liens*
*De si tendres liens. See* Bonds of Affection

BELLOW, SAUL, 1915–2005
*The Last Analysis.* 1964. COTKICO, GAT, SSTY
*Orange Souffle.* 1965. RICK, SANK
*The Wrecker.* 1954? NEWWW6

BELLVIS, GUILLEM DE CASTRO Y. *See* Castro y
Bellvis, Guillem

BELMONT, MRS. O.H.P. (ALVA), 1853–1933, and
MAXWELL, ELSA
*Melinda and Her Sisters.* 1916. FRIED

BELVETT, NAILA. *See* Young, Debbie, joint author

BELY, ANDREI, 1880–1934
*The Jaws of Night.* 1907.
Gerould, D., translator GERO

BEMARRO THEATRE GROUP, THE, 1986–1988? *See*
Jacobs, Pauline, joint author

BEMBA, SYLVAIN, 1934–1995
*Black Wedding Candles for Blessed Antigone.* 1990.
Brewster, T., translator THB
Variant title: *Noces posthumes de Santigone*
*Noces posthumes de Santigone. See* Black Wedding
Candles for Blessed Antigone

BENAVENTE, LUIS QUIÑONES DE. *See* Quiñones de
Benavente, Luis

BENAVENTE Y MARTINEZ, JACINTO, 1866–1954
*The Bias of the World. See* The Bonds of Interest
*The Bonds of Interest.* 1907.
Underhill, J., translator DICDS, FLOS, MOSQ, WHI
Variant titles: *The Bias of the World; Los intereses
creados; Interests Created; Vested Interests*
*Las brujas del domingo. See* The Witches' Sabbath
*His Widow's Husband.* 1908?
Underhill, J., translator MACN
Variant title: *El marido de su viuda*
*Los intereses creados. See* The Bonds of Interest
*Interests Created. See* The Bonds of Interest
*Los malhechores de bien.* 1905. MARLI2
*La malquerida. See* The Passion Flower
*El marido de su viuda. See* His Widow's Husband
*The Nest of Another. See* El nido ajeno
*El nido ajeno.* 1895. BRET
Variant title: *The Nest of Another*
*No fumadores. See* No Smoking
*No Smoking.* 1904.
Underhill, J., translator INGW
Variant title: *No fumadores*
*The Passion Flower.* 1913.
Underhill, J., translator GARZH, TUCG, TUCM,
TUCN, TUCO, WATI, WATL3
Variant title: *La malquerida*
*Vested Interests. See* The Bonds of Interest
*The Witches' Sabbath.* 1903.
Oliver, W., translator COTP
Variant title: *Las brujas del domingo*

BENEDICTO, JOAQUIN DICENTA Y. *See* Dicenta y
Benedicto, Joaquín

BENEDIX, RODERICH, 1811–1873
*Eigensinn. See* Obstinacy
*Obstinacy.* 1864.
Chambers, W., translator BAT11
Variant title: *Eigensinn*

BENELLI, SEM, 1877–1949
*L'amore dei translatore re. See* The Love of the Three
Kings
*La cena delle beffe. See* The Jest
*A Florentine Wager. See* The Jest

*A Fool There Was. See* The Jest
*The Jest.* 1919.
   Sheldon, E., translator and adapter BES19
   Variant titles: *La cena delle beffe; A Florentine Wager;*
     *A Fool There Was; The Jesters' Supper; The Love*
     *Feast; The Love Thief; The Supper of Pranks*
*The Jesters' Supper. See* The Jest
*The Love Feast. See* The Jest
*The Love of the Three Kings.* 1910.
   Jones, H., translator DICDT
   Variant title: *L'amore dei tre re*
*The Love Thief. See* The Jest
*The Supper of Pranks. See* The Jest

BENET, STEPHEN VINCENT, 1898–1943
   *The Devil and Daniel Webster.* 1939. BART, CARMI,
     HEIS, READ1

BENET I JORNET, JOSEP MARIA, 1940–
   *Desig. See* Desire
   *Desire.* 1989.
     Feldman, S., translator LONG
     Variant title: *Desig*
   *La nau. See* The Ship
   *The Ship.* 1969.
     Wellwarth, G., translator WELV
     Variant title: *La nau*

BENGAL, BEN, 1907–1993
   *Plant in the Sun.* 1937? KOZ

BENN, GOTTFRIED, 1886–1956
   *Ithaka.* 1914.
     Ritchie, J.M., translator EXP, SCVG

BENNETT, ALAN, 1934–
   *The Madness of George III.* 1991. BES93

BENNETT, ARNOLD, 1867–1931
   *Flora.* 1933. FIT
   *The Great Adventure.* 1913. CHU, COT

—— and KNOBLOCK, EDWARD
   *Milestones.* 1912. CEU, COD, DICDS, MART, MOD,
     PEN, TUCJ, WAGC4

BENNETT, CLARENCE
   *A Royal Slave.* 1898? AMP8

BENNETT, MICHAEL, 1943–1987
   *A Chorus Line* (conceived by) *See* Kirkwood, James and
     Dante, Nicholas. A Chorus Line

BENNETT, RICHARD R., 1936–
   *The Mines of Sulphur, an Opera* (music by). *See* Cross,
     Beverly
   *The Mines of Sulphur, an Opera.*

BENRIMO, JOSEPH HENRY, 1871–1942. *See* Hazleton,
   George Cochrane, joint author

BENSON, ROBERT HUGH, 1871–1914
   *The Upper Room.* 1914. PRON

BENSON, MRS. SALLY, 1900–1972
   *Junior Miss* (based on the book by). *See* Fields, Joseph
     and Chodorov, Jerome. Junior Miss

BENSUSAN, INEZ, 1871–c.1967
   *The Apple.* 1909. PFIS, VOTE

BENT, ROXXY, 1957–
   *A Trip to the Light Fantastic.* 1991. AROUN
   *Waiting for Annette.* 1987. AROUN

BENTLEY, ERIC RUSSELL, 1916–
   *Are You Now or Have You Ever Been: The*
     *Investigation of Show Business by the Un-*
     *American Activities Committee, 1947–1948.*
     (1972) RICK
   *Celestina; or, The Tragi-comedy of Calisto and*
     *Melibea. See* Rojas, Fernando de. Celestina;
     or, The Tragi-comedy of Calisto and Melibea
     (adapted by)
   *Larry Parks' Day in Court. See* Are You Now or Have
     You Ever Been . . . (excerpt)
   *Mary Stuart. See* Schiller, Johann. Mary Stuart (adapted
     by) Round 2. 1990. GAY4

BENTON, JAMES GRANT, 1949–2002
   *Twelf nite o wateva!* 1974. KUMU

BENTON, ROBERT, 1932–. *See* Newman, David, joint
   author

BEOLCO, ANGELO (called Ruzante or Ruzzante), 1502–
   1542
   *Bilora.* 1527?
     Hughes, B., and G., translators CLF2
   *La moscheta. See* Posh Talk
   *Posh Talk.* c.1532.
     Cairns, C., translator CAIRT
     Variant title: *La moscheta*
   *Il reduce. See* Ruzzante Returns from the Wars
   *Ruzzante Returns from the Wars.* 1522?
     Ingold, A., and Hoffman, T., translators BENR1,
     BENV
     Variant title: *Il reduce*

BERC, SHELLEY
   *A Girl's Guide to the Divine Comedy.* 1994. MARR

BERCOVICI, ERIC, 1933–
   *The Heart of Age.* 1953. NEWWW4

BEREMENYI, GEZA, 1946–
*Halmi*. 1979.
Greist, G., translator TEZ

BERG, GERTRUDE, 1899–1966
*Me and Molly*. 1948. BES47

BERG, ROBERT
*AIDS! The Musical!* (music by). *See* Jones, Wendell.
AIDS! The Musical!

BERGER, ADAM L.
*It's Time for a Change*. 1982. YOUP

BERGMAN, HJALMAR, 1883–1931
*Herr Sleeman kommer*. *See* Mr. Sleeman Is Coming
*Mr. Sleeman Is Coming*. 1917
Alexander, H., translator SCAN1
Variant title: *Herr Sleeman kommer*
*The Swedenhielms*. 1925.
Alexander, H., and Jones, L., translators SCAN3

BERGMAN, INGMAR, 1918–2007
*A Little Night Music* (plot and characters based on the film by)
*A Matter of the Soul* (radio play). 1990.
Martinus, E., translator NEWT
Variant title: *En själslig angelägenhet*
*The Seventh Seal*. 1956.
Anon. translator KNO, KNOJ, KNOK
Malmström, L., and Kushner, D., translators ABCA, ABCB, ABCC, ABCD
*En själslig angelägenhet*. *See* A Matter of the Soul
*Smiles of a Summer Night*. *See* Wheeler, Hugh Callingham
*Wild Strawberries*. (1957)
Malmström, L., and Kushner, D., translators BARK, BARKA, BARKB, BARKC

BERKELEY, REGINALD CHEYNE, 1890–1935
*The Lady with a Lamp*. 1929. FAO, PLAD
*The White Chateau*. 1927. MART

BERKEY, RALPH, 1912– . *See* Denker, Henry, joint author

BERKOFF, STEVEN, 1937–
*Greek*. 1980. WES15/16
*Kvetch*. 1986. BES86

BERKOW, JAY. *See* Hanan, Stephen Mo, joint author

BERMAN, BROOKE
*Dancing with a Devil*. 1999. HUMANA99

BERMAN, SABINA, 1955?–
*Bill*. *See* Yankee
*Yankee*. 1979.

Salas, T., and Vargas, M., translators, SALA
Variant titles: *Bill; Yanqui*
*Yanqui*. *See* Yankee

BERMANGE, BARRY, 1933–
*No Quarter*. 1962. NEWE12
*Scenes from Family Life*. 1969. MESSN

BERNARD, CATHERINE, 1662–1712
*Laodamia, Queen of Epirus*. 1689.
Gethner, P., translator GETH
Variant title: *Laodamie, reine d'Epire*
*Laodamie, reine d'Epire*. *See* Laodamia, Queen of Epirus

BERNARD, JEAN-JACQUES, 1888–1972
*Arver's Secret*. *See* Le secret d'Arvers
*Glamour*. 1924.
Boyd, E., translator DICIN2
Katzin, W., translator KAT
Variant titles: *L'Invitation au voyage; The Years Between*
*L'invitation au voyage*. *See* Glamour
*Martine*. 1922. RHO
Katzin, W., translator KAT
*Le secret d'Arvers*. 1926. GRAF
Variant title: *Arver's Secret*
*The Years Between*. *See* Glamour

BERNARD, KENNETH, 1930–
*The Magic Show of Dr. Ma-Gico*. 1973. MARRA
*The Unknown Chinaman*. 1971. BALLE10

BERNARD, LAWRENCE J.
*Lars Killed His Son*. 1935? TOD

BERNARD, PAUL. *See* Bernard, Tristan, pseudonym

BERNARD, TRISTAN (pseudonym of Paul Bernard), 1866–1947
*L'anglais tel quton le parle*. 1899. SET
Variant titles: *English as It Is Spoken; French without a Master*
*English as It Is Spoken*. *See* L'anglais tel qu'on le parle
*French without a Master*. *See* L'anglais tel qu'on le parle

BERNEY, WILLIAM. 1920–1961. *See* Richardson, Howard, joint author

BERNHARD, EMIL (pseudonym of Emil Cohn), 1881–1948
*The Marranos*. 1935?
Meyer, B., and Arlet, V., translators RUA

BERNSTEIN, ELSA. *See* Rosmer, Ernst, pseudonym

BERNSTEIN, HENRY, 1876–1953
*Le secret.* 1913. HART

BERNSTEIN, LEONARD, 1918–1990
*Candide. See* Hellman, Lillian. *Candide* (music by)
*West Side Story. See* Laurents, Arthur. West Side Story
   (music by)
*Wonderful Town. See* Fields, Joseph and Chodorov,
   Jerome. Wonderful Town (music by)

BERRIGAN, DANIEL J., S.J., 1921–
*The Trial of the Catonsville Nine.* 1971. BES70

BERRY, WENDELL, 1934–
*The Cool of the Day.* 1984. DIX

BESIER, RUDOLF, 1878–1942
*The Barretts of Wimpole Street.* 1930. BES30, CEU,
   FAMAN, GATS, GOW, GOWA, INGH, KNIE,
   PLAD, PLAL2, SPER, THO
*The Virgin Goddess.* 1906. MART

BESSET, JEAN-MARIE, 1959–
*La function. See* The Function
*The Function.* 1986.
   Miller, R., translator GAYIA
   Variant title: *La function*

BETSUYAKU, MINORU, 1937–
*Byōki. See* Sick
*The Cherry in Bloom.* 1980.
   Rolf, R., translator ALTJD
   Variant title: *Ki ni hana saku*
*The Elephant.* 1962.
   Goodman, D., translator AFTAP
   Variant title: *Zō*
*Idō. See* The Move
*Ki ni hana saku. See* The Cherry in Bloom
*The Legend of Noon.* 1973.
   Rolf, R., translator ALTJD
   Variant title: *Shōgo no densetsu*
*The Little Match Girl.* 1966.
   Lawson, R., translator ALTJD
   Variant title: *Matchi-uri no shōjo*
*Matchi-uri no shōjo. See* The Little Match Girl
*The Move.* 1973.
   Takaya, T., translator TAK
   Variant title: *Idō*
*Shōgo no densetsu. See* The Legend of Noon
*Sick.* 1981.
   Poulton, M., translator HACJT6
   Variant title: *Byōki*
*Zō. See* The Elephant

BETTI, UGO, 1892–1953
*Corruption in the Palace of Justice.* 1949.
   Reed, H., translator CONO, COTR, FREG, KERP
   Satin, J., translator SATI
   Variant title: *Corruzione al palazzo di giustizia*
*Corruzione al palazzo di giustizia. See* Corruption in the
   Palace of Justice
*Crime on Goat Island.* 1950.
   Reed, H., translator COTN, TWEI
   Variant titles: *Delitto all' Isola delle Capre; Island of
   Goats*
*Delitto all' Isola delle Capre. See* Crime on Goat Island
*Island of Goats. See* Crime on Goat Island
*The Queen and the Rebels.* 1951.
   Reed, H., translator BRZA, COTQ, REV, ULAN
   Variant title: *La regina e gli insorti*
*Le regina e gli insorti. See* The Queen and the Rebels

BETTS, DORIS, 1932–
*The Ugliest Pilgrim. See* Crawley, Brian. Violet (based on)

BEWS, SAMANTHA, 1969–
*So Wet.* 1998. INSI

BEYNON, RICHARD, 1927–1999
*The Shifting Heart.* 1957. OBSE

BEYZA'I, BAHRAM, 1938–
*Arusakha. See* Marionettes
*Chahar sanduq. See* Four Boxes
*Evening in a Strange Land. See* Three Puppet Shows
*Four Boxes.* 1967.
   Ghanoonparvar, M., translator GHAN
   Variant title: *Chahar sanduq*
*Marionettes.* 1962.
   Bhatt, S., Hoats, J., Nyazee, I., and Oskouee,
   translators GHAN
   Variant title: *Arusakha*
*The Puppets. See* Three Puppet Shows
*Three Puppet Shows.* 1963.
   Kapuscinski, G., translator MOCPD (3 one-act plays:
   *Evening in a Strange Land; The Puppets; The Story
   of the Hidden Moon*)
*The Story of the Hidden Moon. See* Three Puppet Shows

BEZE, THEODORE DE, 1519–1605
*Abraham sacrifiant.* FOUR

BHAGAT, DATTA, 1945–
*Avart. See* Whirlpool
*Whirlpool.* 1986?
   Nagies, G., Thorat, V., and Zelliot, E., translators
   DESH
   Variant title: *Avart*

BHARATI, DHARAMAVIR, 1926–1997
*Andha yug. See* The Blind Age
*The Blind Age.* 1954.
    Sharma, T., translator KAM1
    Variant title: *Andha yug*

BHARTI, BHANU, 1947–
*Katha kahi ek jale pedh ne. See* Tale Told by a
    Scorched Tree
*Tale Told by a Scorched Tree.* 1981?
    Mishra, S., translator KAM3
    Variant title: *Katha kahi ek jale pedh ne*

BHĀSA, 4th century B.C.–1st century A.D.
*The Dream of Vāsavadatta* (supposed author). 4th
    century B.C.–1st century A.D.
    Irwin, V., translator IRW
    Lal, P., translator LAL
    Woolner, A., and Sarup, L., translators ALPJ, ALPJR,
        WEL
    Variant title: *The Vision of Vāsavadatta*
*The Vision of Vāsavadatta. See* The Dream of
    Vāsavadatta

BHAVABHŪTI, 8th century
*The Later Story of Rama.* 8th century
    Josl, C., translator WEL
    Lal, P., translator LAL
    Variant title: *Rama's Later History*
*Mālati and Mādhara.* 8th century
    Coulson, M., translator THWI
*Rama's Later History. See* The Later Story of Rama

BIBBIENA, BERNARDO CARDINAL DOVIZI DA. *See*
    Dovizi da Bibbiena, Bernardo Cardinal

BICKERSTAFFE, ISAAC, 1735?–1812?
*The Hypocrite* (altered from the play by Colley Cibber).
    1768. BELG1
*Lionel and Clarissa* (adapted from Colley Cibber's
    "Nonjuror"). 1768. BELG1, BELK21
    Variant title: *The School for Fathers*
*Love in a Village.* 1762. BELK21
*Maid of the Mill.* 1765. BELK21
*The Padlock.* BELC3
*The Plain Dealer* (altered from the play by William
    Wycherley). 1766. BELG1
*The School for Fathers. See* Lionel and Clarissa
*The Sultan.* BELC1
*Thomas and Sally.* BELC2

BIERCE, AMBROSE, 1842–1914?
*Peaceful Expulsion.* 18??. CHIN

BIGGERS, EARL DERR, 1884–1933
*Seven Keys to Baldpate. See* Cohan, George M. Seven
    Keys to Baldpate (based on the novel by)

BILL, STEPHEN, 1948–
*Curtains.* 1987. BES95

BILLE, S. CORINNA, 1912–1979
*La chemise soufrée. See* The Scent of Sulphur
*The Scent of Sulphur.* 1963. (previously unpublished
    stage version of radio play)
    Makward, C., and Miller, J., translators PLAAG
    Variant title: *La chemise soufrée*

BILLETDOUX, FRANÇOIS, 1927–1991
*Tchin-Tchin. See* Michaels, Sydney. Tchin-Tchin (based
    on the play by)

THE BIM-BOM TROUPE, 1953–1960. *See* Afanasjew,
    Jerzy, joint author

BINGHAM, J. S. *See* MacBeth, George

BINGHAM, SALLIE, 1937–
*Milk of Paradise.* 1980. MIHPW

BINNIE, BRIONY
*Foreshore.* 1987. DEAD

BINNING, SADHU, 1947–
*Lesson of a Different Kind.* 1990. SACL

BIRD, ROBERT MONTGOMERY, 1806–1854
*The Broker of Bogota.* 1834. QUIJ, QUIK, QUIL,
    QUIM, QUIN
*Caridorf; or, The Avenger.* 1827? AMP12
*The Cowled Lover.* 1827? AMP12
*The Gladiator.* 1831. HAL, MONR, RICHE
*News of the Night; or, A Trip to Niagara.* 1829. AMP12
*'Twas All for the Best; or, 'Tis All a Notion.* 1827?
    AMP12

BIRIMISA, GEORGE, 1924–
*Georgie Porgie.* 1968. SME

BIRMELIN, JOHN, 1873–1950
*Der gnopp* (based on the play *Ein knopf* by Julius
    Rosen). 1935. BUFF
*Em Docktor Fogel sei offis schtunn* (based on the farce
    *Dr. Kranichs, sprechstunde*) 1935? BUFF

BISHOP, CONRAD, 1941– , and FULLER, ELIZABETH
*Mine Alone.* 1989. PRIMA89-90
*Okiboji.* 1990. PRIMA91

*The Rose and the Cross.* 1913.
  Green, M., translator GREEN
*The Stranger.* 1907.
  Gerould, D., translator GERO
*The Unknown Woman.* 1906.
  Langen, T., and Weir, J., translators EIGHTRP

BLOUNT, ROY, JR., 1941–
  *Five Ives Gets Named.* 1983. DIX
  *That Dog Isn't Fifteen.* 1984. DIX

BOAKYE, PAUL, 1963–
  *Boy with Beer.* 1992. BREW3

BOBRICK, SAM, 1932–
  *An Eastern Fable.* 1982. *See* Anonymous Plays.
    Twenty-four Hours: P.M.
  *Opening Night.* 1982. *See* Anonymous Plays. Twenty-
    four Hours: P.M.

BOCK, JERRY, 1928–
  *The Apple Tree* (joint author and music by). *See*
    Harnick, Sheldon. *The Apple Tree*
  *Fiddler on the Roof* (music by). *See* Stein, Joseph.
    *Fiddler on the Roof*
  *Fiorello!* (music by). *See* Weidman, Jerome and Abbott,
    George. *Fiorello!*
  *She Loves Me* (music by). *See* Masteroff, Joe. *She Loves
    Me*

BODDY, MICHAEL, 1934– , and ELLIS, BOB
  *The Legend of King O'Malley, or, Never Say Die until a
    Dead Horse Kicks You.* 1970. BRIM1

BODEL, JEAN. *See* Bodel, Jehan

BODEL, JEHAN, ca. 1167–ca. 1210
  *Le jeu de Saint Nicolas. See* The Play of Saint Nicholas
  *The Play of Saint Nicholas.* 1200.
    Axton, R., and Stevens, J., translators AXT
    Mandel, O., translator MARH
    Variant title: *Le jeu de Saint Nicolas*

BODNAROVA, JANA, 1950–
  *Lampiónový sprievod. See* The Lantern Procession
  *The Lantern Procession.* 2002.
    Trebatická, H., translator CONTSL4
    Variant title: *Lampiónový sprievod*

BOER, LODEWIJK DE, 1937–2004
  *The Bouddha van Ceylon. See* The Buddha of Ceylon
  *The Buddha of Ceylon.* 1990.
    Couling, D., translator COUL
    Variant title: *The Bouddha van Ceylon*

BOESING, MARTHA, 1936–
  *The Business at Hand.* 1988. JENN

BOGART, ANNE, 1951–
  *Cabin Pressure: Notes and Excerpts.* 1999. HUMANA99
  *War of the Worlds* (conceived by). *See* Iizuki, Naomi.
    *War of the Worlds*

BOGDANOVSKI, RUSOMIR, 1948–
  *Nothing without Trifolio.* 1985.
    McConnel-Duff, A., translator LUZ

BOGOSIAN, ERIC, 1953–
  *Drinking in America.* BES85
  *Sex, Drugs, Rock & Roll.* 1990. BES89, WETZ
  *SubUrbia.* 1994. BES93.

BOIS ROBERT, FRANÇOIS. *See* Bois-Robert, François
  Le Métel de

BOIS-ROBERT, FRANÇOIS LE METEL DE, 1592–1662
  *L'amant ridicule.* 1655. LANC

BOKER, GEORGE HENRY, 1823–1890
  *The Bankrupt.* 1855. AMP3
  *Francesca da Rimini.* 1855. ELLI1, HAL, KAYS,
    MADI, MASW, MONR, MOSS3, QUIJ, QUIK,
    QUIL, QUIM, QUIN, QUIO1
  *Glacus.* 1886. AMP3
  *The World a Mask.* 1851. AMP3

BOLAND, BRIDGET, 1913–1988
  *Cockpit.* 1948. PLAN1
  *Gordon.* 1961. PLAN25
  *The Prisoner.* 1954. PLAN10
  *The Return.* 1953. PLAN9

BOLGER, DERMOT, 1959–
  *The Lament for Arthur Cleary.* 1989. CRACK

BOLITHO, WILLIAM, 1890–1930 (pseudonym of
    William Bolitho Ryall)
  *Overture.* 1930. BES30

BOLT, CAROL, 1941–2000
  *Buffalo Jump.* 1971. PERKY
    Variant title: *New Year Country*
  *Cyclone Jack* (music by Paul Vigna). 1972. KAL4
  *New Year Country. See* Buffalo Jump
  *Waiting for Sandy.* 1992. ZIMM

BOLT, ROBERT, 1924–1995
  *A Man for All Seasons.* 1960. BES61, CEQA, COTKIT,
    COTR, DIYLA, DIYLB, FOUX, NEWE6
  *Vivat! Vivat Regina!* 1972. BES71

BOLTON, GUY REGINALD, 1884–1979
*Anastasia. See* Maurette, Marcelle. Anastasia (adapted by)
*Chicken Feed.* 1923. BES23
    Variant title: *Wages for Wives*
*Don't Listen Ladies! See* Guitry, Sacha. Don't Listen
    Ladies! (adapted by)
*Wages for Wives. See* Chicken Feed

—— and MIDDLETON, GEORGE
*Adam and Eva.* 1919. BES19

BONAL, DENISE, 1921–
*Beware the Heart.* 1992.
    Miller, R., translator PLABI2
    Variant title: *Féroce comme le coeur*
*A Country Wedding.* 1993.
    Johns, T., translator PLABI3
    Variant title: *Turbulences et petits details*
*Féroce comme le coeur. See* Beware the Heart
*Passions et prairie. See* A Picture Perfect Sky
*A Picture Perfect Sky.* 1987.
    Johns, T., translator PLABI1
    Variant title: *Passions et prairie*
*Turbulences et petits details. See* A Country Wedding

BOND, CHRIS. *See* Bond, Christopher

BOND, CHRISTOPHER, 1945–
*Sweeney Todd. See* Wheeler, Hugh Callingham.
    Sweeney Todd, The Demon Barber of Fleet Street
    (based on Sweeney Todd: the Demon Barber of
    Fleet Street)
    — *See also* Luckham, Claire, joint author

BOND, EDWARD, 1934–
*Bingo: Scenes of Money and Death.* 1974. WOTHM
*Saved.* 1965. COTKB1

BOND, ELISABETH, 1945–
*Lily and Colin* (radio play). 1987. ROBR
*Love and Dissent.* 1983. GRIFG2

BONET, WILMA
*Good Grief, Lolita.* 1993? PURO

BONNER, MARITA, 1899–1971
*Exit: An Illusion.* 1929. PER
*The Pot Maker.* 1927. BRW
*The Purple Flower.* 1928. HARY, HARYB, KEL, PER

BONTEMPELLI, MASSIMO, 1878–1960
*Dea by Dea.* 1925.
    Oldcorn, A., translator TWEI
    Variant title: *Nostra Dea*
*Nostra Dea. See* Dea by Dea

BONTEMPS, ARNA, 1903–1973, and CULLEN,
    COUNTEE
*The St. Louis Woman.* 1946. PATR

BOOTHBY, FRANCES, fl. 1669–1670
*Marcelia: or The Treacherous Friend.* 1669. MISC

BOOTHE, CLARE (married name Clare Boothe Luce),
    1903–1987
*Kiss the Boys Good-bye.* 1938. BES38
*Margin for Error.* 1939. BES39, CER, FIR
*Slam the Door Softly.* 1970. BARIF, BARKD, COLD,
    DIYLB
*The Women.* 1936. BES36, CET, FAMK, GAS, PLAAF,
    SUB

BOPHAVY, KHEM
*A Wound in Her Life.* 2001. SECO

BORCHERT, WOLFGANG, 1921–1947
*Draussen von der Tür. See* The Outsider
*The Man Outside. See* The Outsider
*The Outsider.* 1947.
    Benedikt, M., translator BENB
    Variant titles: *Draussen von der Tür; The Man
    Outside*

BORDEN, WALTER M., 1942–
*Tightrope Time: Ain't Nuthin' more than Some Itty Bitty
    Madness between Twilight & Dawn.* 1986. SEARS1

BORETZ, NICK
*Shelter Area.* 1964. BALLE2

BORGEN, JOHAN, 1902–1979
*The House.*
    Shaw, P., translator MNON
    Variant title: *Huset*
*Huset. See* The House

BORNSTEIN, KATE, 1948–
*Virtually Yours.* 1998. HUGH

BORSOOK, HENRY
*Three Weddings of a Hunchback.* 1924. MAS1

BORUTA, KAZYS, 1905–1965
*Baltaragio malūnas. See* Whitehorn's Windmill
*Whitehorn's Windmill* (dramatization of novel by E.
    Ignatavicius and S. Motiejunas). (1945)
    Sabalis, K., and Abartis, translator and adapter GOLB
    Variant title: *Baltaragio malūnas*

BOSAKOWSKI, PHILIP A., 1946–1994
*Bierce Takes on the Railroad.* 1972. BALLE11
*Chopin in Space.* 1984. WOQ4

BOSE, RANA
*Baba Jacques Dass and Turmoil at Cote-des-Neiges Cemetery.* 1987. SACL
*Five or Six Characters in Search of Toronto.* 1993. SACL

BOSMAN, HERMAN CHARLES, 1905–1951
*Street-woman.* GRAYTO

BOSTON, MICHON, 1962–
*Iola's Letter.* 1994. PERF

BOSTON, STEWART
*Counsellor Extraordinary.* 1971. KAL1

BOTTOMLEY, GORDON, 1874–1948
*Gruach.* 1923. KRE

BOUBLIL, ALAIN, and SCHONBERG, CLAUDE-MICHEL
*Les misérables* (based on the novel by Victor Hugo, lyrics by Herbert Kretzmer, music by Claude-Michel Schonberg, original French text by Alain Boublil and Jean-Marc Natel, additional material by James Fenton). 1985. BES86
*Miss Saigon* (music by Claude-Michel Schonberg; lyrics by Richard Maltby Jr. and Alain Boublil). 1989. BES90

BOUCHARD, JEAN, 1936–
*A Birthday Present for Stalin.* Ward, M., translator PAIS
Variant title: *Un drôle de cadeau*
*Un drôle de cadeau.* See A Birthday Present for Stalin

BOUCHARD, MICHEL MARC, 1958–
*Les muses orphelines.* See The Orphan Muses
*The Orphan Muses.* 1990.
Gaboriau, L., translator NEWFPL, WASCPB2
Variant title: *Les muses orphelines*

BOUCHER, DENISE, 1935–
*Les fées ont soif.* See When Faeries Thirst
*When Faeries Thirst.* 1978.
Makward, C., and Miller, J., translators PLAAG
Variant title: *Les fées ont soif*

BOUCICAULT, DION, 1822–1890
*After Dark; or, Pardon—For a Price* (adapted from a melodrama in three acts). 1868. BAI, MELO
*Belle Lamar.* 1874. LEV, LEVE, MESC
*Boursiquot.* See The Colleen Bawn
*The Colleen Bawn; or, The Brides of Garryowen.* 1860. GREAAI, HUDV, ROWE
Variant title: *Boursiquot*

*The Corsican Brothers.* 1852. BOOA2, BOOM, VICT
*Dot* (adapted from *The Cricket on the Hearth* by Charles Dickens). 1859. AMP1
*Flying Scud; or, A Fourlegged Fortune.* 1866. AMP1, CLA
*Forbidden Fruit.* 1876. AMP1
*London Assurance.* 1841. ASG, BAI, BAT22, BENY, COTKIS, MATTL, MOSN, MOSO
*Louis XI.* 1855. AMP1
*Mercy Dodd; or, Presumptive Evidence.* 1869. AMP1
*The Octoroon; or, Life in Louisiana.* 1859. COY, GARX, MASW, MASX, NILS, QUIJ, QUIK, QUIL, QUIM, QUIN, RICHE, ROGEBD, SIG, WATTAD
*Pardon—For a Price.* See After Dark
*The Poor of New York.* 1857. AMEM, WILMET
*Rip Van Winkle* (adapted by). See Anonymous Plays.
Rip Van Winkle (as played by Joseph Jefferson)
*Robert Emmet.* 1884. AMP1
*The Shaughraun.* 1874. BOOA2

—— and BYRON, HENRY JAMES
*Lost at Sea.* 1869. KILG

BOURDET, GILDAS, 1947–
*The Gas Station.* 1985.
Miller, J., translator WEHL

BOURLET, KATHERINE, SR., 15th century
*The Nativity* (The Chantilly play). 15th century
Sanchez, E., and Robinson, D., translators and adapters ROBM

BOURNE, BETTE, 1939– (b. Peter Bourne) and SHAW, PEGGY, and SHAW, PAUL, and WEAVER, LOIS
*Belle Reprieve.* 1991. CASB, HELB, WOTHB, WOTHM

BOURSAULT, EDME, 1638–1701
*Marie Stuard, reine d'Ecosse.* 1683.
Paulson, M., adapter FALE

BOVASSO, JULIE, 1930–1991
*Down by the River Where Water Lilies Are Disfigured Every Day.* 1972–1973. PLACD
*Schubert's Last Serenade.* 1971. OWER

BOVELL, ANDREW, 1962– , CORNELIUS, PATRICIA, REEVES, MELISSA, TSIOLKAS, CHRISTOS, and VELA, IRINA
*Trash.* See Who's Afraid of the Working Class?
*Who's Afraid of the Working Class?* 1998. MELB (4 one act plays: four following one-act plays: Bovell, A. *Trash*; Cornelius, P. *Money*; Reeves, M. *Dreamtown*; Tsiolkas, C. *Suit*; musical score by I. Vela)

BOWEN, JOHN GRIFFITH, 1924–
*After the Rain.* 1967. BES67
*The Waiting Room.* 1970. RICK

BOWEN, MARGARET ELIZABETH
*Crude and Unrefined.* 193-? PROG

BOWEN, RICHARD, fl. 1570
*Apius and Virginia* (sometimes attributed to). *See*
Anonymous Plays. Apius and Virginia

BOWLES, JANE AUER, 1917–1973
*In the Summer House.* 1953. BES53, PLAAF

BOWMAN, EDWARD
*Salve Regina.* 1969. CONTNZ

BOX, MURIEL, 1905–1991
*Angels of War.* 1935. FIN, TYEW

BOX, SYDNEY, 1907–1983
*The Woman and the Walnut Tree.* 1935? FIN

BOYD, GEORGE ELROY, 1952–
*Consecrated Ground.* 1999. SEARS2

BOYD, PAMELA, 1947–
*Inside Out.* 1986. BERR
*Odd Fish.* 1992. ZIMM

BOYD, POM
*Down onto Blue.* 1994. BOUR

BOYD, SUSAN
*St. Mael and the Maldunkian Penguins.* (1977) NEWP

BOYENGA, JENNIFER TERRY. *See* Terry, Jennifer

BOYER, CLAUDE, 1618–1698
*Le faux Tonaxare. See* Oropastes
*Oropaste; ou, Le faux Tonaxare. See* Oropastes
*Oropastes.* 1662.
    Lockert, L., translator LOCU
    Variant titles: *Le faux Tonaxare; Oropaste*

BRACCO, ROBERTO, 1862–1943
*I fantasmi. See* Phantasms
*Phantasms.* 1906.
    St. Cyr. D., translator TUCG
    Variant title: *I fantasmi*

BRACKENRIDGE, HUGH HENRY, 1748–1816
*The Battle of Bunkers-hill.* 1776? MOSS1, WORN
*The Death of General Montgomery, in Storming the City
    of Quebec.* 1777. PHI

BRACKLEY, ELIZABETH, 1616–1663. *See* Cavendish,
Jane, joint author

BRADBEER, SUZANNE
*Full Bloom.* 2000. WOMP2000

BRADBURY, PAUL. *See* Ball, Alan Egerton, joint
author

BRADDON, MARY ELIZABETH, 1837–1915
*Lady Audley's Secret. See* Hazlewood, Colin. Lady
Audley's Secret (from the novel by)

BRADDON, RUSSELL, 1921–1995
*Naked Island.* 1960. PLAN22

BRADFORD, ROARK, 1896–1948
*Ol' Man Adam and His Chillun. See* Connelly, Marc.
The Green Pastures (based on the novel by)

BRADLEY, BELINDA
*Polly Blue.* 1995. MELB

BRADLEY, JACK
*Everywoman.* (English version by). *See* Kárpáti, Péter.
Everywoman

BRADLEY, JOHN, 1944–
*Irish Stew.* 1979. THUG

BRADLEY, JYLL, 1966–
*Digging for Ladies.* 1996. MYTH (excerpt)
    Variant title: *On the Playing Fields of Her
        Rejection*
*On the Playing Fields of Her Rejection. See* Digging
    for Ladies

BRAMBLE, MARK, 1950– . *See* Stewart, Michael, joint
author

BRANCH, WILLIAM, 1927–
*Baccalaureate.* 1975. BLACTH
*In Splendid Error.* 1954. BPW, HARY, HILEB, PATR
*A Medal for Willie.* 1951. KINH, KINHB

BRAND, MILLEN, 1906–1980
*The Outward Room. See* Kingsley, Sidney. The World
We Make (based on the novel by)

BRAND, MONA, 1915–2007
*Here under Heaven.* 1948. PFIS

BRANDON, JAMES R, 1927– . *See* Nakamura Matagoro,
joint author

Variant titles: *Dreigroschenoper; A Penny for the Poor*
*Das verhor des Lukullus.* 1939? FEFH2

—— and HAUPTMANN, ELISABETH.
*The Threepenny Opera* (based on *The Beggar's Opera* by John Gay; music by Kurt Weill). ·
　　Manheim, R., and Willett, J., translators BES75, LEVY, SCNQ, SSSI

—— and WEILL, KURT.
*He Who Says No.* 1931.
　　Nellhaus, G., translator PLAAC2, SCVDO1
　　Variant title: *Der Neinsager*
*He Who Says Yes.* 1931.
　　Nellhaus, G., translator PLAAC1, SCVDO1
　　Variant title: *Der Jasager*
*Der Jasager. See* He Who Says Yes
*Der Neinsager. See* He Who Says No

BREEN, RICHARD L., 1919–1967, and SCHNIBBE, HARRY
*"Who Ride on White Horses," the Story of Edmund Campion.* 1940. THEC

BREIT, HARVEY, 1909?–1968. *See* Schulberg, Budd, joint author

BRENDLE, THOMAS ROYCE, 1889–1966
*Die hoffning.* 19–? BUFF
*Die mutter.* 1934. BUFF

BRENNAN, KIT, 1957–
*Hunger Striking.* 1997. BREK (excerpt)
*Magpie.* 1993. ZIMM (excerpt)

BRENNER, ALFRED, 1916–
*Survival* (television drama). 1956. SCVDT1

BRENTON, HOWARD, 1942–
*H.I.D. (Hess Is Dead).* 1989. THLA
*Weapons of Happiness.* 1976. COTKB2

BRESLIN, JIMMY, 1930–
*Contract with Jackie.* 1996. HUMANA96

BRETON, ANDRE, 1896–1966, and SOUPAULT, PHILIPPE
*If You Please.* 1920.
　　Wellwarth, G., translator BEN
　　Variant title: *S'il vous plaît*
*S'il vous plaît. See* If You Please

BRETON DE LOS HERREROS, MANUEL, 1796–1873
*Muérete ¡ y verás!* 1837. BRET

BREUER, LEE, 1937–
*The B. Beaver Animation.* 1974. MESSE
*Hajj; the Performance.* 1983. WOQ3
*A Prelude to Death in Venice.* 1979. NEWQ
*The Red Horse Animation.* 1970. THG, THGA

BREWSTER, EMMA E.
*A Bunch of Buttercups.* 1881. CHIN

BRICKS THEATRE GROUP, and MOLAPONG, K.
*The Horizon Is Calling.* 2000. ZEE1

BRICUSSE, LESLIE, 1931– , and NEWLEY, ANTHONY
*Stop the World—I Want to Get Off* (book, lyrics and music by). 1962. BES62

BRIDGEMAN, LAURA
*Maison splendide.* 1996. SETR

BRIDGERS, ANN PRESTON, 1891–1967. *See* Abbott, George, joint author

BRIDIE, JAMES, pseudonym. *See* Mavor, Osborne Henry

BRIEUX, EUGENE, 1858–1932
*The Aim of the Law. See* La robe rouge
*False Gods.* 1909.
　　Fagan, J., translator TUCG
　　Variant title: *La foi*
*La foi. See* False Gods
*The Letter of the Law. See* La robe rouge
*The Red Robe. See* La robe rouge
*La robe rouge.* 1900. GRA
　　Reed, F., translator DICD, DICIN2, WHI
　　Variant titles: *The Aim of the Law; The Letter of the Law; The Red Robe*
*The Three Daughters of M. Dupont. See* Les trois filles de M. Dupont
*Les trois filles de M. Dupont.* 1897. BER, BOR
　　Variant title: *The Three Daughters of M. Dupont*

BRIGADERE, ANNA, 1861–1933
*Maija and Paija.* (1921)
　　Raudsepa, I., translator GOLB
　　Variant title: *Maija un Paija*
*Maija un Paija. See* Maija and Paija

BRIGHOUSE, HAROLD, 1882–1958
*Hobson's Choice.* 1916. MART, TUCD

BRINGSVAERD, TOR ÅGE, 1939–
*The Glass Mountain.* 1975.
　　Beissel, H., and Brask, P., translators BRAK

BRITTON, KENNETH PHILLIPS, and HARGRAVE, ROY
*Houseparty.* 1928? LEV, LEVE

BRIUSOV, VALERII, 1873–1924
*The Wayfarer.* 1911.
Gerould, D., translator GERO

BROCH, HERMANN, 1886–1951
*The Atonement.* 1934.
Wellwarth, G., and Rotherman, H., translators WELG

BROCK, BROCK NORMAN
*Here Is Monster.* 1989. VERI

BROME, RICHARD, 1590–1652
*The Antipodes.* 1638. GAYLE3, KNOW, PARR
*A Jovial Crew.* 1641. LAWS, OLH, OLI2
*A Mad Couple Well Matched.* 1653? KNOW, WALL

BROMLEY, KIRK WOOD, 1966–
*Midnight Brainwash Revival.* 1999. DENT

BRONTË, CHARLOTTE, 1816–1855
*Jane Eyre. See* Jerome, Mrs. Helen (Burton). Jane Eyre (based on the novel by)

BROOK, PETER, 1925– , and CARRIÈRE, JEAN CLAUDE
*Exile in the Forest. See* The Mahabharata
*The Game of Dice. See* The Mahabharata
*The Mahabharata* (three interlocking full-length plays: *The Game of Dice, Exile in the Forest,* and *The War;* adapted from the Sanskrit poem *The Mahabharata*). 1987. BES87
*The War. See* The Mahabharata

——, ——, and CONSTANT, MARIUS
*La tragedie de Carmen,* a full length musical in one act (adapted from the opera *Carmen,* music by Georges Bizet). 1982. BES83

BROOKE, HENRY, 1703?–1783
*The Deliverer of His Country. See* Gustavus Vasa, or, The Deliverer of His Country
*Gustavus Vasa, or, The Deliverer of His Country.* (1739) BELK18
Variant title: *The Deliverer of His Country*

BROOKER, BLAKE, 1955– , and GREEN, MICHAEL
*Alien Bait.* 1994. NEWCAD8

BROOKMAN, ANNE
*Wild about Work.* 1989. AROUN

BROOKS, HARRY, 1876– *See* Malleson, Miles, joint author

BROOKS, HINDI
*The Night the War Came Home.* 1992. COJ

BROOKS, JEREMY, 1926–1994, and MITCHELL, ADRIAN
*A Child's Christmas in Wales* (adapted from the story by Dylan Thomas). 1982. SWO

BROOKS, MEL, 1926– (b. Melvin Kaminsky)
*Of Fathers and Sons.* 1952. READ2

BROPHY, BRIGID, 1929–1995
*The Waste Disposal Unit.* 1964. RICJ

BROSSA, JOAN, 1919–1998
*The Quarrelsome Party.* 1963.
Jové A, Castañé, L., George, D., and London, J., translators LONG
Variant title: *El sarau*
*El sarau. See* Brossa, J. *The Quarrelsome Party*

BROUGH, ROBERT BARNABAS, 1828–1860. *See* Brough, William, joint author

BROUGH, WILLIAM, 1826–1870
*The Field of the Cloth of Gold.* 1868. BOOA5
*Perdita; or, The Royal Milkmaid.* 1856. NIN3

—— and BROUGH, ROBERT BARNABAS
*The Enchanted Isle; or "Raising the Wind" on the Most Approved Principles.* 1848. BOOA5, HUDV (Scene 4 only)
Variant title: *"Raising the Wind" on the Most Approved Principles*
*"Raising the Wind" on the Most Approved Principles. See* The Enchanted Isle; or, "Raising the Wind" on the Most Approved Principles

—— and HALLIDAY, ANDREW
*The Area Belle.* 1864. BOOA4

BROUGHAM, JOHN, 1810–1880
*The Duke's Motto; or, I Am Here!* 1862. AMP14
*The Irish Emigrant, or, Temptation.* 1856. MESCO
*Metamora; or, The Last of the Pollywogs.* 1847. WILMET
*Much Ado about a Merchant of Venice.* 1869. NIN5
*Po-ca-hon-tas. See* Pocahontas; or, The Gentle Savage
*Pocahontas; or, The Gentle Savage.* 1855. AMPA, BAT20, MONR
Variant title: *Po-ca-hon-tas*

BROUGHTON, JOHN, 1947–
*Te hara (The Sin)*. 1988. GARR

BROWER, BROCK, 1931–
*A Little to the Left*. 1959. PAJ

BROWN, AL
*Back to Back*. 1981. WES9

BROWN, ALEX (pseudonym of G. W. Bartram), 1944–
*The Wolf Within*. 1989. WASCT

BROWN, CARLYLE, 1945–
*The African Company Presents Richard III*. 1988.
    SWANS
*The Little Tommy Parker Celebrated Colored Minstrel
    Show*. 1987. ELAM

BROWN, CHARLES, fl. 1814. *See* Keats, John, joint
    author

BROWN, DANIEL GREGORY (b. Kenneth Jeffrey
    Hartman), 1945–1983
*Four in the Morning*. 1982. *See* Anonymous Plays.
    Twenty-four Hours: A.M.

BROWN, DAVID PAUL, 1795–1875
*Sertorius; or, The Roman Patriot*. 1830. MOSS2

BROWN, JASON ROBERT, 1970–
*Parade* (music and lyrics by). *See* Uhry, Alfred. Parade.

BROWN, JEAN H.
*The Honorable Mrs. Ling's Conversion*. 1920. CHIN

BROWN, JOHN, 1715–1766
*Barbarossa*. (1755) BELK10

BROWN, KARL, and MCQUEEN, MATTHEW
*Rimmin' at the Baths*. 1984. *See* Anonymous Plays. The
    AIDS Show . . .
*Safe Livin' in Dangerous Times*. 1984. *See* Anonymous
    Plays. The AIDS Show . . .

BROWN, KENNETH
*Life after Hockey*. 1985. BELLN

BROWN, LENNOX JOHN, 1934–
*Devil Mas'*. 1974. CARR

BROWN, RIWIA
*Irirangi Bay*. 1996. KOU
*Roimata*. 1988. GARR

BROWN, WESLEY, 1945–
*Life during Wartime*. 1992. ALG

BROWN, WILLIAM F., 1928–
*The Wiz* (adapted from *The Wonderful Wizard of Oz*
    by L. Frank Baum; music and lyrics by Charlie
    Smalls). 1975. GREAAR

BROWN, WILLIAM WELLS, 1814–1884
*The Escape; or, A Leap to Freedom*. 1858. HARY,
    HARYB, MESC, RAVIT, ROOTS

BROWN-GUILLORY, ELIZABETH, 1954–
*Mam Phyllis*. 1985. BRW

BROWNE, FELICITY
*The Family Dance*. 1976. PLAN46

BROWNE, MAURICE, 1881–1955. *See* Nichols, Robert
    Malise Boyer, joint author

BROWNE, PORTER EMERSON, 1879–1934
*The Bad Man*. 1920. BES20

BROWNE, ROBERT F. GORE. *See* Gore-Browne,
    Robert F.

BROWNE, THEODORE, 1910–1979
*Natural Man*. 1937. HARY, HARYB

BROWNE, WYNYARD, 1911–1964
*The Holly and the Ivy*. 1950. PLAN3

BROWNING, ROBERT, 1812–1889
*A Blot in the 'Scutcheon*. 1843. ASH, GRE, HARC18,
    MOSN, MOSO, TAT
*In a Balcony*. 1884. GREC2
*King Victor and King Charles*. KAU
*Pippa Passes*. 1841. BAI

BRUCE, LESLEY
*Keyboard Skills*. 1993. BUSHT

BRUCE, RICHARD. *See* Nugent, Richard Bruce

BRUNDAGE, JOHN HERBERT, 1926–2001. *See* Herbert,
    John (pseudonym of)

BRUNO, GIORDANO, 1548–1600
*Il candelaio. See* The Candle Bearer
*The Candle Bearer*. 16th century
    Hale, J., translator BENSA
    Variant title: *Il candelaio*

BRUNSON, BEVERLY
*A Bastard of the Blood.* 1956. NEWWW10

BRUST, ALFRED, 1891–1934
*Die Wölff. See* The Wolves
*The Wolves.* 1922.
    Ritchie, J., and Garten, H., translators RITS
    Variant title: *Die Wölff*

BRUSTEIN, ROBERT, 1927–
*Nobody Dies on Friday.* 1998. NEWR98

BRYDEN, BILL, 1942–
*Willie Rough.* 1973. PLAN43

BRYKS, RACHMIL, 1912–1974
*A Cat in the Ghetto. See* Wincelberg, Shimon. Resort 76
    (based on)

BRYMER, PATRICK. *See* Griffiths, Linda, joint author

BUCHANAN, GEORGE, 1506–1582
*Jephté; ou, Le voeu.* 1552? FOUR

BUCHANAN, WAYNE
*Under their Influence.* 2000. BLAAP

BUCHNER, GEORG, 1813–1837
*Danton's Death.* 1836.
    Holmstrom, J., translator BENT5
    Lustig, T., translator LUST
    Spender, S., and Rees, G., translators BENS1, TREB,
        TREC1, TREE1, TREI1
    Variant title: *Dantons tod*
*Dantons tod. See* Danton's Death
*Leonce and Lena.* 1911.
    Bentley, E., translator BEFOB, BENS3, ESS
*Woyzeck.* 1879.
    Ball, D., adapter 1913. (First performance of
        adaptation, 1972; music by Susan Hesse Keller).
        MIMN
    Hoffman, T., translator BENT1, HILPDH4, SEVT
    Mueller, C., translator COTKIR, COTL, COTQ,
        NORI2, WOTHB
    Schmidt, H., translator COI, GILB, NORGA, SSSIB,
        SSSIC
    Schnitzler, H., and Ulman, S., translators NEWDI50
    Sorell, W., translator ASF
    Wellwarth, G., translator WELT
    Variant title: *Wozzeck*
    — *See* Iizuka, Naomi. Skin (adapted from the play
        *Woyzeck* by)
*Wozzeck. See* Woyzeck

BUCK, PEARL S., 1892–1973
*Will this Earth Hold?* INGA

BUCKHURST, LORD. *See* Sackville, Thomas

BUCKINGHAM, GEORGE VILLIERS, 1628–1687
*The Rehearsal.* 1671. BELK15, FAL, LEV, LEVE,
    MAND, MANF, MOSE1, NET, REST, STM,
    TRUS, WONR

BUCKLAND, ANDREW
*The Ugly Noo Noo.* 1988. KANI

BUCKSTONE, JOHN BALDWIN, 1802–1879
*Luke the Labourer; or, The Lost Son.* 1828. BAI, KILG,
    MOR

BUDBILL, DAVID, 1940–
*Judevine.* 1984. NEWAMP2

BUECHNER, GEORG. *See* Büchner, Georg

BUENAVENTURA, ENRIQUE, 1925–2003
*The Funeral* (from *Documents from Hell*).
    Sampson, A., translator HILET
*In the Right Hand of God the Father.* 1960.
    Oliver, W., translator OLIW
*The Orgy* (from *Documents from Hell*).
    Sampson, A., translator HILET

BUERO VALLEJO, ANTONIO, 1916–2000
*The Basement Window.* 1967.
    O'Connor, P., translator OCONNF
    Variant title: *El tragaluz*
*The Concert at Saint Ovide.* 1962.
    Anderson, F., translator HOLTM
    Variant title: *El concierto de San Ovidio*
*El concierto de San Ovidio. See* The Concert at Saint
    Ovide
*La doble historia del doctor Valmy. See* Two Sides to
    Dr. Valmy's Story
*The Dream Weaver.* 1952.
    Oliver, W., translator COTP
    Variant title: *La tejedora de sueños*
*The Foundation.* 1974.
    Holt, M., translator HOLTS
    Variant title: *La Fundación*
*La Fundación. See* The Foundation
*Irene, o el tesoro.* 1954. MARLI2
*Lázaro en el laberinto. See* Lazarus in the Labyrinth
*Lazarus in the Labyrinth.* 1986.
    Cazorla, H., translator OCONNP
    Variant title: *Lázaro en el laberinto*
*La tejedora de sueños. See* The Dream Weaver

*El tragaluz. See* The Basement Window
*Two Sides to Dr. Valmy's Story.* 1976. Edwards, G.,
    translator BURN
    Variant title: *La doble historia del doctor Valmy*

BUKOWSKI, OLIVER, 1961–
*Jamaica ('Til Denver).* 1997.
    Spencer, D., translator DODGSP
    Variant title: *'Til Denver*
*'Til Denver. See* Jamaica ('Til Denver)

BULGAKOV, MIKHAIL ALFANASE'VICH, 1891–1940
*Adam and Eve.* 1931.
    Glenny, M., translator LOWE2
*Days of the Turbins.* 1926.
    Daglish, R., translator CLKX
    Lyons, E., translator LYK
    Reeve, F., translator REEV2
    Variant title: *Last of the Turbins*
*Dead Souls* (based on the novel by Nikolai Vasilevich
    Gogol). 1980.
    Cole, T., translator and adapter NEWQ
*Heart of a Dog. See* Chervinsky, Alexander. *Heart of
    a Dog* (based on the novel by) Ivan Vasilievich.
    (1935–1936)
    Senelick, L., translator RVI
    Variant title: *Ivan Vasil'evich*
*Last of the Turbins. See* Days of the Turbins

BULKLEY, A. M. (Annette Mabel), 1868–
*The Crown of Light.* 1934. SEVE

BULLINS, ED, 1935–
*Clara's Ole Man.* 1968. BEAN
*The Corner.* 1972. KINH, KINHB
*Dialect Determinism.* 1965. OWER
*Electronic Nigger.* 1968. HOGI, NEWA3, STS
*The Fabulous Miss Marie.* NEWL
*Gentleman Caller.* 1970. BLACQ, OLIV
*Goin' a Buffalo.* 1966. HARY, HARYB
*How Do You Do.* 1969. JONE
*In the Wine Time.* 1968. PATR, SCNPL, TUQTR
*Jo Anne!* 1981. WES9
*The Man Who Dug Fish.* 1967. MESSE
*A Son, Come Home.* 1968. BAIC, BAIE, BAIG, BAIH,
    CLLC, CLN, LITC, LITI
*The Taking of Miss Janie.* 1975. BES74, BLACTH,
    FAMAD
    — *See also* Bass, Kingsley B., Jr. (pseudonym of Ed
    Bullins)

BULLOCK, MICHAEL, 1918–
*Not to Hong Kong.* 1972(?) ALI

BULLY, ALDWYN
*Good Morning, Miss Millie.* 1981. NOEL

BULWER-LYTTON, EDWARD GEORGE EARLE
    LYTTON, 1803–1873
*The Conspiracy. See* Richelieu
*The Lady of Lyons, or, Love and Pride.* 1838. ASG,
    STA, TAT, TAU
    Variant title: *Love and Pride*
*Love and Pride. See* The Lady of Lyons
*Money.* 1840. BAT16, BOOA3, ROWE
*Richelieu; or, The Conspiracy.* 1839. BAI, BOOA1,
    CROS, DUR, MATTL, MOSN, MOSO
    Variant title: *The Conspiracy*

BUMBALO, VICTOR, 1948–
*Tell.* 1991. HELB
*What Are Tuesdays Like?* 1994. ACTOR, JONT

BUNCE, OLIVER BELL, 1828–1890
*Love in '76.* 1857. MOSS3

BUNCH, JIM
*Lay Down by Me.* 1993. BOHV

BUNYAN, H. (HECTOR) JAY, 1947–
*Prodigals in a Promised Land.* 1981. SEARS1
*Thy Creature Blues.* 1996. BEYO

BURGESS, JOHN, and MAROWITZ, CHARLES
*The Chicago Conspiracy* (based on a script by Jonathan
    Cross). 1972. MARP

BURGR, LUBOMIR, 1964–
*Bottom* (script by). *See* Stoka Theatre, *The Bottom*

BURK, JOHN DALY, 1775?–1808
*Bunker-Hill; or, The Death of General Warren.* 1797.
    MONR
    Variant title: *The Death of General Warren*
*The Death of General Warren. See* Bunker-Hill

BURKE, CHARLES ST. THOMAS, 1822–1854
*Rip Van Winkle.* 1850. BAT19, MOSS3
    — *See also* Anonymous Plays. *Rip Van Winkle* (as
    played by Joseph Jefferson)

BURKE, INEZ M.
*Two Races.* 192–? RIR, RIRA

BURKE, KATHY, 1964–
*Mr Thomas.* 1990. FIFHL3

BURKE, KELLEY JO
*Charming and Rose: True Love.* 1992. PRER
*Safe.* 1995. BREK

BURLATSKY, FYODOR, 1927–
*Black Saturday. See* The Burden of Decision
*The Burden of Decision.* 1986.

BYRNES, BURKE, 1937–
*America's Finest.* 1986. WES21/22

BYRON, GEORGE GORDON, 1788–1824
*Cain.* 1821. BARG, ENGL, KOH2
*Harlequin Friday and the King of the Caribee Islands.*
   *See* Robinson Crusoe
*Heaven and Earth.* 1821? KOH2
*Manfred.* 1817. ABRJ2, ABRK2, ABRL2, ABRM2,
   BERN, ENGL, GREB2, HAPT2, HARC18, KAU,
   SML
*Robinson Crusoe, or Harlequin Friday and the King of
   the Caribee Islands.* 1860. BOOA5
   Variant title: *Harlequin Friday and the King of the
      Caribee Islands*
*Sardanapalus.* (1821) ENGL
   — *See also* Boucicault, Dion, joint author

CABANA, AUGUSTIN MORETO Y. *See* Moreto y
   Cavaña, Augustin

CADARIU, ALINA NELEGA, 1960–
*Nascendo.* 1996.
   Nelega, A., and Robson, C., translators EUP, POQ

CADY, PAM
*The Secret Life of Plants.* 1994. TOR

CAHILL, TOM, 1934–
*The Only Living Father.* 1991. LYN

ČAHOJOVA-BERNATOVA, BOZENA, 1949
*Eclipse.* 1992.
   Švecová, M., translator CONTSL3
      Variant title: *Zatmenie*
*Zatmenie. See* Eclipse

CAIGNIEZ, LOUIS CHARLES, 1762–1842, and
   BAUDOUIN, JEAN MARIE THEODORE
   (d'Aubigny, pseudonym)
*La pie voleuse; ou, La servante de Palaiseau. See*
   Payne, John Howard. *Trial without Jury* (adapted
   from)

CAIN, CAITLIN C.
*Thru These Glasses We've Seen Ourselves Each Other a
   Looking Glass.* 1994. TOR

CAJAL, OANA–MARIA, 1955?–
*Exchange at the Café Mimosa.* 2001. LAR

CALCUTT, DAVID, 1950–
*Gifts of Flame.* 1993. SACR

CALDERON DE LA BARCA, PEDRO, 1600–1681
*El alcalde de Zalamea. See* The Mayor of Zalamea
*Amar después de la muerte. See* Love after Death
*Belshazzar's Feast.* 1632.
   MacCarthy, D., translator BAT4
   Variant title: *La cena de Baltasar*
*La cena de Baltasar. See* Belshazzar's Feast
*The Constant Prince.* 1629?
   MacCarthy, D., translator CLF2, STA
   Variant title: *El principe constante*
*El gran teatro del mundo. See* The Great Theater of the
   World
*Elvira. See* No siempre lo peor es cierto
*The Great Theater of the World.* 1642.
   Singleton, M., translator FLOR, MACU
   Variant title: *El gran teatro del mundo*
*Guárdate del ague manse. See* Keep Your Own Secret
*Keep Your Own Secret.* 1649.
   Fitzgerald, E., translator ROB
   Variant title: *Guárdate del ague manse*
*Life a Dream. See* La vida es sueño
*Life Is a Dream. See* La vida es sueño
*Love after Death.* 1651?
   Campbell, R., translator BENR3
   Variant title: *Amar después de la muerte*
*El mágico prodigioso. See* The Wonder-working
   Magician
*The Mayor of Zalamea.* 1651.
   Starkie, W., translator SSTW
   Variant title: *El alcalde de Zalamea*
*El médico y su honra.* 1635. MACU
*No siempre lo peor es cierto.* 1648? HILL
   Variant titles: *Elvira; The Worst Not Always True*
*El postrer duelo de España. See* Payne, John Howard.
   *The Last Duel in Spain* (adapted from)
*El príncipe constante. See* The Constant Prince
*Sometimes Dreams Come True.* 1670.
   McGaha, M., translator STORJ
   Variant title: *Sueños hay que verdad son*
*Such Stuff as Dreams Are Made Of. See* La vida es
   sueño
*Sueños hay que verdad son. See* Sometimes Dreams
   Come True
*La vida es sueño.* 1635. ALP, MARLI1
   Campbell, R., translator BENR3, BENSB1, LIFE,
      MALI1, MALN1, NORG1, NORGA, NORI1,
      NORIB1, NORJ1, WOTHB, WOTHC
   Fitzgerald, E., translator DRAD1, HARC26, PLAB1
   Honig, E., translator HILPDH2, VENA
   Huberman, E., and E., translators FLOS, HOUE,
      TREB
   MacCarthy, D., translator ALPF, MATT, TAV
   Variant titles: *Life a Dream; Life Is a Dream; Such
      Stuff as Dreams Are Made Of*

*The Wonder-working Magician.* 1637?
  Shelley, P., translator BENR3
  Variant title: *El mágico prodigioso*
*The Worst Not Always True. See* No siempre lo peor es
  cierto

CALDOR, M. T.
  *Curiosity.* 1873. CHIN

CALDWELL, BEN, 1937–
  *All White Caste.* (1971) KINH, KINHB
  *Birth of a Blues.* (1989) KINHP
  *The Devil and Otis Redding. See* The King of Soul
  *The First Militant Minister. See* Prayer Meeting
  *The King of Soul; or, The Devil and Otis Redding.*
    (1969) RAVIT
  *Prayer Meeting; or, The First Militant Minister.* (1969)
    BLACQ, HARYB, JONE

CALDWELL, ERSKINE, 1903–1987. *See* Kirkland, Jack,
  joint author

CALDWELL, EVELYN KELLER, 1919–
  *Voice in the Wilderness.* 1944. PERF

CALIBAN, RICHARD
  *Rodents & Radios.* 1990. MESSE

CALLAGHAN, SEAN
  *"No. Please–".* 1996. STN

CALO, ARTURO, 1969–
  *Ang maikling buhay ng apoy.* 2000. JUAN

CAMERON, ANNE, 1938–
  *The Twin Sinks of Allan Sammy.* 1973. FIFVE

CAMERON, KENNETH M., 1931–
  *The Hundred and First.* 1963? NEWA1
  *Papp.* 1969? SCV

CAMERON, RONALD, 1944–
  *Masque* (an adaptation of James Reaney's play *One-
    man Masque*). 1972. KAL4

CAMERON, SILVER DONALD, 1937–
  *The Last Hook* (radio play). 1986. HEID

CAMPANILE, ACHILLE, 1900–1977
  *The Inventor of the Horse.* 1925.
    Senelick, L., translator TWEI
    Variant title: *L'inventore del cavallo*
  *L'inventore del cavallo. See* The Inventor of the Horse

CAMPBELL, ALISTAIR TE ARIKI, 1925–2009
  *When the Bough Breaks.* 1970. CONTNZ

CAMPBELL, BARTLEY, 1843–1888
  *Fairfax.* 1879. AMP19
  *The Galley Slave.* 1879. AMP19
  *My Partner.* 1879. AMP19, CLA
  *The Virginian.* 1873. AMP19
  *The White Slave.* 1882. AMP19

CAMPBELL, GRAEME, 1931–
  *Shouting at Pictures.* 1988? PLACB

CAMPBELL, MARION GURNEY, 1923–1985, and
    ATHAS, DAPHNE SPENCER
  *Ding Dong Bell. See* Sit on the Earth
  *Sit on the Earth.* 1961. OBSE
    Variant title: *Ding Dong Bell*

CAMPBELL, PADDY, 1944–
  *Hoarse Muse.* 1974. WIM

CAMPBELL, WILLIAM EDWARD MARCH. *See* March,
  William (pseudonym)

CAMPION, THOMAS, 1567–1620
  *The Caversham Entertainment.* 1613. LINDC
  *The Lord Hay's Masque.* 1607. LINDC
  *Lords' Masque.* 1613. ETO

CAMPISTRON, JEAN GALBERT DE, 1656–1723
  *Andronica. See* Andronicus
  *Andronicus.* 1685.
    Lockert, L., translator LOCR
    Variant title: *Andronica*
  *Tiridate.* 1691.
    Lockert, L., translator LOCU

CAMPTON, DAVID, 1924–2006
  *The End of the Picnica.* 1964. PLAAC2
  *Incident.* 1965. PLAAC1
  *Soldier from the Wars Returning.* 1963. PLAJI
  *Then . . .* 1960. THOD

CAMUS, ALBERT, 1913–1960
  *Caligula.* 1945.
    Anonymous translator FOUA
    Gilbert, S., translator BLOC, KNIH, KNIJ, MORW,
      MORXB, RAI, TAUJ
    O'Brien, J., translator and adapter BES59
  *Le malentendu.* 1944. PUCC

CANALE, RAYMOND, 1941–
  *The Jingo Ring.* 1971. BRIN

CANDIDUS, CAROLI, ESQ.
*The Female Consistory of Brockville* (a melodrama in
     three acts). (1856) WAGN1

CANETTI, VEZA, 1897–1963
*The Ogre.* ANTHC
     Dixon, R., translator ANTHC
     Variant title: *Der oger*
*Der oger. See* The Ogre

CANNING, GEORGE, 1770–1827, and FRERE, JOHN
     HOOKHAM, and ELLIS, GEORGE
*The Rovers.* 1798. TRUS

CANTH, MINNA, 1844–1897
*Anna-Liisa.* 1895. Flint, A. and A., translators WILM

CAO YU (pseudonym of Wan Chia-Pao), 1910–1996
*Lei-yü. See* Thunderstorm
*Thunderstorm.* 1933.
     Wang, T., and Barnes, A., translators MESH
     Variant title: *Lei-yü*

ČAPEK, JOSEF, 1887–1927. *See* Čapek, Karel, joint
     author

ČAPEK, KAREL, 1890–1938
*R.U.R.* (Rossum's Universal Robots). 1923.
     Anonymous translator BART, BROZ, STAU
     Selver, P., translator BES22, BROF, BROG, BRR3,
       CALN1, COTH, DICDT, DICIN1, HAV, HAVD,
       HAVE, HORN, HUDT, MAD, NAGE, PROX,
       TREBA, TREI2, TUCG, TUCM, TUCN, TUCO,
       WATI, WATL4, WATO
     Selver, P., and Playfair, N., translators CEW, CONG,
       COTKJ, TREC2, TREE2

—— and ČAPEK, JOSEF
*Adam stvoritel. See* Adam the Creator
*Adam the Creator.* 1927.
     Round, D., translator MOSG, MOSH
     Variant title: *Adam stvoritel*
*And so ad infinitum.* 1921.
     Davis, O., translator and adaptor, GARZH
     Selver, P., translator, CHA, CHAN, CLKW, INTE,
       SSTF
     Variant titles: *The Insect Comedy, The Insect Play,
       The Life of the Insects, The World We Live In, Ze
       zivota honyzu*
*The Insect Comedy. See* And so ad infinitum
*The Insect Play. See* And so ad infinitum
*The Life of the Insects. See* And so ad infinitum
*The World We Live In. See* And so ad infinitum
*Za zivota honyzu. See* And so ad infinitum

CAPPELEN, PEDER W., 1931–
*Hvittenland. See* Whittenland
*Whittenland.* 1981
     Sehmsdorf, H., translator NEWNOR
     Variant title: *Hvittenland*

CAPOTE, TRUMAN, 1924–1984
*The Grass Harp.* 1953. WISF

CARBALLIDO, EMILIO, 1925–2008
*The Day the Lions Got Loose. See* The Day They Let the
     Lions Loose
*The Day They Let the Lions Loose.* 1963.
     Oliver, W., translator OLIW
     Variant titles: *The Day the Lions Got Loose; El día
       que se soltaron los leones*
*El día que se soltaron los leones. See* The Day They Let
     the Lions Loose
*I Also Speak of the Rose. See* I Too Speak of Roses
*I Too Speak of Roses.* 1966.
     Oliver, W., translator WOOG
     Variant titles: *I Also Speak of the Rose; Yo también
       hablo de la rosa*
*Yo también hablo de la rosa.* 1966. DAU
     *See also* I Too Speak of Roses

CARBUNARIU, GEANINA, 1977–
*Unrealities from the Immediate Wild East.* 2000.
     Trandafir, CA., translator POQ

CAREW, JAN RYNVELD, 1920–
*Black Horse, Pale Rider.* 1991. NTIR

CAREW, THOMAS, 1595–1639
*Coelum Britannicum.* 1634. LINDC

CAREY, HENRY, 1687?–1743
*Chrononhotonthologos.* 1734. BELC2, TRUS
*The Contrivances.* 1715. BELC4
*The Dragon of Wantley.* 1737. TRUS

CARLEY, DAVE, 1955–
*Hedges.* 1985. SIXA

CARLIN, AVIVA JANE, 1960–
*Jodie's Body.* 1998. WOMP98

CARLOS, LAURIE, 1949–
*White Chocolate for my Father.* 1990. MAQ

—— and HAGEDORN, JESSICA, and McCAULEY,
     ROBBIE
*Teenytown.* 1988. OUT

CARMINES, AL, 1936–
  *Promenade* (music by). *See* Fornés, María Irene.
    *Promenade*

CARNELIA, CRAIG, 1949–
  *Three Postcards* (music and lyrics by). *See* Lucas, Craig.
    *Three Postcards*

CARNEY, SUE
  *Amazon All-Stars* (music by). *See* Gage, Carolyn.
    *Amazon All-Stars*

CARO MALLEN DE SOTO, ANA, 1565?/1600?–1650?
  *El conde Partinuplés*. 1630s–1640s. SOSGA
  *Valor, agravio y mujer*. 1630s–1640s. SOSGA

CARPENTER, BRIDGET
  *Fall*. 1999. WOMP99

CARR, J. COMYNS, 1849–1916 (b. Joseph William
    Comyns Carr)
  *King Arthur*. 1895. LUP

CARR, MARINA, 1964–
  *By the Bog of Cats*. 1998. NEWPAB2
  *Low in the Dark*. 1989. CRACK
  *Portia Coughlan*. 1996. DAZZ

CARR, MARY. *See* Clarke, Mary Carr

CARRERO, JAIME, 1931–
  *The* fm *Safe*. 1979. KANEL

CARRETTE, LOUIS, 1913–. *See* Marceau, Félicien,
    pseudonym

CARRIÈRE, JEAN–CLAUDE, 1931–
  *The Mahabharata*. *See* Brook, Peter, joint author
  *La tragédie de Carmen*. *See* Brook, Peter, joint author

CARRIL, PEPE, d.1992
  *Shango de Ima*. 1966.
    Sherman, S., translator HAPU

CARROLL, PAUL VINCENT, 1900–1968
  *Shadow and Substance*. 1937. BES37, CALM, CEW,
    DUR, FIG, MOSH
  *The Strings, My Lord, Are False*. 1942. NEWS1
  *The White Steed*. 1939. BES38

CARROLL, ROBERT, pseudonym. *See* Alpert, Hollis

CARROLL, SUSANNA. *See* Centlivre, Susanna

CARSON, JO, 1946–
  *Daytrips*. 1988. NEWAMP2
  *A Preacher with a Horse to Ride*. 1990. DEN

CARTER, STEVE, 1929– (b. Horace E. Carter, Jr.)
  *Eden*. 1976. BLACTH
  *Nevis Mountain Dew*. 1978. BES78

CARTER-HARRISON, PAUL. *See* Harrison, Paul Carter

CARTWRIGHT, JIM, 1958–
  *Road*. 1986. BES88

CARUS, PAUL, 1852–1919
  *K'ung Fu Tze*. 1915. CHIN

CARVAJAL, MIGUEL DE, 1480?–1560?
  *The Joseph Tragedy*. 1535.
    McGaha, M., translator STORJ
    Variant title: *Tragedia Josephina*
  *Tragedia Josephina*. *See* The Joseph Tragedy

CARVILLE, DARAGH, 1969–
  *Language Roulette*. 1996. FAIR

CARY, ELIZABETH, 1585–1639
  *The Tragedie of Mariam*. *See* The Tragedy of Mariam,
    the Faire Queene of Jewry.
  *The Tragedy of Mariam, the Faire Queene of Jewry*.
    1613. ABRM1 (excerpts), PURK, RENDW
    Variant title: *The Tragedie of Mariam*

CARY, FALKLAND L., 1897–1989. *See* King, Philip,
    joint author

CASALE, MICHAEL, 1949–
  *Cold*. 1976. GUTR

CASAS, MYRNA, 1934–
  *El gran circo Eukraniano*. *See* The Great USkrainian
    Circus
  *The Great USkrainian Circus*. 1986.
    Salas, T., and Vargas, M., translators SALA
    Variant title: *El gran circo Eukraniano*

CASDAGLI, PENNY (Maro Green, pseudonym), 1948– ,
    and GRIFFIN, CAROLINE
  *More*. 1986. PLABE6

CASILIS, JEANNE DE. *See* De Casalis, Jeanne

CASELLA, ALBERTO, 1891–1957
  *Death Takes a Holiday*. 1929.
    Ferris W., translator and adapter BES29
    Variant title: *La morte in vacanze*
  *La morte in vacanze*. *See* Death Takes a Holiday

CASEY, WARREN, 1935–1988
  *Grease. See* Jacobs, Jim, joint author

CASINO, JESUS. *See* Sicam, Geronimo D., joint author

CASONA, ALEJANDRO (pseudonym of Rodríguez
    Alvarez, Alejandro), 1903–1965
  *La barca sin pescadur. See* The Boat without a
    Fisherman
  *The Boat without a Fisherman.* 1945
    Damar, R., translator HOLTM
    Variant title*: La barca sin pescador*
  *Prohibido suicidarse en primavera. See* Suicide
    Prohibited in Springtime
  *Suicide Prohibited in Springtime.* 1937.
    Horvath, A., translator BENA
    Variant title: *Prohibido suicidarse en primavera*

CASTRO, CONSUELO DE, 1946–
  *Aviso prévio.* 1987. SZO
  *Walking Papers.* 1987.
    Pinto, C., translator SZO
    Variant title: *Aviso prévio*

CASTRO Y BELLVIS, GUILLEM DE, 1569–1631
  *Exploits of the Cid. See* Las mocedades del Cid.
  *Las mocedades del Cid.* 1621. ALP, MACU
    Anonymous translator BENR4, BENSD
    Variant titles: *Exploits of the Cid; The Youthful
      Adventures of El Cid*
  *The Youthful Adventures of El Cid. See* Las mocedades
    del Cid

ČASULE, KOLE, 1921–2009
  *Darkness.* 1961.
    Čašule, I., translator LUZ, MIG

CAULFIELD, ANNE
  *The Ungrateful Dead.* 1987. FEFNV

CAVAN, ROMILLY, 1914?–1975 (pseudonym of Isabelle
    Wilson)
  *All My Own Work.* 1958. OBSE

CAVANA, AUGUSTIN MORETO Y. *See* Moreto y
    Cavana, Augustín

CAVENDISH, JANE, 1621–1669, and BRACKLEY,
    ELIZABETH
  *The Concealed Fancies.* 1645. RENDW

CAVERHILL, ALAN, 1910–1983. *See* Melville, Alan,
    pseudonym

CAYZER, CHARLES WILLIAM, SIR, 1869–1917
  *David and Bathshua.* 1911? KOH2

CELESTE, MICHELE, 1952–
  *Obeah.* 1985. VERI

CELESTINO, AURELIO
  *Say quieo ya angapoy serom.* PHIL
  *A Tree without Shade.*
    Casambre, A., translator PHIL
    Variant title: *Say quieo ya angapoy serom*

CENTLIVRE, SUSANNA, 1667–1723
  *The Adventures of Venice.* 1700. LOQA
  *The Basset Table.* 1705. LYON
  *A Bold Stroke for a Wife.* 1718. BELK6, ROGEW
  *The Busie Body. See* The Busy Body
  *The Busy Body.* 1709. ANTL, BELK8, LYON, POLK,
    WONR
    Variant titles: *The Busie Body, The Busybody*
  *The Busybody. See* The Busy Body
  *The Perjur'd Husband.* 1700. MISC
  *The Wonder.* 1714. BELK4, FEFO
  *The Wonder! A Woman Keeps a Secret. See* The Wonder

CERTEZNI, MONIKA, 1970–
  *Bottom* (script by). *See* Stoka Theatre, The. *Bottom*

CERVANTES SAAVEDRA, MIGUEL DE, 1547–1616
  *The Cave of Salamanca.* 1615?
    Honig, E., translator TREB
    Jagendorf, M., translator CLF2
    Variant title: *La cueva de Salamanca*
  *La cueva de Salamanca.* MARLI1, NOR
    *See also* The Cave of Salamanca
  *Los dos habladores* (atribuído a). NOR
  *Entremés de refranes* (atribuído a). NOR
  *Entremés del retablo de las maravillas.* MACU
  *La guarda cuidadosa. See* The Vigilant Sentinel
  *The Jealous Old Man.* 1611.
    Starkie, W., translator SSTW
    Variant title: *El viejo celoso*
  *La Numance. See* La Numancia
  *La Numancia.* 1585. ALP
    Campbell, R., translator BENR3, LIFE
    Variant titles: *La Numance, The Siege of Numantia*
  *Pedro de Urdemalas. See* Pedro, the Artful Dodger
  *Pedro, the Artful Dodger.* 1615.
    Starkie, W., translator SSTW
    Variant title: *Pedro de Urdemalas*
  *Siege of Numantia. See* La Numancia
  *El viejo celoso. See* The Jealous Old Man
  *The Vigilant Sentinel.* 158–?
    Flores, A., and Lass, J., translators FLOS
    Variant title: *La guarda cuidadosa*

CESAIRE, AIME, 1913–2008
*Une saison au Congo. See* A Season in the Congo
*A Season in the Congo.* 1968. CARR
    Manheim, R., translator THB
    Variant title: *Une saison au Congo*
*A Tempest.* 1969.
    Miller, R., translator WOTHC
    Variant title: *Une tempête*
*Une tempête. See* A Tempest

CESAIRE, INA, 1941–
*Fire's Daughters.* 1992.
    Miller, J., translator NEWFPL
    Variant title: *Rosanie Soleil*
*Island Memories: Mama N. and Mama F.* 1985.
    Makward, C., and Miller, J., translators PLAAG
    Variant title: *Mémoires d'isles: Maman N. et
        Maman F.*
*Mémoires d'isles: Maman N. et Maman F. See* Island
    Memories: Mama N. and Mama F.
*Rosanie Soleil. See* Fire's Daughters

CESAIRE, MICHELE, 1951–
*La nef. See* The Ship
*The Ship.* 1991. Miller, R., translator NEWFPL
    Variant title: *La nef*

CHAFE, RICK
*Zac and Speth.* 1992. RUN

CHAFEE, CLAIRE, 1959–
*Why We Have a Body.* 1993. ACTOR, MIH, WOMP93

CHAIS, PAMELA, 1930–
*Sunny Side Up.* 1982. *See* Anonymous Plays. *Twenty-
    four Hours: A.M.*

CHAMBERS, CHARLES HADDON, 1860–1921
*The Tyranny of Tears.* 1899. BOOA3

CHAMBERS, JANE, 1937–1983
*Last Summer at Bluefish Cove.* 1980. FACO
*A Late Snow.* 1974. HOF, WOLC, WOLCS
*The Quintessential Image.* 1985. CURB

—— and DENNIS, VITA
*Eye of the Gull* (revised and updated by Vita Dennis).
    1971, 1991. HELB

CHAMBERS, WHITTAKER, 1901–1961
*Can You Make Out Their Voices, New Masses, March
    1931. See* Flanagan, Hallie, and Clifford, Margaret
    Ellen, *Can You Hear Their Voices* (based on the
    story by)

CHAMPAGNE, LENORA, 1951–
*Coaticook.* 2000. LAR
*Getting over Tom.* 1982. OUT

CHAMPAGNE, SUSAN
*Bondage.* 1990. MEDN
*Honeymoon.* 1985. WES21/22

CHAN, ANTHONY, 1953–
*American House.* 1991.
    Kwok, H., translator CHEU

CHAN, JOANNA
*Before the Dawn-wind Rises.* 1985.
    Lai, J., translator CHEU

CHAN, MARTY
*"Mom, Dad, I'm Living with a White Girl."* 1995.
    BEYO (excerpt), NOTH, RAVELII

CHANCEL, LA GRANGE. *See* La Grange-Chancel

CHANDEZON, LEOPOLD (Leopold, pseudonym) and
    CUVELIER DE TYRE, JEAN GUILLAUME
    ANTOINE
*Mazeppa, ou, Le cheval Tartare. See* Payne, John
    Howard, *Mazeppa, or, The Wild Horse of Tartary*
    (adapted from)

CHANDRAKHANA, CHUANGCHAN. *See* Phranboon
    (pseudonym of)

CHANG, PAO–HUA. *See* Chao, Chung, joint author

CHAO, CHUNG, CHANG, PAO-HUA, and CHUNG,
    YI-PING
*Yesterday.* (1961)
    Shapiro, S., translator MESE

CHAPIN, HAROLD, 1886–1915
*Augustus in Seach of a Father.* 1910. WEB
*The New Morality.* 1920. MART

CHAPMAN, GEORGE, 1559?–1634
*Bussy D'Ambois.* 1604. BAS, BROC, DPR2, HAPRA1,
    HAPRB1, MAKJ, NEI, NES, ORNT, RYL, SPE
*The Memorable Masque.* 1613. LINDC
*The Revenge of Bussy D'Ambois.* ca. 1609–1610.
    MAUS, WALL
*The Widow's Tears.* 1612. DPR2

—— and JONSON, BEN, and MARSTON, JOHN
*Eastward Ho!* 1605. BROC, GAYLE2, OLI1, RUB,
    SCH, SCI, SCJ, SPE, WALL
*Eastward Hoe. See* Eastward Ho!

CHAPMAN, JOHN, 1927–2001
*Simple Spymen.* 1958. PLAJ2

CHAPMAN, ROBERT HARRIS, 1919–2000. *See* Coxe,
   Louis, joint author

CHARLES, MARTIE
   *Black Cycle.* 1971. KINH, KINHB
   *Job Security.* 1970. HARY

CHARNIN, MARTIN, 1934–
   *Annie* (lyrics by). *See* Meehan, Thomas. *Annie, A
      Musical in Two Acts*

CHASE, MARY COYLE, 1912–1981
   *Bernardine.* 1952. BES52, THEA53
   *Harvey.* 1944. BES44, COLT, CORB, CORBA, GARU,
      GATB3, MIJY, MOST
   *Mr. Thing. See* Mrs. McThing
   *Mrs. McThing.* 1952. BES51
      Variant title: *Mr. Thing*

CHAURETTE, NORMAND, 1954–
   *Provincetown Playhouse, juillet 1919, j'avais 19 ans.*
      *See* Provincetown Playhouse, July 1919
   *Provincetown Playhouse, July 1919.* 1981.
      Boulet, W., translator WALAQ
      Variant title: *Provincetown Playhouse, juillet 1919,
         j'avais 19 ans*

CHAUSEE, PIERRE CLAUDE NIVELLE DE LA. *See* La
   Chauseé, Pierre Claude Nivelle de

CHAVEZ, DENISE, 1948–
   *Novena Narrativas.* 1987. WOMA
   *Plaza.* 1980. JOND
      Variant title: *Santa Fe Charm*
   *Santa Fe Charm. See* Plaza

CHAWAF, CHANTAL, 1943–
   *Chair Chaude. See* Warmth: A Bloodsong
   *Warmth: A Bloodsong.* 1977. PLAAG
      Makward, C., and Miller, J., translators PLAAG
      Variant title: *Chair Chaude*

CHAYEFSKY, PADDY, 1923–1981 (given name
      SIDNEY)
   *The Dybbuk from Woodhaven. See* The Tenth Man
   *Gideon.* 1961. BES61, GARSA
   *The Latent Homosexual.* 1966. SANK
   *Marty.* 1953. BLAH, BLOC, DAVM, DODGE, HEIS,
      MANK, PLAU, SHER, STS
   *The Passion of Josef D.* 1964. BES63
   *The Tenth Man.* 1959. BES59, CEQ, CES, SCL
      Variant title: *The Dybbuk from Woodhaven*

CHECA, PEDRO F., 1900–1974
   *Ang damgohanon kon manginmatu—od.* PHIL
   *When Dreams Come True.* 192?
      Damaso, C., translator PHIL
      Variant title: *Ang damgohanon kon manginmatu—od*

CHEDID, ANDREE, 1920–
   *La déesse lare ou siècles des femmes. See* The Goddess
      Lar or Centuries of Women
   *The Goddess Lar or Centuries of Women.* 1977.
      Makward, C., and Miller, J., translators PLAAG
      Variant title: *La déesse lare ou siècles des femmes*

CHEECHOO, SHIRLEY, 1952–
   *Path with No Moccasins.* 1991. RAVEL

CHEESEMAN, PETER, 1932–
   *Fight for Shelton Bar.* 1974. FAV

CHEKHOV, ANTON, 1860–1904
   *The Anniversary. See* The Jubilee
   *The Bear. See* The Boor
   *The Boor.* 1888.
      Anonymous translator BART, KNIE, KNIF, KNIG
      Banknage, H., translator KNIC, KNID, PATM
      Bentley, E., translator ABCC, BAIK, BAIL, BARIF,
         KIRLA, KIRLB, KIRLC, KIRLD, PERS, PERT,
         PERU, PERV
      Clark, B., and Banknage, H., translators HUD
      Fen, E., translator ROY
      Hingley, R., translator BAIM, BEATA, BOOK
   *The Brute. See* The Boor
   *The Cherry Orchard.* 1904.
      Anonymous translator BARNA, BARR, DIS, DUH,
         EDAD, FOUK, MALN2, SILM, WORP, ZIM
      Ashley, L., translator ASF, MORWA, MORXD
      Bristow, E., translator NORI2, WOTHB
      Calderon, G., translator DICD, HAV, HAVD, MOSG,
         MOSH, SSST, THOM, THON, TUCG, TUCM,
         TUCN, TUCO
      Corrigan, R., translator CLL, CLLC, COTKI,
         COTKICO, COTO, COTQ, DIEA, DIEB
      Cowan, J., translator CARP, CARPA, DEAP, DEAR,
         DEAS, DOLAN, HIG, MOS, SCNN, SCNO,
         SCNP, WHI
      Czerwinski, E., translator (Act I only) RZH
      Daniels, C., and Noyes, G., translators NOY
      Dunnigan, A., translator HAEB, JACOBA, JACOBD,
         JACOBE, MEYD, WOTHA
      Fen, E., translator BARN
      Frayn, M., translator PERW, PERX, PERY, PERZ
      Garnett, C., translator ALLI, ALLJ, ALLK, ALLM,
         ALLN, ALLO, ALT, ALTE, ANTL, BAIH,
         BEATA, CUBE, CUBG, DICIN1, GARZ, GOLD,
         HOUG, HOWM, JACOB, KERN, KERO, KERP,
         KON, LEVY, LID, MEYB, PIC, ROF, SMA, TRE,

CHEN-CHIN HSIUNG. *See* Hsiung, Cheng-chin

CHENG, KIPP ERANTE
*The China Crisis.* 1998. ELLM

CHENG KUANG-TSU. *See* Cheng, The-hui

CHENG, THE-HUI (CHENG, KUANG-TSU,
     pseudonym), ca.1260–ca.1320
*The Soul of Ch'ien–nu Leaves Her Body.*
     Liu, J., translator LIU

CHEONG-LEEN, REGGIE
*The Nanjing Race.* 1994. BES94

CHERVINSKY, ALEXANDER
*Heart of a Dog* (based on the novel by Mikhail
     Bulgakov). 1987.
     Glenny, M., translator SSTX

CHESLEY, ROBERT, 1943–1990
*Jerker, or The Helping Hand.* 1986. SHEW

CHETHAM-STRODE, WARREN, 1897–1974
*Background.* 1950. PLAN4
*Sometimes Even Now.* 1933. FAMD

CHI, CHUN-HSIANG
*The Orphan of Chao.* 13th century
     Liu, J., translator LIU

CHIA, AH. *See* A, Jia

CHIARELLI, LUIGI, 1884–1947
*La maschera ed il volto. See* The Mask and the Face
*The Mask and the Face.* 1916.
     Vic Beamish, N., translator INTE
     Variant title: *La maschera ed il volto*

CHI-HUANG, LI. *See* Li, Chi-huang

CHI-YUAN, MA. *See* Ma, Chih-yuan

CHIC STREET MAN
*Spunk* (music by). *See* Wolfe, George CA. *Spunk*

CHIKAMATSU (SUGIMORI NUBUMORI). *See*
     Chikamatsu, Monzaemon

CHIKAMATSU, MONZAEMON (pseudonym of
     Sugimori Nubumori), 1653–1725
*The Battles of Coxinga.* 1715.
     Keene, D., translator BRAZ (excerpt)
     Variant title: *Kokusen'ya kassen*

*The Courier for Hades. See* The Courier for Hell
*The Courier for Hell.* 1711.
     Keene, D., translator ANDF, ANDI
     Variant titles: *The Courier for Hades; Meido no Hiyaku*
*Four Ladies at a Game of Poem–cards.* 1705.
     Myamora, A., and Nichols, R., translators CLF1
*Kikaigashima no ba. See* Shunkan on Devil Island
*Kokusen'ya kassen. See* The Battles of Coxinga
*Meido no Hiyaku. See* The Courier for Hell
*The Love Suicides at Amijima.* 1721.
     Keene, D., translator BRAZ
     Variant title: *Shinjū ten no Amijima*
*The Love Suicides at Sonezaki.* 1703.
     Keene, D., translator ABCE, KIAN, WOTHB
*Shinjū ten no Amijima. See* The Love Suicides at
     Amijima
*Shunkan on Devil Island.* 1720. (Kabuki adaptation of
     the author's *Heike nyogo no shima*)
     Leiter, S., translator BRAZ (excerpt)
     Variant title: *Kikaigashima no ba*
*Yūgiri and the Straits of Naruto. See* Anonymous Plays.
     *Love Letter from a Licensed Quarter* (based on the
     first act of)

CHILDRESS, ALICE, 1920–1994
*Florence.* 1950. BRW
*Mojo.* 1970. RICK
*Trouble in Mind.* 1955. PATR, PLAAF, TUQTR
*Wedding Band: A Love/Hate Story in Black and White.*
     1972. NEWWT, RIS, SWANS, WILK
*Wine in the Wilderness.* 1969. ABCG, BRW, HARY,
     HARYB, HOEP, SUB, VENA

CHILTON, NOLA
*Naïm* (adapted from the novel, *The Lover*, by A. B.
     Yehoshua). (1978?)
     Auerbach, J., translator MOADE

CHIN, FRANK, 1940–
*The Chickencoop Chinaman.* 1972. VENA, WOLC

CHINA PEKING OPERA TROUPE
*The Red Lantern. See* Anonymous Plays. *The Red
     Lantern* (revised collectively by)
     — *See also* Wong, Ou–hung, and Ah, Chia

CHIRICO, ANDREA DE, 1891–1952. *See* Savinio,
     Alberto, pseudonym

CHISHOLM, MARY–COLIN
*Safe Haven.* 1994. ZIMM (excerpt)

CHLUMBERG, HANS, 1897–1930
*The Miracle at Verdun.* 1931.
     Crankshaw, E., translator FAMC

*Love's Last Shift, or, The Fool in Fashion.* 1696.
 BELK17, JEFF3, MAND, MANF, TUQ, WONR
*Non-juror. See* Bickerstaffe, *I. Lionel and Clarissa*
 (adapted by)
*The Provoked Husband, or, A Journey to London* (from
 an unfinished play by John Vanbrugh). 1727?
 BAT15, TICK
*The Refusal.* 1721. BELK11
*She Wou'd and She Wou'd Not.* 1702. BELK6
*Ximena.* 1718. BELK14

CIBBER, THEOPHILUS, 1703–1758. *See* Jevons,
 Thomas, joint author

CICVAK, MARTIN, 1975–
*Dom, kde sa to robí dobre. See* Frankie Is Ok, Peggy Is
 Fine and the House Is Cool!
*Frankie Is Ok, Peggy Is Fine and the House Is Cool!*
 1995. Cicvák, M., and Paton, CA., translators
 CONTSL1
 Variant title: *Dom, kde sa to robí dobre*

CINQUE, CHRIS
*Growing Up Queer in America.* 1990. JENN

CIXOUS, HELENE, 1937–
*The Name of Oedipus: Song of the Forbidden Body.*
 1978.
 Makward, C., and Miller, J., translators PLAAG
 Variant title: *Le nom d'Oedipe*
*Le nom d'Oedipe. See* The Name of Oedipus: Song of
 the Forbidden Body

CIZMAR, PAULA, 1949–
*Candy & Shelley Go to the Desert.* WOMB, WOMS2

CLARK, BRIAN, 1932–
*Whose Life Is It Anyway?* 1978. BES78, BEST, PERR1

CLARK, JOHN PEPPER. *See* Clark–Bekederemo, John
 Pepper.

CLARK, MRS. MABEL MARGARET (COWIE). *See*
 Storm, Lesley, pseudonym

CLARK, SALLY, 1953–
*Jehanne of the Witches.* 1989. BIG
*Lost Souls and Missing Persons.* 1984. RUDAK
*Moo.* 1988. WASCPA2, WASCPB2, ZIMM (excerpt)

CLARK-BEKEDEREMO, JOHN PEPPER, 1935–
*Song of a Goat.* (1964). LITT

CLARKE, AUSTIN, 1896–1974
*As the Crow Flies.* 1942. OWEC

CLARKE, AUSTIN CHESTERFIELD, 1934–
*When He Was Free and Young He Used to Wear Silks.*
 2000. SEARS1

CLARKE, BREENA, 1951– . *See* Dickerson, Glenda, joint
 author

CLARKE, GEORGE ELLIOTT, 1960–
*Québécité: A Jazz Libretto in Three Cantos.* 2003.
 SEARS2
*Whylah Falls.* 1997. SEARS1

CLARKE, MARGARET, 1941–
*Gertrude and Ophelia.* 1993. ZIMM (excerpt)

CLARKE, MARY CARR, 1790?–1833?
*The Fair Americans: A Play of the War of 1812.* 1815.
 KRIT

CLARKE, WILLIAM KENDALL, 1911–1981
*The Ghost Patrol* (based on a story by Sinclair Lewis).
 1951. INGB

CLARVOE, ANTHONY, 1958–
*Pick Up Ax.* 1990. BES89

CLASS 5 (1990), ECOLE INTERNATIONALE DE
 GENEVE, SWITZERLAND
*Buffalo Dance.* 1993. SACR

CLAUDEL, PAUL, 1868–1955
*L'annonce faite à Marie.* 1912. HART, RHO
 Sill, L., translator DICIN1, HAV, TREBA, TREBJ,
 TREI3, TUCG
 Variant title: *The Tidings Brought to Mary*
*L'histoire de Tobie et de Sara. See* Tobias and Sara
*The Satin Slipper, or, The Worst Is Not the Worst.* 1919?
 O'Connor, J., translator HIBB
 Variant title: *Le soulier de satin, ou, Le père n'est pas
 Toujours sûr*
*The Tidings Brought to Mary. See* L'annonce faite à
 Marie
*Tobias and Sara.* 1942?
 Fiske, A., translator HAYE
 Variant title: *L'histoire de Tobie et de Sara*

CLAUSEN, SVEN, 1893–1961
*The Bird of Contention.* 1933?
 Thornton, P., and A., translators CONT
 Variant title: *Kivflugen*
*Kivflugen. See* The Bird of Contention

CLAVIJO, UVA A., 1944–
*With All and for the Good of All.* 1986. CUB
 Miller, D., translator

CLEAGE, PEARL, 1948–
*Chain.* 1992. MIHPW
*Flyin' West.* 1992. PERC, TUQTR
*Hospice.* 1983. KINHP, WOMA
*Late Bus to Mecca.* 1992. MIHPW

CLELAND, JOHN, 1709–1789
*Fanny Hill, or Memoirs of a Woman of Pleasure.*
See De Angelis, April. John Cleland's *The Life and
Times of Fanny Hill* (based on the novel by)

CLEMENS, SAMUEL, 1835–1910
*Adventures of Huckleberry Finn.* See Myler, Randal.
*Adventures of Huckleberry Finn* (adapted from the
novel by)
*The King and the Duke.* See Fergusson, Francis. *The
King and the Duke* (based on the novel *Huckleberry
Finn* by)
— *See also* Harte, Bret, joint author

CLEMENTS, COLIN CAMPBELL, 1894–1948
*Columbine.* 1922? SHAY
*The Siege.* 1922? SHAY
— *See* Ryerson, Florence, joint author

CLEMENTS, MARIE HUMBER, 1962–
*Age of Iron.* 1993. ZIMM (excerpt)
*Now Look What You Made Me Do.* 1995. PRER

CLIFFORD, JOHN, 1950–
*Great Expectations* (based on the novel by Charles
Dickens). 1988. FRY
*Ines de Castro.* 1990. FIFHL2
*Losing Venice.* 1985. CALE

CLIFFORD, MARGARET ELLEN, 1908–1971. *See*
Flanagan, Hallie, joint author

CLINCH, CHARLES POWELL, 1797–1880
*The Spy, a Tale of the Neutral Ground.* 1822. AMP14

CLONTZ, DENNIS, 1951–2004
*Generations.* 1989. BES88

CLOUD, DARRAH, 1955–
*O Pioneers!* 1989. MIGPW
*The Stick Wife.* 1987. BES86

CLOUGH, DAVID, 1952–
*In Kanada.* 1982. PLACK

CLUM, JOHN M., 1941–
*Dancing in the Mirror.* 1999. CLUM
*Randy's House.* 1995. CLUMS

COBB, JAMES, 1756–1818
*Ramah Droog.* INCA6
*The Wife of Two Husbands.* INCA6

COBURN, D. L., 1938–
*The Gin Game.* 1976. BES77

COCKE, DUDLEY. *See* Baker, Don, joint author

COCTEAU, JEAN, 1891–1963
*Antigone.* See Sophocles. *Antogone* (adapted by)
*The Eiffel Tower Wedding Party.* See Les maries de la
Tour Eiffel
*The Infernal Machine.* See La machine infernale
*Intimate Relations.* 1938
Frank, C., translator BENS3
Variant titles: *Les parents terrible; The Storm Within*
*La machine infernale.* 1934. PUCC
Anonymous translator BOYN, SANO
Wildman, C., translator BENS1, BOY, INTE, LOCL,
LOCLA, LOCLB, TUCN, TUCO
*Les maries de la Tour Eiffel.* 1921.
Benedikt, M., translator BEN
Fitts, D., translator MIJT, NEWDI37
Variant titles: *The Eiffel Tower Wedding Party; The
Wedding on the Eiffel Tower*
*Les parents terrible.* See Intimate Relations
*Orphée.* 1926.
Wildman, C., translator BLOC, HILPDH6
*The Storm Within.* See Intimate Relations
*The Wedding on the Eiffel Tower.* See Les maries de la
Tour Eiffel

CODCO, 1973–1992
*Das capital: or What Do You Want to See the Harbor
for Anyway?* 1975. PETER
*Cod on a Stick.* 1973. PETER
*Sickness, Death, and beyond the Grave.* 1974. PETER
*The Tale Ends.* 1976. PETER
*Would You like to Smell My . . . Pocket Crumbs?* 1975.
PETER

COFFEE, LENORE (Mrs. W. J. Cowen), 1896–1984, and
COWEN, WILLIAM JOYCE
*Family Portrait.* 1939. BES38, PLAN1

COFFEY, CHARLES, 1700?–1745. *See* Jevon, Thomas,
joint author

COHAN, GEORGE MICHAEL, 1878–1942
*Pigeons and People.* 1933. BES32, WAGC3
*Seven Keys to Baldpate* (based on the novel by Earl Derr
Biggers). 1913. BES09, CART, CONG, RICN

COHEN, BENNETT
*Tequila.* 1980. WES8

COHEN, DAVID
*Slice & Dice.* 1985. VICK1

COHEN, JOEL. *See* Cohen, Neil, joint author

COHEN, MARVIN
*Necessary Ends.* 1982. PLACI

COHEN, NEIL, and COHEN, JOEL
*Friends Too Numerous to Mention.* 1982. NEWJV

COHEN, SARAH BLACHER, 1936–2008
*The Ladies Locker Room.* 1989. COJ

COHN, EMIL, 1881–1948. *See* Bernhard, Emil, pseudonym

COKAIN, SIR ASTON, 1608–1684
*Trappolin suppos'd a prince. See* Tate, Nahum. *A Duke or No Duke* (adapted from)

COKAYNE, SIR ASTON. *See* Cokain, Sir Aston

COLE, TOM, 1933–2009 (b. Charles Thomas Cole)
*Dead Souls. See* Bulgakov, Mikhail Alfanasevich
*Medal of Honor Rag.* 1975. COMV

COLEMAN, CY, 1929–
*City of Angels* (music by). *See* Gelbart, Larry. *City of Angels*

COLEMAN, ELIZABETH, 1962–
*It's My Party.* 1993. JONI

COLEMAN, RALF M., 1898–1976
*The Girl from Back Home.* 1929. HARYL

COLEMAN, WIM
*Phaeton and the Sun Chariot.* 1999. SCVDT1

COLERIDGE, SAMUEL TAYLOR, 1820–1894
*Remorse.* 1813. ENGL, KAU

COLETTE, SIDONIE GABRIELLE, 1873–1954
*Gigi. See* Loos, Anita. *Gigi* (from the novel by). *See also* Akalaitis, J. *Dressed like an Egg* (based on the writings of)

COLLEY, PETER, 1949–
*The Donnellys.* 1974. WIM

COLLIE, BRENDA FAYE, 1951–
*Silent Octaves.* 1980. FLET

COLLINGS, PIERRE, 1900–1937. *See* Gibney, Sheridan, joint author

COLLINS, ARTHUR. *See* Wood, J. Hickory, joint author

COLLINS, BARRY, 1941–
*The Ice Chimney.* 1980. SALS

COLLINS, KATHLEEN, 1942–1988
*The Brothers.* 1982. WILK, WOMB, WOMS2
*In the Midnight Hour.* WOMA, WOMS

COLLINS, MARGARET, 1909–2008
*Love Is a Daisy.* COLI
*3 Filosofers in a Fire–tower.* COLI

COLLINSON, LAURENCE, 1925–1986
*Thinking Straight.* 1975. HOM

COLMAN, GEORGE, 1732–1794
*Bonduca* (altered from Beaumont and Fletcher). 1778. BELG3
*Comus* (altered from the masque by John Milton) (1772) BELC4
*The Deuce Is in Him.* 1762. BELC1
*The English Merchant.* 1767. INCA9
*The Jealous Wife.* 1761. BELG3, NET, NIC
*The Musical Lady.* 1762. BELC2
*Polly Honeycombe.* 1760. BELC3, BEVI

—— and GARRICK, DAVID
*The Clandestine Marriage.* 1766. BAT15, BELG7, HAN, MAND, MANF, MOR, MOSE2, TWE

COLMAN, GEORGE, the younger, 1762–1836
*The Iron Chest.* 1796. BOO
*John Bull.* BOOA3, BOOM
*Who Wants a Guinea?* 1805. INCA3

COLON, OSCAR, 1937–
*Siempre en mi corazón.* 1986. ANTU

COLORADO, ELVIRA, and COLORADO, HORTENSIA
*1992: Blood Speaks.* 1992. PERC

COLORADO, HORTENSIA. *See* Colorado, Elvira, joint author

COLTON, JOHN, 1889–1946, and RANDOLPH, CLEMENCE
*Rain* (based on the story, "Miss Thompson," by W. Somerset Maugham). 1922. BES22, GARU, GATB1, TUCD

COLUM, PADRAIC, 1881–1972
*The Land.* 1905. CAP, OWEC
*Thomas Muskerry.* 1910. MOSN

COMDEN, BETTY, 1919–2006, and GREEN, ADOLPH
*Applause* (music by Charles Strouse; lyrics by Lee
Adams). 1970. BES69, RICM
*Wonderful Town* (lyrics by). *See* Fields, Joseph and
Chodorov, Jerome. *Wonderful Town*.

COMMIRE, ANNE, 1940?–
*Starting Monday.* 1988. NEWAMP1

COMMON GROUND, 1981–1991?
*The Fence.* 1984. LOWE

COMPANY THEATRE ENSEMBLE. *See* Opper, Don
Keith (script by)

COMPTON, JENNIFER, 1949–
*Crossfire.* 1975. BRIM3
Variant title: *No Man's Land*
*No Man's Land. See* Crossfire

CONDE, MARYSE, 1937–
*Pension les Alizés. See* The Tropical Breeze Hotel
*The Tropical Breeze Hotel.* 1988.
Lewis, B., translator PLABI2
Variant title: *Pension les Alizés*

CONDON, FRANK, 1943– . *See* Sossi, Ron, joint author

CONE, TOM, 1947–
*Cubistique.* 1974. BRIQ
*Herringbone* (music by Skip Kennon, lyrics by Ellen
Fitzhugh). 1982. PLACF, WASCT
*Stargazing.* 1978. NEWCAD1

CONGDON, CONSTANCE, 1944–
*Dog Opera.* 1995. ACTOR
*Moby Ethan at the Sculptor's Museum.* 2000. *See*
Ackermann, J. *Back Story: A Dramatic
Anthology* HUMANA2000
*No Mercy.* 1986. MESSE, WEJ
*Tales of the Lost Formicans.* 1989. DIXP

CONGREVE, WILLIAM, 1670–1729
*The Double Dealer.* 1693. BELK13
*Love for Love.* 1695. ABRJ1, AUB, BELK8, BENY,
CARP, CARPA, FIS, JEFF3, KRM, MIL, SALR,
STM, THMF, TWE, WONR
*The Mourning Bride.* 1697. BELK3
*The Old Batchelor.* 1693. BELK2
*The Way of the World.* 1700. ABRB1, ABRF1, ABRH1,
ABRK1, ABRL1, ABRM1, ALLK, ARB1, ASH,
BARG, BELK11, BENY, BLON, BLOND, BROJ,
BROK, COLD, COLEL1, COLR, COTKIR,
DEAP, DEAR, FAL, FOUB, FRYEA, GAYLE4,
GOS, GOSA, GREB1, GREC1, HAVHA, HEAB,

HEAC, HILPDH3, JACOBA, JACOBD, JEFF4,
KER, KRM, KRON, LIE, MAND, MANF,
MANH, MATTL, MEN, MOR, MORR, MOSE1,
NET, RES, RESL, REST, ROF, RUB, SHAI1,
SMO, SPD, SPDB, SPEF1, STM, TAT, TAU,
TRE, TREA2, TREB, TREC1, TREE1, TREI1,
TUP, TUQ, TWE, WALJ, WILSR, WONR,
WOOE, WRIE

CONKLE, ELLSWORTH PROUTY, 1899–1994
*Minnie Field.* 1928. GASB
*Prologue to Glory.* 1938. BES37, FEE, SWI

CONN, STEWART, 1936–
*The King.* 1967. NEWE14
*Play Donkey.* 1977. DEC

CONNELLY, MARCUS COOK, 1890–1980
*The Green Pastures* (based on the novel, *Ol' Man
Adam and His Chillun*, by Roark Bradford). 1930.
BES29, CET, CHA, CHAN, CHAP, CONN,
CORD, CORE, CORF, COTE, DUR, FUL, GAS,
GATB1, GRD, KNIC, KNID, KNIE, LOOA,
LOOB, LOOC, LOOD, LOOE, MADG, MOSK,
MOSL, PROI, SIM, SIXD, TRE, TREA1, TREBA,
TREC2, TREE3, TREI3, WATE
*The Wisdom Tooth.* 1926. BES25
— *See also* Elser, Frank Ball, Kaufman, George S.,
joint authors

CONNING, LUEEN. *See* Ndlovu, Malika

CONRAD, JOSEPH (b. Józef Teodor Konrad
Korzeniowski), 1857–1924
*One Day More.* 1905. BENT3

CONRAD, ROBERT TAYLOR, 1810–1858
*Jack Cade, the Commander of the Commons.* MOSS2

CONSTANCE, ZENO OBI, 1941–
*The Ritual.* 1985. NOEL

CONSTANT, MARIUS, 1925–2004
*La tragédie de Carmen. See* Brook, Peter, joint author

CONWAY, HIRAM J., 1800–1860
*The Battle of Stillwater, or, The Maniaca.* 1840. AMP14

COOK, GEORGE CRAM, 1873–1924. *See* Glaspell,
Susan, joint author

COOK, MICHAEL, 1933–1994
*Colour the Flesh the Colour of Dust.* 1972. KAL1
*End of the Road.* 1980. LYN

*The Head, Guts, and Sound Bone Dance.* 1973. CTR, PERKY
*Jacob's Wake.* 1975. WASCP, WASCPA1
*On the Rim of the Curve* (excerpt). 1976. RALPH

COOK, WILL MARION, 1869–1944
*In Dahomey* (music by). 1902. *See* Shipp, Jesse, A. *In Dahomey*

COOKE, BRITTON, d. 1923
*The Translation of John Snaith.* 1923. MAS1

COOKE, TRISH, 1962–
*Back Street Mammy.* 1989. FIFHL2
*Running Dream.* 1993. GEOR

COOKE, VANESSA, and HONEYMAN, JANICE, and KEOGH, DANNY
*This Is for Keeps.* 1983. GRAY
— *See also* Keogh, Danny, joint author

COOPER, DONA, 1950–
*Rules of the House.* 1982. *See* Anonymous Plays. *Twenty-four Hours: P.M.*

COOPER, GILES, 1918–1966
*Everything in the Garden.* 1962. NEWE7
*Happy Family.* 1966. NEWE11
*The Object.* 1964. NEWE12
*Out of the Crocodile.* 1963. PLAN27
*Unman, Wittering, and Zigo.* 1958. ENG

COOPER, JAMES FENIMORE, 1789–1851
*The Wept of the Wish–ton–wish* (based on the novel by). *See* Anonymous Plays. *The Wept of the Wish–ton–wish*

COOPER, J. CALIFORNIA (b. Joan Cooper)
*Loners.* 1979? CEN

COOPER, MARY
*Heartgame* (devised by Leeds Bengali Women's Drama Group). 1988.
Abdullah, M., translator PLABE8
Variant title: *Ridhoy neye keyla*
*Ridhoy neye keyla.* *See* Heartgame

COOPER, SUSAN, 1935– , and CRONYN, HUME
*Foxfire, a Play with Songs in Two Acts* (music and collaboration for lyrics by Jonathan Holtzman). 1980. BES82

COPEAU, JACQUES, 1879–1949
*The Little Poor Man.* 1925.
Thurman, B., translator HAYE
Variant title: *Le petit pauvre*
*Le petit pauvre.* *See* The Little Poor Man

COPI (pseudonym of RAUL DAMONTE), 1939–1987
*Grand Finale.*
Feingold, M., translator GAYIA
Variant title: *Une visite inopportune*
*La tour de la défense.* *See* A Tower near Paris
*A Tower near Paris.* 1987.
O'Donnell, M., translator GAYIA
Variant title: *La tour de la défense*
*Une visite inopportune.* *See* Grand Finale

COPPEE, FRANCOIS EDOUARD JOACHIM, 1842–1908
*Le luthier de Crémone.* *See* The Violin Maker of Cremona
*The Violin Maker of Cremona.* 1877.
Jerome, J., translator BEAC
Lord, I., translator COOK1
Variant title: *Le luthier de Crémone*

COPPEL, ALEC, 1909?–1972
*I Killed the Count.* 1937. SIXP

CORBITT, WAYNE
*Crying Holy.* 1993. ELAM

CORDAY, BARBARA, 1944– . *See* Avedon, Barbara, joint author

CORLETT, WILLIAM, 1938–
*Tinker's Curse.* 1968. PLAN34

CORMACK, BARTLETT, 1898–1942
*The Racket.* BES27, NELSDI

CORMANN, ENZO, 1953–
*Exiles.* 1984.
Strand, J., translator WEHL
Variant title: *Exils*
*Exils.* *See* Exiles

CORMON, EUGENE, 1811–1903. *See* D'Ennery, Adolphe, joint author

CORNEAU, PERRY BOYER
*Masks.* 1922? LAW

CORNEILLE, PIERRE, 1606–1684
*Le cid.* 1636. CLOU1, CLOUD1, CLOUDS1, LYO, SCN, SER, SERD, STJ1
Anonymous translator GAUB
Bryer, D., translator LAQCF
Cooper, F., translator CLF2, CROV, GREA, MATT, SMN, TAV
Fowhe, W., translator FOWL, TREB
Schevill, J., translator BENSD, HILPDH2, HOUE

Schevill, J., Goldsby, R., and A., translators BENR4
  Variant title: *The Cid*
*The Cid. See* Le cid
*Cinna, or, The Mercy of Augustus.* 1639.
  Landus, P., translator KRE
*Horace.* 1639. SER
*The liar. See* Le menteur
*Variant Polyeucte.* 1640. LYO, SER
  Constable, T., translator HARC26, LOGG, STA

CORNEILLE, THOMAS, 1625–1709
  *Ariadne.* 1672.
    Lockert, L., translator LOCU
    Variant title: *Ariane*
  *Ariane. See* Ariadne
  *Le comte d'Essex. See* The Earl of Essex
  *The Earl of Essex.* 1678.
    Lockert, L., translator LOCR
    Variant title: *Le comte d'Essex*
  *Laodice.* 1668.
    Lockert, L., translator LOCR
  *Maximian.* 1662.
    Lockert, L., translator LOCU
  *Timocrate. See* Timocrates
  *Timocrates.* 1656.
    Lockert, L., translator LOCU
    Variant title: *Timocrate*

CORNELIUS, PATRICIA, 1952–
  *Money. See* Bovell, A., Cornelius, P., Reeves, M.,
    Tsiolkas, CA., and Vela, I. *Who's Afraid of the
    Working Class?*

CORNISH, ROGER, 1934–
  *It Hardly Matters Now.* 1978. VORE
  *Open Twenty-four Hours.* 1968. HAVL, WELT

CORTESE, RAIMONDO
  *Features of Blown Youth.* 1997. MELB
  *Inconsolable.* 1996. JONI

CORTHRON, KIA, 1961–
  *Cage Rhythm.* 1993. MAQ
  *Come Down Burning.* 1993. ELAM, PERC

CORWIN, NORMAN LEWIS, 1910–
  *Ann Rutledge.* 1940. LOVR
  *El Capitan and the Corporal.* 1944. NAGE
  *Good Heavens.* 1941. BRS, LOOD
  *My Client Curley.* 1940. STAV, WATS
  *They Fly through the War.* 1939? PROC
  *We Hold these Truths.* 1941. BROZ

COSCOLLUELA, ELSA MARTINEZ
  *In My Father's House.* 1988. JUAN

COTTER, JOSEPH S., SR., 1861–1949
  *Caleb the Degenerate.* 1903. HARY

COTTER, JOSEPH SEAMON, JR., 1895–1919
  *On the Fields of France.* 1920. HARYL

COULTER, JOHN, 1888–1980
  *The House in the Quiet Glen.* 1937. WAGN3
  *Riel.* 1950. PENG, PERKY

COURTELINE, GEORGES (pseudonym of Georges
    Molneaux), 1860–1929
  *Boubouroche.* 1893.
    Bermel, A., translator BERMD
    Shapiro, N., translator FLEA
    Variant title: *Boubouroche, or She Dupes to Conquer*
  *Boubouroche, or She Dupes to Conquer. See*
    Boubouroche
  *Les boulingrin. See* These Cornfields
  *These Cornfields.* 1898.
    Bentley, E., translator BENSC
    Variant title: *Les boulingrin*

—— and LEVY, JULES
  *La commissionaire est bon enfant. See* The
    Commissioner Has a Big Heart
  *The Commissioner. See* The Commissioner Has a Big
    Heart
  *The Commissioner Has a Big Heart.* 1899.
    Bermel, A., translator BERMD, FOUF, THV
    Variant title: *The Police Chief's an Easygoing Guy.
    See* The Commissioner Has a Big Heart. The Police
    Chief's an Easygoing Guy.

COUSSE, RAYMOND, 1942–
  *Enfantillages. See* These Childish Things
  *These Childish Things.* 1984.
    Singleton, B., translator NEWFPA
    Variant title: *Enfantillages*

COWAN, CINDY
  *Spooks: The Mystery of Caledonia Mills.* 1984. HEID
    (excerpt)
  *A Woman from the Sea.* 1986. CTR

COWARD, NOËL PIERCE, 1899–1973
  *Blithe Spirit.* 1941. BES41, FULT, KRM, TREBA,
    TREC2, TREE3, TREI3, WAK, WARI
  *Brief Encounter.* 1946. GREAB
  *Cavalcade.* 1931. CEU, VOAD
  *Come into the Garden, Maude.* 1966. RICJ
  *Conversation Piece.* 1934. SEV
  *Design for Living.* 1932. BES32, SIXH
  *Easy Virtue.* 1925. MOSO
  *Fumed Oak.* 1936. ANDE, COOP
  *Hay Fever.* 1925. MOD, MYB

*Noël Coward in Two Keys.* 1974. BES73
*Point Valaine.* 1934. SIXP
*Private Lives.* 1930. CHA, CHAN, CHAR, COLT,
      COTKIT, FOUX, LONO, PLAL2
*A Song at Twilight.* 1966. RICK
*The Vortex.* 1924. TUCD, TUCM
*Ways and Means.* 1935. WATE
*The Young Idea.* 1923. MART

COWEN, MRS. LENORE (COFFEE). *See* Coffee, Lenore

COWEN, RON, 1944–
   *Summertree.* 1967. HOLP

COWEN, WILLIAM JOYCE, 1883–1964. *See* Coffee,
   Lenore, joint author

COWIE, MABEL MARGARET, 1903–1975. *See* Storm,
   Lesley, pseudonym

COWLEY, ABRAHAM, 1618–1677
   *Cutter of Coleman–street.* 1661. GAYLE4

COWLEY, HANNAH (PARKHOUSE), 1743–1809
   *Albina, Countess Raimond.* 1779. BELG14
   *The Belle's Stratagem.* 1780. BAT15, ROGEW
   *Which Is the Man?* 1782. INCA10

COWLEY, KAY, and TERBLANCHE, TANYA
   *Onele yo kawe (Place of Diamonds).* 2000. ZEE1

COXE, LOUIS O., 1918–1993, and CHAPMAN,
      ROBERT HARRIS
   *Billy Budd* (based on the novel by Herman Melville).
      1949. BES50, COTX, DAVI, GARW, HAVG,
      SSST, SSSU
      Variant title: *Uniform of Flesh*
   *Uniform of Flesh.* *See* Billy Budd

COXON, LUCINDA, 1962–
   *I Am Angela Brazil.* 1998. ONE

COYLE, KEVIN, 1977–
   *Corner Boys.* 1994. COMS

COYLE, MCCARTHY, 1939–2006
   *The Root.* 1973. BALLE12

COYNE, JOSEPH STIRLING, 1803–1868
   *Did You Ever Send Your Wife to Camberwell?* 1846.
      BOOL
   *How to Settle Accounts with Your Laundress.* 1847.
      BOOA4, BOOM

CRABBE, KERRY LEE
   *The Last Romantica.* 1975. PLAN45

CRADDOCK, CHRIS
   *SuperEd.* 1996. STN

CRAIGIE, PEARL. *See* Hobbes, John Oliver

CRAM, CUSI, 1967–
   *Landlocked.* 1998. PLACGH, WOMP2000

CRANE, STEPHEN, 1871–1900
   *The Bride Comes to Yellow Sky.* *See* Agee, James. *The
      Bride Comes to Yellow Sky* (based on the novel by)

CRAVEN, FRANK, 1880–1945
   *The First Year.* 1920. BES20

CRAWLEY, BRIAN, 1962–
   *Violet* (based on *The Ugliest Pilgrim* by Doris Betts,
      lyrics by Brian Crawley, music by Jeanine Tesori).
      1997. BES96

CREA, TERESA, and EBERHARD, JOSIE COMPOSTO,
      and MASTRANTONE, LUCIA, and MORGILLO,
      ANTONIETTA
   *Ricordi.* 1989. AROUN

CREBILLON, CLAUDE PROSPER JOLYOT DE, 1674–
      1762
   *Rhadamiste et Zénobie.* 1711. BRE
      Lockert, L., translator LOCR
      Variant title: *Rhadamistus and Zenobia*
   *Rhadamistus and Zenobia.* *See* Rhadamiste et Zénobie

CREGAN, DAVID, 1931–
   *Transcending.* 1966. CONB

CREIGHTON, ANTHONY, 1920–2005. *See* Osborne,
   John, joint author

CRESSWELL, JANET, and JOHNSON, NIKI
   *The One-sided Wall.* 1989. PLABE8

CREWS, HARRY, 1935–
   *Blood Issue.* 1989. DIX

CRISP, JACK H., 1923–
   *A Wife in the Land.* 1968. WIM

CRISP, SAMUEL, d. 1783
   *Virginia.* 1754? BELK18

CRISTOFER, MICHAEL, 1945–
  *Amazing Grace*. 1995. BES95
  *The Shadow Box*. 1975. BES76

CROCKER, CHARLES TEMPLETON, 1884–1948
  *The Land of Happiness*. 1917. BOH3

CROMELIN, CAROLINE, NIGHTENGALE, ERIC,
    READ, MONICA, REISS, KIMBERLY, TABER,
    TROY W., and WHERRY, TONY
  *Man in the Flying Lawn Chair*. 2000. NEWR2000

CROMMELYNCK, FERNAND, 1885–1970
  *Le sculpteur de masques*. *See* The Sculptor of Masks
  *The Sculptor of Masks*. 1911. ANTM
    Dormoy Savage, N., translator ANTM
    Variant title: *Le sculpteur de masques*

CRONYN, HUME, 1911–2003
  *Foxfire; a Play with Songs in Two Acts*. *See* Cooper,
    Susan, joint author

CROPPER, MARGARET, 1886–1980
  *Two Sides of the Door*. 1925. FED2

CROSS, BEVERLEY, 1931–1998
  *The Mines of Sulphur, an Opera* (music by Richard R.
    Bennett). 1965. PLAN30

CROSS, J.CA., d. 1809
  *Julia of Louvain; or, Monkish Cruelty*. 1797. COXJ
    Variant title: *Monkish Cruelty*
  *Monkish Cruelty*. *See* Julia of Louvain; or, Monkish
    Cruelty

CROSS, JONATHAN
  *The Chicago Conspiracy*. *See* Burgess, John, and
    Marowitz, Charles. *The Chicago Conspiracy* (based
    on a script by)

CROSSLAND, JACKIE
  *Postcards from Hawaii*. 1989. ZIMM (excerpt)

CROTHERS, RACHEL, 1871–1958
  *As Husbands Go*. 1931. BES30, CHA
  *Expressing Willie*. 1924. COT
  *He and She*. 1911. QUIJ, QUIJR, QUIK, QUIL, QUIM,
    QUIN, WATTAD
    Variant title: *The Herfords*
  *The Herfords*. *See* He and She
  *Let Us Be Gay*. 1929. BES28
  *A Man's World*. 1909. AMENW, PLAAD, PLAAE

*Mary the Third*. 1923. BES22, DICEM, TUCD, TUCJ,
  TUCM
*Nice People*. 1921. BES20, MOSJ, MOSK, MOSL, QUI
*Susan and God*. 1937. BES37
*When Ladies Meet*. 1932. BES32

CROUSE, RUSSEL, 1893–1966. *See* Lindsay, Howard,
  joint author

CROWE, RICHARD, and ZAJDLIC, RICHARD
  *Cock & Bull Story*. 1985. GAY3

CROWLEY, MART, 1935–
  *The Boys in the Band*. 1968. BES67, FAMAH, GARTL,
    RICIS

CROWNE, JOHN, 1640?–1712
  *The Destruction of Jerusalem, pt. 2*. 1677. DOA
  *Sir Courtly Nice; or, It Cannot Be*. 1685. JEFF2, SUM

CRUTCHER, JULIE, and McBRIDE, VAUGHN
  *Digging In: The Farm Crisis in Kentucky*. 1987. DIX

CRUZ, MIGDALIA, 1958–
  *Frida: The Story of Frida Kahlo* (monologues and lyrics
    by). *See* Blecher, Hilary. *Frida: The Story of Frida
    Kahlo*
  *Fur*. 1995. SVICH
  *The Have-little*. 1991. PERC
  *Lucy Loves Me*. 1992. ARRIZ
  *Miriam's Flowers*. 1991. FEY

CRUZ, NILO, ca. 1961–
  *Night Train to Bolina*. 1998. ELLM, SVICH

CRUZ CANO Y OLMEDILLA, RAMON (FRANCISCO)
    DE LA, 1731–1794
  *Las tertulias de Madrid*. 1770. NOR

CSURKA, ISTVAN, 1934–
  *Cheese Dumplings*. 1980.
    Brogyányi, E., translator HUNGDC
    Variant title: *Túrógombóc*
  *Túrógombóc*. *See* Cheese Dumplings

CUEVA Y SILVA, LENOR DE LA
  *La firmeza en la auscencia*. 17th century SOSGA

CULBERTSON, ERNEST HOWARD, 1886–
  *Rackey*. 1919. LOC

CULLEN, ALMA
  *Knowing the Score* (television play). 1986? LEAK

CUSACK, DYMPHNA, 1902–1981
*Morning Sacrifice*. 1942. PFIS

CUSHING, ELIZA LANESFORD, 1794–1886
*The Fate; Ring; a Drama*. (1840) WAGN2

CUSTIS, GEORGE WASHINGTON PARKE, 1781–1857
*Pocahontas; or, The Settlers of Virginia*. 1830. QUIJ,
 QUIK, QUIL, QUIM, QUIN

CUTLER, HARRIET
*Fling Away Ambition*. 1989. KEEP

CUVELIER DE TRYE, JEAN GUILLAUME ANTOINE,
 1766–1824. *See* Chandezon, Léopold, joint author

CZAKO, GABOR, 1942–
*Disznójáték. See* Pigs
*Pigs*. 1978.
 Sollosy, J., translator TEZ
 Variant title: *Disznójáték*

CZERKAWSKA, CATHERINE, 1950–
*Wormwood*. 1997. HOWA

DA BIBIENA, BERNARDO CARDINAL DOVIZI. *See*
 Dovizi da Bibiena, Bernardo Cardinal

DABORNE, ROBERT, 158?–1628
*A Christian Turned Turk*. 1612. VIT

D'ABUNDANCE, JEHAN, pseudonym, fl. 16th century
*La farce de la cornette. See* The Farce of the Bonnet
*The Farce of the Bonnet*. 1543–1544.
 Boucquey, T., translator BOUC
 Variant titles: *La farce de la cornette; New Very
 Merry and Very Pleasant Farce of the Bonnet*
*New Very Merry and Very Pleasant Farce of the Bonnet*.
 *See* The Farce of the Bonnet

DACUS, KATY. *See* Pugh, Ann, joint author

DAFYDD, GWENNO
*Llwd bach y baw. See* No Regrets
*No Regrets*. 1988. ONE
 Variant title: *Llwd bach y baw*

DAGERMAN, STIG, 1923–1954
*The Condemned*. 1947.
 Alexander, H., and Jones, L., translators SCAN3
 Variant title: *Den dödsdömde*
*Den dödsdömde. See* The Condemned

D'AGUIAR, FRED, 1960–
*A Jamaican Airman Foresees His Death*. 1991. BREW3

DALE, BRUCE
*White Mountains*. 1985. WOMQ

DALY, AUGUSTIN, 1838–1899
*The Big Bonanza* (adapted from *Ultimo*, by Gustav von
 Moser). 1875. AMP20
*Divorce*. 1871. AMP20
*Horizon*. 1871. HAL
*Man and Wife*. 1870. AMP20
*Needles and Pins* (adapted from *Starke mitteln*, by Julius
 Rosen). 1880. AMP20
*Pique*. 1875. AMP20
*Under the Gaslight*. 1867. AMEM, BOOB, MES,
 VENA, WATTAD

DAMASHEK, BARBARA. *See* Newman, Molly, joint
 author

DAMASO, JIMENO, 1885–1936
*It Withered and Revived*. 1910.
 Damaso, C., translator PHIL
 Variant title: *Nalaya cag manalingsing*
*Nalaya cag manalingsing*. PHIL

DAMEL, CARLOS S., 1890– . *See* Darthes, Juan
 Fernando, joint author

DAMCHENKO, VLADIMIR IVANOVICH
 NEMIROVICH. *See* Nemfrovích Daneheilko,
 Vladímir Ivanovích

DAMONTE, RAUL. *See* Copi (pseudonym)

DANCOURT, FLORENT CARTON, 1661–1725
*Les bourgeoises de qualité. See* Woman's Craze for
 Titles. 1687. BREN
*Woman's Craze for Titles*. 1700.
 Chambers, W., translator BAT8
 Variant title: *Les bourgeoises de qualité*

DANE, CLEMENCE, pseudonym. *See* Ashton, Winifred

DANIEL, SAMUEL, 1562–1619
*Tethys' Festival*. 1610. LINDC
*The Vision of the Twelve Goddesses*. 1604. ETO, PAR

DANIELS, SARAH, 1957–
*Purple Side Coasters* (radio play). 1995. MYTH

DANJURO I, 1660–1704
*The God Fudō*. 1697. *See* Tsunchi, Hanjurō; Yasuda,
 Abun; and Nakada, Mansuke. *Saint Narukami and
 the God Fudō*
*Narukami*. 1684.
 Irwin, V., translator IRW

Variant title: *Saint Narukami*
*Saint Narukami.* See Narukami
  — *See also* Tsuuchi, Hanjurō; Yasuda, Abun; and
    Nakada, Mansuke. *Saint Narukami and the God*
    *Fudō*

DANJURO, ICHIKAWA. *See* Danjuro I

DANNENFELSER, DAVID, 1959–
*When Words Fail.* 1998. DENT

D'ANNUNZIO, GABRIELE. *See* Annunzio, Gabriele d'

DANON, RAMI, and LEVY, AMNON
*Sheindale.* 1993.
  Shlesinger, M., translator BARA

DANTE, NICHOLAS, 1941–1991 (b. Conrado Morales).
  See Kirkwood, James, joint author

DARKE, NICK, 1948–2005
*High Water.* 1980. PLACK

DA PONTE, LORENZO. *See* Ponte, Lorenzo Da

D'ARCY, MARGARETTA, 1934– . *See* Arden, John,
  joint author

DARION, JOSEPH, 1917–2001
*Man of La Mancha* (lyrics by). *See* Wasserman, Dale.
  *Man of La Mancha*

DART, PHILIP. *See* Pickering, Kenneth, joint author

DARTHES, JUAN FERNANDO CAMILO, 1889–1949,
  and DAMEL, CARLOS S.
*La hermana Josefina. See* The Quack Doctor
*The Quack Doctor.* 1938.
  Jones, W., translator JONW
  Variant title: *La hermana Josefina*

DAS, JAGANNATH PRASAD, 1936–
*Before the Sunset.* 1976.
  Das, J., translator KAM2
  Variant title: *Suryast*
*Suryast. See* Before the Sunset

DAS, K., 1929–
*Lela Mayang.* 1968. NEWDR1

DAUMAL, RENE, 1908–1944
*En gggarrrde!* 1924.
  Benedikt, M., translator BEN

DAURIAC, CARLE. *See* Armory, pseudonym

D'AVENANT, SIR WILLIAM, 1606–1668
*Love and Honor.* 1634. WALL
*Salmacida spolia.* 1640. ETO, LINDC
*The Siege of Rhodes, pt. 1.* 1661. MAND, MANF
*The Wits.* 1635. KNOW

————— and DRYDEN, JOHN
*The Tempest; or, The Enchanted Island.* 1667. SUMB

DAVENANT, WILLIAM. *See* D'Avenant, Sir William

DAVENPORT, ROBERT, 1600?–1651?
*The City Night-cap.* 1624? BUL4
*A Crowne for a Conquerour.* 1623? BUL4
*King John and Matilda.* 1655? ARMS, BUL4
*A New Trick to Cheat the Divell.* 1639? BUL4
*A Survey of the Sciences.* BUL4
*Too Late to Call Backe Yesterday.* 1623? BUL4

DAVEY, SHAUN, 1948–
*James Joyce's The Dead* (music and lyrics by). *See*
  Nelson, Richard. *James Joyce's "The Dead"*

DAVID, LARRY, 1947?–
*The Pitch* (a *Seinfeld* episode). 1999. MEYCA,
  MEYCB, MEYF

DAVIDSON, ROBERT, 1808–1876
*Elijah.* 1860? KOH2

DAVIES, HUBERT HENRY, 1865–1917
*The Mollusca.* 1907. DICEM, ROWC

DAVIES, LEWIS, 1967–
*My Piece of Happiness.* 1998. NEWWD1
*Sex and Power at the Beau Rivage.* 2003. NEWWD3

DAVIES, MARY CAROLYN, 1888–
*The Slave with Two Faces.* 1918? PEN

DAVIES, ROBERTSON, 1913–1995
*At My Heart's Core.* 1950. PERKY
*Hope Deferred.* 1948. WAGN3

DAVIN, NICHOLAS FLOOD, 1943–1901
*Advantages of Coalition. See* The Fair Grit
*The Fair Grit; or, The Advantages of Coalition, a Farce.*
  (1876) WAGN1
  Variant title: *Advantages of Coalition*

DAVIOT, GORDON, pseudonym. *See* MacKintosh,
  Elizabeth

DAVIS, ANDRE
*Four Men.* 1958? OBSE

DAVIS, BILL C., 1951–
*Mass Appeal.* 1979. BES81

DAVIS, BOB
*Renaissance Radar: A Performance Landscape* (music by). *See* Finneran, Alan. *Renaissance Radar: A Performance Landscape*

DAVIS, DONALD, 1907–1992. *See* Davis, Owen, joint author

DAVIS, DONNA (D. K. OKLAHOMA, pseudonym)
*Anna's Brooklyn Promise.* 1987. VORE
*Old Flames.* 1987. VORE

DAVIS, ELLEN BROOK
*The Nurse.* 1984. *See* Anonymous Plays. *The AIDS Show . . .*

DAVIS, MRS. IRVING KAYE. *See* Shelley, Elsa (Mrs. Irving Kaye Davis)

DAVIS, JACK, 1917–2000
*The Dreamers.* 1982. PLACC
*No Sugar.* 1985. AUS, WOTHC

DAVIS, LUTHER, 1921–2008
*Grand Hotel* (Songs by Robert Wright and George Forrest, additional music and lyrics by Maury Yeston; based on *Grand Hotel* by Vicki Baum). 1989. BES89

DAVIS, OSSIE, 1917–2005
*Curtain Call, Mr. Aldridge, Sir.* 1963. REAR
*Purlie Victorious.* 1961. ALLK, BRAS, DIS, FAD, OLIV, PATR, TUQT

DAVIS, OWEN, 1874–1956
*And So Ad Infinitum. See* Čapek, Karel, and Čapek, Josef. *And So Ad Infinitum* (adapted by)
*The Detour.* 1921. MOSJ, MOSK, MOSL
*Icebound.* 1923. BES22, CORD, CORE, CORF, DICEM, HAL
*Mr. and Mrs. North* (based on the novel, *The Norths Meet Murder* by Frances and Richard Lockridge). 1941. BES40

—— and DAVIS, DONALD
*Ethan Frome* (based on the novel by Edith Wharton). 1936. BES35, GARU, GATB2

DAVIS, SKOT
*Consider the Banana.* 1999. INCI

DAVIS, THULANI, 1949?–
*X: The Life and Times of Malcolm X.* 1986. MAQ

DAVIS, WIREMU
*Taku mangai.* 1991. KOU

DAY, CLARENCE, 1874–1935
*Life with Father. See* Lindsay, Howard, and Crouse, Russel. *Life with Father* (based on the book by)
*Life with Mother. See* Lindsay, Howard, and Crouse, Russel. *Life with Mother* (based on the book by)

DAY, JOHN, 1574–1640?
*Humour Out of Breath.* 1608? NER
*The Parliament of Bees.* 1641? NER

—— and ROWLEY, WILLIAM, and WILKINS, GEORGE
*The Travels of the Three English Brothers.* 1607. PARR

DAYLEY, GRACE, 1960–
*Rose's Story.* 1984. PLABE4

DAYTON, KATHARINE, 1890–1945, and KAUFMAN, GEORGE S.
*First Lady.* 1935. BES35

DE AMESCUA, ANTONIO MIRA. *See* Mira de Amescua, Antonio

DEAN, ALEXANDER, 1893–1939
*Just Neighborly.* 1921. LAW

DEAN, BASIL, 1888–1978. *See* Kennedy, Margaret, joint author

DEAN, NANCY, 1930–
*Gloria's Visit.* 1990. DEAT

DEAN, PHILIP HAYES, ca. 1938–
*The Owl Killer.* (1972). KINH, KINHB
*Paul Robeson.* 1978. HILEB
*The Sty of the Blind Pig.* 1971. HAPUE

DE ANDA, PETER, 1940– (b. Pedro Deanda)
*Ladies in Waiting.* 1971. BES70, KINH, KINHB

DEANE, HAMILTON, 1891–1958, and BALDERSTON, JOHN
*Dracula* (based on the novel by Bram Stoker). 1927. BRNS, RICI

DE ANGELIS, APRIL, 1960–
*Breathless.* 1986. GRAW
*Crux.* 1990. ROES
*Hush.* 1992. FROLIN1
*Ironmistress.* 1989. PLABE8
John Cleland's *The Life and Times of Fanny Hill* (based on the novel by John Cleland). 1991. FRY

DE BEAUVOIR, SIMONE. *See* Beauvoir, Simone de

DEBENHAM, ARTHUR HENRY, 1881–
  *Good Will toward Men.* 1934. SEVE
  *The Prince of Peace.* 1934. SEVE

DE CAMP, MARIE-THERESE. *See* Kemble, Marie
  Thérèse

DE CASALIS, JEANNE, 1897–1966 (b. Casalis de Pury)
  *See* Sherriff, Robert Cedric, joint author

DECENT, CAMPION
  *Baby X.* 2000. INSI

DECOUR, CHARLES HERBERT, and THEODORE,
  ANNE
  *Le coq de village. See* Smith, Richard Penn (adapted
    from). *The Last Man*

DE CUREL, FRANÇOIS. *See* Curel, François de

DE CURNIEU, GEORGES. *See* Curnieu, Georges de

DEEVY, TERESA, 1894–1963
  *Katie Roche.* 1936. FAMI

DE FILIPPO, EDUARDO. *See* Filippo, Eduardo de

DE GHELDERODE, MICHEL. *See* Ghelderode, Michel de

DE GROEN, ALMA, 1941–
  *The Joss Adams Show.* 1970. BRIM1
  *The Rivers of China.* 1987. AUS
  *Vocations.* 1982. TAIT

DEIKE, TAGGART
  *Waiting for Hiroshima.* 1989. PLACB

DEKKER, THOMAS, ca.1572–1632
  *The Gentle Craft. See* The Shoemakers' Holiday
  *The Magnificent Entertainment.* 1603. KINNR
  *A Pleasant Comedy of a Gentle Craft. See* The
    Shoemakers' Holiday
  *The Pleasant Comedy of Old Fortunatus.* 1599. SCH,
    SCI
  *The Shoemakers' Holiday; or, The Gentle Craft.* 1599.
    BALD, BAS, BENY, BLOO, BROC, CLKW,
    COF, DPR1, DUN, FOUD, GATG, GAYLE3,
    GREC1, HARC47, HAY, HOW, KINNR, LAWR,
    MACL, MAK, MONV, NEI, NES, ORNC, PAR,
    RUB, SCI, SCJ, SCW, SHAJ1, SPD, SPE, SPEF1,
    TAT, TAU, TAV, WHE, WINE, WOO1, WRIH
    Variant titles: *The Gentle Craft; A Pleasant Comedy
    of a Gentle Craft*

— *See* Ford, John, joint author. *The Witch of Edmonton*

—— and MIDDLETON, THOMAS
  *The Honest Whore, Part I.* 1604. BAS, NEI, NES, SPE,
    WALL
  *The Honest Whore, Part II.* 1605. NEI, OLH, OLI1,
    SPE
  *The Roaring Girl.* 1610. DPR2, MAME

DE KOCK, CHARLES PAUL. *See* Kock, Charles Paul de

DE KRUIF, PAUL HENRY, 1890–1971. *See* Howard,
  Sidney Coe, joint author

DE LA BARCA, PEDRO CALDERON. *See* Calderón de
  la Barca, Pedro

DELACOUR, ALFRED CHARLEMAGNE LARTIGNE,
  known as, 1817–1883. *See* Labiche, Eugène Marin,
  joint author

DELAFIELD, E. M., pseudonym. *See* De La Pasture,
  Edmée Elizabeth Monica

DE LANEROLLE, H.CA.N.
  *The Senator.* 1948. GOON (excerpt)

DELANEY, SHELAGH, 1939–
  *A Taste of Honey.* 1958. BES60, POP, SEVD

DE LA PASTURE, EDMEE ELIZABETH MONICA
  (E. M. Delafield, pseudonym), 1890–1943
  *To See Ourselves.* 1930. FAMAN, PLAD

DE LA ROCHE–GUILHEN, ANNE. *See* Roche-Guilhen,
  Anne de la

DE LA TAILLE, JEAN. *See* Taille, Jean de La

DELAVIGNE, CASIMIR. *See* Delavigne, Jean François
  Casimir

DELAVIGNE, JEAN FRANÇOIS CASIMIR, 1793–1843
  *Marino Faliero.* 1829. BOR

DELBO, CHARLOTTE, 1913–1985
  *Who Will Carry the Word?* 1974.
    Haft, C., translator THL

DELDERFIELD, RONALD FREDERICK, 1912–1972
  *Peace Comes to Peckham.* 1947. EMB3
  *Worm's Eye View.* 1945. EMB1

DEL GRANDE, LOUIS, 1942–
  *So Who's Goldberg.* 1973. BRIP

*The Favorite Minister*. 1665.
    Gethner, P., translator GETH
    Variant title: *Le favori*

DESNOS, ROBERT, 1900–1945
  *La Place de l'Etoile*. (1944)
    Benedikt, M., translator BEN

DESSANDRAIS-SEBIRE, FRANÇOIS
  *The Philosopher Duped by Love* (sometimes attributed
    to). *See* Anonymous Plays. *The Philosopher Duped*
    *by Love*

DESTOUCHES, PHILIPPE NERICAULT, 1680–1754
  *The Conceited Count*. *See* Le glorieux
  *Le glorieux*. 1732. BREN
    Aldington, R., translator ALD
    Variant title: *The Conceited Count*

DEVAL, JACQUES, 1895–1972 (b. Jacques Boularan)
  *Tovarich*. 1936.
    Sherwood, R., translator and adapter BES36, CEW

DEVEAUX, ALEXIS, 1948–
  *The Tapestry*. 1976. WILK

DEVERELL, REX, 1941–
  *Medicare!* 1980. SHOW

DEVI, MAHASWETA, 1926–
  *Hajar Churashir Ma*. *See* Mother of 1084
  *Mother of 1084*. 1975.
    Bandopadhyay, S., translator DESH
    Variant title: *Hajar Churashir Ma*

DE VILLEDIEU, MADAME. *See* Villedieu, Madame de,
  pseudonym

DE VISE, JEAN DONNEAU. *See* Donneau de Visé, Jean

DEVLIN, ANNE, 1951–
  *Ourselves Alone*. 1985. KILGC, LAQCW

DEWBERRY, ELIZABETH, 1962–
  *Flesh and Blood*. 1996. HUMANA96
  *Head On*. 1995. DIX, HUMANA95

DE WET, REZA, 1955–
  *A Worm in the Bud*. 1995. HUTCH
  *Crossing*. 1994. GRAV

DEWHURST, KEITH, 1931–
  *Lark Rise* (from the book by Flora Thompson). 1978.
    PLAN48
  *Lark Rise to Candleford*. *See* Lark Rise
  *Rafferty's Chant*. 1967. PLAN33

DEY, JAMES PAUL, 1930–
  *Passacaglia*. 1965. NEWA2

DE ZOYSA, LUCIEN, 1917–1995
  *Fortress in the Sky*. 1956. GOON (excerpt)

DIAGANA, MOUSSA, 1947–
  *The Legend of Wagadu: As Seen by Sia Yatabere*. 1991.
    Mill, R., translator AFRUBU2

DIAMANT-BERGER, MAURICE (André Gillois,
  pseudonym)
  *Paddle Your Own Canoe*. *See* Regnier, Max. A. M.
  (based on)

DIAMOND, DAVID, 1953–
  *No' xya' (Our Footprints)*. 1987. NEWCAD5

DIAZ, JORGE, 1930–2007
  *El cepillo de dientes*. 1966. DAU
  *El luger donde mueren los mamíferos*. *See* The Place
    Where the Mammals Die
  *The Mammals' Graveyard*. *See* The Place Where the
    Mammals Die
  *The Place Where the Mammals Die*. 1963.
    Nelson, N., translator WOOG
    Variant titles: *El luger donde mueren los mamíferos;*
    *The Mammals' Graveyard*

DIBDIN, CHARLES, 1745?–1814
  *The Deserter*. 1782. BELC4

DIBDIN, THOMAS JOHN PITT, 1771–1841
  *Fire, Water, Earth, and Air*. *See* Harlequin in His
    Element
  *Harlequin Harper; or A Jump from Japan*. 1813.
    BOOA5
    Variant title: *A Jump from Japan*
  *A Jump from Japan*. *See* Harlequin Harper
  *Harlequin in His Element, or Fire, Water, Earth, and*
    *Air*. 1807. BOOA5
    Variant title: *Fire, Water, Earth, and Air*
  *The School for Prejudice*. 1801. INCA4

DICENTA Y BENEDICTO, JOAQUIN, 1863–1917
  *Juan José*. 1895.
    Skidmore, M., translator TUR

DICKENS, CHARLES, 1812–1870
  *A Christmas Carol*. *See* Horowitz, Israel. *A Christmas*
    *Carol: Scrooge and Marley* (adapted from the
    story by)
    *See also* Nolte, Charles. *A Christmas Carol* (adapted
    from the story by)
    *See also* Shay, Frank. *A Christmas Carol* (adapted
    from the story by)

*The Cricket on the Hearth. See* Smith, Albert Richard.
    *The Cricket on the Hearth* (adapted from the story
    by)
*Dot. See* Boucicault, Dion. Dot (adapted from *The
    Cricket on the Hearth*)
*Great Expectations. See* Clifford, John. *Great
    Expectations* (based on the novel by)
*The Mystery of Edwin Drood. See* Holmes, Rupert. *The
    Mystery of Edwin Drood* (based on the novel by)
*Nicholas Nickleby. See* Edgar, David. *The Life &
    Adventures of Nicholas Nickleby*; a play in two
    parts with five acts (based on)
*Pickwick Papers. See* Young, Stanley. *Mr. Pickwick*
    (based on)
*The Strange Gentleman.* 1836. KAYF

DICKENS, CHRIS
*Friends.* 1990? MURD

DICKERSON, GLENDA, 1945– , and CLARKE,
    BREENA
*Re/membering Aunt Jemima: A Menstrual Show.* 1992.
    ELAM, PERC

DICKLER, GLORIA JOYCE, 1950–
*The Postcard.* 1994. CURB

DIDEROT, DENIS, 1713–1784
*The Father. See* Le père de famille
*Jacques le fatahste et son maître. See* Kundera, Milan.
    *Jacques and his Master* (adapted from)
*Le père de famille.* 1761. BREN
    Variant title: *The Father*

DIEB, RON, 1932–
*The Mating of Alice May* (1972) PIC

DIETZ, STEVEN, 1958–
*Lonely Planet.* 1993. ACTOR
*Private Eyes.* 1997. HUMANA97

DIFUSCO, JOHN, 1947–
*Tracers.* 1980. BES84

DIGHTON, JOHN, 1909–1989
*The Happiest Days of Your Life.* 1948. PLAN1
*Who Goes There!* 1951. PLAN6

DIKE, FATIMA, 1948–
*The Sacrifice of Kreli.* 1976. GRAYTO
*So What's New?* 1991. PERA

DILLON, DAVID, 1957–
*Party.* 1992. CLUM

DILLON, EILEEN
*Hitch-hiker.* 1984. MALY

DILMEN, GÜNGÖR (KALYONCU), 1930–
*The Ears of Midas.* 1959.
    Graham, C., translator HALM
    Variant title: *Midasin Kulaklari*
*I, Anatolia.* 1991.
    Halman, T., translator KIAN
*Midasin Kulaklari. See* The Ears of Midas

DI MAMBRO, ANN MARIE, 1950–
*Brothers of the Thunder.* 1994. HOWA
*The Letter-box.* 1989. CALE

DING, XILIN, 1893–1974
*Oppression.* (1925)
    Lau, J., translator TWEH
    Variant title: *Ya-p'o Ya-p'o. See* Oppression

DINNER, WILLIAM, and MORUM, WILLIAM
*The Late Edwina Black.* 1949. PLAN2

DINSMAN (pseudonym of Che Shamsuddin Othman),
    1949–
*On Sadandi's Island.* 1993.
    Ishak, S., translator MLAM

DITTON, CORDELIA, and FORD, MAGGIE
*About Face.* 1985. PLABE6

DIYAB, MAHMUD, 1932–1983
*Al-ghuraba' la yashrabun al-qahwa. See* Strangers
    Don't Drink Coffee
*Strangers Don't Drink Coffee.*
    Wright, O., and Brownjohn, A., translators JAY
    Variant title: *Al-ghuraba' la yashrabun al-qahwa*

DIZENZO, CHARLES JOHN, 1938–
*The Drapes Come.* 1965. OFF1
*An Evening for Merlin Finch.* 1968. OFF1

DIZON, LOUELLA, 1966–
*Till Voices Wake Us.* 1994. PERC

DOBIE, LAURENCE, and SLOMAN, ROBERT
*The Tinker.* 1960. PLAN24

DOCKERY, MARTIN, 1968–
*Oh, that Wiley Snake!* 1996. DIYLD

DOCTOROW, E(DGAR).L(AWRENCE)., 1931–
*Ragtime. See* McNally, Terrence. *Ragtime* (based on the
    novel by)

DODD, LEE WILSON, 1879–1933
   *The Changelings.* 1923. BES23

DODD, TERRY
   *Goodnight, Texas.* 1986. PRIMA86

DODSLEY, ROBERT, 1703–1764
   *Cleone.* 1758. BELG15
   *The Miller of Mansfield.* BELC3
   *The Toy Shop.* 1735. BELC3

DODSON, OWEN VINCENT, 1914–1983
   *Bayou Legend.* 1946. TUQT, TUQTR
   *The Confession Stone.* 1960. HARYB
   *Divine Comedy.* 1938. HARY
   *The Shining Town.* 1937. ROOTS

DOGGET, THOMAS, ca.1640–1721
   *Flora; or, Hob in the Well. See* Hob; or, The Country
      Wake
   *Hob; or, The Country Wake* (sometimes attributed to
      Colley Cibber). 1711. HUGL
      Variant titles: *Flora; or, Hob in the Well; The Opera
      of Flora; or, Hob in the Well*
   *The Opera of Flora; or, Hob in the Well. See* Hob; or,
      The Country Wake

DOHERTY, BRIAN, 1906–1974
   *Father Malachy's Miracle* (adapted from the novel by
      Bruce Marshall). 1945. EMB1

DOLAN, HARRY, JR. 1927–1981.
   *Losers Weepers.* (1967) DODGE

DONAHUE, JOHN CLARK
   *The Cookie Jar.* 1972. MIMN

DONALD, SIMON, 1959–
   *The Life of Stuff.* 1992. BROV
   *Prickly Heat.* 1988. FIFHL1

DONLEAVY, JAMES PATRICK (J.P.), 1926–
   *The Interview.* THOD

DONNAY, MAURICE CHARLES, 1859–1945
   *Les amants. See* The Lovers
   *L'autre danger. See* The Other Danger
   *The Lovers.* 1895.
      Clark, B., translator MOSQ
      Steeves, H., translator STE
      Variant title: *Les amants*
   *The Other Danger.* 1902.
      David, C., translator THS
      Variant title: *L'autre danger*

DONNEAU DE VISE, JEAN, 1638?–1710?
   *Le gentilhomme guespin.* 1670? LANC

DONNELLY, NEIL, 1946–
   *The Duty Master.* 1995. NEWPAB1

DORALL, EDWARD, 1936–
   *The Hour of the Dog.* 1970. NEWDR2
   *A Tiger Is Loose in Our Community.* 1967. NEWDR1

DORFMAN, ARIEL, 1942–
   *Death and the Maiden.* 1991. MEYE

DORN, RUDI, 1926–
   *One's a Heifer* (television play; based on a short story
      by Sinclair Ross). 1972. BELLW

DORRAS, JO, and WALKER, PETER
   *The Tale of Mighty Hawk and Magic Fish.* 1993.
      SACR

DORSBT, THOMAS SACKVILLE, 1st earl of. *See*
   Sackville, Thomas

DORST, TANKRED, 1925–
   *The Curve.* 1960.
      Rosenberg, J., translator COTT
      Variant title: *Die Kurve*
   *Die Kurve. See* The Curve
   *Fernando Knapp Wrote Me This Letter: An Assaying of
      the Truth* (based on the novella *Nada menos que
      todo un hombre* by Miguel de Unamuno). 1992.
      Roloff, M., translator WEBER
   *Freedom for Clemens.* 1960.
      Wellwarth, G., translator BENB
      Variant titles: *Freedom for Clement; Freiheit für
      Clemens. See* Freedom for Clemens
   *Freiheit für Clemens. See* Freedom for Clemens

DOSTOEVSKII, FEDOR MIKHAILOVICH, 1821–1881
   *The Brothers Karamazoff. See* S. Nemirovich-
      Danchenko, Vladimir. *The Brothers Karamazoff*
      (based on the novel by)

DOSTOIEVSKY, FEDOR. *See* Dostoevskii, Fedor
   Mikhailovich

DOUGLAS, FELICITY, 1904–1992
   *Rollo. See* Achard, Marcel. *Rollo* (adapted by)

DOUGLAS, GEORGIA. *See* Johnson, Mrs. Georgia
   (Douglas)

DOUGLAS, JAMES, 1929–
   *The Ice Goddess.* 1964. HOGE

DOVIZI DA BIBBIENA, BERNARDO CARDINAL, 1470–1520
*La Calandria. See* The Follies of Calandro
*The Follies of Calandro.* Early 16th century
Evans, O., translator BENSA
Variant title: *La Calandria*

DOWIE, CLAIRE, 1956–
*Adult Child/Dead Child.* 1987. PLABE7

DOWLING, JENNETTE, and LETTON, FRANCIS
*Before the Throne. See* The Young Elizabeth
*Princess Elizabeth. See* The Young Elizabeth
*The Young Elizabeth.* 1951. PLAN7
Variant titles: *Before the Throne; Princess Elizabeth*

DOWLING, MAURICE MATHEW GEORGE, 1793?–
*Othello Travestie.* 1834. NIN2
*Romeo and Juliet, as the Law Directs.* 1837. NIN2

DOWN, OLIPHANT, 1885–1917
*The Maker of Dreams.* 1912. BEAC12

DOWSON, ERNEST CHRISTOPHER, 1867–1900
*The Pierrot of the Minute.* 1902. BENP, SECK

DOYLE, SIR ARTHUR CONAN, 1859–1930
*Sherlock Holmes. See* Gillette, William Hooker.
*Sherlock Holmes* (based on the stories by)

DRAGUN, OSVALDO, 1929–1999
*And They Told Us We Were Immortal.* 1963.
Green, A., translator WOOG
Variant title: *Y nos dijeron que éramos inmortales*
*El amasijo.* 1968. DAU
*Arriba, Corazon! See* Onward, Corazon!
*Onward, Corazon!* 1987.
Glickman, N., and Waldman, G., translators ARGJT
Variant title: *Arriba, Corazon!*
*Y nos dijeron que éramos inmortales. See* And They Told Us We Were Immortal

DRAI, MARTINE, 1953–
*All It Takes Is Something Small.* 1994.
Vogel, S., translator MOGS
Variant title: *Il suffit de peau*
*Il suffit de peau. See* All It Takes Is Something Small

DRAKE, WILLIAM A., 1899–1965
*Grand Hotel* (translator and adapted by). *See* Baum, Vicki. *Grand Hotel*

DRANSFIELD, JANE, 1875–1957
*The Lost Pleiad.* 1910. SHAY

DRAYTON, MICHAEL, 1563–1631
*The Merry Devil of Edmonton* (sometimes attributed to). *See* Anonymous Plays. *The Merry Devil of Edmonton*
*Sir John Oldcastle, Part I* (sometimes attributed to). *See* Anonymous Plays. *Sir John Oldcastle, Part I*

DRAYTON, RONALD
*Notes from a Strange God.* (1968) JONE

DREHER, SARAH, 1937–
*8 × 10 glossy.* 1985. PLA
*Ruby Christmas.* 1981. PLA

DRESSER, RICHARD
*Below the Belt.* 1995. DIXD2, HUMANA95
*The Downside.* 1987. BES88
*Gun-shy.* 1997. HUMANA97
*What Are You Afraid Of?* 1999. HUMANA99

DREXLER, ROSALYN, 1926–
*Occupational Hazard.* 1993. LAMO
*Softly and Consider the Nearness.* 1967. MESSE

DRINKWATER, JOHN, 1882–1937
*Abraham Lincoln.* 1918. BES19, DICDS, PLAP1, SWI
*Cophetua.* 1911. PEN
*Oliver Cromwell.* 1923. DICEM

DRIVER, DONALD, 1922–1988
*Your Own Thing* (suggested by *Twelfth Night* by William Shakespeare; music and lyrics by Hal Hester and Danny Apolinar). 1968. BES67, GREAAR

DRIVER, JOHN, 1947– , and HADDOW, JEFFREY, 1947–
*Chekhov in Yalta* (music composed by Catherine MacDonald). 1981. BES80, WES11/12

DRUMMOND, ALEXANDER MAGNUS, 1884–1956
*The Lake Guns of Seneca and Cayuga.* DRU
— *See also* Baker, E. Irene, joint author

DRUTEN, JOHN VAN. *See* Van Druten, John

DRYDEN, JOHN, 1631–1700
*All for Love; or, The World Well Lost.* 1677. BAUG, BELK5, BENY, CLK1, COTX, DOB, FREG, GOS, GOSA, HARC18, KET, LIE, LIED1, LIEE1, MACL, MAND, MANF, MARG, MATTL, MIL, MOO, MOR, NET, RES, RESL, REST, RET, SHAH1, SHAJ1, SMN, SNYD1, STM, THMF, TUP, TUQ, TWE, WILSR, WONR, WOOE1, WRIR

*Almanzor and Almahide; or, The Conquest of Granada by the Spaniards.* 1670. MOR, NET, TAT, TAU, TUP, TUQ, WONR
　　Variant titles: *The Conquest of Granada; The Conquest of Granada by the Spaniards, Part I*
*Amphitryon.* 1690. BELK11, COTKA
*Aureng-zebe.* 1675. DOA, MEN, STM, TICK
*The Conquest of Granada. See* Almanzor and Almahide
*The Conquest of Granada by the Spaniards, pt. I. See* Almanzor and Almahide
*Don Sebastian, King of Portugal.* (1690) BELK12
*The Feigned Innocence. See* Sir Martin Mar-all
*The Kind Keeper; or, Mr. Limberham.* 1677–1678. JEFF2
　　Variant title: *Mr. Limberham*
*King Arthur.* 1691. LUP
*Marriage a la Mode.* 1672. DAVR
*Mr. Limberham. See* The Kind Keeper
*The Secular Masque.* 1700. ABRA, ABRE, ABRF1, ABRH1, ABRJ1, ABRK1, ABRL1, HAPT1
*Sir Martin Mar-all; or, The Feigned Innocence.* 1667. JEFF1
　　Variant title: *The Feigned Innocence*
*The Spanish Fryer; or, The Double Discovery.* 1679. BELK13, GAYLE4, MOSE1
*The Tempest. See* D'Avenant, Wilham, joint author

—— and HOWARD, SIR ROBERT
*The Indian Queen.* 1663. BENY, MAND, MANF

—— and LEE, NATHANIEL
*Oedipus.* 1679. BELK12

DUARTE-CLARKE, RODRIGO
*Brujerias.* 1972. KANEL

DUBERMAN, MARTIN B., 1930–
*In White America.* 1963. GAT, LAM

DUBIN, AL, 1891–1945
*42nd Street* (music and lyrics by). *See* Stewart, Michael. *42nd Street*

DUBOIS, RENE-DANIEL, 1955–
*Being at Home with Claude.* 1985.
　　Gaboriau, L., translator CTR
*Don't Blame the Bedouins.* 1981.
　　Kevan, M., translator WALAQ
*Ne blâmez jamais les Bédouins. See* Don't Blame the Bedouins

DUBOIS, W.E.B. *See* DuBois, William Edward Burghardt

DUBOIS, WILLIAM EDWARD BURGHARDT, 1868–1963
*Haiti.* 1938. FEE
*Star of Ethiopia.* 1912. HARYB

DUCANGE, VICTOR HENRI JOSEPH BRAHAIN, 1783–1833. *See* Goubaux, Prosper Parfait, joint author

DUDLEY, SIR HENRY BATE, 1745–1824
*The Rival Candidates.* 1775. BELC4

DUDOWARD, VALERIE (WILGOOSG'M NEAX), 1957–2006
*Teach Me the Ways of the Sacred Circle.* 1986. LAND

DUERRENMATT, FRIEDRICH, 1921–1990
*Abendstunde im Spätherbst. See* Incident at Twilight
*Der besuch der alten dame. See* The Visit
*Incident at Twilight.* 1959.
　　Wellwarth, G., translator BENB, WELT
　　Variant title: *Abendstunde im Spätherbst*
*The Old Lady's Visit. See* The Visit
*The Physicists.* 1962.
　　Kirkup, J., translator BES64, HAVHA
　　Variant title: *Die Physiker*
*Die Physiker. See* The Physicists
*Time and Again. See* The Visit
*Trapps. See* Yaffe, James. *The Deadly Game* (adapted from) *The Visit.* 1956.
　　Bowles, P., translator COTQ, NIL
　　Valency, M., translator and adapter BAUL, BES57, BLOC, BOW, CALD, CASK, GOOD, GOODE, KNIF, KNIG, KNIH, KNIJ
　　Variant titles: *Der besuch der alten dame; La visite de la vieille dame; The Old Lady's Visit; Time and Again*
*La visite de la vieille dame. See* The Visit

DUFFET, THOMAS, fl. 1678
*The Mock-tempest; or, The Enchanted Castle.* 1674. SUMB

DUFFIELD, BRAINERD, 1917–1979
*The Lottery* (from the story by Shirley Jackson). 1953? LOVR, SCVDT1

DUFFY, GER, 1962–
*Into the Night.* 1988. GRAW

DUFFY, MAUREEN, 1933–
*Rites.* 1969. PLABE2, SUB

DUGGAN, SHAUN, 1970–
*William.* 1986. DODGS

DUKES, ASHLEY, 1885–1959
*The Man with a Load of Mischief.* 1925. MART, PLAP3
*The Mask of Virtue* (translator and adapted by). *See* Sternheim, Carl. *The Mask of Virtue*

*Such Men Are Dangerous* (adapted from *The Patriot* by Alfred Neumann). 1928. FAO

DUKOVSKI, DEJAN, 1969–
*Powder Keg.* 1994.
    Philipovich, P., translator LUZ

DULLEMEN, INEZ VAN, 1925–
*Schrijf me in het zand. See* Write Me in the Sand
*Write Me in the Sand.* 1989.
    Akerman, A., translator ROET
    Variant title: *Schrijf me in het zand*

DUMAS, ALEXANDRE, père, 1802–1870
*Antony.* 1831. BOR, COM
*The Count of Monte Cristo. See* Fechter, Charles Albert. Monte Cristo (based on the novel, *The Count of Monte Cristo*, by)
*Henry III et sa court.* 1829. BOR, GRA

DUMAS, ALEXANDRE, fils, 1824–1895
*Camilla; or, The Fate of a Coquette. See* La dame aux camélias
*Camille. See* La dame aux camélias
*La dame aux camélias.* 1852. BOR, GRA
    Ashley, L., translator ASF, VICT
    Reynolds, E., and Playfair, N., translators SSTG
    Variant titles: *Camilla; or, The Fate of a Coquette; Camille; The Lady of the Camelias; The Queen of the Camelias*
*Le demi-monde. See* The Outer Edge of Society
*The Ideas of Madame Aubray. See* Les idées de Madame Aubray
*Les idées de Madame Aubray.* 1867. BOR
    Variant title: *The Ideas of Madame Aubray*
*The Lady of the Camelias. See* La dame aux camélias
*The Outer Edge of Society.* 1855.
    Clark, B., translator MATT
    Harper, H., translator CLF2
    Variant title: *Le demimonde*
*The Queen of the Camelias. See* La dame aux camellias

DU MAURIER, DAPHNE, 1907–1989
*The Years Between.* 1945. YEAR

DUMB TYPE, 1984–
*S/N.* 1994.
    Poulton, C., translator HACJT2

DUNBAR, PAUL LAURENCE, 1872–1906
*In Dahomey* (lyrics by). 1902. *See* Shipp, Jesse A. *In Dahomey*

DUNBAR-NELSON, ALICE, 1875–1935
*Mine Eyes Have Seen.* 1918. HARY, HARYB, TYEW

DUNCAN, RONALD FREDERICK (b. Ronald Dunkelsbühler), 1914–1982
*The Death of Satan.* 1954. LOR, SATA
*The Gift.* 1968. RICK

DUNCAN, THELMA M., 1902–
*The Death Dance.* 1923. LOC
*Sacrifice.* (1930) RIR, RIRA

DUNGATE, ROD
*Playing by the Rules.* 1992. GAY5

DUNLAP, WILLIAM, 1766–1839
*André.* 1798. COY, HAL, MOSS1, QUIJ, QUIK, QUIL, QUIM, QUIN, RICHE
*Darby's Return.* 1789. AMPA
*False Shame; or, The American Orphan in Germany* (adapted from *Falsche scham* by August Kotzebue). 1799. AMP2
*The Glory of Columbia: Her Yeomanry!* 1803. MONR
*Thirty Years; or, The Gambler's Fate* (adapted from *Trente ans* by Prosper Goubaux and Victor Ducange). 1828. AMP2
*A Trip to Niagara; or, Travellers in America.* 1828. MONR

DUNN, THEO M.
*Maada and Ulka.* 1974? SHAT

DUNNING, PHILIP HART, 1891–1968, and ABBOTT, GEORGE
*Broadway.* 1926. BES26, CART, GASB

DUNSANY, EDWARD JOHN MORETON DRAX PLUNKETT, 18th BARON of, 1878–1957
*The Glittering Gate.* 1909. WATF1, WATI
*The Gods of the Mountain.* 1911. MOSN, MOSO
*If.* 1921. HAU
*King Argimenes and the Unknown Warrior.* 1911. DICDS
*The Lost Silk Hat.* 1921. CHU, PROM, PRON, SCWI
*A Night at an Inn.* 1916. BEAC11, BLAG, BLAH, COOK3, GATS, HUD, PEN, PROB
*The Queen's Enemies.* 1916. AND

DUPUIS, HERVE, 1941–
*Fugues pour un cheval et un piano. See* Return of the Young Hippolytus
*Return of the Young Hippolytus.* 1988.
    Vigneault, J., translator GAYIA
    Variant title: *Fugues pour un cheval et un piano*

DURANG, CHRISTOPHER, 1949–
*The Actor's Nightmare.* 1981. SCVDT
*Baby with the Bathwater.* 1983. PLACF, RIS

*Laughing Wild.* 1987. OSBW (excerpt)
*Marriage of Bette and Boo.* 1985. BES84, WETZ
*Naomi in the Living Room.* 1991. PERZ
*Sister Mary Ignatius Explains It All for You.* 1979.
     PLACHA

DURAS, MARGUERITE, 1914–1996
*Department of Forestry. See* The Rivers and Forests
*Les eaux et forêts. See* The Rivers and Forests
*Hiroshima, mon amour* (screenplay). 1960.
     Seaver, R., translator BAIL, NORGA, NORIB2
*India Song.* 1972.
     Bray, B., translator WOTHB, WOTHM
*The Rivers and Forests.* 1965.
     Brae, B., translator MIJT·
     Variant titles: *Department of Forestry; Les eaux et
        forêts*
*Vera Baxter or The Atlantic Beaches.* 1980.
     Wehle, P., translator WEHLE
     Variant title: *Vera Baxter ou les plages de
        l'Atlantique*
*Vera Baxter ou les plages de l'Atlantique. See* Vera
     Baxter or The Atlantic Beaches

D'URFEY, THOMAS, 1653–1723
*Madam Fickle; or, The Witty False One.* 1677. JEFF2

DURIVAGE, OLIVER E., 1816 or 1817–1861
*The Stage-struck Yankee.* 1840. MES

DURRENMATT, FRIEDRICH. *See* Duerrenmatt, Friedrich

DURRINGER, XAVIER, 1963–
*A Desire to Kill on the Tip of the Tongue.* 1994.
     Ravenhill, M., and Morris, N., translators NEWFPB
     Variant title: *Une envie de tuer sur le bout de la langue*
*Une envie de tuer sur le bout de la langue. See* A Desire
     to Kill on the Tip of the Tongue

DU RYER, PIERRE, 1606–1658
*Esther.* 1642?
     Lockert, L., translator LOCU
*Saul.* 1640. Lockert, L., translator LOCR
*Scaevola.* 1644? Lockert, L., translator LOCR

DU RYNN, SEBASTIN
*Escape from Bondage.* 1987. MONB4

D'USSEAU, ARNAUD, 1916–1990. *See* Gow, James
     Ellis, joint author

DUTT, UTPAL, 1929–1993
*Hunting the Sun.* 1978.
     Dutt, U., translator DESH, KAM3
     Variant titles: *Surya Shikar, Surya-Shikar*

*Surya Shikar. See* Hunting the Sun
*Surya-Shikar. See* Hunting the Sun

DUVAL, ALEXANDRE VINCENT PINEAUX, 1767–
     1842
*La jeunesse de Henri V. See* Payne, John Howard.
     *Charles the Second* (adapted from *Shakespeare
     amoureux; ou, La pièce á l'étude. See* Smith,
     Richard Penn. *Shakespeare in Love* (adapted
     from)

DUVEYRIER, ANNE-HONORE-JOSEPH. *See*
     Melesville, pseudonym

DYER, CHARLES, 1928–
*Rattle of a Simple Man.* 1961. BES62, PLAN26
*Staircase.* 1966. BES67

DYMOV, OSIP (pseudonym of PERLMAN, YOSEF,
     1878–1959)
*Bronks Ekspres. See* Bronx Express
*Bronx Express.* 1919.
     Sandrow, N., translator SANR
     Variant title: *Bronks Ekspres*

E., A., pseud. *See* Russell, George William

EARLE, LYNDA CHANWAI, 1965–
*Ka-shue (Letters Home)* (original story line by Lynda
     Chanwai Earle and James Littlewood). 1997.
     BREK
     Variant title: *Letters Home*
*Letters Home. See* Ka-shue (Letters Home)

EBB, FRED, 1928–2004
*Cabaret* (lyrics by). *See* Masteroff, Joe. *Cabaret*
*Kiss of the Spider Woman* (lyrics by). *See* McNally,
     Terrence. *Kiss of the Spider Woman*

—— and FOSSE, BOB
*Chicago* (music by John Kander, lyrics by Fred Ebb;
     based on the play by Maurine Dallas Watkins).
     1975. BES75

EBERHARD, JOSIE COMPOSTO. *See* Crea, Teresa,
     joint author

EBERHART, RICHARD, 1904–2005
*The Visionary Forms.* 1952. NEWWW3

EBRAHIMI, NADER, 1936–2008
*Blind Expectation.* 1976.
     Bashir-Elahi, R., Bashir-Elahi, S., Ramazani, S., and
     Ali Takim, L., translators GHAN
     Variant title: *Entezar-e kur*

*Entezar-e kur. See* Blind Expectation
*The Essence of Waiting.* 1976.
    Bashir-Elahi, R., Bashir-Elahi, S., Ramazani, S., and
      Ali Takim, L., translators GHAN
    Variant title: *Nafs-e entezar*
*Nafs-e entezar. See* The Essence of Waiting

ECHEGARAY Y EIZAGUIRRE, JOSE, 1832–1916
*La esposa del vengador. See* The Street Singer
*El gran Galeoto.* 1891. BRET
    Bontecou, E., translator CLDM, DICIN2
    Lynch, H., translator FLOS
    Variant titles: *The Great Galeoto; Slander; The World
      and His Wife*
*The Great Galeoto. See* El gran Galeoto
*Slander. See* El gran Galeoto
*The Street Singer.* 1874.
    Underhill, J., translator MACN
    Variant title: *La esposa del vengador*
*The World and His Wife. See* El gran Galeoto

EDGAR, DAVID, 1948–
*The Life & Adventures of Nicholas Nickleby; A Play in
    Two Parts with Five Acts* (adapted from the novel
    by Charles Dickens). 1980. BES81, PLACHB

EDGREN, ANNE CHARLOTTE LEFFLER. *See* Leffler,
    Anne Charlotte

EDITORS OF THE LIVING NEWSPAPERS. *See* Staff of
    the Living Newspaper

EDMONDS, RANDOLPH, 1900–1983
*Bad Man.* 1934. HARY
*Earth and Stars.* 1946. TUQT
*Nat Turner.* 1935. HILEB
*Old Man Pete.* 1934. HARYB

EDMUNDSON, HELEN, 1964–
*The Mill on the Floss* (based on the novel by George
    Eliot). 1994. FRY

EDSON, MARGARET, 1961–
*Wit.* 1995. BES98, PLACG2

EDWARD, H. F. V., 1898–1973
*Job Hunters.* 1931. HARY, HARYB

EDWARDS, GUS, 1939–
*The Offering.* 1977. HAPUE
*Three Fallen Angels.* (1979) CEN

EDWARDS, JODIE, 1907?–1967. *See* Butterbeans, pseud.

EDWARDS, RICHARD, 1523?–1566
*Damon and Pithias.* 1564? ADA

EDWARDS, SHERMAN, 1919–1981
*1776* (music and lyrics by). *See* Stone, Peter H. *1776*

EDWARDS, SUSIE, d. 1963. *See* Susie, pseud.

EFFINGER, MARTA J.
*Union Station.* 1990. FLET

EFOUI, JOSUE KOSSI, 1962–
*Le carrefour. See* The Crossroads
*The Crossroads.* 1988.
    MacDougall, J., translator AFRUBU2
    Variant title: *Le carrefour*

EFOUI, KOSSI. *See* Efoui, Josue Kossi

EGAN, MICHAEL, 1895–1956
*The Dominant Sex.* 1934. FAMG
*To Love and to Cherish.* 1938. FAML

EGLĪTIS, ANSLAVS, 1906–1993
*Ferdinand and Sybil.* 1980.
    Valters, J., translator BRIDGE
    Variant title: *Ferdinands un Sibila*
*Ferdinands un Sibila. See* Ferdinand and Sybil
*Ludzu ienaciet, ser! See* Please Come In, Sir!
*Please Come In, Sir!* 1983.
    Valters, J., translator BRIDGE
    Variant title: *Ludzu ienaciet, ser!*

EHN, ERIK
*Angel uh God.* 1988. MESSE
*Two Altars, Ten Funerals (All Souls).* 1994. MARR

EICHELBAUM, SAMUEL, 1894–1967
*Aaron the Jew.* 1926.
    Glickman, N., and Waldman, G., translators ARGJT
    Variant title: *El judio Aaron*
*Divorcio nupcial.* 1941. ALPE
*El judio Aaron. See* Aaron the Jew

EICHELBERGER, ETHYL, 1945–1990
*Dasvedanya Mama.* 1990. FEFG

EISELE, ROBERT H., 1948–
*Animals Are Passing from Our Lives.* 1973. WES3

EISENSTEIN, LINDA, 1950–
*At the Root.* 1994. ACTOR

EISENSTEIN, MARK
*The Fighter.* 1958. GARZAL

EISENSTEIN, SERGEI, 1898–1948
*Ivan the Terrible: The Screenplay, Part One.* 1944.
    Montagu, I., and Marshall, H., translators WEIP

EIZAGUIRRE, JOSE ECHEGARAY Y. *See* Echegaray y
     Eizaguirre, José

ELDER, LONNE, III, 1931–1996
     *Ceremonies in Dark Old Men.* 1969. BOGA, GARTL,
          HAPUE, HARYB, HAVHA, PATR
     *Charades on East Fourth Street.* 1967. KINH, KINHB

ELIOT, GEORGE, pseudonym. *See* Evans, Mary Ann.

ELIOT, THOMAS STEARNS, 1888–1965
     *Cats* (words by). *See* Lloyd Webber, Andrew. *Cats*
          (based on the book, *Old Possum's Book of
          Practical Cats* by T. S. Eliot)
     *The Cocktail Party.* 1949. BES49, FEFM
     *The Confidential Clerk.* 1954. BES53, THEA54
     *The Family Reunion.* 1939. BRZ
     *Murder in the Cathedral.* 1935. BALL, BROH, BROI,
          COK, CONP, COTQ, CUBH, DEAP, DEAR,
          HAVG, LEVJ, MALI2, TAUJ, TUCO, WARI,
          WATA
     *Old Possum's Book of Practical Cats. See* Lloyd
          Webber, Andrew. *Cats* (based on)
     *Sweeney Agonistes.* 1926. BENS1

ELIZABETH I, QUEEN OF ENGLAND, 1533–1603
     — *See* Seneca, Lucius Annaeus. *Hercules on Oeta*

ELKUNCHWAR, MAHESH, 1939–
     *Old Stone Mansion.* 1985.
          Sanyal, K., translator KAM2
          Variant title: *Wada chireband*
     *Wada chireband. See* Old Stone Mansion

ELLENBOGEN, NICHOLAS, 1948–
     *Horn of Sorrow.* 1986. GRAV

ELLIOTT, SUMNER LOCKE. See Locke-Elliott, Sumner

ELLIS, BOB, 1942– . *See* Boddy, Michael, joint author

ELLIS, GEORGE, 1753–1815. *See* Canning, George,
     joint author

ELLIS, MICAHEL J., 1950s–
     *Chameleon.* 1985. BREW1

ELLSBURY, CHRIS (aka Chiron, Chris), and TERRY,
     JENNIFER
     *Vietnamese Chess.* 1993. VIET

ELSER, FRANK BALL, 1885–1935, and CONNELLY,
     MARCUS COOK
     *The Farmer Takes a Wife. See* Low Bridge
     *Low Bridge.* 1934. BES34, LEV
          Variant title: *The Farmer Takes a Wife*

EMERY, GILBERT, pseud. *See* Pottle, Emery Bemsley

EMIDIA, LYNN
     *The Revelation Game.* 1994. TOR

EMIG, EVELYN (MELLON), 1895–1982
     *The China Pig.* 1920? SHAY

EMOND, PAUL, 1944–
     *Inaccessibles amours. See* Talk about Love
     *Talk about Love.* 1992.
          Miller, R., translator NEWFPL
          Variant title: *Inaccessibles amours*

ENAMAI NO SAYEMON. *See* Enami Sayemon

ENAMI SAYEMON, fl.1400
     *The Cormorant Fisher.* 15th century
          Waley, A., translator TAV, WAJ
          Variant titles: *The Cormorant-fishers; Ukai*
     *The Cormorant-fisher. See* The Cormorant Fisher
     *Ukai. See* The Cormorant Fisher

ENG, ALVIN
     *The Goong Hay Kid.* 1997. ALG

ENGLAND, BARRY, 1934–
     *Conduct Unbecoming.* 1970. BES70

ENNERY, ADOLPHE D'. *See* D'Ennery, Adolphe

ENRICO, ROBERT, 1931–2001
     *On Owl Creek.* 1961. HAVL

ENRIQUEZ DE GUZMAN, FELICIANA, ca. 1580–1640
     *Entreactos de la segunda parte de la tragicomedia los
          jardines y campos sabeos.* 1620s. SOSGA
     *Segunda parte de la tragicomedia los jardines y campos
          sabeos.* 1620s. SOSGA

ENSLER, EVE, 1953?–
     *Floating Rhoda and the Glue Man.* 1994. WOMP93

EPP, STEVEN, and JONES, FELICITY, and SERRAND,
     DOMINIQUE, and WALSH, PAUL
     *Children of Paradise: Shooting a Dream* (based on the
          work of Marcel Carne and Jacques Prevert). 1992.
          BES92

EPSTEIN, MARTIN
     *Autobiography of a Pearl Diver.* 1979. WES5
     *Mysteries of the Bridal Night.* 1982. PLACE
     *Our Witness.* 1990. MEDN
     *3 Variations on the Theme of Pain.* 1983. WES19/20

ERCKMANN-CHATRAIN (pseud. of Erckmann, Emile, 1822–1899, and Chatrain, Alexandre, 1826–1890, collaborators)
*The Polish Jew. See* Lewis, Leopold David. *The Bells* (adapted from *Le julf polonaise* by)

ERVINE, ST. JOHN GREER, 1883–1971
*The First Mrs. Fraser.* 1929. BES29
*Jane Clegg.* 1913. BES19, PLAP1
*John Ferguson.* 1915. BES09, CHA, CHAN, CHAR, DUR, THF, TUCD, TUCM, TUCN, TUCO
*Mixed Marriage.* 1911. DICDS

ESPARZA, LAURA
*I Dismember the Alamo: A Long Poem for Performance.* 1991. ARRIZ

ESSON, LOUIS, 1879–1943
*The Drovers.* (1919) FIO

ESTABROOK, HOWARD, 1884–1978
*The Human Comedy* (screenplay based on the book by William Saroyan). 1943. NAGE

ESTRIN, MARC, 1939–
*An American Playground Sampler.* (1970). NEWA3

ETHEREGE, SIR GEORGE, 1635?–1691
*The Man of Mode; or, Sir Fopling Flutter.* 1675. CLKW, COLR, FIS, GOSA, JEFF1, JENS, KRM, LID, MAND, MANF, MANH, MOR, MOSE1, NET, REIL, REIWE, RES, RESL, REST, SALR, SSSI, SSSIA, SSSIB, STM, TUQ, WILSR, WONR
*She Would If She Could.* 1668. DAVR, JEFF1

ETHERTON, MICHAEL, 1939–
*Houseboy* (dramatic adaptation by). *See* Oyono, Ferdinand, *Houseboy*

ETIENNE, CHARLES GUILLAUME, 1777–1845
*Les deux gendres. See* Payne, John Howard. *The Two Sons-in-law* (adapted from)

EUBA, FEMI, 1941–
*Abiku.* PIET

EURIPIDES, 480?–406? B.C.
*Alcestis.* 438 B.C.
   Aldington, R., translator ALL1, LIND, LOCK, OAT1, OATH
   Browning, R., translator MAST
   Coleridge, E., translator GRDB5
   Fitts, D., and Fitzgerald, R., translators FEL, FIFR, FIFT

   Lattimore, R., translator GRDBA4, GREP3, GREPA3, GRER3, GRERA3, WEAN
   Murray, G., translator CLKW
   Potter, R., translator CLF1
   Way, A., translator GREE, HOWE, HOWF, THOM, THON
   Williams, F., translator CRY
*Andromache.* 431? B.C.
   Coleridge, E., translator GRDB5, OAT1
   Johnson, V., translator FIFV
   LeRue, J., translator COOA
   Lind, L., translator LIND
   Nims, J., translator GRDBA4, GREP3, GREPA3
*The Bacchae.* 405 B.C.
   Anonymous translator ALLK
   Arrowsmith, W., translator GRDBA4, GREPA3, GRER3, GRERA3, TREB, WOTHA
   Bagg, R., translator COTKICG
   Birkhead, H., translator LIND
   Boer, C., translator COOA
   Cacoyannis, M., translator, HOWM
   Cavander, K., translator COTX, SSSI, SSSIA, SSSIB, SSSIC
   Coleridge, E., translator GRDB5
   Curry, N., translator BENSB1
   Doria, C., translator TENN
   Hadas, M., translator TOU
   Kerr, A., translator DOWS
   Lucas, F., translator LUCA, LUCAB, LUCAF
   Milman, H., translator ROBJ, VONS1
   Murray, G., translator HARC8, OAM, OAT2
   Vellacott, M., translator BAIC
   Vellacott, P., translator ALLJ, ALLM, ALLN, BAIE, BAIG, SANE, WEIS, WELT
   Volanakis, M., translator HAPRL
   Variant titles: *The Bacchantes; The Bacchants; The Bakkhai*
   — *See also* Ferguson, Ian. *Ritual 2378* (based on)
*The Bacchantes. See* The Bacchae
*The Bacchants. See* The Bacchae
*The Bakkhai. See* The Bacchae
*The Children of Heracles. See* The Heracleidae
*The Cyclops.* 5th century B.C.
   Arrowsmith, W., translator GRDBA4, GREP3, GREPA3
   Coleridge, E., translator GRDB5, OAT2
   Eeonomou, G., translator TENN
   Green, R., translator RUSV
   Shelley, P., translator PLAG
   Smith, G., translator BAT1
*Electra.* 413? B.C.
   Coleridge, E., translator GRDB5, OAT2
   Murray, G., translator FGP, TEN, TRE, TREA2
   Vellacott, P., translator FOR

Vermeule, E., translator GRDBA4, GREP4,
    GREPA4, GRER2
Way, A., translator WEAV1
*Hecuba.* 425? B.C.
    Arrowsmith, W., translator GRDBA4, GREP3,
        GREPA3
    Coleridge, E., translator GRDB5, OAT1
*Helen.* 412 B.C.
    Coleridge, E., translator GRDB5, OAT2
    Lattimore, R., translator GRDBA4, GREP3, GREPA3
*The Heracleidae.* 431? B.C.
    Coleridge, E., translator GRDB5, OAT1
    Gladstone, R., translator GRDBA4, GREP3,
        GREPA3
    Variant title: *The Children of Heracles*
*Heracles.* 420? B.C.
    Arrowsmith, W., translator GRDBA4, GREP3,
        GREPA
    Coleridge, E., translator GRDB5, OAT
    Variant titles: *Heracles Mad; The Madness of
        Heracles*
*Heracles Mad. See* Heracles
*Hiketides. See* The Suppliants
*Hippolytus.* 428 B.C.
    Coleridge, E., translator GRDB5, OAT1, THP, WARN1
    Greene, D., translator GRDBA4, HOEP, PERR2
    Grene, G., translator FIFT, GREN, GREP3, GREPA3,
        GRER1, GRERA1
    Hadas, M., and McLean, J., translators GRDG
    Lucas, F., translator BARC, LUCA, LUCAB, LUCAF
    Murray, G., translator FGP, HARC8, MIL, MURP,
        OAM
    Vellacott, P., translator GOLH, SANL
    Warner, R., translator NORG, NORI1, VANV1
    Way, A., translator ATT2, HOUS, ROBI
*Ion.* 5th century B.C.
    Coleridge, E., translator GRDB5
    Doolittle, H., translator KRE
    Potter, R., translator OAT1
    Willetts, R., translator GRDBA4, GREP4, GREPA4
*Iphigenia among the Tauri. See* Iphigenia in Tauris
*Iphigenia at Aulis.* 405 B.C.
    Coleridge, E., translator GRDB5
    Lumley, J., translator and adapter PURK
    Potter, R., translator CROS, ROB
    Stawell, F., translator OAT2
    Walker, C., translator GRDBA4, GREP4, GREPA4
    Way, A., translator BUCK, BUCL, BUCM
    Variant title: *Iphigenia in Aulis*
*Iphigenia in Aulis. See* Iphigenia at Aulis
*Iphigenia in Tauris.* 420? B.C.
    Anonymous translator WED
    Bynner, W., translator GRDBA4, GREP3, GREPA3,
        GRER2
    Coleridge, E., translator GRDB5

Murray, G., translator FGP, TEN
Potter, R., translator OAT1, PLAG
    Variant title: *Iphigenia among the Tauri*
*The Madness of Heracles. See* Heracles
*Medea.* 431 B.C.
    Agard, W., translator MALR1
    Anonymous translator EVB1, SSTF
    Coleridge, E., translator EDAD, GRDB5, LOCM1,
        OAT1, OATH
    Gamel, M., translator BARKF
    Hadas, M., and McLean, J., translators GRDG, SSTF
    Jeffers, R., translator and adapter GARW, GATB3,
        KIN, LOR, SANM
    McLeish, K., translator MAMB
    Murray, G., translator FGP, MATT, ROF, SEBO,
        SEBP, SMP, TEN
    Perrier, R., translator and adapter PERR3
    Prokosch, F., translator FIFT, FREG, GOOD,
        GOODE, HILPDH1 TAUJ
    Robinson, CA., translator ROBK
    Roche, P., translator COLD, JACOBA, JACOBD
    Taylor, J., translator TAV
    Townsend, M., translator COTKICG
    Trevelyan, R., translator ROBI
    Vellacott, P., translator ALLO, HAPRL, SANM
    Warner, R., translator FOT, GRDBA4, GREP3,
        GREPA3, MALC, MALG1, MALI1, MALN1,
        NORG1, NORGA, NORI1, NORIA1, NORIB1,
        NORIC1, NORJ1, NORJA, WOMD, WOTHB,
        WOTHC
    Way, A., translator ATT2, BUCL, BUCM, GREE,
        HOWE, HOWF, LAP, PROW, ROBJA
    Wodhull, M., translator DRAD1, EVA1, EVC1, HIB,
        HIBB, MIK7, PLAB1
*Orestes.* 408 B.C.
    Arrowsmith, W., translator GRDBA4, GREP4,
        GREPA4
    Coleridge, E., translator GRDB5, OAT2
    Kirn, H., translator TAUJ
*The Phoenician Maidens. See* The Phoenissae
*The Phoenician Women. See* The Phoenissae
*The Phoenissae.* 413? B.C.
    Coleridge, E., translator GRDB5, OAT2
    Wyckoff, E., translator GRDBA4, GREP4, GREPA4
    Variant titles: *The Phoenician Maidens; The
        Phoenician Women*
*Rhesus.* 5th century B.C.
    Coleridge, E., translator GRDB5
    Lattimore, R., translator GRDBA4, GREP4, GREPA4
    Murray, G., translator OAT2
*The Suppliants.* 424 B.C.
    Coleridge, E., translator GRDB5, OAT1
    Jones, F., translator GRDBA4, GREP4, GREPA4
    Lind, L., translator LIND
    Variant titles: *Hiketides; The Suppliant Women*

*The Suppliant Women. See* The Suppliants
*Troades. See* The Trojan Women
*The Trojan Women.* 415 B.C.
   Coleridge, E., translator GRDB5
   Doria, C., translator COOA
   Hadas, M., and McLean, J., translators GRDG
   Hamilton, E., translator CLL, HAM, MALI1, SCNR,
     VENA
   Lattimore, R., translator FIFT, GRDBA4, GREP3,
     GREPA3, GRER2, TREB, TREC1, TREE1,
     TREI1, WILLG
   Murray, G., translator CARP, CARPA, OAT1, STA
   Potter, R., translator ROBJA
   Raubitschek, I., and A., translators (assisted by A.
     McCabe) ROBJ
   Sartre, J., adapter, and Duncan, R., translator
     WOLCS
   Williams, F., translator CRY
   Variant titles: *Troades; Women of Troy*
*Women of Troy. See* The Trojan Women

EVANS, DON, 1938–2003
*One Monkey Don't Stop No Show.* 1982. BLAC

EVANS, LISA
*Stamping, Shouting, and Singing Home.* 1986. PLABE7

EVANS, MARY ANN (GEORGE ELIOT, pseud.), 1819–
   1880
*The Mill on the Floss. See* Edmundson, Helen. *The Mill
   on the Floss* (based on the novel by)

EVANS, SIAN
*Little Sister.* 1996. NEWWD2

EVELING, STANLEY, 1925–2008
*Mister.* 1970. DEC

EVREINOV, NIKOLAI NIKOLAEVICH, 1879–1953
*The Back Stage of the Soul. See* The Theatre of the Soul
*The Beautiful Despot.* 1906.
   Roberts, C., translator ROE
*Behind the Curtain of the Soul. See* The Theatre of the
   Soul
*Chetvyortaya stena. See* The Fourth Wall
*The Fourth Wall.* (1915)
   Senelick, L., translator RVI
   Variant title: *Chetvyortaya stena*
*A Merry Death, a Harlequinade.* 1914.
   Collins, M., translator COLI
   Roberts, C. ROE
*Styopic and Maznya.*
   Collins, M., translator COLI
*The Theatre of Soul. See* The Theatre of the Soul
*The Theatre of the Soul.* 1912.

Potapenko, M., and St. John, CA., translators DICDT,
   HIB, HIBA
   Variant titles: *The Back Stage of the Soul; Behind the
     Curtain of the Soul; The Theatre of the Soul*

EWING, THOMAS, 1862–1942
*Jonathan.* 1902? KOH2

EXTON, CLIVE, 1930–2007
*Have You Any Dirty Washing, Mother Dear.* 1969.
   PLAN37

EYEN, TOM, 1940–1991
*Grand Tenement and November 22.* SME
*The White Whore and the Bit Player.* 1964. NEWA2

EYMERY, MARGUERITE. *See* Rachilde (pseud.)

FABIEN, MICHELE, 1945–1999
*Claire Lacombe.* 1989.
   Glasheen, A., translator GLASH
*Jocasta.* 1981.
   Miller, R., PLABI1

FAGAN, JAMES BERNARD, 1873–1933
*The Improper Duchess.* 1931. FAMAN, PLAD

FAGON, ALFRED, 1937–1986
*Lonely Cowboy.* 1985. BREW1

FAIRCHILD, WILLIAM, 1918–2000
*The Sound of Murder.* 1959. PLAN20

FALKLAND, SAMUEL. *See* Heijermans, Herman
   (pseud. of)

FALLON, PADRAIC, 1905–1974
*The Vision of MacConglinne.* 1953. OWEC

FANNIN, HILARY, 1962–
*Mackeral Sky.* 1997. BUSHB

FANNON, CECILIA
*Green Icebergs.* 1994. WOMP95

FANTETTI, EUFEMIA, ca. 1969–
*The Last Moon.* 1986. BELLW

FARABOUGH, LAURA, 1949–
*Surface Tension.* 1981. WES11/12

FARAG, ALFRED, 1929–2005
*`Ali Janah al-Tabrizi and His Servant Quffa.* 1968.
   El-Enany, R., and Doria, C., translators JAY
   Variant title: *`Ali Janah al-Tabrizi wa tabi`uhu Quffa*

`Ali Janah al-Tabrizi wa tabi`uhu Quffa. See `Ali Janah al-Tabrizi and His Servant Quffa

FARGEAU, JEAN-POL, 1950–
*Burn River Burn.* 1989.
MacDougall, J., translator THB
Variant title: *Brûle, rivière, brûle*
*Brûle, rivière, brûle. See* Burn River Burn

FARGO, KATE MILLS
*A Voting Demonstration.* 1912. FRIED

FARHOUD, ABLA, 1945–
*Les filles du 5-10-15. See* The Girls from the Five and Ten
*Game of Patience.* 1994.
MacDougall, J., translator PLABI2
Variant title: *Jeux de patience*
*The Girls from the Five and Ten.* 1986.
MacDougall, J., translator PLABI1
Variant title: *Les filles du 5-10-15*
*Jeux de patience. See* Game of Patience

FARIAS, JOANN, 1963–
*Claudia Meets Fulano Colorado.* 1997. PLACGH

FARIGOULE, LOUIS HENRI JEAN. *See* Romains, Jules

FARJEON, ELEANOR, 1881–1965
*The plane-tree.* 1950. OULD

—— and FARJEON, HERBERT
*The Two Bouquets.* 1936. FAMJ

FARJEON, HERBERT, 1887–1945. *See* Farjeon, Eleanor, joint author

FARMILOE, DOROTHY A., 1920–
*What Do You Save from a Burning Building?* ALI

FARQUHAR, GEORGE, 1678–1707
*The Beaux' Stratagem.* 1707. BAT22, BELK2, BLOO, CLF1, CLK1, COLR, GOS, GOSA, GREAAI, HUD, JEFF4, MAND, MANF, MARK, MARL, MATTL, MOR, MOSE2, NET, RES, RESL, REST, ROGEBD, SIG, STM, TAY, TICK, TUP, TUQ, TWE, UHL, WEAT1, WILSR, WONR, WRIR
*The Constant Couple; or, A Trip to the Jubilee.* 1699. BELK15, JEFF4
Variant title: *A Trip to the Jubilee*
*The Inconstant.* 1702. BELK13
*The Recruiting Officer.* 1706. BELK4, FIS, GAYLE4, JEFF4, RUB, WONR, WOTHC
*Sir Harry Wildair.* 1701. BELK15

*A Trip to the Jubilee. See* The Constant Couple; or, A Trip to the Jubilee
*The Twin Rivals.* 1702. BELK17

FARRELL, BERNARD, 1939–
*Then Moses Met Marconi.* 1983. DRUR

FARRELL, GERALDINE
*Beatrice.* 1989. BREK (excerpts)

FASSBINDER, RAINER WERNER, 1946–1982
*Bremen Coffee.* 1971.
Vivis, A., translator SHAK
Variant title: *Bremer Freibeit*
*Bremer Freibeit. See* Bremen Coffee

FATH'ALI, AKHUND-ZADAH, 1812–1878
*The Alchemist.* 186– ?
Le Strange, G., translator BAT3
*The Magistrates.* 186– ?
Wilson, E., translator TUQH

FATH ALI, MIRZA. *See* Fath'-Ali, Akhund-zadah

FAUCHOIS, RENE, 1882–1962
*The Late Christopher Bean.* 1933.
Howard, S., translator and adapter BES32, GARZH, GATS, SPES, WARH
Williams, E., translator and adapter FAMD
Variant titles: *Muse of All Work; Prenez garde à la peinture*
*Muse of All Work. See* The Late Christopher Bean
*Prenez garde a la peinture. See* The Late Christopher Bean

FAULKNER, WILLIAM, 1897–1962. *See* Ford, Ruth, joint author

FECHTER, CHARLES ALBERT, 1824–1879
*Monte Cristo* (based on the novel, *The Count of Monte Cristo*, by Alexandre Dumas, père). 1883. AMP16, CLA, GARX, SAFM

FEELY, TERENCE, 1928–2000
*Don't Let Summer Come.* 1964. PLAN29

FEIFFER, JULES, 1929–
*Crawling Arnold.* 1961. RICJ
*Grown Ups.* 1981. FAMAB
*Knock Knock.* 1976. BES75, PLACD
*Little Murders.* 1966. GARTL, LIEF, LIEG
*The White House Murder Case.* 1970. BES69, GROV

FEINDEL, JANET, 1952–
*A Particular Class of Women.* 1986. ZIMM

FEINSTEIN, ELAINE, 1930– . *See* Women's Theatre
Group, joint author

FELD, MERLE, 1947–
*Across the Jordan.* 1994. COJ

FELDE, KITTY
*Alice.* 1997. INCI

FELDEK, L'UBOMIR, 1936–
*The Rehearsal.* 1988.
Trebatická, H., translator CONTSL5
Variant title: *Skúška*
*Skúška. See* The Rehearsal

FELDER, LOUIS, 1931–
*The Magic Kingdom.* 1998. ELLM

FELDHAUS-WEBER, MARY, 1942–
*The World Tipped Over and Laying on Its Side.* 1966.
BALLE4

FELDMAN, JACK
*Coming Attractions* (music by). *See* Tally, Ted. *Coming
Attractions*

FELDSHUH, DAVID, 1944–
*The Bremen Town Musicians. See* Fables Here and Then
*The Centipede. See* Fables Here and Then
*Fables Here and Then* (music by Roberta Carlson).
1971. (Made up of: *The Wise Man; The Centipede;
How the Snake Lost His Voice; Gassir the Hero;
The Silver Bell; The Shirt Collar; The Suicide; The
Fisherman and the Sea King's Daughter; The Gas
Company; The Indians and Death; The Bremen
Town Musicians*). MIMN
*The Fisherman and the Sea King's Daughter. See* Fables
Here and Then
*The Gas Company. See* Fables Here and Then
*Gassir the Hero. See* Fables Here and Then
*How the Snake Lost His Voice. See* Fables Here and
Then
*The Indians and Death. See* Fables Here and Then
*The Shirt Collar. See* Fables Here and Then
*The Silver Bell. See* Fables Here and Then
*The Suicide. See* Fables Here and Then
*The Wise Man. See* Fables Here and Then

FELICIANO, GLORIA, 1946–
*Between Blessings.* 1996. ALG

FELIPE, CARLOS, 1911–1975
*The Chinaman.* 1947.
Gonzalez-Cruz, L., and Aker, A., translators THRCD
Variant title: *El chino*
*El chino. See* The Chinaman

FENNARIO, DAVID (b. David Wiper), 1947–
*Balconville.* 1979. WASCP, WASCPA2, WASCPB1

FENTON, ELIJAH, 1683–1730
*Marianne.* 1723. BELK14

FENTON, JAMES, 1949–
*Les misérables* (additional material by). *See* Boubil, A.,
and Schönberg, C. *Les misérables*

FERBER, EDNA, 1887–1968. *See* Kaufman, George S.,
joint author

FERDINAND, VAL, 1947– (aka Kalamu Ya Salaam)
*Blk Love Song #1.* 1969. HARY, HARYB
— *See also* SALAAM, KALAMU YA

FERGUSON, IAN, 1937–
*Ritual 2378* (a modern rendering of *The Bacchae* by
Euripides). 1972. CONTSO

FERGUSSON, FRANCIS, 1904–1986
*The King and the Duke* (based on *Huckleberry Finn* by
Samuel Clemens). 1939? BENS2

FERIANCOVA, VANDA, 1965–
*In the Snow.* 2000.
Cockrell, K., translator CONTSL3
Variant title: *V snehu*
*V snehu. See* In the Snow

FERLINGHETTI, LAWRENCE, 1919–
*Our Little Trip.* FREH

FERNAN-GOMEZ, FERNANDO, 1921–2007
*Las bicicletas son para el verano.* 1977. SEIS2
— *See also* Bikes Are for Summer
*Bikes Are for Summer.* 1982.
Hartkemeyer, D., translator OCONNP
Variant title: *Las bicicletas son para el verano*

FERNANDEZ, EVELINA, 1954–
*How Else Am I Supposed to Know I'm Still Alive.* 1989.
PERC

FERNANDEZ DE MORATIN, LEANDRO. *See* Moratín,
Leandro Fernández de

FERNANDEZ ILAGAN, MARILI, 1964–
*Sanctuary. See* Ugpaanan
*Ugpaanan.* 2001. SECO
Variant title: *Sanctuary*

FERRADAS, RENALDO, 1932–
*Birds without Wings.* 1988. CUB

FERRIS, WALTER, 1882–1949
*Death Takes a Holiday* (translator and adapted by). *See* Casella, Alberto. *Death Takes a Holiday*

FETH-ALI, AKHOUD ZAIDE MIRZA. *See* Fath'Ali, Akhundzadah

FEYDEAU, GEORGES LEON JULES MARIE, 1862–1921
*Breakfast in Bed. See* Keep an Eye on Amélie!
*A Fitting Confusion.*
  Shapiro, N., translator CHARN, FLEA
  Variant title: *Tailleur pour dames*
*The Bug in Her Ear. See* A Flea in Her Rear; or, Ants in Her Pants
*A Flea in Her Rear; or, Ants in Her Pants*
  Parsell, S., translator HILPDH6
  Shapiro, N., translator FLEA
  Variant titles: *La puce à l'oreille, The Bug in Her Ear*
*Feu la mère de Madame. See* My Wife's Dead Mother
*Get Out of My Hair.*
  Davies, F., translator LAB
*Going to Pot.*
  Shapiro, N., translator FLEA
  Variant title: *On purge Bébé*
*"Hey, Cut Out the Parading around Stark Naked!"* 1911.
  Bermel, A., translator BERMD
  Variant title: *"Mais n'te promène donc pas toute nue!"*
*Keep an Eye on Amélie!* 1908.
  Duffield, B., translator BENSC
  Variant titles: *Breakfast in Bed; Occupe-toi d'Amélie; Oh, Amelia*
*"Mais n'te promène donc pas toute nue!" See* "Hey, Cut Out the Parading around Stark Naked!"
*My Wife's Dead Mother.* 1908.
  Bermel, A., translator BERMD
  Variant title: *Feu la mère de Madame*
*Occupe-toi d'Amélie. See* Keep an Eye on Amélie
*Oh, Amelia. See* Keep an Eye on Amélie!
*On purge Bébé. See* Going to Pot
*La puce à l'oreille. See* A Flea in Her Rear; or, Ants in Her Pants
*Tailleur pour dames. See* A Fitting Confusion

FIELD, CHARLES KELLOGG, 1873–1948
*The Cave Man.* 1910. BOH2
*The Man in the Forest.* 1902. BOH1
*The Owl and Cave.* 1906. BOH1

FIELD, EDWARD SALISBURY, 1876–1936
*Wedding Bells.* 1919. BES19

FIELD, JOSEPH M., 1810–1856
*Job and His Children.* 1852. AMP14

FIELD, NATHANIEL, 1587–1633
*Amends for Ladies.* 1611. NER
*Woman Is a Weathercock.* 1609. NER

FIELD, RACHEL, 1894–1942
*The Patchwork Quilt.* 193–? COOK2

FIELDING, HENRY (H. Scriblerus Secundus, pseud.), 1707–1754
*The Covent-Garden Tragedy.* 1732. TRUS
*The Historical Register for Year 1736.* 1737. BEVI
*The Intriguing Chambermaid.* 1781. BELC3
*The Life and Death of Tom Thumb the Great. See* The Tragedy of Tragedies; or, The Life and Death of Tom Thumb the Great.
*The Lottery.* 1732. BELC2
*The Miser. See* Molière, Jean Baptiste Poquilin. *The Miser* (translator and adapted by)
*The Mock Doctor.* 1732. (adapted from Moliére's *Le médecin malgré lui*). BELC1
*Tom Thumb. See* The Tragedy of Tragedies; or, The Life and Death of Tom Thumb the Great
*Tom Thumb the Great. See* The Tragedy of Tragedies; or, The Life and Death of Tom Thumb the Great
*The Tragedy of Tragedies; or, The Life and Death of Tom Thumb the Great.* 1731. COLR, EIGH, HAN, LITI, NET, STM, TAT, TAU, TAY, TRUS, TUP, TUQ
*The Virgin Unmasked.* BELC2

FIELDS, JOSEPH, 1895–1966
*The Doughgirls.* 1942. BES42

—— and CHODOROV, JEROME
*Junior Miss* (based on the book by Mrs. Sally Benson). 1941. BES41, GOW, GOWA
*My Sister Eileen* (based on the stories by Ruth McKenney). 1940. BES40
*The Ponder Heart* (adapted from the story by Eudora Welty). 1956. BES55, THEA56
*Wonderful Town* (based on the play *My Sister Eileen*; music by Leonard Bernstein; lyrics by Betty Comden and Adolph Green). 1953. BES52, RICM, THEA53

FIELDS, W. C., 1879–1946
*Stolen Bonds.* 1923. LITID

FIERSTEIN, HARVEY, 1954–
*La cage aux folles* (based on the French play by the same title by Jean Poiret; music and lyrics by Jerry Herman). 1983. BES83
*Forget Him.* 1982. SHEW

*Fugue in a Nursery. See* Torch Song Trilogy
*The International Stud. See* Torch Song Trilogy
*On Tidy Endings.* 1987. ABCG, ABCH, BARIH,
    BARKE, LITRB, LITRC, LITRD
*Safe Sex.* 1987. OSBW
*Torch Song Trilogy.* 1981. (A program of three one-act
    plays: *The International Stud.* 1976; *Fugue in a
    Nursery.* 1979; and *Widows and Children First!*
    1979.) BES81
*Widows and Children First!* 1979. ABCF *See also* Torch
    Song Trilogy

FIGUEROA, JOHN, 1920–1999
*Everybody's a Jew.* 1974. RAVIT

FILIPPO, EDUARDO DE, 1900–1984
*Filumena Marturano.* 1946.
    Bentley, E., translator BENSA, COTN
    Variant title: *A Mother's a Mother*
*A Mother's a Mother. See* Filumena Marturano
*Natale in casa Cupiello. See* The Nativity Scene
*The Nativity Scene.* 1931.
    Molino, A., and Feinber, B., translators TWEI
    Variant title: *Natale in casa Cupiello*

FILO, VERA, 1973–
*Tulip Doctor.* 1999.
    Nadasi, M., translator EUP

FINEBERG, LARRY, 1945–
*Death.* 1972. BRIP, SCNQCA, SCNQCB

FINK, EDITH ROMIG
*Nooschens duhn viel. See* Noshions duhn
*Noshions duhn.* 1950? BUFF
    Variant title: *Nooschens duhn viel*

FINLAY, IAN HAMILTON, 1925–2006
*The Estate Hunters.* 1956. NEWE14
*Walking through Seaweed.* 1962. NEWE14

FINLAY, SUZANNE
*Monkeyshines.* 1984. FOUNC

FINLEY, KAREN, 1956–
*The Constant State of Desire.* 1986. OUT
*The Theory of Total Blame.* 1989. FEFG
*We Keep Our Victims Ready.* 1989. WATTAD

FINN, WILLIAM, 1952–
*March of the Falsettos.* 1981. PLACF
    — *See also* LAPINE, JAMES, joint author

FINNERAN, ALAN
*Renaissance Radar: A Performance Landscape* (music
    by Bob Davis). 1982. WES13/14

FISCHER, LECK, 1904–1956
*The Mystery Tour.* 1949.
    Pearce, J., translator CONT
    Variant title: *Selskabsrejsen*
*Selskabsrejsen. See* The Mystery Tour

FISCHER, MARGARET
*The Gay Divorcee.* 1990. AUSG

FISCHEROVA, DANIELA, 1948–
*Dog and Wolf.* 1979.
    Turner, G, and Turner, A., translators DAY
    Variant title: *Hodina mezi psem a vlkem*
*Hodina mezi psem a vlkem. See* Dog and Wolf

FITCH, CLYDE, 1865–1909
*Barbara Frietchie.* 1899. BES99
*Beau Brummell.* 1890. COH
*Captain Jinks of the Horse Marines.* 1901. BENT4
*The City.* 1909. MONR, MOSJ, MOSK, MOSL,
    WILMET
*The Climbers.* 1901. BES99, COT
*The Girl with the Green Eyes.* 1902. QUIL, QUIM,
    QUIN, SHA2
*Her Great Match.* 1905. QUIJ, QUIJR, QUIK
*The Moth and the Flame.* 1898. MOSS3
*Nathan Hale.* 1898. COOK2, PROF, PROG, PROM,
    SCWE
*A Trip Abroad. See* Labiche, Eugène Marin and Martin,
    Edouard. *Le voyage de Monsieur Perrichon*
*The Truth.* 1907. DICD, GARX, STA

FITCH, WILLIAM CLYDE. *See* Fitch, Clyde

FITZ-BALL, EDWARD. *See* Fitzball, Edward

FITZBALL, EDWARD, 1792–1873
*The Devil's Elixir.* 1829. HOUR
*The Flying Dutchman; or, The Phantom Ship: A
    Nautical Drama.* 1827. HOUR
    Variant title: *The Phantom Ship: A Nautical Drama*
*The Inchape Bell, or the Dumb Sailor Boy.* 1828.
    BOOL
*The Phantom Ship: A Nautical Drama. See* The Flying
    Dutchman

FITZGERALD, CATHERINE, 1962–
*Just a Little Crooked around the Edge.* 1992. AROUN

FITZHUGH, ELLEN
*Herringbone* (lyrics by). *See* Cone, Tom. *Herringbone*

FITZMAURICE, GEORGE, 1877–1963
*The Dandy Dolls.* 1945. CAP
*The Magic Glasses.* 1913. OWEC

FIVE LESBIAN BROTHERS, THE, 1989–
*Brave Smiles . . . another Lesbian Tragedy.* 1992.
ACTOR

FLACKS, DIANE
*By a Thread.* 1993. ZIMM

FLAHERTY, STEPHEN, 1960–
*Once on This Island* (music by). *See* Ahrens, Lynn.
*Once on This Island*
*Ragtime* (music by). *See* McNally, Terrence. *Ragtime*

FLANAGAN, BRENDA A. 1948–
*When the Jumbie Bird Calls.* (1984) NTIR

FLANAGAN, HALLIE, 1890–1969, and CLIFFORD,
MARGARET ELLEN
*Can You Hear Their Voices?* (based on a story by
Whittaker Chambers). 1931. PLAAF

FLANDERS, MICHAEL, 1922–1975
*No* (lyrics by). *See* Heiberg, Johan. No

FLATHER, PATTI
*West Edmonton Mall.* (1997). BREK (excerpt)

—— and LINKLATER, LEONARD, joint author
*Sixty Below.* 1997. BEYO (excerpt), SSSN, WRIT
(excerpt)

FLAUBERT, GUSTAVE, 1821–1880
*La tentation de Saint Antoine. See* The Wooster Group.
Frank Dell's *The Temptation of St. Antony* (based
on the novel by)

FLAVIN, MARTIN, 1883–1967
*Amaco.* 1933. TOD
*The Criminal Code.* 1929. BES29

FLEISSER, MARIELUISE, 1901–1974
*Fegefeuer in Ingolstadt. See* Purgatory in Ingolstadt
*Pioniere in Ingolstadt. See* Pioneers in Ingolstadt
*Pioneers in Ingolstadt.* 1968 version.
Bond-Pablé, E., and Minter, T., translators PLABE9
Variant title: *Pioniere in Ingolstadt*
*Purgatory in Ingolstadt.* 1926.
Bond-Pablé, E., and Minter, T., translators PLABE9
Honegger, G., translator CAS, HERZ
Variant title: *Fegefeuer in Ingolstadt*

FLEMING, Mrs. DOROTHY (SAYERS). *See* Sayers,
Dorothy

FLEMING, JILL W., 1956–
*The Rug of Identity.* 1986. LES1

FLETCHER, JOHN, 1579–1625
*The Chances.* 1616. BELK15, RUB
—— Buckingham, Duke of, adapter PLAN 25
*An Equal Match. See* Rule a Wife and Have a Wife
*The Faithful Shepherdess.* 1609. BAS, GRE, NEI, SCI,
SCJ
*The Island Princess; or, The Generous Portugal.* 1621.
BROC
*Rule a Wife and Have a Wife.* 1624. BELK4, GAYLE3,
SCH, SCI
Variant title: *An Equal Match*
*The Tragedy of Valentinian.* ca.1614. WIGG
*The Wild-goose Chase.* 1609? BENY, DPR2, NEI, SPE,
TAT, TAU, WALL
*The Woman's Prize; or The Tamer Tamed.* 1633. ADAP
— *See also* Beaumont, Francis, joint author

—— and MASSINGER, PHILIP
*The Sea Voyage.* 1622. PARR

—— and MASSINGER, PHILIP [and BEAUMONT,
FRANCIS]
*Beggars' Bush.* 1609. BROC

—— and SHAKESPEARE, WILLIAM
*The Two Noble Kinsmen.* 1613. BRO, PAR, THA

FLETCHER, JOHN
*Babylon Has Fallen* (radio drama). 1983. PLACK

FLETCHER, LUCILLE, 1912–2000
*The Hitch Hiker.* 1942. SCVDO1
*Sorry, Wrong Number.* 1948. BOOK, HEIS, READ2
(original radio script), WHF

FLISAR, EVALD, 1945–
*Final Innocence.* 1996.
Flisar, E., translator PRED
*Tomorrow.* 1992.
Anonymous translator PRED (summary only)
*What about Leonardo?* 1992.
Anonymous translator PRED (summary only)

FO, DARIO, 1926– . *See* Rame, Franca, joint author

FONG, OTTO
*Cetecea.* 1993. DIRTY

FONSON, FRANTZ, 1870–1924, and WICHELER,
FERNAND
*Le marriage de Mlle Beulemans. See* Miss Bullberg's
Marriage
*Miss Bullberg's Marriage.* 1910.
Willinger, D., translator WILL
Variant title: *Le marriage de Mlle Beulemans*

FONTAINE, ROBERT LOUIS
   *The Happy Time. See* Taylor, Samuel. *The Happy Time*
     (based on the novel by)

FONVIZIN, DINIS IVANOVICH, 1744–1792
   *The Choice of a Tutor.* 1792.
     Roberts, C., translator ROE
   *The Infant.*
     Cooper, J., translator COOPA
   *The Minor.* 1782.
     Reeve, F., translator REEV1
   *The Young Hopeful.* 1782.
     Patrick, G., and Noyes, G., translators NOY

FOOTE, HORTON, 1916–2009
   *The Dancers* (television play). 1954. SCVDO1,
     WAGC2
   *The Trip to Bountiful.* 1953. TEX
   *The Widow Claire.* 1986. BERT, BES86
   *A Young Lady of Property.* 1976. SCVDT1
   *The Young Man from Atlanta.* 1995. BES94

FOOTE, SAMUEL, 1720–1777
   *The Author.* (1757). BELC3
   *The Commissary.* 1765. BELC4, BEVI
   *The Englishman in Paris.* 1753. BELC3
   *The Englishman Return'd from Paris.* (1756) BELC3
   *The Knights.* 1747? BELC1
   *The Liar. See* The Lyar
   *The Lyar.* 1762. BELC2
     Variant title: *The Liar*
   *The Mayor of Garratt.* 1763. BELC2, MOR
   *The Minor.* 1760. BELG15
   *The Orators.* 1762. BELC4
   *The Patron.* 1764. BELC4
   *Taste.* 1752. BELC1

FORBES, JAMES, 1871–1938
   *The Famous Mrs. Fair.* 1919. BES19, MOSJ, MOSK,
     MOSL

FORBES, KATHRYN, 1909–1966
   *Mama's Bank Account. See* Van Druten, John. *I
     Remember Mama* (based on the book by)

FORD, CHARLES, 1932–
   *Wall to Wall.* 1990. KEEP

FORD, DAVID
   *Rush Limbaugh in Night School* (developed with). *See*
     Varon, Charlie. *Rush Limbaugh in Night School*

FORD, FRANK B., 1932–
   *Waterman.* 1976. GUTR

FORD, HARRIET, 1868–1949
   *Youth Must Be Served.* 1926? TOD

FORD, JOHN, 1586–1640?
   *The Broken Heart.* 1629? BALD, BAS, BROC,
     HAPRA2, HAPRB2, NEI, OLH, OLI2, ORNT,
     SCI, SCJ, SPE, WINE
   *The Chronicle History of Perkin Warbeck.* 1633?
     ARMS, BAS, DPR2, LAWT, SCH
     Variant title: *Perkin Warbeck Perkin Warbeck. See*
     The Chronicle History of Perkin Warbeck
   *'Tis a Pity She's a Whore.* 1633. BECK, BENY, DPR2,
     DUN, GIBS, HUST, KINNR, MAKJ, PAR, RUB,
     RYL, WALL

—— DEKKER, THOMAS and ROWLEY, WILLIAM
   *The Witch of Edmonton.* 1621. BAS, COQJW, KAYS,
     LAWS

FORD, MAGGIE. *See* Ditton, Cordelia, joint author

FORD, RUTH, 1911–2009, and FAULKNER, WILLIAM
   *Requiem for a Nun* (adapted from the novel by William
     Faulkner). 1956? BES58

FORDE, NIGEL, 1944–
   *A Winter's Tale: A Christmas Play for Children.* 1979.
     BURB

FOREMAN, FARRELL J.
   *The Ballad of Charlie Sweetlegs Vine.* 1978. FLET (one
     scene only)
   *Daddy's Seashore Blues.* (1979) CEN

FOREMAN, RICHARD, 1937–
   *The Mind King.* 1992. MARR
   *Pandering to the Masses: A Misrepresentation.* 1975.
     THG, THGA
   *Rhoda in Potatoland.* 1975. MESSE

FOREST, LOUIS, 1872–1933
   *Par un jour de pluie.* 192– ? SET

FORESTER, CECIL SCOTT, 1899–1966
   *Payment Deferred. See* Dell, Jeffrey. *Payment Deferred*
     (based on the novel by)

FORNÉS, MARÍA IRENE, 1930–
   *Abingdon Square.* 1987. MESSE, MIHWW, WOLCS
   *And What of the Night? See* What of the Night?
   *Cold Air* (translated and adapted by). *See* Piñera,
     Virgilio. *Cold Air*
   *The Conduct of Life.* 1985. BARN, BARNA, JACOBD,
     OSB, VENA, WOTHM
   *The Danube.* 1982. PLACE, WETZ

*Dr. Kheal.* 1968. GWYN, SMC
*Enter the Night.* 1993. MARR
*Fefu and Her Friends.* 1977. GILB, WOQ1, SSSIB, WOTHB
*Mud.* 1983. WOTHA
*Oscar and Bertha.* 1989. MEDN
*Promenade* (music by Al Carmines). 1965. GREAAR
*Springtime.* 1993. CURB
*The Successful Life of Three.* 1965. BALLE2, ORZ
*Tango Palace.* 1961. BALLE2
*A Vietnamese Wedding.* 1967. LITID
*What of the Night?* 1989. LAMO
   Variant title: *And What of the Night?*

FORREST, GEORGE, 1915–1999
*Grand Hotel* (songs by). *See* Davis, Luther. *Grand Hotel*

FORSSELL, LARS, 1928–2007
*Galenpannan. See* The Madcap
*The Madcap.* (1964)
   Carlson, H., translator MNOS
   Variant title: *Galenpannan*
*Söndags promenader. See* The Sunday Promenade
*The Sunday Promenade.* (1963)
   Carlson, H., translator COTT
   Variant title: *Söndags promenader*

FORSYTH, JAMES, 1913–2004
*Héloise.* 1931. COTK

FORTUNE, MRS. JAN ISABELLE, 1892–1979
*The Cavalier from France.* 194– ? PROG

FOSSE, BOB, 1927–1987
*Fosse* (choreography by). *See* Maltby, Richard, Jr. *Fosse*
   — *See also* Ebb, Fred, joint author

FOSSE, ROBERT LOUIS. *See* Fosse, Bob

FOSTER, CHARLES, 1833–1895
*Bertha, the Sewing Machine Girl, or Death at the Wheel.* 1871. MESCO

FOSTER, PAUL, 1931–
*Balls.* 1964. ORZ
*Tom Paine.* 1967. GARTL

FOSTER, RICK
*The Heroes of Xochiquipa.* 1983. WES19/20

FOUCHER, MICHELE, 1941–
*La table: parole des femmes. See* The Table: Womenspeak

*The Table: Womenspeak.* 1977.
   Makward, C., and Miller, J., translators PLAAG
   Variant title: *La table: parole des femmes*

FOURIE, CHARLES J., 1965–
*Big Boys.* 1989. KANI

FOURIE, TONY
*One Night.* 2000. ZEE2

FOX, ELLEN, 1954–
*Ladies in Waiting.* 1981. PLACK

FOX, STEPHEN
*Never Come Monday. See* Knight, Erica. *Never Come Monday* (adapted by)

FOWLE, WILLIAM BENTLEY, 1795–1865
*Woman's Rights.* 1856. FRIED

FRAGUADA, FEDERICO, 1952–
*Bodega.* 1986. ANTUR, SWANS

FRAME, VIRGINIA. *See* Church, Mrs. Virginia Woodson (Frame)

FRANCE, ANATOLE, 1844–1924
*La comédie de celui qui épousa une femme muette.* 1913. SET
   Jackson, W., and E., translators SMR
   Page, C., translator KAYF, LEV, LEVE
   Variant title: *The Man Who Married a Dumb Wife*
*The Man Who Married a Dumb Wife. See* La comédie de celui qui épousa une femme muette

FRANCIS, ANN, 1738–1800
*The Song of Songs which Is Solomon's.* 1781? KOH2

FRANCIS, MARVIN, 1955–2005
*The Sniffer.* 1996. BEYO

FRANCIS, WILLIAM, 1922–
*Portrait of a Queen.* 1965. PLAN30

FRANCKLIN, THOMAS, 1721–1784
*Earl of Warwick.* 1766. BELG16
*Matilda.* 1775. INCA8

FRANK, ANNE, 1929–1945
*Diary of a Young Girl.* See Goodrich, Frances, and Hackett, Albert. *The Diary of Anne Frank* (based on the book by)

FRANK, FLORENCE KIPER, 1885?–1976
*Cinderelline.* 1913. FRIED

FRANK, MAUDE MORRISON, 1870–1956
*A Mistake at the Manor.* 1915? WEB

FRANK, MIGUEL, 1920–1994
*El hombre del siglo. See* The Man of the Century
*The Man of the Century.* 1958.
Jones, W., translator JONW
Variant title: *El hombre del siglo*

FRANK, WALDO DAVID, 1889–1967
*New Year's Eve.* 1928? AME2

FRANKEN, MRS. ROSE (D. Lewin), 1898–1988
*Another Language.* 1932. BES31
*Claudia.* 1940. BES40, CALN1
*Outrageous Fortune.* 1943. BES43
*Soldier's Wife.* 1944. BES44

FRANKLIN, J.e., 1937–
*Christchild.* 1984. WOMP93
*Miss Honey's Young'uns.* 1989. TUQTR
*Two Mens'es Daughter.* 1990. PERZ

FRANKLIN, JENNIE ELIZABETH, 1937– . *See*
Franklin, J.e.

FRANKLIN, MILES, 1879–1954 (born Stella Maria Sarah
Miles Franklin)
*No Family.* 1946. PFIS

FRANKLIN, THOMAS. *See* Francklin, Thomas

FRATTI, MARIO, 1927–
*The Academy* (1962)
Rosenthal, R., translator COTN, RICJ
Variant title: *L'accademia*
*L'accademia. See* The Academy
*The Bridge.* 1969.
Anonymous translator DIS
Variant title: *Il ponte*
*The Cage* (1961)
Carra, M., and Warner, L., translators COTS
Variant title: *La gabbia*
*La gabbia. See* The Cage
*Nine* (adapted from the Italian by). *See* Kopit, Arthur
Lee. *Nine*
*Il ponte. See* The Bridge
*The Return.* (1960)
Corrigan, R., and Fratti, M., translators COTN
Variant title: *Il ritorno*
*Il ritorno. See* The Return
*The Suicide* (1959)
Carra, M., and Warner, L., translators COTS
Variant title: *Il suicidio*

*Il suicidio. See* The Suicide
Victim. 1968. KAYS

FRAYN, MICHAEL, 1933–
*Benefactors.* BES85
*Copenhagen.* 1998. BES99
*Noises Off.* 1982. BES83
*Wild Honey.* 1984. BES86

FRECHETTE, LOUIS-HONORE, 1839–1908
*Félix Poutré.* 1862.
Doucette, L.E., translator DOUC

FREDERICKS, CLAUDE, 1923–
*A Summer Ghost.* 1961. NEWA1

FREED, AMY, 1958–
*Freedomland.* 1997. PLACG2
*The Psychic Life of Savages.* 1995. PLACJ

FREED, DONALD, 1932–
*Child of Luck.* 1988–89. PRIMA88
*Circe & Bravo.* 1986. PRIMA86
*Inquest.* 1970. FAV
*Veteran's Day.* 1987. PRIMA87

—— and STONE, ARNOLD M.
*Secret Honor: The Last Testament of Richard M. Nixon;
a Political Myth.* 1983. NEWQA

FREEMAN, BRIAN
*Factwino Meets the Moral Majority* (script by). *See* San
Francisco Mime Troupe. *Factwino Meets the Moral
Majority*

FREEMAN, CAROL, 1941–
*The Suicide.* (1968) JON

FREEMAN, DAVID E., 1945–
*Creeps.* 1971. BES73, PENG, WASCP, WASCPA1
*Jesse and the Bandit Queen.* 1975. BES75

FREEMAN, ELEANOR, 1852–1930
*When the Women Vote.* 1885. FRIED

FREEMAN, SANDRA
*Supporting Roles.* 1988. LES2

FREISTADT, BERTA, 1942–2009
*The Celebration of Kokura.* 1970. LOWE

FRENCH, DAVID, 1939–
*Jitters.* 1979. WASCP
*Leaving Home.* 1972. STOTD, STOTLA, STOTLB,
WASCPA1, WASCPB1

*Of the Fields, Lately.* 1973. PENG, PERKY
*Salt-water Moon.* 1984. BELLW
*The Tender Branch* (television play). BELLW

FRERE, JOHN HOOKHAM, 1769–1846. *See* Canning,
     George, joint author

FREYTAG, GUSTAV, 1816–1895
     *The Journalists.* 1853?
          Henderson, E., translator FRA12
          Variant title: *Die journalisten*
     *Die journalisten. See* The Journalists

FRIDELL, FOLKE, 1904–1985
     *Denandresbröd. See* One Man's Bread
     *One Man's Bread.* (1961)
          Austin, P., translator MNOS
          Variant title: *Denandresbröd*

FRIEDMAN, BRUCE JAY, 1930–
     *Scuba Duba.* 1967. BES67, GARTL
     *Steambath.* 1970. ABCE, ABCF, BES70

FRIEDMAN, EVE, 1929– . *See* Singer, Isaac Bashevis,
     joint author

FRIEL, BRIAN, 1929–
     *Aristocrats.* 1989. BES88
     *Dancing at Lughnasa.* 1991. BES91, JACOBA
     *Lovers.* 1968. BES68
     *Molly Sweeney.* 1994. BES95, MEYF (excerpt)
     *Philadelphia, Here I Come!* BES65, RICIS
     *Translations.* 1980. BES80, OWEC, SSSIC, WOTHA,
          WOTHB, WOTHC, WOTHM

FRIESEN, PATRICK, 1946–
     *The Shunning.* 1987. NEWWUX

FRINGS, KETTI (HARTLEY), 1916–1981
     *Look Homeward, Angel* (based on the novel by Thomas
          Wolfe). 1957. BES57, GARSA, GATB4, WATA

FRISBY, TERENCE, 1932–
     *There's a Girl in My Soup.* 1966. PLAN32

FRISCH, MAX, 1911–1991
     *Andorra.* 1961.
          Bullock, M., translator BES62
     *Biedermann and the Firebugs.* 1958.
          Gorelik, M., translator and adapter BLOC, BLOND,
               JOHO, KNIF, KNIG, KNO, RICJ, STY
          Variant titles: *Biedermann und die brandstifter; The
               Fire Raisers; The Firebugs*
     *Biedermann und die brandstifter. See* Biedermann and
          the Firebugs

*The Chinese Wall.* 1946.
     Rosenberg, J., translator COTQ
     Variant title: *Die chinesisehe Mauer*
*Die chinesisehe Mauer. See* The Chinese Wall
*The Fire Raisers. See* Biedermann and the Firebugs
*The Firebugs. See* Biedermann and the Firebugs
*The Great Fury of Philip Hotz.* 1958.
     Benedikt, M., translator BENB
     Variant titles: *The Great Rage of Philip Hotz; Die
          grosse Wut des Philipp Hotz; Philip Hotz's Fury*
*The Great Rage of Philip Hotz. See* The Great Fury of
     Philip Hotz
*Die grosse Wut des Philipp Hotz. See* The Great Fury of
     Philip Hotz
*Philip Hotz's Fury. See* The Great Fury of Philip Hotz

FROLOV, DIANE, and SCHNEIDER, ANDREW
     *"Get Real"* (excerpt from *Northern Exposure* episode).
          1991. MEYC, MEYD, MEYE

FROST, REX, 1914–
     *Small Hotel.* 1955. PLAN13

FROST, ROBERT, 1875–1963
     *A Masque of Reason.* 1945. KNID

FRUET, WILLIAM, 1933–
     *Wedding in White.* 1970. KAL2, PENG

FRUMIN, SUE, 1949–
     *The Housetrample.* 1984. LES2

FRY, CHRISTOPHER, 1907–2005
     *The Boy with a Cart.* 1938. POOL
     *The Dark Is Light Enough.* 1954. BES54
     *Duel of Angels. See* Giraudoux, Jean. *Duel of Angels*
          (adapted by)
     *A Phoenix Too Frequent.* 1946. BAC, BLAH, BRZ,
          FEFL, WARI, WARL
     *A Sleep of Prisoners.* 1951. COTQ
     *Tiger at the Gates. See* Giraudoux, Jean. *Tiger at the
          Gates* (translator and adapted by)
     *Venus Observed.* 1950. BES51, HAVG, WATE

FRY, MICHAEL
     *Emma* (based on the novel by Jane Austen). 1990. FRY

FU, TO. *See* Sha, Seh, joint author

FUENTES, CARLOS, 1928–
     *Orchids in the Moonlight.* 1982. LATIN, WOOGLA

FUERSTENBERG, ANNA, 1948–
     *Why I Sleep Alone* (excerpt from a play in progress titled
          *The Outlet*). 1997. BREK

FUGARD, ATHOL, 1932–
*The Blood Knot.* 1960. NEWE13, WELT
*Boesman and Lena.* 1970. BES70
*The Drummer.* 1980. SCVDO1
*A Lesson from Aloes.* 1980. BES80
*"Master Harold" . . . and the Boys.* 1982. ABCE,
    ABCG, BARKC, BARKE, BARKD, BARKF,
    BES81, BOGA, GILB, HEAC, JACOB, JACOBA,
    JACOBD, JACOBE, KIRLA, KIRLB, KIRLC,
    SSSIA, SSSIB, SSSIC, STOTD, STOTLA,
    STOTLB
*My Children! My Africa!* 1989. BES89, SCVDT1
*Orestes.* 1971. GRAYTO
*The Road to Mecca.* 1984. BES87, HOWM, SCX
*Valley Song.* 1995. BES95, WOTHC

———— and KANI, JOHN; and NTSHONA, WINSTON
*The Island.* 1974. BES74, WOTHM
*Sizwe Bansi Is Dead.* 1972. ALLN, ALLO, WOTHA

FUJITA, DEN, 1932–
*The Amida Black Chant Murder Mystery.* 1971.
    Swain, J., translator HACJT5
    Variant title: *Kuronembutsu satsujin jiken*
*Kuronembutsu satsujin jiken. See* The Amida Black
    Chant Murder Mystery

FUKUDA, TSUNEARI, 1912–1994
*Kenrui dasshu. See* The Siege
*The Siege.* 1950.
    Ingulsrud, L., translator HACJT8
    Variant title: *Kenrui dasshu*

FUKUDA, YOSHIYUKI, 1931–
*Find Hakamadare!* 1964
    Goodman, D., translator JAPDC
    Variant title: *Hakamadare wa doko da*
*Hakamadare wa doko da. See* Find Hakamadare!
*Oppekepe.* 1963.
    Gallimore, D., translator HACJT7

FULDA, LUDWIG, 1862–1939
*Beneath Four Eyes. See* Tête-à-tête
*By Ourselves. See* Tête-à-tête
*Tête-à-tête.* 1886.
    Townsend, E., translator FRA17
    Variant titles: *Beneath Four Eyes; By Ourselves;*
      *Unter vier augen*
*Unter vier augen. See* Tête-a-tête

FULLER, CHARLES, 1939–
*A Soldier's Play.* 1981. BAIK, BES81, HAPUE,
    HARYB, HOWM, MEY, TUQTR, WIEG
*Zooman and the Sign.* 1980. BES80, HAPU

FULLER, ELIZABETH. *See* Bishop, Conrad, joint author

FULLER, HENRY BLAKE, 1857–1929
*At Saint Judas's.* 1896. SELOV

FULLER, WILLIAM HENRY, 1836–1902
*H.M.S. Parliament; or, The Lady Who Loved a*
    *Government Clerk.* 1880. WAGN1

FULWELL, ULPIAN, 1530?–1585?
*Like Will to Like; an enterlude intituled Like wil to like*
    *quod the Deuel to the Colier. . . .* 1568. HAO,
    SOME

FUNT, JULIAN, 1907?–1980
*Child of Grace. See* The Magic and the Loss
*The Magic and the Loss.* 1954. BES53
    Variant title: *Child of Grace*

FURTH, GEORGE, 1932–2008
*Company* (music and lyrics by Stephen Sondheim).
    1970. BES69, RICO

FUSCO, COCO, 1960– , and BUSTAMANTE, NAO
*Stuff.* 1996. SVICH

FYFFE, LAURIE
*The Goldern Horn* (excerpt). 1996. BREK

FYLES, FRANKLIN, 1847–1911. *See* Belasco, David,
    joint author

GAGE, CAROLYN
*Amazon All-Stars* (book and lyrics by Carolyn Gage;
    music by Sue Carney). 1990. CURB

GAGE, NANCY
*Death Row Wedding.* 1985. JOND

GAGLIANO, FRANK, 1931–
*Father Uxbridge Wants to Marry.* 1967. LAH

GAINES, FREDERICK
*The New Chautauqua.* 1968. BALLE5

GAINES, J. E., 1928–
*What If It Had Turned Up Heads.* 1972. NEWL

GAINES-SHELTON, RUTH, 1872–1938
*The Church Fight.* 1925. HARY, HARYB

GALA, ANTONIO, 1936–
*The Green Fields of Eden.* 1963.
    O'Connor, P., translator OCONNC
    Variant title: *Los verdes campos del Eden*

*Los verdes campos del Eden. See* The Green Fields of Eden

GALANTIERE, LEWIS, 1895–1977
  *Antigone. See* Anouilh, Jean. *Antigone* (adapted by)

GALATI, FRANK, 1943–
  *The Grapes of Wrath* (based on the novel by John Steinbeck). 1988. BES89

GALBRAITH, ROBERT. *See* Thury, Fred, joint author

GAŁCZYŃSKI, KONSTANTY ILDEFONS, 1905–1953
  *The Atrocious Uncle.* 1946.
    Gerould, D., and Gerould, E., translators TWEN
  *A Bloody Drama in Three Acts with Vinegar Taken from Life in the Upper Reaches of Academic High Society Entitled "Pickled Alive."* 1947.
    Gerould, D., and Gerould, E., translators TWEN
    Variant title: *Pickled Alive*
  *The Burial of a War Criminal.* 1946.
    Gerould, D., and Gerould, E., translators TWEN
  *Crushed by the Credenza. See* The Drama of a Deceived Husband; or, Crushed by the Credenza
  *The Drama of a Deceived Husband; or, Crushed by the Credenza.* 1949.
    Gerould, D., and Gerould, E., translators TWEN
    Variant title: *Crushed by the Credenza*
  *The End of the World.* 1947.
    Gerould, D., and Gerould, E., translators TWEN
  *Family Happiness; or, Watch Out for Expletives (a Meteorological Drama).* 1947.
    Gerould, D., and Gerould, E., translators TWEN
    Variant title: *Watch Out for Expletives*
  *The Flood that Failed in Winter.* 1947.
    Gerould, D., and Gerould, E., translators TWEN
  *The Frightful Effects of an Illegal Operation. See* In the Clutches of Caffeine; or, The Frightful Effects of an Illegal Operation
  *Greedy Eve.* 1946.
    Gerould, D., and Gerould, E., translators TWEN
  *The Green Goose.*
    Gerould, D., and Gerould, E., translators TWEN
    Variant titles: *Twenty-two Short Plays from The Little Theatre of the Green Goose: A Salvation Army Concert; The Drama of a Deceived Husband; or, Crushed by the Credenza; The Atrocious Uncle; A Bloody Drama in Three Acts with Vinegar Taken from Life in the Upper Reaches of High Society Entitled "Pickled Alive"; The Peculiar Waiter; The Burial of a War Criminal; Judith and Holofernes (Act III of an Opera Called); When Orpheus Played; The Flood that Failed in Winter; In the Clutches of Caffeine; or, The Frightful Effects of an Illegal Operation; Miracle in the Desert; The Poet*

*Is in Bad Form (a Ballet Called); Hamlet and the Waitress (a Play about the Life of the Intellectual Elite Entitled); He Couldn't Wait It Out (a Polish Drama of the so-called "Ponderous" Variety Entitled); The Tragic End of Mythology (Its Author Wielding a Terrible Pen); Principles of the Relay Cure; or, The so-called "Transfer Therapy"; The Seven Sleeping Brothers; Greedy Eve; Rain; Lord Hamilton's Night; Family Happiness; or, Watch Out for Expletives (a Meteorological Drama); The End of the World*
  *Hamlet and the Waitress (a Play about the Life of the Intellectual Elite Entitled).* 1948.
    Gerould, D., and Gerould, E., translators TWEN
  *He Couldn't Wait It Out (a Polish Drama of the So-called "Ponderous" Variety Entitled).* 1947.
    Gerould, D., and Gerould, E., translators TWEN
  *In the Clutches of Caffeine; or, The Frightful Effects of an Illegal Operation.* 1946.
    Gerould, D., and Gerould, E., translators TWEN
    Variant title: *The Frightful Effects of an Illegal Operation*
  *Judith and Holofernes (Act III of an Opera Called).* 1947.
    Gerould, D., and Gerould, E., translators TWEN
  *Lord Hamilton's Night.* 1947.
    Gerould, D., and Gerould, E., translators TWEN
  *Miracle in the Desert.* 1947.
    Gerould, D., and Gerould, E., translators TWEN
  *The Peculiar Waiter.* 1946.
    Gerould, D., and Gerould, E., translators TWEN
  *Pickled Alive. See* A Bloody Drama in Three Acts with Vinegar Taken from Life in the Upper Reaches of Academic High Society Entitled "Pickled Alive"
  *The Poet is in Bad Form (a Ballet Called).* 1950.
    Gerould, D., and Gerould, E., translators TWEN
  *Principles of the Relay Cure; or, The So-called "Transfer Therapy."* 1947.
    Gerould, D., and Gerould, E., translators TWEN
    Variant title: *The So-called "Transfer Therapy"*
  *Rain.* 1949.
    Gerould, D., and Gerould, E., translators TWEN
  *A Salvation Army Concert.* 1946.
    Gerould, D., and Gerould, E., translators TWEN
  *The Seven Sleeping Brothers.* 1946.
    Gerould, D., and Gerould, E., translators TWEN
  *The So-called "Transfer Therapy." See* Principles of the Relay Cure; or, The So-called "Transfer Therapy"
  *The Tragic End of Mythology (Its Author Wielding a Terrible Pen).* 1949.
    Gerould, D., and Gerould, E., translators TWEN
  *Watch Out for Expletives. See* Family Happiness; or, Watch Out for Expletives (a Meteorological Drama)
  *When Orpheus Played.* 1949.
    Gerould, D., and Gerould, E., translators TWEN

GALDOS, BENITO PEREZ. *See* Pérez Galdós, Benito

GALE, LORENA, 1958–
*Angelique*. 1995. BEYO (excerpt), SEARS2
*Je me souviens*. 1997. BREK (excerpt)

GALE, ZONA, 1874–1938
*Miss Lulu Bett*. 1920. CORD, CORE, CORF, PLAAD,
    PLAAE

GALIN, ALEXANDER
*Stars in the Morning Sky*. 1988.
    Glenny, M., and Porter, C., translators SSTX

GALJOUR, ANNE
*Hurricane*. 1993. BES93

GALLAGHER, JODI
*Elegy*. 2000. INSI

GALLAGHER, KATHLEEN, 1957–

—— and RIPPINGALE, GEN
*Banshee Reel*. 1989. GALL
*Offspring*. 1988. GALL

—— and WINSTANLEY, KATE
*Jacaranda*. 1991. GALL
*Mothertongue*. 1986. GALL

GALLAGHER, MARY, 1947–
*Bedtime*. 1984. PLACA
*Windshook*. 1992. WOMP92

GALLAIRE, FATIMA, 1944–
*Ah! Vous êtes venus-là où il y a quelques tombes*. *See*
    You Have Come Back
*Madame Bertin's Testimony*. 1987.
    MacDougall, J., translator MOGS
    Variant title: *Témoignage contre un homme sterile*
*Témoignage contre un homme sterile*. *See* Madame
    Bertin's Testimony
*You Have Come Back*. 1986.
    MacDougall, J., translator PLABI1, PLABI3
    Variant title: *Ah! Vous êtes venus-là où il y a quelques
    tombes*

GALLAIRE-BOUREGA, FATIMA. *See* Gallaire, Fatima

GALLARATI-SCOTTI, TOMMASO, 1878–1966
*Cosi sia*. *See* Thy Will Be Done
*Thy Will Be Done*. 1923.
    Petri, V., translator SAY
    Variant title: *Cosi sia*

GALLICO, PAUL, 1897–1976
*The Snow Goose* (adapted for radio by William A. Bacher
    and Malcolm Meacham). 195– ? INGA, INGB

GALLOWAY, TERRY, 1950–
*Heart of a Dog*. 1983. WOMS2

GALSWORTHY, JOHN, 1867–1933
*Escape*. 1926. BES27, TRE, TREA1, TREBA, TREC2,
    TREE3, TREI3
*Justice*. 1910. BROW, HAU, HAVD, HAVE, ROWC,
    WATF1, WATI, WATO, WATR
*Loyalties*. 1922. ANDE, BES22, BROX, CEU,
    COTKIT, COTKR, LEWI, PEN, SNYD2, SPER,
    WARI, WATF2, WATI
*The Pigeon*. 1912. HARB
*The Silver Box*. 1906. CHAR, CLKW, COTH, CROS,
    MOSN, MOSO, SALE, STAT, TOD
*The Skin Game*. 1920. BES20
*Strife*. 1909. DICD, DUR, INGE, INGG, MACB,
    MACC, MACE, MACF, MART, STEI, WATS,
    WHI, WHK, WOO2

GAMBARO, GRISELDA, 1928–
*El campo*. *See* The Camp
*The Camp*. 1967.
    Oliver, W., translator OLIW
    Variant title: *El campo*
*Decir sí*. *See* Saying Yes
*Información para extranjeros*. *See* Information for
    Foreigners
*Information for Foreigners*. 1973.
    Feitlowitz, M., translator WOTHC, WOTHM
    Variant title: *Información para extranjeros*
*Los siameses*. 1967. DAU
*Saying Yes*. 1981.
    Doggert, S., translator LATIN
    Variant title: *Decir sí*

GAMEL, FRED, 1944–
*Wasted*. 1984. BES83

GANGSTER CHOIR, THE
*Tenement Lover: No Palm Trees/in New York City*
    (music by). *See* Hagedorn, Jessica. *Tenement
    Lover: No Palm Trees/in New York City*

GANNON, LUCY, 1948
*Keeping Tom Nice*. 1988. KILGC, LAQCW

GAO, XINGJIAN, 1940–
*Alarm Signal*. 1985.
    Yu, S., translator YUCHD
    Variant title: *Juedui xinhao*

*Bi an. See* Gao, X. *The Other Side*
*Bus Stop. See* The Bus Stop
*The Bus Stop.* 1983.
   Besio, K., translator THC
   Yu, S., translator YUCHD
   Variant titles: *Bus Stop, Chezhan*
*Chezhan. See* The Bus Stop
*Juedui xinhao. See* Alarm Signal
*The Other Side.* 1986.
   Riley, J., translator CHEU
   Variant title: *Bi an*

GARBEA, HORIA, 1962–
   *Your Coffee, Mr. Secretary!* 1998?
   Rotescu, J., translator POQ

GARCIA-CROW, AMPARO
   *A Roomful of Men: A Radio for the Eyes Performance
     Piece.* 1997. PURO

GARCIA GUTIERREZ, ANTONIO, 1813–1884
   *Juan Lorenzo.* 1865. BRET
   *El trovador.* 1835. TRES

GARCIA LORCA, FEDERICO, 1899–1936
   *Amor de don Perlimplín. See* The Love of Don
     Perlimplín and Belisa in the Garden
   *El amor de don Perlimplín con Belisa en su jardín.*
     *See* The Love of Don Perlimplín and Belisa in the
     Garden
   *Bitter Oleander. See* Blood Wedding
   *Blood Wedding.* 1933.
     O'Connell, R., and Graham-Luján, J., translators
       ALT, ALTE, BIER, BLOC, CLL, FLOS, FOUX,
       HILPDH6, KERP, LITIB, LOCLB, PERS, PERT,
       PERU, PERW, PERX, TREBA, TREBJ, TREC2,
       TREE2, TREI2, WATA, WEIP
     Variant titles: *Bitter Oleander; Bodas de sangre*
   *Bodas de sangre. See* Blood Wedding
   *La casa de Bernarda Alba.* 1945. SEIS1
   — *See also* The House of Bernarda Alba
   *The House of Bernarda Alba.* 1945. PARV
     Anonymous translator CLN
     Graham-Luján, J., and O'Connell, R., translator
       ALLI, ALLJ, ALLK, ALLM, ALLN, BARKD,
       CLM, CLN, DODS, ENC, GILB, HOGF,
       JACOBD, SEN, SSSI, SSSIB, SSSIC, WEIM
     Variant title: *La casa de Bernarda Alba*
     — *See also* Mann, Emily. *The House of Bernarda
      Alba* (adapted from the play by)
   *In the Frame of Don Cristobal.* 193–?
     Honig, E., translator NEWDI44
   *The King of Harlem.*
     Morison, W., translator VANV2
   *Lament for Ignacio Sánchez Mejías.*

     Spender, S., and Gill, J., translators VANV2
     Variant titles: *Lament for the Death of a Bullfighter;
      Llanto por Ignacio Sánchez Mejías*
*Lament for the Death of a Bullfighter. See* Lament for
   Ignacio Sánchez Mejías
*Llanto por Ignacio Sánchez Mejías. See* Lament for
   Ignacio Sánchez Mejías
*The Love of Don Perlimplín and Belisa in the Garden.*
   1931.
   O'Connell, R., and Graham-Lujan, J., translators
     BENS1, CLLC, COTP
   Variant titles: *Amor de Don Perlimplín; El amor de
     Don Perlimplín con Belisa en su jardín*
*The Public (El publico).* 1978. ADAP
*The Shoemaker's Prodigious Wife.* 1930.
   O'Connell, R., and Graham-Luján, J., translators
     BENA
   Variant title: *La zapatera prodigiosa*
*The Tragic-comedy of Don Cristobita and Doña Rosita.*
   1937.
   Oliver, W., translator NEWWW8
*Yerma.* 1934.
   Graham-Luján, J., and O'Connell, R., translators
     COTQ, FREG, ULAN
*La zapatera prodigiosa.* 1930. MARL12
   — *See also* The Shoemaker's Prodigious Wife

GARCIA VILLA, JOSE. *See* Villa, José García

GARD, ROBERT E., 1910–1992
   *Let's Get On with the Marrin'.* DRU
   *Mixing up the Rent.* DRU
   *Raisin' the Devil.* DRU

GARDEL, JULIO SANCHEZ. *See* Sánchez Gardel, Julio

GARDINER, WREY, 1901–1981
   *The Last Refuge.* 1943? NEWS1

GARDNER, MRS. DOROTHY (Butts), 1900–1972
   *Eastward in Eden.* 1947. BES47

GARDNER, HERB, 1934–2003
   *Conversations with My Father.* 1992. BES91, SCM
   *I'm Not Rappaport.* 1985. BES85
   *A Thousand Clowns.* 1962. BES61, ESA, GARSA,
     HOLP

GAREAU, LAURIER
   *The Betrayal.* 1985. BELLN

GARNEAU, MICHEL, 1939–
   *Four to Four.* 1973.
     Bedard, C., and Turnbull, K., translators KAL5
     Variant title: *Quatre à quatre*
   *Quatre à quatre. See* Four to Four

GARNER, HUGH, 1913–1979
*The Magnet. See* Three Women: Some Are So Lucky;
The Magnet; A Trip for Mrs. Taylor
*Some Are So Lucky. See* Three Women: Some Are So
Lucky; The Magnet; A Trip for Mrs. Taylor
*A Trip for Mrs. Taylor. See* Three Women: Some Are
So Lucky; The Magnet; A Trip for Mrs. Taylor
*Three Women: Some Are So Lucky; The Magnet; A Trip
for Mrs. Taylor.* 1966. KAL2
Variant titles: *Some Are So Lucky; The Magnet; A
Trip for Mrs. Taylor*

GARNER, JULIAN, 1956–
*The Awakening.* 1990. FIFHL3
*The Seducer's Diary.* (English version by). *See* Nagy,
András. *The Seducer's Diary*

GARNETT, PORTER, 1871–1950
*The Green Knight.* 1911. BOH2

GARNHUM, KEN
*Beuys bouys Boys: A Monologue.* 1989. WALAG

GARNIER, ROBERT, ca. 1545–1590
*The Hebrew Women.* [1583]
Zoltak, M., translator FOUAF
Variant titles: *Les juifves; Les juives*
*Les juifves. See* The Hebrew Women
*Les juives. See* The Hebrew Women
*Marc Antoine. See* The Tragedy of Antonie
*The Tragedy of Antonie.* 1592.
Pembroke, M., translator PURK, RENDW
Variant title: *Marc Antoine*

GARPE, MARGARETA, 1944–
*For Julia.* 1987.
Carlson, H., translator BRAK

GARRARD, JIM
*Peggy's Song.* 1988. RUDAK

GARRETT, JIMMY, 1944?–
*We Own the Night.* 1968. JONE

GARRICK, DAVID, 1717–1779
*Bon Ton.* 1775. BELC4
*Bucks, Have at Ye All.* BELC4
*Catharine and Petruchio* (alternate of Shakespeare's
*Taming of the Shrew*). 1756. BELC3
*Cymon* (altered from). 1767. BELC3, BELG7
*The Guardian.* 1759. BELC1
*High Life below Stairs.* BELC1
*Lethe.* 1740. BELC1
*The Lying Valet.* 1741. BELC2, KAYF, NET
*Miss in Her Teens.* 1747. BELC1, BEVI

*Neck or Nothing.* 1766. BELC2
— *See also* Colman, George, joint author

GARRO, ELENA, 1920–1998
*El árbol. See* The Tree
*The Tree.* 1967.
Morton, C., translator FFLD
Variant title: *El árbol*

GARSON, JULIET, 1968–
*So What Are We Gonna Do Now?* 1982. YOUP

GARVEY, ELLEN GRUBER, 1954–
*Soup.* 1985. PLA

GARZA, ROBERTO JESUS, 1934–2009
*No nos veneeremos.* CONR

GASBARRA, FELIX. *See* Piscator, Erwin, joint author

GASCOIGNE, GEORGE, 1525?–1577
*Supposes* (adapted from *I suppositi* by Ludovico
Ariosto). 1566. ADA, BAS, BOA, BOND, DPR1,
NES, ORNC

——— and KINWELMERSH, FRANCIS
*Jocasta.* 1566. CUN

GASCOYGNE, GEORGE. *See* Gascoigne, George

GASS, KEN, 1945–
*Hurray for Johnny Canuck.* 1974. FIFVE, SIXA

GASSNER, JOHN, 1903–1967
*Les précieuses ridicules. See* Molière, Jean Baptiste
Poquelin. *Les précieuses ridicules* (translator and
adapted by)
*Then and Now* (adapted from *The Marriage Proposal*
and *The Harmful Effects of Smoking* by Anton
Chekhov). 19–? GATS

GASTEAZORO, EVA
*Amor de mis amores.* 1996. ALG

GAULT, CONNIE, 1949–
*Sky.* 1989. SEUC

GAUP, NILS, 1955– , and WALLE, KNUT
*Gesat.* 1992.
Prask, P., translator BRAKA

GAY, DELPHINE. *See* Girardin, Delphine (Gay) de

GAY, JOHN, 1685–1732
*Achilles.* 1733. BELK9
*The Beggar's Opera.* 1728. ABRM1, ASH, BARB,
BELK9, CASH, CLKJ, EIGH, FEL, HAN,

HILPDH3, KER, KRO, MAL, MAND, MANF,
MOR, MOSE2, NET, ROGEBD, SIG, SMR,
STJM, STM, TAY, TREB, TUP, TUQ, TWE,
UHL, WILSP
— *See also* Brecht, Bertolt, and Hauptmann,
   Elisabeth. *The Threepenny Opera* (based on)
*Polly* (second part of *Beggar's Opera*, suppressed 1728).
   BELK9
*The What d'ye Call It*. 1715. TRUS

—— and POPE, ALEXANDER, and ARBUTHNOT,
   JOHN
*Three Hours after Marriage*. 1717. TRUS

GAY SWEATSHOP, 1974–1997
*Care and Control*. 1977. Wandor, Michelene, scripted
   by. STRI

GAZZO, MICHAEL VINCENTE, 1923–1995
*A Hatful of Rain*. 1956. FAM, FAMAF, GART,
   THEA56

GEAR, BRIAN
*The Sky Is Green*. 1963. PLAN27

GEDDES, VIRGIL, 1897–1989
*The Stable and the Grove*. 1933. AME4

GEIJI, NAMIKI. *See* Namiki, Sōsuke, joint author

GEIOGAMAH, HANAY, 1945–
*Body Indian*. 1972. DAPO, WOLCS
*Foghorn*. 1973. GEIO
*49*. 1975. GEIO
*Grandma*. 1984. (One act play shown on same bill as
   *Grandpa*.) GEIO
*Grandpa*. 1984. (One act play shown on same bill as
   *Grandma*.) GEIO
— *See also* Native American Theater Ensemble, joint
   author

GELBART, LARRY, 1928–2009
*City of Angels* (music by Cy Coleman, lyrics by David
   Zippel). 1989. BES89
*Sly Fox* (based on Ben Jonson's *Volpone*). 1976. BES76
— *See also* Shevelove, Burt, joint author

GELBER, JACK, 1932–2003
*The Connection*. 1959. OBG, SEVD

GÉLINAS, GRATIEN, 1909–1999
*Bousille et les justes*. *See* Bousille and the Just
*Bousille and the Just*. 1961.
   Johnstone, K., and Milville Dechêne J., translators
   PERKY

Variant titles: *Bousille et les justes; The Innocent and
   the Just*
*The Innocent and the Just*. *See* Bousille and the Just
*The Passion of Narcisse Mondoux*. 1986.
   Gaboriau, L., translator BELLW

GELLERT, ROGER, 1927–
*Quaint Honour*. 1958. GAY2

GELMAN, ALEXANDER, 1933–
*A Man with Connections*. 1988.
   Mulrine, S., translator SSTX

GEMS, PAM, 1925–2011
*Aunt Mary; Scenes from Provincial Life*. 1982.
   PLABE3
*Dead Fish*. *See* Dusa, Fish, Stas and Vi
*Dusa, Fish, Stas and Vi*. 1976. PLABE1
   Variant title: *Dead Fish*
*Loving Women*. 1984. ABCF
*Queen Christina*. 1977. PLABE5

GEN'E, 1269?–1350
*The Baby's Mother*. *See* Hōshigahaha
*Hōshigahaha* (attributed to).
   Haynes, C., translator BRAZT
   Variant title: *The Baby's Mother*

GENET, JEAN, 1910–1986
*Le balcon*. *See* The Balcony
*The Balcony*. 1960.
   Frechtman, B., translator NIL, SEVD, WOTHM
   Variant title: *Le balcon*
*The Blacks: A Clown Show*. 1961.
   Frechtman, B., translator GROV, OBG, WOTHA
   Variant title: *Les nègres*
*Les bonnes*. *See* The Maids
*Deathwatch*. 1949.
   Frechtman, B., translator COTQ
   Variant title: *Haute Surveillance*
*Haute Surveillance*. *See* Deathwatch
*The Maids*. 1947.
   Frechtman, B., translator TREBA, TREI3
   Variant title: *Les bonnes*
*Les nègres*. *See* The Blacks: A Clown Show
*The Screens*. 1971.
   Volanakis, M., translator BES71

GENSHICHI, TSUUCHI. *See* Tsuuchi, Genshichi

GEORGE, ERNEST, pseudonym. *See* Wise, Ernst George

GEORGE, GRACE, 1879–1961
*The Nest* (translated and adapted by). *See* Geraldy, Paul.
   *The Nest*

GEORGE, MADELEINE
*The Most Massive Woman Wins.* 1994. PLACA

GERALDY, PAUL, 1885–1983
*The Nest.* 1922.
    George, G., translator and adapter BES21
    Variant titles: *Les noces d'argent; Silver Weddings*
*Les noces d'argent. See* The Nest
*Silver Weddings. See* The Nest

GERSHE, LEONARD, 1922–2002
*Butterflies Are Free.* 1969. BES69

GERSHWIN, GEORGE, 1899–1937
*Crazy for You* (music by). *See* Ludwig, Ken and Mike
    Ockrent. *Crazy for You.*
*Of Thee I Sing* (music by). *See* Kaufman, George S. and
    Ryskind, Morris. *Of Thee I Sing*
*Porgy and Bess* (music by). *See* Heyward, DuBose.
    *Porgy and Bess*

GERSHWIN, IRA, 1896–1983
*Crazy for You* (music by). *See* Ludwig, Ken and Mike
    Ockrent. *Crazy for You.*
*Lady in the Dark* (lyrics by). *See* Hart, Moss. *Lady in
    the Dark*
*Porgy and Bess* (lyrics by). *See* Heyward, DuBose.
    *Porgy and Bess*
    — *See also* Kaufman, George S., joint author

GERSTENBERG, ALICE, 1885–1972
*Ever Young.* 1920? SHAY
*Overtones.* 1915. AMENW, BARKF, EAG, HUD, SUB,
    WAGNOX
*A Patroness.* 1917? SHAY

GESNER, CLARK, 1938–2002
*Animal Fair.* 1989. PRIMA89–90
*You're a Good Man, Charlie Brown* (book, music and
    lyrics by). 1967. BES66

GHELDERODE, MICHEL DE, 1898–1962
*Christophe Colomb.* 1927. PROA
    Hauger, G., translator COTKW
    Valeney, M., translator CASK
    Variant title: *Christopher Columbus*
*Christopher Columbus. See* Christophe Colomb
*The Chronicles of Hell.* 1949.
    Hauger, G., translator DUK, REIT
    Variant title: *Fastes d'enfer*
*Escurial.* 1929.
    Abel, L., translator BENT5
    Gherman, L., translator ANTM
*Fastes d'enfer. See* Chronicles of Hell
*Magie rouge. See* Red Magic

*The Magpie on the Gallows* (1935)
    Dormoy-Savage, N., translator ANTM
    Variant title: *La pie sur le gibes*
*Pantagleize.* 1930.
    Haugher, G., translator COTR
*La pie sur le gibes. See* The Magpie on the Gallows
*Red Magic.* 1934.
    Hauger, G., translator HILPDH6
    Variant title: *Magie rouge*

GHOSE, NANDITA
*Ishtar Descends.* 1987. DEAD, GRAW

GIACOSA, GIUSEPPE, 1847–1908
*As the Leaves Fall. See* Like Falling Leaves
*Come le foglie. See* Like Falling Leaves
*Like Falling Leaves.* 1900.
    Updegraff, E., and A., translators MOSQ
    Variant titles: *As the Leaves Fall; Come le foglie*

GIBBS, WOLCOTT, 1902–1958
*Season in the Sun.* 1950. BES50

GIBNEY, SHERIDAN, 1903–1988, and COLLINGS,
    PIERRE
*The Story of Louis Pasteur.* 1935. STAT, STAU

GIBSON, FLORENCE, 1951–
*Belle.* 1993. ZIMM

GIBSON, P.J., 1952?–
*Brown Silk and Magenta Sunsets.* 1985. WILK
*Konvergence* (1989). KINHP
*Long Time since Yesterday.* 1985. BLACTH

GIBSON, PATRICIA JOANN, 1952?– . *See* Gibson, P.J.

GIBSON, PAULINE, 1908– . *See* Gilsdorf, Frederic, joint
    author

GIBSON, WILFRID WILSON, 1878–1962
*The Family's Pride.* 1914. RICH

GIBSON, WILLIAM, 1914–2008
*Dinny and the Witches.* 1959. KAYT
*The Miracle Worker.* 1960. CARMI, SUT1, WHFA
*Two for the Seesaw.* 1958. GARSA, GATB4

GIDE, ANDRE PAUL GUILLAUME, 1869–1951
*The Immoralist. See* Goetz, Ruth and Goetz, Augustus.
    *The Immoralist* (based on the novel by) Oedipus.
    Russell, J., translator SANO

GIDEON, KILLIAN M.
*England Is de Place for Me.* 1988. GRAW

GIELGUD, VAL HENRY, 1900–1981
*Away from It All.* 1946. EMB3
*Chinese White.* 1928. FIT

GIL Y ZARATE, ANTONIO, 1793–1861
*Guzmán el Bueno.* 185–? BRET

GILBERT, MERCEDES, 1889–1952
*Environment.* 1931. HARYL

GILBERT, MICHAEL FRANCIS, 1912–2006
*The Bargain.* 1961. PLAN23
*A Clean Kill.* 1959. PLAN21

GILBERT, SKY, 1952– (b. Schuyler Lee Gilbert, Jr.)
*Drag Queens on Trial.* 1985. WASCPB1
*Lola Starr Builds Her Dream Home.* 1988. CTR

—— and ALCORN, JOHN
*Capote at Yaddo: A Very Gay Little Musical* (music by John Alcorn, lyrics by Sky Gilbert). 1990. WALAG

GILBERT, STUART REID, 1948–
*A Glass Darkly.* 1972. ALI

GILBERT, WILLIAM SCHWENCK, 1836–1911
*Haste to the Wedding* (adapted from the play *An Italian Straw Hat* by Eugene Labiche and Marc-Michel; music by George Grossmith). 1892. KAYF

—— and SULLIVAN, SIR ARTHUR SEYMOUR, composer
*Dan'l Druce.* 1876. KILG
*Engaged.* 1877. BAI, BOOA3, BOOM
*H.M.S. Pinafore; or, The Lass that Loved a Sailor.* 1878. ASG, COOP, MOSN, MOSO
— *See also* Moss, Alfred Charles. *H.M.S. Pinafore; oder, Das maedle und ihr sailor kerl* (based on)
*Iolanthe; or, The Peer and the Peri.* 1882. BOWY, HUD, LAW
*The Mikado; or, The Town of Titipu.* 1885. HUDV, MIJ2, PROD
*Patience; or, Bunthorne's Bride.* 1881. COTKIS, SMR
*Pygmalion and Galatea.* 1871. MART, MATTL
*Rosencrantz and Guildenstern.* 1891. NIN4
*Ruddigore; or, The Witch's Curse.* 1887. ROGEBD, SIG
*Sweethearts.* 1874. BAT16, COT, WEB
*Tom Cobb.* 1875. BOOA4
*Trial by Jury.* 1875. REIWE

GILBERT, WILLIE, 1916–1980. *See* Burrows, Abram S., and Weinstock, Jack, joint authors

GILBERT-LECOMTE, ROGER, 1907–1943
*L'odyssée d'Ulysse le palmipède. See* The Odyssey of Ulysses the Palmiped

*The Odyssey of Ulysses the Palmiped.* 1924. Wellwarth, G., translator BEN
Variant title: *L'Ulyssée d'Ulysse le palmipède*

GILHOOLEY, JACK, 1940–
*The Time Trial.* 1975. PLACI

GILL, PETER, 1939–
*Mean Tears.* 1987. CLUMS

GILLETTE, WILLIAM HOOKER, 1855–1937
*Secret Service.* 1896. BES94, GARX, MESC, QUIJ, QUIJR, QUIK, QUIL, QUIM, QUIN, SAFM, WILMET
*Sherlock Holmes* (based on the stories by Sir Arthur Conan Doyle). 1899. CART, PLAN44

GILLIATT, PENELOPE, 1932–1993
*Property.* 1979. WOMS

GILLIAT, SIDNEY. 1908–1994. *See* Launder, Frank, joint author

GILLMAN, JONATHAN
*The Marriage Test.* 1968. BALLE6

GILLOIS, ANDRE, pseud. *See* Diamond-Berger, Maurice

GILMAN, CHARLOTTE PERKINS, 1860–1935
*Something to Vote For.* 1911. FRIED

GILMAN, REBECCA, 1965–
*Speech Therapy.* 1999. HUMANA99

GILROY, FRANK D., 1925–
*The Subject Was Roses.* 1964. BES64, GAT, RICT

GILSDORF, FREDERICH, 1903–, and GIBSON, PAULINE
*The Ghost of Benjamin Sweet* (radio play). 1938. WAGC1

GINGOLD, HERMIONE, 1897–1987
*Beauty Beauty* (from *The Gate Revue*). 1939. YEAR
*Bicycling* (from *Sky High*). 1943. YEAR
*Conversation Piece: The Stars Look Down* (from *The Gate Revue*). 1939. YEAR
*I'm Only a Medium Medium* (from *The Gate Revue*). 1939. YEAR
*Madame La Palma* (from *The Gate Revue*). 1939. YEAR
*No Laughing Matter* (from *The Gate Revue*). 1939. YEAR
*Talk on Music* (from *Rise above It*). 1941. YEAR
*What Shall I Wear?* (from *New Ambassadors Revue*). 1941. YEAR

GINGRAS, RENE–DANIEL, 1952–
*Breaks*. 1983.
Gaboriau, L., translator WALAQ
Variant title: *Syncope*
*Syncope*. See Breaks

GINSBURY, NORMAN, 1902–1991 (b. Norman
Ginsberg)
*The First Gentleman*. 1935. FIR
*John Gabriel Borkman*. See Ibsen, Henrik. *John Gabriel
Borkman* (adapted by)
*The Safety Match* (based on a short story by Anton
Pavlovich Chekhov). RICK
*Viceroy Sarah*. 1934. FAMG

GINZBURG, NATALIA, 1916–1991
*The Advertisement*. 1968. SUB

GIPPIUS, ZINAIDA, 1869–1945
*Sacred Blood*. 1901.
Langen, T., and Weir, J., translators EIGHTRP
Zirin, M., and Schuler, C., translators KEL
*Sviataia krov'*. See Sacred Blood

GIRARDIN, DELPHINE (Gay) DE ("Mme. Emile de
Girardin"), 1804–1855
*La joie fait peur*. 1854. BENZ
Variant titles: *Sunshine Follows Rain; Sunshine
through the Clouds*
*Sunshine Follows Rain*. See La joie fait peur
*Sunshine through the Clouds*. See La joie fait peur

"GIRARDIN, MME. EMILE DE." *See* Girardin, Delphine
(Gay) de

GIRAUDOUX, JEAN, 1882–1944
*Amphitryon 38*. See Beheman, Samuel Nathaniel.
*Amphitryon 38* (adapted from)
*The Apollo of Bellaca*. 1942.
Valency, M., adapter COXM, GATS, MIJT
Variant titles: *L'Apollon de Bellac; L'Apollon de
Marsac*
*L'Apollon de Bellac*. See The Apollo of Bellac
*L'Apollon de Marsac*. See The Apollo of Bellac
*Cantique des cantiques*. See Song of Songs
*Duel of Angels*. 1953.
Fry, C., translator and adapter BES59
Variant title: *Pour Lucrece*
*Electra*. 1937.
Smith, W., translator BENS2, BENT1, BLOC,
COTKW, COTQ, FOR, LOR
Variant title: *Electre*
*Electre*. See Electra
*The Enchanted* (adapted by Maurice Valency). 1950.
BES49

Variant title: *Intermezzo*
*La folle de Chaillot*. See The Madwoman of Chaillot
*La guerre de Troie n'aura pas lieu*. See Tiger at the
Gates
*Intermezzo*. See The Enchanted
*Judith*. 1931.
Savacool, J., translator BENT3
*The Madwoman of Chaillot* (adapted by Maurice
Valency). 1948. ALLI, ALLJ, ALLK, BES48,
BLOC, BROX, BROY, COTKICO, FOUAC,
GARZH, GRIF, HAVG, JOHN, PERV, SCAR,
TREBA, TREBJ, TREI3, WATE
Variant title: *La folle de Chaillot*
*Ondine*. 1954? (from the novel *Undine* by Baron de
la Motte Fouque; adapted by Maurice Valency).
CLM, CLN, GARZH, HILPDH6, THEA54, WEIM
*Pour Lucrece*. See Duel of Angels
*Siegfried*. 1928. GRAF
*Sodom and Gomorrah*. 1943.
Anonymous translator SANK
Briffault, H., translator ULAN
*Song of Songs*. 1938?
Briffault, H., translator ULAN
Raikes, J., translator BERMG
Variant title: *Cantique des cantiques*
*Tiger at the Gates*. 1955. CLOU2, CLOUD2,
CLOUDS2, PUCC
Fry, C., translator BES55, CLL, DODS, DOWS,
GARZH, KERO, ROF, SATJ, SCNR, THEA56,
WAIU
Variant title: *La guerre de Troie n'aura pas lieu*

GIRON, ARTHUR, 1937–
*Money*. 1976. HUER

GIVNER, JOAN, 1936–
*Mazo & Caroline*. 1992. ZIMM

GLANCY, DIANE, 1941–
*The Truth Teller*. 1993. GEIO
*Weebjob*. 1987. PERC
*The Woman Who Was a Red Deer Dressed for the Deer
Dance*. 1995. DAPO

GLASPELL, SUSAN, 1882–1948
*Allison's House*. 1930. BES30, CORD, CORE, CORF,
SIXD
*The Outside*. 1917. AMENW
*Trifles*. 1916. ABCE, ABCF, ABCG, ABCH, ACE,
BAIL, BAIM, BARIE, BARIG, BARIH, BARKC,
BARKD, BARKE, BARKF, BEAC11, BEATA,
BOGA, BOOK, BRNS, CARM, DIYL, DIYLB,
DIYLC, DIYLD, DIYRD, EAG, FOL, FREI,
GASB, GEMM, GUTDF, GUTDS, HEAC,
HEAD, HEALB, HEALC, HOEP, HOWM, HUD,

JACOBD, KIRLA, KIRLB, KIRLC, KIRLD,
LITIC, LITID, LITIE, LITIF, LITJ, LITJA,
LITRA, LITRB, LITRC, LITRD, MAO, MEY,
MEYB, MEYC, MEYCA, MEYCB, MEYD,
MEYE, MEYF, MIJH, MOAD, NORALW,
NORALWA, PEN, PERY, PLAAD, PLAAE, PRO,
PROD, PROF, PROG, READ2, SCX, SSSIC,
STAT, STAU, STAV, WAGNOX, WATTAD,
WIEG, WOLC, WOLCS, WOMD, WOTHA,
WOTHB, WOTHC, WOTHM
*The Verge.* 1921. LEVY

—— and COOK, GEORGE CRAM
*Suppressed Desires.* 1915. DIYLA, FRYEA

GLASS, JOANNA, 1936–
*Artichoke.* 1975. SCNQCA
*Play Memory.* 1983. BERR

GLEASON, JAMES, 1885–1959. *See* Abbott, George,
joint author

GLEBOV, ANATOLE GLEBOVITCH, 1899–1964
*Inga.* 1928.
Malamuth, C., translator LYK

GLICKFIELD, CAROLE
*The Challenge of Bureaucracy.* 1987. VORE

GLOVER, EVELYN
*A Chat with Mrs. Chicky.* 1912. VOTE
*Miss Appleyard's Awakening.* 1912. VOTE

GLOVER, HALCOTT, 1877–1949
*The King's Jewry.* 1928. TUCD

GLOVER, RICHARD, 1712–1785
*Boadicia.* 1753. BELK20
*Medea.* 1761. BELG15

GLOVER, SUE, 1943–
*Bondagers.* 1991. BROV

GLOWACKI, JANUSZ, 1938–
*Hunting Cockroaches.* 1985.
Kosicka, J., translator BES85

GODFREY, PAUL, 1960–
*Inventing a New Colour.* 1988. FIFHL1

GODFREY, THOMAS, 1736–1763
*The Prince of Parthia.* 1767? MOSS1, QUIJ, QUIK,
QUIL, QUIM, QUIN

GODLOVITCH, CHARLES Z., 1921–
*Timewatch.* SHAT

GODWIN, PARKE, 1929–
*Cold Journey in the Dark: A Play for Two Voices and
Ideas.* 1973. KAYT
— *See also* Kaye, Marvin. *A Cold Blue Light*
(based on the novel by Marvin Kaye and Parke
Godwin)

GOERING, REINHARD, 1887–1936
*Naval Encounter.* 1917.
Ritchie, J., and Stowell, J., translators RITV
Variant titles: *Sea Flight; Seeschlacht*
*Sea Flight. See* Naval Encounter
*Seeschlacht. See* Naval Encounter

GOETHE, JOHANN WOLFGANG VON, 1749–1832
*Egmont.* 1791.
Hamburger, M., translator BENR2
Lamport, F., translator LAMP
Lustig, T., translator LUST
Swanwick, A., translator CLF2, HARC19
*Faust, Part 1.* 1829. EVB2
Anonymous translator DRAD2, PLAB2
Kauffman, W., translator NORIB2, NORIC2, NORJ2,
NORJA
MacIntyre, C., translator TREB, TREC1, TREE1,
TREI1, VANV2
MacNeice, L., translator MALC, MALG2, MALI2,
MALN2, NORGA, NORIA2
Passage, C., translator HILPDH4
Priest, G., translator EVC2, GRDB47, HOUK
Raphael, A., Jr. GOU2
Swanwick, A., translator BUCK, BUCL, BUCM,
CROV, ESS, EVA2, FRA1, HARC19, ROB,
THOM, THON, WEAV2
Taylor, B., translator HIB, HIBA, LOCM2, TRE,
TREA2, VONS3, WORP
Wayne, P., translator GRDBA45
*Faust, Part II.* 1829.
MacNeice, L., translator MALC, MALG2
Priest, G., translator GRDB47
Swanwick, A., translator BUCM, FRA1
Wayne, P., translator GRDBA45
*Goetz von Berlichinger.* 1774.
Scott, W., translator MATT
*Iphigenia in Tauris.* 1802.
Swanwick, A., translator BAT11, FRA1
Variant titles: *Iphigenia of Tauris; Iphigenie auf
Tauris*
*Iphigenia of Tauris. See* Iphigenia in Tauris
*Iphigenie auf Tauris. See* Iphigenia in Tauris
*Stella.* 1776.
Thompson, B., translator BAT12
*Torquato Tasso.* 1807.
Swanwick, A., translator KRE

GOETZ, AUGUSTUS, 1901–1957. *See* Goetz, Ruth
Goodman, joint author

GOETZ, RUTH GOODMAN, 1908–2001, and GOETZ,
AUGUSTUS
*The Doctor's Daughter. See* The Heiress
*The Heiress* (based on the novel, *Washington Square*, by
Henry James, Jr.). 1947. BES47
Variant titles: *The Doctor's Daughter; Washington
Square*
*The Immoralist* (based on the novel by André Gide).
1954. BES53
*Washington Square. See* The Heiress

GOGGAN, JOHN PATRICK. *See* Patrick, John, pseud.

GOGOL', NIKOLAI VASIL'EVICH, 1809–1852
*Dead Souls. See* Bulgakov, Mikhail Alfanasevich. *Dead
Souls* (based on the novel by)
*Gamblers.* 1833.
Bentley, E., translator BENT3
*The Government Inspector. See* The Inspector
*The Inspector.* 1836.
Anonymous translator COUR
Cooper, J., translator COOPA
Davies, T., translator BAT18
Guerney, B., translator GUE, HOUG
MacAndrew, A., translator GARZE, MAB
Magarshack, D., translator MAP
Reeve, F., translator REEV1
Saffron, R., translator CHARN, SAFF
Seymour, J., and Noyes, G., translators NOY, TREB,
TREC1, TREE1, TREI1
Sykes, A., translator CLKW, COUS
Variant titles: *The Government Inspector; The
Inspector General; Revisor*
*The Inspector General. See* The Inspector
*The Marriage.* 1842.
Bentley, E., translator BENT5
*The Order of Valdimir, Third Class.* 1842.
Green, M., and Katsell, J., translators GREENU
*Revisor. See* The Inspector

GOHEI, NAMIKI, III. *See* Namiki, Gohei III

GOLD, MICHAEL, 1894–1967
*Hoboken Blues; or, The Black Rip Van Winkle.* 1927.
AME1

GOLDBERG, DICK, 1947–
*Family Business.* 1978. BES77

GOLDBERG, JESSICA, 1973–
*Refuge.* 1999. WOMP98

GOLDBERG, LEAH, 1911–1970
*Lady of the Castle.* 1955.
Carmi, T., translator TAUB

GOLDBERG, WHOOPI, 1949/1955?– (born Caryn Elaine
Johnson)
*The Spook Show.* 1982. WES21/22

GOLDEMBERG, ROSE LEIMAN, 1928–
*Letters Home* (based on Sylvia Plath's *Letters Home*,
selected and edited by Aurelia Sehober Plath).
1979. PLABE2, WOMS

GOLDENBERG, JORGE, 1941–
*Krinsky.* 1977.
Glickman, N., and Waldman, G., translators ARGJT

GOLDING, WILLIAM GERALD, 1911–1993
*The Brass Butterfly.* 1958. BARG

GOLDMAN, JAMES, 1927–1998
*Follies* (music and lyrics by Stephen Sondheim). 1971.
BES70
*The Lion in Winter.* 1966. BES65, GAT

GOLDMAN, WILLIAM, 1931–
*Butch Cassidy and the Sundance Kid* (screenplay). 1969.
READ2 (excerpt)

GOLDONI, CARLO, 1707–1793
*Accomplished Maid* (attributed to). BELK21
*Un curioso accidente.* 1757. BIN
Zimmern, H., translator CROV
Variant titles: *A Curious Mishap; A Curious
Misunderstanding*
*A Curious Mishap. See* Un curioso accidente
*A Curious Misunderstanding. See* Un curioso accidente
*The Fan.* 1763.
Fuller, H., translator CLF2
Variant title: *Il ventaglio*
*La locandiera. See* The Mistress of the Inn
*Mirandolina. See* The Mistress of the Inn
*The Mistress of the Inn.* 1753.
Gregory, I., translator BENR1
Lohmann, H., translator LEG
Longman, S., translator HILPDH3
Pierson, M., translator MATT, MOSA
Variant titles: *La locandiera; Mirandolina*
*L'osteria della posta. See* The Post-inn
*The Post-inn.* 1761.
Chambers, W., translator BAT5
Variant title: *L'osteria della posta*
*The Servant of Two Masters.* 1743?
Dent, E., translator BENR1, BENV, BRJA, BRJC,
SMA

Kaye, M., translator KAYF
Lopworth, P., translator PLAN36
Variant title: *Il servitore di due padroni*
*Il servitore di due padroni*. *See* The Servant of Two
 Masters
*Il ventaglio*. *See* The Fan

GOLDSMITH, CLIFFORD, 1899–1971
*What a Life*. 1938. BES37

GOLDSMITH, OLIVER, 1728–1774
*The Good-natured Man*. 1768. BELG8, STM
*She Stoops to Conquer; or, The Mistakes of a Night*.
 1773. BARG, BARU, BEAC11, BELG8, BENN,
 BENY, CLF1, CLKY, COLEL1, COLT, DAI,
 DEM, DOWS, DRAD1, DUH, EIGH, FOUB,
 GOU2, GREAAI, HARC18, HILPDH3, HUD,
 JAFF, KEY, KRM, MAND, MANF, MATTL,
 MOO, MOR, MORR, MOSE2, NET, PERR1,
 PLAB1, POOL, PROM, RUB, SELF, SHAH1,
 SMO, SRY, SRYG, STA, STM, TAT, TAU, TAY,
 THMD, TUP, TUQ, TWE, UHL, VENA, WILSP

GOLL, IWAN, 1891–1950
*The Eternal Bourgeois*. *See* Methusalem
*Der ewige Bürger*. *See* Methusalem
*The Immortal One*. (1920).
 Sokel, W., and J., translators SOK
*Methusalem; oder, Der ewige Bürger*. *See* Methusalem;
 or, The Eternal Bourgeois
*Methusalem; or, The Eternal Bourgeois*. 1922.
 Ritchie, J., and Garten, H., translators RITS
 Wensinger, A., and Atkinson, CA., translators PLAC

GOLL, YVAN. *See* Goll, Iwan

GOLLOBIN, LAURIE BROOKS
*The Match Girl's Gift: A Christmas Story*. 1998. SWO

GOMBAR, JOZEF, 1973–
*Hugo Carp*. 1999.
 Slugenová-Cockrell, K., translator CONTSL2

GOMES, ALFREDO DIAS, 1922–1999
*O pagador de promesas*. *See* Payment as Pledged
*Payment as Pledged*. 1960.
 Fernández, O., translator WOOG
 Variant title: *O pagador de promesas*

GOMEZ, MARGA, 1954–
Excerpts from *Memory Tricks, Marga Gomez Is
 Pretty Witty & Gay*, and *A Line around the
 Block* (Excerpts from three plays, each in one act
 monologues: *Memory Tricks, Marga Gomez Is*

*Pretty Witty & Gay*, and *A Line around the Block*).
 1990–1994. PERC
*A Line around the Block*. 1994. *See* Excerpts from
 *Memory Tricks, Marga Gomez Is Pretty Witty &
 Gay*, and *A Line around the Block*.
*Marga Gomez Is Pretty Witty & Gay*. 1991. *See*
 Excerpts from *Memory Tricks, Marga Gomez Is
 Pretty Witty & Gay*, and *A Line around the Block*.
*Memory Tricks*. 1990. *See* Excerpts from *Memory
 Tricks, Marga Gomez Is Pretty Witty & Gay*, and *A
 Line around the Block*.

GOMEZ, TERRY
*Inter-tribal*. 1994. PERC

GONDINET, EDMOND, 1829?–1888. *See* Labiche,
 Eugène Marin, joint author

GONNE, FRANCIS, 1879–1938
*In the City of David*. 1934. SEVE

GONZALEZ, REUBEN, 1951–
*The Boiler Room*. 1987. ANTU

GONZALEZ-PANDO, MIGUEL, 1941–
*The Great American Justice Game*. 1987. GONZ
*Once upon a Dream*. CUB

GONZALEZ S., SILVIA, 1958–
*The Migrant Farmworker's Son*. 1994. ELLM, SCVDT1

GOOBIE, BETH, 1959–
*The Face Is the Place*. 1998. RAVE

GOODALL, JULIE
*Texas, Queensland*. 1993. JONI

GOODHART, WILLIAM, 1925–1999
*Generation*. 1965. BES65

GOODMAN, KENNETH SAWYER, 1883–1918
*Dust of the Road*. 1912. FED1

—— and HECHT, BEN
*The Hand of Siva*. 1920. STAT, STAU

GOODMAN, PAUL, 1911–1972
*The Tower of Babel*. 1940. NEWDI40

GOODRICH, FRANCES, 1891–1984, and HACKETT,
 ALBERT
*The Diary of Anne Frank* (based on the book by Anne
 Frank). 1955. BES55, CARM, CARME, GARU,
 GATB4, RICT, THEA56, WHFA

GOOLD, MARSHALL NEWTON, 1881–1935
*The Quest Divine.* 1925? FED2
*St. Claudia.* 1924? FED2
*The Shepherds.* 192–? FED2

GORDIN, JACOB, 1853–1900
*God, Man, and Devil.*
Sandrow, N., translator SANR
Variant title: *Got, mentsh, un tayvl*
*Got, mentsh, un tayvl.* See God, Man, and Devil

GORDON, CHARLES F. *See* OyamO (pseud.)

GORDON, DAVID
*The Mysteries* and *What's So Funny?* 1991. FEFG

GORDON, GEORGE, 1788–1824. *See* Byron, George
Gordon

GORDON, RICHARD, and BAUER, IRVIN S.
*The Bulldog and the Bear.* 1996. FLET

GORDON, ROBERT
*And.* 1974. WES2
*The Tunes of Chicken Little.* 1972. BALLE13

GORDON, ROXY, 1945–2000. *See* Howe, LeAnne, joint
author

GORDON, RUTH (MRS. GARSON KANIN), 1896–1985
*Over 21.* 1943. BES43
*Years Ago.* 1946. BES46, WAGC1, WAGE

GORDONE, CHARLES, 1925–1995
*The Breakout.* KINH, KINHB
*No Place to Be Somebody.* 1969. BES68, OLIV, PATR,
WEIP

GORE-BROWNE, ROBERT F., 1893–. *See* Harwood,
Harold Marsh, joint author

GOREING, ANDREW
*Promise.* 1983. BURB

GORIN, GRIGORY, 1940–2000
*Forget Herostratus!* (radio play) 1986.
Glenny, M., translator SSTX

GORKI, MAXIM (pseud. of Aleksîeî Maksimovich
Pîeskov), 1868–1936
*At the Bottom. See* The Lower Depths
*Dans les fonds. See* The Lower Depths
*Down and Out. See* The Lower Depths
*From the Depths. See* The Lower Depths
*In the Depths. See* The Lower Depths

*The Lower Depths.* 1902.
Anonymous translator SMA
Bakshy, A., translator BLOC, FOUM, HILPDH4
Burke, H., translator COTO, COTQ
Chambers, W., translator BAT18
Covan, A., translator CEW, DICIN2, HAV, HOUG,
MOS, TRE, TREA1, TREBA, TREBJ, TREC2,
TREE2, TREI2, TUCN, TUCO, WHI
Guerney, B., translator GUE
Hopkins, E., translator DICDS, MOSG, MOSH, SMP,
TUCG, WATI, WATL3
MacAndrew, W., translator GARZG, MABA
Magarshuck, D., translator MAP
Noyes, G., and Kaun, A., translators NOY
Reeve, F., translator REEV2
Variant titles: *At the Bottom; Dans les fonds; Down
and Out; From the Depths; In the Depths; A Night
Shelter; Night's Lodging; Submerged*
*The Lower Depths: An East End Story* (adapted from the
play by Maxim Gorki). *See* Ikoli, Tundi
*A Night Shelter. See* The Lower Depths
*Night's Lodging. See* The Lower Depths
*Submerged. See* The Lower Depths
*Yegor Bulichov and Others.* 1932. CLKX
Bakshy, A., translator HOGF
Wixley, A., translator FOUS

GORLING, LARS, 1931–1966
*The Sandwiching.* (1962)
Austin, P., translator MNOS
Variant title: *Trängningen*
*Trängningen. See* The Sandwiching

GORMAN, CLEM, 1942–
*A Manual of Trench Warfare.* 1978. AUSG

GOSS, CLAY, 1946–
*Mars: Monument to the Last Black Eunuch.* 1972.
CARR
*On Being Hit.* 1970. NEWL

GOTANDA, PHILIP KAN, 1949–
*Day Standing on Its Head.* 1994. ASIAM, HOUST
*The Dream of Kitamura.* 1982. WES15/16
*The Wash.* 1987. BETW, WES21/22
*Yankee Dawg You Die.* 1986. BRJC, NEWAMP1, RIS,
SWANS

GOUBAUX, PROSPER PARFAIT, 1795–1859,
and DUCANGE VICTOR HENRY JOSEPH
BRAHAIN
*Trente ens; ou, La vie d'un joueur. See* Dunlap,
William. *Thirty Years; or, The Gambler's Fate*
(adapted from)

GOUGH, LUCY
*Red Room.* 1999. ONE
*The Trail.* 1999. ONE

GOULDING, EDMUND, 1891–1959. *See* Selwyn, Edgar,
    joint author

GOW, JAMES ELLIS, 1907–1952, and D'USSEAU,
    ARNAUD
*Deep Are the Roots.* 1945. BES45
*Tomorrow the World.* 1942. BES42, GARZ

GOW, MICHAEL, 1955–
*Away.* 1986. AUS
*Furious.* 1991. AUSG

GOW, RONALD, 1897–1993
*Ann Veronica* (adapted from the novel by H. G. Wells).
    1949. PLAN2
*The Edwardians* (adapted from the novel by Victoria
    Mary Sackville-West). 1959. PLAN20
    Variant title: *Weekend in May*
*Weekend in May. See* The Edwardians

——— and GREENWOOD, WALTER
*Love on the Dole.* 1934. PLAL

GOWANS, ELIZABETH
*Casino.* 1982. FEFNV

GOWER, DOUGLAS
*Daddies.* 1977. WES1

GOZZI, CARLO, CONTE, 1722–1806
*The King Stag.* 1762?
    Wildman, C., translator BENR1, BENV
*The Love of Three Oranges.* 1761. *See* Prokofiev, Serge.
    *The Love of Three Oranges* (based on the play by)
    — *See also* Swortzell, Lowell. *The Love of Three
    Oranges* (adapted from the play by)
*Turandot.* 1761.
    Levy, J., translator BENSA

GRABBE, CHRISTIAN DIETRICH, 1801–1836
*Don Juan and Faust.* (1829)
    Edwards, E., translator MARJ
    Variant title: *Don Juan und Faust*
*Don Juan und Faust. See* Don Juan and Faust
*Jest, Satire, Irony, and Deeper Significance.* 1827?
    Edwards, M., translator BENS2

GRACE-SMITH, BRIAR, 1966–
*Ngā Pou Wāhine.* 1997. BREK (excerpt)

GRAEBNER, GRUBB, 1950–
*Winners of the White Atomic Sweepstakes.* 1984. JOND

GRAFFIGNY, FRANCOISE D'ISSEMBOURG
    D'HAPPONCOURT DE, 1695–1758
*Cenia.* 1750.
    Gethner, P., translator GETH
    Variant title: *Cenie*
*Cenie. See* Cenia

GRAHAM, BARBARA, 1947–
*Jacob's Ladder.* 1987. WES6

GRAHAM, NADINE
*The Basement at the Bottom at the End of the World.*
    1994. ELLM

GRAHAM, SHIRLEY, 1896–1977
*I Gotta Home.* ca.1938–1940. PER
*It's Morning.* ca.1938–1940. BRW, PER, PLAAF
*Tom-tom.* 1932. ROOTS
*Track Thirteen: A Comedy for Radio.* 1940. HARYL

GRAINGER, TOM, 1921–
*The Helper.* 1972. BRIQ

GRANGE, CHANCEL LA. *See* La Grange-Chancel

GRANT, DAVID
*The King Cat.* FRO

GRANT, DAVID MARSHALL, 1955–
*Snakebit.* 1993. NEWR98

GRANT, DIANE
*What Glorious Times They Had: Nellie McClung.* 1974.
    WIM

GRANVILLE-BARKER, HARLEY, 1877–1946
*Deburau* (translated and adapted by). *See* Guitry, Sacha.
    *Deburau*
*The Madras House.* 1910. DICD, MOSN, MOSO,
    WEAL
*Rococo.* 1912. WEAN
*The Voysey Inheritance.* 1905. DICEM, PLAP1,
    ROWC
*Waste.* 1909. TUCD
    — *See* Houseman, Laurence, joint author

GRASS, GUNTER, 1927–
*Beritten hin und zurück. See* Rocking Back and Forth
*Die bösen Köche. See* The Wicked Cooks
*Rocking Back and Forth.* 1960.
    Benedikt, M., and Goradza, J., translators BENB
    Variant title: *Beritten hin und zurück*
*The Wicked Cooks.* 1961.
    Rosenberg, J., translator COTS
    Variant title: *Die bösen Köche*

GRAVES, RUSSELL, 1922–
*The Battle of the Carnival and Lent.* 1967. PAJ

GRAVES, WARREN G., 1933–2008
*The Proper Perspective.* 1974. SHAT
*Would You like a Cup of Tea?* 1984. FOUNC

GRAY, AMLIN, 1946–
*How I Got that Story.* 1979. COMV

GRAY, JOHN, 1866–1934, and RAFFALOVICH,
 MARC-ANDRE
*The Blackmailers.* 1894. SELOV

GRAY, JOHN, 1946– , and PETERSON, ERIC
*Billy Bishop Goes to War.* 1980. WASCP, WASCPA2,
 WASCPB1

GRAY, ORIEL, 1920–2003
*Burst of Summer.* 1960. BRIMA1

GRAY, SIMON, 1936–2008
*Butley.* 1972. BES72
*Otherwise Engaged.* 1975. BES76, BEST
*Quartermaine's Terms; a Play in Two Acts.* 1981.
 BES82, COTKB2

GRAY, STEPHEN, 1941–
*'n Aandjie by die Vernes. See* An Evening at the Vernes
*An Evening at the Vernes* (based on the writings of Jules
 Verne). 1975. CONTSO
 Variant title: *'n Aandjie by die Vernes* (first performed
 as an Afrikaans adaptation by Louis van Rooyen
 and Johann Papendorf)

GRAZIANO, DAVID
*Acorn.* 1997. HUMANA98

GREANIAS, GEORGE, 1948–
*Wilson.* 1973. BALLE12

GREAVES, DONALD, 1943–
*The Marriage.* (1971) KINH, KINHB

GREBAN, ARNOUL, ca. 1420–1471
*Le mistère de la nativité de Nostre Saulveur Jhesu Crist.
 See* Kirkup, James. *The True Mistery of the Nativity*
 (adapted from the French medieval mystery cycle
 by)
*Le vrai mystère de la Passion. See* Kirkup, James. *The
 True Mistery of the Passion* (adapted from the
 French medieval mystery cycle by)

GRECCO, STEPHEN
*The Orientals.* 1969. BALLE7

GREEN, ADOLPH, 1914–2002. *See* Comden, Betty, joint
 author

GREEN, ERMA, 1903–1993. *See* Green, Paul, joint author

GREEN, JANET, 1908–1993
*Murder Mistaken.* 1952. PLAN8

GREEN, JULIEN, 1900–1998
*South.* 1953.
 Anonymous translator PLAN12
 Variant title: *Sud*
*Sud. See* South

GREEN, MARO, pseudonym. *See* Casdagli, Penny

GREEN, MICHAEL, 1957–. *See* Brooker, Blake, joint
 author

GREEN, PAUL, 1894–1981
*The Field God.* 1927. HAL, TUCD, TUCM, TUCN
*The House of Connelly.* 1931. BES31, GARU
*Hymn to the Rising Sun.* 1936. KOZ
*In Abraham's Bosom.* 1927. BES26, CORD, CORE,
 CORF, DICDT, LOC, MOAD, TOD, WHI
*Johnny Johnson* (music by Kurt Weill). 1937. AND,
 ANDE, BES36, GAS
*The Lord's Will.* 1925. LEV, LEVE
*The Man Who Died at Twelve O'clock.* 1925. CHU
*The No'count Boy.* 1924. LOC
*Potter's Field. See* Roll Sweet Chariot
*Roll Sweet Chariot.* 1934. CLKW
 Variant title: *Potter's Field*
*Supper for the Dead.* 1926? AME1
*Tread the Green Grass.* 1928. AME3
*Unto such Glory.* 1926? FLAN, HUDS2
*White Dresses.* 1920. GASB, LOC
 — *See* Wright, Richard, joint author

——— and GREEN, ERMA
*Fixin's: The Tragedy of a Tenant Farm Woman.* 1934.
 RAVIT
 Variant title: *The Renewal*
*The Renewal. See* Fixin's: The Tragedy of a Tenant
 Farm Woman

GREENBERG, DANIEL. *See* Levine, Mark L., joint
 author

GREENBERG, RICHARD, 1958–
*American Plan.* 1990. BES90, FEFG
*Eastern Standard.* 1988. BES89
*The Extra Man.* 1992. BES91
*Night and Her Stars.* 1994. BES94
*Three Days of Rain.* 1997. PLACG2

GREENE, GRAHAM, 1904–1991
  *The Complaisant Lover.* 1959. BES61
  *The Living Room.* 1952. BES54
  *The Potting Shed.* 1957. BES56

GREENE, PATTERSON, 1899–1968
  *Papa Is All.* 1942. GALB

GREENE, ROBERT, 1558–1592
  *Friar Bacon and Friar Bungay. See* The Honorable
    History of Friar Bacon and Friar Bungay
  *George a Greene, The Pinner of Wakefield* (supposed
    author). 1588? ADA, BAS, NES, SCH
    Variant title: *A Pleasant Conceited Comedy of
      [George a Greene] the Pinner of Wakefield*
  *The Honorable History of Friar Bacon and Friar
    Bungay.* 1589? ASH, BAS, BENY, BROC, DPR1,
    GATG, GAYLE1, HEIL, HOW, MAK, MIN2,
    MIO2, NEI, NES, OLH, OLI1, ORNC, PAR, SCI,
    SCJ, SCW, SPE, TICO
    Variant title: *Friar Bason and Friar Bungay*
  *James the Fourth.* 1591? MIN2, MIO2
  *A Pleasant Conceited Comedy of [George a Greene]
    the Pinner of Wakefield. See* George Greene, The
    Pinner of Wakefield
  *Selimus, Emperor of the Turks.* 1588? VIT
    — *See also* Lodge, Thomas, joint author

GREENHORN, STEPHEN, 1964–
  *Passing Places.* 1997. HOWA

GREENLAND, BILL
  *We Three, You and I.* 1970. BRIN

GREENLAND, SETH
  *Jungle Rot.* 1995. BES95

GREENSPAN, DAVID, 1956–
  *Dead Mother, or Shirley Not All in Vain.* 1991. FEFG
  *Jack.* 1987. OSBW
  *Son of an Engineer.* 1994. MESSE
  *Them.* 1999. HUMANA99

GREENSPAN, HANK
  *"Voice"* (monologue from *Remnants*). 1992. VOI

GREENWOOD, WALTER, 1903–1974. *See* Gow, Ronald,
  joint author

GREER, BONNIE, 1948–
  *Munda negra.* 1993. BREW3

GREGG, STEPHEN
  *This Is a Test.* 1988? SCVDO1

GREGORY, ISABELLA AUGUSTA (PERSSE), Lady,
  1859–1932
  *The Canavans.* 1906. BARF
  *Dave.* 1927. POLK
  *The Dragon.* 1917. WEB
  *The Gaol Gate.* 1906. ALLO, OWEC
  *Hyacinth Halvey.* 1906. CAP, MIL, WATF1, WATI,
    WATT2
  *The Rising of the Moon.* 1907. BEAC12, DICD, DIYL,
    DIYLA, DIYLB, DIYLC, DIYLD, DIYRD,
    GREAAI, JACOB, JACOBA, JACOBD, JACOBE,
    PROB, SHAR, SSTA
  *Spreading the News.* 1904. BEAC8, FIG, GREAAI,
    NORALW, NORALWA, OWEC, PEN, PERR2,
    PROC, WATS
  *The Workhouse Ward.* 1908. COD, LITI, LITIA, LITIB,
    LITID, MOSN, MOSO, TOD, TREBA, TREC2,
    TREE2, TREI3

GREIG, DAVID, 1969–
  *Europe.* 1994. FROLIN3
  *One Way Street.* 1995. HOWA

GREIG, NOEL, 1944–2009
  *The Dear Love of Comrades.* 1979. OSME
  *Plague of Innocence.* 1988. GAY5

GREMINA, ELENA, 1956–
  *Behind the Mirror.* (1994)
    Smith, M., translator SMB

GRESSET, JEAN BAPTISTE LOUIS, 1709–1777
  *Le méchant.* 1747. BREN

GRIBOEDOV, ALEXANDER SERGEYEVICH. *See*
  Grib#oîedov, Alexandr Sergîevich

GRIBOIEDOV, ALEXANDER SERGIEVICH, 1795–
  1829
  *Chatsky; or, The Misery of Having a Mind.* 1823.
    Cooper, J., translator COOPA
  *Intelligence Comes to Grief. See* Wit Works Woe
  *The Misery of Having a Mind. See* Chatsky
  *The Misfortune of Being Clever. See* Wit Works Woe
  *The Trouble with Reason.* 1824?
    Reeve, F., translator REEV1
  *Wit Works Woe.* 1831.
    Pares, B., translator NOY
    Variant titles: *Intelligence Comes to Grief; The
      Misfortune of Being Clever; Woe from Wit*
  *Woe from Wit. See* Wit Works Woe

GRIBOYEDOV, ALEXSANDER. *See* Gribôîedov,
  Alexandr Sergîevich

GRIEG, NORDAHL, 1902–1943
*The Defeat: A Play about the Paris Commune.* 1936.
   Watkins, J., translator SCAN2
   Variant title: *Nederlaget*
*Nederlaget. See* The Defeat
*Our Power and Our Glory.*
   Gathorne-Hardy, G., translator FIL

GRIFFIN, ALICE VENEZKY, 1921–
*Oresteia. See* Aeschylus. *Oresteia* (arranged for the stage by)

GRIFFIN, CAROLINE, 1950– . *See* Casagli, Penny, joint author

GRIFFIN, G. W. H.
*Hamlet the Dainty.* (1870?) NIN5
*Othello.* (1870?) NIN5
*Shylock.* (1870?) NIN5

GRIFFITH, ELIZABETH, 1720?–1793
*School for Rakes.* 1769. BELG2

GRIFFITH, HUBERT FREELING, 1896–1953
*Youth at the Helm* (translated and adapted by). *See* Vulpius, Paul. *Youth at the Helm*

GRIFFITH, LOIS
*White Sirens.* 1997. ALG

GRIFFITHS, ELIZABETH. *See* GRIFFITH, ELIZABETH

GRIFFITHS, LINDA, 1956–
*The Darling Family.* 1991. SEUC
*Spiral Woman & the Dirty Theatre.* 1993. ZIMM

—— and BRYMER, PATRICK
*O.D. on Paradise.* 1982. RUDAK

GRIFFITHS, TREVOR, 1935–
*Comedians.* 1975. BES76

GRILLPARZER, FRANZ, 1791–1872
*The Fortunes and Death of King Ottokar. See* König Ottokars glück und ende
*The Jewess of Toledo.* 1873.
   Danton, G., and A., translators FRA6
   Variant title: *Die jüdin von Toledo*
*Die judin von Toledo. See* The Jewess of Toledo
*King Ottocar's Rise and Fall. See* König Ottokars glück und ende
*King Ottakar, His Rise and Fall. See* König Ottokars glück und ende
*König Ottokars glück und ende.* 1825. CAM
   Burkhard, A., translator ANTH

   Stevens, H., translator SCVN
   Variant titles: *The Fortunes and Death of King Ottokar; King Ottocar's Rise and Fall; King Ottokar, His Rise and Fall*
*Medea.* 1821.
   Lamport, F., translator LAMP
   Miller, T., translator FRA6
*Sappho.* 1818. CAM
   Frothingham, E., translator SMN
*Der traum ein leben.* 1834. FEFH1
*Weh dem, der lügt! See* Woe to the Liar!
*Woe to the Liar!* 1837.
   Cardullo, B., translator GERLC
   Variant title: *Weh dem, der lügt!*

GRIMKE, ANGELINA WELD, 1880–1958
*Rachel.* 1916. HARY, HARYB, PERF, WOTHM

GRIMM, HENRY
*The Chinese Must Go.* 1879. CHIN

GRIMM, JACOB, 1785–1863 and GRIMM, WILHELM, 1786–1859
*The Master Thief. See* Sills, Paul. *The Master Thief* (adapted from the tale by)

GRIMSLEY, JIM, 1955–
*Mr. Universe.* 1987. DEN

GROSSMITH, GEORGE, 1847–1912
*Haste to the Wedding* (music by). *See* Gilbert, William Schwenck. *Haste to the Wedding*

GROSSO, NICK, 1968–
*Peaches.* 1995. COMS

GROUNDS, TONY, 1957–
*Made in Spain.* 1987. VER

GROVE, M. ELLIS
*The Land of Counterpane.* 1981. KAYF

GROVER, LEONARD, 1833–1926
*Our Boarding House.* 1877. AMP4

GRUMBERG, JEAN-CLAUDE, 1939–
*L'atelier. See* The Workroom
*The Workroom.* 1976.
   Stein, D., and O'Connor, S., translators WEHL
   Variant title: *L'atelier*

GRUMBINE, EZRA LIGHT, 1845–1880
*Die inschurens bissness. See* Die insurance business
*Die insurance business.* 1880? BUFF
   Variant title: *Die inschurens bissness*

GRUNDY, SYDNEY, 1848–1914
*The New Woman*. 1894. CHOT
*A Pair of Spectacles* (adapted from *Les petite oiseaux* by
    Eugène Labiche and Delacour). 1890. ROWE

GRYPHIUS, ANDREAS, 1616–1664
*Leo Armenius*. 1650.
    Stackhouse, J., translator GILL

GUARE, JOHN, 1938–
*Cop-out*. 1968. OFF1
*The House of Blue Leaves*. 1971. BES70, GARTL
*Marco Polo Sings a Solo*. 1973. PLACHA
*Muzeeka*. 1967. LAH, MESSE, OFF1
*Six Degrees of Separation*. 1990. BES90

—— and SHAPIRO, MEL
*Two Gentlemen of Verona* (music by Galt MacDermot;
    lyrics by John Guare). 1971. GREAAR

GUARINI, GIOVANNI BATTISTA, 1538–1612
*The Faithful Shepherd*. 1595.
    Fanshawe, R., translator FIJ
    Variant title: *Il pastor fido*

GUERDON, DAVID
*The Laundry*. 1962.
    Richardson, H., translator COTT

GUERRERO, WILFRIDO MARIA, 1917–1995
*Forever*. 1947. EDAD
*Forsaken House*. See Uilang Tahanan
*Uilang Tahanan*. 1940. JUAN
    Variant title: *Forsaken House*

GUIMERA, ANGEL, 1847–1924
*Daniela*. 1902.
    Underhill, J., translator CLDM
    Variant titles: *La pecadora*; *The Sinner*
*La pecadora*. See Daniela
*The Sinner*. See Daniela

GUINN, DOROTHY C.
*Out of the Dark*. (1924) RIR, RIRA

GUINNESS, SIR ALEC, 1914–2000, and STRACHAN,
    ALAN
*Yahoo*. 1976. PLAN46

GUINON, ALBERT, 1863–1923, and MARNIERE,
    JEANNE MARIE FRANÇOISE
*Le joug*. See The Yoke
*The Yoke*. 1902.
    Anonymous translator BAT21
    Variant title: *Le joug*

GUIRGIS, STEPHEN ADLY
*Jesus Hopped the "A" Train*. 2000. NEWR2000

GUITRY, SACHA, 1885–1957
*Deburau*. 1920.
    Granville-Barker, H., translator and adapter BES20
*Don't Listen, Ladies!* (adapted by Stephen Powys and
    Guy Bolton). 1948. PLAN1
*Pasteur*. 1919. Brown, I., translator DICDS

GUNAWARDENA, GAMINI, 1930–
*Rama and Sita*. 1964. GOON (excerpt)

GUNNER, FRANCES, 1894–
*The Light of the Women*. 1930. RIR, RIRA

GUNZBURG, DARRELYN
*Water from the Well*. 1990. AROUN

GUO, DAYU, 1948– , and XI, ZHIGAN
*Xu Jiujing sheng guan ji*. See Xu Jiujing's Promotion
*Xu Jiujing's Promotion*. 1981.
    Yu, S., translator YUCHD
    Variant title: *Xu Jiujing sheng guan ji*

GUO, SHIXING, 1952–
*Birdmen*. 1993.
    Lai, J., translator CHEU
    Variant title: *Niaoren*
*Niaoren*. See Birdmen

GURNEY, A. R., Jr., 1930–
*Another Antigone*. 1988. KIRLA, KIRLB, KIRLC
*The Cocktail Hour*. 1989. BERT, BES88
*The Dining Room*. 1982. BES81, PLACHA
*The Golden Fleece*. 1968. BAYM
*Later Life*. 1993. BES92
*Love Letters*. 1988. BES89
*The Perfect Party*. 1986. BES85

GURNEY, RICHARD, 1790–1843
*Romeo and Juliet Travesty*. 1812. NIN1

GUTHRIE, J.
*He Who Gets Slapped*. See Andreev, Leonid
    Nikolaevich. *He Who Gets Slapped* (adapted by)

GUTHRIE, TYRONE, 1900–1971
*Top of the Ladder*. 1950. PLAN3

GUTIERREZ, ANTONIO GARCIA. See García Gutiérrez,
    Antonio

GUTIERREZ, GILBERTO
*Watsonville: Some Place Not Here* (music by Gilberto
    Gutierrez). See Moraga, Cherríe. *Watsonville: Some
    Place Not Here*

GUTWILLIG, STEPHEN
*In the Way.* 1982. YOUP

GUTZKOW, KARL FERDINAND, 1811–1878
*Pigtail and Sword. See* Sword and Queue
*Sword and Queue.* 1843.
   Colbron, G., translator FRA7
   Variant titles: *Pigtail and Sword; Zopf und schwert*
*Zopf und schwert. See* Sword and Queue

GUY, RAY, 1939–
*Young Triffle Have Been Made Away With.* 1985. LYN

GUY, ROSA, 1925–
*My Love, My Love, or the Peasant Girl. See* Ahrens,
   Lynn. *Once on This Island* (based on the novel by)

GUYER, MURPHY
*The World of Mirth.* 1986. PRIMA86

HAAKSKEEN, PETRUS
*Aia makoes.* 2000. ZEE2
*Finders Keepers Losers Weepers.* 2000. ZEE1
*One Night.* 2000. ZEE2

HAASSE, HELLA S., 1918–
*De draad in het donker. See* A Thread in the Dark
*A Thread in the Dark.* 1963.
   Couling, D., translator ROET
   Variant title: *De draad in het donker*

HAAVIKKO, PAAVO, 1931–2008
*The Superintendent.* 1968.
   Binham, P., translator MNOF

HABER, ALEXANDRIA
*Birthmarks* (excerpt) 1995. BREK

HACKETT, ALBERT, 1900–1995. *See* Goodrich, Frances,
   joint author

HACKETT, WALTER, 1876–1944. *See* Megrue, Roi
   Cooper, joint author

HADDOW, JEFFREY, 1947–. *See* Driver, John, joint author

HADLER, WILLIAM
*Flite Cage.* 1969. SME

HAGAN, JAMES, 1888–1947
*One Sunday Afternoon.* 1933. BES32

HAGEDORN, JESSICA TARAHATA, 1949–
*Tenement Lover: No Palm Trees/in New York City*
   (music by Jessica Hatch, the Gangster Choir, and

Lawrence "Butch" Morris; based on a song by
   Jessica Hatch). First performed 1981, published
   version is 1989 revision. BETW
— *See also* Carlos, Laurie, joint author

HAHN, MEDINA. *See* Arnold, Daniel, joint author

HAILEY, ARTHUR, 1920–2004
*Flight into Danger.* 1956. BRNB, BRNS
*Shadow of Suspicion.* GREG

HAILEY, OLIVER, 1932–1993
*About Time.* 1982. *See* Anonymous Plays. *Twenty-four
   Hours: P.M.*
*Hey You, Light Man!* 1961. GASY
*Who's Happy Now?* 1967. LAH, TEX

HAINES, JOHN THOMAS, 1799?–1843
*My Poll and My Partner Joe.* 1835. BOOB
*The Ocean of Life.* 1836. KILG

HAINES, WILLIAM WISTER, 1908–1989
*Command Decision.* 1947. BES47, CLH, MIJY, QUIN,
   TUCN

HAIRSTON, JEROME, 1975?–
*Forty Minute Finish.* 1999. HUMANA99

HAKIM, TAWIQ, 1898–1987. *See* Al-Hakim, Tawfik

HALAC, RICARDO, 1935–
*A Thousand Years, One Day.* 1993.
   Glickman, N., and Waldman, G., translators ARGJT
   Variant title: *Mil anos, un dia*
*Mil anos, un dia. See* A Thousand Years, One Day

HALBE, MAX, 1865–1944
*Mother Earth.* 1897.
   Grummann, P., translator FRA20
   Variant title: *Mutter erde*
*Mutter erde. See* Mother Earth

HALE, JOHN, 1926–
*The Black Swan Winter.* 1969. PLAN37
*Spithead.* 1969. PLAN38

HALEVY, LUDOVIC, 1834–1908. *See* Meilhac, Henri,
   joint author

HALL, BOB, and RICHMOND, DAVID
*The Passion of Dracula* (based on the novel by Bram
   Stoker). 1977. KAYT

HALL, CAROL, 1936?–
*The Best Little Whorehouse in Texas; A Musical
   in Two Acts* (music and lyrics by). *See* King,

Larry L., and Masterson, Peter. *The Best Little Whorehouse in Texas*

HALL, HOLWORTHY, pseud. *See* Porter, Harold Everett

HALL, TONY, 1948– , and SPENCER, RHOMA, and SANDIFORD, SUSAN
*Jean and Dinah Who Have Been Locked Away in a World Famous Calypso since 1956 Speak Their Minds Publicly.* 1994. SEARS2

HALL, WILLIS, 1929–2005
*The Long and the Short and the Tall.* 1959. NEWE3
— *See* Waterhouse, Keith, joint author

HALLDÓRSSON, ERLINGUR E., 1930–
*Mink.* (1965)
    Boucher, A., translator MNOI
    Variant title: *Minkarnir*
*Minkarnir. See* Mink

HALLE, ADAM DE LA. *See* Adam de la Halle

HALLIDAY, ANDREW, 1830–1877
*Romeo and Juliet Travestie; or, The Cup of Cold Poison.* 1859. NIN3
— *See also* BROUGH, WILLIAM, joint author

HALPER, LEIVICK (H. Leivick, pseudonym), 1888–1962
*The Golem.* 1920.
    Landis, J., translator LAO, LAOG, THQ
*Heroic Years. See* Hirsh Lekert
*Hirsh Lekert; or, Heroic Years.* 1928.
    Lifson, D., translator LIFS
    Variant title: *Heroic Years*
*Shap. See* Shop
*Shop.* 1926.
    Sandrow, N., translator SANR
    Variant title: *Shap*

HALPERN, LEIVICK. *See* Halper, Leivick

HAMANJODA, AMINU
*Merchants of Destiny.* 1990. FINBN

HAMBLIN, LOUISA (MEDINA), d.1838
*Nick of the Woods.* 1838. VICT

HAMILTON, CICELY, 1872–1952
*Diana of Dobson's.* 1908. NEWWP, YEAR

—— and ST. JOHN, CHRISTOPHER
*How the Vote Was Won.* 1909. VOTE

HAMILTON, GODFREY
*Kissing Marianne.* 1994. CLUMS

HAMILTON, PATRICK, 1904–1962
*Angel Street.* 1941. BES41, CART, MOST, RICI, SAFM
    Variant title: *Gaslight*
*Gaslight. See* Angel Street

HAMLIN, MARY P., 1871–1964
*The Rock.* 1921? FED1

HAMLISCH, MARVIN, 1944–
*A Chorus Line* (music by). *See* Kirkwood, James and Dante, Nicholas. *A Chorus Line*

HAMMERSTEIN II, OSCAR, 1895–1960
*Allegro* (music by Richard Rodgers). 1947. BES47
*The King and I* (music by Richard Rodgers). 1951. CORB, CORBA
*Oklahoma!* (based on *Green Grow the Lilacs* by Lynn Riggs; music by Richard Rodgers). 1943. BES42, CEY

—— and LOGAN, JOSHUA
*South Pacific* (based on *Tales of the South Pacific* by James A. Michener; music by Richard Rodgers). 1949. QUIN

HAMMOND, MARIE-LYNN
*Beaux gestes et beautiful deeds. See* Beautiful Deeds/De beau gestes
*Beautiful Deeds/De beau gestes.* 1994. RAVELII, ZIMM (excerpt)
    Variant title: *Beaux gestes et beautiful deeds*

HAMMOND, WENDY, 1955–
*Julie Johnson.* 1994. HUMANA94

HAMPTON, CHRISTOPHER, 1946–
*Les liaisons dangereuses.* 1986. BES86
*The Philanthropist.* 1971. BES70
*The Portage to San Cristobal of A. H.* (adapted from the novella by George Steiner). 1982. THLA

—— and BLACK, DAN
*Sunset Boulevard* (book and lyrics by). *See* Black, Dan. *Sunset Boulevard*

HAMSON, LESLIE
*Surfing Blue* (radio play). 1990. WRIT

HAN, LAO-DA (pseudonym of Han, Yong Yuan), 1947–
*Alien.* 1991.
    Sim, B., translator MLAS

HAN, YONG YUAN, 1947–. *See* Han, Lao-Da (pseudonym of)

HAN-CH'ING, KUAN. *See* Kuan, Han-ch'ing

HANAFIAH, ABDUL RAHMAN, 1945– . *See* Sikana, Mana (pseud. of)

HANAN, STEPHEN MO, 1947– and BERKOW, JAY
*Jolson & Company*. 1999. NEWR2000

HANDKE, PETER, 1942–
*Das Mündel will Vormund sein*. *See* My Foot My Tutor
*My Foot My Tutor*. 1969.
Roloff, M., translator SHAK
Variant title: *Das Mündel will Vormund sein*
*Offending the Audience*. 1966. WOTHM
Variant title: *Publikumsbeschimpfung*
*Publikumsbeschimpfung*. *See* Offending the Audience

HANEMON, TSUUCHI. *See* Tsuuchi, Hanemon

HANGULA, VICKSON TABLAH, 1970–
*The Show Isn't over Until*. 1998. ZEE1

HANJURŌ, TSUUCHI. *See* Tsuuchi, Hanjurō

HANKIN, ST. JOHN EMILE CLAVERING, 1869–1909
*The Cassilis Engagement*. 1907. DICEM, MOSN, MOSO, ROWC
*The Last of the De Mullins*. 1908. CHA, CHAN, CHAR, CHOT
*The Return of the Prodigal*. 1905. MART, WEAL

HANLEY, JAMES, 1901–1985
*Say Nothing*. 1962. PLAN27

HANLEY, WILLIAM, 1931–
*Slow Dance on the Killing Ground*. 1964. BES64, GAT

HANNAN, CHRIS, 1958–
*Elizabeth Gordon Quinn*. 1985. CALE

HANSBERRY, LORRAINE, 1930–1965
*The Drinking Gourd*. 1960. HARY
*A Raisin in the Sun*. 1959. ABCH, ALLO, ALS, ANT, BARO, BEATA, BES58, BRIZ, BRJ, BRJA, CASH, CEQ, CEQA, CES, COLD, DIEA, DIEB, DIER, DIYL, DIYLB, DIYLC, DIYLD, DIYRD, FOL, FORD (Act 1 only), FOT, FRYE, GRIH, GUTDF, GUTDS, GWYN, HAPO, HARYB, HEAA, HEAB, HEAC, HEAD, HEALC, HEALD, HEIS, HOEP, HOWM, JACOB, JACOBA, JACOBD, JACOBE, KIN, KIRLA, KLIS, LAV, LEVY, MANCF2, MANCG2, MANCH2, MANCIO, MAO, MEYC, MEYCA, MEYCB, MEYD, MEYE, MEYF, MONA, OLIV, PATR,

PERU, PERV, PLABE5, PLAU, SCNP, SILKI, SSSIC, SYM, WHFM, WILLG
*The Sign in Sidney Brustein's Window*. 1964. GAT, THT
*Toussaint*: excerpt from Act I of a Work in Progress. 1961. WILK

HANSHEW, THOMAS W., 1857–1914
*The Forty-niners*. 1879. BAT20

HAN TIEN. *See* Tien, Han

HANGER, EUNICE, 1911–1972
*Flood*. 1955. PFIS

HAO-KU, LI. *See* Li, Hao-ku

HAPIPI, RORE, 1933– (b. Rowley Habib)
*Death of the Land*. 1991. GARR

HARBURG, EDGAR Y., 1896–1981, and SAIDY, FRED
*Finian's Rainbow*. 1947. HUDE

HARDIE, VICTORIA
*Sleeping Nightie*. 1989. FIFHL2

HARDIN, HERSCHEL, 1936–
*Esker Mike & His Wife, Agiluk*. 1971. SSSN

HARDING, ALEX
*Blood and Honour*. 1990. AUSG

HARDING, MICHAEL, 1953–
*Hubert Murray's Widow*. 1993. NEWPAB1
*Misogynist*. 1990. CRACK
*Sour Grapes*. 1997. NEWPAB2
*Una pooka*. 1989. FIFHL2

HARDMAN, CHRIS
*Vacuum*. 1981. WES17/18

HARDT, ERNST, 1876–1947
*Tantris the Fool*. *See* Tristram the Jester
*Tristram the Jester*. 1907.
Heard, J., translator FRA20
Variant title: *Tantris the Fool*

HARDY, ALEXANDRE, 1575?–1631?
*Mariamne*. 1605–1615?
Lockert, L., translator LOCU

HARDY, THOMAS, 1840–1928
*The Day after the Fair*. *See* Harvey, Frank. *The Day after the Fair* (based on a story by)
*The Play of St. George* (reconstructed from memory by). *See* Anonymous Plays. *The Play of St. George*

HARE, DAVID, 1947–
*Plenty: A Play in Two Acts.* 1978. BES82, PLACHB
*Skylight.* 1996. BES96

HARELIK, MARK, 1951–
*The Immigrant: A Hamilton County Album.* 1985.
PRIMA85
— *See also* Myler, Randal, joint author

HARGRAVE, ROY, 1896–1966. *See* Britton, Kenneth
Phillips, joint author

HARLAN, WALTER, 1867–1931
*The Nüremberg Egg.* 1913.
Katzin, W., translator KAT
Variant title: *Das Nürnburgisch ei*
*Das Nürnburgisch ei. See* The Nüremberg Egg

HARLING, ROBERT, 1951–
*Steel Magnolias.* 1987. BES87, PERR2

HARMON, PEGGY, 1953– , and PEN, POLLY
*Goblin Market* (joint author and music by Polly Pen;
adapted from the poem by Christina Rosetti). 1985.
BES85

HARNICK, SHELDON, 1924–
*The Apple Tree* (joint author and music by Jerry Bock).
1966. BES66
*Fiddler on the Roof* (lyrics by). *See* Stein, Joseph.
*Fiddler on the Roof*
*Fiorello!* (lyrics by). *See* Weidman, Jerome and Abbott,
George. *Fiorello!*
*She Loves Me* (lyrics by). *See* Masteroff, Joe. *She Loves
Me*

HARNWELL, MRS. ANNA JANE (WILCOX), 1872– ,
and MEAKER, MRS. ISABELLE (JACKSON)
*The Alabaster Box.* 1940. FED2

HARRADEN, BEATRICE, 1864–1936
*Lady Geraldine's Speech.* 1911. VOTE

HARRAR, WILLIAM
*Inquest.* 1994. RUN

HARRIGAN, EDWARD, 1844–1911
*The Blue and the Grey.* 1875. MESC
*The Mulligan Guard Ball.* 1879. MONR

HARRIS, ANNE M.
*Coming In.* 1994. TOR

HARRIS, AURAND, 1915–1996
*The Arkansaw Bear.* 1980. SCVDO1

*The Second Shepherd's Play* (modern adaptation). 1991.
SWO

HARRIS, BILL
*Every Goodbye Ain't Gone.* (1989) KINHP
*Robert Johnson: Trick the Devil.* 1995. KINHN
*Up and Gone Again.* 1991. NTIR

HARRIS, TOM, 1930–
*Always with Love.* 1967. NEWA3

HARRISON, JOHN, 1937–
*Knight in Four Acts.* PLAN38
*Unaccompanied Cello.* 1970. PLAN40

HARRISON, PAUL CARTER, 1936–
*Ameri/Cain Gothica.* 1985. HAPU
*The Great MacDaddy.* 1973. CARR, HAPUE
*Tophat.* 1971. KINHP

HARSHA, SON OF HIRA, 12th century
*Naganada.* 12th century.
Boyd, P., translator WEL
*The Necklace. See* Retnavali
*Ratnavali. See* Retnavali
*Retnavali; or, The Necklace.* 12th century.
Lal, P., translator LAL
Wilson, H., translator BAT3
Variant titles: *The Necklace; Ratnavali*

HART, CHARLES, 1961–
*The Phantom of the Opera* (lyrics by). *See* Lloyd
Webber, Andrew. *The Phantom of the Opera*

HART, MOSS, 1904–1961
*Christopher Blake.* 1946. BES46
*The Climate of Eden* (based on the novel *Shadows Move
among Them* by Edgar Mittelhölzer). 1952. BES52,
THEA53
*Lady in the Dark* (music by Kurt Weill; lyrics by Ira
Gershwin). 1941. BES40, RICM
*Light Up the Sky.* 1948. BES48
*Winged Victory* (music by David Rose). 1943. BES43
— *See* Kaufman, George S., joint author

HARTE, BRET, 1836–1902, and TWAIN, MARK
*Ah Sin.* 1876. CHIN

HARTOG, JAN DE, 1914–2002
*The Fourposter.* 1951. BES51, GART, GATB4, RICT
*Skipper Next to God.* 1945. BES47, EMB2

HARTSON, HALL, 1739?–1773
*The Countess of Salisbury* (adapted from the romance
*Longsword, earl of Salisbury,* attributed to Thomas
Leland and John Leland). 1765. BELG11

HARTZENBUSCH, JUAN EUGENIO, 1806–1880
*Los amantes de Teruel*. 1837. BRET
Variant title: *The Lovers of Teruel*
*The Lovers of Teruel*. *See* Los amantes de Teruel

HARVEY, FRANK, 1912–1981
*The Day after the Fair* (based on a story by Thomas
Hardy). 1972. PLAN43

HARVEY, JONATHAN, 1968–
*Mohair*. 1988. DODGS
*Beautiful Thing*. 1993. GAY5

HARWOOD, HAROLD MARSH, 1874–1959
*Old Folks at Home*. 1933. FAMF

―――― and GORE-BROWN, ROBERT F.
*Cynara*. 1930. BES31

HARWOOD, RONALD, 1934– (b. Ronald Horwitz)
*The Dresser*. 1980. BES81

HASEGAWA, SHIGURE. 1879–1941
*Chojo midare*. *See* Wavering Traces
*Wavering Traces*. 1911.
Cavanaugh, C., translator KEL

HASENCLEVER, WALTER, 1890–1940
*Antigone*. 1917.
Ritchie, J., and Stowell, J., translators RITV
*Humanity*. 1918.
Sokel, W., and J., translators SOK
Variant title: *Die Menschen*
*Die Menschen*. *See* Humanity
*The Son*. 1914.
Marx, H., translator EXP, SCVG

―――― and TUCHOLSKY, KARL
*Christopher Columbus*. 1933.
Spalter, M. and Wellwarth, G., translators WELG

HASHIMOTO, SHINOBU, 1918– . *See* Kurosawa, Akira,
joint author

HASSAN, NOORDIN, 1930s–
*Door*. 1993.
Ishak, S., translator MLAM

HASTINGS, BASIL MACDONALD, 1881–1928
*The New Sin*. 1912. PLAP2

HASTINGS, CHARLOTTE
*Bonaventure*. 1949. PLAN3
Variant titles: *Mary Bonaventure; Sister Cecilia*
*Mary Bonaventure*. *See* Bonaventure
*Sister Cecilia*. *See* Bonaventure
*Uncertain Joy*. 1953. PLAN12

HASTINGS, HUGH, 1917–2004 (b. Hugh Williamson)
*Seagulls over Sorrento*. 1950. PLAN4

HASTINGS, MICHAEL, 1938–
*Yes, and After*. 1957. NEWE4

HATCH, JAMES V., 1928– *See* Jackson, C. Bernard, joint
author

HATCHER, JEFFREY, 1957–
*Compleat Female Stage Beauty*. 1999. BES99
*Show Business*. 2000. HUMANA2000
*What Corbin Knew*. 2000. NEWR99

HATHWAY, RICHARD, fl.1602
*Sir John Oldcastle, pt. I* (sometimes attributed to). *See*
Anonymous Plays. *Sir John Oldcastle, Part I*

HAUBOLD, CLEVE, 1930–
*The Big Black Box*. 1965. SCVDO1

HAUPTMAN, WILLIAM, 1942–
*Domino Courts*. 1975. WOQ1

HAUPTMANN, CARL FERDINAND MAXIMILIAN,
1858–1921
*Kreig, ein Te Deum*. *See* War, A Te Deum
*War, a Te Deum*. 1913?
Ritchie, J., and Stowell, J., translators RITV
Variant title: *Kreig, ein Te Deum*

HAUPTMANN, ELISABETH, 1897–1973. *See* Brecht,
Bertolt, joint author

HAUPTMANN, GERHART, 1862–1946
*The Assumption of Hannele*. *See* Hannele
*The Beaver Coat*. 1893.
Cardullo, B., translator GERLC
Lewisohn, L., translator STE, WATI, WATL1
Variant title: *Der biberpelz, eine diebs komödie*
*Der biberpelz, eine diebs komödie*. *See* The Beaver Coat
*The Coming of Peace*. *See* Das friedensfest
*Einsame menschen*. 1891. CAM
Variant title: *Lonely Lives*
*The Festival of Peace*. *See* Das friedensfest
*Das friedensfest*. 1890. STI1
Variant titles: *The Coming of Peace; The Festival of
Peace; The Reconciliation*
*Hannele*. 1893.
Archer, W., translator BAT12
Frenz, H., and Waggoner, M., translators ULAN
Meltzer, C., translator HAV, HUD, INTE
Variant titles: *The Assumption of Hannele; Hannele's
Assumption; Hanneles himmelfahrt; The Journey to
Heaven of Hannele*

*Hannele's Assumption. See* Hannele
*Hanneles himmelfahrt. See* Hannele
*The Journey to Heaven of Hannele. See* Hannele
*Lonely Lives. See* Einsame menschen
*Michael Kramer.* 1900. FEFH2
    Lewisohn, L., translator FRA18
*The Rats.* 1911.
    Lewisohn, L., translator TUCG, TUCM, TUCN,
      TUCO
    Variant title: *Die ratten*
*Die ratten. See* The Rats
*The Reconciliation. See* Das friedens fest
*The Sunken Bell.* 1896.
    Meltzer, C., translator BUCK, BUCL, BUCM,
      FRA18, MACN, MOSQ, WHK
    Variant title: *Die versunkene glocke*
*Die versunkene glocke. See* The Sunken Bell
*The Weavers.* 1892.
    Frenz, H., and Waggoner, M., translators BLOC,
      HOUP
    Huebsch, B., translator THON
    Morison, M., translator CEW, DICD, DICIN1,
      FRA18, SMP, TRE, TREA1, TREBA, TREBJ,
      TREC2, TREE2, TREI2, WHI
    Mueller, C., translator COTL, COTQ
    Variant title: *Die weber*
*Die weber. See* The Weavers
*Der weisse heiland. See* The White Saviour
*The White Saviour.* 1920.
    Muir, W., and E., translators KRE
    Variant titles: *Der weisse heiland; The White Redeemer*

HAUTEROCHE, NOEL LEBRETON, 1617–1707
*Crispin médecin. See* Ravenscroft, Edward, and
    Motteux, P. A. *The Sham Doctor* (based on)

HAVARD, WILLIAM, 1710–1778
*Charles I. See* King Charles I.
*King Charles I.* (1737) BELK12
    Variant title: *Charles I*

HAVEL, VACLAV, 1936–
*Largo desolato.* 1985.
    Stoppard, T., translator BERP, BERPA, VENA
    Winn, M., translator, BES85
*The Memorandum.* 1965.
    Backwell, V., translator THOR
*Protest.* 1978.
    Blackwell, V., translator and adapter DRAC, HEALD,
      HEALE, MEYE
*Temptation.* 1986.
    Winn, M., translator GILB, SSSIA
*Tomorrow!* 1988.
    Day, B., translator DAY
    Variant title: *Zítra to spustíme*

*Unveiling.* Mid-1970s.
    Novak, J., translator PERZ
*Zítra to spustíme. See* Tomorrow!

HAVIARA, ELENI. *See* Kehaidis, Dimitris, joint author

HAVIS, ALLAN, 1951–
*Morocco.* 1985. NEWQB
*A Vow of Silence.* 1994. SCM

HAVREVOLD, FINN, 1905–1988
*The Injustice.* (1955)
    Brown, J., translator MNON
    Variant title: *Uretten*
*Uretten. See* The Injustice

HAWKES, JACQUETTA (HOPKINS), 1910–1996. *See*
    Priestley, John Boynton, joint author

HAWKES, JOHN, 1925–1998
*The Wax Museum.* 1966. PLAC

HAWKESWORTH, JOHN, 1715?–1773
*Edgar and Emmeline.* 1761. BELC4

HAWTHORNE, NATHANIEL, 1804–1864
*Rappacini's Daughter. See* Paz, Octavio. *Rappacini's
    Daughter* (based on the story by)

HAWTHORNE, RUTH (WARREN). *See* Kennedy, Mary,
    joint author

HAY, IAN (pseudonym of John Hay Beith), 1876–1952
*"Let My People Go!"* 1948. EMB3

HAY, JULIUS, 1900–1975
*The Horse.* 1964.
    Hap, P., translator THOR

HAYDEN, JOHN, 1887–1948
*Lost Horizons.* 1935. BES34

HAYES, ALFRED, 1911–1985
*Act of Love. See* The Girl on the Via Flaminia
*The Girl on the Via Flaminia.* 1954. BES53, COTK
    Variant title: *Act of Love*

HAYES, CATHERINE, 1949–
*Not Waving.* 1983. EAG (Act II only)

HAYES, JOSEPH, 1918–2006
*The Desperate Hours.* 1955. BES54, BIER, RICN,
    THEA55

HAYSOM, FINK. *See* Keogh, Danny, joint author

HAZELTON, GEORGE COCHRANE, JR., 1868–1921
*Mistress Nell.* 1900. AMP16

—— and BENRIMO, JOSEPH HENRY
*The Yellow Jacket.* 1912. CHIN, DICDS

HAZLEWOOD, COLIN HENRY, 1823–1875
*Lady Audley's Secret* (from the novel by Mary Elizabeth Braddon). 1863. ROWE

HAZZARD, ALVIRA, 1899–1953
*Mother Liked It.* 1928. HARYL

HE ARA HOU, 1989–1996, and POTIKI, ROMA, joint author
*Whatungarongaro.* 1990. KOU

HE, JIPING, 1951–
*The First House of Beijing Duck.* 1988.
   Yu, S., translator YUCHD
   Variant titles: *Tianxia diyi lou, The World's Top Restaurant*
*Tianxia diyi lou. See* The First House of Beijing Duck
*The World's Top Restaurant. See* The First House of Beijing Duck

HEALEY, FRANCES
*The Copper Pot.* 1919. WEB

HEBBEL, CHRISTIAN FRIEDRICH, 1813–1863
*Agnes Bernauer.* 1852. CAM
   Pattee, L., translator SCVN, SMK
*Herodes und Marianne.* 1849. CAM
*Maria Magdalena. See* Maria Magdalene
*Maria Magdalene.* 1844. CAM
   Fairley, B., translator BUCK, BUCL, BUCM, FEFH1, TREA2, TREB, TREC1, TREE1, TREI1
   Green, P., translator CLKW, GRIF
   Mueller, C., translator COTL, COTQ
   Thomas, P., translator FRA9, SMI
   Variant title: *Maria Magdalena*
*Siegfried's Death.* 1862.
   Royee, K., translator FRA9

HEBERT, JULIE
*Almost Asleep.* 1989. MEDN

HECHT, BEN, 1893–1964
   — *See also* Goodman, Kenneth S., joint author

—— and MacARTHUR, CHARLES
*The Front Page.* 1928. BES28, CET, GASB, GATB1

HEGGEN, THOMAS, 1918–1949, and LOGAN, JOSHUA
*Mister Roberts.* 1948. BES47, CEQA, COLT, GARW, GATB3, HATA, RICT, SIXC

HEIBERG, GUNNAR EDWARD RODE, 1857–1929
*Kjaerlighedens tragedie. See* The Tragedy of Love
*The Tragedy of Love.* 1904.
   Björkman, E., translator DICDS
   Variant title: *Kjaerlighedens tragedie*

HEIBERG, JOHAN LUDVIG, 1791–1860
*No* (adapted by Michael Meyer and Casper Wrede, lyrics by Michael Flanders). 1836.
   Meyer, M., translator THOQ

HEIDE, CHRIS. *See* Heide, Christopher

HEIDE, CHRISTOPHER, 1951–
*"I Ain't Dead Yet!"* 1985. HEID
*Pogie* (music by Al Macdonald). 1980. NEWCAD2

HEIDE, ROBERT, 1939–
*At War with the Mongols.* 1970. NEWA4
*Moon.* 1967. SMC

HEIFNER, JACK, 1946–
*Patio.* 1978. TEX
*Porch.* 1977. TEX

HEIJERMANS, HERMAN (Samuel Falkland, pseud.), 1864–1924
*The Good Hope.* 1900?
   Saunders, L., and Heijermans–Houwink, C., translators GARZH
   Variant title: *Op hoop van zegen*
*Op hoop van zegen. See* The Good Hope

HELLER, JOSEPH, 1923–1999
*We Bombed in New Haven.* 1967. FAMAH

HELLMAN, LILLIAN, 1905–1984
*Another Part of the Forest* (music by Marc Blitzstein). 1946. BES46, WATE
*The Autumn Garden.* 1951. BES50, CLM, FAM, FAMAF, GARW
*Candide* (based on *Candide* by Voltaire; music by Leonard Bernstein; lyrics by Richard Wilbur, John Latouche and Dorothy Parker). 1956. BES56
*The Children's Hour.* 1934. BES34, FIP, GAS, GATB2, LEVY, PLAN5, SUB, WATTAD
*The Lark. See* Anouilh, Jean. *The Lark* (translator and adapted by)
*The Little Foxes.* 1939. BAIL, BAIM, BARNA, BARS, BEATA, BES38, BLOO, CET, CORB, CORBA, COTE, COTH, COTQ, DODS, HARB, HAVE, HILP, KLIS, LITP, LITQ, MIJY, PERR2, PLAAF, SIXC, SIXL, TREBA, TREBJ, TREC2, TREE3, TREI3
   Variant title: *Regina*

*Regina. See* The Little Foxes
*The Searching Wind.* 1944. BES43
*Toys in the Attica.* 1960. BES59, CEQ, CES
*Watch on the Rhine.* 1941. BES40, CALN2, CALP,
    CALQ, CASS, CRIT, CUBE, GARZ, GAVE,
    HAVD, NAGE

HEMRO
*Poor Ostrich.* 1948? RUA

HENG, RUSSELL HIANG KHNG
*Lest the Demons Get to Me.* 1992. FAT

HENLEY, BETH, 1952–
*Abundance.* 1989. PLACG1
*Am I Blue?* 1982. HOEP, MEY
*Crimes of the Heart.* 1979. BERS, BES80, DIXP,
    KIRLC, LITIE, LITJ, PLACHA
*Hymn in the Attica.* 1982. *See* Anonymous Plays.
    *Twenty-four Hours: P.M.*
*The Miss Firecracker Contest; a Play in Two Acts.*
    1981. BES83

HENNESSEY, BRIAN, 1949– . *See* Thomey, Greg, joint
    author

HENSEL, KAREN, 1948– ; JOHNS, PATTI; KENT,
    ALANA; MEREDITH, SYLVIA; SHAW,
    ELIZABETH LLOYD; and TOFFENETTI,
    LAURA
*Going to See the Elephant.* (Original writing and
    structure, Hensel and Kent; character development
    and dialogue, Johns, Meredith, Shaw, Toffenetti;
    concept, Johns). 1982. WES15/16

HENSHAW, JAMES ENE, 1924–2007
*The Jewels of the Shrine.* 1952? HOGN, LITT

HEPBURN, STUART
*Loose Ends.* 1989. FIFHL2

HERBERT, FREDERICK HUGH, 1897–1958
*Kiss and Tell.* 1943. BES42
*The Moon Is Blue.* 1951. GARW

HERBERT, JOHN (pseud. of John Herbert Brundage),
    1926–2001
*Fortune and Men's Eyes.* 1967. MARP, PENG, PERKY,
    WASCP, WASCPA1, WASCPB1

HERMAN, HENRY, 1832–1894. *See* Jones, Henry Arthur,
    joint author; *See also* Wills, W. G., joint author.

HERMAN, JERRY, 1933–
*La cage aux folles* (music and lyrics by). *See* Fierstein,
    Harvey. *La cage aux folles*
*Hello, Dolly!* (music and lyrics by). *See* Stewart,
    Michael. *Hello, Dolly!*

L'HERMITE, FRANÇOIS TRISTAN. *See* Tristan
    l'Hermite, François

HERNANDEZ, ANTONIO ACEVEDO. *See* Acevedo
    Hernández, Antonio

HERNANDEZ, LEOPOLDO M., 1921–
*Martinez.* 1980. CUB
*We Were Always Afraid.* 1987. GONZ

HERNANDEZ, LOUISA JOSEFINA. *See* Hernandez,
    Luisa Josefina

HERNANDEZ, LUISA JOSEFINA, 1928–
*La fiesta del mulato. See* Mullato's Orgy
*Mullato's Orgy.* 1971.
    Oliver, W., translator OLIW
    Variant title: *La fiesta del mulato*

HERNDON, VENABLE, 1927–1999
*Until the Monkey Comes.* 1966. NEWA2

HERNE, JAMES A., 1839–1901
*Drifting Apart.* 1888. AMP7
    Variant title: *The Fisherman's Child*
*The Fisherman's Child. See* Drifting Apart
*Margaret Fleming.* 1890. COY, MASW, MASX, MES,
    NILS, QUIL, QUIM, QUIN, WATTAD
*The Minute Men of 1774–1775.* 1886. AMP7
*The Reverend Griffith Davenport, Act. IV.* 1899. AMP7
*Shore Acres.* 1892. DOWM, MONR, WILMET
*Within an Inch of His Life.* 1879. AMP7

HERRERA, LUIS BAYON. *See* Bayón Herrera, Luis

HERREROS, MANUEL BRETON DE LOS. *See* Bretón
    de los Herreros, Manuel

HERSEY, JOHN, 1914–1993
*A Bell for Adano. See* Osborn, Paul. *A Bell for Adano*
    (based on the novel by)

HERSHADEVA, SRI. *See* Harsha, son of Hira

HERST, BETH, 1962–
*A Woman's Comedy.* 1992. BIG

HERVERA, LUIS BAYON. *See* Bayón Herrera, Luis

HERVIEU, PAUL ERNEST, 1857–1915
*Connais-toi. See* Know Thyself
*La course du flambeau.* 1901. BER
  Variant titles: *The Passing of the Torch; The Torch Race; The Trail of the Torch*
*Know Thyself.* 1909.
  Cerf, B., translator DICD
  Variant title: *Connais-toi*
*The Passing of the Torch. See* La course du flambeau
*The Torch Race. See* La course du flambeau
*The Trail of the Torch. See* La course du flambeau

HERZBERG, JUDITH, 1934–
*De caracal. See* The Caracal
*The Caracal.* 1988.
  Vergano, R., translator ROET
*Leedvermaak. See* The Wedding Party
*The Wedding Party.* 1982. COUL
  Variant title: *Leedvermaak*

HESTER, HAL, 1933–1992
*Your Own Thing* (music and lyrics by). *See* Driver, Donald. *Your Own Thing*

HEVI, JACOB, 1946–
*Amavi.* 1975. AFR1

HEWETT, DOROTHY, 1923–2002
*The Chapel Perilous.* 1971. TAIT
*The Man from Mukinupin.* 1979. TYEW
*This Old Man Comes Rolling Home.* 1967. BRIMA2

HEYWARD, MRS. DOROTHY HARTZELL (KUHNS), 1890–1961

—— and HEYWARD, DuBOSE
*Porgy.* 1927. BES27, GASB, GATB1, MAF, MAFC, MIJY, THF

HEYWARD, DuBOSE, 1885–1940
*Porgy and Bess* (based on *Porgy* by Mrs. Dorothy Hartzell (Kuhns) Heyward and DuBose Heyward; lyries by DuBose Heyward and Ira Gershwin; music by George Gershwin). 1935. RICO
  — *See also* Heyward, Mrs. Dorothy Hartzell (Kuhns), joint author

HEYWOOD, JOHN, 1497?–1580?
*The Four pp.* 1569? ADA, BOA, DPR1, GARZB, HOPP, MED, PARRY, TAV, TICO
  Variant titles: *The Four p's; The Playe Called the Foure pp*
*The Four p's. See* The Four pp
*Gentleness and Nobility.* ca.1525. THW

  Variant title: *Of Gentylnes and Nobylyte a Dyaloge*
*Johan Johan. See* John, Tyb and Sir John
*Johan Johan, the Husbande. See* John, Tyb and Sir John
*Johan, Tyb his wife, and Sir Jhan the Preest. See* John, Tyb and Sir John
*John, Tyb and Sir John.* 1533. ADA, BEVD, CRE, GAYLE1, HOPP, LOOM, PAR, RUB
  Variant titles: *Johan Johan; Johan Johan, the Husbande; Johan, Tyb his Wife and Sir Jhan the Preest; John, Tyb and the Curate; A Merry Play; A Mery Play betweene Johan Johan, the Husbande, Tyb his Wyfe, and Syr Jhan, the Preest; A Mery Play betweene Johan Johan, Tyb, his Wyfe and Syr Jhan, the Preest; A Mery Play betwene Johan Johan the Husbande, Tib his Wife, and Sir Johan the Preest*
*John, Tyb and the Curate. See* John, Tyb and Sir John
*A Merry Play. See* John, Tyb and Sir John
*A Mery Play betweene Johan Johan, the Husbande, Tyb his Wyfe, and Syr Jhan, the Preest. See* John, Tyb, and Sir John
*A Mery Play betweene Johan Johan, Tyb, his Wyfe and Syr Jhan, the Preest. See* John, Tyb and Sir John
*A Mery Play betwene Johan Johan the Husbande, Tib his Wife, and Sir Johan the Preest. See* John, Tyb and Sir John
*A Mery Play betwene Johan Johan, the Husbande, Tyb his Wyfe, and Syr Jhan, the Preest. See* John, Tyb and Sir John
*A Mery Playe betwene the Pardoner and the Frere, the Curate and Neybour Pratte. See* The Pardoner and the Friar
*Of Gentylnes and Nobylyte a Dyaloge. See* Gentleness and Nobility
*The Pardoner and the Friar.* 1521? LOOM, POLL
  Variant title: *A Mery Playe betwene the Pardoner and the Frere, the Curate and Neybour Pratte*
*A Play of Love; A Newe and a Mery Enterlude concerning Pleasure and Payne in Love, Made by Iohn Heywood.* (1533) SOME
*The Play of the Weather. See* The Play of the Wether
*The Play of the Weather a New and a Very Mery Enterlude of All Maner Wethers. See* The Play of the Wether
*The Play of the Wether.* 1525–1533. ADA, BEVD, HAO, GAYLE1, MED, PARRY
*The Playe Called the Foure pp. See* The Four pp

HEYWOOD, THOMAS, 1574?–1641
*The Fair Maid of the West.* 1631. MARG
*A Woman Killed with Kindness.* 1603. ASH, BAS, BROC, CLF1, DPR1, DUN, GATG, KINNR, LAWR, MAKG, MAME, MATTL, NEI, NES, OLH, OLI1, PAR, RYL, SCH, SCI, SCJ, SMI, SPE, STUR, TAT, TAU, WALL

HIBBERD, JACK, 1940–
  *A Stretch of the Imagination.* 1972. BRIM1
  *White with Wire Wheels.* 1967. FOUA
  *Who?* 1968. FOUA

HICKERSON, HAROLD. *See* Anderson, Maxwell, joint
  author

HICKMAN, CRAIG, 1967–
  *Skin & Ornaments.* 1998. HUGH

HIERHOLZER, ALEXANDER
  *Grace and George and God.* 1970. BALLE7

HIGHWAY, TOMSON, 1951–
  *Dry Lips Oughta Move to Kapuskasing.* 1989.
    WASCPA2, WASCPB2, WOTHB, WOTHC

HILARIUS, 12th century
  *Ludus super iconia Sancti Nicolai. See* The Statue of
    Saint Nicholas
  *The Miracle of Saint Nicholas and the Image.* 12th
    century. LOOM
  *The Raising of Lazarus.* 12th century. BEVD
    Variant title: *Suscitatio Lazari*
  *The Statue of Saint Nicholas.* 12th century. MAR
    Variant title: *Ludus super iconia Sancti Nicolai*
  *Suscitatio Lazari. See* The Raising of Lazarus

HILDEGARD OF BINGEN. *See* Hildegard, Saint

HILDEGARD, SAINT, 1098–1179
  *Ordo virtutum. See* The Play of the Virtues
  *The Play of the Virtues.* 1151?
    Dronke, P., translator DRON
    Variant title: *Ordo virtutum*

HILDESHEIMER, WOLFGANG, 1916–1991
  *Nachtstück. See* Nightpiece
  *Nightpiece.* 1962.
    Hildesheimer, W., translator BENB
    Variant title: *Nachtstück*

HILL, AARON, 1685–1750
  *Alzira.* 1736. BELK10
  *Merope.* 1749. BELK10
  *Zara.* 1736. BELK1

HILL, ABRAM, 1911–1986
  *On Strivers Row.* 1938. BLAC, HARYB, ROOTS
  *Walk Hard.* 1944. HARY
  — *See also* Silvera, John D.

HILL, AMY, 1953?–
  *Tokyo Bound.* 1991. ASIAM

HILL, ERROL, 1921–2003
  *Man Better Man.* 1960. GASY, HILEP
  *Strictly Matrimony.* 1959. KINH, KINHB

HILL, FREDERIC STANHOPE, 1805–1851
  *The Six Degrees of Crime.* 1834. SATI

HILL, GARY LEON
  *Back to the Blanket.* 1990. PRIMA91
  *Food from Trash.* 1983. DIXP, NEWQA
  *Soundbite.* 1989. PRIMA89–90

HILL, KAY, 1917–
  *Three to Get Married.* 1964. HEID (excerpt)

HILL, LUCIENNE
  *Paddle Your Own Canoe. See* Regnier, Max Albert
    Marie. *Paddle Your Own Canoe* (translated and
    adapted by)
  *The Waltz of the Toreadors. See* Anouilh, Jean. *The
    Waltz of the Toreadors* (translated and adapted by)

HILL, OLIVIA
  *Mother Spense.* 1992. FLET (one scene only)

HILTON, ARTHUR CLEMENT, 1851–1877
  *Hamlet; or, Not Such a Fool as He Looks.* (1882) NIN4

HINES, BARRY, 1939–
  *Threads* (television play). 1984. MARLC

HINES, KAREN, 1963–
  *Pochsy's Lips.* 1992. ZIMM (excerpt)

HINES, LEONARD JOHN
  *Simon.* 1934. SEVE

HIPPOLYTE, KENDEL, 1952–
  *The Drum-maker.* 1985. NOEL

HIRATA, ORIZA, 1962–
  *Citizens of Seoul.* 1989.
    Swain, J., translator HACJT1
    Variant title: *Sōru shimini*
  *Sōru shimini. See* Citizens of Seoul

HIRSCHBEIN, PERETZ, 1880–1948
  *Farvorfen vinkel.* 1918.
    Lifson, D., translator LIFS
  *Green Fields.* 1917.
    Landis, J., translator LAO, LAOG
    Sandrow, N., translator SANR
    Variant title: *Grine felder*
  *Grine felder. See* Green Fields

HIRSCHBERG, HERBERT, 1881–
  *Fehler. See* "Mistakes"
  *"Mistakes."* 1906.
    Senelick, L., translator SELOV
    Variant title: *Fehler*

HIRSON, DAVID, 1958–
  *La Bete.* 1991. BES90

HITE, BARBARA, 1935–
  *Birdwatchers.* 1973. COLI
  *Sandcastle.* 1973. COLl

HIVNOR, ROBERT, 1916–
  *The Assault upon Charles Sumner.* 1966. PLAC
  *The Ticklish Acrobat.* 1954. PLAA

HIYOSHI, SA-AMI YASUKIYO, 1383?–1458
  *Benkei on the Bridge.* 15th century
    Waley, A., translator ANDF, WAJ
    Variant title: *Hashi-Benki*
  *Hashi-Benki. See* Benkei on the Bridge

HO, CHING-CHIH, and TING, YI
  *The White-haired Girl.* 1945.
    Anonymous translator FIFW
    Yang, H., and Yang, G., translators MESE

HOADLY, BENJAMIN, 1706–1757
  *The Suspicious Husband.* 1747. BELK4, MOR

HOARE, PRINCE, 1755–1834
  *No Song No Supper* (music by Stephen Storace). 1790.
    HUGL

HOBBES, DWIGHT, 1951–
  *You Can't Always Sometimes Never Tell.* (1977) CEN

HOBBES, JOHN OLIVER (pseud. of Pearl Craigie),
    1867–1906
  *The Ambassador.* 1898. FEFNC

HOCHHUTH, ROLF, 1931–
  *The Deputy.* 1963.
    Winston, R., and C., translators BES63
    Variant titles: *The Representative; Der Stellvertreter*
  *The Representative. See* The Deputy
  *Der Stellvertreter. See* The Deputy

HOCHWÄLDER, FRITZ, 1911–1986
  *Das heilige experiment. See* The Strong Are Lonely
  *Die Himbeere Pflücker. See* The Raspberry Picker
  *The Holy Experiment. See* The Strong Are Lonely
  *Der öffentliche ankläger. See* The Public Prosecutor

  *The Public Prosecutor.* 1947.
    Black, K., translator PLAN16
    Variant title: *Der öffentliche ankläger*
  *The Raspberry Picker.* 1965.
    Bullock, M., translator ANTH
    Variant title: *Die Himbeere Pflücker*
  *The Strong Are Lonely.* 1942.
    LeGallienne, E., translator PLAN14
    Wellwarth, G., translator WELT
    Variant titles: *Das heilige experiment; The Holy Experiment*

HODGE, MERTON, 1904–1958
  *As It Was in the Beginning. See* The Wind and the Rain
  *Grief Goes Over.* 1935. FAMH
  *The Island.* 1937. SIXP
  *The Wind and the Rain.* 1933. FAME
    Variant title: *As It Was in the Beginning*

HODSON, JAMES LANSDALE, 1891–1956
  *Harvest in the North.* 1939. FAML
  *Red Night.* 1936. FAMI

HOEM, EDVARD, 1949–
  *God natt, Europa. See* Good Night, Europe
  *Good Night, Europe.* 1983.
    Garton, J., translator NEWNOR
    Variant title: *God natt, Europa*

HOFFE, MONCKTON, 1880–1951 (b. Reaney Monckton
    Hoffe–Miles)
  *Many Waters.* 1926. FAO, PLAD

HOFFMAN, AARON, 1880–1924
  *Welcome Stranger.* 1920. SCL

HOFFMAN, BYRD. *See* Byrd Hoffman School of Byrds

HOFFMAN, E.T.A., 1776–1822 (born Ernst Theodor
    Wilhelm Hoffmann)
  *The Nutcracker and the Mouse King.* SWO

HOFFMAN, WILLIAM M., 1939–
  *As Is.* 1985. BERT, BES84, OSBW, SHEW, WOTHA
  *A Quick Nut Bread to Make Your Mouth Water.* 1970.
    OWER
  *Thank You, Miss Victoria.* 1965. NEWA3
  *X X X X.* 1969. SME

—— and HOLLAND, ANTHONY
  *Cornbury: The Queen's Governnor.* 1976. HOF

HOFMANN, GERT, 1931–1993
  *Our Man in Madras.* 1969. KIRLB

HOFMANNSTHAL, HUGO VON, 1874–1929
  *Death and the Fool. See* Der tor und der tod
  *The Death of Titian.* 1892.
     Heard, J., translator FRA17
     Variant title: *Der tod des Tizian*
  *Electra.* 1904.
     Mueller, C., translator ANTH, COTKJ, COTQ
     Symons, A., translator DICDT
  *Die hochzeit der Sobeide. See* The Marriage of Sobeide
  *The Marriage of Sobeide.* 1899.
     Morgan, B., translator FRA20
     Variant title: *Die hochzeit der Sobeide*
  *Das Salzburger grosse weltheater.* 1920. FEFH2
  *Der tod des Tizian. See* The Death of Titian
  *Der tor und der tod.* 1893. STI1
     Gerould, D., translator GERO
     Hamburger, M., translator BLOC
     Heard, J., translator FRA17
     Variant title: *Death and the Fool*

HOFSISS, JACK, 1950– . *See* Merriam, Eve, joint author

HOGAN, FRANK X.
  *Koozy's Piece.* 1987. PRIMA87
  *Pleasuring Ground.* 1985. PRIMA86
  *Ringers.* 1984. PRIMA85

HOGAN, R., and MOLIN, S. E.
  *The Silent Woman. See* Jonson, Ben. *The Silent Woman*
     (adapted by)

HOIJER, BJORN-ERIK, 1907–1996
  *Isak Juntti hade mänge söner. See* Isak Juntti Had Many
     Sons.
  *Isak Juntti Had Many Sons.* (1954)
     Austin, P., translator MNOS
     Variant title: *Isak Juntti hade mänge söner*

HOLBERG, LUDVIG, 1684–1754
  *Erasmus Montanus. See* Rasmus Montanus
  *Hans Frandsen. See* Jean de France, or, Hans Frandsen
  *Jean de France eller Hans Frandsen. See* Jean de
     France, or, Hans Frandsen
  *Jean de France, or, Hans Frandsen.* 1722.
     Argetsinger, G., translator HILPDH3
     Variant titles: *Hans Frandsen; Jean de France eller
        Hans Frandsen*
  *Jeppe of the Hill, or, A Peasant Translated.* 1722.
     Campbell, O., translator SPR
     Jagendorf, M., translator CLF2
     Meyer, M., translator THOQ
     Variant titles: *Jeppe paa bjerget; A Peasant
        Translated*
  *Jeppe paa bjerget. See* Jeppe of the Hill

  *The Loquacious Barber.* 1723.
     Chambers, W., translator BAT17
     Variant title: *Mester Gert Westphaler eller den meget
        talende barbeer*
  *Mester Gert Westphaler eller den meget talende
     barbeer. See* The Loquacious Barber
  *A Peasant Translated. See* Jeppe of the Hill, or, A
     Peasant Translated
  *Rasmus Montanus.* 1723.
     Campbell, O., and Sehenek, F., translators MATT
     Variant title: *Erasmus Montanus*
  *The Scatterbrain.* 1726.
     Meyer, M., translator THOQ

HOLCROFT, THOMAS, 1745–1809
  *Duplicity.* 1781. INCA4
  *The School for Arrogance.* 1791. INCA4
  *Seduction.* 1787. INCA4
  *A Tale of Mystery.* 1802. ACE, BAI, HOUR, KILG

HOLDEN, JOAN, 1939–
  *Factperson* (script by). *See* San Francisco Mime Troupe.
     *Factperson*
  *Factwino Meets the Moral Majority* (script by). *See* San
     Francisco Mime Troupe. *Factwino Meets the Moral
     Majority*
  *Factwino vs. Armageddonman* (script by). *See*
     San Francisco Mime Troupe. *Factwino vs.
     Armageddonman*

HOLDER, LAURENCE, 1939–
  *Zora.* 1981. KINHP

HOLLAND, ANTHONY, 1933–1988. *See* Hoffman,
     William M., joint author

HOLLAND, ENDESHA IDA MAE, 1944–2006
  *Miss Ida B. Wells.* 1983. PERF
  *Second Doctor Lady.* 1980. FLET

HOLLIDAY, JOYCE, 1932–2002
  *Anywhere to Anywhere.* 1985. GRIFG2

HOLLINGER, MICHAEL, 1962–
  *Tiny Island.* 1997. NEWR99

HOLLINGSWORTH, MARGARET, 1940–
  *Alli Alli Oh.* 1977. ZIMM (excerpt)
  *Ever Loving.* 1980. PENG
  *Operators.* 1974. BRIQ
  *War Babies.* 1984. WASCT

HOLLINGSWORTH, MICHAEL, 1950–
  *Strawberry Fields.* 1972. BRIN

HOLM, JOHN CECIL, 1906–1981, and ABBOTT,
  GEORGE
*Three Men on a Horse*. 1935. GAS

HOLM, SVEN, 1940–
*Leonora*. 1982.
  Anderson, H., translator NEWDAN

HOLMAN, JOSEPH GEORGE, 1764–1817
*The Votary of Wealth*. 1799. INCA3

HOLME, CONSTANCE, 1881?–1955
*"I Want!"* 1933. FIT

HOLMES, RUPERT, 1947–
*The Mystery of Edwin Drood* (music and lyrics by
  Rupert Holmes; based on the novel by Charles
  Dickens). 1985. BES85

HOLMES, SHIRLENE
*A Lady and a Woman*. 1990. CURB

HOLSCLAW, DOUG
*The Baddest of Boys*. 1992. JONT
*It's My Party*. 1984. *See* Anonymous Plays. *The AIDS
  Show*
*Life of the Party*. 1986. WES21/22
*Spice Queen*. 1984. *See* Anonymous Plays. *The AIDS
  Show*

HOLT, BRIAN
*Noah's Ark*. 1963. FRO

HOLTZMAN, JONATHAN, 1953–
*Foxfire; a Play with Songs in Two Acts* (music and
  collaboration for lyrics by). *See* Cooper, Susan, and
  Cronyn, Hume. *Foxfire*

HOLTZMAN, WILLY, 1952–
*Hearts*. 2000. NEWR99

HOME, JOHN, 1722–1808
*Douglas*. 1756. BAT14, BELK20, BOO, MAND,
  MANF, MOR, MOSE2, NET, STM

HOME, WILLIAM DOUGLAS, 1912–1992
*The Jockey Club Stakes*. PLAN40
*Lloyd George Knew My Father*. 1972. PLAN42
*The Queen's Highland Servant*. 1968. PLAN35
*The Secretary Bird*. 1963. PLAN36
*The Thistle and the Rose*. 1949. PLAN4

HONEYMAN, JANICE. *See* Cooke, Vanessa, joint author

HOOD, KEVIN, 1949–
*Sugar Hill Blues*. 1990. FIFHL3

HOOKE, NINA WARNER, 1907–
*The Amazons* (from *New Ambassadors Revue*). 1941.
  YEAR
*Front Door Steps* (from *Rise above It*). 1941. YEAR
*I Wonder How It Feels* (from *Revuedeville*). 1940. YEAR
*Park Meeting* (from *Sky High*). 1943. YEAR
*Reprieve* (from *Sky High*). 1943. YEAR
*Such a Ferocious Bell* (from *New Ambassadors Revue*).
  1941. YEAR

HOOLE, JOHN, 1727–1803
*Cyrus*. 1768. BELG9
*Timanthes*. 1770. BELG9

HOPE, CHRISTOPHER, 1944–
*Ducktails* (television play). 1977. GRAYTT

HOPE, KAREN
*Foreign Lands*. 1993. FROLIN2

HOPGOOD, ALAN, 1934–
*Private Yuk Objects*. 1966. BRIMA2

HOPKINS, ARTHUR MELANCTHON, 1878–1950
*Moonshine*. 1921. PROF, PROG, PROH, PROI, TOD
— *See* Watters, George Manker, joint author

HOPKINS, C.J., 1961–
*Horse Country*. 1997. DENT

HOPKINS, GLENN and LINDBERG, WAYNE, joint
  author
*Dinosaur*. 1980. WES6

HOPKINS, JOHN, 1931–1998
*Find Your Way Home*. 1974. BES73

HOPKINS, PAULINE ELIZABETH, 1859–1930
*Peculiar Sam, or The Underground Railroad*. 1879.
  ROOTS
  Variant title: *The Underground Railroad*
*The Underground Railroad*. See *Peculiar Sam*

HOPKINSON, FRANCIS, 1737–1791
*A Dialogue and Ode*. 1762. MONR
  Variant title: *An Exercise Containing a Dialogue
  and Ode on the Accession of His Present Gracious
  Majesty George III*
*An Exercise Containing a Dialogue and Ode on the
  Accession of His Present Gracious Majesty George
  III*. See *A Dialogue and Ode*

HOPWOOD, AVERY, 1862–1928. *See* Rinehart, Mary
  Roberts, joint author

HORACE. *See* Horatius Flaccus, Quintus

HORAK, KAROL, 1943–
  *The Destruction of Soccer in the City of K.* 1990.
    Cockrell, K., translator CONTSL5
    Variant title: *Skaza futbalu v meste K.*
  *La musica.* 2001.
    Cockrell, K., translator CONTSL4
  *Skaza futbalu v meste K. See* The Destruction of Soccer
    in the City of K.

HORATIUS FLACCUS, QUINTUS, 65–8 B.C.
  *Ars poetica.*
    DeWitt, N., translator COTU
  *The Bore; a Dramatic Version of Horace* (Satires I,9)
    Ullman, B., translator HOWK

HORNE, KENNETH, 1900–1975
  *Trial and Error.* 1953. PLAN9

HOROVITZ, ISRAEL, 1939–
  *A Christmas Carol: Scrooge and Marley* (adapted from
    the story by Charles Dickens). 1979. SWO
  *The Indian Wants the Bronx.* 1968. FAMAH, LAH,
    OBG, OFF1
  *It's Called the Sugar Plum.* 1967. OFF1
  *Line.* 1967. RICK
  *Morning.* 1968. GARTL
  *The Widow's Blind Date.* 1980. WES13/14

HOROWITZ, DAN
  *Cherli ka cherli.*
    Alkalaya, K., and Gut, H., translators MOADE

HORSFIELD, DEBBIE, 1955–
  *Red Devils.* 1983. PLABE3

HORVATH, ODON VON, 1901–1938
  *Geschichten aus dem Wiener Wald. See* Tales from the
    Vienna Woods
  *Tales from the Vienna Woods.* 1931.
    Mueller, C., translator HERZ
    Variant title: *Geschichten aus dem Wiener Wald*

HORVATH, TOMAS, 1971–
  *The Chair.* 1991.
    Trebatická, H., translator CONTSL2
    Variant title: *Stolicka*
  *Stolicka. See* The Chair

HOTTA, KIYOMI, 1922–
  *The Island.* 1957.
    Goodman, D., translator AFTAP

  Variant title: *Shima*
  *Shima. See* The Island

HOUGHTON, STANLEY, 1881–1913
  *Fanny Hawthorne. See* Hindle Wakes
  *Hindle Wakes.* 1912. DICEM, PLAP1, ROWC, TUCD
    Variant title: *Fanny Hawthorne*

HOUSMAN, LAURENCE, 1865–1959
  *A Good Lesson!* (from *Victoria Regina*). 1934. COOP
  *Victoria Regina.* 1935. BES35, CEU

——— and GRANVILLE-BARKER, HARLEY
  *Prunella; or, Love in a Dutch Garden.* 1906. PLAP2

HOUSTON, DIANNE, 1954–
  *The Fishermen.* 1980. CEN

HOUSTON, VELINA HASU, 1957–
  *As Sometimes in a Dead Man's Face.* 1994. ASIAM
  *Asa ga kimashita (Morning Has Broken).* 1981.
    HOUSTP
  *Kokoro (True Heart).* 1994. HOUST
  *Tea.* 1987. UNO, PLACA

HOVEY, RICHARD, 1864–1900
  *The Birth of Galahad.* 1898. LUP

HOWARD, BRONSON CROCKER, 1842–1908
  *The Banker's Daughter.* 1873. AMP10, CLA
  *Baron Rudolph.* 1881. AMP10
  *The Henrietta.* 1887. HAL
  *Hurricanes.* 1878. AMP10
  *Old Love Letters.* 1878. AMP10
  *One of Our Girls.* 1885. AMP10
  *Shenandoah.* 1888. COY, MASW, MESC, MONR,
    MOSS3, QUIJ, QUIJR, QUIK, QUIL, QUIM,
    QUIN, WATTAD
  *Young Mrs. Winthrop.* 1882. MES
    — *See* Young, Sir Charles Lawrence, joint author

HOWARD, ED. *See* Williams, Jaston, joint author

HOWARD, SIR ROBERT, 1626–1698
  *The Committee.* 1662. BELK2
  *The Great Favourite, or The Duke of Lerma.* 1668.
    WONR
    — *See also* Dryden, John, joint author

HOWARD, SIDNEY COE, 1891–1939
  *Alien Corn.* 1933. BES32, FAMD
  *Dodsworth* (based on the novel by Sinclair Lewis).
    1934. BES33, HAT
  *The Ghost of Yankee Doodle.* 1936. NELSDI

HUGHES, JAMES LANGSTON. *See* Hughes, Langston

HUGHES, JOHN, 1677–1720
*Siege of Damascus.* 1720. BELK1

HUGHES, LANGSTON, 1902–1967
*Black Nativity.* 1961. SWO
*Don't You Want to Be Free?* 1937. HARY, HARYB
*The Em-Fuehrer Jones.* 1920. HARYL
*Emperor of Haiti.* 1938. HILEB, TUQT, TUQTR
*Limitations of Life.* 1938. HARY, HARYB
*Little Ham.* 1935. HARY
*Mother and Child.* 1973. KINH, KINHB, PERV, SCNQ
*Mulatto.* 1963. BRAS, HARYB, THT, WATTAD
*The Organizer.* 1938. HARYL
*Scarlet Sister Barry.* 1938. HARYL
*Simply Heavenly.* 1957. BLAC, PATR
*Soul Gone Home.* 1937. RAVIT
*Young Black Joe.* 1940. HARYL

HUGHES, RICHARD ARTHUR WARREN, 1900–1976
*A High Wind in Jamaica. See* Osborn, Paul. *The Innocent Voyage* (based on the novel by)
*The Sister's Tragedy.* 1922. MORT, SUTL

HUGHES, THOMAS, fl.1587
*The Misfortunes of Arthur.* 1588. CUN

HUGO, VICTOR MARIE, 1802–1885
*Hernani.* 1830. BOR, COM, GRA, SEA
  Asher, L., translator BERMG, HOUK, TREB, VENA
  Crosland, Mrs. N., translator CARP, CLF2, MATT
*Les misérables. See* Boubil, A., and Schönberg, C. *Les misérables* (based on the novel by)
*Ruy Blas.* 1838. COM, GRA, SCN, STJ2
  Crosland, Mrs. N., translator GREA

HUIDOBRO, MATIAS MONTES. *See* Montes Huidobro, Matias

HUIE, KAREN, 1952–
*Yasuko and the Young s-s-samurai.* 1998. ELLM

HULCE, TOM, 1953–
*The Cider House Rules, Part II* (conceived for the stage by). *See* Parnell, Peter. *The Cider House Rules, Part II*

HULL, THOMAS, 1728–1808
*The Fall of Rosamond. See* Henry II; or, the Fall of Rosamond
*Henry II; or, The Fall of Rosamond.* 1773. BELG4, INCA9
  Variant title: *The Fall of Rosamond*

HUMPHREY, HUBERT H., 1911–1978. *See* Baldwin, James, joint author

HUNG, SHEN, 1893–1955
*Chao Yen-wang. See* Yama chao
*The Wedded Husband.* 1921. CHIN
*Yama chao.* (1922)
  Brown, C., translator TWEH
  Variant title: *Chao Yen-wang*

HUNKINS, LEE, 1930–
*Revival.* (1980) CEN

HUNT, MAME, 1952–
*Unquestioned Integrity: The Hill-Thomas Hearings.* 1993. FAV

HUNTER, MAUREEN, 1947–
*Footprints on the Moon.* 1988. RUN
*Transit of Venus.* 1992. SEUC, ZIMM (excerpt)

HUNTER, NORMAN CA., 1908–1971
*A Day by the Sea.* 1953. FAMO
*Waters of the Moon.* 1951. FAOS

HUNTER, ROBERT, 1664–1734
*Androboros.* 1714. AMPA

HURLBUT, WILLIAM JAMES, 1883–
*The Bride of the Lamb.* 1926. BES25

HURLEY, JOAN MASON, 1920–2001
*Inukshuk.* 1990. BELLW

HURSTON, ZORA NEALE, 1891–1960
*Color Struck.* 1925. PER
*The First One.* 1927. HARYB, PER, ROOTS
*"The Gilded Six-bits." See* Wolfe, George C. *Spunk* (adapted from the story by)
*"Story in Harlem Slang." See* Wolfe, George C. *Spunk* (adapted from the story by)
*"Sweat." See* Wolfe, George C. *Spunk* (adapted from the story by)

HUSSON, ALBERT, 1912–1978
*La cuisine des anges. See* Spewack, Bella, and Spewack, Samuel. *My Three Angels* (adapted from)

HUSTON, JOHN, 1906–1987
*The Treasure of the Sierra Madre* (screenplay based on the novel by B. Traven). 1948. READ1 (excerpt)
— *See* Koch, Howard, joint author

HUTCHINS, MRS. MAUDE PHELPS MCVEIGH, 1899–1991
*Aunt Julia's Caesar.* 195– ? SPC
*The Case of Astrolable.* 1944? NEWDI44

*A Play about Joseph Smith, Jr.* 1944? NEWDI44
*The Wandering Jew.* 1951? NEWDI51

HUTCHINSON, ALFRED, 1924–1972
*The Rain-killers.* 1968. LITT

HUTCHISON, PATRICK
*The Harvey Milk Show* (music by). *See* Pruitt, Dan. *The Harvey Milk Show*

HUTSELL-MANNING, LINDA, 1940–
*Agnes* (excerpt from play titled *Wolfcall*). 1993. BREK

HUTTON, ARLENE
*Last Train to Nibroca.* 1999. WOMP99

HUTTON, JOSEPH, 1787–1828
*Fashionable Follies.* 1809. MOSS2

HUYNH, QUANG NHUONG, 1946–2001
*Dance of the Wandering Souls.* 1997. HOUST

HWANG, DAVID HENRY, 1957–
*As the Crow Flies.* 1986. BETW
*Bondage.* 1992. ASIAM, HOUST
*The Dance and the Railroad.* 1981. BES81, GUTDS, JACOBD
*FOB.* 1979. KIRLA, KIRLB, KIRLC, NEWQ
*Golden Child.* 1996. PLACG2
*Merchandising.* 1999. HUMANA99
*M. Butterfly.* 1988. ABCF, ABCG, ABCH, BAIL, BES87, BRJB, COI, GILB, HOWM, MEYB, MEYCB, MEYD, MEYE, MEYF, SHRCE, SSSIB, SSSIC, WATTAD, WOTHA, WOTHB, WOTHC, WOTHM
*The Sound of a Voice.* 1983. BARIH, BETW, LITIE, LITIF, LITJ, LITJA
*Trying to Find Chinatown.* 1996. HUMANA96

HWANG, MEI-SHU, 1930–
*Cathay Visions (The Empty Cage).* 1986.
    Hwang, M., translator CHEU
    Variant title: *Konglong gushi*
*Konglong gushi. See* Cathay Visions (The Empty Cage)

HYDE, DOUGLAS, 1860–1949
*The Twisting of the Rope.* 1901. CAP

HYMAN, MAC, 1923–1963
*No Time for Sergeants. See* Levin, Ira. *No Time for Sergeants* (adapted from the novel by)

I-AMI
*Tango-monogurui.*
    Waley, A., translator WAJ (excerpts)

IBBITSON, JOHN, 1955–
*Catalyst.* 1974. KAL4

IBE, SIMON IRO
*The Last of Ala.* 1991. NTIR

IBRAHIM, ALMAHDI AL-HAJ, 1946–. *See* Nadiputra (pseud. of)

IBSEN, HENRIK, 1828–1906
*Bygmester solness. See* The Master Builder
*The Child Wife. See* A Doll's House
*A Doll House. See* A Doll's House
*A Doll's House.* 1879.
    Anonymous translator PRO, SCNPL, SILO, SILS
    Archer, W., translator BERP, BERPA, BRJC, CLF2, COHM, DRAD2, EDAD, FOUX, HOEP, HOUS, HUD, KNIC, KNID, MATT, MAD, PLAB2, PROW, ROSENB, THOM, THON, WATI, WATLI, WHT
    Archer, W., translator, with emendations by Brockett, O. BRJB
    Fjelde, R., translator DIYL, DIYLA, DIYLB, DIYLC, DIYLD, GWYN, JACOBA, JACOBD, JACOBE, KIRLA, KIRLB, KIRLC, KIRLD, LITIA, LITIB, LITIC, LITID, LITQ, MAO, MARK, MARL, MEYC, MEYCA, MEYCB, MEYD, MEYE, MEYF, PERR1, READ2, WOTHA, WOTHB, WOTHC
    LeGallienne, E., translator AUG, COI, DIEB
    McFarlane, J., translator ANT, GRDBA52, LITIE, LITIF, LITJ, LITJA, LITRD
    Meyer, M., translator BARI, BARIA, BARIG, BARIH, BARKE, BARKF, GILB, JACOB, KEN, LITI, LITRC, MEY, MEYB, SCNP, SCNQ, SCNQCA, SCNQCB, SSSI, SSSIA, SSSIB, SSSIC
    Reinert, E., translator BARIC, BARID, BARIE, BARIF, BARKB, BARKD, HEAA, HEAB, HEAC, HEAD, HEALA, HEALB, HEALC, HEALD, REIW, REIWE
    Reinert, O., translator ABCB, ABCC, ABCD, ABCE, BARKC, HEALE, LEVY, LITR, LITRA, LITRB, PERX, PERY, PERZ
    Sharp, R., translator ABCG, ABCH
    Watts, P., translator GUTDF, GUTDS, SEVT
    Variant titles: *The Child Wife; Et dukkehjem; Nora*
*Et dukkehjem. See* A Doll's House
*An Enemy of Society. See* An Enemy of the People
*An Enemy of the People.* 1882.
    Anonymous translator BUCK, BUCL, BUCM, CARLG, DEAR, EVB2, GATS, HARB, JOHO, KNIE, KNIF, KNIG, KON, LAM, MCA, MESSN, OHL, PERS, PERT, PERV, ROGEX, SAND, SHRCF, ZIM
    Archer, W., translator CASH

Farquhorson, R., translator BONB, BONC

Fjelde, R., translator DIYRD

Goodman, R., translator GOODE

Le Gallienne, E., translator PATM

McFarlane, J., translator FRYE, FRYEA

Mark-Aveling, E., translator FREH, HOLM, MOSA,
WALJ, WHK

Miller, A., adapter BURG, HAVH, HAVHA, HOUP,
MERV

Meyer, M., translator CASK

Sharp, R., translator ABCA, ABCF, BONA, COD,
DOLAN, DUR, EVA2, FOT, GOLK, INGW,
PERW, STA, THO

Variant titles: *An Enemy of Society; En folkefiende.*
See An Enemy of the People

*Fruen fra havet. See* The Lady from the Sea

*Gengangere. See* Ghosts

*Ghosts.* 1881.

Anonymous translator DOWN, KNIH, KNIJ, MABC,
SILK, SILM, SILN

Archer, W., translator ALT, ALTE, BARC, BAT17,
BOY, CROW, DEAS, FEL, FREG, GLO, KERP,
LITC, MIL, ROB, SAY, SEBO, SEBP, SHR,
SHRCD, SMP, STE, TREBA, TREBJ, TREC2,
TREE2, TREI2

Fjelde, R., translator VENA

Le Gallienne, E., translator BENU, BLOC, LEVI

Meyer, M., translator BARO, BOW, CLL, CLLC,
COTKIR

Sharp, F., translator ADV, SILKI, WEIS, WEIW,
WHFM

Variant title: *Gengangere*

*Hedda Gabler.* 1890.

Anonymous translator BARNA, BLON, BROI,
HAVL, LOCL, LOR

Arup, J., translator GRDBA52

Ellis-Fermor, U., translator GOLH, SIN, SOM,
SOMA, TAUJ

Fjelde, R., translator HILPDH4, JACOBA, JACOBD

Goodman, R., translator GOO

Gosse, E., translator GPA

Gosse, E., and Archer, W., translators ALLI, ALLJ,
ALLK, ALLM, ALLN, ALLO, BLAG, BLOND,
BLOO, BROF, BROG, BROH, CARP, CARPA,
CLKW, COOP, FOUK, FOUM, GLO, GOU2,
GRIF, HAE, HAEA, HAEB, HAV, HAVD,
HAVE, HOEP, KERN, KERO, SMI, SOUL, TRE,
TREA1, TREBA, TREBJ, TREC2, TREE2, TREI2,
WAK, WATA, WATI, WATL2, WATR, WOLC,
WOLCS

Le Gallienne, E., translator LOCLA, LOCLB

Legallienne, J., and Leysae, P., translators LEG

Meyer, M., translator BAIH, BAIK, BAIL, BAIM,
BARN, BEATA, CLKY, JACOB, NORGA,

NORI2, NORIA2, NORIB2, NORIC2, NORJ2,
NORJA, VANV2

Paulson, A., translator WAIW

Reinert, O., translator ALS, BARJ, BARK, BARKA,
BARKB, BAUL, COLD, COTQ, HEA, KNO,
KNOJ, KNOK, REIO, SILP

*John Gabriel Borkman.* 1897.

Archer, W., translator ULAN

Ginsbury, N., adapter PLAN23

*Kongsemnerna. See* The Pretenders

*The Lady from the Sea.* 1888.

Archer, W., translator SAY

Fjelde, R., translator WOMD

Variant title: *Fruen fra havet*

*Lille Eyolf. See* Little Eyolf

*Little Eyolf.* 1894.

Archer, W., translator LID

Variant title: *Lille Eyolf*

*The Master Builder.* 1892.

Amble, K., translator COTX

Anonymous translator BONB, BRIT, CROS, GUTH,
GUTL, HIB, HIBA, HIBB, SIXB

Archer, W., translator DOWS, VONS3

Fjelde, R., translator SPR, WOTHM

Gosse, E., and Archer, W., translators WARL, WORP

McFarlane, J., translator GRDBA52, SANE

Paulson, A., translator WEIP

Perone, E., translator CALD

Variant titles: *Bygmester solness; Solness, The Master
Builder*

*Nora. See* A Doll's House

*Peer Gynt.* 1876.

Fjelde, R., translator HILPDH4

Ginsbury, N., translator BLOC

*Pillars of Society.* 1877.

Le Gallienne, E., translator MADB

Variant title: *Samfundets støtter*

*The Pretenders.* 1864.

Archer, W., translator SMK

Variant title: *Kongsemnerna*

*Rosmersholm.* 1886.

Anonymous translator BROJ, BROK, LOCM2

Archer, W., translator BENQ, TUCN, TUCO

Jellicoe, A., translator CUBH, FOUM

Le Gallienne, E., JOHN, ROF

McFarlane, J., CLKJ

Meyer, M., translator BENSB2

*Samfundets støtter. See* Pillars of Society

*Solness, the Master Builder. See* The Master Builder

*Vildanden. See* The Wild Duck

*The Wild Duck.* 1885.

Anonymous translator CEW, CLN, SSST, SSSU

Archer, F., translator ASF, BIER, DLM, CUBE,
CUBG, DEAP, GOLD, HOWM, LEV, LEVE,

MALC, MALG2, MALI2, MALN2, MOSQ, SPR, WEAN, WEAV2, WHI
Archer, W., translator BRIX, BRIY, BRIZ, BRJ, BRJA
Christiani, D., translator BAIG
Ellis-Fermor, U., translator LEVJ
Faber, M., translator WEIM
Fjelde, R., translator CLKY, TRI, TRIA, WOTHM
LeGallienne, E., translator DODS, VOLI
McFarlane, J., translator CAPU, GRDBA52, SEN
Meyer, M., translator AUB, BENSB2, SEN
Reinert, O., translator COTQ, DIEA, REIL, REIN, REIP, REIT
Sharp, R., translator BARR
Variant title: *Vildanden*

ICHIDŌ REI (Blue Bird Theater Company), 1974–
*Aoi mi wo tabeta: tsumetai mizu oishii mizu.* See Miss Toyoko's Departure
*Miss Toyoko's Departure.* 1986.
Goodman, D., translator HACJT3
Variant title: *Aoi mi wo tabeta: tsumetai mizu oishii mizu*

ICHIKAWA DANJURO I. *See* Danjuro I

IDRIS, YUSUF, 1927–1991
*The Farfoors.* (1964) ABL

IDZUMO, TAKEDA. *See* Takeda, Izumo

IFFLAND, AUGUST WILHELM, 1759–1814
*Conscience.* 1800?
Thompson, B., translator BAT11
Variant title: *Das gewissen*
*Das gewissen. See* Conscience

IGNATAVICIUS, E., and MOTIEJ ŪNAS, S.
*Whitehorn's Windmill. See* Boruta, Kazys. *Whitehorn's Windmill* (dramatization of the novel by)

IIJIMA, SANAE, 1963– , and SUKI, YUMI
*Hōōchō no Hininhō. See* Rhythm Method
*Rhythm Method.* 1994.
Herbert, S., translator HACJT2
Variant title: *Hōōchō no Hininhō*

IIZAWA, TADASU, 1909–1994
*The Immortals of Mt. Kunlun.* 1955.
Gleason, A., translator HACJT8
Variant title: *Konronzan no hitobito*
*Konronzan no hitobito. See* The Immortals of Mt. Kunlun

IIZUKA, NAOMI, 1965–
*Aloha, Say the Pretty Girls.* 1999. HUMANA99
*Polaroid Stories.* 1997. HUMANA97
*Skin* (adapted from the play *Woyzeck* by Georg Büchner). 1995. SVICH
*Tattoo Girl.* 1994. MESSE
*War of the Worlds* (conceived by Anne Bogart). 2000. HUMANA2000

IJIMERE, OBOTUNDE, 1930– (pseud. of Ulli Beier)
*Born with the Fire on His Head.* THTN

IKHLASI, WALID, 1935–
*The Path.* 1975.
Kenny, O., and Ezzy, T., translators JAY
Variant title: *al-Sirat*
*al-Sirat. See* The Path

IKO, MOMOKO, 1940–
*Gold Watch.* 1972. UNO

IKOLI, TUNDE, 1955–
*The Lower Depths: An East End Story* (adapted from the play by Maxim Gorki). 1986. BREW1
*Scrape Off the Black.* 1981. BREW3

ILAGAN, HERMOGENES E., 1873–1943
*The Barrio Maiden.* 1917.
Zamora, M., translator PHIL
Variant title: *Dalagang bukid*
*Dalagang bukid.* PHIL

ILF, ILYA ARNOLDOVICH, 1897–1937, and PETROV, EVGENY
*The Power of Love* (1933).
Seneliek, L., translator RVI
Variant title: *Silnoe chuvstvo*
*Silnoe chuvstvo. See* The Power of Love

ILYENKOV, VASSILY PAVLOVICH, 1897–1967
*Campo dei fiori. See* The Square of Flowers
*The Square of Flowers.* 1944.
Bakshy, A., translator BAKS
Variant title: *Campo dei fiori*

INCHBALD, MRS. ELIZABETH (SIMPSON), 1753–1821
*Adventures of a Shawl. See* Appearance Is against Them
*Appearance Is against Them.* 1785. HUGL
Variant titles: *Adventures of a Shawl; Mistake upon Mistake; or, Appearance Is against Them*
*Everyone Has His Fault.* 1793. NIC
*I'll Tell You What.* 1785. INCA7

*Mistake upon Mistake; or, Appearance Is against Them.*
　　*See* Appearance Is against Them
*Next Door Neighbors.* INCA7
*Such Things Are.* 1788. POLK, ROGEW
*The Wise Man of the East.* INCA7

INGBRETSON, JONATHAN
　　*Touch* (co-conceived by). *See* Press-Coffman, Toni.
　　　　*Touch*

INGE, WILLIAM, 1913–1973
　　*The Boy in the Basement.* (1950) CAL
　　*Bus Stop.* 1955. BES54, GART, HOGF, THEA55
　　*Come Back, Little Sheba.* 1950. BES49, CEQA, CUBG,
　　　　GARW, GATB4, NEWV, STS, WATA
　　*The Dark at the Top of the Stairs.* 1957. BES57, CES,
　　　　GARSA, HUDE
　　　　Variant title: *Farther Off from Heaven*
　　*The Disposal.* 1972. RICJ
　　*Farther Off from Heaven. See* The Dark at the Top of
　　　　the Stairs
　　*Margaret's Bed.* 1973? RICK
　　*Picnic.* 1953. BES52, GART, GAVE, THEA53

INGHAM, ROBERT E., 1934–
　　*Custer, or Whoever Heard of Fred Benteen?* 1977.
　　　　BES79
　　*A Simple Life.* 1964. GARZAL

INNAURATO, ALBERT, 1948–
　　*Earth Worms.* 1974. WES4
　　*Gemini.* 1976. FAMAD, WOLCS
　　*Gus and Al.* 1987. BES88

INNUINUIT THEATRE COMPANY, 1987–1993, and
　　NALUJUK PLAYERS, joint author
　　*Braindead.* 1993. PETERS

INOUE, HISASHI, 1934–2010
　　*Yabuhara Kengyō. See* Yabuhara, the Blind Master
　　　　Minstrel
　　*Yabuhara, the Blind Master Minstrel.* 1973?
　　　　Wells, M., translator HACJT6
　　　　Variant title: *Yabuhara Kengyō*

INOUYE, BESSIE TOISHIGAWA. *See* Inouye, Lisa
　　Toishigawa

INOUYE, LISA TOISHIGAWA
　　*Reunion.* 1947. KUMU

GL'INTRONATI DI SIENA (16th century literary society)
　　*The Deceived.* (1538)
　　　　Penman, B., translator FIJ
　　　　Variant title: *Gl'Ingannati*
　　*Gl'Ingannati. See* The Deceived

IOBST, CLARENCE F., 1894–1973
　　*Die Calline browierts.* 1930. BUFF
　　*Es Heller's Chrischtdag* (based on the story *Es wasch
　　　　Heller's Chrischtdag's zug* by Charles C. More).
　　　　1931. BUFF

IONESCO, EUGENE, 1912–1994
　　*The Bald Prima Donna. See* The Bald Soprano
　　*The Bald Soprano.* 1950.
　　　　Allen, D., translator AUG, BERP, BERPA, BLOC,
　　　　　　FRYE, NEWWW9, ULAN, WEIM
　　　　Variant titles: *The Bald Prima Donna; La cantatrice
　　　　　　chauve*
　　*La cantatrice chauve. See* The Bald Soprano
　　*The Chairs. See* Les chaises
　　*Les chaises.* 1952. PROA
　　　　Allen, D., translator ALT, ALTE, COTQ, JOHN,
　　　　　　KERP, TREBA, TREI3
　　　　Anonymous translator SILP
　　　　Variant title: *The Chairs*
　　*The Gap.* 1966.
　　　　Lamont, R., translator ACE, BARI, BARIA, BARIC,
　　　　　　BARK, BARKA, DIEB, DIYRD, HEAA, HEAB,
　　　　　　HEALA, HEALB, HOLP, LITP, SEVD, SEVT,
　　　　　　SILKI
　　　　Variant title: *La lacune*
　　*L'impromptu de l'alma. See* Improvisation
　　*Improvisation; or, The Shepherd's Chameleon*
　　　　Watson, D., translator COTKW, SCNO
　　　　Variant titles: *L'impromptu de l'alma; The Shepherd's
　　　　　　Chameleon*
　　*Jack; or, The Submission.* 1955.
　　　　Allen, D. M., translator HOWM, WEIP
　　　　Variant title: *Jacques, ou La soumission*
　　*Jacques, ou La soumission. See* Jack; or, The
　　　　Submission
　　*La jeune fille a marier. See* Maid to Marry
　　*La lacune. See* The Gap
　　*The Leader.* 1953.
　　　　Prouse, D., translator HAVH, HAVHA, RAI
　　　　Variant title: *Le maître*
　　*La leçon. See* The Lesson
　　*The Lesson.* 1951.
　　　　Allen, D., translator ABCB, ABCC, BARKF, DIYLA,
　　　　　　DIYLB, DIYLC, DIYLD, GILB, REIN, REIP,
　　　　　　SSSIC
　　　　Anonymous translator SSSIB
　　　　Variant title: *La leçon*
　　*Macbett.* 1972.
　　　　Marowitz, C., translator KAYT
　　*Maid to Marry.* 1953.
　　　　Calder, J., translator LID
　　　　Variant title: *La jeune fille a marier*
　　*Le maître. See* The Leader
　　*The New Tenant.* 1955.
　　　　Watson, D., translator BRIY, BRIZ, COTY, THOD

Variant title: *Le nouveau locataire*
*Le nouveau locataire. See* The New Tenant
*The Painting.* 1954.
  Watson, D., translator DIER
  Wellwarth, G., translator BEN
  Variant titles: *The Picture; Le tableau*
*The Picture. See* The Painting
*Rhinoceros.* 1959.
  Prouse, D., translator BES60, GROV, LEVY, NIL, SEVD
  Variant title*: Les rhinocéros*
*Les rhinocéros. See* Rhinoceros
*The Shepherd's Chameleon. See* Improvisation
*Le tableau. See* The Painting

IQBAL, OBADIAH, 1958– . *See* Zephaniah, Benjamin

IRELAND, WILLIAM HENRY, 1777–1835
*Vortigern.* 1796. BAT22

IRIZARRY, RICHARD V., 1956?–1994
*Ariano.* 1984. ANTUR

IRVING, JOHN, 1942–
*The Cider House Rules. See* Parnell, Peter. *The Cider House Rules, Part II* (based on the novel by)

IRVING, WASHINGTON, 1783–1859
*Rip Van Winkle. See* Rauch, Edward H. *Rip Van Winkle* (based on the book by)
— *See* Payne, John Howard, joint author

IRWIN, WILL. *See* Irwin, William Henry

IRWIN, WILLIAM HENRY, 1873–1948
*The Hamadryads.* 1904. BOH1
— *See* Howard, Sidney, joint author

ISHERWOOD, CHRISTOPHER, 1904–1986
*The Berlin Stories. See* Van Druten, John. *I Am a Camera* (adapted from the stories by)
— *See also* Masteroff, Joe. *Cabaret* (adapted from the stories by Isherwood and the play by Van Druten)
— *See also* Auden, Wystan Hugh, joint author

ITALLIE, JEAN CLAUDE VAN. *See* Van Itallie, Jean–Claude

ITCHO, ASADA. *See* Asada, Itcho

IVES, ALICE E.
*A Very New Woman.* 1896. FRIED

IVES, DAVID, 1950– (b. David Roszkowski)
*All in the Timing* (6 one-act plays: *The Philadelphia, Philip Glass Buys a Loaf of Bread, Sure Thing, The Universal Language, Variations on the Death of Trotsky, Words, Words, Words*). 1994. BES93
*Arabian Nights.* 2000. HUMANA2000
*Canvas.* 1972. BALLE11 (credited as David Roszkowski)
*The Philadelphia. See* All in the Timing
*Philip Glass Buys a Loaf of Bread. See* All in the Timing
*Sure Thing.* BEATA, LITIF, MEYCA, MEYCB, MEYF, SCVDT1 *See also* All in the Timing
*The Universal Language. See* All in the Timing
*Variations on the Death of Trotsky.* 1994 SCVDO1 *See also* All in the Timing
*Words, Words, Words. See* All in the Timing

IWAMATSU, RYŌ, 1952–
*The Man Next Door.* 1990.
  Yuasa, M., translator HACJT2
  Variant title: *Tonari no otoko*
*Tonari no otoko. See* The Man Next Door

IZUMO, TAKEDA. *See* Takeda, Izumo

JAAFFAR, JOHAN, 1953–
*Surrender.* 1993.
  Ishak, S., translator MLAM

JACK, DONALD L., 1924–2003
*Exit Muttering.* 1962. KAL1

JACKER, CORINNE L., 1933–
*Bits and Pieces.* 1973. NEWWT

JACKMAN, ISAAC, 1752?–1831
*All the World's a Stage.* 1777. BELC4

JACKMAN, MARVIN E. (MARVIN X, pseud.) 1944–
*Flowers for the Trashman.* 1965. JONE

JACKSON, ANGELA, 1951–
*Shango Diaspora.* 1980. BARKF, WOMA

JACKSON, C. BERNARD, 1927–1996
*Iago.* 1979. KINHN

—— and HATCH, JAMES V.
*Fly Blackbird.* 1960. MARY, REAR

JACKSON, CHERRY
*In the Master's House There Are Many Mansions.* (1979) CEN

JACKSON, ELAINE, 1948–
*Paper Dolls.* 1986. HOWM, WILK
*Toe Jam.* (1971) KINH, KINHB

JAYAWARDHANA, BANDULA
*The Tragedy of Musila.* 1984. GOON

JEANS, RONALD, 1887–1973
*Count Your Blessings.* 1951. PLAN5
*Young Wives' Tale.* 1949. PLAN3

JEFFERE, JOHN
*The Buggbears* (supposed author). 1561? BOND

JEFFERS, ROBINSON, 1887–1962
*The Cretan Woman.* 1951. BENS3, SANL
*Medea. See* Euripides. *Medea* (translator and adapted by)

JEFFERSON, JOSEPH, 1829–1905
*Rip Van Winkle. See* Anonymous Plays. *Rip Van Winkle* (as played by); *See also* Burke, Charles. *Rip Van Winkle*

JEFFERY, LAWRENCE, 1953–
*Who Look in Stove.* 1994. SSSN

JEFFREYS, STEPHEN, 1950–
*Valued Friends.* 1989. FIFHL2

JEFFRIES, IRA L.
*Clotel, a Love Story.* 1994. TOR
*Manchild.* 1994. TOR

JELINEK, ELFRIEDE, 1946–
*Pillars of Society. See* What Happened after Nora Left Her Husband
*Präsident Abenwind. See* President Evening Breeze
*President Evening Breeze.* 1987.
    Schreckenberger, H., and Vansant, J., translators LAX
    Variant title: *Präsident Abenwind*
*Totenauberg (Death/Valley/Summit).* 1992.
    Honegger, G., translator WEBER
*What Happened after Nora Left Her Husband, or Pillars of Society.* 1992.
    Minter, T., translator and writer of English version. PLABE10

JELLICOE, ANNE, 1927–
*The Knack.* 1961. AUB, COTKIR, COTKIT
*The Sport of My Mad Mother.* (1957) OBSE

JEN, THE-YΛO
*Magic aster.* (1963)
    White, W., translator MESE

JENKIN, LEN, 1941–
*American Notes.* 1988. MESSE
*Dark Ride.* 1981. WOQ2

*Gogol.* 1978. WEK
*Kid Twist.* 1979. WEJ

JENKINS, MARK
*Strindberg Knew My Father.* 1992. SETR

JENKINS, RAY, 1935–
*Five Green Bottles.* 1968. PLAAC2
*The Whole Truth.* 1975. PLAAC1

JENKINS, RAYMOND LEONARD. *See* Jenkins, Ray

JENNINGS, GERTRUDE E., 1877–1958
*Family Affairs.* 1934. FAMF
*A Woman's Influence.* 1912. VOTE

JENNINGS, TALBOT, 1894–1985
*No More Frontier.* 1929. TOD

JENSEN, JULIE, 1942–
*Two-headed.* 2000. WOMP2000

JENSEN, LORRE, 1941–
*The Mercy Quilt* (radio play). 1996. BEYO (excerpt)

JEPHSON, ROBERT, 1736–1803
*Braganza.* 1775. INCA6
*The Law of Lombardy.* 1779. INCA6

JERMAIN, CLIVE, 1966?–1988
*The Best Years of Your Life* (television play). 1986. LEAK

JEROME, MRS. HELEN (BURTON), 1883–1958
*Charlotte Corday.* 1939. FIP
*Jane Eyre* (based on the novel by Charlotte Brontë). 1936. FOUPL, THH
*Pride and Prejudice* (based on the novel by Jane Austen). 1935. BES35, FOUPL, THH, VOAD

JEROME, V. J. (Victor J.), 1896–1965
*Newsboy. See* Workers' Theatre Movement. *Newsboy* (adapted from the poem by)

JERROLD, DOUGLAS WILLIAM, 1803–1857
*All in the Downs. See* Black Ey'd Susan
*Black Ey'd Susan; or, All in the Downs.* 1829. ASG, BOOA1, MOSN, MOSO, ROWE
    Variant title: *All in the Downs*
*Fifteen Years of a Drunkard's Life.* 1828. KILG
*Mr. Paul Pry.* 1826. BOOA4
*The Rent-day.* 1832. BAI

JESSOP, GEORGE HENRY, 1850?–1915
*Sam'l of Posen; or, The Commercial Drummer.* 1881. AMP4

JESURUN, JOHN, 1951–
  *Deep Sleep.* 1986. WOQ5
  *White Water.* 1986. OSB

JEVON, THOMAS, 1652–1688
  *Devil of a Wife. See* The Devil to Pay; or, The Wives
    Metamorphos'd (adapted from)

—— and COFFEY, CHARLES; MOTTLEY, JOHN;
    GIBBER, THEOPHILUS
  *The Devil to Pay; or, The Wives Metamorphos'd*
    (adapted from *Devil of a Wife* by Thomas Jevon.
    1731. BELC2, HUGH
    Variant title: *The Wives Metamorphos'd* (adapted
      from)
  *The Wives Metamorphos'd. See* The Devil to Pay; or,
    The Wives Metamorphos'd

JI, JUNXIANG. *See* Chi, Chun-Hsiang

JIHEI II, TSUUCHI. *See* Tsuuchí Jihei II

JIMENEZ, ASISCLO
  *Love and Wealth.* 1906.
    Realubit, M., translator PHIL
    Variant title: *Pagkamoot asin cayamanan*
  *Pagkamoot asin cayamanan.* PHIL

JIN, YUN, 1938–
  *Gouerye de niepan. See* The Nirvana of Grandpa Doggie
  *Gou'erye niepan. See* The Nirvana of Grandpa Doggie
  *The Nirvana of Grandpa Doggie.* 1986.
    Ying, R., translator CHEU
    Yu, S., translator YUCHD
    Variant titles: *Gouerye de niepan; Gou'erye niepan;*
      *Uncle Doggie's Nirvana*
  *Uncle Doggie's Nirvana. See* The Nirvana of Grandpa
    Doggie

JINTAN, SORAYA
  *Lalita's Way.* 1988. DODGS

JISUKE II, SAKURADA. *See* Sakurada, Jisuke II

JOAQUIN, NICK, 1917–2004
  *A Portrait of the Artist as Filipino.* 1952. EDAD

JOB, NORMAN
  *Mai jekketti (My Jacket).* 2000. ZEE1

JOB, THOMAS, 1900–1947
  *Uncle Harry.* 1942. BES41, RICN

JODELLE, ÉTIENNE, 1532–1573
  *Didon se sacrifiant.* 1560? FOUR
  *Eugene.* 1552?

    Stabler, A. P., translator FOUAF
    Variant title: *L'Eugene*
  *L'Eugene. See* Eugene

JOHN, ELTON, 1947–
  *The Lion King* (music and lyrics by). *See* Allers, Roger.
    *The Lion King*

JOHN, ERROL, 1924–1988
  *Moon on a Rainbow Shawl.* 1957. OBSE

JOHNS, PATTI. *See* Hensel, Karen, joint author

JOHNSON, BRYAN STANLEY, 1933–1973
  *You're Human like the Rest of Them.* 1967. NEWE14

JOHNSON, CATHERINE, 1957–
  *Boys Mean Business.* 1989. BUSHT

JOHNSON, CHARLES, 1679–1748
  *The Cobler of Preston.* 1716. HUGL
  *Country Lasses; or, The Custom of the Manor.* 1715.
    BELK19
    Variant title: *The Custom of the Manor*
  *The Custom of the Manor. See* Country Lasses; or, The
    Custom of the Manor

JOHNSON, EFFIONG
  *Generous Donors.* 1992. AGOR

JOHNSON, ELIZABETH
  *A Bad Play for an Old Lady.* 1964. BALLE1

JOHNSON, EVA, 1946–
  *Murras.* 1988. PLACC, TAIT
  *What Do They Call Me?* 1990. AUSG

JOHNSON, FRANCINE
  *The Right Reason.* 1991. NTIR

JOHNSON, FRANCIS HALL, 1888–1970
  *Run Little Chillun.* 1933. HARYL

JOHNSON, MRS. GEORGIA (DOUGLAS), 1886–1966
  *Blue Blood.* 1926. BRW, PER
  *Blue-eyed Black Boy.* ca.1930. BRW, PER, PERF
  *Plumes.* 1927. LOC, PER, PLAAE, WORY
  *Safe.* ca.1929. BRW, PERF
  *A Sunday Morning in the South.* 1925. HARY, HARYB,
    PER, PERF

JOHNSON, HESTER N.
  *On to Victory.* 1915. FRIED

JOHNSON, JUDITH, 1962–
*Somewhere.* 1992. FROLIN1
*Uganda.* 1994. FROLIN3

JOHNSON, NIKI. *See* Cresswell, Janet, joint author

JOHNSON, PAMELA HANSFORD, 1912–1981
*The Duchess at Sunset.* 1948. OULD

JOHNSON, PHILIP, 1900–
*Lovers' Leap.* 1934. FAMG

JOHNSON, SAMUEL, 1709–1784
*Irene.* 1749. BELG8, BOO

JOHNSTON, ALEX, 1970–
*Melonfarmer.* 1997. NEWPAB2

JOHNSTON, DENIS, 1901–1984
*The Moon in the Yellow River.* 1931. BRZE
*The Old Lady Says "No!"* 1929. CAN, LAQID, OWEC

JONAS, GEORGE, 1935–
*Pushkin.* 1978. NEWCAD1

JONES, EDITH NEWBOLD. *See* Wharton, Mrs. Edith
    Newbold (Jones)

JONES, FELICITY. *See* Epp, Steven, joint author

JONES, HENRY, 1721–1770
*The Earl of Essex.* 1753. BELK3

JONES, HENRY ARTHUR, 1851–1929
*The Case of Rebellious Susan.* 1894. BES94
*The Dancing Girl.* 1891. MARG
*Dolly Reforming Herself.* 1908. CHA, CHAN, CHAR
*The Goal.* 1898. HUD, PEN
*Judah.* 1894. RUB
*The Liars.* 1897. DUR, MART, MATTL, ROWC, SALE
*The Masqueraders.* 1894. BAI, MOSN, MOSO
*Michael and His Lost Angel.* 1896. ASG, BOWY, DICD
*The Middleman.* 1889. BOOL
*Mrs. Dane's Defence.* BOOA2, BOOM, COT

——— and HERMAN, HENRY
*The Silver King.* 1882. BAI

JONES, JACK, 1884–1970
*Rhondda Roundabout.* 1939. SIXL

JONES, JANE
*The Cider House Rules, Part II* (conceived for the stage
    by). *See* Parnell, Peter. *The Cider House Rules,
    Part II*

JONES, JEFFREY M.
*Der Inka von Peru.* 1984. WEJ
*Night Coil.* 1979. MESSE, WOQ4
*Seventy Scenes of Halloween.* 1980. WEK

JONES, JOSEPH STEVENS, 1809–1877
*The People's Lawyer. See* Solon Shingle
*Solon Shingle.* 1839. BAT20, MOSS2
    Variant title: *The People's Lawyer*
*The Usurper; or, Americans in Tripoli.* 1841? AMP14

JONES, KEN
*Darkside.* 1988. PRIMA88

JONES, LEROI (IMAMU AMIRI BARAKA, pseud.),
    1934–
*Ba-ra-ka.* OWER
*Bloodrites.* (1971) KINH, KINHB
*Dutchman.* 1964. ABCE, ABCF, ALLM, ALLN,
    BARK, BARKA, BARKB, BARKC, BARKD,
    BERP, BERPA, DOLAN, GILB, HARYB,
    HEAC, HOLP, HOWP2, KNO, KNOJ, MANCA2,
    MANCB2, MANCD2, MANCE2, MANCF2,
    MANCG2, OLIV, PATR, REIL, REIW, REIWE,
    SCNT, SSSI, SSSIB, SSSIC, TREBJ, VENA,
    WATTAD, WOTHA, WOTHB, WOTHC,
    WOTHM
*The Election Machine Warehouse.* 1996. ALG
*General Hag's Skeezag.* 1989. BLACTH
*Great Goodness of Life: A Coon Show.* (1967) BLACQ,
    CARR, RAVIT, RICJ, TUQTR
*Home on the Range.* 1968. BEAN
*Junkies Are Full of (SHHH . . .).* KINH, KINHB
*Madheart.* 1967. JONE
*Primitive World: An Anti-nuclear Jazz Musical* (music
    by David Murray; arrangement by Ron McIntire).
    1997. ALG
*Police.* 1968. BEAN
*The Slave.* 1964. HARY, SEVT, TAUJ, THT
*Slave Ship.* 1978. BPW
*Song.* (1989) KINHP
*The Toilet.* 1964. ALLK, BES64, CAL, GAT, GROV,
    MESSE, TUQT

JONES, LISA, 1961–
*Combination Skin.* 1986. PERC

JONES, MARIE, 1951–
*The Hamster Wheel.* 1990. CRACK

JONES, PAUL, d. 1966
*Birthday Honours.* 1953. PLAN9

JONES, PETER, 1920–2000, and JOWETT, JOHN
*The Party Spirit.* 1954. PLAN11

JONES, PRESTON, 1936–1979
*The Last Meeting of the Knights of the White Magnolia*
(part of: *A Texas Trilogy*; a repertory of three
plays). 1973. BES76, PLAN47
*Lu Ann Hampton Laverty Oberlander* (part of: *A Texas
Trilogy*; a repertory of three plays). 1974. TEX
*The Oldest Living Graduate* (part of: *A Texas Trilogy*; a
repertory of three plays). 1974. BES76
*A Texas Trilogy*; a repertory of three plays made up
of: *The Last Meeting of the Knights of the White
Magnolia; Lu Ann Hampton Laverty Oberlander*;
and *The Oldest Living Graduate*. *See* The Last
Meeting of the Knights of the White Magnolia; Lu
Ann Hampton Laverty Oberlander; and The Oldest
Living Graduate.

JONES, RHODESSA
*Big Butt Girls, Hard-headed Women.* 1992. ELAM

JONES, STEPHEN MACK
*Back in the World.* 1987. BES86

JONES, THOMAS W., II
*The Wizard of Hip.* 1987. BLAC

JONES, TOM, 1928–
*Celebration* (music by Harvey Schmidt). 1969. BES68
*The Fantasticks.* 1960. GAT

JONES, WENDELL, and STANLEY, DAVID
*AIDS! The Musical!* (music by Robert Berg). 1991. JONT

JONES-MEADOWS, KAREN, 1953–
*Henrietta.* 1985. KINHN

JONSON, BEN, 1572–1637
*The Alchemist.* 1610. ASH, BAS, BELG16, BELK17,
BENY, BROC, CASK, DEAS, DPR2, GAYLE2,
GRE, HARC47, HOW, KRM, LIE, LIEE1, NEI,
OLH, OLI2, ORNC, REIO, ROF, SPE, TAT, TAU,
THA
*The Alchymist. See* The Alchemist
*Barriers at a Marriage.* 1606. LINDC
*Bartholomew Fair.* 1614. DPR2, KINNR, OLH, OLI2,
SPE
*Chloridia.* 1631. LINDC
*Christmas His Masque.* 1616. LINDC
*The Devil Is an Ass.* 1616. SALF
*Epicoene; or, The Silent Woman.* 1609. BALD, BROC,
CLKW, DPR2, GAYLE2, RUB, STA, WOOD
Hogan, R., and Molin, S., adapters HOGF
*Every Man in His Humour.* 1598. ANG, BAS, BAT14,
BELK2, BROC, CLF1, CLK1, GATG, GAYLE2,
HAPRA1, HAPRB1, MATTL, NEI, ORNC, PAR,
SCI, SCJ, SCW, SPE, WAT

*Fortunate Isles, and Their Union.* 1624. ETO
*The Gipsies Metamorphosed.* 1621. BROC
*Golden Age Restored.* 1616. ETO, LINDC
*The Hue and Cry after Cupid.* 1608. BAS, SCH, SCI,
SCJ
*Love Restored.* 1612. LINDC
*Lovers Made Men.* 1617. ETO
*Love's Welcome at Bolsover.* 1634. LINDC
*Masque at Lord Haddington's Marriage.* 1608. ETO
*Masque of Augurs.* 1622. ETO
*The Masque of Blackness.* 1605. ABRM1, KINNR,
LINDC, WINE
*Masque of Queens.* 1609. ETO, LINDC
*Neptune's Triumph for the Return of Albion.* 1624. ETO,
LINDC
*News from the New World Discovered in the Moon.*
1621. ETO
*Oberon, the Fairy Prince.* 1611. ETO, PAR
*Pan's Anniversary; or, The Shepherd's Holyday.* 1625.
ETO
Variant title: *The Shepherd's Holyday*
*Pleasure Reconciled to Virtue.* 1619. ABRH1, ABRJ1,
ABRK1, ABRL1, LINDC
*The Sad Shepherd; or, A Tale of Robin Hood.* 1641?
BAS, SCH
*Sejanus, His Fall.* 1603. BAS, NEI, PAR
*The Shepherd's Holyday. See* Pan's Anniversary
*The Silent Woman. See* Epicoene
*The Vision of Delight.* 1617. ABRA, ABRB1, ABRE,
ABRF1, TREB
*Volpone; or, The Fox.* 1606. ABRJ1, ABRK1, ABRL1,
ABRM1, ALLI, ALLJ, ALLK, ALLM, ALLN,
ALLO, BAC, BARD, BAS, BECK, BELK19,
BENSB1, BROC, COLD, COTKICO, DEAO,
DEAP, DEAR, DPR2, DUN, FOS, FOUD,
HILPDH2, HOEP, HUD, HUST, KRE, KRM,
LIED1, MORR, NEI, OLH, OLI1, PAR, PARRY,
SCH, SCI, SCJ, SEN, SPE, SSSI, SSSIA, SSSIB,
SSSIC, SUL, TRE, TREA2, TREB, TREC1,
TREE1, TREI1, WAIW, WALL, WINE, WOTHB,
WRIH
— *See* Chapman, George, joint author
— *See also* Celbart, Larry. *Sly Fox* (adapted by)
— *See also* Zweig, Stefan. *Volpone* (adapted by)

JORDAN, JULIA
*Mpls., St. Paul.* 1999. HUMANA99
*Tatjana in Color.* 1998. WOMP97

JOSELOVITZ, ERNEST A., 1942–
*The Inheritance.* 1973. BALLE13

JOSEPH, ALLEN, 1919–
*Anniversary on Weedy Hill.* 1970. BALLE8

JOSEPH, E. M. W.
*The Foreign Expert.* 1979. GOON (excerpt)

JOSEPHSON, RAGNAR, 1891–1966
*Kanske en diktare. See* Perhaps a Poet
*Perhaps a Poet.* 1932.
Lundbergh, H., translator SCAN1
Variant title: *Kanske en diktare*

JOTUNI, MARIA, 1880–1943
*The Golden Calf.* 1918.
Poom, R., translator WILM
Variant title: *Kultainen vasikka*
*Kultainen vasikka. See* The Golden Calf

JOUDRY, PATRICIA, 1921–2000
*Teach Me How to Cry; a Drama in Three Acts.* 1953.
WAGN2

JOVANOVIC, DUSAN, 1939–
*The Liberation of Skopje.* 1978.
Anonymous translator PRED (summary only)
*The Puzzle of Courage.* 1995.
Soule, L., translator PRED
*Wall, Lake.* 1989.
Anonymous translator PRED (summary only)

JOWETT, JOHN. *See* Jones, Peter, joint author

JOYCE, JAMES, 1882–1941
— *See* Barkentin, Majorie
*Ulysses in Nighttown* (based on the novel by)
— *See* Leonard, Hugh. *Stephen D* (based on *Portrait of the Artist as a Young Man* and *Stephen Hero*)
— *See* Nelson, Richard James

JUANA INES DE LA CRUZ, SOR, 1651–1695
*El cetro de José. See* Joseph's Scepter
*Joseph's Scepter.* 1692.
McGaha, M., translator STORJ
Variant title: *El cetro de José*
*Loa to the Divine Narcissus.* 1687.
Peters, P., and Domeier, R., translators WOTHC

JUCHA, BRIAN
*Deadly Virtues.* 1993. HUMANA93

JULLIEN, JEAN, 1854–1919
*The Serenade.* 1887.
Clark, B., translator CLD

JUNCTION AVENUE THEATRE COMPANY, 1976–
*The Fantastical History of a Useless Man.* 1976. ORK
*Randlords and Rotgut.* 1978. GRAYTT, ORK

*Sophiatown.* 1986. GRAV, ORK
*Tooth and Nail.* 1989. ORK

JUPP, KENNETH, 1928–2009
*The Socialites.* 1961? SATA

JURANOVA, JANA, 1957–
*Salome.* 1989.
Trebatická, H., translator CONTSL3

KA, ABDOU ANTA, 1931–
*The Daughter of the Gods.* 1957.
Vogel, S., translator AFRUBU1
Variant title: *La fille des dieux*
*La fille des dieux. See* The Daughter of the Gods

KABAHAR, PIO A., 1892–1977
*Babaye ug lalake. See* Woman and Man
*Marianito.* 1918. PHIL
Ramas, W., translator PHIL
*Miss Dolying.* 1920? RAP
*Woman and Man.* RAP
Variant title: *Babaye ug lalake*

KAFKA, FRANZ, 1883–1924
*The Guardian of the Tomb.* 1916?
Ritchie, J., and Garten, H., translators RITS

KAHN, BARBARA
*Whither thou Goest.* 1995. COJ

KAI, NUBIA
*Harvest the Frost.* 1984. KINHN
*The Last of the Reapers.* 1991. NTIR
*Parting.* 1983. KINHP

KAINY, MIRIAM, 1942–
*The End of the Dream Season.* 1991.
Kaye, H., and Kainy, M., translators BARAM

KAISER, GEORGE, 1878–1945
*Alkibiades Saved.* 1920?
Morgan, B., translator SOK
Variant title: *Der gerettete Alkibiades*
*Der brand im opernhaus. See* The Fire in the Opera House
*The Conflagration of the Opera House. See* The Fire in the Opera House
*The Coral.* 1917.
Katzin, W., translator DICIN2, TUCG, TUCM, TUCN, TUCO
Variant title: *Die koralle*
*The Fire in the Opera House.* 1918.
Katzin, W., translator KAT
Variant titles: *Der brand im opernhaus; The Conflagration of the Opera House*

*Das Floss der Medusa. See* The Raft of the Medusa
*From Morn to Midnight.* 1916.
   Dukes, A., translator BLOC, DICDT, EXP, GARZH,
      HILPDH5, MOSG, MOSH, ROF
   Ritchie, J. M., translator SCVG
   Weisstein, U., translator BRIX, BRIY, BRIZ
   Variant titles: *From Morning to Midnight; Von
      morgens bis mitternachts*
*From Morning to Midnight. See* From Morn to Midnight
*Gas I.* 1918.
   Scheffauer, H., translator SCVG, TUCG, TUCM,
      TUCN, TUCO
*Gas II.* 1920. FEFH2
   Katzin, W., translator SCVG, TUCG, TUCM, TUCN,
      TUCO
*Der gerettete Alkibiades. See* Alkibiades Saved
*Die koralle. See* The Coral
*Der Protagonist. See* The Protagonist
*The Protagonist.* 1922.
   Ritchie, J., and Garten, H., translators RITS
   Variant title: *Der Protagonist*
*The Raft of the Medusa.* 1943.
   Wellwarth, G., translator BENB, ENG
   Variant title: *Das Floss der Medusa*
*Von morgens bis mitternachts. See* From Morn to
   Midnight

KAKO, CHIKAKO (CHIKA), 1835–1893, and
      TOYOZAWA DAMPEI II
*The Miracle of the Tsubosaka Kannon.* 1887.
   Law, J., translator BRAZ
   Variant title: *Tsubosaka Kannon reigenki*
*Tsubosaka Kannon reigenki. See* The Miracle of the
   Tsubosaka Kannon

KALA, SAM
*Akpakaland.* 1990. FINBN

KALCHEIM, LEE H., 1938–
   *. . . and the Boy Who Came to Leave.* 1965. BALLE2

KĀLIDĀSA, 4th century
*Abhijnanashakuntala. See* Shakuntalā
*The Fatal Ring. See* Shakuntalā
*The Hero and the Nymph. See* Vikramorvacie
*Sakoontalā. See* Shakuntalā
*Shakúntalā.* 4th century
   Coulson, M., translator, KIAN, THWI
   Edgren, A., translator, WEL
   Jones, W., translator, TAV
   Lal, P., translator, LAL
   Monier-Williams, M., translator ANDF, BUCK,
      BUCL, BUCM, CLF1, EDAD, ORI3, TRE,
      TREA2, TREB, TREC1, TREE1, TREI1, YOHA,
      YOHB

   Ryder, A., translator ANDI, WARN1
   Variant titles: *Abhijnanashakuntala; The Fatal Ring;
      Sakoontalā; Shakuntala and the Ring of Recognition;
      Shakuntala Recognized by a Ring-token*
*Shakuntala and the Ring of Recognition. See*
   Shakuntalā
*Shakuntala Recognized by a Ring-token. See* Shakuntalā
*Urvashi Won by Valour. See* Vikramorvacie
*Vikramorvacie; or, The Hero and the Nymph.* 4th
      century
   Aurobindo, S., translator WEL
   Variant titles: *The Hero and the Nymph; Urvashi Won
      by Valour; Vikramorvashiya*
*Vikramorvashiya. See* Vikramorvacie

KALINOSKI, RICHARD
*Beast on the Moon.* 1992. HUMANA95

KAMARCK, EDWARD, 1919–1992
*Chenango Crone.* 1940. DRU

KAMBAR, CHANDRASEKHAR, 1938–
*Mahamayi. See* The Mother Supreme
*The Mother Supreme.* 1999.
   Chandrashekar, L., translator KAM1
   Variant title: *Mahamayi*
*Siri sampige.* 1991.
   Hill, B., Vasudevan, K., and Ramaswamy, N.,
      translators DESH

KAN, KIKUCHI, 1888–1948
*Madman on the Roof.* 1916.
   Iwaski, Y., and Hughes, G., translators SCVDT1

KAN'AMI, KANZE KIYOTSUGU. *See* Kanami

KAN-AMI, KIYOTSUGU. *See* Kanami

KANAMI, 1333?–1384?
*Eguchi: A Woman Play. See* Mouth-of-sound
*The Golden Tablet.* 14th century
   Tyler, R., translator TYLG
   Variant title: *Kin'satsu*
*Hanakatami.*
   Waley, A., translator WAJ (excerpts)
*Jinen koji. See* Layman selfsame
*Kayoi Komachi. See* Komachi and the Hundred Nights
*Kin'satsu. See* The Golden Tablet
*Komachi and the Hundred Nights.* 14th century
   Kato, E., translator KEE
   Variant title: *Kayoi Komachi*
*Komachi on the Gravepost. See* Sotoba Komachi
*Lady Shizuka in Yoshino. See* Shizuka at Yoshino
*Layman selfsame.* 14th century
   Shimazaki, C., translator SHIM4, book 2

Tyler, R., translator TYLP
    Variant title: *Jinen koji*
*Motomezuka. See* The Sought-for Grave
*Motomezuka Kayoi Komachi. See* The Sought-for
    Grave
*Mouth-of-sound.* 14th century
    Shimazaki, C., translator SHIM3, book 2
    Tyler, R., translator TYLP
    Variant titles: *Eguchi: A Woman Play; Rivermouth*
*Rivermouth. See* Mouth-of-sound
*Shizuka at Yoshino.* 14th century
    Terasaki, E., translator BRAZT
    Tyler, R., translator TYLG
    Variant title: *Yoshino Shizuka*
*Sotoba Komachi.* 14th century
    Waley, A., translator ANTL, TRE, TREB, TREC1,
        TREE1, TREI1, WAJ
    Tyler, R., translator TYLG
    Variant title: *Komachi on the Gravepost*
*The Sought-for Grave.* 14th century
    Jackman, B., translator KEE
    Variant titles: *Motomezuka, Motomezuka Kayoi*
        *Komachi*
*Yoshino Shizuka. See* Shizuka at Yoshino

—— and ZEAMI
*Matsukase.* 14th century
    Shimazaki, C., translator SHIM3, book 2
    Tyler, R., translator KEE, TYLJ, TYLP, WOTHC
    Waley, A., translator WAJ (excerpts)
    Yasuda, K., translator YASU
    Variant titles: *Matzukaze; Pine Wind; Pining Wind*
*Matzukaze. See* Matsukase
*Pine Wind. See* Matsukase
*Pining Wind. See* Matsukase

KANDER, JOHN, 1927–
    *Cabaret* (music by). *See* Masteroff, Joe. *Cabaret*
    *Chicago* (music by). *See* Ebb, Fred, and Fosse, Bob.
        *Chicago*
    *Kiss of the Spider Woman* (music by). *See* McNally,
        Terrance. *Kiss of the Spider Woman*

KANE, MARGO, 1951–
    *Moonlodge* (excerpt). 1993. BREK

KANE, SARAH, 1971–1999
    *Blasted.* 1995. FROLIN2

KANESHITA, TATSUO, 1964–
    *Ice Blossoms.* 1997.
        Riho, M., translator HACJT1

K'ANG, CHIN-CHIH, fl.1279
    *Li K'uei Carries Thorns* (attributed to).

    Crump, J., translator BIR1, CRU
    Variant title: *Li K'uei fu ching*
*Li K'uei fu ching. See* Li K'uei Carries Thorns

KANG, M. J. *See* Kang, Myung-Jin

KANG, MYUNG-JIN, 1974–
    *Noran Bang: The Yellow Room.* 1993. BEYO (excerpt),
        ZIMM (excerpt)

KANI, JOHN, 1943– . *See* Fugard, Athol, joint author

KANIN, FAY (MITCHELL) (Michael Kanin), 1917–
    *Goodbye, My Fancy.* 1948. BES48, PLAAF
    Variant title: *Most Likely to Succeed*
*Most Likely to Succeed. See* Goodbye, My Fancy

KANIN, GARSON, 1912–1999
    *Born Yesterday.* 1946. BES45, COLT, GARZ, GATB3

KANIN, MRS. GARSON. *See* Gordon, Ruth

KANIN, MICHAEL, 1910–1993. *See* Kanin, Fay
    (Mitchell)

KANNAMI. *See* Kanami

KANZE KIYOTSUGU KAN'AMI. *See* Kwanze,
    Kiyotsugu

KANZE KOJIRŌ NOBUMITSU. *See* Kanze, Kojirō
    Nobumitsu

KANZE, KOJIRŌ NOBUMITSU, 1434–1516
    *Ataka.* 15th century
        Yasuda, K., translator YASU
    *Benkei aboard ship.* 15th century
        Tyler, R., translator TYLJ
        Yasuda, K., translator YASU
        Variant titles: *Funa Benkei; Funabenkai*
    *Butterfly. See* Kochō
    *Chorio.* 15th century
        Pound, E., translator NOH
    *Dōjōji* (attributed to)
        Keene, D., translator KEE, NORJ1, NORJA
    *Funa benkei. See* Benkei aboard ship
    *Funabenkai. See* Benkei aboard ship
    *Kochō.* 15th century
        Shimazaki, C., translator SHIM3, book 1
        Variant title: *Butterfly*
    *The Maple Viewing* (attributed to)
        Weatherby, M., translator ERN
        Variant title: *Momijigari*
    *Momijigari. See* The Maple Viewing
    *The Priest and the Willow.*

Beichman, J., translator KEE
Variant title: *Yugyō Yanagi*
*Yugyō Yanagi. See* The Priest and the Willow

KANZE MOTOKIYO. *See* Zeami

KANZE MOTOKIYO ZEAMI. *See* Zeami

KANZE, MOTOMASA, 1395?–1432?
*Sumida-gawa. See* The Sumida River
*The Sumida River.* 15th century
Tyler, R., translator TYLJ
Variant title: *Sumida-gawa*

KAO, MING, fl.1345
*Pi-Pa-Ki. See* Howard, Sidney, and Irwin, William
Henry. *Lute Song* (adapted from)

KAO TONG-KIA. *See* Kao, Ming

KAPEK, KAREL
*Skin deep.* 1949. MONB2

KAPLAN, BARRY JAY
*Landscape of Desire.* 2001. LAR

KAPP, SHARLEEN
*The Interview.* 1979. VICK1

KAPROW, ALLEN, 1927–2006
*18 Happenings in 6 Parts.* 1959. WILLG

KARA, JURO, 1940–
*A Cry from the City of Virgins.* 1985.
Ingulsrud, L., translator HACJT6
*Futari no onna. See* Two Women
*John Silver: ai no kojiki. See* John Silver: The Beggar of
Love
*John Silver: The Beggar of Love.* 1970.
Goodman, D., translator JAPDC
Variant title: *John Silver: ai no kojiki*
*Shōjo kamen. See* The Virgin's Mask
*Two Women.* 1979.
Gillespie, J., translator ALTJD
Variant title: *Futari no onna*
*The Virgin's Mask.* 1969.
Gillespie, J., and Krieger, P., translators ALTJD
Variant title: *Shōjo kamen*

KARDISH, LAURENCE, 1945–
*Brussels Sprouts.* 1972. BRIN

KARNAD, GIRISH, 1938–
*Death by Beheading.* 1989.
Karnad, G., translator KAM1
Variant title: *Talé-danda*

*Hayavadana.* 1972.
Karnad, G., translator DESH
*Talé-danda. See* Death by Beheading
*Tughlaq.* 1964.
Karnard, G., and Gopalie, S., translators THRIN

KARPATI, PETER, 1961–
*Everywoman* (English version by Jack Bradley; verses
by Tony Curtis). 1993.
Gál, A., translator UPOR

KARTUN, MAURICIO, 1946–
*Sacco-Vanzetti* (*A Dramaturgic Summary Judgment
from Documents on the Case*). 1988.
Thomas, C., translator LATTH
Variant title: *Sacco y Vanzetti: dramaturgia sumario
de documentos sobre el caso*
*Sacco y Vanzetti: dramaturgia sumario de documentos
sobre el caso. See* Sacco-Vanzetti (A Dramaturgic
Summary Judgment from Documents on the Case)
*Salto al cielo.* 1991. PARRI

KASOMA, GODFREY PETER KABWE
*Black Mamba Two.* 1970? AFR2

KASSIN, MICHAEL, 1947–
*Today a Little Extra.* (1977) VORE

KATAEV, VALENTIN PETROVICH, 1897–1986
*Squaring the Circle.* 1928.
Langen, T., and Weir, J., translators EIGHTRP
Malamuth, C., and Lyons, E., translators HAV,
HAVE, LYK

KATAYEV, VALENTIN PETROVICH. *See* Kataev,
Valentin Petrovich

KATES, CHARLES R., 1948–
*The Travels of Heikiki.* 1976. KUMU

KATO, MICHIO, 1918–1953
*The Man Who Sells Memories.* 1953.
Sorgenfrei, C., and Nobuko, A., translators HACJT8
Variant title: *Omoide wo uru otoko*
*Omoide wo uru otoko. See* The Man Who Sells
Memories

KATŌ, TADASHI, 1942– . *See* Satoh, Makoto, joint author

KATZ, L.
*The Three Cuckolds. See* Anonymous Plays. *The Three
Cuckolds* (converted by)

KATZ, LEON, 1919–
*Swellfoot's Tears.* 1976. GUTR

KAUFFMAN, JOHN, 1948–1990
*According to Coyote.* 1987? SWANS

KAUFMAN, GEORGE S., 1889–1961
*The Butter and Egg Man.* 1925. BES25, LEV, LEVE
— *See* Dayton, Katharine; Lardner, Ring; Marquand, John P.; Teichmann, Howard, joint authors

—— and CONNELLY, MARCUS COOK
*Beggar on Horseback.* 1923. BES23, CARP, CARPA, CHAN, CHAP, COT, GASB, WARH, WATC1, WATI
*Dulcy.* 1921. BES21, COH, CONG, MOSJ, MOSK, MOSL
*Merton of the Movies* (based on the novel by Harry L. Wilson). 1922. BEAC12, BES22, PEN
*To the Ladies!* 1922. QUI, TUCD

—— and FERBER, EDNA
*Dinner at Eight.* 1932. RES32, SIXH
*Minick.* 1924. BES24
*The Royal Family.* 1927. BES27
*Stage Door.* 1936. BES36, CLH, GAS

—— and HART, MOSS
*The American Way.* 1939. BES38, PROC
*George Washington Slept Here.* 1940. BES40
*The Man Who Came to Dinner.* 1939. BES39, CET, COLT, DAVK, GARZ, GATB2, SIXC
*Merrily We Roll Along.* 1934. BES34
*Once in a Lifetime.* 1930. BES30, FAMB
*You Can't Take It with You.* 1936. BES36, CLH, CORE, CORF, GAS, GATB2, LAM, LOOC, LOOD, LOOE, LOOF, MERS, SPES

——, RYSKIND, MORRIE, and GERSHWIN, IRA
*Of Thee I Sing* (music by George Gershwin). 1931. BES31, CORD, CORE, CORF, DUR, FAMD, HIL, RICO, ROLF, TRE, VAN

—— and TEICHMANN, HOWARD
*The Solid Gold Cadillac.* 1953. GART

KAUFMAN, LYNNE
*Shooting Simone.* 1993. HUMANA93

KAUFMAN, MOISES, 1963–
*Gross Indecency: The Three Trials of Oscar Wilde.* 1997. BES97

KAUNDU, AINNA
*Now that You Know.* 2000. ZEE2

KAVANAGH, GEOFF
*Ditch.* 1993. SSSN

KAWAMURA, TAKESHI, 1959–
*Nippon uoōzu. See* Nippon Wars
*Nippon Wars.* 1984.
Ingulsrud, L., and Shōicirō, K., translators HACJT4
Variant title: *Nippon uoōzu*

KAWATAKE, MOKUAMI, 1816–1893
*Aoto Zōshi Hana no Nishikie. See* Benten the Thief
*Benten kozō. See* Benten the Thief
*Benten the Thief.* 1862.
Uyehara, Y., translator (English version by Earle Ernst). ERN
Variant titles: *Aoto Zōshi Hana no Nishikie; Benten kozō; Shiranami Gonin Otoko*
*The Hamamatsu-ya Scene.* (from Act 3 of *Benten kozō*) 1862.
Leiter, S., translator BRAZ
*Shiranami Gonin Otoko. See* Benten the Thief

KAY, JACKIE, 1961–
*Chiaroscuro.* 1986. LES1
*Generations* (excerpt from *The Adoption Papers*). 1990. MYTH
*Twice Over.* 1988. OSME

KAY, KWESI, 1940–
*Laughter and Hubbub in the House.* 1972. PIET

KAYE, MARVIN, 1938–
*A Cold Blue Light* (based on the novel by Marvin Kaye and Parke Godwin). 1986. KAYT

KAYLA, LISSELLE, ca.1957–
*When Did I Last See You.* 1987. DEAD

KAZAN, NICHOLAS, 1950–
*Safe House.* 1977. WES3

KEANE, JOHN B., 1928–2002
*Many Young Men of Twenty.* 1961. HOGE
*Sharon's Grave.* 1960. HOGE

KEARNS, MICHAEL
*Attachments.* 1996. HUGH
*Intimacies/More Intimacies.* 1989, 1990. HELB
*Myron, a Fairy Tale in Black and White.* 1993. JONT

KEATS, JOHN, 1795–1821
*King Stephen.* 1819. ADAP, ENGL

—— and BROWN, CHARLES.
*Otho the Great.* 1950. ENGL, KAU

KEEFFE, BARRIE, 1945–
*Gimme Shelter*. Three plays: *Gem, Gotcha*, and
*Getaway*. 1975. BES78

KEHAIDIS, DIMITRIS, 1933– , and HAVIARA, ELENI
*With Power from Kifissia*. 1995.
Karra, N., translator CONTG1

KEILLOR, GARRISON, 1942–
*Prodigal Son* (radio sketch). 1991. LITIE, LITIF, LITJA

KELLER, SUSAN HESSE
*Woyzeck* (music by). *See* Büchner, Georg. *Woyzeck*
(adapted by David Ball)

KELLEY, SAMUEL L., 1948–
*Pill Hill*. 1990. NEWAMP2

KELLEY, SHANNON KEITH, 1948–
*Dennis and Rex*. *See* Hope of the Future
*Hope of the Future*. 1985. PRIMA86
(3 one-act plays: *Dennis and Rex, Rapid Transit,
Practical Magic*)
*Practical Magic*. *See* Hope of the Future
*Rapid Transit*. *See* Hope of the Future

KELLY, GEORGE EDWARD, 1887–1974
*Behold the Bridegroom*. 1927. BES27
*Craig's Wife*. 1925. BES25, CORD, CORE, CORF,
GASB, HARB, MERW, MOSG, MOSH
*Daisy Mayme*. 1926. BES26
*The Fatal Weakness*. 1946. BES46
*Finders-keepers*. 1916? WAGC3
Variant title: *The Lesson*
*The Lesson*. *See* Finders-keepers
*Poor Aubrey*. 1925. GASB, PROH, SCWG, THO
*The Show-off*. 1924. BES23, KRM, MARK, MOAD,
MOSJ, MOSK, MOSL

KELLY, HUGH, 1739–1777
*False Delicacy*. 1768. BELG10, MAND, MANF
*School for Wives*. 1773. BELG10, INCA9
*A Word to the Wise*. 1770. BELG10

KELLY, TIM, 1937–1998
*The Lalapalooza Bird*. 1981. VORE
*The Uninvited*. 1979. KAYT

KEMBLE, FANNY, 1809–1893
*Francis the First*. 1832. FEFNC

KEMBLE, MARIE-THERESE DECAMP, 1774–1838
*Smiles and Tears: or, The Widow's Stratagem*. 1815.
FEFNC
Variant title: *The Widow's Stratagem*

*The Widow's Stratagem*. *See* Smiles and Tears: or, The
Widow's Stratagem

KEMLO, KAREN
*Crazyluv*. 1994. ZIMM (excerpt)
*Mona*. 1997. BREK

KEMP, DAVID, 1936–
*King Grumbletum and the Magic Pie* (1974). KAL4

KEMP, JENNY, 1949–
*Remember*. 1993. TAIT

KEMP, R.
*The Satire of the Three Estates*. *See* Lindsay, Sir David.
*The Satire of the Three Estates* (modernized by)

KENNA, PETER, 1930–1987
*A Hard God*. 1973. BRIM1
*Mates*. 1975. AUSG

KENNAWAY, JAMES PEEBLES EWING, 1928–1968
*Country Dance*. 1967. PLAN33

KENNEDY, ADAM P., and KENNEDY, ADRIENNE,
joint author
*Sleep Deprivation Chamber*. 1996. SSSIC

KENNEDY, ADRIENNE, 1931–
*A Beast Story* (part of *Cities in Bezique*). 1965. CARR
*Cities in Bezique: The Owl Answers* and *A Beast Story*.
(1969) CARR
*The Dramatic Circle*. 1992. MAQ
*Funnyhouse of a Negro*. 1964. BARKF, BRAS,
HARYB, OLIV, WOTHM
*Motherhood 2000*. 1994. MARR
*A Movie Star Has to Star in Black and White*. 1976.
MESSE, WATTAD, WOQ3
*The Ohio State Murders*. 1990. BES90
*The Owl Answers*. 1965. ASF, HARY, NEWA2
*The Owl Answers* (part of *Cities in Bezique*). 1965.
CARR
*A Rat's Mass*. 1966. SME
*Sun* (1972) OWER
— *See* Kennedy, Adam P., joint author

——, LENNON, JOHN, and SPINETTI, VICTOR
*The Lennon Play: In His Own Write*. (1972) RICK

KENNEDY, MARGARET, 1896–1967
*Escape Me Never!* 1933. SEV

—— and DEAN, BASIL
*The Constant Nymph*. 1926. YEAR

KENNEDY, MARY, 1896–1987, AND HAWTHORNE, RUTH (WARREN)
*Mrs. Partridge Presents.* 1925. BES24

KENNEY, JAMES, 1780–1849
*Raising the Wind.* 1803. BOOA4

KENNON, SKIP
*Herringbone* (music by). *See* Cone, Tom. *Herringbone*

KENRICK, WILLIAM, 1725?–1779
*Falstaff's Wedding.* 1766. BELG3

KENT, ALANA. *See* Hensel, Karen, joint author

KENTE, GIBSON, 1932–2004
*Too Late.* 1975. SOUT

KENYON, CHARLES, 1880–1961
*Kindling.* 1911. DICEM

KEOGH, DANNY, 1948– , and COOKE, VANESSA, and HAYSOM, FINK
*The Native Who Caused All the Trouble.* 1986. KANI
— *See also* Cooke, Vanessa, joint author

KERATA, LACO, 1961–
*Dinner about a City.* 1995.
Ruppeldtová, D., translator CONTSL1
Variant title: *Vecera nad mestom*
*Na hladine. See* On the Surface
*On the Surface.* 1997.
Ruppeldtová, D., translator CONTSL2
Variant title: *Na hladine*
*Vecera nad mestom. See* Dinner about a City

KERR, JEAN (COLLINS), 1922–2003
*Finishing Touches.* 1973. BES72
*Lunch Hour.* 1980. BES80
*Mary, Mary.* 1961. BES60, COLT, GARSA, MOST

KERR, LOIS REYNOLDS, 1908–2001
*Open Doors.* 1931. WAGN3

KESSELMAN, WENDY, 1940–
*Maggie Magalita.* 1980. SCVDO1
*My Sister in This House.* 1980. HANNA, KILGC, LAQCW
*Olympe and the Executioner.* 1989. THB

KESSELRING, JOSEPH, 1902–1967
*Arsenic and Old Lace.* 1941. BES40, CEY, COLT, CORB, CORBA, FREE, GARZ, GATB3, MOST, RICI
Variant title: *Bodies in Our Cellar*
*Bodies in Our Cellar. See* Arsenic and Old Lace

KETRON, LARRY, 1947–
*Rachel's Fate.* 1986. PRIMA87

KHAN, HATTA AZAD, 1952–
*Dolls.* 1993.
Ishak, S., translator MLAM

KHAN BEJRA, PHRA (pseudonym of His Highness King Vajiravudh of Siam), 1881–1925
*The Shield.* 1978. MLAT

KHARMS, DANIIL, 1905–1942
*Elizaveta Bam.* 1927.
Langen, T., and Weir, J., translators EIGHTRP
*Makarov and Peterson, No. 3.* 1930s.
Sohonee, R., translator RZH

KIA, KAO TONG. *See* Kao, Ming

KIELLAND, AXEL, 1907–1963
*Herren og hens tjenere. See* The Lord and His Servants
*The Lord and His Servants.* (1955)
Stabell, V., translator MNON
Variant title: *Herren og hens tjenere*

KIELLAND, TRYGVE VON TANGEN, 1893–1987
*Dronningen og hennes menn. See* Queen Margaret of Norway
*Queen Margaret of Norway.* 1950.
Malleson, C., translator MODS

KIFT, ROY, 1943–
*Camp Comedy.* 1999. THLA

KILCOYNE, CATHERINE
*Julie.* 1985. LES2

KILCOYNE, CATHY, and SLOVO, ROBYN
*A Netful of Holes.* 1984. DEAD

KILLIGREW, THOMAS, 1612–1683
*The Parson's Wedding.* 1640. JEFF1, KNOW, SUM

KILLINGWORTH, GERALD
*Days of Cavafy.* 1989. GAY4

KILROY, THOMAS, 1934–
*The Secret Fall of Constance Wilde.* 1997. NEWPAB2

KIMBALL, ROSAMOND
*The Resurrection.* 1917. FED1

KIMBERLAIN, SORA. *See* Terry, Megan, joint author

KIMMEL, HAROLD
*The Cell.* PIET

KIMMINS, ANTHONY, 1901–1964
*The Amorous Prawn*. 1959. PLAN21

KINCAID, JAMAICA, 1949– (b. Elaine Cynthia Potter
     Richardson)
*Girl*. 1978. MYTH

KING, BRUCE, 1950–
*Evening at the Warbonnet*. 1993. GEIO

KING, LARRY L., 1929– , and MASTERSON, PETER
*The Best Little Whorehouse in Texas* (music and lyrics
     by Carol Hall). 1978. BES77

KING, NORMAN, 1921–
*The Shadow of Doubt*. 1955. PLAN12

KING, PHILIP, 1904–1979
*Serious Charge*. 1953. PLAN11

————— and CARY, FALKLAND L.
*Sailor Beware!* 1955. PLAN12
*Watch It, Sailor!* 1960. PLAN22

KING, STEPHEN, 1947–
*Sorry, Right Number*. 1987. SCVDT1

KINGSLEY, SIDNEY, 1906–1995
*Darkness at Noon* (based on the novel by Arthur
     Koestler). 1951. BES50, GARW, GAVE, WISD
*Dead End*. 1935. BES35, CET, FREE, GAS
*Detective Story*. 1949. BES48, GARW, HAVG
*Lunatics and Lovers*. 1954. THEA55
*Men in White*. 1934. BES33, CORD, CORE, CORF,
     FAMF, GARU, GATB1, MERV
*The Patriots*. 1943. AMB, BES42, CRIT, GARZ,
     GAVE
   Variant title: *Thomas Jefferson*
*Thomas Jefferson*. See The Patriots
*The World We Make* (based on the novel *The Outward
     Room* by Millen Brand). 1939. BES39

KINGSLEY-SMITH, TERRY
*I Want to Hold Your Hand*. 1982. *See* Anonymous
     Plays. *Twenty-four Hours: A.M.*

KINOSHITA, JUNJI, 1914–2006
*Okinawa*. 1963.
   Powell, B., translator HACJT8
*Twilight Crane*. 1949.
   Scott, A., translator PLAA
   Variant title: *Yûzuru*
*Yûzuru*. See Twilight Crane

KINROSS, MARTHA
*Tristram and Isoult*. 1913. LUP, LUPW

KINWELMERSH, FRANCIS, 1546?–1580. *See*
     Gascoigne, George, joint author

KIPER, FLORENCE. *See* Frank, Florence Kiper

KIPPHARDT, HEINAR, 1922–1982
*In der Sache J. Robert Oppenheimer*. *See* In the Matter
     of J. Robert Oppenheimer
*In the Matter of J. Robert Oppenheimer*. 1964.
     Speirs, R., translator BES68
     Variant title: *In der Sache J. Robert Oppenheimer*

KIRBY, ANDY
*Compromised Immunity*. 1985. OSME

KIRBY, MICHAEL, 1947–
*Double Gothica*. 1978. VENA

KIRKLAND, JACK, 1904–1969, and CALDWELL,
     ERSKINE
*Tobacco Road*. 1933. CEY, GAS, GATB1, MOST

KIRKUP, JAMES, 1918–2009
*The True Mistery of the Nativity* (adapted from the
     French medieval mystery cycle by Arnoul Gréban).
     1956. TRUE
*The True Mistery of the Passion* (adapted from the
     French medieval mystery cycle by Arnoul Gréban).
     1961. TRUE
*Upon This Rock: A Dramatic Chronicle of Peterborough
     Cathedral*. 1955. TRUE

KIRKWOOD, JAMES, 1924–1989, and DANTE,
     NICHOLAS
*A Chorus Line* (music by Marvin Hamlisch; lyrics by
     Edward Kleban; conceived by Michael Bennett).
     1975. BES74

KIRSHON, VLADIMIR MIKHAILOVICH, 1902–1938
*Bread*. 1930.
     Anonymous translator (excerpt) VONG
     Langen, T., and Weir, J., translators EIGHTRP
     Volochora, S., translator LYK
     Variant title: *Grain*
*Grain*. See Bread

KISARAGI KOHARU, 1956–
*Moral*. 1984–1986. SECO

KISHIDA, RIO, 1950–2003
*Ito jigoku*. See Thread Hell
*Thread Hell*. 1984.
     Sorgenfrei, C., Naomi, T., translators HACJT4
     Variant title: *Ito jigoku*
     — *See also* Terayama, Shuji, joint author

KITAMURA, SŌ, 1952–
  *Eiyaku hogiuta. See* Ode to Joy
  *Ode to Joy*. 1979.
    Riho, M., translator HACJT4
    Variant title: *Eiyaku hogiuta*

KITAS, FRIDA
  *Crossing*. 1999. FOUPAP

KITZBERG, AUGUST, 1855–1927
  *Libahunt. See* The Werewolf
  *The Werewolf*. (1912)
    Lepasaar, M., translator GOLB
    Variant title: *Libahunt*

KIYOTSUGU, KWANAMI. *See* Kwanze, Kiyotsugu
    Kantami

KLEB, WILLIAM, 1939–
  *Honeymoon in Haiti*. 1965. GARZAL

KLEBAN, EDWARD, 1939–1987
  *A Chorus Line* (lyrics by). *See* Kirkwood, James, and
    Dante, Nicholas. *A Chorus Line*

KLEIN, DEBBY
  *Coming Soon*. 1986. LES2

KLEIN, JON
  *Betty the Yeti*. 1994. HUMANA94
  *Something to Do with Bolivia*. 2000. *See* Ackermann,
    J. *Back Story: A Dramatic Anthology*.
    HUMANA2000
  *T Bone n Weasel*. 1986. NEWQC

KLEIN, MAXINE, 1934–
  *The Furies of Mother Jones* (music by James
    Oestereich). 1973. KLEIN
  *New Rise of the Master Race* (music by James
    Oestereich). 1979. KLEIN
  *Split-shift* (music by James Oestereich). 1986. KLEIN
  *Windfall* (music by James Oestereich). 1978. KLEIN

KLEIN, SYBIL, 1939– (b. Consuela Moore)
  *Get Together*. 1970. BRW

KLEIST, HEINRICH VON, 1777–1811
  *The Broken Jug. See* Der zerbrochene krug
  *The Broken Pitcher. See* Der zerbrochene krug
  *Kaethchen of Heilbronn; or, The Test of Fire*. 1810.
    Pierce, F., translator PIE
    Variant titles: *Das Käthchen von Heilbronn; oder, Die
      feuerprobe; Das Käthchen von Heilbronn; oder,
      Die Feuerprobe. See* Kaethchen of Heilbronn; or,
      The Test of Fire

*Penthesilae*. 1876.
    Lamport, F., translator LAMP
    Trevelyan, H., translator BENR2
  *Prince Frederick of Homburg. See* Prinz Friedrich von
    Homburg
  *The Prince of Homburg. See* Prinz Friedrich von
    Homburg
  *Prinz Friedrich von Homburg*. 1821. CAM
    Anonymous translator PLAN36
    Esselin, M., translator ESS
    Hagedorn, H., translator FRA4, SMK
    Kirkup, J., translator BENR2, WEIS
    Lustig, T., translator LUST
    Scheurer, L., translator BENSB1
    Variant titles: *Prince Frederick of Homburg; The
      Prince of Homburg*
  *Der zerbrochene krug*. 1808. CAM
    Cardullo, B., translator GERLC
    Wilson, L., translator ALL
    Variant titles: *The Broken Jug, The Broken Pitcher*

KLIEWER, WARREN, 1931–
  *A Lean and Hungry Priest*. 1973. BALLE12

KLIMA, IVAN, 1931–
  *Games*. (1973)
    Day, B., translator DAY
    Drabek, J., translator DRAC

KLIMACEK, VILIAM, 1958–
  *Axes in Flower*. 2000.
    Trebatická, H., translator CONTSL4
    Variant title: *Rozkvitli sekery*
  *Beach Boredom*. 1993.
    Ruppeldtová, D., translator CONTSL1
    Variant title: *Nuda na plázi*
  *Nuda na plázi. See* Beach Boredom
  *Rozkvitli sekery. See* Axes in Flower

KLING, KEVIN
  *The Ice-fishing Play*. 1993. HUMANA93

KLINGER, FRIEDRICH MAXIMILIAN, 1752–1831
  *Storm and Stress*. 1776.
    Waterhouse, B., translator STURM, WASD

KLONSKY, KENNETH, 1946– , and SHEIN, BRIAN
  *Taking Steam*. 1983. NEWJV

KLOTZ, PHYLLIS
  *You Strike the Woman You Strike the Rock (Wathint'
    abafazi wathint' imbokotho)*. 1986. KANI

KNEE, ALLAN
  *Syncopation*. 1999. BES99

KNEUBUHL, VICTORIA NALANI, 1949–
*The Conversion of Ka'ahumanu.* 1988. HOUST
*The Story of Susanna.* 1998. DAPO

KNIGHT, ERIC MOWBRAY, 1897–1943
*Never Come Monday* (adapted by Stephen Fox). 1939?
    PROC

KNIGHT, VICK, 1908–1984
*Cartwheel* (radio play). 1936. PROC

KNOBLOCK, EDWARD, 1874–1945. *See* Bennett,
    Arnold, joint author

KNOTT, FREDERICK, 1916–2002
*Dial "M" for Murder.* 1952. BES52, FAOS, RICI,
    THEA53

KNOWLES, JAMES SHERIDAN, 1784–1862
*The Love-chase.* 1831. MARG
*Virginius.* 1820. BOOA1, MOSN, MOSO

KNOX, FLORENCE CLAY
*For Distinguished Service.* 1918. SHAY

KOBER, ARTHUR, 1900–1975
*"Having Wonderful Time."* 1937. CET
*Wish You Were Here* (based on *"Having Wonderful
    Time"*; music and lyrics by Harold Rome). 1953.
    THEA53

KOBRIN, LEON, 1872–1946
*Boila. See* Yankel Boyla
*Boile. See* Yankel Boyla
*Boxle. See* Yankel Boyla
*Boxleh. See* Yankel Boyla
*Children of Nature. See* Yankel Boyla
*Dorf's Yung. See* Yankel Boyla
*Yankel Boyla.* 1912.
    Lifson, D., translator LIFS
    Variant titles. *Boila; Boile, Boxle; Boxleh; Children
        of Nature; Dorf's Yung*

KOCH, HOWARD, 1902–1995
*The War of the Worlds* (radio play based on the novel by
    H. G. Wells). 1938. READ1 (excerpt)

———— and HUSTON, JOHN
*In Time to Come.* 1940. AMB, BES41

KOCH, KENNETH, 1925–2002
*The Academic Murders.* 1966. GLI

KOCHERGA, IVAN. *See* Kocherha, Ivan

KOCHERHA, IVAN, 1881–1952
*Masters of Time.* 1934.
    Wixley, A., translator FOUS
    Variant title: *Watchmaker and the Hen*
*Watchmaker and the Hen. See* Masters of Time

KOCK, CHARLES PAUL DE, 1794–1871
*A Happy Day.* 184– ?
    Chambers, W., translator BAT9
    Variant title: *Une journée de bonheur*
*Un journée de bonheur. See* A Happy Day

KOEBNICK, SARAH MONSON
*Fair Beckoning One.* 1967. BALLE5

KOESTLER, ARTHUR, 1905–1983
*Darkness at Noon. See* Kingsley, Sidney. *Darkness at
    Noon* (based on the novel by)

KOFTA, KRYSTYNA, 1942–
*The Umbilical Cord.* 1990.
    Mludzinska, J., translator EUP

KOHOUT, PAVEL, 1928–
*Fire in the Basement.* 1974.
    Stenberg, P., and Goetz-Stankiewicz, M., translators
    DRAC

KŌKAMI, SHŌJI, 1958–
*Lullaby: A Hundred Years of Song.* 2000.
    Boyd, M., translator HACJT3
    Variant title: *Rarabai: matawa hyakunen no
        komori-uta*
*Rarabai: matawa hyakunen no komori-uta. See* Lullaby:
    A Hundred Years of Song

KOKOSCHKA, OSKAR, 1886–1980
*Hiob. See* Job
*Job.* 1917.
    Benedikt, M., translator WELG
    Sokol, W., and J., translators SOK
    Variant title: *Hiob*
*Mörder, Hoffnung der Frauen. See* Murderer Hope of
    Womankind
*Murderer Hope of Womankind.* 1907.
    Hamburger, M., translator SCVG, SOK
    Ritchie, J., and Garten, H., translators RITS
    Variant titles: *Mörder, Hoffnung der Frauen;
        Murderer the Women's Hope*
*Murderer the Women's Hope. See* Murderer Hope of
    Womankind
*Sphinx and Strawman.* 1907.
    Meisel, V., translator EXP

KOLLER, KATHERINE, 1957–
*Cowboy Boots and a Corsage*. 1993. ZIMM (excerpt)
*Madonna of the Wilderness*. 1997. BREK

KOLPAK, DIANA
*Bedtime Stories*. 1990. ZIMM (excerpt)

KOLTES, BERNARD-MARIE, 1948–1989
*Combat de nègre et de chiens*. *See* Struggle of the Dogs and the Black
*Come Dog, Come Night*. *See* Struggle of the Dogs and the Black
*Night just before the Forest*. 1977.
  Johns, T., translator MOGS
  Variant title: *La nuit juste avant les forêts*
*La nuit juste avant les forêts*. *See* Night just before the Forest
*Struggle of the Dogs and the Black*. 1984. Ward, M., translator NEWFPA
  Variant titles: *Combat de nègre et de chiens; Come Dog, Come Night*

KOMATSU, MIKIO, 1941–
*Ame no wanmankā*. *See* Mystery Tour
*Mystery Tour*. 1976.
  Gallimore, D., translator HACJT5
  Variant title: *Ame no wanmankā*

KOMPARU, GONNOKAMI, fl. mid. 14th century
*Ama*. *See* The Diver
*The Diver* (attributed to). 14th century
  Tyler, R., translator TYLJ
  Waley, A., translator WAJ (excerpts)
  Variant title: *Ama*

KOMPARU-ZENCHIKU. *See* Konparu, Zenchiku

KON, STELLA, 1944–
*Emily of Emerald Hill*. 1984. MLAS

KONDOLEON, HARRY, 1955–1994
*The Brides*. 1980. WOQ2
  Variant title: *Disrobing the Bride*
*Disrobing the Bride*. *See* The Brides
*The Fairy Garden*. 1982. SHEW
*Zero Positive*. 1988. OSBW

KONG, SHANGREN. *See* K'ung, Shang-jen

KONGŌ, YAGORO, 16th century?
*The Bird-scaring Boat* (attributed to). 16th century?
  Tyler, R., translator KEE
  Variant title: *Toriolbune*

*Genjo*. 16th century?
  Pound, E., translator NOH
*Toriolbune*. *See* The Bird-scaring Boat

KONPARU, ZENCHIKU, 1405–1468
*Hatsuyuki*
  Waley, A., translator WAJ (excerpts)
*Ikkaku sennin*
  Waley, A., translator WAJ (excerpts)
*Kamo*
  Bethe, M., translator BRAZ
  Shimazaki, C., translator SHIM1
*Kasuga ryujin*. *See* The Kasuga Dragon God
*The Kasuga Dragon God* (attributed to). 15th century
  Tyler, R., translator TYLJ
  Variant title: *Kasuga ryujin*
*Kogō*
  Shimazaki, C., translator SHIM4, bk. 2
*Nonomiya*. *See* The Shrine in the Fields; The Wildwood Shrine
*No-ni-maya*. *See* The Shrine in the Fields
*The Palace in the Fields*. *See* The Shrine in the Fields
*The Queen Mother of the West* (attributed to). 15th century
  Sesar, C., translator KEE
  Shimazaki, C., translator SHIM1
  Variant title: *Seiōbo*
*Seiōbo*. *See* The Queen Mother of the West
*Senju*
  Shimazaki, C., translator SHIM3, book 3
*The Shrine in the Fields* (attributed to). 15th century
  Shimazaki, C., translator SHIM3, book 1
  Varley, H., translator KEE Variant titles: *Nonomiya; No-ni-maya; The Palace in the Fields*
*Tatsuta* (attributed to). 15th century
  Tyler, R., translator TYLJ
*The Wildwood Shrine* (attributed to). 15th century
  Tyler, R., translator TYLJ
  Variant title: *Nonomiya*
*Yamauba*. 15th century
  Waley, A., translator WAJ (excerpts)
*Yokihi*. 15th century
  Sesar, C., translator KEE

KOPIT, ARTHUR LEE, 1937–
*End of the World*. *See* End of the World with Symposium to Follow
*End of the World with Symposium to Follow*. 1984. ABCD, BERT, LOWE
  Variant title: *End of the World*
*The Hero*. 1970. LITI
*Indians*. 1969. BES69, GARTL, HOWM
*Nine* (music and lyrics by Maury Yeston; adaptation from the Italian by Mario Fratti). 1979. BES81

*Oh Dad, Poor Dad, Mamma's Hung You in the Closet*
    *and I'm Feelin' So Sad.* 1960. BES61, CASH,
    FREH, GARSA, GATB4, OFF1, SMA, WHFM
*Road to Nirvana.* 1989. DIXD1
*Wings.* 1978. BERS, BES78, PLACHA
*Y2k.* 1999. HUMANA99

KOPS, BERNARD, 1926–
*Dreams of Anne Frank.* 1992. THLA
*Enter Solly Gold.* 1961? COTKR, SATA
*The Hamlet of Stepney Green.* 1958. NEWE1

KORDER, HOWARD, 1958–
*Search and Destroy.* 1990. PLACG1

KORNBLUTH, JOSH, 1959–
*Red Diaper Baby.* 1992. BES92

KORNEICHUK, ALEKSANDR EVDOKONOVICH,
    1905–1972
*The Front.* 1942.
    Anonymous translator FOUT, VONG
    Kotem, B., and Voynow, M., translators SEVP
*Guerillas of the Ukrainian Steppes.* 1942.
    Anonymous translator FOUT
    Variant titles: *Partisans on the Steppes of the
        Ukraine; Partizany v stepakh Ukrainy*
*Partisans on the Steppes of the Ukraine. See* Guerillas of
    the Ukrainian Steppes
*Partizany v stepakh Ukrainy. See* Guerillas of the
    Ukrainian Steppes
*Platon Krechet.* 1935?
    Prokofieva, R., translator THY

KORNEICHUK, ALEXANDER EVDOKONOVICH. *See*
    Korneichuk, Aleksandr Evdokonovich

KORNIICHUK, OLEKSANDR. *See* Korneichuk,
    Aleksandr Evdokonovich

KORNIS, MIHALY, 1949–
*Kozma.* 1986.
    Brogyányi, E., translator HUNGDC
    Gyorgyey, C., translator GYOR

KORR, DAVID
*Encore.* 1970. BALLE9

KOSACH, LARISA PETROVNA (LESYA UKRAINKA,
    pseudonym), 1871–1913
*The Babylonian Captivity.* 19th century
    Volska, S., translator ROE

KOSSMAN, NINA, 1959–
*Miracles.* 2000. WOMP2000

KOSTROWISKY, GUILLAUME APOLLINAIRE DE
    (GUILLAUME APOLLINAIRE, pseudonym),
    1880–1918
*The Breasts of Tiresius.* 1917.
    Simpson, L., translator BEN
    Slater, M., translator SLAT
    Variant titles: *Les mamelles de Tirésias; The
        Mammaries of Tiresias*
*Les mamelles de Tirésias. See* The Breasts of Tiresius
*The Mammaries of Tiresias. See* The Breasts of Tiresius

KOSTROWITZKI, WILHELM. *See* Kostrowisky,
    Guillaume Apollinaire de

KOTZEBUE, AUGUST FRIEDRICH FERDINAND
    VON, 1761–1819
*Der egoist und kritikus. See* Egotist and Pseudo-critic
    Herr Gottlieb Merks
*Egotist and Pseudo-critic Herr Gottlieb Merks.* 179–?
    Chambers, W., translator BAT11
    Variant title: *Der egoist und kritikus*
*Falsche scham. See* Dunlap, William. *False Shame*
    (adapted from)
*Das kind der liebe. See* Lovers' Vows
*Lovers' Vows; or, The Natural Son.* 1798?
    Thompson, B., translator BAT21
    Variant title: *Das kind der liebe*
*Menschenhass und reue. See* The Stranger
*Pharaoh's Daughter.* 179–?
    Beebe, B., translator WEB
    Variant title: *Die tochter Pharaonis*
*The Stranger.* 1789.
    Thompson, B., translator MAND, MANF
    Variant title: *Menschenhass une reue*
*Die tochter Pharaonis. See* Pharaoh's Daughter

KOUTOUKAS, H. M., 1947–2010 (b. Haralambos
    Monroe Koutoukas, aka Harry)
*Kill, Kaleidoscope, Kill. See* Tidy Passions
*Tidy Passions, or, Kill, Kaleidoscope, Kill.* 1972. SME
    Variant title: *Kill, Kaleidoscope, Kill*

KOVAMEES, RAISSA, 1907–1989
*The Maiden on the Seashore.* 1973.
    Kitching, J., and Kovamees, H., translators BRIDGE
    Variant title: *Piiga rannateel*
*Piiga rannateel. See* The Maiden on the Seashore

KOZAK, PRIMOŽ, 1929–1981
*An Affair.* 1961.
    Anderson, E., and Salamun, T., translators MIG

KOZLENKO, WILLIAM, 1908–1984
*This Earth Is Ours.* 1937? KOZ

KRAL, BRIAN, 1955–
*One to Grow On.* 1980. WES15/16

KRAMER, LARRY, 1935–
*The Destiny of Me.* 1992. BES92, WATTAD

KRAMER, SHERRY
*David's Redhaired Death.* 1991. PLACA

KRAMM, JOSEPH, 1907–1991
*The Shrike.* 1952. BES51

KRANES, DAVID
*Drive-in.* 1970. BALLE7

KRASIŃSKI, ZYGMUNT, 1812–1859
*Nieboska komedia. See* The Un-divine Comedy
*The Un-divine Comedy.* 1902.
   Segel, H., translator POB
   Variant title: *Nieboska komedia*

KRASNA, NORMAN, 1909–1984
*Dear Ruth.* 1944. BES44
*John Loves Mary.* 1947. BES46

KRAUS, JOANNA HALPERT, 1937–
*Angel in the Night.* 1996. VOI
*The Ice Wolf: A Tale of the Eskimos.* 1973. NEWWT

KRAUS, KARL, 1874–1936
*The Last Days of Mankind* (excerpt). 1919–1922.
   Spalter, M., translator WELG
   Variant title: *Die letzten tage der menschheit*
*Die letzten tage der menschheit. See* The Last Days of Mankind

KRETZMER, HERBERT, 1925–
*Les misérables* (lyrics by). *See* Boubil, A., and Schönberg, C. *Les misérables*

KREYMBORG, ALFRED, 1883–1966
*The Dead Are Free.* 1935. AME5
*Hole in the Wall.* 192–? KRE
*Lima Beans.* 1925? LEV, LEVE
*Manikin and Minikin.* 1918. SHAY
*Rocking Chairs.* 1921? SHAY

KRISHNAN, P., 1932–
*After Us.* 1971.
   Elangovan, translator MLAS

KROETZ, FRANZ XAVER, 1946–
*Mensch Meier: A Play of Everyday Life.* 1978.
   Downey, R., translator NEWQA
*Stallerhof.* 1972.
   Hehn, K., translator SHAK

KROG, HELGE, 1889–1962
*Konkylien. See* The Sounding Shell
*The Sounding Shell.* 1929.
   Campbell, R., translator SCAN2
   Variant title: *Konkylien*

KRYLOV, IVAN ANDREEVICH, 1768–1844
*The Milliner's Shop.* (1806)
   Senelick, L., translator RVI
   Variant title: *Modnaya Lavka*
*Modnaya Lavka. See* The Milliner's Shop

KUAN, HAN-CH'ING, 1210?–1298?
*The Butterfly Dream.* MANM
*The Injustice Done to Tou Ngo.*
   Liu, J., translator LIU
*Snow in Midsummer.* 13th century
   Yang, H., and Yang, G., translators MESE
   Variant title: *Tou Ngo*
*Tou Ngo. See* Snow in Midsummer

KUDELKA, JAN, 1952– . *See* Vingoe, Mary, joint author

KUGLER, D. D. *See* Rose, Richard, joint author

KUHNS, DOROTHY HARTZELL. *See* Heyward, Mrs. Dorothy Hartzell (Kuhns)

KULVET, ILMAR, 1920–2002
*Bridge across the Sea.* 1968.
   Kukk, H., translator BRIDGE
   Variant title: *Sild üle mere*
*Sild üle mere. See* Bridge across the Sea

KUMMER, CLARE (BEECHER), 1888–1958
*Chinese Love.* 1922. CHIN
*Good Gracious Annabelle.* 1916. BES09
*Her Master's Voice.* 1933. BES33

KUNDERA, MILAN, 1929–
*Jacques and His Master; an Homage to Diderot in Three Acts.* 1982.
   Heim, M., translator DRAC
   Variant titles: *Jacques et son maître; Jacques le fataliste et son maître*
*Jacques et son maître. See* Jacques and His Master; an Homage to Diderot in Three Acts
*Jacques le fataliste et son maître. See* Jacques and His Master; an Homage to Diderot in Three Acts

KUO, PAO KUN, 1939–2002
*The Silly Little Girl, and the Funny Old Tree.* 1990. MLAS

K'UNG, SHANG-JEN, 1648–1718
*The Peach Blossom Fan.* 1699.
   Chen, S., and Acton, H., and Birch, C., translators
   NORJ2

KURGINIAN, SERGEI, 1949–
*Compensation: A Liturgy of Fact.* 1987.
   Kelson, C., Prokhorov, A., and Prokhorov, H.,
   translators FAV

KURNITZ, HARRY, 1909–1968
*Reclining Figure.* 1954. THEA55

KUROSAWA, AKIRA, 1910–1998, HASHIMOTO,
   SHINOBU, and OGUNI, HIDEO
*Ikiru* (screenplay). 1952.
   Richie, D., translator HIBH
   Variant title: *To Live*
*To Live. See* Ikiru

KURTTI, CASEY
*Catholic School Girls.* 1982. PLACA

KUSHNER, TONY, 1958–
*And the Torso Even More So.* 1999. HUMANA99
*Angels in America, Part I: Millennium Approaches.*
   1991. BES92, JACOBD, OSBW (excerpt), SSSIC,
   WOTHB, WOTHC, WOTHM
*Angels in America, Part II: Perestroika.* 1992. BES93
*A Bright Room Called Day.* 1985. VOI, WEJ
*Reverse Transcription.* 1995. HUMANA96, MESSE
*Slavs! Thinking about the Longstanding Problems of
   Virtue and Happiness.* 1994. HUMANA94

KUZMIN, MIKHAIL, 1872–1936
*The Comedy of Alexis, Man of God.* 1908.
   Green, M., translator GREEN
*The Dangerous Precaution.* 1907.
   Senelick, L., translator SELOV
*The Venetian Madcaps.* 1914.
   Green, M., translator GREEN

KVARES, DONALD, 1936?–1993
*Mushrooms.* 1967. SMC

KWAHULE, KOFFI, 1956–
*Cette vielle magie noire. See* That Old Black Magic
*That Old Black Magic.* 1991.
   MacDougall, J., translator NEWFPL
   Variant title: *Cette vielle magie noire*

KWANAMI. *See* Kanami

KWANAMI KIYOTSUGU. *See* Kanami

KWANZE KIYOTSUGU. *See* Kanami

KWANZE KOJIRŌ NOBUMITSU. *See* Kanze, Kojirō
Nobumitsu

KYD, THOMAS, 1558–1594
*Arden of Feversham* (sometimes attributed to). *See*
   Anonymous Plays. *Arden of Feversham*
*Hieronimo Is Mad Again. See* The Spanish Tragedy; or,
   Hieronimo Is Mad Again *The Spanish Tragedy;
   or, Hieronimo Is Mad Again.* 1589? BAS, BROC,
   DPR1, GATG, GIBS, HEIL, HILPDH2, HOW,
   HUST, KAYS, KINNR, MAKG, MAUS, MATTL,
   MIN1, MIO1, MIR, NEI, NES, OLH, OLI1,
   ORNT, PAR, RUB, SCI, SCJ, SCW, SPE, TICO
   Variant title: *Hieronimo Is Mad Again*

KYLATASKU, JUSSI, 1943–
*Mary Bloom.* 1980.
   Steffa, T., translator BRAK

LABERGE, MARIE, 1950–
*L'homme gris. See* Night
*Night.* 1984.
   Fraticelli, R., translator PLABE7
   Variant title: *L'homme gris*

LABICHE, EUGENE MARIN, 1815–1888
*Eating Crow.* 1853.
   Magruder, J., translator THOS

—— and DELACOUR, ALFRED CHARLEMAGNE
   LARTIGNE
*La cagnotte. See* Pots of Money
*Célimare.* 1863.
   Hoffman, L., and T., and Bentley, E., translators
   BENSC
   Variant title: *Célimare le bien-aimé*
*Célimare le bien-aimé. See* Célimare
*Les petite oiseaux. See* Grundy, Sydney. *A Pair of
   Spectacles* (adapted from)
*The Piggy Bank. See* Pots of Money
*Pots of Money.* 1864.
   Bermel, A., translator BERMD, BERMG, THV
   Variant titles: *La cagnotte; The Piggy Bank*

—— and GONDINET, EDMOND
*The Happiest of the Three.*
   Davies, F., translator LAB

—— and LEVEAUX, ALPHONSE
*La grammaire.* 1867. BENZ, STOC

—— and MARTIN, EDOUARD
*Bluffers. See* La poudre aux yeux
*Cousin Billy. See* Le voyage de Monsieur Perrichon

*Dust in the Eyes.* See La poudre aux yeux
*Perrichon's Voyage.* See Le voyage de Monsieur
    Perrichon
*La poudre aux yeux.* 1861. SCN
    Variant titles: *Bluffers; Dust in the Eyes*
*The 37 Sons of M. Montaudoin.* See Les trente-sept sous
    de M. Montaudoin
*Les trente-sept sous de M. Montaudoin.* 1862. BRN
    Variant title: *The 37 Sons of M. Montaudoin*
*A Trip Abroad.* See Le voyage de Monsieur Perrichon
*Le voyage de Monsieur Perrichon.* 1860. MANA
    Ward, R., translator BENSC
    Variant titles: *Cousin Billy; Perrichon's Voyage; A*
    *Trip Abroad*

—— and MICHEL, MARC ANTOINE AMEDEE
*Haste to the Wedding.* See An Italian Straw Hat
  — See also Gilbert, William Schwenck. *An Italian*
    *Straw Hat.* 1851.
    Hoffman, L., and T., translators BENT3, COTKIR
    Variant title: *The Wedding March*
*It's All Relative.* 1852.
    Shapiro, N., translator FLEA
    Variant title: *Les suites d'un premier lit*
*Les suites d'un premier lit.* See It's All Relative
*The Wedding March.* See An Italian Straw Hat
  — See also Legouve, Ernest, joint author

LA CHAUSEE, PIERRE CLAUDE NIVELLE DE, 1692–
    1754
*Fashionable Prejudice.* See Le préjugé à la mode
*Le préjugé à la mode.* 1735. BREN
    Variant title: *Fashionable Prejudice*

LA FARGE, W. E. R.
*Escape by Balloon.* 1972. BALLE10

LA FOSSE, ANTOINE DE, sieur d'Aubigny, 1653–1708
*Manlius Capitolinus.* 1698.
    Lockert, L., translator LOCR

LAGERKVIST, PAR, 1891–1974
*The Difficult Hour, I–III.* 1918
    Buckman, T., translator SPR
    Variant title: *Den svåra stunden, I–III*
*Låt människan leva.* See Let Man Live
*Let Man Live.* 1949.
    Alexander, H., and Jones, L., translators SCAN3
    Gustafason, W., translator FIL
    Variant titles: *Låt människan leva; The Man Who*
    *Lived His Life Over*
*The Man Who Lived His Life Over.* See Let Man Live
*The Man without a Soul.* 1936.
    Kökeritz, H., translator SCAN1
    Variant title: *Mannen utan själ*

*Mannen utan själ.* See The Man without a Soul
*Den svåra stunden, I–III.* See The Difficult Hour, I–III

LA GRANGE-CHANCEL, 1677–1758
*Ino and Melicertes.* 1713.
    Lockert, L., translator LOCU
    Variant title: *Ino et Mélicerte*
*Ino et Mélicerte.* See Ino and Melicertes

LA HSUN ACADEMY OF ART AND LITERATURE
*The White-haired Girl.* See Ho, Ching-chih, and Ting,
    Yi. *The White-haired Girl* (written by)

LAI, STANLEY SHENG-CH'UAN, 1954–
*Anlian taohuayuan.* See Pining . . . in Peach Blossom
    Land
*Pining . . . in Peach Blossom Land.* 1986.
    Cheung, M., translator CHEU
    Variant title: *Anlian taohuayuan*

LALANDE, FRANCOISE, 1941–
*Alma Mahler.* 1989.
    Glasheen, A., translator GLASH

LAM, DANA, 1953–
*Bernard's Story.* 1992. FAT
*Ordinary Woman.* 1995. PING

LAMB, CHARLES, 1775–1834
*John Woodvil.* 1802. ENGLMI

LAMB, MYRNA, 1935–
*But What Have You Done for Me Lately? See* Scyklon
    Z: But What Have You Done for Me Lately? or,
    Pure Polemic
*I Lost a Pair of Gloves Yesterday.* NEWWT
*Pure Polemic.* See Scyklon Z: But What Have You
    Done for Me Lately?; or, Pure Polemic
*Scyklon Z: But What Have You Done for Me Lately? or,*
    *Pure Polemic.* 1969. BAYM, RAVIT
    Variant titles: *Pure Polemic; But What Have You*
    *Done for Me Lately?*

LAMBERT, ANN, 1957–
*Ask Your Mother.* 1996. BREK
*Parallel Lines.* 2000. ALONG

LAMBERT, BETTY, 1933–1983
*Jennie's Story.* 1981. CTR
*The Song of the Serpent.* RALPH
*Under the Skin.* 1985. WASCT

LANDAU, TINA, 1963–
*1969.* 1994. HUMANA94

LASICA, MILAN, 1940– , and SATINSKY, JULIUS
*Dialogues.* 2003.
　　Cockrell, K., translator CONTSL5

LASK, BERTA, 1878–1967
*Die Befreiung. See* Liberation
*Liberation: 16 Tableaux from the Lives of German and Russian Women, 1914–1920.* 1924.
　　Cardinal, A., translator TYEW
　　Variant title: *Die Befreiung*

LASKER-SCHULER, ELSE, 1869–1945
*IandI.* 1962.
　　Bennett, B., translator CAS
　　Variant title: *IchundIch*
*IchundIch. See* IandI

LASZLO, CARL, 1923– (b. László Károly)
*The Chinese Icebox.* 1956.
　　Wellwarth, G., translator BENB
　　Variant title: *Der Chinesische Kühlschrank*
*Der Chinesische Kühlschrank. See* The Chinese Icebox
*Essen wir Haare. See* Let's Eat Hair!
*Let's Eat Hair!* 1956.
　　Wellwarth, G., translator BENB
　　Variant title: *Essen wir Haare*

LASZLO, MIKLOS, 1904–1973
*She Loves Me. See* Masteroff, Joe. *She Loves Me* (based on a play by)

LA TAILLE, JEAN DE. *See* Taille, Jean de La

LA TEMPA, SUSAN
*The Life of the Party.* (1979) NEWP
*Sunset Beach.* 1982. PLACE

THE LATINO THEATRE GROUP, 1994–2002. *See* Aguirre, Carmen, joint author

LATOUCHE, JOHN TREVILLE, 1917–1956
*Candide. See* Hellman, Lillian. Candide (lyrics by)
*The Golden Apple* (music by Jerome Moross). 1954. BES53, THEA54

LAUCKNER, ROLF T., 1887–1954
*Cry in the Street.* 1922.
　　Edwards, M., and Reich, translators SOK
　　Variant title: *Schrei aus der Strasse*
*Schrei aus der Strasse. See* Cry in the Street

LAUNDER, FRANK, 1907–1997, and GILLIAT, SIDNEY
*The Body Was Well Nourished. See* Meet a Body
*Meet a Body.* 1940. PLAN10
　　Variant title: *The Body Was Well Nourished*

LAURENTS, ARTHUR, 1918–2011
*A Clearing in the Woods.* 1957. BES56
*Gypsy* (music by Jule Styne, lyrics by Stephen Sondheim). 1959. RICO
*Home of the Brave.* 1945. BES45, FAMAF, GARZ, HEWE, SCL
*The Time of the Cuckoo.* 1952. BES52, THEA53
*West Side Story* (music by Leonard Bernstein; lyrics by Stephen Sondheim). 1957. CASH, RICO

LAURO, SHIRLEY, 1933–
*Turn Down.* 2000. *See* Ackermann, J. *Back Story: A Dramatic Anthology* HUMANA2000

LAVEDAN, HENRI LEON EMILE, 1859–1940
*The Prince d'Aureca.* 1892.
　　Clark, B., translator THS

LAVERY, BRYONY, 1947–
*Ophelia.* 1997. MYTH (excerpt)
*Origin of the Species.* 1984. PLABE6
*Witchcraze.* 1985. GRIFG1

LAVERY, EMMET, 1902–1986
*The Magnificent Yankee.* 1946. BES45, MERT, SPES

—— and MURPHY, GRACE
*Kamiano, the Story of Damien.* 1938. THEC

LAVIERA, TATO, 1951– . *See* Algarín, Miguel, joint author

LA VIGNE, ANDRIEU DE, ca.1457–ca.1515
*La farce du munyer. See* The Farce of the Miller
*The Farce of the Miller.* 1496.
　　Boucquey, T., translator BOUC
　　Variant titles: *La farce du munyer; Farce of the Miller Whose Soul the Devil Carries to Hell*
*Farce of the Miller Whose Soul the Devil Carries to Hell. See* The Farce of the Miller
*The Miracle of the Blind Man and the Cripple.* 15th century LOOM

LAVIGNE, LOUIS-DOMINIQUE, 1949–
*Are You Afraid of Thieves?* 1977?
　　Beissel, H., translator KAL5
　　Variant title: *As-tu peur des voleurs?*
*As-tu peur des voleurs? See* Are You Afraid of Thieves?

LAVRIK, SILVESTER, 1964–
*Katarína.* 1996.
　　Slugenová-Cockrell, K., translator CONTSL2

LAW, WARNER
*Indomitable Blacksmith.* 195– ? LOVR

LAWLER, RAY, 1921–
*Summer of the 17th Doll.* 1955. BES57

LAWRENCE, JEROME, 1915–2004, and LEE,
    ROBERT E.
*First Monday in October.* 1978. BES78
*Inherit the Wind.* 1955. AMB, BES54, GART, PLAU,
    REAL, SHER, THEA55
*The Night Thoreau Spent in Jail.* 1971. SCVDT1

LAWRENCE, MAUREEN, 1937–
*Tokens of Affection.* 1986. PLABE9

LAWSON, JOHN HOWARD, 1894–1977
*Processional.* 1925. IFKO, WATC1, WATI
*Roger Bloomer.* 1923. FULT
*Success Story.* 1932. LOO

LAXDAL, VIVIENNE, 1962–
*Cyber:\womb.* 1994. PRER
*Personal Convictions.* 1991. ZIMM (excerpt)

LAXNESS, HALLDOR (b. Halldór Guðjónsson), 1902–
    1998
*Dúfnaveizlan. See* The Pigeon Banquet
*The Pigeon Banquet.* 1966.
    Boucher, A., translator MNOI
    Variant title: *Dúfnaveizlan*

LAYA, JEAN LOUIS, 1761–1833
*L'ami des lois.* 1793. BREN

LAZARUS, JOA. *See* Lazurus, John, joint author

LAZARUS, JOHN, 1947–
*Babel Rap.* 1972. FIFVE, SIXA
*The Late Blumer.* 1984. FOUNC
*Village of Idiots.* 1985. NEWCAD7

—— and LAZARUS, JOA
*Dreaming and Dueling.* 1980. WASCT

LEACOCK, JOHN, 1729–1802
*The Fall of British tyranny; or, American Liberty
    Triumphant.* 1776. MOSS1, PHI

LEAMON, DOROTHY
*Barabas.* 192? FED2

LEAR, NORMAN, 1922–
*Meet the Bunkers.* 1971. MEY

LEARNING, WALTER, 1938– . *See* Nowlan, Alden,
    joint author

LEAVITT, JOHN McDOWELL, 1824–1909
*The Jewish Captives.* 1876? KOH2

LEBOVÍC, DJORDJE, 1928–2004
*Hallelujah.* 1960.
    Koljevío, N., translator MIG

LEBOW, BARBARA, 1936–
*A shayna maidel.* 1985. COJ
*Tiny Tim Is Dead.* 1993. SWO

LECOCQ, ALEXANDRE CHARLES, 1832–1918
*The Daughter of Madame Angot.* 1872.
    Seldes, G., and G., translators PLAH
    Variant title: *La fille de Madame Angot*
*La fille de Madame Angot. See* The Daughter of
    Madame Angot

LEDOUX, PAUL, 1949–
*Sam Slick: The Clockmaker.* 1982. HEID (excerpt)

—— and YOUNG, DAVID
*Love Is Strange.* 1984. CTR

LEE, CHEE KENG
*Breaking Through.* 1993. DIRTY

LEE, CHERYLENE, 1953–
*Arthur and Leila.* 1993. WOMP93
*Carry the Tiger to the Mountain.* 1998. LAR

LEE, JAMES HENRY, 1923–
*Career.* 1956. COTK

LEE, JEANNIE
*On the Corner of Cherry and Elsewhere.* 1969. COLI

LEE, JOO FOR, 1929–
*The Happening in the Bungalow.* 1970. NEWDR1
*When the Sun Sets on the Branches of That Jambu Tree.*
    1972. NEWDR2

LEE, KUO-HSIU, 1955–
*Jiuguo Zhushi Huishe. See* National Salvation
    Corporation Ltd.
*National Salvation Corporation Ltd.* 1991.
    Hung, E., translator CHEU
    Variant title: *Jiuguo Zhushi Huishe*

LEE, LANCE, 1942–
*Fox, Hound, and Huntress.* 1971. BALLE10

LEE, LESLIE, 1942–
*Black Eagles.* 1990. SWANS
*The First Breeze of Summer.* 1975. BLACTH, HAPUE

LEE, LEVI. *See* Larson, Larry, joint author

LEE, NATHANIEL, 1653?–1692
*Alexander the Great; or, The Rival Queens* (an adaptation of *The Rival Queens*). *See* The Rival Queens
*The Death of Alexander the Great. See* The Rival Queens; or, The Death of Alexander the Great
*Lucius Junius Brutus; Father of His Country.* 1680. BELGll, RET, WONR
*The Princess of Cleves.* 1681–1682. COTKA
*The Rival Queens; or, The Death of Alexander the Great.* 1677. BELK7, MAND, MANF
Variant titles: *Alexander the Great; The Death of Alexander the Great*
*Sophonisba.* 1675. DOA
*Theodosius: or, The Force of Love.* (1680) BELK7
— *See also* Dryden, John, joint author

LEE, ROBERT E., 1918–1994. *See* Lawrence, Jerome, joint author

LEE, SOPHIA, 1750–1824
*The Chapter of Accidents.* 1780. BELGll, INCA9

LEEDS BENGALI WOMEN'S DRAMA GROUP, 1988–1989
*Heartgame* (devised by). *See* Cooper, Mary. *Heartgame*

LEEDS, CHARLIE, 1924–1979
*The Love Song of Rotten John Calabrese.* 1970. ALI

LEESON, MICHAEL
*Love Sonnet.* 1982. *See* Anonymous Plays. *Twenty-four Hours: A.M.*

LEFEVRE, ADAM, 1950–
*Waterbabies.* 1997. HUMANA97, PLACA

LEFFLER, ANNE CHARLOTTE, DUCHESS OF CAJANELLO, 1849–1892
*Sanna kvinnor. See* True Women
*True Women.* 1883.
Harvey, A., translator KEL

LEGOUVE, ERNEST, 1807–1903, and LABICHE, EUGENE MARIN
*La cigale chez les fourmis.* 188? BOVE
Variant title: *The Grasshopper at the Home of the Ants*
*The Grasshopper at the Home of the Ants. See* La cigale chez les fourmis

LEGUIZAMO, JOHN, 1964–
*Spic-o-rama.* 1991. BES92

LEICHMAN, SEYMOUR, 1933–
*Freddie the Pigeon.* BALLE7

LEIGH, MIKE, 1943–
*Abigail's Party.* 1977. PLAN47

LEIGH, MITCH (b. Irwin Michnick), 1928–
*Man of La Mancha* (music by). *See* Wasserman, Dale. *Man of La Mancha*

LEIGHT, WARREN, 1957–
*Side Man.* 1998. BES98

LEISEWITZ, JOHANN ANTON, 1752–1806
*Julius of Tarento.* 1776.
Waterhouse, B., translator WASD

LEIVICK, H. *See* Halper, Leiviek

LEIWIK, H. *See* Halper, Leiviek

LELAND, JOHN, 1506?–1552. *See* Leland, Thomas, joint author

LELAND, MICHAEL, II. *See* Moritz, Dennis, joint author

LELAND, THOMAS, 1722–1785, and LELAND, JOHN
*Longsword, Earl of Salisbury* (romance attributed to). *See* Hartson, H. *The Countess of Salisbury* (adapted from)

LEMAITRE, JULES, 1853–1914
*Forgiveness. See* The Pardon
*Le pardon. See* The Pardon
*The Pardon.* 1895.
Clark, B., translator THS
Variant titles: *Forgiveness; Le pardon*

LENERO, VICENTE, 1933–
*Nadie sabe nada. See* No One Knows Anything
*No One Knows Anything.* 1988.
Gann, M., translator GANN2
Variant title: *Nadie sabe nada*

LENERU, MARIE, 1875–1918
*La paix. See* Peace
*Peace.* 1921.
Tyree, C., translator TYEW
Variant title: *La paix*
*La triomphatrice. See* Woman Triumphant
*Woman Triumphant.* 1914.
Hawthorne, M., translator KEL

LENNON, JOHN, 1940–1980. *See* Kennedy, Adrienne, joint author

LENNOX, GILBERT
    *Close Quarters. See* Somin, W. O. *Close Quarters*
        (translator and adapted by)

LENORMAND, HENRI RENE, 1882–1938
    *The Coward.* 1925.
        Orna, D., translator CHA, CHAN
        Variant title: *La lâche*
    *Crépuscle du théâtre. See* In Theatre Street
    *The Devourer of Dreams. See* The Dream Doctor
    *The Dream Doctor.* 1922.
        Orna, D., translator MOSG, MOSH
        Variant titles: *The Devourer of Dreams; Le mangeur*
          *de rêves*
    *L'homme et ses fantômes.* 1924. RHO
        Variant title: *Man and His Phantoms*
    *In Theatre Street.* 1936.
        Dukes, A., translator FAMK
        Variant title: *Crépuscle du théâtre*
    *Le lâche. See* The Coward
    *Man and His Phantoms. See* L'homme et ses fantômes
    *Le mangeur de rêves. See* The Dream Doctor
    *Simoom. See* Le simoun
    *Le simoun.* 1920. HART
        Variant title: *Simoom*
    *Le temps est un songe. See* Time Is a Dream
    *Time Is a Dream.* 1919.
        Katzin, W., translator DICDT, HAV
        Variant title: *Le temps est un songe*

LENSKY, DMITRI, 1805–1860
    *Her First Night (Lev gurych sinichin, or The Provincial*
        *Actress's Debut* based on the play by M. E. G. M.
        Théaulon and J. F. A. Bayard). 1839.
        Senelick, L., translator RUSSCO
        Variant title: *Lev gurych sinichin, or The Provincial*
          *Actress's Debut. See* Her First Night

LENZ, JACOB MICHAEL REINHOLD, 1751–1792
    *The Soldiers.* 1774.
        Waterhouse, B., translator WASD
        Yuill, W., translator STURM
    *The Tutor, or the Advantages of a Private Education: A*
        *Comedy.* 1774.
        Waterhouse, B., translator WASD

LENZ, RICK, 1939–
    *So Long, Mr. Broadway.* 1982. *See* Anonymous Plays.
        *Twenty-four Hours: P.M.*

LEONARD, HUGH, 1926–2009
    *"Da."* 1973. BES77, BEST, OWEC, PLAN44
    *A Life.* 1979. BES80

    *Love in the Title.* 1999. NEWPAB3
    *The Patrick Pearse Motel.* 1971. PLAN41
    *The Poker Session.* 1964. PLAN28
    *Stephen D* (based on James Joyce's *Portrait of the Artist*
        *as a Young Man* and *Stephen Hero*). 1962. ENG

LEONARD, JIM, JR., 1956–
    *The Diviners.* 1980. PLACD

LEONOV, LEONID MAXIMOVICH, 1899–1994
    *Invasion.* 1943.
        Anonymous translator FOUT
        Miller, A., translator CLKX
    *The Orchards of Polovchansk.* 1938.
        Robbins, J., translator SEVP

LEOPOLD, pseudonym. *See* Chandezon, Léopold

LEOW, PUAY TIN, 1957–
    *Family.* 1996. PING
        Variant title: *Mrs. Yang*
    *Letters to a Movie Queen.* 2001. SECO
    *Mrs. Yang. See* Family

LEPAGE, ROBERT, 1957– . *See* Brassard, Marie, joint
    author

LERBERGHE, CHARLES VAN, 1861–1907
    *Pan.* 1904.
        Willinger, D., translator WILL

LERNER, ALAN JAY, 1918–1986
    *Brigadoon* (music by Frederick Loewe). 1947. BES46,
        RICO
    *Camelot* (based on *The Once and Future King* by
        Terence Hanbury White; music by Frederick
        Loewe). 1960. RICM
    *My Fair Lady* (adapted from George Bernard Shaw's
        *Pygmalion*; music by Frederick Loewe). 1956.
        BES55

LERNER, MOTTI, 1949–
    *Kastner.* 1985.
        Goldstein, I., translator TAUB

LEROUX, GASTON, 1868–1927
    *The Phantom of the Opera. See* Lloyd Webber, Andrew.
    *The Phantom of the Opera* (adapted from the novel by)

LE SAGE, ALAIN RENE, 1668–1747
    *Crispin, rival de son maître. See* Crispin, Rival of His
        Master
    *Crispin, Rival of His Master.* 1707.

LEVY, JULES, b. 1857– . *See* Courteline, Georges, joint author

LEWES, GEORGE HENRY, 1817–1878
*The Game of Speculation.* 1851. BOOL

LEWIN, EVA
*Cochon flambé.* 1990. ROES

LEWIN, JOHN
*Five Easy Payments.* 1966. BALLE3

LEWIN, ROSE D. *See* Franken, Mrs. Rose D. (Lewin)

LEWIS, CARTER W.
*The One-eyed Man Is King.* 1993. NEWR98

LEWIS, EMILY SARGENT, 1866–1931
*Election Day: A Suffrage Play.* 1912. FRIED

LEWIS, ERICA
*Man Care.* 1999. FOUPAP

LEWIS, EVE, 1967–
*Ficky Stingers.* 1986. PLABE6

LEWIS, LEOPOLD DAVID, 1828–1890
*The Bells* (adapted from *Le juif Polonais* by Erckmann-Chatrian). 1871. ASG, BOOB, COTKIS, ROWE
Variant title: *The Polish Jew*
*The Polish Jew. See* The Bells

LEWIS, MATTHEW GREGORY "MONK," 1775–1818
*The Captive.* 1803. COXJ
*The Castle Spectre.* 1797. COXJ, HOUR

LEWIS, MICHAEL
*Sunrise on Earth.* 1982. *See* Anonymous Plays. *Twenty-four Hours: P.M.*

LEWIS, SAUNDERS, 1893–1985
*King's Daughter. See* Siwan
*Siwan.* 1954.
Humphreys, E., translator PLAN21
Variant title: *King's Daughter.*

LEWIS, SHARON MAREEKA, 1965– . *See* Bailey, Maxine, joint author

LEWIS, SINCLAIR, 1885–1951
*Dodsworth. See* Howard, Sidney. *Dodsworth* (based on the novel by)
*The Ghost Patrol. See* Clarke, William Kendall. *The Ghost Patrol* (based on the story by)

LEWIS, WILLIAM H.
*Peeling Potatoes.* 1988. STRA
*Road to Black Mesa.* 1988. STRA

LI, CHI-HUANG. *See* Sha, Seh, joint author

LI, CHIEN-WU, 1906–1982
*Ch'ing-ch'un. See* Springtime
*Springtime.* (1944)
Pollard, D., translator TWEH
Variant title: *Ch'ing-ch'un*

LI, HAO-KU, 13th century
*Chang Boils the Sea.* 13th century
Liu, J., translator LIU

LI, SHAOCHUN, 1919–1975
*The Wild Boar Forest.* (1960)
Mitchell, J., and Chang, D., translators MIT

LI, SHOUCHENG. *See* Li, Shou-ching

LI, SHOU-CHING. *See* Sha, Yeh-Hsin, joint author

LI, SYAU-CHWUN. *See* Li, Shaochun

LIANG, BINGKUN, 1936–
*Shuishi qiangzhe. See* Who's the Strongest of Us All?
*Who's the Strongest of Us All?* 1981.
Cheng, S., translator CHEU
Variant title: *Shuishi qiangzhe*

LIANG, CHENYU, 1520–ca.1580
*"Secret Liaison with Chancellor Bo Pi." See* Washing Silk
*Wan-sha ji. See* Washing Silk
*Washing Silk* (Act VII).
Dolby, W., translator EIG
Variant titles: *"Secret Liaison with Chancellor Bo Pi"; Wan-sha ji*

LIBMAN, CARL
*Follow the Leader.* 1968. ALI

LIEBERMAN, EDITH, 1922–1975. *See* Lieberman, Harold, joint author

LIEBERMAN, HAROLD, 1916– , and LIEBERMAN, EDITH
*Throne of Straw.* 1973. THL

LIKING, WEREWERE, 1950–
*La veuve Diyilem. See* The Widow Dylemma
*The Widow Dylemma.* 1993.
Miller, J., translator PLABI2
Variant title: *La veuve Diyilem*

LILL, WENDY, 1950–
*All Fall Down*. 1993. ZIMM (excerpt)
*The Fighting Days*. 1983. TYEW
*The Glace Bay Miners' Museum*. 1995. SEUC
*The Occupation of Heather Rose*. 1986. BERR, SSSN,
 WASCPA2, WASCPB1

LILLFORD, DANIEL R., 1961–
*Dark Heart*. 1993. JONI

LILLO, GEORGE, 1693–1739
*The Fatal Curiosity*. 1736. BELG9
*The London Merchant; or, The History of George
 Barnwell*. 1731. BELK5, BENY, BOO, BROJ,
 BROK, EIGH, GEMM, HAN, MAND, MANF,
 MOR, NET, ROGEBD, SIG, SMI, STM, TAU,
 TREB, TUQ, WILSP, WOTHB

LIM, GENNY, 1946–
*Bitter Cane*. 1989. HOUSTP, WAGNOX
*Paper Angels*. 1980. UNO

LIN, MIN-ZHOU, 1937–
*Inside and Outside the Door*. 1991.
 Sim, B., translator MLAS

LINARES RIVAS, MANUEL, 1867–1938
*The Claws*. 1914.
 Turrell, CA., translator TUR
 Variant title: *La garra*
*La garra*. *See* The Claws

LINDBERG, WAYNE. *See* Hopkins, Glenn, joint author

LINDEN, SONJA
*The Strange Passenger* (music by Derk Barnes). 1995.
 LINDB

LINDSAY, SIR DAVID, 1490–1555
*Ane Satire of the Thrie Estaitis*. *See* The Satire of the
 Three Estates
*Ane Satyre of the Thrie Estaitis*. *See* The Satire of the
 Three Estates
*The Satire of the Three Estates*. 1540. FOUN, MED
 Kemp, R., modernizer ROF
 Variant titles: *Ane Satire of the Thrie Estaitis; Ane
 Satyre of the Thrie Estaitis*

LINDSAY, HOWARD, 1889–1968

—— and CROUSE, RUSSEL
*Life with Father* (based on the book by Clarence Day).
 1939. BES39, CASS, CET, CEY, COLT, COOP,
 GARZ, GATB2, LOVR, MERS, MOST, SPER,
 STRO

*Life with Mother* (based on the book by Clarence Day).
 1948. BES48
*Remains to Be Seen*. 1951. BES51
*State of the Union*. 1945. BES45, GARW, GATB3

—— and RUNYON, DAMON
*A Slight Case of Murder* (based on an unpublished story
 by Damon Runyon). 1935. NELSDI

LINFANTE, MICHELE
*Pizza*. 1980. WES6

LINK, ANN SEYMOUR, 1906–1984
*Lawd, Does You Undahstan'?* 1936. PERF

LINK, DAVID
*Sleeping Together*. 1982. *See* Anonymous Plays.
 *Twenty-four Hours: A.M.*

LINNEY, ROMULUS, 1930–2011
*2*. 1990. BES89, DIX
*Heathen Valley*. 1988. BES87
*Shotgun*. 1994. HUMANA94
*Stars*. 1997. HUMANA97
*A Woman without a Name*. 1985. PRIMA85

LIONHEART, EUSTACE
*What Might Have Happened*. 1985. MONB2

LIPKIN, JOAN
*The Girl Who Lost Her Voice*. 2000. MYTH
*Small Domestic Acts*. 1995. CURB

LIPSCOMB, WILLIAM PERCY, 1887–1958, and
 MINNEY, RUBEIGH J.
*Clive of India*. 1934. FAME

LIPSKEROFF, KONSTANTIN, 1889–1954
*Carmencita and the Soldier* (based on the opera *Carmen*
 by Georges Bizet; libretto by Prosper Mérimée).
 1923.
 Seldes, G., and G., translators PLAH

LIPSKEROV, KONSTANTIN. *See* Lipskeroff, Konstantin

LIPSKY, JON
*The Survivor: A Cambodian Odyssey*. 1993.
 HUMANA94

LISON-LEROY, FRANCOISE, 1951– , and NYS–
 MAZURE, COLETTE
*Tenants All*. 1993.
 Glasheen, A., translator GLASH
 Variant title: *Tous locataires*
*Tous locataires*. *See* Tenants All

LITT, JENNIFER, A., 1965?–
*Epiphany.* 1982. YOUP

LITTLEWOOD, JAMES
*Ka-Shue (Letters Home)* (original storyline by). *See*
Earle, Lynda Chanwai. *Ka-Shue (Letters Home)*

LITTLEWOOD, JOAN, 1914–2002, and MacCOLL,
EWAN
*Last Edition: Extracts from a Living Newspaper.* 1940.
GOOR

LITTLEWOOD, JOAN. *See* Miller, James, H., joint author

LIU, CHING-MIN, 1956–
*Mother's Water Mirror.* 1995.
Lai, J., and Cheung, M., translator CHEU
Variant title: *Muquin de shuijing*
*Muquin de shuijing. See* Mother's Water Mirror

LIU, TANGQING, late 13th or early 14th century
*"The Battling Doctors." See* Cai Shun Shares the
Mulberries
*Cai Shun fen-shen. See* Cai Shun Shares the Mulberries
*Cai Shun Shares the Mulberries* (attributed to). late 13th
or early 14th century
Dolby, W., translator EIG (excerpt)
Variant titles: *"The Battling Doctors"; Cai Shun fen-
shen*

LIVING NEWSPAPER. *See* Staff of the Living Newspaper

LIVINGS, HENRY, 1929–1998
*The Gamecock* (part of *Pongo Plays 1–6*). 1969.
PLAAC1
*Nil carborundum.* 1962. NEWE6
*Rattel* (part of *Pongo Plays 1–6*). 1969. PLAAC2
*Stop It, Whoever You Are.* 1961. NEWE5
*There's No Room for You Here for a Start.* 1963. CONB

LIVINGSTON, MYRTLE SMITH, 1901–1973
*For Unborn Children.* 1926. HARY, HARYB

LIVINGSTONE, DOUGLAS JAMES, 1932–1996
*A Rhino for the Boardroom, a Radio Play.* 1974.
CONTSO
*The Sea My Winding Sheet.* 1964. GRAYTO

LLOYD, DAVID D., 1851–1889, and ROSENFELD,
SYDNEY
*The Senator.* 1889. MESCO

LLOYD, HORACE AMELIUS
*Rummio and Judy; or, Oh, This Love! This Love! This
Love!* (1841) NIN2

LLOYD GEORGE, IAN. *See* Varma, Rahul, joint author

LLOYD WEBBER, ANDREW, 1948–
*Cats, a Musical in Two Acts* (music by Andrew Lloyd
Webber; additional lyrics by Trevor Nunn; based
on *Old Possum's Book of Practical Cats* by T. S.
Eliot). 1980. BES82
*Jesus Christ Superstar* (music by). *See* Rice, Tim. *Jesus
Christ Superstar, a Rock Opera*
*Sunset Boulevard* (music by). *See* Black, Don. *Sunset
Boulevard*

——— and STILLGOE, RICHARD
*The Phantom of the Opera* (music by Andrew Lloyd
Webber, lyrics by Charles Hart, additional lyrics by
Richard Stillgoe; adapted from the novel by Gaston
Leroux). 1986. BES87

LOCHER, JENS, 1889–1952
*Tea for Three.* 1943.
Anonymous translators (revised by Furbank, P., and
Bredsdorff, E.) CONT
Variant title: *Tre mau man vaere*
*Tre maa man vaere. See* Tea for Three

LOCHHEAD, LIZ, 1947–
*Blood and Ice.* 1984. PLABE4
*Quelques fleurs.* 1991. HOWA

LOCKE, ALAIN, 1886–1954. *See* Nugent, Richard Bruce,
joint author

LOCKE-ELLIOTT, SUMNER, 1917–1991
*Rusty Bugles.* 1948. HANG

LOCKRIDGE, FRANCES (MRS. RICHARD
LOCKRIDGE), 1896–1963, and LOCKRIDGE,
RICHARD
*The Norths Meet Murder. See* Davis, Owen. *Mr. and
Mrs. North* (based on the novel by)

LOCKRIDGE, RICHARD, 1898–1982. *See* Lockridge,
Frances, joint author

LODGE, THOMAS, 1558?–1625
*Mucedorus* (sometimes attributed to). *See* Anonymous
Plays. *Mucedorus*
*The Reign of King Edward the Third* (sometimes
attributed to). *See* Anonymous Plays. *The Reign of
King Edward the Third*

——— and GREENE, ROBERT
*A Looking Glass for London and England.* 1592. DPR1

LOESSER, FRANK, 1910–1969
*Guys and Dolls. See* Swerling, Jo, and Burrows, Abe.
    *Guys and Dolls* (music and lyrics by)
*How to Succeed in Business without Really Trying. See*
    Burrows, Abram S. *How to Succeed in Business*
    *without Really Trying* (music and lyrics by)
*The Most Happy Fella* (based on Sidney Howard's play
    *They Knew What They Wanted*). 1956. THEA56

LOEWE, FREDERICK, 1901–1988
*Brigadoon* (music by). *See* Lerner, Alan Jay. *Brigadoon*
*Camelot* (music by). *See* Lerner, Alan Jay. *Camelot*
*My Fair Lady* (music by). *See* Lerner, Alan Jay. *My Fair*
    *Lady*

LOGAN, JOSHUA, 1908–1988
*The Wisteria Trees* (based on *The Cherry Orchard* by
    Anton Chekhov). 1950. BES49
— *See also* Behrman, Samuel Nathaniel;
    Hammerstein II, Oscar; Heggen, Thomas; Kober,
    Arthur, joint authors

LOH, KWUAN
*Fast Cars and Fancy Women*. 1992. FAT

LOHENSTEIN, DANIEL CASPER VON, 1635–1683
*Sophonisba*. 1680.
    Hanak, M., translator GILL

LOHER, DEA, 1964–
*Fremdes haus. See* Stranger's House
*Stranger's House*. 1995.
    Tushingham, D., translator DODGSG
    Variant title: *Fremdes haus*

LOHUISEN, SUZANNE VAN, 1953–
*Dossier: Ronald Akkerman*. 1995.
    Bosch, S., translator ROET

LONERGAN, KENNETH, 1962–
*The Rennings Children*. 1982. YOUP

LONG, JOHN LUTHER, 1861–1927. *See* Belasco, David,
    joint author

LONGFELLOW, HENRY WADSWORTH, 1807–1882
*The Spanish Student*. 1843. BAT19

LONGFIELD, KEVIN, 1950–
*Going Down the River*. 1989. RAVEL

LONGFORD, CHRISTINE, COUNTESS OF, 1900–1980
*Mr. Jiggins of Jigginstown*. 1933. CAN

LONGFORD, EDWARD ARTHUR HENRY. *See*
    Pakenham, Edward Arthur Henry, 6th Earl of
    Longford

LONSDALE, FREDERICK, 1881–1954
*Aren't We All?* 1923. SEV
*Half a Loaf. See* Let Them Eat Cake
*The Last of Mrs. Cheyney*. 1925. BES25
*Let Them Eat Cake*. 1959. PLAN19
    Variant titles: *Half a Loaf; Once Is Enough*
*Once Is Enough. See* Let Them Eat Cake

LOOMER, LISA
*Expecting Isabel*. 1998. BES98
*The Waiting Room*. 1994. BES94

LOON, ROBIN
*Absence Makes the Heart Grow Fonder*. 1992. FAT
*Watching the Clouds Go By*. 1993. DIRTY

LOOS, ANITA, 1893–1981
*Gigi* (from the novel by Colette). 1951. BES51

LOPE DE RUEDA. *See* Rieda, Lope de

LOPE DE VEGA. *See* Vega Carpio, Lope Félix de

LOPEZ, EDUARDO IVAN
*Spanish Eyes*. 1982. ANTU

LOPEZ, EVA
*Marlene*. 1990. ANTU

LOPEZ, JOSEFINA, 1969–
*The American Dream. See* Simply Maria, or The
    American Dream
*Simply Maria, or The American Dream*. 1988? DIYL,
    DIYLD, FEY
    Variant title: *The American Dream*

LOPEZ, SABATINO, 1867–1951
*Il passero. See* The Sparrow
*The Sparrow*. 1918.
    Goldberg, I., translator GOL
    Variant title: *Il passero*

LOPEZ DE AYALA, ADELARDO, 1828–1879
*Consuelo*. 1878. BRET

LOPEZ MOZO, JERONIMO, 1942–
*The Testament*. (1968)
    Wellwarth, M., translator WELK
    Variant title: *El testamento*
*El testamento. See* The Testament

LOPEZ RUBIO, JOSE, 1903–1996
  *The Blindfold.* (1954)
    Holt, M., translator HOLTM
    Variant title: *La venda en los ojos*
  *La venda en los ojos. See* The Blindfold

LORCA, FEDERICO GARCIA. *See* García Lorca,
  Federico

LOS HERREROS, MANUEL BRETON DE. *See* Bretón
  de los Herreros, Manuel

LOUIS, RAY BALDWIN, 1949–
  *Butterfly of Hope (A Warrior's Dream).* 1974. GEIO

LOVEID, CECILIE, 1951–
  *Måkespisere. See* Seagull Eaters
  *Seagull Eaters* (radio play). 1983.
    Sehmsdorf, H., translator NEWNOR
    Variant title: *Måkespisere*

LOVELACE, EARL, 1935–
  *The Dragon Can't Dance.* 1986. BREW2

LOW, SAMUEL, l765–1810?
  *The Politician Out-witted.* 1789. MOSS1

LOWE, STEPHEN, 1947–
  *Keeping Body and Soul Together.* 1984. LOWE

LOWELL, ROBERT, 1917–1977
  *Benito Cereno.* 1964. ABCA, BROTA, BURG,
    DOLAN, FAMAH, GAT, REV, RICJ, TREBJ,
    VONS3
    Variant title: *Old Glory: Beneto Cereno*
  *My Kinsman, Major Molineux.* 1964. ALS, CASH,
    DODGE, SCNR
  *Old Glory: Beneto Cereno. See* Beneto Cereno

LOYA, MARCOS
  *La posada magica* (music by). *See* Solis, Octavio. *La
    posada magica*

LU, HSUN (pseudonym of Cho Shu-Jen), 1881–1936
  *The Passer-by.* (1925)
    Yang, H., and Yang, G., translators MESE

LUCAS, CRAIG, 1951–
  *Bad Dream.* 1992. ACTOR
  *Credo.* 1995. PLACA
  *Good Morning to the Horse.* 2000. *See* Ackermann,
    J. *Back Story: A Dramatic Anthology.*
    HUMANA2000
  *Prelude to a Kiss.* 1990. BES89, PLACG1, WETZ
  *Reckless.* 1983. ANTN, MESSE

*Three Postcards* (music and lyrics by Craig Carnelia).
    1987. BES86
*What I Meant Was.* 1996. HUMANA96

LUCE, CLARE BOOTHE. *See* Boothe, Clare

LUCKHAM, CLAIRE, 1944–
  *The Choice.* 1993. PLABE10
  *Trafford Tanzi.* 1980. PLABE2

——— and BOND, CHRIS
  *Scum.* 1976. HANNA

LUDLAM, CHARLES, 1943–1987
  *Bluebeard.* 1970. SME
  *The Mystery of Irma Vep.* 1984. ANTL
  *Reverse Psychology.* 1980. MESSE
  *Stage Blood.* 1974. MARRA

LUDWIG, KEN, 1950–
  *Lend Me a Tenor.* 1986. BES88

——— and OCKRENT, MIKE
  *Crazy for You* (music by George Gershwin, lyrics by
    Ira Gershwin). 1992. BES91

LUDWIG, OTTO, 1813–1865
  *Der erbförster.* 1850. CAM
    Remy, A., translator FRA9
    Variant title: *The Hereditary Forester*
  *The Hereditary Forester. See* Der erbförster

LUKE, PETER, l919–1995
  *Hadrian VII.* 1967. BES68, PLAN33, RICIS

LUM, DARRELL H. Y., 1950–
  *Oranges Are Lucky.* 1976. KUMU

LUMLEY, JANE, BARONESS LUMLEY, 1537–1576
  — *See* Euripides. *Iphigenia in Aulis*

LUNDEN, JEFFREY, 1958–
  *Wings* (lyrics by). *See* Perlman, Arthur. *Wings*

LUPTON, THOMAS, fl. 1588
  *All for Money.* 1577. SCAT

LUTS, OSKAR, 1887–1953
  *Sootuluke. See* The Will O'the-wisp
  *The Spirit of Lake Ülemiste.* 1916.
    Kukk, H., translator GOLB
    Variant title: *Ülemiste vanake*
  *Ülemiste vanake. See* The Spirit of Lake Ülemiste
  *The Will O'the-wisp.* 1919.
    Kukk, H., translator GOLB
    Variant title: *Sootuluke*

LYLY, JOHN, 1554?–1606
*Alexander and Campaspe. See* Campaspe
Campaspe. 1584. ADA, GAYLE1, MAK, OLH, OLI1
Variant title: *Alexander and Campaspe*
*Endimion. See* Endymion, the Man in the Moon
*Endymion, the Man in the Moon.* 1588. BAS, BROC,
MIN2, MIO2, NEI, NES, ORNC, PAR, SCH, SCI,
SCJ, SCW, SPE
Variant title: *Endimion*
*Gallathea.* 1588. DPRI
*Midas.* 1589. WINN
*Mother Bombie.* 1589? TAT, TAU, TYDE

LYNCH, HAL, 1927–2006
*Three Miles to Poley.* 1971. BALLE10

LYNCH, MICHAEL
*Sylvester the Cat vs. Galloping Billy Bronco.* 1979.
WES6

LYNDON, BARRE, 1896–1972
*The Amazing Dr. Clitterhouse.* 1936. FOUPL, THH
*The Man in Half Moon Street.* 1939. SIXL
*They Came by Night.* 1937. FIP

LYNNE, JAMES BROOM, 1916–1995
*The Trigon.* 1963. NEWE8

LYONS, GARY
*Mohicans.* 1984. ROBR

LYSSA, ALISON, 1947–
*Pinball.* 1981. AUSG, PLABE4

LYSSIOTIS, TES
*The Forty Lounge Café.* 1990. TAIT

LYTTON, EDWARD GEORGE BULWER. *See* Bulwer-
Lytton, Edward George Earle Lytton

M, LEBO
*The Lion King* (additional music and lyrics by). *See*
Allers, Roger. *The Lion King*

MA, CHIH-YUAN, fl. 1251
*Autumn in Han Palace. See* Autumn in the Palace of Han
*Autumn in the Palace of Han.* 13th century
Liu, J., translator BIR1, LIU
Variant titles: *Autumn in Han Palace; Han Kung
Ch'in*
*Han Kung Ch'in. See* Autumn in the Palace of Han

MA, SEN, 1932–
*Flower and Sword.* 1977.
Pollard, D., translator CHEU
Variant title: *Hua yu jian*
*Hua yu jian. See* Flower and Sword

MA, YUNG. *See* Sha, Seh, joint author

MA, ZHONGJUN, 1957–
*Lao fengliu zhen. See* The Legend of Old Bawdy Town
*The Legend of Old Bawdy Town.* 1988.
Wickeri, J., translator CHEU
Variant title: *Lao fengliu zhen*

MAC INTYRE, TOM, 1931–
*Good Evening, Mr. Collins.* 1995. DAZZ
*Sheep's Milk on the Boil.* 1994. NEWPAB1

McANUFF, DES, 1952–
*The Death of von Richthofen as Witnessed from Earth.*
1982. WOQ5
*Leave It to Beaver Is Dead.* 1975. WEK

McARDLE, JOHN, 1938–
*Jacko.* 1979. DRUR

MacARTHUR, CHARLES, 1895–1956. *See* Hecht, Ben,
joint author

MacAULEY, PAULINE, 1937?–
*The Creeper.* 1964. PLAN29
*Monica.* 1970. RICJ

MacBETH, GEORGE, 1932–1992, and BINGHAM, J.
*The Doomsday Show.* 1964. NEWE14

McBRIDE, VAUGHN, 1935–2001. *See* Crutcher, Julie,
joint author

McCABE, JAMES D., JR., 1842–1883
*The Guerillas.* 1862. MESC

McCABE, PATRICK, 1955–
*Frank Pig Says Hello* (based on his novel *The Butcher
Boy*). 1992. FAIR

McCARTHY, JUSTIN HUNTLY, 1860–1936
*If I Were King.* 1901. BES99
Variant title: *The Vagabond King*
*The Vagabond King. See* If I Were King

McCARTHY, NEIL
*Rainshark.* 1991. KANI

McCAULEY, CLARICE VALLETTE
*The Conflict.* 1920. SHAY
*The Seeker.* 1919. FED1

McCAULEY, ROBBIE, 1942–
*Sally's Rape.* 1989. BEAN, HARYB, MAQ
— *See also* Carlos, Laurie, joint author

McCLELLAND, CE, 1940–
  *Blood and Ivy: An American Anthem*. 1999. INCI
    Variant title: *KSU*
  *KSU. See* Blood and Ivy: An American Anthem
  *Time to Go*. 1995. TIME

McCLENAGHAN, TOM
  *Submariners*. 1980. GAY1

McCLINTON, MARION
  *Stones and Bones*. 1994. HUMANA94

McCLOSKEY, JAMES J., 1825–1913
  *Across the Continent; or, Scenes from New York Life
    and the Pacific Railroad*. 1870. AMP4, MONR

McCLURE, MICHAEL, 1932–
  *Goethe: Ein Fragment*. 1978. WES2

MacCOLL, EWAN, 1915–1989
  *Johnny Noble: An Episodic Play with Singing*. 1945.
    GOOR
  *The Other Animals*. 1948. GOOR
  *Uranium 235: An Episodic Play in Two Parts*. 1946.
    GOOR

McCOO, EDWARD J., 1882–1930
  *Ethiopia at the Bar of Justice*. 1924. RIR, RIRA

McCORMICK, DENNY
  *The Incredibly Famous Willy Rivers* (music by). *See*
    Metcalfe, Stephen. *The Incredibly Famous Willy
    Rivers*

McCRACKEN, MRS. ESTHER (ARMSTRONG), 1902–
    1971
  *Quiet Wedding*. 1938. SIXL

McCULLERS, MRS. CARSON (SMITH), 1917–1967
  *The Member of the Wedding*. 1950. BES49, FAMAF,
    GARW, GATB3, GAVE, HEWE, MIJY, PATM,
    PATP, STS

McCULLOCH, CATHARINE WAUGH, 1862–1945
  *Bridget's Sisters; or, The Legal Status of Illinois Women
    in 1868*. 1911. FRIED
    Variant title: *The Legal Status of Illinois Women in
    1868*
  *The Legal Status of Illinois Women in 1868. See*
    Bridget's Sisters; or, The Legal Status of Illinois
    Women in 1868

McCUTCHEON, GEORGE BARR, 1866–1928
  *The Double Doctor: A Farce*. INDI

McDANIEL, CHARLES A., 1930–1997
  *The Ends of Justice* (television play; episode of *Judd for
    the Defense*). 1968. BRNB

MacDERMOT, GALT, 1928–
  *Hair* (music by). *See* Ragni, Gerome and Rado, James.
    *Hair*
  *Two Gentlemen of Verona* (music by). *See* Guare, John
    and Shapiro, Mel. *Two Gentlemen of Verona*

MacDERMOT, ROBERT, 1910?–1964. *See* Morgan,
    Diana, joint author

MacDONAGH, DONAGH, 1912–1968
  *Happy as Larry*. 1947. BRZ, NEWWW6
  *Step-in-the-hollow*. 1957. BRZE

McDONAGH, MARTIN, 1970–
  *The Beauty Queen of Leenane*. 1996. BES97

MacDONALD, ANN-MARIE, 1959–
  *Goodnight Desdemona (Good Morning Juliet)*. 1988.
    ZIMM (excerpt)

McDONALD, AL
  *Pogie* (music by). *See* Heide, Christopher. *Pogie*

MacDONALD, BRUCE
  *What We Do with It*. 1993. HUMANA93

MacDONALD, CATHERINE, 1940–
  *Chekhov in Yalta* (music by). *See* Driver, John and
    Haddow, Jeffrey, *Chekhov in Yalta*

McDONALD, CATHERINE, 1910–2004, and MASON,
    WILTON
  *Spring for Sure*. 1950. PAJ

MacDONALD, GABRIELLE
  *Like a Metaphor*. 2000. INSI

McDONALD, HEATHER, 1959–
  *Dream of a Common Language*. 1992. MIH

McDONALD, IAN, 1933–
  *The Tramping Man*. 1969. HILET

MacDONALD, ROBERT DAVID, 1929–2004
  *Chinchilla*. 1977. DEC

MacDOUGALL, ROGER, 1910–1993
  *The Gentle Gunman*. 1950. PLAN5
  *To Dorothy, a Son*. 1950. PLAN4

McENROE, ROBERT EDWARD, 1916–1998
*Oliver Erwenter. See* The Silver Whistle
*The Silver Whistle.* 1948. BES48
Variant title: *Oliver Erwenter*

McEVOY, CHARLES, 1879–1929
*The Likes of Her.* 1923. MART

MacEWEN, GWENDOLYN, 1941–1987
*Terror and Erebus.* 1975. SSSN

McGEEHAN, MRS. SOPHIE (TREADWELL). *See*
Treadwell, Sophie

McGINN, JIM
*The Termination.* 1982. *See* Anonymous Plays. *Twenty-four Hours: P.M.*

McGOUGH, ROGER, 1937–
*The Puny Little Life Show.* 1970. MARP

McGUIGAN, CAROL
*Inside Uitlander* (excerpt). 1996. BREK

McGUINNESS, FRANK, 1953–
*Borderlands.* 1984. DRUR
*Dolly West's Kitchen.* 1999. NEWPAB3

McGUIRE, JUDY
*Interview* (Angela Sand). 1987. JENN
*Interview* (Dorothy). 1990. JENN

McGUIRE, WILLIAM ANTHONY, 1885–1940
*Six Cylinder Love.* 1921. BES21

MACHADO, EDUARDO, 1953–
*Broken Eggs.* 1984. BARNA, OSB, SWANS
*Fabiola.* 1986. WILLG
*In the Eye of the Hurricane.* 1991. DIXD1
*Trying to Get There.* 2000. *See* Ackermann, J. *Back Story: A Dramatic Anthology* HUMANA2000

McHARDY, AIMEE. *See* Stuart, Mrs. Aimée (McHardy)

MACHIAVELLI, NICCOLO, 1469–1527
*Clizia.* 1524.
Cohen, R., translator COI
*La mandragola. See* Mandragola
*Mandragola.* 1520.
Hale, J., translator BARB
May, F., and Bentley, E., translators BENR1, BENV, HILPDH1
Penman, B., translator FIJ
Richards, K., and Richards, L., translators CAIR
Young, S., translator HAYD

Variant titles: *La mandragola; The Mandrake*
*The Mandrake. See* Mandragola

MACHIN, LEWIS. *See* Barksted, William, joint author

MACIAS, YSIDRO R., 1944?–
*Martir Montezuma.* CONR
*The Ultimate Pendejada.* CONR

MacILWRAITH, BILL
*The Anniversary.* 1966. PLAN31

McILWRAITH, JEAN NEWTON, 1859–1938
*Ptarmigan, or a Canadian Carnival.* 1895. WAGN

McINTIRE, RON
*Primitive World: An Anti-nuclear Jazz Musical* (arrangement by). *See* Jones, Leroi. *Primitive World: An Anti-nuclear Jazz Musical*

McINTYRE, CLARE, 1952–2009
*Low Level Panic.* 1988. FIFHL1

McINTYRE, DENNIS, 1942–1990
*Split Second.* 1984. BES84, RIS

MacINTYRE, ERNEST THALAYASINGHAM
*The Loneliness of the Short-distance Traveler.* 1971. GOON
*A Somewhat Mad and Grotesque Comedy.* 1973. GOON

MacINTYRE, TOM. *See* Mac Intyre, Tom

MACIVOR, DANIEL, 1962–
*Never Swim Alone.* 1991. WASCPB2
*2-2-tango: A-two-man-one-man-show.* 1990. WALAG

MACK, CAROL K., 1941–
*In Her Sight.* 1997. HUMANA97
*Territorial Rites.* 1982. WOMS2

MACKAY, CONSTANCE D'ARCY, 1880–1966
*Benjamin Franklin, Journeyman.* 1924. LAW
*Counsel Retained.* 1915. PEN
*The Prince of Court Painters.* 1915. WEB

MACKAY, MRS. ISABEL ECCLESTONE (MACPHERSON), 1875–1928
*The Second Lie.* 1921. MAS1

McKAY, JOHN, 1965–
*Dead Dad Dog.* 1988. CALE

MacKAY, LOUIS ALEXANDER, 1901–1982
*The Freedom of Jean Guichet.* 1925. MAS2

McKAY, TAMARA
*Pistons.* 1994. ZIMM

MacKAYE, PERCY WALLACE, 1875–1956
*Napoleon Crossing the Rockies.* 1924. CHU
*The Pilgrim and the Book.* 1920. FED1
*Sam Average.* 1911. BEAC11
*The Scarecrow.* 1909. DICD, FLAN, GARX, GATS,
    MOSJ, MOSK, MOSL, QUIJ, QUIJR, QUIK,
    QUIL, QUIM, QUIN

MacKAYE, STEELE, 1842–1894
*Adrift from Her Father's Love. See* Hazel Kirke
*An Arrant Knave.* 1889. AMP11
*Hazel Kirke.* 1880. QUIJ, QUIJR, QUIK, QUIL, QUIM,
    QUIN
*Hazel Kirke; or Adrift from Her Father's Love* (adapted
    into a melodrama in three acts). MELO
*In Spite of All.* 1885. AMP11
*Paul Kauvar, or, Anarchy.* 1890. MOSS3
*Rose Michel.* 1875. AMP11
*Won at Last.* 1877. AMP11

McKENNEY, RUTH, 1911–1972
*My Sister Eileen* (based on the stories by). *See* Fields,
    Joseph and Chodorov, Jerome. *My Sister Eileen*
*Wonderful Town. See* Fields, Joseph and Chodorov,
    Jerome. *Wonderful Town* (based on the stories *My
    Sister Eileen* by)

MacKENZIE, RONALD, 1903–1932
*The Maitlands.* 1934. FAMF
*Musical Chairs.* 1931. FAMB, PLAD

MACKEY, WILLIAM WELLINGTON, 1937–
*Requiem for Brother X.* 1966. KINH, KINHB

MACKIE, PHILIP, 1918–1985
*The Big Killing.* 1962. PLAN25
*The Whole Truth.* 1955. PLAN13

McKILLOP, MENZIES, 1929–
*The Future Pit.* 1972. GUTR

McKINLAY, MICHAEL D. C.
*Walt and Roy.* 1985. NEWWUX

McKINNEY, JACK, 1891–1966
*The Well.* 1960. BRIMA1, HANG

McKINNON, CATH
*A Rose by Any Other Name.* 1989. AROUN

MacKINTOSH, ELIZABETH (GORDON DAVIOT,
    pseudonym), 1897–1952
*The Laughing Woman.* 1934. FAME
*The Pen of My Aunt.* 1954. BRNB, CARME

*Queen of Scots.* 1934. FAMF
*Richard of Bordeaux.* 1933. FAMD, PLAL1

MACKLIN, CHARLES, 1697?–1797
*Man of the World.* 1781. BELG4
*A Will and No Will.* 1746. BEVI

McLAUGHLIN, ROSEMARY
*Horsefeathers.* 1997. DEAT

McLEAN, DIRK, 1956–
*Encore.* 1996. BEYO (excerpt)
*The House on Hermitage Road* (radio play). 1991.
    RAVELII

McLEAN, DUNCAN, 1964–
*Julie Allardyce.* 1993. BROV

McLEAN, LINDA
*One Good Beating.* 1996. HOWA

MacLEISH, ARCHIBALD, 1892–1982
*Air Raid.* 1938. MACE
*The Fall of the City.* 1937. BROZ, BRR3, GAS, KERN,
    KRE, LOOB, LOOC, LOOD, LOOE, NELS,
    VOAD, WAIT
*J. B.* 1958. BES58, COTX, GARSA, HILP, SCNP
*The Music Crept by Me upon the Waters.* 1953? SUL
*The Trojan Horse.* 1952. WHF

McLELLAN, C. M. S. (HUGH MORTON, pseudonym),
    1865–1916
*Leah Kleschna.* 1904. BES99

MacLENNAN, DON, 1929–2009
*An Enquiry into the Voyage of the Santiago.* 1974.
    CONTSO

McLEOD, JENNY, 1963–
*Island Life.* 1988. HANNA

MacLEOD, JOAN, 1954–
*Amigo's Blue Guitar.* 1990. WASCPB2
*The Hope Slide.* 1992. SEUC
*Little Sister.* 1992. ZIMM (excerpt)
*Toronto, Mississippi.* 1987. WASCPA2

MacLEOD, WENDY, 1959–
*The Water Children.* 1997. WOMP98

McLURE, JAMES, 1950–
*Laundry and Bourbon.* 1980. TEX
*Lone Star.* 1979. TEX
*Max and Maxie.* 1984. PRIMA87

MacMAHON, BRYAN, 1909–1998
*Song of the Anvil*. 1960. HOGE

McMAHON, FRANK, 1926–
*Borstal Boy. See* Brendan Behan's Borstal Boy
*Brendan Behan's Borstal Boy*. 1967. RICT
Variant title: *Borstal Boy*

McMANUS, BRUCE, 1948–
*Caffé*. 1985. NEWCAD4
*Calenture*. 1992. RUN

McMASTER, BETH, 1935–
*Put on the Spot*. 1975. WIM
*When Everybody Cares*. (1976) WIM
*Which Witch Is Which?* (1974) KAL4

MacMILLAN, DOUGALD, III, 1897–1975
*Off Nags Head; or, The Bell Buoy*. 1922? LAW

MacMILLAN, HECTOR
*The Rising*. 1973. DEC

MACMILLAN, MARY LOUISE, 1870–1936
*The Pioneers*. 1917? LAW

McMILLAN, MICHAEL
*Brother to Brother*. 1996. BLAAP

McMILLAN, ROSS
*Washing Spider Out*. 1994. RUN

MacNALLY, LEONARD, 1752–1820
*Fashionable Levities*. 1785. INCA10

McNALLY, TERRENCE, 1939–
*And Things That Go Bump in the Night*. 1964. BALLE1
*Andre's Mother*. 1988. DIYL, DIYLD, LITIE, LITIF,
LITJ, OSBW, SCX
*Bad Habits*. 1974. BES73, OBG
*Botticelli*. 1969. BEAS, BOYN, COMV, OFF2
*Frankie and Johnny in the Clair de Lune*. 1987. BERT
*It's Only a Play*. BES85
*Kiss of the Spider Woman* (music by John Kander, lyrics
by Fred Ebb; based on the novel by Manuel Puig).
1993. BES92
*Lips Together, Teeth Apart*. 1992. BES91
*The Lisbon Traviata*. 1985. SHEW
*Love! Valour! Compassion!* 1994. BES94
*Master Class*. 1995. BES95
*Next*. 1969. BES68
*Noon*. 1968. GARTL
*A Perfect Ganesh*. 1994. BES93
*Ragtime* (based on the novel by E. L. Doctorow, lyrics
by Lynn Ahrens, music by Stephen Flaherty). 1998.
BES97

*The Ritz*. 1975. BERS, BES74
*Sweet Eros*. 1968. OFF2
*Tour*. 1968. GLI
*Where Has Tommy Flowers Gone?* 1971. BES71

McNAMARA, JOHN, 1962–
*Present Tense*. 1982. YOUP

McNAMEE, GEORGE C. *See* Levine, Mark L., joint author

MacNEICE, LOUIS, 1907–1963
*The Dark Tower*. 1946. ANDE, BENS2

McNEIL, JOHN, 1935–1982
*How Does Your Garden Grow?* 1974. BRIM2

McNEIL, MARGUERITE
*Island Woman*. 1993. ZIMM (excerpt)

MACOWAN, NORMAN, 1877–1961
*Glorious Morning*. 1938. FAML

McPHEE, FERGUS
*Foxed*. 1983. MONB1
*Merely Players*. 1986. MONB3
*Professor Newman's End*. 1983. MONB1
*The Purple Carnation*. 1983. MONB1
*Rs*. 1983. MONB1

MacPHERSON, ISABEL. *See* Mackay, Mrs. Isabel
Ecclestone (Macpherson)

McPHERSON, SCOTT, 1959–1992
*Marvin's Room*. 1990. BES89, BES91

MacRAE, ARTHUR, 1908–1962
*Both Ends Meet*. 1954. PLAN10

McRAE, MURRAY
*Visiting Hours*. 1985. NEWWUX

MacREADY, WILLIAM, 1755–1829
*The Bank Note*. 1795. INCA9

MACRINICI, RADU, 1964–
*My D(r)ear Country*. 1997?
Rotescu, J., translator POQ

McTAGGART, JAMES, 1928–1974
*Candide* (television script translated and adapted from
*Candide* by Voltaire). 1973. CLKY

MACY, LYNN MARIE
*Crunching Numbers* (3 one-act plays: *Once in a Blue
Moon; The Thrice Three Muses; Twice Blessed*).
1998. DENT

*Once in a Blue Moon. See* Crunching Numbers
*The Thrice Three Muses. See* Crunching Numbers
*Twice Blessed. See* Crunching Numbers

MADANI, `IZZ AL-DIN AL-, 1938–
  *Diwan al-Zanj. See* The Zanj Revolution
  *The Zanj Revolution.* 1973.
    El-Azmeh, N., and Davies, R., translators JAY
    Variant title: *Diwan al-Zanj*

MAETERLINCK, MAURICE, 1862–1949
  *Les avengles. See* The Blind
  *The Blind.* 1891.
    Amoia, A., translator ANTM, WILLG
    Hovey, R., translator HILPDH6
    Slater, M., translator SLAT
  *The Death of Tintagiles.* 1899.
    Sutro, A., translator BAT21, SHAY
    Variant title: *La mort de Tintagiles*
  *Home. See* Interior
  *L'intérieur. See* Interior
  *Interior.* 1894.
    Archer, W., translator MACN, MIL
    Variant titles: *Home; L'intérieur*
  *The Intruder.* 1891.
    Anonymous translator PATM, TREBA, TREBJ,
      TREI2
    Block, H., translator BLOC
    Gerould, D., translator GERO
    Hovey, R., translator BENP, CARP, CARPA, HUD,
      TREC2, TREE2
    Knapp, B. L., translator ANTM
    Variant title: *L'intruse*
  *L'intruse. See* The Intruder
  *The Miracle of St. Anthony.* 1903.
    Willinger, D., translator WILL
  *Monna Vanna.* 1903.
    Sutro, A., translator MOSQ
  *La mort de Tintagiles. See* The Death of Tintagiles
  *Pelléas and Mélisande. See* Pelléas et Mélisande
  *Pelléas et Mélisande.* 1893. RHO
    Amoia, A., translator ANTM
    Hovey, R., translator AUG, DICD, DICIN1, HAV,
      SMN, TUCG, TUCM, TUCN, TUCO, WATI,
      WATL2, WATR, WHI
    Variant title: *Pelléas and Mélisande*

MAGGI, CARLOS, 1922–
  *The Library.* 1959.
    Oliver, W., translator OLIW

MAGNUSON, JIM
  *African Medea.* 1968. NEWA4

MAGTOTO, LIZA
  *Despedida de soltera.* 2001. SECO

MAHARISHI, MOHAN, 1940–
  *Einstein (The Story Till 1905).* 1994.
    Maharishi, M., translator KAM3

MAHFUZ, `ISAM, 1939–
  *The China Tree.* 1968.
    Elmusa, S., and Ezzy, T., translators JAY
    Variant title: *al-Zanalakht*
  *Al-Zanalakht. See* The China Tree

MAHJOEDDIN, INDIJA N., 1963–
  *The Butterfly Seer.* 1999. THUAA

MAHOMED, ISMAIL, 1959–
  *Cheaper than Roses.* 1995. PERA
  *Purdah (The Veil).* 1993. GRAV

MAILLET, ANTONINE, 1929–
  *Les crasseux. See* The Rabble
  *The Rabble.* 1973.
    Makward, CA., and Miller, J., translators
    Variant title: *Les crasseux*

MAIRET, JEAN DE, 1604–1686
  *Sophonisba.* 1634.
    Lockert, L., translator LOCR

MAIS, ROGER, 1905–1955
  *George William Gordon.* 1976. HILET

MAJOR, ALICE, 1949–
  *Saint Marina* (excerpt from poetry collection of dramatic
    monologues, *Some Bones and a Story*, published
    2001). 1997. BREK

MAJUMDAR, DEBASIS, 1950–
  *Amitakshar. See* Unrhymed
  *Unrhymed.* 1999.
    Raha, K., translator KAM2
    Variant title: *Amitakshar*

MAKINO NOZOMI, 1959–
  *Tokyo Atomic Klub.* 1997.
    Swain, J., translator HACJT1
    Variant title: *Tokyo genshikaku kurabu*
  *Tokyo genshikaku kurabu. See* Tokyo Atomic Klub

MALHOTRA, BHUPESH
  *Nature's Revenge.* 1993. SACR

MALIK, AFSHAN
  *Safar.* 1996. NEWWD1

MALINOWITZ, HARRIET
  *Minus One.* 1989. DEAT

MALITI-FRANOVA, EVA, 1953–
*Krcheň Nesmrtel'ný. See* Krcheň the Immortal
*Krcheň the Immortal.* 2001.
   Urbánek, L., translator CONTSL4
   Variant title: *Krcheň Nesmrtel'ný*

MALJEAN, JEAN RAYMOND
*A Message from Cougar.* 1967. NEWA2

MALLESON, MILES, 1888–1969
*La malade imaginaire. See* Molière, Jean Baptiste
   Poquelin. *Le malade imaginaire* (translated and
   adapted by)
*The Misanthrope. See* Molière, Jean Baptiste Poquelin.
   *Le misanthrope* (translated and adapted by)
*The Miser. See* Molière, Jean Baptiste Poquelin. *The
   Miser* (translated and adapted by)
*The Prodigious Snob. See* Molière, Jean Baptiste
   Poquelin. *Le bourgeois gentilhomme* (translated and
   adapted by)
*School for Wives. See* Molière, Jean Baptiste Poquelin.
   *L'école des femmes* (translated and adapted by)
*Sganarelle. See* Molière, Jean Baptiste Poquelin.
   *Sganarelle* (translated and adapted by)
*Tartuffe. See* Molière, Jean Baptiste Poquelin. *Tartuffe*
   (translated and adapted by)

—— and BROOKS, HARRY
*Six Men of Dorset.* 1938. FAML

MALLET, DAVID, 1705–1765
*Elvira.* 1763. BELK20
*Eurydice.* 1731. BELK16

MALONE, BENI, 1954– , and MERCER, RICK, joint
   author
*On Edge.* 1989. PETERS

MALPEDE, KAREN, 1945–
*Us.* 1987. LAMO

MALTBY, RICHARD, JR., 1937–
*Miss Saigon* (lyrics by). *See* Boubil, Alain, and
   Chonberg, Claude-Michel. *Miss Saigon.*

—— and WALKER, CHET, and REINKING, ANN
*Fosse: A Dance Musical in Three Acts* (choreography by
   Bob Fosse; conceived by Richard Maltby, Jr., Chet
   Walker, and Ann Reinking). 1998. BES98

MALTZ, ALBERT, 1908–1985
*Private Hicks.* 1936. KOZ

MAMET, DAVID, 1947–
*American Buffalo.* 1975. BERS, BES76, NIL, OBG
*The Cryptogram.* 1994. BES94, GUTDS

*Edmond.* 1982. WETZ
*The Frog Prince.* 1984. SCVDO1
*Glengarry Glen Ross; a Play in Two Acts.* 1984. BERT,
   BES83, COI
*Goldberg Street.* 1985. SCM
*A Life in the Theater; a Play in One Act and 26 Scenes.*
   1977. BES77
*Oleanna.* 1992. BARIH, BES92, COLD, DIYLD,
   JACOBD, LITRD, SSSIB, SSSIC, WATTAD
*Speed-the-plow.* 1988. BES87, WOTHA
*A Waitress in Yellowstone.* 1990. SCVDT1

MANAKA, MATSEMELA, 1956–1998
*Children of Asazi.* 1985. WOZA
*Pula.* 1982. GRAY

MANCINA, MARK
*The Lion King* (additional music and lyrics by). *See*
   Allers, Roger. *The Lion King*

MANCO, SILVERIO, 1888–1964
*Juan Moreira* (based on 1886 play by Jose J. Podesta).
   Fassett, J., translator 1920. BIES

MANDIELA, AHDRI ZHINA, 1953–
*dark diaspora . . . in dub.* 1991. SEARS1

MANET, EDUARDO, 1930–
*Lady Strass.* 1977.
   Zatlin, P., translator PLAWE

MANHOFF, BILL, 1919–1974
*The Owl and the Pussycat.* 1964. GAT

MANKIEWICZ, HERMAN J., 1897–1953, and WELLES,
   ORSON
*Citizen Kane: The Shooting Script.* 1941. BAIH, SCNQ

MANKOWITZ, WOLF (CYRIL), 1924–1998
*It Should Happen to a Dog.* 1962. THOD

MANLEY, DELARIVIER. *See* Manley, Mary Delarivier

MANLEY, FRANK, 1930–2009, and MURPHY,
   VINCENT
*The Cockfighter* (adapted from the novel by Frank
   Manley). 1999. HUMANA99

MANLEY, MARY DELARIVIER, 1663?–1724
*The Royal Mischief.* 1696. FEFO

MANLEY, MRS. *See* Manley, Mary Delarivier

MANN, EMILY, 1952–
*Annulla, an Autobiography.* 1985. SCM
*Execution of Justice.* 1984. BES85, FAV, NEWQB,
   RIS, SHEW

*The House of Bernard Alba* (adapted from the play by
    Federico Garcia-Lorca). 1997. WOMP97
*Still Life.* 1980. COMV, NEWQ, VENA

MANN, HEINRICH, 1871–1950
*Madame Legros.* 1914.
    Katzin, W., translator KAT

MANN, KLAUS, 1906–1949
*Ania and Esther: A Romantic Play in Seven Tableaux.*
    1925.
    Senelick, L., translator SELOV
    Variant title: *Anja und Esther. Ein romatisches stuck
    in sieben bildern*
*Anja und Esther. Ein romatisches stuck in sieben
    bildern.* See Ania and Esther: A Romantic Play in
    Seven Tableaux
*Mephisto. See* Mnouchkine, Ariane. *Mephisto* (adapted
    from the novel by)

MANNER, EEVA-LIISA, 1921–1995
*Snow in May.* (1966)
    Binham, P., translator MNOF

MANNERS, JOHN HARTLEY, 1870–1928
*Peg O' My Heart.* 1912. CEY

MANNING, LINDA
*Do Something with Yourself! The Life of Charlotte
    Brontë.* 1993. WOMP96

MANNING, MARY, 1905–1999
*Youth's the Season. . . .?* 1931. CAN

MANSUKE, NAKADA. *See* Nakada, Mansuke

MANUEL, VERA, 1948–2010
*The Strength of Indian Women.* 1996. BEYO (excerpt)

MAPA, ALEC, 1965–
*I Remember Mapa.* 1998. HUGH

MAPONYA, MAISHE, 1951–
*Gangsters.* 1985. WOTHC, WOZA
*The Hungry Earth.* 1979. GRAYS
*Umongikazi/The Nurse.* 1983. PERA

MARAINI, DACIA, 1936–
*Veronica Franco, Courtesan and Poet.* 1991.
    Williams, S., and Baraitser, M., translators BARAM

MARANS, JON, 1957–
*Old Wicked Songs.* 1995. BES96

MARASCO, ROBERT, 1936–1998
*Child's Play.* 1970. BES69, RICI

MARBER, ANDREAS, 1961–
*Die lügen der papageien. See* Parrots' Lies
*Parrots' Lies.* 1997.
    Tushingham, D., translator DODGSP
    Variant title: *Die lügen der papageien*

MARBER, PATRICK, 1965–
*Closer.* 1997. BES98

MARCEAU, FELICIEN (pseudonym of LOUIS
    CARRETTE), 1913–
*The Egg.* 1957?
    Schlitt, R., translator and adapter BES61
    Variant title: *L'oeuf*
*L'oeuf. See* The Egg

MARCEL, GABRIEL, 1889–1973
*Ariadne.* 1936?
    Heywood, R., translator ULAN
    Variant title: *Le chemin de Crête*
*Le chemin de Crête. See* Ariadne

MARCH, WILLIAM (pseudonym of WILLIAM
    EDWARD MARCH CAMPBELL), 1894–1954
*The Bad Seed. See* Anderson, Maxwell. *The Bad Seed*
    (based on the novel by)

MARCHAND, SHOSHANA
*Half Fare.* 1982. YOUP

MARCINKEVICIUS, JUSTINAS, 1930–2011
*Mindaugas.* 1969.
    Cerskute-Spidell, O., translator FIFFN

MARC-MICHEL (pseudonym of MARC ANTOINE
    AMÉDEE MICHEL), 1812–1868.
    *See* Labiche, Eugène, joint author

MARCOS, PLINIO, 1935–1999
*Dois perdidos numa note suja.* 1967. SZO
*Two Lost in a Filthy Night.* 1967.
    Szoka, E., translator SZO
    Variant title: *Dois perdidos numa note suja*

MARCUS, FRANK, 1928–1996
*Beauty and the Beast.* 1975. PLAN46
*Formation Dancers.* 1964. PLAN28
*The Killing of Sister George.* 1965. BES66, HOF,
    PLAN31, RICIS
*Mrs. Mouse Are You Within?* 1968. PLAN35
*Notes on a Love Affair.* 1972. PLAN42
*The Window.* RICJ

MARES, E. A. ("Tony"), 1938–
*Lola's Last Dance.* 1979. JOND

MARGOLIN, DEB, 1951– , and SHAW, PEGGY, and
WEAVER, LOIS
*Beauty and the Beast.* 1982. CASB
*Lesbians Who Kill.* 1992. CASB
*Little Women: The Tragedy.* 1988. CASB
*Upwardly Mobile Home.* 1984. CASB

MARGUERITTE, PAUL, 1860–1918
*Pierrot: Assassin of His Wife.* 1882.
Gerould, D., translator GERO

MARGULIES, DONALD, 1954–
*Collected Stories.* 1996. PLACG2
*Dinner with Friends.* 1998. BES98, BES99,
HUMANA98
*July 7, 1994.* 1995. HUMANA95
*The Loman Family Picnic.* 1989. BES89
*Misadventure.* 2000. *See* Ackermann, J. *Back Story: A
Dramatic Anthology.* HUMANA2000
*The Model Apartment.* 1988. THLA
*Sight Unseen.* 1991. BES91, PLACG1, SCM

MARICHAL LUGO, TERESA, 1956–
*Evening Walk.* 1984.
Salas, T., and Vargas, M., translators SALA
Variant title: *Paseo al atardecer*
*Paseo al atardecer. See* Evening Walk

MARINETTI, FILIPPO TOMMASO, 1876–1944
*Le basi. See* Feet
*Connecting Vessels.* 1916.
House, J., translator TWEI
Variant title: *I vasi communicanti*
*Feet.* 1915.
Nes Kirby, V., translator TWEI
Variant title: *Le basi*
*They Are Coming.* 1915.
Nes Kirby, V., translator TWEI
Variant title: *Vengono*
*I vasi communicanti. See* Connecting Vessels
*Vengono. See* They Are Coming

MARINKOVIC, RANKO, 1913–2001
*Gloria.* 1955.
Mladinov, D., and Reeder, R., translators MIG

MARIVAUX, PIERRE CARLET DE CHAMBLAIN DE,
1688–1763
*The False Confessions.* 1737.
Merwin, W., translator BENR4, FOUAD
Variant title: *Les fausses confidences*
*Les fausses confidences. See* (pseudonym of *The False
Confessions*)
*The Game of Love and Chance. See* Le jeu de l'amour et
du hazard

*Le jeu de l'amour et du hazard.* 1730. BREN, SEA,
STJ1, ZDA
Aldington, R., translator ALD
Fowles, J., translator LAQCF
Fowlie, W., translator FOWL
Variant titles: *The Game of Love and Chance; The
Lottery of Love*
*The Lottery of Love. See* Le jeu de l'amour et du hazard
*The Triumph of Love.* 1732.
Magruder, J., translator THOS

MARKOE, MERRILL, 1952–
*A Conversation with My Dogs.* 1992. SCVDO1

MARKS, MRS. L. S. *See* Peabody, Josephine Preston

MARLOWE, CHRISTOPHER, 1564–1593
*Doctor Faustus. See* The Tragical History of Doctor
Faustus
*Edward II. See* The Troublesome Reign and Lamentable
Death of Edward the Second
*Faustus. See* The Tragical History of Doctor Faustus
*The Jew of Malta.* 1589? BROC, DPR1, NEI, PAR,
SPE, THA
*The Reign of King Edward the Third* (sometimes
attributed to). *See* Anonymous Plays. *The Reign of
King Edward the Third*
*Tamburlaine the Great.* 1587? BROC, HOW, HUST,
SCW
*Tamburlaine the Great, Part I.* 1587? BALD, BAS,
DPR1, KRE, NEI, NES, RYL, SCI, SCJ, SPE, TICO
*The Tragical History of Doctor Faustus.* 1588? ABRB1,
ABRF1, ABRH1, ABRJ1, ABRK1, ABRL1,
ABRM1, ASF, BALL, BARD, BARKB, BARKC,
BARKF, BAS, BAUG, BECK, BENY, BROC,
BROK, CLF1, CLK1, COF, COHM, COLD,
COLEL1, CONO, COTX, DEAN, DEAO, DOWN,
DPR1, DUN, FOUD, FREG, GATG, GIBS,
GREB1, GREC1, GRIF, HARCl9, HAY, HEIL,
HOEP, HOW, HUD, JACOB, JACOBD, KER,
KINNR, LIE, LIED1, LIEE1, LOCK, LOCL,
MABC, MADB, MALI1, MALN1, MANN, MIL,
MONV, MOO, NEI, NES, NORG, NORIA1,
NORIB1, NORJ1, OLH, OLI1, ORNT, PAR, RUB,
SCH, SCI, SCJ, SCW, SHAH1, SHAHI1, SHAJ1,
SMI, SNYD1, SPD, SPDB, SPE, SPEF1, SSSIA,
SSSIB, SSSIC, STA, STOTD, STOTLA, SWA,
TOBI, TREB, TREC1, TREE1, TREI1, VENA,
WAT, WEATl, WINE, WOO1, WOOD1, WOOE1,
WOTHA, WOTHB, WOTHC, WRIH
Variant titles: *Doctor Faustus; The Tragical History
of the Life and Death of Doctor Faustus. See* The
Tragical History of Doctor Faustus
*The Troublesome Reign and Lamentable Death of
Edward the Second.* 1592? ASH, BAS, BROC,

CLKW, CLKY, DPR1, GATG, GRE, HARC46, HILPDH2, KINNR, MATTL, NEI, NES, OLH, OLI1, PAR, RUB, SCH, SCI, SCJ, SPE, SSSI, TAT, TAU
Variant title: *Edward II*

MARNI, JEANNE, pseudonym. *See* Marnière, Jeanne Marie Françoise

MARNIERE, JEANNE MARIE FRANÇOISE (JEANNE MARNI, pseudonym), 1854–1910. *See* Guinon, Albert, joint author

MAROWITZ, CHARLES, 1934–
*Measure for Measure.* 1975. ADAP
*An Othello.* 1972. MARP
— *See* Burgess John, joint author
— *See* Burns, Alan, joint author

MARQUAND, JOHN PHILLIPS, 1894–1960, and KAUFMAN, GEORGE S.
*The Late George Apley.* 1944. BES44, COTE, COTH
*Point of No Return. See* Osborn, Paul. *Point of No Return* (adapted from the novel by)

MARQUES, RENE, 1919–1979
*La carreta. See* The Oxcart
*The Fanlights.* 1958.
    Wiezell, R., translator WOOG
    Variant title: *Los soles truncos*
*The Oxcart.* 1953.
    Pilditch, C., translator GRIH
    Variant title: *La carreta*
*Los soles truncos.* 1958. DAU *See also* The Fanlights

MARQUINA, EDUARDO, 1879–1946
*Cuando florezcan las rosales. See* When the Roses Bloom Again
*When the Roses Bloom Again.* 1913.
    Turrell, CA., translator TUR
    Variant title: *Cuando florezcan las rosales*

MARQUIS, DON. *See* Marquis, Donald Robert Perry

MARQUIS, DONALD ROBERT PERRY, 1878–1937
*The Old Soak.* 1922. BES22

MARSHAK, SAMUIL YAKOVLEVICH, 1887–1964
*Twelve Months.* 1943?
    Bakshy, A., translator BAKS

MARSHALL, BRUCE, 1899–1987
*Father Malachy's Miracle. See* Doherty, Brian. *Father Malachy's Miracle* (based on the novel by)

MARSHALL, CHRISTABEL (pseudonym of CHRISTOPHER ST. JOHN), 1875–1960
*See* Hamilton, Cicely, joint author

MARSTON, JOHN, 1576–1634
*The Dutch Courtesan.* 1603. DPR2, SALF, WALL
*The Insatiate Countess. See* Barksted, William, and Machin, Lewis. *The Insatiate Countess* (from the draft by)
*The Malcontent.* 1604. BAS, BROC, GOM, HAPRA1, HAPRB1, LAWR, NEI, NES, SPE
*Sophonisba.* 1606. COQJW

MARSTON, JOHN WESTLAND, 1819–1890
*The Patrician's Daughter.* 1842. BAI

MARTELL, LEON
*Hoss Drawin'.* 1982. PLACE, WES13/14
*Kindling.* 1989. MEDN

MARTENS, ANNE COULTER, 1906–1977
*Blue Beads.* 1938? LOVR

MARTIN, EDOUARD, 1828–1866. *See* Labiche, Eugène Marin, joint author

MARTIN, JANE
*Anton in Show Business.* 2000. HUMANA2000
*Cementville.* 1991. DIXD2
*Clear Glass Marbles.* 1981. WOQ3
*Coup/clucks.* 1982. DIXP
*The Deal.* 2000. *See* Ackermann, J. *Back Story: A Dramatic Anthology.* HUMANA2000
*Jack and Jill.* 1996. BES96, HUMANA96
*Keely and Du.* 1993. BES93, HUMANA93
*Middle-aged White Guys.* 1995. HUMANA95
*Mr. Bundy.* 1998. HUMANA98
*Rodeo.* 1981. MEYC, MEYCA, MEYD, MEYE, MEYF, WOQ3
*Stuffed Shirts.* 1999. HUMANA99
*Twirler.* 1981. MEY, MEYB

MARTIN, MEAH
*White Skates* (excerpt). 1993. BREK

MARTIN, SHARON STOCKARD, 1948–
*The Moving Violation.* 1979? CEN

MARTIN RECUERDA, JOSE, 1926–2007
*Las arrecogias del beaterio de Santa Maria Egipciaca. See* The Inmates of the Convent of Saint Mary Egyptian
*The Inmates of the Convent of Saint Mary Egyptian.* 1977.
    Lima, R., translator HOLTS

Variant title: *Las arrecogias del beaterio de Santa Maria Egipciaca*

MARTINEZ, JACINTO BENAVENTE Y. *See* Benavente y Martínez, Jacinto

MARTINEZ, ROGELIO
*Illuminating Veronica.* 1999. PLACGH

MARTINEZ BALLESTEROS, ANTONIO, 1929–
*The Best of All Possible Worlds.* 1966?
    Salerno, H., and Gross, S., translators WELL, WELT
*The Hero.* 1965.
    Blue, R., translator WELL

MARTINEZ MEDIERO, MANUEL, 1939–
*The Guest.*
    O'Connor, P., translator OCONNF

MARTINEZ SIERRA, GREGORIO, 1881–1947, and MARTINEZ SIERRA, MARIA
*Canción de cuna. See* The Cradle Song
*The Cradle Song.* 1911.
    Underhill, J., translator BES26, CEW, COTP, HAV
    Variant title: *Canción de cuna*
*The Kingdom of God.* 1916.
    Granville-Barker, H., and H., translators BES28
    Variant title: *El reino de Dios*
*A Lily among Thorns.* 1911.
    Granville-Barker, H., and H., translators DICDT
    Variant title: *Lirio entre espinas*
*Lirio entre espinas. See* A Lily among Thorns
*Los pastores. See* The Two Shepherds
*El reino de Dios. See* The Kingdom of God
*The Two Shepherds.* 1913.
    Granville-Barker, H., and H., translators LEV, LEVE
    Variant title: *Los pastores*

MARTINEZ SIERRA, MARIA, 1874–1974. *See* Martínez Sierra, Gregorio, joint author

MARTULA, TANYSS RHEA
*The Three Boys.* 1984. VICK1
*Two Women from Waldo, Arkansas.* 1983. VICK2

MARTYN, EDWARD, 1859–1923
*Maeve.* 1900. CAP

MARY, V. V.
*A Dialogue between a Southern Delegate, and His Spouse, on His Return from the Grand Continental Congress* (attributed to). *See* Anonymous Plays. *A Dialogue, between a Southern Delegate, and His Spouse, on His Return from the Grand Continental Congress*

MASEFIELD, JOHN, 1878–1967
*The Tragedy of Pompey the Great.* 1910. MOSN, PLAP2

MASON, BRUCE, 1921–1982
*Hongi.* 1968. CONTNZ

MASON, CLIFFORD, 1932–
*Gabriel.* KINH, KINHB
*The Verandah.* (1976) CEN

MASON, HARRY SILVERNALE, 1881–
*At the Gate Beautiful.* 1925? FED2

MASON, JUDI ANN, 1955–2009
*Daughters of the Mock.* 1979. HAPUE
*A Star ain't Nothin' but a Hole in Heaven.* 1977. FLET
    (one scene only)

MASON, KEITH ANTAR
*for black boys who have considered homicide when the streets were too much.* 1993. ELAM

MASON, LIBBY, 1949– . *See* Thompson, Tierl, joint author
    — *See also* The Women's Theatre Group, joint author

MASON, TIMOTHY
*Bearclaw.* 1984. GAY2
*Levitation.* 1984. GAY3

MASON, WILLIAM, 1724–1797
*Caractacus.* (1759) BELG12
*Elfrida.* (1752) BELG12

MASON, WILTON, 1916–1994? *See* McDonald, Catherine, joint author

MASSEY, EDWARD MORRELL, 1893–1942
*Plots and Playwrights.* 1915. BAK

MASSINGER, PHILIP, 1583–1640
*The Bondman.* 1623. RUB
*The City Madam.* 1632. PLAN28
*The Fatal Dowry.* 1632. GEMM
*The Maid of Honor.* 1621? BAS
*A New Way to Pay Old Debts.* 1632. ANG, BAS, BAT13, BROC, DPR2, DUN, GAYLE3, HARC47, HOW, KRE, LAWR, MATTL, NEI, OLH, OLI2, ORNC, PAR, RUB, SALF, SCH, SCI, SCJ, SMO, SPE, TAV, WALL, WHE
*The Renegado.* 1624. VIT
    — *See* Fletcher, John, joint author
*The Roman Actor.* 1626. DPR2, MAKJ

MASTEROFF, JOE, 1919–
*Cabaret* (music by John Kander, lyrics by Fred Ebb: based on the play *I Am a Camera* by John van Druten and stories by Christopher Isherwood). 1967. BES66, RICM
*She Loves Me* (based on a play by Miklos Laszlo; music by Jerry Bock, lyrics by Sheldon Harnick). 1963. BES62

MASTERSON, PETER, 1934–
*The Best Little Whorehouse in Texas. See* King, Larry L., joint author

MASTRANTONE, LUCIA. *See* Crea, Teresa, joint author

MASTROSIMONE, WILLLIAM, 1947–
*Extremities; a Play in Two Acts.* 1982. BES82
*Like Totally Weird.* 1998. HUMANA98
*The Undoing.* 1984. DIXP

MATAS, JULIO, 1931–
*Deviations.* 1990.
     Gonzalez-Cruz, L., and Aker, A., translators THRCD
     Variant title: *El extravío*
*Dialogo de Poeta y Maximo. See* Dialogue of the Poet and the Supreme Leader
*Dialogue of the Poet and the Supreme Leader.*
     Gonzalez-Cruz, L., and Colecchia, F., translators GONZ
*El extravío. See* Deviations

MATCHA, JACK, 1919–2003
*Aerobics.* 1982. *See* Anonymous Plays. *Twenty-four Hours: P.M.*

MATHEUS, JOHN FREDERICK, 1887–1983
*Black Damp.* 1929. HARYL
*'Cruiter.* 1926. HARY, HARYB, LOC
*Ti Yette.* 1930. RIR, RIRA

MATHEW, RAY, 1929–2002
*We Find the Bunyip.* 1955. HANG

MATHEWS, CHARLES J., 1803–1878
*Fatter versus Clatter.* 1838. BOOA4

MATHEWS, CORNELIUS, 1817–1889
*Witchcraft, or, the Martyrs of Salem.* 1846. MESCO

MATILLA, LUIS, 1939–
*Post Mortem.* 1968.
     Wellwarth, M., translator WELK

MATSUDA, MASATAKA, 1962–
*Cape Moon.* 1997. Boyd, M., translator HACJT2
     Variant title: *Tsuki no misaki*
*Tsuki no misaki. See* Cape Moon

MATTHEWS, TEDE, d. 1993
*Factwino Meets the Moral Majority* (script by). *See* San Francisco Mime Troupe. *Factwino Meets the Moral Majority*

MATTO, JOSE MARIA RIVAROLA. *See* Rivarola Matto, Jose Maria

MATURIN, CHARLES ROBERT, 1780–1824
*Bertram; or, the Castle of St. Aldobrand.* 1816. BAI, COXJ
     Variant title: *The Castle of St. Aldobrand*
*The Castle of St. Aldobrand. See* Bertram; or, The Castle of St. Aldobrand

MATWYCHUK, PAUL, 1969–
*The Key to Violet's Apartment.* 1996. STN

MAUGHAM, ROBIN, 2nd VICOUNT MAUGHAM OF HARTFIELD, 1916–1981
*Enemy.* 1969. PLAN39

MAUGHAM, W. SOMERSET, 1874–1965
*Before the Party. See* Ackland, Rodney. *Before the Party* (based on a short story by)
*The Breadwinner.* 1930. CHA, CHAN, CHAR
*The Circle.* 1921. BES21, BROH, CEU, CLM, COT, COTH, DICEM, DUR, FOUX, HAVE, KRM, MAD, MART, MOSG, MOSH, MYB, TREBA, TREBJ, TREC2, TREE2, TRE13, TUCD, TUCM, WAK, WATF2, WATI, WATO, WEE
*The Colonel's Lady. See* Sherriff, Robert Cedrica. *The Colonel's Lady* (based on the story by)
*The Constant Wife.* 1927. BES26, HAU, LOR, WARI, WARL
*For Services Rendered.* 1932. MOD
*Jane. See* Behrman, Samuel Nathaniel. *Jane* (based on the story by)
*The Letter.* 1927. RICI, SAFM
*Loaves and Fishes.* 1911. WEAL
*Miss Thompson. See* Colton, John and Randolph, Clemence. *Rain* (based on the story by)
*Our Betters.* 1917. DICDS, MOSO, SALE, SMO, WHI
*Sheppey.* 1933. SIXH

MAUGHAM, WILLIAM SOMERSET. *See* Maugham, W. Somerset

MAUPASSANT, GUY DE, 1850–1893
*The Household Peace.* 1893.
     Chambers, W., translator BAT9
     Variant title: *La paix du ménage*
*La paix du ménage. See* The Household Peace

MAURETTE, MARCELLE, 1903–1972
*Anastasia.* 1953.
     Bolton, G., adapter PLAN9, THEA55

MAUREY, MAX, 1868–1947
*Rosalie.* 1900. SET

MAURIAC, FRANÇOIS, 1885–1970
*Asmodée.* 1938.
Thurman, B., translator HAYE

MAVOR, OSBORNE HENRY (JAMES BRIDIE, pseudonym), 1888–1951
*Tobias and the Angel.* 1930. PLAL1

MAXWELL, ELSA, 1883–1963. *See* Belmont, Mrs. O. H. P. (Alva), joint author

MAY, ELAINE, 1932–
*Adaptation.* 1969. BES68

MAY, VAL, 1927–
*Sixty Thousand Nights* (script and research by George Rowell, music by Julian Slade, lyrics by Julian Slade and George Rowell). 1966. PLAN31

MAYAKOVSKY, VLADIMIR VLADIMIROVICH, 1894–1930
*The Bathhouse.* 1929?
MacAndrew, A., translator GARZG, MABA
*The Bedbug.* 1929.
Hayward, M., translator COTO, GLE, RUSV
Reeve, F., translator REEV2
*Mystery-bouffe.* (Second variant). 1921.
Noyes, G., and Kaun, A., translators NOY
Rottenberg, D., translator CLKX
*Vladimir Mayakovsky: A Tragedy.* 1913.
Langen, T., and Weir, J., translators EIGHTRP

MAYER, EDWIN JUSTUS, 1897–1960
*Children of Darkness.* 1930. GARU, KRM
*The Firebrand.* 1924. BES24

MAYER, JERRY
*The Underachiever.* 1982. *See* Anonymous Plays. *Twenty-four Hours: A.M.*

MAYER, OLIVER, 1964?–
*Ragged Time.* 1994. SVICH

MAYER, TIMOTHY S., 1944–1988. *See* Stone, Peter H., joint author

MAYNE, RUTHERFORD, pseudonym. *See* Waddell, Samuel

MAYOR, BEATRICE, 1886–1971
*The Pleasure Garden.* 1924. PLAP3

MAYORGA, JUAN, 1965–
*El jardín quemado. See* The Scorched Garden

*The Scorched Garden.* 1994.
Drake, N., translator DODGSS
Variant title: *El jardín quemado*

MAZA, BOB, 1939–2000
*The Keepers.* 1988. PLACC

MAZYA, EDNA, 1950–
*A Family Story.* 1996.
Marks, A., translator BARA

MDA, ZAKES, 1948–
*And the Girls in Their Sunday Dresses.* 1988. GRAV
*The Hill.* 1995. HUTCH

MEACHAM, MALCOLM
*The Snow Goose. See* Gallico, Paul. *The Snow Goose* (adapted by)

MEAD, EDWARD SHEPHERD, 1914–1994
*How to Succeed in Business without Really Trying. See* Burrows, Abram S. *How to Succeed in Business without Really Trying* (based on the book by)

MEAKER, MRS. ISABELLE (JACKSON), 1874–
— *See* Harnwell, Mrs. Anna Jane (Wilcox), joint author

MEARA, ANNE, 1929–
*After-play.* 1995. BES94

MECCHI, IRENE. *See* Allers, Roger. *The Lion King*

MEDINA, LOUISA, 1813?–1838
*Ernest Maltravers.* 1838. KRIT

MEDLEY, CASSANDRA, 1949–
*Ma Rose.* 1989. MIHWW

MEDNICK, MURRAY, 1939–
*The Coyote Cycle. See* Coyote V: Listening to Old Nana; Coyote IV: Other Side Camp; Coyote I: Pointing; Coyote VII: He Brings the Waterfall; Coyote VI: The Sacred Dump; Coyote III: Planet of the Spider People; Coyote II: The Shadow Ripens
*Coyote V: Listening to Old Nana.* 1982. PLACE, WES13/14
*Coyote IV: Other Side Camp.* 1981. WES9
*Coyote I: Pointing.* 1978. WES7
*Coyote VII: He Brings the Waterfall.* 1984. WES17/18
*Coyote VI: The Sacred Dump.* 1983. WES17/18
*Coyote III: Planet of the Spider People.* 1980. WES7
*Coyote II: The Shadow Ripens.* 1979. WES7
*He Brings the Waterfall. See* Coyote VII: He Brings the Waterfall
*Listening to Old Nana. See* Coyote V: Listening to Old Nana

*Other Side Camp. See* Coyote IV: Other Side Camp
*Planet of the Spider People. See* Coyote III: Planet of
    the Spider People
*Pointing. See* Coyote I: Pointing
*The Sacred Dump. See* Coyote VI: The Sacred Dump
*The Shadow Ripens. See* Coyote II: The Shadow Ripens
*Shatter 'n Wade.* 1990. MEDN
*Switchback.* 1994. MESSE
*Taxes.* 1976. WOQ3
*Willie the Germ.* 1968. SME

MEDOFF, MARK, 1940–
    *Children of a Lesser God.* 1979. BERP, BERPA, BES79
    *The Kramer.* 1973. BALLE13
    *Kringle's Window.* 1991. SWO
    *The Wager.* 1974. BES74
    *When You Comin' Back, Red Ryder?* 1973. BES73,
        JOND

MEDWALL, HENRY, fl. 1486–1500?
    *Fulgens and Lucrece. See* Fulgens and Lucres
    *Fulgens and Lucres.* 1497? BOA, CRE, HAO (extracts),
        MED
        Variant title: *Fulgens and Lucrece*
    *Nature.* 1495? FARN

MEE, CHARLES L., JR., 1938–
    *Big Love.* 2000. HUMANA2000
    *Constantinople Smith.* 1961. NEWA1
    *The Imperialists at the Club Cave Canem.* 1989.
        MESSE
    *The Investigation of the Murder in El Salvador.* 1984.
        WOQ4

MEEHAN, PAULA, 1955–
    *Mrs. Sweeney.* 1997. BOUR

MEEHAN, THOMAS, 1929–
    *Annie; a Musical in Two Acts* (music by Charles
        Strouse; lyrics by Martin Charnin). 1977. BES76

MEGGED, AHARON, 1920–
    *The First Sin.* (1962)
        Eingad, S., and Arad, M., translators MOADE
    *Hanna Senesh.* 1958.
        Taub, M., translator TAUB

MEGRUE, ROI COOPER, 1883–1927
    *Under Cover.* 1914. CART

—— and HACKETT, WALTER
    *It Pays to Advertise.* 1914. MOSJ, MOSK, MOSL

MEHTA, DINA
    *Getting Away with Murder.* 1990. BODY

MEI, LANFANG, 1894–1961. *See* Anonymous Plays.
    *Hegemon King Says Farewell to His Queen* (Peking
        opera: version by)

MEILHAC, HENRI, 1831–1897, and HALEVY,
        LUDOVIC
    *La mi-carême. See* Mardi Gras
    *Mardi Gras.* 1874.
        Shapiro, N., translator FLEA
        Variant title: *La mi-carême*
    *Signor Nocodemo.* 1867.
        Shapiro, N., translator FLEA
        Variant title: *Tout pour les dames!*
    *Tout pour les dames! See* Signor Nocodemo

MELDON, MAURICE, 1926–1958
    *Purple Path to the Poppy Field.* 1953. NEWWW5

MELESVILLE (pseudonym of ANNE-HONORÉ-JOSEPH
        DUVEYRIER, 1787–1865)
    *See* Scribe, Augustin Eugène, joint author *The Castrata*

MELFI, LEONARD, 1935–2001
    *Birdbath.* 1967. RICJ
    *Cinque.* 1972. OWER
    *Night.* 1968. GARTL

MELL, MAX, 1882–1971
    *The Apostle Play.* 1934.
        White, M., translator SEVE

MELLON, EVELYN EMIG. *See* Emig, Evelyn

MELVILLE, ALAN (pseudonym of ALAN
        CAVERHILL), 1910–1983
    *Castle in the Air.* 1949. PLAN3
    *Dear Charles.* 1952. PLAN8
    *Simon and Laura.* 1954. PLAN11

MELVILLE, HERMAN, 1819–1891
    *Billy Budd. See* Coxe, Louis O., and Chapman, Robert.
        *Billy Budd* (based on the novel by)

MENA, ALICIA
    *Las nuevas tamaleras.* 1993. PURO

MENANDER, OF ATHENS, 342?–292? B.C.
    *The Arbitration.* 4th century B.C.
        Allinson, F., translator HOWE, HOWF
        Casson, L., translator CASU
        Post, L., translator OAM, OAT2
        Variant title: *Epitrepontes*
    *Dyskolos. See* The Grouch
    *Epitrepontes. See* The Arbitration
    *The Girl from Samos.* 4th century B.C.
        Casson, L., translator CASU

Post, L., translator OAT2
   Variant titles: *Samia; The Woman of Samos*
*The Grouch.* 317 B.C.
   Casson, L., translator CASU
   D'Atri, S., translator COTKICC
   Moulton, CA., translator HILPDH1
   Variant title: *Dyskolos*
*The perikeiromene. See* The Shearing of Glycera
*Samia. See* The Girl from Samos
*The Shearing of Glycera.* 4th century B.C.
   Casson, L., translator CASU
   Post, L., translator OAT2
   Variant titles: *The perikeiromene; She Who Was
     Shorn*
*She Who Was Shorn. See* The Shearing of Glycera
*The Woman of Samos. See* The Girl from Samos

MENDEZ, MOSES, d.1758
*The Chaplet.* 1749. BELC1

MENDOZA, JUAN RUIZ DE ALARCON. *See* Ruiz de
   Alarcón y Mendoza, Juan

MENG HAN-CH'ING, fl.1279
*The Mo-ho-lo Doll* (attributed to).
   Crump, J., translator CRU

MENOTTI, GIAN-CARLO, 1911–2007
*Amahl and the Night Visitors.* 1951. SWO
*The Saint of Bleecker Street.* 1954. THEA55

MERCER, DAVID, 1928–1980
*The Governor's Lady.* 1965. RICJ

MERCER, RICK, 1969– . *See* Malone, Beni, joint author

MERCIER, MARY
*Johnny No-trump.* 1967. SSTY

MERCIER, SERGE, 1944–
*Encore un peu. See* A Little Bit Left
*A Little Bit Left.* 1975.
   Van Meer, A., translator KAL5
   Variant title: *Encore un peu*

MEREDITH, SYLVIA, 1908?–1985. *See* Hensel, Karen,
   joint author

MERI, VEIJO, 1928–
*Private Jokinen's Marriage Leave*
   Pitkin, J., translator MNOF

MERIMEE, PROSPER, 1803–1870
*Carmencita and the Soldier* (based on the opera *Carmen*
   by Georges Bizet). *See* Lipakeroff, Konstantin.
   *Carmencita and the Soldier*
*Inez Mendo; or, The Triumph of Prejudice.* 1825. BAT21

MERRIAM, EVE, 1916–1992, WAGNER, PAULA, and
   HOFFSISS, JACK
*Out of Our Fathers' House.* 1975. BARKD, NEWWT

MERRILL, JAMES, 1926–1995
*The Bait.* 1953. MAH
*The Immortal Husband.* 1955. PLAA

MERRITT, CATHARINE NINA, 1859–1926
*When George the Third was King; an Historical Drama
   in Three Acts.* (1897) WAGN

MERRITT, ROBERT J., 1945–
*The Cake Man.* 1975. BRIM2

MESSAGER, CHARLES. *See* Vildrac, Charles,
   pseudonym

METASTASIO, PIETRO ANTONIO DOMENICO
   BUONAVENTURA (pseudonym of PIETRO
   TREPASSI), 1698–1782
*Achilles in Scyros.* 1800?
   Hoole, J., translator JOH
*Attilio Regolo.* 1740. BIN
*The Dream of Scipio.* 1800?
   Hoole, J., translator BAT5
   Variant title: *Il sogno di Scipione*
*Il sogno di Scipione. See* The Dream of Scipio

METCALFE, STEPHEN, 1953–
*The Incredibly Famous Willy Rivers* (music by Denny
   McCormick). 1984. NEWQB
*Strange Snow.* 1982. COMV

MEYER, ANNIE NATHAN, 1867–1951
*Black Souls.* 1932. PERF

MEYER, MARLANE GOMARD, 1951–
*Etta Jenks.* 1986. MIHWW
*Moe's Lucky Seven.* 1994. WOMP94

MEYER, MICHAEL, 1921–2000
*No* (adapted by). *See* Heiberg, Johan. *No*

MEYERS, PATRICK, 1947–
*K2; a Play in One Act.* 1982. BES82

MHAPSEKAR, JYOTI, 1949–
*Bap re bap.* 1994. SECO
   Variant title: *Oh My God!*
*Oh My God! See* Bap re bap

MHLOPHE, GCINA, 1958–
*Have You Seen Zandile?* 1986. PERA

MICHAELS, SIDNEY, 1927–2011
  *Dylan.* 1964. BES63
  *Tchin-Tchin* (based on the play *Chin-Chin* by François
    Billetdoux). 1962. BES62

MICHEL, MARC ANTOINE AMEDEE, 1812–1868. *See*
  Labiche, Eugene, joint author

MICHENER, JAMES, 1907–1997
  *Tales of the South Pacific. See* Hammerstein II, Oscar
    and Logan, Joshua. *South Pacific* (adapted from)

MICINSKI, TADEUSZ, 1873–1918
  *The Ballad of the Seven Sleeping Brothers in China.*
    1934.
    Gerould, D., translator GERO

MICK, HETTIE LOUISE
  *The Maid Who Wouldn't Be Proper.* 1921? LAW

MICKEVICIUS, ADOMAS. *See* Mickiewicz, Adam

MICKIEWICZ, ADAM, 1798–1855
  *Dziady. See* Forefathers' Eve, Part III
  *Forefathers' Eve, Part III.* 1901.
    Segel, H., translator (revised earlier translations edited
      by Noyes, G.) POB

MIDDLEMASS, ROBERT M., 1885–1949. *See* Porter,
  Harold Everett, joint author

MIDDLETON, GEORGE, 1880–1967
  *Back of the Ballot.* 1915. FRIED
  *Nowadays.* 1914. MESCO
  — *See* Bolton, Guy Reginald, joint author

MIDDLETON, THOMAS, 1580–1627
  *A Chaste Maid in Cheapside.* 1612? DPR2, KINNR,
    MAME, WALL
  *A Game at Chess.* 1624. BROC
  *A Mad World, My Masters.* 1608. SALF
  *The Maiden's Tragedy.* ca.1611. WIGG
  *Michaelmas Term.* 1606? SCI, SCJ
  *A Trick to Catch the Old One.* 1608. BAS, LAWS, NEI,
    SPE
  *The Witch.* 1609–1616? COQJW
  *Women Beware Women.* 1622. BECK, GOM, LAWT,
    OLH, OLI2, WOMD
  — *See* Dekker, Thomas, joint author

———— and ROWLEY, WILLIAM
  *The Changeling.* 1622. BAS, BROC, DPR2, GIBS,
    GOM, HAPRA2, HAPRB2, HUST, JACOBA,
    KAYS, KINNR, LAWR, NEI, OLH, OLI2,
    ORNT, SALG, SCH, SCI, SCJ, SPE, TAT, TAU,
    TAUJ, WINE

*A Fair Quarrel.* 1617? OLH, OLI2
*The Spanish Gipsie.* 1623. GAYLE3

MIHURA, MIGUEL. *See* Mihura Santos, Miguel

MIHURA SANTOS, MIGUEL, 1905–1977
  *Ninette and a Gentleman from Murcia.* 1964.
    O'Connor, P., translator OCONNC
    Variant title: *Ninette y un señor de Murcia*
  *Ninette y un señor de Murcia. See* Ninette and a
    Gentleman from Murcia
  *Three Top Hats.* 1932.
    Wellwarth, G., translator BENA
    Variant title: *Tres sombreros de copa*
  *Tres sombreros de copa. See* Three Top Hats

MIKHAILOVA, OLGA, 1953–
  *Russian Dream.* (1994)
    Smith, M., translator SMB

MILAN, ANGIE
  *Dead Proud.* 1987. DEAD

MILES, CRESSIDA
  *Greenheart and the Dragon Pollutant.* 1993. SACR

MILES, KATE
  *I Hate You on Mondays.* 1995. PRER

MILGATE, RODNEY, 1934–
  *A Refined Look at Existence.* 1966. BRIMA3

MILLADO, CHRIS B., 1961–
  *Scenes from an unfinished country.* 1995. JUAN

MILLAN, LORRI, 1965– . *See* Dempsey, Shawna, joint
  author

MILLAR, RONALD, 1919–1998
  *Abelard and Heloise.* 1970. PLAN39
  *The Affair.* 1961. PLAJ2
  *Waiting for Gillian.* 1954. PLAN10

MILLAY, EDNA ST. VINCENT, 1892–1950
  *Aria da capo.* 1919. CHU, GASB, KRE, NORALWA
  *The King's Henchman.* 1927. TUCD
  *The Lamp and the Bell.* 1921. SHAY

MILLER, ALICE DUER, 1874–1942
  *Unauthorized Interviews.* 1917. FRIED

MILLER, ALLAN, 1929–
  *Faro Rides Again.* 1982. *See* Anonymous Plays. *Twenty-
    four Hours: A.M.*
  *The Fox.* 1981. WES13/14

MILLER, ARTHUR, 1915–2005
*After the Fall.* 1964. BES63
*All My Sons.* 1947. BARO, BES46, BROH, CLKJ,
FAMAF, GARW, GAVE, HATA, HEWE, LEVY,
MABC, MADB, PERR3, SILO, SIXB, STS,
WATTAD, WEAN
*The Creation of the World and Other Business.* 1972.
BES72
*The Crucible.* 1953. AMB, BAUL, BES52, COLD,
COOP, DODS, FOT, GART, GATB4, GATT,
GOLK, GUTH, GUTL, LOR, MIJY, MORV,
MORW, MORWA, MORWB, MORX, MORXB,
MORXD, MORXE, SUL, TAUJ, THEA53,
WATA, WOLC, WOTHA
Variant title: *Those Familiar Spirits*
*Death of a Salesman.* 1949. ABCD, ABCE, ABCG,
ALLK, ALLM, ALLN, ALLO, ANT, AUG, BAIH,
BAIK, BAIL, BAIM, BARIC, BARID, BARIE,
BARIF, BARIG, BARIH, BARK, BARKA,
BARKB, BARKC, BARKD, BARKE, BARKF,
BEATA, BENU, BES48, BIER, BLOC, BRIX,
BRIY, BRIZ, BRJ, BRJA, BROX, BROY, CALQ,
CEQA, COTX, DIEB, DIYL, DIYLA, DIYLB,
DIYLC, DIYLD, FOUM, FOUX, FRYE, FRYEA,
GARW, GATB3, GAVE, GILB, GUTDF, GUTDS,
GWYN, HAE, HAEA, HAEB, HAVL, HEA,
HEAA, HEAB, HEAC, HEAD, HEAL, HEALA,
HEALB, HUNT, JACOB, JACOBA, JACOBD,
JACOBE, KIRLA, KIRLB, KIRLC, KIRLD, KLIS,
LITI, LITIB, LITIC, LITID, LITIE, LITIF, LITJ,
LITJA, MANCG2, MANCH2, MANCIU, MANK,
MANL, MEY, MEYB, MEYC, MEYCA, MEYCB,
MEYD, MEYE, MEYF, NEWV, PERS, PERT,
PERU, PERV, PERW, PERX, PERY, PERZ, REIW,
REIWE, SSSI, SSSIA, SSSIB, SSSIC, STEI, STJM,
STJN, TREBA, TREBJ, TREC2, TREE3, TREI3,
TUCO, WARH, WARN, WATE, WISE, WISF
*An Enemy of the People. See* Ibsen, Henrik. *An Enemy
of the People* (adapted by)
*Incident at Vichy.* 1964. BES64, MARO
*The Man Who Had All the Luck.* 1943. CROZ1
*A Memory of Two Mondays.* 1955. ACE, LIEF, MIJH,
SSTF
*The Price.* 1968. BES67, GARTL
*Pussycat and the Expert Plumber Who Was a Man.*
1941. PROX
*The Ride Down Mount Morgan.* 1996 (revised). BES96
*Those Familiar Spirits. See* The Crucible
*A View from the Bridge.* 1956. BAIC, BES55, BRIU,
CLLC, CLM, CLN, COTKIR, COTQ, CUBH,
DIEA, DIYRD, DOWS, GART, HILP, HOGI,
HOGN, MOE, REIN, THEA56, ULAN, WORM

MILLER, CINCINNATUS HEINE, 1841?–1913. *See*
Miller, Joaquin, pseudonym

MILLER, DANIEL, 1843–1909?
*En gespräch zwischer zweb demokrate über politiks.*
18–? BUFF
*Noch eppes vom Peter seim handwerk.* BUFF
*Der Peter soil en handwerk lernen.* 18–? BUFF

MILLER, J. B.
*Bobby Supreme.* 1997. NEWR98

MILLER, J. P. (born James Pinckney Miller), 1919–2001
*The Rabbit Trap* (television play). 1955. READ2

MILLER, JAMES, 1706–1744
*Mahomet.* 1744. BELK7

MILLER, JAMES H., and LITTLEWOOD, JOAN
*John Bullion: A Ballet with Words.* GOOR

MILLER, JASON, 1939–2001
*Lou Gehrig Did Not Die of Cancer.* RICK
*That Championship Season.* 1972. BERS, BES71

MILLER, JOAQUIN (pseudonym of Cincinnatus Hiner
(or Heine) Miller), 1837?–1913
*The Danites in the Sierras.* 1877. HAL, RAVIT

MILLER, MAY, 1899–1995
*Christophe's Daughters.* PER
*Graven Images.* 1929. HARY, HARYB, RIR, RIRA
*Harriet Tubman.* 1935. HILEB, PER
*Nails and Thorns.* 1933. PERF, ROOTS
*Riding the Goat.* 1930. BRW, PER, RIR, RIRA
*Stragglers in the Dust.* 1930. PER

MILLER, SIGMUND STEPHEN, 1917–1998
*Cross Country.* 1975. WES1
*One Bright Day.* 1956. PLAN14

MILLER, SUSAN, 1944–
*Confessions of a Female Disorder.* 1973. HOF
*Cross Country.* 1975. WES1
*Introducing Dad.* 2000. *See* Ackermann, J. *Back Story:
A Dramatic Anthology.* HUMANA2000
*It's Our Town, Too.* 1993. ACTOR
*My Left Breast.* 1993. HUGH, HUMANA94
*Nasty Rumors and Final Remarks.* 1979. CURB

MILLER, TIM, 1958–
*My Queer Body.* 1992. JONT
*Naked Breath.* 1994. HUGH

MILLS, HUGH, 1913–1971
*The House by the Lake.* 1956. PLAN14
*The Little Glass Clock.* 1954. PLAN11

MILMAN, HENRY HART, 1791–1868
  *Belshazzar.* 1822? KOH2
  *The Fall of Jerusalem.* 1820. KOH2

MILNE, A. A. (ALAN ALEXANDER), 1882–1956
  *The Boy Comes Home.* 1918. SRY, SRYG
  *The Dover Road.* 1922. BES21, DICDT, MOD, WATT2
  *The Great Broxopp.* 1923. CHU
  *The Ivory Door.* 1927. TUCJ
  *Michael and Mary.* 1929. BES29
  *Mr. Pim Passes By.* 1919. CALM, CEU, MAD, THF,
    WATF2, WATI
  *Success.* 1923. COT, MYB
  *The Truth about Blayds.* 1921. MOSG, MOSH, TUCD,
    TUCM
  *The Ugly Duckling.* (1941) BART, PERR2, READ1

MILNER, ARTHUR, 1950–
  *Learning to Live with Personal Growth.* 1987.
    NEWCAD5
  *Zero Hour.* 1986. CTR

MILNER, HENRY M.
  *The Demon of Switzerland. See* Frankenstein; or, The
    Man and the Monster
  *Frankenstein; or, The Demon of Switzerland. See*
    Frankenstein; or, The Man and the Monster
  *Frankenstein; or, The Man and the Monster.* 1823.
    HOUR
    Variant titles: *Frankenstein; or, The Demon of
      Switzerland; The Demon of Switzerland; The Man
      and the Monster*
  *The Man and the Monster. See* Frankenstein; or, The
    Man and the Monster
  *Mazeppa.* 1831. VICT

MILNER, ROGER, 1925–
  *How's the World Treating You?* 1965. PLAN30

MILNER, RONALD, 1938–2004
  *Roads of the Mountaintop.* 1986. HILEB
  *The Warning—a Theme for Linda.* 1969. BLACQ
  *Who's Got His Own.* 1966. KINH, KINHB

MILTON, DAVID SCOTT, 1934–
  *Skin.* 1985. WOMQ

MILTON, JOHN, 1608–1674
  *Comus.* 1634. CLK1, HARC4, OLH, OLI2, PAR, RICH
  *Comus. See also* Colman, G. (altered by). BELK9
  *Samson Agonistes.* 1670? BARD, BELG12, FREG,
    GREB1, GREC1, GREAB, HAPT2, HARC4,
    KOH2, SML

MINNEY, RUBEIGH J., 1895–1979. *See* Lipscomb,
  William Percy, joint author

MIRA DE AMESCUA, ANTONIO, 1570?–1644
  *La adversa fortuna de don Alvaro de Luna.* 1624.
    MACU
  *El esclavo del demonio.* 1612. ALP

MIRBEAU, OCTAVE, 1850–1917
  *Les affaires sont les affaires.* 1903. BER
    Variant title: *Business Is Business*
  *Business Is Business. See* Les affaires sont les affaires
  *The epidemica.* 1898?
    Barzun, J., translator BENS2
    Variant title: *L'epidémie L'epidémie. See* The
      Epidemic

MIRCEA, ION, 1947–
  *Noah Sailing across Our Memory Is a Woman.* 1998?
    Ieronim, I., and McClinton, C., translator POQ

MIRCEVSKA, ŽANINA, 1967–
  *A Place I've Never Been To.* 1996.
    Mišić, S., translator LUZ

MIRZA FATH-ALI. *See* Fath'Al-, Akhundzadah

MIRZA FETH-ALI AKHOUD ZAIDE. *See* Fath'Al-,
  Akhundzadah

MISHIMA YUKIO, 1925–1970
  *The Lady Aoi.* 1956.
    Keene, D., translator WOTHC
  *Yoroboshi. See* Yoroboshi: The Blind Young Man
  *Yoroboshi: The Blind Young Man.* 1965.
    Takaya, T. T., translator TAK
    Variant title: *Yoroboshi*

"MR. PUNCH," pseudonym
  *A Dramatic Sequel to Hamlet; or, The New Wing at
    Elsinor.* 19th century BAT22
  *A Dramatic Sequel to The Lady of Lyons; or, In the
    Lyons Den.* 19th century BAT22
  *Omar and Oh My!* 19th century BAT21

"MR. S. MR. OF ART," pseudonym. *See* Stevenson,
  William

MITCHELL, ADRIAN, 1932–2008
  *The Tragedy of King Real.* 1983. LOWE
    — *See also* Brooks, Jeremy, jt. au.

MITCHELL, JOSEPH S., 1891–195?
  *Help Wanted.* 1929. ROOTS
  *Son-boy.* 1928. HARYL

MITCHELL, JULIAN, 1935–
  *A Family and a Fortune.* PLAN45
  *A Heritage and Its History.* 1965. PLAN30

MOLETTE, CARLTON, 1939– , and MOLETTE,
    BARBARA
*Noah's Ark.* 1974. CEN


MOLIERE, JEAN BAPTISTE POQUELIN, 1622–1673
*The Affected Young Ladies. See* Les précieuses ridicules
*L'amour médecin. See* Love Is the Best Doctor
*L'avare. See* The Miser
*Le bourgeois gentilhomme.* 1670. CLOUDS1, SCN
    Anonymous translator GAUB
    Baker, H., and Miller, J., translators CLF2, MALC,
        MALG2
    Bishop, M., translator BAUL, GRDBA31, TOU
    Cohen, R., translator EIGHT
    Malleson, M., translator and adapter PLAN6
    Porter, M., translator LOCLA
    Taylor, H., translator SAFF
    Wood, J., translator WELT
    Variant titles: *The Bourgeois Gentleman; The Cit
        Turned Gentleman; The Prodigious Snob; The
        Would-be Gentleman*
*The Bourgeois Gentleman. See* Le bourgeois
    gentilhomme
*The Cit Turned Gentleman. See* Le bourgeois
    gentilhomme
*The Critique of the School for Wives.* 1663.
    Bishop, M., translator GRDBA31
*The Doctor in Spite of Himself.* 1666.
    Anonymous translator COPB, INGW, KNIE, KNIF,
        KNIJ, SHAR
    Bishop, M., translator FRYE, LITIC
    Clark, B., translator LEV, LEVE
    Frame, D., translator BAIL, DIYRD
    Van Laun, H., translator SATI, WEAV2
    Wall, C., translator SMR
    Variant titles: *Le médecin malgré lui; The Physician
        in Spite of Himself*
*Doctor's Delight. See* Le malade imaginaire
*Dom Juan, ou les festin de Pierre. See* Don Juan
*Don John; or, The Libertine. See* Don Juan
*Don Juan.* 1665.
    Calder, J., translator LID
    Frame, D., translator BENSB1
    Ozell, J., translator and Mandel, O., adapter MARJ
    Wood, J., translator GRDBA31
    Variant titles: *Dom Juan, ou le festin de Pierre; Don
        John; or, The Libertine; Don Juan; or, The Stone
        Guest; The Libertine*
*Don Juan; or, The Stone Guest. See* Don Juan
*L'école de maris.* 1661.
    Anonymous translator BAT7
    Variant title: *School for Husbands*
*L'école des femmes.* 1662.
    Bishop, M., translator GRDBA31
    Malleson, M., translator and adapter PLAN10

    Van Laun, H., translator, and Dukore, B., adapter
        SEVT
    Wilbur, R., translator LITQ
    Variant title: *School for Wives*
*Les femmes savantes. See* The Intellectual Ladies
*The Flying Doctor.* 1645.
    Bermel, A., translator WILLG
    Variant title: *Le médecin volant.*
*The Forced Marriage.* 1664.
    Bermel, A., translator MIJT
    Variant title: *Le mariage forcé*
*Les fourberies de Scapin. See* Scapin
*The Gay Invalid. See* Le malade imaginaire
*The High-brow Ladies. See* Les précieuses ridicules
*The Hypochondriac. See* Le malade imaginaire
*The Hypocrite. See* Le Tartuffe
*The Imaginary Invalid. See* La malade imaginaire
*The Imposter. See* Le Tartuffe
*The Intellectual Ladies.* 1672.
    Fowlie, W., translator FOWL
    Variant title: *Les femmes savantes*
*The Libertine. See* Don Juan
*Love as a Doctor. See* Love Is the Best Doctor
*The Love Doctor. See* Love Is the Best Doctor
*Love Is the Best Doctor.* 1665.
    Kaye, M., adapter KAYF, SCVDT1
    Van Laun, H., translator RUSV
    Variant titles: *L'amour médecin; Love as a Doctor;
        The Love Doctor*
*Le malade imaginaire.* 1673.
    Anonymous translator KNIG, KNIH
    Baker, H., and Miller, J., translators BERP, BERPA,
        LOGG
    Bermel, A., translator BERMD
    Bishop, M., translator DEAR, GRDBA31
    Jackson, B., translator and adapter PLAN5
    Malleson, M., translator and adapter PLAN19
    Marmur, M., translator BERMG
    Variant titles: *Doctor's Delight; The Gay Invalid;
        The Hypochondriac; The Imaginary Invalid; The
        Robust Invalid; The Would-be Invalid*
*Le mariage forcé. See* The Forced Marriage
*Le médecin malgré lui. See* The Doctor in Spite of
    Himself
*Le médecin volant. See* The Flying Doctor
*Le misanthrope.* 1666. CLOU1, CLOUD1, LYO, SER,
    STJ1
    Anonymous translator BLON, CARP, CARPA,
        CROV, EDAD, GRIF, HOUS, SCNPL
    Baker, H., and Miller, J., translators ROB
    Bentley, G., translator MIL
    Bishop, M., translator BURG, DOWS
    Cohen, R., translator COI
    Frame, D., translator CHARN
    Grebanier, D., translator GREC1

Guth, H., translator GUTDF, GUTDS, GUTH

Malleson, M., translator and adapter PLAN11

Page, C., translator KRE, WALJ

Van Laun, H., translator BUCK, BUCL, BUCM, DEAP, HIB, HIBA, LOCM2, TRE, TREA2, TREB, TREC1, TREE1, TREI1

Wall, C., translator DRAD1, PLAB1

Wilbur, R., translator ABCA, ABCB, ABCD, ADV, ALTE, BAIC, BAIK, BARI, BARIA, BARID, BARJ, BARK, BARKA, BARKB, BARKC, BARKD, BARKE, BARKF, BENR4, BENSB1, BENSD, BLOND, COLD, CONO, DIEA, DIEB, DOLAN, FEFL, GOLD, GOOD, GOODE, HEA, HEAA, HEAB, HOUE, JACOB, JACOBA, JACOBD, JACOBE, KERN, KERO, LITC, PERS, PERT, PERU, PERV, PERW, PERX, PERZ, REIO, ROF, SCNQ, SSSI, SSSIA, SSSIB, SSSIC, VENA, VONS2, WAIW, WEIS, WEIW

Variant title: *The Misanthrope*

*The Misanthrope. See* Le misanthrope

*The Miser.* 1668.

Anonymous translator ASF, CARLO, CASH, CROS, THO

Baker, H., and Miller, J., translators ALT, BARU

Barnet, S., Berman, M., and Burto, W., translators BARB

Fielding, H., adapter BELK6

Fowlie, W., translator GRDBA31

Malleson, M., translator and adapter MARK, PLAN1

Nolte, C., translator and adapter PERR3

Ozell, J., translator THMF

Parks, L. C., translator ALLI, ALLJ, ALLK, ALLM, BENU, HAVH, HAVHA, SOUL

Sutherland, D., translator COTKIR

Van Laun, H., translator THOM, THON

Wall, C., translator CLKW

Wood, J., translator GOLH

Wormeley, K., translator STA

Variant title: *L'avare*

*The Mock Doctor. See* The Doctor in Spite of Himself

*The Physician in Spite of Himself. See* The Doctor in Spite of Himself

*Les précieuses ridicules.* 1659. LYO, SER, SERD

Anonymous translator COOP, SEBO, SEBP

Gassner, J., translator and adapter GATS

Variant titles: *The Affected Young Ladies; The High-brow Ladies; The Pretentious Ladies; The Ridiculous précieuses*

*The Pretentious Ladies. See* Les précieuses ridicules

*The Prodigious Snob. See* Le bourgeois gentilhomme

*The Ridiculous précieuses. See* Les précieuses ridicules

*The Robust Invalid. See* Le malade imaginaire

*Scapin.* 1671.

Parsell, D., translator HILPDH2

Quinn, M., translator WOLCS

Roth, M., translator CASH

Variant title: *Les fourberies de Scapin*

*School for Husbands. See* L'école de maris

*School for Wives. See* L'école des femmes

*Sganarelle.* 1660.

Malleson, M., translator and adapter PLAN11

Sweetkind, M., translator HOBI

*Le Tartuffe; ou, L'imposteur.* 1664. LYO, SER

Anonymous translator EVB2, MARL, SMO

Bishop, M., translator GRDBA31, VOLI

Brown, C., translator EVC2

Clare, M., translator THMF

Hampton, C., translator LAQCF

Hartle, R., translator DOWN

Hogan, R., and Molin, S., translators HOGF

Malleson, M., translator and adapter PLAN3

Page, C., translator HARC26, HOWM, HUD, MATT

Rosenberg, J., translator CALD, COTKICO, COTY, SMA

Van Laun, H., translator BUCK, BACL, BUCM, EVA2, WEAV2

Waldinger, R., translator REIN, SANE

Wall, C., translator BLAG, GREA

Waller, A., translator HOEP

Wilbur, R., translator ALLN, ALLO, ANTL, BRJA, BRJB, BRJC, CLLC, DEAS, DIYLA, DIYLB, DIYLC, DIYLD, HEAC, HEAD, HEALC, HILP, HILPDH2, JOHO, KINNS, LITIB, MALI2, MALN2, MEY, MEYB, MEYD, MEYE, MORWB, MORXE, NORGA, NORI2, NORIA2, NORIB2, NORIC2, NORJ2, NORJA, PERY, REIL, REIW, REIWE, SHRO, VANV2, WHFM, WOTHA, WOTHB, WOTHC

Wood, J., translator BRIX, BRIY, BRIZ, BRJ

Variant titles: *The Hypocrite; The Imposter; Tartuffe.*

*Tartuffe. See* Le Tartuffe

*The Would-be Gentleman. See* Le bourgeois gentilhomme

*The Would-be Invalid. See* Le malade imaginaire

MOLIN, S. E. *See* Hogan, R., joint author

MOLINA, TIRSO DE, pseudonym. *See* Téllez, Gabriel

MOLINARO, URSULE, 1916–2000

*The Abstract Wife.* 1961. NEWA2

*Breakfast Past Noon.* 1971. EAG, NEWWT

MOLLOY, M. J. *See* Molloy, Michael Joseph

MOLLOY, MICHAEL JOSEPH, 1917–1994

*The King of Friday's Men.* 1948. PLAN2

*The Paddy Pedlar.* 1953. OWEC

*The Visiting House.* 1946. HOGE

MOLNAR, FERENC, 1878–1952
*Csendélet. See* Still Life
*The Daisy. See* Liliom
*Liliom.* 1909.
  Glazer, B., translator BES20, CEW, DICDT, DICIN1,
    HAV, LEV, LEVE, MOSG, MOSH, STE, THF,
    TRE, TREA1, TREBA, TREC2, TREE2, TREI2,
    TUCG, TUCM, TUCN, TUCO, WHI
  Variant titles: *The Daisy; The Lily*
*The Lily. See* Liliom
*The Play in the Castle. See* The Play's the Thing
*The Play's the Thing.* 1926.
  Wodehouse, P., translator and adapter BES26,
    COTKJ, GARZH
  Variant title: *The Play in the Castle*
*Still Life.* 1937.
  Anonymous translator CHR
  Variant title: *Csendélet*
*The Swan.* 1914.
  Baker, M., translator BES23
  Glazer, P., translator CHA, CHAN

MONCRIEFF, WILLIAM THOMAS, 1794–1857
*Giovanni in London; or, The Libertine Reclaimed.* 1828.
  MARJ
  Variant title: *The Libertine Reclaimed*
*The Libertine Reclaimed. See* Giovanni in London

MONGE-RAFULS, PEDRO R., 1943–
*Trash: A Monologue.* 1995. SVICH

MONKHOUSE, ALLAN NOBLE, 1858–1936
*The Conquering Hero.* 1924. HAU
*First Blood.* 1926. MOSO
*The Grand Cham's Diamond.* 1924. BEAC10, COOK2,
  PROB
  Variant title: *The Grand Cham's Necklace*
*The Grand Cham's Necklace. See* The Grand Cham's
  Diamond
*Mary Broome.* 1911. PLAP2

MONROE, MICHAEL
*Politesse: A Piece for Tape and Landscape.* 1982.
  PLACE

MONSON, WILLIAM N.
*The Nihilist.* 1971. BALLE8

MONTANO, SEVERINO, 1915–1980
*Sabina.* 1953. EDAD

MONTCHRESTIEN, ANTOINE DE, ca.1575–1621
*L'Ecossaise. See* La Reine d'Ecosse
*The Queen of Scots. See* La Reine d'Ecosse

*La Reine d'Ecosse.* (1601) FALE
  Bourque, J. H., translator FOUAF
  Variant titles: *L'Ecossaise; The Queen of Scots*

MONTCHRÉTIEN, ANTOINE DE. *See* Montchrestien,
  Antoine de

MONTELLANO, BERNARDO ORTIZ DE. *See* Ortiz de
  Montellano, Bernardo

MONTENOY, CHARLES PALISSOT DE. *See* Palissot de
  Montenoy, Charles

MONTERO, GLORIA, 1933–
*Frida K.* 1994. BREK

MONTES HUIDOBRO, MATIAS, 1931–
*La navaja de Olofe. See* Olofe's Razor
*Olofe's Razor.* 1982.
  Gonzalez-Cruz, L., and Colecchia, F., translators
    GONZ
*Your Better Half.* 1991.
  Miller, D., and Cortina, L., translators CUB

MONTGOMERY, ROBERT, 1946–
*Subject to Fits.* 1971. GARTL

MONTHERLANT, HENRY DE, 1896–1972
*Le cardinal d'Espagne. See* The Cardinal of Spain
*The Cardinal of Spain.* 1969.
  Griffin, J., translator PLAN37
  Variant title: *Le cardinal d'Espagne*
*Le maître de Santiago. See* The Master of Santiago
*The Master of Santiago.* 1947.
  Griffin, J., translator ULAN
  Variant title: *La maître de Santiago*
*Port-Royal.* 1954.
  Griffin, J., translator HAYE
*The Queen after Death. See* La reine morte
*La reine morte.* 1942. PUCC
  Griffin, J., translator COTKW
  Variant title: *The Queen after Death*

MONTI, RICARDO, 1944–
*Una noche con Magnus e hijos.* 1970. PARRI

MONTLEY, PATRICIA, 1942–
*Sisters.* 1981. CURB

MONZAEMON CHIKAMATSU. *See* Chikamatsu,
  Monzaemon

MOOCK, ARMANDO. *See* Moock Bousquet, Armando

MOOCK BOUSQUET, ARMANDO, 1894–1942
*La serpeinte.* 1920. ALPE

MOODIE, ANDREW, 1967–
*A Common Man's Guide to Loving Women.* 1999.
SEARS2
*Riot.* 1995. BEYO (excerpt), SEARS1

MOODY, WILLIAM VAUGHN, 1869–1910
*The Death of Eve.* 1912? KRE
*The Faith Healer.* 1909. QUIJ, QUIJR, QUIK, QUIL,
QUIN
*The Great Divide.* 1906. AMENW, BES99, DICD,
DOWM, GARX, MONR, WATTAD
Variant title: *A Sabine Woman*
*A Sabine Woman. See* The Great Divide

MOORE, CHARLES MICHAEL, 1948–2003
*Love's Light in Flight.* 1984. KINHN

MOORE, EDWARD, 1712–1757
*The Foundling.* 1748. BELK13
*The Gamester.* 1753. BELK12, BOO

MOORE, EDWARD J., 1935–
*The Sea Horse.* 1974. BES73

MOORE, ELISE, 1975–
*Live with It.* 1994. RUN

MOORE, ELVIE A., 1942–
*Angela Is Happening.* 1971. RAVIT

MOORE, HONOR, 1945–
*Mourning Pictures.* 1974. NEWWT

MOORE, MARSHALL
*The Charioteers; or, A Roman Holiday.* 1905. MAYER

MOORE, MAVOR, 1919–2006
*Customs.* BELLW, RALPH
*Inside Out. See* The Pile, the Store, Inside Out
*The Pile. See* The Pile, the Store, Inside Out
*The Pile, the Store, Inside Out* (three short plays).
(1971–73) KAL2
Variant titles: *The Pile; The Store; Inside Out*
*The Store. See* The Pile; the Store; Inside Out

MOORE, PAUL T., 1956–
*Daddy* (television play). 1988. HEID

MOOTSENG, BOLI
*"Social Avenue."* 2000. ZEE1

MORAD, GOWAR-E, pseudonym. *See* Sa'edi,
Gholamhoseyn

MORAGA, CHERRIE, 1952–
*Giving up the Ghost.* 1989. ACTOR, WATTAD, WIEG
*Heart of the Earth: A Popol Vuh Story.* 1994. PURO
*Heroes and Saints.* 1992. PERC
*The Hungry Woman: A Mexican Medea.* 1995. SVICH
*Mexican Medea: La Llorona Retold* (work in progress).
1994. ARRIZ
*Shadow of a Man.* 1990. FEY
*Watsonville: Some Place Not Here* (music by John
Santos with Gilberto Gutierrez). 1995. PLACGH

MORAL, JOSE ZORILLA Y. *See* Zorrilla y Moral, José

MORATIN, LEANDRO FERNANDEZ DE, 1760–1828
*The Girls' Acquiescence. See* El sí de las niñas
*El sí de las niñas.* 1805. BRET, MARLI1
Davis, W., translator FLOS
Variant titles: *The Girls' Acquiescence; When a Girl
Says Yes*
*When a Girl Says Yes. See* El sí de las niñas

MORE, CHARLES CA., 1851–1940
*Die verrechelte rechler. See* Barba, Preston Albert. *Die
verrechelte rechler* (adapted from the novel by)
*Es wasch Heller's Chrischtdag's zug. See* Iobst,
Clarence F. *Es Heller's Chrischtdag* (based on the
story by)

MORE, HANNAH, 1745–1833
*Belshazzar.* 1782? KOH2
*Daniel.* 1782? KOH2
*David and Goliath.* 1782? KOH2
*Moses in the Bulrushes.* 1782? KOH2
*Percy.* 1780. INCA7

MORETO Y CABANA, AGUSTIN. *See* Moreto y
Cavana, Agustín

MORETO Y CAVANA, AGUSTIN, 1618–1669
*El desdén con el desdén.* 1654. ALP, MACU
Variant titles: *Donna Diana; Love's Victory; or, The
School for Pride*
*Donna Diana. See* El desdén con el desdén
*Love's Victory; or, The School for Pride. See* El desdén
con el desdén

MORGAN, CHRIS, 1958– . *See* Ross, Lesley, joint author

MORGAN, DIANA, 1908–1996
*A House in the Square.* 1940. FIR

—— and MacDERMOT, ROBERT
*All Smart Women Must* (from *The Gate Revue*). 1939.
    YEAR
*–And Friend* (from *The Gate Revue*). 1939. YEAR
*The Bacchante* (from *Swinging the Gate*). 1940. YEAR
*Folk Songs* (from *New Ambassadors Revue*). 1941.
    YEAR
*The Guardsman.* YEAR
*Kensington Girls* (from *The Gate Revue*). 1939. YEAR
*South Coast Women* (from *Swinging the Gate*). 1940.
    YEAR

MORGAN, SHARON
*Ede hud. See* Magic Threads
*Magic Threads.* 1996. ONE
    Variant title: *Ede hud*

MORGILLO, ANTONIETTA
*The Olive Tree.* 1990. AROUN *See* Crea, Teresa, joint
    author

MORI, BRIAN
*Adult Fiction.* 2000. NEWR2000

MORITZ, DENNIS, and LELAND, MICHAEL, II
*Just the Boys.* 1997. ALG

MORLEY, CHRISTOPHER DARLINGTON, 1890–1957
*Good Theatre.* 1926? CHU
*Really, My Dear . . .* 1928? WEE
*Rehearsal.* 1922? SHAY
*Thursday Evening.* 1922? PEN
*Wagon-lits.* 1928? WEE

MORLEY, JILL
*True Confessions of a Go-go Girl.* 1998. WOMP98

MORLEY, ROBERT, 1908–1992, and LANGLEY,
    NOEL
*Edward, My Son.* 1948. BES48

MORNIN, DANIEL, 1956–
*Müller's Dancers* (English version by). *See* Németh,
    Ákos. *Müller's Dancers*

MOROSS, JEROME, 1913–1983
*The Golden Apple. See* Latouche, John. *The Golden
    Apple* (music by)

MORRIS, MRS. ELIZABETH (WOODBRIDGE), 1870–
    1964
*The Crusade of the Children.* 1923? FED1

MORRIS, LAWRENCE "BUTCH", 1947–
*Tenement Lover: No Palm Trees/in New York City*
    (music by).

*See* Hagedorn, Jessica. *Tenement Lover: No Palm Trees/
    in New York City*

MORRIS, LLOYD R., 1893–1954. *See* Van Druten, John,
    joint author

MORRIS, MARKLEY
*Alice.* 1984. *See* Anonymous Plays. *The AIDS Show . . .*
*Nobody's Fool.* 1984. *See* Anonymous Plays. *The AIDS
    Show . . .*

MORRIS, ROBERT J., 1945–
*Paradise Tours.* 1976. KUMU

MORRISON, CONALL, 1966–
*Hard to Believe.* 1995. FAIR

MORRISSEY, KIM, 1955–
*Poems for Men Who Dream of Lolita.* 1992. MYTH
    (excerpt)

MORSE, CARL, 1934–2008
*Annunciation.* 1991. HELB

MORSELLI, ERCOLE LUIGI, 1882–1921
*Acqua sul fuoco. See* Water upon Fire
*Il domatore Gastone. See* Gastone the Animal Tamer
*Gastone the Animal Tamer.* 1923.
    Goldberg, I., translator GOL
    Variant title: *Il domatore Gastone*
*Water upon Fire.* 1920.
    Goldberg, I., translator GOL
    Variant title: *Acqua sul fuoco*

MORTIMER, SIR JOHN CLIFFORD, 1923–2009
*Bermondsey.* 1970. RICK
*David and Broccoli.* 1960. CONB1
*The Dock Brief.* 1957. LOND1, PLAN17
*What Shall We Tell Caroline?* 1958. PLAN17

MORTIMER, LILLIAN, ca.1870–1946
*No Mother to Guide Her.* 1905. AMP8

MORTON, CARLOS, 1947–
*El jardin.* 1974. TEX
*Las many muertes de Richard Morales. See* The Many
    Deaths of Danny Rosales
*The Many Deaths of Danny Rosales.* 1976. BARKF
    Variant title: *Las many muertes de Richard Morales*
*Rancho Hollywood.* 1979. HOWM, KANEL

—— and VIGIL, ANGEL
*Cuentos.* 1988. PRIMA88

MORTON, HUGH, pseudonym. *See* McClellan, C. M. S.

MORTON, JOHN MADDISON, 1811–1891
*Box and Cox.* 1847. BOOA4, BOOM, THO

MORTON, THOMAS, 1764?–1838
*Secrets Worth Knowing.* 1798. INCA3
*Speed the Plough.* 1800. MOR, NIC
*Zorinski.* 1795. INCA3

MORUM, WILLIAM. *See* Dinner, William, joint author

MOSAKOWSKI, SUSAN
*Cities Out of Print.* 1989. MEDN

MOSALELE, LUCKY 'PIETERS', 1969–
*Mogomotsiemang? (Who Will Comfort Me?).* 2000.
ZEE2

MOSEL, TAD (b. George Ault Mosel, Jr.), 1922–2008
*All the Way Home* (based on *A Death in the Family* by
James Agee). 1960. BES60, GARSA

MOSER, GUSTAV VON, 1825–1903
*Ultimo.* 1875. *See* Daly, Augustin. *The Big Bonanza*
(adapted from)

MOSES, DANIEL DAVID, 1952–
*Kyotopolis.* 1993. BEYO (excerpt)

MOSS, ALFRED CHARLES and NEWHARD,
ELWOOD L.
*H.M.S. Pinafore*; *oder, Das maedle und ihr sailor kerl*
(based on the opera by W. S. Gilbert and Sir A. S.
Sullivan). 1882. BUFF

MOSS, HOWARD, 1922–1987
*No Strings Attached.* 1944? NEWDI44

MOSS, LELAND, d.1990
*Murray 1981.* 1984. *See* Anonymous Plays. *The AIDS
Show . . .*
*Murray 1983.* 1984. *See* Anonymous Plays. *The AIDS
Show . . .*
*Murray 1982.* 1984. *See* Anonymous Plays. *The AIDS
Show . . .*
*Murray Now.* 1984. *See* Anonymous Plays. *The AIDS
Show . . .*

MOTOKIYO, SEAMI. *See* Zeami

MOTOYASU, ZEMBO. *See* Zembo, Motoyasu

MOTTE FOUQUE, HENRI AUGUSTE, BARON DE LA,
1698–1774
*Undine. See* Giraudoux, Jean. *Ondine* (from the novel by)

MOTTEUX, PETER ANTHONY, 1663–1718. *See*
Ravenscroft, Edward, joint author

MOTTLEY, JOHN, 1692–1750. *See* Jevon, Thomas, joint
author

MOUAWAD, WAJDI, 1968–
*Journée de noces chez les Cro-Magnons. See* Wedding
Day at the Cro-Magnons'
*Wedding Day at the Cro-Magnons'.* 1994.
Tepperman, S., translator PLAWE
Variant title: *Journée de noces chez les Cro-
Magnons*

MOWATT, MRS. ANNA CORA (OGDEN)
RITCHIE. *See* Ritchie, Mrs. Anna Cora (Ogden)
Mowatt

MOXLEY, GINA
*Danti-Dan.* 1995. BOUR, DAZZ

MOYES, PATRICIA, 1923–2000
*Time Remembered. See* Anouilh, Jean. *Time
Remembered* (translator and adapted by)

MOZART, WOLFGANG AMADEUS, 1756–1791
*Eine Kleine Nachtmusik. See* Wheeler, Hugh. *A Little
Night Music* (title from)

MROZEK, SŁAWOMIR, 1930–
*Joy in Earnest. See* Afanasjeu, J., and the Bim-Bom
Troupe *Faust*; Afanasjew, J., and the Bim-Bom
Troupe. *Snouts*; and Mrozek, S., *The Professor*
*The Police.* 1958.
Bethell, N., translator SCNP
Variant title: *Policja*
*Policja. See* The Police
*The Professor* (part of *Joy in Earnest*). 1956.
Gerould, D., and Gerould, E., translators TWEN
*Striptease.*
Gruenthal, L., translator 1961. WOTHA
*Tango.* 1965.
Bethell, N., and Stoppard, T., translators THOR
Manheim, R., and Dzieduscycka, T., translators
GROV, NIL

MSOMI, WELCOME, 1943–
*uMabatha.* 1995. ADAP

MTSHALI, THULANI S., ca.1963–2002
*Weemen* 1996. PERA

MTWA, PERCY, 1954–
*Bopha.* 1986. WOZA

—— and NGEMA, MBONGENI, and SIMON,
  BARNEY
*Woza Albert!* 1982. BANH, BPW, HOWM, WOZA

MUELLER, LAVONNE
*Fire in the Killing Zone.* 1989. MIHWW
*Killings on the Last Line.* 1979. WOMS
*Little Victories.* 1983. WOMS2
*Violent Peace.* 1990. MIHPW

MUELLER, ROSS, 1967–
*No Man's Island.* 1997. JONI

MUKERJI, DHAN GOPEL, 1890–1936
*The Judgment of Indra.* 1920. PATM3, PATP

MUKHERJEE, ARUN, 1937–
*Mareech, the Legend.* 1973.
  Mohanty, U., translator DESH

MULCASTER, RICHARD, ca.1530–1611
*The Queen's Majesty's Passage.* 1559. KINNR

MULLER, HEINER, 1929–1995
*Hamletmachine.* 1978.
  Weber, C., translator ADAP, BARN, BARNA,
    WOTHC, WOTHM
*Mommsen's Block.* 1994.
  Weber, C., translator WEBER

MULLER, ROMEO, 1928–1992
*The Great Git-away.* 1966. BALLE3

MULLETT, ANDREW
*A Right Wally.* 1989. PLACB

MULVEY, TIMOTHY J.
*Letter to Tuffy.* 194–? PROI

THE MUMMERS TROUP, 1972–1982
*Makin' Time with the Yanks.* 1981. PETERS
*They Club Seals, Don't They?* 1978. PETERS

MUNDAY, ANTHONY, 1553–1633
*The Death of Robert, Earle of Huntington.* 1599.
  KNIRH (excerpts)
*The Downfall of Robert, Earle of Huntington.* 1599.
  KNIRH
*Sir John Oldcastle, Part I* (sometimes attributed to). *See*
  Anonymous Plays. *Sir John Oldcastle, Part I*
*Sir Thomas More* (sometimes attributed to). *See*
  Anonymous Plays. *Sir Thomas More*
*The Triumphs of Re-united Britannia.* 1605. KINNR

MUNFORD, ROBERT (COLONEL), 1730?–1784
*The Candidates; or, The Humours of a Virginia
  Election.* (1798) MONR
  Variant title: *The Humours of a Virginia Election*
*The Humours of a Virginia Election. See* The Candidates
*The Patriots.* 1778. PHI

MUNGIU-PIPPIDI, ALINA, 1964–
*The Evangelists.* 2000.
  Mungiu-Pippidi, A., and Taub, M., translator POQ

MUNIZ, CARLOS, 1927–
*The Inkwell.* O'Connor, P., translator OCONNF

MUNK, KAJ (b. Kaj Petersen), 1898–1944
*E gelykke.* 1939.
  Jones, L., translator MODS
*Herod the King.* 1933.
  Keigwin, R., translator CONT
  Variant title: *En idealist*
*En idealist. See* Herod the King
*Niels Ebbesen.* 1942.
  Larsen, H., translator SCAN2

MUNRO, CHARLES KIRKPATRICK, 1889–1973
*At Mrs. Beam's.* 1923. MART, MOSO, PLAP3
*The Rumour.* 1922. MYB

MUNRO, RONA, 1959–
*Bold Girls.* 1990. FIFHL3
*Piper's Cave.* 1985. PLABE5
*Saturday at the Commodore.* 1989. CALE

MUNROE, JAN, 1952–
*Alligator Tails.* 1983. WES19/20

MURDOCH, FRANK HITCHCOCK, 1843–1872
*Davy Crockett; or, Be Sure You're Right, Then Go
  Ahead.* 1872. AMP4, CLA

MURDOCH, IRIS, 1919–1999, and PRIESTLEY, JOHN
  BOYNTON
*A Severed Head.* 1963. PLAJ2

MURPHY, ARTHUR, 1727–1805
*All in the Wrong.* 1761. MOR
*The Apprentice.* 1756. BELC1
*The Citizen.* 1761. BELC3
*Grecian Daughter.* 1772. BELG13
*The Old Maid.* 1761. BELC2
*The Orphan of China.* 1759. BELG14
*School for Guardians.* 1767. BELG14
*Three Weeks after Marriage; or, What We Must All
  Come To.* 1764. BELC4

*The Upholsterer.* 1758. BELC1, BEVI
*The Way to Keep Him.* 1760. BELG13, BEVI, NIC
*Zenobia.* 1768. BELG13

MURPHY, DALLAS
*The Terrorists.* 1979. PLACF

MURPHY, GRACE, 1888–1975. *See* Lavery, Emmet, joint author

MURPHY, JIMMY, 1962–
*The Muesli Belt.* 2000. NEWPAB3
*A Picture of Paradise.* 1997. DAZZ

MURPHY, PETER
*Bluffing.* 1982. YOUP

MURPHY, VINCENT. *See* Manley, Frank, joint author

MURRAY, DAVID, 1955–
*Primitive World: An Anti-nuclear Jazz Musical* (music by). *See* Jones, Leroi. *Primitive World: An Anti-nuclear Jazz Musical*

MURRAY, JUDITH SARGENT, 1751–1820
*The Traveler Returned.* 1796. KRIT

MURRAY, ROBERT BRUCE
*The Good Lieutenant.* 1965. GARZAL

MURRAY, STEVE
*Rescue and Recovery.* 1999. CLUM

MURRAY, THOMAS C., 1873–1959
*Birthright.* 1910. CAP
*Maurice Harte.* 1912. OWEC

MURRAY, WILLIAM HENRY, 1790–1852
*Diamond Cut Diamond.* 1838. BOOA4

MURRELL, JOHN, 1945–
*Memoir.* 1977. DOOL, PLAN48

MUSINGA, VICTOR ELAME, 1946–
*The Tragedy of Mr. No-Balance.* 1966. AFR2

MUSSET, ALFRED DE, 1810–1857
*Camille and Perdican.*
    Meyer, P., translator WEAN
*Les caprices de Marianne.* 1851. BOR
    Variant title: *The Follies of Marianne*
*The Chandelier.* 1847.
    Chambers, W., translator BAT9
*A Door Should Be either Open or Shut.* 1848.

Barzun, J., translator BENS3
    Variant title: *Il faut qu'une porte soit ouverte ou fermée*
*Fantasio.* 1834. CLOU2, CLOUD2, CLOUDS2
    Baring, M., translator BENS1, BENT2
*The Follies of Marianne. See* Les caprices de Marianne
*Il faut qu'une porte soit ouverte ou fermée. See* A Door Should Be either Open or Shut
*Lorenzaccio.* 1896.
    Bruce, R., translator BENT6
*No Trifling with Love. See* On ne badine pas avec l'amour
*On ne badine pas avec l'amour.* 1861. COM, GRA
    Pellissier, R., translator TREB, TREC1, TREE1, TREI1
    Variant title: *No Trifling with Love*

MUTWA, CREDO, 1921–
*uNosilemela.* 1973. SOUT

MWANSA, DICKSON M.
*The Family Question.* 1989. NTIR

MYERS, CAROLYN. *See* Baum, Terry, joint author

MYGATT, TRACY DICKINSON, 1885–1973
*The Sword of the Samurai.* 1925? FED2

MYLER, RANDAL
*Adventures of Huckleberry Finn* (adapted from the novel by Mark Twain). 1990. PRIMA89–90

—— and HARELIK, MARK
*Lost Highway: The Music and Legend of Hank Williams.* 1987. PRIMA 89–90

MYRTLE, FREDERICK S., 1868?–
*Gold.* 1916. BOH3

NABBES, THOMAS, 1605–1946
*Covent Garden.* 1632–3? BUL3
*Hannibal and Scipio.* 1635. BUL3
*Tottenham Court.* 1633. BUL3

NADIPUTRA (pseudonym of Almahdi Al-Haj Ibrahim), 1946–
*Encong.* 1985. MLAS

NAGAI AI, 1951–
*Time's Storeroom.* 1994.
    Shapiro, D., translator HACJT1

NAGLE, URBAN, FATHER, O. P., 1905–1965
*Savonarola, the Flame of Florence.* 1941. THEC

NAGY, ANDRAS, 1956–
   *The Seducer's Diary* (English version by Julian Garner).
      1992.
      Pathy, I., translator UPOR

NAGY, PHYLLIS, 1962–
   *Trip's Cinch*. 1994. HUMANA94
   *Weldon Rising*. 1992. PLABE10

NAHARRO, BARTHOLOME TORRES DE. *See* Torres
   de Naharro, Bartholomé de

NAIDOO, MUTHAL, 1935–
   *Flight from the Mahabarath*. 1998. PERA

NAJAC, EMILE DE, 1828–1889. *See* Sardou, Victorien,
   joint author

NAKADA, MANSUKE. *See* Tsuuchi, Hanjurō, joint
   author

NAKAMURA, MATAGORŌ, 1913–2009, and
      BRANDON, JAMES
   *Chūshigura: The Forty-seven Samurai*. 1979.
      Brandon, J., Berberich, J., and Feldman, M.,
      translators WOTHC

NA'LBANDIAN, ABBAS, 1947–1989
   *A Modern, Profound and Important Research in the
      Fossils of the 25th Geological Era*. 1968.
      Kapuscinski, G., translator MOCPD

NALUJUK PLAYERS, 1985– . *See* Innuinuit Theatre
   Company, joint author

NAMBOKU IV, TSURUYA. *See* Tsuruya, Namboku IV

NAMIKI, GEIJI. *See* Namiki, Sōsuke, joint author

NAMIKI, GOHEI III, 1789–1855
   *Kanjinchō. See* The Subscription List
   *The Subscription List*. 1840.
      Scott, A., translator ANDF, ASF, BRA
      Variant titles: *Kanjinchō; The Subscription Scroll*
   *The Subscription Scroll. See* The Subscription List

NAMIKI, SENRYŪ, pseudonym. *See* Namiki, Sōsuke

NAMIKI, SHŌZŌ I. *See* Namiki, Sōsuke, joint author

NAMIKI, SŌSUKE (Namiki Senryū, pseudonym), 1695–
      1751
   *Suma Bay*. 1751. (Kabuki adaptation of scene from Act
      2 of *Ichonotani futaba gunki*)
      Brandon, J., BRAZ

—— and NAMIKI, SHŌZŌ I; NAMIKI, GEIJI; and
      ASADA, ITCHO
   *Chronicle of the Battle of Ichinotani*. 1751.
      Brandon, J., translator KAB
      Variant title: *Ichinotani Futaba Gunki*
   *Ichinotani Futaba Gunki. See* Chronicle of the Battle of
      Ichinotani
   — *See also* Takeda, Izumo, joint author

NARUI, YUTAKA, 1961–
   *Farewell to Huckleberry*. 1991.
      Shapiro, D., translator HACJT2
      Variant title: *Hakkuruberii ni sayonara wo*
   *Hakkuruberii ni sayonara wo. See* Farewell to
      Huckleberry

NASCIMENTO, ABDIAS DO, 1914–
   *Sortilege II: Zumbi Returns*. 1991.
      Nascimento, E., translator BPW

NASEV, SASKO, 1966–
   *Who Do You Belong To?* 1991.
      Dinevska, T., translator LUZ

NASH, N. RICHARD, 1916–2000
   *The Rainmaker*. 1954. CORB, CORBA

NASH, OGDEN, 1902–1971. *See* Perelman, S. J., joint
   author

NASHE, THOMAS, 1567–1601
   *Summer's Last Will and Testament*. (1600) DPR1

NATEL, JEAN-MARC, 1942–
   *Les misérables* (original French text by). *See* Boubil, A.,
      and Schönberg, C. *Les misérables*

NATIVE AMERICAN THEATER ENSEMBLE, 1972–
      1975?, and GEIOGAMAH, HANEY, joint author
   *Coon Cons Coyote*. 1973. GEIO

NAUGHTON, BILL, 1910–1992
   *A Special Occasion* (radio play). 1982. LEAK

N'DEBEKA, MAXIME, 1944–
   *Equatorium*. 1986.
      Brewster, T., translator AFRUBU1

NDJAVERA, DAWID STONE
   *The Bride and the Broom*. 2000. ZEE1

NDLOVU, DUMA
   *Sheila's Day*. 1989. PERA

NDLOVU, MALIKA, 1971–
   *A Coloured Place*. 1996. PERA

NEAL, JENNIFER
*Strawberries and Cream.* 1988. STRA

NEALE-KENNERLEY, JAMES. *See* Shaw, Peggy, joint
author

NEILHARDT, JOHN G., 1881–1973
*Black Elk Speaks. See* Sergel, Christopher. *Black Elk
Speaks* (based on the book by)

NEILSON, KEITH
*The End of the World; or, Fragments from a Work in
Progress.* 1968. BALLE6
Variant title: *Fragments from a Work in Progress*
*Fragments from a Work in Progress. See* The End of
the World

NEIPRIS, JANET, 1936–
*A Small Delegation.* 1992. WOMP99

NELEGA, ALINA, 1960– . *See* Cadariu, Alina Nelega

NELSON, MARIAH BURTON, 1956–
*Out of Bounds.* 1984. PLA

NELSON, RICHARD J., 1950–
*Bal.* 1979. ANTN
*Between East and West.* 1984. NEWQB
*Conjuring an Event.* 1976. MESSE
*James Joyce's The Dead* (based on the story by
James Joyce; lyrics by Richard Nelson and
Shaun Davey, music by Shaun Davey). 1999.
BES99
*Jungle Coup.* 1978. PLACF
*New England.* 1995. BES95
*Vienna Notes.* 1978. WOQ1

NEMEROV, HOWARD, 1920–1991
*Cain.* 1959? FAD

NEMETH, ÁKOS, 1964–
*Müller's Dancers* (English version by Daniel Mornin).
1992.
Melis, P., and Upor, L., translators UPOR

NEMETH, SALLY, 1960–
*Holy Days.* 1988. PLACG1
*Mill Fire.* 1989. MIHWW

NEMIROVICH–DANCHENKO, VLADIMIR
IVANOVICH, 1858–1943
*The Brothers Karamazoff* (based on the novel by Fedor
Dostoevskii). 1922?
Covan, J., translator MOSA

*Love and Death,* featuring "Aleko" by Rachmaninoff
(based on the story by Aleksandr Pushkin). 1891.
Seldes, G. and G., translators PLAH

NESTROY, JOHANN, 1802–1862
*The Talisman.* 1840.
Harrison, R., and Wilson, K., translators SCVN
Knight, M., and Fabry, J., translator and adapter
ANTH
Variant title: *Der talisman*
*Der talisman. See* The Talisman

NEUMANN, ALFRED, 1895–1952
*The Patriot. See* Dukes, Ashley. *Such Men Are
Dangerous* (adapted from)

NEVEUX, GEORGES, 1900–1982
*Juliette ou la cié des songes.* (1930) PROA

NEWBOUND, BERNARD SLADE. *See* Slade, Bernard

NEWHARD, ELWOOD L., 1858–193? *See* Moss, Alfred
Charles, joint author

NEWLEY, ANTHONY, 1931–1999. *See* Bricusse, Leslie,
joint author

NEWMAN, DAVID, 1937–2003, and BENTON,
ROBERT
*"It's a Bird, It's a Plane, It's Superman"* (music by
Charles Strouse, lyrics by Lee Adams). 1966. BES65

NEWMAN, MOLLY
*Shooting Stars.* 1986. PRIMA87

—— and DAMASHEK, BARBARA
*Quilters.* 1982. FAV

NEWSPAPER, STAFF OF THE LIVING. *See* Staff of the
Living Newspaper

NGEMA, MBONGENI, 1955–
*Asinamali.* 1987. WOZA
— *See* Mtwa, Percy, joint author

NGOC, NGUYEN THI MINH
*Beyond the Truth.* 2001. SECO

NHU, HO THI AI
*The Story of Mother.* 2001. SECO

NICCODEMI, DARIO, 1877–1934
*The Poet.*
Rietty, R., translator ALL
Variant title: *Il poeta*
*Il poeta. See* The Poet

NICHOLAS, DENISE, 1944–
*Buses*. 1988. KINHN

NICHOLS, ANNE, 1891–1966
*Abie's Irish Rose*. 1922. CEY, MOST

NICHOLS, DUDLEY, 1895–1960
*The Informer*. See O'Flaherty, Liam. *The Informer* (adapted by)

NICHOLS, PETER, 1927–
*A Day in the Death of Joe Egg*. 1968. BES67, DIEB
Variant title: *Joe Egg*
*Joe Egg*. See A Day in the Death of Joe Egg
*The National Health*. 1969. BES74
*Passion Play*. 1981. COTKB2

NICHOLS, ROBERT MALISE BOWYER, 1893–1944, and BROWNE, MAURICE
*Wings over Europe*. 1928. BES28, CHU, MACF, MOSG, MOSH

NICHOLSON, WILLIAM, 1948–
*Shadowlands*. 1989. BES90

NICOL, ERIC PATRICK, 1919–
*The Clam Made a Face*. 1967. KAL4

NICOLAU, VALENTIN, 1960–
*The Ghost from the First Class Waiting Room*. 2000. Stoian, G., translator POQ

NIEVA, FRANCISCO, 1927–
*Coronada and the Bull*. 1985. Signes, E., translator HOLTS
Variant title: *Coronada y el toro*
*Coronada y el toro*. See Coronada and the Bull
*La Señora Tártara*. 1980. SEIS2

NIGGLI, JOSEFINA, 1910–1983
*The Ring of General Macías*. BRNB
*Singing Valley*. 1936. PAJ
*This Bull Ate Nutmeg*. 1937? GALB

NIGHTENGALE, ERICA. See Cromelin, Caroline, joint author

NIGRO, DON
*Quint and Miss Jessel at Bly*. 2000. NEWR2000

NILSSON, REIDAR, and the TUKAK' THEATER ENSEMBLE
*Inuit—the People*. 1992. Brask, P., translator BRAKA

NIRDLINGER, CHARLES FREDERIC, 1863–1940
*The World and His Life*. See Echegaray y Eizaguirre, José. *The Great Galeoto* (translated and adapted by)

NISHIKAWA, LANE, and TALMADGE, VICTOR
*The Gate of Heaven*. 1996. ASIAM

NISSEN, KAJ, 1941–
*Fair Kirsten* (radio play). 1988. Garner, J., translator NEWDAN
Variant title: *Liden Kirsten*
*Liden Kirsten*. See Fair Kirsten

NIVELLE DE LA CHAUSEE, PIERRE CLAUDE. See La Chausée, Pierre Claude Nivelle de

NIVOIX, PAUL, 1893–1958. See Pagnol, Marcel, joint author

NKOSI, LEWIS, 1936–
*The Rhythm of Violence*. 1964. GREJ, LITT, WELT

NO SAYEMON, ENAMAI. See Enami Sayemon

NOAH, MORDECAI MANUEL, 1785–1851
*She Would Be a Soldier; or, The Plains of Chippewa*. 1819. MONR, MOSS1

NOBLE, JANET, 1939?–
*Away Alone*. 1989. NEWAMP2

NOBUMITSU, KANZE KOJIRO. See Kanze, Kojirō Nobumitsu

NOBUMORI, SUGIMORI. See Chikamatsu, Monzaemon

NODA, HIDEKI, 1955–
*Akaoni*. See The Red Demon Akaoni
*The Red Demon Akaoni*. 1996. Pulvers, R., translator HACJT4
Variant title: *Akaoni*

NODA, KŌGŌ, 1893–1968. See Ozu, Yasujirō, joint author

NOLAN, YVETTE, 1961–
*Annie Mae's Movement*. 1997. BREK (excerpt)
*Blade*. 1990. RUN
*Child*. 1996. BEYO (excerpt)

NOLTE, CHARLES M., 1923–2010
*A Christmas Carol* (adapted from the novel by Charles Dickens). PERR1
*Dracula* (adapted from the novel by Bram Stoker). PERR1

*Do Not Pass Go.* 1965. MIMN
*The Strange Case of Dr. Jekyll and Mr. Hyde* (adapted from the novel by Robert Louis Stevenson). PERR3

NOREN, LARS, 1944
*München-Athen. See* Munich-Athens
*Munich-Athens.* 1987.
    Anderman, G., translator NEWT
    Variant title: *München-Athen*

NORMAN, MARSHA (WILLIAMS), 1947–
*Getting Out.* 1977. BAIM, BES77, BES78, DIXP, GUTDS, HOWM, KILGC, LAQCW, WATTAD
*Loving Daniel Boone.* 1992. DIX
*'night, Mother.* 1981. BARIE, BARIF, BARIH, BARKC, BARKD, BARKE, BES82, COLD, GILB, HAEA, HAEB, HEAD, JACOB, JACOBA, JACOBD, JACOBE, KIRLD, LEVY, SSSIA, SSSIB, SSSIC, WOLC
*Third and Oak: The Laundromat.* 1978. BAIK
*Trudy Blue.* 1995. DIXD2, HUMANA95

NORTH, FRANCIS, 1761–1817
*The Kentish Barons.* 1791. COXJ

NORTON, THOMAS, 1532–1584. *See* Sackville, Thomas, joint author

NOTTAGE, LYNN, 1964–
*Poof!* 1993. HUMANA93, PLACA

NOVION, ALBERTO, 1881–1937
*Petroff's Junkshop.* 1934.
    Glickman, N., and Waldman, G., translators ARGJT

NOWLAN, ALDEN, 1933–1983, and LEARNING, WALTER
*The Dollar Woman.* 1977. NEWCAD2

NOWRA, LOUIS, 1950–
*The Golden Age.* 1985. AUS
*Inner Voices.* 1977. BRIM3

NTSHONA, WINSTON. *See* Fugard, Athol, joint author

N'TUMB, DIUR
*Lost Voices.* 1986.
    MacDougall, J., translator AFRUBU1
    Variant title: *Qui hurle dans la nuit?*
*Qui hurle dans la nuit? See* Lost Voices

NÜ, CH'I-CHIEH
*A Girl Setting Out for Trial.*
    Scott, A., translator SCY3

NUGENT, ELLIOTT, 1896–1980. *See* Thurber, James, joint author

NUGENT, RICHARD BRUCE, 1906–1987, and LOCKE, ALAIN
*Sahdji, an African Ballet* (music by William Grant Still). 1927. LOC

NUNEZ DE ARCE, GASPAR, 1834–1903
*The Face of Wood. See* El haz de leña
*El haz de leña.* 1872. BRET
    Variant title: *The Face of Wood*

NUNN, TREVOR, 1940–
*Cats* (additional lyrics by). *See* Lloyd Webber, Andrew. *Cats*

NUYDA, JUSTINO
*Anti Cristo.* 1910. PHIL
    Realubit, M., translator PHIL

NYATHI, FRANCIS SIFISO
*Tears of Fear in the Era of Terror.* 2000. ZEE2

NYS-MAZURE, COLETTE, 1939– . *See* Lison-Leroy, Françoise, joint author

NYSWANER, RON, 1956–
*Reservoir.* 1994. ACTOR

OAKES, MEREDITH, 1946–
*Mind the Gap.* 1995. PERZ

OATES, JOYCE CAROL, 1938–
*Black.* 1994. MIH
*Tone Clusters.* 1990. BARIG, BARKE, SCX

OBEY, ANDRE, 1892–1975
*Noah.* 1931.
    Wilmurt, A., translator and adapter GARZH
*Venus and Adonis.* 1932?
    Becker, W., translator BENS2

OBOLENSKY, KIRA
*Lobster Alice.* 1999. WOMP99

OBRENOVÍC, ALEKSANDAR, 1928–
*The Bird.* 1958. (part of his *Variations*)
    Drndíc, D., translator MIG

O'BRIEN, EDNA, 1932–
*A Cheap Bunch of Nice Flowers.* 1962. PLAN26

O'BRIEN, JUSTIN, 1906–1968
*Caligula. See* Camus, Albert. *Caligula* (adapted by)

O'HARA, KANE, 1722–1782
*The Golden Pippin*. 1773. BELC3
*Midas*. 1762. BELC2

ŌHASHI, YASUHIKO, 1956–
*Godzilla*. 1987.
    Gillespie, J., translator HACJT3
    Variant title: *Gojira*
*Gojira. See* Godzilla

OHNET, GEORGES, 1848–1918
*The Forge Master. See* The Iron Manufacturer
*The Iron Manufacturer*. 1883.
    Leslie, G., translator BAT9
    Variant titles: *The Forge Master; The Iron Master; Le maître de forges*
*The Iron Master. See* The Iron Manufacturer
*Le maître de forges. See* The Iron Manufacturer

OKABE, KŌDAI, 1945–
*Ayako: Cherry Blossoms Never Fall*. 1988.
    Kenny, D., translator HACJT5
    Variant title: *Ayako: haha no sakura wa chiranai sakura*
*Ayako: haha no sakura wa chiranai sakura. See* Ayako: Cherry Blossoms Never Fall

OKAMURA, SHIKO, 1881–1925
*The Zen Substitute*. 1963.
    Brandon, J., and Niwa, T., translators BRA

O'KEEFE, JOHN, 1747–1833
*Lie of a Day*. 1796. INCA10

O'KEEFE, JOHN, 1941–
*All Night Long*. MESSE, WOQ2
*Azteca*. 1984. WES19/20
*Bercilak's Dream*. 1982. PLACE
*Chamber Piece*. 1972. BALLE11
*Don't You Ever Call Me Anything but Mother*. 1983. WES19/20
*The Man in the Moon*. 1983. WES19/20

O'KELLY, DONAL
*Asylum! Asylum!* 1994. NEWPAB1
*Bat the Father Rabbit the Son*. 1988. FAIR
*The Dogs*. 1992. BOUR

OKITA, DWIGHT, 1958–
*The Rainy Season*. 1993. ASIAM

OKLAHOMA, D. K., pseudonym. *See* Davis, Donna

OKO, ATABO
*The Spoiler*. 1990. FINBN

OKONKWO, RUFUS
*The Game of Love*. 1964? OBI

OLDENBURG, CLAES, 1929–
*Fotodeath*. 1961. HILP

OLEKSAK, ROMAN, 1978–
*Niečoho viac, niečoho menej. See* Something More, Something Less
*Something More, Something Less*. 2000.
    Cockrell, K., translator CONTSL4
    Variant title: *Niečoho viac, niečoho menej*

OLESHA, YURI, 1899–1960
*The Conspiracy of Feelings*. 1929.
    Gerould, D. C., and Gerould, E. S., translators DUK
    Variant title: *Zagovor chyvstv*
*A List of Assets*. 1931?
    MacAndrew, A., translator GARZG, MABA
*Zagovor chyvstv. See* The Conspiracy of Feelings

OLIANSKY, JOEL, 1935–2002
*Here Comes Santa Claus!* 1962. GASY

OLIVE, JOHN, 1949–
*Star Skating*. 2000. *See* Ackermann, J. *Back Story: A Dramatic Anthology* HUMANA2000
*The Voice of the Prairie*. 1987. BES87

OLIVER, BRYAN
*Sector Three*. 1989. PLACB

OLIVIER-SAMPSON, LAURINDA, 1955–
*Gebroke onskuld (She Was Innocent)*. 2000. ZEE2
*A Moment in Our Lives*. 2000. ZEE1

OLMO, LAURO, 1922–1994
*La camisa. See* The Shirt
*The News Item*. 1963.
    Wellwarth, M., translator BENA
*The Shirt*. 1962.
    O'Connor, P., translator OCONNF
    Variant title: *La camisa*

OLMOS, CARLOS, 1947–2003
*Juegos profanos. See* Profane Games
*Profane Games*. 1970.
    Morton, CA., translator FFLD
    Variant title: *Juegos profanos*

OLSEN, ERNST BRUUN, 1923–
*The Bookseller Cannot Sleep*. (1963)
    Shaw, P., translator MNOD
    Variant title: *Men bog handleren ken ikke sove*
*Men bog handleren ken ikke sove. See* The Bookseller Cannot Sleep

O'MALLEY, MARY, 1941–
  *Once a Catholic.* 1977. BEST, PLAN47

OMATA, GARRETT H., 1958?–1997
  *S.A.M. I Am.* 1995. ASIAM

O'MORRISON, KEVIN, 1916–
  *The Long War.* 1966. BALLE4

O'NEAL, JOHN, 1940– , and WATKINS, NAYO
    BARBARA
  *You Can't Judge a Book by Looking at the Cover:
    Sayings from the Life and Writings of junebug
    jabbo jones, Volume II.* 1986. DEN

O'NEIL, DEBORAH, 1951–
  *Worm Moon.* 1990. RUN

O'NEILL, EUGENE GLADSTONE, 1888–1953
  *Ah, Wilderness!* 1933. BES33, CET, DAVK, HAVG,
    HIL, HOLM, JAFF, REIWE, WATA, WOLC,
    WOTHB
  *All God's Chillun Got Wings.* 1925. RAVIT
  *Anna Christie.* 1921. ASH, BES21, BLAG, CASS,
    CHAN, CHAP, CORD, CORE, CORF, COTE,
    COTH, CUBG, MOAD, RIL2, TRE, TREA1,
    TREBA, TREC2, TREE3, TREI3
  *Before Breakfast.* 1916. SHAY
  *Beyond the Horizon.* 1920. BES19, CORB, CORD,
    CORE, CORF, FULT, GORDP, HAPD, HAT,
    HAVD, HAVE, LOOA, LOOB, LOOC, LOOD,
    LOOE, LOOF, MIKL, QUIJR, QUIK, QUIL,
    QUIM, QUIN, ROB, WHK
  *Bound East for Cardiff.* 1916. BLAH, CONP, ELKE,
    GPA, NELS, SAND
  *Desire under the Elms.* 1924. ABCB, ALLK, ALLM,
    ALLN, ALLO, ALT, ALTE, BAC, BARC,
    BARKB, BARKE, BES24, BONB, BONC, BOW,
    BROE, CAPU, COTQ, CUBH, FREG, GASB,
    GATB1, GOO, HAVH, HEA, HEAA, HEAB,
    HEALC, HOEP, HOWP2, JACOB, JACOBA,
    JACOBD, JACOBE, KLIS, LEVY, LIEF, LIEG,
    LITC, MACN, MANCF2, MANCIO, MIJY,
    MOSG, MOSH, PERR2, RAY2, SANL, SCNT,
    SDQ, SEN, SSSF, VOLI, VOLP, WALJ, WARL,
    WEIM, WEIS, WHFM
  *Diff'rent.* 1920. COT
  *The Dreamy Kid.* 1919. LOC
  *The Emperor Jones.* BARK, BARKA, BARKD,
    BARKF, BES20, BLOC, BROX, CHU, CLK2,
    COHM, COLD, CUBE, DEAP, DICDT, DOWN,
    ELLK, FOUK, FOUM, HARB, HAVHA, HAVL,
    HATA, HUBA2, HUD, HUTC, LOC, LOCK,
    MAC, MACB, MACC, MACE, MACF, MAD,

    MIJA1, MOSJ, MOSK, MOSL, QUI, REIL,
    SCWG, SIXC, STS, TUCJ, UNTE2, WARF,
    WATC1, WATI, WORP, WOTHA, WOTHM
  *The Great God Brown.* 1926. BES25, DUR, FOUX,
    HAL, POCH2, STE, STEI, TAUJ, TUCD, TUCM,
    TUCN, TUCO
  *The Hairy Ape.* 1922. AND, ANDE, ANT, BERP,
    BERPA, BLA12, BLAJ, BLON, BLOND, BLOO,
    BPD, BRJ, BRJA, BRJB, BRJC, BROZ, CASH,
    CLH, CLKW, CORBA, DAV1, DICEM, DIEB,
    DOWM, FUL, GASB, GATB1, HARA, HEAC,
    HIB, HIBA, HIBB, HOWM, LEVG, LEVI,
    LITI, LITP, MANCA2, MANCB2, MANCD2,
    MANCE2, MANCG2, MANCH2, MANCI,
    MANCIA, MANCIU, MIL, RAI, SCX, SHA2,
    STL4, TREBA, TREBJ, TREC2, TREE3, TREI3,
    VENA, WAIT, WAIU, WAK, WATC2, WATO,
    WEIP, WHI, WOTHC
  *Hughie.* 1958. CASH, CLLC, GAT, GOLH, MIJH,
    ROY, SILS
  *The Iceman Cometh.* 1946. BES46, BLOC, CEQA,
    COK, GARW, KLIS, MIKE2, WATTAD
  *"Ile."* 1916. BEAC12, GASB, HOGN, KNIC,
    KNID, KNIE, KNIF, KNIG, KNIH, KNIJ, PEN,
    ROSENB, SUT3
  *In the Zone.* 1917. BROW, BURG, CARL, GREAB,
    HAP, MIJB, THO, WAGC2
  *Lazarus Laughed.* 1928. NELS, OXF, QUIO2
  *Long Day's Journey into Night.* 1956. BES56
  *The Long Voyage Home.* 1919. ASF, CARPA, COOP,
    LOCL, LOCLA, LOCLB, RAY2, ULAN
  *Marco Millions.* 1928. CHA, HUB, HUDS2, HUDT
  *A Moon for the Misbegotten.* 1947. BES56, GART,
    GILB, LOR, SSSI, SSSIA, SSSIB, SSSIC, TREBJ
  *The Moon of the Caribbees.* 1918. LEV, LEVE, LOO,
    MAF, MAFC
  *Mourning becomes Electra.* 1931. BES31, GRDBA60,
    WARH
  *The Rope.* 1919. ELLI2
  *Strange Interlude.* 1928. BES27, CORD, CORE, CORF,
    THF
  *A Touch of the Poet.* 1957. BES58, COXM, FOT,
    GARSA
  *Where the Cross Is Made.* 1918. BENP, COD, ING,
    INGA, PROW, SCWE, TOD

ONETTI, ANTONIO, 1962–
  *Bleeding Heart.* 1991.
    Ceballos, O., and Peate, M., translators DODGSS
    Variant title: *La puñalá*
  *La puñalá. See* Bleeding Heart

ONWUEME, (OSONYE) TESS AKAEKE, 1955–
  *Parables for a Season.* 1991. NTIR

OPEN THEATER, 1963–1973
*The Mutation Show.* 1970. OPE
*Nightwalk.* 1973. OPE

OPPENHEIMER, JOEL, 1930–1988
*The Great American Desert.* 1961. ORZ

OPPER, DON KEITH, 1949– , and the COMPANY
    THEATRE ENSEMBLE
*Children of the Kingdom* (script by Don Keith Opper).
    1970. BALLE9

ÖRKENY, ISTVAN, 1912–1979
*Pisti a vérzivatarban. See* Stevie in the Bloodbath
*Stevie in the Bloodbath.* 1979.
    Györgyey, C., translator GYOR
    Variant title: *Pisti a vérzivatarban*

ORLOV, STEPHEN. *See* Varma, Rahul, joint author

ØRNSBO, JESS, 1931–
*Odysseus fra Vraa. See* Odysseus from Vraa
*Odysseus from Vraa.* 1993.
    Matthews, H., translator NEWDAN
    Variant title: *Odysseus fra Vraa*

ORRERY, ROGER BOYLE, 1st Earl of, 1621–1679
*The Tragedy of Mustapha, the Son of Solyman the
    Magnificent.* 1665. DOA

ORS, FRANCISCO, 1933–
*Contradance.* 1980.
    Edwards, G., translator BURN
    Variant title: *Contradanza*
*Contradanza. See* Contradance

ORTIZ DE MONTELLANO, BERNARDO, 1899–1949
*Saloma's Head.* 1944?
    Mallan, L., translator NEWDI44

ORTON, JOE, 1933–1967
*Entertaining Mr. Sloan.* 1964. CALD, HOF, NEWE8
*Loot.* 1966. COTKB1, NEWE13
*What the Butler Saw.* 1970. BES69, PLACHB, RIS

OSBORN, PAUL, 1901–1988
*A Bell for Adano* (based on the novel by John Hersey).
    1944. BES44
*The Innocent Voyage* (based on the novel *A High Wind
    in Jamaica* by Richard Hughes). 1943. BES43
*Morning's at Seven.* 1939. BES39, GARU, KRM
*On Borrowed Time* (based on the novel by Lawrence E.
    Watkin). 1938. BES37, GARU, GATB2, GOW,
    GOWA

*Point of No Return* (adapted from the novel by John P.
    Marquand). 1950. BES51, WAGC3

OSBORNE, JOHN, 1929–1994
*The Entertainer.* 1957. BES44, TAUJ
*Inadmissible Evidence.* 1964. BES65, COTT
*Look Back in Anger.* 1956. BES57, BLOC, CEQA,
    COK, HAVHA
*Luther.* 1961. BES63, DIEA, RICT
*A Patriot for Me.* 1965. COTKB1
*A Subject of Scandal and Concern.* 1960. BARU, RICJ

—— and CREIGHTON, ANTHONY
*Epitaph for George Dillon.* 1958. BES58, NEWE2,
    TREBJ

OSBORNE, MARIAN, 1871–1931
*The Point of View.* 1923. MAS1

OSGOOD, PHILLIPS ENDECOTT, 1882–1956
*A Sinner Beloved.* 1924? FED1

OSHODI, MARIA, 1964–
*Blood Sweat and Fears.* 1988. BREW2
*'S'bend.* 1984. MALY

OSMENT, PHILIP
*This Island's Mine.* 1987. ADAP, OSME

OSOFISAN, FEMI, 1946–
*The Chattering and the Song.* 1976. BANH

OSTEREICH, JAMES
*The Furies of Mother Jones* (music by). *See* Klein,
    Maxine. *The Furies of Mother Jones*
*New Rise of the Master Race* (music by). *See* Klein,
    Maxine. *New Rise of the Master Race*
*Split-shift* (music by). *See* Klein, Maxine. *Split-shift*
*Windfall* (music by). *See* Klein, Maxine. *Windfall*

OSTROVSKII, ALEKSANDR NIKOLAEVICH, 1823–
    1886
*The Diary of a Scoundrel.* 1868.
    Ackland, R., translator BENT2
    Kasherman, P., translator MOSA
    Variant titles: *Enough Stupidity in Every Wise Man;
        Even a Wise Man Stumbles*
*A Domestic Picture.* 18–?
    Voynich, E., translator COUR
*Easy Money.* 1870?
    Magarshack, D., translator BENS2
    Variant title: *Fairy Gold*
*Enough Stupidity in Every Wise Man. See* The Diary of
    a Scoundrel

*Even a Wise Man Stumbles. See* The Diary of a
    Scoundrel
*Fairy Gold. See* Easy Money
*Larisa.* 1879.
    Green, M., and Katsell, J., translators GREENU
*The Poor Bride.* 1852.
    Seymour, J., and Noyes, G., translators NOY
*The Storm. See* The Thunderstorm
*Thunder. See* The Thunderstorm
*The Thunderstorm.* 1880.
    Cooper, J., translator COOPA
    MacAndrew, A., translator GARZE, MAB, TREB
    Magarshack, D., translator MAP
    Reeve, F., translator REEV1
    Whyte, F., and Noyes, G., translators CLF2
    Variant titles: *The Storm; Thunder*

OSTROVSKY, ALEKSANDER. *See* Ostrovskii,
    Aleksandr Nikolaevich

ŌTA, SHŌGO, 1939–2007
*Komachi fūden. See* The Tale of Komachi Told by the
    Wind
*The Tale of Komachi Told by the Wind.* 1977.
    Boyd, M., translator HACJT6
    Variant title: *Komachi fūden*

OTHMAN, CHE SHAMSUDDIN, 1949–. *See* Dinsman
    (pseudonym of)

OTIS, MERCY. *See* Warren, Mrs. Mercy (Otis)

OTWAY, THOMAS, 1652–1685
*The Orphan.* 1680. BELK5
*The Soldiers' Fortune.* 1680. COTKA
*Venice Preserv'd; or, A Plot Discover'd.* 1682. BELK1,
    DOB, GOS, GOSA, MAND, MANF, MATTL,
    MEN, MOR, MOSE1, NET, RES, RESL, REST,
    RET, RUB, STM, TAT, TAU, TICK, TUP, TUQ,
    TWE, WILSR, WONR

OULESS, E. U.
*Our Pageant.* 1926? THU

OULTON, BRIAN, 1908–1992
*Mr. Sydney Smith Coming Upstairs.* 1972. PLAN42

OU-YANG YÜ CHIEN. *See* Ouyang Yuqian

OUYANG YUQIAN, 1889–1962
*P'an Chin-lien.* 1928.
    Swatek, C., translator TWEH

OUZOUNIAN, RICHARD, 1950–
*British Properties. See* Westmount
*Once upon a Time in Old Westmount. See* Westmount

*Westmount.* 1977. NEWCAD1
    Variant titles: *British Properties; Once upon a Time
    in Old Westmount*

OVERMYER, ERIC, 1951–
*Dark Rapture.* 1992. BES92
*In a Pig's Valise.* 1986. WEJ
*Native Speech.* 1983. MESSE, WOQ3
*On the Verge.* 1985. ANTN, BARNA
    Variant title: *On the Verge or The Geography of
    Yearning*
*On the Verge or The Geography of Yearning. See*
    On the Verge

OWA, 1944–
*The Soledad tedrad, Part II: Transitions for a Mime
    Poem.* 1975. CEN

OWEN, ALUN DAVIES, 1925–1994
*Male of the Species.* 1969. RICK
*Progress to the Park.* 1961. NEWE5

OWEN, RENA, 1962?–
*Te awa I tahuti.* 1987. GARR

OWENS, DANIEL WALTER, 1948–
*The Box.* 1989. KINHP

OWENS, ROCHELLE, 1936–
*Chucky's Lunch.* WOQ2
*Futz.* 1967. NEWA2
*He Wants Shih.* 1972. OWER

OXENFORD, JOHN, 1812–1877
*East Lynne.* 1866. KILG

OYAMO, 1943– (b. Charles F. Gordon)
*His First Step.* 1972. NEWL
*Mary Goldstein.* 1989. KINHP
*The Resurrection of Lady Lester.* 1981. MESSE

OYIN ADEJOBI COMPANY, 1963–
*Kuye* (adapted from the novel by J. F. Odunjo). 1964.
    Barber, K., and Ogundijo, B., translators YORU
*Laniyonu.* 1967.
    Barber, K., and Ogundijo, B., translators YORU
*Ona Ola.* 1981.
    Barber, K., and Ogundijo, B., translators YORU

OYONO, FERDINAND L., 1929–2010
*Houseboy* (dramatic adaptation by Michael Etherton).
    PIET
    Reed, J., translator HUTCH

OYONO-MBIA, GUILLAUME, 1939–
*Three Suitors: One Husband.* 1968.
Wake, C., translator FACES
Variant title: *Trois prétendants, un mari*
*Trois prétendants, un mari. See* Three Suitors: One
Husband
*Until Further Notice.* 1967. FACES

OZU, YASUJIRO, 1903–1963, and NODA, KOGO
*Tokyo Story.* 1953.
Richie, D., and Klestadt, E., translators HIBH
Variant title: *Tokyo monogatari*
*Tokyu monogatari. See* Tokyo Story

PADMANABHAN, MANJULA, 1953–
*Harvest.* 1999. BLAAP
*Lights Out.* 1986. BODY

PAGE, ALEX
*The Cancelled Sky* (radio play). 1986. VICK2
*Once in a Golden Hour* (radio play). 1984. VICK1

PAGE, LOUISE, 1955–
*Real Estate.* 1987. BES87
*Tissue.* 1978. PLABE1
*Toby and Donna.* 1989. ROBR

PAGNOL, MARCEL, 1899–1974
*Marius, Fanny and Céssr. See* Behrman, Samuel
Nathaniel and Logan, Joshua. *Fanny* (based on the
trilogy by)

—— and NIVOIX, PAUL
*Les marchands de gloire.* 1925. GRAF

PAICE, ERIC, and WODDIS, ROGER
*World on Edge.* 1956. FAV

PAILLERON, ÉDOUARD JULES HENRI, 1834–1899
*The Art of Being Bored. See* Le monde où l'on s'ennuie
*The Cult of Boredom. See* Le monde où l'on s'ennuie
*Le monde où l'on s'ennuie.* 1881. BOR, BOV
Variant titles: *The Art of Being Bored; The Cult
of Boredom; This Bored World; The World of
Boredom*
*This Bored World. See* Le monde où l'on s'ennuie
*The World of Boredom. See* Le monde où l'on s'ennuie

PAKENHAM, EDWARD ARTHUR HENRY, 6th EARL
OF LONGFORD, 1902–1961
*Yahoo.* 1933. CAN

PAKINGTON, MARY AUGUSTA, HON., 1878–1949
*The Queen of Hearts.* 1926. THU

PALACIOS, MONICA, 1959–
*Describe Your Work.* 2000. PURO
*Greetings from a Queer Señorita.* 1995. SVICH
*Latin lezbo comica.* 2000. ARRIZ

PALAFOX, FILEMON M., d. 1933 or 1934
*Dalusapi.* 1915. PHIL
Tupas, F., translator PHIL

PALARCA, JULIA
*Other Tomorrows.* 195? EDAD

PALISSOT DE MONTENOY, CHARLES, 1730–1814
*Les philosophes.* 1760. BREN

PALMER, JOHN, 1943–
*Before the Guns.* 1969. RUDAK
Variant title: *Memories for My Brother, Part I:
Before the Guns*
*Henrik Ibsen on the Necessity of Producing Norwegian
Drama.* 1976. CTR
*Memories for My Brother, Part I: Before the Guns. See*
Before the Guns

PALMER, T. A., 1838–1905
*East Lynne.* 1874. ASG, FEFNC

PALMER, TANYA
*Barbra Live at Canyon Ranch.* 2000. *See* Ackermann,
J. *Back Story: A Dramatic Anthology.*
HUMANA2000

PAM-GRANT, SUSAN, 1962–
*Curl Up and Dye.* 1989. GRAYS

PANIKKAR, K. N., 1928–
*The Lone Tusker.* 1988.
Pillai, K., translator DESH
Variant title: *Ottayan*
*Ottayan. See* The Lone Tusker

PANYCH, MORRIS, 1952–
*7 Stories.* 1989. WASCPB2

PARAMESWARAN, UMA, 1938–
*Meera: A Dance Drama.* 1972. SACL
*Rootless but Green Are the Boulevard Trees.* 1987.
SACL
*Sita's Promise.* 1981. SACL

PARKER, DOROTHY (ROTHSCHILD), 1893–1967
*Candide. See* Hellman, Lillian. *Candide* (lyrics by)
*Here We Are.* 1931? BOOK

PARKER, LOUIS NAPOLEON, 1852–1944
*Disraeli.* 1911. BES09
*A Minuet.* 1915. CAR
*The Monkey's Paw* (adapted from the novel by W. W.
     Jacobs). 1903. BRNS, LITRA, LITRB

PARKHOUSE, HANNAH. *See* Cowley, Mrs. Hannah
     (Parkhouse)

PARKINGTON-EDWARDS, DUDLEY
*Request Stop.* 1983. MONB1

PARKS, STEPHEN DAVIS, 1949–
*When the Sun Slides.* 1985. PRIMA85

PARKS, SUZAN-LORI, 1963–
*The America Play.* 1994. BEAN, WOTHC
*The Death of the Last Black Man in the Whole Entire
     World.* 1990. JACOBA, JACOBD, LAMO, MAQ
*Imperceptible Mutabilities in the Third Kingdom.* 1989.
     ELAM, MESSE, WETZ

PARLATO, CALVERT
*Billings for the Defense.* 1983. WOMQ

PARNELL, PETER, 1953–
*The Cider House Rules, Part II* (adapted from the novel
     by John Irving, conceived for the stage by Tom
     Hulce, Jane Jones, and Peter Parnell). 1997. BES97

PARNES, UZI. *See* Tropicana, Carmelita, joint author

PARONE, EDWARD
*The Way We Live Now* (adapted from the short story by
     Susan Sontag). 1989. OSBW

PARRA, MARCO ANTONIO DE LA, 1952–
*The Dead Father.* 1991.
     Thomas, C., translator LATTH
     Variant title: *El padre muerto*
*Killer Tangos.* 1978.
     Thomas, C., translator LATTH
     Variant title: *Matatangos*
*Matatangos. See* Killer Tangos
*El padre muerto. See* The Dead Father

PARRIS-BAILEY, LINDA
*Dark Cowgirls and Prairie Queens.* 1983. DEN

PARTHASARATHI, INDIRA. *See* Parthasarathy, Indira

PARTHASARATHY, INDIRA, 1930–
*Aurangzeb.* 1974.
     Ramanathan, K., translator DESH
*Nandan kathai. See* The Story of Nandan

*The Story of Nandan.* 2001.
     Indra, C., translator KAM2
     Variant title: *Nandan kathai*

PASCAL, FRANCOISE, 1632–1698?
*The Lunatic Lover.* 1664.
     Gethner, P., translator GETH
     Variant title: *L'amoreaux extravagant*
*L'amoreaux extravagant. See* The Lunatic Lover

PASCAL, JULIA, 1949–
*Theresa.* 1990. MYTH

PASKANDI, GEZA, 1933–1995
*Sojourn.* 1984.
     Brogyányi, G., translator HUNGDC
     Variant title: *Vendégség*
*Vendégség. See* Sojourn

PASO, ALFONSO, 1925–1978
*La corbata. See* The Necktie
*The Necktie.* 1963.
     O'Connor, P., translator OCONNC
     Variant title: *La corbata*

PASSEUR, STEVE (b. Étienne Morin), 1899–1966
*L'acheteuse. See* A Measure of Cruelty
*A Measure of Cruelty.* 1930.
     Mitchell, Y., translator PLAN29
     Variant title: *L'acheteuse*

PATON, ALAN, 1903–1988
*Cry, the Beloved Country. See* Anderson, Maxwell and
     Weill, Kurt. *Lost in the Stars* (based on the novel by)

PATRICK, JOHN (pseudonym of John Patrick Goggan),
     1907–1995
*The Hasty Heart.* 1945. HES44, GARZ
*The Story of Mary Surratt.* 1947. DES46
     Variant title: *This Gentle Ghost*
*The Teahouse of the August Moon* (based on the novel
     by Vern Sneider). 1953. BES53, CORB, CORBA,
     GARU, GATB4, GAVE, RICT, THEA54
*This Gentle Ghost. See* The Story of Mary Surratt

PATRICK, ROBERT, 1937–
*Fred and Harold.* 1975. HOM
*The Golden Circle.* 1969. NEWA3
*The Haunted Host.* 1974. HOM
*Judas.* 1978. WES5
*One Person.* 1975. HOM
*T-shirts.* 1978. HOF

PATRIKAREAS, THEODORE, 1930–
*Peta tee fyssarmonica, Pepino. See* The Promised
     Woman

*The Promised Woman.* 1963. BRIMA1
    Variant titles: *Peta tee fyssarmonica, Pepino; Throw*
      *Away Your Harmonica, Pepino*
*Throw Away Your Harmonica, Pepino. See* The
    Promised Woman

PATTERSON, CHARLES, 1941–
*Black Ice.* 1968. JONE

PAUL, MRS. CLIFFORD
*The Fugitive King.* 1926? THU

PAULDING, JAMES KIRKE, 1778–1860
*The Bucktails; or, Americans in England.* 1947. HAL

PAVLOVSKY, EDUARDO, 1933–
*El Señor Galindez.* 1973. DAUR

PAWLEY, THOMAS, 1917–
*The Tumult and the Shouting.* 1969. HARY, HARYB

PAYNE, ALICIA
*The Troubleshooter.* 1996. BEYO (excerpt)

PAYNE, JOHN HOWARD, 1791–1852
*The Black Man; or, The Spleen.* 181–? AMP6
*The Boarding Schools; or, Life among the Little Folks.*
    1841? AMP5
*Brutus; or, The Fall of Tarquin.* 1818. GRE, MOSS
*The Italian Bride.* 1832? AMP6
*The Last Duel in Spain* (adapted from *El postrer duelo*
    *de España* by Calderón de la Barca). 1822? AMP6
*Mazeppa; or, The Wild Horse of Tartary* (adapted from
    *Mazeppa* by Léopold Chandezon and Jean Cuvilier
    de Trye). 1825? AMP5
*Mount Savage* (adapted from *Le mont sauvage* by René
    Pixérécourt). 1822. AMP5
*Romulus, the Shepherd King.* 1839? AMP6
*The Spanish Husband: or, First and Last Love.* 1830.
    AMP5
*Thérèse, the Orphan of Geneva.* 1821. BAT19
*Trial without Jury; or, The Magpie and the Maid*
    (adapted from *La pie voleuse* by Louis Caigniez
    and Jean Marie Théodore Baudoin). 1815? AMP5
*The Two Sons-in-law* (adapted from *Les deux gendres*
    by Charles Etienne). 1824? AMP5
*Woman's Revenge.* 1832. AMP6

—— and IRVING, WASHINGTON
*Charles the Second; or, The Merry Monarch* (adapted
    from the book *La jeunesse de Henri V* by
    Alexandre Duval). 1824. GARX, QUIJ, QUIK,
    QUIL, QUIM, QUIN, TAFT

PAYNE, RHONDA, 1950?–2002
*Stars in the Sky Morning.* 1978. PETERS

PAZ, OCTAVIO, 1914–1998
*La hija de Rappacini. See* Rappacini's Daughter
*Rappacini's Daughter* (based on the story by Nathaniel
    Hawthorne). 1956.
    Doggert, S., translator LATIN
    Variant title: *La hija de Rappacini*

PEABODY, JOSEPHINE PRESTON (MRS. L. S.
    MARKS), 1874–1922
*The Piper.* 1910. BRIK, DICDS, MOSJ, MOSK, MOSL

PEACOCK, MRS. BARBARA (BURNHAM). *See*
    Burnham, Barbara

PEACOCK, JOHN
*Children of the Wolf.* 1971. PLAN40

PEACOCK, THOMAS LOVE, 1785–1866
*Nightmare Abbey. See* Sharp, Anthony. *Nightmare*
    *Abbey* (adapted from *The Frolic* by)

PEAKE, RICHARD BRINKSLEY, 1792–1847
*The Fate of Frankenstein. See* Presumption; or, The Fate
    of Frankenstein
*Presumption; or, The Fate of Frankenstein.* 1823. COXJ
    Variant title: *The Fate of Frankenstein*

PEARSE, PADRAIC, 1879–1916
*The Singer.* 1915. CAP

PEARSE, PATRICK. *See* Pearse, Padraic

PEARSON, SYBILLE, 1937–
*Unfinished Stories.* 1992. BES92, WOMP92

PECHANTRE, 1638?–1709
*Geta.* 1687.
    Lockert, L., translator LOCU

PECHANTRES. *See* Péchantré

PEDRERO, PALOMA, 1957–
*Besos de lobo. See* Wolf Kisses
*Wolf Kisses.* 1987.
    Silbert, R., translator DODGSS
    Variant title: *Besos de lobo*

PEDROLO, MANUEL DE, 1918–1990
*Cruma.* 1957.
    Wellwarth, G., translator WELV
*Full Circle.* 1958.
    Steel, B., translator WELV
    Variant title: *Situació bis*
*The Room.* 1959.
    Webster, J., translator WELV
    Variant title: *Tècnica de cambra*

*Situació bis. See* Full Circle
*Tècnica de cambra. See* The Room

PEELE, GEORGE, 1558?–1597?
*The Arraignment of Paris.* 1584? BAS, BROC, NES
*David and Bethsabe.* 1593. DPR1, MIN1, MIO1
*The Lamentable Tragedy of Locrine* (sometimes attributed to).
    *See* Anonymous Plays. *The Lamentable Tragedy of Locrine*
*The Old Wife's Tale. See* The Old Wives' Tale
*The Old Wives' Tale.* 1593? BAS, BROC, GAYLE1, MAK, MIN2, MIO2, NEI, NES, OLH, OLI1, PAR, PARRY, RUB, SCI, SCJ, SCW, THWO
    Variant title: *The Old Wife's Tale*

PELFREY, MATT
*Drive Angry.* 1999. HUMANA99

PELLET, CHRISTOPHE
*Encore une année pour rien. See* One More Wasted Year
*One More Wasted Year.* 1998.
    Crimp, M., translator NEWFPB
    Variant title: *Encore une année pour rien*

PELUSO, EMANUEL
*Good Day.* 1965. OFF2
*Little Fears.* 1967? OFF2
*Moby Tick.* 1970. NEWA4

PEMBROKE, MARY SIDNEY HERBERT, COUNTESS OF, 1561–1621
   — *See* Garnier, Robert. *The Tragedie of Antonie*

PEN, POLLY, 1959– . *See* Harmon, Peggy, joint author

PENDARK, ROBERT
*The Case of Red Diamonds.* 1986. MONB3
*The Faces of Lust.* 1987. MONB4

PENGILLY, GORDON, 1953–
*Swipe.* 1981. NEWCAD3

PENHALL, JOE, 1967–
*Some Voices.* 1994. FROLIN3
*Wild Turkey.* 1993. SETR

PENNY, ROB, 1941–2003
*Good Black Don't Crack.* 1995. KINHN
*Pain in My Heart.* 1987. KINHP

PERCY, EDWARD, 1891–1968, and DENHAM, REGINALD
*Ladies in Retirement.* 1940. RICN

PEREIRAS, MANUEL, 1950–
*The Marriage of Hippolyta.* 1984. GONZ

PERELMAN, S. J. (SIDNEY JOSEPH), 1904–1979
*The Beauty Part.* 1962. SSTY

—— and NASH, OGDEN
*One Touch of Venus* (music by Kurt Weill; lyrics by Ogden Nash). 1943. RICO

PEREZ, FRANK
*Estorias del Barrio: Special People of International Character.* 1997. ALG

PEREZ, HECTOR, 1957–
*Perhaps the Marshland.* 1982. GONZ

PEREZ, JUDITH, 1945– , and PEREZ, SEVERO
*Soldierboy.* 1982. HUER

PEREZ, SEVERO, 1941– . *See* Perez, Judith, joint author

PEREZ, TONY, 1951–
*North Diversion Road.* 1988.
    Fernandez, D., and Perez, T., translators MLAP

PEREZ DE SAAVEDRA RIVAS, ANGEL. *See* Rivas, Angel Pérez de Saavedra

PEREZ GALDOS, BENITO, 1845–1920
*La de San Quintín.* 1894. BRET
    Hayden, P., translator CLDM
    Variant title: *The Duchess of San Quentin*
*The Duchess of San Quentin. See* La de San Quintín
*Electra.* 1901.
    Anonymous translator BUCK
    Turrell, C., translator TUCG, TUR
    Variant title: *The Nun and the Barbarian*
*The Nun and the Barbarian. See* Electra

PERINELLI, ROBERTO, 1940–
*Miembro del jurado.* 1979. PARRI

PERKINS, ALAN DAVID, 1962–
*Nobody Knows I'm a Dog.* 1999. INCI

PERLMAN, ARTHUR, 1958–
*Wings* (music by Jeffrey Lunden, lyrics by Fred Ebb; based on *Wings* by Arthur Kopit). 1993. BES92

PERLMAN, YOSEF. *See* Dymov, Osip, pseudonym

PERR, HARVEY
*Afternoon Tea.* 1976. GUTR

PERRY, SHAUNEILLE, 1930–
*In Dahomey*. 1990. KINHN

PERRY-RYDER, SHAUNEILLE. *See* Perry, Shauneille

PERTWEE, MICHAEL, 1916–1991. *See* Pertwee, Roland, joint author

PERTWEE, ROLAND, 1885–1963
*Heat Wave*. 1929. FIT

—— and PERTWEE, MICHAEL
*The Paragon*. 1948. PLAN1

PERYALIS, NOTIS, 1920–2009
*Masks of Angels*. 195?
Finer, L., translator COTR

PESCHINA, HELMUT, 1943–
*Ich doch nicht. See* Straight as a Corkscrew
*Straight as a Corkscrew*. 1982.
Foster, P., and Dixon, R., translators LAXC
Variant title: *Ich doch nicht*

PESHKEV, ALEXEI MAXIMOVITCH. *See* Pieskov, Aleksiei Maksimovich

PETCH, STEVE, 1952–
*Another Morning*. 1987. BELLW
*The General*. 1972. BRIP

PETERS, KIER, 1947–
*The Confirmation*. 1994. MESSE

PETERS, PAUL
*Nat Turner*. 1940. CROZ1

PETERSON, ERIC, 1946– . *See* Gray, John, joint author

PETERSON, LEONARD, 1917–
*Billy Bishop and the Red Baron*. (1974) KAL4

PETERSON, LOUIS STAMFORD, 1922–1998
*Take a Giant Step*. 1953. BES53, FORD, HARY, HARYB, PATR, TUQT, TUQTR, WOLCS

PETITCLAIR, PIERRE, 1813–1860
*A Country Outing*. 1857.
Doucette, L. E., translator DOUC
Variant title: *Une partie de campagne*
*La donation. See* The Donation
*The Donation*. 1842.
Doucette, L. E., translator DOUC
Variant title: *La donation*
*Une partie de campagne. See* A Country Outing

PETROLINI, ETTORE, 1886–1936
*Fortunello*. 1915.
House, J., translator TWEI
Variant title: *Tale of an Idiot*
*Tale of an Idiot. See* Fortunello

PETROV, EVGENY. *See* Ilf, Ilya Arnoldovich, joint author

PETROVSKI, JUGOSLAV, 1969–
*Porcelain Vase*. 1995.
Roman, G., and Petrovski, J., translators LUZ

PETRUSHEVSKAYA, LUDMILA, 1938–
*Three Girls in Blue*. 1988.
Aukin, L. and Glenny, M., translators SSTX

PEZZULO, TED, 1936–1979
*Skaters*. 1978. WES4

PHELPS, MAUDE. *See* Hutchins, Mrs. Maude Phelps McVeigh

PHILIP, M. NOURBESE, 1947–
*Coups and Calypsos*. 1996. BEYO (excerpt), SEARS1

PHILIP, MARLENE NOURBESE. *See* Philip, M. Nourbese

PHILLIPS, AMBROSE, 1675–1749
*Distressed Mother*. 1712. BELK1

PHILLIPS, DAVID GRAHAM, 1867–1911
*The Worth of a Woman*. 1908. INDI

PHILLIPS, LOUIS, 1942–
*The Last of the Marx Brothers' Writers*. 1977. WES2

PHILLIPS, STEPHEN, 1868–1915
*Paolo and Francesca*. 1902. DICEM, SMN

PHILLIPS, WATTS, 1825–1874
*Lost in London*. 1867? BOOB

PHILON, FREDERIC
*He Would Be a Soldier*. 1786. INCA8

PHIRI, MASAUTO
*Waiting for Sanctions*. 1991. NTIR

PHRANBOON (pseudonym of Chandrakhana, Chuangchan)
*Chan chao kha. See* Dear Moon
*Dear Moon*. 1931.
Poolthupya, S., translator MLAT
Variant title: *Chan chao kha*

*The Magistrate.* 1885. BENS3, BOOA4, BOOM, PLAN38, SMR
*Mid-channel.* 1909. HAU, SMI, WATF1, WATI, WEAL, WHI
*The Notorious Mrs. Ebbsmith.* 1895. BAI, CHOT
*The Second Mrs. Tanqueray.* 1893. ASG, BENY, BOOA2, BOWY, CEU, CLK2, COF, COTKIS, DICD, DUR, FULT, HUD, HUDV, MATTL, ROWC, SALE, STE, TAU, WATT2
*The Thunder-bolt.* 1908. CHA, CHAN, CHAR, TUCD, TUCM, TUCN, TUCO
*Trelawny of the "Wells."* 1898. BES94, CLKY, MART
— *See also* Woods, Aubrey. *Trelawny* (based on)

PIÑERO, MIGUEL, 1946–1988
*Playland Blues.* 1997. ALG
*Short Eyes.* 1974. BES73, PLACI
*The Sun Always Shines for the Cool.* 1977. KANEL

PING, CHIN WOO
*Diary of a Madwoman.* 1996. PING

PINGET, ROBERT, 1919–1997
*Architruc.* 1961.
Benedikt, M., translator BEN
*La manivelle. See* The Old Tune
*The Old Tune.* 1962
Beckett, S., translator GOO
Variant title: *La manivelle*

PINNER, DAVID, 1940–
*Dickon.* 1966. NEWE10
*The Drums of Snow.* 1969. NEWE13, PLAN42

PINNOCK, WINSOME, 1961–
*A Hero's Welcome.* 1989. GEOR
*Leave Taking.* 1987. FIFHL1
*A Rock in Water.* 1989. BREW2
*Talking in Tongues.* 1991. BREW3

PINSKI, DAVID, 1872–1959
*King David and His Wives.* 1923.
Landis, J., translator LAO, LAOG
*Der Oytser. See* The Treasure
*The Treasure.* 1906.
Sandrow, N., translator SANR
Variant title: *Der Oytser*

PINTAURO, JOE, 1930–
*Lenten Puddings. See* Wild Blue
*Pony Ride. See* Wild Blue
*The Real Dark Night of the Soul. See* Wild Blue
*Rex. See* Wild Blue
*Rosen's Son.* 1989. ACTOR
— *See also* Wild Blue

*Rules of Love. See* Wild Blue
*Seymour in the Very Heart of Winter. See* Wild Blue
*Snow Orchid.* 1981. GAY5, PLACD
*Uncle Chick. See* Wild Blue
*Wild Blue.* 1987. GAY4
(8 short plays: *Lenten Puddings; Pony Ride; The Real Dark Night of the Soul; Rex; Rosen's Son; Rules of Love; Seymour in the Very Heart of Winter; Uncle Chick*)

PINTER, HAROLD, 1930–2008
*Applicant.* 1959. PLAAC2
*Betrayal.* 1979. BES79, JACOBD, PLACHB
*The Birthday Party.* 1958. BARKF, LEVY, NIL, MORWB, MORXE, SEVD, VENA
*The Black and White.* 1959. BAIK, BAIL, BAIM, THOD
*The Caretaker.* 1960. ALLN, ALLO, BES61, COTKB1, POP
*The Collection.* 1962. BES62
*The Dumb Waiter.* 1960. ABCB, ABCC, ABRJ1, ABRK1, ABRL2, ABRM2, BAIH, BARKB, BARKC, BARKD, CLLC, COK, COLD, HEA, HEAD, JACOB, JACOBA, LITIA, MEY, MEYB, MEYD, MEYE, NEWE3, REIW, REIWE, SOUL
*The Homecoming.* 1965. BES66, GILB, SSSI, SSSIA, SSSIB, STOTD, STOTLA, WOTHA, WOTHB, WOTHC, WOTHM
*Landscape.* 1967. SSSIC
*Last to Go.* 1959. THOD
*A Night Out.* 1960. CONB, MAE
*Request Stop.* 1959. PLAAC1
*A Slight Ache.* 1961. AUB, SCNPL, SDQ, TREBJ
*Trouble in the Works.* 1959. GLI

PIRANDELLO, LUIGI, 1867–1936
*And That's the Truth. See* Right You Are! If You Think So
*As You Desire Me.* 1931.
Alba, M., translator GARZH
Putnam, S., translator HAV
Variant title: *Come tu mi vuoi*
*Bellavita.*
Murray, W., translator RICJ
*Ciascuno a suo modo. See* Each in His Own Way
*Come tu mi vuoi. See* As You Desire Me
*Cosi è se vi pare! See* Right You Are! If You Think So
*Each in His Own Way.* 1924.
Livingston, A., translator CHA, CHAN, DUK, SEVT
Variant title: *Ciascuno a suo modo*
*The Emperor. See* Henry IV
*Enrico IV. See* Henry IV
*La giara. See* The Jar
*Henry IV.* 1922.
Bentley, E., translator BENSA, COTQ

Caputi, A., translator CAPU
Storer, E., translator BARJ, BARK, BLOC, DODS,
  DOLAN, FREG, JOHN, MALN2, NORI2, SANE,
  ULAN, WATA, WATI, WATL4, WEIP, WELT
  Variant titles: *The Emperor; Enrico IV; The Living
    Mask; The Mock Emperor*
*It Is So (If You Think So). See* Right You Are! If You
  Think So
*The Jar.* 1917.
  Anonymous translator CHR
  Livingston, A., translator FRYE, HIBB
  May, F., translator ALL
  Variant title: *La giara*
*The Living Mask. See* Henry IV
*Lumie di Sicilia. See* Sicilian Limes
*The Man with the Flower in His Mouth.* (1928)
  Bentley, E., translator HOGN
*The Mock Emperor. See* Henry IV
*Naked.* 1922.
  Livingston, A., translator CLKW, DICDT
  Variant title: *Vestire gl'ignudi*
*Our Lord of the Ships.* 1925.
  Anonymous translator MACN
  Variant title: *La sagra del signore della nave*
*Perché? See* Why?
*Il placere dell' onestà. See* The Pleasure of Honesty
*The Pleasure of Honesty.* 1917.
  Murray, W., translator COTN
  Variant title: *Il placere dell' onestà*
*Questa sera si recita a soggetto. See* Tonight We
  Improvise
*Right You Are! If You Think So.* 1918.
  Bentley, E., translator BENSB2
  Livingston, A., translator ALT, ALTE, MOSG,
    MOSH
  Variant titles: *And That's the Truth; Cosí è se vi
    pare!; It Is So (If You Think So)*
*La sagra del signore della nave. See* Our Lord of the
  Ships
*Sei personaggi in cerca d'autore. See* Six Characters in
  Search of an Author
*Sicilian Limes.* 1910.
  Goldberg, I., translator GOL
  Variant title: *Lumie di Sicilia*
*Six Characters in Search of an Author.* 1921.
  Anonymous translator ALLK, ALLM, ALLN, ALLO,
    MANL
  Bentley, E., translator BENSB2
  Caputi, A., translator WOTHA
  Linstrum, J., translator NORIC2, NORJ2, NORJA,
    WOTHB, WOTHC, WOTHM
  Longman, S., translator HILPDH6
  May, F., translator GILB, HOEP, SSSI, SSSIA,
    SSSIB, SSSIC, STY
  Mayer, P., translator COTN, COTQ

Storer, E., translator ASF, AUG, BAIC, BAIE,
  BAIG, BARKA, BARKB, BARKC, BARKE,
  BARN, BARR, CEW, COLD, DEAS, DICIN2,
  DIEA, DIEB, DIER, DOWS, GOLD, GRDBA59,
  HAVL, HEA, HEAA, HEAB, JACOB, JACOBA,
  JACOBD, JACOBE, KEN, KERP, KINNS, LEVY,
  LITI, NORGA, NORIA2, NORIB2, REIO, REIP,
  REIT, REIW, REIWE, SEN, TRE, TREAT,
  TREBA, TREBJ, TREC2, TREE2, TREI2, TRI,
  TRIA, VONS3, WAIW, WEIM, WEIS, WEIW,
  WHFM, WHI
  Variant title: *Sei personaggi in cerca d'autore*
*Such Is Life.* (1925)
  Duplaix, L., translator VANV2
  Variant title: *La vita che ti diedi*
*Tonight We Improvise.* 1930.
  Abba, M., translator WEAN
  Campbell, J., and Sbrocchi, L., translators TWEI
  Variant title: *Questa Sera si recita a soggetto*
*Vestire gl'ignudi. See* Naked
*La vita che ti diedi. See* Such Is Life
*Why?* 1892.
  House, J., translator TWEI
  Variant title: *Perché?*

PISCATOR, ERWIN, 1893–1966, and GASBARRA,
    FELIX
*In Spite of Everything.* 1925. FAV

PISEMSKII, ALEKSIEI FEOFILAKTOVICH, 1820–1881
*Baal.* 1873.
  Green, M., and Katsell, J., translator GREENU
*A Bitter Fate.* 1859.
  Kagan, A., and Noyes, G., translators NOY
  Variant titles: *Cruel Fate; A Hard Fate*
*Cruel Fate. See* A Bitter Fate
*A Hard Fate. See* A Bitter Fate

PISEMSKY, ALEXEI. *See* Pisemskii, Aleksiei
    Feofilaktovich

PITCHER, OLIVER, 1924– .
*The One* (1971) KINH, KINHB

PITT, GEORGE DIBDIN, 1799–1855
*The Fiend of Fleet Street. See* The String of Pearls
    (Sweeney Todd)
*The String of Pearls (Sweeney Todd).* 1847. KILG
  Variant titles: *The Fiend of Fleet Street; Sweeney
    Todd; Sweeney Todd, the Barber of Fleet Street*
*Sweeney Todd* (revised and restructured by Marvin
    Kaye). 1992. KAYS
  — *See* The String of Pearls (Sweeney Todd)
*Sweeney Todd, the Barber of Fleet Street. See* The
    String of Pearls (Sweeney Todd)

POGODIN, NIKOLAI FEDEROVICH, 1900–1962
(pseudonym of Stukalov, N. F.)
*Aristocrats*. 1935.
Wixley, A., and Carr, R., translators FOUS
Variant title: *Aristokraty*
*Aristokraty. See* Aristocrats
*The Chimes of the Kremlin*. 1941.
Bakshy, A., translator BAKS
Shoett, A., translator CLKX, THY
Variant titles: *Kremlevskie kuranty; Kremlin Chimes*
*Kremlevskie kuranty. See* The Chimes of the Kremlin
*Kremlin Chimes. See* The Chimes of the Kremlin
*Temp. See* Tempo
*Tempo*. 1930.
Talmadg, I., translator LYK
Variant title: *Temp*

POGSON, SARAH. *See* Smith, Sarah Pogson

POHL, KLAUS, 1952–
*The Beautiful Stranger*. 1991.
Weber, C., translator WEBER
*Waiting Room Germany*. 1995
Tushingham, D., translator DODGSG
Variant title: *Wartesaal Deutschland*
*Wartesaal Deutschland. See* Waiting Room Germany

POIRIER, LEONIE M.
*The White Night*. 1988. HEID

POIRET, JEAN, 1926–1992
*La cage aux folles. See* Fierstein, Harvey. *La cage aux folles* (adaptation of)

POLLOCK, CHANNING, 1880–1946
*The Enemy*. 1925. BES25
*The Fool*. 1922. BES22

POLLOCK, RICHARD
*Zoo in Silesia*. 1945. EMB1

POLLOCK, SHARON, 1936–
*Blood Relations*. 1980. BAIL, BAIM, PENG, PLABE3, STOTD, STOTLA, STOTLB
Variant title: *My Name Is Lisbeth*
*Doca*. 1984. SCNQCB, WASCPA2, WASCPB1
*Generations*. 1980. PERKY
*Getting It Straight*. 1989. DOOL
*The Komagata Maru Incident*. 1976. SIXA
*My Name Is Lisbeth. See* Blood Relations
*Walsh*. 1973. WASCP, WASCPA1
*Whiskey Six Cadenza*. 1983. BERR

POMERANCE, BERNARD, 1940–
*The Elephant Man*. 1977. BERS, BES78, BEST

POMO AFRO HOMOS (Postmodern African-American Homosexuals), 1990–1995
*Dark Fruit*. 1994. CLUMS
*Fierce Love*. 1991. ELAM

PONTCHARRA, NATACHA DE, 1960–
*Mickey la torche. See* Mickey the Torch
*Mickey the Torch*. 1993.
Arden, A., translator NEWFPB
Variant title: *Mickey la torche*

PONTE, LORENZO DA, 1749–1838
*Don Giovanni. See* The Punished Libertine
*The Punished Libertine; or, Don Giovanni*. 1787.
Schizzano, A., and Mandel, O., translators MARJ

POOLE, JOHN, 1786?–1872
*Hamlet Travestie*. 1811. NIN1
*Ye Comedie of Errours*. late 1850s?. NIN5

POPE, ALEXANDER, 1688–1744. *See* Gay, John, joint author

POPOVA, ELENA
*The Chosen Ones*. 1999.
Harvey, S., translator EUP

POPPLE, WILLIAM, 1701–1764?
*A Cure for Jealousy. See* The Double Deceit
*The Double Deceit*. 1735. PLAN26
Variant title: *A Cure for Jealousy*

POPPLEWELL, JACK, 1911–1996
*Dead on Nine*. 1955. PLAN13
*Dear Delinquent*. 1957. PLAN16

POPPLEWELL, OLIVE M.
*This Bondage*. 1935. FIN

PORTER, COLE, 1891–1964
*Kiss Me Kate* (music and lyrics by). *See* Spewack, Mrs. Bella (Cohen) and Spewack, Samuel. *Kiss Me Kate*
*Leave It to Me!* (music and lyrics by). *See* Spewack, Mrs. Bella (Cohen) and Spewack, Samuel. *Leave It to Me!*

PORTER, DEBORAH, 1959–
*Flowers*. 1993. ZIMM (excerpt)

PORTER, HAL, 1911–1984
*The Tower*. 1963. THOP

Variant titles: *Cambyses; The Life of Cambises, King of Persia*
*Cambyses. See* Cambises, King of Persia
*The Life of Cambises, King of Persia. See* Cambises, King of Persia

PREVELAKIS, PANDELIS, 1909–1986
*The Last Tournament.* 1966.
Gianos, M., translator GIA

PREVERT, JACQUES, 1900–1977
*La famille tuyare de poile; ou, Une famille bien unie.*
*See* A United Family
*A United Family.* 1955?
Allen, J., translator BENSC
Variant title: *La famille tuyare de poile; ou, Une famille bien unie*

PRICHARD, KATHARINE SUSANNAH, 1883–1969
*Forward One.* 1935. PFIS

PRICHARD, REBECCA, 1971–
*Essex Girls.* 1994. COMS

PRIDA, DOLORES, 1943–
*Botanica.* 1991. PURO
*Pantellas. See* Screens
*Screens.* 1986–1987.
Gonzalez-Cruz, L., and Colecchia, F., translators GONZ

PRIEDE, GUNARS, 1928–2000
*The Blue One.* 1972.
Sedriks, A., translator CONF
Variant title: *Zila*
*Zila. See* The Blue One

PRIESTLEY, JOHN BOYNTON, 1894–1984
*Cornelius.* 1935. SIXP
*Dangerous Corner.* 1932. CEU, RICI, SIXH
*An Inspector Calls.* 1945. BES47, FOUX, HUDE, RICN
*Laburnum Grove.* 1933. SEV
*They Came to the City.* 1943. BARV

—— and HAWKES, JACQUETTA
*Dragon's Mouth.* 1952. COTK, FAOS
— *See* Murdoch, Iris, joint author

PRINCE, HAROLD, 1928 . *See* Uhry, Alfred, joint author

PRITCHARD, BARRY
*Captain Fantastic Meets the Ectomorph.* 1965. SCAR
*The Day Roosevelt Died.* 1980. WES10
*Visions of Sugar Plums.* 1966. BALLE4

PROKOFIEV, SERGE, 1891–1953
*L'amour de trois oranges. See* The Love of Three Oranges
*The Love of Three Oranges* (libretto by; based on a play by Carlo Gozzi). 1919.
Bermel, A., translator BERMD

PROVIDENCE, TIEN
*Blues for My Grandfather.* 1995. BEYO

THE PROVISIONAL THEATRE, 1972–
*Inching through the Everglades.* 1978. WES10

PRUITT, DAN
*The Harvey Milk Show* (book and lyrics by Dan Pruitt; music by Patrick Hutchison). 1991. CLUMS

PRUTKOV, KOZ'MA (pseudonym of Aleksiei Konstantinovich Tolstoi; Aleksandr Mikhailovich Zhemchuzhnikov; Aleksei Mikhailovich Zhemchuzhnikov; and Vladimir Mikhailovich Zhemchuzhnikov)
*Evening of Books for Youth Clubs.* 1924.
Anonymous translator VONG (excerpt)
Variant title: *Vecher knigi v klubakhmolodezhi (opyt massovoi khudozhestvennoi agitatsii za knigu)*
*Fantasy.* 1851.
Senelick, L., translator RUSSCO
*The Headstrong Turk, or, Is It Nice to Be a Grandson?* (1854)
Senelick, L., translator RVI
Variant title: *Oprometchiviy turka: ili Plilichno li byt vnukom?*
*Oprometchiviy turka: ili Plilichno li byt vnukom?*
*See* The Headstrong Turk, or, Is It Nice to Be a Grandson?
*Vecher knigi v klubakhmolodezhi (opyt massovoi khudozhestvennoi agitatsii za knigu). See* Evening of Books for Youth Clubs

PRYCE, RICHARD, 1864–1942
*Frolic Wind.* 1935. FAMG

PRZYBYSZEWSKI, STANISLAW, 1868–1927
*Visitors.* 1901.
Gerould, D., and Kosicka, J., translators GERO

PUCCIONI, MADELINE
*Laundromat.* 1975. NEWP
*Two O'clock Feeding.* 1978. WES4

PUGH, ANN, and DACUS, KATY
*The Day They Kidnapped Blanche.* 1987. VORE

PUIG, MANUEL, 1932–1990
  *Kiss of the Spider Woman* (adapted from the novel by).
    1981.
    Barker, A., translator COLD, JACOBD
    Feingold, M., translator WOOGLA
    — *See* McNally, Terrence. *Kiss of the Spider Woman*
      (based on the novel by)
    — *See also* Schrader, Leonard. *Kiss of the Spider
      Woman* (based on the novel by)

PULMAN, JACK, 1925–1979
  *The Happy Apple*. 1967. PLAN34

"PUNCH." *See* "Mr. Punch," pseudonym

PURDUE, ROBERT L.
  *Family Reunion*. 1991. NTIR

PURSCELL, PHYLLIS, 1934–
  *Separate Ceremonies*. 1979. WOMS

PUSHKIN, ALEKSANDR SERGIEEVICH, 1799–1837
  *Boris Godunov*. 1870.
    Reeve, F., translator REEV1
    Rzhevsky, N., translator RZH
  *Love and Death featuring "Aleko"* by Rachmaninoff
    (based on the story by). *See* Nemirovich-
    Danchenko, Vladimír Ivanovích. *Love and Death*
  *The Stone Guest*. 1847.
    MacAndrew, A., translator GARZE, MAB

QUAN, BETTY, 1964–
  *Nancy Chew Enters the Dragon*. 1993. ZIMM (excerpt)
  *One Ocean* (radio play). 1994. BEYO

QUARRELL, JOHNNIE, 1935–
  *Smith*. 1987. VER

QUEER STREET YOUTH, 1991–1993
  *friendly fire*. 1993. BOWL
  *people who live in glass houses . . .* 1991. BOWL
  *street dish*. 1992. BOWL

QUESNEL, JOSEPH, 1746–1809
  *Anglomania, or Dinner, English-style*. 1932.
    Doucette, L. E., translator DOUC
    Variant title: *L'anglomanie ou le le dîner à
      l'angloise*
  *L'anglomanie ou le le dîner à l'angloise*. *See*
    Anglomania, or Dinner, English-style

QUILES, EDUARDO, 1940
  *El asalariado*. *See* The Employee
  *The Bridal Chamber*. (1972)
    Wellwarth, M., translator WELK

  Variant title: *El tálamo*
  *The Employee*. (1969)
    Wellwarth, M., translator WELK
    Variant title: *El asalariado*
  *El frigorífico*. *See* The Refrigerator
  *The Refrigerator*. (1972)
    Wellwarth, M., translator WELK
    Variant title: *El frigorífico*
  *El tálamo*. *See* The Bridal Chamber

QUINAULT, PHILIPPE, 1635–1688
  *Astrate*. *See* Astrates
  *Astrates*. 1664–1665.
    Lockert, L., translator LOCU
    Variant title: *Astrate*

QUIÑONES DE BENAVENTE, LUIS, 1589?–1651
  *The Doctor and the Patient*. *See* El doctor y el enfermo.
  *El doctor y el enfermo*. (1644) NOR
    Variant title: *The Doctor and the Patient*

QUINTANA, EDUARDO DE ZAMACOIS Y. *See*
  Zamacois, Eduardo

QUINTERO, HECTOR, 1942–
  *The Booby Prize*. (1965)
    Quintero, H., et al., translators HILET
    Variant title: *El premio flaco*
  *El premio flaco*. *See* The Booby Prize

QUINTERO, JOAQUIN ALVAREZ. *See* Alvarez
  Quintero, Joaquín

QUINTERO, SERAFIN ALVAREZ. *See* Alvarez
  Quintero, Serafin

QUINTOS, FLOY, 1961–
  *. . . And St. Louis Loves dem Filipinos*. 1993. JUAN

RABE, DAVID (WILLIAM), 1940–
  *The Basic Training of Pavlo Hummel*. 1971. FAMAD,
    OBG
  *Hurlyburly*. 1984. BERT, BES84
  *Sticks and Bones*. 1971. BES71, BRIY, BRIZ, GARTL,
    HEAD, RICT
  *Streamers*. 1976. BES75, BEST, BRIZ, BRJ, COMV,
    PLACGA, PLACI, WATTAD

RABINDRANATH TAGORE. *See* Tagore, Rabindranath

RACHILDE (pseudonym of Marguerite Eymery),
    1860–1953
  *The Crystal Spider*. 1892.
    Gerould, D., translator GERO
    Gounaridou, K., and Lively, F., translators KEL

RACHMANINOFF, SERGEI, 1873–1943
*Aleko. See* Nemirovich–Danchenko, Vladímír
    Ivanovích. *Love and Death featuring "Aleko"* by
    Rachmaninoff

RACINE, JEAN BAPTISTE, 1639–1699
*Andromache. See* Andromaque
*Andromaque.* 1667. CLOU1, CLOUD1, CLOUDS1,
    LYO, SCN, SER, SERD, SIJ1
    Abel, L., translator BERMG
    Boswell, R., translator CLKW
    Variant title: *Andromache*
*Athaliah.* 1691.
    Anonymous translator GAUB, HOUS
    Boswell, R., translator BUCK, BUCL, BUCM,
        GREA, KOH2, KRE
    Muir, K., translator ENC
*Bérénice.* 1670.
    Boswell, R., translator CLF2
    Masefield, J., translator STA
    Solomon, S., translator GRDBA31
*Esther.* 1689. SER
*Phaedra. See* Phèdre
*Phèdre.* 1677. LYO, SER
    Anonymous translator EVB2, GAUB, THMF,
        WORM
    Arnott, P., translator REIWE
    Boswell, R., translator CARP, CARPA, DRAD1,
        HARC26, LOCM2, LOGO, MALC, MALG2,
        MATT, MIL, PLAB1, ROB, SEBO, SEBP, SMP
    Cairncross, J., translator ALLM, ALLN, ALLO
    Fowlie, W., translator DOLAN, FOWL
    Goddard, W., translator CALD, WEIS
    Henderson, R., translator EVA2, EVC2, HIB, HIRE,
        THOM, THON, TRE, TREA2, TREB, TREC1,
        TREE1, TREI1, WALJ
    Knight, R. C., translator COLD, WOTHA, WOTHB,
        WOTHC
    Lockert, L., translator WEAV2
    Lowell, R., translator ALLK, AUB, BENR4, BENS1,
        BENSD, BOW, COTX, FREC, HILPDH2, HOUE,
        MALI2, MALN2, NORI2, SANL, VANV2
    MacDonald, R., translator LAQCF
    Muir, K., translator GOUZ, NORGA, NORIA2,
        ROF
    Packard, W., translator VENA
    Solomon, S., translator GRDBA31
    Wilbur, R., translator NORIB2, NORIC2, NORJ2,
        NORJA
    Variant title: *Phaedra*
*Phèdre and Hippolyte. See* Phèdre
*Les plaideurs.* 1668.
    Browne, I., translator BAT7
    Variant title: *The Suitors*
*The Suitors. See* Les plaideurs

RADIGUET, RAYMOND, 1903–1923
*Les pélican. See* The Pelicans
*The Pelicans.* 1921.
    Benedikt, M., translator BEN
    Variant title: *Les pélican*

RADO, JAMES, 1939?–
*Hair. See* Ragni, Gerome, joint author

RADSTROM, NIKLAUS, 1953–
*Hitlers Barndom. See* Hitler's Childhood
*Hitler's Childhood.* 1984.
    Perry, F., translator VOI
    Variant title: *Hitlers Barndom*

RAFENOMANJATO, CHARLOTTE–ARRISOA, 1936–
    2008
*The Herd.* 1990.
    De Jager, M., translator AFRUBU2

RAFFALOVICH, MARC-ANDRE, 1864–1934. *See* Gray,
    John, joint author

RAGNI, GEROME, 1942–1991, and RADO, JAMES
*Hair* (music by Galt MacDermot). 1967. GREAAR

RAHARIMANANA, JEAN-LUC, 1967–
*The Prophet and the President.* 1991.
    Vogel, S., translator AFRUBU2

RAHBAR, MAHMUD
*Law.* 1979.
    Godec, J., Ibsen, L., and Nyce, C., translators
        GHAN
    Variant title: *Qanun*
*Qanun. See* Law

RAHMAN, AISHAH, 1936–
*The Mojo and the Sayso.* 1989. HARYB, MAQ
*Unfinished Women Cry in No Man's Land while a Bird
    Dies in a Gilded Cage.* 1977. WILK

RAIF, AYSHE, 1952–
*Caving In.* 1989. PLABE8
*Fail/safe.* 1986. ROES

RAINIS, JĀNIS (pseudonym of Jānis Pliekšàns), 1865–
    1929
*Fire and Night.* 1911.
    Straumanis, A., translator FIFFN
    Variant title: *Uguns un nakts*
*The Golden Steed.* 1910.
    Barbina Stahnke, A., translator GOLB
    Variant title: *Zelta zirgs*
*Uguns un nakts. See* Fire and Night
*Zelta zirgs. See* The Golden Steed

RATTIGAN, SIR TERENCE MERVYN. *See*
  RATTIGAN, TERENCE

RATTIGAN, TERENCE, 1911–1977
  *After the Dance.* 1939. SIXL
  *The Browning Version.* 1949. HAMI
  *The Deep Blue Sea.* 1952. FAOS
  *French without Tears.* 1936. FIP, PLAL2, THH
  *Love in Idleness. See* O Mistress Mine
  *O Mistress Mine.* 1946. BES45
    Variant title: *Love in Idleness*
  *Ross.* 1960. PLAJ1
  *Separate Tables.* 1954. BES56 (2 one-act plays: *Table
    by the Window: Table Number Seven*)
  *Table Number Seven* (part of *Separate Tables*). 1956.
    BENPB
  *The Winslow Boy.* 1946. BES47, BOGO, LOND1, RED,
    REDM, SPER, WAGC2

RAUCH, EDWARD H. (Pit Schweffelbrenner,
    pseudonym).
  *Rip Van Winkle; oder, Die shpooks fun Blowa Barrick*
    (based on the book by Washington Irving). 18–?
    BUFF

RAVEL, AVIVA, 1928–
  *Black Dreams.* 1973. SHAT
  *Dance like a Butterfly.* 1993. RAVEL
  *Dispossessed.* 1977. PERKY
  *Gently down the Stream.* 1990. RAVELII
  *Moon People.* 1988. RALPH, SIXA
  *Soft Voices. See* Two short plays: *The Twisted Loaf;
    Soft Voices*
  *The Twisted Loaf. See* Two short plays: *The Twisted
    Loaf; Soft Voices*
  Two short plays: *The Twisted Loaf; Soft Voices.* 1966.
    KAL3
    Variant titles: *Soft Voices; The Twisted Loaf*

RAVEL FAMILY, THE
  *Kim-Ka!* 1852. CHIN

RAVENSCROFT, EDWARD, fl. 1671–1697
  *The London Cuckolds.* 1681. JEFF2, SUM

———— and MOTTEUX, PETER ANTHONY
  *The Anatomist; or, The Sham Doctor . . . with the Loves
    of Mars and Venus* (based upon *Crispin médecin* by
    Hautroche). 1696. BELC1, HUGL

RAYFIEL, DAVID, 1923–
  *P.S. 193.* 1962. BES62

RAYMOND, ANN
  *Lifeline.* 1982. *See* Anonymous Plays. *Twenty-four
    Hours: P.M.*

RAYNAL, PAUL, 1890–1971
  *The Tomb beneath the Arc de triomphe. See* Le tombeau
    sous l'Arc de triomphe
  *Le tombeau sous l'Arc de triomphe.* 1924. RHO
    Variant titles: *The Tomb beneath the Arc de triomphe;
    The Unknown Warrior*
  *The Unknown Warrior. See* Le tombeau sous l'Arc de
    triomphe

RAZNOVICH, DIANA, 1945–
  *Casa matriz. See* Dial-a-Mom
  *Dial-a-Mom.* 1980.
    Salas, T., and Vargas, M., translators SALA
    Variant title: *Casa matriz*
  *Lost Belongings.* 1988.
    Glickman, N., and Waldman, G., translators ARGJT
    Variant title: *Objetos perdidos*
  *Objetos perdidos. See* Lost Belongings

RCA THEATRE COMPANY, 1980–
  *Land of Cod. See* Terras de bacalhau (Land of Cod)
  *Terras de bacalhau (Land of Cod).* 1980. PETERS
    Variant title: *Land of Cod*
  *Time before Thought.* 1991. PETERS

READ, MONICA. *See* Cromelin, Caroline, joint author

READE, CHARLES, 1814–1884. *See* Taylor, Tom, joint
    author

REAL, PHILIP
  *Stronger and Stronger.* 1984. *See* Anonymous Plays.
    The AIDS Show . . .

REANEY, JAMES CRERAR, 1926–2008
  *The Canadian Brothers, or, The Prophecy Fulfilled.*
    1983. PERKY
  *Handcuffs* (part three of *The Donnellys*). 1975. PENG
  *The St. Nicholas Hotel, Wm. Donnelly, prop.* (The
    Donnellys, Part Two) 1974. WASCP, WASCPA1,
    WASCPB1
  — *See also* Cameron, Ronald. *Masque* (adapted from
    One-man Masque)

REARDON, DENNIS J., 1944–
  *The Leaf People.* 1975. PLACI

REBAR, KELLY-JEAN, 1956–
  *Bordertown Café.* 1987. WASCPB2
  *Checkin' Out.* 1981. NEWCAD3

REBECK, THERESA
  *Abstract Expression.* 1998. WOMP99
  *The Butterfly Collection.* 2000. WOMP2000
  *The Family of Mann.* 1994. WOMP94

*Spike Heels.* 1992. WOMP92
*View of the Dome.* 1996. WOMP96

REBHUN, PAUL, 1500?–1546
*Susanna.* 1535.
    Hanak, M., translator GILL

RECKORD, BARRY, 1928–
*Skyvers.* 1963. NEWE9

RED LADDER THEATRE COMPANY, 1968–
*Strike while the Iron Is Hot.* 1974. STRI
    Variant title: *A Woman's Work Is Never Done; or,*
    *Strike while the Iron Is Hot*
*A Woman's Work Is Never Done. See* Strike while the
    Iron Is Hot

REDDIN, KEITH, 1956–
*Highest Standard of Living.* 1986. ANTN

REDDING, JOSEPH DEIGHN, 1859–1932
*The Attonement of Pan.* 1912. BOH2

REDFORD, JOHN, 1486?–1547
*The Play of Wit and Science.* 1541? ADA, BEVD,
    FARN, HAO, SCAT
    Variant titles: *Wit and Science; Wyt and Science*
*Wit and Science. See* The Play of Wit and Science
*Wyt and Science. See* The Play of Wit and Science
    — *See also* Anonymous Plays. *The Marriage of Wit*
    *and Science*

REDMOND, EUGENE B. 1937–
*A Funky-grace.* 1991. NTIR

REDWOOD, JOHN HENRY, 1942–2003
*The Old Settler.* 1997. BES97

REED, BILL, 1939–
*Burke's Company.* 1968. BRIMA3

REED, ISHMAEL, 1938–
*Hubba City.* 1996. ALG
*The Preacher and the Rapper.* 1994. ALG
*Savage Wilds.* 1990. ALG

REED, JOSEPH, 1723–1787
*The Register-office.* 1761. BELC3

REED, MARK WHITE, 1890?–1969
*Yes, My Darling Daughter.* 1937. BES36, GAS

REELY, MARY KATHARINE, 1881–1959
*Flittermouse.* 1927. GALB

REEVES, MELISSA
*Dream-town. See* Bovell, A., Cornelius, P., Reeves, M.,
    Tsiolkas, CA., and Vela, I. *Who's Afraid of the*
    *Working Class?*

REGAN, SYLVIA, 1908–2003
*Morning Star.* 1940. SCL

REGNARD, JEAN FRANÇOIS, 1655–1709
*Le légataire universel.* 1708. BREN
    Aldington, R., translator ALD
    Variant title: *The residuary légatee*
*The residuary légatee. See* Le légataire universel

REGNAULT, CHARLES, fl.1640
*Marie Stuard, reyne d'Écosse.* 1639.
    Paulson, M. (rendered into modern French by). FALE

REGNIER, MAX ALBERT MARIE, 1908–
*The Headshrinkers. See* Paddle Your Own Canoe
*Paddle Your Own Canoe* (based on the scenario by
    Andre Gillois). 1957?
    Hill, L., translator and adapter PLAN17
    Variant title: *The Headshrinkers*

REID, ARTHUR
*People in Love.* 1937. FAMK

REID, BEN
*The Fourth Room.* 1944? NEWDI44

REID, CHRISTINA, 1942–
*My Name, Shall I Tell You My Name* (radio play). 1988.
    TYEW

REID, LESLIE, 1895–
*Trespassers.* 1923. MAS2

REILLY, CLAUDIA
*Astronauts.* 1986. DIXD1

REINGOLD, JACQUELYN
*Acapulco.* 2001. LAR
*Girl Gone.* 1994. WOMP94

REINKING, ANN, 1949– . *See* Maltby, Richard, Jr., joint
    author

REINSHAGEN, GERLIND, 1926–
*Eisenherz. See* Ironheart
*Ironheart.* 1982.
    Case, S., and Teraoka, A., translators CAS
    Variant title: *Eisenherz*

REISS, KIMBERLY. *See* Cromelin, Caroline, joint author

REIZENSTEIN, ELMER. *See* Rice, Elmer L.

RELLAN, MIGUEL ANGEL, 1943–
*The Blind Warrior.* 1967.
Wellwarth, M., translator WELK
Variant title: *El guerrero ciego*
*El guerrero ciego. See* The Blind Warrior

REMIZOV, ALEKSEI, 1877–1957
*The Tragedy of Judas, Prince of Iscariot.* 1908.
Green, M., translator GREEN

RENAUDE, NOELLE, 1949–
*The Northern Fox.* 1989.
Hanna, G, translator NEWFPB
Variant title: *Le renard du nord*
*Le renard du nord. See* The Northern Fox

RENDERS, KIM
*Motherhood, Madness, and the Shape of the Universe*
(excerpts). 1992–1993. BREK

RENEE, 1929–
*Tiggy Tiggy Touch Wood.* 1992. DEAT

REXROTH, KENNETH, 1905–1982
*Iphigenia at Aulis.* 1944? NEWDI44
*Phaedra.* 1944? NEWDI44

REYES, GUILLERMO
*Chilean Holiday.* 1996. HUMANA96
*Deporting the Divas.* 1996. CLUM
*Men on the Verge of a His–panic Breakdown.* 1994.
CLUMS

REYES, SEVERINO, 1861–1942
*R.I.P.* 1902. PHIL
Zamora, M., translator PHIL

REYNOLDS, FREDERICK, 1764–1841
*The Delinquent.* 1805. INCA2
*The Dramatist; or, Stop Him Who Can!* 1789. MOR,
NIC
*Folly as It Flies.* 1802. INCA2
*Fortune's Fool.* 1796. INCA2
*The Fugitive.* INCA8
*How to Grow Rich.* 1793. INCA1
*Laugh When You Can.* 1798. INCA2
*Life.* 1800. INCA1
*Notoriety.* 1792. INCA1
*The Rage.* 1794. INCA1
*Speculation.* 1795. INCA2
*Werter.* 1786. INCA3
*The Will.* INCA1

REYNOLDS, JEAN
*Dance with Me.* 1995. WOMP95

REYNOLDS, REBECCA
*Visitation.* 1999. HUMANA99

REZA, YASMINA, 1960–
*Art.* 1996.
Hampton, C., translator BES97, SSSIC

REZNIK, LIPE, 1890–1943? *See* Axenfeld, Israel, joint
author

RHODES, CRYSTAL
*The Trip.* 1979. CEN

RHODES, WILLIAM BARNES, 1772–1826
*Bombastes furioso.* 1810. TRUS

RHYS, ERNEST, 1859–1946
*The Masque of the Grail.* 1908. LUP

RIBES, JEAN-MICHEL, 1946–
*The Rest Have Got It Wrong.* 1976.
Watson, D., translator PAIS
Variant title: *Tout contre un petit bois*
*Tout contre un petit bois. See* The Rest Have Got It
Wrong

RIBMAN, RONALD, 1932–
*Buck.* 1983. NEWQA
*fingernails blue as flowers.* 1971. SCV

RICARDO DE LA VEGA. *See* Vega, Ricardo de la

RICE, ELMER L. (formerly Elmer Reizenstein), 1892–
1967
*The Adding Machine.* 1923. BERP, BERPA, DAV1,
DICEM, DUR, GARU, HAT, HATA, JORG,
MOSJ, MOSK, MOSL, RAVIT, SCNN, SMA,
SSSF, THF
*Counsellor-at-law.* 1931. FAMC, SCL
*Dream Girl.* 1945. BES45, GARZ, GATB3
*Flight to the West.* 1940. BES40
*Judgment Day.* 1934. FAMK
*The Left Bank.* 1931. BES31
*On Trial.* 1914. BES09, CART
*See Naples and Die.* 1929. FAMB
*Street Scene.* 1929. BES28, CER, CHA, CHAN, CHAP,
CLH, CORD, CORE, CORF, COTE, COTH,
FULT, GASB, GATB1, GRIF, MAF, MAFC,
MERU, SIXD, WATC2, WATI, WATO
*We, the People.* 1933. BES32

RICE, GEORGE EDWARD, 1822–1861
*Hamlet, Prince of Denmark.* 1852. NIN5

RICE, TIM, 1944–
*Jesus Christ Superstar, a Rock Opera* (music by Andrew
    Lloyd Webber). 1971. GREAAR
*The Lion King* (music and lyrics by). *See* Allers, Roger.
    *The Lion King*

RICHARDS, BEAH, 1920–2000
*A Black Woman Speaks.* 1950. WILK

RICHARDS, GILLIAN
*In His 80th Year.* 1987. WEJ

RICHARDS, IVOR ARMSTRONG, 1893–1979
*A Leak in the Universe.* 1954. PLAA

RICHARDS, STANLEY, 1918–1980
*District of Columbia.* 1945. HARY

RICHARDSON, HOWARD, 1917–1984, and BERNEY,
    WILLIAM
*Barbara Allen. See* Dark of the Moon
*Dark of the Moon.* 1945. PLAN2
    Variant title: *Barbara Allen*

RICHARDSON, JACK CARTER, 1935–
*Gallows Humor.* 1961. DODGE, MARO, MESSE,
    WELT
*The Prodigal.* 1960. FOR
*Xmas in Las Vegas.* 1965. SSTY

RICHARDSON, WILLIS, 1889–1977
*The Black Horseman.* 1931. RIR, RIRA
*The Broken Banjo.* 1925. LOC
*The Chip Woman's Fortune.* 1923. ROOTS, TUQT,
    TUQTR
*The Deacon's Awakening.* 1920. HARYB
*The Flight of the Natives.* 1927. HARY, LOC
*The House of Sham.* 1929. RIR, RIRA
*The Idle Head.* 1927. HARY
*The King's Dilemma.* 1929. RIR, RIRA
*A Pillar of the Church.* 1929. HARYL

RICHE, GEORGES DE PORTO. *See* Porto-Riche,
    Georges de

RICHMAN, ARTHUR, 1886–1944
*Ambush.* 1921. BES21

RICHMOND, DAVID. *See* Hall, David, joint author

RICHMOND, SAMUEL S.
*Career for Ralph.* 1949? LOVR

RICKERT, VAN DUSEN, JR.
*The Bishop's Candlesticks.* 1945? GALB

RIDER, JENNIFER
*Methusalife and Escapism.* 1988. STRA

RIFBJERG, KLAUS, 1931–
*Developments.* 1963.
    Shaw, P., translator MNOD
    Variant title: *Udviklinger*
*Udviklinger. See* Developments

RIFKIN, JAY
*The Lion King* (additional music and lyrics by). *See*
    Allers, Roger. *The Lion King*

RIGGS, LYNN, 1899–1954
*The Cherokee Night.* 1932. GEIO
*Green Grow the Lilacs.* 1931. BES30, CLH, GARU,
    LEV, LEVE, SIM
    — *See also* Hammerstein II, Oscar. *Oklahoma!* (based
        on)
*Knives from Syria.* 1927. BENP, TOD
*Roadside.* 1930. TUCN, TUCO

RILEY, WILBERFORCE
*The Missing Ingredient.* 1983. MONB1

RIMMER, CHRISTINE, 1950–
*Pelicans.* 1982. *See* Anonymous Plays. *Twenty-four
    Hours: A.M.*

RIML, MICHELLE
*Miss Teen.* 1993. ZIMM (excerpt)

RINEHART, MRS. MARY (ROBERTS), 1876–1958, and
    HOPWOOD, AVERY
*The Bat.* 1920. CART, CEY
    Variant title: *The Circular Staircase*
*The Circular Staircase. See* The Bat

RINGWOOD, GWEN PHARIS, 1910–1984
*Drum Song.* 1982. PERKY
*Garage Sale.* 1981. PENG
*Mirage.* 1979. NEWCAD2
*Pasque Flower; a Play of the Canadian Prairie.* 1939.
    WAGN2
*The Rainmaker.* 1945. WAGN3

RINTOUL, HARRY, 1956–2002
*Between Then and Now.* 1993. RUN
*Brave Hearts.* 1990. WALAG

RIORDAN, ARTHUR
*Hidden Charges.* 1994. BOUR

RIORDAN, MICHAEL
*A Jungle Out There.* 1989. NEWCAD5

RIPPINGALE, GEN, 1956– . *See* Gallagher, Kathleen,
joint author

RISING TIDE THEATRE, 1978–
*Joey.* 1981. PETERS

RISPEL, KUBBE
*The Child.* 2000. ZEE2
*Die droom (The Dream).* 2000. ZEE2
*Die stoel (The Chair).* 2000. ZEE1

RISTESKI, BLAGOJA, 1949–
*Lepa Angelina.* 1994.
Mihajlovski, D., and Gaughran, R., translators LUZ

RITCHIE, MRS. ANNA CORA (OGDEN MOWATT),
1819–1870
*Fashion; or, Life in New York.* 1845. COY, FEFNC,
GARX, HAL, MASW, MASX, MES, MONR,
MOSS2, PLAAD, QUIJ, QUIK, QUIL, QUIM,
QUIN, RICHE, WATTAD, WILMET

RITTER, ERIKA, 1948–
*Automatic Pilot.* 1980. WASCP, WASCPA1

RITZ, JOSEPH P., 1929–
*Abbey of the Monanghalia. See* Trappists
*Acts of Contrition. See* Trappists
*Trappists.* 2001. INCI
Variant Titles: *Abbey of the Monanghalia; Acts of
Contrition*

RIVAROLA MATTO, JOSE MARIA, 1917–1998
*The Fate of Chipí González.* 1954.
Jones, W., translator JONW
Variant title: *El fin de Chipí Gonzáles*
*El fin de Chipí Gonzáles. See* The Fate of Chipí
González

RIVAS, ANGEL PEREZ DE SAAVEDRA, 1791–1865
*Don Alvaro; ó la fuerza del sino.* 1835. BRET, PATT,
TRES
Variant titles: *Don Alvaro; or, The Force of Destiny;
La forza del destino*
*Don Alvaro; or, The Force of Destiny. See* Don Alvaro
ó la fuerza del sino
*La forza del destino. See* Don Alvaro

RIVAS, MANUEL LINARES. *See* Linares Rivas, Manuel

RIVERA, CARMEN
*Julia.* 1992. ANTU

RIVERA, JOSE, 1955–
*Cloud Tectonics.* 1995. HUMANA95
*The House of Ramon Iglesia.* 1983. OSB
*Lovers of Long Red Hair.* 2000. HUMANA2000
*Maricela de la Luz Lights the World.* 1998. ELLM
*Marisol.* 1992. ANTU
*References to Salvador Dali Make Me Hot.* 1999.
PLACGH
*Tape.* 1993. HUMANA93
*The Winged Man.* 1993. PLACA

RIVERS, LOU. *See* Rivers, Louis

RIVERS, LOUIS, 1922–
*More Bread and the Circus* (1976). CEN
*This Piece of Land.* 1975. GEMM

RIVERS, SUSAN, 1954–
*Maud Gonne Says No to the Poet.* 1978. WES3

RIVES, AMELIE. *See* Troubetskoy, Amélie (Rives)
Chanler

RIVINGTON, JAMES, 1724–1802
*"The Battle of Brooklyn." See* Anonymous Plays. *The
Battle of Brooklyn*

RNO, SUNG, 1967–
*Cleveland Raining.* 1997. HOUST

ROBERT, FRANÇOIS LE METEL DE BOIS. *See* Bois—
Robert, François Le Mètel de

ROBERTS, CYRIL, 1892–
*Tails Up.* 1935? GALB

ROBERTS, DMAE, 1957–
*Breaking Glass.* 1997. HOUST

ROBERTS, SHEILA, 1942–
*Weekend* (Scene I only). CONTSO

ROBERTS, TED, 1931–
*Lindsay's Boy* (TV play). 1974. FIO

ROBERTSON, LOUIS ALEXANDER, 1856–1910
*Montezuma.* 1903. BOH1

ROBERTSON, THOMAS WILLIAM, 1829–1871
*Caste.* 1867. ASG, BAI, BOWY, COD, COT, DUR,
MART, MATTL, MOSN, MOSO, ROWE, TAU
*Society.* 1865. BAT16, HUDV, RUB

ROBINS, ELIZABETH, 1862–1952
*Votes for Women.* 1907. CHOT, KEL, VOTE, WOTHM
— *See also* Bell, Florence, joint author

*Comedia de Calisto y Melibea. See* Celestina
*Tragicomedia de Calixto y Melibea. See* Celestina

ROJAS, RICARDO, 1882–1957
*Ollántay.* 1938. ALPE

ROJAS ZORRILLA, FRANCISCO DE, 1607–1648
*Del rey abajo, ninguno.* 1650. ALP
  Goldberg, I., translator ALPF
  Variant title: *None beneath the King*
*Entre bobos anda el juego.* 1638. MACU
*None beneath the King. See* del rey abajo, ninguno

ROKK, VSEVOLOD, d. 1953 (b. Vsevolod Merkulov)
*Engineer Sergeyev.* 1941.
  Moss, H., translator SEVP

ROMAINS, JULES (formerly Louis Henri Jean Farigoule),
  1885–1972
*Cromedeyre-le-vieilo.* 1920. RHO
*Dr. Knock.* 1923
  Granville-Barker, H., translator BENS3

ROMAN, MIKHAIL
*The New Arrival.* 1965. ABL

ROMCEVIC, NEBOJSA, 1962–
*Cordon.* 2000.
  Vujovic, S., translator ROEB

ROME, HAROLD JACOB, 1908–1993
*Fanny. See* Behrman, Samuel Nathaniel and Logan,
  Joshua. *Fanny* (music and lyrics by)
*Wish You Were Here. See* Kober, Arthur and Logan,
  Joshua. *Wish You Were Here* (music and lyrics by)

ROMERIL, JOHN, 1945–
*Chicago, Chicago. See* The Man from Chicago
*The Man from Chicago.* 1969. BRIMA3, FOUA
*Mrs Thally F.* 1971. BRIM1

ROMERO, ELAINE
*¡Curanderas! Serpents of the Clouds.* 1996. WOMP2000
*The Fat-free Chicana & the Snow Cap Queen.* 2000.
  PURO

ROMERO, MARIELA, 1949–
*Esperando al italiano. See* Waiting for the Italian
*Waiting for the Italian.* 1988.
  Salas, T., and Vargas, M., translators SALA
  Variant title: *Esperando al italiano*

RONDER, JACK, 1924–
*This Year, Next Year.* 1960. PLAN22
  Variant title: *Wedding Day*
*Wedding Day. See* This Year, Next Year

RONILD, PETER, 1928–2001
*Boxing for One Person. See* Boxing for One
*Boxing for One.* 1964.
  Shaw, P., translator MNOD
  Variant titles: *Boxing for One Person; Boxning for en
  person*
*Boxning for en person. See* Boxing for One

ROPER, TONY
*The Steamie.* 1987. CALE

ROPES, BRADFORD
*42nd Street. See* Stewart, Michael. *42nd Street* (from the
  novel by)

ROSE, DAVID, 1910–1990
*Winged Victory* (music by). *See* Hart, Moss. *Winged
  Victory*

ROSE, REGINALD, 1920–2002
*Dino.* 1957. GRIH
*Thunder on Sycamore Street.* BOOK, BRNB
*Twelve Angry Men.* 1954. BOOK, CARL, CARLE

ROSE, RICHARD, and KUGLER, D. D.
*Newhouse.* 1989. CTR

ROSEI, PETER, 1946–
*Blameless.* 1990.
  Hutchinson, H., translator LAX
  Variant title: *Die Schuldlosen*
*Die Schuldlosen. See* Blameless

ROSEN, JULIUS, 1833–1892
*Ein knopf. See* Birmelin, John. *Der gnopp* (based on the
  play by)
*Starke mitteln. See* Daly, Augustin. *Needles and Pins*
  (adapted from)

ROSEN, SHELDON, 1943–
*The Box.* 1974. BRIQ
*Love Mouse. See* Two plays: *Love Mouse; Meyer's
  Room*
*Meyer's Room. See* Two plays: *Love Mouse; Meyer's
  Room*
*Ned and Jack.* 1977. WASCT
Two plays: *Love Mouse; Meyer's Room.* 1971. KAL1
  Variant titles: *Love Mouse; Meyer's Room*

ROSENBERG, JAMES L., 1921–
*The Death and Life of Sneaky Fitch.* NEWA1

ROSENBERG, JEROLD. *See* Ross, Jerry (pseudonym)

ROSENFELD, SYDNEY, 1855–1931. *See* Lloyd, David
  D., joint author

ROSENTHAL, ANDREW, 1917–1979
*Third Person.* 1951. PLAN7

ROSENTHAL, RACHEL, 1926–
*My Brazil.* 1979. OUT
*Pangaean Dreams: A Shamanic Journey.* 1990. MARR

ROSENZWEIG, BARNEY, 1937– . *See* Avedon, Barbara,
    joint author

ROSMER, ERNST (pseudonym of Elsa Bernstein),
    1866–1949
*Maria Arndt.* 1908.
    Kord, S., translator KEL

ROSS, GEORGE, 1907–1982, and SINGER, CAMPBELL
*Any Other Business.* 1957. PLAN18
*Difference of Opinion.* 1965. PLAN27
*Guilty Party.* 1960. PLAN24
    Variant title: *Refer to Drawer*
*Refer to Drawer. See* Guilty Party
*The Sacking of Norman Banks.* 1969. PLAN37

ROSS, IAN, 1968–
*fareWel.* 1996. BEYO (excerpt)
*Heart of a Distant Tribe.* 1996. RUN

ROSS, JERRY (pseudonym of JEROLD ROSENBERG),
    1926–1955
*The Pajama Game. See* Abbott, George and Bissell,
    Richard. *The Pajama Game* (lyrics and music by)

ROSS, LESLEY (pseudonym of GREG ASHTON), 1969– ,
    and MORGAN, CHRIS
*Inside Out.* 2001. NEWWD3

ROSS, SINCLAIR, 1908–1996
*"One's a Heifer" in The Lamp at Noon and Other
    Stories. See* Dorn, Rudi. *One's a Heifer* (based on
    the short story by)

ROSSELLI, AMELIA, 1870–1954
*Her Soul.* 1898.
    Costa-Zalessow, N., and Borelli, J., translators KEL

ROSSETTI, CHRISTINA, 1830–1894
*"Goblin Market." See* Harmon, Peggy. *Goblin Market*
    (adapted from the poem by)

ROSSI, VITTORIO, 1961–
*Little Blood Brother.* 1986. PASS

ROSSO DI SAN SECONDO, PIER MARIA, 1889–1956
*Marionette, che passionel! See* Puppets of Passion!
*Puppets of Passion!* 1918.

House, J., translator TWEI
    Variant title: *Marionette, che passionel!*
*La scale. See* The Stairs
*The Stairs.* 1925.
    Katzin, W., translator KAT
    Variant title: *La scale*

ROSTAND, EDMOND, 1868–1918
*Cyrano de Bergerac.* 1897. BOR, GRA, SEA
    Anonymous translator LAM, WISD, ZIM
    Dole, H., translator SMN, STRO
    Hall, G., translator COTH, DICDS, DICIN2, HAV,
        HUDS2, MACC, MACE, MACF, MOSQ, TUCG,
        TUCM, TUCN, TUCO, WATI, WATL2, WATO,
        WATR, WHI, WHK
    Henderson, D., translator HUD
    Hooker, B., translator BLOO, CARPA, CEW, GATT,
        GOLK, HILP, HILPDH4, KNIC, TREBA, TREBJ,
        TREC2, TREE2, TRE12, WALJ, WISE
    Kingsbury, H., translator BLOD1, COHM, HOUK,
        KON, LEV, LEVE, SHRO, TRE, TREA1
    Thomas, G., and Guillemard, M., translators MIL
    Whitehall, H., translator WORP
    Wolfe, H., translator BENU, FOUM
*La dernière nuit de Don Juan. See* The Last Night of
    Don Juan
*Don Juan's Last Night. See* The Last Night of Don Juan
*The Fantasticks. See* The Romancers
*The Last Night of Don Juan.* 1922.
    Bagley, D., translator MARJ
    Kaye, M., translator KAYD
    Riggs, T., translator KRE
    Variant titles: *La dernière nuit de Don Juan; Don
        Juan; Don Juan's Final Night, Don Juan's Last
        Night*
*The Romancers.* 1894.
    Anonymous translator COOK2
    Clark, B., translator BERMG, PATM
    Hendee, M., translator COD
    Variant titles: *The Fantasticks; The Romantics; Les
        romanesques*
*Les romanesques. See* The Romancers
*The Romantics. See* The Romancers

ROSTEN, NORMAN, 1914–1995
*Mister Johnson.* 1955. THEA56

ROSWITHA VON GANDERSHEIM. *See* Hrotsvit, of
    Gandersheim

ROSZKOWSKI, DAVID. *See* Ives, David

ROTH, BEATRICE, 1919–
*The Father.* 1985. OUT

ROTH, FRIEDERIKE, 1948–
*Klavierspiele. See* Piano Plays
*Piano Plays.* 1980.
Weddington, A., translator CAS
Variant title: *Klavierspiele*

ROTROU, JEAN DE, 1609–1650
*Chosroes.* 1648.
Lockert, L., translator LOCR
Variant title: *Cosroés*
*Coeroés. See* Chosroes
*Le feint véritable. See* Saint Genesius
*Saint Genesius.* 1646?
Lockert, L., translator LOCU
Variant titles: *Le feint véritable; Saint Genest; Le
véritable Saint Genest*
*Saint Genest. See* Saint Genesius
*Venceslas. See* Wenceshaus
*Le véritable Saint Genest. See* Saint Genesius
*Wenceshaus.* 1647.
Lockert, L., translator LOCR
Variant title: *Venceslas*

ROTTER, FRITZ, 1900–1984, and VINCENT, ALLEN
*Letters to Lucerne.* 1941. BES41

ROUSSIN, CLAUDE, 1941–
*Une job. See* Looking for a Job
*Looking for a Job.* 1972.
Van Meer, A., translator KAL5
Variant title: *Une job*

ROVNER, EDUARDO, 1942–
*Compañía. See* Company
*Company.* 1993.
Thomas, C., translator LATTH
Variant title: *Compañía*
*Cuarteto.* 1991. PARRI
*She Returned One Night.* 1991.
Thomas, C., translator LATTH
Variant title: *Volvió una noche*
*Volvió una noche. See* She Returned One Night

ROWE, NICHOLAS, 1674–1718
*Ambitious step-mother.* (1700) BELK16
*The fair penitent.* 1703. BELK3, DOB, MAND, MANF,
WILSP
*Lady Jane Gray.* 1715. BELK7
*The Royal Convert.* 1707. BELK7
*Tamerlane.* 1701. BELK3
*The Tragedy of Jane Shore.* 1713. BELK1, EIGH, HAN,
MOSE2, NET, STM, TUQ
*Ulysses.* 1705. BELK18

ROWE, ROSEMARY
*Benedetta Carlini: Lesbian Nun of Renaissance Italy.*
1996. STN

ROWELL, GEORGE, 1923–2001
*Sixty Thousand Nights* (script, research and lyrics by).
*See* May, Val. *Sixty Thousand Nights*
— *See* Woods, Aubrey, joint author

ROWLEY, WILLIAM, 1585?–1642?
*The Birth of Merlin* (sometimes attributed to). *See*
Anonymous Plays. *The Birth of Merlin*
— *See also* Day, John; Ford, John; Middleton,
Thomas, joint authors

ROWSON, SUSANNA HASWELL, 1762–1828
*Slaves in Algiers, or a Struggle for Freedom.* 1794.
KRIT
Variant title: *A Struggle for Freedom*
*A Struggle for Freedom. See* Slaves in Algiers

ROY, EDWARD
*The Other Side of the Closet.* 1997. RAVE

ROYCE, CHERYL
*My Son Susie.* 1994. WOMP93

ROYLE, EDWIN MILTON, 1862–1942
*The Squaw Man.* 1905. BES99

ROZENMACHER, GERMAN, 1936–1971
*Simon Brumelstein, Knight of the Indies.* 1970.
Glickman, N., and Waldman, G., translators ARGJT
Variant title: *Simon, el caballero de Indies*
*Simon, el caballero de Indies. See* Simon Brumelstein,
Knight of the Indies

RÓZEWICZ, TADEUSZ, 1921–
*Birth Rate: The Biography of a Play for the Theatre.*
1968.
Gerould, D., and Gerould, E., translators TWEN
Variant title: *Przyrost Naturalny*
*Przyrost Naturalny. See* Birth Rate: The Biography of a
Play for the Theatre

ROZOV, VICTOR SERGEEVICH, 1913–2004
*In Search of Happiness.* 1955.
Daglish, R., translator CLKX
Variant title: *V poiskach radosti*
*V poiskach radosti. See* In Search of Happiness

RUBENSTEIN, KEN
*Icarus.* NEWA4

RUSSELL, LAWRENCE, 1941–
*Penetration.* 1969. ALI

RUSSELL, WILLY, 1947–
*Shirley Valentine.* 1986. BES88

RUST, D., 1959–
*Jennifer Klemm.* 1995.
    Riggs, R., translator DODGSG

RUSTEBUEF. *See* Rutebeuf

RUTEBEUF, fl.1248–1277
*Le miracle de Theophile.* 13th century AXT

RUTEBUEF. *See* Rutebeuf

RUTHERFORD, STANLEY
*The Chinese Art of Placement.* 1998. PLACJ

RUX, CARL HANCOCK, 1970–
*Chapter & Verse* (a poem in progress). 1997. ALG

RUZANTE. *See* Beolco, Angelo

RUZZANTE. *See* Beolco, Angelo

RYE, ELIZABETH
*The Three-fold Path.* 1935. FIN

RYERSON, FLORENCE, 1892–1965 (MRS. COLIN
    CLEMENTS), and CLEMENTS, COLIN
    CAMPBELL
*Harriet.* 1943. BES42

RYGA, GEORGE, 1932–1987
*The Ecstasy of Rita Joe.* 1967. SCNQCA, SCNQCB,
    WASCP, WASCPA1, WASCPB1
*Indian* (television play). 1962. OXFC, PENG

RYLSKI, NIKA
*Just like a kommedia.* 1984. RAVEL

RYSKIND, MORRIE, 1895–1985. *See* Kaufman, George
    S., joint author

RYTON, ROYCE, 1924–2009
*Crown Matrimonial.* 1972. PLAN43

RYUM, ULLA, 1937–
*And the Birds Are Singing Again* (radio drama). 1980.
    Brask, P., translator BRAK

"S., MR., MR. OF ART." *See* Stevenson, William

SA-AMI-YASUKIYO, HIYOSHI. *See* Hiyoshi, Sa-Ami
    Yasukiyo

SAADAWI, NAWAL EL, 1931–
*Twelve Women in a Cell.* 1984.
    Baraitser, M., and Robson, C., translators BARAM

SAALBACH, ASTRID, 1955–
*Morgen og aften. See* Morning and Evening
*Morning and Evening.* 1993.
    Madsen, M., translator NEWDAN
    Variant title: *Morgen og aften*

SAAVEDRA, GUADALUPE DE, 1936?–
*Justice.* ASF

SAAVEDRA, MIGUEL DE CERVANTES. *See* Cervantes
    Saavedra, Miguel

SAAVEDRA RIVAS, ANGEL PEREZ DE. *See* Rivas,
    Angel Pérez de Saavedra

SACHS, HANS, 1494–1576
*Der fahrende schüller im Paradies. See* The Wandering
    Scholar from Paradise
*Der fahrende schüller mit dem teufelbanner. See* Raising
    the Devil
*Fool Surgery.* 1557.
    Walsh, M., translator GILL
*The Horse Thief.* 1553.
    Leighton, W., translator INGW
*Raising the Devil.* 155–?
    Chambers, W., translator BAT10
    Variant titles: *Der fahrende schüller mit dem
        teufelbanner; The Wandering Scholar and Exorcist*
*The Wandering Scholar and Exorcist. See* Raising the
    Devil
*The Wandering Scholar from Paradise.* 1550.
    Eliot, S., translator CLF1, KRE, PROW
    Variant title: *Der fahrende schüller im Paradies*

SACHS, NELLY, 1891–1970
*Eli: A Mystery Play of the Sufferings of Israel.* 1950.
    Holme, CA., translator FUCHS

SACK, LEENY, 1951–
*The Survivor and the Translator* 1980. OUT, THLA

SACKLER, HOWARD, 1929–1982
*The Great White Hope.* 1968. BES68, GARTL, RICIS

SACKVILLE, THOMAS (LORD BUCKHURST, 1st
    EARL OF DORSET), 1536–1608, and NORTON,
    THOMAS
*Gorboduc; or, Ferrex and Porrex.* 1561. ADA, BAS,
    CRE, CUN, DPR1, GARZB, MAKG, MIN1,
    MIO1, MIR, NES, SCW, TAV

Variant title: *The Tragidie of [Gorboduc; or, of]*
*Ferrex and Porrex*
*The Tragidie of [Gorboduc; or, of] Ferrex and Porrex.*
*See* Gorboduc; or, Ferrex and Porrex

SACKVILLE WEST, VICTORIA MARY, 1892–1962
*The Edwardians. See* Gow, Ronald. *The Edwardians*
(adapted from)

SA'EDI, GHOLAMHOSEYN (Morad, Gowar-e,
pseudonym), 1935–1985
*Honeymoon.* 1978.
Clark, J., Ghanoonparvar, M., Hajibashi, Z., Phillips,
M., and Salmon, P., translators GHAN
Variant title: *Mah-e asal*
*Karbafakha dar sangar. See* Workaholics in the
Trenches
*Mah-e asal. See* Honeymoon
*O Fool! O Fooled!* 1967.
Kapuscinski, G., translator MOCPD
*Workaholics in the Trenches.* 1960.
Chambers, D., Childs, L., Consolvi, P., and Putril, S.,
translators GHAN
Variant title: *Karbafakha dar sangar*

SAENZ, DIANA, 1949–
*A Dream of Canaries.* FEY

SAFRAN, STEVEN A.
*Not One of Us.* 1988. STRA (excerpt)

SAHNI, BHISHAM, 1915–2003
*Hanush.* 1977.
Sahni, B., translator KAM2

SAIDY, FRED, 1907–1982. *See* Harburg, Edgar Y., joint
author

SAINER, ARTHUR, 1924–2007
*The Thing Itself.* 1967. BALLE6

ST. GERMAIN, MARK, 1955–
*Camping with Henry and Tom.* 1995. BES94

ST. JAMES, ANN
*Queen of Spades* (excerpt from an untitled work in
progress). 1997. BREK

ST. JOHN, CHRISTOPHER, pseudonym. *See* Marshall,
Christabel.

SAINT-JOHN, JOHN, 1746–1793
*Mary Queen of Scots.* 1789. INCA8

ST. JOSEPH, ELLIS, 1911–1993
*A Passenger to Bali.* 1940. HAT

ST. PETER'S YOUTH GROUP, SCOTLAND
*Persephone and the Rubbish Bin.* 1993. SACR

SAITŌ, REN, 1940–
*Asayake no Manhattan. See* Red Dawn over
Manhattan
*Red Dawn over Manhattan.* 1993.
Goodman, D., translator HACJT6
Variant title: *Asayake no Manhattan*
— *See also* Satoh, Makoto, joint author

SAJA, KAZYS, 1932–
*Devynbédžiai. See* The Village of Nine Woes
*The Village of Nine Woes.* 1974.
Juodvalkis, E., translator GOLB
Variant title: *Devynbédžiai*

SAKAMOTO, EDWARD, 1940–
*In the Alley.* 1961. KUMU

SAKATE, YŌJI, 1962–
*Epitaph for the Whales.* 1993.
Masako, Y., translator HACJT1

SAKURADA, JISUKE II, 1768–1829. *See* Tsuruya,
Namboku IV, joint author

SALAAM, KALAMU YA, 1947– (b. Vallery Ferdinand
III)
*The Quest.* 1989. KINHP
— *See also* FERDINAND, VAL

SALACROU, ARMAND, 1899–1989
*A Circus Story.* 1922.
Benedikt, M., translator BEN
Variant title: *L'histoire du cirque*
*L'histoire du cirque. See* A Circus Story
*Marguerite.* 1944.
Voysey, M., translator RICK
Variant title: *La Marguerite*
*La Marguerite. See* Marguerite

SALIM, `ALI, 1936–
*The Comedy of Oedipus: You're the One Who Killed the*
*Beast.* 1970.
Cacchia, P., and O'Grady, D., translators JAY
Variant title: *Inta 'l-li qatalt al-wahsh*
*Inta 'l-li qatalt al-wahsh. See* The Comedy of Oedipus:
You're the One Who Killed the Beast

SALOM, JAIME, 1925–
*Almost a Goddess.* 1993.
Edwards, G., translator BURN
*Bitter Lemon.* 1976.
O'Connor, P., translator OCONNP

SANTIAGO, DANNY, pseudonym. *See* James, Dan

SANTOS, AL
*Ang sistema ni Propesor Tuko. See* The System of
    Professor Tuko
*The System of Professor Tuko.* 1981.
    Santos, A., translator MLAP
    Variant title: *Ang sistema ni Propesor Tuko*

SANTOS, JOHN
*Watsonville: Some Place Not Here* (music by John
    Santos).
    *See* Moraga, Cherríe. *Watsonville: Some Place Not
    Here*

SANTOS, JUAN D.
*Kar-Na-Na.* PHIL
*Yesterday, Today, Tomorrow.*
    Casambre, A., translator PHIL
    Variant title: *Kar-Na-Na*

SAPERGIA, BARBARA, 1943–
*Roundup.* 1990. ZIMM (excerpt)

SAPINSLEY, ALVIN, 1921–2002
*Even the Weariest River.* 1957? GREAB

SARACHCHANDRA, EDIRIWIRA, 1914–1996
*The Golden Swan, or Beyond the Curtain.* 1989. GOON

SARDOU, VICTORIEN, 1831–1908
*Fatherland. See* Patrie!
*For Love or Money.* 1861.
    Shapiro, N., translator FLEA
    Variant title: *L'Ecureuil*
*L'Ecureuil. See* For Love or Money
*Patrie!* 1869.
    Clark, B., translator LEV, LEVE
    Variant title: *Fatherland*
*Les pattes de mouche.* 1860.
    Gilmour, L., translator DRAD2, PLAB2, SSTG
    Variant title: *A Scrap of Paper*
*A Scrap of Paper. See* Les pattes de mouche

—— and NAJAC, EMILE DE
*Divorçons. See* Let's Get a Divorce!
*Let's Get a Divorce!* 1880.
    Davies, F., translator LAB
    Goldsby, A., and R., translators BENSC, PLAN31
    Variant title: *Divorçons*

SARGENT, LYDIA, 1942–
*Daughter of Earth* (adapted from the novel by Agnes
    Smedley). 1984. KLEIN
*I Read about My Death in Vogue Magazine.* 1986.
    KLEIN

SARMA, ARUN, 1931–
*Aahar. See* Food
*Food.* 1964.
    Sharma, A., translator KAM3
    Variant title: *Aahar*

SARMENT, JEAN, 1897–1976
*The Most Beautiful Eyes in the World. See* Les plus
    beaux yeux du monde
*Le pécheur d'ombres.* 1921. HART
    Variant title: *The Shadow Fisher*
*Les plus beaux yeux du monde.* 1925. RHO
    Variant title: *The Most Beautiful Eyes in the World*
*The Shadow Fisher. See* Le pécheur d'ombres

SARO-WIWA, KEN, 1941–1995
*The Transistor Radio* (television play). 1987. HUTCH

SAROYAN, WILLIAM, 1908–1981
*The Cave Dwellers.* 1956. GARSA
*Hello Out There.* 1942. ELKE, HOLP, WATE
*The Human Comedy. See* Estabrook, Howard. *The
    Human Comedy* (screenplay based on the book by)
*The Man with the Heart in the Highlands. See* My
    Heart's in the Highlands
*My Heart's in the Highlands.* 1930. BART, BENT4,
    ROYE, TREBA, TREBJ, TREC2, TREE3, TRE13,
    VOAD
    Variant title: *The Man with the Heart in the
    Highlands*
*The Oyster and the Pearl.* 1953. THOD
*The People with Light Coming Out of Them.* 1942.
    GALB
*The Time of Your Life.* 1939. BES39, BIER, BLOC,
    CET, CLUR, COTQ, CRIT, DAVM, FAMAL,
    GARZ, GATB3, GAVE, HATA, KERN, LAV,
    MAFC, MERU, SCAR, SILS, STEI

SARRAUTE, NATHALIE, 1900–1999
*Over Nothing at All.* 1982.
    Wehle, P., translator WEHLE

SARTRE, JEAN-PAUL, 1905–1980
*Crime Passional. See* Les mains sales
*Dirty Hands. See* Les mains sales
*The Flies.* 1943.
    Gilbert, S., translator TREBA, TREBJ, TREC2,
    TREE2, TREI2
    Variant title: *Les mouches*
*Huis clos.* 1944. CLOU2, CLOUD2, CLOUDS2
    Anonymous translator ABCF, FOUAC
    Gilbert, S., translator BRZA, CLKJ, MALI2,
    MALN2, NORI2
    Stuart, S., translator BLOC, GARZH, HAMI
    Variant titles: *In Camera; No Exit*

*The Faithful Friend.* 17th century?
  Chambers, W., translator BAT5
  Variant title: *Il fido amico*
*Il fido amico. See* The Faithful Friend
*The Portrait.* 1575?
  Leverton, G., translator TREB
  Van Der Meer, E., translator CLF2, LEV, LEVE
  Variant title: *Il rittrato*
*Il rittrato. See* The Portrait
  — *See also* Anonymous Plays. *The Pedant*

SCANLON, PATRICIA
*What Is This Everything?* 1992. WOMP92

SCHARY, DORE, 1905–1980
*The Devil's Advocate* (based on the novel by Morris L.
    West). 1961. BES60
*Sunrise at Campobello.* 1958. AMB, BES57, CES

SCHAUFFLER, MRS. ELSIE (TOUGH), 1888–1935
*Parnell.* 1936. FAMJ

SCHEFFAUER, HERMAN GEORGE, 1878–1927
*The Sons of Baldur.* 1908. BOH1

SCHEFFER, WILL
*Falling Man.* 1994. ACTOR

SCHEHADE, GEORGES, 1910–1989
*Histoire de Vasco. See* Vasco
*The History of Vasco. See* Vasco
*Vasco.* 1956.
    Victor, L., translator and adapter COTS
    Variant titles: *Histoire de Vasco; The History of Vasco*

SCHEIN, DAVID
*Out Comes Butch.* 1981. WES17/18

SCHENKAR, JOAN, 1946–
*The Lodger.* 1988. CURB
*Signs of Life.* 1979. WOMS
*The Universal Wolf.* 1991. LAMO

SCHENKKAN, ROBERT, 1953–
*The Kentucky Cycle.* 1991. BES93

SCHEVILL, JAMES ERWIN, 1920–2009
*American Power. See* The Master; The Space Fan (cover
    title of two unrelated one-act plays)
*Cathedral of Ice.* 1975. FUCHS
*The Master.* 1964. BALLE1
*The Space Fan.* 1964. BALLE1

SCHILDT, RUNAR, 1888–1925
*Galgamannen; en midvintersaga. See* The Gallows Man:
    A Midwinter Story

*The Gallows Man; a Midwinter Story.* 1922.
  Alexander, H., translator SCAN1
  Variant title: *Galgamannen: en midvintersaga*

SCHILLER, FRIEDRICH. *See* Schiller, Johann Christoph
    Friedrich von

SCHILLER, JOHANN CHRISTOPH FRIEDRICH VON,
    1759–1805
*The Camp of Wallenstein.* 1798.
  Churchill, J., translator BAT10
  Variant titles: *Das lager; Wallenstein; Wallensteins
    lager*
*The Death of Wallenstein.* 1799.
  Coleridge, S., translator ESS, FRA3, KRE
  Variant titles: *Wallenstein; Wallensteins tod*
*Don Carlos.* 1787.
  Kirkup, J., translator BENR2
*The Homage of the Arts.* 1804.
  Coleman, A., translator FRA3
  Variant title: *Die huldigung des künste*
*Die huldigung des künste. See* The Homage of the Arts
*Das lager. See* The Camp of Wallenstein
*Mary Stuart.* 1801.
  Goldstone, J., and Reich, J., translators HOUK
  Lamport, F., translator LAMP
  Lustig, T., translator LUST, TREB
  Mellish, J., translator and Bentley, E., adapter
    BENR2, DRAD2, PLAB2
*The Robbers.* 1782.
  Lamport, F., translator STURM
*Wallenstein* (trilogy). *See* The Camp of Wallenstein; The
    Death of Wallenstein
*Wallensteins lager. See* The Camp of Wallenstein
*Wallensteins tod. See* The Death of Wallenstein
*Wilhelm Tell. See* William Tell
*William Tell.* 1804.
  Jordan, G., translator HILPDH4
  Martin, T., translator CLF2, FRA3, GREA, HARC26,
    MATT, SMK, STA, WEAV2
  Variant title: *Wilhelm Tell*

SCHISGAL, MURRAY, 1926–
*All over Town.* 1974. BES74
*The Chinese.* 1970. RICK
*Luv.* 1963. BES64, CEQA
*The Typists.* 1960. MARO

SCHLEGEL, JOHANN ELIAS, 1719–1749
*The Dumb Beauty.* 1747.
  Lefevere, A., translator GILL

SCHLITT, R.
*The Egg. See* Marceau, Felicien. *The Egg* (translated and
    adapted by)

SCHLOSS, MARTIN F.
  *Totentanz. See* Anonymous Plays. *Totentanz* (from the German text of)

SCHLUTER, KARL, 1883–1960
  *Afsporet. See* Off the Rails
  *Off the Rails.* 1932.
    Born, A., translator CONT
    Variant title: *Afsporet*

SCHMIDHUBER DE LA MORA, GUILLERMO, 1943–
  *Los heroes inútiles. See* The Useless Heroes
  *Obituary.* 1993.
    Thomas, C., translator LATTH
    Variant title: *Obituario*
  *Obituario. See* Obituary
  *The Secret Friendship of Juana and Dorothy.* 1995.
    Thomas, C., translator LATTH
    Variant title: *La secreta amistad de Juana y Dorotea*
  *La secreta amistad de Juana y Dorotea. See* The Secret Friendship of Juana and Dorothy
  *The Useless Heroes.* 1979.
    Thomas, C., translator LATTH
    Variant title: *Los heroes inútiles*

SCHMIDMAN, JO ANN, 1948– . *See* Terry, Megan, joint author
  *Babes in the Big House* (structure by). *See* Terry, Megan. *Babes in the Big House*
  *Running Gag.* 1979 (lyrics by Megan Terry; music by Marianne de Pury and Lynn Herrick). HIJ

SCHMIDT, HARVEY, 1929–
  *Celebration* (music by). *See* Jones, Tom. *Celebration*

SCHMIEDL, ADAORA NZELIBE. *See* Bush, Max.
  *Ezigbo, the Spirit Child* (dramatized for the stage from an Igbo story as told by)

SCHNEEMANN, CAROLEE, 1939–
  *Meat Joy.* ASF

SCHNEIDER, ANDREW. *See* Frolov, Diane, joint author

SCHNEIDER, DAVID
  *The Eleventh Commandment.* 1996. LINDB

SCHNEIDER, PAT
  *After the Applebox.* 1989. VICK2
  *A Question of Place.* 1983. VICK1

SCHNEIDER, SIMONE, 1962–
  *Malaria.* 1998.
    Black, P., translator DODGSP

SCHNIBBE, HARRY. *See* Breen, Richard, joint author

SCHNITZLER, ARTHUR, 1862–1931
  *The Affairs of Anatol. See* Anatol
  *Anatol.* 1893.
    Colbron, G., translator CEW
    Granville-Barker, H., translator BENS3
    Variant title: *The Affairs of Anatol*
    — *See also* A Farewell Supper (from *Anatol*)
  *The Duke and the Actress. See* The Green Cockatoo
  *Der einsame weg. See* The Lonely Way
  *A Farewell Supper* (from *Anatol*). 1893.
    Granville-Barker, H., translator MIKL
  *Flirtation. See* Light-o'-love
  *Die frage an das schicksal. See* Questioning the Irrevocable
  *The Game of Love. See* Light-o'-love
  *The Green Cockatoo. See* Der gruene kakadu
  *Der gruene kakadu.* 1899. FEFH2
    Samuel, H., translator FRA20
    Van Der Meer, E., translator LEV, LEVE
    Variant titles: *The Duke and the Actress; The Green Cockatoo*
  *Hands Around. See* Round Dance
  *Intermezzo.* 1905.
    Björkman, E., translator STE
    Variant title: *Zwischenspiel*
  *Lebendige stunden.* 1902. STI1
    Colbron, G., translator DICDS
    Variant title: *Living Hours*
  *Liebelei. See* Light-o'-love
  *Light-o'-love.* 1895.
    Morgan, B., translator DICIN1, TUCG, TUCM, TUCN, TUCO, WATI, WATL1
    Mueller, C., translator COTKJ
    Variant titles: *Flirtation; The Game of Love; Liebelei; Playing with Love; The Reckoning*
  *Literatur. See* Literature
  *Literature.* 1902.
    Coleman, A., translator FRA20
    Variant title: *Literatur*
  *Living Hours. See* Lebendige stunden
  *The Lonely Way.* 1904.
    Björkman, E., translator MOSQ
    Leigh, J., translator WHI
    Variant title: *Der einsame weg*
  *Merry Go Round. See* Round Dance
  *Playing with Love. See* Light-o'-love
  *Professor Bernhardi.* 1912.
    Borell, L., and Adam, R., translators FAMJ
  *Questioning the Irrevocable.* 1893.
    Chambers, W., translator BAT12
    Variant title: *Die frage an das schicksal*
  *The Reckoning. See* Light-o'-love
  *Reigen. See* Round Dance

*La ronde. See* Round Dance
*Round Dance.* 1897.
  Bentley, E., translator BEFOB, BENT2, WELT
  Mueller, C., translator ANTH, COTKJ, COTQ, WEIP
  Wallis, K., translator BENS1
  Weigert, H., and Newhall, P., translators BLOC
  Variant titles: *Hands Around; Merry Go Round;*
    *Reigen; La ronde*
*Zwischenspiel. See* Intermezzo

SCHONBERG, CLAUDE-MICHEL, 1944–
  *Les misérables* (music by). *See* Boubil, A., and
    Schönberg, C. *Les misérables*
  *Miss Saigon* (music by). *See* Boubil, A., and Schönberg,
    C. *Miss Saigon*

SCHONHERR, KARL, 1869–1943
  *Faith and Fireside.* 1910.
    Mach, E., translator FRA16
    Variant title: *Glaube und heimat*
  *Glaube und heimat. See* Faith and Fireside

SCHOTTER, RICHARD, 1944–
  *Benya the King.* 1979. NEWJV

SCHRADER, CLARE
  *Corryvrecken.* FEFNV

SCHRADER, LEONARD, 1943–2006
  *Kiss of the Spider Woman* (screenplay by; based on the
    novel by Manual Puig). 1987. WOTHA

SCHREYER, LOTHAR, 1886–1966
  *The Crucifixion.* 1920.
    Gordon, M., translator EXP

SCHROCK, GLADDEN
  *Glutt. See* Two for the Silence
  *Madam Popov.* 1970. BALLE9
  *Taps. See* Two for the Silence
  *Two for the Silence* (2 one-act plays *Glutt, Taps*). 1976.
    GUTR

SCHULBERG, BUDD, 1914–2009, and BREIT,
    HARVEY
  *The Disenchanted* (adapted from the novel by Budd
    Schulberg). 1958. BES58

SCHULL, (JOHN) JOSEPH. *See* Schull, Joseph

SCHULL, JOSEPH, 1916–1980
  *The Vice President.* (1973) KAL3

SCHULMAN, SARAH, 1958–
  *Promenade.* 1995. DEAT

SCHUYLER, GEORGE S., 1895–1977
  *The Yellow Peril.* 1925. HARYL

SCHWAB, WERNER, 1958–1994
  *Holy Mothers.* 1990.
    Oakes, M., translator DODGSP
    Variant title: *Die präsidentinnen*
  *People Annihilation or My Liver Is Senseless.* 1991.
    Roloff, M., translator LAXC
    Variant title: *Volksvernichtung oder meine leber ist*
      *sinnlos*
  *Die präsidentinnen. See* Holy Mothers
  *Volksvernichtung oder meine leber ist sinnlos. See*
    People Annihilation or My Liver Is Senseless

SCHWAIGER, BRIGITTE, 1949–2010
  *Führer, befiehl! See* Yes, My Führer!
  *Yes, My Führer!* 1987.
    Black, P., translator LAXC
    Variant title: *Führer, befiehl!*

SCHWARTZ, DELMORE, 1913–1966
  *Choosing Company.* 1936? AME5
  *Paris and Helen.* 1941? NEWDI41
  *Shenandoah.* 1941? KRE

SCHWARTZ, JOEL
  *Psalms for Two Davids.* 1971. BALLE9

SCHWARTZ, YEVGENY, 1896–1958
  *The Dragon.* 1944.
    Hayward, M., and Shukman, H., translators GLE

SCHWARZ-BART, SIMONE, 1938–
  *Ton beau capitaine. See* Your Handsome Captain
  *Your Handsome Captain.* 1987.
    Harris, J., and Temerson, C., translators PLABI1,
      PLABI3
    Variant title: *Ton beau capitaine*

SCHWEFFELBRENNER, PIT. *See* Rauch, Edward H.
    (pseudonym of)

SCOTT, DENNIS, 1939–1991
  *The Crime of Anabel Campbell.* 1985. NOEL
  *An Echo in the Bone.* 1974. HILEP

SCOTT, DUNCAN CAMPBELL, 1862–1947
  *Pierre.* 1921. MAS1

SCOTT, MUNROE, 1927–
  *Wu-feng.* 1970. KAL1

SCOTT, PAUL, 1920–1978
  *Pillars of Salt.* 1947? RUA

SCOTT, VIRGINIA
*The Living Exhibition of Sweeney Todd.* 1981. VICK2

SCOTT, SIR WALTER, 1771–1832
*Halidon Hill.* 1822. ENGLMI

SCOTTI, TOMMASO GALLARATI. *See* Gallarati-Scotti, Tommaso

"SCRIBBLE, SAM"
*Dolorsolatio, a Local Political Burlesque.* 1865. WAGN1

SCRIBE, AUGUSTIN EUGENE, 1791–1861
*Les doigts de fée.* 1858. BENZ
   Variant titles: *Frocks and Thrills; Lady Margaret*
*Frocks and Thrills. See Les doigts de fée*
*A Glass of Water. See Le verre d'eau*
*The Glass of Water, or Effects and Causes. See Le verre d'eau*
*Lady Margaret. See Les doigts de fée*
*Le verre d'eau.* 1840. BOR
   Bodee, D., translator SSTG
   Parsell, S., translator HILPDH4
   Variant titles: *A Glass of Water; The Glass of Water, or Effects and Causes*

——— and BAYARD, J. F. A.
*La frontière de savoir. See A Peculiar Position*
*A Peculiar Position.* 1837.
   Planche, J., translator SSTG
   Variant title: *La frontière de savoie*

——— and MELESVILLE
*The Castrata.* 1831.
   Shapiro, N., translator FLEA
   Variant title: *Le soprano*
*Le soprano. See The Castrata*

SCRIBE, EUGENE. *See* Scribe, Augustin Eugène

SCRIBLERUS SECUNDUS, pseudonym. *See* Fielding, Henry

SEAMI MOTOKIYO. *See* Zeami

SEARLE, JAMES, 1938–
*The Lucky Streak.* 1966. BRIMA2

SEARS, DJANET, 1959–
*The Adventures of a Black Girl in Search of God.* 2002. SEARS2
*Afrika Solo.* 1987. BREK (excerpt)
*Harlem Duet.* 1997. ADAP, SEARS1, WASCPB2

*The Madwoman and the Fool: A Harlem Duet.* 1997. BEYO (excerpt)
*Who Killed Katie Ross?* 1994. ZIMM

SEARS, JOE, 1949– . *See* Williams, Jaston, joint author

SEATON, SANDRA, 1942–
*The Bridge Party.* 1989. PERF

SEBASTIAN, ELLEN V.
*Your Place Is No Longer with Us.* 1962. WES13/14

SEBAZCO, RAUL SANTIAGO, 1952– . *See* Wright, Glenn, joint author

SEBBAR, LEILA, 1941–
*My Mother's Eyes.* 1994.
   Vogel, S., translator PLAWE
   Variant title: *Les yeux de ma mère*
*Les yeux de ma mère. See My Mother's Eyes*

SEBIRE, FRANÇOIS DESSANDRAIS. *See* Dessandrais-Sebire, François

SEBREE, CHARLES, 1914–1985
*The Dry August.* 1949. HARY

SECOND, LOUIS, pseudonym
*Apollinaris.* 1942? NEWDI42

SECONDO, PIERMARIA ROSSO DI SAN. *See* Rossi di San Secondo, Piermaria

SECUNDUS, H. SCRIBLERUS, pseudonym. *See* Fielding, Henry

SEDAINE, MICHEL JEAN, 1719–1797
*Le philosophe sans le savoir.* 1765. BREN, ZDA

SEDLEY, SIR CHARLES, 1639–1701
*The Mulberry Garden.* 1668. DAVR, JEFF1

SEDLEY, WILLIAM HENRY. *See* Smith, William Henry

SEEBRING, WILLIAM, 1956–
*The Original Last Wish Baby.* 1995. MEYCB, MEYF

SEGURA, MANUEL ASCENSIO, 1805–1871
*Na Catita.* 1856. ALPE

SEIAMI
*Michimori* (revised by Zeami).
   Shimazaki, C., translator SHIM2, book 2

SEIBEL, BEATRIZ, 1934–
*Seven Times Eve.* 1980.
Salas, T., and Vargas, M., translators SALA
Variant title: *7 veces Eva*
*7 veces Eva. See* Seven Times Eve

SEIDEL, GEORG, 1945–1990
*Carmen Kittel.* 1989.
Heibert, F., in collaboration with Seven Stages,
translators WEBER

SEILER, CONRAD, 1897–
*Darker Brother.* 1938. HARYL

SEJAVKA, SAM, 1960–
*The Hive.* 1989. JONI

SEJOUR, VICTOR, 1817–1874
*The Brown Overcoat.* 1858. HARY, HARYB

SELBY, CHARLES, 1802?–1863
*Kinge Richard ye Third; or, Ye Battel of Bosworth
Field.* 1844. NIN2
*London by Night* (sometimes attributed to). *See*
Anonymous Plays. *London by Night*

SELIG, PAUL
*Terminal Bar.* 1985. GAY3

SELIGO, RUDI, 1935–2004
*Beautiful Vida. See* Lepa Vida
*Ana.* 1984.
Anonymous translator PRED (summary only)
*Lepa Vida (Beautiful Vida).* 1979.
Anonymous translator PRED (summary only)
Variant title: *Beautiful Vida*
*The Wedding.* 1981.
Kravanja, S., translator PRED

SELKIRK, GORDON. *See* Selkirk, John, joint author

SELKIRK, JOHN, and SELKIRK, GORDON
*The Land Called Morning.* 1985. BELLN, LAND

SELLECK, ROGER, and LARMAN, CLAIRE
*Juliet and Romeo.* MURD

SELWYN, EDGAR, 1875–1944, and GOULDING,
EDMUND
*Dancing Mothers.* 1924. BES24

SENECA, LUCIUS ANNAEUS, 4? B.C.–65 A.D.
*Agamemnon.* 1st century
Miller, F., translator DUC2
*Hercules furens. See* Mad Hercules

*Hercules Oetaeus. See* Hercules on Oeta
*Hercules on Oeta.* 1st century
Elizabeth I, translator (fragment) RENDW
Harris, E., translator DUC2
Variant title: *Hercules Oetaeus*
*Mad Hercules.* 1st century
Miller, F., translator DUC2
Variant title: *Hercules furens*
*Medea.* 1st century
Ahl, F., translator COTKICG
Anonymous translator MALR2
Hadas, M., translator COTU, ROM
Harris, E., translator CROS, CROV, CUIN, HAPV
Miller, F., translator CLF1, DUC2, LIDE, SANM
Taylor, J., translator TAV
*Octavia.* 1st century
Miller, F., translator DUC2, HOWJ, HOWK
*Oedipus.* 1st century
Hadas, M., translator ROM
Mendell, C., translator LEVI
Miller, F., translator DUC2, LIDE, SANO
Turner, D., translator COTKICG
*Phaedra.* 1st century
Bradshaw, W., translator MIK8
Harris, E., translator HAPV
Miller, F., translator DUC2, LIDE, SANL
*The Phoenician Women.* 1st century
Harris, E., translator DUC2
Variant title: *Phoenissae*
*Phoenissae. See* The Phoenician Women
*Thyestes.* 1st century
Hadas, M., translator ROM
Harris, E., translator DUC2, HAPV, PAR
Harris, E., translator, and Gassner, J., adapter TREB
Heywood, L., translator MAKG
Parker, D., translator TENN
*Troades. See* The Trojan Women
*The Trojan Women.* 1st century
Miller, F., translator DUC2, HILPDH1
Variant title: *Troades*

SENGUPTA, POILE (AMBIKA), 1948–
*Mangalam.* 1994. BODY

SENTONGO, NUWA
*The Invisible Bond.* 1972. AFR1

SEREMBA, GEORGE BWANIKA
*Come Good Rain.* 1992. ALONG, SEARS1
*Napoleon of the Nile.* 1996. BEYO (excerpt)

SERGEL, CHRISTOPHER, 1918–1993
*Black Elk Speaks* (based on the book by John G.
Neilhardt). 1976. BES93

SERLING, ROD, 1924–1975
  *Back There.* 1961. SCVDT1
  *I Shot an Arrow.* 1960. BRNS
  *Patterns.* 1955. HUNT
  *Requiem for a Heavyweight.* 1957. CORB, CORBA,
    SUT3
  *The Shelter.* 1961. SUT2

SERRAND, DOMINIQUE. *See* Epp, Steven, joint author

SERRANO, LYNNETTE M., 1964–
  *The Bronx Zoo.* 1982. YOUP

SERREAU, COLINE, 1947–
  *Lapin lapin.* 1985.
    Wright, B., translator PLABI3

SETTLE, ELKANAH, 1648–1724
  *The Empress of Morocco.* 1673. DOA

SEWELL, STEPHEN, 1953–
  *The Father We Loved on a Beach by the Sea.* 1978.
    THUG

SEYMOUR, ALAN, 1927–
  *The One Day of the Year.* 1961. FIO, THOP

SHA, CH'ING-CH'IEN. *See* Lao, Sheh, pseudonym

SHA, SEH; FU, TO; MA, YUNG; and LI, CHI–HUANG
  *Letters from the South.* 1964.
    Shapiro, S., translator MESE

SHA, YEH-HSIN, 1939– ; LI, SHOU–CH'ENG; and
    YAO, MING-TE
  *Chia-ju wo shih chen-ti. See* If I Were Real
  *If I Were Real.* 1979.
    Gunn, E., translator TWEH (Scene 5 only; others
      summarized)
    Variant title: *Chia-ju wo shih chen-ti*

SHA YEXIN. *See* Sha, Yeh-hsin

SHABAKA
  *Blow This Mother Up* (song by). *See* San Francisco
    Mime Troupe. *Factwino vs. Armageddonman*

SHADOW PLAYS. *See* Anonymous Plays. *The Death of
    Karna: Irawan's Wedding; The Reincarnation of
    Rama*

SHADWELL, CHARLES, 1675?–1726
  *The Fair Quaker of Deal; or The Humours of the Navy.*
    1710. BELK17
  *The Humours of the Navy. See* The Fair Quaker of Deal

SHADWELL, THOMAS, 1642?–1692
  *Bury Fair.* 1689? MOR, STM
  *The Lancashire Witches and Tegue O. Divelly, the Irish
    Priest.* 1681? BAT22
  *The Libertine.* 1676. MARJ
  *The Squire of Alsatia.* 1688. JEFF3, MAND, MANF
  *The Virtuoso.* 1676. JENS

SHAFFER, ANTHONY, 1926–2001
  *Murderer.* 1975. KAYS
  *Sleuth.* 1970. BES70, BEST, RICI

SHAFFER, DIANE
  *Sacrilege.* 1995. WOMP95

SHAFFER, PETER LEVIN, 1926–
  *Amadeus.* 1979. BES80, COTKB, HOEP
  *Black Comedy.* 1967. BES66, HAVL
  *Equus.* 1973. ALLM, ALLN, BARID, BARKA,
    BARKB, BARKC, BARKD, BES74, SSSI, SSSIA
  *Five Finger Exercise.* 1958. BES59, NEWE4
  *The Private Ear.* 1962. ENG
  *The Royal Hunt of the Sun.* 1964. BES65, PLAJ1, RICIS
  *White Liars. See* White Lies
  *White Lies.* 1967. RICJ
    Variant title: *White Liars*

SHAH, B. M., 1933–1998
  *Trishanku.* 1967.
    Kaushal, J., translator KAM3

SHAIRP, MORDAUNT, 1887–1939
  *The Green Bay Tree.* 1933. BES33, CEU, GAY1

SHAKESPEARE, WILLIAM, 1564–1616
  *All's Well That Ends Well.* 1602? GRDB27, GRDBA25
  *Antony and Cleopatra.* 1606? BROG, BROH, BROI,
    BURG, CROS, DIEA, DOWN, ELK, EVC2,
    GOLH, GRDB27, GRDBA25, GUTH, GUTL,
    LID, MANP, MIL, OLI2, SHR, STOTD, STOTLA,
    STOTLB, WELT, WOOE1
    Variant title: *The Tragedy of Antony and Cleopatra*
  *Arden of Feversham* (sometimes attributed to).
    *See* Anonymous Plays. *Arden of Feversham*
  *As You Like It.* 1599? BARJ, BARK, BRIK, CASH,
    DIYLC, GRDB26, GRDBA24, HOUS, OLI1,
    SCW1, SOUL, WOLCS
  *The Birth of Merlin* (sometimes attributed to). *See*
    Anonymous Plays. *The Birth of Merlin*
  *The Comedy of Errors.* 1592? CHARN, GRDB26,
    GRDBA24, TAV
  *Coriolanus.* 1607? GRDB27, GRDBA25, LEVJ, OLI2,
    REV
  *Cymbeline.* 1609. GRDB27, GRDBA25, OLI2
  *Florizel and Perdita* (altered from). BELC1

*Hamlet.* 1600? ALTE, ANTL, BAC, BAIC, BAIE, BAIG, BAIH, BAIK, BAIL, BAIM, BARI, BARIA, BARID, BARIE, BARIF, BARIH, BARN, BARNA, BEATA, BOGA, BRJ, BRJA, BRJB, BRJC, CLL, CLLC, COI, COLD, DAVK, DIYL, DIYLD, FRYEA, GORE, GRDB27, GRDBA25, GUTDF, GUTDS, HAPD, HAPS1, HAPT1, HARC26, HAVH, HEA, HEAA, HEAB, HEAC, HEAD, HEAL, HEALA, HEALB, HEALC, HEALD, HEALE, HIG, HOWM, JACOB, JACOBA, JACOBD, JACOBE, JOHO, JORH, KAYS, KERN, KERO, KIRLB, KIRLC, KIRLD, KNIH, KNIJ, LITC, LITI, LITIE, LITIF, LITJ, LITQ, LITR, LITRA, LITRB, LITRC, LITRD, LOCM1, MABC, MALG1, MALI2, MALN1, MAO, MEY, MEYB, MEYC, MEYCA, MEYD, MEYE, MEYF, MONA, NORG, NORIA1, NORIB1, NORJ1, NORJA, OLI1, PERR3 (altered from), PRO, REIL, REIW, REIWE, RICH, ROGEX, SEVT, SHRO, SMA, STA, THOM, THON, TRE, TREA2, TREB, TREC1, TREE1, TREI1, WALJ, WARN2, WHFM, WOTHB, WOTHC

  Variant titles: *Hamlet, Prince of Denmark; The Tragedy of Hamlet, Prince of Denmark*

*Hamlet, Prince of Denmark. See* Hamlet

*Henry IV. See* King Henry the Fourth

*Julius Caesar.* 1599? BEAC11, BENP, CARM, CARME, COOK3, GRDB26, GRDBA24, KET, MAEC, OLI1, READ1, RED, REDM, SUT2, WORL2

*King Henry the Eighth.* 1613? GRDB27, GRDBA25

*King Henry the Fifth.* 1598? GRDB26, GRDBA24, WHF, WHFA

*King Henry the Fourth, Part I.* 1597? ABRA, ABRB1, ABRE, ABRF1, ABRH1, ABRJ1, ABRK1, ABRL1, ALLM, BEAL, BEAM, BOGO, BOY, BROJ, BROK, CALD, CASH, COLEL1, DAV1, DEAN, DEAS, GATT, GRDB26, GRDBA24, HAPS1, HAPT1, KERN, MEY, OLI1, PRAT1, SMK, STJM, STJN

  Variant title: *Henry IV*

*King Henry the Fourth, Part II.* 1596? GRDB26, GRDBA24, STJN

*King Henry VI, Part I.* 1591? GRDB26, GRDBA24

*King Henry VI, Part II.* GRDB26, GRDBA24

*King Henry VI, Part III.* GRDB26, GRDBA24

*King John.* 1596? GRDB26, GRDBA24

*King Lear.* 1605? ABRH1, ABRJ1, ABRK1, ABRL1, ABRM1, BARC, BARK, BARKA, BARKB, BARKC, BARKD, BARKE, BARKF, BENQ, BENSB1, BONB, BONC, BRIX, BRIY, BRIZ, BROK, BROTA, COTX, CRAF, DEAN, DEAO, FOS, GOLD, GRDB27, GRDBA25, GREAB, HARC46, HAVHA, HIB, HIBA, HIBB, HILPDH2,

HOGF, HOUS, JOHN, KINNS, KNOJ, MORWB, MORXE, OLI1, PRAT1, ROB, RUSS, SCNQCA, SCNQCB, SOUL, STY, TRI, TRIA, WAIW, WOTHA

  Variant title: *The Tragedy of King Lear*

*King Richard II.* 1595? DUH, GRDB26, GRDBA24

  Variant titles: *Richard II; The Tragedy of King Richard II*

*King Richard III.* 1592? CONG, GRDB26, GRDBA24

  Variant title: *The Tragedy of King Richard III*

*The Lamentable Tragedy of Locrine* (sometimes attributed to). *See* Anonymous Plays. *The Lamentable Tragedy of Locrine*

*The London Prodigal* (sometimes attributed to). *See* Anonymous Plays. *The London Prodigal*

*Love's Labour's Lost.* 1594? GRDB26, GRDBA24

*Macbeth.* 1605? BARD, BARIF, BARU, BEAC12, BENN, BRIG, CALD, CARLG, CARN, CLKJ, CLKY, COTY, DAI, DIYRD, FRYE, GOOD, GOODE, GRDB27, GRDBA25, HARC46, HOGI, INGE, INGG, KIN, KNID, KNIE, MAE, MARL, MIJ2, MIJA2, NEVI, OLI2, PATM, PATP, PERR2, POOL, PROM, PRON, REIN, ROHR, ROSS, SANK, SEN, SHAR, SHAV, SRY, SRYG, SUT4, WAGC4, WORL4, WORM

  Variant title: *The Tragedy of Macbeth*

*Measure for Measure.* 1604? GEMM, GRDB27, GRDBA25, KRE, SIN, VENA

*The Merchant of Venice.* 1596? BEAC10, GEMM, GRDB26, GRDBA24, GREJ, HOWM, OLI1

*The Merry Wives of Windsor.* 1600? GRDB27, GRDBA25

*A Midsummer Night's Dream.* 1595? ALS, AUB, BAIL, BAIM, BARIG, BARIH, BARKA, BARKB, BARKC, BARKD, BARKE, BARKF, BART, BEAC9, BEATA, BONA, BONB, COLD, GRDB26, GRDBA24, GUTDF, GUTDS, HEAC, HOEP, HUDE, JACOB, JACOBA, JACOBD, JACOBE, KIRLA, KIRLB, KNOK (excerpt from Act V, Scene I only), MEYC, MEYCA, MEYD, MEYE, MEYF, OLI1, SEN

*Mucedorus* (sometimes attributed to). *See* Anonymous Plays. *Mucedorus*

*Much Ado about Nothing.* 1598? GRDB26, GRDBA24, HEALD, HEALE, KIRLC

*Othello, the Moor of Venice.* 1604? ABCA, ABCB, ABCC, ABCD, ABCE, ABCF, ABCG, ABCH, ACE, ALLN, ALLO, ANT, AUB, BARIC, BARIG, BARJ, BEAR, BENU, BERP, BERPA, BIER, BLON, BLOND, BLOO, BOW, COOP, COTKIR, DIYL, DIYLA, DIYLB, DIYLC, DIYLD, DOLAN, FREG, GLO, GRDB27, GRDBA25, GREC1, GWYN, HAE, HAEA, HAEB, HAVL, HOEP, HOGN, HOWM, JAFF, KIRLA, KNIF, KNIG, LEVI, LITIA, LITIB, LITIC, LITID, LITIE, LITIF,

LITJA, LITP, MARK, MESSN, MEYB, MEYCB, MOE, MON, NORIC1, OLI1, PERS, PERT, PERU, PERV, PERW, PERX, PERY, PERZ, PES, REIO, SCNN, SCNO, SCNP, SCNPL, SCNQ, SIN, SMP, SSSI, SSSIA, SSSIB, SSSIC, SUTL, TAUJ, VOLI, VOLP, VONS2

Variant title: *The Tragedy of Othello*

*Pericles, Prince of Tyre.* 1609? BELG7, GRDB27, GRDBA25

*The Puritan; or, The Widow of Watling Street* (sometimes attributed to). *See* Anonymous Plays. *The Puritan; or, The Widow of Watling Street*

*The Reign of King Edward the Third* (sometimes attributed to). *See* Anonymous Plays. *The Reign of King Edward the Third*

*Richard II. See* King Richard II

*Romeo and Juliet.* 1594? BARO, BLAH, CARMI, EDAD, EIGHT, EVA2, EVB2, GATS, GLO, GPA, GRDB26, GRDBA24, GRIF, HOLP, JORG, OLI1, PERR1, PIC, REF, SHAW, SMN, SOM, SOMA, STS, THO, TOB

*The Taming of the Shrew.* 1593? GRDB26, GRDBA24, LITRA, LITRB, SMR

*The Tempest.* 1611? ADV, CALD, CONN, FEFM, FRYEA, GRDB27, GRDBA25, HAPS1, HAPT1, HARC46, JACOBA, JACOBD, KER, LITIC, LITRC, MEYD, MEYE, MEYF, ROSENB, SSST, SSSU, STOTD, STOTLA, STOTLB, TOU, WOTHA, WOTHB, WOTHC

*Timon of Athens.* 1607? GRDB27, GRDBA25

*Titus Andronicus.* 1593? GRDB26, GRDBA24

*The Tragedy of Antony and Cleopatra. See* Antony and Cleopatra

*The Tragedy of Hamlet, Prince of Denmark. See* Hamlet

*The Tragedy of King Lear. See* King Lear

*The Tragedy of King Richard II. See* King Richard II

*The Tragedy of King Richard III. See* King Richard III

*The Tragedy of Macbeth. See* Macbeth

*The Tragedy of Othello. See* Othello, the Moor of Venice

*The Tragedy of Othello: The Moor of Venice. See* Othello, the Moor of Venice

*Troilus and Cressida.* 1602? BENSB1, GRDB27, GRDBA25, WEAN

*Twelfth Night; or, What You Will.* 1599. ABRM1, BARB, BENU, BIER, COTKICO, DIEB, FEFL, FOT, GOLD, GRDB27, GRDBA25, HILP, HILPDH2, JOHO, MEY, MIL, OLI1, SSSIA, SSSIB, SSSIC, STY, WALJ
— *See also* Driver, D. *Your Own Thing*

*The Two Gentlemen of Verona.* 1594? GRDB26, GRDBA24

*The Winter's Tale.* 1610. GRDB27, GRDBA25, OLI2, PRAT1

*A Yorkshire Tragedy* (sometimes attributed to). *See* Anonymous Plays. *A Yorkshire Tragedy*
— *See* Fletcher, John, joint author

SHAMIR, MOSHE, 1921–2004
*He Walked through the Fields.* 1948
Hodes, A., translator MOADE

SHANGE, NTOZAKE (b. Paulette Williams), 1948–
*Daddy Says.* 1989. KINHP
*for colored girls who have considered suicide/when the rainbow is enuf.* 1976. BERS, HAPU, HARYB, PLACI
*I Live in Music* (a work in progress). 1995. ALG
*The Resurrection of the Daughter: Liliane* (excerpt). 1995. MAQ
*Spell #7.* 1979. GILB, SSSIB, WATTAD, WILK, WOTHA, WOTHB, WOTHM

SHANK, ADELE EDLING, 1940–
*Or Maybe Not.* 2000. *See* Ackermann, J. *Back Story: A Dramatic Anthology.* HUMANA2000
*Sand Castles.* 1982. WES15/16
*Sunset/sunrise.* 1979. WES4
*Winter Play; a Hyperreal Comedy in Two Acts.* 1980. NEWQ

SHANLEY, JOHN PATRICK, 1950–
*Kissing Christine.* 1996. HUMANA96
*Missing Marisa.* 1996. HUMANA96

SHANMUGAM, S.V., 1933–
*Singapore Bridegroom.* 1984.
Elangovan, translator MLAS
Variant title: *Singapore mappillai*
*Singapore mappillai. See* Singapore Bridegroom

SHAPIRO, MEL, 1935– . *See* Guare, John, joint author

SHARIF, BINA, 1940–
*My Ancestor's House.* 1992. PERC

SHARP, ALAN, 1934–
*The Long-distance Piano Player.* 1962. NEWE12

SHARP, ANTHONY, 1915–1984
*Nightmare Abbey* (adapted from the frolic by Thomas Love Peacock). 1952. PLAN7

SHAW, ELIZABETH LLOYD. *See* Hensel, Karen, joint author

SHAW, GEORGE BERNARD, 1856–1950
*Androcles and the Lion.* 1913. CARN, KRM, SAND, STRO, WISF

SHEASBY, DAVE, 1940–2010
*Welcome to the Times* (radio play). 1985. MARLC

SHEEAN, JOHN J.
*Babes in the Bighouse* (music by). *See* Terry, Megan.
*Babes in the Bighouse*

SHEH, LU. *See* Lao, Sheh

SHEILA'S BRUSH THEATRE COMPANY, 1977–
*Jack's Christmas. See* JAXMASS (Jack's Christmas)
*JAXMASS (Jack's Christmas)*. 1979. PETERS
Variant title: *Jack's Christmas*

SHEIN, BRIAN, 1947–
*Cowboy Island*. (1972) FIFVE

—— and KLONSKY, KENNETH, joint author
*Taking Steam*. 1983. NEWJV

SHEINEN, LEV ROMANOVICH, 1906–1967. *See* Tur,
Leonid Davidovich, joint author

SHELDON, EDWARD BREWSTER, 1886–1946
*The Boss*. 1911. QUIJ, QUIJR, QUIK, QUIL, QUIM,
QUIN
*The Jest. See* Benelli, Sem. *The Jest* (translated and
adapted by)
*"Man's Extremity Is God's Opportunity." See* Salvation
Nell
*The Nigger*. 1909. MESCO
*Romance*. 1913. BAK, BES09
*Salvation Nell*. 1908. GARX, GATB1
Variant title: *"Man's Extremity Is God's
Opportunity"*

SHELLEY, ELSA (MRS. IRVING KAYE DAVIS),
1905?–
*Pick-up Girl*. 1944. BES43

SHELLEY, PERCY BYSSHE, 1792–1822
*The Cenci*. 1886. ASG, ENGL, HARC18, KAU, KRE,
MOSE2, SMP, TAT, TAU, TRE
*Prometheus Unbound*. 1820. ABRM2 (excerpts), BERN,
ENGL, GREB2, HAPT2, PRAT2, SML

SHEN, TUAN-HSIEN. *See* Hsia, Yen

SHENGOLD, NINA
*Lives of the Great Waitresses*. 1995. PLACA

SHEPARD, SAM (pseudonym of Samuel Shepard
Rogers), 1943–
*Action*. 1975. MESSE, MIJH

*Buried Child*. 1978. BARN, BARNA, BERS, FAMAD,
JACOBA, JACOBD, LEVY, MARK, MARL,
SILS, WOTHM
*Chicago*. 1965. ORZ
*Curse of the Starving Class*. 1976. KNOK
*Fool for Love; A Full-length Play in One Act*. 1983.
BES83, BRJA, EIGHT, FAMAB, GILB, HAEA,
SSSIB
*Forensic and the Navigators*. 1967. SMC
*The Holy Ghostly*. 1972. OFF2, RICK
*Red Cross*. 1968. OFF2
*The Tooth of Crime*. 1973. OBG, VENA, WATTAD
*True West*. 1980. COLD, DIYRD, HOEP, JACOB,
KIRLC, MEY, WOTHA, WOTHB, WOTHC

SHEPHARD-MASSAT, S. M. (Sherry)
*Waiting to Be Invited*. 1996. WOMP2000

SHEPHERD, CATHERINE, 1912–1976
*Jane, My Love*. 1951. PFIS

SHEPP, ARCHIE, 1937–
*Junebug Graduates Tonight*. KINH, KINHB

SHERIDAN, MRS. FRANCES, 1724–1766
*The Discovery*. 1763. BELG4

SHERIDAN, RICHARD BRINSLEY BUTLER, 1751–
1816
*The Critic; or, A Tragedy Rehearsed*. 1779. ASH,
COLR, COP, COPC1, FEFL, NET, STM
*The Duenna*. 1775. STM
*The Rivals*. 1775. ALLI, ALLJ, ALLK, ALLM, ALLN,
ALLO, ANT, BENP, CLK1, CLKY, COLR, DEM,
DRAD2, EIGH, HIG, HOUS, HOWM, KEY,
LITP, MOR, NET, PLAB2, REIO, ROB, SCAR,
SELF, SHAI2, SHAJ2, SNYD1, STM, THMD,
TUP, TUQ, TWE, UHL, WEAT1, WOO1
*Saint Patrick's Day, or The Scheming Lieutenant*. 1775.
GOODE
Variant title: *The Scheming Lieutenant*
*The Scheming Lieutenant. See* Saint Patrick's Day, or
the Scheming Lieutenant
*The School for Scandal*. 1777. ABRB1, ALT, ALTE,
BAC, BARNA, BAUG, BENY, BONC, BRIG,
BRIX, BRIY, BRIZ, BRJ, BROJ, BROK, CLF1,
CLKW, COF, COHM, COLR, CONP, COTKICO,
DAV1, DEM, FOUB, GATS, GRE, GREAAI,
GREB1, GREC1, HARC18, HAVH, HEAD,
HILPDH3, HUD, KRM, KRO, LIE, LIED1,
LIKE1, MACL, MAND, MANF, MANH, MATTL,
MON, MOO, MORR, MOSE2, NET, PIC,
ROGEBD, RUB, RUSS, SCNQCB, SHRO, SIG,
SMO, SPD, SPDB, SPEF1, SSSI, SSSIA, SSSIB,
SSSIC, STA, STM, TAT, TAU, THO, TREB,

TREC, TREE1, TREI1, TUP, TUQ, TWE, UHL,
WATT2, WILSP, WOOD1, WOOE1
*A Trip to Scarborough.* 1777. INCA7

SHERIDAN, THOMAS, 1719–1788
*The Brave Irishman; or, Captain O'Blunder* (sometimes
   attributed to John Preston). 1746. BELC3, HUGL
   Variant title: *Captain O'Blunder; or, The Brave
   Irishman*
*Captain O'Blunder; or, The Brave Irishman. See* The
   Brave Irishman
*The Spirit of Contradiction (by a Gentleman of
   Cambridge).* 1760. BELC4

SHERIFF, JACK
*The Bruce Curtis Story: Journey to Bordentown.* 1988.
   HEID (excerpt)

SHERMAN, MARTIN, 1938–
*Bent.* 1978. BES79, JACOB, SHEW
*Cracks.* 1975. GAY2
*A Madhouse in Goa.* 1989. CLUMS
*Messiah.* 1982. HOWM
*Passing By.* 1974. GAY1

SHERRIFF, ROBERT CEDRIC, 1896–1975
*Badger's Green.* 1930. SIXD
*The Colonel's Lady* (screenplay based on the story by
   W. Somerset Maugham). JORG
*Home at Seven.* 1950. BARV
*Journey's End.* 1928. BES28, CEU, CHA, CHAN,
   CHAR, FAO, FREI, FUL, HUDS2, LOV, MOD,
   PLAD, STAT, STAU, STAV, TRE, TREA1,
   TREBA, TREC2, TREE3, TREI3
*The Long Sunset.* 1955. PLAN12
*A Shred of Evidence.* 1960. PLAN22
*The Telescope.* 1957. PLAN15

—— and DE CASALIS, JEANNE
*St. Helena.* 1935. BES36, FAMI

SHERWOOD, ROBERT EMMET, 1896–1955
*Abe Lincoln in Illinois.* 1938. BES38, BIER, BROX,
   CALG, CALP, CASS, CLH, COOJ, CORF, COTE,
   COTH, GARZ, GATB2, GOW, GOWA, HAT,
   HATA, HAVD, HAVE, NAGE, PROD, ROLF,
   WATI, WATO
*Idiot's Delight.* 1936. BES35, CLUR, CORE, CORF,
   FAMAL, GAS, HIL, MAFC, MERU, MOSH,
   SIXP
*The Petrified Forest.* 1935. BES34, CET, DOWM,
   MOSL, WATC2
*Reunion in Vienna.* 1931. BES31, FAME, THF
*The Road to Rome.* 1926. BES26, GASB

*The Rugged Path.* 1945. BES45
*Second Threshold. See* Barry, Philip. *Second Threshold*
   (revised by)
*There Shall Be No Night.* 1940. BES39, CORB,
   CORBA, DUR
*Tovarich. See* Deval, Jacques. *Tovarich* (translated and
   adapted by)

SHEVELOVE, BURT, 1915–1982, and GELBART,
   LARRY
*A Funny Thing Happened on the Way to the Forum.*
   1962. (adapted from Plautus' *Pseudolus.*) GOODE

SHEZI, MTHULI, d.1972
*Shanti.* 1973. SOUT

SHI, JUNBAO, 1192–1276
*Qui Hu Tries to Seduce His Own Wife.* 13th century
   Dolby, W., translator EIG
   Variant title: *Qiu Hu xi-gi*
*Qiu Hu xi-gi. See* Qui Hu Tries to Seduce His Own Wife

SHIELS, GEORGE, 1886–1949
*The New Gossoon.* 1930. CAN

SHIELS, JOHN WILSON, 1871–1929
*Nec-natama.* 1914. BOH3

SHIH, YÜ-CHO
*Picking Up the Jade. See* Picking Up the Jade Bracelet
*Picking Up the Jade Bracelet.*
   Scott, A., translator SCY3
   Variant title: *Picking Up the Jade*

SHIKO, OKAMURA. *See* Okamura, Shiko

SHIMIZU, KUNIO, 1936–
*Ano hitachi. See* Those Days: A Lyrical Hypothesis on
   Time and Forgetting
*The Dressing Room: That Which Flows Away Ultimately
   Becomes Nostalgia.* 1977.
   Miyagawa, C., and Gillespie, J., translators ALTJD
   Variant title: *Gakuya*
*Gakuya. See* The Dressing Room: That Which Flows
   Away Ultimately Becomes Nostalgia
*The Sand of Youth, How Quickly.* 1980. Rolf, R.,
   translator ALTJD
   Variant title: *Seishun no suna no nan to hayaku*
*Seishun no suna no nan to hayaku. See* The Sand of
   Youth, How Quickly
*Shinjō afururu keihakusa. See* Such a Serious Frivolity
*Such a Serious Frivolity.* 1969.
   Rimer, J., translator HACJT7
   Variant title: *Shinjō afururu keihakusa*

*Those Days: A Lyrical Hypothesis on Time and*
*Forgetting.* 1966.
Gillespie, J., translator ALTJD
Variant title: *Ano hitachi*

SHIN, ROB
*The Art of Waiting.* 1993. ASIAM

SHINE, TED, 1931–
*Contribution.* 1969. BLAC, BRAS, HARYB
*Herbert III.* 1974. HARY
*Morning, Noon, and Night.* 1964. REAR
*The Woman Who Was Tampered with in Youth.* 1980.
CEN

SHIOMI, R. A., 1947–
*Yellow Fever.* 1982. SWANS, WES13/14

SHIPLEY, LISA
*The Bathtub.* 1979. WES5

SHIPP, JESSE A., 1869–1934
*In Dahomey* (music by Will Marion Cook; lyrics by
Paul Laurence Dunbar). 1902. HARYB

SHIRLEY, JAMES, 1596–1666
*The Cardinal.* 1641. BAS, BROC, LAWT, NEI, PAR,
WALL
*The Gamester. See* Gamesters
*Gamesters.* 1634. BELK19
*Hyde Park.* 1637. DPR2
*The Lady of Pleasure.* 1635. BAS, HAPRA2, HAPRB2,
KNOW, NEI, SCH, SCI, SCJ, SPE
*The Royall Master.* 1638. GAYLE3
*The Traitor.* 1631. OLH, OLI2, TAV
*Triumph of Peace.* 1634. ETO
*The Wedding.* 1626. KNOW

SHIRLEY, WILLIAM, 1739–1780
*Edward the Black Prince.* 1750. BELK16

SHKVARKIN, VASILII VASIL-'EVICH, 1893–1967
*Father Unknown.* 1933.
Bakshy, H., translator BAKS

SHORTY, SHARON
*Trickster Visits the Old Folks Home.* 1996. SSSN

SHOTLANDER, SANDRA, 1941–
*Is that You Nancy?* 1991. AUSG

SHOVELLER, BROCK
*Westhound 12:01.* 1970. KAL2

SHŌZŌ I NAMIKI. *See* Namiki Shōzō I

SHUDRAKA (KING), 1st century B.C.–1st century
A.D.?
*The Little Clay Cart* (attributed to). 1st century B.C.–
1st century A.D.?
Lal, P., translator BRA, LAL
Oliver, R., translator WEL, PLAN29
Ryder, A., translator ANDF
Wilson, H., translator DOWS
Variant title: *The Toy Cart*
*The Toy Cart. See* The Little Clay Cart

SHUE, LARRY, 1946–1985
*The Foreigner.* 1983. BES84
*Wenceslas Square.* 1984. BES87

SHULMAN, MAX, 1919–1988, and SMITH, ROBERT
PAUL
*The Tender Trap.* 1954. THEA55

SHVARTS, EVGENII L'VOVICH, 1897–1958
*The Shadow.* 1940.
Reeve, F., translator REEV2

SICAM, GERONIMO D., 1908–1987, and CASINO,
JESUS
*Mir-i-nisa* (based on the story by José García Villa).
195– ? EDAD

SIDDONS, HENRY, 1774–1815
*Time's a Tell-tale.* 1807. INCA10

SIDHU, CA. D., 1938–
*Indumati and Satyadev.* 2007.
Sidhu, C., translator KAM3

SIDNEY, MARY. *See* Pembroke, Mary Sidney Herbert,
Countess of

SIDNEY, SIR PHILIP, 1554–1586
*The Lady of May.* 1579? KINNR, PAR

SIEFERT, LYNN
*Coyote Ugly.* 1985. KILGC, LAQCW

SIERENS, ARNE
*De drumleraar. See* Drummers
*Drummers.* 1994.
Malfait, N., translator COUL
Variant title: *De drumleraar*

SIERRA, GREGORIO MARTINEZ. *See* Martínez Sierra,
Gregorio

SIERRA, MARIA MARTINEZ. *See* Martínez Sierra, María

SIERRA, RUBÉN, 1946–1998
  *Manolo.* 1976. KANEL
  *La raze pura, or racial, racial.* 1969. CONR

SIEVEKING, LANCELOT DE GIBERNE, 1896–1972
  *The Strange Case of Dr. Jekyll and Mr. Hyde* (adapted
    from the novel by Robert Louis Stevenson). 1956.
    PLAN15

SIFTON, CLAIRE, 1897–1980, and SIFTON, PAUL
  *Give All Thy Terrors to the Wind.* 1936? KOZ

SIFTON, PAUL, 1898–1972. *See* Sifton, Claire, joint author

SIGLEY, MARJORIE, 1928–1997
  *Saint George and the Dragon at Christmas Tide*
    (modern adaptation). 1991. SWO

SIGURJONSSON, JOHANN, 1880–1919
  *Bjaerg-Ejvind og hens hustru. See* Eyvind of the Hills
  *Eyvind of the Hills.* 1911.
    Schanche, H., translator DICDT
    Variant title: *Bjaerg-Ejvind og hans hustru*
  *Galtra-Loftur. See* The Wish
  *Loftur the Magician. See* The Wish
  *Ønsket. See* The Wish
  *The Wish.* 1914.
    Haugen, E., translator HAVHN
    Variant titles: *Galtra–Loftur; Loftur the Magician;
      Ønsket*

SIKANA, MANA (pseudonym of Abdul Rahman
    Hanafiah), 1945–
  *Mustaqima.* 1985.
    Ishak, S., translator MLAM

SILAS, SHELLEY
  *Calcutta Kosher* (first broadcast on radio, later a stage
    play). 2000, 2004. BLAAP

SILLS, PAUL, 1927–2008
  *The Master Thief* (adapted from the tale by Jacob
    Grimm and Wilhelm Grimm). 1971. READ1

SILVER, ALF
  *Climate of the Times.* 1983. NEWCAD4
  *Dud Shuffle. See* Thimblerig
  *Thimblerig.* 1978. RUN
    Variant title: *Dud Shuffle*

SILVER, SUSAN
  *The Five Minute Romance.* 1982. *See* Anonymous Plays.
  *Twenty-four Hours: A.M.*

SILVERA, JOHN D., 1909–2002, and HILL, ABRAM
  *Liberty Deferred.* 1938. BRP, HARYB (Part I only)

SIM, DESMOND
  *Blood and Snow.* 1992. FAT

SIMARD, ANDRÉ, 1949–1990
  *En attendant Gaudreault. See* Waiting for Gaudreault
  *Waiting for Gaudreault.* 1976.
    Beissel, H., and Francière, A., translators KAL5
    Variant title: *En attendant Gaudreault*

SIMMONS, ALEXANDER
  *Sherlock Holmes and the Hands of Othello.* 1987.
    BLACTH

SIMON, BARNEY, 1932–1995
  *Born in the R.S.A.* 1986. BES86, KANI, WOZA
  *Hey, Listen . . .* 1974. GRAY
    — *See also* Mtwa, Percy, joint author

SIMON, MAYO
  *What Became of the Polar Bear?* 2000. *See*
    Ackermann, J. *Back Story: A Dramatic Anthology.*
    HUMANA2000

SIMON, (MARVIN) NEIL, 1927–
  *Barefoot in the Park.* 1963. BES63, MOST
  *Biloxi Blues.* 1985. BES84
  *Brighton Beach Memoirs.* 1982. BERT
  *Broadway Bound.* 1986. BES86
  *California Suite; a Comedy in Two Acts and Four
    Playlets: Visitor from New York; Visitor from
    Philadelphia; Visitors from London; Visitors from
    Chicago.* 1976. BES76
  *Chapter Two.* 1977. BERS, BES77
  *Come Blow Your Horn.* 1961. LITIA
  *The Gingerbread Lady.* 1970. BES70
  *The Good Doctor.* 1973. BES73
  *I Ought to Be in Pictures.* 1980. BES79
  *Last of the Red Hot Lovers.* 1969. BES69
  *Laughter on the 23rd Floor.* 1993. BES93
  *Lost in Yonkers.* 1991. BES90, SCVDT1
  *The Odd Couple.* 1965. BES64, COLT, GAT, GATB4,
    RICIS, SSSI
  *Plaza Suite* (3 one-act plays: *Visitor from Forest
    Hills; Visitor from Hollywood; Visitor from
    Mamaroneck*). 1968. BES67
  *The Prisoner of Second Avenue.* 1971. BES71, GARTL
  *The Sunshine Boys.* 1972. BES72, BEST, KNIH, KNIJ
  *Visitor from Forest Hills* (part of *Plaza Suite*). 1968.
    RICK
  *Visitor from Hollywood. See* Plaza Suite
  *Visitor from Mamaroneck. See* Plaza Suite
  *Visitor from New York. See* California Suite

*Visitor from Philadelphia. See* California Suite
*Visitors from Chicago. See* California Suite
*Visitors from London. See* California Suite

SIMONARSON, OLAFUR HAUKUR, 1947–
*Under Your Skin.* 1984.
    Jónsdóttir, I., translator, BRAK

SIMONES, PAMELA S.
*Sins of the Mothers.* 1994. TOR

SIMONOV, KONSTANTIN MIKHAILOVICH, 1915–
    1979
*The Russian People. See* The Russians
*The Russian Question.* 1947.
    Manning, E., and Kozelsky, S., translator VONG
        (excerpt)
*The Russians.* 1942.
    Odets, C., translator SEVP
    Shelley, G., and Guthrie, T., translators FOUT
    Variant titles: *The Russian People; Russkie liudi*
*Russkie liudi. See* The Russians

SIMONSON, ROBERT, 1964–
*Café Society.* 1998. DENT

SIMPSON, ELIZABETH. *See* Inchbald, Mrs. Elizabeth
    (Simpson)

SIMPSON, NORMAN FREDERICK, 1919–
*Gladly Otherwise.* PLAAC2
*Oh!* 1961. PLAAC1
*One Way Pendulum.* 1959. POP
*A Resounding Tinkle.* 1957. NEWE2, OBSE

SIMS, GEORGE ROBERT, 1847–1922
*The Lights o' London.* 1881. BOOL

SINCLAIR, CAROL
*Old Boots.* 1988. RALPH
*Sabrina's Splendid Brain.* 1995. BREK

SINGER, CAMPBELL, 1909–1976. *See* Ross, George,
    joint author

SINGER, ISAAC BASHEVIS, 1902–1991, and
    FRIEDMAN, EVE
*Teibele and Her Demon.* 1979. KAYT

SINGH, LAKVIAR
*Manjit.* 1984. MALY

SIRCAR, BADAL, 1925–
*Evam Indrajit.* 1965.
    Karnard, G., translator DESH, THRIN

*Shesh Nei. See* There's No End
*There's No End.* 1970.
    Raha, K., translator KAM1
    Variant title: *Shesh Nei*

SIRERA, RODOLF, 1948–
*The Audition.* 1978.
    London, J., translator LONG, OCONNP
    Variant title: *El veri del teatre*
*El veri del teatre. See* The Audition

SIRIWARDENA, REGGIE, 1929–2004
*Prometheus: An Argumentative Comedy for Two*
    *Characters.* 1989. GOON

SIROIS, SERGE, 1953–
*Dodo.* 1971?
    Van Burek, J., translator KAL5
    Variant title: *Dodo l'enfant do*
*Dodo l'enfant do. See* Dodo

SISSON, ROSEMARY ANNE, 1923–
*The Queen and the Welshman.* 1957. PLAN18
*The Splendid Outcasts.* 1959. PLAN19

SJOERDSMA, AL, JR., 1957–
*The 82nd Shepherds' Play.* 2000. INCI

SKARMETA, ANTONIO, 1940–
*Burning Patience.* 1982.
    Holt, M., translator WOOGLA

SKELTON, JOHN, 1460–1529
*Magnyfycence.* 1516? FOUN, MED, POLL

ŠKEMA, ANTANAS, 1911–1961
*Ataraxia.*
    Škema-Snyder, K., translator BRIDGE
*The Awakening; a Play in Three Sequences: Footsteps;*
    *La Cumparsita; The Awakening.* 1956.
    Škema-Snyder, K., translator CONF
    Variant titles: *La Cumparsita; Footsteps; Pabudimas*
*La Cumparsita. See* The Awakening
*Footsteps. See* The Awakening
*Pabudimas. See* The Awakening

SKINNER, CORNELIA OTIS, 1901–1979. *See* Taylor,
    Samuel, joint author

SKOLNIK, WILLIAM, 1950–
*Hoarse Muse* (music by). *See* Campbell, Paddy. *Hoarse*
    *Muse*

SKOURTIS, GEORGE
*Love Thriller.* 1998.
    Panagiotakou, A., translator CONTG

SKRYWER-AFRIKANER, MARTHA LAURENCIA
  *Homecoming.* 2000. ZEE2

SLABOLEPSZY, PAUL, 1948–
  *Mooi Street Moves.* 1992. GRAV
  *Over the Hill.* 1985. GRAYS

SLADE, BERNARD, 1930–
  *Same Time, Next Year.* 1975. BERS, BES74, FAMAD,
    MOST
  *Tribute.* 1978. BES77

SLADE, JULIAN, 1930–2006
  *Sixty Thousand Nights* (music and lyrics by). *See* May,
    Val. *Sixty Thousand Nights*
  *Trelawny, a Musical Play* (music by). *See* Woods,
    Aubrey, and Rowell, George. *Trelawny, a Musical
    Play*

SLOBODA, RUDOLF, 1938–1995
  *Armageddon in Grba.* 1993.
    Trebatická, H., translator CONTSL5
    Variant title: *Armagedon na Grbe*
  *Armagedon na Grbe. See* Armageddon in Grba

SLOMAN, ROBERT, 1926–2005. *See* Dobie, Laurence,
    joint author

SLOVES, CHAIM, 1905– (aka Henri Sloves)
  *Haman's Downfall.* 1944.
    Rosenfeld, M., translator LIFS

SLOVO, ROBYN. *See* Kilcoyne, Cathy, joint author

SŁOWACKI, JULIUSZ, 1809–1849
  *Fantazy.* 1867.
    Segel, H., translator POB
    Variant titles: *The Incorrigible; The New Deianira;
      Niepoprawni; Nowa Deianira*
  *The Incorrigible. See* Fantazy
  *The New Deianira. See* Fantazy
  *Niepoprawni. See* Fantazy
  *Nowa Deianira. See* Fantazy

SMALL CHANGE THEATRE, 1982–
  *One Beautiful Evening.* 1982. BELLN

SMALLS, CHARLIE, 1943–1987
  *The Wiz* (music and lyrics by). *See* Brown, William F.
    The Wiz

SMARTT, DOROTHEA, 1963–
  *Medusa? Medusa Black!* 1991. MYTH (excerpt)

SMEDLEY, AGNES, 1890–1950
  *Daughter of Earth. See* Sargent, Lydia. *Daughter of
    Earth* (based on the novel by)

SMEE, AMANDA
  *Fleas.* 1985. MONB2

SMEE, LILLIAN
  *No Thoroughfare.* 1935. FIN

SMITH, ALBERT RICHARD, 1816–1860
  *The Cricket on the Hearth* (adapted from the story by
    Charles Dickens). 1859. CARP

SMITH, ALI, 1962–
  *Trace of Arca.* 1989. MYTH

SMITH, ANNA DEAVERE, 1950–
  *Aye Aye Aye I'm Integrated.* 1984. MIH
  *Fires in the Mirror: Crown Heights, Brooklyn, and
    Other Identities.* 1992. BES91, HARYB, MAQ
    (excerpt), WOTHC, WOTHM
  *Twilight Los Angeles.* 1992 (excerpts). 1993. ANTL,
    BES93, JACOBD, MEYCA, MEYCB, MEYE,
    MEYF, PERC

SMITH, BETTY, 1904–1972
  *Fun after Supper.* 1940. GALB

SMITH, BEVERLY A.
  *Family Portrait.* 1984. WES17/18

SMITH, CEDRICA. *See* Winter, Jack, joint author

SMITH, CHARLES
  *Knock Me a Kiss.* 2000. NEWR2000
  *Takunda.* 1987. ELLM

SMITH, CHARLOTTE (TURNER), 1749–1806
  *What Is She?* 1799. INCA10

SMITH, DODIE, pseudonym. *See* Smith, Dorothy Gladys

SMITH, DOROTHY GLADYS (Dodie Smith; C. L.
    Anthony, pseudonyms), 1896–1990
  *Autumn Crocus.* 1931. FAMAN, PLAD, PLAL2
  *Call It a Day.* 1935. BES35, FAMI
  *Dear Octopus.* 1938. PLAL1
  *Service.* 1932. FAMC
  *Touch Wood.* 1934. FAMF

SMITH, EDMUND (Edmund "Rag" Smith), 1672–1710
  *Phaedra and Hippolitus.* 1706. BELK10

SMITH, EVAN, 1967–
*Remedial English.* 1986. SHEW
*The Uneasy Chair.* 1998. NEWR98

SMITH, HARRY JAMES, 1880–1918
*Mrs. Bumpstead-Leigh.* 1911. BES09, MOSJ, MOSK, MOSL

SMITH, HOWARD FORMAN
*Blackberryin'.* 1922? SHAY

SMITH, IAIN CRICHTON, 1928–1998
*Lazybed.* 1997. HOWA

SMITH, JACK, 1932–
*The Rehearsal for the Destruction of Atlantis.* 1965. MARRA

SMITH, JOHN, 1752–1809
*A Dialogue between an Englishman and an Indian.* 1781? MONR
*A Little Teatable Chitchat, ala-mode; or an Ancient Discovery Reduced to Modern Practice;—Being a Dialogue, and a Dish of Tea.* 1781? MONR

SMITH, LILLIAN, 1897–1966
*Strange Fruit.* 1945. PERF

SMITH, MARIAN SPENCER
*An American Grandfather.* 1924. IFKO

SMITH, MICHAEL, 1935–
*Captain Jack's Revenge.* 1970. NEWA4
*The Next Thing.* 1966. SMC

SMITH, OTHNIEL, 1962–
*Giant Steps.* 1998. NEWWD2

SMITH, PATRICK
*Driving around the House.* 1990. JENN

SMITH, RICHARD PENN, 1799–1854
*The Bombardment of Algiers.* 1829? AMP13
*The Last Man; or, The Cock of the Village* (adapted from *Le coq de village* by Charles Decour and Anne Théodore). 1822. AMP13
*The Sentinels; or, The Two Sergeants.* 1829. AMP13
*Shakespeare in Love* (adapted from *Shakespeare amoureux* by Alexandre Duval). 1804. AMP13
*The Triumph at Plattsburg.* 1830. QUIJ, QUIK
*A Wife at a Venture.* 1829. AMP13
*William Penn.* 1829. AMP13

SMITH, ROBERT PAUL, 1915–1977. *See* Shulman, Max, joint author

SMITH, RONN
*Nothing but the Truth* (adapted from the novel by Avi). 1997. SCVDO1

SMITH, SARAH POGSON, 1774–1870
*The Female Enthusiast.* 1807. KRIT

SMITH, VAL
*Dead Men Make No Dollars.* 2000. *See* Ackermann, J. *Back Story: A Dramatic Anthology.* HUMANA2000
*Marguerite Bonet.* 1997. WOMP98
*Meow.* 1998. HUMANA98

SMITH, WILLIAM HENRY, 1806–1872
*The Drunkard; or, The Fallen Saved.* 1844. MESCO, MONR, RICHE, VICT

SMITH, WINCHELL, 1871–1933, and BACON, FRANK
*Lightnin'.* 1918. CEY

SMOLIN, DMITRY
*Lysistrata. See* Aristophanes. *Lysistrata* (translated and adapted by)

SMOLLETT, TOBIAS GEORGE, 1721–1771
*The Reprisal.* 1757. BELC2

SNEAL, PATRICIA
*Is There Any Body There?* 1983. MONB1

SNEIDER, VERN, 1916–1981
*The Teahouse of the August Moon. See* Patrick, John. *The Teahouse of the August Moon* (adapted from the novel by)

SNODGRASS, KATHERINE
*Haiku.* 1995. SCVDT1

SNOW, ANDREA
*Factperson* (script and songs by). *See* San Francisco Mime Troupe. *Factperson*

SOBOL, JOSHUA (YEHOSHUA), 1939–
*Adam.* 1989.
  Jenkins, R., translator TAUB
*Ghetto.* 1983. FUCHS, LAS
*The Night of the Twentieth.*
  Salkind, M., translator MOADE
*The Palestinian Girl.* 1985. LINDB

SOD, TED, 1951–
*Satan and Simon Desoto.* 1991. JONT

SOLIS, OCTAVIO, 1958–
*Man of the Flesh.* 1990. PLACG1
*El Otro.* 1997. PLACGH
*La posada magica* (music by Marcos Loya). 1994.
    PLACG2

SOLLY, BILL, 1931– , and WARD, DONALD
*Boy Meets Boy.* 1975. HOF

SOLOGUB, FYODOR, 1863–1927
*The Triumph of Death.* 1907.
    Green, M., translator GREEN
*Vanka the Steward and Jehan the Page.* 1908.
    Green, M., and Katsell, J., translators GREENU

SOLOMON, PETER
*Factwino Meets the Moral Majority* (script by). *See* San
    Francisco Mime Troupe. *Factwino Meets the Moral
    Majority*

SOLORZANO, CARLOS, 1922–
*Crossroads: A Sad Vaudeville.* 1966.
    Collecchia, F., and Matas, J., translators ROSENB

SOLOVEV, VLADIMIR ALEKSANDROVICH, 1907–
    1978
*Field Marshal Kutuzov.* 1939.
    Robbins, J., translator SEVP

SOLOVYOV, VLADIMIR A. *See* Solovev, Vladimir
    Aleksandrovich

SOMIN, WILLI OSCAR, 1898–
*Attentat. See* Close Quarters
*Close Quarters.* 1935.
    Lennox, G., translator and adapter FAMH
    Variant title: *Attentat*

SOMSEN, PENNELL
*One Tit, a Dyke, & Gin!* 1992. HELB

SON, DIANA, 1965–
*Happy Birthday Jack.* 1999. HUMANA99
*R.A.W. ('cause I'm a Woman).* 1993. PERC

SØNDERBY, KNUD, 1909–1966
*En kvinde er overflødig. See* A Woman Too Many
*A Woman Too Many.* 1942.
    Roughton, A., translator CONT
    Variant title: *En kvinde er overflødig*

SONDHEIM, STEPHEN, 1930–
*Company* (music and lyrics by). *See* Furth, George.
    *Company*
*Follies* (music and lyrics by). *See* Goldman, James.
    *Follies*
*A Funny Thing Happened on the Way to the Forum*
    (music and lyrics by). *See* Shevelove, Burt. *A
    Funny Thing Happened on the Way to the Forum*
*Gypsy* (lyrics by). *See* Laurents, Arthur. *Gypsy*
*Into the Woods* (music and lyrics by). *See* Lapine,
    James. *Into the Woods*
*A Little Night Music* (music and lyrics by). *See* Wheeler,
    Hugh. *A Little Night Music*
*Pacific Overtures* (music and lyrics by). *See* Weidman,
    John. *Pacific Overtures*
*Passion* (music and lyrics by). *See* Lapine, James.
    Passion
*Sunday in the Park with George* (music and lyrics by).
    *See* Lapine, James. *Sunday in the Park with George*
*Sweeney Todd, the Demon Barber of Fleet Street* (music
    and lyrics by). *See* Wheeler, Hugh. *Sweeney Todd,
    the Demon Barber of Fleet Street*
*West Side Story* (lyrics by). *See* Laurents, Arthur. *West
    Side Story*

SONTAG, SUSAN, 1933–2004
*The Way We Live Now. See* Parone, Edward. *The Way
    We Live Now* (adapted from the short story by)

SONY LAB'OU TANSI, 1947–1995
*Conscience de tracteur. See* The Second Ark
*The Second Ark.* 1979.
    Miller, R., translator AFRUBU1
    Variant title: *Conscience de tracteur*

SOPHOCLES, 496–406 B.C.
*Ajax.* 5th century B.C.
    Jebb, R., translator GRDB5
    Moore, J., translator GREP2, GREPA2
    Trevelyan, R., translator OAT1
*Antigone.* 441 B.C.
    Anonymous translator BLON, BRIT, CARN, EVB1,
        WORM
    Arnott, P., translator ANTL, HAVH, HAVHA
    Banks, T., translator MALI1, MALN1, NORG,
        NORI1, SOM, SOMA, VON
    Cocteau, J., adapter, and Wildman, C., translator
        BENU, CLM
    Fagles, R., translator GUTDF, GUTDS, MEY,
        MEYB, MEYD, MEYE, MEYF, NORIA1,
        NORIB1, NORJ1, ROSENB
    Fitts, D., and Fitzgerald, R., translators ABCA,
        ABCB, ABCC, ABCD, ABCE, ABCF, ABCG,
        ABCH, ADV, ALT, ALTE, ANT, BARI, BARIA,

BARIC, BARID, BARIE, BARIG, BARIH,
BARKF, BARU, BAUL, BEAR, BONA, BONB,
BONC, CONG, CONP, COOP, COTKICG,
COXM, CRAF, DIEA, DIYL, DIYLA, DIYLB,
DIYLC, DIYLD, DIYRD, DOLAN, DOWS, FIFT,
GOLD, GOLH, GUTH, GUTL, HEALA, HEALB,
HEALC, HEALD, HEALE, HIG, HOEP, HOGF,
HOLP, JACOB, JACOBA, JACOBD, JACOBE,
JOHO, KERN, KERO, KIRLA, KIRLB, KIRLC,
LEVJ, LITIC, LITID, LITIE, LITIF, LITP, LITR,
LITRA, LITRB, LITRC, LITRD, MARK, MON,
MONA, MORT, MORV, MORW, MORWA,
MORWB, MORX, MORXB, MORXD, MORXE,
PERU, REIO, ROHR, SCNP, SHRCD, SHRCE,
SIN, SSST, SSSU, SUL, TAUJ, WOTHB
Francklin, T., translator MIK7
Gassner, J., translator GATS
Grene, D., translator BAIM, BEATA, GREPA2,
GRERA1
Jebb, R., translator GEMM, GLO, GRDB5, GREE,
HUD, KNID, KNIE, OAT1, OAM, OATH, SHAV,
SHAX, THO, TRE, TREA2
Jebb, R., translator and Rapp, A., modifier GRDG,
KNIF, KNIG, KNIH, KNIJ
Kitto, H., translator BARIF, BARKD, BARKE,
CARLG
Lucas, F., translator LUCA, LUCAB, LUCAF
Moore, J., translator GRDBA4
Neufeld, M., translator MALR1
O'Sheel, S., translator FREH, LIND
Plumptre, E., translator BAT1, BUCK, BUCL,
BUCM, EVA1, HARC8, HAVI, HIB, HIBB,
HOUS, HUDS2, HUDT, INGW, MAST, THOM,
THON
Robinson, C., translator ROBK
Roche, P., translator BARH
Townsend, M., translator CASE, KNOK, KOTKIR,
COTY, SUTL
Watling, E., translator BLOND, BLOO, KON,
PATM, PATP, REF
Way, A., translator STA
Whitelaw, R., translator ATTI, CLM, FGP, ROBI,
ROBJA, TEN
Williams, F., translator CRY
Wyckoff, E., translator GRDBA4, GREP2, GRER1,
LITM
Young, G., translator CLF1, CROS, PLAG, SEBO,
SEBP

*Electra*. 5th century B.C.
Anonymous translator HAPD, WED
Campbell, L., translator FGP
Ferguson, F., translator FIFT, FOR
Grene, D., translator GRDBA4, GREP2, GREPA2,
GRER2

Jebb, R., translator GRDB5, OAT1
Kitto, H., translator CLL, REAL
Plumptre, E., translator CLKW
Whitelaw, R., translator ATT3
Williams, F., translator CRY
Young, G., translator PLAG
*King Oedipus. See* Oedipus the King
*Oedipus at Colonus.* 401 B.C.
Anonymous translator GRER3
Campbell, L., translator FGP, ROBJA
Fitzgerald, R., translator FIFT, GRDBA4, GREP2,
MALI1
Grene, D., translator GREPA2, GRERA3
Jebb, R., translator GRDB5, OAT1
Kitto, H., translator CLLC
Moebius, W., translator COOA
Plumptre, E., translator ROBJ
Williams, F., translator CRY
Young, G., translator KRE
Variant title: *Oedipus coloneus*
*Oedipus coloneus. See* Oedipus at Colonus
*Oedipus, King of Thebes. See* Oedipus the King
*Oedipus Rex. See* Oedipus the King
*Oedipus the King.* 5th century B.C.
Anonymous translator BEAS, BERP, BERPA, CASH,
EVB1, MABC, SANK, SATJ, SCNN, SCNPL,
STS
Arnott, P., translator HAPRL, MOE, REIW, REIWE
Bagg, R., translator HOWM
Banks, T., translator BOY, MALI1
Berkowitz, L., translator BAIC, MALN1
Berkowitz, L., and Brunner, T., translators BAIG,
BAIH, BAIK, EIGHT, NORG, NORI1
Bywater, I., translator SCNO
Cavender, K., translator COTKICG, GOU1, SEVT,
SMA, WEIS, WEIW
Cook, A., translator COOA, DAVK, HAPO, LIND
Fagles, R., translator BAIL, GUTDF, GUTDS, MEY,
MEYB, MEYC, MEYCA, MEYCB, MEYD,
MEYE, MEYF, NORGA, NORIA1, NORIB1,
NORIC1, NORJ1, NORJA, WOTHC
Fitts, D., and Fitzgerald, R., translators ABCB,
ABCC, ABCD, ABCE, ABCF, ABCG, ACE,
ALLI, ALLJ, ALLK, ALLM, ALLN, ALLO, ALS,
BARI, BARIA, BARIC, BARID, BARIE, BARIG,
BARIH, BARJ, BARKF, BEAM, BIER, BOGA,
BOW, BRIX, BRIY, BRIZ, BRJ, BRJA, BRJB,
BRJC, BROI, BURG, CALD, CLKJ, COLD,
CONO, DEAR, DEAS, DIEA, DIEB, DIEF, DIYL,
DIYLA, DIYLB, DIYLC, DIYLD, DOLAN,
DOWN, DUH, ELK, FIFR, FREG, FRYE,
FRYEA, GOLD, GORE, GWYN, HAEA, HAEB,
HEA, HEAA, HEAB, HEAC, HEAD, HEAL,
HEALA, HEALB, HEALC, HEALD, HEALE,

HILPDH, HOGI, HOGN, JACOB, JACOBA,
JACOBD, JACOBE, JAFF, JOHN, KINNS, KNO,
KNOJ, KNOK, LEVI, LID, LITC, LITI, LITIA,
LITIB, LITIC, LITID, LITIE, LITIF, LITJ, LITJA,
LITQ, LITR, LITRA, LITRB, LITRC, LITRD,
MADB, MARL, MORXB, MORXD, PERS, PERT,
PERV, PERW, PERX, PERY, PERZ, PRO, REIL,
REIN, SHRCF, SCNQ, SCNQCA, SCNQCB, SEN,
SIN, SSSI, SSSIA, SSSIB, SSSIC, STY, TOU,
TRI, TRIA, VANV1, VOLI, VOLP, VONS1,
WAIW, WOTHA, WOTHB

Francklin, T., translator GREE

Gassner, J., translator TREB, TREC1, TREE1, TREI1

Glasser, J., translator HILP

Gould, T., translator KIRLA, KIRLB, KIRLC,
KIRLD, MAO

Grene, D., translator AUB, BEAL, BAIM, BARN,
BARNA, BEATA, BLAG, BLAH, GPA,
GRDBA4, GREN, GREP2, GREPA2, GRER1,
GRERA1, LITM, LOCL, LOCLA, LOCLB, ROBI

Jebb, R., translator BROK, GATT, GRDB5, GRDG,
GREC1, LOCM1, MATT, MURP, OAM, OAT1,
OATH, THP, WARN1

Kitto, H., translator BARIF, BARK, BARKA,
BARKB, BARKC, BARKD, BARKE, CLLC

Knox, B., translator GORDP, PERR1

Lucas, F., translator LUCA, LUCAB, LUCAF

Mendell, C., translator ROBJA, WALJ

Murray, G., translator CARP, CARPA, COHM, FGP,
MIL, TEN

Petalas, U., translator PIC

Plumptre, E., translator BUCK, BUCL, BUCM,
DRAD1, EVA1, EVC1, HARC8, PLAB1, SMP

Roach, P., translator JORH

Sheppard, J., translator BARC, GLO, WEAV1

Starr, F., translator LAP

Watling, E., translator BENQ, BROTA, SANO

Whitelaw, R., translator ATT1, HOWE, HOWF

Williams, F., translator CRY

Yeats, W., translator DEAP, ESA, FIFT, HOEP,
MALC, MALG1, MIJB, PES, ROF, SHR, SHRO,
WHFM

Young, G., translator PLAG

Variant titles: *King Oedipus; Oedipus, King of
Thebes; Oedipus Rex; Oedipus tyrannos; Oedipus
tyrannus*

*Oedipus tyrannos. See* Oedipus the King

*Oedipus tyrannos. See* Oedipus the King

*Philoctetes.* 409 B.C.

Cavender, K., translator HAPRL

Chase, A., translator FIFV

Dolin, E., and Sugg, A., translators COOA

Francklin, T., translator OAT1

Freeman, K., translator LIND

Grene, D., translator GRDBA4, GREP2, GREPA2,
GRER3, GRERA3

Jebb, R., translator GRDB5, GRDG

Schwerner, A., translator TENN

Workman, J., translator ROBJ

*The Searching Satyrs.* 5th century B.C.

Green, R., translator TREB

*The Trachiniae.* 5th century B.C.

Jameson, M., translator GRDBA4, GREP2, GREPA2

Jebb, R., translator GRDB5, OAT1

Variant title: *The Women of Trachis*

*The Women of Trachis. See* The Trachiniae

SORGE, REINHARD JOHANNES, 1895–1944
*The Beggar.* 1912.
Sokel, W., and J., translators SOK
Variant title: *Die Bettler*
*Die Bettler. See* The Beggar

SOSSI, RON, 1939– , and CONDON, FRANK
*The Chicago Conspiracy Trial.* 1979. WES7

SŌSUKE, NAMIKI. *See* Namiki, Sōsuke

SOTO, GARY, 1952–
*Novio Boy.* 1997. SCVDO1

SOUCY, PETE
*Flux.* 1993. LYN

SOULE, CHARLES CARROLL, 1842–1913
*Hamlet Revamped; a Travesty without a Pun.* 1874.
NIN5

SOUPAULT, PHILIPPE, 1897–1990. *See* Breton, Andrè,
joint author

SOUTHERNE, THOMAS, 1660–1746
*The Fatal Marriage. See* Isabella.
*Isabella.* 1694. BELK5
*Oroonoko.* 1696. BELK10, DOB, RET
*The Wives' Excuse.* 1691–1692. COTKA

SOUTHEY, ROBERT, 1774–1843
*Wat Tyler.* 1794. ENGLMI

SOWERBY, GITHA, 1876–1970
*Rutherford and Son.* 1912. DICEM, NEWWP, PLAP2

SOWERBY, KATHERINE GITHA. *See* Sowerby, Githa

SOYA, CARL ERIK, 1896–1983
*Lion with Corset.*
Knudson, B., translator FIL

*To Trade. See* Two Threads
*Two Threads.* 1943.
 Anonymous translator (revised by P. N. Furbank)
 CONT
 Variant title: *To Trade*

SOYINKA, WOLE, 1934–
 *Death and the King's Horseman.* 1975. BANH, BPW,
 GUTDF, GUTDS, NORJ2, SSSIC, VENA,
 WOTHA, WOTHB, WOTHC
 *The Lion and the Jewel.* 1959. HOWM, KIAN, LEVY,
 NORGA, NORIA2, WOTHM
 *The Strong Breed.* 1964. BARKF, COLD, HAPU,
 HOEP, JACOBA, JACOBD, MEYB, MEYD,
 MEYE, MEYF
 *The Trials of Brother Jero.* 1964. ROSENB

SPARK, MURIEL SARAH, 1918–2006
 *Doctors of Philosophy.* 1962. RHE
 *The Dry River Bed* (radio play). 1959. PLAAC2
 *The Party through the Wall* (radio play). 1957. PLAAC1

SPEARS, STEVE J., 1951–
 *King Richard.* 1978. THUG

SPECHT, KERSTIN, 1956–
 *Das glühend männla. See* The Little Red-hot Man
 *The Little Red-hot Man.* 1990.
 Weber, G., translator CAS
 Variant title: *Das glühend männla*

SPENCE, EULALIE, 1894–1981
 *Episode.* 1928. BRW
 *Fool's Errand.* 1927. PER
 *Her.* 1927. PER
 *Hot Stuff.* 1927. BRW
 *The Start*er. 1927. LOC
 *Undertow.* 1928. HARY, HARYB, PER

SPENCE, JANIS, 1946?–2008
 *Catlover.* 1990. LYN

SPENCE, MARJORIE ELLEN
 *Stars at the Break of Day.* 1995. TIME

SPENCER, DAVID, 1958–
 *Hurricane Roses.* 1994. FROLIN2
 *Releevo.* 1987. VER

SPENCER, JAMES
 *A Bunch of the Gods Were Sitting around One Day.*
 1973. BALLE12

SPENCER, RHOMA. *See* Hall, Tony, joint author

SPENCER, STUART, 1957–
 *Resident Alien.* 1998. HUMANA98

SPENSLEY, PHILIP
 *Hell's Bells.* 1967. ALI

SPEWACK, MRS. BELLA (COHEN), 1899–1990, and
 SPEWACK, SAMUEL
 *Boy Meets Girl.* 1935. BES35, CET, FAMJ, GAS,
 SAFF
 *Kiss Me Kate* (adapted from *The Taming of the Shrew*
 by William Shakespeare; music and lyrics by Cole
 Porter). 1948. RICO
 *Leave It to Me!* (music and lyrics by Cole Porter). 1938.
 RICM
 *My Three Angels* (adapted from *La cousine des anges* by
 Albert Husson). 1953. BES52, GARZH, THEA53

SPEWACK, SAMUEL, 1899–1971
 *Two Blind Mice.* 1949. BES49
 *Under the Sycamore Tree.* 1952. PLAN7
 — *See also* Spewack, Mrs. Bella (Cohen), joint
 author

SPIDERWOMAN THEATRE, 1975–
 *Power Pipes.* 1993. DAPO
 *Sun Moon and Feather.* 1981. GEIO, PERC
 *Winnetou's Snake Oil Show from Wigwam City.* 1988.
 SWANS

SPINETTI, VICTOR, 1933–. *See* Kennedy, Adrienne, joint
 author

SPIRO, GYORGY, 1946–
 *Chicken Head.* 1987.
 Brogyányi, E., translator HUNGDC
 Variant title: *Csirkefei*
 *Csirkefei. See* Chicken Head
 *The Imposter.* 1982.
 Györgyey, C., translator GYOR
 Sollosy, J., translator TEZ
 Variant title: *Az imposztor*
 *Az imposztor. See* The Imposter
 *Soap Opera.* 2000.
 Bock, A., translator ROEB

SPIRO, PETER
 *Howya Doin' Freaky Banana?* 1997. ALG

SPUNDE, WALTER G.
 *The Mercenary.* 1974. SHAT

SPUNNER, SUZANNE, 1951–
 *Running Up a Dress.* 1986. TAIT

SRBLJANOVIC, BILJANA, 1970–
  *Belgrade Trilogy.* 1997.
    Ellis, translator EUP

SRI-HARSHADEVA. *See* Harsha, son of Hira

SRIRANGA. *See* Rangachar, Adya (pseudonym of)

SRUOGA, BALYS, 1896–1947
  *Kazimieras Sapiega.* 1940.
    Sabalis, K., translator FIFFN

STAFF OF THE LIVING NEWSPAPER
  *Injunction Granted.* 1936. BRP
  *Medicine Show.* 1940. BRP
  *1935.* 1936. BRP
  *Triple-A Plowed Under.* 1936. FEF

STALLINGS, LAURENCE, 1894–1968. *See* Anderson,
    Maxwell, joint author

STANESCU, SAVIANA, 1967–
  *Outcast.* 1998.
    Nelega, A., translator POQ

STANLEY, DAVID. *See* Jones, Wendell, joint author

STAPLETON, BERNI
  *Offensive to Some* (excerpt). 1997. BREK
  *Woman in a Monkey Cage.* 1993. LYN

STARKWEATHER, DAVID, 1935–
  *The Poet's Papers.* 1970. NEWA3

STAYTON, RICHARD, 1946–
  *After the First Death.* 1985. LOWE2

STEARNS, SHARON, 1954–
  *Hunter of Peace.* 1993. ZIMM (excerpt)

STEELE, SIR RICHARD, 1672–1729
  *The Conscious Lovers.* 1722. BELK4, COF, EIGH,
    JEFF4, MAND, MANF, MANH, MOR, MOSE1,
    NET, ROGEBD, SIG, STM, TAT, TAU, TAY,
    TUP, TUQ, WILSP
  *The Funeral, or Grief a la mode.* 1701. BELK8
  *Grief a la mode. See* The Funeral.
  *The Tender Husband.* 1705. BELK8, SIG

STEELE, RUFUS, 1877–1935
  *The Fall of Ug.* 1913. BOH3

STEELE, SILAS SEXTON
  *The Crock of Gold; or, The Toiler's Trials.* 1845.
    AMP14

STEELE, WILBUR DANIEL, 1886–1970
  *The Giant's Stair.* 1924? THO

STEFANOVSKI, GORAN, 1952–
  *Proud Flesh.* 1979.
    Stefanovska, P., translator LUZ
  *Sarajevo (Tales from a City).* 1993. LABO

STEFANSSON, DAVID JOHANN, 1895–1964
  *The Golden Gate.* 1941.
    Gathorne-Hardy, G., translator FIL, HAVHN
    Variant title: *Gullna hlidid*
  *Gullna hlidid. See* The Golden Gate

STEIN, GERTRUDE, 1874–1946
  *Accents in Alsace: A Reasonable Tragedy.* 1919. TYEW
  *Daniel Webster Eighteen in America.* 1937? NEWDI37,
    SPC
  *The Mother of Us All.* 1947. BARKE, PLAAF
  *Please Do Not Suffer.* 1916. TYEW
  *Yes Is for a Very Young Man.* 1946. WOLCS

STEIN, JOSEPH, 1912–2010
  *Fiddler on the Roof* (music by Jerry Bock, lyrics by
    Sheldon Harnick). 1964. BES64, GAT, GATB4,
    RICIS, RICO

STEINBECK, JOHN, 1902–1968
  *The Grapes of Wrath. See* Galati, Frank. *The Grapes of
    Wrath* (based on the novel by)
  *The Moon Is Down.* 1942. BES41
  *Of Mice and Men.* 1937. BENPB, BES37, CLUR, CRIT,
    FAMAL, GAS, GAVE, MAFC, PERR3, SATI

STEINER, GEORGE, 1929– (b. Francis George Steiner)
  *The Portage to San Cristobal of A. H. See* Hampton,
    Christopher. *The Portage to San Cristobal of A. H.*
    (adapted from the novella by)

STEINWACHS, GINKA, 1942–
  *George Sand.* 1980.
    Daniel, J., and Sieg, K., translators CAS

STEPHENS, HENRY MORSE, 1857–1919
  *St. Patrick at Tara.* 1909. BOH2

STEPKA, STANISLAV, 1944–
  *The Black Sheep.* 1983.
    Trebatická, H., translator CONTSL5
    Variant title: *Čierna ovca*
  *Čierna ovca. See* The Black Sheep

STEPPLING, JOHN, 1951–
  *The Dream Coast.* 1986. WES21/22
  *Neck.* 1982. PLACE

*Standard of the Breed.* 1988. MESSE
*Storyland.* 1990. MEDN
*Theory of Miracles.* 1989. MEDN

STERLING, GEORGE, 1869–1926
*The Triumph of Bohemia.* 1906. BOH1

STERNER, JERRY, 1938–2001
*Other People's Money.* 1989. BERT, BES88

STERNHEIM, CARL, 1878–1942
*The Bloomers. See* The Underpants
*Die hose. See* The Underpants
*Die Kassette. See* The Strongbox
*Die marquise von Arcis. See* The Mask of Virtue
*The Mask of Virtue.* 1920.
　Dukes, A., translator and adapter FAMH
　Variant title: *Die marquise von Arcis*
*A Pair of Drawers. See* The Underpants
*A Place in the World.* 1913.
　Bentley, E., translator BENS1
　Clark, B., and Katzin, W., translators KAT
　Variant titles: *Der snob; The Snob*
*Der snob. See* A Place in the World
*The Snob. See* A Place in the World
*The Strongbox.* 1912.
　Edwards, M., and Reich, V., translators SOK
　Variant title: *Die Kassette*
*The Underpants.* 1911.
　Bentley, E., translator BEFOB, BENT6
　McHaffie, M., translator SCVG
　Variant titles: *The Bloomers; Die hose; A Pair of
　Drawers*

STETSON, JEFF
*The Meeting.* 1990. KINHN

STEVENS, DAVID, 1940–
*The Sum of Us.* 1990. BES90

STEVENS, GEORGE ALEXANDER, 1710–1784
*Distress upon Distress.* 1752. TRUS

STEVENS, WALLACE, 1879–1955
*Carlos among the Candles.* 1917. GERO

STEVENSON, ROBERT LOUIS, 1850–1894
*The Strange Case of Jekyll and Mr. Hyde. See* Nolte,
　Charles. *The Strange Case of Dr. Jekyll and Mr.
　Hyde* (adapted from the novel by)
　*— See also* Sieveking, Lance. *The Strange Case
　of Dr. Jekyll and Mr. Hyde* (adapted from the
　novel by)

STEVENSON, WILLIAM (Mr. S. Mr. of Art.
　pseudonym), 1521–1575
*Gammer Gurton's nedle. See* Gammer Gurton's needle
*Gammer Gurton's needle* (supposed author). 1552?
　ADA, BAS, BOA, CRE, DPR1, FAR, GARZB,
　GAYLE1, HEIL, LEV, LEVE, MARG, NES,
　THWO, TYDE, WATT2
　Variant title: *Gammer Gurton's nedle*

STEWART, DONALD OGDEN, 1894–1980
*Rebound.* 1930. BES29

STEWART, DOUGLAS ALEXANDER, 1913–1985
*The Golden Lover* (radio play). 1943. FIO
*Ned Kelly.* 1943? THOP

STEWART, ENA LAMONT, 1912–2006
*Towards Evening.* 1985. PLABE8
　*— See also* Will You Still Need Me
*Walkies Time.* 1985. PLABE8
　*— See also* Will You Still Need Me
*Will You Still Need Me* (trilogy consisting of *Knocking
　on the Wall, Towards Evening, Walkies Time*).
　1985.

STEWART, MICHAEL, 1924–1987
*Hello, Dolly!* (music and lyrics by Jerry Herman; based
　on *The Matchmaker* by Thornton Wilder). 1964.
　BES63

——— and BRAMBLE, MARK
*42nd Street* (music and lyrics by Harry Warren and Al
　Dubin; based on the novel by Bradford Ropes).
　1980. BES80

STEWART-BROWN, CHRISTI
*The Gene Pool.* 1998. PLACJ

STICKNEY, PHYLLIS YVONNE
*Big Momma n''em.* 1994. BLAC

STILES, THELMA JACKSON, 1939–
*No One Man Show.* 1971. CEN

STILGOE, RICHARD, 1943– , joint author. *See* Lloyd
　Webber, Andrew. *The Phantom of the Opera*

STILL, WILIAM GRANT, 1895–1977
*Sahdji, an African Ballet* (music by). *See* Bruce, Richard
　and Locke, Alain. *Sahdji, an African Ballet*

STITT, MILAN, 1941–2009
*The Runner Stumbles.* 1976. BES75

*There Are Crimes and Crimes.* 1899.
    Björkman, E., translator MOSG, MOSH, TREBA,
      TREC2, TREE2, TREI2
    Sprinchorn, E., translator SPR
    Variant titles: *Brott och brott; Crimes and Crimes*
*To Damascus, Part 1.* 1900.
    Paulson, A., translator ULAN
    Sprinchorn, E., translator SPR

**STRINGER, VIRGINIA BURTON**
*Can You Hear Them Crying?* 1994. VOI

**STRODE, WARREN CHETHAM.** *See* Chetham-Strode,
    Warren

**STROMAN, SUSAN, 1954– , and WEIDMAN, JOHN**
*Contact: A Dance Play with Music in Three Short*
    *Stories: Swinging, Did You Move?, Contact*
    (choreography by Susan Stroman). 1999. BES99
*Did You Move? See* Contact
*Swinging. See* Contact

**STRONG, AUSTIN, 1881–1952**
*The Drume of Oude.* 1906. LEV, LEVE, MIL

**STROUSE, CHARLES, 1928–**
*Annie* (music by). *See* Meehan, Thomas. *Annie; a*
    *Musical in Two Acts*
*Applause* (music by). *See* Comden, Betty and Green,
    Adolph. *Applause*
*"It's a Bird, It's a Plane, It's Superman"* (music by).
    *See* Newman, David and Benton, Robert. *"It's a Bird,*
    *It's a Plane, It's Superman"*

**STUART, MRS. AIMEE (McHARDY), 1886?–1981**
*Jeannie.* 1940. FIR
*Lace on Her Petticoat.* 1950. PLAN5
*Sixteen.* 1934. FAME

**STUART, KELLY**
*Ball and Chain.* 1990. MEDN
*A Shoe Is Not a Question.* 2001. LAR

**STUKALOV, N. F.** *See* Pogodin, Nikolai Federovich,
    pseudonym

**STURGES, PRESTON, 1898–1959**
*Strictly Dishonorable.* 1929. BES29, GASB, NELSDI

**STYNE, JULE, 1905–1994**
*Gypsy* (music by). *See* Laurents, Arthur. *Gypsy*

**SUDERMANN, HERMANN, 1857–1928**
*Casa paterna. See* Magda
*The Fires of St. John.* 1900.

    Swickard, C., translator MOSQ
    Variant title: *Johannisfeuer*
*Das glück im winkel. See* The Vale of Content
*Happiness in a Nook. See* The Vale of Content
*Heimat. See* Magda
*Home. See* Magda
*Johannes. See* John the Baptist
*Johannisfeuer. See* The Fires of St. John
*John the Baptist.* 1898.
    Marshall, B., translator FRA17
    Variant title: *Johannes*
*Magda.* 1893.
    Winslow, C., translator WATI, WATL2
    Variant titles: *Casa paterna; Heimat; Home*
*The Vale of Content.* 1895.
    Leonard, W., translator DICD
    Variant titles: *Das glück im winkel; Happiness in a*
    *Nook*

**SUDRAKA (KING).** *See* Shudraka (King)

**SUGIMORI, NOBUMORI.** *See* Chikamatsu, Monzaemon

**SULLIVAN, SIR ARTHUR SEYMOUR, 1842–1900**
    (composer). *See* Gilbert, William Schwenck

**SULLIVAN, L. M.**
*Baron's Night, or Catch as Catch-can.* 1973. NEWP

**SUMMERS, DAVID.** *See* Ruderman, Gary, joint author

**SUN, YU, 1900–1990**
*The Women's Representative.* 1953.
    Tang, S., translator MESE

**SUNDGAARD, ARNOLD, 1909–2006**
*Spirochete.* 1938. FEF

**SUNDUKIANTS, GAVRILL NIKITOVICH, 1825–1911**
*The Ruined Family.* 1888.
    Collins, F., translator ARM
    Variant title: *Die ruinerte Familie*
*Die ruinerte Familie. See* The Ruined Family

**SURAYYI','ABD al-'AZIZ al-, 1939–**
*The Bird Has Flown.* 1972.
    Jabseh, S., and Ezzy, T., translators JAY
    Variant title: *Tara 'l-dik*
*Tara 'l-dik. See* The Bird Has Flown

**SURRIDGE, ANDRE, 1951–**
*Children of the Rainbow.* 1993. SACR

**SUSIE (pseudonym of Susie Edwards), d. 1967.** *See*
    Butterbeans, joint author

SUSSMAN, BRUCE
*Coming Attractions* (lyrics by Bruce Sussman and Ted Tally). *See* Tally, Ted. *Coming Attractions*

SUTHERLAND, EFUA THEODORA, 1924–1996
*Edufa.* 1964. BPW, LITT

SUTO, ANDRAS, 1927–2006
*Egy lócsiszár virágvasárnapja. See* The Palm Sunday of a Horse Dealer
*The Palm Sunday of a Horse Dealer.* 1976.
    Brogyányi, E., translator HUNGDC
    Variant title: *Egy lócsiszár virágvasárnapja*

SUTRO, ALFRED, 1863–1933
*John Glayde's Honour.* 1907. DICEM
*A Marriage Has Been Arranged.* 1902. PEN
*The Walls of Jericho.* 1904. MART

SUZUKI, YUMI, 1963– . *See* Iijima, Sanae, joint author

SVEINBJORNSSON, TRYGGVI, 1891–1964
*Bishop Jón Arason.* 1950.
    Hollander, L., translator MODS

SVETINA, IVO, 1948–
*Babylon. See* The Gardens and the Dove
*The Gardens and the Dove.* 1995.
    Anonymous translator PRED (summary only)
    Variant titles: *Babylon; Vrtovi in golobica*
*Šeherezada, vzhodno-zahodna opera. See* Sheherezade
*Sheherezade.* 1989.
    Anonymous translator PRED (summary only)
    Variant title: *Šeherezada, vzhodno-zahodna opera*
*Thus died Zarathushtra.* 1997.
    McConnell–Duff, A., Svetina, I., and Potpara, L., translators PRED
    Variant title: *Tako je umrl Zarathushtra*
*Tako je umrl Zarathushtra. See* Thus died Zarathushtra
*Vrtovi in golobica. See* The Gardens and the Dove

SVEVO, ITALO, 1861–1928
*Con la penna d'oro. See* With Gilded Pen
*With Gilded Pen.* 1926.
    Oldcorn, A., translator TWEI
    Variant title: *Con la penna d'oro*

SVICH, CARIDAD, 1963–
*Alchemy of Desire/Dead Man's Blues.* 1994. SVICH
*Gleaning/Rebusca.* 1990. FEY
*Prodigal Kiss.* 1999. NEWR99
*Scar.* 1997. ARRIZ

SWADOS, ELIZABETH, 1951–
*Esther, a Vaudeville Megillah.* 1988. SCM

SWADOS, ROBIN, 1953–
*A Quiet End.* 1986. HELB

SWAIN, ELIZABETH
*Half Return.* 1985. DODGS

SWAYZE, MRS. J.C.
*Ossawattomie Brown.* 1859. MESC

SWEET, JEFFREY, 1950–
*American Enterprise.* 1991. BES91, BES93
*The Value of Names.* 1982. SCM

SWERLING, JOSEPH, 1897–1964; BURROWS, ABRAM; and LOESSER, FRANK
*Guys and Dolls* (based on the story "Idyll of Miss Sarah Brown" by Damon Runyan). 1950. BENT4, BES50

SWINBURNE, ALGERNON CHARLES, 1837–1909
*Atlanta in Calydon.* 1865. KAU

SWORTZELL, LOWELL, 1930–2004
*The Love of Three Oranges* (adapted from the play by Carlo Gozzi). 1997. SCVDO1
*A Partridge in a Pear Tree.* 1966. SWO
*The Shepherds of Saint Francis.* 1995. SWO
*A Visit from St. Nicholas or The Night before Christmas.* 1991. SWO

SYAL, MEERA, 1961–
*My Sister-wife.* 1994. GEOR

SYLVAINE, VERNON, 1897–1957
*As Long as They're Happy.* 1953. PLAN9

SYLVANUS, ERWIN, 1917–1985
*Dr. Korczak and the Children.* 1957.
    Wellwarth, G., translator BENB
    Variant title: *Korczak und die Kinder*
*Korczak und die Kinder. See* Dr. Korczak and the Children

SYNGE, JOHN MILLINGTON, 1871–1909
*Deirdre of the Sorrows.* 1910. BARF
*In the Shadow of the Glen.* 1903. BALL, LOCLA, MERC, STY
*The Playboy of the Western World.* 1907. AUG, BAC, BENSB2, BLOC, CEW, CLKW, CLKWI, CLKY, CLLC, COK, COLEL2, COTKICO, COTM, COTQ, CUBE, CUBG, DODS, DUR, FIG, FOS, FOUX, GREAAI, GREAB, GREC2, HAU, KNIH, KNIJ, KRM, LAQID, LEVY, LIED2, LIEE2, MALG2, MORV, MORW, MORX, MORXB, OWEC, PLAAB, REIO, REIT, SALE, SOM, SOMA, SSSI, STEI, TREBJ, WALJ, WEIM

*Riders to the Sea.* 1904. ALLI, ALLJ, ALLK, ALLM, ALLN, ALLO, ALT, ALTE, BARI, BARIA, BARIC, BARID, BARIE, BARKB, BARKC, BARKF, BLOC, BOGA, BONC, BOOK, BRIG, BRIU, CAP, CARP, CARPA, CASH, CLL, COD, COLD, CONN, COTM, COTQ, COTY, DAI, DAV1, DICD, DIYL, DIYLC, DIYLD, DIYRD, FIG, GREAAI, GREG, HAVI, HEALB, HILPDH5, HOGI, HUD, INGE, INGG, INGH, JACOB, JACOBA, JACOBD, KERO, LITID, LITIE, LITIF, LOOA, LOOB, LOOC, LOOD, LOOE, LOOF, MAC, MACB, MIKL, MOSN, MOSO, PATM (1 act only), PATP, PERR3, PROW, REIL, REIWE, ROY, ROYE, SANK, SEN, SEVT, SILK, SILKI, SILN, SILO, SSTA, STEI, STJN (1 act only), STS, TAUJ, TOBI, TRE, TREA1, TREBA, TREBJ, TREC2, TREE3, TREI3, TUCN, TUCO, VENA, WARI, WARL, WATA, WATF1, WATI, WATT2, WEAT2, WEIP, WHI, WHK, WOOD2, WOOE2
*The Well of the Saints.* 1905. ULAN

SZABLOWSKI, JERZY
*Subsidiary Vice-president.* 1969. ALI

SZAJNA, JOZEF, 1922–2008
*Replika.* 1973.
　Czerwinski, E., translator FUCHS

SZILÁGYI, ANDOR, 1955–
*Unsent Letters.* 1993.
　Patthy, I., translator UPOR

SZYSZKOWITZ, GERALD, 1938–
*Friedemann Puntigam or The Delicate Art of Losing One's Memory.* ANTHC

TA, BINH DUY
*The Monkey Mother.* 1998. THUAA

TABER, TROY W. *See* Cromelin, Caroline, joint author

TABORI, GEORGE, 1914–2007
*The Cannibals.* 1968. SCV, THL
*The Emperor's Clothes.* 1953. BES52
*Mein kampf.* 1987. WEBER

TAGORE, RABINDRANATH, 1861–1941
*Karna and Kunti.* 1899. GERO
*Muktdhara. See* The River Unbound
*The Post Office.* 1914. BART, SCVDT1
*The River Unbound.* 1922.
　Tagore, R., translator KAM1
　Variant title: *Muktdhara*

TAHIR, PENGIRAN HAJI
*Ray of Hope.* 1994.
　Abdullah, K., translator MLAB

TAILLE, JEAN DE LA, 1533?–1608?
*Saul le furieux.* 1572? FOUR

TAKEDA, IZUMO, 1691–1756
*Bushido.* 1746.
　Eliot, S., translator LAW

——— and MIYOSHI, SHORAKU; and NAMIKI, SENRYU
*At the Farmhouse.* 1748. (Act 6 of *Kandehon chūshingura*)
　Keene, D., translator BRAZ
*The First Note of Spring.* 1747. (travel scene from Act 4 of *Yoshitsune sembon zakura*)
　Goff, J., translator BRAZ
*The House of Sugawara.* 1746.
　Miyasato, A., and Yamaguchi, S., translators (English version by Louis M. Steed and Earle Ernst). ERN
　Variant title: *Sugawara Denju Tenarai Kagami*
*Mount Tempai.* 1746. (Act 4, Scene 1 of *Sugawara Denju Tenarai Kagami*)
　Jones, S., translator BRAZ
*Sugawara Denju Tenarai Kagami. See* The House of Sugawara; Mount Tempai; Tumult in the Palace
*Tumult in the Palace.* 1746. (Act 5, Scene 1 of *Sugawara Denju Tenarai Kagami*)
　Jones, S., translator BRAZ

TAKEUCHI, JŪICHIRŌ, 1947–
*Claire de lune.* 1996.
　Poulton, M., translator HACJT5
　Variant title: *Tsuki no hikari*
*Tsuki no hikari. See* Claire de lune

TALEBI, FARAMARZ
*Barracks in the Evening.* 1979.
　Godeca, J., Ibsen, L., and Nyce, C., translators GHAN
　Variant title: *Padegan dar shamgah*
*Padegan dar shamgah. See* Barracks in the Evening

TALFOURD, FRANCIS, 1828–1862
*Hamlet Travestie* (attributed to). 1849. NIN3
*Macbeth, Somewhat Removed from the Text of Shakespeare.* 1853. NIN3
*Shylock; or, The Merchant of Venice Preserved.* 1853. NIN3

TALLMAN, JAMES, 1947–
*Trans-Canada Highway.* SHAT

TALLMAN, ROBERT
*The Man Who Liked Dickens* (television adaptation of the short story by Evelyn Waugh). 1953. SUT1

TALLY, TED, 1952–
*Coming Attractions* (music by Jack Feldman, lyrics by Bruce Sussman and Jack Feldman). 1980. PLACF

TALMADGE, VICTOR. *See* Nishikawa, Lane, joint author

TAMAYO Y BAUS, MANUEL, 1829–1898
*Un drama nuevo.* 1967. BRET

TAN, MEI CHING
*Quiet the Gorilla.* 1995. PING

TAN, TARN HOW
*Home.* 1991. FAT
*Undercover.* 1994. DIRTY

TAN, THERESA, ca.1968–
*Bra Sizes.* 1992. FAT
*Dirty Laundry.* 1993. DIRTY

TANAKA, CHIKAO, 1905–1995
*Far Fringes of the Clouds.* 1947.
Swain, J., translator HACJT8
Variant title: *Kumo no hatate*
*The Head of Mary: A Nagasaki Fantasia.* 1959.
Goodman, D., translator AFTAP
Variant title: *Maria no kubi*
*Kumo no hatate. See* Far Fringes of the Clouds
*Maria no kubi. See* The Head of Mary: A Nagasaki Fantasia

TANER, HALDUN, 1915–1986
*The Ballad of Ali of Keshan.* 1964.
Özdogru, N., translator HALM

T'ANG, HSIEN-TSU, 1550–1617
*Huan hun chi. See* Peony Pavilion
*Mu-tan t'ing. See* Peony Pavilion
*Peony Pavilion* (scenes 7, 10, 14, 20). 1598?
Anonymous translator BIR2
Variant titles: *Huan hun chi; Mu-tan chi; The Soul's Revenge*
*The Soul's Revenge. See* Peony Pavilion

TANKRED-DORST. *See* Dorst, Tankred

TANTAR, NINA, 1961–
*Ubu and Milena.* 2000.
Voiculescu, M., translator POQ

TANVIR, HABIB, 1923–2009
*Agra Bazaar.* 1954.
Malick, J., translator KAM3

TARCHETTI, IGNIO UGO, 1839–1869
*Fosca. See* Lapine, James Passion (based on the novel *Fosca* by)

TARDIEU, JEAN, 1903–1995
*La cite sans sommeil. See* The Sleepless City
*One Way for Another.* 1951.
Wellwarth, G., translator BEN
Variant title: *Un geste pour un autre*
*The Sleepless City.* 1987.
Lamont, R., translator PAIS
Variant title: *La cite sans sommeil*
*Un geste pour un autre. See* One Way for Another

TARKINGTON, BOOTH, 1869–1946
*Clarence.* 1919. BES19, GARU
*The Intimate Strangers.* 1921. COH
*Monsieur Beaucaire.* 1919. PEN, PROB
*The Trysting-place.* 1923. SCWE, SCWG

—— and WILSON, HARRY LEON
*The Gibson Upright.* 1919. WEB
*The Man from Home.* 1908. BES99, CEY

TARLO, LUNA. *See* Aaron, Joyce, joint author

TARLTON, RICHARD, d.1588
*The Famous Victories of Henry the Fifth* (sometimes attributed to). *See* Anonymous Plays. *The Famous Victories of Henry the Fifth*

TASSO, TORQUATO, 1544–1595
*Aminta.* 1573.
Hunt, L., translator BENSA
Oldmixon, J., translator HAYD
Variant title: *Amyntas*
*Amyntas. See* Aminta

TATE, NAHUM, 1652–1715
*A Duke and No Duke; or, Trapolin's Vagaries* (adapted from *Trappolin Suppos'd a Prince* by Sir Aston Cokain). 1684. HUGL
*The History of King Lear.* 1681? ADAP, SUMB

TATHAM, JOHN, fl.1600
*Grim the Collier of Croydon; or, The Devil and His Dame* (sometimes attributed to). *See* Anonymous Plays. *Grim the Collier of Croydon; or, The Devil and His Dame*

TAVEL, RONALD, 1936–2009
  *Boy on a Straight-back Chair. See* Boy on the Straight-
    back Chair
  *Boy on the Straight-back Chair.* 1969. MESSE, WOQ1
    Variant title: *Boy on a Straight-back Chair*
  *Gorilla Queen.* 1967. SMC
  *The Life of Lady Godiva.* 1966. MARRA

TAYLEURE, CLIFTON W., 1832–1891
  *Horse-shoe Robinson.* 1856. MOSS2

TAYLOR, CECIL PHILIP (C. P.), 1929–1981
  *And a Nightingale Sang . . . a Play in Two Acts.* 1977.
    BES83
  *Bread and Butter.* 1966. NEWE10
  *Getting by, and Going Home. See* Walter Good; a Play
    with Music in Two Acts. 1981. BES82
  *Happy Days Are Here Again.* 1967. NEWE12
  *Lies about Vietnam.* 1969. GAY2
  *Walter.* 1977. DEC
    Variant title: *Getting by, and Going Home*

TAYLOR, CHARLES A., 1864–1942
  *From Rags to Riches.* 1903. AMP8

TAYLOR, CHRISTOPHER
  *The Wings of the Dove* (based on the novel by Henry
    James). 1963. PLAN28

TAYLOR, DON, 1936–2003
  *Paradise Restored.* 1972. CLKY

TAYLOR, DREW HAYDEN, 1962–
  *Only Drunks and Children Tell the Truth.* 1996. DAPO
  *Someday.* 1991. BEYO (excerpt)
  *Toronto at Dreamer's Rock.* 1990. BELLW

TAYLOR, JOHN
  *My Three Dads.* 1992. PETERS

TAYLOR, REGINA, 1960–
  *Beside Every Good Man.* 2000. HUMANA2000
  *Between the Lines.* 1995. HUMANA95
  *Escape from Paradise.* 1997. WOMP97
  *Oo-bla-dee.* 1999. BES99
  *Watermelon Rinds.* 1993. DIXD2, HUMANA93

TAYLOR, RON
  *The Unreasonable Act of Julian Waterman.* 1974. KAL3

TAYLOR, SAMUEL, 1912–2000
  *The Happy Time* (based on the novel by Robert
    Fontaine). 1950. BES49
  *Sabrina Fair.* 1953. THEA54

—— and SKINNER, CORNELIA OTIS
  *The Pleasure of His Company.* 1958. BES58

TAYLOR, TOM, 1817–1880
  *New Men and Old Acres.* 1869. BOOA3
  *Our American Cousin.* 1858. BAI
  *The Ticket-of-leave Man.* 1863. BOOA2, MELO,
    MOSN, MOSO, ROWE

—— and READE, CHARLES
  *Masks and Faces; or, Before and Behind the Curtain.*
    1852. ROWE

TAYMOR, JULIE, 1952–
  *The Lion King* (additional music and lyrics by). *See*
    Allers, Roger. *The Lion King*

TCHEKOFF, ANTON. *See* Chekhov, Anton Pavlovich

TCHING, TSE. *See* Kao, Ming

TEALE, POLLY
  *Fallen* (developed with Carole Pluckrose). 1987. DEAD

EL TEATRO DE LA ESPERANZA, 1969–
  *Guadalupe.* 1974. HUER
  *La victim.* 1976. HUER

TEH-HUI, CHENG. *See* Cheng, Teh-Hui

TEH-YAO, JEN. *See* Jen, Teh-Yao

TEICHMANN, HOWARD, 1916–1987, and KAUFMAN,
  GEORGE S.
  *The Solid Gold Cadillac.* 1953. GART, THEA54

TEIXIDOR, JORDI, 1941–
  *The Legend of the Piper.* 1972.
    Wellwarth, G., translator WELV
    Variant title: *El retaule del flautista*
  *El retaule del flautista. See* The Legend of the Piper

TEJADA, LUIS VARGAS. *See* Vargas Tejada, Luis

TELLEZ, GABRIEL (Tirso De Molina, pseudonym),
  1570?–1648
  *El burlador de Sevilla.* 1630. ALP, HILL, MACU
    Campbell, R., translator BENR3, FLOR, HILPDH2,
      LIFE, MALI1
    O'Brien, R., translator FLOS
    Schizzano, A., and Mandel, O., translators MARJ
    Starkie, W., translator SSTW
    Variant titles: *The Love-rogue; The Playboy of
      Seville; or, Supper with a statue; The Rogue of*

*Babes in the Big House* (structure by JoAnn
    Schmidman; music by John J. Sheean). 1974. HIJ
*Calm Down, Mother.* 1965. BAYM, ORZ, SUB
*Ex-Miss Copper Queen on a Set of Pills.* 1963. BALLE1
*The Gloaming, Oh My Darling.* 1965. BAIC, BAIE
*The Magic Realists.* 1968. DIS
*Running Gag* (lyrics by). *See* Schmidman, JoAnn.
    *Running Gag*
*Sanibel and Captiva.* 1968. OWER
*Willa Willie Bill's Dope Garden.* 1975. CURB

—— and SCHMIDMAN, JO ANN, and KIMBERLAIN,
    SORA
*Body Leaks* (music by Marianne De Pury, Luigi Waites,
    and Jeremy Arakara; lyrics by Megan Terry). 1990.
    BERPA

TERSON, PETER, 1932– (b. Peter Patterson)
*The Mighty Reservoy.* 1964. NEWE14
*A Night to Make the Angels Weep.* 1964. NEWE11

TESFAI, ALEMSEGED, 1944–
*The Other War.* 1984.
    Warwick, P., Gebregzhier, and Tesfai, A., translators
    BANH

TESICH, STEVE, 1942–1996 (born Stojan Tešić)
*The Carpenters.* 1970. SCV

TESORI, JEANINE, 1961–
*Violet* (music by). *See* Crawley, Brian. *Violet*

THANISEB, AXARO W.
*To Live a Better Life.* 2000. ZEE2

THARP, NEWTON J., 1867–1909
*The Quest of the Gorgon* (music by Theodore Vogt).
    1905. BOH1

THATCHER, KRISTINE, 1950–
*Emma's Child.* 1995. WOMP95

THAYER, ELLA CHEEVER
*Lords of Creation.* 1883. FRIED

THEATRE PASSE MURAILLE, 1968–
*The West Show.* 1975. SHOW
    — *See* Salutin, Rick, joint author
    — *See also* Wiebe, Rudy, joint author

THEAULON, MARIE EMMANUEL GUILLAUME
    MARGUERITE, 1787–1841, and BAYARD, JEAN
    FRANCOIS ALFRED
*Le père de la debutante. See* Lensky, Dimitri. *Her First
    Night* (based on the play by)

THEOBALD, LEWIS, 1688–1744
*Electra.* 1714. BELK16

THEODORE, ANNE. *See* Décour, Charles Hébert, joint
    author

THEOTOKAS, GEORGE, 1906–1966
*The Game of Folly vs. Wisdom.*
    Gianos, M., translator GIA

THERRIAULT, DANIEL, 1953–
*The White Death.* 1986. ANTN

THIYAM, RATAN, 1948–
*Chakravyuha.* 1984.
    Thiyam, R., translator KAM3

THOMA, LUDWIG, 1867–1921
*Champions of Morality. See* Moral
*Moral.* 1908.
    Recht, C., translator DICDS
    Variant title: *Champions of Morality*

THOMAS, ALBERT ELLSWORTH, 1872–1947
*No More Ladies.* 1934. BES33

THOMAS, AUGUSTUS, 1857–1934
*As a Man Thinks.* 1911. AMENW, BAK
*The Copperhead.* 1918. COH
*In Mizzoura.* 1893. MOSS3
*The Witching Hour.* 1907. BES99, DICD, GARX,
    MOSJ, MOSK, MOSL, QUIJ, QUIJR, QUIK,
    QUIL, QUIM, QUIN

THOMAS, COLIN, 1952–
*Flesh and Blood.* 1991. WALAG

THOMAS, DYLAN, 1914–1953
*A Child's Christmas in Wales. See* Brown, Jeremy, and
    Mitchell, Adrian (adapted from the short story by)
*The Doctor and the Devils.* 1959. BEAR
*Under Milk Wood.* 1953. BES57

THOMAS, EDWARD, 1961–
*East from the Gantry.* 1992. FROLIN1

THOMAS, GWYN, 1913–1981
*Jackie the Jumper.* 1963. PLAN26
*The Keep.* 1961. PLAN24

THOMAS, LEE
*Joe's Not Home.* 1982. *See* Anonymous Plays. *Twenty-
    four Hours: A.M.*

THOMEY, GREG, 1961– , and HENNESSEY, BRIAN
*Hanlon House.* 1988, 1991. LYN

THOMPSON, ALICE CALLENDER
*A Suffragette Baby.* 1912. FRIED

THOMPSON, BEVERLY
*Yardlights Ahead.* 1993. DEAT

THOMPSON, DENMAN, 1833–1911
*Joshua Whitcomb. See* The Old Homestead
*The Old Homestead.* 1875. CEY, MES
    Variant title: *Joshua Whitcomb*

THOMPSON, ERNEST, 1949–
*On Golden Pond.* 1978. BES78, PERR1

THOMPSON, FLORA JANE (TIMMS), 1876–1948
*Lark Rise to Candleford* (v. 1 of her trilogy, *Lark Rise*).
    *See* Dewhurst, Keith. *Lark Rise* (based on)

THOMPSON, JUDITH, 1954–
*I Am Yours.* 1987. WASCPA2
*Lion in the Streets.* 1990. SEUC, WASCPB2
*Pink.* 1986. ZIMM (excerpt)

THOMPSON, TIERL, and MASON, LIBBY
*Dear Girl.* 1983. GRIFG2

THOMSON, JAMES, 1700–1748
*Edward and Eleonora.* 1739. BELG2
*Sophonisba.* 1729. BELK18
*Tancred and Sigismunda.* 1745. BELK5

THORDARSON, AGNAR, 1917–2006
*Atoms and Madams.* 1955.
    Haugen, E., translator HAVHN
    Variant title: *Kjarnorka og kvenkylli*
*Kjarnorka og kvenkylli. See* Atoms and Madams

THORNE, JOAN VAIL
*The Exact Center of the Universe.* 1999. WOMP99

THUNA, LEONORA, 1929–
*Fugue.* 1986. BES85

THURBER, JAMES, 1894–1961
*A Thurber Carnival.* 1960. BES59

—— and NUGENT, ELLIOTT
*The Male Animal.* 1940. BES39, BLOO, GARZ, HARB,
    KRM, LOCK, MIJY, ROLF, WISD

THURSTON, ELLA L.
*Family Cooperative.* DRU

THURY, FRED, 1945–2006, and GALBRAITH, ROBERT
*Nuts and Bolts and Rusty Things.* 1974. KAL4

TIECK, JOHANN LUDWIG, 1773–1853
*Der gestiefelte kater.* 1844. CAM
    Winter, L., translator FRA4
    Variant title: *Puss in Boots*
*Puss in Boots. See* Der gestiefelte kater

TIEMPO, CESAR (pseudonym of Israel Zeitlin), 1906–
    1975
*La alfarada. See* The Tithe
*The Tithe.* 1938.
    Glickman, N., and Waldman, G., translators ARGJT
    Variant title: *La alfarada*

TIEN, HAN
*The White Snake.*
    Chang, D., translator, and Packard, W. (English verse
    adaptation) MIT

T'IEN, HAN. *See* T'ien, Shou-ch'ang

T'IEN, SHOU-CH'ANG, 1898–1968
*Kuan Han-ch'ing.* 1958–1961. Foreign Languages
    Press, Peking, translator TWEH (Scenes 3, 5, 9, and
    11 have been omitted)

TIKKANEN, MARTA, 1935–
*Arhundradets kärlekssaga. See* Love Story of the
    Century
*Love Story of the Century.* Adapted for the stage by
    Clare Venables.
    Katchadourian, S., translator HANNA
    Variant title: *Arhundradets kärlekssaga*

TILLMAN, KATHERINE D. CHAPMAN, 1870–193?
*Aunt Betsy's Thanksgiving.* 1914. ROOTS

TILLY, 1946–
*Les trompettes de la mort. See* Trumpets of Death
*Trumpets of Death.* 1986.
    Johns, T., translator PAIS
    Variant title: *Les trompettes de la mort*

TING, HIS-LIN. *See* Ding, Xilin

TING, YI. *See* Ho Ching-chih, joint author

TIRADO, CANDIDO
*First Class.* 1987. ANTUR
*Some People Have All the Luck.* 1990. ANTU

TIRSO DE MOLINA, pseudonym. *See* Téllez, Gabriel

TISON, PASCALE, 1961–
*La rapporteuse. See* The Telltale
*The Telltale.* 1989.
Glasheen, A., translator GLASH
Variant title: *La rapporteuse*

TO, FU. *See* Fu, To

TO, RAYMOND K. W., 1946–
*Where Love Abides.* 1986.
Cheng, Y., translator CHEU

TOBIN, JOHN, 1770–1804
*The Honeymoon.* 1805. BAT16

TOFFENETTI, LAURA. *See* Hensel, Karen, joint author

TOLAN, KATHLEEN, 1950–
*Approximating Mother.* 1991. MIHPW
*A Weekend near Madison.* 1983. SHEW

TOLLER, ERNST, 1893–1939
*Hinkelmann.* 1922?
Ritchie, J., and Stowell, J., translators RITV
*Hoppla! See* Hoppla! Such Is Life!
*Hoppla! Such Is Life!* 1927?
Ould, H., translator ULAN
Variant titles: *Hoppla!; Hoppla, wir leben*
*Hoppla, wir leben. See* Hoppla! Such Is Life!
*The Machine-wreckers.* 1922.
Dukes, A., translator MOSG, MOSH
Variant title: *Die maschinen-stuermer*
*Man and the Masses. See* Masse mensch
*Die maschinen-stuermer. See* The Machine-wreckers
*Masse mensch.* 1921. STI2
Mendel, V., translator SCVG
Untermeyer, L., translator DUK, WATI, WATL4
Variant titles: *Man and the Masses; Masses and Man*
*Masses and Man. See* Masse mensch
*Nie wieder friede. See* No More Peace!
*No More Peace!* 1937.
Crankshaw, E., and Auden, W., translators CALM, WELG
Variant title: *Nie wieder friede*
*Transfiguration.* 1919
Crankshaw, E., translator EXP, HAV
Variant titles: *Transformation; Wandlung*
*Transformation. See* Transfiguration
*Wandlung. See* Transfiguration

TOLSTOI, ALEKSEI KONSTANTINOVICH, 1817–1875
*The Death of Iván the Terrible.* 1867.
Noyes, G., translator NOY
*Tsar Fyodor Ivanovitch.* 1868.
Covan, J., translator MOS
— *See* also Prutkov, Koz'ma, pseudonym

TOLSTOI, LEV NICHOLAEVICH, 1828–1910
*Condemnation.* 18–?
Maude, L., and Aylmer, translators COUR
*The Dominion of Darkness. See* The Power of Darkness
*The Live Corpse.* 1911.
Anonymous translator GARZH
Maude, L., and A., translators CHA, CHAN
Variant titles: *The Living Corpse; The Man Who Was Dead; Redemption*
*The Living Corpse. See* The Live Corpse
*The Man Who Was Dead. See* The Live Corpse
*The Power of Darkness; or, If a Claw Is Caught the Bird Is Lost.* 1895.
Anonymous translator DICIN1
MacAndrew, A., translator GARZE, MAB
Magarshack, D., translator MAP
Noyes, G., and Patrick, G., translators HOUG, NOY, TREBA, TREBJ, TREC2, TREE2, TREI2
Reeve, F., translator REEV1
Variant title: *The Dominion of Darkness*
*Redemption. See* The Live Corpse
*Taxes.* 18–?
Maude, L., and Aylmer, translators COUR
*What Men Live By. See* Church, Mrs. Virgina Woodson Frame. *What Men Live By* (based on the story by)

TOLSTOY. *See* Tolstoi

TOMER, BEN-ZION, 1928–1998
*Children of the Shadows.* 1962.
Halkin, H., translator TAUB

TOMPKINS, FRANK GEROW, 1879–1940
*Sham.* 1920. MIJA1

TONG KIA, KAO. *See* Kao, Ming

TOOMER, JEAN, 1894–1967
*Balo.* 1924. HARY, HARYB, LOC
*Kabnis.* (1923) CARR

TOPOL, JOSEF, 1935–
*Cat on the Rails.* 1965.
Voskovec, G., and Voskovec, C., translators DAY
Variant title: *Kočka na kolejích*
*Kočka na kolejích. See* Cat on the Rails

TOPOR, TOM, 1938–
*Nuts.* 1980. BES79

TORRENCE, FREDERICK RIDGELY, 1875–1950
*The Dense Calinda.* 1922. LOC
*Granny Maumee.* 1917. LOC
*The Rider of Dreams.* 1917. LOC

TORRES NAHARRO, BARTOLOME DE, fl.1517
*Comedia Himenea. See* Hymen
*Hymen.* 1517?
    Chambers, W., translator BAT6
    Variant title: *Comedia Himenea*

TOSHIRŌ, SUZUE, 1963–
*Fireflies.* 1995.
    Goodman, D., translator HACJT1
    Variant title: *Kami wo Kakiageru*
*Kami wo Kakiageru. See* Fireflies

TOTHEROH, DAN, 1894–1976
*Wild Birds.* 1925. BES24

TOUGH, ELSIE. *See* Schauffler, Mrs. Elsie (Tough)

TOULOUKIAN, CHRISTOPHER
*Celestial music.* 1988. STRA (excerpt)

TOURNEUR, CYRIL, 1575?–1626
*The Atheist's Tragedy.* 1610? GOM, MAUS
*The Revenger's Tragedy.* 1606? DPR2, GIBS, GOM,
    HAPRA2, HAPRB2, HUST, KAYS, MAUS, OLH,
    OLI2, RYL, SALG

TOWBIN, FREDI, 1946–
*Love in a Pub.* 1982. *See* Anonymous Plays. *Twenty-
    four Hours: P.M.*

TOWLE, W. RAY
*The Golden Door.* 1996. RAVELII

TOWNLEY, JAMES, 1714–1778
*High Life below Stairs.* 1759. BAT16, MOR

TOWNS, GEORGE A., 1870–1960
*The Sharecropper.* 1932. ROOTS

TOWNSHEND, AURELIAN, ca. 1583–1643?
*Tempe Restored.* 1632. LINDC

TOWNSHEND, PETER, 1945– , and THE WHO
*Tommy, a Rock Opera.* 1969. GREAAR

TOYOZAWA DAMPEI II, 1827–1898. *See* Kaka Chikajo
    (Chika), joint author

TOZZI, FEDERIGO, 1883–1920
*The Casting.* 1919.
    D'Aponte, M., and House, J., translators TWEI
    Variant title: *L'Incalco*
*L'Incalco. See* The Casting

TRAVEN, B., 1882?–1969
*The Treasure of the Sierra Madre. See* Huston, John.
    *The Treasure of the Sierra Madre* (based on the
    novel by)

TREADWELL, SOPHIE (MRS. SOPHIE McGEEHAN),
    1891–1970
*Hope for a Harvest.* 1941. BES41
*Machinal.* 1928. BES28, GASB, PLAAD, PLAAE,
    WATTAD

TREMBLAY, JOEY. *See* Christenson, Jonathan, joint
    author

TREMBLAY, LARRY, 1954–
*Anatomy Lesson.* 1992.
    Fischman, S., translator MOGS
    Variant title: *Leçon d'anatomie*
*Leçon d'anatomie. See* Anatomy Lesson

TREMBLAY, MICHEL, 1942–
*Les belles-soeurs.* 1968.
    Van Burek, J., and Glassco, B., translators
    WASCPA1, WASCPB1
*Hosanna.* 1974.
    Van Burek, J., and Glassco, B., translators DOOL

TREMBLAY, RENALD, 1943–
*La céleste Gréta. See* Greta, the Divine
*Greta, the Divine.* 1973.
    Van Meer, A., translator KAL5
    Variant title: *La céleste Gréta*

TRENEV, KONSTANTIN ANDREIVICH, 1884–1945
*Lyubov Yarovaya.* 1926.
    Bakshy, A., translator BAKS

TREPASSI, PIETRO. *See* Metastasilo, Pietro Antonio
    Domenico Buonaventura, pseudonym

TRIANA, JOSE, 1931–
*The Criminals.* 1964.
    Doggert, S., translator LATIN
    Fernandez, P., and Kustow, M., translators WOOG
    Variant titles: *The Night of the Assassins; La noche de
    los asesinos*
*The Night of the Assassins. See* The Criminals
*La noche de los asesinos.* 1964. DAU
    — *See also* The Criminals

TRISSINO, GIAN GIORGIO, 1478–1550
*Sophonisba.* 1524.
    Sharman, G., translator LET

TRISTAN L'HERMITE, FRANÇOIS, 1601–1655
*The Death of Seneca.* 1643?
   Lockert, L., translator LOCU
     Variant title: *La mort de Seneque*
*Mariamne.* 1636.
   Lockert, L., translator LOCR
     Variant title: *La mariane*
*La mariane. See* Mariamne
*La mort de Seneque. See* The Death of Seneca
*La mort du grand Osman. See* Osman
*Osman.* 1646–1647?
   Lockert, L., translator LOCU
     Variant title: *La mort du grand Osman*

TROCHIM, DENNIS
*Better Looking Boys.* 1997. RUN

TROPICANA, CARMELITA, 1957–
*Milk of Amnesia—Leche de amnesia.* 1998. ARRIZ, HUGH

—— and PARNES, UZI
*Memorias de la revolucion.* 2000. PURO

TROTTER, CATHERINE, 1679–1749
*The Fatal Friendship.* 1698. FEFO
*Love at a Loss, or, Most Votes Carry It.* 1700. LOQA
   Variant title: *Most Votes Carry It.*
   *See* Love at a Loss, or, Most Votes Carry It

TROUBETSKOY, AMELIE (RIVES) CHANLER, 1863–1945
*Herod and Mariamne.* 1888? KOH2

TROWBRIDGE, J. T., 1827–1916
*Neighbor Jackwood.* 1857. MESC

TRUMBO, DALTON, 1905–1976
*Opening Sequence.* 1969. BAYM

TRYE, JEAN GUILLAUME ANTOINE CUVELIER DE.
   *See* Cuvelier de Trye, Jean Guillaume Antoine

TRZEBIŃSKI, ANDRZEJ, 1922–1943
*Aby podnie podnieść różę. See* To Pick Up the Rose
*To Pick Up the Rose.* 1942.
   Gerould, D., and Gerould, E., translators TWEN
     Variant title: *Aby podnie podnieść różę*

TS'AO, YÜ. *See* Cao, Yu

TSE-TCHING. *See* Kao, Ming

TSIOLKAS, CHRISTOS, 1965–
*Suit. See* Bovell, A., Cornelius, P., Reeves, M., Tsiolkas, C., and Vela, I. *Who's Afraid of the Working Class?*

TSUKA, KŌHEI, 1948–2010
*The Atami Murder Case.* 1973.
   Ingulsrud, L., translator HACJT5
     Variant title: *Atami satsujin jiken*
*Atami satsujin jiken. See* The Atami Murder Case

TSUNG, FU-HSIEN, 1947?–
*In a Land of Silence.* (1978)
   Shu-ying, T., translator TWEH
     Variant title: *Yü wu-sheng ch'u*
*Yü wu-sheng ch'u. See* In a Land of Silence

TSURUYA, NAMBOKU IV, 1755–1829
*Tōkaidō Yotsuya kaidan. See* Yotsuya Ghost Stories
*Yotsuya Ghost Stories.* 1825.
   Oshima, M., translator BRAZ (Act 2 only)
     Variant title: *Tōkaidō Yotsuya kaidan*

—— and SAKURADA JISUKE II, and TSUUCHI GENSHICHI
*The Scarlet Princess of Edō.* 1817.
   Brandon, J., translator KAB
     Variant title: *Sakura Hime Azuma Bunshō*
*Sukara Hime Azuma Bunshō. See* The Scarlet Princess of Edō

TSUUCHI GENSHICHI. *See* Tsuruya, Namboku IV, joint author

TSUUCHI HANEMON. *See* Tsuuchi, Jihei II, joint author

TSUUCHI HANJURO, YASUDA ABUN, and NAKADA MANSUKE
*Narukami Fudō Kityama Zakura. See* Saint Narukami and the God Fudō
*Saint Narukami and the God Fudō.* 1684 (based on: *Saint Narukami* by Danjūrō I; *The God Fudo* by Danjūrō I; and *The Whisker Tweezers*, Anonymous Plays).
   Brandon, J., translator BRAZ, KAB
     Variant titles: *The God Fudo; Narukami Fudō Kityama Zakura; Saint Narukami; The Whisker Tweezers*

TSUUCHI, JIHEI II, and TSUUCHI HANEMON
*Protection of the Cherries of Flower Mansion. See* Sukeroku: Flower of Edo
*Sukeroku: Flower of Edo.* 1713.
   Brandon, J., translator KAB
     Variant titles: *Protection of the Cherries of Flower*

*Mansion; Sukeroku yukari no Edo zakura*
*Sukeroku yukari no Edo zakura. See* Sukeroku Flower
     of Edo

TUCHOLSKY, KURT, 1890–1935. *See* Hasenclever,
     Walter, joint author

TUCKER, WALLACE HAMPTON, 1939–
*At the Sweet Gum Bridge.* 1978. GEIO

TUKAK' THEATER ENSEMBLE. *See* Nilsson, Reidar,
     joint author

TUKE, SIR SAMUEL, 1610–1673
*The Adventures of Five Hours.* 1662. WONR

TUNG, YANG-SHENG. *See* Chou, Wei-po, joint author

TUNOONIQ THEATRE, 1986–
*Changes.* 1986. SSSN
*In Search of a Friend.* 1988. SSSN

TUR, LEONID DAVIDOVICH, 1905–1961, TUR,
     PETR DAVIDOVICH, and SHEININ, LEV
     ROMANOVICH
*Smoke of the Fatherland.* 1942.
     Feinberg, A., translator SEVP

TUR, PETR DAVIDOVICH, 1907–. *See* Tur, Leonid
     Davidovich, joint author

TURGENEV, IVAN SERGIEEVICH, 1818–1883
*A Friendly Delusion. See* Luncheon with the Marshal of
     Nobility, or A Friendly Delusion
*A Month in the Country.* 1872.
     MacAndrew, A., translator GARZE, MAB
     Mandell, M., translator FAMK
     Newnham, R., translator COTO
     Nicolaeff, A., translator PLAN45
     Noyes, G., translator NOY, TREB, TREC1, TREE1,
          TREI1
     Williams, E., adapter GARZH, HOUG
*Luncheon with the Marshal of Nobility, or A Friendly
     Delusion.* 1856.
     Senelick, L., translator RUSSCO
     Variant title: *A Friendly Delusion*
*The Weakest Link.* 1848.
     Green, M., and Katsell, J., translators GREENU

TURNER, DAN, d. 1990
*Invitation* (Part One). 1984. *See* Anonymous Plays. *The
     AIDS Show . . .*
*Invitation* (Part Two). *See* Anonymous Plays. *The AIDS
     Show . . .*

TURNER, GRAEME, 1947–
*Super Cool.* 1990. MURD

TURNEY, CATHERINE, 1906–1998
*Bitter Harvest.* 1936. FOUPL

TURNEY, ROBERT, 1900–1972
*Daughters of Atreus.* 1936. BES36

TURQUE, MICHAEL, 1933–2002
*Shoptalk.* 19–? GREAB

TURRINI, PETER, 1944–
*Alpenglüen. See* Alpine Glow
*Alpine Glow.* 1993.
     Dixon, R., translator LAXC
     Variant title: *Alpenglüen*
*Sauschlachten. See* Swine
*Swine.* 1972.
     Dixon, R., translator ANTHC
     Variant title: *Sauschlachten*

TUWHARE, HONE, 1922–2008
*In the Wilderness without a Hat.* 1985. GARR
     Variant title: *On ilkla moor b'aht 'at*
*On ilkla moor b'aht 'at. See* In the Wilderness without
     a Hat

TWAIN, MARK. *See* Clemens, Samuel Langhorne

TYAN, HAN. *See* Tien, Han

TYLER, ROYALL, 1757–1826
*The Contrast.* 1787. BLAI1, BPD1, CADY, DOWM,
     ELLI1, GARX, GATB1, HAL, HOWP1,
     MANCD1, MANCE1, MANCF1, MES, MIJH,
     MONR, MOSS1, QUIJ, QUIK, QUIL, QUIM,
     QUIN, QUIO1, RICHE, SPI, STL1, WATTAD,
     WILMET
*The Island of Barrataria.* 18th century AMP15
*Joseph and His Brethren.* 18th century AMP15
*The Judgment of Solomon.* 18th century AMP15
*The Origin of the Feast of Purim; or, The Destinies of
     Haman and Mordecai.* 18th century AMP15

TZARA, TRISTAN, 1896–1963
*Le coeur à gaz. See* The Gas Heart
*The Gas Heart.* 1920.
     Benedikt, M., translator BEN
     Variant title: *Le coeur à gaz*

UDALL, NICHOLAS, 1505–1556
*Jack Juggler* (attributed to). *See* Anonymous Plays. *Jack
     Juggler*

*The Dark Root of a Scream.* 1967. WES19/20
*I Don't Have to Show You No Stinking Badges!* 1986. WATTAD
*The Shrunken Head of Pancho Villa.* 1965. HUER, WES11/12
*Soldado razo.* 1971. WES19/20
*Los vendidos.* 1967. BARIG, BARIH, BARKE, BARKF, CHG, CONR, PERZ, SSSIC, SWANS, WOTHA, WOTHB, WOTHC, WOTHM
*Zoot Suit.* 1978. ANTL

VALEAN, ANDREEA, 1972–
*When I Want to Whistle, I Whistle . . .* 2000. Robson, C., and Trandafir, C., translators ROEB
Trandafir, C., translator POQ

VALENCY, MAURICE JACQUES, 1903–1996
*The Apollo of Bellac. See* Giraudoux, Jean. *The Apollo of Bellac* (adapted by)
*The Enchanted. See* Giraudoux, Jean. *The Enchanted* (adapted by)
*The Madwoman of Chaillot. See* Giraudoux, Jean. *The Madwoman of Chaillot* (adapted by)
*Ondine. See* Giraudoux, Jean. *Ondine* (adapted by)
*The Visit. See* Duerrenmatt, Friedrich. *The Visit* (translator and adapted by)

VALLE, FRED
*I Am a Winner.* 1987. ANTU

VALLE-INCLAN, RAMON MARIA DEL, 1870–1936
*La cabeza del Bautista.* 1924. MARLI2
*Divinas palabras. See* Divine Words
*Divine Words.* 1933.
Williams, E., translator BENA
Variant title: *Divinas palabras*
*Dream Comedy.* 1905.
Weiss, R., translator GERO

VALLEJO, ANTONIO BUERO. *See* Buero Vallejo, Antonio

VANBRUGH, SIR JOHN, 1664–1726
*City Wives Confederacy. See* The Confederacy
*The Confederacy.* 1705. BELK15, KRM
Variant title: *City Wives Confederacy*
*A Journey to London* (ms. completed by C. Cibber). 1728. BAT15, BELK6, TICK
Variant title: *The Provoked Husband*
*Mistake.* 1705. BELK19
*The Provoked Husband. See* A Journey to London
*The Provok'd Wife.* 1697. BELK2, FIS, GAYLE4, GOS, GOSA, JEFF3, MATTL, MOSE1, RES, RESL, RUB, TWE

*The Relapse; or, Virtue in Danger.* 1696. BELK11, DAVR, JEFF3, MAND, MANF, MOR, NET, REST, TUQ, WONR

VAN DOREN, MARK, 1894–1972
*The Last Days of Lincoln.* 1961. AMB, SWI

VAN DRUTEN, JOHN, 1902–1957
*After All.* FAMAN, MYB, PLAD
*Behold We Live.* 1932. FAMC
*Bell, Book, and Candle.* 1950. BES50, GARW
*The Distaff Side.* 1933. BES34, FAME
*Flowers of the Forest.* 1934. FAMG
*I Am a Camera* (adapted from the Berlin stories by Christopher Isherwood). 1951. BES51, FAMO, GART, GAVE
Variant title: *Sally Bowles*
— *See also* Masteroff, Joe. *Cabaret* (adapted from *I Am a Camera* and the stories of Christopher Isherwood)
*I Remember Mama* (based on the book *Mama's Bank Account* by Kathryn Forbes). 1949. BES44, DAVI, GARZ, GRIH, MERS, REDM, SPES, STAV
*London Wall.* 1931. FAMAN
*Sally Bowles. See* I Am a Camera
*Somebody Knows.* 1932. FAMB
*There's Always Juliet.* 1931. FAMB
*The Voice of the Turtle.* 1943. BES43, GARZ, KRM
*Young Woodley.* 1925. BES25, FAO, PLAD

——— and MORRIS, LLOYD
*The Damask Cheek.* 1942. BES42

VAN ITALLIE, JEAN-CLAUDE, 1936–
*America Hurrah.* 1966. ASF, BES66, CLN, ORZ, SANE
*Ancient Boys.* 1989. GAYIA
*Interview.* 1966. BAIC, GLI
Variant title: *Pavane Produced . . .*
*A Masque for Three Dolls. See* Motel
*Motel; a Masque for Three Dolls* (part of *America Hurrah*). 1965. HAVL, RAVIT
*Naropa* [being the incredibly frustrating adventures of a middle-aged university professor on his way to perfect enlightenment]; a play for puppets and people adapted from the translation by Herbert V. Guenther of *Tibeton Texts.* WOQ1
*Pavane Produced. . . . See* Interview
*The Serpent: A Ceremony.* 1970. BES69
*Where Is de Queen?* 1966. BALLE3

VANCE, DANITRA, 1959–1994
*Live and in Color!* 1991. MAQ

VANE, SUTTON, 1888–1943
*Outward Bound.* 1923. BES23, CEU, MART

VENTURA DE LA VEGA. *See* Vega, Ventura de la

VERBITSKAYA, ANASTASIYA, 1861–1928
*Mirage.* 1895–1896. WOMR

VERDECCHIA, GUILLERMO, 1962–
*Fronteras Americanas.* 1993. WASCPB2

VERGA, GIOVANNI, 1840–1922
*La caccia al lupo. See* The Wolf-hunt
*Cavalleria rusticana.* 1880?
Bentley, E., translator BENT1
*The Wolf-hunt.* 1901.
Goldberg, I., translator GOL
Variant title: *La caccia al lupo*

VERHAEREN, EMILE, 1855–1916
*Les aubes. See* The Dawn
*The Dawn.* 1898.
Symons, A., translator MOSQ
Variant title: *Les aubes*

VERMA, SURENDRA, 1941–
*From Sunset to Sunrise.* 1981.
Krishnamachari, J., translator DESH
*Qaid-e-hayat. See* Wings in Chains
*Wings in Chains.* 1983.
Futehally, S., translator KAM2
Variant title: *Qaid-e-hayat*

VERNEUIL, LOUIS, 1893–1952
*Affairs of State.* 1950. BES50, PLAN8
Variant title: *Irene*
*Irene. See* Affairs of State

VESAAS, TARJEI, 1897–1970
*The Bleaching Yard.* 1953.
Brown, J., translator MNON

VETEMAA, ENN, 1936–
*Illuminations; for a Globe of Lightning and Nine Actors (with a Bang at the End).* 1969?
Kurman, G., translator CONF
Variant titles: *Illuminations for Ball Lightning and Nine Actors (with a Bang at the End); Illuminatsioonid; Illuminatsioonid keravälyule ja uheksale naitlejale (pauguga lopus)*
*Illuminations for Ball Lightning and Nine Actors (with a Bang at the End). See* Illuminations; for a Globe of Lightning and Nine Actors (with a Bang at the End)
*Illuminatsioonid. See* Illuminations; for a Globe of Lightning and Nine Actors (with a Bang at the End)
*Illuminatsioonid keravälgule ja uheksale naitlejule (pauguga lopus). See* Illuminations; for a Globe of Lightning and Nine Actors (with a Bang at the End)

VIAN, BORIS, 1920–1959
*Les bâttisseurs d'empire. See* The Empire Builders
*The Empire Builders.* 1959.
Taylor, S., translator PLAN25
Variant titles: *Les bâttisseurs d'empire; Le Schmürz*
*L'équarrissage pour tous. See* Knackery for All
*The Knacker's ABC. See* Knackery for All
*Knackery for All.* 1944.
Estrin, M., translator PLAC
Variant titles: *L'équarrissage pour tous; The Knacker's ABC*
*Le Schmürz. See* The Empire Builders

VICHITVADAKARN, LUANG, 1898–1962
*Luad Suphan.* 1936.
Poolthupya, S., translator MLAT
Variant title: *Suphan's Blood*
*Suphan's Blood. See* Luad Suphan

VICK, SUSAN, 1945–
*ord-Way ames-Gay.* 1982. VICK2
*When I Was Your Age.* 1982. VICK1

VIDAL, GORE, 1925–
*The Best Man.* 1960. BES59, GARSA
*The Death of Billy the Kid* (television play). READ1 (excerpt)
*Visit to a Small Planet.* 1957. BES56, KIN, OHL

VIGIL, ANGEL, 1947–. *See* Morton, Carlos, joint author

VIGNA, PAUL
*Cyclone Jack* (music by). *See* Bolt, Carol. *Cyclone Jack*

VIGNE, ANDRIEU DE LA. *See* La Vigne, Andrieu de

VIGNY, ALFRED VICTOR, COMTE DE, 1797–1863
*Chatterton.* 1835. BOR, GOM, GRA

VIK, BJORG, 1935–
*Døtre. See* Daughters
*Daughters* (radio play). 1979.
Garton, J., translator NEWNOR
Variant title: *Døtre*

VILALTA, MARUXA, 1932–
*Una mujer, dos hombres y un balazo. See* A Woman, Two Men, and a Gunshot
*A Woman, Two Men, and a Gunshot.* 1981.
Nigro, K., translator SALA
Variant title: *Una mujer, dos hombres y un balazo*

VILDRAC, CHARLES (pseudonym of Charles Messager), 1882–1971
*Michel Auclair.* 1922.
Howard, S., translator LEV, LEVE

*Le paquebot Tenacity.* 1920. HART, HARV
    Howard, S., translator TUCG, TUCM
    Newberry, J., translator DICDT
    Variant titles: S. *S. Tenacity; The Steamer Tenacity;*
       *The Steamship Tenacity*
*S.S. Tenacity. See* Le paquebot Tenacity
*The Steamer Tenacity. See* Le paquebot Tenacity
*The Steamship Tenacity. See* Le paquebot Tenacity

VILLA, JOSE GARCIA, 1914–1997
    *Mir-i-nisa. See* Sicam, Geronimo D., and Casino, Jesús.
       *Miri-nisa* (based on the story by)

VILLA, LILIA A.
    *Educating Josefina.* 193–? EDAD

VILLANUEVA, RENE O., 1954–2007
    *Hiblang abo. See* Strands of Gray
    *Strands of Gray.* 1980.
       Fernandez, D., translator MLAP
       Variant title: *Hiblang abo*

VILLAREAL, EDIT, 1944–
    *My Visits with MGM.* 1989. FEY

VILLAURRUTIA, XAVIER, 1903–1950
    *Invitacion a la muerte.* 1947. DAU

VILLEDIEU, MADAME DE, pseudonym
    *See* Desjardins, Marie-Catherine

VILLIERS, CLAUDE DESCHAMPS, 1600?–1681
    *L'apoticaire devalisé.* 1658? LANC

VILLIERS, GEORGE. *See* Buckingham, George Villiers

VINAVER, MICHEL, 1927–
    *Chamber Theatre.* 1978.
       Antal, P., translator WEHLE
       (2 one-act plays *Dissident, Goes without Saying;*
         *Nina, It's Different*)
       Variant titles: *Dissident, il va sans dire; Nina c'est*
         *autre chose*
    *Dissident, Goes without Saying. See* Chamber Theatre
    *Dissident, il va sans dire. See* Chamber Theatre
    *The Neighbors.* 1987.
       Antal, P., translator PAIS
       Variant title: *Les voisins*
    *Nina c'est autre chose. See* Chamber Theatre
    *Nina, It's Different. See* Chamber Theatre
    *Portrait d'une femme. See* Portrait of a Woman
    *Portrait of a Woman.* 1988.
       Watson, D., translator NEWFPA
       Variant title: *Portrait d'une femme*
    *Les voisins. See* The Neighbors

VINCENT, ALLEN, 1903–1979. *See* Rotter, Fritz, joint
    author

VINEBERG, DORIS M., 1925–2009
    *Emissary.* 1987. VORE

VINGOE, MARY, 1955– , and KUDELKA, JAN
    *Hooligans.* 1982. NEWCAD6

VISAWANATHAN, PADMA, 1968–
    *House of Sacred Cows.* 1997. NOTH

VISDEI, ANCA, 1954–
    *Always Together.* 1994.
       Vogel, S., translator PLABI3
       Variant title: *Toujours ensemble*
    *Class Photo.* 1996.
       Vogel, S., translator PLAWE
       Variant title: *Photo de classe*
    *Photo de classe. See* Class Photo
    *Toujours ensemble. See* Always Together

VISE, JEAN DONNEAU DE. *See* Donneau de Visé,
    Jean

VISHAKADATTA. 9th century
    *Rākshasa's Ring. See* The Signet Ring of Rakshasa
    *The Signet Ring of Rakshasa.* 9th century
       Coulson, M., translator THWI
       Lal, P., translator LAL
       Variant title: *Rākshasa's Ring*

VISHĀKHADATTA. *See* Vishakadatta

VISHNEVSKII, VSEVOLOD VITALEVICII, 1900–1951
    *Optimicheskaya tragediya. See* An Optimistic Tragedy
    *An Optimistic Tragedy.* 1933.
       Scott, H., and Carr, R., translators FOUS
       Variant title: *Optimicheskaya tragediya*

VISNIEC, MATEI, 1956–
    *The Body of a Woman as a Battlefield in the Bosnian*
       *War.* 2000.
       Sinclair, A., translator ROEB

VITRAC, ROGER, 1899–1952
    *Les mystères de l'amour. See* The Mysteries of Love
    *The Mysteries of Love.* 1927.
       Goldstone, R., translator BEN
       Variant title: *Les mystères de l'amour*

VITTACHCHI, NEDRA
    *Bed and Bored.* 1986. GOON
    *Cave Walk.* 1986. GOON

VIVIANI, RAFFAELE, 1888–1950
*Via Toledo by Night.* 1918.
King, M., translator TWEI
Variant title: *Via Toledo di note*
*Via Toledo di note. See* Via Toledo by Night

VIZIN, DENIS VON. *See* Fonvízin, Dinís Ivanovich

VLACHOS, HELEN. *See* Varma, Rahul, joint author

VLIET, R. G. (Russell Gordon), 1929–1984
*The Regions of Noon.* 1960. TEX

VOADEN, HERMAN, 1903–1991
*Hill-land.* 1934. PERKY
*Murder Pattern.* 1936. WAGN3
*Wilderness; a Play of the North.* 1931. WAGN3

VODÁNOVIC, SERGIO, 1926–2001
*Three Beach Plays.* 1964.
Oliver, W., translator OLIW

VOGEL, PAULA, 1951–
*The Baltimore Waltz.* 1992. ACTOR, BRJB, OSBW
(excerpt), WOMP92
*Desdemona.* 1993. ADAP, CURB, PLACA
*Hot 'n' Throbbing.* 1994. WOMP94
*How I Learned to Drive.* 1997. BES96

VOGT, THEODORE, 1835–1906
*The Quest of the Gorgon* (music by). *See* Tharp, Newton
J. *The Quest of the Gorgon*

VOLLMER, LULA, 1898–1955
*Sun-up.* 1923. BES23, LOW, QUIJR, QUIK, QUIL,
QUIM, QUIN, TUCD, TUCM

VOLLMÖLLER, KARL GUSTAV, 1878–1948
*Uncle's Been Dreaming.* 1918.
Katzin, W., translator KAT

VOLSKY, PAULA
*The Bastard of Bologna.* 1992. KAYS

VOLTAIRE, FRANÇOIS MARIE AROUET DE, 1694–
1778
*Candide. See* Hellman, Lillian. *Candide* (based on)
— *See also* McTaggart, James. *Candide* (translated
and adapted for television by)
*Mahomet.* 1741.
Leigh, O., translator BAT8
*Nanine.* 1749. BREN
*Oedipe. See* Oedipus
*Oedipus.* 1718.
Smollett, T., translator SANO
Variant title: *Oedipe*

*Socrates.* 1759.
Leigh, O., translator BAT8
*Zaire.* 1732. BREN, LOCR, SEA

VONNEGUT, KURT, JR., 1922–2007
*Fortitude.* 1968. REAL

VUJOVIC, SLADJANA, 1958–
*The Tender Mercies.* 1993. EUP

VULPIUS, PAUL (pseudonym of Hans Adler)
*Youth at the Helm.* 1934.
Griffith, H., translator and adapter FAMH

WADDELL, SAMUEL (Rutherford Mayne, pseudonym),
1878–1967
*Bridge Head.* 1934. CAN

WAGER, WILLIAM, fl. 1566
*Enough Is as Good as a Feast.* ca.1560–1570. SCAT

WAGNER, COLLEEN, 1949–
*The Monument.* 1995. SEUC

WAGNER, HEINRICH LEOPOLD, 1747–1779
*The Child Murderess.* 1777.
Waterhouse, B., translator STURM, WASD

WAGNER, JANE, 1935–
*The Search for Signs of Intelligent Life in the Universe.*
1986. COI

WAGNER, PAULA, 1946– . *See* Merriam, Eve, joint
author

WAITES, LUIGI, 1927–2010
*Body Leaks* (music by). *See* Terry, Megan. *Body Leaks*

WAKEFIELD, JACQUES
*Perceptual Movement.* 1979. CEN

WAKEFIELD, LOU, and THE WOMEN'S THEATRE
GROUP
*Time Pieces.* 1982. PLABE3

WAKEMAN, ALAN, 1936–
*Ships.* 1975. HOM

WALCOTT, DEREK, 1930–
*Dream on Monkey Mountain.* 1971. HAPUE, NORJ2
*Pantomime.* 1980. BPW, HOWM
*Ti-Jean and His Brothers.* 1958. HAPU, HILEP

WALCOTT, RODERICK, 1930–2001
*The Banjo Man.* 1971. HILET

WALDRON, SHARON
*The Night Moon Went Fishing.* 1999. FOUPAP

WALKER, CHET. *See* Maltby, Richard, Jr., joint author

WALKER, GEORGE F., 1947–
*Ambush at Tether's End.* 1971. BRIN
*The Art of War.* 1982. PENG
*Prince of Naples.* 1971. BRIP
*Problem Child.* 1997. WASCPB2
*Rumours of Our Death: A Parable in 25 Scenes.* 1980.
    CTR
*Zastrozzi: The Master of Discipline.* 1977. WASCP,
    WASCPA2, WASCPB1

WALKER, JOHN
*The Factory Lad.* 182?. BOOA1, BOOM, HUDV, VICT

WALKER, JOSEPH A., 1935–2003
*Ododo.* 1970. KINH, KINHB
*The River Niger.* 1973. BERS, BES72, HAPUE, RICT

WALKER, PETER. *See* Dorras, Jo, joint author

WALKER, STUART, 1880–1941
*The Medicine Show.* 1917. BEAC11

WALLACE, LEW, 1827–1905
*Ben-Hur. See* Young, William. *Ben-Hur* (adapted from
    the novel by)

WALLACE, NAOMI, 1960–
*In the Fields of Aceldama.* 1993. SETR
*In the Heart of America.* 1994. CLUMS
*Manifesto.* 1999. HUMANA99
*One Flea Spare.* 1995. BUSHT, HUMANA96
*Standard Time.* 2000. HUMANA2000
*The Trestle at Pope Lick Creek.* 1998. HUMANA98

WALLACK, LESTER, 1820–1888
*Rosedale; or, The Rifle Ball.* 1863. AMP4

WALLE, KNUT, 1949– . *See* Gaup, Nils, joint author

WALLEY, RICHARD, 1953–
*Coordah.* 1987. PLACC

WALMSLEY, TOM, 1948–
*Something Red.* 1978. WASCT

WALPOLE, SIR HUGH, 1884–1941
*Kind Lady. See* Chodorov, Edward. *Kind Lady* (adapted
    from a story by)

WALSH, DES, 1954–
*Tomorrow Will Be Sunday.* 1992. LYN

WALSH, ENDA, 1967–
*Disco Pigs.* 1996. FAIR

WALSH, PAUL, 1951– . *See* Epp, Steven, joint author

WALTER, EUGENE, 1874–1941
*The Easiest Way.* 1908. BES09, DICDS, GARX,
    MOSS3

WALTER, NANCY, 1939–
*Rags.* 1969. BALLE7

WAN, CHIA-PAO. *See* Ts'ao, Yü, pseudonym

WANDOR, MICHELENE, 1940–
*Aurora Leigh.* 1979. PLABE1
*Care and Control* (scripted by). *See* Gay Sweatshop

WANG, CHING-HSIEN, 1940–
*Wu Feng.* 1979.
    Kwok, C., and Yang, M., translators TWEH

WANG, CHIU-SSU, 1468–1551
*Wolf of Mount Zhong.*
    Dulby, W., translator EIG
    Variant title: *Zhong-shan lang*
*Zhong-shan lang. See* Wolf of Mount Zhong

WANG, JIUSI. *See* Wang, Chiu-ssu

WANG, LUCY, 1963–
*Junk Bonds.* 1995. HOUST

WANG, PEIGONG, 1943–
*WM(WE).* 1985.
    Revised for performance by Gui Wang.
    Moran, T., translator THC
    Yu, S., translator YUCHD

WANG, SHIH-FU, fl. 13th century
*The West Chamber.* 13th century
    Irwin, V., translator IRW

WANNUS, SA'DALLAH, 1941–1997
*The King Is the King.* 1977.
    Maleh, G., and Ezzy, T., translators JAY
    Variant title: *Al-malik huwa 'l-malik*
*Al-malik huwa 'l-malik. See* The King Is the King

WAPUL, GEORGE. *See* Wapull, George

WAPULL, GEORGE, fl.1576
*The Tide Tarrieth No Man.* 1576. SCAT

WARD, DONALD. *See* Solly, Bill, joint author

WARD, DOUGLAS TURNER, 1930– (b. Roosevelt
    Ward, Jr.)
*Brotherhood.* 1970. KINH, KINHB
*Day of Absence.* 1965. ACE, BAC, BLAC, BOYN,
    BRAS, CORBA, GRIH, HARY, HARYB, OLIV,
    PES, RAI, RICK, SWANS
*Happy Ending.* 1965. BARI, BARIA, BARIC, BRAS,
    HOLP, OLIV

WARD, FREDERICK, 1937–
*Somebody Somebody's Returning.* 1986. SEARS2

WARD, JULIA. *See* Howe, Mrs. Julia (Ward)

WARD, THEODORE, 1902–1983
*Big White Fog.* 1938. HARY, HARYB
*Our Lan'.* 1946. TUQT, TUQTR

WARKENTIN, VERALYN
*Like the Sun.* 1995. RAVELII

WARREN, HARRY, 1893–1981
*42nd Street* (music and lyrics by). *See* Stewart, Michael.
    *42nd Street*

WARREN, MERCY (OTIS), 1728–1814
*The Blockheads; or, The Affrighted Officers* (attributed
    to). *See* Anonymous Plays. *The Blockheads; or,*
    *The Affrighted Officers*
*The Group.* 1775. KRIT, MOSS1, ROGEW
*The Motley Assembly* (attributed to). *See* Anonymous
    Plays. *The Motley Assembly*

WARREN, RUTH. *See* Hawthorne, Ruth (Warren)

WASHBURN, DERIC
*Ginger Anne.* 1961. NEWA1

WASHINGTON, ERWIN CHARLES
*Oh Oh Freedom.* 1977. FLET (one scene only)

WASHINGTON, VON H., SR., 1943–
*The Operation.* 1991. NTIR

WASSERMAN, DALE, 1917–2008
*Man of La Mancha* (music by Mitch Leigh, lyrics by Joe
    Darion). 1965. BES65, RICM

WASSERSTEIN, WENDY, 1950–2006
*An American Daughter.* 1997. BRJC
*The Heidi Chronicles.* 1988. BES88, PERR3

*Isn't It Romantic.* 1981. COJ
*The Man in a Case.* 1986. BARIH, BARKE, DIYLC,
    LITID, LITRC, LITRD, SCVDO1, SHRCG,
    SSSIA, SSSIB
*The Sisters Rosensweig.* 1992. BES92, LEVY
*Tender Offer.* 1991. DIYL, DIYLD, GUTDS, KIRLD,
    MEYC, MEYD, MEYF
*To t or not to t.* 1999. HUMANA99
*Uncommon Women and Others.* 1977. WOTHM
*Workout.* 1997. PLACA

WATADA, TERRY, 1951–
*The Tale of a Mask.* 1993. RAVEL

WATANABE, ERIKO, 1955–
*Gegege no ge: Ōma ga toki ni yureru buranko. See*
    Kitarō the Ghost-buster
*Kitarō the Ghost-buster.* 1982.
    Herbert, S., translator HACJT3
    Variant title: *Gegege no ge: Ōma ga toki ni yureru*
    *buranko*

WATERHOUSE, KEITH, 1929–2009, and HALL,
    WILLIS
*Billy Liar.* 1960. PLAJ1

WATKIN, LAWRENCE EDWARD, 1901–1981
*On Borrowed Time. See* Osborn, Paul. *On Borrowed*
    *Time* (based on the novel by)

WATKINS, ARTHUR THOMAS LEVY. *See* Watkyn,
    Arthur, pseudonym

WATKINS, CHRISTINE
*Queen of Hearts.* 1998. ONE (excerpt)
*Welcome to My World.* 1998. ONE

WATKINS, MAURINE DALLAS, 1901–1969
*Chicago.* 1926. BES26
    — *See also* Ebb, Fred, and Fosse, Bob. *Chicago*
    (adapted from)

WATKINS, NAYO BARBARA, 1939–2008. *See* O'Neal,
    John, joint author

WATKYN, ARTHUR (pseudonym of Arthur Thomas
    Levy Watkins), 1907–1965
*For Better, for Worse.* 1952. PLAN8
*Not in the Book.* 1958. PLAN17

WATSON, HARMON C., 1943–
*Those Golden Gates Fall Down.* 1971. FORD

WATSON, MARJORIE R.
*The Dogs of War.* 1937. BRNB, BRNS

WATSON-TAYLOR, GEORGE, d.1841
*England Preserved.* 1795. INCA8

WATTERS, GEORGE MANKER, 1892–1943, and
        HOPKINS, ARTHUR MELANCTHON
*Burlesque.* 1927. BES27

WATTS, MURRAY
*Catwalk.* 1976. BURB
*A Gentleman's Agreement.* 1979. BURB
*St. John's Gospel* (adapted for the stage by). *See*
        Anonymous Plays. *St. John's Gospel*

WAUGH, EVELYN, 1903–1966
*The Man Who Liked Dickens. See* Tallman, Robert. *The
        Man Who Liked Dickens* (television adaptation
        from the short story by)

WEAVER, LOIS, 1949–
*Faith and Dancing.* 1996. MYTH (excerpt)
        — *See* Bourne, Bette, joint author

WEBBER, CECIL EDWIN
*Be Good, Sweet Maid.* 1957. PLAN15

WEBBER, JAMES PLAISTED, 1878–1930
*Frances and Francis.* 1923. WEB

WEBER, MARY FELDHAUS. *See* Feldhaus-Weber, Mary

WEBSTER, CONVEY
*I Was a Grand Piano.* 1987. MONB4

WEBSTER, JOHN, 1580?–1625?
*The Duchess of Malfi.* 1613. ABRH1, ABRJ1, ABRK1,
        ABRL1, ABRM1, ALLK, ALLM, BALD, BAS,
        BAUL, BECK, BENQ, BROC, CLKY, COTKIR,
        DEAN, DEAO, DOWS, DPR2, DUN, FOUD,
        GIBS, HARC47, HILPDH2, HOW, HUST,
        KINNR, MAKJ, MATTL, NEI, OLH, OLI2,
        ROET, SCH, SCI, SCJ, SEN, SPD, SPDB, SPEF1,
        SSSI, SSSIA, SSSIB, TAT, TAU, THA, TRE,
        TREA2, TREB, TREC1, TREE1, TREI1, WATT2,
        WHE, WINE, WRIH
        Variant title: *The Tragedy of the Duchess of Malfi*
*The Tragedy of the Duchess of Malfi. See* The Duchess
        of Malfi
*The White Devil; or, Vittoria Corombona.* 1612? BENY,
        DPR2, HAPRA1, HAPRB1, KRE, OLH, OLI2,
        ORNT, PAR, RUB, RYL, SALG, SPE, WALL,
        WHE

WEDEKIND, FRANK, 1864–1918
*The Court Singer. See* Der kammersänger
*The Earth-spirit. See* Erdgeist

*The Epicurean. See* The Marquis of Keith
*Erdgeist.* 1895.
        Eliot, S., translator DICIN2
        Variant title: *The Earth-spirit*
*Frühlingserwachen. See* Spring's Awakening
*Der kammersänger.* 1899. STI1
        Boesche, A., translator FRA20
        Tridon, A., translator HUDE, TREBA, TREBJ,
        TREC2, TREE2, TREI2
        Variant titles: *The Court Singer; The Tenor*
*King Nicolo. See* Such Is Life
*König Nikolo. See* Such Is Life
*The Marquis of Keith.* 1900?
        Gottlieb, B., translator BENS2, BLOC
        Mueller, C., translator COTL, COTQ, HERZ
        Variant title: *The Epicurean*
*So ist das leben. See* Such Is Life
*Spring Awakening. See* Spring's Awakening
*Spring's Awakening.* 1906.
        Bentley, E., translator BEFOB, BENT6
        Bond, E., translator HERZ
        Variant titles: *Frühlingserwachen; Spring Awakening*
*Such Is Life.* 1902.
        Esslin, M., translator ESS
        Ziegler, F., translator DICDT, TUCG
        Variant titles: *King Nicolo; König Nikolo; So ist das
        leben*
*The Tenor. See* Der kammersänger

WEETMAN, MARTIN
*Estonia You Fall.* 1983. WES13/14

WEI, MINGLUN, 1941–
*Pan Jinlian.* 1986.
        Williams, D., and Williams, X., translators THC
        Yu, S., translator YUCHD
        Variant titles: *Pan Jinlian: The History of a Fallen
        Woman; Pan Jinlian: yige nuren de chenlunshi*
*Pan Jinlian: The History of a Fallen Woman. See* Pan
        Jinlian
*Pan Jinlian: yige nuren de chenlunshi. See* Pan Jinlian

WEIDMAN, JEROME, 1913–1998, and ABBOTT,
        GEORGE
*Fiorello!* (music by Jerry Bock; lyrics by Sheldon
        Harnick). 1959. BES59, RICM

WEIDMAN, JOHN, 1946–
*Pacific Overtures* (additional material by Hugh
        Callingham Wheeler). 1976. BES75
        — *See also* Stroman, Susan, joint author

WEIGAND, RANDY
*Ricky.* 1984. *See* Anonymous Plays. *The AIDS Show . . .*

WHITE, ROBERT
*Cupid's Banishment: A Maske Presented to Her Majesty by the Younge Gentlewomen of the Ladies Hall in Deptford at Greenwich*. 1617. RENDW

WHITE, TERENCE HANBURY, 1906–1964
*The Once and Future King. See* Lerner, Alan Jay. *Camelot* (based on the novel by)

WHITEHEAD, WILLIAM
*And If That Mockingbird Don't Sing*. 1977. WES3

WHITEHEAD, WILLIAM, 1715–1785
*Creusa, Queen of Athens*. 1754. BELK20
*The Roman Father*. 1750. BELK20
*School for Lovers*. 1762. BELG16

WHITEMORE, HUGH, 1936–
*Pack of Lies*. 1983. BES84, PLACHB

WHITING, JOHN, 1917–1963
*The Devils*. 1961. NEWE6
*Marching Song*. 1954. NEWE3
*Saint's Day*. 1951 PLAN6

WHITTINGTON, ROBERT, 1912–
*The Death of Garcia Lorca*. 1940. CROZ1

WHO, THE
*Tommy, a Rock Opera. See* Townshend, Peter, joint author

WHYLE, JAMES
*National Madness*. 1982. GRAY

WICHELER, FERNAND, 1874–1935. *See* Fonson, Frantz, joint author

WIDEMAN, ANGELA
*The Hard to Serve*. 1991. NTIR

WIEAND, PAUL R., 1907–1993
*Die huchzich um kreitz waig?* BUFF
*Der parra kumpt.* BUFF
*Tzu forwitsich.* BUFF

WIEBE, RUDY, 1934– , and THEATRE PASSE MURAILLE
*Far as the Eye Can See*. 1977. SHOW

WIECHERT, ERNST EMIL, 1887–1950
*Das spiel vom deutschen bettelmann*. 1933. STI2

WIED, GUSTAV JOHANNES, 1858–1914
*Ranke viljer. See* $2 \times 2 = 5$

$2 \times 2 = 5$. 1906.
Boyd, E., and Koppel, H., translators LEG
Variant title: *Ranke viljer*

WIESE, ANNE PIERSON, 1964–
*Coleman, S.D.* 1982. YOUP

WILBRANDT, ADOLF VON, 1837–1911
*The Master of Palmyra*. 1889.
Stork, C., translator FRA16
Variant title: *Der meister von Palmyra*
*Der meister von Palmyra. See* The Master of Palmyra

WILBUR, RICHARD, 1921–
*Candide. See* Hellman, Lillian. *Candide* (lyrics by)

WILCOX, ANNA JANE. *See* Harnwell, Mrs. Anna Jane (Wilcox)

WILCOX, DESMOND, 1931–2000
*The Year Two Billion*. 1985. MONB2

WILCOX, MICHAEL, 1943–
*Accounts*. 1981. GAY1

WILDE, OSCAR, 1854–1900
*An Ideal Husband*. 1895. JAFF
*The Importance of Being Earnest*. 1895. ABRJ2, ABRK2, ABRL2, ABRM2, ACE, ALLM, ALLN, ALLO, ANT, ASG, ASH, BAIG, BAIH, BAIK, BAIL, BAIM, BARB, BARG, BARIE, BARKC, BARKD, BARKE, BARKF, BARR, BEATA, BENSB2, BENU, BOWY, BROG, CARP, CARPA, CASH, CEU, COLD, COLT, COTKICO, COTKIS, COTKR, COTY, CRAF, CRAN2, EDAD, FEFL, FOUM, GREAAI, GREB2, GREC2, HAEA, HAEB, HEAC, HEALB, HEALC, HILP, HILPDH5, HOUS, JACOBA, JACOBD, KER, KRM, LEVY, LOO, LOOA, MON, MOSN, MOSO, NEVI, PERR2, PERR3, PRO, REIWE, ROGEBD, SAFF, SALE, SATI, SCNQCB, SHAJ2, SIG, SMR, STE, STEI, STJN, STOTD, STOTLA, STOTLB, STRO, STY, THOM, THON, TRE, TREA1, TREBA, TREBJ, TREC2, TREE3, TREI3, TUCD, TUCM, TUCN, TUCO, WATA, WHFM, WHI, WOLC, WOLCS, WOO2, WOOD2, WOOE2, WOTHB, WOTHM
*Lady Windermere's Fan*. 1892. BAUG, BENY, BROJ, BROK, DAV1, DICD, HUD, LIE, LIED2, LIEE2, MACL, MATTL, MOO, RUB, SMO, TAT, TAU
*A Woman of No Importance*. 1893. COT

WILDE, PATRICK
*What's Wrong with Angry?* 1993. CLUM

WILLIAMS, JESSE LYNCH, 1871–1929
*And So They Were Married. See* Why Marry?
*Why Marry?* 1917. AMENW, BES09, CORD, CORE,
    CORF, QUI
        Variant title: *And So They Were Married*
*Why Not?* 1922. BES22

WILLIAMS, KARIN D.
*Quiz.* 1990. BREK

WILLIAMS, LAUREN
*Over Fourteen: and Single.* DRU

WILLIAMS, MAGI NONINZI
*Kwa-landlady.* 1993. PERA

WILLIAMS, MARGARET (VYNER), 1914–1993. *See*
    Williams, Hugh, joint author

WILLIAMS, MARY ANN, 1945–
*Cinder, Tell-It.* (1976) AUB

WILLIAMS, NIALL, 1958–
*A Little like Paradise.* 1995. NEWPAB1

WILLIAMS, NORMAN, 1923–
*The Mountain.* GREG

WILLIAMS, PAULETTE. *See* Shange, Ntozake

WILLIAMS, ROD, ca.1964–
*The Life of the World to Come.* 1994. FROLIN2

WILLIAMS, ROGER, 1974–
*Gulp.* 1997. NEWWD1
*Killing Kangaroos.* 1999. NEWWD2

WILLIAMS, SAMUEL ARTHUR. *See* Samm-Art
    Williams

WILLIAMS, SAMM-ART (b. Samuel Arthur Williams),
    1946–
*Home.* 1979. BES79, HAPUE

WILLIAMS, TENNESSEE (b. Thomas Lanier Williams),
    1914–1983
*Camino Real.* 1953. CES, FAM, FAMAF, MIJY,
    SANK, ULAN
*The Case of the Crushed Petunias.* 1941? COOF
*Cat on a Hot Tin Roof.* 1955. BAIK (from Act II only),
    BERP, BES54, BRJB, BRJC, COI, COLD, GART,
    GAVE, GILB, GOODE, JACOBA, JACOBD,
    LITQ, SCNPL, SCNQ, SSSI, SSSIA, SSSIB,
    SSSIC, STOTD, STOTLA, STOTLB, THEA55,
    VENA,WATTAD

*The Confessional.* 1966. RICK
*Dos Ranchos; or, The Purification.* 1944. NEWDI44
*The Glass Menagerie.* 1944. ABCB, ABCC, ABCD,
    ABCE, ABCG, ABCH, ALLM, ALLN, ALLO,
    ANTL, AUB, BAIG, BAIH, BAIK (Scene 7
    only), BARI, BARIA, BARIC, BARID, BARIE,
    BARIG, BARIH, BARKD, BARKE, BARKF,
    BARN, BARNA, BARS, BES44, BLOC, BLON,
    BLOND, BONA, BONB, BONC, BOYN,
    BOOK, BPD2, BPE, BROY, CASH, CLH,
    COK, COOP, CORB, CORBA, COTQ, CUBE,
    CUBG, CUBH, DEAS, DIEA, DIYLC, DIYRD,
    DOWM, ELK, FRYEA, GARZ, GATB3, GATS,
    GAVE, GUTDF, GUTDS, GWYN, HAEA,
    HAEB, HAPO, HATA, HAVH, HAVI, HEA,
    HEAA, HEAB, HEAC, HEAD, HEALC, HEALD,
    HEALE, HOEP, HOWM, JACOB, JACOBA,
    JACOBD, JACOBE, KIRLA, KIRLB, KIRLC,
    KIRLD, KLIS, KNIC, KNID, KNIF, KNIG,
    LAV, LEVY, LIEG, LITC, LITIA, LITIB, LITIC,
    LITID, LITIE, LITIF, LITJ, LITJA, LITRB,
    LITRC, LITRD, MABC, MAEC, MANCD2,
    MANCE2, MANCF2, MANCG2, MANCH2,
    MANCIA, MANCIO, MANK, MANL, MAO,
    MARK, MARL, MEY, MEYB, MEYC, MEYCA,
    MEYCB, MEYD, MEYE, MEYF, MON, MONA,
    PERR2, PERS, PERT, PERW, PERX, PERY,
    PERZ, PIC, PRO, REIP, REIT, ROHR, SCNQCA,
    SCNQCB, SDQ, SHRO, SILK, SILKI, SILN,
    SILO, SILP, SIXB, SIXC, SOM, SOMA, SOUL,
    SPES, SSSF, STEI, STY, TREBA, TREBJ,
    TREC2, TREE3, TREI3, WAIT, WAIU, WAK,
    WARH, WARL, WATE, WEIM, WEIS, WEIW,
    WOTHA, WOTHB, WOTHC, WOTHM
*The gnädiges fräulein.* 1966. MESSE
*Hello from Bertha.* RAVIT
*I Rise in Flame, Cried the Phoenix.* 1951. NEWWW1
*The Last of My Solid Gold Watches.* 1947. BURG,
    PLAAC1
*The Long Goodbye.* 1940. BAIG, BAIH
*A Lonely Sunday for Creve Coeur.* 1979. BERS
*The Milk Train Doesn't Stop Here Anymore.* 1962.
    BES62
*The Night of the Iguana.* 1961. BES61, GARSA,
    PERR1, RICIS, SEVT
*Not about Nightingales.* 1999. BES98
*Orpheus Descending.* 1957. BES56, GARSA, GORE
*Period of Adjustment.* 1960. BES60
*Portrait of a Madonna.* 1945. MIJH
*The Rose Tattoo.* 1951. BES50, CLM, CLN, COTY,
    GART, GREAB, RICT
*Small Craft Warnings.* 1972. BES71
*Something Unspoken.* 1953? SUL
*A Streetcar Named Desire.* 1947. BAIK, BAIL, BAIM,
    BARJ, BEATA, BES47, CEQA, CLL, CLLC,

FOUX, GARW, GATB3, GAVE, GOOD, NEWV, TUCO
*Suddenly Last Summer*. 1958. LIEF, MESSN, PERR3
*Summer and Smoke*. 1948. GARW, GOLH, HAVG, TAUJ
*Sweet Bird of Youth*. 1959. BES58
*Talk to Me like the Rain and Let Me Listen*. 1970. RAVIT
*This Property Is Condemned*. 1946. PLAAC2, READ2
*27 Wagons Full of Cotton*. 1955. HALU, SPC

WILLIAMS, THOMAS LANIER. *See* Williams, Tennessee

WILLIAMS, TOM
*New Business*. 1990. PRIMA91

WILLIAMS, WILLIAM CARLOS, 1883–1963
*The First President*. 1936? AME5
*Trial Horse No. 1: Many Loves*. 1942? NEWDI42

WILLIAMSON, DAVID, 1942–
*Emerald City*. 1987. BES88
*The Removalists*. 1971. BRIM1
*Travelling North*. 1979. AUS
*What If You Died Tomorrow*. 1973. FIO

WILLIAMSON, GAYLE WEAVER
*Mirror, Mirror*. 1993. FLET (one scene only)

WILLIAMSON, HAROLD
*Peggy*. 1919. HUD

WILLIAMSON, HUGH ROSS, 1901–1978
*Diamond Cut Diamond*. 1952. PLAN7
*Gunpowder, Treason, and Plot*. 1951. PLAN6
*Heart of Bruce*. 1959. PLAN20
*A Question of Obedience*. *See* Teresa of Avila
*Teresa of Avila*. 1961. PLAN24
    Variant title: *A Question of Obedience*

WILLIAMSON, LAIRD, and POWERS, DENNIS
*Christmas Miracles*. 1985. PRIMA85

WILLIS, ANTHONY ARMSTRONG (Anthony Armstrong, pseudonym), 1897–1976
*Ten Minute Alibi*. 1933. FAMD

WILLIS, JULIA, 1949–
*Going Up*. 1979. PLA

WILLIS, NATHANIEL PARKER (N.P.), 1806–1867
*Bianca Visconti; or, The Heart Overtasked*. 1837. HAL
*Tortesa, the Usurer*. 1839. MOSS2, QUIJ, QUIK, QUIL, QUIM, QUIN

WILLMOTT, KEVIN, 1959– , and AVERILL, RIC
*T-money & Wolf*. 1993. VOI

WILLS, W. G. *See* Wills, William Gorman

WILLS, WILLIAM GORMAN, 1828–1891
*Eugene Aram*. 1873. KILG

—— and HERMAN, HENRY, joint author
*Claudian*. 1883. MAYER

WILMOT, ROBERT, fl. 1568–1608
*Tancred and Gismund; or, Gismond of Salerne*. 1691? CUN

WILMURT, ARTHUR. *See* Obey, André, Noah (translated and adapted by)

WILNER, SHERI
*Hunger*. 2000. NEWR99
*Labor Day*. 1999. HUMANA99

WILSON, SIR ANGUS FRANK JOHNSTONE, 1913–1991
*The Mulberry Bush*. 1955. RHE

WILSON, AUGUST, 1945–2005
*Fences*. 1985. BAIL, BAIM, BARIG, BARIH, BARKD, BARKE, BARN, BARNA, BES85, BES86, DIYL, DIYLC, DIYLD, HAEB, HEAD, JACOB, JACOBA, JACOBD, JACOBE, KIRLC, KIRLD, LITRC, LITRD, MARK, MARL, MEYB, MEYC, MEYD, PERY, PERZ, SCX, WOLC, WOTHB, WOTHC, WOTHM
*The Janitor*. 1985. SCVDT1
*Jitney*. 1996. BES97, BES99
*Joe Turner's Come and Gone*. 1988. ANTL, BERT, BES87, BPW, COI, HOWM, LITID, LITIE, LITIF, LITJA
*Ma Rainey's Black Bottom*. 1985. BES84, BLACTH, FAMAB, GILB, HAPU, PLACGA, SSSIA, SSSIB, SSSIC, TUQTR, WATTAD
*The Piano Lesson*. 1988. BES88, BES89, COLD, JACOBD, LEVY, MEYCA, MEYE, MEYF
*Seven Guitars*. 1995. BES95
*Two Trains Running*. 1992. ABCG, BES90, BES91

WILSON, DORIC, 1939–2011
*Street Theater*. 1982. SHEW

WILSON, ERIC
*Strands*. 1991. FLET

WILSON, ERIN CRESSIDA, 1964–
*Cross-dressing in the Depression*. 1994. WOMP93
*Hurricane*. 1999. WOMP98

WILSON, FRANK H., 1886–1956
*Sugar Cane.* 1925. LOC

WILSON, HARRY LEON, 1867–1939
*Merton of the Movies. See* Kaufman, George S., and
Connelly, Marca. *Merton of the Movies* (based
on the novel by)
— *See* Tarkington, Booth, joint author

WILSON, JOHN, 1785–1854
*The City of the Plague.* 1816. ENGLMI

WILSON, JOHN, 1921–
*Hamp.* 1964. BES66

WILSON, LANFORD, 1937–2011
*Angels Fall.* 1982. BES82
*Book of Days.* 1998. BES98
*Burn This.* 1987. BERT
*The Fifth of July.* 1978. BES77
*The Hot L Baltimore.* 1973. BES72, OBG
*Lemon Sky.* 1970. GARTL
*The Madness of Lady Bright.* 1964. HOF, ORZ
*The Mound Builders.* 1975. PLACD
*A Poster of the Cosmos.* 1988. OSBW
*Serenading Louie.* 1976. BES75
*Talley's Folly.* 1979. BERS, BES79

WILSON, MARIE ELAINE, ca.1966–
*Shopping Spree.* 1987. DEAD

WILSON, ROBERT, d.1600
*Sir John Oldcastle, Part I* (sometimes attributed to).
*See* Anonymous plays. *Sir John Oldcastle, Part I*

WILSON, ROBERT, 1941–
*A Letter for Queen Victoria.* 1974. THG, THGA
— *See also* Byrd Hoffman School of Byrds, joint
author

WILSON, SANDY (b. Alexander Galbraith Wilson),
1924–
*The Boyfriend.* 1953. BES54

WILSON, THEODORA WILSON, d.1941
*Champion North.* 1933. FIT

WILTSE, DAVID, 1940–
*Doubles.* 1985. BES84

WIN, TIN TIN
*Place for a Woman.* 2001. SECO

WINCELBERG, SHIMON, 1924–2004
*The Enemy. See* Kataki

*Kataki.* 1959. BES58
Variant title: *The Enemy*
*Resort 76* (based on the novella, *A Cat in the Ghetto* by
Racbmil Bryks). 1969. THL
Variant title: *The Windows of Heaven*
*The Windows of Heaven. See* Resort 76

WINDSOR, VALERIE
*Effie's Burning.* 1987. PLABE7

WING, PAULA, 1957–
*Lydia.* 1987. ZIMM (excerpt)

WINGFIELD, GARTH
*Are We There Yet?* 1999. DENT

WINSLOE, CHRISTA, 1888–1944
*Children in Uniform.* 1932.
Burnham, B., translator and adapter FAMC
Variant titles: *Gestern und heute; Girls in Uniform;
Maedchen in Uniform*
*Gestern und heute. See* Children in Uniform
*Girls in Uniform. See* Children in Uniform
*Maedchen in Uniform. See* Children in Uniform

WINSOR, MARY
*A Suffrage Rummage Sale.* 1913. FRIED

WINSTANLEY, KATE, d. 1993. *See* Gallagher, Kathleen,
joint author

WINTER, JACK, and SMITH, CEDRIC
*Ten Lost Years.* 1974. CTR

WINTER, JOHN KEITH, 1906–1983
*The Rats of Norway.* 1933. SIXH
*The Shining Hour.* 1934. BES33, SEV

WISE, ERNEST GEORGE (Ernest George, pseudonym),
1894–
*Down Our Street.* 1930. SIXD

WISEMAN, JANE, fl. 1682–1717
*Antiochus the Great, or, The Fatal Relapse.* 1701.
LOQA
Variant title: *The Fatal Relapse*
*The Fatal Relapse. See* Antiochus the Great, or, The
Fatal Relapse

WISHENGRAD, MORTON, 1913–1963
*The Rope Dancers.* 1957. BES57, GARSA

WITHERSPOON, KATHLEEN
*Jute.* 1929. THX

WITKIEWICZ, STANISŁAW IGNACY, 1885–1939
*The Anonymous Work: Four Acts of a Rather Nasty
    Nightmare.* 1921.
        Gerould, D., and Gerould, E., translators TWEN
*The Cuttlefish.* 1922.
        Gerould, D., and Gerould, E., translators TREBJ
*Kurka wodna. See* The Water Hen
*The Water Hen.* 1922.
        Gerould, D., and Durer, C., translators DUK
        Variant title: *Kurka wodna*

WITTEN, MATTHEW
*The Deal.* 1987. BES87

WODDIS, ROGER, 1917–1993. *See* Paice, Eric, joint
    author

WODEHOUSE, PELLHAM GRENVILLE (P.G.), 1881–
    1975
*The Play's the Thing. See* Molnár, Ferenca. *The Play's
    the Thing* (adapted by)

WOLFE, GEORGE C., 1954–
*The Colored Museum.* 1985. BARNA, BLAC,
    BLACTH, BRJB, BRJC, HEALE, KIRLB,
    NEWQC
*Spunk* (adapted from the stories "Sweat," "Story in
    Harlem Slang," and "The Gilded Six-bits" by Zora
    Neale Hurston; music by Chic Street Man). 1989.
    SWANS

WOLFE, HUMBERT, 1885–1940
*The Silent Knight.* 1939. SIXP

WOLFE, THOMAS, 1900–1938
*Look Homeward, Angel. See* Frings, Ketti. *Look
    Homeward, Angel* (based on the novel by)

WOLFF, EGON, 1926–
*Flores de papel.* 1970. DAU

WOLFF, RUTH, 1932–
*The Abdication.* 1971? NEWWT

WOLFSON, VICTOR, 1910–1990
*Excursion.* 1937. BES36

WOLK, MICHAEL
*Femme Fatale.* 1983. WOMQ

WOLLENWEBER, LUDWIG AUGUST, 1807–1888
*Ein gesprach.* 18–? BUFF
*Das lied von der union.* 18–? BUFF
*Die margareth und die Lea.* 18–? BUFF

*Eb Refschneider und Susu Leimbach.* 18–? BUFF
*Die Sara und die Bets.* 18–? BUFF

WOLTON, JOAN
*Motherlove.* 1987. PLABE8

WOMEN'S THEATRE GROUP, 1974–1991
*My Mother Says I Never Should.* 1975. STRI
    — *See also* Wakefield, Lou, joint author

——— and FEINSTEIN, ELAINE, joint author
*Lear's Daughters.* 1987. ADAP, GRIFG1, MYTH

——— and MASON, LIBBY, joint author
*Double Vision.* 1982. LES1

WONG, ELEANOR, 1962–
*Mergers and Accusations.* 1993. DIRTY
*Wills and Secession.* 1995. PING

WONG, ELIZABETH, 1958–
*China Doll.* 1991. PERC
*Kimchee and Chitlins.* 1993. HOUST
*Let the Big Dog Eat.* 1998. HUMANA98
*Letters to a Student Revolutionary.* 1991. ELLM,
    LAMO, SWANS, UNO

WONG OU-HONG. *See* Weng, Ou-hong, and A, Jia

WOOD, CHARLES, 1932–1980
*Cockade.* 1963. NEWE8
*Fill the Stage with Happy Hours.* 1966. NEWE11

WOOD, MRS. HENRY, 1813–1887
*East Lynne.* 1864. BAI, CEY
    Variant title: *The Marriage Bells; or, The Cottage on
        the Cliff*
*The Marriage Bells; or, The Cottage on the Cliff. See*
    East Lynne

WOOD, J. HICKORY, 1858–1913, and COLLINS,
    ARTHUR
*The Sleeping Beauty and the Beast.* 1900. BOOA5

WOOD, KEVIN. *See* Pickering, Kenneth, joint author

WOOD, SILVIANA, 1940–
*And Where Was Pancho Villa When You Really Needed
    Him?* 2000. PURO

WOODBRIDGE, ELIZABETH. *See* Morris, Elizabeth
    (Woodbridge)

WOODES, NATHANIEL, fl.1580?
*The Conflict of Conscience.* 1581. SCAT

WOODS, AUBREY, 1928– , and ROWELL, GEORGE
*Trelawny, a Musical Play* (based on *Trelawny of the Wells* by Sir Arthur Wing Pinero; music and lyrics by Julian Slade). 1972. PLAN41

WOODS, GRAHAME, 1934–
*Vicky.* KAL3

WOODS, VINCENT, 1960–
*At the Black Pig's Dyke.* 1992. FAIR

WOODS, W.
*The Twins; or, Which Is Which?* 1780. BELC4

WOODS, WALTER, d. 1942
*Billy the Kid.* 1906. AMP8

WOODWORTH, SAMUEL, 1785–1842
*The Forest Rose.* 1825. MONR

WOOLF, BENJAMIN EDWARD, 1836–1901
*The Almighty Dollar. See* The Mighty Dollar
*The Mighty Dollar.* 1875. CLA
    Variant title: *The Almighty Dollar*
*Off to the War!* 1861. MESC

WOOLL, EDWARD, 1878–1970
*Libel!* 1934? SEV

THE WOOSTER GROUP, 1975–
*Frank Dell's The Temptation of St. Antony* (based on the novel by Gustave Flaubert). 1988. MARR

WOOTEN, JOHN J., 1965–
*The Role of Della.* 1995. PLACA

WORDSWORTH, WILLIAM, 1770–1850
*The Borderers.* 1797. ENGL, KAU

WORKERS THEATRE MOVEMENT
*Newsboy* (co-ordinated and planned by Workers Laboratory Theatre, New York; adapted from the poem by V. J. Jerome). 1934.
    Blumentahl, G., English adaptation GOOR

WORKSHOP '71 THEATRE COMPANY, 1975–
*Survival.* 1976. SOUT

WORSLEY, VICTORIA, 1966–
*Lift and Separate.* 1993. MYTII

WOUDSTRA, KARST, 1947–
*Burying the Dog.* 1989.
    Couling, D., translator COUL
    Variant title: *Een hond begraven*
*Een hond begraven. See* Burying the Dog

WOUK, HERMAN, 1915–
*The Caine Mutiny Court-martial.* 1953. BES53, GART, NEWV, RED, THEA54

WOUTERS, LILIANE, 1930–
*Charlotte or Mexican Night.* 1989.
    Glasheen, A., translator GLASH
    Variant title: *Charlotte ou la nuit mexicaine*
*Charlotte ou la nuit mexicaine. See* Charlotte or Mexican Night
*The Lives and Deaths of Miss Shakespeare.* 1979.
    Glasheen, A., translator GAYIA
    Variant title: *Vies et morts de Mademoiselle Shakespeare. See* The Lives and Deaths of Miss Shakespeare

WRAY, ELIZABETH, 1950–
*Border* (Part 2 of 3-part *Mobile Homes*). 1981. WEK
    Variant title: *Mobile Homes*
*Forecast.* 1982. WEK
*Mobile Homes. See* Border

WREDE, CASPER, 1955–
*No* (adapted by). *See* Heiberg, Johan. *No*

WRIGHT, DOUG, 1962–
*Interrogating the Nude.* 1989. NEWAMP1

WRIGHT, FRANCES, 1795–1852
*Altorf: A Tragedy.* 1819. KRIT

WRIGHT, GLENN, 1960– , and SEBAZCO, RAUL SANTIAGO
*The Crime.* 1980. ALG

WRIGHT, NICHOLAS, 1940–
*Mrs. Klein.* 1988. BES95

WRIGHT, RICHARD, 1908–1960, and GREEN, PAUL
*Native Son.* 1941. AMB, BES40, BRAS, HARY, HARYB

WRIGHT, ROBERT, 1914–2005
*Grand Hotel* (songs by). *See* Davis, Luther. *Grand Hotel*

WROTH, LADY MARY, ca.1587–ca.1651
*Love's Victory.* ca.1620. RENDW

WU, CH'UN-HAN, 1909–1966
*Hai Jui Dismissed from Office.* 1961.
    Huang, C., and Gunn, E., translators TWEH (Acts III, VI and IX in full; others summarized)
    Variant title: *Hai Jui pa-kuan*
*Hai Jui pa-kuan. See* Hai Jui Dismissed from Office

WU, HAN. *See* Wu, Ch'un-han

WUCHTER, ASTOR CLINTON, 1856–1933
*An der lumpa parti. See* Barba, Preston Albert (based on the poem by)

WUOLIJOKI, HELLA, 1886–1954
*Hulda Juurakko*. 1937.
   Poom, R., translator KEL
*Law and Order*. 1933.
   Wilmer, M. and S., translators WILM

WYATT, RACHEL, 1929–
*Getting Out*. 1993. ZIMM

WYCHERLEY, WILLIAM, 1640?–1716
*The Country Wife*. 1674? ALLK, ALLM, ALLN,
   ALLO, BAUL, BELK17, COLR, DAVR, ENC,
   FAL, FOUB, GOS, GOSA, HAVL, JEFF1, KRM,
   MANH, RES, RESL, REST, SALR, SEN, SEVT,
   TAUJ, THMF, TUQ, TWE, WEAN, WILSR,
   WONR, WRIR
*The Plain Dealer*. 1676. COLR, FIS, GAYLE4, JEFF2,
   JENS, MANF, MATTL, MOR, MOSE1, NET,
   WONR
   — *See* also Bickerstaffe, I. *The Plain Dealer*
   (altered by)

WYMARK, OLWEN, 1932–
*Find Me*. 1977. PLABE2

WYNNE, MICHAEL, 1973–
*The Knocky*. 1994. COMS

X, MARVIN, pseudonym. *See* Jackman, Marvin

XENOPOULOS, GREGORIUS, 1867–1951
*Divine Dream*.
   Gianos, M., translator GIA

XI, ZHIGAN, 1947– . *See* Guo, Dayu, joint author

XIA, YAN, 1900–1995
*Shanghai wu-Yen hsia. See* Under Shanghai Eaves
*Under Shanghai Eaves*. (1937)
   Hayden, G., translator TWEH
   Variant title*: Shanghai wu-yen hsia*

XU, PINLI, 1953–
*Laolin. See* Old Forest
*Old Forest*. 1991.
   Cheung, M., and Lai, J., translator CHEU
   Variant title: *Laolin*

YAFA, STEVEN H. 1941–
*Passing Shots*. 1976. WES1

YAFFE, JAMES, 1927–
*The Deadly Game* (adapted from the novel *Trapps* by
   Friedrich Deurrenmatt). 1960. BES59

YAGI, SHŌICHIRŌ, 1928–2004
*Kono shōni. See* The Little One
*The Little One*. 1955.
   Gallimore, D., translator HACJT8
   Variant title: *Kono shōni*

YAGORO, KONGO. *See* Kongō, Yagorō

YALFANI, MOHSEN
*Dar sahel. See* On the Shore
*On the Shore*. 1977.
   Godec, J., Ibsen, L., and Nyce, C., translators GHAN
   Variant title: *Dar sahel*

YAMAMOTO, KIYOKAZU, 1939– . *See* Satoh, Makoto,
   joint author

YAMAUCHI, WAKAKO, 1924–
*And the Soul Shall Dance*. 1977. BARKF, BETW,
   BOGA, WES11/12, WOLCS, WOMA
*The Chairman's Wife*. 1990. HOUSTP
*The Music Lessons*. 1980. UNO
*12-1-A*. 1982. HOUSTP, SWANS

YAMAZAKI, MASAKAZU, 1934–
*At Play with a Lion*. 1977.
   Poulton, M., translator HACJT7
   Variant titles: *Crucifixion of a Wooden Statue, Shisi
      wo kau*
   *Crucifixion of a Wooden Statue. See* At Play with a Lion
   *Shisi wo kau. See* At Play with a Lion

YAMAZAKI, TETSU, 1947–
*The Family Adrift: The Jesus Ark Incident*. 1982.
   Boyd, M., translator HACJT5
   Variant title: *Hyōryō kazoku: Iesu no hakobune*
   *Hyōryō kazoku: Iesu no hakobune. See* The Family
      Adrift: The Jesus Ark Incident

YANG, CHIANG. *See* Yang, Chi-K'ang

YANG, CHI-K'ANG, 1911–
*Feng-hsü. See* Windswept Blossoms
*Windswept Blossoms*. 1945–1946.
   Gunn, E., translator TWEH
   Variant title: *Feng-Hsu*

YANG, HSIEN-CHIH, fl.1246
*Rain on the Hsiao-Hsiang* (attributed to).
   Crump, J., translator CRU

YANG, JIAN. *See* Chen, Zidu, joint author

YANG, JIANG. *See* Yang, Chi-K'ang

YANG, LÜ-FANG
*Cuckoo Sings Again.* 1957.
Talmadge, D., and Gunn, E., translators TWEH (Acts
I–III in full; Act IV summarized)
Variant title: *Pu-ku-niao yu chiao-le*
*Pu-ku-nino yu chiao-le. See* Cuckoo Sings Again

YANG MU, pseudonym. *See* Wang, Ching-Ksien

YANKOWITZ, SUSAN, 1941–
*Alarms.* 1986. FEFNV
*Boxes.* 1972. BALLE11
*Night Sky.* 1991. MIHPW
*Slaughterhouse.* 1971? NEWA4
*Terminal.* ca. 1974. OPE

YAO, HSIN-NUNG, 1905–1991
*Ch'ing kung yüan. See* The Malice of Empire
*The Malice of Empire* (Act I, Scene 1). 1941?
Anonymous translator BIR2
Variant title: *Ch'ing kung yüan*

YAO, MINGDE. *See* Yao, Ming-te

YAO, MING-TE. *See* Sha, Yeh-Hsin, joint author

YASHIRO, SEIICHI, 1927–1998
*The Courtesan Miyagino.* 1966.
Boyd, M., translator HACJT8
Variant title: *Miyagino*
*Miyagino. See* The Courtesan Miyagino

YASUDA, ABUN, fl. 1720s–1740s. *See* Tsuuchi, Hanjurō,
joint author

YASUDA, KENNETH, 1914–
*Martin Luther King, Jr.: A Nōh Play.* 1989. YASU

YASUKIYO, HYOSHI SA-AMI. *See* Hiyoshi, Sa-ami
Yasukiyo

YEATON, DANA
*Helen at Risk.* 1995. HUMANA95

YEATS, JACK BUTLER, 1871–1957
*La la noo.* 1942. BARF

YEATS, WILLIAM BUTLER, 1865–1939
*At the Hawk's Well.* 1916? BLOC
Variant title: *The Well of Immortality*
*The Cat and the Moon.* 1926. HAE
*Cathleen ni Houlihan.* 1902. DUR, MERC, MIKL,
MOSN, MOSO

*The Countess Cathleen.* 1892. ASG, BOWY, CLKWI,
COTM, PLAAB, SECK
*Deirdre.* 1906. SALE, SSTA
*The Dreaming of the Bones.* 1931. STEI
*A Full Moon in March.* 1935. BENS1
*The Hour-glass.* 1903. DICD, REIT
*The King's Threshold.* 1903. KRE
*The Land of Heart's Desire.* 1894. BURR, GREAAI,
HUD, MACN, WATT2
*On Baile's Strand.* 1904. AUG, BARC, CAP, COTQ,
GREAAI, LAQID, OWEC, ULAN, WOTHA
*The Only Jealousy of Emer.* 1922. CAP, COK, OWEC
*Purgatory.* 1938. ALT, BARH, BEAM, BENT2,
CALD, DIYLB, DIYRD, DOLAN, HILPDH5,
KAYT, LITIC, LITP, REIN, REIP, REIWE, TAUJ,
TREBJ, TRI, TRIA, ULAN
*The Resurrection.* 1934. MERC
*The Shadowy Waters.* 1900. GERO
*The Well of Immortality. See* At the Hawk's Well
*The Words upon the Windowpane.* 1935. ALT, BARF,
CAN, SHR

YEGER, SHEILA
*Variations on a Theme by Clara Schumann.* 1991.
PLABE9

YEH, HSIAO-NAN. *See* Chou, Wei-po, joint author

YEHOSHUA, A. B. *See* Yehoshua, Abraham B.

YEHOSHUA, ABRAHAM B., 1936–
*The Lover. See* Chilton, Nora. *Naim* (based on the
novel by)
*Mr Mani.* 1988.
Simpson, P., and Harshav, B., translators BARA

YELLOW ROBE, WILLIAM S., JR., 1960–
*The Independence of Eddie Rose.* 1986. DAPO
*Sneaky.* 1990. JENN

YELVINGTON, RAMSEY, 1913–1973
*A Cloud of Witnesses.* 1955. TEX

YEN, ANNA
*Chinese Take Away.* 1997. THUAA

YEOH, PATRICK, 1941–
*The Need to Be.* 1970. NEWDR2

YEP, LAURENCE, 1948–
*Pay the Chinaman.* 1987. BETW

YERBY, LOREES, 1930–
*The Golden Bull of Boredom.* NEWA1

YESTON, MAURY, 1945–
  *Grand Hotel* (additional music and lyrics by). *See* Davis,
    Luther. *Grand Hotel*
  *Nine* (music and lyrics by). *See* Kopit, Arthur Lee. *Nine*
  *Titanic* (music and lyrics by). *See* Stone, Peter H.
    *Titanic*

YEVREINOV, NIKOLAI. *See* Evreinov, Nikolai

YEW, CHAY, 1965–
  *A Language of Their Own.* 1994. HOUST
  *Porcelain.* 1992. CLUM

YHAP, BEVERLEY.
  *Body Blows.* 1996. BEYO (excerpt)

YI-PING, CHUNG. *See* Chung, Yi-ping

YOKOUCHI, KENSUKE, 1961–
  *Gusha niwa mienai Ra-Mancha no hadaka: Yokouchi
    Kensuke gikyoku-syō. See* The King of La
    Mancha's Clothes
  *The King of La Mancha's Clothes.* 1991.
    Rimer, J., translator HACJT3
    Variant title: *Gusha niwa mienai Ra-Mancha no
    hadaka: Yokouchi Kensuke gikyoku-syō*

YOON, JEAN, 1962–
  *Sliding for Home.* 1996. BEYO (excerpt)

YORDAN, PHILIP, 1914–2003
  *Anna Lucasta.* 1944. BES44

YOSHIMURA, JAMES, 1950–
  *Mercenaries.* 1982. NEWQA

YOUNG, SIR CHARLES LAWRENCE, 1839–1887, and
    HOWARD, BRONSON CROCKER
  *Knave and Queen.* 1882? AMP10

YOUNG, DAVID. *See* Ledoux, Paul, joint author

YOUNG, DEBBIE, 1978– , and BELVETT, NAILA
  *yagayah: two.womyn.black.griots.* 2001. SEARS2

YOUNG, EDWARD, 1683–1765
  *The Brothers.* 1753. BELK14
  *Busiris.* 1719. BELK16
  *The Revenge.* 1721. BELK12

YOUNG, ROBERT. *See* Roemer, Michael, joint author

YOUNG, STANLEY, 1906–1975
  *Mr. Pickwick* (based on Charles Dickens' *Pickwick
    Papers*). 1952. THEA53

YOUNG, WILLIAM, 1847–1920
  *Ben-Hur* (adapted from the novel by Lew Wallace).
    1899. MAYER

YOUNG, WILLIAM R.
  *Eden's Moon* (story conceived by Sasha Wentges).
    1998. NEWCAD8

YOUNG LADY, A. *The Unnatural Mother.* 1697. MISC

YOUNG.ANITAFRIKA, D'BI. *See* Young, Debbie

YOUNGBLOOD, SHAY, 1959–
  *Movie Music.* 1993. FLET (one scene only)
    Variant title: *Talking Bones*
  *Shakin' the Mess Outta Misery.* 1992. ELAM
  *Talking Bones. See* Movie Music
  *There Are Many Houses in My Tribe.* 1992. ACTOR

YŪ, MIRI, 1968–
  *Festival for the Fish.* 1992.
    Masako, Y., translator HACJT2
    Variant title: *Uo no matsuri*
  *Uo no matsuri. See* Festival for the Fish

YU, OVIDIA, 1960–
  *Three Fat Virgins Unassembled.* 1991. FAT
  *The Woman in a Tree on the Hill.* 1992. PING

YUNG, DANNY N. T., 1943–
  *Chronicle of Women—Liu Sola in Concert.* 1991.
    Cheung, M., translator CHEU

YUSOF, ABDUL RAHMAN
  *Eye.* 1994.
    Abdullah, K., translator MLAB

ZACHARKO, LARRY, 1950–
  *Land of Magic Spell.* 1974. KAL4

ZADI ZAOUROU, BERNARD, 1938–
  *The Eye.* 1974.
    MacDougall, J., translator AFRUBU1
    Variant title: *L'Oeil*
  *L'Oeil. See* The Eye

ZAHN, CURTIS, 1912–1990
  *The Reactivated Man.* 1965. WES11/12

ZAIN, SHUKRI, 1936–
  *Seri Begawan I.* 1994.
    Abdullah, K., translator MLAB

ZAJC, DANE, 1929–2005
  *Kalevala.* 1986.

*Grmače. See* Rocky Peak
    Anonymous translator PRED (summary only)
*Medea.* 1988.
    Anonymous translator PRED (summary only)
*Rocky Peak.* 1995.
    Flisar, E., translator PRED
    Variant title: *Grmače*

ZAJDLIC, RICHARD, 1962–
    *Infidelities.* 1990. FIFHL3
    — *See also* Crowe, Richard, joint author

ZAMACOIS, EDUARDO (EDUARDO DE ZAMACOIS
    Y QUINTANA), 1873–1971
    *The Passing of the Magi.* 1912
    Turrell, C., translator TUR
    Variant title: *Los reyes pasan*
    *Los reyes pasan. See* The Passing of the Magi

ZAMACOIS Y QUINTANA, EDUARDO DE. *See*
    Zamacois, Eduardo

ZAOUROU, BERNARD ZADI. *See* Zadi Zaourou,
    Bernard

ZARATE, ANTONIO GIL Y. *See* Gil y Zárate, Antonio

ZAUNER, FRIEDRICH CH., 1936–
    *A Handful of Earth.* 1996.
    Bernelle, A., and Mattivi, J., translators LAX
    Variant title: *Land*
    *Land. See* A Handful of Earth

ZAYAS Y SOTOMAYOR, MARIA DE, 1590–1661
    *La traction en la Amistad.* 1628–1632. SOSGA

ZEAMI, 1363–1443
    *Aoi no Uye* (sometimes attributed to). *See* Zenchiku,
      Ujinobu. *Aoi no Uye.*
    *Ashikara. See* The Reed Cutter
    *Atsumori.* 14th century
    Brazell, K., translator BRAZ
    Shimazaki, C., translator SHIM2
    Tyler, R., translator TYLJ
    Waley, A., translator ANDI, BOGA, NORJ1, TAV,
      WAJ, YOHA, YOHB
    Yasuda, K., translator YASU
    *Aya no tsuzumi. See* The Damask Drum
    *The Boat Bridge.*
    Shimazaki, C., translator SHIM4, book 1
    Tyler, R., translator TYLP
    Variant title: *Funabashi*
    *The Brocade Tree.*
    French, C., translator KEE

Pound, E., translator NOH
    Variant title: *Nishikigi*
*Cormorant Plumes. See* Unoha
*The Damask Drum.*
    Tyler, R., translator TYLJ
    Waley, A., translator ROSENB, WAJ
    Variant title: *Aya no tsuzumi*
*The Deserted Crone.*
    Jones, S., translator ANDI, KEE
    Shimazaki, C., translator SHIM3, book 2
    Yasuda, K., translator YASU
    Variant titles: *Obasute; Mt. Obasute*
*The Dwarf Trees.*
    Waley, A., translator ANDI, PATM, PATP, WAJ
    Variant title: *Hachi no ki*
*Eguchi.* 14th century
    Tyler, R., translator TYLJ
*The Fulling Block.* Pound, E., translator NOH
    Tyler, R., translator TYLJ, TYLP
    Variant titles: *The Block; Kinuta*
*Funabashi. See* The Boat Bridge
*Futari Shizuka* (attributed to).
    Shimazaki, C., translator SHIM3, book 3
    Variant title: *The Two Shizukas*
*Granny Mountains. See* Yamamba
*Hachi no ki. See* The Dwarf Trees
*Hagoromo.*
    Waley, A., translator WAJ
*Haku Rakuten.* 14th century
    Waley, A., translator ANDF, NORJ1, WAJ
*Hanjo. See* Lady Han
*Higaki.* 14th century
    Yasuda, K., translator YASU
*Hotoke no hara* (attributed to).
    Shimazaki, C., translator SHIM3, book 3
    Waley, A., translator WAJ (excerpts)
*Hyakuman. See* Million
*Ikeniye.*
    Waley, A., translator WAJ
*The Imperial Visit to Ohara* (attributed to).
    Hochstedler, C., translator KEE
    Shimazaki, C., translator SHIM3, book 3
    Variant title: *Ohara gokō*
*Iris. See* Kakitsubata
*Iris, The. See* Kakitsubata
*Izutsu. See* The Well-cradle
*Kagekiyo.*
    Anonymous translator WOLCS
    Pound, E., translator NOH
    Waley, A., translator WAJ
*Kakitsubata.* 14th century (attributed to)
    Klein, S., translator BRAZT
    Pound, E., translator NOH
    Shimazaki, C., translator SHIM3, book 2
    Variant titles: *Iris; The Iris*

Variant titles: *Granny Mountains; The Mountain Crone*
*Yashima.*
   Shimazaki, C., translator SHIM2, book 2
   Tyler, R., translator TYLJ, TYLP
*Yorimasa.*
   Shimazaki, C., translator SHIM2, book 2
   Tyler, R., translator TYLG
*Yoro.*
   Shimazaki, C., translator SHIM1
*Yuya* (attributed to).
   Shimazaki, C., translator SHIM2, book 3
   *See also* Kanami, joint author
   *See also* Seiami, Michimori (revised by)

ZEAMI MOTOKIYO. *See* Zeami

ZEITLIN, ISRAEL, 1906–1975. *See* Tiempo, Cesar, pseudonym

ZELL, ALLISON EVE
*Come to Leave.* 1994. WOMP94

ZEMBO, MOTOYASU, 1453–1532
*Atsumori at Ikuta.*
   Waley, A., translator ANDF
   Variant titles: *Ikuta; Ikuta Atsumori*
*Early Snow.*
   Waley, A., translator ANDF, ANDI, KINNS
   Variant title: *Hatsuyuki*
*Hatsuyuki. See* Early Snow
*Ikkaku sennin.* 1524.
   Hoff, F., translator BRA
   Irwin, V., translator IRW
   Variant title: *The Holy Hermit Unicorn*
*Ikuta. See* Atsumori at Ikuta
*Ikuta Atsumori. See* Atsumori at Ikuta

ZENCHIKU KOMPARU-. *See* Komparu-Zenchiku

ZENCHIKU UJINOBU, 1414–1499?
*Aoi no Uye* (sometimes attributed to Seami Motokiyo; adapted from Genji Monogatari (*Romance of Genji or Tale of Genji*) by Lady Murasaki Shikubu, 1004 A.D.). 15th century
   Pound, E., translator NOH
   Walcy, A., translator ANDF, ANDI, WAJ
   Variant titles: *Awoi no uye; Lady Aoi; Princess Hollyhock*
*Awoi no uye. See* Aoi no Uye
*The Hoka Priests.*
   Waley, A., translator WAJ

*Kumasaka.*
   Pound, E., translator NOH
   Waley, A., translator WAJ
*Lady Aoi. See* Aoi no Uye
*Princess Hollyhock. See* Aoi no Uye
*Taniko* (attributed to).
   Waley, A., translator WAJ

ZEPHANIAH, BENJAMIN, 1958–
*Job Rocking.* 1987. BREW2

ZHEMCHUZHNIKOV, ALEKSANDR MIKHAILOVICH, 1826–1896.
   *See* Prutkov, Koz'ma, pseudonym

ZHEMCHUZHNIKOV, ALEKSEI MIKHAILOVICH, 1821–1908.
   *See* Prutkov, Koz'ma, pseudonym

ZHEMCHUZHNIKOV, VLADIMIR MIKHAILOVICH, 1830–1884.
   *See* Prutkov, Koz'ma, pseudonym

ZHENG, YI, 1947–
*Laojing. See* Old Well
*Old Well* (screenplay). 1986.
   Yu, S., translator THC
   Variant title: *Laojing*

ZHOU, WEI-BO. *See* Chou, Wei-Po

ZHU, XIAOPING, 1952– . *See* Chen, Zidu, joint author

ZIMMER, HANS, 1957–
*The Lion King* (additional music and lyrics by). *See* Allers, Roger. *The Lion King*

ZINDEL, BONNIE, 1943– , and ZINDEL, PAUL, joint authors
*Lemons in the Morning.* 1982. *See* Anonymous plays. *Twenty-four Hours: A.M.*

ZINDEL, PAUL, 1936–2003
*The Effect of Gamma Rays on Man-in-the-moon Marigolds.* 1970. BARK, BARKA, BES69, BEST, DIEB, HAVL, OBG
   — *See* Zindel, Bonnie, joint author

ZINDIKA
*Leonora's Dance.* 1992. GEOR

ZINN, HOWARD, 1922–2010
*Emma.* 1976. KLEIN

ZINSOU, SENOUVO AGBOTA, 1946–
  *The Singing Tortoise.* 1986.
    Brewster, T., translator AFRUBU2
    Variant title: *La tortue qui chante*
  *La tortue qui chante. See* The Singing Tortoise
  *Yevi's Adventures in Monsterland.* 1988.
    Brounon, D., translator AFRUBU2

ZIPPEL, DAVID, 1954–
  *City of Angels* (music by). *See* Gelbart, Larry. *City of
    Angels*

ZĪVERTS, MĀRTINS, 1903–1990
  *Mad Christopher, Mad; a Northern Legend in Seven
    Scenes.* 1960.
    Straumanis, A., translator and adapter CONF
    Variant titles: *The ore; Rūda*
  *The ore. See* Mad Christopher, Mad, a Northern Legend
    in Seven Scenes
  *Power.* 1945. Straumanis, A., translator FIFFN
    Variant title: *Vara*
  *Rūda. See* Mad Christopher, Mad; a Northern Legend in
    Seven Scenes
  *Vara. See* Power

ZOGRAFI, VLAD, 1955–
  *Peter or The Sun Spots.* 1996?
    Solomon, A., translator POQ

ZOLA, EMILE, 1840–1902
  *Thérèse Raquin.* 1873.
    Boutall, K., translator BENS3, HOUP
    Parsell, S., translator HILPDH4

ZORIN, LEONID, 1924–
  *The Guests.* 1953.
    Langen, T., and Weir, J., translators EIGHTRP

ZORRILLA, FRANCISCO DE ROJAS. *See* Rojas
  Zorrilla, Francisco de

ZORRILLA Y MORAL, JOSE, 1817–1893
  *Don Juan Tenorio.* 1844. BRET, MARLIN, TRES
    Oliver, W., translator MARJ

ZOSHCHENKO, MIKHAIL, 1895–1958
  *Crime and Punishment: A Comedy in One Act.* 1933.
    Rzhevsky, N., translator RZH

ZUBER, RON
  *Three X Love.* KINH, KINHB

ZUCKMAYER, CARL, 1896–1977
  *The Captain from Koepenick. See* The Captain of
    Köpenick.
  *The Captain of Köpenick.* 1931
    Mueller, C., translator WELG
    Variant titles: *The Captain from Koepenick; Der
      Hauptmann von Koepenick*
  *The Devil's General.* 1946.
    Gilbert, I., and W., translators BLOC
    Variant title: *Des Teufels General*
  *Der Hauptmann von Koepenick. See* The Captain of
    Köpenick
  *Des Teufels General. See* The Devil's General

ZUSY, JEANNIE
  *Kicking Inside.* 1996. WOMP96

ZWEIG, STEFAN, 1881–1942
  *Volpone* (adapted from the play by Ben Jonson).
    Langner, R., translator GARZH

ZYLIN, SVETLANA, 1948–2002
  *Obsidian.* 1995. BREK
  *Taking Care of Numero Uno.* 1997. BREK

# List of Collections Analyzed and Key to Symbols

ABCA Abcarian, Richard, and Klotz, Marvin, eds.
Literature: The Human Experience. New York: St.
Martin's, 1973. 971pp.
Bergman, I. The Seventh Seal
Everyman
Ibsen, H. An Enemy of the People
Lowell, R. Benito Cereno
Molière, J. The Misanthrope
Shakespeare, W. Othello
Shaw, G. Major Barbara
Sophocles. Antigone

ABCB Abcarian, Richard, and Klotz, Marvin, eds.
Literature: The Human Experience. 2nd ed. New
York: St. Martin's, 1978. 1180pp.
Bergman, I. The Seventh Seal
Everyman
Ibsen, H. A Doll's House
Ionesco, E. The Lesson
Molière, J. The Misanthrope
O'Neill, E. Desire under the Elms
Pinter, H. The Dumb Waiter
Shakespeare, W. Othello
Sophocles. Antigone
Sophocles. Oedipus Rex
Williams, T. The Glass Menagerie

ABCC Abcarian, Richard, and Klotz, Marvin, eds.
Literature: The Human Experience. 3rd ed. New
York: St. Martin's, 1982. 1260pp.
Allen, W. Death Knocks
Bergman, I. The Seventh Seal
Chekhov, A. The Brute
Ibsen, H. A Doll's House
Ionesco, E. The Lesson
Pinter, H. The Dumb Waiter
Shakespeare, W. Othello
Shaw, G. Pygmalion

Sophocles. Antigone
Sophocles. Oedipus Rex
Williams, T. The Glass Menagerie

ABCD Abcarian, Richard, and Klotz, Marvin, eds.
Literature: The Human Experience. 4th ed. New
York: St. Martin's, 1986. 1405pp.
Allen, W. Death Knocks
Bergman, I. The Seventh Seal
Ibsen, H. A Doll's House
Kopit, A. End of the World
Miller, A. Death of a Salesman
Molière, J. The Misanthrope
O'Casey, S. The Shadow of a Gunman
Shakespeare, W. Othello
Shaw, G. Pygmalion
Sophocles. Antigone
Sophocles. Oedipus Rex
Strindberg, A. The Stronger
Williams, T. The Glass Menagerie

ABCE Abcarian, Richard, and Klotz, Marvin, eds.
Literature: The Human Experience. 5th ed. New
York: St. Martin's, 1990. 1379pp.
Albee, E. Who's Afraid of Virginia Woolf?
Allen, W. Death Knocks
Baraka, I. Dutchman
Chikamatsu, M. The Love Suicides at Sonezaki
Friedman, B. Steambath
Fugard, A. "Master Harold" . . . and the Boys
Glaspell, S. Trifles
Ibsen, H. A Doll's House
Miller, A. Death of a Salesman
Shakespeare, W. Othello
Sophocles. Antigone
Sophocles. Oedipus Rex
Strindberg, A. The Stronger
Williams, T. The Glass Menagerie

ABCF Abcarian, Richard, and Klotz, Marvin, eds.
    *Literature: The Human Experience.* 6th ed. New
    York: St. Martin's, 1994. 1397pp.
  Allen, W. *Death Knocks*
  Baraka, I. *Dutchman*
  Fierstein, H. *Widows and Children First!*
  Friedman, B. *Steambath*
  Gems, P. *Loving Women*
  Glaspell, S. *Trifles*
  Hwang, D. *M. Butterfly*
  Ibsen, H. *An Enemy of the People*
  Sartre, J. *No Exit*
  Shakespeare, W. *Othello*
  Shaw, G. *Major Barbara*
  Sophocles. *Antigone*
  Sophocles. *Oedipus Rex*


ABCG Abcarian, Richard, and Klotz, Marvin, eds.
    *Literature: Reading and Writing, The Human
    Experience.* 7th ed. New York: St. Martin's, 1998.
    1460pp.
  Allen, W. *Death Knocks*
  Childress, A. *Wine in the Wilderness*
  Fierstein, H. *On Tidy Endings*
  Fugard, A. *"Master Harold" . . . and the Boys*
  Glaspell, S. *Trifles*
  Hwang, D. *M. Butterfly*
  Ibsen, H. *A Doll's House*
  Miller, A. *Death of a Salesman*
  Shakespeare, W. *Othello*
  Sophocles. *Antigone*
  Sophocles. *Oedipus Rex*
  Williams, T. *The Glass Menagerie*
  Wilson, A. *Two Trains Running*


ABCH Abcarian, Richard, and Klotz, Marvin, eds.
    *Literature: Reading and Writing, The Human
    Experience.* Shorter 7th ed. New York: Bedford/St.
    Martin's, 2000. 1192pp.
  Fierstein, H. *On Tidy Endings*
  Glaspell, S. *Trifles*
  Hansberry, L. *A Raisin in the Sun*
  Hwang, D. *M. Butterfly*
  Ibsen, H. *A Doll's House*
  Shakespeare, W. *Othello*
  Sophocles. *Antigone*
  Williams, T. *The Glass Menagerie*


ABL Abdel Wahab, Farouk, comp. *Modern Egyptian
    Drama: An Anthology* / Farouk Abdel Wahab.
    Minneapolis, Biblioteca Islamica, 1974. 493pp.
    (Studies in Middle Eastern Literature; No. 3)
  al-Hakim, T. *The Sultan's Dilemma*
  Idris, Y. *The Farfoors*

  Roman, M. *The New Arrival*
  Rushdy, R. *A Journey outside the W*all


ABRA Abrams, Meyer Howard; Donaldson, E. Talbot;
    Smith, Hallett; Adams, Robert M.; Monk, Samuel
    Holt; Ford, George H. and Daiches; David, eds.
    *The Norton Anthology of English Literature*; Major
    Authors Edition. New York: W. W. Norton [c1962]
    2024pp.
  Dryden, J. *The Secular Masque*
  Jonson, B. *The Vision of Delight*
  Shakespeare, W. *King Henry the Fourth, Part I*
  Shaw, G. *Arms and the Man*


ABRB Abrams, Meyer Howard; Donaldson, E. Talbot;
    Smith, Hallett; Adams, Robert M.; Monk, Samuel
    Holt; Ford, George H. and Daiches, David, eds. *The
    Norton Anthology of English Literature.* New York:
    W. W. Norton [ca. 1962] 2 vols.
  Congreve, W. *The Way of the World* 1
  *Everyman* 1
  Jonson, B. *The Vision of Delight* 1
  Marlowe, C. *The Tragical History of the Life and Death
    of Doctor Faustus* 1
  *The Second Shepherds' Play* 1
  Shakespeare, W. *King Henry the Fourth, Part I* 1
  Shaw, G. *Arms and the Man* 2
  Sheridan, R. *The School for Scandal* 1


ABRE Abrams, Meyer Howard, et al., eds. *The Norton
    Anthology of English Literature.* Rev. ed. New
    York: Norton [ca. 1968] 2658pp.
  Dryden, J. *The Secular Masque*
  Jonson, B. *Vision of Delight*
  Shakespeare, W. *Henry IV, Part I*
  Shaw, G. *Arms and the Man*


ABRF Abrams, Meyer Howard, ed. *The Norton Anthology
    of English Literature.* Rev. ed. New York: Norton,
    1968. 2 vols.
  Congreve, W. *The Way of the World* 1
  Dryden, J. *The Secular Masque* 1
  *Everyman* 1
  Jonson, B. *The Vision of Delight* 1
  Marlowe, C. *Dr. Faustus* 1
  *Second Shepherds' Play* 1
  Shakespeare, W. *Henry IV, Part I* 1
  Shaw, G. *Arms and the Man* 2


ABRH Abrams, Meyer Howard, ed. *The Norton Anthology
    of English Literature.* 3rd ed. New York: W. W.
    Norton, 1974. 2 vols.
  *The Brome Play of Abraham and Isaac* 1
  Congreve, W. *The Way of the World* 1
  Dryden, J. *The Secular Masque* 1
  *Everyman* 1

Jonson, B. *Pleasure Reconciled to Virtue* 1
Marlowe, C. *Dr. Faustus* 1
*The Second Shepherds' Play* 1
Shakespeare, W. *Henry IV, Part. I* 1
Shakespeare, W. *King Lear* 1
Shaw, G. *Major Barbara* 2
Webster, J. *The Duchess of Malfi* 1

ABRJ Abrams, Meyer Howard, ed. *The Norton Anthology of English Literature.* 4th ed. New York: W. W. Norton, 1979. 2 vols.
Byron, G. *Manfred* 2
Congreve, W. *Love for Love* 1
Dryden, J. *The Secular Masque* 1
*Everyman* 1
Jonson, B. *Pleasure Reconciled to Virtue* 1
Jonson, B. *Volpone* 1
Marlowe, C. *Dr. Faustus* 1
Pinter, H. *The Dumb Waiter* 2
*The Second Shepherds' Play* 1
Shakespeare, W. *Henry IV, Part I* 1
Shakespeare, W. *King Lear* 1
Shaw, G. *Mrs. Warren's Profession* 2
Webster, J. *The Duchess of Malfi* 1
Wilde, O. *The Importance of Being Earnest* 2

ABRK Abrams, Meyer Howard, ed. *The Norton Anthology of English Literature.* 5th ed. New York: W. W. Norton, 1986. 2 vols.
Beckett, S. *Happy Days* 2
Byron, G. *Manfred* 2
Congreve, W. *The Way of the World* 1
Dryden, J. *The Secular Masque* 1
*Everyman* 1
Jonson, B. *Pleasure Reconciled to Virtue* 1
Jonson, B. *Volpone* 1
Marlowe, C. *Dr. Faustus* 1
Pinter, H. *The Dumb Waiter* 2
*The Second Shepherds' Play* 1
Shakespeare, W. *Henry IV, Part I* 1
Shakespeare, W. *King Lear* 1
Shaw, G. *Mrs. Warren's Profession* 2
Webster, J. *The Duchess of Malfi* 1
Wilde, O. *The Importance of Being Earnest* 2
*The York Play of the Crucifixion* 1

ABRL Abrams, Meyer Howard, ed. *The Norton Anthology of English Literature.* 6th ed. New York: W. W. Norton, 1993. 2 vols.
Beckett, S. *Happy Days* 2
Byron, G. *Manfred* 2
*The Chester Play of Noah's Flood* 1
Congreve, W. *The Way of the World* 1
Dryden, J. *The Secular Masque* 1
*Everyman* 1
Jonson, B. *Pleasure Reconciled to Virtue* 1

Jonson, B. *Volpone* 1
Marlowe, C. *Dr. Faustus* 1
Pinter, H. *The Dumb Waiter* 2
Shakespeare, W. *Henry IV, Part I* 1
Shakespeare, W. *King Lear* 1
Shaw, G. *Mrs. Warren's Profession* 2
Stoppard, T. *The Real Inspector Hound* 2
*The Wakefield Second Shepherds' Play* 1
Webster, J. *The Duchess of Malfi* 1
Wilde, O. *The Importance of Being Earnest* 2

ABRM Abrams, Meyer Howard, and Greenblatt, Stephen, eds. *The Norton Anthology of English Literature.* 7th ed. New York: W. W. Norton, 2000. 2 vols.
Beckett, S. *Endgame* 2
Byron, G. *Manfred* 2
Cary, E. *The Tragedy of Mariam, the Faire Queene of Jewry* (excerpts) 1
*The Chester Play of Noah's Flood* 1
Congreve, W. *The Way of the World* 1
*Everyman* 1
Gay, J. *The Beggar's Opera* 1
Jonson, B. *The Masque of Blackness* 1
Jonson, B. *Volpone* 1
Marlowe, C. *Dr. Faustus* 1
Pinter, H. *The Dumb Waiter* 2
Shakespeare, W. *King Lear* 1
Shakespeare, W. *Twelfth Night* 1
Shaw, G. *Mrs. Warren's Profession* 2
Shelley, P. *Prometheus Unbound* (excerpts) 2
Stoppard, T. *The Real Inspector Hound* 2
*The Wakefield Second Shepherds' Play* 1
Webster, J. *The Duchess of Malfi* 1
Wilde, O. *The Importance of Being Earnest* 2

ACE *Access to Literature: Understanding Fiction, Drama, and Poetry*; ed. by Elliott L. Smith and Wanda V. Smith. New York: St. Martin's Press, 1981. 819pp.
Chekhov, A. *A Marriage Proposal*
Glaspell, S. *Trifles*
Holcroft, T. *A Tale of Mystery*
Ionesco, E. *The Gap*
Miller, A. *A Memory of Two Mondays*
Shakespeare, W. *Othello*
Sophocles. *Oedipus Rex*
Ward, D. *Day of Absence*
Wilde, O. *The Importance of Being Earnest*

ACTOR *Actor's Book of Gay and Lesbian Plays*; ed. by Eric Lane and Nina Shengold. New York: Penguin Books, 1995. 344pp.
Bumbalo, V. *What Are Tuesdays Like?*
Chafee, C. *Why We Have a Body*
Congdon, C. *Dog Opera*
Curran, K. *The Stand-in*
Dietz, S. *The Lonely Planet*

Eisenstein, L. *At the Root*
Five Lesbian Brothers, The. *Brave Smiles . . . another Lesbian Tragedy*
Lane, E. *Cater-waiter*
Lucas, C. *Bad Dream*
Miller, S. *It's Our Town, Too*
Moraga, C. *Giving up the Ghost*
Nyswaner, R. *Reservoir*
Pintauro, J. *Rosen's Son*
Sanchez, E. *Trafficking in Broken Hearts*
Scheffer, W. *Falling Man*
Vogel, P. *The Baltimore Waltz*
Youngblood, S. *There Are Many Houses in My Tribe*

ADA Adams, Joseph Quincy, ed. *Chief Pre-Shakespearean Dramas.* Boston: Houghton Mifflin [ca. 1924] 712pp.
*Banns*
*The Betraying of Christ*
*The Birth of Jesus*
*The Castle of Perseverance*
*Christ's Ministry*
*The Conversion of St. Paul*
*The Creation of Eve, with the Expelling of Adam and Eve Out of Paradise*
*The Deluge*
*Duk Moraud*
Edwards, R. *Damon and Pithias*
*Everyman*
*The Fall of Lucifer*
*The Famous Victories of Henry the Fifth*
*Gammer Gurton's Nedle*
Gascoygne, G. *Supposes*
*George a Greene, the Pinner of Wakefield*
*The Harrowing of Hell*
Heywood, J. *A Mery Play betwene Johan Johan, the Husband, Tyb His Wife and Syr Johan the Preest*
Heywood, J. *The Playe Called the Four pp*
Heywood, J. *The Play of the Wether*
*The Judgment Day*
*The Killing of Abel*
*Leicestershire St. George Play*
Lyly, J. *Campaspe*
*The Magi, Herod, and the Slaughter of the Innocents*
*Mankind*
*Mary Magdalene*
*Noah*
Norton, T., and Sackville, T. *Gorboduc; or, Ferrex and Porrex*
*Oxfordshire St. George Play*
*Pharaoh*
*The Play of the Sacrament*
Preston, T. *Cambises, King of Persia*
*The Prophets*
*The Resurrection of Christ*

*The Revesby Sword Play*
*Robin Hood and the Friar*
*Robin Hood and the Sheriff of Nottingham*
*The Sacrifice of Isaac*
*The Salutation and Conception*
*The Shepherds*
*Shetland Sword Dance*
*The Trial of Christ*
Udall, N. *Roister Doister*
*Wyt and Science*

ADAP *Adaptations of Shakespeare: A Critical Anthology of Plays from the Seventeenth Century to the Present.* Edited by Daniel Fischlin and Mark Fortier. London and New York: Routledge, 2000. 320pp.
Brecht, B. *The Resistable Rise of Arturo Ui*
Fletcher, J. *The Woman's Prize; or the Tamer Tamed*
Garcia Lorca, F. *The Public (El publico)*
Keats, J. *King Stephen: A Dramatic Fragment*
Marowitz, C. *Measure for Measure*
Msomi, W. *uMabatha*
Müller, H. *Hamletmachine*
Osment, P. *This Island's Mine*
Sears, D. *Harlem Duet*
Tate, N. *The History of King Lear*
Vogel, P. *Desdemona: A Play about a Handkerchief*
The Women's Theatre Group and Feinstein, E. *Lear's Daughters*

ADV *Adventures in World Literature,* [by] James Earl Applegate [and Others] Classic Edition. New York: Harcourt, Brace, Jovanovich, 1970. 1046pp.
Ibsen, H. *An Enemy of the People*
Molière, J. *The Misanthrope*
Shakespeare, W. *The Tempest*
Sophocles. *Antigone*

AFR *African Plays for Playing*; selected and edited by Michael Etherton. London: Heinemann, 1975–1976. 2 vols. (African Writers Series).
Ajibade, S. *Rakinyo* 1
Hevi, J. *Amavi* 1
Kasoma, G. *Black Mamba Two* 2
Musinga, V. *The Tragedy of Mr. No-Balance* 2
Sentongo, N. *The Invisible Bond* 1
Udensi, U. *Monkey on the Tree* 2

AFRUBU *Afrique: New Plays.* New York: Ubu Repertory Theater Publications, 1987–1991. 2 vols. Vol. 1 New Plays: Congo, Ivory Coast, Senegal, Zaire. Vol. 2. New Plays. Madagascar, Mauretania, Togo.
Diagana, M. *The Legend of Wagadu: As Seen by Sia Yataere* 2
Efoui, J. *The Crossroads* 2

Ka, A. *The Daughter of the Gods* 1
N'Debeka, M. *Equatorium* 1
N'Tumb, D. *Lost Voices* 1
Rafenomanjato, C. *The Herd* 2
Raharimanana, J. *The Prophet and the President* 2
Sony Lab'ou Tansi. *The Second Ark* 1
Zadi Zaourou, B. *The Eye* 1
Zinsou, S. *The Singing Tortoise* 2
Zinsou, S. *Yevi's Adventures in Monsterland* 2

AFTAP *After Apocalypse: Four Japanese Plays of Hiroshima and Nagasaki*. Selected and translated by David G. Goodman. New York: Columbia University Press, 1986. 325pp.
Betsuyaku, M. *The Elephant*
Hotta, K. *The Island*
Satoh, M. *Nezumi kozo: The Rat*
Tanaka, C. *The Head of Mary: A Nagasaki Fantasia*

AGOR Agoro, S.N.A., ed. *Generous Donors: A Dramatic Expose on AIDS and Other Plays*. Port Harcourt, Nigeria: Linnet Paul Publications, 1997. 138pp.
Adesina, F. *A Nest in a Cage*
Agoro, S. *Co-tenants*
Johnson, E. *Generous Donors*

ALD Aldington, Richard, ed. *French Comedies of the XVIIIth Century*. London: Routledge [1923] 347pp.
Destouches, P. *The Conceited Count*
Le Sage, A. *Turcaret; or, the Financier*
Marivaux, P. *The Game of Love and Chance*
Regnard, J. *The Residuary Legatee*

ALG Algarin, Miguel, and Griffith, Lois, eds. *Action: The Nuyorican Poets Café Theater Festival*. New York: Simon & Schuster, 1997.
Astor del Valle, J. *Transplantations: Straight and Other Jackets para Mi*
Baraka, A. *The Election Machine Warehouse*
Baraka, A. *Primitive World: An Anti-nuclear Jazz Musical*
Brown, W. *Life during Wartime*
Eng, A. *The Goong Hay Kid*
Feliciano, G. *Between Blessings*
Gasteazoro, E. *Amor de mis amores*
Griffith, L. *White Sirens*
Moritz, D. *Just the Boys*
Perez, F. *Estorias del Barrio: Special People of International Character*
Pietri, P. *El cabron*
Pinero, M. *Playland Blues*
Reed, I. *Hubba City*
Reed, I. *The Preacher and the Rapper*
Reed, I. *Savage Wilds*
Rodriguez, E. *Estorias del Barrio: un ghost*

Rux, C. *Chapter & Verse* (a poem in progress)
Shange, N. *I Live in Music* (a work in progress)
Spiro, P. *Howya Doin' Freaky Banana?*
Wright, G., and Sebazco, R. *The Crime*

ALI Alive Theatre Workshop. *Dialogue and Dialectic: A Canadian Anthology of Short Plays*. Guelph, Ontario: Alive Press [1972] 199pp.
Bullock, M. *Not to Hong Kong*
Farmiloe, D. *What Do You Save from a Burning Building?*
Gilbert, S. *A Glass Darkly*
Leeds, C. *The Love Song of Rotten John Calabrese*
Libman, C. *Follow the Leader*
Pluta, L. *Little Guy Napoleon*
Russell, L. *Penetration*
Spensley, P. *Hell's Bells*
Szablowski, J. *Subsidiary Vice-president*

ALL Allen, John, ed. *Four Continental Plays*. London: Heinemann [1964] 149pp.
Chekhov, A. *A Wedding*
Kleist, H. *The Broken Jug*
Niccodemi, D. *The Poet*
Pirandello, L. *The Jar*

ALLE Allen, John, ed. *Three Medieval Plays*. London, Heineman [ca. 1953] 54pp.
*The Farce of Master Pierre Pathelin*
*The Pageant of the Shearmen and Taylors*
*The Summoning of Everyman*

ALLI Allison, Alexander W.; Carr, Arthur J.; and Eastman, Arthur M., eds. *Masterpieces of the Drama*. New York: Macmillan [ca. 1957] 693pp.
Chekhov, A. *The Cherry Orchard*
Euripides. *Alcestis*
García Lorca, F. *The House of Bernarda Alba*
Giraudoux, J. *The Madwoman of Chaillot*
Ibsen, H. *Hedda Gabler*
Jonson, B. *Volpone; or, the Fox*
Molière, J. *The Miser*
O'Casey, S. *Juno and the Paycock*
Sheridan, R. *The Rivals*
Sophocles. *Oedipus Rex*
Synge, J. *Riders to the Sea*

ALLJ Allison, Alexander Ward; Carr, Arthur J.; and Eastman, Arthur M., eds. *Masterpieces of the Drama*. 2nd ed. New York: Macmillan [1966] 814pp.
Beckett, S. *Act without Words*
Beckett, S. *All that Fall*
Brecht, B. *The Caucasian Chalk Circle*
Chekhov, A. *The Cherry Orchard*

Euripides. *The Bacchae*
García Lorca, F. *The House of Bernarda Alba*
Giraudoux, J. *The Madwoman of Chaillot*
Ibsen, H. *Hedda Gabler*
Jonson, B. *Volpone; or, the Fox*
Molière, J. *The Miser*
O'Casey, S. *Juno and the Paycock*
Sheridan, R. *The Rivals*
Sophocles. *Oedipus*
Synge, J. *Riders to the Sea*

ALLK Allison, Alexander Ward; Carr, Arthur J.; and
Eastman, Arthur M., eds. *Masterpieces of the
Drama.* 3rd ed. New York: Macmillan, 1974. 937pp.
Aeschylus. *Agamemnon*
Aristophanes. *Lysistrata*
Beckett, S. *Act without Words*
Beckett, S. *All that Fall*
Brecht, B. *Good Woman of Setzuan*
Chekhov, A. *The Cherry Orchard*
Congreve, W. *The Way of the World*
Davis, O. *Purlie Victorious*
Euripides. *The Bacchae*
García Lorca, F. *The House of Bernarda Alba*
Giraudoux, J. *The Madwoman of Chaillot*
Ibsen, H. *Hedda Gabler*
Jones, L. *The Toilet*
Jonson, B. *Volpone; or, the Fox*
Miller, A. *Death of a Salesman*
Molière, J. *The Miser*
O'Casey, S. *Juno and the Paycock*
O'Neill, E. *Desire under the Elms*
Pirandello, L. *Six Characters in Search of an Author*
Racine, J. *Phaedra*
*The Second Shepherds' Play*
Shaw, G. *Saint Joan*
Sheridan, R. *The Rivals*
Sophocles. *Oedipus Rex*
Strindberg, A. *The Ghost Sonata*
Synge, J. *Riders to the Sea*
Webster, J. *The Duchess of Malfi*
Wycherley, W. *The Country Wife*

ALLM Allison, Alexander W., Carr, Arthur J., and Eastman,
Arthur M., eds. *Masterpieces of the Drama.* 4th ed.
New York: Macmillan, 1979. 985pp.
Aeschylus. *Agamemnon*
Aristophanes. *Lysistrata*
Beckett, S. *Act without Words*
Beckett, S. *All that Fall*
Brecht, B. *The Good Woman of Setzuan*
Chekhov, A. *The Cherry Orchard*
Euripides. *The Bacchae*
García Lorca, F. *The House of Bernarda Alba*
Ibsen, H. *Hedda Gabler*

Jones, L. *Dutchman*
Jonson, B. *Volpone; or, the Fox*
Miller, A. *Death of a Salesman*
Molière, J. *The Miser*
O'Casey, S. *Juno and the Paycock*
O'Neill, E. *Desire under the Elms*
Pirandello, L. *Six Characters in Search of an Author*
Racine, J. *Phaedra*
*The Second Shepherds' Play*
Shakespeare, W. *Henry IV, Part 1*
Shaffer, P. *Equus*
Shaw, G. *Saint Joan*
Sheridan, R. *The Rivals*
Sophocles. *Oedipus Rex*
Strindberg, A. *Ghost Sonata*
Synge, J. *Riders to the Sea*
Webster, J. *Duchess of Malfi*
Wilde, O. *The Importance of Being Earnest*
Williams, T. *The Glass Menagerie*
Wycherley, W. *The Country Wife*

ALLN Allison, Alexander W., Carr, Arthur J., and
Eastman, Arthur M., eds. *Masterpieces of the
Drama.* 5th ed. New York: Macmillan, 1986.
995pp.
Aeschylus. *Agamemnon*
Aristophanes. *Lysistrata*
Baraka, I. *Dutchman*
Beckett, S. *All that Fall*
Brecht, B. *The Good Woman of Setzuan*
Chekhov, A. *The Cherry Orchard*
Euripides. *The Bacchae*
Fugard, A., Kani, J., and Ntshona, W. *Siswe Bansi Is
Dead*
García Lorca, F. *The House of Bernarda Alba*
Ibsen, H. *Hedda Gabler*
Jonson, B. *Volpone; or, the Fox*
Miller, A. *Death of a Salesman*
Molière, J. *Tartuffe*
O'Casey, S. *Juno and the Paycock*
O'Neill, E. *Desire under the Elms*
Pinter, H. *The Caretaker*
Pirandello, L. *Six Characters in Search of an Author*
Racine, J. *Phaedra*
*The Second Shepherds' Play*
Shaffer, P. *Equus*
Shakespeare, W. *Othello*
Shaw, G. *Saint Joan*
Sheridan, R. *The Rivals*
Sophocles. *Oedipus Rex*
Strindberg, A. *Miss Julie*
Synge, J. *Riders to the Sea*
Wilde, O. *The Importance of Being Earnest*
Williams, T. *The Glass Menagerie*
Wycherley, W. *The Country Wife*

ALLO Allison, Alexander W., Carr, Arthur J., and
Eastman, Arthur M., eds. *Masterpieces of the
Drama*. 6th ed. New York: Macmillan, 1991.
1036pp.
Aeschylus. *Agamemnon*
Aristophanes. *Lysistrata*
Beckett, S. *All that Fall*
Brecht, B. *The Good Woman of Setzuan*
Chekhov, A. *The Cherry Orchard*
Churchill, C. *Top Girls*
Euripides. *Medea*
Fugard, A., Kani, J., and Ntshona, W. *Siswe Bansi Is
Dead*
Gregory, I. *The Gaol Gate*
Hansberry, L. *A Raisin in the Sun*
Ibsen, H. *Hedda Gabler*
Jonson, B. *Volpone; or, the Fox*
Miller, A. *Death of a Salesman*
Molière, J. *Tartuffe*
O'Casey, S. *Juno and the Paycock*
O'Neill, E. *Desire under the Elms*
Pinter, H. *The Caretaker*
Pirandello, L. *Six Characters in Search of an Author*
Racine, J. *Phaedra*
*The Second Shepherds' Play*
Shakespeare, W. *Othello*
Shaw, G. *Pygmalion*
Sheridan, R. *The Rivals*
Sophocles. *Oedipus Rex*
Stoppard, T. *Travesties*
Strindberg, A. *Miss Julie*
Synge, J. *Riders to the Sea*
Wilde, O. *The Importance of Being Earnest*
Williams, T. *The Glass Menagerie*
Wycherley, W. *The Country Wife*

ALONG *Along Human Lines: Dramas from Refugee Lives*.
Winnipeg and Niagara Falls: Blizzard Publishing,
2000. 157pp.
Aguirre, C., and The Latino Theatre Group. *¿Que pasa
with La Raza, eh?*
Lambert, A. *Parallel Lines*
Seremba, G. *Come Good Rain*

ALP Alpern, Hymen, and Martel, José, eds. *Diez comedies
del siglo de oro*. New York: Harper [ca. 1939]
859pp.
Calderón de la Barca, P. *La vida es sueño*
Castro y Bellvis, G. *Las mocedades del Cid*
Cervantes Saavedra, M. *La Numancia*
Mira de Amescua, A. *El esclavo del demonio*
Moreto y Cabaña, A. *El desdén con el desdén*
Rojas Zorrilla, F. *Del rey abajo, ninguno*
Ruiz de Alarcón y Mendoza, J. *La verdad sospechosa*
Téllez, G. *El burlador de Sevilla*

Vega Carpio, L. *La estrella de Sevilla*
Vega Carpio, L. *Fuenteovejuna*

ALPE Alpern, Hymen, and Martel, José, eds. *Teatro
hispanoamericano*. New York: Odyssey Press [ca.
1956] 412pp.
Alsina, A. *La marca de fuego*
Eichelbaum, S. *Divorcio nupcial*
Moock Bousquet, A. *La serpiente*
Rojas, R. *Ollántay*
Sánchez, F. *Los derechos de la salud*
Segura, M. *Na Catita*

ALPF Alpern, Hymen, ed. *Three Classic Spanish Plays*.
New York: Washington Square Press [1963] 229pp.
(The ANTA Series of Distinguished Plays)
Calderón de la Barca, P. *Life Is a Dream*
Rojas Zorrilla, F. *None beneath the King*
Vega Carpio, L. *The Sheep Well*

ALPJ Alphonso-Karkala, John Baptist, ed. *An Anthology
of Indian Literature*. Harmondsworth, Middlesex:
Penguin, 1971. 630pp.
Bhāsa. *The Vision of Vāsavadatta*

ALPJR Alphonso-Karkala, John Baptist, ed. *An
Anthology of Indian Literature*. 2nd rev. ed. New
Delhi: Indian Council for Cultural Relations,
1987. 593pp.
Bhāsa. *The Vision of Vāsavadatta*

ALS Altenbernd, Lynn, ed. *Exploring Literature: Fiction,
Poetry, Drama, Criticism*. New York: Macmillan,
1970. 702pp.
Hansberry, L. *A Raisin in the Sun*
Ibsen, H. *Hedda Gabler*
Lowell, R. *My Kinsman, Major Molineux*
Shakespeare, W. *A Midsummer Night's Dream*
Sophocles. *Oedipus Rex*

ALT Altenbernd, Lynn, and Lewis, Leslie L., eds.
*Introduction to Literature: Plays*. New York:
Macmillan, 1963. 440pp.
Anouilh, J. *Becket; or, the Honor of God*
Chekhov, A. *The Cherry Orchard*
*Everyman*
García Lorca, P. *Blood Wedding*
Ibsen, H. *Ghosts*
Ionesco, E. *The Chairs*
Molière, J. *The Miser*
O'Neill, E. *Desire under the Elms*
Pirandello, L. *It Is So (If You Think So)*
Sheridan, R. *The School for Scandal*
Sophocles. *Antigone*

Synge, J. *Riders to the Sea*
Yeats, W. *Purgatory*
Yeats, W. *The Words upon the Window-pane*

ALTE Altenberndt, Lynn, and Lewis L. L., eds.
      *Introduction to Literature: Plays*. 2nd ed. New
      York: Macmillan, 1969. 546pp.
   Anouilh, J. *Becket or, the Honor of God*
   Chekhov, A. *The Cherry Orchard*
   *Everyman*
   García Lorca, F. *Blood Wedding*
   Ibsen, H. *Ghosts*
   Ionesco, E. *The Chairs*
   Molière, J. *The Misanthrope*
   O'Neill, E. *Desire under the Elms*
   Pirandello, L. *It Is So (If You Think So)*
   Plautus, T. *Amphitryon*
   Shakespeare, W. *The Tragedy of Hamlet, Prince of
      Denmark*
   Shaw, G. *The Man of Destiny*
   Sheridan, R. *The School for Scandal*
   Sophocles. *Antigone*
   Synge, A. *Riders to the Sea*

ALTJD *Alternative Japanese Drama: Ten Plays*. Edited
      by Robert T. Rolf and John K. Gillespie. Honolulu:
      University of Hawaii Press, 1992. 364pp.
   Betsuyaku, M. *The Cherry in Bloom*
   Betsuyaku, M. *The Legend of Noon*
   Betsuyaku, M. *The Little Match Girl*
   Kara, J. *Two Women*
   Kara, J. *The Virgin's Mask*
   Satoh, M. *Ismene*
   Shimizu, K. *The Dressing Room: That Which Flows
      Away Ultimately becomes Nostalgia*
   Shimizu, K. *The Sand of Youth, How Quickly*
   Shimizu, K. *Those Days: A Lyrical Hypothesis on Time
      and Forgetting*
   Terayama, S., and Kishida, R. *Knock: Street Theater*

AMB *America on Stage: 10 Great Plays of American
      History*. Edited with preface and introductory note
      by Stanley Richards. New York: Doubleday, 1976.
      939pp.
   Anderson, M. *Valley Forge*
   Kingsley, S. *The Patriots*
   Koch, H. *In Time to Come*
   Lawrence, J., and Lee, R. *Inherit the Wind*
   Levitt, S. *The Andersonville Trial*
   Miller, A. *The Crucible*
   Schary, D. *Sunrise at Campobello*
   Shaw, I. *Bury the Dead*
   Van Doren, M. *The Last Days of Lincoln*
   Wright, R. *Native Son*

AME *American Caravan: A Yearbook of American
      Literature*. Edited by Van Wyck Brooks, Alfred
      Kreymborg, Lewis Mumford and Paul Rosenfeld.
      New York: Macaulay [ca. 1927, ca. 1936] 5 vols.
      Title varies: 1927, The American Caravan; 1928,
      The Second American Caravan; 1929, The New
      American Caravan; 1931, American Caravan IV;
      1936, The New Caravan
   Basshe, E. *The Dream of the Dollar* 5
   Frank, W. *New Year's Eve* 2
   Geddes, V. *The Stable and the Grove* 4
   Gold, M. *Hoboken Blues* 1
   Green, P. *Supper for the Dead* 1
   Green, P. *Tread the Green Grass* 3
   Kreymborg, A. *The Dead Are Free* 5
   Schwartz, D. *Choosing Company* 5
   Williams, W. *The First President* 5

AMEM *American Melodrama*. Edited by Daniel C.
      Gerould. New York: Performing Arts Journal
      Publications, 1983. 247pp.
   Aiken, G. *Uncle Tom's Cabin*
   Belasco, D. *The Girl of the Golden West*
   Boucicault, D. *The Poor of New York*
   Daly, A. *Under the Gaslight*

AMENW *American Plays of the New Woman*. Edited with
      an introduction by Keith Newlin. Chicago: Ivan R.
      Dee, 2000. 294pp.
   Crothers, R. *A Man's World*
   Gerstenberg, A. *Overtones*
   Glaspell, S. *The Outside*
   Moody, W. *The Great Divide*
   Thomas, A. *As a Man Thinks*
   Willliams, J. *Why Marry?*

AMERICAN LITERATURE: *A Period Anthology*; Oscar
      Cargill, general editor. See MCDO McDowell,
      Tremaine, ed. *The Romantic Triumph*. NELS
      Nelson, John Herbert, and Cargill, Oscar, eds.
      *Contemporary Trends*. SPI Spiller, Robert Ernest,
      ed. *The Roots of National Culture*.

AMERICAN PROFILE. See CATH Catholic University
      of America. Committee for the Revision of English
      Curricula

AMP *America's Lost Plays*. Barrett H. Clark, general
      editor. Princeton, NJ: Princeton University Press.
      1940–1941. 20 vols.
   Alfriend, E., and Wheeler, A. *The Great Diamond
      Robbery* 8
   Belasco, D. *La belle russe* 18
   Belasco, D. *The Heart of Maryland* 18
   Belasco, D. *Naughty Anthony* 18

Belasco, D. *The Stranglers of Paris* 18
Belasco, D., and De Mille, H. *The Charity Ball* 17
Belasco, D., and De Mille, H. *The Wife* 17
Belasco, D., and Fyles, F. *The Girl I Left behind Me* 18
Bennett, C. *A Royal Slave* 8
Bird, R. *Caridorf; or, The Avenger* 12
Bird, R. *The Cowled Lover* 12
Bird, R. *News of the Night; or, A Trip to Niagara* 12
Bird, R. *'Twas All for the Best; or, 'Tis All a Notion* 12
Boker, G. *The Bankrupt* 3
Boker, G. *Glaucus* 3
Boker, G. *The World a Mask* 3
Boucicault, D. *Dot* 1
Boucicault, D. *Flying Scud* 1
Boucicault, D. *Forbidden Fruit* 1
Boucicault, D. *Louis XI* 1
Boucicault, D. *Mercy Dodd* 1
Boucicault, D. *Robert Emmet* 1
Brougham, J. *The Duke's Motto: or, I Am Here!* 14
Campbell, B. *Fairfax* 19
Campbell, B. *The Galley Slave* 19
Campbell, B. *My Partner* 19
Campbell, B. *The Virginian* 19
Campbell, B. *The White Slave* 19
Clinch, D. *The Spy: or, A Tale of the Neutral Ground* 14
Conway, H. *The Battle of Stillwater; or, the Maniac* 14
Daly, A. *The Big Bonanza* 20
Daly, A. *Divorce* 20
Daly, A. *Man and Wife* 20
Daly, A. *Needles and Pins* 20
Daly, A. *Pique* 20
De Mille, H., and Barnard, C. *The Main Line* 17
De Mille, H., and Belasco, D. *Lord Chumley* 17
De Mille, H., and Belasco, D. *Men and Women* 17
De Mille, W. *The Warrens of Virginia* 16
Dunlap, W. *False Shame; or, the American Orphan in Germany* 2
Dunlap, W. *Thirty Years; or, the Gambler's Fate* 2
Fechter, C. *Monte Cristo* 16
Field, J. *Job and His Children* 14
Grover, L. *Our Boarding House* 4
Hazelton, G. *Mistress Nell* 16
Herne, J. *Drifting Apart* 7
Herne, J. *"The Minute Men" of 1774–1775* 7
Herne, J. *The Reverend Griffith Davenport, Act IV* 7
Herne, J. *Within an Inch of His Life* 7
Howard, B. *The Banker's Daughter* 10
Howard, B. *Baron Rudolph* 10
Howard, B. *Hurricanes* 10
Howard, B. *Old Love Letters* 10
Howard, B. *One of Our Girls* 10
Howe, J. *Hippolytus* 16
Hoyt, C. *A Bunch of Keys* 9
Hoyt, C. *A Midnight Bell* 9
Hoyt, C. *A Milk White Flag* 9

Hoyt, C. *A Temperance Town* 9
Hoyt, C. *A Trip to Chinatown* 9
Jessop, G. *Sam'l of Posen; or, the Commercial Drummer* 4
Jones, J. *The Usurper; or, Americans in Tripoli* 14
McCloskey, J. *Across the Continent; or, Scenes from New York Life and the Pacific Railroad* 4
MacKaye, S. *An Arrant Knave* 11
MacKaye, S. *In Spite of All* 11
MacKaye, S. *Rose Michel* 11
MacKaye, S. *Won at Last* 11
Mitchell, L. *Becky Sharp* 16
Mortimer, L. *No Mother to Guide Her* 8
Murdock, F. *Davy Crockett; or, Be Sure You're Right, then Go Ahead* 4
Payne, J. *The Black Man; or, the Spleen* 6
Payne, J. *The Boarding Schools or, Life among the Little Folk* 5
Payne, J. *The Italian Bride* 6
Payne, J. *The Last Duel in Spain* 6
Payne, J. *Mazeppa; or, the Wild Horse of Tartary* 5
Payne, J. *Mount Savage* 5
Payne, J. *Romulus, the Shepherd King* 6
Payne, J. *The Spanish Husband or, First and Last Love* 5
Payne, J. *Trial without Jury; or the Magpie and the Maid* 5
Payne, J. *The Two Sons-in-law* 5
Payne, J. *Woman's Revenge* 6
Smith, R. *The Bombardment of Algiers* 13
Smith, R. *The Last Man; or, the Cock of the Village* 13
Smith, R. *The Sentinels; or, the Two Sergeants* 13
Smith, R. *Shakespeare in Love* 13
Smith, R. *A Wife at a Venture* 13
Smith, R. *William Penn* 13
Steele, S. *The Crock of Gold; or, the Toiler's Trials* 14
Stone, J. *Metamora; or, the Last of the Wampanoags* 14
Stone, J. *Tancred, King of Sicily; or, the Archives of Palermo* 14
Taylor, C. *From Rags to Riches* 8
Tyler, R. *The Island of Barrataria* 15
Tyler, R. *Joseph and His Brethren* 15
Tyler, R. *The Judgment of Solomon* 15
Tyler, R. *The Origin of the Feast of Purim; or, the Destinies of Haman & Mordecai* 15
Wallach, L. *Rosedale; or, the Rifle Ball* 4
Wilkins, J. *Signor Marc* 14
Woods, W. *Billy the Kid* 8
Young, C., and Howard, B. *Knave and Queen* 10

AMPA *America's Lost Plays.* V21. Satiric Comedies; Meserve, Walter J., and Reardon, William R., eds. Bloomington, IN: Indiana University Press, 1969. 158pp.
*The Battle of Brooklyn*
Brougham, J. *Po-ca-hon-tas*

Dunlap, W. *Darby's Return*
Hunter, R. *Androboros*
*The Trial of Atticus before Judge Beau, for a Rape*

AND Anderson, George Kumler and Walton, Edna Lou,
    eds. *This Generation*. Chicago: Scott, Foresman
    [ca. 1939] 975pp.
Dunsany, E. *The Queen's Enemies*
Green, P. *Johnny Johnson*
O'Neill, E. *The Hairy Ape*
Shaw, I. *Bury the Dead*

ANDE Anderson, George Kumler and Walton, Edna Lou,
    eds. *This Generation*. Revised edition. Chicago:
    Scott, Foresman [ca. l949] 1065pp.
Coward, N. *Fumed Oak*
Galsworthy, J. *Loyalties*
Green, P. *Johnny Johnson*
MacNeice, L. *The Dark Tower*
O'Neill, E. *The Hairy Ape*

ANDF Anderson, George Lincoln, ed. *The Genius of
    the Oriental Theatre*. New York: New American
    Library [1966] 416pp.
Chikamatsu, M. *The Courier for Hell*
Hiyoshi, S. *Benkei on the Bridge*
Kalidisa. *Shakuntala and the Ring of Recognition*
Miyamasu. *The Hatmaker*
Namiki, G., III. *The Subscription List*
Seami, M. *Haku Rakuten*
Shudraka. *The Little Clay Cart*
Zembo, M. *Atsumori at Ikuta*
Zembo, M. *Early Snow*
Zenchiku, U. *Aoi no Uye*

ANDI Anderson, George L., ed. *Masterpieces of the
    Orient*. Enlarged edition. New York: W. W.
    Norton, 1977. 834pp.
Chikamatsu, M. *The Courier for Hell*
*The Deserted Crone*
*The Dwarf Tree*
Kalidisa. *Shakuntala and the Ring of Recognition*
*Komachi at Sekidera*
*The Red Lantern*
Seami, M. *Atsumori*
Zembo, M. *Early Snow*
Zenchiku, U. *Princess Hollyhock*

ANG Andrews, John Douglass and Smith, Albert Reginald
    Wilson, eds. *Three Elizabethan Plays*. London:
    Nelson [1929] 287pp.
Beaumont, F., and Fletcher, J. *The Knight of the Burning
    Pestle*
Jonson, B. *Everyman in His Humour*
Massinger, P. *A New Way to Pay Old Debts*

ANSORGE, ELIZABETH FRANCES. See PROC *Prose
    and Poetry for Appreciation.*

ANT *Anthology: An Introduction to Literature: Fiction,
    Poetry, Drama*. Edited by Lynn Altenbernd. New
    York: Macmillan, 1977. 1669pp.
Arrabal, F. *Picnic on the Battlefield*
Brecht, B. *Mother Courage and Her Children*
Hansberry, L. *A Raisin in the Sun*
Ibsen, H. *A Doll's House*
Miller, A. *Death of a Salesman*
O'Neill, E. *The Hairy Ape*
Shakespeare, W. *Othello*
Shaw, G. *Arms and the Man*
Sheridan, R. *The Rivals*
Sophocles. *Antigone*
Wilde, O. *The Importance of Being Earnest*

ANTH *An Anthology of Austrian Drama*, ed. with an
    introduction by Douglas A. Russell. Rutherford,
    NJ: Fairleigh Dickinson University Press, ca. 1982.
    442pp.
Grillparzer, F. *King Ottocar, His Rise and Fall*
Hochwälder, F. *The Raspberry Picker*
Hofmannsthal, H. *Electra*
Nestroy, J. *The Talisman*
Schnitzler, A. *La Ronde*
Werfel, F. *Goat Song*

ANTHC *Anthology of Contemporary Austrian Folk
    Drama*. Translated and with an afterword by
    Richard Dixon. Riverside, CA: Ariadne Press,
    1993. 397pp.
Canetti, V. *The Ogre*
Mitterer, F. *No Place for Idiots*
Preses, P. and Becher, U. *Our Mr. Bockerer*
Szyszkowitz, G. *Friedemann Puntigam or the Delicate
    Art of Losing One's Memory*
Turrini, P. *Swine*

ANTL *Anthology of Living Theater*. Edited by Edwin
    Wilson and Alvin Goldfarb. Boston: McGraw-Hill,
    1998. 520pp.
Beckett, S. *Krapp's Last Tape*
Brecht, B. *The Good Woman of Setzuan*
Brome. *Abraham and Isaac*
Centlivre, S. *The Busy Body*
Chekhov, A. *The Cherry Orchard*
Kwananami, K. *Sotoba Komachi*
Ludlam, C. *The Mystery of Irma Vep*
Molière, J. *Tartuffe*
Plautus, T. *The Menaechmus Brothers*
Shakespeare, W. *Hamlet*
Smith, A.D. *Twilight Los Angeles, 1992*
Sophocles. *Antigone*

Strindberg, A. *A Dream Play*
Valdez, L. *Zoot Suit*
Williams, T. *The Glass Menagerie*
Wilson, A. *Joe Turner's Come and Gone*

ANTM *An Anthology of Modern Belgian Theatre: Maurice Maeterlinck, Fernand Crommelynck, and Michel de Ghelderode.* Troy, NY: Whitston Pub. Co., 1981. 288pp.
Crommelynck, F. *The Sculptor of Masks*
Ghelderode, M. *Escurial*
Ghelderode, M. *The Magpie on the Gallows*
Maeterlinck, M. *The Blind*
Maeterlinck, M. *The Intruder*
Maeterlinek, M. *Pelleas and Melisande*

ANTN *Anti-Naturalism: Six Full-Length Contemporary American Plays.* New York: Broadway Play Publishing, 1989. 335pp.
Lucas, C. *Reckless*
Nelson, R. *BAL*
Overmayer, E. *On the Verge*
Reddin, K. *Highest Standard of Living*
Therriault, D. *The White Death*
Wellman, M. *Harm's Way*

ANTU Antush, John V., ed. *Nuestro New York: An Anthology of Puerto Rican Plays.* New York: Mentor, 1994. 566pp.
Colón, O. *Siempre en mi corazón*
Gonzalez, R. *The Boiler Room*
López, E. *Marlene*
López, E. I. *Spanish Eyes*
Rivera, C. *Julia*
Rivera, J. *Marisol*
Rodríguez, Y. *Rising Sun, Falling Star*
Rodríguez Suárez, R. *The Betrothal*
Shamsul Alám, J. *Zookeeper*
Tirado, C. *Some People Have All the Luck*
Valle, F. *I Am a Winner*

ANTUR Antush, John V., ed. *Recent Puerto Rican Theater: Five Plays from New York.* Houston, TX: Arte Publico Press, 1991. 255pp.
Fraguada, F. *Bodega*
Irizarry, R. *Ariano*
Ramírez, I. *Family Scenes*
Shamsul Alám, J. *Midnight Blues*
Tirado, C. *First Class*

ARGJT *Argentine Jewish Theatre: A Critical Anthology.* Edited and translated by Nora Glickman and Gloria F. Waldman. Lewisburg, NJ: Associated University Presses, 1996. 346pp.
Dragun, O. *Onward, Corazon!*

Eichelbaum, S. *Aaron the Jew*
Goldenberg, J. *Krinsky*
Halac, R. *A Thousand Years, One Day*
Novion, A. *Petroff's Junkshop*
Raznovich, D. *Lost Belongings*
Rozenmacher, G. *Simon Brumelstein, Knight of the Indies*
Tiempo, C. *The Tithe*

ARM *Armenian Literature Comprising Poetry, Drama, Folklore, and Classic Traditions.* Introduction by Robert Arnot. Rev. ed. New York: Colonial Press [c1901] 142pp. (The World's Great Classics)
Sundukianz, G. *The Ruined Family*

ARMS Armstrong, William A., ed. *Elizabethan History Plays.* New York: Oxford University Press, 1965. 428pp.
Bale, J. *King John*
Davenport, R. *King John and Matilda*
*Edward the Third*
Ford, J. *Perkin Warbeck*
*Woodstock*

ARNOT, ROBERT. See ARM *Armenian Literature.*

AROUN *Around the Edge: Women's Plays.* Adelaide, South Australia: Tantrum Press, 1992. 472pp.
Bent, R. *A Trip to the Light Fantastic*
Bent, R. *Waiting for Annette*
Brookman, A. *Wild about Work*
Crea, T., Eberhard, J., Mastratone, L, and Morgillo, A. *Ricordi*
Fitzgerald, C. *Just a Little Crooked around the Edge*
Gunzburg, D. *Water from the Well*
McKinnon, C. *A Rose by Any other Name*
Morgillo, A. *The Olive Tree*

ARRIZ Arrizón, Alicia, and Manzor, Lillian, eds. *Latinas on Stage.* Berkeley, CA: Third Woman Press, 2000. 444pp. (Series in Chicana/Latina Studies)
Arce, E. *My Grandmother Never Past Away*
Cruz, M. *Lucy Loves Me*
Esparza, L. *I Dismember the Alamo*
Moraga, C. *Mexican Medea: La Llorona retold*
Palacios, M. *Latin lezbo comic*
Svich, C. *Scar*
Tropicana, C. *Milk of Amnesia-Leche de amnesia*

ASF Ashley, Leonard R. N., comp. *Mirrors for Man: 26 Plays of World Drama.* Cambridge, MA: Winthrop Pub., 1974. 967pp.
Anouilh, J. *Antigone*
Brecht, B. *The Three Penny Opera*
Büchner, G. *Woyzeck*

Chekhov, A. *The Cherry Orchard*
Dumas, A., fils. *Lady of the Camellias*
*Everyman*
Ibsen, H. *The Wild Duck*
Jarry, A. *Ubu the King*
Kennedy, A. *The Owl Answers*
Marlowe, C. *The Tragical History of Doctor Faustus*
Molière, J. *The Miser*
Namiki, G., III. *The Subscription Scroll*
O'Neill, E. *The Long Voyage Home*
Pirandello, L. *Six Characters in Search of an Author*
Plautus. *Pot of Gold*
Saavedra, G. *Justice*
Schneeman, C. *Meat Joy*
Shakespeare, W. *Macbeth*
Shaw, G. *Mrs. Warren's Profession*
Sheridan, R. *The School for Scandal*
Sophocles. *Antigone*
Strindberg, A. *Miss Julie*
Synge, J. *Riders to the Sea*
Van Itallie, J. *America Hurrah*
Williams, T. *The Glass Menagerie*
Wycherley, W. *The Country Wife*

ASG Ashley, Leonard R. N., comp. *Nineteenth-Century British Drama*. Glenview, IL: Scott, Foresman [1967] 700pp.
Boucicault, D. *London Assurance*
Bulwer-Lytton, E. *The Lady of Lyons*
Gilbert W. *H.M.S. Pinafore*
Jerrold, D. *Black-ey'd Susan*
Jones, H. *Michael and His Lost Angel*
Lewis, L. *The Bells*
Palmer, T. *East Lynne*
Pinero, A. *The Second Mrs. Tanqueray*
Robertson, T. *Caste*
Shelley, P. *The Cenci*
Wilde, O. *The Importance of Being Earnest*
Yeats, W. *The Countess Cathleen*

ASH Ashton, John William, ed. *Types of English Drama*. New York: Macmillan, 1940. 750pp.
*Abraham and Melchizedek and Lot, with the Sacrifice of Isaac*
Browning, R. *A Blot in the 'Scutcheon*
Congreve, W. *The Way of the World*
*Everyman*
Gay, J. *The Beggar's Opera*
Greene, R. *Friar Bacon and Friar Bungay*
Heywood, T. *A Woman Killed with Kindness*
Jonson, B. *The Alchemist*
Marlowe, C. *Edward II*
O'Neill, E. *Anna Christie*
Sheridan, R. *The Critic*
Wilde, O. *The Importance of Being Earnest*

ASIAM *Asian American Drama: 9 Plays from the Multiethnic Landscape*. Edited by Brian Nelson. New York: Applause, 1997. 421pp.
Gotanda, P. *Day Standing on Its Head*
Hill, A. *Tokyo Bound*
Houston, V. *As Sometimes in a Dead Man's Face*
Hwang, D. *Bondage*
Nishikawa, L., and Talmadge, V. *The Gate of Heaven*
Okita, D. *The Rainy Season*
Omata, G. *S.A.M. I Am*
Shin, R. *The Art of Waiting*
Uyehara, D. *Hiro*

ATKINSON, BROOKS. See FOUB *Four Great Comedies of the Restoration and 18th Century*; NEWV *New Voices in the American Theatre*.

ATT *Attic Tragedies*. Boston: Bibliophile Society, 1927. 3 vols.
Aeschylus. *Prometheus Bound* 3
Euripides. *Hippolytus* 2
Euripides. *Medea* 2
Sophocles. *Antigone* 1
Sophocles. *Electra* 3
Sophocles. *Oedipus the King* 1

AUB Auburn, Mark S., and Burkman, Katherine H., comps. *Drama through Performance*. Boston: Houghton Mifflin, 1977. 775pp.
Chekhov, A. *The Cherry Orchard*
Congreve, W. *Love for Love*
Ibsen, H. *The Wild Duck*
Jellicoe, A. *The Knack*
Pinter, H. *A Slight Ache*
Racine, J. *Phaedra*
*Second Shepherds' Play*
Shakespeare, W. *A Midsummer Night's Dream*
Shakespeare, W. *Othello*
Sophocles. *Oedipus the King*
Williams, M. *Cinder, Tell-it*
Williams, T. *The Glass Menagerie*

AUDE Auden, Wystan Hugh, ed. *The Portable Greek Reader*. New York: Viking, 1948. 726pp.
Aeschylus. *Agamemnon*
Aeschylus. *Choephoroe*
Aeschylus. *Eumenides*

AUG Aughtry, Charles Edward, ed. *Landmarks in Modern Drama, from Ibsen to Ionesco*. Boston: Houghton Mifflin [ca. 1963]. 726pp.
Brecht, B. *The Good Woman of Setzuan*
Ibsen, H. *A Doll's House*
Ionesco, E. *The Bald Soprano*
Maeterlinck, M. *Pelléas and Mélisande*

Miller, A. *Death of a Salesman*
Pirandello, L. *Six Characters in Search of an Author*
Shaw, G. *Man and Superman*
Strindberg, A. *A Dream Play*
Strindberg, A. *Miss Julie*
Synge, J. *The Playboy of the Western World*
Yeats, W. *On Baile's Strand*

AUS *Australia Plays: New Australian Drama*. Introduced
    by Katherine Brisbane. London: Nick Hern, 1989.
    397pp.
Davis, J. *No Sugar*
De Groen, A. *The Rivers of China*
Gow, M. *Away*
Nowra, L. *The Golden Age*
Williamson, D. *Travelling North*

AUSG *Australian Gay and Lesbian Plays*. Edited by Bruce
    Parr. Sydney: Currency Press, 1996. 384pp.
Fischer, M. *The Gay Divorcee*
Gorman, C. *A Manual of Trench Warfare*
Gow, M. *Furious*
Harding, A. *Blood and Honour*
Johnson, E. *What Do They Call Me?*
Kenna, P. *Mates*
Lyssa, A. *Pinball*
Shotlander, S. *Is That You Nancy?*

AXT Axton, Richard, and Stevens, John, compilers and
    translators. *Medieval French Plays*. Oxford:
    Blackwell, 1971. 313pp.
Adam de la Halle. *Le jeu de la feuillée*
Adam de la Halle. *Le jeu de Robin et Marion*
Bodel, J. *Le jeu de Saint Nicolas*
*Courtois d'Arras*
*Le garçon et l'aveugle*
*Le je d'Adam: Adam and Eve; Cain and Abel*
Rutebeuf. *Le miracle de Théophile*
*La seinte resureccion*

AYLIFF, H. K. See MAL *Malvern Festival Plays*.

BAC Bach, Bert C., and Browning, Gordon, compiler.
    *Drama for Composition*. Glenview, IL: Scott,
    Foresman, 1973. 507pp.
*Everyman*
Fry, C. *A Phoenix Too Frequent*
Jonson, B. *Volpone; or, the Fox*
O'Neill, E. *Desire under the Elms*
Shakespeare, W. *Hamlet*
Shaw, G. *Arms and the Man*
Sheridan, R. *The School for Scandal*
Synge, J. *The Playboy of the Western World*
Ward, D. *Day of Absence*

BAI Bailey, James Osler, ed. *British Plays of the
    Nineteenth Century*. New York: Odyssey Press
    [1966] 535pp.
Boucicault, D. *After Dark*
Boucicault, D. *London Assurance*
Browning, R. *Pippa Passes*
Buckstone, J. *Luke the Labourer; or, the Lost Son*
Bulwer-Lytton, E. *Richelieu; or, the Conspiracy*
Gilbert, W. *Engaged*
Holcroft, T. *A Tale of Mystery*
Jerrold, D. *The Rent-day*
Jones, H. *The Masqueraders*
Jones, H. *The Silver King*
Marston, J. *The Patrician's Daughter*
Maturin, C. *Bertram; or, the Castle of St. Aldobrand*
Pinero, A. *The Notorious Mrs. Ebbsmith*
Robertson, T. *Caste*
Shaw, G. *Widowers' Houses*
Taylor, T. *Our American Cousin*
Wood, H. *East Lynne*

BAIC Bain, Carl E., ed. *Drama*. New York: W. W.
    Norton, 1973. 592pp.
Bullins, E. *A Son, Come Home*
Chekhov, A. *The Three Sisters*
Euripides. *The Bacchae*
Ibsen, H. *The Wild Duck*
Miller, A. *A View from the Bridge*
Molière, J. *The Misanthrope*
Pirandello, L. *Six Characters in Search of an Author*
Shakespeare, W. *Hamlet*
Shaw, G. *Caesar and Cleopatra*
Shaw, G. *Major Barbara*
Sophocles. *Oedipus Tyrannus*
Terry, M. *The Gloaming, Oh My Darling*
Van Itallie, C. *Interview*

BAIE Bain, Carl E., and Others, compiler. *The Norton
    Introduction to Literature*. New York: W. W.
    Norton, 1973. 1191pp.
Bullins, E. *A Son, Come Home*
Chekhov, A. *The Three Sisters*
Euripides. *The Bacchae*
Ibsen, H. *The Wild Duck*
Pirandello, L. *Six Characters in Search of an Author*
Shakespeare, W. *Hamlet*
Shaw, G. *Major Barbara*
Terry, M. *The Gloaming, Oh My Darling*

BAIG Bain, Carl E., et al., eds. *The Norton Introduction
    to Literature*. 2nd ed. New York: W. W. Norton,
    1977. 1403pp.
Bullins, E. *A Son, Come Home*
Chekhov, A. *The Three Sisters*
Euripides. *The Bacchae*

Ibsen, H. *The Wild Duck*
Pirandello, L. *Six Characters in Search of an Author*
*The Sacrifice of Isaac*
Shakespeare, W. *Hamlet*
Sophocles. *Oedipus Tyrannus*
Wilde, O. *The Importance of Being Earnest*
Williams, T. *The Glass Menagerie*
Williams, T. *The Long Goodbye*

BAIH Bain, Carl E., et al., eds. *The Norton Introduction to Literature*. 3rd ed. New York: W. W. Norton, 1981. 1540pp.
Bullins, E. *A Son, Come Home*
Chekhov, A. *Three Sisters*
Ibsen, H. *Hedda Gabler*
Mankiewicz, H., and Welles, O. *Citizen Kane*
Miller, A. *Death of a Salesman*
Pinter, H. *The Dumb Waiter*
*The Sacrifice of Isaac*
Shakespeare, W. *Hamlet*
Sophocles. *Oedipus Tyrannus*
Wilde, O. *The Importance of Being Earnest*
Williams, T. *The Glass Menagerie*
Williams, T. *The Long Goodbye*

BAIK Bain, Carl E., et al., eds. *The Norton Introduction to Literature*. 4th ed. New York: W. W. Norton, 1986. 1561p
Beckett, S. *Krapp's Last Tape*
Chekhov, A. *The Brute*
Fuller, C. *A Soldier's Play*
Ibsen, H. *Hedda Gabler*
Miller, A. *Death of a Salesman*
Molière, J. *The Misanthrope*
Norman, M. *Third and Oak: The Laundromat*
Pinter, H. *The Black and White*
*The Sacrifice of Isaac*
Shakespeare, W. *Hamlet*
Sophocles. *Oedipus Tyrannus*
Wilde, O. *The Importance of Being Earnest*
Williams, T. *Cat on a Hot Tin Roof* (from Act II only)
Williams, T. *The Glass Menagerie* (Scene 7 only)
Williams, T. *A Streetcar Named Desire*

BAIL Bain, Carl E., et al., eds. *The Norton Introduction to Literature*. 5th ed. New York: W. W. Norton, 1991. 1985pp.
Aristophanes. *Lysistrata*
Beckett, S. *Krapp's Last Tape*
Chekhov, A. *The Brute*
Duras, M. *Hiroshima, mon amour*
Glaspell, S. *Trifles*
Hellman, L. *The Little Foxes*
Hwang, D. *M. Butterfly*
Ibsen, H. *Hedda Gabler*

Miller, A. *Death of a Salesman*
Molière, J. *The Doctor in Spite of Himself*
Pinter, H. *The Black and White*
Pollock, S. *Blood Relations*
Shakespeare, W. *Hamlet*
Shakespeare, W. *A Midsummer Night's Dream*
Sophocles. *Oedipus the King*
Wilde, O. *The Importance of Being Earnest*
Williams, T. *A Streetcar Named Desire*
Wilson, A. *Fences*

BAIM Bain, Carl E., et al., eds. *The Norton Introduction to Literature*. 6th ed. New York: W. W. Norton, 1995. 2165pp.
Chekhov, A. *The Bear*
Chekhov, A. *The Cherry Orchard*
Churchill, C. *Top Girls*
Glaspell, S. *Trifles*
Hellman, L. *The Little Foxes*
Ibsen, H. *Hedda Gabler*
Miller, A. *Death of a Salesman*
Norman, M. *Getting Out*
Pinter, H. *The Black and White*
Pollock, S. *Blood Relations*
Shakespeare, W. *Hamlet*
Shakespeare, W. *A Midsummer Night's Dream*
Shaw, G. *Pygmalion*
Sophocles. *Antigone*
Sophocles. *Oedipus the King*
Wilde, O. *The Importance of Being Earnest*
Williams, T. *A Streetcar Named Desire*
Wilson, A. *Fences*

BAK Baker, George Pierce, comp. *Modern American Plays*. New York: Harcourt, Brace and Howe, 1920. 544pp.
Anspacher, L. *The Unchastened Woman*
Belasco, D. *The Return of Peter Grimm*
Massey, E. *Plots and Playwrights*
Sheldon, E. *Romance*
Thomas, A. *As a Man Thinks*

BAKS Bakshy, Alexander, comp. and tr. *Soviet Scene: Six Plays of Russian Life*. New Haven: Yale University Press, 1946. 348pp.
Afinogenov, A. *Far Taiga*
Ilyenkov, V. *The Square of Flowers*
Marshak, S. *Twelve Months*
Pogodin, N. *The Chimes of the Kremlin*
Shkvarkin, V. *Father Unknown*
Trenyov, K. *Lyubov Yarovaya*

BALD Bald, Robert Cecil, ed. *Six Elizabethan Plays*. Boston: Houghton Mifflin [c. 1963]
Beaumont, F., and Fletcher, J. *The Knight of the Burning Pestle*

Dekker, T. *The Shoemakers' Holiday*
Ford, J. *The Broken Heart*
Jonson, B. *Epicoene; or, the Silent Woman*
Marlowe, C. *Tamburlaine the Great (Part 1)*
Webster, J. *The Duchess of Malfi*

BALL Ball, John, ed. *From Beowulf to Modern British Writers. Based on Robert Shafer's from Beowulf to Thomas Hardy* [One-volume ed.]. New York: Odyssey Press [1959] 1364pp.
Eliot, T. *Murder in the Cathedral*
*Everyman*
Marlowe, C. *The Tragical History of Doctor Faustus*
Shaw, G. *Don Juan in Hell*
Synge, J. *In the Shadow of the Glen*

BALLE Ballet, Arthur Harold, ed. *Playwrights for Tomorrow: A Collection of Plays.* Minneapolis: University of Minnesota Press, c. 1966–1975. 13 vols.
Auletta, R. *Stops* 10
Ball, D. *Assassin* 7
Barber, P. *I, Elizabeth Otis, Being of Sound Mind* 3
Bernard, K. *The Unknown Chinaman* 10
Boretz, N. *Shelter Area* 2
Bosakowski, P. *Bierce Takes on the Railroad* 11
Coyle, M. *The Root* 12
Feldhaus-Weber, M. *The World Tipped Over, and Laying on Its Side* 4
Fornés, M. *The Successful Life of Three* 2
Fornés, M. *Tango Palace* 2
Gaines, F. *The New Chautauqua* 5
Gillman, J. *The Marriage Test* 6
Gordon, R. *The Tunes of Chicken Little* 13
Greanias, G. *Wilson* 12
Grecco, S. *The Orientals* 7
Hierholzer, A. *Grace and George and God* 7
Johnson, E. *A Bad Play for an Old Lady* 1
Joselovitz, E. *The Inheritance* 13
Joseph, A. *Anniversary on Weedy Hill* 8
Kalcheim, L. *. . . and the Boy Who Came to Leave* 3
Kliewer, W. *A Lean and Hungry Priest* 12
Koebnick, S. *Fair Beckoning One* 5
Korr, D. *Encore* 9
Kranes, D. *Drive-in* 7
LaFarge, W. *Escape by Balloon* 10
Landon, J. *Blessing* 13
Lee, L. *Fox, Hound, and Huntress* 10
Leichman, S. *Freddie the Pigeon* 7
Lewin, J. *Five Easy Payments* 3
Lynch, H. *Three Miles to Poley* 10
McNally, T. *And Things That Go Bump in the Night* 1
Medoff, M. *The Kramer* 13
Monson, W. *The Nihilist* 8
Muller, R. *The Great Gitaway* 3

Neilson, K. *The End of the World; or, Fragments from a Work in Progress* 6
O'Keefe, J. *Chamber Piece* 11
O'Morrison, K. *The Long War* 4
Opper, D. *Children of the Kingdom* 9
Powell, A. *The Strangler* 4
Pritchard, B. *Visions of Sugar Plums* 4
Roszkowski, D. *Canvas* 11
Sainer, A. *The Thing Itself* 6
Schevill, J. *American Power: The Master* 1
Schevill, J. *American Power: The Space Fan* 1
Schrock, G. *Madam Popov* 9
Schwartz, J. *Psalms for Two Davids* 9
Spencer, J. *A Bunch of the Gods Were Sitting around One Day* 12
Stranack, J. *With Malice Aforethought* 3
Terry, M. *Ex-Miss Cooper Queen on a Set of Pills* 1
Udoff, Y. *A Gun Play* 8
Van Itallie, J. *Where Is de Queen?* 3
Walter, N. *Rags* 7
Yankowitz, S. *Boxes* 11

BANH Banham, Martin, and Plastow, Jane, eds. *Contemporary African Plays.* London: Methuen Drama, 1999. 382pp.
Aidoo, A. *Anowa*
Mtwa, P., Ngema, M., and Simon, B. *Woza Albert!*
Osofisan, F. *The Chattering and the Song*
Soyinka, W. *Death and the King's Horseman*
Tesfai, A. *The Other War*
Whaley, A. *The Rise and Shine of Comrade Fiasco*

BARA Baraitser, Marion, ed. *Echoes of Israel: Contemporary Drama.* London: Loki Books, 1999. 267pp.
Danon, R., and Levy, A. *Sheindale*
Levin, H. *Murder*
Mazya, E. *A Family Story*
Yehoshua, A. *Mr. Mani*

BARAM Baraitser, Marion, ed. *Plays by Mediterranean Women.* London: Aurora Metro Publications, 1994. 295pp.
Avraamidou, M. *Harsh Angel*
Cunillé, L. *Libration*
Kainy, M. *The End of the Dream Season*
Maraini, D. *Veronica Franco, Courtesan and Poet*
Mnouchkine, A. *Mephisto*
Saadawi, N. *Twelve Women in a Cell*

BARNES, JOHN R. *See* PROW *Prose and Poetry of the World.*

BARB Barnet, Sylvan; Berman, Morton; and Burto, William, eds. *Eight Great Comedies.* New York: New American Library [c. 1958] 472pp.

Aristophanes. *The Clouds*
Chekhov, A. *Uncle Vanya*
Gay, J. *The Beggar's Opera*
Machiavelli, N. *Mandragola*
Molière, J. *The Miser*
Shakespeare, W. *Twelfth Night; or, What You Will*
Shaw, G. *Arms and the Man*
Wilde, O. *The Importance of Being Earnest*

BARC Barnet, Sylvan; Berman, Morton; and Burto, William, eds. *Eight Great Tragedies.* New York: New American Library, 1957. 443pp.
Aeschylus. *Prometheus Bound*
Euripides. *Hippolytus*
Ibsen, H. *Ghosts*
O'Neill, E. *Desire under the Elms*
Shakespeare, W. *King Lear*
Sophocles. *Oedipus, the King*
Strindberg, A. *Miss Julie*
Yeats, W. *On Baile's Strand*

BARD Barnet, Sylvan; Berman, Morton; and Burto, William, eds. *The Genius of the Early English Theatre.* New York: New American Library [c. 1962] 453pp.
*Abraham and Isaac*
*Everyman*
Jonson, B. *Volpone*
Marlowe, C. *Doctor Faustus*
Milton, J. *Samson Agonistes*
*The Second Shepherds' Play*
Shakespeare, W. *Macbeth*

BARF Barnet, Sylvan; Berman, Morton; and Burto, William, eds. *The Genius of the Irish Theatre.* New York: New American Library [c. 1960] 366pp.
Gregory, I. *The Canavans*
O'Casey, S. *Purple Dust*
O'Donovan, M. *In the Train*
Shaw, G. *John Bull's Other Island*
Synge, J. *Deirdre of the Sorrows*
Yeats, J. *La la noo*
Yeats, W. *The Words upon the Windowpane*

BARG Barnet, Sylvan; Berman, Morton; and Burto, William eds. *The Genius of the Later English Theater.* New York: New American Library [c.1962] 536pp.
Byron, G. *Cain*
Congreve, W. *The Way of the World*
Golding, W. *The Brass Butterfly*
Goldsmith, O. *She Stoops to Conquer; or, the Mistakes of a Night*
Shaw, G. *Major Barbara*
Wilde, O. *The Importance of Being Earnest*

BARII Barnet, Sylvan; Berman, Morton; and Burto, William, eds. *An Introduction to Literature.* Boston: Little, Brown [c.1961] 491pp.
*Quem quaeritis*
Sophocles. *Antigone*
Shaw, G. *The Shewing up of Blanco Posnet*
Yeats, W. *Purgatory*

BARI Barnet, Sylvan, [and Others] compiler. *An Introduction to Literature.* 4th ed. Boston: Little, Brown, 1971. 961pp.
Ibsen, H. *A Doll's House*
Ionesco, E. *The Gap*
Molière, J. *The Misanthrope*
*Quem quaeritis*
Shakespeare, W. *The Tragedy of Hamlet: Prince of Denmark*
Sophocles. *Antigone*
Sophocles. *Oedipus Rex*
Synge, J. *Riders to the Sea*
Ward, D. *Happy Ending*
Williams, T. *The Glass Menagerie*

BARIA Barnet, Sylvan, et al., eds. *An Introduction to Literature: Fiction, Poetry, Drama.* 5th ed. Boston: Little, Brown, 1973. 963pp.
Ibsen, H. *A Doll's House*
Ionesco, E. *The Gap*
Molière, J. *The Misanthrope*
*Quem quaeritis*
Shakespeare, W. *The Tragedy of Hamlet: Prince of Denmark*
Sophocles. *Antigone*
Sophocles. *Oedipus Rex*
Synge, J. *Riders to the Sea*
Ward, D. *Happy Ending*
Williams, T. *The Glass Menagerie*

BARIC Barnet, Sylvan, et al., ed. *An Introduction to Literature: Fiction, Poetry, Drama.* 6th ed. Boston: Little, Brown, 1977. 1092pp.
Ibsen, H. *A Doll's House*
Ionesco, E. *The Gap*
Miller, A. *Death of a Salesman*
*Quem quaeritis*
Shakespeare, W. *The Tragedy of Othello*
Shaw, B. *Pygmalion*
Sophocles. *Antigone*
Sophocles. *Oedipus Rex*
Synge, J. *Riders to the Sea*
Ward, D. *Happy Ending*
Williams, T. *The Glass Menagerie*

BARID Barnet, Sylvan, et al., ed. *An Introduction to Literature: Fiction, Poetry, Drama.* 7th ed. Boston: Little, Brown, 1981. 1179pp.
Ibsen, H. *A Doll's House*
Miller, A. *Death of a Salesman*
Molière, J. *The Misanthrope*
*Quem quaeritis*
Shaffer, P. *Equus*
Shakespeare, W. *The Tragedy of Hamlet*
Sophocles. *Antigone*
Sophocles. *Oedipus Rex*
Synge, J. *Riders to the Sea*
Williams, T. *The Glass Menagerie*

BARIE Barnet, Sylvan, et al., ed. *An Introduction to Literature: Fiction, Poetry, Drama.* 8th ed. Boston: Little, Brown, 1985. 1219pp.
Glaspell, S. *Trifles*
Ibsen, H. *A Doll's House*
Miller, A. *Death of a Salesman*
Norman, M. *'Night, Mother*
*Quem quaeritis*
Shakespeare, W. *The Tragedy of Hamlet*
Sophocles. *Antigone*
Sophocles. *Oedipus Rex*
Synge, J. *Riders to the Sea*
Wilde, O. *The Importance of Being Earnest*
Williams, T. *The Glass Menagerie*

BARIF Barnet, Sylvan, et al., ed. *An Introduction to Literature: Fiction, Poetry, Drama.* 9th ed. Glenview, IL: Scott, Foresman, and Company, 1989. 1244pp.
Albee, E. *The Sandbox*
Chekhov, A. *The Brute*
Ibsen, H. *A Doll's House*
Luce, C. *Slam the Door Softly*
Miller, A. *Death of a Salesman*
Norman, M. *'Night, Mother*
*Quem quaeritis*
Shakespeare, W. *The Tragedy of Hamlet*
Shakespeare, W. *The Tragedy of Macbeth*
Sophocles. *Antigone*
Sophocles. *Oedipus the King*
Williams, T. *The Glass Menagerie*

BARIG Barnet, Sylvan, et al., ed. *An Introduction to Literature: Fiction, Poetry, Drama.* 10th ed. New York: HarperCollins College Publishers, 1993. 1304pp.
Glaspell, S. *Trifles*
Ibsen, H. *A Doll's House*
Miller, A. *Death of a Salesman*
Oates, J. *Tone Clusters*

Shakespeare, W. *A Midsummer Night's Dream*
Shakespeare, W. *Othello*
Sophocles. *Antigone*
Sophocles. *Oedipus Rex*
Valdez, L. *Los vendidos*
Williams, T. *The Glass Menagerie*
Wilson, A. *Fences*

BARIH Barnet, Sylvan, et al., ed. *An Introduction to Literature: Fiction, Poetry, Drama.* 11th ed. New York: Longman, 1997. 1574pp.
Fierstein, H. *On Tidy Endings*
Glaspell, S. *Trifles*
Hwang, D. *The Sound of a Voice*
Ibsen, H. *A Doll's House*
Mamet, D. *Oleanna*
Miller, A. *Death of a Salesman*
Norman, M. *'Night, Mother*
Shakespeare, W. *Hamlet*
Shakespeare, W. *A Midsummer Night's Dream*
Sophocles. *Antigone*
Sophocles. *Oedipus Rex*
Valdez, L. *Los vendidos*
Wasserstein, W. *The Man in a Case*
Williams, T. *The Glass Menagerie*
Wilson, A. *Fences*

BARJ Barnet, Sylvan; Berman, Morton; and Burto, William, eds. *Tragedy and Comedy.* Boston: Little, Brown [1967] 764pp.
Aristophanes. *The Birds*
Ibsen, H. *Hedda Gabler*
Molière, J. *The Misanthrope*
Pirandello, L. *Henry IV*
Shakespeare, W. *As You like It*
Shakespeare, W. *The Tragedy of Othello*
Shaw, G. *Major Barbara*
Sophocles. *Oedipus the King*
Wilder, T. *The Matchmaker*
Williams, T. *A Streetcar Named Desire*

BARK Barnet, Sylvan, Berman, Morton, and Burto, William, eds. *Types of Drama: Plays and Essays.* Boston: Little, Brown, 1972. 674pp.
Aristophanes. *The Birds*
Bergman, I. *Wild Strawberries*
Brecht, B. *The Good Woman of Setzuan*
Chekhov, A. *The Cherry Orchard*
Ibsen, H. *Hedda Gabler*
Ionesco, E. *The Gap*
Jones, L. *Dutchman*
Miller, A. *Death of a Salesman*
Molière, J. *The Misanthrope*
O'Neill, E. *The Emperor Jones*
Pirandello, L. *Henry IV*

Shakespeare, W. *As You like It*
Shakespeare, W. *King Lear*
Shaw, G. *Major Barbara*
Sophocles. *Oedipus the King*
Zindel, P. *The Effect of Gamma Rays on Man-in-the-
    moon Marigolds*

BARKA Barnet, Sylvan, et al., compiler. *Types of Drama:
    Plays and Essays.* 2nd ed. Boston: Little, Brown,
    1977. 708pp.
Aristophanes. *Lysistrata*
Bergman, I. *Wild Strawberries*
Brecht, B. *The Good Woman of Setzuan*
Chekhov, A. *The Cherry Orchard*
Ibsen, H. *Hedda Gabler*
Ionesco, E. *The Gap*
Jones, L. *Dutchman*
Miller, A. *Death of a Salesman*
Molière, J. *The Misanthrope*
O'Neill, E. *The Emperor Jones*
Pirandello, L. *Six Characters in Search of an Author*
Shaffer, P. *Equus*
Shakespeare, W. *King Lear*
Shakespeare, W. *A Midsummer Night's Dream*
Shaw, G. *Major Barbara*
Sophocles. *Oedipus the King*
Zindel, P. *The Effect of Gamma Rays on Man-in-the-
    moon Marigolds*

BARKB Barnet, Sylvan, et al., compiler. *Types of Drama:
    Plays and Essays.* 3rd ed. Boston: Little, Brown,
    1981. 836pp.
Aristophanes. *Lysistrata*
Beckett, S. *Happy Days*
Bergman, I. *Wild Strawberries*
Chekhov, A. *The Cherry Orchard*
Ibsen, H. *A Doll's House*
Ibsen, H. *Hedda Gabler*
Jones, L. *Dutchman*
Marlowe, C. *Doctor Faustus*
Miller, A. *Death of a Salesman*
Molière, J. *The Misanthrope*
O'Neill, E. *Desire under the Elms*
Pinter, H. *The Dumb Waiter*
Pirandello, L. *Six Characters in Search of an Author*
Shaffer, P. *Equus*
Shakespeare, W. *A Midsummer Night's Dream*
Shakespeare, W. *The Tragedy of King Lear*
Shaw, G. *Major Barbara*
Sophocles. *Oedipus the King*
Strindberg, A. *The Ghost Sonata*
Synge, J. *Riders to the Sea*
Wilder, T. *The Matchmaker*

BARKC Barnet, Sylvan, et al., compiler. *Types of Drama:
    Plays and Essays.* 4th ed. Boston: Little, Brown,
    1985. 784pp.
Aristophanes. *Lysistrata*
Beckett, S. *Happy Days*
Bergman, I. *Wild Strawberries*
Chekhov, A. *The Cherry Orchard*
Fugard, A. *"Master Harold" . . . and the Boys*
Glaspell, S. *Trifles*
Ibsen, H. *A Doll's House*
Jones, L. *Dutchman*
Marlowe, C. *Doctor Faustus*
Miller, A. *Death of a Salesman*
Molière, J. *The Misanthrope*
Norman, M. *'Night, Mother*
Pinter, H. *The Dumb Waiter*
Pirandello, L. *Six Characters in Search of an Author*
Shaffer, P. *Equus*
Shakespeare, W. *A Midsummer Night's Dream*
Shakespeare, W. *The Tragedy of King Lear*
Shaw, G. *Arms and the Man*
Sophocles. *Oedipus the King*
Synge, J. *Riders to the Sea*
Wilde, O. *The Importance of Being Earnest*

BARKD Barnet, Sylvan, et al., compiler. *Types of Drama:
    Plays and Essays.* 5th ed. Glenview, IL: Scott,
    Foresman, and Company, 1989. 834pp.
Aristophanes. *Lysistrata*
Beckett, S. *Happy Days*
Chekhov, A. *The Cherry Orchard*
Fugard, A. *"Master Harold" . . . and the Boys*
Garcia Lorca, F. *The House of Bernarda Alba*
Glaspell, S. *Trifles*
Ibsen, H. *A Doll's House*
Jones, L. *Dutchman*
Luce, C. *Slam the Door Softly*
Merriam, E., Wagner, P., and Hofsiss, J. *Out of Our
    Fathers' House*
Miller, A. *Death of a Salesman*
Molière, J. *The Misanthrope*
Norman, M. *'Night, Mother*
O'Neill, E. *The Emperor Jones*
Pinter, H. *The Dumb Waiter*
Shaffer, P. *Equus*
Shakespeare, W. *A Midsummer Night's Dream*
Shakespeare, W. *The Tragedy of King Lear*
Shaw, G. *Arms and the Man*
Sophocles. *Antigone*
Sophocles. *Oedipus the King*
Wilde, O. *The Importance of Being Earnest*
Williams, T. *The Glass Menagerie*
Wilson, A. *Fences*

BARKE Barnet, Sylvan, et al., compiler. *Types of Drama:
Plays and Essays.* 6th ed. New York: HarperCollins
College Publishers, 1993. 806pp.
Albee, E. *The Sandbox*
Aristophanes. *Lysistrata*
Barrie, J. *The Twelve-pound Look*
Beckett, S. *Happy Days*
Brecht, B. *The Good Woman of Setzuan*
Chekhov, A. *The Cherry Orchard*
Fierstein, H. *On Tidy Endings*
Fugard, A. *"Master Harold" . . . and the Boys*
Glaspell, S. *Trifles*
Ibsen, H. *A Doll's House*
Miller, A. *Death of a Salesman*
Molière, J. *The Misanthrope*
Norman, M. *'Night, Mother*
Oates, J. *Tone Clusters*
O'Neill, E. *Desire under the Elms*
Pirandello, L. *Six Characters in Search of an Author*
*The Second Shepherds' Play*
Shakespeare, W. *A Midsummer Night's Dream*
Shakespeare, W. *The Tragedy of King Lear*
Shaw, G. *Arms and the Man*
Sophocles. *Antigone*
Sophocles. *Oedipus the King*
Stein, G. *The Mother of Us All*
Synge, J. *Riders to the Sea*
Valdez, L. *Los vendidos*
Wasserstein, W. *The Man in a Case*
Wilde, O. *The Importance of Being Earnest*
Williams, T. *The Glass Menagerie*
Wilson, A. *Fences*

BARKF Barnet, Sylvan, et al., compiler. *Types of Drama:
Plays and Essays.* 7th ed. New York: Longman,
1997. 1078pp.
Albee, E. *The Sandbox*
Aristophanes. *Lysistrata*
Beckett, S. *Happy Days*
Behn, A. *The Rover*
Brecht, B. *The Good Woman of Setzuan*
Chekhov, A. *The Cherry Orchard*
Euripides. *Medea*
*Everyman*
Fugard, A. *"Master Harold" . . . and the Boys*
Gerstenberg, A. *Overtones*
Glaspell, S. *Trifles*
Ibsen, H. *A Doll's House*
Ionesco, E. *The Lesson*
Jackson, A. *Shango Diaspora*
Kennedy, A. *Funnyhouse of a Negro*
Marlowe, C. *Doctor Faustus*
Miller, A. *Death of a Salesman*

Molière, J. *The Misanthrope*
Morton, C. *The Many Deaths of Danny Rosales*
O'Neill, E. *The Emperor Jones*
Pinter, H. *The Birthday Party*
*The Second Shepherds' Play*
Shakespeare, W. *A Midsummer Night's Dream*
Shakespeare, W. *The Tragedy of King Lear*
Shaw, G. *Major Barbara*
Sophocles. *Antigone*
Sophocles. *Oedipus Rex*
Soyinka, W. *The Strong Breed*
Strindberg, A. *Miss Julie*
Synge, J. *Riders to the Sea*
Valdez, L. *Los vendidos*
Wilde, O. *The Importance of Being Earnest*
Williams, T. *The Glass Menagerie*
Yamauchi, W. *And the Soul Shall Dance*

BARN Barranger, Milly S. *Understanding Plays.* Boston:
Allyn & Bacon, 1990. 720pp.
Brecht, B. *Mother Courage and Her Children*
Chekhov, A. *The Cherry Orchard*
Fornes, M. *The Conduct of Life*
Ibsen, H. *Hedda Gabler*
Müller, H. *Hamletmachine*
Pirandello, L. *Six Characters in Search of an Author*
Shakespeare, W. *The Tragedy of Hamlet, Prince of
Denmark*
Shepard, S. *Buried Child*
Sophocles. *Oedipus the King*
Williams, T. *The Glass Menagerie*
Wilson, A. *Fences*

BARNA Barranger, Milly S. *Understanding Plays.* 2nd ed.
Boston: Allyn & Bacon, 1994. 758pp.
Beckett, S. *Footfalls*
Brecht, B. *Galileo*
Chekhov, A. *The Cherry Orchard*
Churchill, C. *Fen*
Fornes, M. *The Conduct of Life*
Hellman, L. *The Little Foxes*
Ibsen, H. *Hedda Gabler*
Machado, E. *Broken Eggs*
Müller, H. *Hamletmachine*
Overmayer, E. *On the Verge or the Geography of
Yearning*
Shakespeare, W. *The Tragedy of Hamlet, Prince of
Denmark*
Shepard, S. *Buried Child*
Sheridan, R. *The School for Scandal*
Sophocles. *Oedipus the King*
Williams, T. *The Glass Menagerie*

Wilson, A. *Fences*
Wolfe, G. *The Colored Museum*

BARO Barranger, Milly Slater, and Dodson, Daniel B.
        *Generations: An Introduction to Drama.* New
        York: Harcourt, Brace, Jovanovich, 1971. 431pp.
    Arrabal, F. *Picnic on the Battlefield*
    Hansberry, L. *A Raisin in the Sun*
    Ibsen, H. *Ghosts*
    Miller, A. *All My Sons*
    Molière, J. *The Miser*
    Shakespeare, W. *Romeo and Juliet*
    Sophocles. *Antigone*

BARR Barrows, Herbert; Heffner, Hubert; Ciardi, John
        and Douglas, Wallace, eds. *An Introduction to
        Literature.* Boston: Houghton Mifflin [c. 1959]
        1331pp.
    Chekhov, A. *The Cherry Orchard*
    Ibsen, H. *The Wild Duck*
    O'Casey, S. *Juno and the Paycock*
    Pirandello, L. *Six Characters in Search of an Author*
    Shaw, G. *Candida*
    Wilde, O. *The Importance of Being Earnest*

BARS Barrows, Marjorie Wescott, and others, eds.
        *The American Experience: Drama.* New
        York: Macmillan, 1968. 371pp. (Rev. ed. of
        *Contemporary American Drama*)
    Albee, E. *The Sandbox*
    Anderson, M. *Barefoot in Athens*
    Hellman, L. *The Little Foxes*
    Wilder, T. *The Matchmaker*
    Williams, T. *The Glass Menagerie*

BART Barrows, Marjorie Wescott, compilers . . . *Currents
        in Drama.* Rev. ed. New York: Macmillan [1968]
        327pp.
    Benét, S. *The Devil and Daniel Webster*
    Čapek, K. *R.U.R.*
    Chekhov, A. *The Boor*
    Milne, A. *The Ugly Duckling*
    Saroyan, W. *The Man with the Heart in the Highlands*
    Shakespeare, W. *A Midsummer Night's Dream*
    Tagore, R. *The Post Office*

BARU Barrows, Marjorie Wescott, ed. *The English
        Tradition: Drama.* New York: Macmillan, 1968.
        477pp.
    Goldsmith, O. *She Stoops to Conquer*
    O'Casey, S. *The Plough and the Stars*
    Osborne, J. *A Subject of Scandal and Concern*
    Shakespeare, W. *Macbeth*
    Shaw, G. *Arms and the Man*

BARV Barrows, Marjorie Wescott, and Dolkey, Matthew,
        eds. *Modern English Drama.* New York:
        Macmillan [c. 1964] 358pp.
    Dane, C. *Wild Decembers*
    Priestley, J. *They Came to the City*
    Shaw, G. *Arms and the Man*
    Sherriff, R. *Home at Seven*

BAS Baskervill, Charles Read; Heltzel, Virgil B.; and
        Nethercot, Arthur H., eds. *Elizabethan and Stuart
        Plays.* New York: Holt [c. 1934] 1660pp.
    *Arden of Feversham*
    *Attowell's Jig (Francis' New Jig)*
    Beaumont, F., and Fletcher, J. *The Knight of the Burning
        Pestle*
    Beaumont, F., and Fletcher, J. *The Maid's Tragedy*
    Beaumont, F., and Fletcher, J. *Philaster*
    Chapman, G. *Bussy d'Ambois*
    Dekker, T. *The Honest Whore, Part I*
    Dekker, T. *The Shoemakers' Holiday*
    Fletcher, J. *The Faithful Shepherdess*
    Ford, J. *The Broken Heart*
    Ford, J. *Perkin Warbeck*
    Ford, J., Dekker, T., and Rowley, W. *The Witch of
        Edmonton*
    Gascoigne, G. *Supposes*
    Greene, R. *Friar Bacon and Friar Bungay*
    Greene, R. *George a Greene*
    Heywood, T. *A Woman Killed with Kindness*
    Jonson, B. *The Alchemist*
    Jonson, B. *Every Man in His Humour*
    Jonson, B. *The Hue and Cry after Cupid*
    Jonson, B. *The Sad Shepherd*
    Jonson, B. *Sejanus, His Fall*
    Jonson, B. *Volpone*
    Kyd, T. *The Spanish Tragedy*
    Lyly, J. *Endymion*
    Marlowe, C. *Doctor Faustus*
    Marlowe, C. *Edward II*
    Marlowe, C. *Tamburlaine, Part I*
    Marston, J., and Webster, J. *The Malcontent*
    Massinger, P. *The Maid of Honor*
    Massinger, P. *A New Way to Pay Old Debts*
    Middleton, T. *A Trick to Catch the Old One*
    Middleton, T., and Rowley, W. *The Changeling*
    Norton, T., and Sackville, T. *Gorboduc*
    Peele, G. *The Arraignment of Paris*
    Peele, G. *The Old Wives' Tale*
    Preston, T. *Cambises*
    Shirley, J. *The Cardinal*
    Shirley, J. *The Lady of Pleasure*
    Stevenson, W. *Gammer Gurton's Needle*
    Udall, N. *Roister Doister*
    Webster, J. *The Duchess of Malfi*

BAT Bates, Alfred. *The Drama: Its History, Literature, and Influence on Civilization.* London: Athenian Society, 1903–1904. 22 vols.

Aeschylus. *Eumenides* 1
Alfieri, V. *Myrrha* 5
Aristophanes. *The Clouds* 2
Aristophanes. *Ecclesiazusae* 21
Babo, J. *Dagobert, King of the Franks* 12
Beaumont, F., and Fletcher, J. *The Knight of the Burning Pestle* 14
Benedix, R. *Obstinacy* 11
Bjørnson, B. *A Gauntlet* 17
Boucicault, D. *London Assurance* 22
Brougham, J. *Pocahontas* 20
Bulwer-Lytton, E. *Money* 16
Burke, C. *Rip Van Winkle* 19
Calderón de la Barca, P. *Belshazzar's Feast* 4
Chekhov, A. *A Marriage Proposal* 18
Colman, G., and Garrick D. *The Clandestine Marriage* 15
Cowley, Mrs. H. *The Belle's Stratagem* 15
Dancourt, F. *Woman's Craze for Titles* 8
*The Death Stone* 3
Euripides. *The Cyclops* 1
*Everyman* 4
Farquhar, G. *The Beaux' Stratagem* 22
*The Fatal Error* 21
Fath-Ali, M. *The Alchemist* 3
Gazul, C. [pseudonym] *Ines Mendo; or, the Triumph of Prejudice* 21
Gilbert, W. *Sweethearts* 16
Goethe, J. *Iphigenia in Tauris* 11
Goethe, J. *Stella* 12
Gogol, N. *The Inspector (Revisor)* 18
Goldoni, C. *The Post-inn* 5
Gorki, M. *In the Depths* 18
Guinon, A., and Marni, J. *The Yoke* 21
Hanshew, T. *The Fortyniners* 20
Hauptmann, G. *Hannele* 12
Hersha Deva, S. *Retnavali* 3
Holberg, L. *The Loquacious Barber* 17
Home, J. *Douglas* 14
Ibsen, H. *Ghosts* 17
Iffland, A. *Conscience* 11
Ireland, W. *Vortigern* 22
Jones, J. *Solon Shingle* 20
Jonson, B. *Every Man in His Humour* 14
Kock, P. *A Happy Day* 9
Kotzebue, A. *Egotist and Pseudo-critic (Herr Gottlieb Merks)* 11
Kotzebue, A. *Lover's Vows; or, the Natural Son* 21
Le Sage, A. *Crispin, Rival of His Master* 8
Lessing, G. *The Soldier's Fortune (Minna von Barnhelm)* 10

Longfellow, H. *The Spanish Student* 19
Maeterlinck, M. *The Death of Tintagiles* 21
*The Martyrdom of Ali* 3
Massinger, P. *A New Way to Pay Old Debts* 13
Maupassant, G. *The Household Peace* 9
Metastasio, P. *The Dream of Scipio* 5
"Mr. Punch." *A Dramatic Sequel to the Lady of Lyons; or, In the Lyons Den* 22
"Mr. Punch." *A Dramatic Sequel to Hamlet; or, the New Wing at Elsinore* 22
"Mr. Punch." *Omar and Oh My!* 21
Molière, J. *L'école des maris (School for Husbands)* 7
Musset, A. *The Chandelier* 9
Ohnet, G. *The Iron Manufacturer* 9
Payne, J. *Therese, the Orphan of Geneva* 19
*The Philosopher Duped by Love* 7
Plautus. *Amphitryon; or, Jupiter in Disguise* 21
*The Printer's Apprentice* 4
Racine, J. *Les plaideurs (The Suitors)* 7
Robertson, T. *Society* 16
Rueda, L. *The Seventh Farce* 6
Sachs, H. *Raising the Devil* 10
Scala, F. *The Faithful Friend* 5
Schiller, F. *The Camp of Wallenstein* 10
Schnitzler, A. *Questioning the Irrevocable* 12
Shadwell, T. *The Lancashire Witches, and Tegue O. Divelly* 22
Sophocles. *Antigone* 1
Terence. *The Eunuch* 2
Tobin, J. *The Honeymoon* 16
Torres Naharro, B. *Hymen* 6
Townley, J. *High life below Stairs* 16
Udall, N. *Ralph Roister Doister* 13
Vanbrugh, J. *The Provoked Husband* 15
Vega Carpio, L. *The Dog in the Manger* 6
Voltaire, F. *Mahomet* 8
Voltaire, F. *Socrates* 8
*The Wept of the Wish-ton-wish* 19
Werner, F. *The Twenty-fourth of February* 10

BAUG Baugh, Albert C., and McClelland, George W., eds. *English Literature.* New York: Appleton-Century-Crofts [c. 1954] 1480pp.

Dryden, J. *All for Love*
Marlowe, C. *The Tragical History of Doctor Faustus*
Wilde, O. *Lady Windermere's Fan*

BAUL Bauland, Peter, and Ingram, William, compiler. *The Tradition of the Theatre.* Boston: Allyn and Bacon, 1971. 633pp.

Brecht, B. *The Caucasian Chalk Circle*
Chekhov, A. *The Cherry Orchard*
Dürrenmatt, F. *The Visit*
Ibsen, H. *Hedda Gabler*

Miller, A. *The Crucible*
Molière, J. *The Would-be Gentleman*
*The Second Shepherds' Play*
Shaw, G. *The Devil's Disciple*
Sophocles. *Antigone*
Strindberg, A. *A Dream Play*
Webster, J. *The Duchess of Malfi*
Wycherley, W. *The Country Wife*

BAYLISS, JOHN *See* NEWR *New Road.*

BAYM Baylor, Robert, and Moore, James, ed. *In the
    Presence of This Continent: American Themes and
    Ideas.* New York: Holt, Rinehart and Winston,
    1971. 551pp.
Gurney, A. *The Golden Fleece*
Humphrey, H., and Baldwin, J. *My Childhood*
Lamb, M. *But What Have You Done for Me Lately?*
Terry, M. *Calm Down, Mother*
Trumbo, D. *Opening Sequence*

BEAC *Beacon Lights of Literature.* [Edited by] Marquis
    E. Shattuck, Rudolph W. Chamberlain, Edwin
    B. Richards. [Books six-twelve] Syracuse, NY:
    Iroquois, 1940. 7 vols.
Coppée, F. *The Violin Maker of Cremona* 8
Down, O. *The Maker of Dreams* 12
Dunsany, R. *A Night at an Inn* 11
Glaspell, S. *Trifles* 11
Goldsmith, O. *She Stoops to Conquer* 11
Gregory, I. *The Rising of the Moon* 12
Gregory, I. *Spreading the News* 8
Hall, H., and Middlemass, R. *The Valiant* 10
Kaufman, G., and Connelly, M. *Merton of the Movies*
    12
MacKaye, P. *Sam Average* 11
Moeller, P. *Helena's Husband* 12
Moorhouse, A. *The Grand Cham's Diamond* 10
O'Neill, E. *Ile* 12
Saunders, L. *The Knave of Hearts* 7
Shakespeare, W. *Julius Caesar* 11
Shakespeare, W. *Macbeth* 12
Shakespeare, W. *The Merchant of Venice* 10
Shakespeare, W. *A Midsummer Night's Dream* 9
Walker, S. *The Medicine Show* 11

BEAD Beadle, Richard, and King, Pamela M., eds. *York
    Mystery Plays: A Selection in Modern Spelling.*
    Oxford: Clarendon Press, 1984. 279pp.
*Christ before Annas and Caiaphas (The Bowers and
    Fletchers)*
*Christ before Herod (The Litsters)*
*Christ before Pilate (1): The Dream of Pilate's Wife
    (The Tapiters and Couchers)*

*Christ before Pilate (2): The Judgement*
*The Conspiracy (The Cutlers)*
*The Crucifixion (The Pinners)*
*The Death of Christ (The Butchers)*
*The Entry into Jerusalem (The Skinners)*
*The Fall of Man (The Coopers)*
*The Fall of the Angels (The Barkers)*
*The Flight into Egypt (The Marshals)*
*The Flood (The Fishers and the Mariners)*
*The Harrowing of Hell (The Saddlers)*
*Herod and the Magi (The Masons; the Goldsmiths)*
*Joseph's Trouble about Mary (The Pewterers and
    Founders)*
*The Last Judgement (The Mercers)*
*Moses and Pharoah (The Hosiers)*
*The Nativity (The Tilethatchers)*
*The Resurrection (The Carpenters)*
*The Slaughter of the Innocents (The Girdlers and
    Nailers)*
*The Temptation (The Smiths)*

BEAL Beal, Richard S., and Korg, Jacob, eds. *The
    Complete Reader.* Englewood Cliffs, NJ: Prentice-
    Hall, 1961. 630pp.
Shakespeare, W. *The Chronicle History of King Henry
    the IV, Part 1*
Shaw, G. *Arms and the Man*
Sophocles. *Oedipus the King*

BEAM Beal, Richard S., and Korg, Jacob, eds. *The
    Complete Reader.* 2nd ed. Englewood Cliffs, NJ:
    Prentice-Hall, 1967. 627pp.
Shakespeare, W. *Henry IV, Part 1*
Shaw, G. *Arms and the Man*
Sophocles. *Oedipus*
Yeats, W. *Purgatory*

BEAN Bean, Annemarie, ed. *A Sourcebook of African-
    American Performance: Plays, People, Movements.*
    London and New York: Routledge, 1999. 360pp.
Baraka, A. *Home on the Range*
Baraka, A. *Police*
Bullins, E. *Clara's Ole Man*
McCauley, R. *Sally's Rape*
Parks, S. *The America Play*
Sanchez, S. *The Bronx Is Next*

BEAR Beardsley, Monroe C.; Daniel, Robert; and Leggett,
    Glenn, eds. *Theme and Form.* Englewood Cliffs,
    NJ: Prentice-Hall, 1956. 725pp.
Shakespeare, W. *Othello*
Shaw, G. *Arms and the Man*
Sophocles. *Antigone*
Thomas, D. *The Doctor and the Devils*

BEAS Beardsley, Monroe C., et al., eds. *Theme and Form: An Introduction to Literature.* 4th ed. Englewood Cliffs, NJ: Prentice-Hall, 1975. 711pp.
Brecht, B. *Life of Galileo*
McNally, T. *Botticelli*
Sophocles. *Oedipus the King*

BEATA Beaty, Jerome, and Hunter, J. Paul, eds. *The Norton Introduction to Literature.* 7th ed. New York: W. W. Norton & Company, 1998. 2132pp.
Chekhov, A. *The Bear*
Chekhov, A. *The Cherry Orchard*
Glaspell, S. *Trifles*
Hansberry, L. *A Raisin in the Sun*
Hellman, L. *The Little Foxes*
Ibsen, H. *Hedda Gabler*
Ives, D. *Sure Thing*
Miller, A. *Death of a Salesman*
Shakespeare, W. *Hamlet*
Shakespeare, W. *A Midsummer Night's Dream*
Shaw, G. *Pygmalion*
Sophocles. *Antigone*
Sophocles. *Oedipus the King*
Wilde, O. *The Importance of Being Earnest*
Williams, T. *A Streetcar Named Desire*

BECHHOFER, CARL ERIC. *See* ROE Roberts, Carl Eric Bechhofer, translator. *Five Russian Plays*

BECK Beckerman, Bernard, ed. *Five Plays of the English Renaissance.* New York: Meridian, 1993. 533pp.
Ford, J. *'Tis Pity She's a Whore*
Jonson, B. *Volpone, or, the Fox*
Marlowe, C. *The Tragical history of Doctor Faustus*
Middleton, T. *Women Beware Women*
Webster, J. *The Duchess of Malfi*

BEFOB *Before Brecht: Four German Plays.* Edited and translated by Eric Bentley. New York: Applause Theatre Book Publishers, 1985. 267pp. (Eric Bentley's Dramatic Repertoire vol. 1)
Büchner, G. *Leonce and Lena*
Schnitzler, A. *La ronde*
Sternheim, C. *The Underpants*
Wedekind, F. *Spring's Awakening*

BELC Bell, John, ed. *Bell's British Theatre, Farces—1784*; with a new introduction by Byrne R. S. Fone; and with new author and play indexes. New York: AMS Press, 1977. 4 vols.
Bate, H. *The Rival Candidates* 4
Bickerstaffe, I. *The Padlock* 3
Bickerstaffe, I. *The Sultan* 1

Bickerstaffe, I. *Thomas and Sally* 2
Burney, C. *The Cunning Man* 2
Carey, H. *Chrononhotonthologos* 2
Carey, H. *The Contrivances* 4
Cibber, C. *Flora* 4
Coffey, C. *The Devil to Pay* 2
Colman, G. *Comus* 4
Colman, G. *The Deuce Is in Him* 1
Colman, G. *The Musical Lady* 2
Colman, G. *Polly Honeycombe* 3
Dibdin, C. *The Deserter* 4
Dodsley, R. *The Miller of Mansfield* 3
Dodsley, R. *The Toy-shop* 3
Fielding, H. *The Intriguing Chambermaid* 3
Fielding, H. *The Lottery* 2
Fielding, H. *The Mock Doctor* 1
Fielding, H. *The Virgin Unmasked* 2
Foote, S. *The Author* 3
Foote, S. *The Commissary* 4
Foote, S. *The Englishman in Paris* 3
Foote, S. *The Englishman Return'd from Paris* 3
Foote, S. *The Knights* 1
Foote, S. *The Lyar* 2
Foote, S. *The Mayor of Garrat* 2
Foote, S. *The Orators* 4
Foote, S. *The Patron* 4
Foote, S. *Taste* 1
Garrick, D. *Bon Ton* 4
Garrick, D. *Bucks, Have at Ye All* 4
Garrick, D. *Catharine and Petruchio* 3
Garrick, D. *Cymon* 3
Garrick, D. *The Guardian* 1
Garrick, D. *High Life below Stairs* 1
Garrick, D. *Lethe* 1
Garrick, D. *The Lying Valet* 2
Garrick, D. *Miss in Her Teens* 1
Garrick, D. *Neck or Nothing* 2
Hawkesworth, J. *Edgar and Emmeline* 4
Jackman, I. *All the World's a Stage* 4
Mendez, M. *The Chaplet* 1
Murphy, A. *The Apprentice* 1
Murphy, A. *The Citizen* 3
Murphy, A. *The Old Maid* 2
Murphy, A. *Three Weeks after Marriage* 4
Murphy, A. *The Upholsterer* 1
O'Hara, K. *The Golden Pippin* 3
O'Hara, K. *Midas* 2
Ravenscroft, E. *The Anatomist* 1
Reed, J. *The Register office* 3
Shakespeare, W. *Florizel and Perdita* (altered from) 1
Sheridan, T. *Captain O'Blunder* 3
*The Spirit of Contradiction (by a Gentleman of Cambridge)* 4
Smollet, T. *The Reprisal* 2
Woods, W. *The Twins* 4

BELG Bell, John, ed. *Bell's British Theatre: Selected Plays, 1791–1802, 1797*; 49 plays unrepresented in eds. of 1776–1781 and 1784; with a new introduction and preface by Byrne R. S. Fone and with new author and play indexes. New York: AMS Press, 1977. 16 vols.

Bickerstaffe, I. *The Hypocrite*, altered from Colley Cibber 1

Bickerstaffe, I. *The Plain Dealer*, altered from William Wycherley 1

Bickerstaffe, I. *The School for Fathers* 1

Cibber, C. *Love Makes a Man* 2

Colman, G. *Bonduca*, altered from Beaumont and Fletcher 3

Colman, G. *The Jealous Wife* 3

Cowley, H. *Albina, Countess Raimond* 14

Cumberland, R. *Battle of Hastings* 6

Cumberland, R. *The Brothers* 5

Cumberland, R. *The Carmelite* 5

Cumberland, R. *The Choleric Man* 6

Cumberland, R. *The Fashionable Lover* 6

Cumberland, R. *The Natural Son* 6

Cumberland, R. *The West Indian* 5

Dodsley, R. *Cleone* 15

Foote, S. *The Minor* 15

Franklin, T. *Earl of Warwick* 16

Garrick, D. *The Clandestine Marriage* 7

Garrick, D. *Cymon* 7

Glover, R. *Medea* 15

Goldsmith, O. *The Good Natured Man* 8

Goldsmith, O. *She Stoops to Conquer* 8

Griffiths, E. *School for Rakes* 2

Hartson, H. *The Countess of Salisbury* 11

Hoole, J. *Cyrus* 9

Hoole, J. *Timanthes* 9

Hull, T. *Henry II* 4

Johnson, S. *Irene* 8

Jonson, B. *The Alchemist* 16

Kelly, H. *False Delicacy* 10

Kelly, H. *School for Wives* 10

Kelly, H. *A Word to the Wise* 10

Kendrick, W. *Falstaff's Wedding* 3

Lee, N. *Lucius Junius Brutus* 11

Lee, S. *Chapter of Accidents* 11

Lillo, G. *The Fatal Curiosity* 9

Macklin, C. *Man of the World* 4

Mason, W. *Caractacus* 12

Mason, W. *Elfrida* 12

Milton, J. *Samson Agonistes* 12

Murphy, A. *Grecian Daughter* 13

Murphy, A. *The Orphan of China* 14

Murphy, A. *School for Guardians* 14

Murphy, A. *A Way to Keep Him* 13

Murphy, A. *Zenobia* 13

Shakespeare, W. *Pericles* (altered from) 7

Sheridan, F. *The Discovery* 4

Thomson, J. *Edward and Eleonora* 2

Whitehead, W. *School for Lovers* 16

BELK Bell, John, ed. *Bell's British theatre, 1776–1781*; with a new introduction and preface by Byrne R. S. Fone and with new author and play indexes. New York: AMS Press, 1977. 21 vols. contains 105 plays, each with special title page and separate pagination. [Repr. of the 1776–1781 ed. pub. by J. Bell, London]

Addison, J. *Cato* 3

Addison, J. *The Drummer* 11

Banks, J. *The Albion Queens* 7

Banks, J. *Anna Bullen* 14

Beaumont, F., and Fletcher, J. *Jovial Crew* 21

Beaumont, F., and Fletcher, J. *Philaster* 18

Beaumont, F., and Fletcher, J. *Rule a Wife and Have a Wife* 4

Bickerstaffe, I. *Lionel and Clarissa* 21

Bickerstaffe, I. *Love in a Village* 21

Bickerstaffe, I. *Maid of the Mill* 21

Brooke, H. *Gustavus Vasa* 18

Brown, J. *Barbarossa* 10

Centlivre, S. *A Bold Stroke for a Wife* 6

Centlivre, S. *The Busy Body* 8

Centlivre, S. *The Wonder* 4

Cibber, C. *The Careless Husband* 8

Cibber, C. *The Double Gallant* 13

Cibber, C. *The Lady's Last Stake* 19

Cibber, C. *Love's Last Shift* 17

Cibber, C. *The Refusal* 11

Cibber, C. *She Wou'd and She Wou'd Not* 6

Cibber, C. *Ximena* 14

Congreve, W. *The Double Dealer* 13

Congreve, W. *Love for Love* 8

Congreve, W. *The Mourning Bride* 3

Congreve, W. *The Old Batchelor* 2

Congreve, W. *The Way of the World* 11

Crisp, S. *Virginia* 18

Dryden, J. *All for Love* 5

Dryden, J. *Amphitryon* 11

Dryden, J. *Don Sebastian, King of Portugal* 12

Dryden, J. *The Spanish Fryar* 13

Dryden, J., and Lee, N. *Oedipus* 12

Farquhar, G. *The Beaux' Stratagem* 2

Farquhar, G. *The Constant Couple* 15

Farquhar, G. *The Inconstant* 13

Farquhar, G. *The Recruiting Officer* 4

Farquhar, G. *Sir Harry Wildair* 15

Farquhar, G. *The Twin Rivals* 17

Fenton, E. *Marianne* 14

Fielding, H. *The Miser* 6

Fletcher, J. *The Chances* 15
Gay, J. *Achilles* 9
Gay, J. *The Beggar's Opera* 9
Gay, J. *Polly* 9
Glover, R. *Boadicia* 20
Goldoni, C. *Accomplished Maid* 21
Havard, W. *King Charles I* 12
Hill, A. *Alzira* 10
Hill, A. *Merope* 10
Hill, A. *Zara* 1
Hoadly, J. *The Suspicious Husband* 4
Home, J. *Douglas* 20
Howard, R. *The Committee* 2
Hughes, J. *Siege of Damascus* 1
Johnson, C. *Country Lasses* 19
Jones, H. *The Earl of Essex* 3
Jonson, B. *The Alchymist* 17
Jonson, B. *Every Man in His Humour* 2
Jonson, B. *Volpone* 19
Lee, N. *Alexander the Great* 7
Lee, N. *Theodosius* 7
Lillo, G. *George Barnwell* 5
Mallet, D. *Eurydice* 16
Mallet, D. *Elvira* 20
Miller, J. *Mahomet* 7
Milton, J. *Comus* 9
Moore, E. *The Foundling* 13
Moore, E. *The Gamester* 12
Otway, T. *The Orphan* 5
Otway, T. *Venice Preserv'd* 1
Phillips, A. *Distressed Mother* 1
Ramsay, A. *The Gentle Shepherd* 9
Rowe, N. *Ambitious Step-mother* 16
Rowe, N. *The Fair Penitent* 3
Rowe, N. *Jane Shore* 1
Rowe, N. *Lady Jane Gray* 7
Rowe, N. *The Royal Convert* 7
Rowe, N. *Tamerlane* 3
Rowe, N. *Ulysses* 18
Shadwell, C. *The Fair Quaker of Deal; or, the Humours of the Navy* 17
Shirley, J. *Gamesters* 19
Shirley, W. *Edward the Black Prince* 16
Smith, E. *Phaedra and Hippolitus* 10
Southerne, T. *Isabella* 5
Southerne, T. *Oroonoko* 10
Steele, R. *The Conscious Lovers* 4
Steele, R. *The Funeral: or, Grief a la Mode* 8
Steele, R. *The Tender Husband* 8
Theobald, L. *Electra* 16
Thomson, J. *Sophonisba* 18
Thomson, J. *Tancred and Sigismunda* 5
Vanbrugh, J. *City Wives Confederacy* 15
Vanbrugh, J. *Mistake* 19

Vanbrugh, J. *The Provok'd Wife* 2
Vanbrugh, J. *The Relapse* 11
Vanbrugh, J., and Cibber, C. *The Provok'd Husband* 6
Villiers, G. *The Rehearsal* 15
Whitehead, W. *Creusa, Queen of Athens* 20
Whitehead, W. *The Roman Father* 20
Wycherley, W. *The Country Wife* 17
Young, E. *The Brothers* 14
Young, E. *Busiris* 16
Young, E. *The Revenge* 12

BELLN Bell, Nancy, with Bessai, Diane, eds. *Five from the Fringe: A Selection of Five Plays First Performed at the Fringe Theatre Event.* Edmonton: NeWest Press, 1986. 159pp.
Albert, L. *Cut!*
Brown, K. *Life after Hockey*
Gareau, L. *The Betrayal*
Selkirk, J., and Selkirk, G. *The Land Called Morning*
Small Change Theatre. *One Beautiful Evening*

BELLW Bell, William, ed. *Contours: Plays from across Canada.* Toronto: Irwin Publishing, 1993. 331pp.
Dorn, R. *One's a Heifer*
Fanetti, E. *The Last Moon*
French, D. *Salt-water Moon*
French, D. *The Tender Branch*
Gélinas, G. *The Passion of Narcisse Mondoux*
Hurley, J. *Inukshuk*
Moore, M. *Customs*
Petch, S. *Another Morning*
Taylor, D. *Toronto at Dreamer's Rock*

BEN Benedikt, Michael, and Wellwarth, George E., eds. and trs. *Modern French Theatre: The Avant-garde, Dada, and Surrealism, An Anthology of Plays.* New York, Dutton, 1964. 406pp.
Anouilh, J., and Aurenche, J. *Humulus the Mute*
Apollinaire, G. *The Breasts of Tiresias*
Aragon, L. *The Mirror-wardrobe One Fine Evening*
Artaud, A. *Jet of Blood*
Breton, A., and Soupault, P. *If You Please*
Cocteau, J. *The Wedding on the Eiffel Tower*
Daumal, R. *En gggarrrde!*
Desnos, R. *La Place de l'Etoile*
Gilbert-Lecomte, R. *The Odyssey of Ulysses the Palmiped*
Ionesco, E. *The Painting*
Jarry, A. *King Ubu*
Pinget, R. *Architruc*
Radiguet, R. *The Pelicans*
Salacrou, A. *A Circus Story*
Tardieu, J. *One Way for Another*

Tzara, T. *The Gas Heart*
Vitrac, R. *The Mysteries of Love*

BENA Benedikt, Michael, and Wellwarth, George E., eds.
     *Modern Spanish Theatre: An Anthology of Plays.*
     New York, Dutton, 1968. 416pp.
     Alberti, R. *Night and War in the Prado Museum*
     Arrabal, F. *First Communion*
     Bellido, J. *Football*
     Casona, A. *Suicide Prohibited in Springtime*
     García Lorca, F. *The Shoemaker's Prodigious Wife*
     Mihura, M. *Three Top Hats*
     Olmo, L. *The News Item*
     Valle-Inclán, R. *Divine Words*

BENB Benedikt, Michael, and Wellwarth, George E., eds.
     and trs. *Postwar German Theatre: An Anthology of
     Plays.* New York: Dutton, 1967. 348pp.
     Borchert, W. *The Outsider*
     Dorst, T. *Freedom for Clemens*
     Dürrenmatt, F. *Incident at Twilight*
     Frisch, M. *The Great Fury of Philip Hotz*
     Grass, G. *Rocking Back and Forth*
     Hildesheimer, W. *Nightpiece*
     Kaiser, G. *The Raft of the Medusa*
     Laszlo, C. *The Chinese Icebox*
     Laszlo, C. *Let's Eat Hair!*
     Sylvanus, E. *Dr. Korczak and the Children*
     Weiss, P. *The Tower*

BENET, WILLIAM ROSE. *See* OXF *Oxford Anthology
     of American Literature.* Edited by William Rose
     Benét and Norman Holmes Pearson

BENN Bennett, Henry Garland, ed. *English Literature.*
     NY: American Book Company [c. 1935] 603pp.
     Goldsmith, O. *She Stoops to Conquer*
     Shakespeare, W. *Macbeth*

BENP Bennett, Henry Garland. *On the High Road.* NY:
     American Book Company [c. 1935] 600pp.
     Dowson, E. *The Pierrot of the Minute*
     *Everyman*
     Maeterlinck, M. *The Intruder*
     O'Neill, E. *Where the Cross Is Made*
     Riggs, L. *Knives from Syria*
     Shakespeare, W. *Julius Caesar*
     Sheridan, R. *The Rivals*
     Wilde, P. *Confessional*

BENPB Bens, John H., ed. *Facing Some Problems.* New
     York: Holt, Rinehart, and Winston, 1970. 306pp.
     Rattigan, T. *Table Number Seven*
     Shaw, I. *Bury the Dead*
     Steinbeck, J. *Of Mice and Men*

BENQ Benson, Carl Frederick, and Littleton, Taylor, eds.
     *The Idea of Tragedy.* Glenview, IL: Scott Foresman
     [1966] 370pp.
     Aeschylus. *Agamemnon*
     Chekhov, A. *Uncle Vanya*
     Ibsen, H. *Rosmersholm*
     Shakespeare, W. *King Lear*
     Sophocles. *King Oedipus*
     Webster, J. *The Duchess of Malfi*

BENR Bentley, Eric Russell, ed. *The Classic Theatre.* [1st
     ed.]. Garden City, NY: Doubleday [1958–1961]
     4 vols.
     Beaumarchais, P. *Figaro's Marriage; or, One Mad
     Day* 4
     Beolco, A. *Ruzzante Returns from the Wars* 1
     Calderón de la Barca, P. *Life Is a Dream* 3
     Calderón de la Barca, P. *Love after Death* 3
     Calderón de la Barca, P. *The Wonder-working
     Magician* 3
     Castro y Bellvis, G. *Exploits of the Cid* 4
     Cervantes Saavedra, M. *The Siege of Numantia* 3
     Corneille, P. *The Cid* 4
     Goethe, J. *Egmont* 2
     Goldoni, C. *Mirandolina* 1
     Goldoni, C. *The Servant of Two Masters*
     Gozzi, C. *The King Stag* 1
     Kleist, H. *Penthesilea* 2
     Kleist, H. *The Prince of Homburg* 2
     Lesage, A. *Turcaret* 4
     Machiavelli, N. *The Mandrake* 1
     Marivaux, P. *The False Confessions* 4
     Molière, J. *The Misanthrope* 4
     Racine, J. *Phaedra* 4
     Rojas, F. *Celestina; or, the Tragi-comedy of Calisto and
     Melibea* 3
     Schiller, J. *Don Carlos* 2
     Schiller, J. *Mary Stuart* 2
     Téllez, G. *The Trickster of Seville and His Guest of
     Stone* 3
     *The Three Cuckolds* 1
     Vega Carpio, L. *Fuente ovejuna* 3

BENS Bentley, Eric Russell, ed. *From the Modern
     Repertoire.* Series one-three. [Denver, CO]:
     University of Denver Press; Bloomington, IN:
     Indiana University Press. [c. 1949–1956] 3 vols.
     Anouilh, J. *Cecile; or, The School for Fathers* 3
     Becque, H. *La Parisienne* 1
     Brecht, B. *Galileo* 2
     Brecht, B. *Saint Joan of the Stockyards* 3
     Brecht, B. *The Threepenny Opera* 1
     Büchner, G. *Danton's Death* 1
     Büchner, G. *Leonce and Lena* 3
     Cocteau, J. *The Infernal Machine* 1

Cocteau, J. *Intimate Relations* 3
Cummings, E. *Him* 2
Eliot, T. *Sweeney Agonistes* 1
Fergusson, F. *The King and the Duke* 2
García Lorca, F. *The Love of Don Perlimplin and Belisa in the Garden* 1
Giraudoux, J. *Electra* 2
Grabbe, C. *Jest, Satire, Irony, and Deeper Significance* 2
Jeffers, R. *The Cretan Woman* 3
MacNeice, L. *The Dark Tower* 2
Mirbeau, O. *The Epidemic* 2
Musset, A. *A Door Should Be either Open or Shut* 3
Musset, A. *Fantasio* 1
Obey, A. *Venus and Adonis* 2
Ostrovsky, A. *Easy Money* 2
Pinero, A. *The Magistrate* 3
Romains, J. *Dr. Knock* 3
Schnitzler, A. *Anatol* 3
Schnitzler, A. *Round Dance* 1
Sternheim, C. *The Snob* 1
Wedekind, F. *The Marquis of Keith* 2
Yeats, W. *A Full Moon in March* 1
Zola, E. *Thérèse Raquin* 3

BENSA Bentley, Eric Russell, ed. *The Genius of the Italian Theater*. New York: New American Library [1964] 584pp.
Bruno, C. *The Candle Bearer*
*The Deceived*
Dovizi da Bibiena, B. *The Follies of Calandro*
Filippo, E. *Filumena Marturano*
Gozzi, C. *Turandot*
Pirandello, L. *The Emperor*
Tasso, T. *Amyntas*

BENSB Bentley, Eric Russell, ed. *The Great Playwrights: 25 Plays with Commentaries by Critics and Scholars*. Garden City, NY: Doubleday, 1972. 2 vols.
Aeschylus. *Prometheus Bound* 1
Brecht, B. *The Caucasian Chalk Circle* 2
Brecht, B. *Mother Courage* 2
Calderón de la Barca, P. *Life Is a Dream* 1
Chekhov, A. *The Three Sisters* 2
Euripides. *The Bacchae* 1
Ibsen, H. *Rosmersholm* 2
Ibsen, H. *The Wild Duck* 2
Jonson, B. *Volpone; or, the Fox* 1
Kleist, H. *Prince Frederick of Hamburg* 1
Molière, J. *Don Juan; or, the Stone Guest* 1
Molière, J. *The Misanthrope* 1
Pirandello, L. *Right You Are* 2
Pirandello, L. *Six Characters in Search of an Author* 2
Racine, J. *Phaedra* 1
Shakespeare, W. *King Lear* 1

Shakespeare, W. *Troilus and Cressida* 1
Shaw, G. *Major Barbara* 2
Shaw, G. *Saint Joan* 2
Sophocles. *Antigone* 1
Sophocles. *King Oedipus* 1
Strindberg, A. *Miss Julie* 2
Synge, J. *The Playboy of the Western World* 2
Vega Carpio, L. *Fuente ovejuna* 1
Wilde, O. *The Importance of Being Earnest* 2

BENSC Bentley, Eric Russell, ed. *Let's Get a Divorce! and Other Plays*. New York: Hill and Wang [c. 1958] 364pp.
Courteline, G. *These Cornfields*
Feydeau, G. *Keep an Eye on Amélie!*
Labiche, E., and Delacour, A. *Célimare*
Labiche, E., and Martin, E. *A Trip Abroad*
Prévert, J. *A United Family*
Sardou, V., and Najac, E. *Let's Get a Divorce!*

BENSD Bentley, Eric Russell, ed. *The Misanthrope and Other French Classics*. New York: Applause Theatre Book Publishers, 1986. 332pp. (Eric Bentley's Dramatic Repertoire, vol. 3)
Beaumarchais, P. *Figaro's Marriage; or, One Mad Day*
Castro y Bellvis, G. *Exploits of the Cid*
Corneille, P. *The Cid*
Molière, J. *The Misanthrope*
Racine, J. *Phaedra*

BENT Bentley, Eric Russell, ed. *The Modern Theatre*. [Plays] Garden City, NY: Doubleday [c. 1955–1960] 6 vols.
Anouilh, J. *Medea* 5
Anouilh, J. *Thieves' Carnival* 3
Becque, H. *Woman of Paris* 1
Beerbohm, M. *A Social Success* 6
Brecht, B. *The Measures Taken* 6
Brecht, B. *Mother Courage* 2
Brecht, B. *The Threepenny Opera* 1
Büchner, G. *Woyzeck* 1
Büchner, G. *Danton's Death* 5
Conrad, J. *One Day More* 3
Fitch, C. *Captain Jinks of the Horse Marines* 4
Ghelderode, M. *Escurial* 5
Giraudoux, J. *Electra* 1
Giraudoux, J. *Judith* 3
Gogol, N. *Gamblers* 3
Gogol, N. *The Marriage* 5
Labiche, E., and Marc-Michel. *An Italian Straw Hat* 3
Mitchell, L. *The New York Idea* 4
Musset, A. *Fantasio* 2
Musset, A. *Lorenzaccio* 6
O'Casey, S. *Cock-a-doodle Dandy* 5
Ostrovsky, A. *The Diary of a Scoundrel* 2

Saroyan, W. *The Man with the Heart in the Highlands* 4
Schnitzler, A. *La ronde* 2
Sternheim, C. *The Underpants* 6
Swerling, J., Burrows, A., and Loesser, F. *Guys and Dolls* 4
Verga, G. *Cavalleria rusticana* 1
Wedekind, F. *Spring's Awakening* 6
Wilder, T. *Pullman Car Hiawatha* 4
Yeats, W. *Purgatory* 2


BENU Bentley, Eric Russell, ed. *The Play: A Critical Anthology.* New York: Prentice-Hall, 1951. 774pp.
Ibsen, H. *Ghosts*
Miller, A. *Death of a Salesman*
Molière, J. *The Miser*
Rostand, E. *Cyrano de Bergerac*
Shakespeare, W. *Othello*
Shakespeare, W. *Twelfth Night*
Sophocles. *Antigone*
Strindberg, A. *The Ghost Sonata*
Wilde, O. *The Importance of Being Earnest*


BENV Bentley, Eric Russell, ed. *The Servant of Two Masters: And Other Italian Classics.* New York: Applause Theatre Book Publishers, 1986. 262pp. (These four plays, along with two additional plays, were originally published in 1958 as vol.1 of Classic Theatre with the title of *Six Italian Plays.*)
Beolco, A. *Ruzzante Returns from the Wars*
Goldoni, C. *The Servant of Two Masters*
Gozzi, C. *The King Stag*
Machiavelli, N. *The Mandrake*


BENY Bentley, Gerald Eades, ed. *The Development of English Drama.* New York: Appleton-Century-Crofts [c. 1950] 823pp.
*Abraham and Isaac*
Beaumont, F., and Fletcher, J. *The Knight of the Burning Pestle*
Boucicault, D. *London Assurance*
Congreve, W. *Love for Love*
Congreve, W. *The Way of the World*
Cumberland, R. *The West Indian*
Dekker, T. *The Shoemakers' Holiday*
*The Deluge; or, Noah's Flood*
Dryden, J. *All for Love; or, the World Well Lost*
Dryden, J., and Howard, R. *The Indian Queen*
*Everyman*
Fletcher, J. *The Wild-goose Chase*
Ford, J. *'Tis a Pity She's a Whore*
Goldsmith, O. *She Stoops to Conquer*
Greene, R. *Friar Bacon and Friar Bungay*
Jonson, B. *The Alchemist*
Lillo, G. *The London Merchant*

Marlowe, C. *Doctor Faustus*
Pinero, A. *The Second Mrs. Tanqueray*
*The Second Shepherds' Play*
Sheridan, R. *The School for Scandal*
Webster, J. *The White Devil*
Wilde, O. *Lady Windermere's Fan*


BENZ Benton, Charles William, ed. *Easy French Plays.* Chicago: Scott, Foresman, 1901. 236pp.
Girardin, E. de. *La joie fait peur*
Labiche, E. *La grammaire*
Scribe, E. *Les doigts de fée*


BERGH, ALBERT ELLERY. *See* DRA *Dramatic Masterpieces.*


BER Bergin, Thomas Goddard and Anderson, Theodore, eds. *French Plays.* New York: American Book Co. [c. 1941] 452pp.
Brieux, E. *Les trois filles de M. Dupont*
Hervieu, P. *La course du flambeau*
Mirbeau, O. *Les affaires sont les affaires*


BERKLEY, JAMES. *See* PATM, PATP *Patterns of Literature.*


BERMD Bermel, Albert, ed. *A Dozen French Farces: Medieval to Modern.* New York: Limelight Editions, 1997. 405pp.
Adamov, A. *Professor Taranne*
Beaumarchais, P. *The Barber of Seville*
Courteline, G. *Boubouroche*
Courteline, G. *The Police Chief's an Easygoing Guy*
Feydeau, G. *"Hey, Cut Out the Parading around Stark Naked!"*
Feydeau, G. *My Wife's Dead Mother*
Jarry, A. *Ubu cocu*
Labiche, E., and Delacour, A. *The Piggy Bank*
Languirand, J. *Autumn Violins*
Molière, J. *The Imaginary Invalid*
Prokofiev, S. *The Love of Three Oranges*
*The Washtub*


BERMG Bermel, Albert, ed. *The Genius of the French Theater.* New York: New American Library [c. 1961] 574pp.
Anouilh, J. *The Lark*
Beaumarchais, P. *The Barber of Seville*
Giraudoux, J. *Song of Songs*
Hugo, V. *Hernani*
Labiche, E., and Delacour. A. *Pots of Money*
Molière, J. *The Imaginary Invalid*
Racine, J. *Andromache*
Rostand, E. *The Romantics*

BERN Bernbaum, Ernest, ed. *Anthology of Romanticism.* New York: Ronald [c. 1948] 1238pp.
  Byron, G. *Manfred*
  Shelley, P. *Prometheus Unbound*

BERP Bert, Norman, A., ed. *Theatre Alive! An Introductory Anthology of World Drama.* Colorado Springs, CO: Meriwether Publishing Ltd., 1991. 796pp.
  Aiken, G. *Uncle Tom's Cabin, or, Life among the Lowly*
  Baraka, I. *Dutchman*
  *Everyman*
  Havel, V. *Largo desolato*
  Ibsen, H. *A Doll's House*
  Ionesco, E. *The Bald Soprano*
  Medoff, M. *Children of a Lesser God*
  Molière, J. *The Hypochondriac*
  Odets, C. *Waiting for Lefty*
  O'Neill, E. *The Hairy Ape*
  Rice, E. *The Adding Machine*
  Shakespeare, W. *The Tragedy of Othello, the Moor of Venice*
  Sophocles. *Oedipus the King*
  Williams, T. *Cat on a Hot Tin Roof*
  Zeami, M. *Izutsu (The Well-curb)*

BERPA Bert, Norman, A., ed. *Theatre Alive! An Introductory Anthology of World Drama.* Colorado Springs, CO: Meriwether Publishing Ltd., 1995. 831pp.
  Aiken, G. *Uncle Tom's Cabin, or, Life among the Lowly*
  Baraka, I. *Dutchman*
  *Everyman*
  Havel, V. *Largo desolato*
  Ibsen, H. *A Doll's House*
  Ionesco, E. *The Bald Soprano*
  Medoff, M. *Children of a Lesser God*
  Molière, J. *The Hypochondriac*
  Odets, C. *Waiting for Lefty*
  O'Neill, E. *The Hairy Ape*
  Rice, E. *The Adding Machine*
  Shakespeare, W. *The Tragedy of Othello, the Moor of Venice*
  Sophocles. *Oedipus the King*
  Terry, M., Schmidman, J., and Kimberlain, S. *Body Leaks*
  Williams, T. *Cat on a Hot Tin Roof*
  Zeami, M. *Izutsu (The Well-curb)*

BERR Bessai, Diane, and Kerr, Don, eds. *NeWest Plays by Women.* Edmonton: NeWest Press, 1987. 251pp.
  Boyd, P. *Inside Out*
  Glass, J. *Play Memory*
  Lill, W. *The Occupation of Heather Rose*
  Pollock, S. *Whiskey Six Cadenza*

BERS *Best American Plays: Eighth Series, 1974–1982.* Edited by Clive Barnes. New York: Crown Publishers, Inc., 1983. 548pp.
  Babe, T. *A Prayer for My Daughter*
  Henley, B. *Crimes of the Heart*
  Kopit, A. *Wings*
  McNally, T. *The Ritz*
  Mamet, D. *American Buffalo*
  Miller, J. *That Championship Season*
  Pomerance, B. *The Elephant Man*
  Rabe, D. *Streamers*
  Shange, N. *for colored girls who have considered suicide/when the rainbow is enuf*
  Shepard, S. *Buried Child*
  Simon, N. *Chapter Two*
  Slade, B. *Same time, Next Year*
  Walker, J. *The River Niger*
  Weller, M. *Loose Ends*
  Wheeler, H. *A Little Night Music*
  Williams, T. *A Lovely Sunday for Creve Coeur*
  Wilson, L. *Talley's Folly*

BERT *Best American Plays: Ninth Series, 1983–1992.* Edited by Clive Barnes. New York: Crown Publishers, Inc., 1993. 526p
  Foote, H. *The Widow Claire*
  Gardner, H. *I'm Not Rappaport*
  Gurney, A. *The Cocktail Hour*
  Hoffman, W. *As Is*
  Howe, T. *Painting Churches*
  Kopit, A. *End of the World*
  Mamet, D. *Glengarry Glen Ross*
  McNally, T. *Frankie and Johnny in the Clair de Lune*
  Rabe, D. *Hurlyburly*
  Simon, N. *Brighton Beach Memoirs*
  Sondheim, S., and Lapine, J. *Into the Woods*
  Sterner, J. *Other People's Money*
  Uhry, A. *Driving Miss Daisy*
  Weller, M. *Spoils of War*
  Wilson, A. *Joe Turner's Come and Gone*
  Wilson, L. *Burn This*

BES *Best Plays of 1894/1899–1999/2000; and The Yearbook of the Drama in America.* Edited by R. B. Mantle, G. P. Sherwood, John Chapman, Louis Kronenberger, Henry Hewes, Otis L. Guernsey, Jr., Jeffrey Sweet. New York: Dodd, Mead, 1920–1989; New York: Applause Theatre Book Publishers, 1990 1992. New York: Limelight Editions: Proscenium Publishers, 1993–2000. ?v Note: Volumes contain excerpts and synopses only. Numbers following titles indicate volumes by years, e.g., 27 indicates volume for 1927/28; 28 for 1928/29; etc. Plays appearing in the years from 1894–1900 and 1994–2000 are given by full date,

Black, D., and Hampton, C. *Sunset Boulevard* 1994

Blessing, L. *A Walk in the Woods* 86, 87

Bogosian, E. *Drinking in America* 85

Bogosian, E. *Sex, Drugs, Rock & Roll* 89

Bogosian, E. *SubUrbia* 93

Bolitho, W. *Overture* 30

Bolt, R. *A Man for All Seasons* 61

Bolt, R. *Vivat! Vivat! Regina* 71

Bolton, G. *Chicken Feed* 23

Bolton, G., and Middleton, G. *Adam and Eva* 19

Boothe, C. *Kiss the Boys Goodbye* 38

Boothe, C. *Margin for Error* 39

Boothe, C. *The Women* 36

Boublil, A., and Schonberg, C. *Les Misérables* 86

Boublil, A., and Schonberg, C. *Miss Saigon* 90

Bowen, J. *After the Rain* 67

Bowles, J. *In the Summer House* 53

Brecht, B. *Mother Courage and Her Children* 62

Brecht, B. *Threepenny Opera* 75

Bricusse, L., and Newley, A. *Stop the World—I Want to Get Off* 62

Brook, P., and Carrière, J. *The Mahabharata* 87

Brook, P., Carrière, J., and Constant, M. *La tragédie de Carmen* 83

Browne, P. *The Bad Man* 20

Bullins, E. *The Taking of Miss Janie* 74

Burrows, A. *Cactus Flower* 65

Burrows, A., Weinstock, J., and Gilbert, W. *How to Succeed in Business without Really Trying* 61

Butler, R. *Mamma's Affair* 19

Butterfield, C. *Joined at the Head* 92

Camus, A. *Caligula* 59

Čapek, K. *R.U.R.* 22

Carroll, P. *Shadow and Substance* 37

Carroll, P. *The White Steed* 38

Carter, S. *Nevis Mountain Dew* 78

Cartwright, J. *Road* 88

Casella, A. *Death Takes a Holiday* 29

Chase, M. *Bernardine* 52

Chase, M. *Harvey* 44

Chase, M. *Mrs. McThing* 51

Chayefsky, P. *Gideon* 61

Chayefsky, P. *The Passion of Josef D.* 63

Chayefsky, P. *The Tenth Man* 59

Cheong-Leen, R. *The Nanjing Race* 1994

Chodorov, E. *Decision* 43

Christie, A. *Witness for the Prosecution* 54

Churchill, C. *Cloud 9* 80

Churchill, C. *Mad Forest* 91

Churchill, C. *The Skriker* 1995

Clark, B. *Whose Life Is It Anyway?* 78

Clarvoe, A. *Pick Up Ax* 89

Clontz, D. *Generations* 88

Cloud, D. *The Stick Wife* 86

Coburn, D. *The Gin Game* 77

Coffee, L., and Cowen, W. *Family Portrait* 38

Cohan, G. *Pigeons and People* 32

Cohan, G. *Seven Keys to Baldpate* 09

Colton, J., and Randolph, C. *Rain* 22

Comden, B., and Green, A. *Applause* 69

Conkle, E. *Prologue to Glory* 37

Connelly, M. *Green Pastures* 29

Connelly, M. *The Wisdom Tooth* 25

Cooper, S., and Cronyn, H. *Foxfire* 82

Cormack, B. *The Racket* 27

Coward, N. *Blithe Spirit* 41

Coward, N. *Design for Living* 32

Coward, N. *Noel Coward in Two Keys* 73

Coxe, L., and Chapman, R. *Billy Budd* 50

Craven, F. *The First Year* 20

Crawley, B. *Violet* 1996

Cristofer, M. *Amazing Grace* 1995

Cristofer, M. *The Shadow Box* 76

Crothers, R. *As Husbands Go* 30

Crothers, R. *Let Us Be Gay* 28

Crothers, R. *Mary the 3rd* 22

Crothers, R. *Nice People* 20

Crothers, R. *Susan and God* 37

Crothers, R. *When Ladies Meet* 32

Crowley, M. *The Boys in the Band* 67

Dane, C. *A Bill of Divorcement* 21

Davis, B. *Mass Appeal* 81

Davis, L. *Grand Hotel* 89

Davis, O. *Icebound* 22

Davis, O. *Mr. and Mrs. North* 40

Davis, O., and Davis, D. *Ethan Frome* 35

Dayton, K., and Kaufman, G. *First Lady* 35

De Anda, P. *Ladies in Waiting* 70

Delaney, S. *A Taste of Honey* 60

Dell, F., and Mitchell, T. *Little Accident* 28

Denker, H. *A Far Country* 60

Deval, J. *Tovarich* 36

DiFusco, J. *Tracers* 84

Dodd, L. *The Changelings* 23

Dresser, R. *The Downside* 88

Drinkwater, J. *Abraham Lincoln* 19

Driver, D. *Your Own Thing* 67

Driver, J., and Haddow, J. *Chekhov in Yalta* 80

Duerrenmatt, F. *The Physicists* 64

Duerrenmatt, F. *The Visit* 57

Dunning, P., and Abbott, G. *Broadway* 26

Durang, C. *Marriage of Bette and Boo* 84

D'Usseau, A., and Gow, J. *Deep Are the Roots* 45

Dyer, C. *Rattle of a Simple Man* 62

Dyer, C. *Staircase* 67

Ebb, F., and Fosse, B. *Chicago* 75

Edgar, D. *The Life and Adventures of Nicholas Nickleby* 81

Edson, M. *Wit* 1998

Eliot, T. *Cats* 82

Patrick, J. *The Teahouse of the August Moon* 53
Pearson, S. *Unfinished Stories* 92
Perlman, A. *Wings* 92
Peterson, L. *Take a Giant Step* 53
Pielmeier, J. *Agnes of God* 81
Pinero, A. *Trelawny of the Wells* 1994
Pinero, M. *Short Eyes* 73
Pinter, H. *Betrayal* 79
Pinter, H. *The Caretaker* 61
Pinter, H. *The Collection* 62
Pinter, H. *The Homecoming* 66
Pollock, C. *The Enemy* 25
Pollock, C. *The Fool* 22
Pomerance, B. *The Elephant Man* 78
Priestley, J. *An Inspector Calls* 47
Rabe, D. *Hurlyburly* 84
Rabe, D. *Sticks and Bones* 71
Rabe, D. *Streamers* 75
Randall, B. *6 rms riv vu* 72
Raphaelson, S. *Accent on Youth* 34
Raphaelson, S. *Jason* 41
Raphaelson, S. *Skylark* 39
Rattigan, T. *O Mistress Mine* 45
Rattigan, T. *Separate Tables* 56
Rattigan, T. *The Winslow Boy* 47
Rayffel, D. *P.S. 193* 62
Redwood, J. *The Old Settler* 1997
Reed, M. *Yes, My Darling Daughter* 36
Reizenstein, E. *On Trial* 09
Reza, Y. *Art* 1997
Rice, E. *Dream Girl* 45
Rice, E. *Flight to the West* 40
Rice, E. *The Left Bank* 31
Rice, E. *Street Scene* 28
Rice, E. *We, the People* 32
Richman, A. *Ambush* 21
Riggs, L. *Green Grow the Lilacs* 30
Rotter, F., and Vincent, A. *Letters to Lucerne* 41
Royle, E. *The Squaw Man* 1899
Rudkin, D. *Ashes* 76
Rudnick, P. *Jeffrey* 92
Russell, W. *Shirley Valentine* 88
Ryerson, F., and Clements, C. *Harriet* 42
Sackler, H. *The Great White Hope* 68
St. Germain, M. *Camping with Henry and Tom* 1994
Saroyan, W. *The Time of Your Life* 39
Saunders, J. *Next Time I'll Sing to You* 63
Schary, D. *The Devil's Advocate* 60
Schary, D. *Sunrise at Campobello* 57
Schenkkan, R. *The Kentucky Cycle* 93
Schisgal, M. *All over Town* 74
Schisgal, M. *Luv* 64
Schulberg, B., and Breit, H. *The Disenchanted* 58
Selwyn, E., and Goulding, E. *Dancing Mothers* 24
Sergel, C. *Black Elk Speaks* 93

Shaffer, A. *Sleuth* 70
Shaffer, P. *Amadeus* 80
Shaffer, P. *Black Comedy* 66
Shaffer, P. *Equus* 74
Shaffer, P. *Five Finger Exercise* 59
Shaffer, P. *The Royal Hunt of the Sun* 65
Shairp, M. *The Green Bay Tree* 33
Shaw, R. *The Man in the Glass Booth* 68
Shawn, W. *Aunt Dan and Lemon* 85
Shawn, W. *The Designated Mourner* 1999
Sheldon, E. *Romance* 09
Shelley, E. *Pick-up Girl* 43
Shepard, S. *Fool for Love* 83
Sherman, M. *Bent* 79
Sherriff, R. *Journey's End* 28
Sherriff, R., and Casalis, J. *St. Helena* 36
Sherwood, R. *Abe Lincoln in Illinois* 38
Sherwood, R. *Idiot's Delight* 35
Sherwood, R. *The Petrified Forest* 34
Sherwood, R. *Reunion in Vienna* 31
Sherwood, R. *The Road to Rome* 26
Sherwood, R. *The Rugged Path* 45
Sherwood, R. *There Shall Be No Night* 39
Shue, L. *The Foreigner* 84
Shue, L. *Wenceslas Square* 87
Simon, B. *Born in the R.S.A.* 86
Simon, N. *Barefoot in the Park* 63
Simon, N. *Biloxi Blues* 84
Simon, N. *Broadway Bound* 86
Simon, N. *California Suite* 76
Simon, N. *Chapter Two* 77
Simon, N. *The Gingerbread Lady* 70
Simon, N. *The Good Doctor* 73
Simon, N. *I Ought to Be in Pictures* 79
Simon, N. *Last of the Red Hot Lovers* 69
Simon, N. *Laughter on the 23rd Floor* 93
Simon, N. *Lost in Yonkers* 90
Simon, N. *The Odd Couple* 64
Simon, N. *Plaza Suite* 67
Simon, N. *The Prisoner of Second Avenue* 71
Simon, N. *The Sunshine Boys* 72
Slade, B. *Same Time, Next Year* 74
Slade, B. *Tribute* 77
Smith, A.D. *Fires in the Mirror* 91
Smith, A.D. *Twilight: Los Angeles, 1992* 93
Smith, D. *Call It a Day* 35
Smith, H. *Mrs. Bumpstead-Leigh* 09
Spewack, B., and Spewack, S. *Boy Meets Girl* 35
Spewack, B., and Spewack, S. *My 3 Angels* 52
Spewack, S. *Two Blind Mice* 48
Stein, J. *Fiddler on the Roof* 64
Steinbeck, J. *The Moon Is Down* 41
Steinbeck, J. *Of Mice and Men* 37
Sterner, J. *Other People's Money* 88
Stevens, D. *The Sum of Us* 90

Wilson, A. *Jitney* 1997, 1999
Wilson, A. *Joe Turner's Come and Gone* 87
Wilson, A. *Ma Rainey's Black Bottom* 84
Wilson, A. *The Piano Lesson* 88, 89
Wilson, A. *Seven Guitars* 1995
Wilson, A. *Two Trains Running* 90, 91
Wilson, J. *Hamp* 66
Wilson, L. *Angels Fall* 82
Wilson, L. *Book of Days* 1998
Wilson, L. *The 5th of July* 77
Wilson, L. *The Hot L Baltimore* 72
Wilson, L. *Serenading Louie* 75
Wilson, L. *Talley's Folly* 79
Wilson, S. *The Boy Friend* 54
Wiltse, D. *Doubles* 84
Wincelberg, S. *Kataki* 58
Winter, K. *The Shining Hour* 33
Wishengrad, M. *The Rope Dancers* 57
Witten, M. *The Deal* 87
Wolfson, V. *Excursion* 36
Wouk, H. *The Caine Mutiny Court-martial* 53
Wright, N. *Mrs. Klein* 1995
Yaffe, J. *The Deadly Game* 59
Yordan, P. *Anna Lucasta* 44
Zindel, P. *The Effect of Gamma Rays on Man-in-the-moon Marigolds* 69

BEST *Best Plays of the Seventies*. Edited by Stanley
    Richards. New York: Doubleday, 1980. 814pp.
Ayckbourn, A. *Absurd Person Singular*
Clark, B. *Whose Life Is It Anyway?*
Gray, S. *Otherwise Engaged*
Leonard, H. *"Da"*
O'Malley, M. *Once a Catholic*
Pomerance, B. *The Elephant Man*
Rabe, D. *Streamers*
Shaffer, A. *Sleuth*
Simon, N. *The Sunshine Boys*
Zindel, P. *The Effect of Gamma Rays on Man-in-the-moon Marigolds*

BEST PLAYS SERIES; See GARSA, GART, GARTL,
    GARU, GARW, GARX, GARZ, GAS, GASB,
    GATB. Gassner, John, ed.

BETW *Between Worlds: Contemporary Asian-American
    Plays*. Edited by Misha Berson. New York: Theatre
    Communications Group, 1990. 196pp.
Chong, P. *Nuit blanche: A Select View of Things*
Gotanda, P. *The Wash*
Hagedorn, J. *Tenement Lover: No Palm Trees/in New
    York City*
Hwang, D. *As the Crow Flies*
Hwang, D. *The Sound of a Voice*

Yamauchi, W. *And the Soul Shall Dance*
Yep, L. *Pay the Chinaman*

BEV Bevington, David Martin, ed. *The Macro; The Castle
    of Perseverance; Wisdom, Mankind*. New York:
    Johnson Reprint, 1972. 305pp.
*The Castle of Perseverance*
*Mankind*
*Wisdom; or, Mind, Will, and Understanding*

BEVD Bevington, David Martin, comp. *Medieval
    Drama*. Boston: Houghton Mifflin, 1975. 1075pp.
    [Selections in Latin or Anglo-Norman French have
    English translators in parallel columns; selections
    in Middle English have marginal glosses.]
*The Annunciation (Wakefield)*
*The Banns (N Town)*
*The Birth of Jesus (York)*
*The Buffeting (Wakefield)*
*The Castle of Perseverance*
*Christ Appears to the Disciples (Chester)*
*The Christmas Play (Luaus de nativitate)
    (Benediktbeuern)*
*Christ's Death and Burial (York)*
*The Conversion of St. Paul (Digby)*
*The Creation and the Fall of the Angels (Wakefield)*
*The Crucifixion of Christ (York)*
*The Death of Herod (N Town)*
*Everyman*
*The Fall of Man (York)*
*The Flight into Egypt (York)*
*For Representing How Saint Nicholas Freed the Son of
    Getron (Fleury)*
*For Representing the Conversion of the Blessed Apostle
    Paul (Fleury)*
*For Representing the Scene at the Lord's Sepulchre
    (Fleury)*
*For the Mass of Our Lord (Limoges)*
*The Harrowing of Hell (Wakefield)*
*Herod the Great (Wakefield)*
Heywood, J. *A Mery Play betwene Johan Johan the
    Husbande, Tib His Wife, and Sir Johan the Preest*
Heywood, J. *The Play of the Weather; a New and a Very
    Mery Enterlude of all Maner Wethers*
Hilarius. *The Raising of Lazarus*
*The Holy Resurrection*
*The Killing of Abel (Wakefield)*
*The Last Judgment (Wakefield)*
*Mankind*
*Mary Magdalene (Digby)*
*Noah (Wakefield)*
*Of the Resurrection of the Lord (St. Gall)*
*The Offering of the Magi (Wakefield)*
*The Passion Play (Benediktbeuern)*

*The Passion Play I (N Town)*
*The Passion Play II (N Town)*
*Pharaoh (Wakefield)*
*The Play of Daniel (Beauvais)*
*The Play of the Sacrament (Croxton)*
*The Raising of Lazarus (Wakefield)*
Redford, J. *Wit and Science*
*The Resurrection of the Lord (Wakefield)*
*The Sacrifice of Isaac (Brome)*
*The Salutation of Elizabeth (Wakefield)*
*The Scourging (Wakefield)*
*The Second Shepherds' Pageant (Wakefield)*
*The Service for Representing Adam*
*The Service for Representing Herod (Fleury)*
*The Service [for representing] the Pilgrim, at Vespers of*
  *the Second Holy Day of Easter (Beauvais)*
*The Shepherds (York)*
*The Slaughter of the Innocents (Fleury)*
*The Ten Commandments, Balaam and Balak, and the*
  *Prophets (Chester)*
*Trope for Easter*
*The Visit to the Sepulchre (Aquileia?)*
*The Visit to the Sepulchre (from The Regularis*
  *Concordia of St. Ethelwold)*
*The Visit to the Sepulchre (from St. Lambrecht)*
*The Visit to the Sepulchre (from the Tenth-Century*
  *troper of Winchester)*
*The Woman Taken in Adultery (N Town)*

BEVI Bevis, Richard W., ed. *Eighteenth Century Drama:*
  *Afterpieces.* London: Oxford University Press,
  1970. 286pp.
  Colman, G. *Polly Honeycombe*
  Fielding, H. *The Historical Register for Year 1736*
  Foote, S. *The Commissary*
  Garrick, D. *Miss in Her Teens*
  *The Kept Mistress*
  Macklin, C. *A Will and No Will*
  Murphy, A. *The Upholsterer*
  Murphy, A. *The Way to Keep Him*

BEYO *Beyond the Pale: Dramatic Writing from First*
  *Nations Writers & Writers of Colour.* Editors
  Yvette Nolan, Betty Quan, George Bwanika
  Seremba. Toronto: Playwrights Canada Press, 1996,
  234pp. [All selections in this work are excerpts
  from full-length plays, or short performance pieces.
  There are so few anthologies containing Canadian
  playwrights of color that many of the authors
  listed below would not be represented in this index
  otherwise if it was not included.]
  Bunyan, H. *Thy Creature Blues*
  Chan, M. *Mom, Dad, I'm Living with a White Girl*
  Francis, M. *The Sniffer*

Gale, L. *Angelique*
Jacob, B. *Man You Mus'*
Jensen, L. *The Mercy Quilt*
Kang, M. *Noran Bang: The Yellow Room*
Linklater, L., and Flather, P. *Sixty Below*
McLean, D. *Encore*
Manuel, V. *The Strength of Indian Women*
Mojica, M. *This Is for Aborelia Dominguez*
Moodie, A. *Riot*
Moses, D. *Kyotopolis*
Nolan, Y. *Child*
Odhiambo, D. *afrocentric*
Payne, A. *The Troubleshooter*
Philip, M. *Coups and Calypsos*
Providence, T. *Blues for My Grandfather*
Quan, B. *One Ocean*
Ross, I. *fareWel*
Sears, D. *The Madwoman and the Fool: A Harlem Duet*
Seremba, G. *Napoleon of the Nile*
Taylor, D. *Someday*
Yhap, B. *Body Blows*
Yoon, J. *Sliding for Home*

BIER Bierman, Judah; Hart, James; and Johnson, Stanley,
  eds. *The Dramatic Experience.* Englewood Cliffs,
  NJ: Prentice Hall, 1958. 549pp.
  *Everyman*
  García Lorca, F. *Blood Wedding*
  Ibsen, H. *The Wild Duck*
  Hayes, J. *The Desperate Hours*
  Miller, A. *Death of a Salesman*
  Saroyan, W. *The Time of Your Life*
  Shakespeare, W. *Othello*
  Shakespeare, W. *Twelfth Night; or, What You Will*
  Shaw, G. *Caesar and Cleopatra*
  Sherwood, R. *Abe Lincoln in Illinois*
  Sophocles. *Oedipus Rex*

BIES Bierstadt, Edward Hale, ed. *Three Plays of the*
  *Argentine.* New York: Duffield, 1920. 147pp.
  Bayón Herrera, L. *Santos Vega*
  Manco, S. *Juan Moreira*
  Sánchez Gardel, P. *The Witches' Mountain*

BIG *Big-time Women from Way Back When.* Toronto:
  Playwrights Canada Press, 1993. 236pp.
  Clark, S. *Jehanne of the Witches*
  Herst, B. *A Woman's Comedy*

BIN Bingham, Joel Foote, comp. *Gemme della letteratura*
  *italiane.* London: Frowde, 1904. 1016pp.
  Alfieri, V. *Saul*
  Goldoni, C. *Un curioso accidente*
  Metastasio, P. *Attilio Regolo*

BIR Birch, Cyril, ed. *Anthology of Chinese Literature.*
New York: Grove, 1972. 2 vols. (v1, From early
times to the 14th century; v2, From the 14th
century to the present day)
K'ang, C. *Li K'uei Carries Thorns* 1
Ma, C. *Autumn in the Palace of Han* 1
T'ang, H. *Peony Pavilion* 1
Yao, H. *The Malice of Empire* 2

BLAAP *Black and Asian Plays Anthology.* Introduced by
Afia Nkrumah with a bibliography by Susan Croft.
London: Aurora Metro Press, 2000. 320pp.
Bancil, P. *Made in England*
Buchanan, W. *Under Their Influence*
McMillan, M. *Brother to Brother*
Padmanabhan, M. *Harvest*
Silas, S. *Calcutta Kosher*

BLAC *Black Comedy: Nine Plays: A Critical Anthology,
with Interviews and Essays.* Edited by Pamela Faith
Jackson and Karimah. New York: Applause, 1997.
500pp.
Evans, D. *One Monkey Don't Stop No Show*
Hill, A. *On Strivers Row*
Hughes, L. *Simply Heavenly*
Jones, T. *The Wizard of Hip*
Russell, C. *Five on the Black Hand Side*
Shine, T. *Contribution*
Stickney, P. *Big Momma n''em*
Ward, D. *Day of Absence*
Wolfe, G. *The Colored Museum*

BLACQ *A Black Quartet: 4 New Black Plays by Ben
Caldwell, and Others.* New York: New American
Libraries, 1970. 158pp.
Bullins, E. *The Gentleman Caller*
Caldwell, B. *Prayer Meeting; or, the First Militant
Minister*
Jones, L. *Great Goodness of Life*
Milner, R. *The Warning, a Theme for Linda*

BLACTH *Black Thunder: An Anthology of Contemporary
African-American Drama.* Edited and with an
introduction by William B. Branch. New York:
Mentor, 1992. 520pp.
Baraka, A. *General Hag's Skeezag*
Branch, W. *Baccalaureate*
Bullins, E. *The Taking of Miss Janie*
Carter, S. *Eden*
Gibson, P. *Long Time since Yesterday*
Lee, L. *The First Breeze of Summer*
Simmons, A. *Sherlock Holmes and the Hands of Othello*
Wilson, A. *Ma Rainey's Black Bottom*
Wolfe, G. *The Colored Museum*

BLAG Blair, Walter, and Gerber, John C., eds. *Literature*
(Better Reading vol. 2). Chicago, Scott, Foresman
[c. 1949] 778pp. Note: Also published in one
volume under the title *The College Anthology*
Chekhov, A. *The Swan Song*
Dunsany, E. *A Night at an Inn*
Ibsen, H. *Hedda Gabler*
Molière, J. *Tartuffe*
O'Neill, E. *Anna Christie*
Sophocles. *Oedipus the King*

BLAH Blair, Walter, and Gerber, John, eds. *Repertory.*
Chicago: Scott, Foresman [1960] 1173pp.
Chekhov, A. *The Cherry Orchard*
Chekhov, A. *The Swan Song*
Chayefsky, P. *Marty*
Dunsany, E. *A Night at an Inn*
Fry, C. *A Phoenix Too Frequent*
O'Neill, E. *Bound East for Cardiff*
Shakespeare, W. *Romeo and Juliet*
Sophocles. *Oedipus the King*

BLAI Blair, Walter; Hornberger, Theodore; and Stewart,
Randall, eds. *The Literature of the United States.*
Chicago: Scott, Foresman [c. 1946–1947] 2 vols.
Aiken, G. *Uncle Tom's Cabin; or, Life among the
Lowly* 2
Mitchell, L. *The New York Idea* 2
O'Neill, E. *The Hairy Ape* 2
Tyler, R. *The Contrast* 1

BLAJ Blair, Walter; Hornberger, Theodore; and Stewart,
Randall. *The Literature of the United States.* Single
volume edition. Chicago: Scott, Foresman [c. 1949]
1313pp.
O'Neill, E. *The Hairy Ape*

BLOC Block, Haskell M., and Shedd, Robert G., eds.
*Masters of Modern Drama.* New York: Random
House [c. 1962] 1198pp.
Anouilh, J. *Antigone*
Anouilh, J. *Thieves' Carnival*
Beckett, S. *Endgame*
Brecht, B. *The Good Woman of Setzuan*
Brecht, B. *Mother Courage and Her Children*
Camus, A. *Caligula*
Chayefsky, P. *Marty*
Chekhov, A. *The Cherry Orchard*
Chekhov, A. *The Sea Gull*
Cocteau, J. *Orphée*
Duerrenmatt, F. *The Visit*
Frisch, M. *Biedermann and the Firebugs*
García Lorca, F. *Blood Wedding*
Giraudoux, J. *Electra*
Giraudoux, J. *The Madwoman of Chaillot*

Gorki, M. *The Lower Depths*
Hauptmann, G. *The Weavers*
Hofmannsthal, H. *Death and the Fool*
Ibsen, H. *Ghosts*
Ibsen, H. *Peer Gynt*
Ionesco, E. *The Bald Soprano*
Kaiser, G. *From Morn to Midnight*
Maeterlinck, M. *The Intruder*
Miller, A. *Death of a Salesman*
O'Casey, S. *Cock-a-doodle Dandy*
O'Casey, S. *Juno and the Paycock*
Odets, C. *Awake and Sing!*
O'Neill, E. *The Emperor Jones*
O'Neill, E. *The Iceman Cometh*
Osborne, J. *Look Back in Anger*
Pirandello, L. *Henry IV*
Saroyan, W. *The Time of Your Life*
Sartre, J. *No Exit*
Schnitzler, A. *La ronde*
Shaw, G. *Major Barbara*
Shaw, G. *Man and Superman*
Strindberg, A. *The Ghost Sonata*
Strindberg, A. *Miss Julie*
Synge, J. *The Playboy of the Western World*
Synge, J. *Riders to the Sea*
Wedekind, F. *The Marquis of Keith*
Wilder, T. *The Matchmaker*
Williams, T. *The Glass Menagerie*
Yeats, W. *At the Hawk's Well*
Zuckmayer, C. *The Devil's General*

BLOD Blodgett, Harold William, and Johnson, Burges, eds. *Readings for Our Times.* Boston, Ginn [c. 1942] 2 vols.
Rostand, E. *Cyrano de Bergerac* 1
Wilder, T. *Our Town* 1

BLON Bloomfield, Morton Wilfred, and Elliott, Robert C., eds. *Great Plays, Sophocles to Brecht.* New York: Holt, Rinehart and Winston [1965] 614pp.
Brecht, B. *The Caucasian Chalk Circle*
Chekhov, A. *Three Sisters*
Congreve, W. *The Way of the World*
Ibsen, H. *Hedda Gabler*
Molière, J. *The Misanthrope*
O'Neill, E. *The Hairy Ape*
Shakespeare, W. *Othello*
Shaw, G. *Arms and the Man*
Sophocles. *Antigone*
Strindberg, A. *Miss Julie*
Williams, T. *The Glass Menagerie*

BLOND Bloomfield, Morton Wilfred, and Elliott, Robert C., eds. *Great Plays, Sophocles to Albee.* 3rd ed. New York, Holt 1975. 701pp.

Albee, E. *The American Dream*
Brecht, B. *The Caucasian Chalk Circle*
Chekhov, A. *Three Sisters*
Congreve, W. *The Way of the World*
Frisch, M. *The Firebugs*
Ibsen, H. *Hedda Gabler*
Molière, J. *The Misanthrope*
O'Neill, E. *The Hairy Ape*
Shakespeare, W. *Othello*
Shaw, G. *Arms and the Man*
Sophocles. *Antigone*
Strindberg, A. *Miss Julie*
Williams, T. *The Glass Menagerie*

BLOO Bloomfield, Morton Wilfred, and Elliott, Robert C., eds. *Ten Plays.* New York: Rinehart [c. 1951] 719pp.
Chekhov, A. *Three Sisters*
Dekker, T. *The Shoemakers' Holiday*
Farquhar, G. *The Beaux' Stratagem*
Hellman, L. *The Little Foxes*
Ibsen, H. *Hedda Gabler*
O'Neill, E. *The Hairy Ape*
Rostand, E. *Cyrano de Bergerac*
Shakespeare, W. *Othello*
Sophocles. *Antigone*
Thurber, J., and Nugent, E. *The Male Animal*

BOA Boas, Frederick Samuel, ed. *Five Pre-Shakespearean Comedies (Early Tudor Period).* London: Oxford University Press [1934] 343pp. (The World's Classics)
Gascoigne, G. *Supposes*
Heywood, J. *The Four pp*
Medwall, H. *Fulgens and Lucrece*
"Mr. S. Mr. of Art." *Gammer Gurton's Needle*
Udall, N. *Ralph Roister Doister*

BODY *Body Blows: Women, Violence, and Survival: Three Plays.* With an introductory essay by C. S. Lakshmi ("Ambai"). Calcutta: Seagull Books, 2000. 155pp.
Mehta, D. *Getting Away with Murder*
Padmanabhan, M. *Lights Out*
Sengupta, P. *Mangalam*

BOGA Bogarad, Carley Rees, and Schmidt, Jan Zlotnik, eds. *Legacies: Fiction, Poetry, Drama, Nonfiction.* Fort Worth, TX: Harcourt Brace College Publishers, 1995. 1380pp.
Elder, L. *Ceremonies in Old Dark Men*
Fugard, A. *"Master Harold" . . . and the Boys*
Glaspell, S. *Trifles*
Seami, M. *Atsumori*
Shakespeare, W. *Hamlet*

Sophocles. *Oedipus Rex*
Synge, J. *Riders to the Sea*
Yamauchi, W. *And the Soul Shall Dance*

BOGO Bogorad, Samuel N., and Trevithick, Jack, eds. *The College Miscellany.* New York: Rinehart [c. 1952] 621pp.
Barrie, J. *The Twelve-pound Look*
Rattigan, T. *The Winslow Boy*
Shakespeare, W. *King Henry IV, Part I*

BOH Bohemian Club, San Francisco. *The Grove Plays of the Bohemian Club.* Edited by Porter Garnett. San Francisco: The Club, 1918. 3 vols.
Crocker, C. *The Land of Happiness* 3
Field, C. *The Cave Man* 2
Field, C. *The Man in the Forest* 1
Field, C. *The Owl and Cave* 1
Garnett, P. *The Green Knight* 2
Irwin, W. *The Hamadryads* 1
Myrtle, F. *Gold* 3
Pixley, F. *Apollo* 3
Redding, J. *The Atonement of Pan* 2
Robertson, L. *Montezuma* 1
Scheffauer, H. *The Sons of Baldur* 1
Shiels, J. *Nec-natama* 3
Steele, R. *The Fall of Ug* 3
Stephens, H. *St. Patrick at Tara* 2
Stirling, G. *The Triumph of Bohemia* 1
Tharp, N. *The Quest of the Gorgon* 1

BOHV *Bohemian Verses: An Anthology of Contemporary English Language Writings from Prague.* Selected and edited by Scott H. Rogers. Prague: Modrá músa, 1993. 215pp.
Bunch, J. *Lay Down by Me*

BONA Bonazza, Blaze O., and Roy, Emil, eds. *Studies in Drama.* New York: Harper & Row [c. 1963] 344pp.
Ibsen, H. *An Enemy of the People*
Shakespeare, W. *A Midsummer Night's Dream*
Shaw, G. *Candida*
Sophocles. *Antigone*
Williams, T. *The Glass Menagerie*

BONB Bonazza, Blaze Odell, and Roy, Emil, eds. *Studies in Drama.* New York: Harper & Row [c. 1964] 378pp.
Chekhov, A. *The Cherry Orchard*
Ibsen, H. *The Master Builder*
O'Neill, E. *Desire under the Elms*
Shakespeare, W. *King Lear*
Shaw, G. *Heartbreak House*
Wilder, T. *Our Town*

BONC Bonazza, Blaze Odell, and Roy, Emil, eds. *Studies in Drama.* 2nd ed. New York: Harper and Row [1968] 583pp.
Brecht, B. *Mother Courage and Her Children*
Chekhov, A. *The Cherry Orchard*
Ibsen, H. *An Enemy of the People*
O'Neill, E. *Desire under the Elms*
Shakespeare, W. *King Lear*
Shaw, G. *Heartbreak House*
Sheridan, R. *The School for Scandal*
Sophocles. *Antigone*
Strindberg, A. *Miss Julie*
Synge, J. *Riders to the Sea*
Wilder, T. *Our Town*
Williams, T. *The Glass Menagerie*

BOND Bond, Richard Warwick, ed. *Early Plays from the Italian.* Oxford: Clarendon Press, 1911. 332pp.
*The Buggbears*
Gascoigne, G. *Supposes*
*Misogonus*

BOO Booth, Michael R., ed. *Eighteenth Century Tragedy.* London, New York: Oxford University Press, 1965. 394pp.
Colman, G., the Younger. *The Iron Chest*
Home, J. *Douglas*
Johnson, S. *Irene*
Lillo, G. *The London Merchant*
Moore, E. *The Gamester*

BOOA Booth, Michael, R., ed. *English Plays of the Nineteenth Century.* New York: Oxford University Press, 1969–1976. 5 vols.
Blanchard, E. *Aladdin; or, Harlequin and the Wonderful Lamp* 5
Boucicault, D. *The Corsican Brothers* 2
Boucicault, D. *The Shaughraun* 2
Brough, W. *The Field of the Cloth of Gold* 5
Brough, W., and Brough, R. *The Enchanted Isle* 5
Brough, W., and Halliday, A. *The Area Belle* 4
Bulwer-Lytton, E. *Richelieu; or the Conspiracy* 1
Bulwer-Lytton, E. *Money* 3
Byron, G. *Robinson Crusoe; or, Harlequin Friday and the King of the Caribbee Islands* 5
Chambers, C. *The Tyranny of Tears* 3
Colman, G., the Younger. *John Bull* 3
Coyne, J. *How to Settle Accounts with Your Laundress* 4
Dibdin, T. *Harlequin Harper; or, a Jump from Japan* 5
Dibdin, T. *Harlequin in His Element* 5
Gilbert, W. *Engaged* 3
Gilbert, W. *Tom Cobb* 4
Jerrold, D. *Black-eyed Susan; or, All in the Downs* 1
Jerrold, D. *Mr. Paul Pry* 4
Jones, H. *Mrs. Dane's Defence* 2

Kenney, K. *Raising the Wind* 4
Knowles, J. *Virginius* 1
Mathews, C. *Patter versus Clatter* 4
Morton, J. *Box and Cox* 4
Murray, W. *Diamond Cut Diamond* 4
Pinero, A. *The Magistrate* 4
Pinero, A. *The Second Mrs. Tanqueray* 2
Planché, J. *Fortunio and His Seven Gifted Servants* 5
Planché, J. *The Island of Jewels* 5
Pocock, I. *The Miller and His Men* 1
Taylor, T. *New Men and Old Acres* 3
Taylor, T. *The Ticket-of-leave Man* 2
Walker, J. *The Factory Lad* 1
Wood, J., and Collins, A. *The Sleeping Beauty and the Beast* 5

BOOB Booth, Michael R., comp. *Hiss the Villain: Six English and American Melodramas*. New York: Benjamin Blom, 1964. 390pp.
Daly, A. *Under the Gaslight*
Haines, J. *My Poll and My Partner Joe*
Lewis, L. *The Bells*
Phillips, W. *Lost in London*
Pocock, I. *The Miller and His Men*
Pratt, W. *Ten Nights in a Barroom*

BOOK *A Book of Plays*. Austin, TX: Holt, Rinehart, and Winston, 2000. 341pp. (HRW Library)
Chekhov, A. *The Bear*
Fletcher, L. *Sorry, Wrong Number*
Glaspell, S. *Trifles*
Parker, D. *Here We Are*
Rose, R. *Thunder on Sycamore Street*
Rose, R. *Twelve Angry Men*
Synge, J. *Riders to the Sea*
Wilder, T. *Our Town*
Wilder, T. *The Happy Journey to Trenton and Camden*
Williams, T. *The Glass Menagerie*

BOOL Booth, Michael, R., ed. *The Lights o' London and Other Victorian Plays*. (Variant title used by some libraries: *The Inchape Bell*). New York: Oxford University Press, 1995. 251pp.
Coyne, J. *Did You Ever Send Your Wife to Camberwell?*
Fitz-ball, E. *The Inchape bell, or the Dumb Sailor Boy*
Jones, H. *The Middleman*
Lewes, G. *The Game of Speculation*
Sims, G. *The Lights o' London*

BOOM Booth, Michael R., ed. *The Magistrate, and Other Nineteenth-century Plays*. London: Oxford University Press, 1974. 464pp.
Boucicault, D. *The Corsican Brothers*
Colman, G., the Younger. *John Bull*
Coyne, J. *How to Settle Accounts with Your Laundress*

Gilbert, W. *Engaged*
Jones, H. *Mrs. Dane's Defence*
Morton, J. *Box and Cox*
Pinero, A. *The Magistrate*
Pocock, I. *The Miller and His Men*
Walker, J. *The Factory Lad*

BOR Borgerhoff, Joseph Leopold, ed. *Nineteenth Century French Plays*. New York: Century [c. 1931] 790pp.
Augier, E. *Le mariage d'Olympe*
Augier, E., et Sandeau, J. *Le gendre de M. Poirier*
Balzac, H. *Mercadet*
Becque, H. *Les corbeaux*
Brieux, E. *Les trois filles de M. Dupont*
Curel, F. *L'envers d'une sainte*
Delavigne, C. *Marino Faliero*
Dumas, A. père. *Antony*
Dumas, A. père. *Henri III et sa cour*
Dumas, A. fils. *La dame aux camélias*
Dumas, A. fils. *Les idées de Madame Aubray*
Hugo, V. *Hernani*
Musset, A. *Les caprices de Marianne*
Pailleron, E. *Le monde où l'on s'ennuie*
Picard, L. *Les ricochets*
Pixérécourt, R. *Coelina; ou, L'enfant du mystère*
Rostand, E. *Cyrano de Bergerac*
Scribe, E. *Le verre d'eau*
Vigny, A. *Chatterton*

THE BORZOI READER. *See* VAN Van Doren, Carl Clinton, ed.

BOUC Boucquey, Thierry, ed., and trans. *Six Medieval French Farces*. Lewiston, NY: Edwin Mellen Press, 1999. 241pp. (Medieval Studies, vol. 11)
D'Abundance, J. *The Farce of the Bonnet*
*The Farce of Calbain*
*The Farce of the Chimney Sweep*
*The Farce of the Gentleman and Naudet*
*The Farce of the Kettle Maker*
La Vigne, A. *The Farce of the Miller*

BOUR Bourke, Siobhán, ed. *Rough Magic: First Plays*. Dublin: New Island Books, 1999. 464pp.
Boyd, P. *Down onto Blue*
Hughes, D. *I Can't Get Started*
Meehan, P. *Mrs. Sweeney*
Moxley, G. *Danti-Dan*
O'Kelly, D. *The Dogs*
Riordan, A. *Hidden Charges*

BOV Bovée, Arthur Gibbon; Cattanès, Hélènc; and Robert, Osmond Thomas, eds. *Promenades littéraires et historiques*. New York: Harcourt, Brace, 1940. 750pp.

Beaumarchais, P. *Le barbier de Séville*
Paulleron, E. *Le monde où l'on s'ennuie*

BOVE Bovée, Arthur Gibbon; Cattanès, Hélène; and
Robert, Osmond Thomas, eds. *Promenades
littéraires et historiques*. Nouvelle édition. New
York: Harcourt Brace, 1948. 658pp.
Beaumarchais, P. *Le barbier de Séville*
Legouvé, E., and Labiche, E. *La cigale chez les
fourmis*

BOVI Bovie, Smith Palmer, ed. *Five Roman Comedies: In
Modern English Verse*. New York: Dutton, 1970.
329pp.
Plautus. *Amphitryon*
Plautus. *Mostellaria*
Plautus. *Poenulus; or, the Little Carthaginian*
Terence. *The Eunuch*
Terence. *Phormio*

BOW Bowen, James K., and Van Der Beets, Richard,
compilers. *Drama*. New York: Harper and Row,
1971. 761pp.
Aristophanes. *Lysistrata*
Chekhov, A. *The Cherry Orchard*
Dürrenmatt, F. *The Visit*
*Everyman*
Ibsen, H. *Ghosts*
Molière, J. *The Misanthrope*
O'Neill, E. *Desire under the Elms*
Racine, J. *Phaedra*
Shakespeare, W. *Othello*
Shaw, G. *Major Barbara*
Sophocles. *Oedipus Rex*
Strindberg, A. *Miss Julie*

BOWL Bowles, Norma, ed. *friendly fire: An Anthology
of Plays by Queer Street Youth*. Los Angeles, CA:
A.S.K. Theater Projects, 1997. 218pp.
Queer Street Youth. *friendly fire*
Queer Street Youth. *people who live in glass houses . . .*
Queer Street Youth. *street dish*

BOWY Bowyer, John Wilson, and Brooks, John Lee, eds.
*The Victorian Age*. 2nd ed. New York: Appleton
Century-Crofts [c. 1954] 1188pp.
Gilbert, W. *Iolanthe; or, the Peer and the Peri*
Jones, H. *Michael and His Lost Angel*
Pinero, A. *The Second Mrs. Tanqueray*
Robertson, T. *Caste*
Shaw, G. *Arms and the Man*
Wilde, O. *The Importance of Being Earnest*
Yeats, W. *The Countess Cathleen*

BOY Boynton, Robert Whitney, and Mack, Maynard, eds.
*Introduction to the Play*. New York: Hayden Book,
1969. 386pp.
Cocteau, J. *The Infernal Machine*
Ibsen, H. *Ghosts*
Shakespeare, W. *Henry the IV, Part I*
Shaw, G. *The Devil's Disciple*
Sophocles. *Oedipus the King*

BOYN Boynton, Robert Whitney, and Mack, Maynard,
compilers. *Introduction to the Play: In the Theater
of the Mind*. Rev. 2nd ed. Rochelle Park, NJ:
Hayden Book Company, 1976. 262pp.
Cocteau, J. *The Infernal Machine*
McNally, T. *Botticelli*
Shaw, G. *The Devil's Disciple*
Ward, D. *Day of Absence*
Williams, T. *The Glass Menagerie*

BPD Bradley, Edward Sculley, et al., eds. *The American
Tradition in Literature*. 4th ed. New York: Grosset
and Dunlap, 1974. 2 vols.
O'Neill, E. *The Hairy Ape* 2
Tyler, R. *The Contrast* 1
Williams, T. *The Glass Menagerie* 2

BPE Bradley, Edward Sculley, et al., eds. *The American
Tradition in Literature*. 4th ed. Shorter ed. in one
volume. New York: Grosset and Dunlap, 1974.
2001pp.
Williams, T. *The Glass Menagerie*

BPW Branch, William B., ed. *Crosswinds: An Anthology
of Black Dramatists in the Diaspora*. Bloomington,
IN: Indiana University Press, 1993. 416pp.
Baraka, A. *Slave Ship*
Branch, W. *In Splendid Error*
Mtwa, P., Ngema, M., and Simon, B. *Woza Albert!*
Nascimento, A. *Sortilege II: Zumbi Returns*
Soyinka, W. *Death and the King's Horseman*
Sutherland, E. *Edufa*
Walcott, D. *Pantomime*
Wesley, R. *The Talented Tenth*
White, E. *Lament for Rastafari*
Wilson, A. *Joe Turner's Come and Gone*

BQA Brandon, James R., ed. *On Thrones of Gold: Three
Javanese Shadow Plays*. Cambridge, MA: Harvard
University Press, 1970. 407pp.
*Death of Karna*
*Irawan's Wedding*
*The Reincarnation of Rama*

BRA Brandon, James R., compiler . . . *Traditional Asian
Plays*. New York: Hill and Wang, 1972. 308pp.

*Manohra*
Namiki G., III. *The Subscription List*
Okamura, S. *The Zen Substitute*
The Price of Wine
Shudraka, K. *The Toy Cart*
Zembo, M. *Ikkaku sennin*

BRAK Brask, Per, ed. *Scandinavia: Plays.* New York: PAJ
Publications, 1996. 213pp. (Dramacontemporary:
Scandinavia)
Bringsvaerd, T. *The Glass Mountain*
Garpe, M. *For Julia*
Kylätasku, J. *Mary Bloom*
Ryum, U. *And the Birds Are Singing Again*
Simonarson, O. *Under Your Skin*

BRAKA Brask, Per, and Morgan William, eds. *Aboriginal
Voices: Amerindian, Inuit, and Sami Theater.*
Baltimore, MD: Johns Hopkins University Press,
1992. 145pp.
Gaup, N., and Walle K. *Gesat*
Nilson, R., and the Tukak Theater Ensemble. *Inuit—the
People*
Weiser, J. *Homecoming: An Alaskan Native's Quest for
Self-esteem*

BRAS Brasmer, William, and Consolo, Dominick Peter,
eds. *Black Drama: An Anthology.* Columbus, OH:
Charles E. Merrill Publishing Company, 1970.
393pp.
Davis, O. *Purlie Victorious*
Green, P. *Native Son*
Hughes, L. *Mulatto*
Kennedy, A. *Funny House of a Negro*
Shine, T. *Contribution*
Ward, D. *Day of Absence*
Ward, D. *Happy Ending*

BRAZ Brazell, Karen, ed. *Traditional Japanese Theater:
An Anthology of Plays.* New York, Columbia
University Press, 1998. 561pp.
Chikamatsu, M. *The Battles of Coxinga*
Chikamatsu, M. *The Love Suicides at Amijima*
Chikamatsu, M. *Shunkan on Devil Island*
*The Cicada*
*The Delicious Poison*
*Dōjōji*
Kako, C., and Toyozawa, D. *The Miracle of the
Tsubosaka Kannon*
*Kanaoka*
Kawatake, M. *The Hamamatsu-ya Scene*
*A Maiden at Dōjōji*
*Miidera*
*Mushrooms*
Namiki, S. *Suma Bay*

*Shunkan*
*The "Sickley" Stomach*
*The Snail*
*The Song of Sambasō*
Takeda, I., Miyoshi, S., and Namiki, S. *At the
Farmhouse*
Takeda, I., Miyoshi, S., and Namiki, S. *The First Note
of Spring*
Takeda, I., Miyoshi, S., and Namiki, S. *Mount Tempai*
Takeda, I., Miyoshi, S., and Namiki, S. *Tumult in the
Palace*
*Thunderbolt*
Tsuruya, N. *Yotsuya Ghost Stories*
Tsuuchi, H., Yasuda, A., and Nakada, M. *Saint
Narukami*
*Two daimyō*
Zeami. *Atsumori*
Zeami. *Izutsu*
Zeami. *Yamamba*
Zenchiku. *Kamo*

BRAZT Brazell, Karen, ed. *Twelve Plays of the Noh
and Kyōgen Theaters.* Ithaca, NY: East Asia
Program: Cornell University, 1988. 253pp. (Cornell
University East Asia Papers No. 50). Revised
edition of this title published in 1990 is a reprint of
this edition.
*Bōshibari (Tied to a Stick)*
Gen'e. *Hōshigahaha (The Baby's Mother)*
*Genji kuyō (A Memorial Service for Genji)*
*Ikarikazuki (The Anchor Draping)*
Kanami. *Yoshino Shizuka (Lady Shizuka in Yoshino)*
Miyamasu. *Ōeyama (The Demon of Ōeyama)*
*Semi (The Cicada)*
*Unrin'in (The Unrin Temple)*
Zeami. *Kakitsubata (The Iris)*
Zeami. *Miwa (Three Circles)*
Zeami. *Saigyōzakura (Saigyō and the Cherry Tree)*
Zeami. *Unoha (Cormorant Plumes)*

BREK Brennan, Kit, ed. *Going It Alone: Plays by Women
for Solo Performers.* Winnipeg: Nuage Editions,
1997. 196pp.
Ackerman, M. *Meanwhile, Goodbye*
Barrie, S. *Transition*
Brennan, K. *Hunger Striking*
Burke, K. *Safe*
Curran, C. *A Brave Girl*
Derbyshire, J. *Joke You*
Earle, L. *Ka-Shue (Letters Home)*
Farell, G. *Beatrice*
Flather, P. *West Edmonton Mall*
Fuerstenberg, A. *Why I Sleep Alone*
Fyffe, L. *The Golden Horn*
Gale, L. *Je me souviens*

Grace-Smith, B. *Ngā Pou Wāhine*
Haber, A. *Birthmarks*
Hutsell-Manning, L. *Agnes*
Kane, M. *Moonlodge*
Kemlo, K. *Mona*
Koller, K. *Madonna of the Wilderness*
Lambert, A. *Ask Your Mother*
Langeberg, S. *Maija of Chaggaland*
McGuigan, C. *Inside Uitlander*
Major, A. *Saint Marina*
Martin, M. *White Skates*
Montero, G. *Frida K*
Nolan, Y. *Annie Mae's Movement*
Renders, K. *Motherhood, Madness, and the Shape of
    the Universe*
St. James, A. *Queen of Spades*
Sears, D. *Afrika Solo*
Sinclair, C. *Sabina's Splendid Brain*
Stapleton, B. *Offensive to Some*
Williams, K. *Quiz*
Zylin, S. *Obsidian*
Zylin, S. *Taking Care of Numero Uno*

BREN Brenner, Clarence Dietz, and Goodyear, Nolan, A.,
    eds. *Eighteenth Century French Plays.* New York:
    Century [c. 1927] 561pp.
Beaumarchais, P. *Le mariage de Figaro*
Crébillon, P. *Rhadamiste et Zénobie*
Dancourt, F. *Le chevalier à la mode*
Destouches, P. *Le glorieux*
Diderot, D. *Le père de famille*
Gresset, J. *Le mèchant*
La Chaussée, P. *Le préjugé à la mode*
Laya, J. *L'ami des lois*
Lesage, A. *Turcaret*
Marivaux, P. *Le jeu de l'amour et du hazard*
Palissot de Montenoy, C. *Les philosophes*
Regnard, J. *Le légataire universel*
Sedaine, M. *Le philosophe sans le savoir*
Voltaire, F. *Nanine*
Voltaire, F. *Zaire*

BRET Brett, Lewis Edward, ed. *Nineteenth Century
    Spanish Plays.* New York: Appleton-Century
    [c. 1935] 889pp.
Benavente y Martínez, J. *El nido ajeno*
Bréton de los Herreros, M. *Muérete ¡y verás!*
Echegaray y Eizaguirre, J. *El gran Galeoto*
García Gutiérrez, A. *Juan Lorenzo*
Gil y Zárate, A. *Guzman el Bueno*
Hartzenbusch, J. *Los amantes de Teruel*
López de Ayala, A. *Consuelo*
Moratín, L. *El sí de las niñas*
Nuñez de Arce, G. *El haz de leña*
Pérez Galdós, B. *La de San Quintín*

Rivas, A. *Don Alvaro*
Tamayo y Baus, M. *Un drama nuevo*
Vega, R. *Pepa la frescachona*
Vega, V. *El hombre de mundo*
Zorrilla y Moral, J. *Don Juan Tenorio*

BREW Brewster, Yvonne, ed. *Black Plays.* London:
    Methuen, 1987–1995. 3 vols.
Boakye, P. *Boy with Beer* 3
D'Aguiar, F. *A Jamaican Airman Forsees His Death* 3
Ellis, M. *Chameleon* 1
Fagon, A. *Lonely Cowboy* 1
Greer, B. *Munda negra* 3
Ikoli, T. *The Lower Depths: An East End Story* 1
Ikoli, T. *Scrape Off the Black* 3
Lovelace, E. *The Dragon Can't Dance* 2
Oshodi, M. *Blood Sweat and Fears* 2
Pinnock, W. *A Rock in Water* 2
Pinnock, W. *Talking in Tongues* 3
Rudet, J. *Basin* 1
Zephaniah, B. *Job Rocking* 2

BRIDGE *Bridge across the Sea: Seven Baltic Plays.*
    Edited by Alfreds Straumanis. Prospect Heights,
    IL: Waveland Press, 1983. 368pp.
Eglītis, A. *Ferdinand and Sybil*
Eglītis, A. *Please Come In, Sir!*
Kulvet, I. *Bridge across the Sea*
Kõvamees, R. *The Maiden on the Seashore*
Landsbergis, A. *The School for Love*
Škema, A. *Ataraxia*
Straumanis, A. *It's Different Now, Mr. Abele*

BRIG Briggs, Thomas Henry; Herzberg, Max J.; and
    Bolenius, Emma Miller, eds. *English Literature.*
    Boston: Houghton Mifflin [c. 1934] 770pp.
    (Literature in the Senior High School. Vol. 4)
Shakespeare, W. *The Tragedy of Macbeth*
Sheridan, R. *The School for Scandal*
Synge, J. *Riders to the Sea*

BRIK Briggs, Thomas Henry; Herzberg, Max J.; and
    Bolenius, Emma Miller, eds. *Romance.* Boston:
    Houghton Mifflin [c. 1932] 770pp. (Literature in the
    Senior High School. Vol. 2)
Peabody, J. *The Piper*
Shakespeare, W. *As You like It*

BRIM Brisbane, Katharine, ed. *Plays of the 70s.* Sydney:
    Currency Press, 1998. 3 vols.
Blair, R. *The Christian Brothers* 3
Boddy, M., and Ellis, B. *The Legend of King O'Malley* 1
Buzo, A. *Coralie Lansdowne Says No* 2

Compton, J. *Crossfire* 3
De Groen, A. *The Joss Adams Show* 1
Hibberd, J. *A Stretch of the Imagination* 1
Kenna, P. *A Hard God* 2
McNeil, J. *How Does Your Garden Grow?* 2
Merritt, R. *The Cake Man* 2
Nowra, L. *Inner Voices* 3
O' Donoghue, J. *A Happy and Holy Occasion* 3
Romeril, J. *Mrs. Thally F* 1
Williamson, D. *The Removalists* 1

BRIMA Brisbane, Katharine, ed. *Plays of the 60s.* Sydney:
     Currency Press, 1998. 3 vols.
Buzo, A. *The Front Room Boys* 3
Buzo, A. *Norm and Ahmed* 2
Gray, O. *Burst of Summer* 1
Hewett, D. *This Old Man Comes Rolling Home* 2
Hopgood, A. *Private Yuk Objects* 2
McKinney, J. *The Well* 1
Milgate, R. *A Refined Look at Existence* 3
Patrikareas, T. *The Promised Woman* 1
Reed, B. *Burke's Company* 3
Romeril, J. *Chicago, Chicago* 3
Searle, J. *The Lucky Streak* 2
White, P. *The Season at Sarsaparilla* 1

BRIN Brissenden, Connie, ed. *The Factory Lab Anthology.*
     Vancouver: Talon Books, Ltd., 1974. 316pp.
Canale, R. *The Jingo Ring*
Greenland, B. *We Three, You and I*
Hollingsworth, M. *Strawberry Fields*
Kardish, L. *Brussels Sprouts*
Walker, G. *Ambush at Tether's End*

BRIP Brissenden, Connie, ed. *Now in Paperback: Six
     Canadian Plays of the 1970's.* Toronto: Fineglow
     Plays, 1973. 102pp.
Alianak, H. *Mathematics*
Alianak, H. *Western*
Del Grande, L. *So Who's Goldberg*
Fineberg. L. *Death*
Petch, S. *The General*
Walker, G. *Prince of Naples*

BRIQ Brissenden, Connie, ed. *West Coast Plays.*
     Vancouver: New Play Centre. 1975. 160pp.
Angel, L. *Forthcoming Wedding*
Cone, T. *Cabistique*
Grainger, T. *The Helper*
Hollingsworth, M. *Operators*
Rosen, S. *The Box*

BRIT Britsch, Ralph A., and Others. *Literature as Art.*
     Provo, UT: Brigham Young University Press, 1972.
     743pp.

Ibsen, H. *The Master Builder*
Sophocles. *Antigone*

BRIU Brittin, Norman A., comp. *A Reading
     Apprenticeship Literature.* New York: Holt,
     Rinehart, and Winston, 1971. 469pp.
Miller, A. *A View from the Bridge*
O'Casey, S. *Bedtime Story*
Synge, J. *Riders to the Sea*

BRIX Brockett, Oscar Gross, and Brockett, Lenyth, eds.
     *Plays for the Theatre: An Anthology of World
     Drama.* New York, Holt, Rinehart and Winston
     [1967] 503pp.
Brecht, B. *The Good Woman of Setzuan*
Ibsen, H. *The Wild Duck*
Kaiser, G. *From Morn to Midnight*
Miller, A. *Death of a Salesman*
Molière, J. *Tartuffe; or, the Imposter*
Plautus, T. *The Menaechmi*
*The Second Shepherds' Play*
Shakespeare, W. *King Lear*
Sheridan, R. *The School for Scandal*

BRIY Brockett, Oscar G., and Brockett, Lenyth, eds. *Plays
     for the Theatre: An Anthology of World Drama.*
     2nd ed. New York: Holt, 1974. 580pp.
Brecht, B. *The Good Woman of Setzuan*
Ibsen, H. *The Wild Duck*
Ionesco, E. *The New Tenant*
Kaiser, G. *From Morn to Midnight*
Miller, A. *Death of a Salesman*
Molière, J. *Tartuffe, or the Imposter*
Plautus. *The Menaechmi*
Rabe, D. *Sticks and Bones*
*The Second Shepherds' Play*
Shakespeare, W. *King Lear*
Sheridan, R. *The School for Scandal*
Sophocles. *Oedipus Rex*

BRIZ Brockett, Oscar G., and Brockett, Lenyth, eds. *Plays
     for the Theatre: An Anthology of World Drama.* 3rd
     ed. New York: Holt, 1979. 638pp.
Brecht, B. *The Good Woman of Setzuan*
Hansberry, L. *A Raisin in the Sun*
Ibsen, H. *The Wild Duck*
Ionesco, E. *The New Tenant*
Kaiser, G. *From Morn to Midnight*
Miller, A. *Death of a Salesman*
Molière, J. *Tartuffe, or the Imposter*
Plautus. *The Menaechmi*
Rabe, D. *Sticks and Bones*
Rabe, D. *Streamers*
*The Second Shepherds' Play*
Shakespeare, W. *King Lear*

Sheridan, R. *The School for Scandal*
Sophocles. *Oedipus Rex*

BRJ Brockett, Oscar G., ed. *Plays for the Theatre: An Anthology of World Drama.* 4th ed. New York: Holt, 1984. 652pp.
Beckett, S. *Happy Days*
Brecht, B. *Mother Courage and Her Children*
Hansberry, L. *A Raisin in the Sun*
Ibsen, H. *The Wild Duck*
Miller, A. *Death of a Salesman*
Molière, J. *Tartuffe, or the Imposter*
O'Neill, E. *The Hairy Ape*
Plautus. *The Menaechmi*
Rabe, D. *Streamers*
*The Second Shepherds' Play*
Shakespeare, W. *Hamlet*
Sheridan, R. *The School for Scandal*
Sophocles. *Oedipus Rex*

BRJA Brockett, Oscar G., ed. *Plays for the Theatre: A Drama Anthology.* 5th ed. New York: Holt, 1988. 614pp.
Beckett, S. *Happy Days*
Brecht, B. *The Good Woman of Setzuan*
Goldoni, C. *The Servant of Two Masters*
Hansberry, L. *A Raisin in the Sun*
Ibsen, H. *The Wild Duck*
Miller, A. *Death of a Salesman*
Molière, J. *Tartuffe, or the Imposter*
O'Neill, E. *The Hairy Ape*
Plautus. *The Menaechmi*
*The Second Shepherds' Play*
Shakespeare, W. *Hamlet*
Shepard, S. *Fool for Love*
Sophocles. *Oedipus Rex*
Zeami. *The Shrine in the Fields*

BRJB Brockett, Oscar G., ed. *Plays for the Theatre: A Drama Anthology.* 6th ed. Fort Worth, TX: Harcourt Brace College Publishers, 1996. 568pp.
Beckett, S. *Happy Days*
Brecht, B. *The Good Woman of Setzuan*
Hwang, D. *M. Butterfly*
Ibsen, H. *A Doll's House*
Molière, J. *Tartuffe*
*Noah and His Sons*
O'Neill, E. *The Hairy Ape*
Sanchez-Scott, M. *Roosters*
Scala, F. *The Dentist*
Shakespeare, W. *Hamlet*
Sophocles. *Oedipus Rex*
Vogel, P. *The Baltimore Waltz*
Williams, T. *Cat on a Hot Tin Roof*
Wolfe, G. *The Colored Museum*

BRJC Brockett, Oscar G., with Ball, Robert J. *Plays for the Theatre: A Drama Anthology.* 7th ed. Fort Worth, TX: Harcourt Brace College Publishers, 2000. 624pp.
Beckett, S. *Happy Days*
Brecht, B. *The Good Woman of Setzuan*
Goldoni, C. *The Servant of Two Masters*
Gotanda, P. *Yankee Dawg You Die*
Ibsen, H. *A Doll's House*
Molière, J. *Tartuffe*
*Noah and His Sons*
O'Neill, E. *The Hairy Ape*
Sanchez-Scott, M. *Roosters*
Shakespeare, W. *Hamlet*
Sophocles. *Oedipus Rex*
Williams, T. *Cat on a Hot Tin Roof*
Wasserstein, W. *An American Daughter*
Wolfe, G. *The Colored Museum*

BRN Brodin, Sylvie Bostsarron, and Vigneras, Marcel, eds. *En scène: Trois comédies avec musique.* New York: Dryden Press [c. 1942] 295pp.
Beaumarchais, P. *Le barbier de Séville*
Labiche, E., and Martin, E. *Les trente-sept sous de M. Montaudoin*
*Le savetier Calbain*

BRNB Brodkin, Sylvia Z., and Person, Elizabeth J., eds. *Close-up: A Collection of Short Plays.* New York: Globe, 1970. 282pp.
Arno, O. *The Other Player*
Carroll, R. *Heat Lightning*
Daviot, G. *The Pen of My Aunt*
Hailey, A. *Flight into Danger*
McDaniel, C. *The Ends of Justice*
Niggli, J. *The Ring of General Macías*
Rose, R. *Thunder on Sycamore Street*
Watson, M. *The Dogs of War*

BRNS Brodkin, Sylvia Z., and Person, Elizabeth J., eds. *Seven Plays of Mystery and Suspense with Writing Manual.* New York: Globe Book Company, 1982. 212pp.
Carroll, R. *Heat Lightning*
Deane, H., and Balderston, J. *Dracula*
Glaspell, S. *Trifles*
Hailey, A. *Flight into Danger*
Parker, L. *The Monkey's Paw*
Serling, R. *I Shot an Arrow*
Watson, M. *The Dogs of War*

BRO Brooke, Charles Frederick Turner, ed. *The Shakespeare Apocrypha.* Oxford: Clarendon Press, 1918. 455pp.

*Arden of Feversham*
*The Birth of Merlin*
*Edward III*
*Fair Em*
*Locrine*
*The London Prodigal*
*The Merry Devil of Edmonton*
*Mucedorus*
*The Puritan*
*Sir John Oldcastle*
*Sir Thomas More*
*Thomas, Lord Cromwell*
*The Two Noble Kinsmen*
*A Yorkshire Tragedy*

BROC Brooke, Charles Frederick Tucker, and Paradise, Nathaniel Burton, eds. *English Drama, 1580–1642.* Boston: Heath [c. 1933] 1044pp.
Beaumont, F., and Fletcher, J. *The Knight of the Burning Pestle*
Beaumont, F., and Fletcher, J. *The Maid's Tragedy*
Beaumont, F., and Fletcher, J. *Philaster*
Chapman, G. *Bussy d'Ambois*
Chapman, G., Johnson, B., and Marston, J. *Eastward Ho!*
Dekker, T. *The Shoemakers' Holiday*
Fletcher, J. *The Island Princess*
Fletcher, J., and Massinger, P. *Beggars' Bush*
Ford, J. *The Broken Heart*
Greene, R. *Friar Bacon and Friar Bungay*
Heywood, T. *A Woman Killed with Kindness*
Jonson, B. *The Alchemist*
Jonson, B. *Epicoene; or, the Silent Woman*
Jonson, B. *Every Man in His Humour*
Jonson, R. *The Gipsies Metamorphosed*
Jonson, B. *Volpone, or, the Fox*
Kyd, T. *The Spanish Tragedy*
Lyly, J. *Endymion*
Marlowe, C. *Doctor Faustus*
Marlowe, C. *Edward II*
Marlowe, C. *The Jew of Malta*
Marlowe, C. *Tamburlaine, Part I*
Marston, J. *The Malcontent*
Massinger, P. *A New Way to Pay Old Debts*
Middleton, T. *A Game at Chess*
Middleton, T., and Rowley, W. *The Changeling*
Peele, G. *The Arraignment of Paris*
Peele, G. *The Old Wives' Tale*
Shirley, J. *The Cardinal*
Webster, J. *The Duchess of Malfi*

BROE Brooks, Cleanth, et al., compiler. *American Literature: The Makers and the Making.* New York: St. Martins, 1974. 2 vols.
Odets, C. *Waiting for Lefty* 2

O'Neill, E. *Desire under the Elms* 2
Wilder, T. *The Skin of Our Teeth* 2

BROF Brooks, Cleanth; Purser, John Thibaut; and Warren, Robert Penn. *An Approach to Literature.* Baton Rouge, LA: Lousiana State University Press, 1936. 578pp.
Čapek, K. *R.U.R. (Rossum's Universal Robots)*
Ibsen, H. *Hedda Gabler*

BROG Brooks, Cleanth; Purser, John Thibaut; and Warren, Robert Penn. *An Approach to Literature.* Rev. ed. New York: Crofts, 1939. 634pp.
Čapek, K. *R.U.R. (Rossum's Universal Robots)*
Ibsen, H. *Hedda Gabler*
Shakespeare, W. *Antony and Cleopatra*
Wilde, O. *The Importance of Being Earnest*

BROH Brooks, Cleanth; Purser, John Thibaut; and Warren, Robert Penn. *An Approach to Literature.* 3rd ed. New York: Appleton-Century-Crofts [c. 1952] 820pp.
Eliot, T. *Murder in the Cathedral*
Ibsen, H. *Hedda Gabler*
Maugham, W. *The Circle*
Miller, A. *All My Sons*
Shakespeare, W. *Antony and Cleopatra*

BROI Brooks, Cleanth, et al., compilers. *An Approach to Literature.* 5th ed. Englewood Cliffs, NJ: Prentice-Hall, 1975. 902pp.
Beckett, S. *Act without Words*
Eliot, T. *Murder in the Cathedral*
Ibsen, H. *Hedda Gabler*
Shakespeare, W. *Antony and Cleopatra*
Shaw, G. *Pygmalion*
Shaw, G. *Saint Joan*
Sophocles. *Oedipus Rex*
Wilder, T. *The Skin of Our Teeth*

BROJ Brooks, Cleanth, and Heilman, Robert B., eds. *Understanding Drama.* New York: Holt [c. 1945] 515pp.
Congreve, W. *The Way of the World*
*Everyman*
Lillo, G. *The London Merchant*
Ibsen, H. *Rosmersholm*
Plautus. *The Twin Menaechmi*
Shakespeare, W. *Henry IV, Part I*
Sheridan, R. *The School for Scandal*
Wilde, O. *Lady Windermere's Fan*

BROK Brooks, Cleanth, and Heilmar, Robert B. *Understanding Drama: Twelve Plays.* New York: Holt [c. 1948] 674, +64pp.

Chekhov, A. *The Sea Gull*
Congreve, W. *The Way of the World*
*Everyman*
Ibsen, H. *Rosmersholm*
Lillo, G. *The London Merchant; or, the History of George Barnwell*
Marlowe, C. *Dr. Faustus*
Plautus. *The Twin Menaechmi*
Shakespeare, W. *Henry IV, Part I*
Shakespeare, W. *King Lear*
Sheridan, R. *The School for Scandal*
Sophocles. *Oedipus the King*
Wilde, O. *Lady Windermere's Fan*

BROOKS, VAN WYCK. *See* AME *American Caravan.*

BROTA Brown, Ashley, and Kimmey, J. L., eds. *Tragedy.* Columbus, OH: Merrill, 1968. 268pp.
Lowell, R. *Benito Cereno*
Shakespeare, W. *King Lear*
Sophocles. *King Oedipus*

BROV Brown, Ian, and Fisher, Mark, eds. *Made in Scotland: An Anthology of New Scottish Plays.* London: Methuen Drama, 1995. 238pp.
Cullen, M. *The Cut*
Donald, S. *The Life of Stuff*
Glover, S. *Bondagers*
Mclean, D. *Julie Allardyce*

BROWN, IVOR. *See* FOUP *Four Plays of 1936.*

BROW Brown, Leonard Stanley, and Perrin, Porter Gale, eds. *A Quarto of Modern Literature.* New York, Scribner [c. 1935] 436pp.
Barrie, J. *Dear Brutus*
Galsworthy, J. *Justice*
Howard, S. *The Silver Cord*
O'Neill, E. *In the Zone*

BROX Brown, Leonard Stanley, and Perrin, Porter Gale, eds. *A Quarto of Modern Literature.* 3rd ed. New York: Scribner [c. 1950] 631pp.
Galsworthy, J. *Loyalties*
Giraudoux, J. *The Madwoman of Chaillot*
Howard, S. *The Silver Cord*
Miller, A. *Death of a Salesman*
O'Neill, E. *The Emperor Jones*
Sherwood, R. *Abe Lincoln in Illinois*

BROY Brown, Leonard Stanley, and Perrin, P. G., eds. *A Quarto of Modern Literature.* 5th ed. New York, Scribner, 1964. 606pp.
Giraudoux, J. *The Madwoman of Chaillot*
Miller, A. *Death of a Salesman*

Shaw, G. *Pygmalion*
Williams, T. *The Glass Menagerie*

BROZ Brown, Leonard Stanley; Waite, Harlow O.; and Atkinson, Benjamin P., eds. *Literature for Our Time.* New York: Holt [c. 1947] 951pp.
Anderson, M. *Winterset*
Barry, P. *The Philadelphia Story*
Behrman, S. *Biography*
Capek, K. *R.U.R.*
Corwin, N. *We Hold These Truths*
MacLeish, A. *The Fall of the City*
O'Neill, E. *The Hairy Ape*

BRP Brown, Lorraine, ed. *Liberty Deferred and Other Living Newspapers of the 1930s Federal Theatre Project.* Fairfax, VA: George Mason University Press. 1989, 316pp.
Editors of the Living Newspapers. *Medicine Show*
Hill, A., and Silvera, J. *Liberty Deferred: A Living Newspaper*
Living Newspaper Unit. *1935*
Living Newspaper Unit. *Injunction Granted*

BRR Brown, Sharon Osborne, ed. *Present Tense.* New York: Harcourt, Brace, 1941. 3 vols.
Čapek, K. *R.U.R. (Rossum's Universal Robots)* 3
MacLeish, A. *The Fall of the City* 3
Wilder, T. *Our Town* 1

BRS Brown, Sharon Osborne, ed. *Present Tense.* Rev. ed. New York: Harcourt, Brace, 1945. 762pp.
Corwin, N. *Good Heavens*
Wilder, T. *Our Town*

BRW Brown-Guilllory, Elizabeth, ed. *Wines in the Wilderness: Plays by African-American Women from the Harlem Renaissance to the Present.* New York: Greenwood Press, 1990. 251pp. (Contributions in Afro-American and African Studies, Number 135)
Bonner, M. *The Pot Maker*
Brown-Guillory, E. *Mam Phyllis*
Childress, A. *Florence*
Childress, A. *Wine in the Wilderness*
Graham, S. *It's Mornin'*
Johnson, G. *Blue Blood*
Johnson, G. *Blue-eyed Black Boy*
Johnson, G. *Safe*
Klein, S. *Get Together*
Miller, M. *Riding the Goat*
Sanchez, S. *Sister Son/ji*
Spence, E. *Episode*
Spence, E. *Hot Stuff*

BRZ Browne, Elliott Martin, ed. *Four Modern Verse Plays*. Harmondsworth, Middlesex: Penguin Books [1957] 269pp.
  Eliot, T. *The Family Reunion*
  Fry, C. *A Phoenix Too Frequent*
  MacDonagh, D. *Happy as Larry*
  Williams, C. *Thomas Cranmer of Canterbury*

BRZA Browne, Elliott Martin, ed. *Three European Plays*. Harmondsworth, Middlesex: Penguin Books [1958] 190pp.
  Anouilh, J. *Ring round the Moon*
  Betti, U. *The Queen and the Rebels*
  Sartre, J. *In Camera*

BRZE Browne, Elliott Martin, ed. *Three Irish Plays*. Baltimore, MD: Penguin Books [1960, c. 1959] 236pp.
  Johnston, D. *The Moon in the Yellow River*
  MacDonagh, D. *Step-in-the-hollow*
  O'Conor, J. *The Iron Harp*

BROWNE, ELLIOTT MARTIN. *See also* NEWE *New English Dramatists*.

BRYSON, LYMAN. *See* THP *Three Great Greek Plays*.

BUCK Buck, Philo M., Jr., ed. *An Anthology of World Literature*. New York: Macmillan, 1934. 1016pp.
  Aeschylus. *Agamemnon*
  Aeschylus. *Prometheus Bound*
  Aristophanes. *The Frogs*
  Euripides. *Iphigenia at Aulis*
  Goethe, J. *Faust, Parts I and II*
  Hauptmann, G. *The Sunken Bell*
  Hebbel, F. *Maria Magdalena*
  Ibsen, H. *An Enemy of the People*
  Kälidäsa. *Sakoontalá*
  Molière, J. *The Misanthrope*
  Molière, J. *Tartuffe*
  Pèrez Galdós, B. *Electra*
  Racine, J. *Athaliah*
  Sophocles. *Antigone*
  Sophocles. *Oedipus the King*

BUCL Buck, Philo M., Jr., and Albertson, Hazel, eds. *An Anthology of World Literature*. Revised edition. New York: Macmillan, 1940. 1148pp.
  Aeschylus. *Agamemnon*
  Aeschylus. *Prometheus Bound*
  Aristophanes. *The Frogs*
  *Book of Job*
  Euripides. *Iphigenia at Aulis*
  Euripides. *Medea*
  Goethe, J. *Faust, Parts I and II*

  Hauptmann, G. *The Sunken Bell*
  Hebbel, F. *Maria Magdalena*
  Ibsen, H. *An Enemy of the People*
  Kälidäsa. *Sakoontalá*
  Molière, J. *The Misanthrope*
  Molière, J. *Tartuffe*
  Racine, J. *Athaliah*
  Sophocles. *Antigone*
  Sophocles. *Oedipus the King*

BUCM Buck, Philo M., Jr., and Albertson, Hazel Stewart, eds. *An Anthology of World Literature*. 3rd ed. New York: Macmillan [c. 1951] 1150pp.
  Aeschylus. *Agamemnon*
  Aeschylus. *Prometheus Bound*
  Aristophanes. *The Frogs*
  *Book of Job*
  Euripides. *Iphigenia at Aulis*
  Euripides. *Medea*
  Goethe, J. *Faust Parts I & II*
  Hauptmann, G. *The Sunken Bell*
  Hebbel, F. *Maria Magdalena*
  Ibsen, H. *An Enemy of the People*
  Kälidäsa. *Shakuntalä*
  Molière, J. *The Misanthrope*
  Molière, J. *Tartuffe*
  Plautus. *Aulularia*
  Racine, J. *Athaliah*
  Sophocles. *Antigone*
  Sophocles. *Oedipus the King*

BUFF Bufffngton, Albert F., ed. *The Reichard Collection of Early Pennsylvania German Plays*. Lancaster, PA, 1962. 439pp. (vol. 61, Pennsylvania German Society)
  Barba, P. *An der lumpa parti*
  Barba, P. *Die verrechelte rechler*
  Birmelin, J. *Der gnopp*
  Birmelin, J. *Em Docktor Fogel sei offis schtunn*
  Brendle, T. *Die hoffning*
  Brendle, T. *Die mutter*
  Fink, E. *Noshions duhn*
  Grumbine, E. *Die insurance business*
  Iobst, C. *Die Calline browierts*
  Iobst, C. *Es Heller's Chrischtdag*
  Miller, D. *Per Peter soll en handwerk lernen*
  Miller, D. *En gespräch zwischen zweb demokrate über politiks*
  Miller, D. *Noch eppes vom Peter seim handwerk*
  Moss, A., and Newhard, E. *H.M.S. Pinafore; oder, Das maedle und ihr sailor kerl*
  Rauch, E. *Rip Van Winkle; oder, Die shpooks fum Blowa Barrick*
  Wieand, P. *Der parra kumpt*
  Wieand, P. *Die huchzich um kreitz waig*

Wieand, P. *Tzu forwitsich*
Wollenweber, L. *Das lied von der union*
Wollenweber, L. *Die Margareth und die Lea*
Wollenweber, L. *Die Sära und die Betz*
Wollenweber, L. *Eb Refschneider un Susi Leimbach*
Wollenweber, L. *Ein gespräch*

BUL Bullen, Arthur Henry, ed. *A Collection of Old English Plays*. New York: B. Blom, 1964. 7 vol. in 4 vols.
Davenport, R. *The City Nightcap* 4
Davenport, R. *A Crowne for a Conquerour* 4
Davenport, R. *King John and Matilda* 4
Davenport, R. *A New Trick to Cheat the Divell* 4
Davenport, R. *A Survey of the Sciences* 4
Davenport, R. *Too Late to Call Backe Yesterday* 4
*The Distracted Emperor* 2
*The Martyr'd Souldier* 1
*The Mayde's Metamorphosis* 1
Nabbes, T. *Covent Garden* 3
Nabbes, T. *Hannibal and Scipio* 3
Nabbes, T. *Tottenham Court* 3
*The Noble Souldier* 1
*Sir Gyles Goosecappe* 2
*Tragedy of Nero* 1
*The Tryall of Chevalry* 2
*The Wisdom of Dr. Dodypoll* 2

BURB Burbridge, Paul, ed. *Playing with Fire: Five Stageplays from Riding Lights Theatre Co.* Bromley, Kent: MARC Europe, 1987. 245pp.
Forde, N. *A Winter's Tale*
Goreing, A. *Promise*
*St. John's Gospel*
Watts, M. *Catwalk*
Watts, M. *A Gentleman's Agreement*

BURG Burgess, Charles Owen. *Drama: Literature on Stage*. Philadelphia: Lippincott, 1969. 598pp.
Beach, L. *The Clod*
Brecht, B. *The Good Woman of Setzuan*
Chekhov, A. *The Sea-gull*
Ibsen, H. *An Enemy of the People*
Lowell, R. *Benito Cereno*
Molière, J. *The Misanthrope*
O'Neill, E. *In the Zone*
Shakespeare, W. *Antony and Cleopatra*
Shaw, G. *Major Barbara*
Sophocles. *Oedipus Rex*
Strindberg, A. *The Stronger*
Williams, T. *The Last of My Solid Gold Watches*

BURN *Burning the Curtain: Four Revolutionary Spanish Plays*. Translated and introduced by Gwynne Edwards. New York: Marion Boyars, 1995. 254pp.

Buero Vallejo, A. *Two Sides to Dr. Valmy's Story*
Ors, F. *Contradance*
Salom, J. *Almost a Goddess*
Sastre, A. *Tragic Prelude*

BURNS Burns, Edward, ed. *The Chester Mystery Cycle: A New Staging Text*. Liverpool: Liverpool University Press, 1987. 171pp.
*Abraham, Melchisedec and Isaac*
*The Ascension*
*The Blind Chelidonian*
*Cain and Abel*
*Christ's Passion*
*Christ's Resurrection*
*The Creation of Man: Adam and Eve*
*The Deluge*
*Epilogue*
*The Fall of Lucifer*
*The Harrowing of Hell*
*Interlude*
*Judas' Plot*
*The Last Judgment*
*The Last Supper*
*The Nativity*
*The Raising of Lazarus*
*The Resurrection*
*The Shepherds*
*The Slaying of the Innocents*
*The Temptation*
*The Trial and Flagellation*
*The Woman Taken in Adultery*

THE BURNS MANTLE YEARBOOK.
*See* BES *Best Plays of 1894/99*, etc.

BURR Burrows, David James, and others, eds. *Myth and Motifs in Literature*. New York: Free Press, 1973. 470pp.
Aeschylus. *Prometheus Bound*
Büchner, G. *Woyzeck*
Yeats, W. *The Land of the Heart's Desire*

BUSHB *The Bush Theatre Book*. Edited by Mike Bradwell. London: Methuen Drama, 1997. 271pp. (Frontline Drama 5; Continuation of Frontline Intelligence)
Blakeman, H. *Caravan*
Fannin, H. *Mackeral Sky*

BUSHT *Bush Theatre Plays*. Boston: Faber and Faber, 1996. 345pp.
Bruce, L. *Keyboard Skills*
Johnson, C. *Boys Mean Business*
Oglesby, T. *Two Lips Indifferent Red*
Wallace, N. *One Flea Spare*

CADY Cady, Edwin H., ed. *Literature of the Early Republic*. New York: Rinehart [c. 1950] 495pp.
Tyler, R. *The Contrast*

CAIR Cairns, Christopher, ed. *Ariosto's The Supposes, Machiavelli's The Mandrake, Intronati's The Deceived: Three Renaissance Comedies*. Lewiston, NY: Edwin Mellen Press, 1996. 439pp.
Accademia degli Intronati. *The Deceived*
Ariosto, L. *The Supposes*
Machiavelli, N. *The Mandrake*

CAIRT Cairns, Christopher, ed. *Three Renaissance Comedies*. Lewiston, NY: Edwin Mellen Press, 1991. 353pp.
Aretino, P. *Talanta*
Ariosto, L. *Lena*
Ruzante. *Posh Talk*

CAL *Calamus; Male Homosexuality in Twentieth Century Literature, an International Anthology*. Edited by David Galloway and Christian Sabisch. New York: William Morrow, 1982. 503pp.
Inge, W. *The Boy in the Basement*
Jones, L. *The Toilet*

CALD Calderwood, James Lee, and Tollver, H. E., eds. *Forms of Drama*. Englewood Cliffs, NJ: Prentice-Hall, 1969. 601pp.
Beckett, S. *All that Fall*
Chekhov, A. *The Cherry Orchard*
Dürrenmatt, F. *The Visit*
*Everyman*
Ibsen, H. *The Master Builder*
Molière, J. *Tartuffe*
Orton, J. *Entertaining Mr. Sloane*
Racine, J. *Phaedra*
*The Second Shepherds' Pageant*
Shakespeare, W. *Henry the IV, Part I*
Shakespeare, W. *The Tempest*
Shakespeare, W. *The Tragedy of Macbeth*
Shaw, G. *Arms and the Man*
Sophocles. *Oedipus Rex*
Yeats, W. *Purgatory*

CALE Cameron, Alasdair, ed. *Scot-free: New Scottish Plays*. London: Nick Hern Books, 1990. 275pp.
Byrne, J. *Writer's Cramp*
Clifford, J. *Losing Venice*
Di Mambro, A. *The Letter-box*
Hannan, C. *Elizabeth Gordon Quinn*
McKay, J. *Dead Dad Dog*
Munro, R. *Saturday at the Commodore*
Roper, T. *The Steamie*

CALG Campbell, Gladys, and Thomas, Russell Brown, eds. *Reading American Literature*. Boston: Little, Brown, 1944. 912pp.
Sherwood, R. *Abe Lincoln in Illinois*

CALM Campbell, Oscar James; Van Gundy, Justine; and Shrodes, Caroline, eds. *Patterns for Living*. New York: Macmillan, 1940. 1306pp.
Anderson, M. *Winterset*
Carroll, P. *Shadow and Substance*
Milne, A. *Mr. Pim Passes By*
Toller, E. *No More Peace!*

CALN Campbell, Oscar James; Van Gundy, Justine; and Shrodes, Caroline, eds. *Patterns for Living*. Alternate edition. New York: Macmillan [c1943, c1947] 2 vols.
Anderson, M. *Winterset* 2
Čapek, K. *R.U.R.* 1
Franken, R. *Claudia* 1
Hellman, L. *Watch on the Rhine* 2

CALP Campbell, Oscar James; Van Gundy, Justine; and Shrodes, Caroline, eds. *Patterns for Living*. 3rd ed. New York: Macmillan, 1949. 951pp.
Hellman, L. *Watch on the Rhine*
Sherwood, R. *Abe Lincoln in Illinois*

CALQ Campbell, Oscar James; Van Gundy, Justine; and Shrodes, Caroline, eds. *Patterns for Living*. 4th ed. New York: Macmillan [c1955] 975pp.
Hellman, L. *Watch on the Rhine*
Miller, A. *Death of a Salesman*

CAM Campbell, Thomas Moody, ed. *German Plays of the Nineteenth Century*. New York: Crofts, 1930. 437pp.
Anzengruber, L. *Das vierte gebot*
Grillparzer, F. *König Ottokars glück und ende*
Hauptmann, G. *Einsame menschen*
Hebbel, C. *Agnes Bernauer*
Hebbel, C. *Herodes und Mariamne*
Hebbel, C. *Maria Magdalene*
Kleist, B. *Der zerbrochene krug*
Kleist, B. *Prinz Friedrich von Homburg*
Ludwig, O. *Der erbförster*
Tieck, J. *ner gestiefelte kater*
Werner, Z. *Der vierundzwanzigste Februar*

CANADIAN PLAYS FROM HART HOUSE THEATRE. *See* MAS Massey, Vincent, ed.

CAN Canfield, Curtis, ed. *Plays of Changing Ireland*. New York: Macmillan, 1936. 481pp.
Johnston, D. *The Old Lady Says "No!"*

Longford, C. *Mr. Jiggins of Jigginstown*
Longford, E. *Yahoo*
Manning, M. *Youth's the Season . . .?*
Mayne, R. *Bridge Head*
Robinson, L. *Church Street*
Shiels, G. *The New Gossoon*
Yeats, W. *The Words upon the Windowpane*

CAP Canfield, Curtis, ed. *Plays of the Irish Renaissance,
    1880–1930.* New York: Ives Washburn, 1929.
    436pp.
Colum, P. *The Land*
Fitzmaurice, G. *The Dandy Dolls*
Gregory, I. *Hyacinth Halvey*
Hyde, D. *The Twisting of the Rope*
Martyn, E. *Maeve*
Murray, T. *Birthright*
O'Casey, S. *Juno and the Paycock*
Pearse, P. *The Singer*
Robinson, L. *The Big House*
Russell, G. *Deirdre*
Synge, J. *Riders to the Sea*
Yeats, W. *On Baile's Strand*
Yeats, W. *The Only Jealousy of Emer*

CAPU Caputi, Anthony Francis, ed. *Modern Drama:
    Authoritative Texts, Backgrounds, and Criticism.*
    New York: W. W. Norton [1966] 494pp.
Chekhov, A. *The Three Sisters*
Ibsen, H. *The Wild Duck*
O'Neill, E. *Desire under the Elms*
Pirandello, L. *Henry IV*
Shaw, G. *The Devil's Disciple*
Strindberg, A. *A Dream Play*

CARGILL, OSCAR. *See American Literature: A Period
    Anthology*; Oscar Cargill, general editor

CARL Carlsen, George Robert. *American Literature:
    Themes and Writers.* St. Louis, MO: Webster,
    1967. 788pp.
Lardner, R. *Thompson's Vacation*
O'Neill, E. *In the Zone*
Rose, R. *Twelve Angry Men*
Wilder, T. *Our Town*

CARLE Carlsen, George Robert, et al., compilers
    *American Literature: Themes and Writers.* 3rd ed.
    New York: McGraw-Hill, 1978. 787pp.
Lardncr, R. *Thompson's Vacation*
Rose, R. *Twelve Angry Men*
Wilder, T. *Our Town*

CARLG Carlsen, George Robert, and Folkert, Miriam,
    compilers. *British and Western Literature.* 3rd ed.
    New York, McGraw-Hill, 1979. 786pp.
Ibsen, H. *An Enemy of the People*
Molière, J. *The Miser*
Shakespeare, W. *Macbeth*
Sophocles. *Antigone*

CARM Carlsen, George Robert. *Encounters: Themes in
    Literature.* St. Louis, MO: Webster, 1967. 758pp.
Glaspell, S. *Trifles*
Goodrich, F., and Hackett, A. *The Diary of Anne Frank*
Shakespeare, W. *Julius Caesar*

CARME Carlsen, George Robert, and Carlsen, Ruth
    Christoffer, compilers. *Encounters: Themes in
    Literature.* 3rd ed. New York: McGraw-Hill, 1979.
    754pp.
Daviot, G. *The Pen of My Aunt*
Goodrich, F., and Hackett, A. *The Diary of Anne Frank*
Shakespeare, W. *Julius Caesar*

CARMI Carlsen, George Robert, et al., compilers.
    *Insights: Themes in Literature.* 3rd ed. New York:
    McGraw-Hill, 1979. 757pp.
Benét, S. *The Devil and Daniel Webster*
Gibson, W. *The Miracle Worker*
Shakespeare, W. *Romeo and Juliet*

CARN Carlsen, George Robert. *Western Literature:
    Themes and Writers.* St. Louis, MO: Webster,
    1967. 786pp.
Shakespeare, W. *Macbeth*
Shaw, G. *Androcles and the Lion*
Sophocles. *Antigone*

CARP Carpenter, Bruce, compiler. *A Book of Dramas: An
    Anthology of Nineteen Plays.* New York: Prentice-
    Hall, 1929. 1111pp.
Aeschylus. *Agamemnon*
Archer, W. *The Green Goddess*
Behrman, S. *The Second Man*
Chekhov, A. *The Cherry Orchard*
Congreve, W. *Love for Love*
Dickens, C. *The Cricket on the Hearth*
Euripides. *The Trojan Women*
*The Farce of the Worthy Master Pierre Patelin*
Hugo, V. *Hernani*
Ibsen, H. *Hedda Gabler*
Kaufman, G., and Connelly, M. *Beggar on Horseback*
Maeterlinck, M. *The Intruder*
Molière, J. *The Misanthrope*
Parker, L. *A Minuet*
Racine, J. *Phaedra*

Sophocles. *Oedipus, King of Thebes*
Strindberg, A. *Miss Julia*
Synge, J. *Riders to the Sea*
Wilde, O. *The Importance of Being Earnest*

CARPA Carpenter, Bruce, ed. *A Book of Dramas*. Rev. ed. New York: Prentice-Hall, 1949. 992pp.
Aeschylus. *Agamemnon*
Behrman, S. *The Second Man*
Chekhov, A. *The Cherry Orchard*
Congreve, W. *Love for Love*
Euripides. *The Trojan Women*
Ibsen, H. *Hedda Gabler*
Kaufman, G., and Connelly, M. *Beggar on Horseback*
Maeterlinck, M. *The Intruder*
Molière, J. *The Misanthrope*
O'Neill, E. *The Long Voyage Home*
Racine, J. *Phaedra*
Rostand, E. *Cyrano de Bergerac*
Sophocles. *Oedipus, King of Thebes*
Synge, J. *Riders to the Sea*
Wilde, O. *The Importance of Being Earnest*

CARR Carter-Harrison, Paul, comp. *Kuntu Drama: Plays of the African Continuum*. New York: Grove, 1974. 352pp.
Brown, L. *Devil Mas'*
Carter-Harrison, P. *The Great MacDaddy*
Césaire, A. *A Season in the Congo*
Goss, C. *Mars: Monument of the Last Black Eunuch*
Jones, L. *Great Goodness of Life: A Coon Show*
Kennedy, A. *Cities in Bezique: The Owl Answers and a Beast Story*
Toomer, J. *Kabnis*

CART Cartmell, Van H., and Cerf, Bennett Alfred, compilers. *Famous Plays of Crime and Detection*. Philadelphia: Blakiston, 1946. 910pp.
Cohan, G. *Seven Keys to Baldpate*
Chodorov, E. *Kind Lady*
Dell, J. *Payment Deferred*
Dunning, P., and Abbott, G. *Broadway*
Gillette, W. *Sherlock Holmes*
Hamilton, P. *Angel Street*
Megrue, R. *Under Cover*
Rice, E. *On Trial*
Rinehart, M., and Hopwood, A. *The Bat*
Veiller, B. *The Thirteenth Chair*
Veiller, B. *Within the Law*
Willard, J. *The Cat and the Canary*
Williams, E. *Night Must Fall*

CARTMELL, VAN H. *See also* CET Cerf, Bennett Alfred, and Cartmell, Van H., compilers

CAS Case, Sue-Ellen, ed. *The Divided Home/Land: Contemporary German Women's Plays*. Ann Arbor: University of Michigan Press, 1992. 350pp.
Fleisser, M. *Purgatory in Ingolstadt*
Lasker-Schüler, E. *IandI*
Reinshagen, G. *Ironheart*
Roth, F. *Piano Plays*
Specht, K. *The Little Red-hot Man*
Steinwachs, G. *George Sand*

CASB Case, Sue-Ellen, ed. *Split Britches: Lesbian Practice/Feminist Performance*. London and New York: Routledge, 1996. 276pp.
Bourne, B, Shaw, P., Shaw, P., and Weaver, L. *Belle Reprieve: A Collaboration*
Margolin, D., Shaw, P., and Weaver, L. *Beauty and the Beast*
Margolin, D., in collaboration with P. Shaw and L. Weaver. *Lesbians Who Kill*
Margolin, D., Shaw, P., and Weaver, L. *Little Women: The Tragedy*
Margolin, D., Shaw, P., and Weaver, L. *Upwardly Mobile Home*
Shaw, P., Margolin, D., and Weaver, L. *Split Britches: A True Story*
Shaw, P., Weaver, L., and Neale-Kennerley, J. *Lust and Comfort*

CASH Cassady, Mershall, and Cassady, Pat, compilers. *An Introduction to Theatre and Drama*. Skokie, IL: National Textbook Company, 1975. 618pp.
*Everyman*
Gay, J. *The Beggar's Opera*
Hansberry, L. *A Raisin in the Sun*
Ibsen, H. *An Enemy of the People*
Kopit, A. *Oh Dad, Poor Dad, Mamma's Hung You in the Closet and I'm Feelin' So Sad*
Laurents, A. *West Side Story*
Molière, J. *The Miser*
O'Neill, E. *The Hairy Ape*
Shakespeare, W. *As You like It*
Sophocles. *Oedipus Rex*
Synge, J. *Riders to the Sea*
Wilde, O. *The Importance of Being Earnest*
Williams, T. *The Glass Menagerie*

CASK Cassell, Richard A., and Knepler, Henry, eds. *What is the Play?* Glenview, IL: Scott, Foresman [1967] 751pp.
Anouilh, J. *Antigone*
Dürrenmatt, F. *The Visit*
Ghelderode, M. *Christopher Columbus*
Ibsen, H. *An Enemy of the People*
Jonson, B. *The Alchemist*

Lowell, R. *My Kinsman, Major Molineux*
Molière, J. *Scapin*
O'Neill, E. *Hughie*
Shakespeare, W. *King Henry the IV, Part I*
Shaw, G. *Arms and the Man*
Sophocles. *Antigone*
Wilder, T. *The Matchmaker*

CASS Cassidy, Frederic G., ed. *Modern American Plays.*
New York: Longmans, Green, 1949. 501pp.
Anderson, M. *Winterset*
Hellman, L. *Watch on the Rhine*
Lindsay, H., and Crouse, R. *Life with Father*
Odets, C. *Waiting for Lefty*
O'Neill, E. *Anna Christie*
Sherwood, R. *Abe Lincoln in Illinois*

CASU Casson, Lionel, ed. and tr. *Masters of Ancient
Comedy.* New York: Macmillan, 1960. 424pp.
Aristophanes. *The Acharnians*
Menander. *The Arbitration*
Menander. *The Grouch*
Menander. *She Who Was Shorn*
Menander. *The Woman of Samos*
Plautus, T. *The Haunted House*
Plautus, T. *The Rope*
Terentius Afer, P. *The Brothers*
Terentius Afer, P. *Phormio*

CATH Catholic University of America. *Committee for the
Revision of English Curricula: American Profile.*
(The Catholic High School Literature series. Book
III) New York: W. H. Sadlier [c1944] 752pp.
Barry, P. *The Joyous Season*
Wilder, T. *Our Town*

CAWL Cawley, Arthur C., ed. *Everyman and Medieval
Miracle Plays.* New York: Dutton [c1959] 266pp.
*Abraham and Isaac* (Brome)
*The Annunciation* (Coventry)
*Cain and Abel* (N Town)
*The Creation, and the Fall of Lucifer* (York)
*The Creation of Adam and Eve* (York)
*The Crucifixion* (York)
*The Death of Pilate* (Cornish)
*Everyman*
*The Fall of Man* (York)
*The Harrowing of Hell* (Chester)
*Herod the Great* (Wakefield)
*The Judgment* (York)
*Noah's Flood* (Chester)
*The Resurrection* (York)
*The Second Shepherds' Pageant* (Wakefield)
*The Woman Taken in Adultery* (N Town)

CAWM Cawley, Arthur C., ed. *The Wakefield Pageants
in the Towneley Cycle.* Manchester: Manchester
University Press [c1958] 187pp. (Old and Middle
English texts)
*Coliphizacio*
*Mactacio Abel*
*Magnus Herodes*
*Prima pastorum*
*Processus Noe cum filiis*
*Secundus pastorum*

CEN *Center Stage: An Anthology of 21 Contemporary
Black-American Plays.* Edited by Eileen Joyce
Ostrow. Oakland, CA: Sea Urchin Press [c1981]
309pp.
Alexander, R. *The Hourglass*
Cooper, J. *Loners*
Edwards, G. *Three Fallen Angels*
Foreman, F. *Daddy's Seashore Blues*
Hobbes, D. *You Can't Always Sometimes Never Tell*
Houston, D. *The Fishermen*
Hunkins, L. *Revival*
Jackson, C. *In the Master's House There Are Many
Mansions*
Martin, S. *The Moving Violation*
Mason, C. *The Verandah*
Molette, C., and Molette, B. *Noah's Ark*
Owa. *The Soledad tedrad, Part II: Transitions for a
Mime Poem*
Rhodes, C. *The Trip*
Rivers, L. *More Bread and the Circus*
Shine, T. *The Woman Who Was Tampered with in Youth*
Stiles, T. *No One Man Show*
Wakefield, J. *Perceptual Movement*
Welch, L. *Hands in the Mirror*
Wesley, R. *The Sirens*
Wesson, K. *Miss Cegenation*
Williams, A. *A Christmas Story (A Turkey Tale)*

CERF, BENNETT ALFRED. *See also* CART Cartmell,
Van H., and Cerf, Bennett Alfred, compilers
*Famous Plays of Crime and Detection*

CEQ Cerf, Bennett Alfred, comp. *Four Contemporary
American Plays.* New York: Vintage Books
[c1961] 386pp.
Chayefsky, P. *The Tenth Man*
Hansberry, L. *A Raisin in the Sun*
Hellman, L. *Toys in the Attic*
Levitt, S. *The Andersonville Trial*

CEQA Cerf, Bennett Alfred, comp. *Plays of Our Time.*
New York: Random House [1967] 782pp.
Bolt, R. *A Man for All Seasons*
Hansberry, L. *A Raisin in the Sun*

Heggen, T., and Logan, J. *Mister Roberts*
Inge, W. *Come Back, Little Sheba*
Miller, A. *Death of a Salesman*
O'Neill, E. *The Iceman Cometh*
Osborne, J. *Look Back in Anger*
Schisgal, M. *Luv*
Williams, T. *A Streetcar Named Desire*

CER Cerf, Bennett Alfred, ed. *The Pocket Book of Modern American Plays*. New York: Pocket Books [1942] 430pp.
Behrman, S. *No Time for Comedy*
Boothe, C. *Margin for Error*
Odets, C. *Awake and Sing*
Rice, E. *Street Scene*

CES Cerf, Bennett Alfred, ed. *Six American Plays for Today*. New York: Modern Library [c1961] 599pp.
Chayefsky, P. *The Tenth Man*
Hansberry, L. *A Raisin in the Sun*
Hellman, L. *Toys in the Attic*
Inge, W. *The Dark at the Top of the Stairs*
Schary, D. *Sunrise at Campobello*
Williams, T. *Camino Real*

CET Cerf, Bennett Alfred, and Cartmell, Van H., eds. *Sixteen Famous American Plays*. Garden City, NY: Garden City Publishing Co. [c1941] 1049pp.
Behrman, S. *Biography*
Boothe, C. *The Women*
Connelly, M. *The Green Pastures*
Hart, M., and Kaufman, G. *The Man Who Came to Dinner*
Hecht, B., and MacArthur, C. *The Front Page*
Hellman, L. *The Little Foxes*
Howard, S. *They Knew What They Wanted*
Kingsley, S. *Dead End*
Kober, A. *"Having Wonderful Time"*
Lindsay, H., and Crouse, R. *Life with Father*
Odets, C. *Waiting for Lefty*
O'Neill, E. *Ah, Wilderness!*
Saroyan, W. *The Time of Your Life*
Sherwood, R. *The Petrified Forest*
Spewack, B., and Spewack, S. *Boy Meets Girl*
Wilder, T. *Our Town*

CEU Cerf, Bennett Alfred, and Cartmell, Van H., compilers *Sixteen Famous British Plays*. Garden City, NY: Garden City Publishing Co. [1942] 1000pp.
Archer, W. *The Green Goddess*
Barrie, J. *What Every Woman Knows*
Bennett, A., and Knobluck, E. *Milestones*
Besier, R. *The Barretts of Wimpole Street*
Coward, N. *Cavalcade*

Galsworthy, J. *Loyalties*
Housman, L. *Victoria Regina*
Maugham, W. *The Circle*
Milne, A. *Mr. Pim Passes By*
Pinero, A. *The Second Mrs. Tanqueray*
Priestley, J. *Dangerous Corner*
Shairp, M. *The Green Bay Tree*
Sherriff, R. *Journey's End*
Vane, S. *Outward Bound*
Wilde, O. *The Importance of Being Earnest*
Williams, E. *The Corn Is Green*

CEW Cerf, Bennett Alfred, and Cartmell, Van H., compilers. *Sixteen Famous European Plays*. Garden City, NY: Garden City Publishing Co. [1943] 1052pp.
Ansky, S. *The Dybbuk*
Baum, V. *Grand Hotel*
Čapek, K. *R.U.R.*
Carroll, P. *Shadow and Substance*
Chekhov, A. *The Sea Gull*
Deval, J. *Tovarich*
Giraudoux, J. *Amphitryon 38*
Gorky, M. *The Lower Depths*
Hauptmann, G. *The Weavers*
Ibsen, H. *The Wild Duck*
Martínez Sierra, G. *The Cradle Song*
Molnár, F. *Liliom*
Pirandello, L. *Six Characters in Search of an Author*
Rostand, E. *Cyrano de Bergerac*
Schnitzler, A. *Anatol*
Synge, J. *The Playboy of the Western World*

CEY Cerf, Bennett Alfred, and Cartmell, Van H., compilers. *S.R.O.: The Most Successful Plays in the History of the American Stage*. Garden City, NY: Doubleday, Doran, 1944. 920pp.
Aiken, G. *Uncle Tom's Cabin*
Boucicault, D. *Rip Van Winkle*
D'Ennery, A., and Cormon, E. *The Two Orphans*
Hammerstein, O., and Rodgers, R. *Oklahoma!*
Kesselring, J. *Arsenic and Old Lace*
Kirkland, J. *Tobacco Road*
Lindsay, H., and Crouse, R. *Life with Father*
Manners, J. *Peg O' My Heart*
Nichols, A. *Abie's Irish Rose*
Rinehart, M., and Hopwood, A. *The Bat*
Smith, W., and Bacon, F. *Lightnin'*
Tarkington, B., and Wilson, H. *The Man from Home*
Thompson, D. *The Old Homestead*
Wood, Mrs. H. *East Lynne*

CHA Chandler, Frank Wadleigh, and Cordell, Richard Albert, eds. *Twentieth Century Plays*. New York: Nelson, 1934.

Alvarez Quintero, S., and Alvarez, Quintero, J. *Doña Clarines*
Anderson, M., and Stallings, L. *What Price Glory*
Čapek, K., and Čapek, J. *And So Ad Infinitum*
Chlumberg, H. *The Miracle at Verdun*
Connelly, M. *The Green Pastures*
Coward, N. *Private Lives*
Crothers, R. *As Husbands Go*
Ervine, St. J. *John Ferguson*
Hankin, St. J. *The Last of the De Mullins*
Jones, H. *Dolly Reforming Herself*
Lenormand, H. *The Coward*
Maugham, W. *The Breadwinner*
Molnár, F. *The Swan*
O'Neill, E. *Marco Millions*
Pinero, A. *The Thunderbolt*
Pirandello, L. *Each in His Own Way*
Rice, E. *Street Scene*
Robinson, L. *The Far-off Hills*
Sherriff, R. *Journey's End*
Tolstoy, L. *The Live Corpse*

CHAN Chandler, Frank Wadleigh, and Cordell, Richard Albert, eds. *Twentieth Century Plays.* Rev. ed. New York: Nelson, 1939.
Alvarez Quintero, S., and Alvarez Quintero, J. *Doña Clarines*
Anderson, M. *Winterset*
Behrman, S. *Rain from Heaven*
Čapek, K., and Čapek, J. *And So Ad Infinitum*
Chlumberg, H. *The Miracle at Verdun*
Connelly, M. *The Green Pastures*
Coward, N. *Private Lives*
Ervine, St. J. *John Ferguson*
Hankin, St. J. *The Last of the De Mullins*
Howard, S. *The Silver Cord*
Jones, H. *Dolly Reforming Herself*
Kaufman, G., and Connelly, M. *Beggar on Horseback*
Lenormand, H. *The Coward*
Maugham, W. *The Breadwinner*
Molnár, F. *The Swan*
O'Neill, E. *Anna Christie*
Pinero, A. *The Thunderbolt*
Pirandello, L. *Each in His Own Way*
Rice, E. *Street Scene*
Robinson, L. *The Far-off Hills*
Sherriff, R. *Journey's End*
Tolstoy, L. *The Live Corpse*

CHAP Chandler, Frank Wadleigh, and Cordell, Richard Albert, eds. *Twentieth Century Plays, American.* Rev. ed. New York: Nelson, 1939. 295pp.
Anderson, M. *Winterset*
Behrman, S. *Rain from Heaven*
Connelly, M. *The Green Pastures*

Howard, S. *The Silver Cord*
Kaufman, G., and Connelly, M. *Beggar on Horseback*
O'Neill, E. *Anna Christie*
Rice, E. *Street Scene*

CHAR Chandler, Frank Wadleigh, and Cordell, Richard Albert, eds. *Twentieth Century Plays, British.* Rev. and enl. ed. New York: Nelson, 1941. 399pp.
Barrie, J. *The Admirable Crichton*
Coward, N. *Private Lives*
Ervine, St. J. *John Ferguson*
Galsworthy, J. *The Silver Box*
Hankin, St. J. *The Last of the De Mullins*
Jones, H. *Dolly Reforming Herself*
Maugham, S. *The Breadwinner*
Pinero, A. *The Thunderbolt*
Robinson, L. *The Far-off Hills*
Sherriff, R. *Journey's End*

CHAPMAN, JOHN ARTHUR. *See* BES *Best Plays of 1894/99 . . .* etc.; THEA *Theater, 1953/56;* PLAJ *Plays of the Sixties;* PLAL *Plays of the Thirties*

CHARN Charney, Maurice, ed. *Classic Comedies.* New York: Mentor, 1995. 596pp.
Aristophanes. *Lysistrata*
Feydeau, G. *A Fitting Confusion*
Gogol, N. *The Inspector General*
Molière, J. *The Misanthrope*
Plautus. *The Menaechmus Twins*
Shakespeare, W. *The Comedy of Errors*
Shaw, G. *Candida*

CHEL *The Chester Mystery Cycle.* Edited by Robert M. Lumiansky and David Mills. V.1, Text: published for the Early English Text Society. London: Oxford, 1974. 624pp.
*Abraham and Isaac—The Barbers*
*Abraham, Lot and Melchysedeck—The Barbers*
*Adam and Eve—The Drapers*
*The Annunciation and the Nativity—The Wrights*
*Antichrist—The Dyers*
*The Ascension—The Tailors*
*Balaack and Balaam—The Cappers*
*The Betrayal of Christ—The Bakers*
*The Blind Chelidonian—The Glovers*
*Cain and Abel—The Drapers*
*Christ and the Doctors—The Blacksmiths*
*Christ and the Moneylenders—The Corvisors*
*Christ at the House of Simon the Leper—The Corvisors*
*Christ on the Road to Emmaus—The Saddlers*
*Doubting Thomas—The Saddlers*
*The Fall of Lucifer—The Tanners*
*The Harrowing of Hell—The Cooks*
*Judas' Plot—The Corvisors*

*The Last Judgment—The Websters*
*The Last Supper—The Bakers*
*Moses and the Law—The Cappers*
*Noah's Flood—The Waterleaders and Drawers of Dee*
*The Offerings of the Three Kings—The Mercers*
*The Passion—The Ironmongers*
*The Pentecost—The Fishmongers*
*The Prophets of Antichrist—The Clothworkers*
*The Purification—The Blacksmiths*
*The Raising of Lazarus—The Glovers*
*The Resurrection—The Skinners*
*The Slaughter of the Innocents—The Goldsmiths*
*The Shepherds—The Painters*
*The Temptation—The Butchers*
*The Three Kings—The Vintners*
*The Trial and Flagellation—The Fletchers, Bowyers,*
*  Coopers, and Stringers*
*The Woman Taken in Adultery—The Butchers*

CHELM *The Chester Mystery Cycle: A New Edition*
*with Modernized Spelling.* By David Mills. East
Lansing, MI: Colleagues Press, 1992. 444pp.
*Abraham and Isaac—The Barbers*
*Abraham, Lot and Melchysedeck—The Barbers*
*Adam and Eve—The Drapers*
*The Annunciation and the Nativity—The Wrights*
*The Ascension—The Tailors*
*Balaack and Balaam—The Cappers*
*The Betrayal of Christ—The Bakers*
*Cain and Abel—The Drapers*
*Christ and the Moneylenders—The Shoemakers*
*Christ at the House of Simon the Leper—The*
*  Shoemakers*
*Christ's Appearance before the Doctors—The*
*  Blacksmiths*
*The Coming of Antichrist—The Dyers*
*The Crucifixion—The Ironmongers*
*Emmaus—The Saddlers*
*The Fall of Lucifer—The Tanners*
*The Harrowing of Hell—The Cooks*
*The Healing of the Blind Man—The Glovers*
*Judas' Plot—The Shoemakers*
*The Last Judgment—The Websters*
*The Last Supper—The Bakers*
*The Massacre of the Innocents—The Goldsmiths*
*Moses and the Law—The Cappers*
*Noah's Flood—The Waterleaders and Drawers of Dee*
*The Offerings of the Three Kings—The Mercers*
*Pentecost—The Fishmongers*
*The Post-Reformation Banns*
*The Prophets of Antichrist—The Clothworkers*
*The Purification of the Virgin Mary—The Blacksmiths*
*The Raising of Lazarus—The Glovers*
*The Resurrection—The Skinners*
*The Shepherds—The Printers*

*The Temptation of Christ—The Butchers*
*The Three Kings—The Vintners*
*The Trial and flagellation of Christ—The Fletchers,*
*  Bowers, Coopers, and Stringers*
*The Woman Taken in Adultery—The Butchers*

CHES *The Chester Mystery Plays.* Adapted into Modern
English by Maurice P. Hussey. London: William
Heinemann [c1957] 160pp.
*Abraham and Isaac*
*The Adoration of the Magi*
*The Adoration of the Shepherds*
*Antichrist*
*The Betrayal of Christ*
*Christ's Ascension*
*Christ's Passion*
*Christ's Resurrection*
*The Creation of Man: Adam and Eve*
*The Fall of Lucifer*
*The Last Judgment*
*The Magi's Oblation*
*The Nativity*
*Noah's Deluge*
*Simon the Leper*
*The Slaying of the Innocents*

CHESE *The Chester Mystery Plays: Seventeen Pageant*
*Plays from the Chester Craft Cycle.* Adapted
into modern English by Maurice Hussey. 2nd ed.
London, Heinemann, 1975. 170pp.
*Abraham and Isaac*
*The Adoration of the Magi*
*The Adoration of the Shepherds*
*Antichrist*
*The Betrayal of Christ*
*Christ's Ascension*
*Christ's Passion*
*Christ's Resurrection*
*The Creation of Man: Adam and Eve*
*The Fall of Lucifer*
*The Last Judgment*
*The Magi's Oblation*
*The Nativity*
*Noah's Deluge*
*Simon the Leper*
*The Slaying of the Innocents*
*The Temptation*

CHEU Cheung, Martha P.Y., and Jane C.C. Lai, ed.
*An Oxford Anthology of Contemporary Chinese*
*Drama.* Hong Kong: Oxford University Press; New
York: Oxford, 1997. 873pp.
Chan, A. *American House*
Chan, J. *Before the Dawn-wind Rises*
Gao, X. *The Other Side*

Guo, S. *Birdmen*
Hwang, M. *Cathay Visions (The Empty Cage)*
Jin, Y. *Uncle Doggie's Nirvana*
Lai, S. *Pining . . . in Peach Blossom Land*
Lee, K. *National Salvation Corporation Ltd.*
Liang, B. *Who's the Strongest of Us All?*
Liu, C. *Mother's Water Mirror*
Ma, S. *Flower and Sword*
Ma, Z. *The Legend of Old Bawdy Town*
To, R. *Where Love Abides*
Xu, P. *Old Forest*
Yung, D. *Chronicle of Women—Liu Sola in Concert*

CHG *Chicano Voices.* ed. by Carlota Cardenas de Dwyer;
    Tino Villaneuva, editorial adviser. Boston:
    Houghton Mifflin, 1975. 189pp. (Multi-ethnic
    Literature Series)
Valdez, L. *Los vendidos*

CHI Child, Clarence Griffin, ed. and tr. *The Second
    Shepherds' Play, Everyman, and Other Early
    Plays.* Boston: Houghton Mifflin [cl910] 138pp.
*The Brome Abraham and Isaac*
*Everyman*
*The Oxfordshire St. George Play*
*The Quem quaeritis*
*Robin Hood and the Friar*
*Robin Hood and the Knight*
*Robin Hood and the Potter*
*The Second Shepherds' Play*

CHIN *The Chinese Other 1850–1925: An Anthology of
    Plays.* Edited by Dave Williams. Lanham, MD:
    University Press of America, 1997. 432pp.
Baker, G. *New Brooms Sweep Clean*
Bierce, A. *Peaceful Expulsion*
Brewster, E. *A Bunch of Buttercups*
Brown, J. *The Honorable Mrs. Ling's Conversion*
Caldor, M. *Curiosity*
Carus, P. *K'ung Fu Tze*
Denison, T. *Patsy O' Wang*
Grimm, H. *The Chinese Must Go*
Harte, B., and Twain, M. *Ah Sin*
Hazelton, G., and Benrimo, J. *The Yellow Jacket*
Hung, S. *The Wedded Husband*
Jarrow, J. *The Queen of Chinatown*
Kummer, C. *Chinese Love*
Powers, F. *The First Born*
Ravel Family, The. *Kim-Ka!*

CHOT Chothia, Jean, ed. *The New Woman and Other
    Emancipated Woman Plays.* Oxford; New York:
    Oxford University Press, 1998. 303pp.

Grundy, S. *The New Woman*
Hankin, S. *The Last of the De Mullins*
Pinero, A. *The Notorious Mrs. Ebbsmith*
Robins, E. *Votes for Women*

CHR Christy, Arthur, and Wells, Henry Willis, eds. *World
    Literature.* Freeport, NY: Books for Libraries,
    1971. 1115pp. (Reprint)
Aeschylus. *Agamemnon*
Andreyev, L. *An Incident*
Molnár, F. *Still Life*
Pirandello, L. *The Jar*

CHU Church, Mrs. Virginia Woodson (Frame), ed.
    *Curtain! A Book of Modern Plays.* New York:
    Harper, 1932. 504pp.
Bennett, A. *The Great Adventure*
Church, V. *What Men Live By*
Dunsany, E. *The Lost Silk Hat*
Green, P. *The Man Who Died at Twelve O'clock*
MacKaye, P. *Napoleon Crossing the Rockies*
Millay, E. *Aria da capo*
Milne, A. *The Great Broxopp*
Morley, C. *Good Theatre*
Nichols, R., and Brown, M. *Wings over Europe*
O'Neill, E. *The Emperor Jones*
Wilder, T. *The Angel on the Ship*

CLARK, BARRETT HARPER. *See also* AMP *America's
    Lost Plays.*

CLA Clark, Barrett Harper, ed. *Favorite American Plays
    of the Nineteenth Century.* Princeton, NJ: Princeton
    University Press, 1943. 553pp.
Alfriend, E., and Wheeler, A. *The Great Diamond
    Robbery*
Belasco, D. *The Heart of Maryland*
Boucicault, D. *Flying Scud; or, A Four-legged Fortune*
Campbell, B. *My Partner*
Fechter, C. *Monte Cristo*
Howard, B. *The Banker's Daughter*
Hoyt, C. *A Trip to Chinatown; or, an Idyll of San
    Francisco*
Murdoch, F. *Davy Crockett; or, Be sure You're Right,
    then Go Ahead*
Stone, J. *Metamora; or, the Last of the Wampanoags*
Woolf, B. *The Mighty Dollar*

CLD Clark, Barrett Harper, tr. *Four Plays of the Free
    Theater.* Cincinnati: Stewart & Kidd, 1915. 257pp.
Ancey, G. *The Dupe*
Curel, F. *The Fossils*
Julien, J. *The Serenade*
Porto-Riche, G. *Françoise' Luck*

CLDM Clark, Barrett Harper, ed. *Masterpieces of Modern Spanish Drama*. New York: Cuffield, 1917. 290pp.

Echegaray [y Eizaguirre], J. *The Great Galeoto*

Guimerá, A. *Daniela*

Pérez Galdós, B. *The Duchess of San Quentin*

CLF Clark, Barrett Harper, ed. *World Drama*. New York: Appleton, 1933. 2 vols.

*Abstraction* 1

*Adam* 1

Aeschylus. *Prometheus Bound* 1

Alfieri, V. *Saul* 2

Aristophanes. *The Clouds* 1

Augier, E., and Sandeau, J. *M. Poirier's Son-in-law* 2

Beaumarchais, P. *The Barber of Seville* 2

Beaumont, F., and Fletcher, J. *The Maid's Tragedy* 1

Beolco, A. *Bilora* 2

Calderón de la Barca, P. *The Constant Prince* 2

Cervantes Saavedra, M. *The Cave of Salamanca* 2

*The Chalk Circle* 1

Chikamatsu Monzaemon. *Fair Ladies at a Game of Poemcards* 1

Corneille, P. *The Cid* 2

Dumas, A. fils. *The Demimonde* 2

Euripides. *Alcestis* 1

*Everyman* 1

*The Farce of the Worthy Master Pierre Patelin* 1

Farquhar, G. *The Beaux' Stratagem* 1

Goethe, J. *Egmont* 2

Goldoni, C. *The Fan* 2

Goldsmith, O. *She Stoops to Conquer* 1

Heywood, T. *A Woman Killed with Kindness* 1

Holberg, L. *Jeppe of the Hill* 2

Hugo, V. *Hernani* 2

Ibsen, H. *A Doll's House* 2

Jonson, B. *Every Man in His Humour* 1

Kālidāsa. *Sakoontalá* 1

Lessing, G. *Miss Sara Sampson* 2

Marlowe, C. *The Tragical History of Dr. Faustus* 1

Molière, J. *The Cit Turned Gentleman* 2

Ostrovsky, A. *The Thunderstorm* 2

Plautus, T. *The Captives* 1

*The Play of St. George* 1

Racine, J. *Berenice* 2

Sachs, H. *The Wandering Scholar from Paradise* 1

Scala, F. *The Portrait* 2

Schiller, J. *William Tell* 2

Seami, M. *Nakamitsu* 1

*The Second Shepherds' Play* 1

Seneca. *Medea* 1

Sheridan, R. *The School for Scandal* 1

Sophocles. *Antigone* 1

Terence. *Phormio* 1

Vega Carpio, L. *The King, the Greatest Alcalde* 2

*The Wise Virgins and the Foolish Virgins* 1

CLH Clark, Barrett Harper, and Davenport, William H., eds. *Nine Modern Plays*. New York: Appleton-Century-Crofts [c1951] 432pp.

Anderson, M. *High Tor*

Ferber, E., and Kaufman, G. *Stage Door*

Haines, W. *Command Decision*

Hart, M., and Kaufman, G. *You Can't Take It with You*

O'Neill, E. *The Hairy Ape*

Rice, E. *Street Scene*

Riggs, L. *Green Grow the Lilacs*

Sherwood, R. *Abe Lincoln in Illinois*

Williams, T. *The Glass Menagerie*

CLK Clark, David Lee; Gates, William Bryan; and Leisy, Ernest Erwin, eds. *The Voices of England and America*. New York: Nelson, 1939. 2 vols.

Dryden, J. *All for Love* 1

*Everyman* 1

Farquhar, G. *The Beaux' Stratagem* 1

Jonson, B. *Every Man in His Humour* 1

Marlowe, C. *The Tragical History of Doctor Faustus* 1

Milton, J. *Comus* 1

O'Neill, E. *The Emperor Jones* 2

Pinero, A. *The Second Mrs. Tanqueray* 2

*The Second Shepherds' Play* 1

Sheridan, R. *The Rivals* 1

CLKJ Clark, Justus Kent and Piper, Henry D., eds. *Dimensions in Drama: Six Plays of Crime and Punishment*. New York, Scribner [1964] 573pp.

Gay, J. *The Beggar's Opera*

Ibsen, H. *Rosmersholm*

Miller, A. *All My Sons*

Sartre, J. *No Exit*

Shakespeare, W. *Macbeth*

Sophocles. *Oedipus Rex*

CLKW Clark, William Smith II, ed. *Chief Patterns of World Drama*. Boston: Houghton Mifflin [c1946] 1152pp.

Aeschylus. *Prometheus Bound*

Anderson, M. *Mary of Scotland*

Aristophanes. *The Birds*

Barrie, J. *The Admirable Crichton*

Beaumont, F., and Fletcher, J. *The Maid's Tragedy*

Čapek, J., and Čapek, K. *The Life of the Insects*

Chekhov, A. *The Sea-gull*

Dekker, T. *The Shoemakers' Holiday*

Euripides. *Alcestis*

Etherege, G. *The Man of Mode; or, Sir Fopling Flutter*

Galsworthy, J. *The Silver Box*

Gogol, N. *The Inspector-general*

Green, P. *Roll Sweet Chariot*

Hebbel, J. *Maria Magdalena*

Ibsen, H. *Hedda Gabler*

Jonson, B. *Epicoene; or, the Silent Woman*
Marlowe, C. *The Troublesome Reign and Lamentable
  Death of Edward the Second*
Molière, J. *The Miser*
*Nice Wanton*
O'Neill, E. *The Hairy Ape*
Pirandello, L. *Naked*
Plautus. *The Pot of Gold*
Racine, J. *Andromache*
*The Second Shepherds' Play*
Sheridan, R. *The School for Scandal*
Sophocles. *Electra*
Synge, J. *The Playboy of the Western World*
Terence. *Phormio*
Vega, Lope de. *The Star of Seville*

CLKWI *Classic Irish Drama*, introduced by W. A.
  Armstrong. Harmondsworth: Penguin, 1964 (1979
  [printing]) 224pp. (Penguin Plays)
O'Casey, S. *Cock-a-doodle Dandy*
Synge, J. *The Playboy of the Western World*
Yeats, W. *The Countess Cathleen*

CLKX *Classic Soviet Plays*; compiled by Alla Mikhailova;
  translated from the Russian. Moscow: Progress
  Publishers, 1979. 829pp. [Distributed in U.S. by
  Imported Pubs.]
Arbuzov, A. *Tanya*
Bulgakov, M. *The Days of the Turbins*
Gorky, M. *Yegor Bulychov and Others*
Leonov, L. *Invasion*
Mayakovsky, V. *Mystery-bouffe*
Pogodin, N. *Kremlin Chimes*
Rozov, V. *In Search of Happiness*

CLKY *Classic Theatre: The Humanities in Drama*. ed. by
  Sylvan Barnet [and Others]. Boston: Educ. Assocs.,
  1975. 682pp.
Chekhov, A. *Three Sisters*
Goldsmith, O. *She Stoops to Conquer*
Ibsen, H. *Hedda Gabler*
Ibsen, H. *The Wild Duck*
Marlowe, C. *Edward the Second*
Pinero, A. *Trelawny of the Wells*
Shakespeare, W. *The Tragedy of Macbeth*
Shaw, G. *Mrs. Warren's Profession*
Sheridan, R. *The Rivals*
Synge, J. *The Playboy of the Western World*
Taylor, D. *Paradise Restored*
Voltaire, F. *Candide*
Webster, J. *The Duchess of Malfi*

CLL Clayes, Stanley A., ed. *Drama and Discussion*. New
  York: Appleton-Century-Crofts [1967] 651pp.

Aeschylus. *Libation Bearers*
Anouilh, J. *The Lark*
Beckett, S. *All that Fall*
Brecht, B. *Mother Courage and Her Children*
Chekhov, A. *The Cherry Orchard*
Euripides. *The Trojan Women*
García Lorca, F. *Blood Wedding*
Giraudoux, J. *Tiger at the Gates*
Ibsen, H. *Ghosts*
Shakespeare, W. *Hamlet*
Shaw, G. *Saint Joan*
Sophocles. *Electra*
Synge, J. *Riders to the Sea*
Williams, T. *A Streetcar Named Desire*

CLLC Clayes, Stanley A., ed. *Drama and Discussion*. 2nd
  ed. Englewood Cliffs, NJ: Prentice-Hall, 1978.
  664pp.
Aeschylus. *The Libation Bearers (Chöephori)*
Beckett, S. *All that Fall*
Brecht, B. *Mother Courage and Her Children*
Bullins, E. *A Son, Come Home*
Chekhov, A. *The Cherry Orchard*
García Lorca, F. *The Love of Don Perlimplín*
Ibsen, H. *Ghosts*
Miller, A. *A View from the Bridge*
Molière, J. *Tartuffe*
O'Neill, E. *Hughie*
Pinter, H. *The Dumb Waiter*
Shakespeare, W. *Hamlet*
Shaw, G. *Major Barbara*
Sophocles. *Oedipus Rex*
Synge, J. *The Playboy of the Western World*
Williams, T. *A Streetcar Named Desire*

CLM Clayes, Stanley A., and Spencer, David G., eds.
  *Contemporary Drama*. New York: Scribner [c1962]
  512pp.
Chekhov, A. *Uncle Vanya*
García Lorca, F. *The House of Bernarda Alba*
Giraudoux, J. *Ondine*
Hellman, L. *The Autumn Garden*
Ibsen, H. *The Wild Duck*
Maugham, W. *The Circle*
Miller, A. *A View from the Bridge*
O'Casey, S. *Juno and the Paycock*
Odets, C. *The Country Girl*
Shaw, G. *The Devil's Disciple*
Sophocles. *Antigone* (Cocteau, J., adapter)
Sophocles. *Antigone*
Strindberg, A. *Miss Julie*
Williams, T. *The Rose Tattoo*

CLN Clayes, Stanley, and Spencer, David G., eds. *Contemporary Drama: 13 Plays.* 2nd ed. New York: Scribner, 1970. 512pp.
Brecht, B. *The Caucasian Chalk Circle*
Bullins, E. *A Son Come Home*
Chekhov, A. *Uncle Vanya*
García Lorca, F. *The House of Bernarda Alba*
Giraudoux, J. *Ondine*
Ibsen, H. *The Wild Duck*
Itallie, J. *America Hurrah*
Miller, A. *A View from the Bridge*
O'Casey, S. *Juno and the Paycock*
Odets, C. *The Country Girl*
Shaw, G. *The Devil's Disciple*
Strindberg, A. *Miss Julie*
Williams, T. *The Rose Tattoo*

CLOU Clouard, Henri, and Leggewie, Robert, eds. *Anthologie de la litterature française.* New York: Oxford University Press, 1960. 2 vols.
Corneille, P. *Le cid* 1
Giraudoux, J. *La guerre de Troie n'aura pas lieu* 2
Molière, J. *Le misanthrope* 1
Musset, A. *Fantasio* 2
Racine, J. *Andromaque* 1
Sartre, J. *Huis clos* 2

CLOUD Clouard, Henri, and Leggewie, Robert, eds. *Anthologie de la litterature française.* New York: Oxford University Press, 1975. 2nd ed. 2 vols.
Anouilh, J. *Ardele, ou la Marguerite* 2
Corneille, P. *Le cid* 1
Giraudoux, J. *La guerre de Troie n'aura pas lieu* 2
Molière, J. *Le misanthrope* 1
Musset, A. *Fantasio* 2
Racine, J. *Andromaque* 1
Sartre, J. *Huis clos* 2

CLOUDS Clouard, Henri, and Leggewie, Robert, eds. *Anthologie de la litterature française.* New York: Oxford University Press, 1990. 3rd ed. 2 vols.
Anouilh, J. *Ardele, ou la Marguerite* 2
Corneille, P. *Le cid* 1
Giraudoux, J. *La guerre de Troie n'aura pas lieu* 2
Molière, J. *Le bourgeois gentilhomme* 1
Musset, A. *Fantasio* 2
Racine, J. *Andromaque* 1
Sartre, J. *Huis clos* 2

CLUM Clum, John M., ed. *Asking and Telling: A Collection of Gay Drama for the 21st Century.* Garden City, NY: Stage & Screen, 2000. 458pp.
Adamson, S. *Clocks and Whistles*
Bell, N. *Somewhere in the Pacific*

Clum, J. *Dancing in the Mirror*
Dillon, D. *Party*
Murray, S. *Rescue and Recovery*
Reyes, G. *Deporting the Divas*

CLUMS Clum, John M., ed. *Staging Gay Lives: An Anthology of Contemporary Gay Theater.* Foreword by Tony Kushner. Boulder, CO: Westview Press, 1996. 471pp.
Clum, J. *Randy's House*
Gill, P. *Mean Tears*
Hamilton, G. *Kissing Marianne*
Pomo Afro Homos. *Dark Fruit*
Pruitt, D., and Hutchison, P. *The Harvey Milk Show*
Reyes, G. *Men on the Verge of a His-panic Breakdown*
Sherman, M. *A Madhouse in Goa*
Wallace, N. *In the Heart of America*
Wilde, P. *What's Wrong with Angry?*
Yew, C. *Porcelain*

CLUR Clurman, Harold, ed. *Famous American Plays of the 1930s.* New York: Dell Publishing Co. c1959. 480pp. (Lauren Drama Series)
Behrman, S. *End of Summer*
Odets, C. *Awake and Sing!*
Saroyan, W. *The Time of Your Life*
Sherwood, R. *Idiot's Delight*
Steinbeck, J. *Of Mice and Men*

CLURMAN, HAROLD. *See also* SEVD *Seven Plays of the Modern Theatre*

COD Coffman, George Raleigh, ed. *A Book of Modern Plays.* Chicago: Scott, Foresman [c1925] 490pp.
Bennett, A., and Knoblock, E. *Milestones*
Gregory, I. *The Workhouse Ward*
Ibsen, H. *An Enemy of the People*
O'Neill, E. *Where the Cross Is Made*
Robertson, T. *Caste*
Rostand, E. *The Romancers*
Synge, J. *Riders to the Sea*

COF Coffman, George Raleigh, ed. *Five Significant English Plays.* New York: Nelson, 1930. 433pp.
Dekker, T. *The Shoemakers' Holiday*
Marlowe, C. *Dr. Faustus*
Pinero, A. *The Second Mrs. Tanqueray*
Sheridan, R. *The School for Scandal*
Steele, R. *The Conscious Lovers*

COH Cohen, Helen Louise, ed. *Longer Plays by Modern Authors (American).* New York: Harcourt, Brace [c1922] 353pp.
Fitch, C. *Beau Brummell*

Kaufman, G., and Connelly, M. *Dulcy*
Tarkington, B. *The Intimate Strangers*
Thomas, A. *The Copperhead*

COHM Cohen, Helen Louise, ed. *Milestones of the Drama.*
New York: Harcourt, Brace [1940] 580pp.
*Everyman*
Ibsen, H. *A Doll's House*
Marlowe, C. *Doctor Faustus*
O'Neill, E. *The Emperor Jones*
Rostand, E. *Cyrano de Bergerac*
Sheridan, R. *The School for Scandal*
Sophocles. *Oedipus, King of Thebes*

COI Cohen, Robert, ed. *Twelve Plays for Theatre.*
Mountain View, CA: Mayfield Publishing
Company, 1994. 626pp.
Aeschylus. *Prometheus Bound*
Büchner, G. *Woyzeck*
Hwang, D. *M. Butterfly*
Ibsen, H. *A Doll's House*
Machiavelli, N. *Clizia*
Mamet, D. *Glengarry Glen Ross*
Molière, J. *The Misanthrope*
Shakespeare, W. *Hamlet*
Shaw, G. *Major Barbara*
Wagner, J. *The Search for Signs of Intelligent Life in the Universe*
Williams, T. *Cat on a Hot Tin Roof*
Wilson, A. *Joe Turner's Come and Gone*

COJ Cohen, Sarah Blacher, ed. *Making a Scene: The Contemporary Drama of Jewish-American Women.*
Syracuse, NY: Syracuse University Press, 1997. 370pp.
Brooks, H. *The Night the War Came Home*
Cohen, S. *The Ladies Locker Room*
Feld, M. *Across the Jordan*
Kahn, B. *Whither thou Goest*
Lebow, B. *A shayna maidel*
Roisman, L. *Nobody's gilgul*
Wasserstein, W. *Isn't It Romantic*

COK Cohn, Ruby; Dukore, Bernard F.; and Block, Haskett
M., eds. *Twentieth Century Drama: England,
Ireland [and] The United States.* New York:
Random House [1966] 692pp.
Albee, E. *The Zoo Story*
Beckett, S. *Embers*
Eliot, T. *Murder in the Cathedral*
Odets, C. *Awake and Sing!*
O'Neill, E. *The Iceman Cometh*
Osborne, J. *Look Back in Anger*
Pinter, H. *The Dumb Waiter*
Shaw, G. *Major Barbara*

Synge, J. *The Playboy of the Western World*
Wilder, T. *Our Town*
Williams, T. *The Glass Menagerie*
Yeats, W. *The Only Jealousy of Emer*

COLD Coldewey, John C., and Streitberger, compilers.
*Drama: Classical to Contemporary.* Upper Saddle
River, NJ: Prentice-Hall, 1998. 1382pp.
Aeschylus. *Agamemnon*
Albee, E. *Three Tall Women*
Aristophanes. *Lysistrata*
Barker, H. *Hated Nightfall*
Beckett, S. *Endgame*
Brecht, B. *Mother Courage and Her Children*
Chekhov, A. *The Cherry Orchard*
Congreve, W. *The Way of the World*
Euripides. *Medea*
*Everyman*
Hansberry, L. *A Raisin in the Sun*
Howe, T. *Painting Churches*
Ibsen, H. *Hedda Gabler*
Jonson, B. *Volpone*
Luce, C. *Slam the Door Softly*
Mamet, D. *Oleanna*
Marlowe, C. *Dr. Faustus*
Miller, A. *The Crucible*
Molière, J. *The Misanthrope*
Norman, M. *'Night, Mother*
O'Neill, E. *The Emperor Jones*
Pinter, H. *The Dumb Waiter*
Pirandello, L. *Six Characters in Search of an Author*
Puig, M. *Kiss of the Spider Woman*
Racine, J. *Phaedra*
*The Second Shepherd's Play*
Shakespeare, W. *Hamlet*
Shakespeare, W. *A Midsummer Night's Dream*
Shaw, G. *Major Barbara*
Shepard, S. *True West*
Sophocles. *Oedipus Rex*
Soyinka, W. *The Strong Breed*
Stoppard, T. *Rosencrantz and Guildenstern Are Dead*
Strindberg, A. *Miss Julie*
Synge, J. *Riders to the Sea*
Wilde, O. *The Importance of Being Earnest*
Williams, T. *Cat on a Hot Tin Roof*
Wilson, A. *The Piano Lesson*

COLDE Coldewey, John C., ed. *Early English Drama:
An Anthology.* New York: Garland Publishing, Inc,
1993. 379pp.
*Abraham and Isaac* (from the Chester cycle)
*The Brome Abraham and Isaac*
*The Croxton Play of the Sacrament*
*The Crucifixion of Christ* (from the York Cycle)
*The Digby Conversion of St. Paul*

*The Digby Killing of the Children*
*The Digby Mary Magdalene*
*The Durham Prologue*
*Dux Moraud*
*Everyman*
*Mankind*
*The Norwich Grocers Play*
*The Pride of Life*
*The Reynes Extracts*
*The Second Shepherds' Play* (from the Wakefield Cycle)
*The Wakefield Noah*
*Wisdom*

THE COLLEGE OMNIBUS. *See also* MCCA, MCCB, MCCD, MCCF, MCCG McCallum, James Dow, ed. *See also* FUL Fullington, James Fitz-James. *The New College Omnibus*

COLEL *College Survey of English Literature.* Edited by B. J. Whiting; Fred B. Millett; Alexander M. Whitherspoon and Others. New York: Harcourt, Brace, 1942. 2 vols.
Congreve, W. *The Way of the World* 1
Goldsmith, O. *She Stoops to Conquer* 1
Marlowe, C. *The Tragical History of Doctor Faustus* 1
*The Second Play of the Shepherds* (Wakefield) 2
Shakespeare, W. *King Henry IV, Part I* 1
Synge, J. *The Playboy of the Western World* 2

COLLETTE, ELIZABETH. *See* WORL *The World in Literature*

COLI Collins, Margaret, and Collins, Fletcher, eds. *Theater Wagon Plays of Place and Any Place.* Charlottesville: University Press of Virginia, 1973. 299pp.
Collins, M. *Love Is a Daisy*
Collins, M. *3 Filosofers in a Firetower*
Evreinov, N. *A Merry Death*
Evreinov, N. *Styopik and Manya*
Hite, B. *Birdwatchers*
Hite, B. *Sandcastle*
Lee, J. *On the Corner of Cherry and Elsewhere*

COLR *Comedy Restored or Ten English Plays of Manners.* Garden City, NY: Doubleday, 1986. 756pp.
Congreve, W. *The Way of the World*
Etherege, G. *The Man of Mode*
Farquhar, G. *The Beaux' Stratagem*
Fielding, H. *Tom Thumb the Great*
Goldsmith, O. *She Stoops to Conquer*
Sheridan, R. *The Critic*
Sheridan, R. *The Rivals*
Sheridan, R. *The School for Scandal*

Wycherley, W. *The Country Wife*
Wycherley, W. *The Plain-dealer*

COLT *Comedy Tonight! Broadway Picks its Favorite Plays.* Edited by Mary Sherwin. New York: Doubleday, 1977. 850pp.
Chase, M. *Harvey*
Coward, N. *Private Lives*
Hart, M., and Kaufman, G. *The Man Who Came to Dinner*
Heggen, T., and Logan, J. *Mister Roberts*
Kanin, G. *Born Yesterday*
Kerr, J. *Mary, Mary*
Kesselring, J. *Arsenic and Old Lace*
Lindsay, H., and Crouse, R. *Life with Father*
Simon, N. *The Odd Couple*
Wilde, O. *The Importance of Being Earnest*

COMFORT, ALEX. *See* NEWR *New Road.*

COM Comfort, William Wistar, ed. *French Romantic Plays.* New York: Scribner [cl933] 628pp.
Dumas, A. père. *Antony*
Hugo, V. *Hernani*
Hugo, V. *Ruy Blas*
Musset, A. *On ne badine pas avec l'amour*
Vigny, A. *Chatterton*

COMS *Coming on Strong: New Writing from the Royal Court Theatre.* London: Faber and Faber, 1995. 280pp.
Coyle, K. *Corner Boys*
Grosso, N. *Peaches*
Prichard, R. *Essex Girls*
Wynne, M. *The Knocky*

COMV *Coming to Terms: American Plays and the Vietnam War.* Introduction by James Reston, Jr. New York: Theatre Communications Group, Inc., 1985. 372pp.
Cole, T. *Medal of Honor Rag*
Gray, A. *How I Got that Story*
McNally, T. *Botticelli*
Mann, E. *Still Life*
Metcalfe, S. *Strange Snow*
Rabe, D. *Streamers*
Weller, M. *Moonchildren*

CONB *Conflict in Social Drama: Plays for Education.* London: Methuen, 1972. 2 vols. (v1, *The Personal Conflict*; v2, *The Social Conflict*)
Arden, J. *Soldier, Soldier* 2
Cregan, D. *Transcending* 1
Livings, H. *There's No Room for You Here for a Start* 2
Mortimer, J. *David and Broccoli* 1

Pinter, H. *A Night Out* 1
Wesker, A. *The Kitchen* 2

CONF *Confrontations with Tyranny: Six Baltic Plays with Introductory Essays.* Edited by Alfreds Straumanis. Prospect Hills, IL: Waveland Press, 1977. 363pp.
Landabergis, A. *Five Posts in a Market Place*
Priède, G. *The Blue One*
Rummo, P. *Cinderellagame*
Škema, A. *The Awakening*
Vetemaa, E. *Illuminations; For a Globe of Lightning and Nine Actors (with a Bang at the End)*
Zīverts, M. *Mad Christopher, Mad; a Northern Legend in Seven Scenes*

CONG Congdon, S. Perry, ed. *The Drama Reader.* New York: Odyssey Press [c1962] 418pp.
Čapek, K. *R.U.R.*
Cohan, G. *Seven Keys to Baldpate*
Kaufman, G., and Connelly, M. *Dulcy*
Shakespeare, W. *Richard III*
Sophocles. *Antigone*

CONN Connolly, Francis Xavier, ed. *Literature, the Channel of Culture.* New York: Harcourt, Brace, 1948. 714pp.
Connelly, M. *The Green Pastures*
Shakespeare, W. *The Tempest*
Synge, J. *Riders to the Sea*

CONO Connolly, Francis Xavier, ed. *Man and His Measure.* New York: Harcourt, Brace & World [1964] 139pp.
Betti, U. *Corruption in the Palace of Justice*
Marlowe, C. *The Tragical History of Doctor Faustus*
Molière, J. *The Misanthrope*
Sophocles. *Oedipus Rex*

CONP Connolly, Francis X., ed. *The Types of Literature.* New York: Harcourt, Brace [c1955] 810pp.
Barrie, J. *The Twelve-pound Look*
Eliot, T. *Murder in the Cathedral*
O'Neill, E. *Bound East for Cardiff*
Sheridan, R. *The School for Scandal*
Sophocles. *Antigone*

CONR *Contemporary Chicano Theatre.* Roberto J. Garza, editor. Notre Dame, IN: University of Notre Dame Press, 1976. 248pp.
Alurista. *Dawn*
Garza, R. *No nos venceremos*
Macias, Y. *Mdrtlr Montezuma*
Macias, Y. *The ultimate pendejada*
Portillo, E. *The Day of the Swallows*
Sierra, R. *La raze pura, or racial, racial*

Valdez, L. *Bernabé*
Valdez, L. *Los vendidos*

CONT *Contemporary Danish Plays.* London: Thames and Hudson, 1955. 557pp.
Abell, K. *The Queen on Tour*
Branner, H. *The Judge*
Clausen, S. *The Bird of Contention*
Fischer, L. *The Mystery Tour*
Locher, J. *Tea for Three*
Munk, K. *Herod the King*
Schlüter, K. *Off the Rails*
Sønderby, K. *A Woman Too Many*
Soya, C. *Two Threads*

CONTG *Contemporary Greek Theatre.* London: Arcadia Books, 1999.
Anagnostaki, L. *The Parade*
Kehaidis, D., and Haviara, E. *With Power from Kifissia*
Skourtis, G. *Love Thriller*

CONTNZ *Contemporary New Zealand Plays.* Selected by Howard McNaughton. Wellington and London: Oxford, 1974. 153pp.
Baxter, J. *The Wide Open Cage*
Bowman, E. *Salve Regina*
Campbell, A. *When the Bough Breaks*
Mason, B. *Hongi*

CONTSL *Contemporary Slovak Drama.* Bratislava: The Theatre Institute, 1999–2004. 5 vols.
Bodnárová, J. *The Lantern Procession* 4
Čahojová-Bernátová, B. *Eclipse* 3
Cicvák, M. *Frankie Is Ok, Peggy Is Fine and the House Is Cool!* 1
Feldek, L. *The Rehearsal* 5
Feriancová, V. *In the Snow* 3
Gombár, J. *Hugo Carp* 2
Horák, K. *The Destruction of Soccer in the City of K.* 5
Horák, K. *La musica* 4
Horváth, T. *The Chair* 2
Juráňová, J. *Salome* 3
Kerata, L. *Dinner about a City* 1
Kerata, L. *On the Surface* 2
Klimáček, V. *Axes in Flower* 4
Klimáček, V. *Beach Boredom* 1
Lasica, M., and Satinský, J. *Dialogues* 5
Lavrík, S. *Katarína* 2
Maliti-Fraňová, E. *Krcheň the Immortal* 4
Olekšák, R. *Something More, Something Less* 4
Piussi, L. *Scenes from Illegitimate Life* 3
Sloboda, R. *Armageddon in Grba* 5
Štepka, S. *The Black Sheep* 5
The Stoka Theatre. *Bottom* 1
Uličianska, Z. *Emotional Mix* 3

CONTSO *Contemporary South African Plays*. Edited and introduced by Ernest Pereira. Johannesburg: Ravan Press, 1977. 293pp.
Ferguson, I. *Ritual 2378*
Gray, S. *An Evening at the Vernes*
Leshoai, B. *Lines Draw Monster* (Act I only)
Livingstone, D. *A Rhino for the Boardroom; a Radio Play*
Maclennan, D. *An Enquiry into the Voyage of the Santiago*
Roberts, S. *Weekend*
Wilhelm, P. *Frame Work*

CONTINENTAL DRAMA. *See* HARC *Harvard Classics*, v26

COOA Cook, Albert Spaulding, and Dolin, Edwin, eds. *An Anthology of Greek Tragedy*. Indianapolis: Bobbs-Merrill, 1972. 400pp.
Aeschylus. *Agamemnon*
Aeschylus. *Prometheus Bound*
Euripides. *Andromache*
Euripides. *The Bacchae*
Euripides. *The Trojan Women*
Sophocles. *Oedipus at Colonus*
Sophocles. *Oedipus Rex*
Sophocles. *Philoctetes*

COOF Cook, David M., and Wanger, Craig G., compilers. *The Small Town in American Literature*. New York: Dodd, Mead, 1969. 253pp.
Wilder, T. *Our Town*
Williams, T. *The Case of the Crushed Petunias*

COOJ Cook, Luella Bussey; Loban, Walter; McDowell, Tremaine; and Stauffer, Ruth M., eds. *America through Literature*. Harcourt, Brace, 1948. 750pp. (Living Literature)
Sherwood, R. *Abe Lincoln in Illinois*
Wilder, T. *Our Town*

COOK Cook, Luella Bussey; Norvell, George W., and McCall, William A., eds. *Hidden Treasures in Literature*. New York: Harcourt, Brace, 1934. 3 vols.
Coppée, F. *The Violin-maker of Cremona* 1
Dunsany, E. *A Night at an Inn* 3
Field, R. *The Patchwork Quilt* 2
Fitch, C. *Nathan Hale* 2
Monkhouse, A. *The Grand Cham's Necklace* 2
Pillot, E. *Two Crooks and a Lady* 3
Rostand, E. *The Romancers* 2
Saunders, L. *The Knave of Hearts* 1
Shakespeare, W. *Julius Caesar* 3

COOP Cooper, Charles W. *Preface to Drama*. New York: Ronald Press [c1955] 773pp.
Coward, N. *Fumed Oak*
Gilbert, W. *H.M.S. Pinafore*
Housman, L. *"A Good Lesson!"*
Ibsen, H. *Hedda Gabler*
Lindsay, H., and Crouse, R. *Life with Father*
Miller, A. *The Crucible*
Molière, J. *The Ridiculous précieuses*
O'Neill, E. *The Long Voyage Home*
Shakespeare, W. *Othello*
Shaw, G. *Candida*
Sophocles. *Antigone*
Wilder, T. *The Happy Journey to Trenton and Camden*
Williams, T. *The Glass Menagerie*

COOPA Cooper, Joshua, ed., and tr. *Four Russian Plays*. Harmondsworth, Middlesex: Penguin, 1972. 394pp.
Fonvizin, D. *The Infant*
Gogol, N. *The Inspector*
Griboiedov, A. *Chatsky*
Ostrovskii, A. *Thunder*

COOPER, LANE. *See* TEN *Ten Greek Plays*

COP Copeland, Charles Townsend, ed. *The Copeland Reader*. New York: Scribner, 1926. 1687pp.
Sheridan, R. *The Critic; or, a Tragedy Rehearsed*

COPB Copeland, Charles Townsend, ed. *The Copeland Translations*. New York: Scribner, 1934. 1080pp.
Molière, J. *The Physician in Spite of Himself*

COPC Copeland, Charles Townsend, ed. *Copeland's Treasury for Booklovers*. New York: Scribner, 1927. 5 vols.
Sheridan, R. *The Critic; or, a Tragedy Rehearsed* 1

COQJW Corbin, Peter, and Sedge, Douglas, eds. *Three Jacobean Witchcraft Plays*. Manchester: Manchester University Press, 1986. 259pp.
Ford, J., Dekker, T., and Rowley, W. *The Witch of Edmonton*
Marston, J. *Sophonisba*
Middleton, T. *The Witch*

CORB Corbin, Richard K., and Balf, Miriam, eds. *Twelve American Plays, 1920–1960*. New York: Scribner, 1969. 480pp.
Albee, E. *The Sandbox*
Chase, M. *Harvey*
Hellman, L. *The Little Foxes*
Kesselring, J. *Arsenic and Old Lace*
Nash, R. *The Rainmaker*
O'Neill, E. *Beyond the Horizon*

Patrick, J. *The Teahouse of the August Moon*
Rodgers, R. and Hammerstein, O. *The King and I*
Serling, R. *Requiem for a Heavyweight*
Sherwood, R. *There Shall Be No Night*
Wilder, T. *Our Town*
Williams, T. *The Glass Menagerie*

CORBA Corbin, Richard K., and Balf, Miriam, eds. *Twelve American Plays*. New York: Scribner, 1973. 475pp.
Chase, M. *Harvey*
Hellman, L. *The Little Foxes*
Kesselring, J. *Arsenic and Old Lace*
Nash, R. *The Rainmaker*
O'Neill, E. *The Hairy Ape*
Patrick, J. *The Teahouse of the August Moon*
Rodgers, R. and Hammerstein, O. *The King and I*
Serling, R. *Requiem for a Heavyweight*
Sherwood, R. *There Shall Be No Night*
Ward, D. *Day of Absence*
Wilder, T. *Our Town*
Williams, T. *The Glass Menagerie*

CORD Cordell, Kathryn (Coe), and Cordell, Wilham Howard, eds. *The Pulitzer Prize Plays, 1918–1934*. New York: Random House, [1935] 856pp.
Anderson, M. *Both Your Houses*
Connelly, M. *The Green Pastures*
Davis, O. *Icebound*
Gale, Z. *Miss Lulu Bett*
Glaspell, S. *Alison's House*
Green, P. *In Abraham's Bosom*
Howard, S. *They Knew What They Wanted*
Hughes, H. *Hell-bent fer Heaven*
Kaufman, G., and Ryskind, M. *Of Thee I Sing*
Kelly, G. *Craig's Wife*
Kingsley, S. *Men in White*
O'Neill, E. *Anna Christie*
O'Neill, E. *Beyond the Horizon*
O'Neill, E. *Strange Interlude*
Rice, E. *Street Scene*
Williams, J. *Why Marry?*

CORE Cordell, Kathryn (Coe), and Cordell, William Howard, eds. *The Pulitzer Prize Plays*. New ed. New York: Random House [1938?] 983pp.
Anderson, M. *Both Your Houses*
Connelly, M. *The Green Pastures*
Davis, O. *Icebound*
Gale, Z. *Miss Lulu Bett*
Glaspell, S. *Alison's House*
Green, P. *In Abraham's Bosom*
Hart, M., and Kaufman, G. *You Can't Take It with You*
Howard, S. *They Knew What They Wanted*
Hughes, H. *Hell-bent fer Heaven*
Kaufman, G., and Ryskind, M. *Of Thee I Sing*

Kelly, G. *Craig's Wife*
Kingsley, S. *Men in White*
O'Neill, E. *Anna Christie*
O'Neill, E. *Beyond the Horizon*
O'Neill, E. *Strange Interlude*
Rice, E. *Street Scene*
Sherwood, R. *Idiot's Delight*
Williams, J. *Why Marry?*

CORF Cordell, Kathryn (Coe), and Cordell, William Howard, eds. *A New Edition of the Pulitzer Prize Plays*. New York: Random House [1940] 1091pp.
Anderson, M. *Both Your Houses*
Connelly, M. *The Green Pastures*
Davis, O. *Icebound*
Gale, Z. *Miss Lulu Bett*
Glaspell, S. *Alison's House*
Green, P. *In Abraham's Bosom*
Hart, M., and Kaufman, G. *You Can't Take It with You*
Howard, S. *They Knew What They Wanted*
Hughes, H. *Hell-bent fer Heaven*
Kaufman, G., and Ryskind, M. *Of Thee I Sing*
Kelly, G. *Craig's Wife*
Kingsley, S. *Men in White*
O'Neill, E. *Anna Christie*
O'Neill, E. *Beyond the Horizon*
O'Neill, E. *Strange Interlude*
Rice, E. *Street Scene*
Sherwood, R. *Abe Lincoln in Illinois*
Sherwood, R. *Idiot's Delight*
Wilder, T. *Our Town*
Williams, J. *Why Marry?*

COT Cordell, Richard Albert, ed. *Representative Modern Plays*. New York: Nelson, 1929. 654pp.
Ade, G. *The College Widow*
Bennett, A. *The Great Adventure*
Crothers, R. *Expressing Willie*
Dane, C. *A Bill of Divorcement*
Fitch, C. *The Climbers*
Gilbert, W. *Sweethearts*
Hughes, H. *Hell-bent fer Heaven*
Jones, H. *Mrs. Dane's Defence*
Kaufman, G., and Connelly, M. *Beggar on Horseback*
Maugham, W. *The Circle*
Milne, A. *Success*
O'Casey, S. *Juno and the Paycock*
O'Neill, E. *Diff'rent*
Pinero, A. *Iris*
Robertson, T. *Caste*
Wilde, O. *A Woman of No Importance*

COTE Cordell, Richard Albert, ed. *Twentieth Century Plays, American*. 3rd ed. New York: Ronald Press [c1947] 329pp.

Anderson, M. *Winterset*
Connelly, M. *The Green Pastures*
Hellman, L. *The Little Foxes*
Howard, S. *The Silver Cord*
Marquand, J., and Kaufman, G. *The Late George Apley*
O'Neill, E. *Anna Christie*
Rice, E. *Street Scene*
Sherwood, R. *Abe Lincoln in Illinois*

COTH Cordell, Richard Albert, ed. *Twentieth Century Plays, British, American, Continental*. 3rd ed. New York: Ronald Press [c1947] 447pp.
Anderson, M. *Winterset*
Barrie, J. *The Admirable Crichton*
Čapek, K. *R.U.R.*
Galsworthy, J. *The Silver Box*
Hellman, L. *The Little Foxes*
Marquand, J., and Kaufman, G. *The Late George Apley*
Maugham, W. *The Circle*
O'Neill, E. *Anna Christie*
Rice, E. *Street Scene*
Rostand, E. *Cyrano de Bergerac*
Sherwood, R. *Abe Lincoln in Illinois*

COTK Cordell, Richard Albert, and Matson, Lowell, eds. *The Off-Broadway Theatre*. New York: Random House [c1959] 481pp.
Anouilh, J. *Ardèle*
Barkentin, M. *Ulysses in Nighttown*
Forsyth, J. *Heloise*
Hayes, A. *The Girl on the Via Flaminia*
Lee, J. *Career*
O'Casey, S. *Purple Dust*
Priestley, J., and Hawkes, J. *Dragon's Mouth*

CORDELL, RICHARD ALBERT. *See also* CHA, CHAN, CHAP, CHAR Chandler, Frank Wadleigh, and Cordell, Richard Albert, eds. *Twentieth Century Plays*.

COTKA Cordner, Michael, and Clayton, Ronald, eds. *Four Restoration Marriage Plays*. Oxford: Oxford University Press, 1995. 439pp.
Dryden, J. *Amphitryon*
Lee, N. *The Princess of Cleves*
Otway, T. *The Soldiers' Fortune*
Southerne, T. *The Wives' Excuse*

COTKB Cornish, Roger, and Ketels, Violet, compilers. *Landmarks of Modern British Drama: The Plays of the Sixties*, vol. 1; *The Plays of the Seventies*, vol. 2. London; New York: Methuen, 1986. 2 vols.
Arden, J. *Serjeant Musgrave's Dance* 1
Ayckbourn, A. *Just between Ourselves* 2
Barnes, P. *The Ruling Class* 1

Bond, E. *Saved* 1
Brenton, H. *Weapons of Happiness* 2
Churchill, C. *Top Girls* 2
Gray, S. *Quartermaine's Terms* 2
Nichols, P. *Passion Play* 2
Orton, J. *Loot* 1
Osborne, J. *A Patriot for Me* 1
Pinter, H. *The Caretaker* 1
Shaffer, P. *Amadeus* 2
Stoppard, T. *Every Good Boy Deserves Favour* 2
Wesker, A. *Roots* 1

COTKICC Corrigan, Robert W., ed. *Classical Comedy Greek and Roman*. New York: Applause, 1987. 484pp.
Aristophanes. *The Birds*
Aristophanes. *Lysistrata*
Menander. *The Grouch*
Plautus, T. *The Menaechmi*
Plautus, T. *Mostellaria (The Haunted House)*
Terence. *The Self-tormentor*

COTKICG Corrigan, Robert W., ed. *Classical Tragedy Greek and Roman: Eight Plays in Authoritative Modern Translations*. New York: Applause, 1990. 556pp.
Aeschylus. *The Oresteia*
Aeschylus. *Prometheus Bound*
Euripides. *The Bakkhai*
Euripides. *Medea*
Seneca, L. *Medea*
Seneca, L. *Oedipus*
Sophocles. *Antigone*
Sophocles. *Oedipus the King*

COTKICO Corrigan, Robert Willoughby, ed. *Comedy: A Critical Anthology*. Boston: Houghton Mifflin, 1971. 769pp.
Aristophanes. *Lysistrata*
Bellow, S. *The Last Analysis*
Brecht, B. *Puntila and His Hired Man*
Chekhov, A. *The Cherry Orchard*
Giraudoux, J. *The Madwoman of Chaillot*
Jonson, B. *Volpone*
Molière, J. *Tartuffe*
Shakespeare, W. *Twelfth Night*
Shaw, G. *Misalliance*
Sheridan, R. *The School for Scandal*
Synge, J. *The Playboy of the Western World*
Wilde, O. *The Importance of Being Earnest*

COTKIR Corrigan, Robert Willoughby, comp. *The Forms of Drama*. Boston: Houghton Mifflin, 1972. 746pp.
Buchner, G. *Woyzeck*
Congreve, W. *The Way of the World*

Ibsen, H. *Ghosts*
Jellicoe, A. *The Knack*
Labiche, E., and Michel, M. *An Italian Straw Hat*
Miller, A. *A View from the Bridge*
Molière, J. *The Miser*
Plautus, T. *The Menaechmi*
Shakespeare, W. *Othello*
Shaw, G. *Arms and the Man*
Sophocles. *Antigone*
Webster, J. *The Duchess of Malfi*

COTKIS Corrigan, Robert Willoughby, comp. *Laurel British Drama: The Nineteenth Century.* New York: Dell, 1967. 464pp.
Boucicault, D. *London Assurance*
Gilbert, W. *Patience*
Lewis, L. *The Bells*
Pinero, A. *The Second Mrs. Tanqueray*
Shaw, G. *Arms and the Man*
Wilde, O. *The Importance of Being Earnest*

COTKIT Corrigan, Robert Willoughby, ed. *Laurel British Drama: The Twentieth Century.* New York: Dell, 1965. 511pp.
Bagnold, E. *The Chalk Garden*
Bolt, R. *A Man for All Seasons*
Coward, N. *Private Lives*
Galsworthy, L. *Loyalties*
Jellicoe, A. *The Knack*
Shaw, G. *Heartbreak House*

COTKJ Corrigan, Robert Willoughby, ed. *Masterpieces of the Modern Central European Theatre: Five Plays.* New York: Collier Books, 1967. 382pp.
Čapek, K. *R.U.R.*
Hofmannstal, H. *Electra*
Molnár, F. *The Play's the Thing*
Schnitzler, A. *The Game of Love*
Schnitzler, A. *La ronde*

COTKR Corrigan, Robert Willoughby, ed. *Masterpieces of the Modern English Theatre.* New York: Collier Books, 1967. 476pp.
Barrie, J. *Dear Brutus*
Galsworthy, J. *Loyalties*
Kops, B. *Enter Solly Gold*
Shaw, G. *Major Barbara*
Wilde, O. *The Importance of Being Earnest*

COTKW Corrigan, Robert Willoughby, ed. *Masterpieces of the Modern French Theatre: Six Plays.* New York: Collier Books, 1967. 442pp.
Anouilh, J. *Euridice*
Becque, H. *The Parisian Woman*
Ghelderode, M. *Christopher Columbus*

Giraudoux, J. *Electra*
Ionesco, E. *Improvisation; or, the Shepherd's Chameleon*
Montherlant, H. *Queen after Death*

COTL Corrigan, Robert Willoughby, ed. *Masterpieces of the Modern German Theatre: Five Plays.* New York: Collier Books, 1967. 416pp.
Brecht, B. *The Caucasian Chalk Circle*
Büchner, G. *Woyzeck*
Hauptmann, G. *The Weavers*
Hebbel, F. *Maria Magdalena*
Wedekind, F. *The Marquis of Keith*

COTM Corrigan, Robert Willoughby, ed. *Masterpieces of the Modern Irish Theatre: Five Plays.* New York: Collier Books, 1967. 317pp.
O'Casey, S. *Cock-a-doodle Dandy*
O'Casey, S. *The Silver Tassie*
Synge, J. *The Playboy of the Western World*
Synge, J. *Riders to the Sea*
Yeats, W. *The Countess Cathleen*

COTN Corrigan, Robert Willoughby, ed. *Masterpieces of the Modern Italian Theatre: Six Plays.* New York: Collier Books, 1967. 352pp.
Betti, U. *Crime on Goat Island*
Filippo, E. *Filumena Marturano*
Fratti, M. *The Academy*
Fratti, M. *The Return*
Pirandello, L. *The Pleasure of Honesty*
Pirandello, L. *Six Characters in Search of an Author*

COTO Corrigan, Robert Willoughby, ed. *Masterpieces of the Modern Russian Theatre: Five Plays.* New York: Collier Books, c1967. 414pp.
Chekhov, A. *The Cherry Orchard*
Chekhov, A. *Uncle Vanya*
Gorki, M. *The Lower Depths*
Mayakovsky, V. *The Bed Bug*
Turgenev, I. *A Month in the Country*

COTP Corrigan, Robert Willoughby, ed. *Masterpieces of the Modern Spanish Theatre.* New York: Collier Books, 1967. 384pp.
Benavente y Martínez, J. *The Witches' Sabbath*
Buero Vallejo, A. *The Dream Weaver*
García Lorca, F. *The Love of Don Perlimplín and Belisa in the Garden*
Martínez Sierra, G. *The Cradle Song*
Sastre, A. *Death Thrust*

COTQ Corrigan, Robert Willoughby, ed. *The Modern Theatre.* New York: Macmillan, 1964. 1267pp.

Anouilh, J. *Eurydice*
Beckett, S. *Endgame*
Betti, U. *The Queen and the Rebels*
Brecht, B. *The Caucasian Chalk Circle*
Büchner, G. *Woyzeck*
Chekhov, A. *The Cherry Orchard*
Chekhov, A. *Uncle Vanya*
Duerrenmatt, F. *The Visit*
Eliot, T. *Murder in the Cathedral*
Frisch, M. *The Chinese Wall*
Fry, C. *A Sleep of Prisoners*
García Lorca, F. *Yerma*
Genêt, J. *Deathwatch*
Giraudoux, J. *Electra*
Gorki, M. *The Lower Depths*
Hauptmann, G. *The Weavers*
Hebbel, F. *Maria Magdalena*
Hellman, L. *The Little Foxes*
Hofmannsthal, H. *Electra*
Ibsen, H. *Hedda Gabler*
Ibsen, H. *The Wild Duck*
Ionesco, E. *The Chairs*
Miller, A. *A View from the Bridge*
O'Casey, S. *The Plough and the Stars*
O'Neill, E. *Desire under the Elms*
Pirandello, L. *The Emperor*
Pirandello, L. *Six Characters in Search of an Author*
Saroyan, W. *The Time of Your Life*
Sartre, J. *The Victors*
Sastre, A. *Anna Kleiber*
Schnitzler, A. *La ronde*
Shaw, G. *Major Barbara*
Strindberg, A. *The Ghost Sonata*
Strindberg, A. *Miss Julie*
Synge, J. *Playboy of the Western World*
Synge, J. *Riders to the Sea*
Wedekind, F. *The Marquis of Keith*
Wilder, T. *The Skin of Our Teeth*
Williams, T. *The Glass Menagerie*
Yeats, W. *On Baile's Strand*

COTR Corrigan, Robert W., ed. *The New Theatre of Europe*. New York: Dell Publishing Co., c1962. 399pp.
Betti, U. *Corruption in the Palace of Justice*
Bolt, R. *A Man for All Seasons*
Ghelderode, M. *Pantagleize*
Peryalis, N. *Masks of Angels*
Sastre, A. *Anna Kleiber*

COTS Corrigan, Robert Willoughby, ed. *The New Theatre of Europe, 2: 5 Contemporary Plays from the European Stage*. New York: Dell, 1964. 320pp.
Brecht, B. *Mother Courage*
Fratti, M. *The Cage*

Fratti, M. *The Suicide*
Grass, G. *The Wicked Cooks*
Schehadé, G. *Vasco*

COTT Corrigan, Robert Willoughby, ed. *The New Theatre of Europe, 3: 4 Contemporary Plays from the European Stage*. New York: Dell, 1968. 309pp.
Dorst, T. *The Curve*
Forssell, L. *The Sunday Promenade*
Guerdon, D. *The Laundry*
Osborne, J. *Inadmissible Evidence*

COTU Corrigan, Robert Willoughby, ed. *Roman Drama, in Modern Translations*. New York: Dell, 1966. 380pp.
Horatius Flaccus, Q. *Ars poetica*
Plautus, T. *The Menaechmi*
Plautus, T. *The Merchant*
Seneca, L. *Medea*
Terentius Afer, P. *Adelphi*
Terentius Afer, P. *Phormio*

COTX Corrigan, Robert Willoughby, comp. *Tragedy: A Critical Anthology*. Boston: Houghton Mifflin, 1971. 787pp.
Coxe, L., and Chapman, R. *Billy Budd*
Dryden, J. *All for Love*
Euripides. *The Bacchae*
Ibsen, H. *The Master Builder*
MacLeish, A. *J. B.*
Marlowe, C. *Doctor Faust*
Miller, A. *Death of a Salesman*
Racine, J. *Phaedra*
Shakespeare, W. *The Tragedy of King Lear*
Shaw, G. *Saint Joan*
Sophocles. *Oedipus the King*
Strindberg, A. *Miss Julie*

COTY Corrigan, Robert Willoughby, and Rosenberg, James L., eds. *The Art of the Theatre: A Critical Anthology of Drama*. San Francisco: Chandler, 1964. 609pp.
Aristophanes. *Lysistrata*
Chekhov, A. *Uncle Vanya*
Ionesco, E. *The New Tenant*
Molière, J. *Tartuffe*
Shakespeare, W. *Macbeth*
Sophocles. *Antigone*
Strindberg, A. *Miss Julie*
Synge, J. *Riders to the Sea*
Wilde, O. *The Importance of Being Earnest*
Williams, T. *The Rose Tattoo*

CORRIGAN, ROBERT WILLOUGHBY. *See also* NEWA *New American Plays.*

COUL Couling, Delia, comp. *Dutch and Flemish Plays.*
    London: Nick Hern Nooks, 1997. 295pp.
    Boer, L. *The Buddha of Ceylon*
    Herzberg, J. *The Wedding Party*
    Sierens, A. *Drummers*
    Strijards, F. *The Stendhal Syndrome*
    Woudstra, K. *Burying the Dog*

COUR Cournos, John, ed. *A Treasury of Classic Russian
    Literature.* New York: Capricorn Books [c1961]
    580pp.
    Gogol, N. *The Inspector-general*
    Ostrovskii, A. *A Domestic Picture*
    Tolstoi, L. *Condemnation*
    Tolstoi, L. *Taxes*

COUS Cournos, John, ed. *A Treasury of Russian Life
    and Humor.* New York: Coward-McCann [c1943]
    676pp.
    Gogol, N. *The Inspector*

COV *The Coventry Corpus Christi Plays.* Edited
    by Pamela M. King and Clifford Davidson.
    Kalamazoo, MI: Medieval Institute Publications,
    Western Michigan University, 2000. 326pp. (Early
    Drama, Art, and Music Monograph Series 27)
    *The Pageant of the Company of Shearmen and Taylors
    in Coventry*
    *The Weavers' Pageant*

COXJ Cox, Jeffrey, N., ed. *Seven Gothic Dramas, 1789–
    1825.* Athens: Ohio State University Press, 1992.
    425pp.
    Baillie, J. *De Monfort*
    Cross, J. *Julia of Louvain; or, Monkish Cruelty*
    Lewis, M. *The Captive*
    Lewis, M. *The Castle Spectre*
    Maturin, C. *Bertram; or, the Castle of St. Aldobrand*
    North, F. *The Kentish Barons*
    Peake, R. *Presumption; or, the Fate of Frankenstein*

COXM Cox, Martha Heasley, ed. *Image and Value: An
    Invitation to Literature.* New York: Harcourt, Brace
    & World [1966] 630pp.
    Arrabal, F. *Picnic on the Battlefield*
    Giraudoux, J. *The Apollo of Bellac*
    O'Neill, E. *A Touch of the Poet*
    Shaw, G. *Pygmalion*
    Sophocles. *Antigone*

COY Coyle, William, and Damaser, H. G., eds. *Six Early
    American Plays, 1798–1890.* Columbus, OH:
    Merrill, 1968. 313pp.
    Boucicault, D. *The Octoroon*
    Dunlap, W. *André*

Herne, J. *Margaret Fleming*
Howard, B. *Shenandoah*
Mowatt, A. *Fashion*
Stone, J. *Metamora*

CRACK *The Crack in the Emerald: New Irish Plays.*
    Selected and introduced by David Grant. London:
    Nick Hern Books, 1990. 258pp.
    Bolger, D. *The Lament for Arthur Cleary*
    Carr, M. *Low in the Dark*
    Harding, M. *Misogynist*
    Jones, M. *The Hamster Wheel*

CRAF Craft, Harry M., comp. *Logic, Style and
    Arrangement.* Beverly Hills, CA: Glencoe Press,
    1971. 501pp.
    Shakespeare, W. *King Lear*
    Sophocles. *Antigone*
    Wilde, O. *The Importance of Being Earnest*

CRAN Crane, William Garrett [and others] eds. *Twelve
    Hundred Years: The Literature of England.*
    Harrisburg, PA: Stackpole and Heck [c1949]
    2 vols.
    Wilde, O. *The Importance of Being Earnest* 2

CRE Creeth, Edmund, compiler. *Tudor Plays: An
    Anthology of Early English Drama.* Garden City,
    NY: Anchor Books (Doubleday), [1966] 569pp.
    Bale, J. *Kyng Johan*
    Heywood, J. *Johan Johan the Husbande*
    Medwall, H. *Fulgens and Lucres*
    Preston, T. *Cambises*
    Sackville, T., and Norton, T. *Ferrex and Porrex; or,
    Gorboduc*
    Stevenson, W. *Gammer Gurton's Nedle*
    Udall, N. *Royster Doyster*

CRIT *The Critics' Prize Plays.* Introduction by George
    Jean Nathan. Cleveland, OH: World Publishing Co.
    [c1945] 377pp.
    Anderson, M. *High Tor*
    Anderson, M. *Winterset*
    Hellman, L. *Watch on the Rhine*
    Kingsley, S. *The Patriots*
    Saroyan, W. *The Time of Your Life*
    Steinbeck, J. *Of Mice and Men*

CROS Cross, Ethan Allan, ed. *World Literature.* New
    York: American Book Co. [c1935] 1396pp.
    Aeschylus. *Prometheus Bound*
    Bulwer-Lytton, E. *Richelieu; or, the Conspiracy*
    Euripides. *Iphigenia in Aulis*
    Galsworthy, J. *The Silver Box*
    Ibsen, H. *The Master Builder*

Molière, J. *The Miser*
Plautus. *Menaechmi; or, the Twin Brothers*
Seneca. *Medea*
Shakespeare, W. *Antony and Cleopatra*
Sophocles. *Antigone*
Terence. *Andria*

CROV Cross, Tom Peete, and Slover, Clark H., eds. *Heath Readings in the Literature of Europe*. Boston: Heath [c1933] 1194pp.
*Adam, The Play of*
Aeschylus. *Prometheus Bound*
Aristophanes. *The Birds*
Corneille, P. *Le cid*
Goethe, J. *Faust, Part I*
Goldoni, C. *A Curious Mishap*
Ibsen, H. *Ghosts*
Lessing, G. *Minna von Barnhelm*
Molière, J. *The Misanthrope*
Plautus. *The Captives*
Seneca. *Medeu*
Vega Carpio, L. *The Star of Seville*

CROX Cross, Tom Peete; Smith, Reed; Stauffer, Elmer C.; and Collette, Elizabeth. *American Writers*. Rev. ed. Boston: Ginn [c1955] 708pp.
Wilder, T. *Our Town*

CROZ *Cross-Section*. Edited by Edwin Seaver. New York: L. B. Fischer [c1944–1948] 4 vols.
Miller, A. *The Man Who Had All the Luck* 1
Peters, P. *Nat Turner* 1
Whittington, R. *The Death of García Lorca* 1

CRU Crump, James Irving, compiler. *Chinese Theater in the Days of Kublai Khan*. Tucson: University of Arizona Press, 1980. 429pp.
K'ang, C. *Li K'uei Carries Thorns*
Meng, H. *The Mo-ho-lo Doll*
Yang, H. *Rain on the Hsiao-hsiang*

CRY *A Cry of Kings: Six Greek Dramas in Modern English*. Edited and translated by Frederic Williams. Champaign, IL: Stipes Publishing LLC, 1999. 199pp.
Euripides. *Alcestis*
Euripides. *Women of Troy*
Sophocles. *Antigone*
Sophocles. *Electra*
Sophocles. *Oedipus at Colonus*
Sophocles. *Oedipus the King*

CTR *The CTR Anthology: Fifteen Plays from Canadian Theatre Review*. Edited by Alan Filewod. Toronto: University of Toronto Press, 1993. 683pp.

Alianak, H. *Passion and Sin*
The Anna Project. *This Is for You, Anna*
Brassard, M., and Lepage, R. *Polygraph*
Cook, M. *The Head, Guts, and Sound Bone Dance*
Cowan, C. *A Woman from the Sea*
Dubois, R. *Being at Home with Claude*
Gilbert, S. *Lola Starr Builds Her Dream Home*
Lambert, B. *Jennie's Story*
Ledoux, P., and Young, D. *Love Is Strange*
Milner, A. *Zero Hour*
Palmer, J. *Henrik Ibsen on the Necessity of Producing Norwegian Drama*
Rose, R., and Kugler, D. *Newhouse*
Rubess, B. *Boom, Baby, Boom!*
Walker, G. *Rumours of Our Death*
Winter, J., and Smith, C. *Ten Lost Years*

CUB *Cuban American Theater*. Edited by Rodolfo J. Cortina. Houston, TX: Arte Publico Press, 1991. 280pp.
Aloma, R. *A Little Something to Ease the Pain*
Clavijo, U. *With All and For the Good of All*
Ferradas, R. *Birds without Wings*
Gonzalez-Pando, M. *Once upon a Dream*
Hernandez, L. *Martinez*
Montes Huidobro, M. *Your Better Half*

CUBE Cubeta, Paul M., ed. *Modern Drama for Analysis*. New York: William Sloane Associates [c1950] 584pp.
Chekhov, A. *The Cherry Orchard*
Hellman, L. *Watch on the Rhine*
Ibsen, H. *The Wild Duck*
O'Casey, S. *Juno and the Paycock*
O'Neill, E. *The Emperor Jones*
Synge, J. *The Playboy of the Western World*
Wilder, T. *The Skin of Our Teeth*
Williams, T. *The Glass Menagerie*

CUBG Cubeta, Paul M. *Modern Drama for Analysis*. Rev. ed. New York: Dryden, c1955. 785pp.
Chekhov, A. *The Cherry Orchard*
Ibsen, H. *The Wild Duck*
Inge, W. *Come Back, Little Sheba*
O'Casey, S. *Juno and the Paycock*
O'Neill, E. *Anna Christie*
Shaw, G. *Arms and the Man*
Synge, J. *The Playboy of the Western World*
Wilder, T. *The Skin of Our Teeth*
Williams, T. *The Glass Menagerie*

CUBH Cubeta, Paul M. *Modern Drama for Analysis*. 3rd ed. New York: Holt, Rinehart and Winston [c1962] 613pp.

Albee, E. *The Sandbox*
Anouilh, J. *Becket: or, the Honor of God*
Chekhov, A. *The Cherry Orchard*
Eliot, T. *Murder in the Cathedral*
Ibsen, H. *Rosmersholm*
Miller, A. *A View from the Bridge*
O'Neill, E. *Desire under the Elms*
Shaw, G. *The Devil's Disciple*
Wilder, T. *The Skin of Our Teeth*
Williams, T. *The Glass Menagerie*

CUN Cunliffe, John William, ed. *Early English Classical Tragedies*. Oxford: Clarendon Press, 1912. 352pp.
Gascoigne, G., and Kinwelmersh, F. *Jocasta*
Hughes, T. *The Misfortunes of Arthur*
Norton, T., and Sackville, T. *Gorboduc; or, Ferrex and Porrex*
[Wilmot, R., and Others] *Gismond of Salerne*

CURB Curb, Rosemary, ed. *Amazon All Stars: 13 Lesbian Plays*. New York: Applause Books, 1996. 482pp.
Astor del Valle, J. *I'll Be Home para la Navidad*
Chambers, J. *The Quintessential Image*
Dickler, G. *The Postcard*
Fornes, M. *Springtime*
Gage, C. *Amazon All-stars*
Holmes, S. *A Lady and a Woman*
Lipkin, J. *Small Domestic Acts*
Miller, S. *Nasty Rumors and Final Remarks*
Montley, P. *Sisters*
Sam, C. *The Dissident*
Schenkar, J. *The Lodger*
Terry, M. *Willa Willie Bill's Dope Garden*
Vogel, P. *Desdemona*

DAI Daiches, David; Jewett, Arno; Havighurst, Walter; and Searles John, compilers. *English Literature*. Boston: Houghton Mifflin, 1968. 848p.
Goldsmith, O. *She Stoops to Conquer*
Shakespeare, W. *Macbeth*
Shaw, G. *Pygmalion*
Synge, J. *Riders to the Sea*

DANA, H. W. L. See SEVP *Seven Soviet Plays*.

DANI Daniel, Robert Woodham, and Leggett, G. H., eds. *The Written Word*. Englewood Cliffs, NJ: Prentice-Hall, 1960. 726pp.
Shaw, G. *The Man of Destiny*

DAPO D'Aponte, Mimi Gisolfi, ed. *Seventh Generation: An Anthology of Native American Plays*. New York: Theatre Communications Group, 1999. 385pp.

Geiogamah, H. *Body Indian*
Glancy, D. *The Woman Who Was a Red Deer Dressed for the Deer Dance*
Howe, L., and Gordon, R. *Indian Radio Days*
Kneubuhl, V. *The Story of Susanna*
Spiderwoman Theater. *Power Pipes*
Taylor, D. *Only Drunks and Children Tell the Truth*
Yellow Robe, W. *The Independence of Eddie Rose*

DAU Dauster, Frank, Lyday, Leon, and Woodyard, George, eds. *9 Dramaturgos Hispanoamericanos: Antología del Teatro HispanoAmericano del Diglo XX*. 2nd ed. Ottawa: Girol Books, 1983. 3 vols. (Colección Telón. Antologías 1–3; same title with identical authors and plays also published in 1979, 1994, 1995, and 1997–1998.)
Carballido, E. *Yo también hablo de la rosa* 3
Diaz, J. *El cepillo de dientes* 3
Dragun, O. *El amasijo* 1
Gambaro, G. *Los siameses* 2
Marqués, R. *Los soles truncos* 3
Triana, J. *La noche de los asesinos* 1
Usigli, R. *Corona de sombra* 1
Villaurrutia, X. *Invitacion a la muerte* 2
Wolff, E. *Flores de papel* 2

DAUR Dauster, Frank, Lyday, Leon, and Woodyard, George, eds. *3 Dramaturgos Rioplatenses: Antología del Teatro Hispanoamericano del Siglo XX*. Ottawa: Girol Books, 1983. 212pp. (Colección Telón. Antología IV; 2nd ed. with same authors and titles published in 1994.)
Arlt, R. *Savierio el cruel*
Pavlovsky, E. *El Señor Galindez*
Sánchez, F. *Barranca Abajo*

DAV Davenport, William H.; Wimberley, Lowry C.; and Shaw, Harry, eds. *Dominant Types in British and American Literature*. New York: Harper [c1949] 2 vols.
Anderson, M. *Winterset* 1
Barrie, J. *The 12-pound Look* 1
O'Neill, E. *The Hairy Ape* 1
Rice, E. *The Adding Machine* 1
*The Second Shepherds' Play* 1
Shakespeare, W. *King Henry IV* 1
Sheridan, R. *The School for Scandal* 1
Synge, J. *Riders to the Sea* 1
Wilde, O. *Lady Windermere's Fan* 1

DAVI David, Sister Mary Agnes. *Modern American Drama*. New York: Macmillan [c1961] 235pp. (The Pageant of Literature)

Barry, P. *The Joyous Season*
Coxe, L., and Chapman, R. *Billy Budd*
Van Druten, J. *I Remember Mama*

DAVJ Davies, Reginald Trevor, ed. *The Corpus Christi Play of the English Middle Ages*. Totowa, NJ: Rowman and Littlefield, 1972. 458pp.
*Abraham* (Wakefield)
*Abraham* (York)
*Abraham and Isaac* (Brome)
*Abraham and Isaac* (Dublin)
*Abraham and Isaac* (Ludus Coventriae)
*Abraham, Melchisedec, and Isaac* (Chester)
*The Apostles at the Tomb*
*Appearance to Cleopas and Luke*
*Appearance to Mary Magdalen*
*Appearance to Thomas*
*Ascension*
*Assumption*
*Birth of the Son*
*Cain and Abel*
*Creation and Fall of Lucifer*
*Creation and Fall of Man*
*Doomsday*
*Harrowing of Hell II*
*Herod and the Three Kings*
*Jesse*
*Jesus and the Doctors*
*Matthias*
*Moses*
*Mother of Mercy: Conception*
*Mother of Mercy: Joseph*
*Mother of Mercy: Parliament of Heaven and Annunciation*
*Mother of Mercy: Salutation*
*Noah*
*Passion I: Agony at Olivet*
*—I: Betrayal*
*—I: Council of Jews I*
*—I: Council of Jews II*
*—I: Entry into Jerusalem*
*—I: Maundy I*
*—I: Maundy II*
*—I: Maundy III*
*—I: Prologues*
*—I: Taking of Jesus*
*Passion II: before Annas and Caiphas*
*—II: before Herod II*
*—II: before Pilate*
*Passion II: before Pilate II*
*—II: Centurion*
*—II: Crucifixion*
*—II: Dream of Pilate's Wife*
*—II: Harrowing of Hell I*
*—II: Jesus before Herod*

*—II: Longeus and Burial*
*—II: Peter's Denial*
*—II: Prologue*
*—II: Setting of Watch*
*—II: Way of the Cross*
*Pentecost*
*Presentation and Purification*
*Raising of Lazarus*
*Resurrection and Appearance to Mother*
*The Shepherds Play*
*Slaughter of the Innocents*
*Story of the Watch*
*Three Marys at the Tomb*
*Trial of Joseph and Mary*
*Woman Taken in Adultery*

DAVK Davis, Earle R., and Hummel, William C., eds. *Readings for Enjoyment*. Englewood Cliffs, NJ: Prentice-Hall, 1959. 611pp.
*The Book of Job*
Kaufman, G., and Hart, M. *The Man Who Came to Dinner*
O'Neill, E. *Ah, Wilderness*
Shakespeare, W. *Hamlet, Prince of Denmark*
Sophocles. *Oedipus Rex*

DAVM Davis, Muriel, comp. *Inscape: Stories, Plays, Poems*. Philadelphia, Lippincott, 1971. 632p
Aristophanes. *Lysistrata*
Chayefsky, P. *Marty*
Saroyan, W. *The Time of Your Life*
Williams, T. *The Glass Menagerie*

DAVN Davis, Norman, ed. *Noncycle Plays and Fragments*. Edited by N. Davis. Supplementary Text No. 1; published for the Early English Text Society. London: Oxford, 1970. 168pp.
*Abraham and Isaac* (Brome)
*Abraham and Isaac* (Northampton)
*The Ashmole Fragment*
*The Cambridge Prologue*
*The Durham Prologue*
*Dux moraud*
*The Newcastle Play* (Noah's Ark; or, the Shipwrights Ancient Play, or Dirge).
*The Norwich Grocers' Play* (The Story of the Creation of Eve, or the Expelling of Adam and Eve Out of Paradise); Text A and Text B
*The Play of the Sacrament*
*The Pride of Life*
*The Shrewsbury Fragments: Officium pastorum; Officium resurrectionis; Officium peregrinorum*
*The Reynes Extracts*
*The Rickinghall* (Bury St. Edmunds) *Fragment*

DAVR Davison, Dennis, ed. *Restoration Comedies.*
    London: Oxford, 1970. 399pp.
  Dryden, J. *Marriage a la mode*
  Etherege, G. *She Would If She Could*
  Sedley, C. *The Mulberry Garden*
  Vanbrugh, J. *The Relapse*
  Wycherley, W. *The Country Wife*

DAY Day, Barbara, ed. *Czech Plays: Modern Czech
    Drama.* London: Nick Hern Books, 1994. 224pp.
  Fischerova, D. *Between Dog and Wolf*
  Havel, V. *Tomorrow!*
  Klíma, I. *Games*
  Topol, J. *Cat on the Rails*

DAZZ *The Dazzling Dark: New Irish Plays.* Selected and
    introduced by Frank McGuinness. London: Faber
    and Faber, 1996. 311pp.
  Carr, M. *Portia Coughlan*
  MacIntyre, T. *Good Evening, Mr. Collins*
  Moxley, G. *Danti-Dan*
  Murphy, J. *A Picture of Paradise*

DEAD *Dead Proud: From Second Wave Young Women
    Playwrights.* Edited by Ann Considine and Robin
    Slovo. London: Livewire from the Women's Press,
    Ltd., 1987. 186pp.
  Baptiste, R. *Back Street Mammy*
  Baptiste, R. *No Place like Home*
  Binnie, B. *Foreshore*
  Ghose, N. *Ishtar Descends*
  Jacobs, P., and Bemarro Theatre Group. *A Slice of Life*
  Kayla, L. *When Did I Last See You*
  Kilcoyne, C., and Slovo, R. *A Netful of Holes*
  Milan, A. *Dead Proud*
  Teale, P. *Fallen*
  Wilson, M. *Shopping Spree*

DEAN Dean, Leonard [Fellows], ed. *Elizabethan Drama.*
    New York: Prentice-Hall, 1950. 334pp. (English
    masterpieces. Vol. 2)
  Marlowe, C. *Doctor Faustus*
  Shakespeare, W. *Henry IV, Part I*
  Shakespeare, W. *King Lear*
  Webster, J. *The Duchess of Malfi*

DEAO Dean, Leonard Fellows, ed. *Elizabethan Drama.*
    2nd ed. Englewood Cliffs, NJ: Prentice-Hall, 1961.
    364pp. (English masterpieces. Vol. 2)
  Jonson, B. *Volpone; or, the Fox*
  Marlowe, C. *The Tragical History of Doctor Faustus*
  Shakespeare, W. *King Lear*
  Webster, J. *The Duchess of Malfi*

DEAP Dean, Leonard Fellows, ed. *Nine Great Plays from
    Aeschylus to Eliot.* New York: Harcourt, Brace
    [c1950] 595pp.
  Aeschylus. *Agamemnon*
  Chekhov, A. *The Cherry Orchard*
  Congreve, W. *The Way of the World*
  Eliot, T. *Murder in the Cathedral*
  Ibsen, H. *The Wild Duck*
  Jonson, B. *Volpone; or, the Fox*
  Molière, J. *The Misanthrope*
  O'Neill, E. *The Emperor Jones*
  Sophocles. *King Oedipus*

DEAR Dean, Leonard [Fellows], ed. *Nine Great Plays
    from Aeschylus to Eliot.* Rev. ed. New York:
    Harcourt Brace [c1956] 695pp.
  Aeschylus. *Agamemnon*
  Chekhov, A. *The Cherry Orchard*
  Congreve, W. *The Way of the World*
  Eliot, T. *Murder in the Cathedral*
  Ibsen, H. *An Enemy of the People*
  Jonson, B. *Volpone*
  Molière, J. *The Would-be Invalid*
  Shaw, G. *Pygmalion*
  Sophocles. *Oedipus Rex*

DEAS Dean, Leonard [Fellows], ed. *Twelve Great Plays.*
    New York: Harcourt, Brace, Jovanovich, 1970.
    789pp.
  Abse, D. *House of Cowards*
  Aeschylus. *Agamemnon*
  Brecht, B. *The Caucasian Chalk Circle*
  Chekhov, A. *The Cherry Orchard*
  Ibsen, H. *Ghosts*
  Jonson, B. *The Alchemist*
  Marlowe, C. *The Jew of Malta*
  Molière, J. *Tartuffe*
  Pirandello, L. *Six Characters in Search of an Author*
  Shakespeare, W. *Henry IV, Part 1*
  Sophocles. *Oedipus Rex*
  Williams, T. *The Glass Menagerie*

DEAT Dean, Nancy, and Soares, M.G., eds. *Intimate Acts:
    Eight Contemporary Lesbian Plays.* New York:
    Brito & Lair, 1997. 253pp.
  Astor del Valle, J. *Fuchsia*
  Baum, T. *Two Fools*
  Dean, N. *Gloria's Visit*
  McLaughlin, R. *Horsefeathers*
  Malinowitz, H. *Minus One*
  Renee. *Tiggy Tiggy Touch Wood*
  Schulman, S. *Promenade*
  Thompson, B. *Yardlights Ahead*

DEBENHAM, A. H. See SEVE *Seven Sacred Plays*

DEC *A Decade's Drama: Six Scottish Plays*. Todmorden,
    Lancashire: Woodhouse Books, 1980. 330pp.
  Byrne, J. *Threads*
  Conn, S. *Play Donkey*
  Eveling, S. *Mister*
  Macdonald, R. *Chinchilla*
  MacMillan, H. *The Rising*
  Taylor, C. *Walter*

DEM De Mille, Alban Bertram, ed. *Three English
    Comedies*. Boston: Allyn and Bacon [c1924]
    479pp.
  Goldsmith, O. *She Stoops to Conquer*
  Sheridan, R. *The Rivals*
  Sheridan, R. *The School for Scandal*

DEN DeNobriga, Kathie, and Valetta Anderson, eds.
    *Alternate Roots: Plays from the Southern Theater*.
    Portsmouth, NH: Heinemann, 1994. 340pp.
  Baker, D., and Cocke, D. *Red Fox/Second Hangin'*
  Carson, J. *A Preacher with a Horse to Ride*
  Grimsley, J. *Mr. Universe*
  Members of the Road Company Ensemble. *Blind Desire*
  O'Neal, J., and Watkins, N. B. *You Can't Judge a Book
    by Looking at the Cover: Sayings from the Life and
    Writings of junebug jabbo jones, Volume II*
  Parris-Bailey, L. *Dark Cowgirls and Prairie Queens*
  Ransom, R. *Blood on Blood*

DENSMORE, H. B. See TEN *Ten Greek Plays*

DENT Denton, Martin, ed. *Plays and Playwrights for the
    New Millennium*. New York: Theatre Experience,
    2000. 366pp.
  Bromley, K. *Midnight Brainwash Revival*
  Dannenfelser, D. *When Words Fail*
  De Santis, E. *Making Peter Pope*
  Hopkins, C. *Horse Country*
  Macy, L. *Crunching Numbers*
  Ruderman, G., and Summers, D. *"So, I Killed a Few
    People . . ."*
  Simonson, R. *Café Society*
  Wingfield, G. *Are We There Yet?*

DESH Deshpande, G. P. ed. *Modern Indian Drama: An
    Anthology*. New Delhi: Sahitya Akademi, 2000.
    754pp.
  Alekar, S. *Mahapoor*
  Bhagat, D. *Whirlpool*
  Deshpande, G. *Roads*
  Devi, M. *Mother of 1084*

  Dutt, U. *Hunting the Sun*
  Kambar, C. *Siri sampige*
  Karnad, G. *Hayavadana*
  Mukherjee, A. *Mareech, the Legend*
  Panikkar, K. *The Lone Tusker*
  Parthasarathi, I. *Aurangzeb*
  Rakesh, M. *One Day in Ashadha*
  Sircar, B. *Evam Indrajit*
  Sriranga. *Listen, Janamejaya*
  Tendulkar, V. *The Vultures*
  Verma, S. *From Sunset to Sunrise*

DICD Dickinson, Thomas Herbert. *Chief Contemporary
    Dramatists*. First Series. Boston: Hougton, Mifflin
    [c1915] 676pp.
  Bjørnson, B. *Beyond Human Power*
  Brieux, E. *The Red Robe*
  Chekhov, A. *The Cherry Orchard*
  Fitch, C. *The Truth*
  Galsworthy, J. *Strife*
  Granville-Barker, H. *The Madras House*
  Gregory, I. *The Rising of the Moon*
  Hauptmann, G. *The Weavers*
  Hervieu, P. *Know Thyself*
  Jones, H. *Michael and His Lost Angel*
  MacKaye, P. *The Scarecrow*
  Maeterlinck, M. *Pélléas and Mélisande*
  Moody, W. *The Great Divide*
  Pinero, A. *The Second Mrs. Tanqueray*
  Strindberg, A. *The Father*
  Sudermann, H. *The Vale of Content*
  Synge, J. *Riders to the Sea*
  Thomas, A. *The Witching Hour*
  Wilde, O. *Lady Windermere's Fan*
  Yeats, W. *The Hour-glass*

DICDS Dickinson, Thomas Herbert, ed. *Chief
    Contemporary Dramatists*. Second Series. Boston:
    Houghton Mifflin [c1921] 734pp.
  Annunzio, G. d'. *Gioconda*
  Bahr, H. *The Concert*
  Benavente y Martínez, J. *The Bonds of Interest*
  Bennett, A., and Knoblock, E. *Milestones*
  Drinkwater, J. *Abraham Lincoln*
  Dunsany, E. *King Argimenes and the Unknown
    Warrior*
  Ervine, St. J. *Mixed Marriage*
  Gorki, M. *The Lower Depths*
  Guitry, S. *Pasteur*
  Hazelton, G., and Benrimo, J. *The Yellow Jacket*
  Heiberg, G. *The Tragedy of Love*
  Maugham, W. *Our Betters*
  Peabody, J. *The Piper*
  Porto-Riche, G. de. *A Loving Wife*

Rostand, E. *Cyrano de Bergerac*
Schnitzler, A. *Living Hours*
Thomas, L. *Moral*
Walter, E. *The Easiest Way*

DICDT Dickinson, Thomas Herbert, ed. *Chief
  Contemporary Dramatists*. Third Series. Boston:
  Houghton, Mifflin [c1930] 698pp.
  Alvarez Quintero, S., and Alvarez Quintero, J.
    *Malvaloca*
  Andreyev, L. *He Who Gets Slapped*
  Ansky, S. *The Dybbuk*
  Benelli, S. *The Love of the Three Kings*
  Čapek, K. *R.U.R.*
  Green, P. *In Abraham's Bosom*
  Hofmannsthal, H. von. *Electra*
  Howard, S. *The Silver Cord*
  Kaiser, G. *From Morn to Midnight*
  Lenormand, H. *Time Is a Dream*
  Martínez Sierra, G., and Martínez Sierra, M. *A Lily
    among Thorns*
  Milne, A. *The Dover Road*
  Molnár, F. *Liliom*
  O'Casey, S. *Juno and the Paycock*
  O'Neill, E. *The Emperor Jones*
  Pirandello, L. *Naked*
  Sigurjónsson, J. *Eyvind of the Hills*
  Vildrac, C. *The Steamship Tenacity*
  Wedekind, F. *Such Is Life*
  Yevreinov, N. *The Theatre of Soul*

DICEM Dickinson, Thomas Herbert, and Crawford,
  Jack Randall, eds. *Contemporary Plays*. Boston:
  Houghton Mifflin [c1925] 650pp.
  Anspacher, L. *The Unchastened Woman*
  Baker, E. *Chains*
  Crothers, R. *Mary the Third*
  Davies, H. *The Mollusc*
  Davis, O. *Icebound*
  Drinkwater, J. *Oliver Cromwell*
  Granville-Barker, H. *The Voysey Inheritance*
  Hankin, St. J. *The Cassilis Engagement*
  Houghton, S. *Hindle Wakes*
  Kenyon, C. *Kindling*
  Maugham, W. *The Circle*
  O'Neill, E. *The Hairy Ape*
  Phillips, S. *Paolo and Francesca*
  Rice, E. *The Adding Machine*
  Sowerby, G. *Rutherford and Son*
  Sutro, A. *John Glayde's Honour*

DICIN Dickinson, Thomas Herbert, ed. *Continental Plays*.
  Boston: Houghton Mifflin [c1935] 2 vols. (Types
  contemporary drama)

Alvarez Quintero, S., and Alvarez Quintero, J. *A Bright
    Morning* 1
Andreyev, L. *The Life of Man* 2
Annunzio, G. d'. *Francesca da Rimini* 1
Bernard, J. *L'invitation au voyage* 2
Brieux, E. *The Red Robe* 2
Čapek, K. *R.U.R.* 1
Chekhov, A. *The Cherry Orchard* 1
Claudel, P. *The Tidings Brought to Mary* 1
Echegaray [y Eizaguirre], J. *The Great Galeoto* 2
Gorky, M. *The Lower Depths* 2
Hauptmann, G. *The Weavers* 1
Kaiser, G. *The Coral* 2
Maeterlinck, M. *Pelléas and Mélisande* 1
Molnár, F. *Liliom* 1
Pirandello, L. *Six Characters in Search of an Author* 2
Rostand, E. *Cyrano de Bergerac* 2
Schnitzler, A. *Light-O-love* 1
Strindberg, A. *A Dream Play* 2
Tolstoy, L. *The Power of Darkness* 1
Wedekind, F. *Erdgeist* 2

DIEA Dietrich, Richard Farr, and others, compilers. *The
  Art of Drama*. New York: Holt, 1969. 669pp.
  Brecht, B. *The Caucasian Chalk Circle*
  Chekhov, A. *The Cherry Orchard*
  Hansberry, L. *A Raisin in the Sun*
  Ibsen, H. *The Wild Duck*
  Miller, A. *A View from the Bridge*
  Molière, J. *The Misanthrope*
  Osborne, J. *Luther*
  Pirandello, L. *Six Characters in Search of an Author*
  Shakespeare, W. *Antony and Cleopatra*
  Shaw, G. *Caesar and Cleopatra*
  Sophocles. *Antigone*
  Sophocles. *Oedipus*
  Williams, T. *The Glass Menagerie*

DIEB Dietrich, Richard F., et al., compilers. *The Art of
  Drama*. 2nd ed. New York: Holt, 1976. 781pp.
  Beckett, S. *Act without Words* II
  Chekhov, A. *The Cherry Orchard*
  Hansberry, L. *A Raisin in the Sun*
  Ibsen, H. *A Doll's House*
  Ionesco, E. *The Gap*
  Miller, A. *Death of a Salesman*
  Molière, J. *The Misanthrope*
  Nichols, P. *Joe Egg*
  O'Neill, E. *The Hairy Ape*
  Pirandello, L. *Six Characters in Search of an Author*
  Shakespeare, W. *Twelfth Night*
  Shaw, G. *Candida*
  Sophocles. *Oedipus Rex*
  Strindberg, A. *The Stronger*
  Weiss, P. *Marat/Sade*

Zindel, P. *The Effect of Gamma Rays on man-in-the-moon Marigolds*

DIER Dietrich, Richard Farr, compiler. *The Realities of Literature*. Waltham, MA: Xerox College Publications, 1971. 656pp.
Hansberry, L. *A Raisin in the Sun*
Ionesco, E. *The Picture*
Pirandello, L. *Six Characters in Search of an Author*
Shaw, G. *Caesar and Cleopatra*
Sophocles. *Oedipus Rex*

DIGBY *The Digby Plays: Rendered into Modern English*. By Alice J. Brock and David G. Byrd. Dallas, TX: Paon Press, 1973. 144pp.
*Christ's Burial and Resurrection*
*The Conversion of St. Paul*
*Herod's Killing of the Children*
*Mary Magdalene*
*A Morality of Wisdom, Who Is Christ*

DIRTY *Dirty Laundry, Mergers & Undercover: Plays from TheatreWorks' Writers' Lab*. Singapore: TheatreWorks, Singapore Press Holdings, 1995. 352pp.
Fong, O. *Cetecea*
Lee, C. *Breaking Through*
Loon, R. *Watching the Clouds Go By*
Tan, T. H. *Undercover*
Tan, T. *Dirty Laundry*
Varella, E. *Others*
Wong, E. *Mergers and Accusations*

DIS Disch, Robert, and Schwartz, Barry N., eds. *Killing Time: A Guide to Life in the Happy Valley*. Englewood Cliffs, NJ: Prentice-Hall, 1972. 500pp.
Aeschylus. *Agamemnon*
Chekhov, A. *The Cherry Orchard*
Davis, O. *Purlie Victorious*
Fratti, M. *The Bridge*
Terry, M. *The Magic Realists*

DIX Dixon, Michael Bigelow, and Volansky, Michele, eds. *By Southern Playwrights: Plays from Actors Theatre of Louisville*. Lexington: University Press of Kentucky, 1996. 240pp.
Berry, W. *The Cool of the Day*
Blount, R. *Five Ives Gets Named*
Blount, R. *That Dog Isn't Fifteen*
Crews, H. *Blood Issue*
Crutcher, J., and McBride, V. *Digging in: the Farm Crisis in Kentucky*
Dewberry, E. *Head On*
Larson, L., Lee, L., and Wackler, R. *Tent Meeting*

Linney, R. *2*
Norman, M. *Loving Daniel Boone*

DIXD Dixon, Michael Bigelow, and Volansky, Michele, eds. *A Decade of New Comedy: Plays from the Humana Festival*. Portsmouth, NH: Heinemann, 1996. 2 vols.
Ackermann, J. *Zara Spook and Other Lures* 1
Dresser, R. *Below the Belt* 2
Kopit, A. *Road to Nirvana* 1
Larson, L., and Levi, L. *Some Things You Need to Know before the World Ends (A Final Evening with the Illuminati)* 1
Machado, E. *In the Eye of the Hurricane* 1
Martin, J. *Cementville* 2
Norman, M. *Trudy Blue* 2
Reilly, C. *Astronauts* 1
Strand, R. *The Death of Zukasky* 2
Taylor, R. *Watermelon Rinds* 2

DIXP Dixon, Michael Bigelow, and Kathleen Chopin, eds. *Plays from Actors Theatre of Louisville*. New York: Broadway Play Publishing Inc., 1989. 406pp.
Congdon, C. *Tales of the Lost Formicans*
Henley, B. *Crimes of the Heart*
Hill, G. *Food from Trash*
Martin, J. *Coup/clucks*
Mastrosimone, W. *The Undoing*
Norman, M. *Getting Out*

DIYL DiYanni, Robert, ed. *Literature: Reading Fiction, Poetry, and Drama*. Compact ed. New York: McGraw-Hill, 2000. 1482pp.
Glaspell, S. *Trifles*
Gregory, I. *The Rising of the Moon*
Hansberry, L. *A Raisin in the Sun*
Ibsen, H. *A Doll's House*
López, J. *Simply Maria*
McNally, T. *Andre's Mother*
Miller, A. *Death of a Salesman*
Shakespeare, W. *Hamlet, Prince of Denmark*
Shakespeare, W. *The Tragedy of Othello*
Sophocles. *Antigone*
Sophocles. *Oedipus Rex*
Synge, J. *Riders to the Sea*
Wasserstein, W. *Tender Offer*
Wilson, A. *Fences*

DIYLA DiYanni, Robert, ed. *Literature: Reading Fiction, Poetry, Drama, and the Essay*. New York: Random House, 1986. 1563pp.
Bolt, R. *A Man for All Seasons*
Chekhov, A. *The Cherry Orchard*
Glaspell, S. *Suppressed Desires*
Gregory, I. *The Rising of the Moon*

Ibsen, H. *A Doll's House*
Ionesco, E. *The Lesson*
Miller, A. *Death of a Salesman*
Molière, J. *Tartuffe*
Shakespeare, W. *Othello*
Shaw, G. *Arms and the Man*
Sophocles. *Antigone*
Sophocles. *Oedipus Rex*
Strindberg, A. *The Father*

DIYLB DiYanni, Robert, ed. *Literature: Reading Fiction,*
    *Poetry, Drama, and the Essay.* 2nd ed. New York:
    McGraw-Hill, 1990. 1746pp.
    Bolt, R. *A Man for All Seasons*
    Chekhov, A. *The Cherry Orchard*
    Glaspell, S. *Trifles*
    Gregory, I. *The Rising of the Moon*
    Hansberry, L. *A Raisin in the Sun*
    Ibsen, H. *A Doll's House*
    Ionesco, E. *The Lesson*
    Luce, C. *Slam the Door Softly*
    Miller, A. *Death of a Salesman*
    Molière, J. *Tartuffe*
    Shakespeare, W. *The Tragedy of Othello*
    Shaw, G. *Arms and the Man*
    Sophocles. *Antigone*
    Sophocles. *Oedipus Rex*
    Yeats, W. *Purgatory*

DIYLC DiYanni, Robert, ed. *Literature: Reading Fiction,*
    *Poetry, Drama, and the Essay.* 3rd ed. New York:
    McGraw-Hill, 1994. 1777pp.
    Chekhov, A. *The Cherry Orchard*
    Glaspell, S. *Trifles*
    Gregory, I. *The Rising of the Moon*
    Hansberry, L. *A Raisin in the Sun*
    Ibsen, H. *A Doll's House*
    Ionesco, E. *The Lesson*
    Miller, A. *Death of a Salesman*
    Molière, J. *Tartuffe*
    Shakespeare, W. *As You like It*
    Shakespeare, W. *The Tragedy of Othello*
    Shaw, G. *Arms and the Man*
    Sophocles. *Antigone*
    Sophocles. *Oedipus Rex*
    Strindberg, A. *The Stronger*
    Synge, J. *Riders to the Sea*
    Wasserstein, W. *The Man in the Case*
    Williams, T. *The Glass Menagerie*
    Wilson, A. *Fences*

DIYLD DiYanni, Robert, ed. *Literature: Reading Fiction,*
    *Poetry, Drama, and the Essay.* 4th ed. New York:
    McGraw-Hill, 1998. 2036pp.

Dockery, M. *Oh, that Wiley Snake!*
Glaspell, S. *Trifles*
Gregory, I. *The Rising of the Moon*
Hansberry, L. *A Raisin in the Sun*
Howe, T. *Painting Churches*
Ibsen, H. *A Doll's House*
Ionesco, E. *The Lesson*
López, J. *Simply Maria*
McNally, T. *Andre's Mother*
Mamet, D. *Oleanna*
Miller, A. *Death of a Salesman*
Molière, J. *Tartuffe*
Shakespeare, W. *Hamlet, Prince of Denmark*
Shakespeare, W. *The Tragedy of Othello*
Shaw, G. *Arms and the Man* (Scene II only)
Sophocles. *Antigone*
Sophocles. *Oedipus Rex*
Synge, J. *Riders to the Sea*
Wasserstein, W. *Tender Offer*
Wilson, A. *Fences*

DIYRD DiYanni, Robert, ed. *Reading Drama: An*
    *Anthology of Plays.* New York: Macmillan/
    McGraw-Hill School Publishing Company, 1990.
    655pp.
    Chekhov, A. *A Marriage Proposal*
    Glaspell, S. *Trifles*
    Gregory, I. *The Rising of the Moon*
    Hansberry, L. *A Raisin in the Sun*
    Ibsen, H. *An Enemy of the People*
    Ionesco, E. *The Gap*
    Miller, A. *A View from the Bridge*
    Molière, J. *The Doctor in Spite of Himself*
    Shakespeare, W. *The Tragedy of Macbeth*
    Shepard, S. *True West*
    Sophocles. *Antigone*
    Strindberg, A. *The Stronger*
    Synge, J. *Riders to the Sea*
    Williams, T. *The Glass Menagerie*
    Yeats, W. *Purgatory*

DOA Dobrée, Bonamy, ed. *Five Heroic Plays.* London:
    Oxford University Press, 1960. 417pp.
    Crowne, J. *The Destruction of Jerusalem*
    Dryden, J. *Aureng-zebe*
    Lee, N. *Sophonisba*
    Orrery, R. *The Tragedy of Mustapha, the Son of*
        *Solyman the Magnificent*
    Settle, E. *The Empress of Morocco*

DOB Dobrée, Bonamy, ed. *Five Restoration Tragedies.*
    London: Oxford University Press [1928] 450pp.
    (The World's Classics)
    Addison, J. *Cato*
    Dryden, J. *All for Love*

Otway, T. *Venice Preserv'd*
Rowe, N. *The Fair Penitent*
Southerne, T. *Oroonoko*

DODGE Dodge, Richard H., and Lindblom, Peter D.,
 compilers. *Of Time and Experience: Literary
 Themes*. Cambridge, MA: Winthrop Publishers,
 1972. 725pp.
Chayefsky, P. *Marty*
Dolan, H. *Losers Weepers*
Lowell, R. *My Kinsman, Major Molineaux*
Richardson, J. *Gallows Humor*
Shaw, G. *Arms and the Man*

DODGS Dodgson, Elyse, ed. *First Lines: Young Writers
 at the Royal Court*. London: Hodder & Stoughton,
 1990. 149pp.
Duggan, S. *William*
Harvey, J. *Mohair*
Jintan, S. *Lalita's Way*
Swain, E. *Half Return*

DODGSG Dodgson, Elyse, ed. *German Plays: New
 Drama from a Changing Country*. London: Nick
 Hearn Books in association with the Goethe-Institut
 and the Royal Court Theatre. 1997. 234pp.
Langhoff, A. *The Table Laid*
Loher, D. *Stranger's House*
Pohl, K. *Waiting Room Germany*
Rust, D. *Jennifer Klemm*

DODGSP Dodgson, Elyse, ed. *German Plays 2*. London:
 Nick Hearn Books in association with the Goethe-
 Institut and the Royal Court Theatre. 1999. 208pp.
Bukowski, O. *Jamaica ('Til Denver)*
Marber, A. *Parrots' Lies*
Schneider, S. *Malaria*
Schwab, W. *Holy Mothers*

DODGSS Dodgson, Elyse, and Peate, Mary, eds. *Spanish
 Plays: New Spanish and Catalan Drama*. London:
 Nick Hearn Books in association with the British
 Council. 1999. 288pp.
Belbel, S. *Caresses*
Cunille, L. *Roundabout*
Mayorga, J. *The Scorched Garden*
Onetti, A. *Bleeding Heart*
Pedrero, P. *Wolf Kisses*
Planell, D. *Bazaar*

DODS Dodson, Daniel Boone, comp. *Twelve Modern
 Plays*. Belmont, CA: Wadsworth Publishers, 1970.
 471pp.
Anouilh, J. *Antigone*
Brecht, B. *The Good Woman of Setzuan*

Chekhov, A. *The Three Sisters*
García Lorca, F. *The House of Bernarda Alba*
Giraudoux, J. *Tiger at the Gates*
Hellman, L. *The Little Foxes*
Ibsen, H. *The Wild Duck*
Miller, A. *The Crucible*
Pirandello, L. *Henry IV*
Shaw, G. *Heartbreak House*
Strindberg, A. *Miss Julie*
Synge, J. *The Playboy of the Western World*

DOLAN Dolan, Paul J., and Dolan, Grace M., eds.
 *Introduction to Drama*. New York: Wiley, 1974.
 642pp.
Chekhov, A. *The Cherry Orchard*
Ibsen, H. *An Enemy of the People*
Jones, L. *Dutchman*
Lowell, R. *Benito Cereno*
Molière, J. *The Misanthrope*
Pirandello, L. *Henry IV*
Racine, J. *Phaedre*
*The Second Shepherds' Play*
Shakespeare, W. *Othello*
Shaw, G. *Saint Joan*
Sophocles. *Antigone*
Sophocles. *Oedipus*
Strindberg, A. *Miss Julie*
Yeats, W. *Purgatory*

DOOL Doolittle, Joyce, ed. *Heroines: Three Plays*. Red
 Deer, AB: Red Deer College Press, 1992. 191pp.
Murrell, J. *Memoir*
Pollock, S. *Getting It Straight*
Tremblay, M. *Hosanna*

DOUC Doucette, L. E., ed. *The Drama of our Past: Major
 Plays from Nineteenth-Century Quebec*. Toronto:
 University of Toronto Press, 1997. 327pp.
*Archibald Cameron of Locheill, or an Episode in the
 Seven Year's War in Canada.*
Frechette, L. *Félix Poutré*
Petitclair, P. *A Country Outing*
Petitclair, P. *The Donation*
Quesnel, J. *Anglomania, or Dinner, English Style*
The *Status Quo* comedies, 5 playlets: the first *Status
 Quo* comedy, the second *Status Quo* comedy, the
 third *Status Quo* comedy, the fourth *Status Quo*
 comedy, the fifth *Status Quo* comedy

DOWM Downer, Alan S., ed. *American Drama*. New
 York: Thomas Y. Crowell [c1960] 261pp.
 (American Literary Forms)
Herne, J. *Shore Acres*
Moody, W. *The Great Divide*
O'Neill, E. *The Hairy Ape*

Sherwood, R. *The Petrified Forest*
Tyler, R. *The Contrast*
Wilder, T. *The Long Christmas Dinner*
Williams, T. *The Glass Menagerie*

DOWN Downer, Alan S. *The Art of the Play*. New York:
    Henry Holt [c1955] 451pp.
Aeschylus. *Prometheus Bound*
Chekhov, A. *The Sea-gull*
Ibsen, H. *Ghosts*
Marlowe, C. *Doctor Faustus*
Molière, J. *Tartuffe*
O'Neill, E. *The Emperor Jones*
Shakespeare, W. *Antony and Cleopatra*
Sophocles. *Oedipus Rex*
Vega Carpio, L. *Fuente ovejuna*

DOWS Downer, Seymour, ed. *Great World Theatre: An
    Introduction to Drama*. New York: Harper & Row
    [1964] 867pp.
Chekhov, A. *The Three Sisters*
Euripides. *The Bacchae*
*Everyman*
Ibsen, H. *Solness, the Master Builder*
Giraudoux, J. *Tiger at the Gates*
Goldsmith, O. *She Stoops to Conquer*
Miller, A. *A View from the Bridge*
Molière, J. *The Misanthrope*
Pirandello, A. *Six Characters in Search of an Author*
Plautus, T. *The Little Ghost*
Shudraka. *The Toy Cart*
Sophocles. *Antigone*
Webster, J. *The Duchess of Malfi*
Wilder, T. *The Skin of Our Teeth*

DPR *Drama of the English Renaissance*. Edited by Russell
    A. Fraser and Norman C. Rabkin. New York:
    Macmillan, 1976. 2 vols. (Vol.1, Tudor period;
    Vol. 2, Stuart period)
*Arden of Feversham* 1
Beaumont, F., and Fletcher, J. *A King and No King* 2
Beaumont, F., and Fletcher, J. *The Knight of the Burning
    Pestle* 2
Chapman, G. *Bussy D'Ambois* 2
Chapman, G. *The Widow's Tears* 2
Dekker, T., and Middleton, T. *The Roaring Girl* 2
Dekker, T. *The Shoemakers' Holiday* 1
Fletcher, J. *The Wild-goose Chase* 2
Ford, J. *Perkin Warbeck* 2
Ford, J. *'Tis a Pity She's a Whore* 2
Gascoigne, G. *Supposes* 1
Greene, R. *Friar Bacon and Friar Bungay* 1
Heywood, J. *The Four pp* 1
Heywood, T. *A Woman Killed with Kindness* 1
Jonson, B. *The Alchemist* 2

Jonson, B. *Bartholomew Fair* 2
Jonson, B. *Epicoene* 2
Jonson, B. *Volpone* 2
Kyd, T. *Spanish Tragedy* 1
Lodge, T., and Greene, R. *A Looking Glass for London
    and England* 1
Lyly, J. *Gallathea* 1
Marlowe, C. *The Jew of Malta* 1
Marlowe, C. *Tamburlaine the Great, Part 1 and Part 2*
    1
Marlowe, C. *The Tragical History of Doctor Faustus* 1
Marlowe, C. *The Troublesome Reign and Lamentable
    Death of Edward the Second* 1
Marston, J. *The Dutch Courtesan* 2
Massinger, P. *A New Way to Pay Old Debts* 2
Massinger, P. *The Roman Actor* 2
Middleton, T. *A Chaste Maid in Cheapside* 2
Middleton, T., and Rowley, W. *The Changeling* 2
*Mucedorus* 1
Nashe, T. *Summer's Last Will and Testament* 1
Peele, G. *David and Bethsabe* 1
Preston, T. *Cambyses* 1
Sackville, T., and Norton, T. *Gorboduc* 1
Shirley, J. *Hyde Park* 2
Stevenson, W. *Gammer Gurton's Needle* 1
Tourneur, C. *The Revenger's Tragedy* 2
Webster, J. *The Duchess of Malfi* 2
Webster, J. *The White Devil* 2

DRAC *Drama Contemporary Czechoslovakia*. Plays by
    Milan Kundera, Václav Havel, Pavel Kohout,
    Milan Uhde, Pavel Landovský, Ivan Klíma.
    Edited with an introduction by Marketa Goetz-
    Stankiewicz. New York: Performing Arts Journal
    Publications, 1985. 224pp.
Havel, V. *Protest*
Klíma, I. *Games*
Kohout, P. *Fire in the Basement*
Kundera, M. *Jacques and His Master*
Landovský, P. *The Detour*
Uhde, M. *A Blue Angel*

DRAD *Dramatic Masterpieces by Greek, Spanish, French,
    German and English Dramatists*. With a special
    introduction by Albert Ellery Bergh. Rev. ed.
    New York: Collier [c1900] 2 vols. (The World's
    Greatest Literature)
Aeschylus. *Prometheus Bound* 1
Aristophanes. *The Knights* 1
Calderón de la Barca, P. *Life Is a Dream* 1
Euripides. *Medea* 1
Goethe, J. *Faust* 2
Goldsmith, O. *She Stoops to Conquer* 1
Ibsen, H. *A Doll's House* 2
Molière, J. *The Misanthrope* 1

Racine, J. *Phaedra* 1
Sardou, V. *Les pattes de mouche* 2
Schiller, F. *Mary Stuart* 2
Sophocles. *Oedipus Rex* 1
Sheridan, R. *The Rivals* 2

DRAF *Dramatic Representations of Filial Piety: Five Noh in Translation.* With an introduction by Mae J. Smethurst. Ithaca, NY: East Asia Program, Cornell University, 1998. 172pp. (Number 97 in the Cornell East Asia Series)
*Dampu*
*Nakamitsu*
*Nishikido*
*Shichikiochi*
*Shun'ei*

DRON Dronke, Peter, ed. *Nine Medieval Latin Plays.* Cambridge, England; and New York: Cambridge University Press, 1994. 237pp.
*Danielis ludus*
*Hildegard of Bingen. Ordo virtutum*
*Ludus de passione*
*Officium stele*
*Sponsus*
*Tres clerici*
*Tres filie*
*Verses pascales de tres Maries*
*Versus de pelegrino*

DRU Drummond, Alexander Magnus, and Gard, Robert E., eds. *The Lake Guns of Seneca and Cayuga and Eight Other Plays of Upstate New York.* Port Washington, NY: Kennikat Press, 1972. 273pp. (Reprint)
Baker, E., and Drummond, A. *A Day in the Vineyard*
Drummond, A. *The Lake Guns of Seneca and Cayuga*
Gard, R. *Let's Get On with the Marrin'*
Gard, R. *Raisin' the Devil*
Gard, R. *Mixing Up the Rent*
Kamarck, E. *Chenango Crone*
O'Connell, L. *Donalds O'Rourk*
Thurston, E. *Family Cooperative*
Williams, L. *Over Fourteen: and Single*

DRUR Drury, Martin, ed. *Three Team Plays.* Dublin: Wolfhound Press, 1988. 223pp.
Farrell, B. *Then Moses Met Marconi*
McArdle, J. *Jacko*
McGuinness, F. *Borderlands*

DUC Duckworth, George Eckel, ed. *The Complete Roman Drama.* New York: Random House [c1942] 2 vols.
Plautus. *Amphytryon* 1
Plautus. *The Braggart Warrior* 1

Plautus. *The Captives* 1
Plautus. *The Carthaginian* 1
Plautus. *Casina* 1
Plautus. *The Casket* 1
Plautus. *The Comedy of Asses* 1
Plautus. *Curculio* 1
Plautus. *Epidicus* 1
Plautus. *The Girl from Persia* 1
Plautus. *The Haunted House* 1
Plautus. *The Merchant* 1
Plautus. *The Pot of Gold* 1
Plautus. *Pseudolus* 1
Plautus. *The Rope* 1
Plautus. *Stichus* 2
Plautus. *The Three Penny Day* 2
Plautuu. *Truculentus* 2
Plautus. *The Twin Menaechmi* 1
Plautus. *The Two Bacchides* 1
*Querolus* 2
Seneca. *Agamemnon* 2
Seneca. *Hercules on Oeta* 2
Seneca. *Mad Hercules* 2
Seneca. *Medea* 2
Seneca. *Octavia* 2
Seneca. *Oedipus* 2
Seneca. *Phaedra* 2
Seneca. *The Phoenician Women* 2
Seneca. *Thyestes* 2
Seneca. *The Trojan Women* 2
Terence. *The Brothers* 2
Terence. *The Eunuch* 2
Terence. *The Mother-in-law* 2
Terence. *Phormio* 2
Terence. *The Self-tormentor* 2
Terence. *The Woman of Andros* 2

DUH Duhamel, Pierre Albert and Hughes, Richard E., eds. *Literature: Form and Function.* Englewood Cliffs, NJ: Prentice-Hall, 1965. 634pp.
Chekhov, A. *The Cherry Orchard*
Goldsmith, O. *She Stoops to Conquer*
Shakespeare, W. *Richard II*
Sophocles. *Oedipus Rex*

DUK Dukore, Bernard F., and Gerould, Daniel C., eds. *Avant Garde Drama: A Casebook, 1918–1939.* New York: Thomas Y. Crowell, 1976. 592pp. (Originally published by Bantam in 1969 as *Avant-Garde Drama: Major Plays and Documents Post World War I*)
Brecht, B. *St. Joan of the Stockyards*
Cummings, E. *him*
Ghelderode, M. *Chronicles of Hell*
Olesha, Y. *The Conspiracy of Feelings*
Pirandello, L. *Each in His Own Way*

Toller, E. *Man and the Masses*
Witkiewicz, S. *The Water Hen*

DUN Dunn, Esther Cloudman, ed. *Eight Famous
        Elizabethan Plays*. New York: Modern Library
        [1932] 721pp.
    Beaumont, F., and Fletcher, J. *The Maid's Tragedy*
    Dekker, T. *The Shoemakers' Holiday*
    Ford, J. *'Tis a Pity She's a Whore*
    Heywood, T. *A Woman Killed with Kindness*
    Jonson, B. *Volpone; or, the Fox*
    Marlowe, C. *The Tragical History of Doctor Faustus*
    Massinger, P. *A New Way to Pay Old Debts*
    Webster, J. *The Duchess of Malfi*

DUP Duran, Lee, tr. *Plays of Old Japan*. Folcroft, PA:
        Folcro Library Editions, 1973. 127pp. (Reprint)
    *The Daimyo*
    *Forsaken Love*
    *The Hands in the Box*
    *The Honor of Danzo*
    *The Horns*

DUR Durham, Willard Higley, and Dodds, John W., eds.
        *British and American Plays. 1830–1945*. New
        York: Oxford University Press, 1947. 796pp.
    Anderson, M. *Winterset*
    Barrie, J. *The Admirable Crichton*
    Bulwer-Lytton, E. *Richelieu*
    Carroll, P. *Shadow and Substance*
    Connelly, M. *The Green Pastures*
    Ervine, St. J. *John Ferguson*
    Galsworthy, J. *Strife*
    Ibsen, H. *An Enemy of the People*
    Jones, H. *The Liars*
    Kaufman, G., and Ryskind, M. *Of Thee I Sing*
    Maugham, W. *The Circle*
    O'Casey, S. *Juno and the Paycock*
    Odets, C. *Waiting for Lefty*
    O'Neill, E. *The Great God Brown*
    Pinero, A. *The Second Mrs. Tanqueray*
    Rice, E. *The Adding Machine*
    Robertson, T. *Caste*
    Sherwood, R. *There Shall Be No Night*
    Synge, J. *The Playboy of the Western World*
    Yeats, W. *Cathleen ni Houlihan*

DUSE, ELEONORA. See SAY Sayler, Oliver Martin, ed.
    *The Eleonora Duse Series of Plays*.

EAG Eagleton, Sandra, compiler. *Women in Literature:
        Life Stages through Stories, Poems, and Plays*.
        Englewood Cliffs, NJ: Prentice Hall, 1988. 472pp.
    Gerstenberg, A. *Overtones*

Glaspell, S. *Trifles*
Hayes, C. *Not Waving*
Molinaro, U. *Breakfast Past Noon*

EAVE Eaves, Thomas Cary Duncan, and Kimpe, Ben D.,
        eds. *The Informal Reader*. New York: Appleton-
        Century-Crofts [c1955] 743pp.
    Shaw, G. *Pygmalion*

EDAD Edades, Jean, and Fosdick, Carolyn E., eds. *Drama
        of the East and West*. Manila: Bookman, 1956.
        656pp.
    Alvarez Quintero, S., and Alvarez Quintero, J. *A Sunny
        Morning*
    Chekhov, A. *The Cherry Orchard*
    Euripides. *Medea*
    Guerrero, W. *Forever*
    Ibsen, H. *A Doll's House*
    Joaquín, N. *A Portrait of the Artist as Filipino*
    Kalidisa. *Shakuntala*
    Molière, J. *The Misanthrope*
    Montano, S. *Sabina*
    Palarca, J. *Other Tomorrows*
    Plautus. *The Menaechmi*
    Shakespeare, W. *Romeo and Juliet*
    Shaw, I. *Bury the Dead*
    Sicam, G., and Casiño, J. *Mir-i-nisa*
    *The Sorrows of Han*
    Villa, L. *Educating Josefina*
    Wilde, O. *The Importance of Being Earnest*
    Wilder, T. *Our Town*
    Williams, E. *The Corn Is Green*

EDMON Edmonson, Munro S., ed. *Quiché Dramas and
        Divinatory Calendars*. New Orleans: Middle
        American Research Institute, Tulane University,
        1997. 171pp. (Publication # 66: Parallel Columns
        in English and Quiché, a Maya Dialect of Spanish)
    *The Bull Dance*
    Zaqi Q'oxol and Cortés: *The Conquest of Mexico*

EIG *Eight Chinese Plays: From the 13th Century to
        the Present*. Translated with an introduction by
        William Dolby. New York: Columbia University
        Press, 1978. 164pp.
    *Buying Rouge*
    *Grandee's Son Takes the Wrong Career*
    *Hegemon King Says Farewell to His Queen*
    *Identifying Footprints in the Snow*
    Liang, C. *Washing Silk*
    Liu, T. *Cai Shun Shares the Mulberries*
    Shi, J. *Qiu Hu Tries to Seduce His Own Wife*
    Wang, J. *Wolf of Mount Zhong*

EIGH *Eighteenth-Century Plays*, with an introduction by
    Ricardo Quintana. New York: Modern Library
    [c1952] 484pp.
  Addison, J. *Cato*
  Fielding, H. *The Tragedy of Tragedies*
  Gay, J. *The Beggar's Opera*
  Goldsmith, O. *She Stoops to Conquer*
  Lillo, G. *The London Merchant*
  Rowe, N. *The Tragedy of Jane Shore*
  Sheridan, R. *The Rivals*
  Steele, R. *The Conscious Lovers*

EIGHT *Eight Plays for Theatre*. Edited and with
    introductions by Robert Cohen. Mountain View,
    CA: Mayfield Publishing Company, 1988. 275pp.
  Beckett, S. *Happy Days*
  Chekhov, A. *The Three Sisters*
  Molière, J. *The Bourgeois Gentleman*
  *The Plaie Called Corpus Christi Part I: The Beginnings*
  Shakespeare, W. *Romeo and Juliet*
  Shepard, S. *Fool for Love*
  Sophocles. *Oedipus Tyrannos*
  Strindberg, A. *Miss Julie*

EIGHTRP *Eight Twentieth-Century Russian Plays*.
    Edited, translated from the Russian, and with an
    introduction by Timothy Langen and Justin Weir.
    Evanston, IL: Northwestern University Press, 2000.
    354pp.
  Ardov, V. *The Case of the Entry Room*
  Blok, A. *The Unknown Woman*
  Gippius, Z. *Sacred Blood*
  Kataev, V. *Squaring the Circle*
  Kharms, D. *Elizaveta Bam*
  Kirshon, V. *Grain*
  Mayakovsky, V. *Vladimir Mayakovsky: A Tragedy*
  Zorin, L. *The Guests*

ELAM Elam, Harry J., and Alexander, Robert. *Colored
    Contradictions: An Anthology of African-American
    Plays*. New York: Plume Books, 1996. 643pp.
  Alexander, R. *I Ain't Yo' Uncle*
  Brown, C. *The Little Tommy Parker Celebrated Colored
    Minstrel Show*
  Corbitt, W. *Crying Holy*
  Corthron, K. *Come Down Burning*
  Dickerson, G., and Clarke, B. *Re/membering Aunt
    Jemima: A Menstrual Show*
  Jones, R. *Big Butt Girls, Hard-headed Women*
  Mason, K. *for black boys who have considered homicide
    when the streets were too much*
  Parks, S. *Imperceptible Mutabilities in the Third
    Kingdom*
  Pomo Afro Homos. *Fierce Love*

  West, C. *Before It Hits Home*
  Wilks, T. *Tod, the Boy, Tod*
  Youngblood, S. *Shakin' the Mess Outta Misery*

THE ELEONORA DUSE SERIES OF PLAYS. See SAY
  Sayler, Oliver Martin, ed.

ELEVEN PLAYS OF THE GREEK DRAMATISTS. See
  PLAG *Plays of the Greek Dramatists*.

ELIOT, CHARLES W. See HARC *Harvard Classics*.

ELIZABETHAN DRAMA. See HARC *Harvard Classics,
  v46–47*

ELK Elkins, William R., and Others, compilers. *Literary
    Reflections*. New York: McGraw, 1967. 757pp.
  Shakespeare, W. *Antony and Cleopatra*
  Sophocles. *Oedipus Rex*
  Williams, T. *The Glass Menagerie*

ELKE Elkins, William R., and Others, compilers. *Literary
    Reflections*. 3rd ed. New York: McGraw, 1976.
    501pp.
  Anouilh, J. *Antigone*
  O'Neill, E. *Bound East for Cardiff*
  Saroyan, W. *Hello Out There*
  Wilder, T. *Pullman Car Hiawatha*

ELLI Ellis, Harold Milton; Pound, Louise; and Spohn,
    George Weida, eds. *A College Book of American
    Literature*. New York: American Book Co. [c1939]
    2 vols.
  Boker, G. *Francesca da Rimini* 1
  O'Neill, E. *The Rope* 2
  Tyler, R. *The Contrast* 1

ELLK Ellis, Harold Milton; Pound, Louise; Spohn, George
    Weida; and Hoffman, Frederick J., eds. *A College
    Book of American Literature*. 2nd ed. New York:
    American Book Co. [c1949] 1107pp.
  O'Neill, E. *The Emperor Jones*

ELLIS, HAVELOCK. See NER Nero (Tragedy); *Nero and
  Other Plays*.

ELLM Ellis, Roger, ed. *Multicultural Theatre II:
    Contemporary Hispanic, Asian, and African-
    American Plays*. Colorado Springs, CO:
    Meriwether Publishing, Ltd., 1998. 380pp.
  Bush, M. *Ezigbo, the Spirit Child*
  Cheng, K. *The China Crisis*
  Cruz, N. *Night Train to Bolina*
  Felder, L. *The Magic Kingdom*

Gonzalez S., S. *The Migrant Farmworker's Son*
Graham, N. *The Basement at the Bottom at the End of
     the World*
Huie, K. *Yasuko and the Young s-s-samurai*
Rivera, J. *Maricela de la Luz Lights the World*
Smith, C. *Takunda*
Wong, E. *Letters to a Student Revolutionary*

EMB *Embassy Successes*. London: Sampson, Low,
     Marston [1946–1948] 3 vols.
Bagnold, E. *National Velvet* 2
Delderfield, R. *Peace Comes to Peckham* 3
Delderfield, R. *Worm's Eye View* 1
Doherty, B. *Father Malachy's Miracle* 1
Gielgud, V. *Away from It All* 3
Hartog, J. *Skipper Next to God* 2
Hay, I. *"Let My People Go!"* 3
Pollock, R. *Zoo in Silesia* 1
Temple, J. *No Room at the Inn* 2

ENC *Enclosure: A Collection of Plays*. Edited by Robert
     J. Nelson and Gerald Weales. New York: McKay,
     1975. 282pp.
García Lorca, F. *The House of Bernarda Alba*
Odets, C. *Awake and Sing!*
Racine, J. *Athaliah*
Wycherley, W. *The Country Wife*

ENG England, Alan Wilham, ed. *Two Ages of Man*.
     Edinburgh: Oliver and Boyd, 1971. 206pp.
Cooper, G. *Unman, Wittering and Zigo*
Kaiser, G. *The Raft of Medusa*
Leonard, H. *Stephen D*
Shaffer, P. *The Private Ear*

ENGLISH MASTERPIECES. v2. See DEAN Dear,
     Leonard, ed. *Elizabethan Drama: vol. 5*. See MACI
     Mack, Maynard, ed. *The Augustans*

ENGE *English Mystery Plays: A Selection*. Edited by Peter
     Happé. Baltimore: Penguin, 1975. 713pp.
*Abraham and Isaac* (Brome)
*Abraham and Isaac* (Chester)
*The Adoration* (York)
*The Ascension* (Chester)
*The Assumption and coronation of the Virgin* (York)
*Balaam, Balak, and the Prophets* (Chester)
*Banns* (Chester)
*The Buffeting* (Towneley)
*Christ's Appearances to the Disciples* (N Town)
*The Creation, and Adam and Eve* (Chester)
*The Crucifixion* (York)
*The Death and Burial* (York)

*The Death of Herod* (N Town)
*The Dream of Pilate's Wife* (York
*The Fall of Lucifer* (Chester)
*The First Shepherds' Play* (Towneley)
*The Flight into Egypt* (Towneley
*The Harrowing of Hell* (York)
*John the Baptist* (York)
*Joseph* (N Town)
*Judgement Day* (York)
*The Killing of Abel* (Towneley)
*Lazarus* (Towneley)
*Moses* (York)
*The Nativity* (N Town)
*Noah* (Chester)
*Noah* (Towneley)
*The Parliament of Heaven, the Salutation and
     Conception* (N Town)
*The Passion Play I: The Council of the Jews; The Last
     Supper; The Betrayal* (N Town)
*Pentecost* (York)
*The Purification, and Christ with the Doctors* (Chester)
*The Resurrection* (Towneley)
*The Scourging* (Towneley)
*The Second Shepherds' Play* (Towneley)
*The Shearmen and Tailors' Play* (Coventry)
*The Temptation of Christ, and the Woman Taken in
     Adultery* (Chester)
*The Three Kings* (introduction to) (York)

ENGL *English Romantic Drama: An Anthology, the Major
     Romantics*. Edited by Charles J. Clancy. Norwood,
     1976. 414pp.
Blake, W. *The Ghost of Abel*
Blake, W. *King Richard the Third*
Byron, G. *Cain*
Byron, G. *Manfred*
Byron, G. *Sardanapalus*
Coleridge, S. *Remorse*
Keats, J. *King Stephen*
Keats, J., and Brown, C. *Otho the Great*
Shelley, P. *The Cenci*
Shelley, P. *Prometheus Unbound*
Wordsworth, W. *The Borderers*

ENGLMI *English Romantic Drama: An Anthology, the
     Minor Romantics*. Edited by Charles J. Clancy.
     Norwood, 1978. 315pp.
Baillie, J. *De Monfort*
Beddoes, T. *Death's Jest Book, or, the Fool's Tragedy*
Lamb, C. *John Woodvil*
Scott, W. *Halidon Hill*
Southey, R. *Wat Tyler*
Wilson, J. *The City of the Plague*

ERN Ernst, Earle, ed. *Three Japanese Plays from the Traditional Theatre*. Westport, CT: Greenwood, 1976. 199pp.
  Kanze, K. *The Maple Viewing*
  Kawatake, M. *Benten the Thief*
  Takeda, I.; Miyoshi, S.; and Namiki, S. *The House of Sugawara*

ESA *The Essential Self: An Introduction to Literature*. Edited by Paul Berry. New York: McGraw, 1976. 439pp.
  Gardner, H. *A Thousand Clowns*
  *In an Oval Office* (from the Watergate transcripts)
  Sophocles. *King Oedipus*

ESS Esslin, Martin, ed. *The Genius of the German Theater*. New York: New American Library, 1968. 638pp.
  Brecht, B. *The Caucasian Chalk Circle*
  Büchner, G. *Leonce and Lena*
  Goethe, J. *Faust, a Tragedy, Part I*
  Kleist, H. *Prince Frederick of Homburg*
  Lessing, G. *Emilia Galotti*
  Schiller, J. *The Death of Wallenstein*
  Wedekind, F. *King Nicolo; or, Such Is Life*

ETO Evans, Herbert A., ed. *English Masques*. Norwood, 1976. 245pp.
  Beaumont, F. *Masque of the Inner-Temple and Gray's Inn*
  Campion, T. *Lords' Masque*
  Daniel, S. *Vision of the Twelve Goddesses*
  D'Avenant, W. *Salmacida spolia*
  Jonson, B. *Fortunate Isles, and Their Union*
  Jonson, B. *Golden Age Restored*
  Jonson, B. *Lovers Made Men*
  Jonson, B. *Masque at Lord Haddington's Marriage*
  Jonson, B. *Masque of Augurs*
  Jonson, B. *Masque of Queens*
  Jonson, B. *Neptune's Triumph for the Return of Albion*
  Jonson, B. *News from the New World Discovered in the Moon*
  Jonson, B. *Oberon*
  Jonson, B. *Pan's Anniversary, or the Shepherd's Holyday*
  *The Masque of Flowers*
  Shirley, J. *Triumph of Peace*

EUP Evans, Sian, and Robson, Cheryl, eds. *Eastern Promise: Seven Plays from Central and Eastern Europe*. London: Aurora Metro Press, 1999. 311pp.
  Filo, V. *Tulip Doctor*
  Kofta, K. *The Umbilical Cord*
  Nelega, A. *Nascendo*
  Popova, E. *The Chosen Ones*

  Preissova, G. *Janufa (Her Step-daughter)*
  Srbljanovic, B. *Belgrade Trilogy*
  Vujovic, S. *The Tender Mercies*

EVA Everett, Edwin Mallard; Brown, Calvin S.; and Wade, John D., eds. *Masterworks of World Literature*. New York: Dryden Press [c1947] 2 vols.
  Euripides. *Medea* 1
  Goethe, J. *Faust, Part I* 2
  Ibsen, H. *An Enemy of the People* 2
  Molière, J. *Tartuffe* 2
  Racine, J. *Phaedra* 2
  Shakespeare, W. *Romeo and Juliet* 2
  Sophocles. *Antigone* 1
  Sophocles. *Oedipus the King* 1

EVB Everett, Edwin Mallard; Brown, Calvin S.; and Wade, John D., eds. *Masterworks of World Literature*. Rev. ed. New York: Dryden [c1955] 2 vols.
  Aeschylus. *Agamemnon* 1
  Euripides. *Medea* 1
  Goethe, J. *Faust, Part I* 2
  Ibsen, H. *An Enemy of the People* 2
  Molière, J. *Tartuffe* 2
  Racine, J. *Phaedra* 2
  Shakespeare, W. *Romeo and Juliet* 2
  Sophocles. *Antigone* 1
  Sophocles. *Oedipus the King* 1

EVC Everett, Edwin Mallard, and Others, ed. *Masterworks of World Literature*. 3rd ed. New York: Holt, Rinehart, and Winston, 1970. 2 vols.
  Aeschylus. *Agamemnon* 1
  Aristophanes. *Lysistrata* 1
  Euripides. *Medea* 1
  Goethe, J. *Faust* 2
  Molière, J. *Tartuffe* 2
  Racine, J. *Phaedra* 2
  Shakespeare, W. *Antony and Cleopatra* 2
  Sophocles. *Oedipus the King* 1

EVEM *Everyman and Other Miracle and Morality Plays*. New York: Dover Publications, Inc., 1995. 88pp.
  *Everyman*
  *Hickscorner*
  *Noah's Flood*
  *The Second Shepherds' Play*

EVEP *Everyman and Other Plays*. London: Chapman and Hall, 1925. 201pp.
  *Everyman*
  *The Nativity* (Wakefield)
  *The Shepherds' Play*

EVER *"Everyman," with Other Interludes, Including Eight Miracle Plays.* London: Dent [1928] 198pp. (Everyman's Library)
*Abraham, Melchisedec, and Isaac*
Bale, J. *God's Promises*
*The Crucifixion*
*The Deluge*
*Everyman*
*The Harrowing of Hell*
*Mary Magdalene*
*Pageant of Shearmen and Taylors*
*St. George and the Dragon*
*Second Shepherds' Play*
*The Three Maries*

EXP *Expressionist Texts.* Edited by Mel Gordon. New York: PAJ Publications, 1986. 220pp.
Benn, G. *Ithaka*
Hasenclever, W. *The Son*
Kaiser, G. *From Morn to Midnight*
Kokoschka, O. *Sphinx and Strawman*
Schreyer, E. *Crucifixion*
Stramm, A. *Sancta Susanna*
Toller, E. *The Transfiguration*

FACES *Faces of African Independence: Three Plays.* Translated by Clive Wake. Introduction by Richard Bjornson. Charlottesville: University Press of Virginia, 1988. 127p
Badian, S. *The Death of Chaka*
Oyono-Mbia, G. *Three Suitors: One Husband*
Oyono-Mbia, G. *Until Further Notice*

FACO Faderman, Lillian, compiler. *Chloe Plus Olivia: An Anthology of Lesbian Literature from the Seventeenth Century to the Present.* New York: Viking, 1994. 812pp.
Chambers, J. *Last Summer at Bluefish Cove*

FAD Faderman, Lillian, and Bradshaw, Barbara, compilers. *Speaking for Ourselves: American Ethnic Writing.* 2nd ed. Glenview, IL: Scott Foresman, 1975. 625pp.
Davis, O. *Purlie Victorious*
Nemerov, H. *Cain*

FAIR Fairleigh, John, ed. *Far from the Land: New Irish Plays.* London: Methuen Drama, 1998. 340pp.
Carville, D. *Language Roulette*
McCabe, P. *Frank Pig Says Hello*
Morrison, C. *Hard to Believe*
O'Kelly, D. *Bat the Father Rabbit the Son*
Walsh, E. *Disco Pigs*
Woods, V. *At the Black Pig's Dyke*

FAL Falle, George C., ed. *Three Restoration Comedies.* London: Macmillan, 1964. 342pp.
Buckingham, G. *The Rehearsal*
Congreve, W. *The Way of the World*
Wycherley, W. *The Country Wife*

FALE *The Fallen Crown: Three French Mary Stuart Plays of the Seventeenth Century.* Introductory notes, critical comments, and editing, Michael G. Paulson. Washington: University Press of America, c1980. 199pp.
Boursault, E. *Marie Stuard, reine d'Ecosse*
Montchrestien, A. *La reine d'Ecosse*
Regnault, C. *Marie Stuard, reyne d'Ecosse*

FAM *Famous American Plays of the 1950s.* Selected and introduced by Lee Strasberg. New York: Dell, c1962. 415pp.
Albee, E. *The Zoo Story*
Anderson, R. *Tea and Sympathy*
Gazzo, M. *A Hatful of Rain*
Hellman, L. *The Autumn Garden*
Williams, T. *Camino Real*

FAMAB *Famous American Plays of the 1980s.* Selected and introduced by Robert Marx. New York: Dell, 1988. 520pp. (The Laurel Drama Series)
Feiffer, J. *Grown Ups*
Shawn, W. *Aunt Dan and Lemon*
Shepard, S. *Fool for Love*
Sondheim, S., and Lapine, J. *Sunday in the Park with George*
Wilson, A. *Ma Rainey's Black Bottom*

FAMAD *Famous American Plays of the 1970s.* With an introduction by Ted Hoffman. New York: Dell, 1981. 460pp. (The Laurel Drama Series)
Bullins, E. *The Taking of Miss Janie*
Innaurato, A. *Gemini*
Rabe, D. *The Basic Training of Pavlo Hummel*
Shepard, S. *Buried Child*
Slade, B. *Same Time, Next Year*
Weller, M. *Moonchildren*

FAMAF *Famous American Plays of the 1940s and 1950s.* Selected and introduced by Henry Hewes and Lee Strasberg. Garden City, NY: The Fireside Theatre, 1988. 608pp.
Albee, E. *The Zoo Story*
Anderson, M. *Lost in the Stars*
Anderson, R. *Tea and Sympathy*
Gazzo, M. *A Hatful of Rain*
Hellman, L. *The Autumn Garden*
Laurents, A. *Home of the Brave*
McCullers, C. *Member of the Wedding*

Miller, A. *All My Sons*
Wilder, T. *The Skin of Our Teeth*
Williams, T. *Camino Real*

FAMAH *Famous American Plays of the 1960s*. Selected
and introduced by Harold Clurman. New York:
Dell, 1972. 395pp. (The Laurel Drama Series)
Alfred, W. *Hogan's Goat*
Crowley, M. *The Boys in the Band*
Heller, J. *We Bombed in New Haven*
Horovitz, I. *The Indian Wants the Bronx*
Lowell, R. *Benito Cereno*

FAMAL *Famous American Plays of the 1930s*. Selected
and introduced by Harold Clurman. New York:
Dell, c1959. 480pp.
Behrman, S. *End of Summer*
Odets, C. *Awake and Sing!*
Saroyan, W. *The Time of Your Life*
Sherwood, R. *Idiot's Delight*
Steinbeck, J. *Of Mice and Men*

FAMAN *Famous Plays of 1931*. London: Gollancz [1931]
672pp.
Anthony, C. *Autumn Crocus*
Besier, R. *The Barretts of Wimpole Street*
Delafield, E. *To See Ourselves*
Fagan, J. *The Improper Duchess*
Van Druten, J. *After All*
Van Druten, J. *London Wall*

FAMB *Famous Plays of 1932*. London: Gollancz, 1932.
654pp.
Bax, C. *The Rose without a Thorn*
Hart, M., and Kaufman, G. *Once in a Life Time*
Mackenzie, R. *Musical Chairs*
Rice, E. *See Naples and Die*
Van Druten, J. *Somebody Knows*
Van Druten, J. *There's Always Juliet*

FAMC *Famous Plays of 1932–1933*. London: Gollancz.
1933. 727pp.
Ackland, R. *Strange Orchestra*
Anthony, C. *Service*
Chlumberg, H. *Miracle at Verdun*
Rice, E. *Counsellor at-law*
Van Druten, J. *Behold We Live*
Winsloe, C. *Children in Uniform*

FAMD *Famous Plays of 1933*. London: Gollancz, 1933.
702pp.
Armstrong, A. *Ten-minute Alibi*
Chetham Strode, W. *Sometimes even Now*
Daviot, G. *Richard of Bordeaux*

Fauchois. R. *The Late Christopher Bean*
Howard, S. *Alien Corn*
Kaufman, G., and Ryskind, M. *Of Thee I Sing*

FAME *Famous Plays of 1933–1934*. London: Gollancz,
1934. 712pp.
Daviot, G. *The Laughing Woman*
Hodge, M. *The Wind and the Rain*
Lipscomb, W., and Minney, R. *Clive of India*
Sherwood, R. *Reunion in Vienna*
Stuart, A., and Stuart, P. *Sixteen*
Van Druten, J. *The Distaff Side*

FAMF *Famous Plays of 1934*. London: Gollancz, 1934.
688pp.
Anthony, C. *Touch wood*
Daviot, G. *Queen of Scots*
Harwood, H. *Old Folks at Home*
Jennings, G. *Family Affairs*
Kingsley, S. *Men in White*
Mackenzie, R. *The Maitlands*

FAMG *Famous Plays of 1934–1935*. London: Gollancz,
1935. 695pp.
Ackland, R. *The Old Ladies*
Egan, M. *The Dominant Sex*
Ginsbury, M. *Viceroy Sarah*
Johnson, P. *Lovers' Leap*
Pryce, R. *Frolic Wind*
Van Druten, J. *Flowers of the Forest*

FAMH *Famous Plays of 1935*. London: Gollancz, 1935.
622pp.
Hodge, M. *Grief Goes Over*
Raphaelson, S. *Accent on Youth*
Somin, W. *Close Quarters* (Attentat)
Sternheim, C. *The Mask of Virtue*
Vulpius, P. *Youth at the Helm*
Williams, E. *Night Must Fall*

FAMI *Famous Plays of 1935–1936*. London: Gollancz,
1936. 701pp.
Ackland, R. *After October*
Anthony, C. *Call It a Day*
Deevy, T. *Katie Roche*
Hodson, J. *Red Night*
Odets, C. *Awake and Sing!*
Sherriff, R., and De Casalis, J. *St. Helena*

FAMJ *Famous Plays of 1936*. London: Gollancz, 1936.
568pp.
Farjeon, E., and Farjeon, H. *The Two Bouquets*
Odets, C. *Till the Day I Die*
Schauffler, E. *Parnell*

Schnitzler, A. *Professor Bernhardi*
Shaw, I. *Bury the Dead*
Spewack, B., and Spewack, S. *Boy Meets Girl*

FAMK *Famous Plays of 1937*. London: Gollancz, 1937.
    775pp.
Boothe, C. *The Women*
Lenormand, H. *In Theatre Street*
Reid, A. *People in Love*
Rice, E. *Judgment Day*
Sayers, D., and Byrne, M. *Busman's Honeymoon*
Turgenev, I. *A Month in the Country*

FAML *Famous Plays of 1938–1939*. London: Gollancz,
    1939. 661pp.
Egan, M. *To Love and to Cherish*
Hodson, J. *Harvest in the North*
MacOwan, N. *Glorious Morning*
Malleson, M., and Brooks, H. *Six Men of Dorset*
Odets, C. *Golden Boy*
Sayers, D. *The Zeal of Thy House*

FAMO *Famous Plays of 1954*. London: Gollancz, 1954.
    592pp.
Christie, A. *Witness for the Prosecution*
Christie, D., and Christie, C. *Carrington. V. C.*
Hunter, N. *A Day by the Sea*
Odets, C. *The Big Knife*
Van Druten, J. *I Am a Camera*

FAO *Famous Plays of To-day*. London: Gollancz, 1929.
    671pp.
Berkeley, R. *The Lady with a Lamp*
Dukes, A. *Such Men Are Dangerous*
Hoffe, M. *Many Waters*
Levy, B. *Mrs. Moonlight*
Sherriff, R. *Journey's End*
Van Druten, J. *Young Woodley*

FAOS *Famous Plays of Today*. London: Golluncz, 1953.
    373pp.
Hunter, N. *Waters of the Moon*
Knott, F. *Dial "M" for Murder*
Priestley, J., and Hawkes, J. *Dragon's Mouth*
Rattigan, T. *The Deep Blue Sea*

FAR Farmer, John Stephen, ed. *Anonymous Plays*. 3rd
    series. London: Early English Drama Society, 1906.
    302pp. (Early English Dramatists)
*Gammer Gurton's Needle*
*Jack Juggler*
*King Dadus*
*New Custom*
*Trial of Treasure*

FARM Farmer, John Stephen, ed. *Five Anonymous Plays*.
    4th series. London: Early English Drama Society,
    1908. 328pp. (Early English Dramatists)
*Appius and Virginia*
*Common Conditions*
*Grim the Collier of Croydon*
*The Marriage of Wit and Science*
*The Marriage of Wit and Wisdom*

FARN Farmer, John Stephen, ed. *Recently Recovered
    "Lost" Tudor Plays with Some Others*. London:
    Early English Drama Society, 1907. 427pp. (Early
    English Dramatists)
*An Interlude of Impatient Poverty*
*The Interlude of John the Evangelist*
*An Interlude of Wealth and Health*
*Mankind*
*Medwall, H. Nature*
*Redford, J. The Play of Wit and Science*
*Respublica*

FARO Farmer, John Stephen, ed. *Six Anonymous Plays*.
    1st Series (cl510–1537). London: Early English
    Drama Society, 1905. 286pp. (Early English
    Dramatists)
*The Beauty and Good Properties of Women* (commonly
    called *Calisto and Melibaea*)
*Hickscorner*
*The Nature of the Four Elements*
*The Summoning of Everyman*
*Thersites*
*The World and the Child*

FARP Farmer, John Stephen, ed. *Six Anonymous Plays*.
    2nd Series. London: Early English Drama Society,
    1906. 478pp. (Early English Dramatists)
*A Comedy Called Misogonus*
*The History of Jacob and Esau*
*An Interlude of Godly Queen Hester*
*The Interlude of Youth*
*A Moral Play of Albion, Knight*
*Tom Tyler and His Wife*

FAT *Fat Virgins, Fast Cars, and Asian Values: A
    Collection of Plays from Theatreworks Writers'
    Lab*. Singapore: Times Books International, 1993.
    359pp.
Chng, S. *Good Asian Values*
Heng, R. *Lest the Demons Get to Me*
Lam, D. *Bernard's Story*
Loh, K. *Fast Cars and Fancy Women*
Loon, R. *Absence Makes the Heart Grow Fonder*
Sim, D. *Blood and Snow*

Tan, T.H. *Home*
Tan, T. *Bra Sizes*
Yu, O. *Three Fat Virgins Unassembled*

FAV Favorini, Attilio, ed. *Voicings: Ten Plays from the Documentary Theater.* Hopewell, NJ: Ecco Press, 1995. 376pp.
Arent, A. *Ethiopia*
Cheeseman, P., et al. *Fight for Shelton Bar*
Freed, D. *Inquest*
Hunt, M. *Unquestioned Integrity: The Hill-Thomas Hearings*
Kurginian, S. *Compensation*
Mann, E. *Execution of Justice*
Newman, M., and Damashek, B. *Quilters*
Paice, E., and Woddis, R. *World on Edge*
Piscator, E., and Gasbarra, F. *In Spite of Everything*
Weiss, P. *The Investigation*

FAY, W. G. *See* FIT *Five Three-Act Plays.*

FED Federal Council of the Churches of Christ in America. Committee on Religious Drama. *Religious Dramas, 1924–1925.* New York: Century [c1923–1026] 2 vols.
Bates, E. *The Two Thieves* 2
Cropper, M. *Two Sides of the Door* 2
Currie, C. *Whither Goest Thou?* 2
Goodman, K. *Dust of the Road* 1
Goold, M. *The Quest Divine* 2
Goold, M. *St. Claudia* 2
Goold, M. *The Shepherds* 2
Hamlin, M. *The Rock* 1
Harnwell, A., and Meaker, I. *The Alabaster Box* 2
Kimball, R. *The Resurrection* 1
Leamon, D. *Barabas* 2
McCauley, C. *The Seeker* 1
MacKaye, P. *The Pilgrim and the Book* 1
Mason, H. *At the Gate Beautiful* 2
Mygatt, T. *The Sword of the Samurai* 2
Osgood, P. *A Sinner Beloved* 1
Willcox, H. *Larola* 1
Woodbridge, E. *The Crusade of the Children* 1

FEDERAL THEATRE PLAYS. *See* FEE, FEF Federal Theatre Project

FEE Federal Theatre Project. *Federal Theatre Plays.* Edited for the Federal Theatre by Pierre de Rohan. New York: Random House [c1938] v.p.
Arent, A., ed. *One-third of a Nation*
Conkle, E. *Prologue to Glory*
Dubois, W. *Haiti*

FEF Federal Theatre Project. *Federal Theatre Plays.* Edited for the Federal Theatre by Pierre de Rohan. New York: Random House [c1938] v.p.
Arent, A. *Power, a Living Newspaper*
Sundgaard, A. S*pirochete*
*Triple-A Plowed Under, by the Staff of the Living Newspaper*

FEFG Feingold, Michael, ed. *Grove New American Theater.* New York: Grove Press, 1993. 386pp.
Eichelberger, E. *Dasvedanya Mama*
Finley, K. *The Theory of Total Blame*
Gordon, D. *The Mysteries and What's So Funny?*
Greenberg, R. *The American Plan*
Greenspan, D. *Dead Mother, or Shirley Not All in Vain*
Wellman, M. *Sincerity Forever*

FEFH Feise, Ernst, and Steinhauer, Harry, eds. *German Literature since Goethe.* Boston: Houghton Mifflin [c1958] 2 vols.
Brecht, B. *Das verhör des Lukullus* 2
Grillparzer, F. *Der traum ein leben* 1
Hauptmann, G. *Michael Kramer* 2
Hebbel, F. *Maria Magdalene* 1
Hofmannsthal, H. *Das Salzburger grosse welttheater* 2
Kaiser, G. *Gas II* 2
Schnitzler, A. *Der grüne kakadu* 2

FEFL Felheim, Marvin, ed. *Comedy: Plays, Theory, and Criticism.* New York: Harcourt, Brace [c1962] 288pp.
Aristophanes. *The Birds*
Chekhov, A. *A Wedding; or, a Joke in One Act*
Fry, C. *A Phoenix Too Frequent*
Molière, J. *The Misanthrope*
Shakespeare, W. *Twelfth Night; or, What You Will*
Shaw, G. *The Man of Destiny*
Sheridan, R. *The Critic; or, Tragedy Rehearsed*
Wilde, O. *The Importance of Being Earnest*

FEFM Felperin, Howard Michael, ed. *Dramatic Romance.* New York: Harcourt, Brace, Jovanovich, 1973. 258pp.
Brecht, B. *The Caucasian Chalk Circle*
Eliot, T. *The Cocktail Party*
Euripides. *Alcestis*
Gay, J. *The Beggar's Opera*
Ibsen, H. *When We Dead Awaken*
Shakespeare, W. *The Tempest*

FEFNC *Female Playwrights of the Nineteenth Century.* Edited by Adrienne Scullion. London: J. M. Dent; Rutland, VT: Charles Tuttle, 1996. 478pp.

Baillie, J. *The Family Legend*
Bell, F., and Robins, E. *Alan's Wife*
De Camp, M. *Smiles and Tears*
Hobbes, J. *The Ambassador*
Kemble, F. *Francis the First*
Mowatt, A. *Fashion*
Palmer, T. *East Lynne*

FEFNV *Female Voices*. London: Playwrights Press, 1987.
    150pp.
    Aykroyd, J. *The Clean-up*
    Caulfield, A. *The Ungrateful Dead*
    Gowans, E. *Casino*
    Schrader, C. *Corryvrecken*
    Yankowitz, S. *Alarms*

FEFO *The Female Wits: Women Playwrights on the
    London Stage, 1660–1720*. By Fidelis Morgan.
    London: Virago Press, 1981. 468pp. [cover title:
    *The Female Wits: Women Playwrights of the
    Restoration*]
    Behn, A. *The Lucky Chance, or: An Alderman's Bargain*
    Centlivre, S. *The Wonder: A Woman Keeps a Secret*
    Manley, M. *The Royal Mischief*
    Pix, M. *The Innocent Mistress*
    Trotter, C. *The Fatal Friendship*

FENELLOSA, ERNEST FRANCISCO, and POUND,
    EZRA. *See* NOH 'Noh' or Accomplishment

FEY Feyder, Linda, ed. *Shattering the Myth: Plays by
    Hispanic Women*. Houston, TX: Arte Publico Press,
    1992. 255pp.
    Cruz, M. *Miriam's Flowers*
    López, J. *Simply Maria, or the American Dream*
    Moraga, C. *Shadow of a Man*
    Sáenz, D. *A Dream of Canaries*
    Svich, C. *Gleaning/Rebusca*
    Villarreal, E. *My Visits with MGM*

FFLD *The Fickle Finger of Lady Death and other Plays*.
    Translated by Carlos Morton. New York: Peter
    Lang, 1996. 133pp. (Taft Memorial Fund and
    University of Cincinnati Studies in Latin American,
    Chicano, and U.S. Latino Theatre vol. 5)
    Garro, E. *The Tree*
    Olmos, C. *Profane Games*
    Rascon Banda, V. *Murder with Malice (The Case of
        Santos Rodríguez)*
    Rodríguez Solís, E. *The Fickle Finger of Lady Death*

FGP *Fifteen Greek Plays Translated into English*. New
    York: Oxford University Press, 1943. 794pp.
    Aeschylus. *Agamemnon*
    Aeschylus. *Choephoroe*

Aeschylus. *The Eumenides*
Aeschylus. *Prometheus Bound*
Aristophanes. *The Birds*
Aristophanes. *The Clouds*
Aristophanes. *The Frogs*
Euripides. *Electra*
Euripides. *Hippolytus*
Euripides. *Iphigenia in Tauris*
Euripides. *Medea*
Sophocles. *Antigone*
Sophocles. *Electra*
Sophocles. *Oedipus at Colonus*
Sophocles. *Oedipus, King of Thebes*

FIF *Fifteenth Century Prose and Verse*. With an
    introduction by Alfred W. Pollard. New York:
    Dutton [1903] 324pp. (An English Garner. [vol. 1])
    *Everyman*
    *The Pageant of the Shearmen and Tailors*

FIFFN *Fire and Night: Five Baltic Plays*. Edited by
    Alfreds Straumanis. Prospect Heights, IL:
    Waveland Press, Inc., 1986. 386pp.
    Alliksaar, A. *The Nameless Island*
    Marcinkevicius, J. *Mindaugas*
    Rainis, J. *Fire and Night*
    Sruoga, B. *Kazimieras sapiega*
    Ziverts, M. *Power*

FIFHL *First Run: New Plays by New Writers*. Edited by
    Kate Harwood (vols. 1 and 2); edited by Matthew
    Lloyd (vol. 3). London: Nick Hern Books, 1989–
    1991. 3 vols.
    Burke, K. *Mr Thomas* 3
    Clifford, J. *Ines de Castro* 2
    Cooke, T. *Back Street Mammy* 2
    Donald, S. *Prickly Heat* 1
    Garner, J. *The Awakening* 3
    Godfrey, P. *Inventing a New Colour* 1
    Hardie, V. *Sleeping Nightie* 2
    Harding, M. *Una pooka* 2
    Hepburn, S. *Loose Ends* 2
    Hood, K. *Sugar Hill Blues* 3
    Jeffreys, S. *Valued Friends* 2
    McIntyre, C. *Low Level Panic* 1
    Munro, R. *Bold Girls* 3
    Pinnock, W. *Leave Taking* 1
    Roche, B. *A Handful of Stars* 1
    Zajdlic, R. *Infidelities* 3

FIFR Fitts, Dudley, ed. *Four Greek Plays*. New York:
    Harcourt, Brace [cl960] 310pp.
    Aeschylus. *Agamemnon*
    Aristophanes. *The Birds*

Euripides. *Alcestis*
Sophocles. *Oedipus Rex*

FIFT Fitts, Dudley, ed. *Greek Plays in Modern
    Translation*. New York: Dial Press, 1947. 596pp.
    (The Permanent Library Series)
Aeschylus. *Agamemnon*
Aeschylus. *Eumenides*
Aeschylus. *Prometheus Bound*
Euripides. *Alcestis*
Euripides. *Hippolytus*
Euripides. *Medea*
Euripides. *The Trojan Women*
Sophocles. *Antigone*
Sophocles. *King Oedipus*
Sophocles. *Oedipus at Colonus*

FIFV Fitts, Dudley, ed. *Six Greek Plays in Modern
    Translation*. New York: Dryden [c1955] 294pp.
Aeschylus. *Agamemnon*
Aeschylus. *Choephoroe*
Aeschylus. *Eumenides*
Aristophanes. *The Birds*
Euripides. *Andromache*
Sophocles. *Philoctetes*

FIFVE *Five Canadian Plays*. Toronto: Playwrights Co-op,
    1978. 152pp.
Gass, K. *Hurray for Johnny Canuck*
Hubert, C. *The Twin Sinks of Allan Sammy*
Lazarus, J. *Babel Rap*
Mitchell, K. *Heroes*
Shein, B. *Cowboy Island*

FIFW *Five Chinese Communist Plays*. Edited by Martin
    Ebon. New York: Day, 1975. 328pp.
*Azalea Mountain*
Ho, C., and Ting, Y. *The White-haired Girl*
*The Red Detachment of Women*
*The Red Lantern*
*Taking the Bandits' Stronghold*

FIG *Five Great Modern Irish Plays*. With a foreword by
    George Jean Nathan. New York: Modern Library
    [1941] 332pp.
Carroll, P. *Shadow and Substance*
Gregory, I. *Spreading the News*
O'Casey, S. *Juno and the Paycock*
Synge, J. *The Playboy of the Western World*
Synge, J. *Riders to the Sea*

FIJ *Five Italian Renaissance Comedies*. Edited by Bruce
    Penman. Harmondsworth, Middlesex: Penguin,
    1978. 443pp.

Aretino, P. *The Stablemaster*
Ariosto, L. *Lena*
Gl'Intronati de Siena. *The Deceived*
Guarini, G. *The Faithful Shepherd*
Machiavelli, N. *Mandragola*

FIL *Five Modern Scandinavian Plays*. New York: Twayne
    Publishers, 1971. 424pp.
Chorell, W. *The Sisters*
Grieg, N. *Our Power and Our Glory*
Lagerkvist, P. *The Man Who Lived His Life Over*
Soya, C. *Lion with Corset*
Stefánsson, D. *The Golden Gate*

FIN *Five New Full-Length Plays for All-Women Casts*.
    London: Dickson & Thompson [1935] 375pp.
Box, M. *Angels of War*
Box, S. *The Woman and the Walnut Tree*
Popplewell, O. *This Bondage*
Rye, E. *The Three-fold Path*
Smee, L. *No Thoroughfare*

FINBN *5 Plays: British Council/Association of Nigerian
    Authors* (1989 Drama Prize). Ibadan, Nigeria:
    Heinemann Educational Books, 1990. 256pp.
Atai, U. *SAP Rites*
Hamanjoda, A. *Merchants of Destiny*
Kala, S. *Akpakaland*
Ogunrinde, F. *The Woman with a Past*
Oko, A. *The Spoiler*

FIO *Five Plays for Stage, Radio, and Television*. Edited by
    Alrene Sykes. Brisbane: University of Queensland
    Press, 1977. 279pp.
Esson, L. *The Drovers*
Roberts, T. *Lindsay's Boy*
Seymour, A. *The One Day of the Year*
Stewart, D. *The Golden Lover*
Williamson, D. *What If You Died Tomorrow*

FIP *Five Plays of 1937*. London: Hamilton [1937] v.p.
Hellman, L. *The Children's Hour*
Jerome, H. *Charlotte Corday*
Lyndon, B. *They Came by Night*
Rattigan, T. *French without Tears*
Savory, G. *George and Margaret*

FIR *Five Plays of 1940*. London: Hamilton [1940] v.p.
Ardrey, R. *Thunder Rock*
Boothe, C. *Margin for Error*
Ginsbury, N. *The First Gentleman*
Morgan, D. *A House in the Square*
Stuart, A. *Jeannie*

FIS *Five Restoration Comedies*. Introduced by Brian
       Gibbon. London: A. & C. Black [c1984] 727pp.
       (The New Mermaids)
    Congreve, W. *Love for Love*
    Etherege, G. *The Man of Mode*
    Farquhar, G. *The Recruiting Officer*
    Vanbrugh, J. *The Provok'd Wife*
    Wycherley, W. *The Plain-dealer*

FIT *Five Three-Act Plays*. Foreword by W. G. Fay.
       London: Rich and Cowan [1933] 448pp.
    Bennett, A. *Flora*
    Gielgud, V. *Chinese White*
    Holme, C. *"I Want!"*
    Pertwee, R. *Heat Wave*
    Wilson, T. *Champion North*

FLAN Flanagan, John Theodore, and Hudson, Arthur
       Palmer, eds. *Folklore in American Literature*.
       Evanston, IL: Rowe, Peterson [c1958] 511pp.
    Green, P. *Unto such Glory*
    MacKaye, P. *The Scarecrow; or, the Glass of Truth*

FLEA *A Flea in Her Rear; or, Ants in Her Pants and
       Other Vintage French Farces*. English versions by
       Norman R. Shapiro. New York: Applause Books,
       1994. 479pp.
    Allais, A. *The Poor Beggar and the Fairy Godmother*
    Courteline, G. *Boubouroche, or She Dupes to Conquer*
    Feydeau, G. *A Fitting Confusion*
    Feydeau, G. *A Flea in Her Rear; or, Ants in Her Pants*
    Feydeau, G. *Going to Pott*
    Labiche, E., and Michel, M. *It's All Relative*
    Meilhac, H., and Halévy, L. *Mardi Gras*
    Meilhac, H., and Halévy, L. *Signor Nicodemo*
    Sardou, V. *For Love or Money*
    Scribe, E., and Mélesville. *The Castrata*

FLET Fletcher, Winona, ed. *The Lorraine Hansberry
       Playwriting Award: An Anthology of Prize-Winning
       Plays*. Topeka, KS: Clark Publishing Co., 1996.
       419pp.
    Collie, B. *Silent Octaves*
    Effinger, M. *Union Station*
    Foreman, F. *The Ballad of Charlie Sweetlegs Vine*
    Gordon, R., and Bauer, I. *The Bulldog and the Bear*
    Hill, O. *Mother Spense*
    Holland, E. *Second Doctor Lady*
    Mason, J. *A Star Ain't Nothin' but a Hole in Heaven*
    Washington, E. *Oh Oh Freedom*
    Williamson, G. *Mirror, Mirror*
    Wilson, E. *Strands*
    Youngblood, S. *Movie Music*

FLOR Flores, Angel, ed. *Masterpieces of the Spanish
       Golden Age*. New York: Rinehart [c1957] 395pp.
    Calderón de la Barca, P. *The Great Theater of the World*
    Téllez, G. *The Trickster of Seville and the Guest of
       Stone*
    Vega Carpio, L. *Fuente ovejuna*

FLOS Flores, Angel, ed. *Spanish Drama*. New York:
       Bantam Books [c1962] 473pp. (Library of World
       Drama)
    Benavente y Martínez, J. *The Bonds of Interest*
    Calderón de la Barca, P. *Life Is a Dream*
    Cervantes Saavedra, M. *The Vigilant Sentinel*
    Echegaray y Eizaguirre, J. *The Great Galeoto*
    García Lorca, F. *Blood Wedding*
    Moratín, L. *When a Girl Says Yes*
    Rueda, L. *The Olives*
    Ruiz de Alarcón y Mendoza, J. *The Truth Suspected*
    Téllez, G. *The Rogue of Seville*
    Vega Carpio, L. *Fuente ovejuna*

FOL Folsom, Marcia McClintock and Kirschner, Linda
       Heinlein, eds. *By Women: An Anthology of
       Literature*. Boston: Houghton Mifflin, 1976. 478pp.
    Glaspell, S. *Trifles*
    Hansberry, L. *A Raisin in the Sun*

FOR Force, William M., comp. *Orestes and Electra: Myth
       and Dramatic Form*. Boston: Houghton Mifflin
       [1968] 329pp.
    Aeschylus. *The Libation-bearers*
    Euripides. *Electra*
    Giraudoux, J. *Electra*
    Richardson, J. *The Prodigal*
    Sophocles. *Electra*

FORD Ford, Nick Aaron, ed. *Black Insights: Significant
       Literature by Black Americans 1760 to the Present*.
       Boston: Ginn, 1971. 373pp.
    Hansberry, L. *A Raisin in the Sun* (Act I only)
    Peterson, L. *Take a Giant Step*
    Watson, H. *Those Golden Gates Fall Down*

FOS Foulke, Robert, and Smith, Paul, compilers. *An
       Anatomy of Literature*. New York: Harcourt, Brace,
       Jovanovich, 1972. 1125pp.
    Jonson, B. *Volpone; or, the Fox*
    Shakespeare, W. *King Lear*
    Synge, J. *The Playboy of the Western World*

FOT *Foundations of Drama*. Ed. by C. J. Gianakaris.
       Boston: Houghton Mifflin, 1975. 437pp.
    Euripides. *Medea*
    Hansberry, L. *A Raisin in the Sun*

Ibsen, H. *An Enemy of the People*
Miller, A. *The Crucible*
O'Neill, E. *A Touch of the Poet*
Shakespeare, W. *Twelfth Night*

**FOUA** *Four Australian Plays*. Harmondsworth, Middlesex: Penguin, 1977. 320pp.
Buzo, A. *The Front Room Boys*
Hibberd, J. *White with Wire Wheels*
Hibberd, J. *Who?*
Romeril, J. *Chicago, Chicago*

**FOUAC** *Four Contemporary French Plays*. New York: Modern Library, 1967. 265pp.
Anouilh, J. *Antigone*
Camus, A. *Caligula*
Giraudoux, J. *The Madwoman of Chaillot*
Sartre, J. *No Exit*

**FOUAD** *Four French Plays*. Translations by W. S. Merwin; with a foreword by the translator. New York: Atheneum, 1985. 247pp.
Le Sage, A. *The Rival of His Master*
Le Sage, A. *Turcaret*
Marivaux, P. *The False Confessions*
*Robert the Devil*

**FOUAF** *Four French Renaissance Plays*; in translation with introductions and notes. By Arthur P. Stabler, general editor. Pullman: Washington State University Press, 1978. 368pp.
Garnier, R. *The Hebrew Women*
Jodelle, E. *Eugene*
Larivey, P. *The Spirits*
Montchrestien, A. *The Queen of Scots*

**FOUB** *Four Great Comedies of the Restoration and 18th Century*. With an introduction by Brooks Atkinson. New York: Bantam Books [c1958] 321pp.
Congreve, W. *The Way of the World*
Goldsmith, O. *She Stoops to Conquer; or, the Mistakes of a Night*
Sheridan, R. *The School for Scandal*
Wycherley, W. *The Country Wife*

**FOUD** *Four Great Elizabethan Plays*. With an introduction by John Gassner. New York: Bantam Books [c1960] 316pp.
Dekker, T. *The Shoemakers' Holiday; or, a Pleasant Comedy of the Gentle Craft*
Jonson, B. *Volpone; or, the Fox*
Marlowe, C. *The Tragical History of Doctor Faustus*
Webster, J. *The Duchess of Malfi*

**FOUF** *Four Modern French Comedies*. With an introduction by Wallace Fowlie. New York: Capricorn Books [c1960] 256pp.
Adamov, A. *Professor Toranne*
Aymé, M. *Clérambard*
Courteline, G. *The Commissioner*
Jarry, A. *Ubu Roi*

**FOUK** *Four Modern Plays*; first series. rev. ed. New York: Holt, Rinehart and Winston, 1963. 292pp.
Chekhov, A. *The Cherry Orchard*
Ibsen, H. *Hedda Gabler*
O'Neill, E. *The Emperor Jones*
Shaw, G. *Pygmalion*

**FOUM** *Four Modern Verse Plays*. First [and] second series. Edited by Henry Popkin. New York: Holt, Rinehart and Winston [c1957, 1961] 2 vols.
Gorky, M. *The Lower Depths*
Ibsen, H. *Hedda Gabler*
Ibsen, H. *Rosmersholm*
Miller, A. *Death of a Salesman*
O'Neill, E. *The Emperor Jones*
Rostand, E. *Cyrano de Bergerac*
Shaw, G. *Pygmalion*
Wilde, O. *The Importance of Being Earnest*

**FOUN** *Four Morality Plays*. Edited with an introduction and notes. By Peter Happé. Harmondsworth, Middlesex, England: Penguin Books. c1979. 709pp.
Bale, J. *King Johan*
*The Castle of Perseverance*
Lindsay, D. *Ane Satire of the Thrie Estaitis*
Skelton, J. *Magnyfycence*

**FOUNC** *Four New Comedies*. Toronto: Playwrights Canada, 1987. 364pp.
Curran, C. *Cake-walk*
Finlay, S. *Monkeyshines*
Graves, W. *Would You Like a Cup of Tea?*
Lazarus, J. *The Late Blumer*

**FOUPAP** *4 Plays by Young Australian Playwrights*. Queanbeyan: Queanbeyan Cultural Centre, 1999. 112pp.
Bishop, S. *This Little Piggy*
Kitas, F. *Crossing*
Lewis, E. *Man Care*
Waldron, S. *The Night Moon Went Fishing*

**FOUPL** *Four Plays of 1936*. With an introduction by Ivor Brown. London: Hamilton [1936] 624pp.
Jerome, H. *Jane Eyre*
Jerome, H. *Pride and Prejudice*

Lyndon, B. *The Amazing Dr. Clitterhouse*
Turney, C. *Bitter Harvest*

FOUR *Four Renaissance Tragedies*. With an introduction
  and glossary by Donald Stone, Jr. Cambridge, MA:
  Harvard University Press, 1966. 224pp.
  Bèze, T. *Abraham sacrifiant*
  Buchanan. *G. Jephté; ou, Le voeu*
  Jodelle, E. *Didon se sacrifiant*
  Taille, J. *Saul le furieux*

FOUS *Four Soviet Plays*. New York: International
  Publishers, 1937. 427pp.
  Gorky, M. *Yegor Bulichov and Others*
  Kocherga, I. *Masters of Time*
  Pogodin, N. *Aristocrats*
  Vishnevskii, V. *An Optimistic Tragedy*

FOUT *Four Soviet War Plays*. London: Hutchinson [1944]
  208pp.
  Korneichuk, A. *The Front*
  Korneichuk, A. *Guerillas of the Ukranian Steppes*
  Leonov, L. *Invasion*
  Simonov, K. *The Russians*

FOUX *Fourteen Great Plays*. London: Heinemann,
  Octopus Books, 1977. 859pp. (jointly published
  by Heinemann, Octopus, and Martin Seeker and
  Warburg, Ltd.)
  Albee, E. *Who's Afraid of Virginia Woolf?*
  Bolt, R. *A Man for All Seasons*
  Chekhov, A. *The Sea-gull*
  Coward, N. *Private Lives*
  García Lorca, F. *Blood Wedding*
  Ibsen, H. *A Doll's House*
  Maugham, W. *The Circle*
  Miller, A. *Death of a Salesman*
  O'Neill, E. *The Great God Brown*
  Priestley, J. *An Inspector Calls*
  Shaw, G. *Heartbreak House*
  Strindberg, A. *The Father*
  Synge, J. *The Playboy of the Western World*
  Williams, T. *A Streetcar Named Desire*

FOWL Fowlie, Wallace, ed., and tr. *Classical French
  Drama*. New York: Bantam Books [c1962] 277pp.
  Beaumarchais, P. *The Barber of Seville*
  Corneille, P. *The Cid*
  Marivaux, P. *The Game of Love and Chance*
  Molière, J. *The Intellectual Ladies*
  Racine, J. *Phaedra*

FOWLIE, WALLACE. *See also* FOUF *Four Modern
  French Comedies*

FRA Francke, Kuno, ed. *The German Classics of the
  Nineteenth and Twentieth Centuries*. New York:
  German Publication Society [c1913–1914] 20 vols.
  Anzengruber, L. *The Farmer Foresworn* 16
  Freytag, G. *The journansts* 12
  Fulda, L. *Tête-à-tête* 17
  Goethe, J. *Faust, Part I* 1
  Goethe, J. *Faust, Part II* 1
  Goethe, J. *Iphigenia in Tauris* 1
  Grillparzer, F. *The Jewess of Toledo* 6
  Grillparzer, F. *Medea* 6
  Gutzkow, K. *Sword and Queue* 7
  Halbe, M. *Mother Earth* 20
  Hardt, E. *Tristram the Jester* 20
  Hauptmann, G. *Michael Kramer* 18
  Hauptmann, G. *The Sunken Bell* 18
  Hauptmann, G. *The Weavers* 18
  Hebbel, F. *Maria Magdalena* 9
  Hebbel, F. *Siegfried's Death* 9
  Hofmannsthal, H. *Death and the Fool* 17
  Hofmannsthal, H. *The Death of Titian* 17
  Hofmannsthal, H. *The Marriage of Sobeide* 20
  Kleist, H. *The Prince of Homburg* 4
  Ludwig, O. *The Hereditary Forester* 9
  Schiller, F. *The Death of Wallenstein* 3
  Schiller, F. *The Homage of the Arts* 3
  Schiller, F. *William Tell* 3
  Schnitzler, A. *The Green Cockatoo* 20
  Schnitzler, A. *Literature* 20
  Schönherr, K. *Faith and Fireside* 16
  Sudermann, H. *John the Baptist* 17
  Tieck, J. L. *Puss in Boots* 4
  Wedekind, F. *The Court Singer* 20
  Wilbrandt, A. *The Master of Palmyra* 16
  Wildenbruch, E. *King Henry* 17

FRAN Franklin, Alexander, ed. *Seven Miracle Plays*. New
  York: Oxford University Press, 1963. 158pp.
  *Abraham and Isaac*
  *Adam and Eve*
  *Cain and Abel*
  *King Herod*
  *Noah's Flood*
  *The Shepherds*
  *The Three Kings*

FREE Freedley, George, ed. *Three Plays About Crime and
  Criminals*. New York: Washington Square Press
  [c1962] 278pp.
  Chodorov, E. *Kind Lady*
  Kesselring, J. *Arsenic and Old Lace*
  Kingsley, S. *Detective Story*

FREG Freedman, Morris, ed. *Tragedy: Texts and
  Commentary*. New York: Scribner, 1969. 641pp.

Aeschylus. *Agamemnon*
Betti, U. *Corruption in the Palace of Justice*
Chekhov, A. *The Three Sisters*
Dryden, J. *All for Love*
Euripides. *Medea*
*Everyman*
García Lorca, F. *Yerma*
Ibsen, H. *Ghosts*
Marlowe, C. *The Tragic History of Doctor Faustus*
Milton, J. *Samson Agonistes*
O'Neill, E. *Desire under the Elms*
Pirandello, L. *Henry IV*
Racine, J. *Phaedra*
Shakespeare, W. *Othello, the Moor of Venice*
Sophocles. *Oedipus Rex*
Strindberg, A. *The Father*


FREH Freedman, Morris, and Davis, P. B., eds.
    *Controversy in Literature: Fiction, Drama and
    Poetry with Related Criticism.* New York: Scribner,
    1968. 750pp.
    *Abraham and Isaac* (Brome)
    Ferlinghetti, L. *Our Little Trip*
    Ibsen, H. *An Enemy of the People*
    Kopit, A. *Oh Dad, Poor Dad, Mamma's Hung You in
        the Closet and I'm Feelin' So Sad*
    Shaw, G. *The Devil's Disciple*
    Sophocles. *Antigone*


FREI Freier, Robert; Lazarus, Arnold Leslie; and Potell,
    Herbert, eds. *Adventures in Modern Literature.*
    4th ed. New York: Harcourt Brace [c1956] 690pp.
    (Adventures in Literature Series)
    Glaspell, S. *Trifles*
    O'Casey, S. *The End of the Beginning*
    Shaw, G. *Caesar and Cleopatra*
    Sherriff, R. *Journey's End*


FRIED Friedl, Bettina, ed. *On to Victory: Propaganda
    Plays of the Woman Suffrage Movement.* Boston:
    Northeastern University Press, 1987. 378pp.
    Belmont, Mrs. O.H.P., and Maxwell, E. *Melinda and
        Her Sisters*
    Curtis, A., and Curtis, D. *The Spirit of Seventy-six; or,
        the Coming Woman*
    Fargo, K. *A Voting Demonstration*
    Fowle, W. *Woman's Rights*
    Freeman, E. *When the Women Vote*
    Gilman, C. *Something to Vote For*
    Howe, M. *An Anti-suffrage Monologue*
    Ives, A. *A Very New Woman*
    Johnson, H. *On to Victory*
    Kiper, F. *Cinderelline*
    Lewis, E. *Election Day: A Suffrage Play*

McCulloch, C. *Bridget's Sisters; or, the Legal Status of
    Illinois Women in 1868*
Middleton, G. *Back of the Ballot*
Miller, A. *Unauthorized Interviews*
Rugg, G. *The New Woman*
Shaw, M. *The Parrot Cage*
Shaw, M. *The Woman of It*
Thayer, E. *Lords of Creation*
Thompson, A. *A Suffragette Baby*
Winsor, M. *A Suffrage Rummage Sale*


FRO *From Classroom to Stage: Three New Plays.* London:
    Longmans, 1966. 214pp.
    Grant, D. *The King Cat*
    Holt, B. *Noah's Ark*
    Mitson, R. *Beyond the Bourn; or, the Night Time Stood
        Still*


FROLIN *Frontline Intelligence: New Plays for the
    Nineties.* Selected and introduced by Pamela
    Edwardes. London: Methuen, 1993–1995. 3 vols.
    De Angelis, A. *Hush* 1
    Greig, D. *Europe* 3
    Hope, K. *Foreign Lands* 2
    Hughes, D. *Digging for Fire* 1
    Johnson, J. *Somewhere* 1
    Johnson, J. *Uganda* 3
    Kane, S. *Blasted* 2
    Penhall, J. *Some Voices* 3
    Spencer, D. *Hurricane Roses* 2
    Thomas, E. *East from the Gantry* 1
    Upton, J. *Ashes and Sand* 3
    Williams, R. *The Life of the World to Come* 2


FRY Fry, Michael, ed. *Adapting Classics.* London:
    Methuen Drama, 1996. 340pp. (Frontline Drama 4;
    this series continues Frontline Intelligence 1–3)
    Clifford, J. Charles Dicken's *Great Expectations*
    De Angelis, A. John Cleland's *The Life and Times of
        Fanny Hill*
    Edmundson, H. George Eliot's *The Mill on the Floss*
    Fry, M. Jane Austen's *Emma*


FRYE Frye, Northrup, Baker, Sheridan, and Perkins,
    George, eds. *The Practical Imagination: Stories,
    Poems, Plays.* New York: Harper & Row,
    Publishers, 1980. 1514pp.
    Albee, E. *The American Dream*
    Beckett, S. *Not I*
    Aristophanes. *Lysistrata*
    Chekhov, A. *The Cherry Orchard*
    Hansberry, L. *A Raisin in the Sun*
    Ibsen, H. *An Enemy of the People*
    Ionesco, E. *The Bald Soprano*
    Miller, A. *Death of a Salesman*

Molière, J. *The Physician in Spite of Himself*
Pirandello, L. *It Is So! (If You Think So)*
Sophocles. *Oedipus Rex*
Shakespeare, W. *Macbeth*
Strindberg, A. *Miss Julie*

FRYEA Frye, Northrup, Baker, Sheridan, Perkins,
     George, and Perkins, Barbara, eds. *The Practical
     Imagination: Stories, Poems, Plays*. Revised
     Compact Edition. New York: Harper & Row,
     Publishers, 1987. 1445pp.
   Aristophanes. *Lysistrata*
   Beckett, S. *Not I*
   Chekhov, A. *The Cherry Orchard*
   Congreve, W. *The Way of the World*
   Glaspell, S., and Cook, G. *Suppressed Desires*
   Ibsen, H. *An Enemy of the People*
   Miller, A. *Death of a Salesman*
   Shakespeare, W. *Hamlet, Prince of Denmark*
   Shakespeare, W. *The Tempest*
   Sophocles. *Oedipus Rex*
   Williams, T. *The Glass Menagerie*

FUCHS Fuchs, Elinor, ed. *Plays of the Holocaust: An
     International Anthology*. New York: Theatre
     Communications Group, 1987. 310pp. (Includes
     annotated bibliography of Holocaust plays by Alvin
     Goldfarb)
   Atlan, L. *Mister Fugue or Earth Sick*
   Barnes, P. *Auschwitz*
   Sachs, N. *Eli: A Mystery Play of the Sufferings of Israel*
   Schevill, J. *Cathedral of Ice*
   Sobol, J. *Ghetto*
   Szajna, J. *Replika*

FUL Fullington, James Fitz-James; Reed, Harry B.; and
     McCorkle, Julia Norton, eds. *The New College
     Omnibus*. New York: Harcourt, Brace, 1938.
     1241pp.
   Connelly, M. *The Green Pastures*
   Howard, S. *The Silver Cord*
   O'Neill, E. *The Hairy Ape*
   Sherriff, R. *Journey's End*

FULLINGTON, JAMES FITZ-JAMES. *See also* MCCA,
     MCCB, MCCD, MCCF, MCCG McCallum, James
     Dow, ed. *The College Omnibus*.

FULT Fulton, Albert Rondthaler, ed. *Drama and Theatre:
     Illustrated by Seven Modern Plays*. New York: Holt
     [c1946] 556pp.
   Barrie, J. *A Well-remembered Voice*
   Coward, N. *Blithe Spirit*
   Lawson, J. *Roger Bloomer*
   O'Neill, E. *Beyond the Horizon*

Pinero, A. *The Second Mrs. Tanqueray*
Rice, E. *Street Scene*
Wilder, T. *Our Town*

GALB Galbraith, Esther E., ed. *Plays without Footlights*.
     New York: Harcourt, Brace [c1945] 358pp.
   Anderson, M. *Journey to Jerusalem*
   Greene, P. *Papa Is All*
   Niggli, J. *This Bull Ate Nutmeg*
   Reely, M. *Flittermouse*
   Rickert, V. *The Bishop's Candlesticks*
   Roberts, C. *Tails Up*
   Saroyan, W. *The People with Light Coming Out of Them*
   Smith, B. *Fun after Supper*
   Upson, W. *The Master Salesman*
   Wilder, T. *The Happy Journey to Trenton and Camden*

GALL Gallagher, Kathleen, Winstanley, Kate, and
     Rippingale, Gen. *Mothertongue: Four Plays of
     the Women's Action Theatre*. Christchurch, NZ:
     Publishing Giant Press, 1999. 176pp.
   Gallagher, K., and Rippingale, G. *Banshee Reel*
   Gallagher, K., and Rippingale, G. *Offspring*
   Gallagher, K., and Winstanley, K. *Jacaranda*
   Gallagher, K., and Winstanley, K. *Mothertongue*

GANN Gann, Myra S., ed. *Contemporary Mexican Drama
     in Translation*. Potsdam, NY: Danzon Press,
     1994–1995. 2 vols. (Vol. 1 Azcárate, Rascón,
     Urtusástegui. Vol. 2 *No One Knows Anything*.)
   Azcárate, L. *Margarita Came Back to Life* 1
   Leñero, V. *No One Knows Anything* 2
   Rascón Banda, V. *Blue Beach* 1
   Urtusástegui, T. *Do You Smell Gas?* 1

GARNETT, PORTER. *See* BOH Bohemian Club, San
     Francisco. *The Grove Plays of the Bohemian Club*.

GARR Garrett, Simon, ed. *He reo hou: 5 Plays by Maori
     Playwrights*. Wellington, NZ: Playmarket, 1991.
     239pp.
   Broughton, J. *Te hara (The Sin)*
   Brown, R. *Roimata*
   Hapipi, R. *Death of the Land*
   Owen, R. *Te awa I tahuti*
   Tuware, H. *In the Wilderness without a Hat*

GARSA Gassner, John, ed. *Best American Plays: Fifth
     Series, 1957–1963*. New York: Crown, 1963.
     678pp.
   Albee, E. *Who's Afraid of Virginia Woolf?*
   Anderson, R. *Silent Night, Lonely Night*
   Chayefsky, P. *Gideon*
   Frings, K. *Look Homeward, Angel*
   Gardner, H. *A Thousand Clowns*

Gibson, W. *Two for the See-saw*
Inge, W. *The Dark at the Top of the Stairs*
Kerr, J. *Mary, Mary*
Kopit, A. *Oh Dad, Poor Dad, Mamma's Hung You in the Closet and I'm Feelin' So Sad*
MacLeish, A. *J. B.*
Mosel, T. *All the Way Home*
O'Neill, E. *A Touch of the Poet*
Saroyan, W. *The Cave Dwellers*
Vidal, G. *The Best Man*
Williams, T. *The Night of the Iguana*
Williams, T. *Orpheus Descending*
Wishengrad, M. *The Rope Dancers*

GART Gassner, John, ed. *Best American Plays: Fourth Series, 1951–1957*. New York: Crown [c1958] 648pp.
Anderson, R. *Tea and Sympathy*
Axelrod, G. *The Seven-year Itch*
Gazzo, M. *A Hatful of Rain*
Hartog, J. *The Fourposter*
Inge, W. *Bus Stop*
Inge, W. *Picnic*
Kaufman, G., and Teichman, H. *The Solid Gold Cadillac*
Lawrence, J., and Lee, R. *Inherit the Wind*
Levin, I. *No Time for Sergeants*
Miller, A. *The Crucible*
Miller, A. *A View from the Bridge*
O'Neill, E. *A Moon for the Misbegotten*
Van Druten, J. *I Am a Camera*
Wilder, T. *The Matchmaker*
Williams, T. *Cat on a Hot Tin Roof*
Williams, T. *The Rose Tattoo*
Wouk, H. *The Caine Mutiny*

GARTL [Gassner, John] ed. *Best American Plays: Seventh Series, 1967–1973*. Edited with an introduction by Clive Barnes. New York: Crown, 1975. 585pp.
Albee, E. *All Over*
Allen, W. *Play It Again, Sam*
Crowley, M. *The Boys in the Band*
Elder, L. *Ceremonies in Dark Old Men*
Feiffer, J. *Little Murders*
Foster, P. *Tom Paine*
Friedman, B. *Scuba Duba*
Guare, J. *The House of Blue Leaves*
Horovitz, I. *Morning*
Kopit, A. *Indians*
McNally, T. *Noon*
Melfi, L. *Night*
Miller, A. *The Price*
Montgomery, R. *Subject to Fits*
Rabe, D. *Sticks and Bones*
Sackler, H. *The Great White Hope*

Simon, N. *The Prisoner of Second Avenue*
Stone, P., and Edwards, S. *1776*
Wilson, L. *Lemon Sky*

GARU Gassner, John, ed. *Best American Plays: Supplementary Vol., 1918–1958*. New York: Crown [c1961] 687pp.
Barry, P. *Here Come the Clowns*
Behrman, S. *Biography*
Chase, M. *Harvey*
Colton, J. *Rain*
Davis, O., and Davis, D. *Ethan Frome*
Goodrich, F., and Hackett, A. *The Diary of Anne Frank*
Green, P. *The House of Connelly*
Howard, S., and DeKruif, P. *Yellow Jack*
Kingsley, S. *Men in White*
Mayer, E. *Children of Darkness*
Odets, C. *Awake and Sing*
Osborn, P. *Morning's at Seven*
Osborn, P. *On Borrowed Time*
Patrick, J. *The Teahouse of the August Moon*
Rice, E. *The Adding Machine*
Riggs, L. *Green Grow the Lilacs*
Tarkington, B. *Clarence*

GARW Gassner, John, ed. *Best American Plays: Third Series, 1945–1951*. New York: Crown [c1952] 707pp.
Anderson, M. *Anne of the Thousand Days*
Coxe, L., and Chapman, R. *Billy Budd*
Euripides. *Medea*
Heggen, T., and Logan, J. *Mister Roberts*
Hellman, L. *The Autumn Garden*
Herbert, F. *The Moon Is Blue*
Inge, W. *Come Back, Little Sheba*
Kingsley, S. *Darkness at Noon*
Kingsley, S. *Detective Story*
Lindsay, H., and Crouse, R. *State of the Union*
McCullers, C. *The Member of the Wedding*
Miller, A. *All My Sons*
Miller, A. *Death of a Salesman*
O'Neill, E. *The Iceman Cometh*
Van Druten, J. *Bell, Book, and Candle*
Williams, T. *A Streetcar Named Desire*
Williams, T. *Summer and Smoke*

GARX Gassner, John, compiler. *Best Plays of the Early American Theatre: From the Beginning to 1916*. New York: Crown [1967] 716pp.
Aiken, G. *Uncle Tom's Cabin*
Barker, J. *Superstition*
Boucicault, D. *The Octoroon*
Fechter, C. *The Count of Monte Cristo*
Fitch, C. *The Truth*
Gillette, W. *Secret Service*

Howells, W. *The Mousetrap*
MacKaye, P. *The Scarecrow*
Mitchell, L. *The New York Idea*
Moody, W. *The Great Divide*
Mowatt, A. *Fashion*
Payne, J. and Irving, W. *Charles the Second*
Sheldon, E. *Salvation Nell*
Thomas, A. *The Witching Hour*
Tyler, R. *The Contrast*
Walter, E. *The Easiest Way*

GARZ Gassner, John, ed. *Best Plays of the Modern
    American Theatre: Second Series.* New York:
    Crown [c1947] 776pp.
Barry, P. *The Philadelphia Story*
Gow, J., and D'Usseau, A. *Tomorrow the World*
Hellman, L. *Watch on the Rhine*
Kanin, G. *Born Yesterday*
Kaufman, G., and Hart, M. *The Man Who Came to
    Dinner*
Kesselring, J. *Arsenic and Old Lace*
Kingsley, S. *The Patriots*
Laurents, A. *Home of the Brave*
Lindsay, H., and Crouse, R. *Life with Father*
Patrick, J. *The Hasty Heart*
Rice, E. *Dream Girl*
Saroyan, W. *The Time of Your Life*
Sherwood, R. *Abe Lincoln in Illinois*
Thurber, J., and Nugent, E. *The Male Animal*
Van Druten, J. *I Remember Mama*
Van Druten, J. *The Voice of the Turtle*
Williams, T. *The Glass Menagerie*

GARZAL Gassner, John, ed. *Four New Yale Playwrights.*
    New York: Crown [1965] 235pp.
Eisenstein, M. *The Fighter*
Ingham, R. *A Simple Life*
Kleb, W. *Honeymoon in Haiti*
Murray, R. *The Good Lieutenant*

GARZB Gassner, John, ed. *Medieval and Tudor Drama.*
    New York: Bantam Books [c1963] 457pp. (Library
    of World Drama)
*Abraham and Isaac*
*The Betrayal of Christ*
*A Christmas Mumming; the Play of Saint (Prince)
    George*
*The Creation and the Fall of Lucifer*
*The Crucifixion*
*The Death of Herod*
*The Death of Pilate*
*The Deluge*
*An Easter Resurrection Play*
*Everyman*
*Man's Disobedience and the Fall of Man*

*The Murder of Abel*
*The Orléans Sepulcher*
*The Pageant of the Shearmen and Tailors*
*A Pantomime for Easter Day*
*The quem quaeritis*
*The Resurrection, Harrowing of Hell, and the Last
    Judgment*
*The Second Shepherds' Play*
Heywood, J. *The Play Called the Four pp*
Hrotsvit. *Dulcitius*
Hrotsvit. *Paphnutius*
Sackville, T., and Norton, T. *Gorboduc*
Stevenson, W. *Gammer-Gurton's Needle*
Udall, N. *Ralph Roister Doister*

GARZE Gassner, John, ed. *19th Century Russian Drama.*
    With introduction and prefaces by Marc Slonin.
    New York: Bantam Books [c1963] 342pp. (Library
    of World Drama)
Gogol, N. *The Inspector General*
Ostrovsky, A. *The Thunderstorm*
Pushkin, A. *The Stone Guest*
Tolstoy, L. *The Power of Darkness*
Turgenev, I. *A Month in the Country*

GARZG Gassner, John, ed. *20th Century Russian Drama.*
    Translated with an introduction and prefaces by
    Andrew R. MacAndrew. New York: Bantam Books
    [c1963] 376pp. (Library of World Drama)
Andreyev, L. *He Who Gets Slapped*
Chekhov, A. *The Three Sisters*
Gorky, M. *The Lower Depths*
Mayakóvsky, V. *The Bathhouse*
Olesha, Y. *A List of Assets*

GARZH Gassner, John, ed. *Twenty Best European Plays
    on the American Stage.* New York: Crown [c1957]
    733pp.
Anouilh, J. *The Lark*
Behrman, S. *Jacobowsky and the Colonel*
Benavente y Martínez, J. *The Passion Flower*
Capek, J., and Capek, K. *The World We Live In*
Chekhov, A. *The Seagull*
Giraudoux, J. *The Madwoman of Chaillot*
Giraudoux, J. *Ondine*
Giraudoux, J. *Tiger at the Gates*
Heijermans, H. *The Good Hope*
Howard, S. *The Late Christopher Bean*
Kaiser, G. *From Morn to Midnight*
Molnar, F. *The Play's the Thing*
Obey, A. *Noah*
Pirandello, L. *As You Desire Me*
Rappaport, S. *The Dybbuk*
Sartre, J. *No Exit*

Spewack, S. *My Three Angels*
Tolstoy, L. *Redemption*
Turgenev, I. *A Month in the Country*
Zweig, S. *Volpone*

GAS Gassner, John, ed. *Twenty Best Plays of the Modern American Theatre.* New York: Crown [c1939] 874pp.
Abbott, G., and Holm, J. *Three Men on a Horse*
Anderson, M. *High Tor*
Anderson, M. *Winterset*
Barry, P. *The Animal Kingdom*
Behrman, S. *End of Summer*
Boothe, C. *The Women*
Connelly, M. *Green Pastures*
Ferber, E., and Kaufman, G. *Stage Door*
Green, P. *Johnny Johnson*
Hart, M., and Kaufman, G. *You Can't Take It with You*
Hellman, L. *The Children's Hour*
Kingsley, S. *Dead End*
Kirkland, J., and Caldwell, E. *Tobacco Road*
MacLeish, A. *The Fall of the City*
Odets, C. *Golden Boy*
Reed, M. *Yes, My Darling Daughter*
Shaw, I. *Bury the Dead*
Sherwood, R. *Idiot's Delight*
Spewack, B., and Spewack, S. *Boy Meets Girl*
Steinbeck, J. *Of Mice and Men*

GASB Gassner, John, ed. *Twenty-five Best Plays of the Modern American Theatre: Early Series.* New York: Crown [c1949] 756pp.
Anderson, M., and Hickerson, H. *Gods of the Lightning*
Anderson, M. *Saturday's Children*
Balderston, J. *Berkeley Square*
Barry, P. *Paris Bound*
Beach, L. *The Clod*
Behrman, S. *The Second Man*
Conkle, E. *Minnie Field*
Dunning, P., and Abbott, G. *Broadway*
Glaspell, S. *Trifles*
Green, P. *White Dresses*
Hecht B., and MacArthur, C. *The Front Page*
Heyward, D., and Heyward, D. *Porgy*
Howard, S. *They Knew What They Wanted*
Kaufman, G., and Connelly, M. *Beggar on Horseback*
Kelly, G. *Craig's Wife*
Kelly, G. *Poor Aubrey*
Millay, E. *Aria da Capo*
O'Neill, E. *Desire under the Elms*
O'Neill, E. *The Hairy Ape*
O'Neill, E. *Ile*
Rice, E. *Street Scene*
Sherwood, R. *The Road to Rome*
Stallings, L., and Anderson, M. *What Price Glory?*

Sturges, P. *Strictly Dishonorable*
Treadwell, S. *Machinal*

GASSNER, JOHN. *See also* FOUD *Four Great Elizabethan Plays*; TRE, TREA, TREB, TREBA, TREC, TREE, TREI *A Treasury of the Theatre*

GASY Gassner, John, ed. *The Yale School of Drama Presents.* 1st ed. New York: Dutton, 1964. 315p
Hailey, O. *Hey You, Light Man!*
Hill, E. *Man Better Man*
Oliansky, J. *Here Comes Santa Claus*

GAT Gassner, John, and Barnes, Clive, eds. *Best American Plays: Sixth Series, 1963–1967.* New York: Crown, 1971. 594p
Albee, E. *Tiny Alice*
Alfred, W. *Hogan's Goat*
Anderson, R. *You Know I Can't Hear You When the Water's Running*
Baldwin, J. *Blues for Mister Charlie*
Bellow, S. *The Last Analysis*
Duberman, M. *In White America*
Gilroy, F. *The Subject Was Roses*
Goldman, J. *The Lion in Winter*
Hanley, W. *Slow Dance on the Killing Ground*
Hansberry, L. *The Sign in Sidney Brustein's Window*
Jones, L. *The Toilet*
Jones, T. *The Fantasticks*
Lowell, R. *Benito Cereno*
Manhoff, B. *The Owl and the Pussycat*
O'Neill, E. *Hughie*
Simon, N. *The Odd Couple*
Stein, J. *Fiddler on the Roof*

GATB Gassner, John, and Barnes, Clive, compilers. *50 Best Plays of the American Theater.* New York: Crown, 1969. 4 vols.
Aiken, G. *Uncle Tom's Cabin* 1
Albee, E. *Who's Afraid of Virginia Woolf?* 4
Anderson, M. *High Tor* 2
Anderson, R. *Tea and Sympathy* 4
Axelrod, G. *The Seven Year Itch* 4
Barry, P. *The Philadelphia Story* 2
Chase, M. *Harvey* 3
Colton. J. and Randolph, C. *Rain* 1
Connolly, M. *Green Pastures* 1
Davis, O. and Davis, D. *Ethan Frome* 2
Frings, K. *Look Homeward, Angel* 4
Gibson, W. *Two for the Seesaw* 4
Goodrich, F. and Hackett, A. *The Diary of Anne Frank* 4
Hartog, J. *The Fourposter* 4
Hecht, B. and MacArthur, C. *The Front Page* 1
Heggen, T. and Logan, J. *Mister Roberts* 3
Hellman, L. *The Children's Hour* 2

Heyward, D. and Heyward, D. *Porgy* 1
Inge, W. *Come Back, Little Sheba* 4
Jeffers, R. *Medea* 3
Kanin, G. *Born Yesterday* 3
Kaufman, G., and Hart, M. *The Man Who Came to Dinner* 2
Kaufman, G., and Hart, M. *You Can't Take It with You* 2
Kesselring, J. *Arsenic and Old Lace* 3
Kingsley, S. *Men in White* 1
Kirkland, J. *Tobacco Road* 1
Kopit, A. *Oh Dad, Poor Dad, Mamma's Hung You in the Closet and I'm Feelin' So Sad* 4
Lindsay, H., and Crouse, R. *Life with Father* 2
Lindsay, H., and Crouse, R. *The State of the Union* 3
McCullers, C. *The Member of the Wedding* 3
Miller, A. *The Crucible* 4
Miller, A. *Death of a Salesman* 3
Odets, C. *Awake and Sing* 2
Odets, C. *Golden Boy* 2
O'Neill, E. *Desire under the Elms* 1
O'Neill, E. *The Hairy Ape* 1
Osborn, P. *On Borrowed Time* 2
Patrick, J. *The Teahouse of the August Moon* 4
Rice, E. *Dream Girl* 3
Rice, E. *Street Scene* 1
Saroyan, W. *The Time of Your Life* 3
Shaw, I. *Bury the Dead* 2
Sheldon, E. *Salvation Nell* 1
Sherwood, R. *Abe Lincoln in Illinois* 2
Simon, N. *The Odd Couple* 4
Stein, J. *Fiddler on the Roof* 4
Tyler, R. *The Contrast* 1
Wilder, T. *The Matchmaker* 2
Williams, T. *The Glass Menagerie* 3
Williams, T. *A Streetcar Named Desire* 3

GATG Gassner, John, and Green, William, compilers *Elizabethan Drama.* New York: Bantam Books, 1967. 639pp.
*Arden of Feversham*
Dekker, T. *The Shoemaker's Holiday*
Greene, R. *Friar Bacon and Friar Bungay*
Heywood, T. *A Woman Killed with Kindness*
Jonson, B. *Everyman in His Humour*
Kyd, T. *The Spanish Tragedy*
Marlowe, C. *Doctor Faustus*
Marlowe, C. *Edward II*

GATS Gassner, John, and Sweetkind, Morris, eds. *Introducing the Drama: An Anthology.* New York: Holt, Rinehart and Winston [1963] 583pp.
Besier, R. *The Barretts of Wimpole Street*
Chekhov, A. *Then and Now*
Dunsany, E. *A Night at an Inn*
*Everyman*

Giraudoux, J. *The Apollo of Bellac*
Howard, S. *The Late Christopher Bean*
Ibsen, H. *An Enemy of the People*
Mackaye, P. *The Scarecrow*
Molière, J. *The Pretentious Ladies*
Shakespeare, W. *Romeo and Juliet*
Shaw, G. *Arms and the Man*
Sheridan, R. *The School for Scandal*
Sophocles. *Antigone*
Williams, T. *The Glass Menagerie*

GATT Gassner, John, and Sweetkind Morris, compilers. *Tragedy, History and Romance.* New York: Holt, Rinehart and Winston, 1968. 419pp.
Miller, A. *The Crucible*
Rostand, E. *Cyrano de Bergerac*
Shakespeare, W. *Henry IV, Part I*
Sophocles. *Oedipus the King*

GAUB Gaubert, Helen A. *Four Classic French Plays.* New York: Washington Square Press, 1961. 260pp.
Corneille, P. *The Cid*
Molière, J. *The Would-be Gentleman*
Racine, J. *Athaliah*
Racine, J. *Phaedra*

GAVE Gaver, Jack, ed. *Critics' Choice: New York Drama Critics' Circle Prize Plays 1935–1955.* New York: Hawthorn Books, 1955. 661pp.
Anderson, M. *High Tor*
Anderson, M. *Winterset*
Hellman, L. *Watch on the Rhine*
Inge, W. *Picnic*
Kingsley, S. *Darkness at Noon*
Kingsley, S. *The Patriots*
McCullers, C. *The Member of the Wedding*
Miller, A. *All My Sons*
Miller, A. *Death of a Salesman*
Patrick, J. *The Teahouse of the August Moon*
Saroyan, W. *The Time of Your Life*
Steinbeck, J. *Of Mice and Men*
Van Druten, J. *I Am a Camera*
Williams, T. *Cat on a Hot Tin Roof*
Williams, T. *The Glass Menagerie*
Williams, T. *A Streetcar Named Desire*

GAY *Gay Plays.* Edited and introduced by Michael Wilcox. London: Methuen, 1984–1994. 5 vols.
Ackerley, J. *The Prisoners of War* 3
Bartlett, N. *A Vision of Love Revealed in Sleep (Part Three)* 4
Bentley, E. *Round 2* 4
Crowe, R., and Zajdlic, R. *Cock & Bull Story* 3
Dungate, R. *Playing by the Rules* 5

Gellert, R. *Quaint Honour* 2
Greig, N. *Plague of Innocence* 5
Harvey, J. *Beautiful Thing* 5
Killingworth, G. *Days of Cavafy* 4
McClenaghan, T. *Submariners* 1
Mason, T. *Bearclaw* 2
Mason, T. *Levitation* 3
Pintauro, J. *Snow Orchid* 5
Pintauro, J. *Wild Blue* 4
Selig, P. *Terminal Bar* 3
Shairp, M. *The Green Bay Tree* 1
Sherman, M. *Cracks* 2
Sherman, M. *Passing By* 1
Taylor, C. *Lies about Vietnam* 2
Wilcox, M. *Accounts* 1


GAYIA *Gay Plays: An International Anthology.* New
York: Ubu Repertory Theater Publications, 1989.
471pp.
Besset, J. *The Function*
Copi. *Grand Finale*
Copi. *A Tower near Paris*
Dupuis, H. *Return of the Young Hippolytus*
Van Itallie, J. *Ancient Boys*
Wouters, L. *The Lives and Deaths of Miss Shakespeare*


GAYLE Gayley, Charles Mills, ed. *Representative English
Comedies.* New York: Macmillan, 1903–1936.
4 vols.
Brome, R. *The Antipodes* 3
Chapman, G.; Jonson, B.; and Marston, J. *Eastward
Hoe* 2
Congreve, W. *The Way of the World* 4
Cowley, A. *Cutter of Coleman-street* 4
Dekker, T. *The Shoemaker's Holiday* 3
Dryden, J. *The Spanish Fryer* 4
Farquhar, G. *The Recruiting Officer* 4
Fletcher, J. *Rule a Wife and Have a Wife* 3
Greene, R. *The Honorable Historie of Frier Bacon and
Frier Bungay* 1
Heywood, J. *A Mery Play betweene Johan Johan, Tyb,
His Wyfe, and Syr Jhan the Preest* 1
Heywood, J. *The Play of the Wether* 1
Jonson, B. *The Alchemist* 2
Jonson, B. *Epicoene; or, the Silent Woman* 2
Jonson, B. *Every Man in His Humour* 2
Lyly, J. *Alexander and Campaspe* 1
Massinger, P. *A New Way to Pay Old Debts* 3
*The Merry Devill of Edmonton* 2
Middleton, T., and Rowley, W. *The Spanish Gipsie* 3
Peele, G. *The Old Wives' Tale* 1
Porter, H. *The Two Angry Women of Abington* 1
Shirley, J. *The Royall Master* 3
Stevenson, W. *Gammer Gurton's Nedle* 1

Udall, N. *Roister Doister* 1
Vanbrugh, J. *The Provok'd Wife* 4
Wycherley, W. *The Plain-dealer* 4


GEIO Geiogamah, Hanay, and Darby, Jaye T., eds. *Stories
of Our Way: An Anthology of American Indian
Plays.* Los Angeles: UCLA American Indian
Studies Center, 1999. 503pp.
Arkeketa, A. *Hokti*
Geiogamah, H. *Foghorn*
Geiogamah, H. *49*
Geiogamah, H. *Grandma*
Geiogamah, H. *Grandpa*
Glancy, D. *The Truth Teller*
King, B. *Evening at the Warbonnet*
Louis, R. *Butterfly of Hope (A Warrior's Dream)*
Native American Theater Ensemble and Geiogamah, H.
*Coon Cons Coyote*
Riggs, L. *The Cherokee Night*
Spiderwoman Theater. *Sun Moon and Feather*
Tucker, W. *At the Sweet Gum Bridge*


GEMM Gemmette, Elizabeth Villiers, ed. *Law in
Literature: Legal Themes in Drama.* Troy, NY:
Whitston Publishing Company, 1995. 554pp.
Aeschylus. *The Eumenides*
Glaspell, S. *Trifles*
Lillo, G. *The London Merchant, or, the History of
George Barnwell*
Massinger, P. *The Fatal Dowry*
Rivers, L. *This Piece of Land*
Shakespeare, W. *Measure for Measure*
Shakespeare, W. *The Merchant of Venice*
Sophocles. *Antigone*


GEOR George, Kadija, ed. *Six Plays by Black and Asian
Women Writers.* London: Aurora Metro Press,
1993. 227pp.
Ahmad, R. *Song for a Sanctuary*
Chowdhry, M. *Monsoon*
Cooke, T. *Running Dream*
Pinnock, W. *A Hero's Welcome*
Syal, M. *My Sister-wife*
Zindika. *Leonora's Dance*


GERLC *German-Language Comedy: A Critical Anthology.*
Translated and with a historical introduction by
Bert Cardullo. Selinsgrove, PA: Susquehanna
University Press; London and Toronto: Associated
University Presses, 1992. 299pp.
Grillparzer, F. *Woe to the Liar!*
Hauptmann, G. *The Beaver Coat*
Kleist, H. *The Broken Pitcher*
Lessing, G. *Minna von Barnhelm*

GERO Gerould, Daniel, ed. *Doubles, Demons, and Dreamers: An International Collection of Symbolist Drama.* New York: Performing Arts Journal Publications, 1985. 223pp.
 Andreyev, L. *Requiem*
 Bely, A. *The Jaws of Night*
 Blok, A. *The Stranger*
 Briusov, V. *The Wayfarer*
 Hoffmansthal, H. *Death and the Fool*
 Maeterlinck, M. *The Intruder*
 Margueritte, P. *Pierrot: Assassin of His Wife*
 Micinski, T. *The Ballad of the Seven Sleeping Brothers in China*
 Przybyszewski, S. *Visitors*
 Rachilde. *The Crystal Spider*
 Stevens, W. *Carlos among the Candles*
 Strindberg, A. *Coram populo!*
 Tagore, R. *Karna and Kunti*
 Valle-Inclán, R. *Dream Comedy*
 Yeats, W. *The Shadowy Waters*

GEST, MORRIS. See MOSA *Moscow Art Theatre Series of Russian Plays.*

GETH Gethner, Perry, ed. *The Lunatic Lover and Other Plays by French Women of the 17th and 18th Centuries.* Portsmouth, NH: Heinemann, 1994. 344pp.
 Barbier, M. *Arria and Paetus*
 Bernard, C. *Laodamia, Queen of Epirus*
 Desjardins, M. *The Favorite Minister*
 Graffigny, F. *Cenia*
 Pascal, F. *The Lunatic Lover*
 Roche-Guilhen, A. *All-wondrous*

GHAN Ghanoonparvar, M. R., and Green, John, eds. *Iranian Drama: An Anthology.* Costa Mesa, CA: Mazdâ Publishers, 1989. 302pp.
 Beyza'i, B. *Four Boxes*
 Beyza'i, B. *Marionettes*
 Chubak, S. *Sly*
 Ebrahimi, N. *Blind Expectation*
 Ebrahimi, N. *The Essence of Waiting*
 Rahbar, M. *Law*
 Sa'edi, G. *Honeymoon*
 Sa'edi, G. *Workaholics in the Trenches*
 Talebi, F. *Barracks in the Evening*
 Yalfani, M. *On the Shore*

GIA Gianos, Mary P., ed. and tr. *Introduction to Modern Greek Literature: An Anthology of Fiction, Drama, and Poetry.* New York: Twayne, 1969. 548pp.
 Akritas, L. *Hostages*
 Prevelakis, P. *The Last Tournament*

Theotokas, G. *The Game of Folly vs. Wisdom*
Xenopoulos, G. *Divine Dream*

GIBS Gibson, Colin, ed. *Six Renaissance Tragedies.* New York: St. Martin's Press, 1997. 527pp.
 Ford, J. *'Tis a Pity She's a Whore*
 Kyd, T. *The Spanish Tragedy*
 Marlowe, C. *The Tragical History of Doctor Faustus*
 Middleton, T., and Rowley, W. *The Changeling*
 Tourneur, C. *The Revenger's Tragedy*
 Webster, J. *The Duchess of Malfi*

GILB Gilbert, Miriam, Klaus, Carl H., and Field, Bradford, S., Jr., compilers. *Modern and Contemporary Drama.* New York: St. Martin's Press, 1994. 888pp.
 Albee, E. *The Zoo Story*
 Baraka, I. *Dutchman*
 Beckett, S. *Endgame*
 Brecht, B. *Galileo*
 Büchner, G. *Woyzeck*
 Chekhov, A. *The Cherry Orchard*
 Churchill, C. *Top Girls*
 Fornes, M. *Fefu and Her Friends*
 Fugard, A. *"Master Harold" . . . and the Boys*
 Garcia Lorca, F. *The House of Bernarda Alba*
 Havel, V. *Temptation*
 Hwang, D. *M. Butterfly*
 Ibsen, H. *A Doll's House*
 Ionesco, E. *The Lesson*
 Miller, A. *Death of a Salesman*
 Norman, M. *'Night, Mother*
 O'Casey, S. *Juno and the Paycock*
 O'Neill, E. *A Moon for the Misbegotten*
 Pinter, H. *The Homecoming*
 Pirandello, L. *Six Characters in Search of an Author*
 Shange, N. *Spell # 7*
 Shaw, G. *Major Barbara*
 Shepard, S. *Fool for Love*
 Stoppard, T. *Professional Foul*
 Strindberg, A. *Miss Julie*
 Wertenbaker, T. *Our Country's Good*
 Williams, T. *Cat on a Hot Tin Roof*
 Wilson, A. *Ma Rainey's Black Bottom*

GILL Gillespie, Gerald, ed. *German Theater before 1750.* New York: Continuum, 1992. (The German Library, vol. 8)
 Gryphius, A. *Leo Armenius*
 Hrotsvitha of Gandersheim. *Dulcitius*
 Lohenstein, D. *Sophonisba*
 Rebhun, P. *Susanna*
 Sachs, H. *Fool Surgery*
 Schlegel, J. *The Dumb Beauty*

GLASH Glasheen, Anne-Marie, trans. *The Key to Our Aborted Dreams: Five Plays by Contemporary Belgian Women Writers*. New York: Peter Lang Publishing, Inc., 1998. 203pp. (Belgian Francophone Library, vol. 9)
Fabien, M. *Claire Lacombe*
Lalande, F. *Alma Mahler*
Lison-Leroy, F., and Nys-Mazure, C. *Tenants All*
Tison, P. *The Telltale*
Wouters, L. *Charlotte or Mexican Night*

GLE Glenny, Michael, ed. *Three Soviet Plays*. Middlesex, England: Penguin Books [1966] 217pp.
Babel, I. *Marya*
Mayakóvsky, V. *The Bedbug*
Schwartz, Y. *The Dragon*

GLI Gliner, Robert, and Raines, Robert Arnold, eds. *Munching on Existence: Contemporary American Society through Literature*. New York: Free Press, 1971. 465pp.
Koch, K. *The Academic Murders*
McNally, T. *Tour*
Pinter, H. *Trouble in the Works*
Van Itallie, J. *Interview*

GLO Glorfeld, Louis E., and others, eds. *Plays by Four Tragedians*. Columbus, OH: Merrill, 1968. 529pp.
Ibsen, H. *Ghosts*
Ibsen, H. *Hedda Gabler*
Shakespeare, W. *Othello*
Shakespeare, W. *Romeo and Juliet*
Sophocles. *Antigone*
Sophocles. *Oedipus the King*
Strindberg, A. *The Father*
Strindberg, A. *Miss Julie*

GOL Goldberg, Isaac, translator. *Plays of the Italian Theatre*. Boston: Luce, 1921. 202pp.
Lopez, S. *The Sparrow*
Morselli, E. *Gastone the Animal Tamer*
Morselli, E. *Water upon Fire*
Pirandello, L. *Sicilian Limes*
Verga, G. *The Wolf-hunt*

GOLB *The Golden Steed: Seven Baltic Plays*. Edited by Alfreds Straumanis. Prospect Heights, IL: Waveland Press, c1979. 383pp.
Boruta, K. *Whitehorn's Windmill*
Brigadere, A. *Maija and Paija*
Kitzberg, A. *The Werewolf*
Luts, O. *The Spirit of Lake Ulemiste*
Luts, O. *The Will-o'-the-wisp*

Rainis, J. *The Golden Steed*
Saja, K. *The Village of Nine Woes*

GOLD Goldman, Mark, and Traschen, Isadore, eds. *The Drama: Traditional and Modern*. Rockleigh, NJ: Allyn and Bacon [1968] 690pp.
Beckett, S. *Happy Days*
Brecht, B. *Mother Courage*
Chekhov, A. *The Cherry Orchard*
Ibsen, H. *The Wild Duck*
Molière, J. *The Misanthrope*
Pirandello, L. *Six Characters in Search of an Author*
Shakespeare, W. *King Lear*
Shakespeare, W. *Twelfth Night*
Shaw, G. *Arms and the Man*
Sophocles. *Oedipus Rex*

GOLH Goldstone, Richard Henry, compiler. *Contexts of the Drama*. New York: McGraw-Hill [1968] 775pp.
Albee, E. *The Zoo Story*
Anouilh, J. *Becket*
Chekhov, A. *Three Sisters*
Euripides. *Hippolytus*
Ibsen, H. *Hedda Gabler*
Molière, J. *The Miser*
O'Neill, E. *Hughie*
Shakespeare, W. *Antony and Cleopatra*
Shaw, G. *Caesar and Cleopatra*
Sophocles. *Antigone*
Wilder, T. *The Matchmaker*
Williams, T. *Summer and Smoke*

GOLK Goldstone, Richard Henry, compiler. *Mentor Masterworks of Modern Drama: Five Plays*. New York: New American Library, 1969. 478pp.
Ibsen, H. *An Enemy of the People*
Miller, A. *The Crucible*
Rostand, E. *Cyrano de Bergerac*
Shaw, G. *Pygmalion*
Wilder, T. *Our Town*

GOM Gomme, Andor Harvey, ed. *Jacobean Tragedies*. New York: Oxford University Press, 1969. 398pp.
Marston, J. *The Malcontent*
Middleton, T. *Women Beware Women*
Middleton, T., and Rowley, W. *The Changeling*
Tourneur, C. *The Atheist's Tragedy*
Tourneur, C. *The Revenger's Tragedy*

GONZ Gonzalez-Cruz, Luis F., and Colecchia, Francesca M., eds. and trans. *Cuban Theater in the United States: A Critical Anthology*. Tempe, AZ: Bilingual Press/Editorial Bililngue, 1992. 186pp.

Arenas, R. *Traitor*
Ariza, R. Four Minidramas (*The Meeting, Doll's Play, Declaration of Principles, and A Flower Vendor for These Times*)
Gonzalez-Pando, M. *The Great American Justice Game*
Hernandez, L. *We Were Always Afraid*
Matas, J. *Dialogue of the Poet and the Supreme Leader*
Montes Huidobro, M. *Olofe's Razor*
Pereiras, M. *The Marriage of Hippolyta*
Perez, H. *Perhaps the Marshland*
Prida, D. *Screens*

GOODMAN, DAVID, G. *See* AFAP *After Apocalypse*; JAPDC *Japanese Drama and Culture*

GOO Goodman, G., ed. *From Script to Stage: Eight Modern Plays*. San Francisco: Rinehart Press, 1971. 623pp.
Aspenström, W. *The Apes Shall Inherit the Earth*
Brecht, B. *The Seven Deadly Sins of the Lower Middle Classes*
Chekhov, A. *The Seagull*
Ibsen, H. *Hedda Gabler*
O'Neill, E. *Desire under the Elms*
Pinget, R. *The Old Tune*
Shaw, G. *Pygmalion*
Strindberg, A. *A Dream Play*

GOOD Goodman, Randolph, ed. *Drama on Stage*. New York: Holt, Rinehart and Winston [c1961] 475pp.
Duerrenmatt, F. *The Visit*
Euripides. *Medea*
*Everyman*
Molière, J. *The Misanthrope*
Shakespeare, W. *The Tragedy of Macbeth*
Williams, T. *A Streetcar Named Desire*

GOODE Goodman, Randolph, ed. *Drama on Stage*. 2nd ed. New York: Holt, 1978. 658pp.
Beckett, S. *Krapp's Last Tape*
Duerrenmatt, F. *The Visit*
Euripides. *Medea*
*Everyman*
Ibsen, H. *An Enemy of the People*
Molière, J. *Le misanthrope*
Shakespeare, W. *Macbeth*
Sheridan, R. *St. Patrick's Day, or the Scheming Lieutenant*
Shevelove, B., and Gelbart, L. *A Funny Thing Happened on the Way to the Forum*
Strindberg, A. *The Ghost Sonata*
Williams, T. *Cat on a Hot Tin Roof*

GOON Goonetilleke, D.C.R.A., ed. *Modern Sri Lankan Drama: An Anthology*. Delhi, India: Sri Satguru

Publications, 1991. 228pp. (Studies on Sri Lanka Series No. 15)
Abeysinghe, R. *Family Bonds*
De Lanerolle, H.C.N. *The Senator* (excerpt)
De Zoysa, L. *Fortress in the Sky* (excerpt)
Gunawardena, G. *Rama and Sita* (excerpt)
Jayawardhana, B. *The Tragedy of Musila*
Joseph, E. M. W. *The Foreign Expert* (excerpt)
MacIntyre, E. *The Loneliness of the Short-distance Traveler*
MacIntyre, E. *A Somewhat Mad and Grotesque Comedy*
Sarachchandra, E. *The Golden Swan, or Beyond the Curtain*
Siriwardena, R. *Prometheus: An Argumentative Comedy for Two Characters*
Vittachchi, N. *Bed and Bored*
Vittachchi, N. *Cave Walk*

GOOR Goorney, Howard, and MacColl, Ewan, eds. *Agit-Prop to Theatre Workshop: Political Playscripts 1930–1950*. Manchester: Manchester University Press, 1986. 205pp.
Littlewood, J., and MacColl, E. *Last Edition* (extracts)
MacColl, E. *Johnny Noble*
MacColl, E. *The Other Animals*
MacColl, E. *Uranium 235*
Miller, J., and Littlewood, J. *John Bullion*
Worker's Theatre Movement. *Newsboy*

GORDON, DUDLEY CHADWICK. *See* TOD *Today's Literature*

GORDP Gordon, Edward J., compiler. *Introduction to Tragedy*. Rochelle Park, NJ: Hayden Books, 1973. 349pp.
Anouilh, J. *Antigone*
Ibsen, H. *Hedda Gabler*
O'Neill, E. *Beyond the Horizon*
Sophocles. *Oedipus the King*

GORE Gordon, Walker K., ed. *Literature in Critical Perspectives: An Anthology*. New York: Appleton-Century-Crofts, 1968. 795pp.
Shakespeare, W. *The Tragedy of Hamlet, Prince of Denmark*
Shaw, G. *Major Barbara*
Sophocles. *Oedipus Rex*
Williams, T. *Orpheus Descending*

GOS Gosse, Edmund William. *Restoration Plays from Dryden to Farquhar*. London: Dent [1929] 431pp. (Everyman's Library)
Congreve, W. *The Way of the World*
Dryden, J. *All for Love*
Farquhar, G. *The Beaux' Stratagem*

Otway, T. *Venice Preserved*
Vanbrugh, J. *The Provok'd Wife*
Wycherley, W. *The Country Wife*

GOSA Gosse, Edmund William. *Restoration Plays from Dryden to Farquhar.* London: Dent [1932] 509pp. (Everyman's Library)
Congreve, W. *The Way of the World*
Dryden, J. *All for Love*
Etherege, G. *The Man of Mode*
Farquhar, G. *The Beaux' Stratagem*
Otway, T. *Venice Preserved*
Vanbrugh, J. *The Provok'd Wife*
Wycherley, W. *The Country Wife*

GOSS Gossett, Suzanne, and Berger, Thomas, L., eds. *Jacobean Academic Plays.* Oxford: Printed for the Malone Society by David Syanford at the University Printing House, 1988. 147pp.
*Boot and Spurre*
*A Christmas Messe*
*Gigantomachia, or Worke for Jupiter*
*Gowne, Hood, and Capp*
*Heteroclitanomalonomia*
*Preist the Barbar, Sweetball His Man*
*Ruff, Band, and Cuff*

GOU Gould, James Adams, and Kiefer, Harry Christian, eds. *The Western Humanities.* New York: Holt, Rinehart, and Winston, 1971. 2 vols.
Aristophanes. *Lysistrata* 1
Brecht, B. *The Caucasian Chalk Circle* 2
Goethe, J. *Faust, Part I* 2
Goldsmith, O. *She Stoops to Conquer; or, the Mistakes of a Night* 2
Ibsen, H. *Hedda Gabler* 2
Racine, J. *Phaedra* 2
Sophocles. *Oedipus the King* 1

GOW Gow, J. Rodger, and Hanlon, Helen J., eds. *Five Broadway Plays.* New York: Harper [c1948] 432pp.
Anderson, M. *High Tor*
Besier, R. *The Barretts of Wimpole Street*
Chodorov, J., and Fields, J. *Junior Miss*
Osborn, P. *On Borrowed Time*
Sherwood, R. *Abe Lincoln in Illinois*

GOWA Gow, J. Rodger, and Hanlon, Helen J., eds. *Five Broadway Plays.* 2nd ed. New York: Globe Book Co., 1968. 432pp.
Anderson, M. *High Tor*
Besier, R. *The Barretts of Wimpole Street*
Chodorov, J., and Fields, J. *Junior Miss*

Osborn, P. *On Borrowed Time*
Sherwood, R. *Abe Lincoln in Illinois*

GPA Graham, Gary B. *Freshman English Program.* Chicago: Scott, Foresman [c1960] 946pp.
Ibsen, H. *Hedda Gabler*
O'Neill, E. *Bound East for Cardiff*
Shakespeare, W. *Romeo and Juliet*
Sophocles. *Oedipus the King*

GRA Grant, Elliott Mansfield, ed. *Chief French Plays of the Nineteenth Century.* New York: Harper, 1934. 934pp.
Augier, E. *Le gendre de M. Poirier*
Becque, H. *Les corbeaux*
Brieux, E. *La robe rouge*
Dumas, A. fils. *La dame aux camélias*
Dumas, A. père. *Henri III et sa cour*
Hugo, V. *Hernani*
Hugo, V. *Ruy Blas*
Musset, A. *On ne badine pas avec l'amour*
Rostand, E. *Cyrano de Bergerac*
Vigny, A. *Chatterton*

GRAF Grant, Elliott Mansfield, ed. *Four French Plays of the Twentieth Century.* New York: Harper [c1949] 338pp.
Anouilh, J. *Antigone*
Bernard, J. *Le secret d'Arvers*
Giraudoux, J. *Siegfried*
Pagnol, M., and Nivoix, P. *Les marchands de gloire*

GRAV Graver, David, ed. *Drama for a New South Africa: Seven Plays.* Bloomington: Indiana University Press, 1999. 228pp.
Bailey, B. *Ipi Zombi?*
De Wet, R. *Crossing*
Ellenbogen, N. *Horn of Sorrow*
Junction Avenue Theatre Company. *Sophiatown*
Mahomed, I. *Purdah (The Veil)*
Mda, Z. *And the Girls in Their Sunday Dresses*
Slabolepszy, P. *Mooi Street Moves*

GRAW Gray, Frances, ed. *Second Wave Plays: Women at the Albany Empire.* Sheffield: Sheffield Academic Press, 1990. (Critical Stages, vol. 4)
De Angelis, A. *Breathless*
Duffy, G. *Into the Night*
Ghose, N. *Ishtar Descends*
Gideon, K. *England Is de Place for Me*

GRAY Gray, Stephen, ed. *Market Plays.* Craighall, South Africa: A.D. Donker Ltd., 1986. 190pp.
Cooke, V., Honeyman, J., and Keogh, D. *This Is for Keeps*

Manaka, M. *Pula*
Picardie, M. *Shades of Brown*
Simon, B. *Hey, Listen . . .*
Uys, P. *Appassionata*
Whyle, J. *National Madness*

GRAYS Gray, Stephen, ed. *South Africa Plays*. London:
  Nick Hern Books, 1993. 241pp.
Akerman, A. *Somewhere on the Border*
Maponya, M. *The Hungry Earth*
Pam-Grant, S. *Curl Up and Dye*
Slabolepszy, P. *Over the Hill*
Uys, P. *Just like Home*

GRAYTO Gray, Stephen, ed. *Theatre One: New South
  African Drama*. Johannesburg: Ad. Donker (Pty)
  Ltd., 1978. 181pp.
Bosman, H. *Street-woman*
Dike, F. *The Sacrifice of Kreli*
Fugard, A. *Orestes*
Livingstone, D. *The Sea My Winding Sheet*
Uys, P. *Paradise Is Closing Down*

GRAYTT Gray, Stephen, ed. *Theatre Two: New South
  African Drama*. Johannesburg: Ad. Donker (Pty)
  Ltd., 1981. 190pp.
Aron, G. *Mickey Kannis Caught My Eye*
Hope, C. *Ducktails*
Junction Avenue Theatre Co. *Randlords and Rotgut*
Uys, P. *God's Forgotten*

GRD *Great American Parade*. Garden City, NY:
  Doubleday Doran, 1935. 611pp.
Connelly, M. *The Green Pastures*

GRDB *Great Books of the Western World*. Robert
  Maynard Hutchins, editor in chief. Chicago: W.
  Benton [1952] 54 vols.
Aeschylus. *Agamemnon* 5
Aeschylus. *Choephoroe* 5
Aeschylus. *Eumenides* 5
Aeschylus. *The Persians* 5
Aeschylus. *Prometheus Bound* 5
Aeschylus. *The Seven against Thebes* 5
Aeschylus. *The Suppliant Maidens* 5
Aristophanes. *Acharnians* 5
Aristophanes. *Birds* 5
Aristophanes. *Clouds* 5
Aristophanes. *Ecclesiazusae* 5
Aristophanes. *Frogs* 5
Aristophanes. *Knights* 5
Aristophanes. *Lysistrata* 5
Aristophanes. *Peace* 5
Aristophanes. *Plutus* 5
Aristophanes. *Thesmaphoriazusse* 5

Aristophanes. *Wasps* 5
Euripides. *Alcestis* 5
Euripides. *Andromache* 5
Euripides. *The Bacchantes* 5
Euripides. *The Cyclops* 5
Euripides. *Electra* 5
Euripides. *Hecuba* 5
Euripides. *Helen* 5
Euripides. *Heracleidae* 5
Euripides. *Heracles Mad* 5
Euripides. *Hippolytus* 5
Euripides. *Ion* 5
Euripides. *Iphigenia among the Tauri* 5
Euripides. *Iphigenia at Aulis* 5
Euripides. *Medea* 5
Euripides. *The Phoenician Maidens* 5
Euripides. *Rhesus* 5
Euripides. *The Suppliants* 5
Euripides. *The Trojan Women* 5
Goethe, J. *Faust* 47
Shakespeare, W. *All's Well that Ends Well* 27
Shakespeare, W. *Antony and Cleopatra* 27
Shakespeare, W. *As You like It* 26
Shakespeare, W. *The Comedy of Errors* 26
Shakespeare, W. *Coriolanus* 27
Shakespeare, W. *Cymbeline* 27
Shakespeare, W. *Hamlet, Prince of Denmark* 27
Shakespeare, W. *Julius Caesar* 26
Shakespeare, W. *King Henry VIII* 27
Shakespeare, W. *King Henry V* 26
Shakespeare, W. *King Henry IV, Part 1* 26
Shakespeare, W. *King Henry IV, Part 2* 26
Shakespeare, W. *King Henry VI, Part 1* 26
Shakespeare, W. *King Henry VI, Part 2* 26
Shakespeare, W. *King Henry VI, Part 3* 26
Shakespeare, W. *King John* 26
Shakespeare, W. *King Lear* 27
Shakespeare, W. *King Richard II* 26
Shakespeare, W. *King Richard III* 26
Shakespeare, W. *Love's Labour's Lost* 26
Shakespeare, W. *Macbeth* 27
Shakespeare, W. *Measure for Measure* 27
Shakespeare, W. *The Merchant of Venice* 26
Shakespeare, W. *The Merry Wives of Windsor* 27
Shakespeare, W. *A Midsummer Night's Dream* 26
Shakespeare, W. *Much Ado about Nothing* 26
Shakespeare, W. *Othello, the Moor of Venice* 27
Shakespeare, W. *Pericles, Prince of Tyre* 27
Shakespeare, W. *Romeo and Juliet* 26
Shakespeare, W. *The Taming of the Shrew* 26
Shakespeare, W. *The Tempest* 27
Shakespeare, W. *Timon of Athens* 27
Shakespeare, W. *Titus Andronicus* 26
Shakespeare, W. *Troilus and Cressida* 27
Shakespeare, W. *Twelfth Night* 27

Shakespeare, W. *The Two Gentlemen of Verona* 26
Shakespeare, W. *The Winter's Tale* 27
Sophocles. *Ajax* 5
Sophocles. *Antigone* 5
Sophocles. *Electra* 5
Sophocles. *Oedipus at Colonus* 5
Sophocles. *Oedipus the King* 5
Sophocles. *Philoctetes* 5
Sophocles. *Trachiniae* 5

GRDBA *Great Books of the Western World.* Mortimer
    J. Adler, editor in chief. Chicago: Encyclopedia
    Britannica, Inc., 2nd ed. 1990. 61 vols.
Aeschylus. *Agamemnon* 4
Aeschylus. *Eumenides* 4
Aeschylus. *The Libation Bearers* 4
Aeschylus. *The Persians* 4
Aeschylus. *Prometheus Bound* 4
Aeschylus. *Seven against Thebes* 4
Aeschylus. *The Suppliant Maidens* 4
Aristophanes. *The Acharnians* 4
Aristophanes. *The Assemblywomen* 4
Aristophanes. *The Birds* 4
Aristophanes. *The Clouds* 4
Aristophanes. *The Frogs* 4
Aristophanes. *The Knights* 4
Aristophanes. *Lysistrata* 4
Aristophanes. *Peace* 4
Aristophanes. *The Poet and the Women* 4
Aristophanes. *The Wasps* 4
Aristophanes. *Wealth* 4
Beckett, S. *Waiting for Godot* 60
Brecht, B. *Mother Courage and Her Children* 60
Chekhov, A. *Uncle Vanya* 59
Euripides. *Alcestis* 4
Euripides. *Andromache* 4
Euripides. *The Bacchae* 4
Euripides. *The Cyclops* 4
Euripides. *Electra* 4
Euripides. *Hecuba* 4
Euripides. *Helen* 4
Euripides. *The Heracleidae* 4
Euripides. *Heracles* 4
Euripides. *Hippolytus* 4
Euripides. *Ion* 4
Euripides. *Iphigenia at Aulis* 4
Euripides. *Iphigenia in Tauris* 4
Euripides. *The Medea* 4
Euripides. *Orestes* 4
Euripides. *The Phoenician Women* 4
Euripides. *Rhesus* 4
Euripides. *The Suppliant Women* 4
Euripides. *The Trojan Women* 4
Goethe, J. *Faust* 45
Ibsen, H. *A Doll's House* 52

Ibsen, H. *Hedda Gabler* 52
Ibsen, H. *The Master Builder* 52
Ibsen, H. *The Wild Duck* 52
Molière, J. *The Critique of the School for Wives* 31
Molière, J. *Don Juan* 31
Molière, J. *The Miser* 31
Molière, J. *The School for Wives* 31
Molière, J. *Tartuffe* 31
Molière, J. *The Would-be Gentleman* 31
Molière, J. *The Would-be Invalid* 31
O'Neill, E. *Mourning becomes Electra* 60
Pirandello, L. *Six Characters in Search of an Author* 59
Racine, J. *Bérénice* 31
Racine, J. *Phaedra* 31
Shakespeare, W. *All's Well that Ends Well* 25
Shakespeare, W. *Antony and Cleopatra* 25
Shakespeare, W. *As You like It* 24
Shakespeare, W. *The Comedy of Errors* 24
Shakespeare, W. *Coriolanus* 25
Shakespeare, W. *Cymbeline* 25
Shakespeare, W. *Hamlet, Prince of Denmark* 25
Shakespeare, W. *Julius Caesar* 24
Shakespeare, W. *King Henry VIII* 25
Shakespeare, W. *King Henry V* 24
Shakespeare, W. *King Henry IV, Part 1* 24
Shakespeare, W. *King Henry IV, Part 2* 24
Shakespeare, W. *King Henry VI, Part 1* 24
Shakespeare, W. *King Henry VI, Part 2* 24
Shakespeare, W. *King Henry VI, Part 3* 24
Shakespeare, W. *King John* 24
Shakespeare, W. *King Lear* 25
Shakespeare, W. *King Richard II* 24
Shakespeare, W. *King Richard III* 24
Shakespeare, W. *Love's Labour's Lost* 24
Shakespeare, W. *Macbeth* 25
Shakespeare, W. *Measure for Measure* 25
Shakespeare, W. *The Merchant of Venice* 24
Shakespeare, W. *The Merry Wives of Windsor* 25
Shakespeare, W. *A Midsummer Night's Dream* 24
Shakespeare, W. *Much Ado about Nothing* 24
Shakespeare, W. *Othello, the Moor of Venice* 25
Shakespeare, W. *Pericles, Prince of Tyre* 25
Shakespeare, W. *Romeo and Juliet* 24
Shakespeare, W. *The Taming of the Shrew* 24
Shakespeare, W. *The Tempest* 25
Shakespeare, W. *Timon of Athens* 25
Shakespeare, W. *Titus Andronicus* 24
Shakespeare, W. *Troilus and Cressida* 25
Shakespeare, W. *Twelfth Night* 25
Shakespeare, W. *The Two Gentlemen of Verona* 24
Shakespeare, W. *The Winter's Tale* 25
Shaw, G. *Saint Joan* 59
Sophocles. *Ajax* 4
Sophocles. *Antigone* 4
Sophocles. *Electra* 4

Sophocles. *Oedipus at Colonus* 4
Sophocles. *Oedipus the King* 4
Sophocles. *Philoctetes* 4
Sophocles. *The Women of Trachis* 4

GRDG *Greek Drama.* Edited by Moses Hadas. Toronto;
    London: Bantam, 1965 (1982 printing). 337pp. (A
    Bantam Classic)
Aeschylus. *Agamemnon*
Aeschylus. *Eumenides*
Aristophanes. *Frogs*
Euripides. *Hippolytus*
Euripides. *Medea*
Euripides. *Trojan Women*
Sophocles. *Antigone*
Sophocles. *Oedipus the King*
Sophocles. *Philoctetes*

GRE *Great Plays* (English). With biographical notes
    and a critical introduction by Joseph O'Connor.
    Aldine ed. New York: Appleton, 1900. 421pp. (The
    World's Great Books)
Browning, R. *A Blot in the 'Scutcheon*
Fletcher, J. *The Faithful Shepherdess*
Jonson, B. *The Alchemist*
Marlowe, C. *Edward the Second*
Payne, J. *Brutus; or, the Fall of Tarquin*
Sheridan, R. *The School for Scandal*

GREA *Great Plays* (French and German). With
    biographical notes, and a critical introduction
    by Brander Matthews. Aldine ed. New York:
    Appleton, 1901. 504pp. (The World's Great Books)
Corneille, P. *The Cid*
Hugo, V. *Ruy Blas*
Lessing, G. *Minna von Barnhelm*
Molière, J. *Tartuffe*
Racine, J. *Athaliah*
Schiller, J. *Wilhelm Tell*

GREAAI *Great Irish Plays.* New York: Gramercy Books,
    1995. 712pp.
Boucicault, D. *The Colleen Bawn*
Farquhar, G. *The Beaux' Stratagem*
Goldsmith, O. *She Stoops to Conquer*
Gregory, I. *The Rising of the Moon*
Gregory, I. *Spreading the News*
Shaw, G. *Pygmalion*
Sheridan, R. *The School for Scandal*
Synge, J. *The Playboy of the Western World*
Synge, J. *Riders to the Sea*
Wilde, O. *The Importance of Being Earnest*
Yeats, W. *The Land of Heart's Desire*
Yeats, W. *On Baile's Strand*

GREAAR *Great Rock Musicals.* Edited with an
    introduction by Stanley Richards. New York: Stein
    and Day, 1979. 562pp.
Brown, W. *The Wiz*
Driver, D. *Your Own Thing*
Fornés, M. *Promenade*
Guare, J., and Shapiro, M. *Two Gentlemen of Verona*
Jacobs, J., and Casey, W. *Grease*
Ragni, G., and Rado, J. *Hair*
Rice, T. *Jesus Christ Superstar*
Townshend, P., and The Who. *Tommy*

GREAB Grebanier, Bernard D. N., and Reiter, Seymour,
    eds. *Introduction to Imaginative Literature.* New
    York: Thomas Y. Crowell Company. [c1960]
    969pp.
Coward, N. *Brief Encounter*
Milton, J. *Samson Agonistes*
O'Neill, E. *In the Zone*
Sapinsley, A. *Even the Weariest River*
Shakespeare, W. *King Lear*
Shaw, G. *Caesar and Cleopatra*
Synge, J. *The Playboy of the Western World*
Turque, M. *Shoptalk*
Williams, T. *The Rose Tattoo*

GREB Grebanier, Bernard D. N., and Thompson, Stith,
    eds. *English Literature and Its Backgrounds.* New
    York: Cordon Co. [c1939–1940] 2 vols.
Aeschylus. *Prometheus Bound* 2
Byron, G. *Manfred* 2
Congreve, W. *The Way of the World* 1
*Everyman* 1
Marlowe, C. *The Tragical History of Doctor Faustus* 1
Milton, J. *Samson Agonistes* 1
Molière, J. *The Misanthrope* 1
Shelley, P. *Prometheus Unbound* 2
Sheridan, R. *The School for Scandal* 1
Wilde, O. *The Importance of Being Earnest* 2

GREC Grebanier, Bernard D. N.; Middlebrook, Samuel;
    Thompson, Stith; and Watt, William, eds. *English
    Literature and its Backgrounds.* Rev. ed. New
    York: Dryden Press [c1949] 2 vols.
*Abraham and Isaac* 1
Browning, R. *In a Balcony* 2
Congreve, W. *The Way of the World* 1
Dekker, T. *The Shoemaker's Holiday* 1
*Everyman* 1
Marlowe, C. *Doctor Faustus* 1
Milton, J. *Samson Agonistes* 1
Molière, J. *The Misanthrope* 1
Shakespeare, W. *Othello* 1
Sheridan, R. *The School for Scandal* 1

Sophocles. *Oedipus the King* 1
Synge, J. *The Playboy of the Western World* 2
Wilde, O. *The Importance of Being Earnest* 2
Williams, E. *The Corn Is Green* 2

GREE *Greek Dramas.* With biographical notes and a
   critical introduction by Bernadotte Perrin. Aldine
   ed. New York: Appleton, 1900. 390pp. (The
   World's Great Books)
Aeschylus. *Agamemnon*
Aeschylus. *Prometheus Bound*
Aristophanes. *The Clouds*
Aristophanes. *Plutus*
Euripides. *Alcestis*
Euripides. *Medea*
Sophocles. *Antigone*
Sophocles. *Oedipus Tyrannus*

GREEN Green, Michael, ed. and trans. *The Russian
   Symbolist Theatre: An Anthology of Plays and
   Critical Texts.* Ann Arbor: Adis Publishers, 1986.
   371pp.
Annensky, I. *Thamyris Kitharodos*
Blok, A. *The Puppet Show*
Blok, A. *The Rose and the Cross*
Kuzmin, M. *The Comedy of Alexis, Man of God*
Kuzmin, M. *The Venetian Madcaps*
Remizov, A. *The Tragedy of Judas, Prince of Iscariot*
Sologub, F. *The Triumph of Death*

GREENU Green, Michael, and Katsell, Jerome, eds.
   and trans. *The Unknown Russian Theater: An
   Anthology.* Vol. 1. Ann Arbor: Adis Publishers,
   1991. 221pp. (Volume 2 was never published.)
Gogol, N. *The Order of Vladimir, Third Class*
Ostrovsky, A. *Larisa*
Pisemsky, A. *Baal*
Sologub, F. *Vanka the Steward and Jehan the Page*
Turgenev, I. *The Weakest Link*

GREG Greenfield, Ralph, and Side, Ronald K., eds.
   *Temper of the Times.* New York: McGraw-Hill,
   1969. 557pp.
Hailey, A. *Shadow of Suspicion*
Odets, C. *Waiting for Lefty*
Synge, J. *Riders to the Sea*
Williams, N. *The Mountain*

GREJ Greenspan, Charlotte L., and Hirsch, Lester M., eds.
   *All Those Voices: The Minority Experience.* New
   York: Macmillan, 1971. 484pp.
Nkosi, L. *The Rhythm of Violence*
Shakespeare, W. *The Merchant of Venice*
Shaw, G. *John Bull's other Island* (Act I only)

GREN Grene, David, translator. *Three Greek Tragedies in
   Translation.* Chicago: University of Chicago Press
   [c1942] 228pp.
Aeschylus. *Prometheus Bound*
Euripides. *Hippolytus*
Sophocles. *Oedipus the King*

GREP Grene, David, and Lattimore, Richmond, eds. *The
   Complete Greek Tragedies.* Chicago: University of
   Chicago Press [1959] 4 vols.
Aeschylus. *Agamemnon* 1
Aeschylus. *The Eumenides* 1
Aeschylus. *The Libation Bearers* 1
Aeschylus. *The Persians* 1
Aeschylus. *Prometheus Bound* 1
Aeschylus. *Seven against Thebes* 1
Aeschylus. *The Suppliant Maidens* 1
Euripides. *Alcestis* 3
Euripides. *Andromache* 3
Euripides. *The Bacchae* 4
Euripides. *The Cyclops* 3
Euripides. *Electra* 4
Euripides. *Hecuba* 3
Euripides. *Helen* 3
Euripides. *The Heracleidae* 3
Euripides. *Heracles* 3
Euripides. *Hippolytus* 3
Euripides. *Ion* 4
Euripides. *Iphigenia in Aulis* 4
Euripides. *Iphigenia in Tauris* 3
Euripides. *The Medea* 3
Euripides. *Orestes* 4
Euripides. *The Phoenician Women* 4
Euripides. *Rhesus* 4
Euripides. *The Suppliant Women* 4
Euripides. *The Trojan Women* 3
Sophocles. *Ajax* 2
Sophocles. *Antigone* 2
Sophocles. *Electra* 2
Sophocles. *Oedipus at Colonus* 2
Sophocles. *Oedipus the King* 2
Sophocles. *Philoctetes* 2
Sophocles. *The Women of Trachis* 2

GREPA Grene, David, and Lattimore, Richmond, eds. *The
   Complete Greek Tragedies.* Centennial Edition.
   Chicago: University of Chicago Press, 1992. 4 vols.
Aeschylus. *Agamemnon* 1
Aeschylus. *The Eumenides* 1
Aeschylus. *The Libation Bearers* 1
Aeschylus. *The Persians* 1
Aeschylus. *Prometheus Bound* 1
Aeschylus. *Seven against Thebes* 1
Aeschylus. *The Suppliant Maidens* 1

Euripides. *Alcestis* 3
Euripides. *Andromache* 3
Euripides. *The Bacchae* 4
Euripides. *Cyclops* 3
Euripides. *Electra* 4
Euripides. *Hecuba* 3
Euripides. *Helen* 3
Euripides. *The Heracleidae* 3
Euripides. *Heracles* 3
Euripides. *Hippolytus* 3
Euripides. *Ion* 4
Euripides. *Iphigenia in Aulis* 4
Euripides. *Iphigenia in Tauris* 3
Euripides. *The Medea* 3
Euripides. *Orestes* 4
Euripides. *The Phoenician Women* 4
Euripides. *Rhesus* 4
Euripides. *The Suppliant Women* 4
Euripides. *The Trojan Women* 3
Sophocles. *Ajax* 2
Sophocles. *Antigone* 2
Sophocles. *Electra* 2
Sophocles. *Oedipus at Colonus* 2
Sophocles. *Oedipus the King* 2
Sophocles. *Philoctetes* 2
Sophocles. *The Women of Trachis* 2

GRER Grene, David, and Lattimore, Richmond, eds.
    *Greek Tragedies.* Chicago: University of Chicago
    Press, 1960. 3 vols.
Aeschylus. *Agamemnon* 1
Aeschylus. *The Eumenides* 3
Aeschylus. *The Libation Bearers* 2
Aeschylus. *Prometheus Bound* 1
Euripides. *Alcestis* 3
Euripides. *The Bacchae* 3
Euripides. *Electra* 2
Euripides. *Hippolytus* 1
Euripides. *Iphigenia in Tauris* 2
Euripides. *The Trojan Women* 2
Sophocles. *Antigone* 1
Sophocles. *Electra* 2
Sophocles. *Oedipus at Colonus* 3
Sophocles. *Oedipus the King* 1
Sophocles. *Philoctetes* 3

GRERA Grene, David, and Lattimore, Richmond, eds.
    *Greek Tragedies.* 2nd ed. Chicago: University of
    Chicago Press, 1991. 3 vols.
Aeschylus. *Agamemnon* 1
Aeschylus. *The Eumenides* 3
Aeschylus. *The Libation Bearers* 1
Aeschylus. *The Persians* 2
Aeschylus. *Prometheus Bound* 2
Aeschylus. *Seven against Thebes* 2

Aeschylus. *The Suppliant Maidens.* 2
Euripides. *Alcestis* 3
Euripides. *The Bacchae* 3
Euripides. *Hippolytus* 1
Sophocles. *Antigone* 1
Sophocles. *Oedipus at Colonus* 3
Sophocles. *Oedipus the King* 1
Sophocles. *Philoctetes* 3

GRIF Griffin, Alice Sylvia (Venezky), ed. *Living Theatre.*
    New York: Twayne [c1953] 510pp.
Aeschylus. *Oresteia*
Anderson, M. *Winterset*
Chekhov, A. *The Seagull*
*Everyman*
Giraudoux, J. *The Madwoman of Chaillot*
Hebbel, F. *Maria Magdalena*
Ibsen, H. *Hedda Gabler*
Marlowe, C. *Faustus*
Molière, J. *The Misanthrope*
Odets, C. *Awake and Sing!*
Plautus, T. *Mostellaria*
Rice, E. *Street Scene*
Shakespeare, W. *Romeo and Juliet*

GRIFG Griffin, Gabriele, and Aston, Elaine, eds. *Herstory:*
    *Plays by Women for Women.* Sheffield, England:
    Sheffield Academic Press, 1991. 2 vols. (Critical
    Stages 5–6)
Bond, E. *Love and Dissent* 2
Holliday, J. *Anywhere to Anywhere* 2
Lavery, B. *Witchcraze* 1
Thompson, T., and Mason, L. *Dear Girl* 2
Wilkinson, J. *Pinchdice & Co.* 1
The Women's Theatre Group and Feinstein, E. *Lear's*
    *Daughters* 1

GRIH Griffith, Francis, and Mersand, Joseph, eds. *Eight*
    *American Ethnic Plays.* New York: Scribner's,
    1974. 386pp.
Alfred, W. *Hogan's Goat*
Apstein, T. *Wetback Run*
Hansberry, L. *A Raisin in the Sun*
Marqués, R. *The Oxcart*
Rose, R. *Dino*
Van Druten, J. *I Remember Mama*
Ward, D. *Day of Absence*

GROS Gross, Theodore, L. *The Literature of American*
    *Jews.* New York: Free Press, 1973. 510pp.
Odets, C. *Awake and Sing!*

GROV *Grove Press Modern Drama: 6 Plays by Brecht,*
    *Baraka, Feiffer, Genêt, Mrozek, Ionesco.* John
    Lahr, editor. New York: Grove, 1975. 446pp.

Brecht, B. *The Caucasian Chalk Circle*
Feiffer, J. *The White House Murder Case*
Genêt, J. *The Blacks: A Clown Show*
Ionesco, E. *Rhinoceros*
Jones, L. *The Toilet*
Mrozek, S. *Tango*

THE GROVE PLAYS OF THE BOHEMIAN CLUB. See
BOH Bohemian Club, San Francisco

GUE Guerney, Bernard Guilbert, ed. *A Treasury of
Russian Literature.* New York: Vanguard Press
[c1943] 1048pp.
Chekhov, A. *The Three Sisters*
Gogol, N. *The Inspector General*
Gorki, M. *The Lower Depths*

GUI Guinagh, Kevin, and Dorjahn, Alfred Paul, eds. *Latin
Literature in Translation.* New York: Longmans,
Green, 1942. 822pp.
Platus, T. *The Menaechmi*
Plautus, T. *The Rudens; or, the Rope*
Terence. *The Adelphi; or, the Brothers*
Terence. *The Phormio*

GUIN Guinagh, Kevin, and Dorjahn, Alfred P., eds. *Latin
Literature in Translation.* 2nd ed. New York:
Longmans, Green [c1952] 822pp.
Plautus. *The Menaechmi*
Plautus. *The Rudens*
Seneca. *Medea*
Terence. *The Adelphi*
Terence. *The Phormio*

GUSTAFSON, ALRIK. *See SCAN Scandinavian Plays of
the Twentieth Century*

GUTDF Guth, Hans P., and Rico, Gabriele L., compilers
*Discovering Literature: Fiction, Poetry, and
Drama.* Englewood Cliffs, NJ: Prentice-Hall, 1993.
1637pp.
Churchill, C. *Objections to Sex and Violence*
*Everyman: A Modern Abridgement*
Glaspell, S. *Trifles*
Hansberry, L. *A Raisin in the Sun*
Ibsen, H. *A Doll's House*
Miller, A. *Death of a Salesman*
Molière, J. *The Misanthrope*
Shakespeare, W. *Hamlet*
Shakespeare, W. *A Midsummer Night's Dream*
Sophocles. *Antigone*
Sophocles. *Oedipus the King*
Soyinka, W. *Death and the King's Horseman*
Valdez, L. *The Buck Private*
Williams, T. *The Glass Menagerie*

GUTDS Guth, Hans P., and Rico, Gabriele L., compilers.
*Discovering Literature: Stories, Poems, Plays.* 2nd
ed. Upper Saddle River. NJ: Prentice-Hall, 1996.
1876pp.
*Everyman: A Modern Abridgement*
Glaspell, S. *Trifles*
Hansberry, L. *A Raisin in the Sun*
Hwang, D. *The Dance and the Railroad*
Ibsen, H. *A Doll's House*
Mamet, D. *The Cryptogram*
Miller, A. *Death of a Salesman*
Molière, J. *The Misanthrope*
Norman, M. *Getting Out*
Shakespeare, W. *Hamlet*
Shakespeare, W. *A Midsummer Night's Dream*
Sophocles. *Antigone*
Sophocles. *Oedipus the King*
Soyinka, W. *Death and the King's Horseman*
Valdez, L. *The Buck Private*
Wasserstein, W. *Tender Offer*
Williams, T. *The Glass Menagerie*

GUTH Guth, Hans Paul. *Idea and Image.* Belmont, CA:
Wadsworth Pub. Co. [c1962] 838pp.
Ibsen, H. *The Master Builder*
Miller, A. *The Crucible*
Molière, J. *The Misanthrope*
Shakespeare, W. *Antony and Cleopatra*
Sophocles. *Antigone*

GUTL Guth, Hans Paul, compiler. *Literature.* 2nd ed.
Belmont, CA: Wadsworth Pub. Co. [1968] 923pp.
Ibsen, H. *The Master Builder*
Miller, A. *The Crucible*
Shakespeare, W. *Antony and Cleopatra*
Sophocles. *Antigone*

GUTR *Guthrie New Theater.* Volume I. Edited by Eugene
Lion and David Ball. New York: Grove Press,
1976. 316pp. (No further volumes were published.)
Casale, M. *Cold*
Ford, F. *Waterman*
Katz, L. *Swellfoot's Tears*
McKillop, M. *The Future Pit*
Perr, H. *Afternoon Tea*
Schrock, G. *Two for the Silence*

GWYN Gwynn, R. S., compiler. *Drama: A HarperCollins
Pocket Anthology.* New York: HarperCollins
College Publishers, 1993. 498pp.
Chekhov, A. *The Three Sisters*
Fornes, M. *Dr. Kheal*
Hansberry, L. *A Raisin in the Sun*
Ibsen, H. *A Doll's House*
Miller, A. *Death of a Salesman*

Shakespeare, W. *Othello*
Sophocles. *Oedipus Rex*
Williams, T. *The Glass Menagerie*

GYOR Györgyey, Clara, ed. *A Mirror to the Cage: Three Contemporary Hungarian Plays.* Fayetteville: University of Arkansas Press, 1993. 245pp.
Kornis, M. *Kozma*
Örkény, I. *Stevie in the Bloodbath*
Spiro, G. *The Imposter*

HACJT *Half a Century of Japanese Theater.* Edited by Japan Playwrights Assocation. Tokyo: Konokuniya, 1999–2006. 8 vols. (Vol. 1, 1990s, Part 1; Vol. 2, 1990s, Part 2; Vol. 3, 1980s, Part 1; Vol. 4, 1980s, Part 2; Vol. 5, 1970s; Vol. 6, 1960s, Part 1; Vol. 7, 1960s, Part 2; Vol. 8, 1950s)
Akihama, S. *Comedy Duo in Hibernation* 7
Akimoto, M. *Our Lady of the Scabs* 7
Betsuyaku, M. *Sick* 6
Chong, W. *A Legend of Mermaids* 4
Dumb Type. *S/N* 2
Fujita, D. *The Amida Black Chant Murder Mystery* 5
Fukuda, T. *The Siege* 8
Fukada, Y. *Oppekepe* 7
Hirata, O. *Citizens of Seoul* 1
Ichidō, R. *Miss Toyoko's Departure* 3
Iijima, S., and Suzuki, Y. *Rhythm Method* 2
Iizawa, T. *The Immortals of Mt. Kunlun* 8
Inoue, H. *Yabuhara, the Blind Master Minstrel* 6
Iwamatsu, R. *The Man Next Door* 2
Kaneshita, T. *Ice Blossoms* 1
Kara, J. *A Cry from the City of Virgins* 6
Kato, M. *The Man Who Sells Memories* 8
Kawamura, T. *Nippon Wars* 4
Kinoshita, J. *Okinawa* 8
Kishida, R. *Thread Hell* 4
Kitamura, S. *Ode to Joy* 4
Kōkami, S. *Lullaby: A Hundred Years of Song* 3
Komatsu, M. *Mystery Tour* 5
Makino, N. *Tokyo Atomic Klub* 1
Matsuda, M. *Cape Moon* 2
Miyamoto, K. *The Meiji Coffin* 7
Miyazawa, A. *Hinemi* 2
Miyoshi, J. *In the Womb* 8
Nagai, A. *Time's Storeroom* 1
Narui, Y. *Farewell to Huckleberry* 2
Noda, H. *The Red Demon Akaoni* 4
Ōhashi, Y. *Godzilla* 3
Okabe, K. *Ayako: Cherry Blossoms Never Fall* 5
Ōta, S. *The Tale of Komachi Told by the Wind* 6
Saitō, R. *Red Dawn over Manhattan* 6
Sakate, Y. *Epitaph for the Whales* 1
Satoh, M. *Abe Sada's Dogs* 6
Shimizu, K. *Such a Serious Frivolity* 7

Takeuchi, J. *Claire de lune* 5
Tanaka, C. *Far Fringes of the Clouds* 8
Terayama, S. *La Marie-vison* 6
Toshirō, S. *Fireflies* 1
Tsuka, K. *The Atami Murder Case* 5
Watanabe, E. *Kitarō the Ghost-buster* 3
Yagi, S. *The Little One* 8
Yamazaki, M. *At Play with a Lion* 7
Yamazaki, T. *The Family Adrift: The Jesus Ark Incident* 5
Yashiro, S. *The Courtesan Miyagino* 8
Yokouchi, K. *The King of La Mancha's Clothes* 3
Yū, M. *Festival for the Fish* 2

HAE Hall, Donald, compiler. *To Read Literature: Fiction, Poetry, Drama.* New York: Holt, Rinehart & Winston, 1981. 1508pp.
Albee, E. *The Zoo Story*
Ibsen, H. *Hedda Gabler*
Miller, A. *Death of a Salesman*
Shakespeare, W. *Othello, the Moor of Venice*
Shaw, G. *Saint Joan*
Yeats, W. *The Cat and the Moon*

HAEA Hall, Donald, compiler. *To Read Literature: Fiction, Poetry, Drama.* 2nd ed. New York: Holt, Rinehart & Winston, 1987. 1281pp.
Beckett, S. *Krapp's Last Tape*
Chekhov, A. *The Cherry Orchard*
Ibsen, H. *Hedda Gabler*
Miller, A. *Death of a Salesman*
Norman, M. *'Night, Mother*
Shakespeare, W. *Othello, the Moor of Venice*
Shepherd, S. *Fool for Love*
Sophocles. *Oedipus Rex*
Wilde, O. *The Importance of Being Earnest*
Williams, T. *The Glass Menagerie*

HAEB Hall, Donald, compiler. *To Read Literature: Fiction, Poetry, Drama.* 3rd ed. Fort Worth, TX: Harcourt Brace Jovanovich College Publishers, 1992. 1340pp.
Beckett, S. *Krapp's Last Tape*
Chekhov, A. *The Cherry Orchard*
Ibsen, H. *Hedda Gabler*
Miller, A. *Death of a Salesman*
Norman, M. *'Night, Mother*
Shakespeare, W. *Othello, the Moor of Venice*
Sophocles. *Oedipus Rex*
Wilde, O. *The Importance of Being Earnest*
Williams, T. *The Glass Menagerie*
Wilson, A. *Fences*

HAH Halliday, Frank Ernest, ed. *The Legend of the Rood.* London: Gerald Duckworth [c1955] 142pp.

*The Death of Pilate*
*The Legend of the Rood*
*The Three Maries*

HAL Halline, Allan Gates, ed. *American Plays*. New York:
    American Book Co. [c1935] 787pp.
Barker, J. *Superstition*
Barry, P. *You and I*
Bird, R. *The Gladiator*
Boker, G. *Francesca da Rimini*
Daly, A. *Horizon*
Davis, O. *Icebound*
Dunlap, W. *André*
Green, P. *The Field God*
Howard, B. *The Henrietta*
Miller, J. *The Danites in the Sierras*
Mitchell, L. *The New York Idea*
Moeller, P. *Madame Sand*
Mowatt, A. *Fashion*
O'Neill, E. *The Great God Brown*
Paulding, J. *The Bucktails; or, Americans in England*
Tyler, R. *The Contrast*
Willis, N. *Bianca Visconti*

HALLINE, ALLAN GATES. See also SIXC *Six Modern
    American Plays*.

HALM Halman, Talat Sait, ed. *Modern Turkish Drama:
    An Anthology of Plays in Translation*. Edited
    with an introduction by T. Halman. Minneapolis:
    Bibliotheca Islamica, 1976. 415pp.
Cumali, N. *Dry Summer*
Dilmen, G. *The Ears of Midas*
Oflazoğlu, A. *Ibrahim the Mad*
Taner, H. *The Ballad of Ali of Keshan*

HALU Hamahan, Leo, and Volpe, Edmond L., eds.
    *Pulitzer Prize Reader*. New York: Popular Library
    [c1961] 607pp.
Williams, T. *27 Wagons Full of Cotton*

HAM Hamilton, Edith, translator. *Three Greek Plays*. New
    York: W. W. Norton [c1937] 239pp.
Aeschylus. *Agamemnon*
Aeschylus. *Prometheus Bound*
Euripides. *The Trojan Women*

HAMI Hamilton (Hamfish) ltd., *London Majority: 1931–
    52*. London: Hamish Hamilton [1952] 1035pp.
Rattigan, T. *The Browning Version*
Sartre, J. *In Camera*

HAN Hampden, John, compiler. *Eighteenth Century Plays*.
    London: Dent [1928] 408pp. (Everyman's Library)
Addison, J. *Cato*

Colman, G., and Garrick, D. *The Clandestine Marriage*
Cumberland, R. *The West Indian*
Fielding, H. *The Tragedy of Tragedies; or, Tom Thumb
    the Great*
Gay, J. *The Beggar's Opera*
Lillo, G. *The London Merchant; or, George Barnwell*
Rowe, N. *Jane Shore*

HANG Hanger, Eunice, compiler. *Three Australian Plays*.
    Minneapolis: University of Minnesota Press, 1968.
    274pp.
Elliott, S. *Rusty Bugles*
McKinney, J. *The Well*
Mathew, R. *We Find the Bunyip*

HANNA Hanna, Gillian, compiler. *Monstrous Regiment:
    Four Plays and a Collective Celebration*. London:
    Nick Hern Books, 1991. 270pp.
Kesselman, W. *My Sister in This House*
Luckham, C., and Bond, C. *Scum*
McLeod, J. *Island Life*
Tikkanen, M. *Love Story of the Century*

HAO Happé, Peter, ed. *Tudor Interludes*. New York:
    Penguin, 1972. 434pp.
*Apius and Virginia*
Fulwell, U. *Like Will to Like*
Heywood, J. *The Play of the Wether*
Medwall, H. *Fulgens and Lucres* (Extracts)
Redford, J. *Wit and Science*
*Respublica* (Extracts)
*Youth*

HAP *Harbrace Omnibus*. Edited by H. B. Reed, J. N.
    McCorcle, W. H. Hildreth, and J. D. McCallum.
    New York: Harcourt, Brace, 1942. v.p.
Anderson, M. *High Tor*
O'Neill, E. *In the Zone*

HAPD Harding, Helen Elizabeth, ed. *Tragedies Old and
    New*. New York: Noble & Noble [c1939] 486pp.
    Note: Also published under the title, *Hamlet and
    Other Tragedies*
O'Neill, E. *Beyond the Horizon*
Shakespeare, W. *Hamlet*
Sophocles. *Electra*

HAPO Hardison, Osborne Bennett, and Mills, Jerry Leath,
    eds. *The Forms of Imagination*. Englewood Cliffs,
    NJ: Prentice-Hall, 1972. 615pp.
Chekhov, A. *Uncle Vanya*
Hansberry, L. *A Raisin in the Sun*
Sophocles. *Oedipus Rex*
Williams, T. *The Glass Menagerie*

HAPRA Harrier, Richard C., ed. *The Anchor Anthology of Jacobean Drama.* Garden City, NY: Doubleday (Anchor Books). 1963. 2 vols.
Chapman, G. *Bussy D'Ambois* 1
Ford, J. *The Broken Heart* 2
Jonson, B. *Everyman in His Humour* 1
Marston, J., and Webster, J. *The Malcontent* 1
Middleton, T., and Rowley, W. *The Changeling* 2
Shirley, J. *The Lady of Pleasure* 2
Tourneur, C. *The Revenger's Tragedy* 2
Webster, J. *The White Devil* 1

HAPRB Harrier, Richard C., ed. *Jacobean Drama: An Anthology.* New York: W. W. Norton, 1968. 2 vols.
Chapman, G. *Bussy D'Ambois* 1
Ford, J. *The Broken Heart* 2
Jonson, B. *Everyman in His Humour* 1
Marston, J., and Webster, J. *The Malcontent* 1
Middleton, T., and Rowley, W. *The Changeling* 2
Shirley, J. *The Lady of Pleasure* 2
Tourneur, C. *The Revenger's Tragedy* 2
Webster, J. *The White Devil* 1

HARRIS, BRICK. *See* REST *Restoration Plays . . .*

HAPRL Harris, Stephen LeRoy, compiler. *The Humanist Tradition in World Literature: An Anthology of Masterpieces from Gilgamesh to the Divine Comedy.* Columbus, OH: Merrill, 1970. 1008pp.
Aeschylus. *Agamemnon*
Aeschylus. *Prometheus Bound*
Aristophanes. *Lysistrata*
Euripides. *The Bacchae*
Euripides. *Medea*
Sophocles. *Oedipus the King*
Sophocles. *Philoctetes*

HAPS Harrison, G. B., ed. *Major British Writers.* New York: Harcourt [c1954] 2 vols.
Shakespeare, W. *Hamlet, Prince of Denmark* 1
Shakespeare, W. *King Henry IV, Part I* 1
Shakespeare, W. *The Tempest* 1
Shaw, G. *Man and Superman* 2

HAPT Harrison, George Bagshawe [and Others], eds. *Major British Writers.* Enl. ed. New York: Harcourt, Brace [c1959] 2 vols.
Byron, G. *Manfred* 2
Dryden, J. *The Secular Masque* 1
Milton, J. *Samson Agonistes* 1
Shakespeare, W. *Hamlet* 1
Shakespeare, W. *Henry IV, Part I* 1
Shakespeare, W. *The Tempest* 1

Shaw, G. *Man and Superman* 2
Shelley, P. *Prometheus Unbound* 2

HAPU Harrison, Paul Carter, ed. *Totem Voices: Plays from the Black World Repertory.* New York: Grove Press, 1998. 523pp.
Carril, P. *Shango de Ima*
Fuller, C. *Zooman and the Sign*
Harrison, P. *Ameri/Cain Gothic*
Mofokeng, Z. *A New Song*
Shange, N. *for colored girls who have considered suicide when the rainbow is enuf*
Soyinka, W. *The Strong Breed*
Walcott, D. *Ti-Jean and His Brothers*
Wilson, A. *Ma Rainey's Black Bottom*

HAPUE Harrison, Paul Carter, and Gus Edwards, eds. *Classic Plays from the Negro Ensemble Company.* Pittsburgh: University of Pittsburgh Press, 1995. 594pp.
Dean, P. *The Sty of the Blind Pig*
Edwards, G. *The Offering*
Elder, L. *Ceremonies in Dark Old Men*
Fuller, C. *A Soldier's Play*
Harrison, P. *The Great MacDaddy*
Lee, L. *The First Breeze of Summer*
Mason, J. *Daughters of the Mock*
Walcott, D. *Dream on Monkey Mountain*
Walker, J. *The River Niger*
Williams, S. *Home*

HAPV Harsh, Philip Whaley, ed. *An Anthology of Roman Drama.* New York: Holt, Rinehart and Winston [c1960] 317pp.
Plautus, T. *The Rope*
Plautus, T. *The Twin Menaechmi*
Seneca, L. *The Medea*
Seneca, L. *The Phaedra*
Seneca, L. *The Thyestes*
Terentius Afer, P. *The Brothers*
Terentius Afer, P. *The Phormio*

HARA Hart, James David, and Gohdes, Clarence, eds. *America's Literature.* New York: Dryden [c1955] 958pp.
O'Neill, E. *The Hairy Ape*

HARB Hartley, Lodwick Charles, and Ladu, Arthur Irish, eds. *Patterns in Modern Drama.* New York: Prentice-Hall, 1948. 496pp.
Chekhov, A. *Uncle Vanya*
Galsworthy, J. *The Pigeon*
Hellman, L. *The Little Foxes*
Ibsen, H. *An Enemy of the People*

Kelly, G. *Craig's Wife*
O'Neill, E. *The Emperor Jones*
Thurber, J., and Nugent, E. *The Male Animal*

HARC *Harvard Classics.* Edited by Charles W. Eliot. New
     York: Collier [c1909–1910] 50 vols.
Aeschylus. *Agamemnon* 8
Aeschylus. *The Furies* 8
Aeschylus. *The Libation-bearers* 8
Aeschylus. *Prometheus Bound* 8
Aristophanes. *The Frogs* 8
Beaumont, F., and Fletcher, J. *Philaster* 47
Browning, R. *A Blot in the 'Scutcheon* 18
Byron, R. *Manfred* 18
Calderón de la Barca, P. *Life Is a Dream* 26
Corneille, P. *Polyeucte* 26
Dekker, T. *The Shoemaker's Holiday* 47
Dryden, J. *All for Love; or, the World Well Lost* 18
Euripides. *The Bacchae* 8
Euripides. *Hippolytus* 8
Goethe, J. *Egmont* 19
Goethe, J. *Faust, Part I* 19
Goldsmith, O. *She Stoops to Conquer* 18
Jonson, B. *The Alchemist* 47
Lesslng, G. *Minna von Barnhelm; or, the Soldier's
     Fortune* 26
Marlowe, C. *Doctor Faustus* 19
Marlowe, C. *Edward the Second* 46
Massinger, P. *A New Way to Pay Old Debts* 47
Milton, J. *Comus* 4
Milton, J. *Samson Agonistes* 4
Molière, J. *Tartuffe; or, the Hypocrite* 26
Racine, J. *Phaedra* 26
Schiller, J. *Wilhelm Tell* 26
Shakespeare, W. *The Tempest* 46
Shakespeare, W. *The Tragedy of Hamlet Prince of
     Denmark* 46
Shakespeare, W. *The Tragedy of King Lear* 46
Shakespeare, W. *The Tragedy of Macbeth* 46
Shelley, P. *The Cenci* 18
Sheridan, R. *The School for Scandal* 18
Sophocles. *Antigone* 8
Sophocles. *Oedipus the King* 8
Webster, J. *The Duchess of Malfi* 47

THE HARVARD DRAMATIC CLUB MIRACLE
     PLAYS. *See* ROHD Robinson, Donald Fay, ed.

HART Harvitt, Hélène Joséphine, ed. *Representative Plays
     from the French Theatre of Today.* Boston: Heath
     [c1940] 442pp.
Bernstein, H. *Le secret*
Claudel, P. *L'annonce faite à Marie*
Lenormand, H. *Le simoun*

Sarment, J. *Le pêcheur d'ombres*
Vildrac, C. *Le paquebot Tenacity*

HARV Harvitt, Hélène Joséphine, and Schwartz, H.
     Stanley, eds. *Promenade littéraire au vintième
     siècle.* New York: Dryden Press [c1949] 407pp.
Vildrac, C. *Le paquebot Tenacity*

HARW Harwood, A. C., translator. *Christmas Plays from
     Oberufer.* London: Anthroposophical Publishing
     Co. [1944] 64pp.
*The Paradise Play*
*The Shepherds' Play*
*The Three Kings' Play*

HARY Hatch, James Vernon, ed. *Black Theatre, U.S.A.:
     45 Plays by Black Americans, 1847–1974.* New
     York: Free Press, 1974. 886pp.
Aldridge, I. *The Black Doctor*
Anderson, G. *Appearances*
Baldwin, J. *The Amen Corner*
Bonner, M. *The Purple Flower*
Branch, W. *In Splendid Error*
Brown, W. *The Escape; or, a Leap to Freedom*
Browne, T. *Natural Man*
Bullins, E. *Goin' a Buffalo*
Burrill, M. *They That Sit in Darkness*
Charles, M. *Job Security*
Childress, A. *Wine in the Wilderness*
Cotter, J. *Caleb the Degenerate*
Dodson, O. *Divine Comedy*
Dunbar-Nelson, A. *Mine Eyes Have Seen*
Edmonds, R. *Bad Man*
Edward, H. *Job Hunters*
Ferdinand, V. *Blk Love Song #1*
Gaines-Shelton, R. *The Church Fight*
Grimke, A. *Rachel*
Hansberry, L. *The Drinking Gourd*
Hill, A. *Walk Hard*
Hughes, L. *Don't You Want to Be Free*
Hughes, L. *Limitations of Life*
Hughes, L. *Little Ham*
Jackson, C. *Fly Blackbird*
Johnson, G. *A Sunday Morning in the South*
Jones, L. *The Slave*
Kennedy, A. *The Owl Answers*
Livingston, M. *For Unborn Children*
Matheus, J. *'Cruiter*
Miller, M. *Graven Images*
Mitchell, L. *Star of the Morning*
Pawley, T. *The Tumult and the Shouting*
Peterson, L. *Take a Giant Step*
Richards, S. *District of Columbia*
Richardson, W. *The Flight of the Natives*

Richardson, W. *The Idle Head*
Sebree, C. *The Dry August*
Sejour, V. *The Brown Overcoat*
Shine, T. *Herbert III*
Spence, E. *Undertow*
Toomer, J. *Balo*
Ward, D. *Day of Absence*
Ward, T. *Big White Fog*
Wright, R., and Green P. *Native Son*

HARYB Hatch, James Vernon, and Shine, Ted. *Black Theatre, USA: Plays by African Americans, 1847 to Today*. Revised and expanded edition. New York: Free Press, 1996. 916pp.
Aldridge, I. *The Black Doctor*
Anderson, G. *Appearances*
Baldwin, J. *The Amen Corner*
Baraka, A. *Dutchman*
Bonner, M. *The Purple Flower*
Brown, W. *The Escape; or, a Leap to Freedom*
Browne, T. *Natural Man*
Bullins, E. *Goin' a Buffalo*
Burrill, M. *Aftermath*
Burrill, M. *They That Sit in Darkness*
Caldwell, B. *Prayer Meeting*
Childress, A. *Wine in the Wilderness*
Dodson, O. *The Confession Stone*
Du Bois, W. *Star of Ethiopia*
Dunbar, P., and Shipp, J. *In Dahomey*
Dunbar-Nelson, A. *Mine Eyes Have Seen*
Edward, H. *Job Hunters*
Edmonds, R. *Old Man Pete*
Elder, L. *Ceremonies in Old Dark Men*
Fuller, C. *A Soldier's Play*
Gaines-Shelton, R. *The Church Fight*
Grimke, A. *Rachel*
Hansberry, L. *A Raisin in the Sun*
Hill, A. *On Strivers Row*
Hughes, L. *Don't You Want to Be Free*
Hughes, L. *Limitations of Life*
Hughes, L. *Mulatto*
Hurston, Z. *The First One*
Johnson, G. *A Sunday Morning in the South*
Kalamu ya Salaam. *Blk Love Song #1*
Kennedy, A. *Funnyhouse of a Negro*
Livingston, M. *For Unborn Children*
Matheus, J. *'Cruiter*
McCauley, R. *Sally's Rape*
Miller, M. *Graven Images*
Pawley, T. *The Tumult and the Shouting*
Peterson, L. *Take a Giant Step*
Rahman, A. *The Mojo and the Sayso*
Richardson, W. *The Deacon's Awakening*

Sejour, V. *The Brown Overcoat*
Shange, N. *for colored girls who have considered suicide . . .*
Shine, T. *Contribution*
Silvera, J., and Hill, A. *Liberty Deferred*
Smith, A. D. *Fires in the Mirror*
Spence, E. *Undertow*
Toomer, J. *Balo*
Ward, D. *Day of Absence*
Ward, T. *Big White Fog*
Wolfe, G. *The Colored Museum*
Wright, R., and Green P. *Native Son*

HARYL Hatch, James Vernon, and Hamalian, Leo, eds. *Lost Plays of the Harlem Renaissance, 1920–1940*. Detroit: Wayne State University Press, 1996. 467p.
Burris, A. *You Mus' Be Bo'n Ag'in*
Coleman, R. *The Girl from Back Home*
Cotter, J. *On the Fields of France*
Gilbert, M. *Environment*
Graham, S. *Track Thirteen*
Hazzard, A. *Mother Liked It*
Hughes, L. *The Em-Fuehrer Jones*
Hughes, L. *The Organizer*
Hughes, L. *Scarlet Sister Barry*
Hughes, L. *Young Black Joe*
Johnson, F. *Run Little Chillun*
Matheus, J. *Black Damp*
Mitchell, J. *Son-boy*
Richardson, W. *A Pillar of the Church*
Schuyler, G. *The Yellow Peril*
Seiler, C. *Darker Brother*

HAT Hatcher, Harlan Henthorne, ed. *Modern American Dramas*. New York: Harcourt, Brace, 1941. 394p.
Anderson, M. *Winterset*
Howard, S. *Dodsworth*
Odets, C. *Awake and Sing*
O'Neill, E. *Beyond the Horizon*
Rice, E. *The Adding Machine*
St. Joseph, E. *A Passenger to Bali*
Sherwood, R. *Abe Lincoln in Illinois*
Wilder, T. *Our Town*

HATA Hatcher, Harlan Henthorne, ed. *Modern American Dramas*. New ed. New York: Harcourt, Brace [c1949] 378pp.
Anderson, M. *Winterset*
Heggen, T. *Mister Roberts*
Miller, A. *All My Sons*
O'Neill, E. *The Emperor Jones*
Rice, E. *The Adding Machine*

Saroyan, W. *The Time of Your Life*
Sherwood, R. *Abe Lincoln in Illinois*
Williams, T. *The Glass Menagerie*

HAU Hatcher, Harlan Henthorne, ed. *Modern British
    Dramas*. New York: Harcourt, Brace, 1941. 374pp.
Dunsany, E. *If*
Galsworthy, J. *Justice*
Maugham, W. *The Constant Wife*
Monkhouse, A. *The Conquering Hero*
O'Flaherty, L. *The Informer*
Pinero, A. *Mid-channel*
Synge, J. *The Playboy of the Western World*

HAV Hatcher, Harlan Henthorne, ed. *Modern Continental
    Dramas*. New York: Harcourt Brace, 1941. 747pp.
Čapek, K. *R.U.R.*
Chekhov, A. *The Cherry Orchard*
Claudel, P. *The Tidings Brought to Mary*
Gorky, M. *The Lower Depths*
Hauptmann, G. *Hannele*
Ibsen, H. *Hedda Gabler*
Katayev, V. *Squaring the Circle*
Lenormand, H. *Time Is a Dream*
Maeterlinck, M. *Pelléas and Mélisande*
Martínez Sierra, G. *The Cradle Song*
Molnár, F. *Liliom*
Pirandello, L. *As You Desire Me*
Rostand, E. *Cyrano de Bergerac*
Strindberg, A. *The Ghost Sonata*
Strindberg, A. *Miss Julia*
Toller, E. *Transfiguration*

HAVD Hatcher, Harlan Henthorne, ed. *Modern Dramas.*
    Shorter ed. New York: Harcourt Brace [c1944]
    495pp.
Anderson M. *Winterset*
Čapek, K. *R.U.R.*
Chekhov, A. *Cherry Orchard*
Galsworthy, J. *Justice*
Hellman, L. *Watch on the Rhine*
Ibsen, H. *Hedda Gabler*
O'Flaherty, L. *The Informer*
O'Neill, E. *Beyond the Horizon*
Sherwood, R. *Abe Lincoln in Illinois*

HAVE Hatcher, Harlan Henthorne, ed. *Modern Dramas.*
    New shorter ed. New York. Harcourt, Brace
    [c1948] 479pp.
Anderson, M. *Winterset*
Čapek, K. *R.U.R.*
Galsworthy, J. *Justice*

Hellman, L. *The Little Foxes*
Ibsen, H. *Hedda Gabler*
Katayev, V. *Squaring the Circle*
Maugham, W. *The Circle*
O'Neill, E. *Beyond the Horizon*
Sherwood, R. *Abe Lincoln in Illinois*

HAVG Hatcher, Harlan Henthorne. *A Modern Repertory.*
    New York: Harcourt, Brace [c1953] 714pp.
Coxe, L., and Chapman, R. *Billy Budd*
Eliot, T. *Murder in the Cathedral*
Fry, C. *Venus Observed*
Giraudoux, J. *The Madwoman of Chaillot*
Kingsley, S. *Detective Story*
O'Casey, S. *Juno and the Paycock*
O'Neill, E. *Ah, Wilderness!*
Shaw, G. *Candida*
Williams, T. *Summer and Smoke*

HAVH Hatlen, Theodore W., compiler. *Drama: Principles
    and Plays*. New York: Appleton-Century-Crofts
    [1967] 552pp.
Beckett, S. *Act without Words, I*
Brecht, B. *The Caucasian Chalk Circle*
Ibsen, H. *An Enemy of the People*
Ionesco, E. *The Leader*
Molière, J. *The Miser*
O'Neill, E. *Desire under the Elms*
Shakespeare, W. *Hamlet*
Shaw, G. *Major Barbara*
Sheridan, R. *The School for Scandal*
Sophocles. *Antigone*
Strindberg, A. *Miss Julie*
Williams, T. *The Glass Menagerie*

HAVHA Hatlen, Theodore W., ed. *Drama: Principles and
    Plays*. 2nd ed. Englewood Cliffs, NJ: Prentice-Hall,
    1975. 660pp.
Beckett, S. *Act without Words*
Brecht, B. *The Caucasian Chalk Circle*
Congreve, W. *The Way of the World*
Durrenmatt, F. *The Physicists*
Elder, L. *Ceremonies in Dark Old Men*
Ibsen, H. *An Enemy of the People*
Ionesco, E. *The Leader*
Molière, J. *The Miser*
O'Neill, E. *The Emperor Jones*
Osborne, J. *Look Back in Anger*
Shakespeare, W. *King Lear*
Shaw, G. *Major Barbara*
Sophocles. *Antigone*
Strindberg, A. *Miss Julie*

HAVHN Haugen, Einar Ingvald, ed. *Fire and Ice: 3 Icelandic Plays*. Madison: University of Wisconsin Press, 1967. 266pp.
Sigurjónsson, J. *The Wish*
Stefánsson, D. *The Golden Gate*
Thórdarson, A. *Atoms and Madams*

HAVI Havighurst, Walter; Almy, Robert F.; Wilson, Gordon D.; and Middlebrook, L. Ruth, eds. *Selection: A Reader for College Writing*. New York: Dryden [c1955] 740pp.
Shaw, G. *Arms and the Man*
Sophocles. *Antigone*
Synge, J. *Riders to the Sea*
Williams, T. *The Glass Menagerie*

HAVL Hay, David L., and Howell, James F., compilers. *Contact with Drama*. Chicago: Science Research Associates, 1974. 550pp.
Cornish, R. *Open Twenty-four Hours*
Enrico, R. *On Owl Creek*
Ibsen, H. *Hedda Gabler*
Miller, A. *Death of a Salesman*
O'Neill, E. *The Emperor Jones*
Pirandello, L. *Six Characters in Search of an Author*
Shaffer, P. *Black Comedy*
Shakespeare, W. *Othello*
Synge, J. *Riders to the Sea*
Van Itallie, J. *Motel*
Wycherley, W. *The Country Wife*
Zindel, P. *The Effect of Gamma Rays on Man-in-the-moon Marigolds*

HAY Haydn, Hiram Collins, ed. *The Portable Elizabethan Reader*. New York: Viking, 1946. 688pp.
Dekker, T. *The Shoemaker's Holiday; or, a Pleasant Comedy of the Gentle Craft*
Marlowe, C. *Doctor Faustus*

HAYD Haydn, Hiram Collins, and Nelson, John Charles, eds. *A Renaissance Treasury*. New York: Doubleday, 1953. 432pp.
Machiavelli, N. *Mandragola*
Tasso, T. *Aminta*

HAYES, HELEN. *See* GRIF Grifffn, Alice Sylvia (Venezky), ed. *Living Theatre*.

HAYE Hayes, Richard, ed. *Port-Royal and Other Plays*. New York: Hill and Wang [c1962] 267pp. (Mermaid Dramabook)
Claudel, P. *Tobias and Sara*
Copeau, J. *The Little Poor Man*
Mauriac, F. *Asmodée*
Montherlant, H. *Port-Royal*

HEA *The Heath Introduction to Drama*. With a preface on drama and introductory notes by Jordan Y. Miller. Lexington, MA: Heath, 1976. 907pp.
Aristophanes. *Lysistrata*
Brecht, B. *Mother Courage*
Chekhov, A. *The Cherry Orchard*
Ibsen, H. *Hedda Gabler*
Miller, A. *Death of a Salesman*
Molière, J. *The Misanthrope*
O'Neill, E. *Desire under the Elms*
Pinter, H. *The Dumb Waiter*
Pirandello, L. *Six Characters in Search of an Author*
*The Second Shepherds' Play*
Shakespeare, W. *Hamlet*
Shaw, G. *Major Barbara*
Sophocles. *Oedipus Rex*
Strindberg, A. *Miss Julie*
Williams, T. *The Glass Menagerie*

HEAA *The Heath Introduction to Drama*. With a preface on drama and introductory notes by Jordan Y. Miller. 2nd ed. Lexington, MA: Heath, 1983. 977pp.
Aristophanes. *Lysistrata*
Brecht, B. *The Caucasian Chalk Circle*
Chekhov, A. *The Cherry Orchard*
Hansberry, L. *A Raisin in the Sun*
Ibsen, H. *A Doll's House*
Ionesco, E. *The Gap*
Miller, A. *Death of a Salesman*
Molière, J. *The Misanthrope*
O'Neill, E. *Desire under the Elms*
Pirandello, L. *Six Characters in Search of an Author*
*The Second Shepherds' Play*
Shakespeare, W. *Hamlet*
Shaw, G. *Major Barbara*
Sophocles. *Oedipus Rex*
Strindberg, A. *Miss Julie*
Williams, T. *The Glass Menagerie*

HEAB *The Heath Introduction to Drama*. With a preface on drama and introductory notes by Jordan Y. Miller. 3rd ed. Lexington, MA: Heath, 1988. 1054pp.
Aristophanes. *Lysistrata*
Brecht, B. *The Good Woman of Setzuan*
Chekhov, A. *The Cherry Orchard*
Congreve, W. *The Way of the World*
Hansberry, L. *A Raisin in the Sun*
Ibsen, H. *A Doll's House*
Ionesco, E. *The Gap*
Miller, A. *Death of a Salesman*
Molière, J. *The Misanthrope*
O'Neill, E. *Desire under the Elms*
Pirandello, L. *Six Characters in Search of an Author*

Shakespeare, W. *Hamlet*
Shaw, G. *Major Barbara*
Sophocles. *Oedipus Rex*
Strindberg, A. *Miss Julie*
Williams, T. *The Glass Menagerie*

HEAC *The Heath Introduction to Drama*. With a preface
    on drama and introductory notes by Jordan Y.
    Miller. 4th ed. Lexington, MA: Heath, 1992.
    1131pp.
Aristophanes. *Lysistrata*
Chekhov, A. *The Cherry Orchard*
Congreve, W. *The Way of the World*
Fugard, A. *"Master Harold" . . . and the Boys*
Glaspell, S. *Trifles*
Hansberry, L. *A Raisin in the Sun*
Ibsen, H. *A Doll's House*
Jones, L. *Dutchman*
Miller, A. *Death of a Salesman*
Molière, J. *Tartuffe*
O'Neill, E. *The Hairy Ape*
Shakespeare, W. *A Midsummer Night's Dream*
Shakespeare, W. *Hamlet*
Shaw, G. *Major Barbara*
Sophocles. *Oedipus Rex*
Wilde, O. *The Importance of Being Earnest*
Williams, T. *The Glass Menagerie*

HEAD *The Heath Introduction to Drama*. With a preface
    on drama and introductory notes by Jordan Y.
    Miller. 5th ed. Lexington, MA: Heath, 1996.
    1114pp.
Aristophanes. *Lysistrata*
Chekhov, A. *The Cherry Orchard*
Glaspell, S. *Trifles*
Hansberry, L. *A Raisin in the Sun*
Ibsen, H. *A Doll's House*
Miller, A. *Death of a Salesman*
Molière, J. *Tartuffe*
Norman, M. *'Night Mother*
O'Neill, E. *Desire under the Elms*
Pinter, H. *The Dumb Waiter*
Rabe, D. *Sticks and Bones*
*The Second Shepherds' Play*
Shakespeare, W. *Hamlet*
Shaw, G. *Major Barbara*
Sheridan, R. *The School for Scandal*
Sophocles. *Oedipus Rex*
Williams, T. *The Glass Menagerie*
Wilson, A. *Fences*

HEAL *The Heath Introduction to Literature*. Compiled
    by Alice S. Landy. Lexington, MA: Heath, 1980.
    949pp.

Miller, A. *Death of a Salesman*
*The Second Shepherds' Play*
Shakespeare, W. *Hamlet*
Shaw, G. *Major Barbara*
Sophocles. *Oedipus Rex*

HEALA *The Heath Introduction to Literature*. Compiled
    by Alice S. Landy. 2nd ed. Lexington, MA: Heath,
    1984. 1090pp.
Chekhov, A. *A Marriage Proposal*
Ibsen, H. *A Doll's House*
Ionesco, E. *The Gap*
Miller, A. *Death of a Salesman*
Shakespeare, W. *Hamlet*
Shaw, G. *Pygmalion*
Sophocles. *Antigone*
Sophocles. *Oedipus Rex*

HEALB *The Heath Introduction to Literature*. Compiled
    by Alice S. Landy. 3rd ed. Lexington, MA: Heath,
    1988. 1104pp.
Chekhov, A. *A Marriage Proposal*
Glaspell, S. *Trifles*
Ibsen, H. *A Doll's House*
Ionesco, E. *The Gap*
Miller, A. *Death of a Salesman*
Shakespeare, W. *Hamlet*
Sophocles. *Antigone*
Sophocles. *Oedipus Rex*
Strindberg, A. *The Stronger*
Synge, J. *Riders to the Sea*
Wilde, O. *The Importance of Being Earnest*

HEALC *The Heath Introduction to Literature*. Compiled
    by Alice S. Landy. 4th ed. Lexington, MA: Heath,
    1992. 1142pp.
Glaspell, S. *Trifles*
Hansberry, L. *A Raisin in the Sun*
Ibsen, H. *A Doll's House*
Molière, J. *Tartuffe*
O'Neill, E. *Desire under the Elms*
Shakespeare, W. *Hamlet*
Sophocles. *Antigone*
Sophocles. *Oedipus Rex*
Wilde, O. *The Importance of Being Earnest*
Williams, T. *The Glass Menagerie*

HEALD *The Heath Introduction to Literature*. Compiled
    by Alice S. Landy. 5th ed. Lexington, MA: Heath,
    1996. 1035pp.
Hansberry, L. *A Raisin in the Sun*
Havel, V. *Protest*
Ibsen, H. *A Doll's House*
Shakespeare, W. *Hamlet*
Shakespeare, W. *Much Ado about Nothing*

Sophocles. *Antigone*
Sophocles. *Oedipus Rex*
Williams, T. *The Glass Menagerie*

HEALE *The Heath Introduction to Literature.* Compiled by
      Alice S. Landy and William Rodney Allen. 6th ed.
      Boston: Houghton Mifflin Company, 2000. 1009pp.
Havel, V. *Protest*
Ibsen, H. *A Doll's House*
Shakespeare, W. *Hamlet*
Shakespeare, W. *Much Ado about Nothing*
Sophocles. *Antigone*
Sophocles. *Oedipus Rex*
Williams, T. *The Glass Menagerie*
Wolfe, G. *The Colored Museum*

HEID Heide, Christopher, ed. *Maritime Lines: An
      Anthology of Contemporary Plays.* Halifax, NS:
      Nimbus Publishing Limited, 1988. 175pp.
Cameron, S. *The Last Hook*
Cowan, C. *Spooks: The Mystery of Caledonia Mills*
      (excerpt)
Heide, C. *"I Ain't Dead Yet!"*
Hill, K. *Three to Get Married* (excerpt)
Ledoux, P. *Sam Slick: The Clockmaker* (excerpt)
Moore, P. *Daddy*
Poirer, L. *The White Night*
Sheriff, J. *The Bruce Curtis Story: Journey to
      Bordentown* (excerpt)

HEIL Heilman, Robert B., ed. *An Anthology of English
      Drama before Shakespeare.* New York: Rinehart
      [c1952] 405pp.
*The Betrayal*
*The Crucifixion*
*Everyman*
Greene, R. *The Honorable History of Friar Bacon and
      Friar Bungay*
Kyd, T. *The Spanish Tragedy*
Marlowe, C. *The Tragical History of Dr. Faustus*
*Noah*
*The Second Shepherds' Play*
Stevenson, W. *Gammer Gurton's Needle*

HEIS Heisch, Elizabeth, ed. *Discovery and Recollection:
      An Anthology of Literary Types.* New York: Holt,
      Rinehart and Winston, 1970. 566pp.
Benet, S. *The Devil and Daniel Webster*
Chayevsky, P. *Marty*
Fletcher, L. *Sorry, Wrong Number*
Hansberry, L. *A Raisin in the Sun*
Shaw, G. *Pygmalion*

HELB Helbing, Terry, ed. *Gay and Lesbian Plays Today.*
      Portsmouth, NH: Heinemann, 1993. 288p

Bourne, B., and Shaw, P., and Shaw, P., and Weaver,
      W. *Belle Reprieve*
Bumbalo, V. *Tell*
Chambers, J., and Dennis, V. *Eye of the Gull*
Kearns, M. *Intimacies/More Intimacies*
Morse, C. *Annunciation*
Somsen, P. *One Tit, a Dyke, & Gin!*
Swados, R. *A Quiet End*

HERZ Herzfeld-Sander, Margaret, ed. *Early 20th-Century
      German Plays.* (The German Library, vol. 58) New
      York: Continuum, 1998. 267pp.
Fleisser, M. *Purgatory in Ingolstadt*
Horváth, Ö. *Tales from the Vienna Woods*
Wedekind, F. *The Marquis of Keith*
Wedekind, F. *Spring Awakening*

HEWE Hewes, Henry, ed. *Famous American Plays of the
      1940s.* New York: Dell, c1960. 447pp. (Laurel
      Drama Series)
Anderson, M., and Weil, K. *Lost in the Stars*
Laurents, A. *Home of the Brave*
McCullers, C. *The Member of the Wedding*
Miller, A. *All My Sons*
Wilder, T. *The Skin of Our Teeth*

HEWES, HENRY. *See also BES Best Plays of 1894/99-,
      1961/62.*

HIB Hibbard, Clarence Addison, ed. *Writers of the
      Western World.* Boston: Houghton, Mifflin [c1942]
      1261pp.
Aeschylus. *Agamemnon*
Aristophanes. *The Frogs*
Euripides. *Medea*
Evreinov, N. *The Theatre of the Soul*
Goethe, J. *Faust, Part I*
Ibsen, H. *The Master Builder*
Molière, J. *The Misanthrope*
O'Neill, E. *The Hairy Ape*
Racine, J. *Phaedra*
Shakespeare, W. *King Lear*
Sophocles. *Antigone*

HIBA Hibbard, Clarence Addison, ed. *Writers of the
      Western World.* Rev. ed. Boston: Houghton, Mifflin
      [c1946] 1033pp. (United States Naval Academy
      edition edited by Cyril B. Judge)
Aeschylus. *Agamemnon*
Aristophanes. *The Frogs*
Evreinov, N. *The Theatre of the Soul*
Goethe, J. *Faust, Part I*
Ibsen, H. *The Master Builder*
Molière, J. *The Misanthrope*

O'Neill, E. *The Hairy Ape*
Shakespeare, W. *King Lear*

HIBB Hibbard, Clarence Addison, and Frenz, Horst, eds.
 *Writers of the Western World.* 2nd ed. Boston:
 Houghton Mifflin [c1954] 1239pp.
Aeschylus. *Agamemnon*
Aristophanes. *The Frogs*
Chekhov, A. *The Cherry Orchard*
Claudel, P. *The Satin Slipper; or, the Worst Is Not the
 Surest*
Euripides. *Medea*
Goethe, J. *Faust, Part I*
Ibsen, H. *The Master Builder*
Molière, J. *The Misanthrope*
O'Neill, E. *The Hairy Ape*
Pirandello, L. *The Jar*
Racine, J. *Phaedra*
Shakespeare, W. *King Lear*
Sophocles. *Antigone*

HIBH Hibbett, Howard, ed. *Contemporary Japanese
 Literature: An Anthology of Fiction, Film, and
 other Writing since 1945.* New York: Knopf, 1977.
 468pp.
Abe, Kōbō (Kimifusa). *Friends*
Kurosawa, Akira. *Ikiru*
Ozu, Yasujirō. *Tokyo Story*

HIG Higgins, V. Louise, and Kerr, Walter, eds. *Five World
 Plays.* New York: Harcourt, Brace and World,
 1964. 550pp.
Chekhov, A. *The Cherry Orchard*
Shakespeare, W. *Hamlet*
Shaw, G. *Saint Joan*
Sheridan, R. *The Rivals*
Sophocles. *Antigone*

HIJ *High Energy Musicals from the Omaha Magic
 Theatre.* New York: Broadway Play Publishing,
 c1983. 212pp.
Schmidman, J. *Running Gag*
Terry, M. *American King's English for Queens*
Terry, M. *Babes in the Big House*

HILDRETH, WILLIAM HENRY. *See also* HAP *Harbrace
 Omnibus.*

HIL Hildreth, William Henry, and Dumble, Wilson
 Randle, eds. *Five Contemporary American Plays.*
 New York: Harper [c1939] 410pp.
Anderson, M. *Winterset*
Kaufman, G., and Ryskind, M. *Of Thee I Sing*
Odets, C. *Waiting for Lefty*

O'Neill, E. *Ah, Wilderness*
Sherwood, R. *Idiot's Delight*

HILEB Hill, Errol, ed. *Black Heroes: Seven Plays.* New
 York: Applause Theatre Book Publishers, 1989.
 426pp.
Branch, W. *In Splendid Error*
Dean, P. *Paul Robeson*
Edmonds, R. *Nat Turner*
Hughes, L. *Emperor of Haiti*
Miller, M. *Harriet Tubman*
Milner, R. *Roads of the Mountaintop*
White, E. *I, Marcus Garvey (and the Captivity of
 Babylon)*

HILEP Hill, Errol, ed. *Plays for Today.* Harlow, UK:
 Longman, 1985. 233pp.
Hill, E. *Man Better Man*
Scott, D. *An Echo in the Bone*
Walcott, D. *Ti-Jean and His Brothers*

HILET Hill, Errol, ed. *A Time . . . and a Season: 8
 Caribbean Plays.* Trinidad: School of Continuing
 Studies, the University of the West Indies, 1996.
 450pp.
Arrivi, F. *Masquerade*
Buenaventura, E. *The Funeral*
Buenaventura, E. *The Orgy*
James, C. *The Black Jacobins*
Mais, R. *George William Gordon*
McDonald, I. *The Tramping Man*
Quintero, H. *The Booby Prize*
Walcott, R. *The Banjo Man*

HILL Hill, John McMurray, and Harlan, Mabel Margaret,
 eds. *Cuatro Comedies.* New York: Norton [c1941]
 699pp.
Calderón de la Barca, P. *No siempre lo peor es cierto*
Ruiz de Alarcón y Mendoza, J. *No hay mal que por bien
 no venga (Don Domingo de Don Blas)*
Téllez, G. (Tirso de Molina [pseudonym]). *El burlador
 de Sevilla*
Vega [Carpio], L. de. *Peribáñez y el comendador de
 Ocaña*

HILP Hill, Philip George, compiler. *The Living Art: An
 Introduction to Theatre and Drama.* New York:
 Holt, Rinehart and Winston, 1971. 578pp.
Brecht, B. *Galileo*
Hellman, L. *The Little Foxes*
MacLeish, A. *J. B.*
Miller, A. *A View from the Bridge*
Molière, J. *Tartuffe*
Oldenburg, C. *Fotodeath*
Rostand, E. *Cyrano de Bergerac*

Shakespeare, W. *Twelfth Night*
Sophocles. *Oedipus Rex*
Wilde, O. *The Importance of Being Earnest*

HILPDH Hill, Philip George, ed. *Our Dramatic Heritage.*
Rutherford, NJ: Fairleigh Dickinson University
Press; London and Toronto: Associated University
Presses, 1983–1992. 6 vols. (Vol. 1: Classical
Drama and the Early Renaissance; Vol. 2: The
Golden Age; Vol. 3: The Eighteenth Century; Vol.
4: Romanticism and Realism; Vol. 5: Reactions to
Realism; Vol. 6: Expressing the Inexpressible)
Aeschylus. *Agamemnon* 1
Aeschylus. *Choephoroe* 1
Aeschylus. *Eumenides* 1
Anouilh, J. *Thieves' Carnival* 6
Aristophanes. *Lysistrata* 1
Beaumarchais, P. *Figaro's Marriage* 3
Beaumont, F., and Fletcher, J. *The Knight of the Burning
Pestle* 2
Brecht, B. *Galileo* 5
Brecht, B. *The Threepenny Opera* 5
Büchner, G. *Woyzeck* 4
Calderón de la Barca, P. *Life Is a Dream* 2
Chekhov, A. *The Cherry Orchard* 4
Cocteau, J. *Orphée* 6
Congreve, W. *The Way of the World* 3
Corneille, P. *The Cid* 2
*The Doubles according to Plautus* 1
Euripides. *Medea* 1
*Everyman* 1
Feydeau, G. *The Bug in Her Ear* 6
García Lorca, F. *Blood Wedding* 6
Gay, J. *The Beggar's Opera* 3
Ghelderode, M. *Red Magic* 6
Giraudoux, J. *Ondine* 6
Goethe, J. *Faust, Part 1* 4
Goldoni, C. *The Mistress of the Inn* 3
Goldsmith, O. *She Stoops to Conquer* 3
Gorky, M. *The Lower Depths* 4
Holberg, L. *Jean de France* 3
Hrotsvitha. *Abraham* 1
Ibsen, H. *Hedda Gabler* 4
Ibsen, H. *Peer Gynt* 4
Jarry, A. *King Ubu* 6
Jonson, B. *Volpone* 2
Kaiser, G. *From Morn to Midnight* 5
Kyd, T. *The Spanish Tragedy* 2
Machiavelli, N. *The Mandrake* 1
Maeterlinck, M. *The Blind* 6
Marlowe, C. *Edward II* 2
Menander, *The Dyskolos* 1
Molière, J. *Scapin* 2
Molière, J. *Tartuffe* 2
Molina, T. *The Trickster of Seville* 2

O'Casey, S. *Juno and the Paycock* 5
*Pierre Pathelin* 1
Pirandello, L. *Six Characters in Search of an Author* 6
Plautus, T. *Miles gloriosus (Major Bull-shot Gorgeous)* 1
Racine, J. *Phaedra* 2
Rostand, E. *Cyrano de Bergerac* 4
Schiller, F. *Wilhelm Tell* 4
Scribe, E. *The Glass of Water* 4
*The Second Shepherds' Play* 1
Seneca, L. *The Trojan Women* 1
Shakespeare, W. *King Lear* 2
Shakespeare, W. *Twelfth Night* 2
Shaw, G. *Arms and the Man* 5
Shaw, G. *Saint Joan* 5
Sheridan, R. *The School for Scandal* 3
Sophocles. *Oedipus Rex* 1
Strindberg, A. *A Dream Play* 5
Synge, J. *Riders to the Sea* 5
Terentius Afer, P. *The Brothers* 1
Vega, L. *The Dog in the Manger* 2
Webster, J. *The Duchess of Malfi* 2
Wilde, O. *The Importance of Being Earnest* 5
Yeats, W. *Purgatory* 5
Zola, E. *Thérèse Raquin* 4

HOEP Hoeper, Jeffrey D., Pickering, James H., and
Chappel, Deborah K., compilers. *Drama.* New
York: Macmillan Publishing Company, 1994.
1469pp.
Aeschylus. *Agamemnon*
Aristophanes. *Lysistrata*
Beckett, S. *All that Fall*
Chekhov, A. *The Cherry Orchard*
Childress, A. *Wine in the Wilderness*
Euripides. *Hippolytus*
*Everyman*
Glaspell, S. *Trifles*
Hansberry, L. *A Raisin in the Sun*
Henley, B. *Am I Blue?*
Ibsen, H. *A Doll's House*
Ibsen, H. *Hedda Gabler*
Jonson, B. *Volpone*
Marlow, C. *Dr. Faustus*
Molière, J. *Tartuffe*
O'Neill, E. *Desire under the Elms*
Pirandello, L. *Six Characters in Search of an Author*
*The Second Shepherd's Play*
Shaffer, P. *Amadeus*
Shakespeare, W. *A Midsummer Night's Dream*
Shakespeare, W. *Othello*
Shaw, G. *Mrs. Warren's Profession*
Shepard, S. *True West*
Sophocles. *Antigone*
Sophocles. *King Oedipus*
Soyinka, W. *The Strong Breed*

Stoppard, T. *The Real Inspector Hound*
Strindberg, A. *Miss Julia*
Williams, T. *The Glass Menagerie*

HOF Hoffman, William M., ed. *Gay Plays: The First
    Collection*. New York: Avon, 1979. 493p
  Chambers, J. *A Late Snow*
  Hoffman, W., and Holland, A. *Cornbury: The Queen's
    Governor*
  Marcus, F. *The Killing of Sister George*
  Miller, S. *Confessions of a Female Disorder*
  Orton, J. *Entertaining Mr. Sloane*
  Patrick, R. *T-shirts*
  Solly, B., and Ward, D. *Boy Meets Boy*
  Wilson, L. *The Madness of Lady Bright*

HOFFMAN, WILLIAM M. *See* NEWA *New American
    Plays.*

HOGE Hogan, Robert Goode, compiler. *Seven Irish Plays,
    1946–1964*. Minneapolis: University of Minnesota
    Press [1967] 472pp.
  Byrne, S. *Design for a Headstone*
  Douglas, J. *The Ice Goddess*
  Keane, J. *Many Young Men of Twenty*
  Keane, J. *Sharon's Grave*
  MacMahon, B. *Song of the Anvil*
  Molloy, M. *The Visiting House*
  O'Donovan, J. *Copperfaced Jack*

HOGF Hogan, Robert Goode and Molin, Sven Eric, eds.
    *Drama: The Major Genres*. New York: Dodd,
    Mead, 1962. 652pp.
  Chekhov, A. *The Three Sisters*
  García Lorca, F. *The House of Bernarda Alba*
  Gorky, M. *Yegor Bulychov and the Others*
  Inge, W. *Bus Stop*
  James, H. *The American*
  Jonson, B. *The Silent Woman*
  Molière, J. *Tartuffe*
  O'Casey, S. *The Plough and the Stars*
  Shakespeare, W. *The Tragedy of King Lear*
  Shaw, G. *The Six of Calais*
  Sophocles. *Antigone*

HOGI Hogins, James B., compiler. *Literature: A
    Collection of Mythology and Folklore, Short
    Stories, Poetry, Drama*. Chicago: Science
    Research Associates, 1973. 962pp.
  Arrabal, F. *Picnic on the Battlefield*
  Bullins, E. *The Electronic Nigger*
  Miller, A. *A View from the Bridge*
  Molière, J. *Sganarelle*
  Shakespeare, W. *Macbeth*
  Shaw, G. *How He Lied to Her Husband*

Sophocles. *Oedipus Rex*
Synge, J. *Riders to the Sea*

HOGN Hogins, James B., compiler. *Literature: A
    Collection of Mythology and Folklore, Short
    Stories, Poetry, and Drama*. 2nd ed. Chicago:
    Science Research Associates, 1977. 974pp.
  Arrabal, F. *Picnic on the Battlefield*
  Henshaw, J. *The Jewels of the Shrine*
  Miller, A. *A View from the Bridge*
  O'Neill, E. *Ile*
  Pirandello, L. *The Man with the Flower in His Mouth*
  Shakespeare, W. *Othello*
  Sophocles. *Oedipus Rex*
  Strindberg, A. *Miss Julie*

HOLM Holmes, John Albert, and Towle, Carroll S., eds.
    *A Complete College Reader*. Boston: Houghton,
    Mifflin [c1950] 1063pp.
  Anderson, M. *Winterset*
  Ibsen, H. *An Enemy of the People*
  O'Neill, E. *Ah, Wilderness!*

HOLP Holmes, Paul C., and Lehman, A. J., eds. *Keys to
    Understanding: Receiving and Sending; Drama*.
    New York: Harper and Row, 1970. 459pp.
  Aristophanes. *Lysistrata*
  Cowen, R. *Summertree*
  Gardner, H. *A Thousand Clowns*
  Ionesco, E. *The Gap*
  Jones, L. *Dutchman*
  Saroyan, W. *Hello Out There*
  Shakespeare, W. *Romeo and Juliet*
  Sophocles. *Antigone*
  Ward, D. *Happy Ending*

HOLTM Holt, Marion P., ed. *The Modern Spanish Stage:
    Four Plays*. New York: Hill and Wang, 1970.
    388pp.
  Buero Vallejo, A. *The Concert at Saint Ovide*
  Casona, A. *The Boat without Fisherman*
  López Rubio, J. *The Blindfold*
  Sastre, A. *Condemned Squad*

HOLTS Holt, Marion P., ed. *Spain: Plays
    (Dramacontemporary Series)*. New York:
    Performing Arts Journal Publications, 1985. 229pp.
  Buero Vallejo, A. *The Foundation*
  Martin Recuerda, J. *The Inmates of the Convent of Saint
    Mary Egyptian*
  Nieva, F. *Coronada and the Bull*
  Salom, J. *The Cock's Short Flight*

HOM *Homosexual Acts: Five Short Plays from the Gay
    Season at the Almost Free Theatre*. Edited by

Ed Berman. London: Inter-Action Inprint, 1975.
142pp. (Ambiance/Almost Free playscripts, 1)
Collinson, L. *Thinking Straight*
Patrick, R. *Fred and Harold*
Patrick, R. *The Haunted Host*
Patrick, R. *One Person*
Wakeman, A. *Ships*

HOPP Hopper, Vincent Foster, and Lahey, Gerald B.,
eds. *Medieval Mystery Plays, Morality Plays, and
Interludes.* Great Neck, NY: Barron's Educational
Series [c1962] 299pp.
*Abraham and Isaac*
*The Castle of Perseverance*
*Everyman*
*Noah's Flood*
*The Second Shepherds' Play*
Heywood, J. *Johan Johan*
Heywood, J. *The Play Called the Four pp*

HORN Horn, Gunnar. *A Cavalcade of World Writing.*
Boston: Allyn and Bacon, 1961. 718pp.
Čapek, K. *R.U.R. (Rossum's Universal Robots)*

HORNE, HERBERT P. *See* NER Nero (Tragedy). *Nero &
Other Plays*

HOUE Houghton, Norris, ed. *The Golden Age.* New
York: Dell, 1963. 349pp. (Laurel Masterpieces of
Continental Drama, vol. 1)
Calderón de la Barca, P. *Life Is a Dream*
Corneille, P. *The Cid*
Molière, J. *The Misanthrope*
Racine, J. *Phaedra*
Vega Carpio, L. *The Sheep Well*

HOUG Houghton, Norris, ed. *Great Russian Plays.* New
York: Dell, c1960. 511pp. (Laurel Drama Series)
Andreyev, L. *He Who Gets Slapped*
Chekhov, A. *The Cherry Orchard*
Gogol, N. *The Inspector General*
Gorky, M. *The Lower Depths*
Tolstoy, L. *The Power of Darkness*
Turgenev, I. *A Month in the Country*

HOUK Houghton, Norris, ed. *The Romantic Influence.*
New York: Dell, 1963. 542pp. (Laurel
Masterpieces of Continental Drama, vol. 2)
Goethe, J. *Faust, Part 1*
Hugo, V. *Hernani*
Rostand, E. *Cyrano de Bergerac*
Schiller, F. *Mary Stuart*

HOUP Houghton, Norris, ed. *Seeds of Modern
Drama.* New York: Dell, 1963. 413pp. (Laurel
Masterpieces of Continental Drama, vol. 3)

Chekhov, A. *The Sea Gull*
Hauptmann, G. *The Weavers*
Ibsen, H. *An Enemy of the People*
Strindberg, A. *Miss Julie*
Zola, E. *Thérèse Raquin*

HOUR *The Hour of One: Six Gothic Melodramas.* Edited
and introduced by Stephen Wischhusen. London:
Gordon Fraser Gallery, 1975. 173pp.
Fitz-Ball, E. *The Devil's Elixir*
Fitz-Ball, E. *The Flying Dutchman; or, the Phantom
Ship; a Nautical Drama*
Holcroft, T. *A Tale of Mystery*
Lewis, M. *The Castle Spectre*
Milner, H. *Frankenstein; or, the Man and the Monster*
Planché, J. *The Vampire; or, the Bride of the Isles*

HOUS Houston, Percy Hazen, and Smith, Robert Metcalf,
eds. *Types of World Literature.* Garden City, NY:
Doubleday, Doran [c1930] 1200pp.
Aeschylus. *Agamemnon*
Aristophanes. *The Birds*
Euripides. *Hippolytus*
*Everyman*
Ibsen, H. *A Doll's House*
Molière, J. *The Misanthrope*
Plautus, T. *The Captives*
Racine, J. *Athaliah*
Shakespeare, W. *As You like It*
Shakespeare, W. *King Lear*
Sheridan, R. *The Rivals*
Sophocles. *Antigone*
Wilde, O. *The Importance of Being Earnest*

HOUST Houston, Velina Hasu, ed. *But Still, Like Air, I'll
Rise: New Asian American Plays.* Philadelphia:
Temple University Press, 1997. 520pp.
Barroga, J. *Talk-story*
Gotanda, P. *Day Standing on Its Head*
Houston, V. *Kokoro (True Heart)*
Huynh, Q. *Dance of the Wandering Souls*
Hwang, D. *Bondage*
Kneubuhl, V. *The Conversion of Ka'ahumanu*
Rno, S. *Cleveland Raining*
Roberts, D. *Breaking Glass*
Wang, L. *Junk Bonds*
Wong, E. *Kimchee and Chitlins*
Yew, C. *A Language of Their Own*

HOUSTP Houston, Velina Hasu, ed. *The Politics of
Life: Four Plays by Asian-American Women.*
Philadelphia: Temple University Press, 1993.
274pp. ("In the series Asian American History and
Culture edited by Sucheng Chan")

Houston, V. *Asa ga kimashita (Morning Has Broken)*
Lim, G. *Bitter Cane*
Yamauchi, W. *The Chairman's Wife*
Yamauchi, W. *12-1-A*

HOW Howard, Edwin Johnson, ed. *Ten Elizabethan Plays.*
New York: Nelson, 1931. 451pp.
Beaumont, F., and Fletcher, J. *The Knight of the Burning
Pestle*
Beaumont, F., and Fletcher, J. *Philaster*
Dekker, T. *The Shoemaker's Holiday*
Greene, R. *The Honorable History of Friar Bacon and
Friar Bungay*
Jonson, B. *The Alchemist*
Kyd, T. *The Spanish Tragedy*
Marlowe, C. *Tamburlaine the Great*
Marlowe, C. *The Tragical History of Dr. Faustus*
Massinger, P. *A New Way to Pay Old Debts*
Webster, J. *The Duchess of Malfi*

HOWA Howard, Philip, ed. *Scotland Plays: New Scottish
Drama.* London: Nick Hern Books, 1998. 369pp.
Czerkawska, C. *Wormwood*
Di Mambro, A. *Brothers of the Thunder*
Greenhorn, S. *Passing Places*
Greig, D. *One Way Street*
Lochhead, L. *Quelques fleurs*
McLean, L. *One Good Beating*
Smith, I. *Lazybed*

HOWE Howe, George, and Harrer, Gustave Adolphus,
eds. *Greek Literature in Translation.* New York:
Harper [c1924] 642pp.
Aeschylus. *Agamemnon*
Aristophanes. *The Clouds*
Euripides. *Alcestis*
Euripides. *Medea*
Menander. *The Arbitration*
Sophocles. *Oedipus the King*

HOWF Howe, George, and Harrer, Gustave Adolphus, eds.
*Greek Literature in Translation.* Revised edition by
Preston Herschel Epps. New York: Harper [c1948]
903pp.
Aeschylus. *Agamemnon*
Aristophanes. *The Clouds*
Aristophanes. *The Frogs*
Euripides. *Alcestis*
Euripides. *Medea*
Menander. *The Arbitration*
Sophocles. *Oedipus the King*

HOWJ Howe, George, and Harrer, Gustave, eds. *Roman
Literature in Translation.* New York: Harper, 1924.
630pp.

Plautus. *Menaechmi*
Seneca. *Octavia*
Terence. *Phormio*

HOWK Howe, George, and Harrer, Gustave, eds. *Roman
Literature in Translation.* Revised by Albert
Suskin. New York: Harper [c1959] 649pp.
Horatius Flaccus, Q. *The Bore; a Dramatic Version of
Horace* (Satires I, 9)
Plautus, T. *The Braggart Soldier*
Seneca, L. *Octavia*
Terentius Afer, P. *The Brothers*

HOWM Howe, James, and Stephany, William, A.,
compilers. *The McGraw-Hill Book of Drama.* New
York: McGraw-Hill, 1995. 1101pp.
Aristophanes. *Lysistrata*
Baldwin, J. *Blues for Mister Charlie*
Beckett, S. *Rough for Theatre I*
Behn, A. *The Rover*
Chekhov, A. *The Cherry Orchard*
Churchill, C. *Vinegar Tom*
Euripides. *The Bacchae*
Fugard, A. *The Road to Mecca*
Fuller, C. *A Soldier's Play*
Glaspell, S. *Trifles*
Hansberry, L. *A Raisin in the Sun*
Hwang, D. *M. Butterfly*
Ibsen, H. *The Wild Duck*
Ionesco, E. *Jack; or, the Submission*
Jackson, E. *Paper Dolls*
Kopit, A. *Indians*
Molière, J. *Tartuffe*
Mtwa, P., Ngema, M., and Simon, B. *Woza Albert!*
Morton, C. *Rancho Hollywood*
Norman, M. *Getting Out*
O'Neill, E. *The Hairy Ape*
Shakespeare, W. *Hamlet*
Shakespeare, W. *The Merchant of Venice*
Shakespeare, W. *Othello*
Shaw, G. *Pygmalion*
Sheridan, R. *The Rivals*
Sherman, M. *Messiah*
Sophocles. *Oedipus the King*
Soyinka, W. *The Lion and the Jewel*
Walcott, D. *Pantomime*
Williams, T. *The Glass Menagerie*
Wilson, A. *Joe Turner's Come and Gone*

HOWP Howe, Irving, [and Others], compilers. *The
Literature of America.* New York: McGraw-Hill,
1971. 2 vols.
Albee, E. *The Zoo Story* 2
Jones, L. *Dutchman* 2
O'Neill, E. *Desire under the Elms* 2

Tyler, R. *The Contrast* 1
Wilder, T. *The Skin of Our Teeth* 2

HUB Hubbell, Jay Broadus, ed. *American Life in
    Literature.* New York: Harper [c1936] 849pp.
    O'Neill, E. *Marco Millions*

HUBA Hubbell, Jay Broadus, ed. *American Life in
    Literature.* New York: Harper [c1949] 2 vols.
    O'Neill, E. *The Emperor Jones* 2

HUD Hubbell, Jay Broadus, and Beatty, John Owen, eds.
    *An Introduction to Drama.* New York: Macmillan,
    1927. 838pp.
    *Abraham and Isaac*
    Beaumont, F., and Fletcher, J. *Philaster*
    Chekhov, A. *The Boor*
    Dunsany, E. *A Night at an Inn*
    *Everyman*
    Farquhar, G. *The Beaux' Stratagem*
    Gerstenberg, A. *Overtones*
    Gilbert, W., and Sullivan, A. *Iolanthe*
    Glaspell, S. *Trifles*
    Goldsmith, O. *She Stoops to Conquer*
    Hauptmann, G. *The Assumption of Hannele*
    Ibsen, H. *A Doll's House*
    Jones, H. *The Goal*
    Jonson, B. *Volpone*
    Maeterlinck, M. *The Intruder*
    Marlowe, C. *Doctor Faustus*
    Molière, J. *Tartuffe*
    O'Neill, E. *The Emperor Jones*
    Pinero, A. *The Second Mrs. Tanqueray*
    Plautus, T. *Menaechmi*
    *Quem quaeritis*
    Rostand, E. *Cyrano de Bergerac*
    *The Second Shepherds' Play*
    Sheridan, R. *The School for Scandal*
    Sophocles. *Antigone*
    Synge, J. *Riders to the Sea*
    Wilde, O. *Lady Windermere's Fan*
    Williamson, H. *Peggy*
    Yeats, W. *The Land of Heart's Desire*

HUDE Huberman, Edward, and Raymo, Robert R.,
    eds. *Angels of Vision.* Boston: Houghton Mifflin
    [c1962] 679pp.
    Harburg, E., and Saidy, F. *Finian's Rainbow*
    Inge, W. *The Dark at the Top of the Stairs*
    Priestley, J. *An Inspector Calls*
    Shakespeare, W. *A Midsummer Night's Dream*
    Wedekind, F. *The Tenor*

HUDS Hudson, Arthur Palmer; Hurley, Leonard Buswell;
    and Clark, Joseph Deadrick, eds. *Nelson's College
    Caravan.* New York: Nelson, 1936. 4 vols.

Green, P. *Unto such Glory* 2
O'Neill, E. *Marco Millions* 2
Rostand, E. *Cyrano de Bergerac* 2
Sherriff, R. *Journey's End* 2
Sophocles. *Antigone* 2

HUDT Hudson, Arthur Palmer; Hurley, Leonard Buswell;
    and Clark, Joseph Deadrick, eds. *Nelson's College
    Caravan.* 3rd ed. New York: Nelson, 1942. 1418pp.
    (4 vols. in 1)
    Čapek, K. *R.U.R.*
    O'Neill, E. *Marco Millions*
    Sophocles. *Antigone*

HUDV Hudston, Sara, compiler. *Victorian Theatricals:
    From Menageries to Melodramas.* London:
    Methuen, 2000. 431pp.
    Boucicault, D. *The Colleen Bawn*
    Brough, R., and Brough, W. *The Enchanted Isle,
    or, "Raising the Wind" on the Most Approved
    Principles*
    Gilbert, W. *The Mikado; or, the Town of Titipu*
    Pinero, A. *The Second Mrs. Tanqueray*
    Planché, J. *Jason in Colchis. The First Part*
    Robertson, T. *Society*
    Walker, J. *The Factory Lad*

HUER Huerta, Jorge, A., compiler. *Necessary Theater: Six
    Plays about the Chicano Experience.* Houston: Arte
    Publico Press, 1989. 368pp.
    Girón, A. *Money*
    Pérez, J., and Pérez, S. *Soldierboy*
    Sanchez-Scott, M., and Blahnik, J. *Latina*
    El Teatro de la Esperanza. *Guadalupe*
    El Teatro de la Esperanza. *La víctima*
    Valdez, L. *The Shrunken Head of Pancho Villa*

HUGH Hughes, Holly, and Román, David, eds. *O Solo
    Homo: The New Queer Performance.* New York:
    Grove Press, 1998. 481pp.
    Alfaro, L. *Downtown*
    Barfield, T. *Without Skin or Breathlessness*
    Bornstein, K. *Virtually Yours*
    Hickman, C. *skin & ornaments*
    Hughes, H. *Clit Notes*
    Kearns, M. *Attachments*
    Mapa, A. *I Remember Mapa*
    Miller, S. *My Left Breast*
    Miller, T. *Naked Breath*
    Shaw, P. *You're Just like My Father*
    Tropicana, C. *Milk of Amnesia—Leche de amnesia*
    Uyehara, D. *Hello (Sex) Kitty: Mad Asian Bitch on
    Wheels*
    Vawter, R. *Roy Cohn/Jack Smith*

HUGL Hughes, Leo, and Scouten, A. H., eds. *Ten English Farces.* Austin, TX: University of Texas Press, 1948. 286pp.

Behn, A. *The Emperor of the Moon*

*The Bilker Bilk'd*

Dogget, T. *Hob; or, the Country Wake*

Hoare, P. *No Song No Supper*

Inchbald, E. *Appearance Is against Them*

Jevon, T.; Coffey, C.; Mottley, J.; and Cibber, T. *The Devil to Pay; or, the Wives Metamorphos'd*

Johnson, C. *The Cobler of Preston*

Ravenscroft, E., and Motteux, P. *The Anatomist; or, the Sham Doctor*

Sheridan, T. *The Brave Irishman*

Tate, N. *A Duke and No Duke*


HUMANA *Humana Festival: The Complete Plays 1993–2000.* Edited by Marisa Smith, Michael Bigelow Dixon, Liz Engelman, Amy Wegener. Lyme, NH: Smith and Kraus, 1993–2000. 8 vols.

Ackermann, J., et al. *Back story: A Dramatic Anthology* 00

(Consists of the following nineteen brief plays: Ackermann, J. *Norman Rockwell's Thanksgiving in the Year* 2000; Ackermann, J. *Time to Think*; Baron, C. *Blackfish*; Beber, N. *The Reluctant Instrument*; Congdon, C. *Moby Ethan at the Sculptor's Museum*; Klein, J. *Something to Do with Bolivia*; Lauro, S. *Turn Down*; Lucas, C. *Good Morning to the Horse*; Machado, E. *Trying to Get There*; Margulies, D. *Misadventure*; Martin, J. *The Deal*; Miller, S. *Introducing Dad*; Olive, J. *Star Skating*; Palmer, T. *Barbra Live at Canyon Ranch*; Rambo, D. *Maid of Athens*; Sanchez, E. *Ethan's Got Get*; Shank, A. *Or Maybe Not*; Simon, M. *What Became of the Polar Bear?*; Smith, V. *Dead Men Make No Dollars*)

Ackermann, J. *The Batting Cage* 96

Ackermann, J. *Norman Rockwell's Thanksgiving in the Year 2000.* See Ackermann, J. *Back Story: A Dramatic Anthology* 00

Ackermann, J. *Stanton's Garage* 93

Ackermann, J. *Time to Think.* See Ackermann, J. *Back Story: A Dramatic Anthology* 00

Aerenson, B. *Lighting Up the Two-year Old* 97

Akalaitis, J. *Ti Jean Blues* 98

Anderson, J. *The Last Time We Saw Her* 94

Anderson, J. *The Reprimand* 00

Anderson, J. *Tough Choices for the New Century* 95

Badlam, R. *Slop-culture* 99

Baron, C. *Blackfish.* See Ackermann, J. *Back Story: A Dramatic Anthology* 00

Baron, C. *The Blue Room* 99

Beber, N. *Misreadings* 97

Beber, N. *The Reluctant Instrument.* See Ackermann, J. *Back Story: A Dramatic Anthology* 00

Belber, S. *Tape* 00

Bell, N. *Will You Accept the Charges?* 99

Berman, B. *Dancing with a Devil* 99

Bogart, A. *Cabin Pressure* 99

Breslin, J. *Contract with Jackie* 96

Congdon, C. *Moby Ethan at the Sculptor's Museum.* See Ackermann, J. *Back Story: A Dramatic Anthology* 00

Cummings, B. *Your Obituary Is a Dance* 95

Cunningham, A. *No. 11 (Blue and White)* 00

Dewberry, E. *Flesh and Blood* 96

Dewberry, E. *Head On* 95

Dietz, S. *Private Eyes* 97

Dresser, R. *Below the Belt* 95

Dresser, R. *Gun-shy* 97

Dresser, R. *What Are You Afraid Of?* 99

Gilman, R. *Speech Therapy* 99

Graziano, D. *Acorn* 98

Greenspan, D. *Them* 99

Hairston, J. *Forty Minute Finish* 99

Hammond, W. *Julie Johnson* 94

Hatcher, J. *Show Business* 00

Howe, T. *The Divine Fallacy* 00

Hwang, D. *Merchandising* 99

Hwang, D. *Trying to Find Chinatown* 96

Iizuka, N. *Aloha, Say the Pretty Girls* 99

Iizuka, N. *Polaroid Stories* 97

Iizuka, N. *War of the Worlds* 00

Ives, D. *Arabian Nights* 00

Jordan, J. *Mpls., St. Paul* 99

Jucha, B. *Deadly Virtues* 93

Kalinoski, R. *Beast on the Moon* 95

Kaufman, L. *Shooting Simone* 93

Klein, J. *Betty the Yeti* 94

Klein, J. *Something to Do with Bolivia.* See Ackermann, J. *Back Story: A Dramatic Anthology* 00

Kling, K. *The Ice-fishing Play* 93

Kopit A. *Y2k* 99

Kushner, T. *And the Torso Even More So* 99

Kushner, T. *Reverse Transcription* 96

Kushner, T. *Slavs! Thinking about the Longstanding Problems of Virtue and Happiness* 94

Landau, T. *1969.* 94

Lauro, S. *Turn Down.* See Ackermann, J. *Back Story: A Dramatic Anthology* 00

LeFevre, A. *Waterbabies* 97

Linney, R. *Shotgun* 94

Linney, R. *Stars* 97

Lipsky, J. *The Survivor; A Cambodian Odyssey* 94

Lucas, C. *Good Morning to the Horse.* See Ackermann, J. *Back Story: A Dramatic Anthology* 00

Lucas, C. *What I Meant Was* 96

MacDonald, B. *What We Do with It* 93

Machado, E. *Trying to Get There.* See Ackermann, J. *Back Story: A Dramatic Anthology* 00

Mack, C. *In Her Sight* 97

McClinton, M. *Stones and Bones* 94
Manley, F., and Murphy, V. *The Cockfighter* 99
Margulies, D. *Dinner with Friends* 98
Margulies, D. *July 7, 1994* 95
Margulies, D. *Misadventure. See* Ackermann, J. *Back Story: A Dramatic Anthology* 00
Martin, J. *Anton in Show Business* 00
Martin, J. *The Deal. See* Ackermann, J. *Back Story: A Dramatic Anthology* 00
Martin, J. *Jack and Jill* 96
Martin, J. *Keely and Du* 93
Martin, J. *Middle-aged White Guys* 95
Martin, J. *Mr. Bundy* 98
Martin, J. *Stuffed Shirts* 99
Mastrosimone, W. *Like Totally Weird* 98
Mee, C. *Big Love* 00
Miller, S. *Introducing Dad. See* Ackermann, J. *Back Story: A Dramatic Anthology* 00
Miller, S. *My Left Breast* 94
Nagy, P. *Trip's Cinch* 94
Norman, M. *Trudy Blue* 95
Nottage, L. *Poof!* 93
O'Donnell, M. *Trespassion* 00
Olive, J. *Star Skating. See* Ackermann, J. *Back Story: A Dramatic Anthology* 00
Palmer, T. *Barbra Live at Canyon Ranch. See* Ackermann, J. *Back Story: A Dramatic Anthology* 00
Pelfrey, M. *Drive Angry* 99
Press-Coffman, T. *Touch* 00
Rambo, D. *God's Man in Texas* 99
Rambo, D. *Maid of Athens. See* Ackermann, J. *Back Story: A Dramatic Anthology* 00
Reyes, G. *Chilean Holiday* 96
Reynolds, R. *Visitation* 99
Rivera, J. *Cloud Tectonics* 95
Rivera, J. *Lovers of Long Red Hair* 00
Rivera, J. *Tape* 93
Sanchez, E. *Ethan's Got Get. See* Ackermann, J. *Back Story: A Dramatic Anthology* 00
Sanchez, E. *Icarus* 97
Shank, A. *Or Maybe Not. See* Ackermann, J. *Back Story: A Dramatic Anthology* 00
Shanley, J. *Kissing Christine* 96
Shanley, J. *Missing Marisa* 96
Simon, M. *What Became of the Polar Bear? See* Ackermann, J. *Back Story: A Dramatic Anthology* 00
Smith, V. *Dead Men Make No Dollars. See* Ackermann, J. *Back Story: A Dramatic Anthology* 00
Smith, V. *Meow* 98
Son, D. *Happy Birthday Jack* 99
Spencer, S. *Resident Alien* 98
Taylor, R. *Beside Every Good Man* 00
Taylor, R. *Between the Lines* 95

Taylor, R. *Watermelon Rinds* 93
Wallace, N. *Manifesto* 99
Wallace, N. *One Flea Spare* 96
Wallace, N. *Standard Time* 00
Wallace, N. *The Trestle at Pope Lick Creek* 98
Wasserstein, W. *To t or Not to t* 99
Wellman, M. *The Fez* 99
Williams, C. *Just Be Frank* 99
Wilner, S. *Labor Day* 99
Wong, E. *Let the Big Dog Eat* 98
Yeaton, D. *Helen at Risk* 95

HUNG Hung, Josephine Huang, compiler. *Classical Chinese Plays*. 2nd ed. London: Vision Press, 1972. 277pp.
*The Faithful Harlot*
*One Missing Head*
*The Price of Wine*
*Twice a Bride*
*Two Men on a String*

HUNGDC *Hungary: Plays*. Edited with an introduction, by Eugene Brogyányi. New York: PAJ Publications, 1991. 247pp. (DramaContemporary Series)
Csurka, I. *Cheese Dumplings*
Kornis, M. *Kozma*
Páskándi, G. *Sojourn*
Spiró, G. *Chicken Head*
Süto, A. *The Palm Sunday of a Horse Dealer*

HUNT Hunt, Kellogg, W., and Stoakes, Paul, eds. *Our Living Language*. Boston: Houghton Mifflin [c1961] 631pp.
Miller, A. *Death of a Salesman*
Serling, R. *Patterns*

HUSSEY, MAURICE P. *See* CHES *Chester Mystery Plays*

HUST Huston, John Dennis, and Kernan, A. B., compilers. *Classics of the Renaissance Theater: English Plays*. New York: Harcourt, 1969. 735pp.
Ford, J. *'Tis a Pity She's a Whore*
Jonson, B. *Volpone*
Kyd, T. *The Spanish Tragedy*
Marlowe, C. *Tamburlaine the Great*
Middleton, T., and Rowley, W. *The Changeling*
Tourneur, C. *The Revenger's Tragedy*
Webster, J. *The Duchess of Malfi*

HUTC Hutchens, John K., ed. *The American Twenties*. Philadelphia: Lippincott [c1952] 480pp.
O'Neill, E. *The Emperor Jones*

HUTCHINS, RORERT MAYNARD. *See* GRDB *Great Books of the Western World*.

HUTCH Hutchison, Yvette, and Omotoso, Kole, eds.
　　　*Open Space: Six Contemporary Plays from Africa.*
　　　Groote Schuur, South Africa: Kagiso Publishers,
　　　1995. 199pp.
　　Al-Hakim, T. *The Donkey Market*
　　De Wet, R. *A Worm in the Bud*
　　Mda, Z. *The Hill*
　　Oyono, F. *Houseboy*
　　Rugyendo, M. *The Contest*
　　Saro-Wiwa, K. *The Transistor Radio*

IFKO Ifkovic, Edward, compiler. *American Letter:*
　　　*Immigrant and Ethnic Writing.* Edited by Edward
　　　Ifkovic. Englewood Cliffs, NJ: Prentice-Hall [1975]
　　　386pp.
　　Lawson, J. *Processional*
　　Smith, M. *An American Grandfather*

INCA Inchbald, Mrs. Elizabeth (Simpson), compiler.
　　　*The Modern Theatre: A Collection of Plays.*
　　　(First published in London, 1811, in ten volumes;
　　　reissued in 1968 in five volumes). New York:
　　　Benjamin Blom, Inc., 1968. 10 vols in 5
　　Cobb, J. *Ramah Droog* 6
　　Cobb, J. *The Wife of Two Husbands* 6
　　Colman, G. *The English Merchant* 9
　　Colman, G., the younger. *Who Wants a Guinea?* 3
　　Cowley, Mrs. H. *Which Is the Man?* 10
　　Cumberland, R. *The Box-lobby Challenger* 5
　　Cumberland, R. *The Carmelite* 5
　　Cumberland, R. *False Impressions* 5
　　Cumberland, R. *The Imposters* 6
　　Cumberland, R. *The Mysterious Husband* 5
　　Cumberland, R. *The Natural Son* 5
　　Dibdin, T. *The School for Prejudice* 4
　　Francklin, T. *Matilda* 8
　　*He's Much to Blame* 4
　　Holcroft, T. *Duplicity* 4
　　Holcroft, T. *The School for Arrogance* 4
　　Holcroft, T. *Seduction* 4
　　Holman, J. *The Votary of Wealth* 3
　　Hull, T. *Henry the Second, or the Fall of Rosamond* 9
　　Inchbald, Mrs. E. *I'll Tell You What* 7
　　Inchbald, Mrs. E. *Next Door Neighbors* 7
　　Inchbald, Mrs. E. *The Wise Man of the East* 7
　　Jephson, R. *Braganza* 6
　　Jephson, R. *The Law of Lombardy* 6
　　Kelly, H. *School for Wives* 9
　　Lee, Miss. *The Chapter of Accidents* 9
　　Macnally, L. *Fashionable Levities* 10
　　Macready, W. *The Bank Note* 9
　　More, H. *Percy* 7
　　Morton, T. *Secrets Worth Knowing* 3
　　Morton, T. *Zorinski* 3
　　O'Keeffe, J. *Lie of a Day* 10

　　Philon, F. *He Would Be a Soldier* 8
　　Reynolds, F. *The Delinquent* 2
　　Reynolds, F. *Folly as It Flies* 2
　　Reynolds, F. *Fortune's Fool* 2
　　Reynolds, F. *The Fugitive* 8
　　Reynolds, F. *How to Grow Rich* 1
　　Reynolds, F. *Laugh When You Can* 2
　　Reynolds, F. *Life* 1
　　Reynolds, F. *Notoriety* 1
　　Reynolds, F. *The Rage* 1
　　Reynolds, F. *Speculation* 2
　　Reynolds, F. *Werter* 3
　　Reynolds, F. *The Will* 1
　　St. John, J. *Mary Queen of Scots* 8
　　Sheridan, R. *A Trip to Scarborough* 7
　　Siddon, H. *Time's a Tell-tale* 10
　　Smith, C. *What Is She?* 10
　　Watson, G. *England Preserved* 8

INCI *Incisions.* Edited by Marvin Kaye. With a foreword by
　　　John Jakes. Garden City, NY: Stage & Screen, the
　　　Book Club for the Performing Arts, 2000. 303pp.
　　Davis, S. *Consider the Banana*
　　Felde, K. *Alice*
　　McClellan, C. *Blood and Ivy: An American Anthem*
　　Perkins, A. *Nobody Knows I'm a Dog*
　　Ritz, J. *Trappists*
　　Sjoersdma, A. *The 82nd Shepherds' Play*

INDI *The Indiana Experience: An Anthology.* Compiled
　　　and edited by Arnold Leslie Lazarus. Bloomington:
　　　Indiana University Press, 1977. 426pp.
　　McCutcheon, G. *The Double Doctor: A Farce*
　　Phillips, D. *The Worth of a Woman*

ING Inglis, Rewey Belle; Gehlmann, John; Bowman, Mary
　　　Rives; and Foerster, Norman, eds. *Adventures in*
　　　*American Literature.* 3rd ed. New York: Harcourt,
　　　Brace, 1941. v.p.
　　Anderson, S. *Textiles*
　　O'Neill, E. *Where the Cross Is Made*
　　Wilder, T. *Our Town*

INGA Inglis, Rewey Belle; Bowman, Mary Rives;
　　　Gehlmann, John; and Schramm, Wilbur.
　　　*Adventures in American Literature.* 4th ed. New
　　　York: Harcourt, Brace [c1947] 811pp.
　　Buck, P. *Will This Earth Hold?*
　　Gallico, P. *The Snow Goose*
　　O'Neill, E. *Where the Cross Is Made*
　　Wilder, T. *Our Town*

INGB Inglis, Rewey Belle; Gehlmann, John; Bowman,
　　　Mary Rives; and Schramm, Wilbur, eds. *Adventures*

*in American Literature*. Mercury edition. [5th edition] New York: Harcourt, Brace, 1952. 783pp.
Clarke, W. *The Ghost Patrol*
Gallico, P. *The Snow Goose*
Wilder, T. *Our Town*

INGE Inglis, Rewey Belle; Cooper, Alice Cecilia; Sturdevant, Marion A.; and Benét, William Rose, eds. *Adventures in English Literature*. Rev. ed. New York: Harcourt, Brace, 1938. 1178pp.
Galsworthy, J. *Strife*
Shakespeare, W. *Macbeth*
Synge, J. *Riders to the Sea*

INGG Inglis, Rewey Belle; Cooper, Alice Cecilia; Oppenheimer, Celia; and Benét, William Rose, eds. *Adventures in English Literature*. 4th ed. New York: Harcourt, Brace [c1946] 775pp.
Barrie, J. *The Old Lady Shows Her Medals*
Galsworthy, J. *Strife*
Shakespeare, W. *Macbeth*
Synge, J. *Riders to the Sea*

INGH Inglis, Rewey Belle; Stauffer, Donald A.; and Larsen, Cecil Evva, eds. *Adventures in English Literature*. Mercury edition. New York: Harcourt, Brace. 1952. 782pp.
Barrie, J. *The Old Lady Shows Her Medals*
Besier, R. *The Barretts of Wimpole Street*
Synge, J. *Riders to the Sea*

INGW Inglis, Rewey Belle, and Stewart, William Kilbourne, eds. *Adventures in World Literature*. New York: Harcourt, Brace, 1936. 1268pp.
Benavente y Martínez, J. *No Smoking*
*The Bird-catcher in Hell*
Ibsen, H. *An Enemy of the People*
Molière, J. *The Physician in Spite of Himself*
Sachs, H. *The Horse Thief*
Sophocles. *Antigone*

INSI *Inside 2000*. Sydney: Curency Press, 2000. 220pp. (Current Theatre Series)
Bews, S. *So Wet*
Decent, C. *Baby X*
Gallagher, J. *Elegy*
Leversha, P. *Violet Inc.*
Macdonald, G. *Like a Metaphor*

INTE *International Modern Plays*. London: Dent [1950] 304pp. (Everyman's Library)
Čapek, K., and Čapek, J. *The Life of the Insects*
Chiarelli, I.. *The Mask and the Face*
Cocteau, J. *The Infernal Machine*
Hauptmann, G. *Hannele*
Strindberg, A. *Lady Julie*

IRW Irwin, Vera Rusforth, compiler and translator. *Four Classical Asian Plays in Modern Translation*. Baltimore: Penguin, 1972. 333pp.
Bhāsa. *The Vision of Vāsavandatta*
Danjuro I. *Narukami*
Wang, S. *The West Chamber*
Zembō, M. *Ikkaku sennin*

JACKSON, SIR BARRY. *See* MAL *Malvern Festival Plays*.

JACKSON, PAMELA FAITH. *See* BLAC *Black Comedy*.

JACOB Jacobus, Lee, A., ed. *The Bedford Introduction to Drama*. New York: St. Martin's Press, 1989. 1126pp.
Aristophanes. *Lysistrata*
Beckett, S. *Happy Days*
Beckett, S. *Krapp's Last Tape*
Brecht, B. *Mother Courage and Her Children*
Chekhov, A. *The Cherry Orchard*
Chekhov, A. *Three Sisters*
Churchill, C. *Top Girls*
*Everyman*
Fugard, A. *"Master Harold" . . . and the Boys*
Gregory, A. *The Rising of the Moon*
Hansberry, L. *A Raisin in the Sun*
Ibsen, H. *A Doll's House*
Ibsen, H. *Hedda Gabler*
Marlowe, C. *Doctor Faustus*
Miller, A. *Death of a Salesman*
Molière, J. *The Misanthrope*
Norman, M. *'Night, Mother*
O'Neill, E. *Desire under the Elms*
Pinter, H. *The Dumb Waiter*
Pirandello, L. *Six Characters in Search of an Author*
Shakespeare, W. *Hamlet*
Shakespeare, W. *A Midsummer Night's Dream*
Shaw, G. *Major Barbara*
Shepard, S. *True West*
Sherman, M. *Bent*
Sophocles. *Antigone*
Sophocles. *Oedipus Rex*
Strindberg, A. *Miss Julie*
Synge, J. *Riders to the Sea*
Williams, T. *The Glass Menagerie*
Wilson, A. *Fences*

JACOBA Jacobus, Lee, A., ed. *The Bedford Introduction to Drama*. 2nd ed. Boston: Bedford Books of St. Martin's Press, 1993. 1435pp.
Aristophanes. *Lysistrata*
Beckett, S. *All that Fall*
Beckett, S. *Endgame*

Behn, A. *The Rover; or the Banished Cavaliers*
Brecht, B. *Galileo*
Chekhov, A. *The Cherry Orchard*
Congreve, W. *The Way of the World*
*Everyman*
Euripides. *Medea*
Friel, B. *Dancing at Lughnasa*
Fugard, A. *"Master Harold" . . . and the Boys*
Gregory, I. *The Rising of the Moon*
Hansberry, L. *A Raisin in the Sun*
Ibsen, H. *A Doll's House*
Ibsen, H. *Hedda Gabler*
Middleton, T., and Rowley, W. *The Changeling*
Miller, A. *Death of a Salesman*
Molière, J. *The Misanthrope*
Norman, M. *'Night, Mother*
O'Neill, E. *Desire under the Elms*
Parks, S. *The Death of the Last Black Man in the Whole Entire World*
Pinter, H. *The Dumb Waiter*
Pirandello, L. *Six Characters in Search of an Author*
Shakespeare, W. *Hamlet*
Shakespeare, W. *A Midsummer Night's Dream*
Shakespeare, W. *The Tempest*
Shaw, G. *Major Barbara*
Shepard, S. *Buried Child*
Sophocles. *Antigone*
Sophocles. *Oedipus Rex*
Soyinka, W. *The Strong Breed*
Strindberg, A. *Miss Julie*
Synge, J. *Riders to the Sea*
Wilde, O. *The Importance of Being Earnest*
Williams, T. *Cat on a Hot Tin Roof*
Williams, T. *The Glass Menagerie*
Wilson, A. *Fences*

JACOBD Jacobus, Lee, A., ed. *The Bedford Introduction to Drama*. 3rd ed. Boston: Bedford Books, 1997. 1797pp.
Aeschylus. *Agamemnon*
Aeschylus. *The Eumenides*
Aeschylus. *The Libation Bearers*
Aristophanes. *Lysistrata*
Beckett, S. *Endgame*
Behn, A. *The Rover; or the Banished Cavaliers*
Brecht, B. *Mother Courage*
Chekhov, A. *The Cherry Orchard*
Churchill, C. *Top Girls*
Congreve, W. *The Way of the World*
Euripides. *Medea*
*Everyman*
Fornes, M. *The Conduct of Life*
Fugard, A. *"Master Harold" . . . and the Boys*
García Lorca, F. *The House of Bernarda Alba*
Glaspell, S. *Trifles*

Gregory, I. *The Rising of the Moon*
Hansberry, L. *A Raisin in the Sun*
Hwang, D. *The Dance and the Railroad*
Ibsen, H. *A Doll's House*
Ibsen, H. *Hedda Gabler*
Kushner, T. *Angels in America: Millennium Approaches*
Mamet, D. *Oleanna*
Marlowe, C. *Doctor Faustus*
Miller, A. *Death of a Salesman*
Molière, J. *The Misanthrope*
Norman, M. *'Night, Mother*
O'Neill, E. *Desire under the Elms*
Parks, S. *The Death of the Last Black Man in the Whole Entire World*
Pinter, H. *Betrayal*
Pirandello, L. *Six Characters in Search of an Author*
Puig, M. *Kiss of the Spider Woman*
Shakespeare, W. *Hamlet*
Shakespeare, W. *A Midsummer Night's Dream*
Shakespeare, W. *The Tempest*
Shaw, G. *Pygmalion*
Shepard, S. *Buried Child*
Smith, A. D. *Twilight: Los Angeles, 1992*
Sophocles. *Antigone*
Sophocles. *Oedipus Rex*
Soyinka, W. *The Strong Breed*
Strindberg, A. *Miss Julie*
Synge, J. *Riders to the Sea*
Wilde, O. *The Importance of Being Earnest*
Williams, T. *Cat on a Hot Tin Roof*
Williams, T. *The Glass Menagerie*
Wilson, A. *Fences*
Wilson, A. *The Piano Lesson*

JACOBE Jacobus, Lee, A., ed. *The Compact Bedford Introduction to Drama*. 2nd ed. Boston: Bedford Books of St. Martin's Press, 1996. 917pp.
Aristophanes. *Lysistrata*
Beckett, S. *Endgame*
Brecht, B. *Galileo*
Chekhov, A. *The Cherry Orchard*
*Everyman*
Fugard, A. *"Master Harold" . . . and the Boys*
Gregory, I. *The Rising of the Moon*
Hansberry, L. *A Raisin in the Sun*
Ibsen, H. *A Doll's House*
Miller, A. *Death of a Salesman*
Molière, J. *The Misanthrope*
Norman, M. *'Night, Mother*
O'Neill, E. *Desire under the Elms*
Pirandello, L. *Six Characters in Search of an Author*
Shakespeare, W. *Hamlet*
Shakespeare, W. *A Midsummer Night's Dream*
Shaw, G. *Major Barbara*
Sophocles. *Antigone*

Sophocles. *Oedipus Rex*
Strindberg, A. *Miss Julie*
Williams, T. *The Glass Menagerie*
Wilson, A. *Fences*

JAFF Jaffe, Adrian H., and Weisinger, Herbert, eds. *The Laureate Fraternity*. Evanston, IL: Row, Peterson [c1960] 720pp.
Goldsmith, O. *She Stoops to Conquer; or, the Mistakes of a Night*
O'Neill, E. *Ah, Wilderness!*
Shakespeare, W. *Othello, the Moor of Venice*
Sophocles. *Oedipus Rex*
Wilde, O. *An Ideal Husband*

JAPDC *Japanese Drama and Culture in the 1960s: The Return of the Gods*. By David G. Goodman. Armonk, NY; London, England: M.E. Sharpe, 1988. 363pp.
Akimoto, M. *Kaison the Priest of Hitachi*
Fukuda, Y. *Find Hakamadare!*
Kara, J. *John Silver: The Beggar of Love*
Satoh, M. *My Beatles*
Satoh, M., Yamamoto, K., Kato, T., and Saito, R. *The Dance of Angels Who Burn Their Own Wings*

JAY Jayyusi, Salma Khadra, and Allen, Roger, eds. *Modern Arabic Drama: An Anthology*. Bloomington: Indiana University Press, 1995. 416pp.
`Abd al-Sabur, S. *Night Traveler*
`Ani, Y. *The Key*
Balalin Company of Jerusalem. *The. Darkness*
Diyab, M. *Strangers Don't Drink Coffee*
Farag, A. `*Ali Janah al-Tabrizi and His Servant Quffa*
Ikhlasi, W. *The Path*
Madani, `I. *The Zanj Revolution*
Mahfuz,`I. *The China Tree*
Salim,`A. *The Comedy of Oedipus: You're the One Who Killed the Beast*
Surayyi`,`A. *The Bird Has Flown*
`Udwan, M. *That's Life*
Wannus, S. *The King Is the King*

JEFF Jeffares, Alexander N., ed. *Restoration Comedy*. Totowa, NJ: Rowman & Littlefield, 1974. 4 vols.
Behn, A. *The Lucky Chance; or an Alderman's Bargain* 3
Behn, A. *The Rover; or, the Banished Cavaliers* 2
Cibber, C. *The Careless Husband* 4
Cibber, C. *Love's Last Shift* 3
Congreve, W. *Love for Love* 3
Congreve, W. *The Way of the World* 4
Crowne, J. *Sir Courtly Nice* 2
Dryden, J. *The Kind Keeper, or Mr. Limberham* 2

Dryden, J. *Sir Martin Mar-all, or, the Feigned Innocence* 1
D'Urfey, T. *Madam Fickle, or, the Witty False One* 2
Etherege, G. *The Man of Mode* 1
Etherege, G. *She Would If She Could* 1
Farquhar, G. *The Beaux' Stratagem* 4
Farquhar, G. *The Constant Couple, or, a Trip to the Jubilee* 4
Farquhar, G. *The Recruiting Officer* 4
Killigrew, T. *The Parson's Wedding* 1
Ravenscroft, E. *The London Cuckolds* 2
Sedley, C. *The Mulberry Garden* 1
Shadwell, T. *The Squire of Alsatia* 3
Steele, R. *The Conscious Lovers* 4
Vanbrugh, J. *The Provok'd Wife* 3
Vanbrugh, J. *The Relapse* 3
Wycherley, W. *The Country Wife* 1
Wycherley, W. *The Plain Dealer* 2

JENN Jenness, Morgan, Richardson, John, and Wellman, Mac, eds. *Slant Six: New Theater from Minnesota's Playwrights' Center*. Minneapolis: New Rivers Press, 1990. 206pp.
Boesing, M. *The Business at Hand*
Cinque, C. *Growing Up Queer in America*
Lappin, T. *Hit by a Cab*
McGuire, J. *Interview* (Angela Sand)
McGuire, J. *Interview* (Dorothy)
Smith, P. *Driving around the House*
Yellow Robe, W. *Sneaky*

JENS Jensen, H. James, ed. *The Sensational Restoration*. Bloomington, IN: Indiana University Press, 1996. 450pp.
Behn, A. *The Rover*
Etherege, G. *The Man of Mode*
Shadwell, T. *The Virtuoso*
Wycherley, W. *The Plain Dealer*

THE JOHNS HOPKINS STUDIES IN ROMANCE LITERATURE AND LANGUAGES vol. 29. *See* LAN Lancaster, Henry Carrington, ed. *Five French Farces, 1655–1694?*

JOH [Johnson, Rossiter] ed. *An Anthology of Italian Authors from Cavalcanti to Fogazzaro* (1270–1907). New York: National alumni [c1907] 388pp. (The Literature of Italy, 1265–1907)
Metastasio, P. *Achilles in Scyros*

JOHN Johnson, Stanley Lewis; Bierman, Judah; and Hart, James, eds. *The Play and the Reader*. Englewood Cliffs, NJ: Prentice-Hall, 1966. 442pp.
Aristophanes. *Lysistrata*
Brecht, B. *Mother Courage*

Giraudoux, J. *The Madwoman of Chaillot*
Ibsen, H. *Rosmersholm*
Ionesco, E. *The Chairs*
Pirandello, L. *Henry IV*
Shakespeare, W. *King Lear*
Shaw, G. *Caesar and Cleopatra*
Sophocles. *Oedipus Rex*

JOHO Johnson, Stanley Lewis, [and Others], eds. *The Play and the Reader*. Englewood Cliffs, NJ: Prentice-Hall, 1971. 583pp.
Anouilh, J. *Antigone*
Brecht, B. *The Caucasian Chalk Circle*
Frisch, M. *Firebugs*
Ibsen, H. *An Enemy of the People*
Molière, J. *Tartuffe*
Pirandello, L. *Right You Are If You Think You Are*
Shakespeare, W. *Hamlet*
Shakespeare, W. *Twelfth Night*
Sophocles. *Antigone*
Wilder, T. *The Skin of Our Teeth*

JOND Jones, David Richard, ed. *New Mexico Plays*. Albuquerque: University of New Mexico Press, 1989. 231pp.
Anaya, R. *Who Killed Don José?*
Chávez, D. *Plaza*
Gage, N. *Death Row Wedding*
Graebner, G. *Winners of the White Atomic Sweepstakes*
Mares, E. *Lola's Last Dance*
Medoff, M. *When You Comin' Back, Red Ryder?*

JONE Jones, Le Roi, and Neal, Larry, eds. *Black Fire: An Anthology of Afro-American Writing*. New York: Apollo Eds., 1969. 670pp.
Bullins, E. *How Do You Do*
Caldwell, B. *Prayer Meeting; or, the First Militant Minister*
Drayton, R. *Notes from a Strange God*
Freeman, C. *The Suicide*
Garrett, J. *We Own the Night*
Jackman, M. *Flowers for the Trash-man*
Jones, L. *Madheart*
Patterson, C. *Black Ice*
White, J. *The Leader*

JONI Jones, Liz, ed. *The La Mama Collection: 6 Plays for the 1990s*. Sydney: Currency Press, 1997. 298pp.
Coleman, E. *It's My Party*
Cortese, R. *Inconsolable*
Goodall, J. *Texas, Queensland*
Lillford, D. *Dark Heart*
Mueller, R. *No Man's Island*
Sejavka, S. *The Hive*

JONT Jones, Teresa, ed. *Sharing the Delirium: Second Generation AIDS Plays and Performances*. Portsmouth, NH: Heinemann, 1994. 342pp.
Bumbalo, V. *What Are Tuesdays Like?*
Holsclaw, D. *The Baddest of Boys*
Jones, W., and Stanley, D. *AIDS! The Musical!*
Kearns, M. *Myron, a Fairy Tale in Black and White*
Miller, T. *My Queer Body*
Pickett, J. *Queen of the Angels*
Sod, T. *Satan and Simon Desoto*

JONW Jones, Willis Knapp, translator and compiler. *Men and Angels: Three South American Comedies*. Carbondale, IL: Southern Illinois University Press, 1970. 191pp.
Darthes, J., and Damel, C. *The Quack Doctor*
Frank, M. *The Man of the Century*
Matto, J. *The Fate of Chipi González*

JORG Jorgenson, Paul A., and Shroyer, Frederick B., eds. *A College Treasury*. New York: Charles Scribner's Sons [c1956] 598pp.
Howard, S. *The Silver Cord*
Rice, E. *The Adding Machine*
Shakespeare, W. *Romeo and Juliet*
Shaw, G. *Arms and the Man*
Sherriff, R. *The Colonel's Lady*

JORH Jorgensen, Paul A., and Shroyer, Frederick B., eds. *A College Treasury: Prose, Fiction, Drama, Poetry*. 2nd ed. New York: Scribner [1967] 604pp.
Shakespeare, W. *The Tragedy of Hamlet, Prince of Denmark*
Shaw, G. *Arms and the Man*
Sophocles. *Oedipus Rex*
Wilder, T. *The Skin of Our Teeth*

JUAN Juan, Anton, ed. *The Likhaan Book of Philippine Drama, 1991–1996: From Page to Stage*. Quezon City, Likhaan: Creative Writing Center and University of the Philippines Press, 2000. 447pp.
Calo, A. *Ang maikling buhay ng apoy*
Coscolluela, E. *In My Father's House*
Guerrero, W. *Uilang Tahanan*
Millado, C. *scenes from an unfinished country*
Quintos, F. *. . . And St. Louis Loves dem Filipinos*

KAB *Kabuki: 5 Classic Plays*. Translated by James R. Brandon. Cambridge, MA: Harvard University Press, 1975. 378pp.
*Love Letter from the Licensed Quarter*
Namiki, S.; Namiki, S. I.; Namiki, G.; and Asada, I. *Chronicle of the Battle of Ichinotani*
Tsuruya, N. IV; Sakurada, J. II; and Tsuuchi, G. *The Scarlet Princess of Edo*

Tsuuchi, H.; Yasuda, A.; and Nakada, M. *Saint
    Narukami and the God Fudō*
Tsuuchi, J. II, and Tsuuchi, H. *Sukeroku: Flower of Edo*

KAL Kalman, Rolf, ed. *A Collection of Canadian Plays.*
    Toronto: Basset Books, 1972–1978. 5 vols.
Ball, A., and Bradbury, P. *Professor Fuddle's Fantastic
    Fairy-tale Machine* 4
Bolt, C. *Cyclone Jack* 4
Boston, S. *Counsellor Extraordinary* 1
Cameron, R. *Masque* 4
Cook, M. *Colour the Flesh the Colour of Dust* 1
Denison, M. *Marsh Hay* 3
Fruet, W. *Wedding in White* 2
Gerneau, M. *Four to Four* 5
Gorner, H. *Three Women* 2
Ibbitson, J. *Catalyst* 4
Jack, D. *Exit Muttering* 1
Kemp, D. *King Grumbletum and the Magic Pie* 4
Lavigne, L. *Are You Afraid of Thieves?* 5
McMaster, B. *Which Witch Is Which?* 4
Mercier, S. *A Little Bit Left* 5
Mitchell, W. *The Devil's Instrument* 2
Moore, M. *The Pile, the Store, Inside Out* 2
Nicol, E. *The Clam Made a Face* 4
Peterson, L. *Billy Bishop and the Red Baron* 4
Ravel, A. *The Twisted Loaf; Soft Voices* (two short
    plays) 3
Rosen, S. *Two plays: Love Mouse; Meyer's Room* 1
Roussin, C. *Looking for a Job* 5
Schull, J. *The Vice President* 3
Scott, M. *Wu-feng* 1
Shoveller, B. *Westbound 12:01* 2
Simard, A. *Waiting for Gaudreault* 5
Sirois, S. *Dodo* 5
Taylor, R. *The Unreasonable Act of Julian Waterman* 3
Thury, F., and Galbraith, R. *Nuts and Bolts and Rusty
    Things* 4
Tremblay, R. *Greta, the Divine* 5
Woods, G. *Vicky* 3
Zacharko, L. *Land of Magic Spell* 4

KAM Kambar, Chandrasekhar, and J. N. Kausal, eds.
    *Modern Indian Plays.* New Delhi: National School
    of Drama, Bahawalpur House, 2000–2007. 3 vols.
    (Vols. 1–2 edited by Chandrasekhar Kambar, and
    vol. 3 edited by J. N. Kausal.)
Alekar, S. *Begum Barve* 2
Bharati, D. *The Blind Age* 1
Bharti, B. *Tale Told by a Scorched Tree* 3
Das, J. *Before the Sunset* 2
Deshpande, G. *A Man in Dark Times* 2
Dutt, U. *Hunting the Sun* 3
Elkunchwar, M. *Old Stone Mansion* 2
Kambar, C. *The Mother Supreme* 1

Karnad, G. *Death by Beheading* 1
Maharishi, M. *Einstein* 3
Majumdar, D. *Unrhymed* 2
Parthasarathy, I. *The Story of Nandan* 2
Prasanna. *Way Beyond* 3
Rakesh, M. *One Day in Ashadha* 1
Sahni, B. *Hanush* 2
Sarma, A. *Food* 3
Shah, B. *Trishanku* 3
Sidhu, C. *Indumati and Satyadev* 3
Sircar, B. *There's No End* 1
Sriranga. *Listen! Oh, Janmejaya!* 1
Tagore, R. *The River Unbound* 1
Tanvir, H. *Agra Bazaar* 3
Tendulkar, V. *Ghasiram kotwal* 1
Thiyam, R. *Chakravyuha* 3
Verma, S. *Wings in Chains* 2

KANEL Kanellos, Nicolás, and Huerta, Jorge A., eds.
    *Nuevos Pasos: Chicano and Puerto Rican Drama.*
    Houston, TX: Arte Público Press, 1989, 1979.
    204pp.
Algarín, M. and Laviera, T. *Olú Clemente*
Arias, R. *The Interview*
Carrero, J. *The Fm Safe*
Duarte-Clarke, R. *Brujerias*
Morton, C. *Rancho Hollywood*
Piñero, M. *The Sun Always Shines for the Cool*
Portillo-Trambley, E. *Sun Images*
Sierra, R. *Manolo*

KANI Kani, John, compiler. *More Market Plays.*
    Parklands, South Africa: Ad Donker, 1994. 256pp.
Buckland, A. *The Ugly Noo noo*
Fourie, C. *Big Boys*
Keogh, D., and Cooke, V., and Haysom, F. *The Native
    Who Caused All the Trouble*
Klotz, P. *You Strike the Woman You Strike the Rock
    (Wathint' abafazi wathint' imbokotho)*
McCarthy, N. *Rainshark*
Simon, B. *Born in the RSA*

KAT Katzin, Winifred, compiler. *Eight European Plays.*
    New York: Brentano, 1927. 426pp.
Bernard, J. *Glamour*
Bernard, J. *Martine*
Harlan, W. *The Nüremberg Egg*
Kaiser, G. *The Fire in the Opera House*
Mann, H. *Madame Legros*
Rosso di san Secondo, P. *The Stairs*
Sternheim, C. *A Place in the World*
Vollmoller, K. *Uncle's Been Dreaming*

KAU Kauver, Gerald B., and Sorensen, Gerald Charles,
    compilers. *Nineteenth Century English Verse*

*Drama*. Cranbury, NJ: Fairleigh Dickinson
University Press, 1973. 355pp.
Arnold, M. *Empedocles on Etna*
Browning, R. *King Victor and King Charles*
Coleridge, S. *Remorse*
Gordon, G. *Manfred*
Keats, J. *Otho the Great*
Shelley, P. *The Cenci*
Swinburne, A. *Atlanta in Calydon*
Tennyson, A. *Becket*
Wordsworth, W. *The Borderers*

KAYD Kaye, Marvin, and Saralee Kaye, compilers. *Devils
& Demons: A Treasury of Fiendish Tales Old &
New*. Garden City, NY: Doubleday, 1987. 587pp.
Rostand, E. *Don Juan's Final Night*

KAYF Kaye, Marvin, compiler. *Frantic Comedy: Eight
Plays of Knockabout Fun*. Garden City, NY: The
Fireside Theatre, 1993. 209pp.
Dickens, C. *The Strange Gentleman*
France, A. *The Man Who Married a Dumb Wife*
Garrick, D. *The Lying Valet*
Gilbert, W. *Haste to the Wedding*
Goldoni, C. *The Servant of Two Masters*
Grove, M. *The Land of Counterpane*
Molière, J. *The Love Doctor*
Plautus, T. *Assinine*

KAYS Kaye, Marvin, compiler. *Sweet Revenge: 10 Plays
of Bloody Murder*. Garden City, NY: The Fireside
Theatre, 1992. 818pp.
Boker, G. *Francesca da Rimini*
Dekker, T. *The Witch of Edmonton*
Fratti, M. *Victim*
Kyd, T. *The Spanish Tragedy*
Middleton, T., and Rowley, W. *The Changeling*
Pitt, G. *Sweeney Todd*
Shaffer, A. *Murderer*
Shakespeare, W. *Hamlet*
Tourneur, C. *The Revenger's Tragedy*
Volsky, P. *The Bastard of Bologna*

KAYT Kaye, Marvin, compiler. *13 Plays of Ghosts and
the Supernatural*. Garden City, NY: Doubleday
Book and Music Clubs, 1990. 617pp.
Barrie, J. *When Wendy Grew Up*
Gibson, W. *Dinny and the Witches*
Godwin, P. *Cold Journey in the Dark*
Hall, B., and Richmond, D. *The Passion of Dracula*
Howard, S. *Madam, Will You Walk?*
Ionesco, E. *Macbett*
Kaye, M. *A Cold Blue Light*
Kelly, T. *The Uninvited*
Leslie, F. *The Haunting of Hill House*

Singer, I., and Friedman, E. *Teibele and Her Demon*
Wilder, T. *Mozart and the Gray Steward*
Williams, E. *Pen Don*
Yeats, W. *Purgatory*

KEE Keene, Donald, ed. and compiler. *Twenty Plays of the
Nō Theatre*. New York: Columbia University Press,
1970. 336pp.
*The Iron Crown*
Komparu-Zenchiku. *The Queen Mother of the West*
Komparu-Zenchiku. *Yōkihi*
Kongō, Y. *The Bird-scaring Boat*
Kwanze, K. K. *Komachi and the Hundred Nights*
Kwanze, K. K. *Matsukaze*
Kwanze, K. K. *The Sought-for Grave*
Kwanze, K. N. *Dōjōji*
Kwanze, K. N. *The Priest and the Willow*
Seami, M. *The Brocade Tree*
Seami, M. *The Deserted Crone*
Seami, M. *The Imperial Visit to Ohara*
Seami, M. *Kanehira*
Seami, M. *Komachi at Sekidera*
Seami, M. *Lady Han*
Seami, M. *The Reed Cutter*
Seami, M. *Semimaru*
*Shōkun*
*The Shrine in the Fields*
*The Valley Rite*

KEEP *Keeping On: Four Plays About Senior Citizens*.
London: The Ecounters Press, 1990. 115pp.
Cutler, H. *Fling Away Ambition*
Ford, C. *Wall to Wall*
Levine, M. *Mutual Bond*
West, D. *Breakfast with Bridy*

KEL Kelly, Katherine, E., ed. *Modern Drama by Women
1880s–1930s*. New York: Routledge, 1996. 319pp.
Barnes, D. *The Dove*
Bernstein, E. *Maria Arndt*
Bonner, M. *The Purple Flower*
Gippius, Z. *Sacred Blood*
Hasegawa, S. *Wavering Traces*
Leffler, A. *True Women*
Leneru, M. *Woman Triumphant*
Rachilde. *The Crystal Spider*
Robins, E. *Votes for Women*
Rosselli, A. *Her Soul*
Storni, A. *The Master of the World*
Wuolijoki, H. *Hulda Juurakko*

KER Kermode, John Frank, ed. *The Anthology of English
Literature*. New York: Oxford University Press,
1973. 2 vols.

Congreve, W. *The Way of the World* 1
*Everyman* 1
Gay, J. *The Beggar's Opera* 1
Marlowe, C. *Doctor Faustus* 1
*The Second Shepherds' Play* 1
Shakespeare, W. *The Tempest* 1
Shaw, G. *Saint Joan* 2
Wilde, O. *The Importance of Being Earnest* 2

KERN Kernan, Alvin B., ed. *Character and Conflict: An Introduction to Drama.* New York: Harcourt, Brace [c1963] 757pp.
Brecht, B. *Mother Courage and Her Children*
Chekhov, A. *The Cherry Orchard*
*Everyman*
Ibsen, H. *Hedda Gabler*
MacLeish, A. *The Fall of the City*
Molière, J. *The Misanthrope*
Saroyan, W. *The Time of Your Life*
Shakespeare, W. *King Henry IV, Part 1*
Shakespeare, W. *The Tragedy of Hamlet, Prince of Denmark*
Sophocles. *Antigone*
Strindberg, A. *The Stronger*

KERO Kernan, Alvin Bernard, ed. *Character and Conflict: An Introduction to Drama.* 2nd ed. New York: Harcourt, Brace and World, 1969. 721pp.
Arrabal, F. *Picnic on the Battlefield*
Brecht, B. *Mother Courage and Her Children*
Chekhov, A. *The Cherry Orchard*
*Everyman*
Giraudoux, J. *Tiger at the Gates*
Ibsen, H. *Hedda Gabler*
Molière, J. *The Misanthrope*
Shakespeare, W. *Hamlet*
Sophocles. *Antigone*
Strindberg, A. *The Stronger*
Synge, J. *Riders to the Sea*
Wilder, T. *The Skin of Our Teeth*

KERP Kernan, Alvin Bernard, ed. *Classics of the Modern Theater, Realism and After.* New York: Harcourt, Brace and World [1965] 538pp.
Albee, E. *The Zoo Story*
Betti, U. *Corruption in the Palace of Justice*
Brecht, B. *Mother Courage and Her Children*
Chekhov, A. *The Cherry Orchard*
García Lorca, F. *Blood Wedding*
Ibsen, H. *Ghosts*
Ionesco, E. *The Chairs*
Pirandello, L. *Six Characters in Search of an Author*
Shaw, G. *Arms and the Man*
Strindberg, A. *The Father*
Strindberg, A. *The Ghost Sonata*

KET Ketchum, Roland, and Billis, Adolph, eds. *Three Masters of English Drama.* New York: Dodd, Mead, 1934. 469pp.
Dryden, J. *All for Love*
Shakespeare, W. *Julius Caesar*
Shaw, G. *Caesar and Cleopatra*

KEY Keyes, Rowena Keith, and Roth, Helen M., eds. *Comparative Comedies Present and Past.* New York: Noble & Noble [c1935] 628pp.
Barry, P. *Holiday*
Beach, L. *The Goose Hangs High*
Goldsmith, O. *She Stoops to Conquer*
Sheridan, R. *The Rivals*

KIAN Kiani, Ali, ed. *An Anthology of Non-Western Drama.* Lido Beach, NY: Whittier Publications, 1993. 492pp.
*The Butterfly Dream*
Chikamatsu, M. *The Love Suicides at Sonezaki*
Dilmen, G. I. *Anatolia*
Hakim, T. *The Sultan's Dilemma*
Kālidāsa. *Shakuntalā*
*The Martyrs of Karbala*
Soyinka, W. *The Lion and the Jewel*

KILG Kilgarriff, Michael, compiler. *The Golden Age of Melodrama: Twelve 19th Century Melodramas.* Abridged and introduced by the author. London: Wolfe Pub., 1974. 499pp.
Buckstone, J. *Luke the Labourer*
Byron, H., and Boucicault, D. *Lost at Sea*
Gilbert, W. *Dan'l Druce*
Haines, J. *The Ocean of Life*
Holcroft, T. *A Tale of Mystery*
Jerrold, D. *Fifteen Years of a Drunkard's Life*
*Maria Martin; or, the Murder in the Red Barn*
Oxenford, J. *East Lynne*
Pitt, G. *The String of Pearls (Sweeney Todd)*
Planché, J. *The Vampire*
Potter, P. *Trilby*
Wills, W. *Eugene Aram*

KILGC Kilgore, Emilie S., ed. *Contemporary Plays by Women: Outstanding Winners and Runners-up for the Susan Smith Blackburn Prize (1978–1990).* New York: Prentice Hall, 1991. 504pp.
Churchill, C. *Serious Money*
Devlin, A. *Ourselves Alone*
Gannon, L. *Keeping Tom Nice*
Howe, T. *Painting Churches*
Kesselman, W. *My Sister in This House*
Norman, M. *Getting Out*
Siefert, L. *Coyote Ugly*

KIN Kincheloe, Isabel Mary, and Cook, Lester H.,
  compilers. *Adventures in Values*. New York:
  Harcourt, Brace, Jovanovich, 1969. 784pp.
  Anderson, M. *Feast of Ortolans*
  Hansberry, L. *A Raisin in the Sun*
  Jeffers, R. *Medea*
  Shakespeare, W. *Macbeth*
  Shaw, G. *Devil's Disciple*
  Vidal, G. *Visit to a Small Planet*

KING, VERNON RUPERT. *See* TOD *Today's Literature.*

KINH King, Woodie, Jr., and Milner, Ron, compilers.
  *Black Drama Anthology*. New York: Columbia
  University Press. 1971. 671pp.
  Branch, W. *A Medal for Willie*
  Bullins, E. *The Corner*
  Caldwell, B. *All White Caste*
  Charles, M. *Black Cycle*
  Dean, P. *The Owl Killer*
  DeAnda, P. *Ladies in Waiting*
  Elder, L. *Charades on East Fourth Street*
  Gordone, C. *The Breakout*
  Greaves, D. *The Marriage*
  Hill, E. *Strictly Matrimony*
  Hughes, L. *Mother and Child*
  Jackson, E. *Toe Jam*
  Jones, L. *Bloodrites*
  Jones, L. *Junkies Are Full of (SHHH . . .)*
  Mackey, W. *Requiem for Brother X*
  Mason, C. *Gabriel*
  Milner, R. *Who's Got His Own*
  Mitchell, L. *Star of the Morning*
  Pitcher, O. *The One*
  Shepp, A. *Junebug Graduates Tonight*
  Walker, J. *Ododo*
  Ward, D. *Brotherhood*
  Zuber, R. *Three X Love*

KINHB King, Woodie, Jr., and Milner, Ron, compilers.
  *Black Drama Anthology*. New York: Meridian,
  1986. 671pp.
  Baraka, A. *Bloodrites*
  Baraka, A. *Junkies are full of (SHHH . . .)*
  Branch, W. *A Medal for Willie*
  Bullins, E. *The Corner*
  Caldwell, B. *All White Caste*
  Charles, M. *Black Cycle*
  Dean, P. *The Owl Killer*
  DeAnda, P. *Ladies in Waiting*
  Elder, L. *Charades on East Fourth Street*
  Gordone, C. *The Breakout*
  Greaves, D. *The Marriage*
  Hill, E. *Strictly Matrimony*
  Hughes, L. *Mother and Child*

  Jackson, E. *Toe Jam*
  Mackey, W. *Requiem for Brother X*
  Mason, C. *Gabriel*
  Milner, R. *Who's Got His Own*
  Mitchell, L. *Star of the Morning*
  Pitcher, O. *The One*
  Shepp, A. *Junebug Graduates Tonight*
  Walker, J. *Ododo*
  Ward, D. *Brotherhood*
  Zuber, R. *Three X Love*

KINHN King, Woodie, Jr., ed. *The National Black Drama
  Anthology: Eleven Plays from America's Leading
  African-American Theaters*. New York: Applause
  Books, 1995. 515pp.
  Harris, B. *Robert Johnson: Trick the Devil*
  Jackson, C. *Iago*
  Jackson, M. *Sisters*
  Jones-Meadows, K. *Henrietta*
  Kai, N. *Harvest the Frost*
  Moore, C. *Love's Light in Flight*
  Nicholas, D. *Buses*
  Penny, R. *Good Black Don't Crack*
  Perry, S. *In Dahomey*
  Stetson, J. *The Meeting*
  Wilks, T. *Tod, the Boy, Tod*

KINHP King, Woodie, Jr., ed. *New Plays for the Black
  Theatre*. Chicago: Third World Press, 1989.
  312pp.
  Baraka, A. *Song*
  Beasley, E. *The Fallen Angel*
  Caldwell, B. *Birth of a Blues*
  Cleage, P. *Hospice*
  Gibson, P. *Konvergence*
  Harris, B. *Every Goodbye Ain't Gone*
  Harrison, P. *Tophat*
  Holder, L. *Zora*
  Kai, N. *Parting*
  Owens, D. *The Box*
  OyamO. *Mary Goldstein*
  Penny, R. *Pain in My Heart*
  Salaam, K. *The Quest*
  Shange, N. *Daddy Says*
  Wesley, R. *The Past Is the Past*

KINNR Kinney, Arthur Frederick. *Renaissance Drama: An
  Anthology of Plays and Entertainments*. Malden,
  MA: Blackwell Publishers, 1999. 744pp.
  *Arden of Faversham*
  Beaumont, F. *The Knight of the Burning Pestle*
  Dekker, T. *The Magnificent Entertainment*
  Dekker, T. *The Shoemaker's Holiday*
  Ford, J. *'Tis Pity She's a Whore*
  Heywood, T. *A Woman Killed with Kindness*

*The Honorable Entertainment Given to the Queen's*
    *Majesty in Progress, at Elvetham in Hampshire*
Jonson, B. *Bartholomew Fair*
Jonson, B. *The Masque of Blackness*
Kyd, T. *The Spanish Tragedy*
Marlowe, C. *The Tragical History of Doctor Faustus*
Marlowe, C. *The Troublesome Reign and Lamentable*
    *Death of Edward II*
Middleton, T. *A Chaste Maid in Cheapside*
Middleton, T., and Rowley, W. *The Changeling*
Mulcaster, R. *The Queen's Majesty's Passage*
Munday, A. *The Triumphs of Re-united Britannia*
Sidney, P. *The Lady of May*
Webster, J. *The Duchess of Malfi*

KINNS Kinney, Arthur Frederick, and others, eds.
    *Symposium on Love.* Boston: Houghton, Mifflin,
    1970. 268pp.
*Abraham and Isaac*
Molière, J. *Tartuffe*
Pirandello, L. *Six Characters in Search of an Author*
Shakespeare, W. *The Tragedy of King Lear*
Sophocles. *Oedipus the King*
Zembō, M. *Early Snow*

KIRLA Kirzner, Laurie G., and Mandell, Stephen G., eds.
    *Literature: Reading, Reacting, Writing.* Fort Worth:
    Holt, Rinehart, and Winston, 1991. 1784pp.
Albee, E. *The Sandbox*
Chekhov, A. *The Brute*
Fugard, A. *"Master Harold" . . . and the Boys*
Glaspell, S. *Trifles*
Gurney, A. *Another Antigone*
Hansberry, L. *A Raisin in the Sun*
Hwang, D. *FOB*
Ibsen, H. *A Doll's House*
Miller, A. *Death of a Salesman*
Shakespeare, W. *A Midsummer Night's Dream*
Shakespeare, W. *Othello*
Sophocles. *Antigone*
Sophocles. *Oedipus the King*
Williams, T. *The Glass Menagerie*

KIRLB Kirzner, Laurie G., and Mandell, Stephen G., eds.
    *Literature: Reading, Reacting, Writing.* 2nd ed.
    Fort Worth: Harcourt Brace College Publishers,
    1994. 1843p
Albee, E. *The Sandbox*
Chekhov, A. *The Brute*
Fugard, A. *"Master Harold" . . . and the Boys*
Glaspell, S. *Trifles*
Gurney, A. *Another Antigone*
Hofmann, G. *Our Man in Madras*
Hwang, D. *FOB*
Ibsen, H. *A Doll's House*

Miller, A. *Death of a Salesman*
Sanchez-Scott, M. *The Cuban Swimmer*
Shakespeare, W. *Hamlet*
Shakespeare, W. *A Midsummer Night's Dream*
Sophocles. *Antigone*
Sophocles. *Oedipus the King*
Williams, T. *The Glass Menagerie*
Wolfe, G. *The Colored Museum*

KIRLC Kirzner, Laurie G., and Mandell, Stephen G., eds.
    *Literature: Reading, Reacting, Writing.* 3rd ed. Fort
    Worth: Harcourt Brace College Publishers, 1997.
    2095pp.
Albee, E. *The Sandbox*
Chekhov, A. *The Brute*
Fugard, A. *"Master Harold" . . . and the Boys*
Glaspell, S. *Trifles*
Gurney, A. *Another Antigone*
Henley, B. *Crimes of the Heart*
Hwang, D. *FOB*
Ibsen, H. *A Doll's House*
Miller, A. *Death of a Salesman*
Sanchez-Scott, M. *The Cuban Swimmer*
Shakespeare, W. *Hamlet*
Shakespeare, W. *Much Ado about Nothing*
Shepard, S. *True West*
Sophocles. *Antigone*
Sophocles. *Oedipus the King*
Williams, T. *The Glass Menagerie*
Wilson, A. *Fences*

KIRLD Kirzner, Laurie G., and Mandell, Stephen G., eds.
    *Literature: Reading, Reacting, Writing.* Compact
    4th ed. Fort Worth: Harcourt College Publishers,
    2000. 1546pp.
Chekhov, A. *The Brute*
Glaspell, S. *Trifles*
Ibsen, H. *A Doll's House*
Miller, A. *Death of a Salesman*
Norman, M. *'Night, Mother*
Sanchez-Scott, M. *The Cuban Swimmer*
Shakespeare, W. *Hamlet*
Sophocles. *Oedipus the King*
Strindberg, A. *The Stronger*
Wasserstein, W. *Tender Offer*
Williams, T. *The Glass Menagerie*
Wilson, A. *Fences*

KLEIN Klein, Maxine, Sargent, Lydia, and Zinn, Howard.
    *Playbook.* Boston, MA: South End Press, 1986.
    501pp.
Klein, M. *The Furies of Mother Jones*
Klein, M. *New Rise of the Master Race*
Klein, M. *Split-shift*
Klein, M. *Windfall*

Sargent, L. *Daughter of Earth*
Sargent, L. *I Read about My Death in Vogue Magazine*
Zinn, H. *Emma*

KLIS Klisurska, Natalia, and Grinberg, Boukitsa, eds. *An Anthology of American Drama.* Sofia, Rumania: Sofia University Press, 1993. 2 vols.
Albee, E. *Who's Afraid of Virginia Woolf?* 2
Hansberry, L. *A Raisin in the Sun* 2
Hellman, L. *The Little Foxes* 1
Miller, A. *Death of a Salesman* 2
Odets, C. *Waiting for Lefty* 1
O'Neill, E. *Desire under the Elms* 1
O'Neill, E. *The Iceman Cometh* 1
Wilder T. *Our Town* 1
Williams, T. *The Glass Menagerie* 2

KNIC Knickerbocker, Kenneth L., and Reninger, H. Willard, eds. *Interpreting Literature.* New York: Henry Holt [c1955] 850pp.
Chekhov, A. *The Boor*
Connelly, M. *The Green Pasture*
Ibsen, H. *A Doll's House*
O'Neill, E. *Ile*
Rostand, E. *Cyrano de Bergerac*
Shaw, G. *Candida*
Williams, T. *The Glass Menagerie*

KNID Knickerbocker, Kenneth L., and Reninger, H. Willard, eds. *Interpreting Literature.* Rev. ed. New York: Holt, Rinehart and Winston [c1960] 832pp.
Chekhov, A. *The Boor*
Connelly, M. *The Green Pastures*
Frost, R. *A Masque of Reason*
Ibsen, H. *A Doll's House*
O'Neill, E. *Ile*
Shakespeare, W. *The Tragedy of Macbeth*
Shaw, G. *Candida*
Sophocles. *Antigone*
Williams, T. *The Glass Menagerie*

KNIE Knickerbocker, Kenneth L., and Reninger, H. Willard. *Interpreting Literature.* 3rd ed. New York: Holt, Rinehart and Winston, 1965. 908p
Besier, R. *The Barretts of Wimpole Street*
Chekhov, A. *The Boor*
Connelly, M. *The Green Pastures*
Ibsen, H. *An Enemy of the People*
Molière, J. *The Physician in Spite of Himself*
O'Neill, E. *Ile*
Shakespeare, W. *The Tragedy of Macbeth*
Shaw, G. *Arms and the Man*
Sophocles. *Antigone*

KNIF Knickerbocker, Kenneth L., and Reninger, H. Willard. *Interpreting Literature.* 4th ed. New York: Holt, Rinehart and Winston, 1969. 893pp.
Brecht, B. *The Caucasian Chalk Circle*
Chekhov, A. *The Boor*
Duerrenmatt, F. *The Visit*
Frisch, M. *Biedermann and the Firebugs*
Ibsen, H. *An Enemy of the People*
Molière, J. *The Physician in Spite of Himself*
O'Neill, E. *Ile*
Shakespeare, W. *The Tragedy of Othello: The Moor of Venice*
Shaw, G. *Arms and the Man*
Sophocles. *Antigone*
Williams, T. *The Glass Menagerie*

KNIG Knickerbocker, Kenneth L., and Reninger, H. Willard, eds. *Interpreting Literature: Preliminaries to Literary Judgment.* 5th ed. New York: Holt, 1974. 909pp.
Brecht, B. *The Caucasian Chalk Circle*
Chekhov, A. *The Boor*
Duerrenmatt, F. *The Visit*
Frisch, M. *Biedermann and the Firebugs*
Ibsen, H. *An Enemy of the People*
Molière, J. *The Physician in Spite of Himself*
O'Neill, E. *Ile*
Shakespeare, W. *The Tragedy of Othello*
Shaw, G. *Arms and the Man*
Sophocles. *Antigone*
Williams, T. *The Glass Menagerie*

KNIH Knickerbocker, Kenneth L., and Reninger, H. Willard, eds. *Interpreting Literature.* 6th ed. New York: Holt, 1978. 852pp.
Camus, A. *Caligula*
Duerrenmatt, F. *The Visit*
Ibsen, H. *Ghosts*
O'Neill, E. *Ile*
Shakespeare, W. *The Tragedy of Hamlet, Prince of Denmark*
Simon, N. *The Sunshine Boys*
Sophocles. *Antigone*
Strindberg. A. *Miss Julie*
Synge, J. *The Playboy of the Western World*

KNIJ Knickerbocker, Kenneth L., and Reninger, H. Willard, eds. *Interpreting Literature.* 7th ed. New York: Holt, 1985. 1184pp.
Camus, A. *Caligula*
Duerrenmatt, F. *The Visit*
Ibsen, H. *Ghosts*
Molière, J. *The Physician in Spite of Himself*
O'Neill, E. *Ile*

Shakespeare, W. *The Tragedy of Hamlet, Prince of Denmark*
Simon, N. *The Sunshine Boys*
Sophocles. *Antigone*
Strindberg. A. *Miss Julie*
Synge, J. *The Playboy of the Western World*

KNIRH Knight, Stephen, and Ohlgren, eds. *Robin Hood and Other Outlaw Tales*. Kalamazoo, MI: Published for TEAMS in association with the University of Rochester by Medieval Institute Publications, Western Michigan University, 1997. 723pp. (Middle English Texts Series)
Munday, A. *The Death of Robert, Earle of Huntington* (excerpts)
Munday, A. *The Downfall of Robert, Earle of Huntington*
*Robin Hood and His Crew of Soldiers*
*Robin Hood and the Friar and Robin Hood and the Potter*
*Robyn Hod and the Shryff of Notyngham*

KNO Knott, John Ray, and Reaske, Christopher Russell, eds. *Mirrors: An Introduction to Literature*. San Francisco: Canfield Press, 1972, 508pp.
Bergman, I. *The Seventh Seal*
Frisch, M. *Biedermann and the Firebugs*
Ibsen, H. *Hedda Gabler*
Jones, L. *Dutchman*
Sophocles. *Oedipus Rex*

KNOJ Knott, John Ray, and Reaske, Christopher Russell, eds. *Mirrors: An Introduction to Literature*. 2nd ed. San Francisco: Canfield Press, 1975. 542pp.
Bergman, I. *The Seventh Seal*
Ibsen, H. *Hedda Gabler*
Jones, L. *Dutchman*
Shakespeare, W. *King Lear*
Sophocles. *Oedipus Rex*

KNOK Knott, John Ray, and Reaske, Christopher Russell, eds. *Mirrors: An Introduction to Literature*. 3rd ed. New York: Harper and Row, 1988. 801pp.
Bergman, I. *The Seventh Seal*
Ibsen, H. *Hedda Gabler*
Shakespeare, W. *A Midsummer Night's Dream* (excerpt from Act V, Scene 1)
Shepard, S. *Curse of the Starving Class*
Sophocles. *Antigone*
Sophocles. *Oedipus Rex*

KNOW Knowland, A. S., ed. *Six Caroline Plays*. London. Oxford University Press, 1962. 553pp.
Brome, R. *The Antipodes*
Brome, R. *The Mad Couple Well Matched*

D'Avenant, W. *The Wits*
Killigrew, T. *The Parson's Wedding*
Shirley, J. *The Lady of Pleasure*
Shirley, J. *The Wedding*

KOH Kohut, George Alexander, ed. *A Hebrew Anthology*. Cincinnati: Bacharach, 1913. 2 vols.
Byron, G. *Cain* 2
Byron, G. *Heaven and Earth* 2
Cayzer, C. *David and Bathshua* 2
Davidson, R. *Elijah* 2
Ewing, T. *Jonathan* 2
Francis, A. *The Song of Songs which Is Solomon's* 2
Leavitt, J. *The Jewish Captives* 2
Lessing, G. *Nathan the Wise* 2
Milman, H. *Belshazzar* 2
Milman, H. *The Fall of Jerusalem* 2
Milton, J. *Samson Agonistes* 2
More, H. *Belshazzar* 2
More, H. *Daniel* 2
More, H. *David and Goliath* 2
More, H. *Moses in the Bulrushes* 2
Racine, J. *Athaliah* 2
Rives, A. *Herod and Mariamne* 2

KON Konick, Marcus, ed. *Six Complete World Plays and a History of the Drama*. New York: Globe [c1963] 701pp.
Chekhov, A. *The Cherry Orchard*
*Everyman*
Ibsen, H. *An Enemy of the People*
Rostand, E. *Cyrano de Bergerac*
Shaw, G. *Caesar and Cleopatra*
Sophocles. *Antigone*

KOU Kouka, Hone, ed. *Ta Matou Mangai: Our Own Voice*. Wellington, NZ: Victoria University of Wellington, 1999. 133pp.
Brown, R. *Irirangi Bay*
Davis, W. *Taku mangai*
He Ara Hou, and R. Potiki. *Whatungarongaro*

KOZ Kozlenko, William, ed. *The Best Short Plays of the Social Theatre*. New York: Random House [c1939] 456pp.
Auden, W., and Isherwood, C. *The Dog beneath the Skin*
Bengal, B. *Plant in the Sun*
Blitzstein, M. *The Cradle Will Rock*
Green, P. *Hymn to the Rising Sun*
Kozlenko. W. *This Earth Is Ours*
Maltz, A. *Private Hicks*
Odets, C. *Waiting for Lefty*
Shaw, I. *Bury the Dead*

Sifton, C., and Sifton, P. *Give All Thy Terrors to the Wind*
Wesley, J. *Running Dogs*

KREYMBORG, ALFRED. *See also* AME *American Caravan.*

KRE Kreymborg, Alfred, ed. *Poetic Drama.* New York: Modern Age [c1941] 855pp.
*Abraham, Melchisedec, and Isaac*
*Adam*
Aeschylus. *Agamemnon*
Aristophanes. *The Acharnians*
Auden, W., and Isherwood, C. *The Dog beneath the Skin*
Bottomley, G. *Gruach*
*The Chalk Circle*
Corneille, P. *Cinna*
Euripides. *Ion*
*Everyman*
Goethe, J. *Torquato Tasso*
Hauptmann, G. *The White Saviour*
Jonson, B. *Volpone*
Kreymborg, A. *Hole in the Wall*
MacLeish, A. *The Fall of the City*
Marlowe, C. *Tamburlaine the Great, Part I*
Massinger, P. *A New Way to Pay Old Debts*
Millay, E. *Aria da capo*
Molière, J. *The Misanthrope*
Moody, W. *The Death of Eve*
Racine, J. *Athaliah*
Rostand, E. *The Last Night of Don Juan*
Sachs, H. *The Wandering Scholar from Paradise*
Schiller, F. *The Death of Wallenstein*
Schwartz, D. *Shenandoah*
Seami, M. *Nakamitsu*
*The Second Shepherds' Play*
Shakespeare, W. *Measure for Measure*
Shelley, P. *The Cenci*
Sophocles. *Oedipus Coloneus*
Vega Carpio, L. de. *The Sheep Well*
Webster, J. *The White Devil*
Yeats, W. *The King's Threshold*

KRIT Kritzer, Amelia Howe, ed. *Plays by Early American Women, 1775–1850.* Ann Arbor: University of Michigan Press, 1995. 444pp.
Barnes, C. *The Forest Princess, or Two Centuries Ago*
Clarke, M. *The Fair Americans: A Play of the War of 1812*
Medina, L. *Ernest Maltravers*
Murray, J. *The Traveller Returned*
Rowson, S. *Slaves in Algiers*
Smith, S. *The Female Enthusiast*
Warren, M. *The Group*
Wright, F. *Altorf*

KRONENBERGER, LOUIS. *See also* BES *Best Plays of 1894/99–1961/62*

KRM Kronenberger, Louis, ed. *Cavalcade of Comedy.* New York: Simon and Schuster [c1953] 715pp.
Congreve, W. *Love for Love*
Congreve, W. *The Way of the World*
Coward, N. *Blithe Spirit*
Etherege, G. *The Man of Mode*
Goldsmith, O. *She Stoops to Conquer*
Jonson, B. *The Alchemist*
Jonson, B. *Volpone*
Kelly, G. *The Show-off*
Maugham, W. *The Circle*
Mayer, E. *Children of Darkness*
O'Casey, S. *Juno and the Paycock*
Osborn, P. *Morning's at Seven*
Shaw, G. *Androcles and the Lion*
Shaw, G. *Pygmalion*
Sheridan, R. *The School for Scandal*
Synge, J. *The Playboy of the Western World*
Thurber, J., and Nugent, E. *The Male Animal*
Vanbrugh, J. *The Confederacy*
Van Druten, J. *The Voice of the Turtle*
Wilde, O. *The Importance of Being Earnest*
Wycherley, W. *The Country Wife*

KRO Kronenberger, Louis, ed. *An Eighteenth Century Miscellany.* New York: Putnam, 1936. 578pp.
Gay, J. *The Beggar's Opera*
Sheridan, R. *The School for Scandal*

KRON Kronenberger, Louis, ed. *The Pleasure of Their Company.* New York: Knopf, 1946. 653pp.
Congreve, W. *The Way of the World*

KUMU *Kumu Kahua Plays.* Edited by Dennis Carroll. Honolulu: University of Hawaii Press, c1983. 249pp.
Amano, L. *Ashes*
Aw, A. *All Brand New Classical Chinese Theatre*
Benton, J. *Twelf nite o wateva!*
Inouye, B. *Reunion*
Kates, C. *The Travels of Heikiki*
Lum, D. *Oranges Are Lucky*
Morris, R. *Paradise Tours*
Sakamoto, E. *In the Alley*

LAB Labiche, Eugène, and Gondinet, Edmond, eds. *Three French Farces.* [*Le plus heureux des trois*] *The Happiest of the Three.* Harmondsworth, Middlesex: Penguin, 1973. 288pp.
Feydeau, G. *Get Out of My Hair*
Labiche, E., and Gondinet, E. *The Happiest of the Three*
Sardou, V., and Najac, E. *Let's Get a Divorce!*

LABO Labon, Joanna, ed. *Balkan Blues: Writing Out of Yugoslavia*. Evanston, IL: Northwestern University Press, 1995. 268pp. Originally published as: *Out of Yugoslavia*. London: Storm, 1994. (Storm # 6)
Stefanovski, G. *Sarajevo (Tales from a City)*

LAH Lahr, John, ed. *Showcase 1: Plays from Eugene O'Neill Foundation*. New York: Grove, 1970. 220pp.
Gagliano, F. *Father Uxbridge Wants to Marry*
Guare, J. *Muzeeka*
Hailey, O. *Who's Happy Now?*
Horovitz, I. *The Indian Wants the Bronx*

LAL Lal, Paul, ed. and tr. *Great Sanscrit Plays*. New York: New Directions, 1964. 396pp.
Bhāsa. *The Dream of Vāsavandatta*
Bhavabhāti. *The Later Story of Rama*
Harsha. *Ratnavali*
Kālidāsa. *Shakuntalā*
Shudraka, K. *The Toy Cart*
Vishakadatta. *The Signet Ring of Rakshasa*

LAM Lambert, Robert, and Lynn, Kenneth S., eds. *The Range of Literature: Drama*. Boston: Houghton, Mifflin, 1969. 502pp.
Duberman, M. *In White America*
Hart, M., and Kaufman, G. *You Can't Take It with You*
Ibsen, H. *An Enemy of the People*
Rostand, E. *Cyrano de Bergerac*
Wilder, T. *Our Town*

LAMO Lamont, Rosette, C. ed. *Women on the Verge: 7 Avant-garde American Plays*. New York; London: Applause, 1993. 366pp.
Drexler, R. *Occupational Hazard*
Fornes, M. *What of the Night?*
Howe, T. *Birth and After Birth*
Malpede, K. *Us*
Parks, S. *The Death of the Last Black Man in the Whole Entire World*
Schenkar, J. *The Universal Wolf*
Wong, E. *Letters to a Student Revolutionary*

LAMP Lamport, Francis John, ed. and tr. *Five German Tragedies*. Harmondsworth, Middlesex: Penguin, 1969. 503pp.
Goethe, J. *Egmont*
Grillparzer, F. *Medea*
Kleist, H. *Penthesilea*
Lessing, G. *Emelia Galotti*
Schiller, J. *Mary Stuart*

LANC Lancaster, Henry Carrington, ed. *Five French Farces, 1655–1694?* Baltimore: Johns Hopkins

Press, 1937. 141pp. (The Johns Hopkins Studies in Romance Literatures and Languages, vol. 29)
Bois-Robert, F. *L'amant ridicule*
*Le docteur amoureux*
Donneau de Visé, J. *Le gentilhomme guespin*
Raisin, J. *Merlin gascon*
Villiers, C. *L'apoticaire devalisé*

LAND *The Land Called Morning: Three Plays*. Edited by Caroline Heath. Saskatoon, SK: Fifth House, 1986. 112pp.
Dudoward, V. *Teach Me the Ways of the Sacred Circle*
Selkirk, J., and Selkirk, G. *The Land Called Morning*
Upisasik Theatre of Rossignol School. *Gabrielle*

LAO Landis, Joseph C., ed. and tr. *The Dybbuk, and Other Great Yiddish Plays*. New York: Bantam Books [1966] 356pp.
Anski, S. *The Dybbuk*
Asch, S. *God of Vengeance*
Hirschbein, P. *Green Fields*
Leivick, H. *The Golem*
Pinski, D. *King David and His Wives*

LAOG Landis, Joseph C., ed. and tr. *The Great Jewish Plays*. New York: Horizon, 1972. 356pp.
Asch, S. *God of Vengeance*
Halper, L. *The Golem*
Hirschbein, P. *Green Fields*
Pinski, D. *King David and His Wives*
Rappoport, S. *The Dybbuk*

LAP Landis, Paul Nissley, ed. *Four Famous Greek Plays*. New York: Modern Library [1929] 285pp.
Aeschylus. *Agamemnon*
Aristophanes. *The Frogs*
Euripides. *Medea*
Sophocles. *Oedipus the King*

LAQCF *Landmarks of Classical French Drama*. Introduced by David Bradby. London: Methuen Drama, 1991. 393pp.
Beaumarchais, P. *The Marriage of Figaro*
Corneille, P. *The Cid*
Marivaux, P. *The Lottery of Love*
Molière, J. *Tartuffe*
Racine, J. *Phedra*

LAQCW *Landmarks of Contemporary Women's Drama*. Edited by Emilie S. Kilgore. London: Methuen Drama, 1992. 504pp.
Churchill, C. *Serious Money*
Devlin, A. *Ourselves Alone*
Gannon, L. *Keeping Tom Nice*
Howe, T. *Painting Churches*

Kesselman, W. *My Sister in This House*
Norman, M. *Getting Out*
Siefert, L. *Coyote Ugly*

LAQID *Landmarks of Irish Drama*. London: Methuen
    Drama, 1988. With an introduction by Brendan
    Kennelly. 538pp.
Beckett, S. *All that Fall*
Behan, B. *The Quare Fellow*
Johnston, D. *The Old Lady Says "No"!*
O'Casey, S. *The Silver Tassie*
Shaw, G. *John Bull's Other Island*
Synge, J. *The Playboy of the Western World*
Yeats, W. *On Baile's Strand*

LAR Landon, Todd, ed. *New Dramatists, 2000: Best Plays
    by the Graduating Class*. Hanover, NH: Smith and
    Kraus, 2001. 285pp. (Contemporary Playwrights
    Series)
Cajal, O. *Exchange at the Café Mimosa*
Champagne, L. *Coaticook*
Kaplan, B. *Landscape of Desire*
Lee, C. *Carry the Tiger to the Mountain*
Reingold, J. *Acapulco*
Stuart, K. *A Shoe Is Not a Question*

LANE, ERIC. *See* ACTOR *The Actor's Book.*

LAS Langer, Lawrence L., ed. *Art from the Ashes: A
    Holocaust Anthology*. New York: Oxford Univ.
    Press, 1995. 694pp.
Sobol, J. *Ghetto*

LAT *The Late Medieval Religious Play of Bodleian MSS
    Digby 133 and e Museo 160*. Edited by Donald
    C. Baker, John L. Murphy, and Louis B. Hall
    Jr. Oxford: Published for the Early English Text
    Society by the Oxford University Press, 1982.
    284pp. (Early English Text Society; no. 283)
*Christ's Burial*
*Christ's Resurrection*
*The Conversion of St. Paul* (Digby)
*Killing of the Children*
*Mary Magdalen* (Digby)
*Wisdom*

LATIN *Latin American Plays: New Drama from
    Argentina, Cuba, Mexico, and Peru*. Selected,
    translated, and introduced by Sebastian Doggert.
    London: Nick Hern Books in Association with
    Visiting Arts, 1996. 230pp.
Fuentes, C. *Orchids in the Moonlight*
Gambaro, G. *Saying Yes*
Paz, O. *Rappacini's Daughter*

Triana, J. *Night of the Assassins*
Vargas Llosa, M. *Mistress of Desires*

LATTH *Latin American Theatre in Translation: An
    Anthology of Works from Mexico, the Caribbean,
    and the Southern Cone: Plays*. Compiled and
    translated by Charles Philip Thomas. United States:
    Xlibris Corporation, 2000. 539pp.
Kartun, M. *Sacco-Vanzetti (A Dramaturgic Summary
    Judgement from Documents on the Case)*
Parra, M. *The Dead Father*
Parra, M. *Killer Tangos*
Ramos-Perea, R. *Bad Blood: The New Emigration*
Ramos-Perea, R. *Family Secrets*
Ramos-Perea, R. *Forever Yours, Julita*
Rovner, E. *Company*
Rovner, E. *She Returned One Night*
Santana, R. *The Ladies Room*
Santana, R. *Looking into the Stands*
Santana, R. *Never Lose Your Head over a Swedish Doll*
Schmidhuber de la Mora, G. *Obituary*
Schmidhuber de la Mora, G. *The Secret Friendship of
    Juana and Dorothy*
Schmidhuber de la Mora, G. *The Useless Heroes*

LAUGHLIN, JAMES. *See* NEWD *New Directions in
    Prose and Poetry.*

LAUREL DRAMA SERIES. *See* FAM *Famous American
    Plays of the 1950s*; FAMAD *Famous American
    Plays of the 1970s*; FAMAH *Famous American
    Plays of the 1960s*; FAMAL *Famous American
    Plays of the 1930s*; HEWE Hewes, Henry, ed.
    *Famous American Plays of the 1940s*; HOUG
    Houghton, Norris, ed. *Great Russian Plays*; MACG
    Macgowan, Kenneth, ed. *Famous American Plays
    of the 1920s*.

LAUREL MASTERPIECES OF CONTINENTAL
    DRAMA, vols. 1–3. *See* HOUE, HOUK, NOUP
    Houghton, Norris, ed.

LAV Laverty, Carroll D., and Others, compilers. *The Unity
    of English*. New York: Harper, 1971. 556pp.
Hansberry, L. *A Raisin in the Sun*
Saroyan, W. *The Time of Your Life*
Williams, T. *The Glass Menagerie*

LAW Law, Frederick Houk, ed. *Modern Plays, Short and
    Long*. New York: Century, 1924. 429pp.
Archer, W. *The Green Goddess*
Church, V. *What Men Live By*
Corneau, P. *Masks*
Dean, A. *Just Neighborly*
Gilbert, W. *Iolanthe*

Mackay, C. *Benjamin Franklin Journeyman*
MacMillan, D. *Off Nags Head*
Macmillan, M. *The Pioneers*
Mick, H. *The Maid Who Wouldn't Be Proper*
*Rip van Winkle*
Takeda, I. *Bushido*

LAWR Lawrence, Robert Gilford, ed. *Early Seventeenth
        Century Drama.* New York: Dutton [c1963] 390pp.
Dekker, T. *The Shoemaker's Holiday; or, the Gentle
        Craft*
Heywood, T. *A Woman Killed with Kindness*
Marston, J., and Webster, J. *The Malcontent*
Massinger, P. *A New Way to Pay Old Debts*
Middleton, T., and Rowley, W. *The Changeling*

LAWS Lawrence, Robert Gilford, ed. *Jacobean and
        Caroline Comedies.* London: Dent, 1973. 241pp.
Brome, R. *A Jovial Crew*
Ford, J., and Rowley, W. *The Witch of Edmonton*
Middleton, T. *A Trick to Catch the Old One*

LAWT Lawrence, Robert Gilford, ed. *Jacobean and
        Caroline Tragedies.* London: Dent, 1975. 265pp.
Ford, J. *Perkin Warbeck*
Middleton, T. *Women Beware Women*
Shirley, J. *The Cardinal*

LAX Lawson, Richard H., ed. *New Anthology of
        Contemporary Austrian Folk Plays.* Riverside, CA:
        Ariadne Press, 1996. 354pp.
Baum, T. *Cold Hands*
Jelinek, E. *President Evening Breeze*
Rosei, P. *Blameless*
Unger, H. *The Bell Tolls at Twelve*
Zauner, F. *A Handful of Earth*

LAXC Lawson, Richard H., ed. *Seven Contemporary
        Austrian Plays.* Riverside, CA: Ariadne Press,
        1995. 283pp. (Studies in Austrian Literature,
        Culture, and Thought Translation Series)
Barylli, G. *Buttered Bread*
Barylli, G. *Honeymoon*
Bauer, W. *Insalata mista*
Peschina, H. *Straight as a Corkscrew*
Schwab, W. *People Annihilation or My Liver Is
        Senseless*
Schwaiger, B. *Yes, My Führer!*
Turrini, P. *Alpine Glow*

LEAK Leake, Alison, ed. *A Special Occasion: Three Plays
        by Clive Jermain, Alma Cullen, Bill Naughton.*
        Harlow: Longman, 1988. 142pp.
Cullen, A. *Knowing the Score*

Jermain, C. *The Best Years of Your Life*
Naughton, B. *A Special Occasion*

LEG Le Gallienne, Eva, ed. *Eva Le Gallienne's Civic
        Repertory Plays.* New York: W. W. Norton [c1928]
        327pp.
Chekhov, A. *Three Sisters*
Goldoni, C. *La locandiera*
Ibsen, H. *Hedda Gabler*
Wied, G. $2 \times 2 = 5$

LEIS Leishman, J. B., ed. *The Three Parnassus Plays
        (1598–1601).* London: Ivor Nicholson & Watson,
        1949. 398pp.
*The First Part of the Return from Parnassus*
*The Pilgrimage to Parnassus*
*The Second Part of the Return from Parnassus*

LES *Lesbian Plays.* Selected and introduced by Jill Davis.
        London: Methuen, 1987–1989. 2 vols.
Fleming, J. *The Rug of Identity* 1
Freeman, S. *Supporting Roles* 2
Frumin, S. *The Housetrample* 2
Kay, J. *Chiaroscuro* 1
Kilcoyne, C. *Julie* 2
Klein, D. *Coming Soon* 2
Moch, C. *Cinderella: The Real True Story* 2
Posener, J. *Any Woman Can* 1
The Women's Theatre Group with Libby Mason.
        *Double Vision* 1

LET Lettieri, Michael, and Ukas, Michael, eds. *Trissino's*
        Sophonisba *and Aretino's* Horatia*: Two Italian
        Renaissance Tragedies.* Lewiston, NY: Edwin
        Mellen Press, 1997. 262pp.
Aretino, P. *Horatia*
Trissino, G. *Sophonisba*

LEV Leverton, Garrett Hasty, ed. *Plays for the College
        Theater.* New York: French, 1932. 629pp.
Ames, W. *A Kiss in Xanadu*
Atlas, L. *"L"*
Barry, P. *Hotel Universe*
Boucicault, D. *Belle Lamar*
Britton, K., and Hargrave, R. *Houseparty*
Buckingham, G. *The Rehearsal*
Wiser, F. *Low Bridge*
*Everyman*
France, A. *The Man Who Married a Dumb Wife*
*Gammer Gurton's Needle*
Green, P. *The Lord's Will*
Ibsen, H. *The Wild Duck*
Kaufman, G. *The Butter and Egg Man*
Kreymborg, A. *Lima Beans*
Levy, B. *Springtime for Henry*

Martínez Sierra, G. *The Two Shepherds*
Molière, J. *The Doctor in Spite of Himself*
Molnár, F. *Liliom*
O'Neill, E. *The Moon of the Caribbees*
Riggs, L. *Green Grow the Lilacs*
Rostand, E. *Cyrano de Bergerac*
Sardou, V. *Patrie!*
Scala, F. *The Portrait*
Schnitzler, A. *The Green Cockatoo*
Shay, F. *A Christmas Carol*
Strong, A. *The Drums of Oude*
Vildrac, C. *Michel Auclair*
*The York Nativity*

LEVE Leverton, Garrett Hasty, ed. *Plays for the College
  Theater*. New York: French, 1934. 601pp.
  Ames, W. *A Kiss in Xanadu*
  Atlas, L. *"L"*
  Barry, P. *Hotel Universe*
  Boucicault, D. *Belle Lamar*
  Britton, K., and Hargrave R. *Houseparty*
  Buckingham, G. *The Rehearsal*
  *Everyman*
  France, A. *The Man Who Married a Dumb Wife*
  *Gammer Gurton's Needle*
  Green, P. *The Lord's Will*
  Ibsen, H. *The Wild Duck*
  Kaufman, G. *The Butter and Egg Man*
  Kreymborg, A. *Lima Beans*
  Levy, B. *Springtime for Henry*
  Martínez Sierra, G. *The Two Shepherds*
  Molière, J. *The Doctor in Spite of Himself*
  Molnar, F. *Liliom*
  O'Neill, E. *The Moon of the Caribbees*
  Riggs, L. *Green Grow the Lilacs*
  Rostand, E. *Cyrano de Bergerac*
  Sardou, V. *Patrie!*
  Scala, F. *The Portrait*
  Schnitzler, A. *The Green Cockatoo*
  Shay, F. *A Christmas Carol*
  Strong, A. *The Drums of Oude*
  Vildrac, C. *Michel Auclair*
  *The York Nativity*

LEVG Levin, David, and Gross, Theodore L., compilers.
  *America in Literature*. New York: Wiley [c1978] 2
  vols.
  Albee, E. *The American Dream*
  O'Neill, E. *The Hairy Ape*

LEVI Levin, Richard Louis, ed. *Tragedy: Plays, Theory,
  Criticism*. New York: Harcourt Brace & World
  [c1960] 217pp.
  Ibsen, H. *Ghosts*
  O'Neill, E. *The Hairy Ape*

Seneca, L. *Oedipus*
Shakespeare, W. *Othello*
Sophocles. *Oedipus Rex*

LEVJ Levin, Richard Louis, ed. *Tragedy: Plays, Theory
  and Criticism*. Alternate ed. New York: Harcourt
  Brace and World [1965] 233pp.
  Eliot, T. *Murder in the Cathedral*
  Ibsen, H. *The Wild Duck*
  Shakespeare, W. *Coriolanus*
  Sophocles. *Antigone*

LEVY Levy, Walter, ed. *Modern Drama: Selected Plays
  from 1879 to the Present*. Upper Saddle River, NJ:
  Prentice-Hall, 1999. 985pp.
  Albee, E. *The Zoo Story*
  Beckett, S. *Endgame*
  Brecht, B. *The Threepenny Opera*
  Chekhov, A. *The Cherry Orchard*
  Glaspell, S. *The Verge*
  Hansberry, L. *A Raisin in the Sun*
  Hellman, L. *The Children's Hour*
  Ibsen, H. *A Doll's House*
  Ionesco, E. *Rhinoceros*
  Miller, A. *All My Sons*
  Norman, M. *'Night, Mother*
  O'Neill, E. *Desire under the Elms*
  Pinter, H. *The Birthday Party*
  Pirandello, L. *Six Characters in Search of an Author*
  Shaw, G. *Pygmalion*
  Shepard, S. *Buried Child*
  Soyinka, W. *The Lion and the Jewel*
  Stoppard, T. *Rosencrantz and Guildenstern Are Dead*
  Strindberg, A. *Miss Julie*
  Synge, J. *The Playboy of the Western World*
  Wasserstein, W. *The Sisters Rosensweig*
  Wilde, O. *The Importance of Being Earnest*
  Wilder, T. *Our Town*
  Wilson, A. *The Piano Lesson*
  Williams, T. *The Glass Menagerie*

LEWI Lewisohn, Ludwig, ed. *Among the Nations*. New
  York: Farrar, Strauss [c1948] 270pp.
  Galsworthy, J. *Loyalties*

LIBRARY OF BEST AMERICAN PLAYS. See GARW,
  GARZ, GAS, GASB Gassner, John, ed.

LIBR *Library of Universal Literature*. New York: Alden
  Bros. [c1906] 701pp.
  Addison, J. *Cato*

LIBRARY OF WORLD DRAMA. See FLOS Flores,
  Angel, ed. *Spanish Drama*; GARZB Gassner,
  John, ed. *Medieval and Tudor Drama*; GARZE

Gassner, John, ed. *19th Century Russian Drama*;
GARZJ Gassner, John, ed. *20th Century Russian
Drama*; MACD MacAndrew, Andrew Robert, tr.
*19th Century Russian Drama*; MACE MacAndrew,
Andrew Robert, tr. *20th Century Russian Drama*

LID Lid, Richard Wald, and Bernd, Daniel, compilers.
*Plays, Classic and Contemporary*. Philadelphia:
Lippincott, [1967] 623pp.
Chekhov, A. *The Cherry Orchard*
Etherege, G. *The Man of Mode; or, Sir Fopling Flutter*
Ibsen, H. *Little Eyolf*
Ionesco, E. *Maid to Marry*
Molière, J. *Don Juan*
Shakespeare, W. *The Tragedy of Antony and Cleopatra*
Shaw, G. *The Doctor's Dilemma*
Sophocles. *Oedipus Rex*

LIDE Lieberman, Samuel, and Miller, Frank Justus, eds.
and trs. *Roman Drama*. New York: Bantam Books
[1964] 376pp.
Plautus, T. *Menaechmi Twins*
Plautus, T. *Prisoners of War*
Plautus, T. *The Rope*
Seneca, L. *Medea*
Seneca, L. *Oedipus*
Seneca, L. *Phaedra*
Terence, P. *Adelphi*
Terence, P. *Phormio*
Terence, P. *The Woman of Andros*

LIE Lieder, Paul Robert; Lovett, Robert Morss; and Root,
Robert Kilburn, eds. *British Drama*. Boston:
Houghton Mifflin [c1929] 374pp.
Beaumont, F., and Fletcher, J. *Philaster; or, Love Lies
A-bleeding*
*The Brome Abraham and Isaac*
Congreve, W. *The Way of the World*
Dryden, J. *All for Love; or, the World Well Lost*
*Everyman*
Jonson, B. *The Alchemist*
Marlowe, C. *The Tragical History of Dr. Faustus*
*The Second Shepherds' Play*
Sheridan, R. *The School for Scandal*
Wilde, O. *Lady Windermere's Fan*

LIED Lieder, Paul Robert; Lovett, Robert Morss; and Root,
Robert Kilburn, eds. *British Prose and Poetry*. Rev.
ed. Boston: Houghton Mifflin [c1938] 2 vols.
Dryden, J. *All for Love* 1
Jonson, B. *Volpone* 1
Marlowe, C. *Dr. Faustus* 1
*Second Shepherds' Play* 1
Sheridan, R. *The School for Scandal* 1

Synge, J. *The Playboy of the Western World* 2
Wilde, O. *Lady Windermere's Fan* 2

LIEE Lieder, Paul Robert; Lovett, Robert Morss; and Root,
Robert Kilburn, eds. *British Poetry and Prose*. 3rd
ed. Boston: Houghton Mifflin [c1950] 2 vols.
Dryden, J. *All for Love* 1
Jonson, B. *Alchemist* 1
Marlowe, C. *Dr. Faustus* 1
*The Second Shepherds' Play* 1
Sheridan, R. *The School for Scandal* 1
Synge, J. *Playboy of the Western World* 2
Wilde, O. *Lady Windermere's Fan* 2

LIEF Lief, Leonard, and Light, James Forest, eds. *The
Modern Age: Literature*. 2nd ed. New York: Holt,
1972. 744pp.
Feiffer, J. *Little Murders*
Miller, A. *A Memory of Two Mondays*
O'Neill, E. *Desire under the Elms*
Shaw, G. *Major Barbara*
Wilder, T. *The Skin of Our Teeth*
Williams, T. *Suddenly Last Summer*

LIEG Lief, Leonard, and Light, James Forest, compilers.
*The Modern Age: Literature*. 3rd ed. New York:
Holt, 1976.
Feiffer, J. *Little Murders*
O'Neill, E. *Desire under the Elms*
Shaw, G. *Major Barbara*
Wilder, T. *The Skin of Our Teeth*
Williams, T. *The Glass Menagerie*

LIFE *Life Is a Dream, and Other Spanish Classics*. Edited
by Eric Bentley; translated by Roy Campbell.
New York: Applause Books, 1985. 297pp. (Eric
Bentley's Dramatic Repertoire, vol. 2)
Calderon de la Barca, P. *Life Is a Dream*
Cervantes, M. *Siege of Numantia*
Molina, T. *The Trickster of Seville*
Vega, L. *Fuente ovejuna*

LIFS Lifson, David S., ed. and tr. *Epic and Folk Plays
of the Yiddish Theatre*. Rutherford, NJ: Fairleigh
Dickinson University Press, 1975. 224pp.
Axenfeld, I., and Reznik, L. *Recruits; or, That's How It
Was*
Hirschbein, P. *Farvorfen vinkel*
Kobrin, L. *Yankel Boyla*
Leivick, H. *Hirsh Lekert*
Sloves, C. *Haman's Downfall*

LIND Lind, Levi Robert, ed. *Ten Greek Plays in
Contemporary Translations*. Boston: Houghton
Mifflin [c1957] 419pp.

Aeschylus. *Agamemnon*
Aeschylus. *Prometheus Bound*
Aristophanes. *Lysistrata*
Euripides. *Alcestis*
Euripides. *Andromache*
Euripides. *Bacchae*
Euripides. *Suppliants*
Sophocles. *Antigone*
Sophocles. *Oedipus Rex*
Sophocles. *Philoctetes*


LINDB Linden, Sonja, and Baraitser, eds. *Bottled Notes
    from Underground: Contemporary Plays by Jewish
    Writers.* London: Loki Books, 1998. 309pp.
Baraitser, M. *LOUIS/lui*
Braverman, C. *The Yiddish Trojan Women*
Linden, S. *The Strange Passenger*
Schneider, D. *The Eleventh Commandment*
Sobol, J. *The Palestinian Girl*


LINDC Lindley, David, ed. *Court Masques: Jacobean and
    Caroline Entertainments, 1605–1640.* New York:
    Oxford University Press, 1995. 286pp.
Anonymous. *The Coleorton Masque*
Campion, T. *The Caversham Entertainment*
Campion, T. *The Lord Hay's Masque*
Carew, T. *Coelum Britannicum*
Chapman, G. *The Memorable Masque*
Daniel, S. *Tethys' Festival*
Davenant, W. *Salmacida spolia*
Jonson, B. *Barriers at a Marriage*
Jonson, B. *Chloridia*
Jonson, B. *Christmas His Masque*
Jonson, B. *The Golden Age Restored*
Jonson, B. *Love Restored*
Jonson, B. *Love's Welcome at Bolsover*
Jonson, B. *The Masque of Blackness*
Jonson, B. *The Masque of Queens*
Jonson, B. *Neptune's Triumph for the Return of Albion*
Jonson, B. *Pleasure Reconciled to Virtue*
Townshend, A. *Tempe Restored*


LITC *Literature: A College Anthology.* Ed. by Patrick W.
    Shaw. Boston: Houghton Mifflin, 1977. 1255pp.
Albee, E. *The American Dream*
Brecht, B. *The Caucasian Chalk Circle*
Bullins, E. *A Son, Come Home*
Ibsen, H. *Ghosts*
Molière, J. *The Misanthrope*
O'Neill, E. *Desire under the Elms*
Shakespeare, W. *The Tragedy of Hamlet, Prince of
    Denmark*
Shaw, B. *Major Barbara*
Sophocles. *Oedipus Rex*
Williams, T. *The Glass Menagerie*

LITI *Literature: An Introduction to Fiction, Poetry and
    Drama.* Compiled by X. J. Kennedy. Boston: Little,
    Brown, 1976. 1447pp.
Albee, E. *The Zoo Story*
Bullins, E. *A Son, Come Home*
Chekhov, A. *The Cherry Orchard*
Fielding, H. *Tom Thumb*
Gregory, I. *The Workhouse Ward*
Ibsen, H. *A Doll's House*
Kopit, A. *The Hero*
Miller, A. *Death of a Salesman*
O'Neill, E. *The Hairy Ape*
Pirandello, L. *Six Characters in Search of an Author*
Shakespeare, W. *The Tragedy of Hamlet, Prince of
    Denmark*
Shaw, G. *Pygmalion*
Sophocles. *Oedipus Rex*


LITIA *Literature: An Introduction to Fiction, Poetry
    and Drama.* Compiled by X. J. Kennedy. 2nd ed.
    Boston: Little, Brown, 1979. 1412pp.
Albee, E. *The Zoo Story*
Brecht, B. *Mother Courage and Her Children*
Chekhov, A. *The Marriage Proposal*
Gregory, I. *The Workhouse Ward*
Ibsen, H. *A Doll's House*
Pinter, H. *The Dumb Waiter*
Shakespeare, W. *The Tragedy of Othello*
Shaw, G. *Pygmalion*
Simon, N. *Come Blow Your Horn*
Sophocles. *Oedipus Rex*
Stoppard, T. *The Real Inspector Hound*
Williams, T. *The Glass Menagerie*


LITIB *Literature: An Introduction to Fiction, Poetry,
    and Drama.* Compiled by X. J. Kennedy. 3rd ed.
    Boston: Little, Brown, 1983. 1461pp.
Albee, E. *The Zoo Story*
Garcia Lorca, F. *Blood Wedding*
Gregory, I. *The Workhouse Ward*
Ibsen, H. *A Doll's House*
Miller, A. *Death of a Salesman*
Molière, J. *Tartuffe*
Shakespeare, W. *The Tragedy of Othello*
Shaw, G. *Pygmalion*
Sophocles. *Oedipus Rex*
Williams, T. *The Glass Menagerie*


LITIC *Literature: An Introduction to Fiction, Poetry,
    and Drama.* Compiled by X. J. Kennedy. 4th ed.
    Boston: Little, Brown, 1987. 1447pp.
Albee, E. *The Zoo Story*
Allen, W. *Death Knocks*
Glaspell, S. *Trifles*
Ibsen, H. *A Doll's House*

Miller, A. *Death of a Salesman*
Molière, J. *The Physician in Spite of Himself*
Shakespeare, W. *The Tempest*
Shakespeare, W. *The Tragedy of Othello*
Sophocles. *Antigone*
Sophocles. *Oedipus Rex*
Williams, T. *The Glass Menagerie*
Yeats, W. *Purgatory*

LITID *Literature: An Introduction to Fiction, Poetry and Drama.* Compiled by X. J. Kennedy. 5th ed. New York: HarperCollins College Publishers, 1991. 1572pp.
Fields, W. C. *Stolen Bonds*
Fornes, M. *A Vietnamese Wedding*
Glaspell, S. *Trifles*
Gregory, I. *The Workhouse Ward*
Ibsen, H. *A Doll's House*
Miller, A. *Death of a Salesman*
Shakespeare, W. *The Tragedy of Othello*
Sophocles. *Antigone*
Sophocles. *Oedipus the King*
Stoppard, T. *The Real Inspector Hound*
Synge, J. *Riders to the Sea*
Wasserstein, W. *The Man in a Case*
Williams, T. *The Glass Menagerie*
Wilson, A. *Joe Turner's Come and Gone*

LITIE *Literature: An Introduction to Fiction, Poetry and Drama.* Compiled by X. J. Kennedy and Dana Gioia. 6th ed. New York: HarperCollins College Publishers, 1995. 1854pp.
Albee, E. *The Sandbox*
Glaspell, S. *Trifles*
Henley, B. *Crimes of the Heart*
Hwang, D. *The Sound of a Voice*
Ibsen, H. *A Doll's House*
Keillor, G. *Prodigal Son*
McNally, T. *Andre's Mother*
Miller, A. *Death of a Salesman*
Shakespeare, W. *The Tragedy of Hamlet, Prince of Denmark*
Shakespeare, W. *The Tragedy of Othello*
Sophocles. *Antigone*
Sophocles. *Oedipus the King*
Synge, J. *Riders to the Sea*
Williams, T. *The Glass Menagerie*
Wilson, A. *Joe Turner's Come and Gone*

LITIF *Literature: An Introduction to Fiction, Poetry and Drama.* Compiled by X. J. Kennedy and Dana Gioia. 7th ed. New York: Longman, 1999. 2029pp.
Albee, E. *The Sandbox*
Glaspell, S. *Trifles*
Hwang, D. *The Sound of a Voice*

Ibsen, H. *A Doll's House*
Ives, D. *Sure Thing*
Keillor, G. *Prodigal Son*
McNally, T. *Andre's Mother*
Miller, A. *Death of a Salesman*
Sanchez-Scott, M. *The Cuban Swimmer*
Shakespeare, W. *The Tragedy of Hamlet, Prince of Denmark*
Shakespeare, W. *The Tragedy of Othello*
Sophocles. *Antigone*
Sophocles. *Oedipus the King*
Synge, J. *Riders to the Sea*
Williams, T. *The Glass Menagerie*
Wilson, A. *Joe Turner's Come and Gone*

LITJ *Literature: An Introduction to Fiction, Poetry and Drama.* Compiled by X. J. Kennedy and Dana Gioia. Compact ed. New York: HarperCollins, 1995. 1444pp.
Glaspell, S. *Trifles*
Henley, B. *Crimes of the Heart*
Hwang, D. *The Sound of a Voice*
Ibsen, H. *A Doll's House*
McNally, T. *Andre's Mother*
Miller, A. *Death of a Salesman*
Shakespeare, W. *The Tragedy of Hamlet, Prince of Denmark*
Sophocles. *Oedipus the King*
Williams, T. *The Glass Menagerie*

LITJA *Literature: An Introduction to Fiction, Poetry, and Drama.* Compiled by X. J. Kennedy and Dana Gioia. 2nd Compact ed. New York: Longman, 2000. 1531pp.
Glaspell, S. *Trifles*
Hwang, D. *The Sound of a Voice*
Ibsen, H. *A Doll's House*
Keillor, G. *Prodigal Son*
Miller, A. *Death of a Salesman*
Sanchez-Scott, M. *The Cuban Swimmer*
Shakespeare, W. *The Tragedy of Othello*
Sophocles. *Oedipus the King*
Williams, T. *The Glass Menagerie*
Wilson, A. *Joe Turner's Come and Gone*

LITP *Literature: Fiction, Poetry, Drama.* Compiler, Joseph K. Davis, et al. Glenview, IL: Scott, Foresman, 1977. 1157pp.
Chekhov, A. *The Cherry Orchard*
Hellman, L. *The Little Foxes*
Ionesco, E. *The Gap*
O'Neill, E. *The Hairy Ape*
Shakespeare, W. *Othello*
Sheridan, R. *The Rivals*
Sophocles. *Antigone*

Strindberg, A. *Miss Julie*
Yeats, W. *Purgatory*

LITQ *Literature as Experience: An Anthology.* Edited
by Irving Howe, John Hollander, and David
Bromwich. New York: Harcourt Brace Jovanovich,
1979. 1104pp.
Hellman, L. *The Little Foxes*
Ibsen, H. *A Doll's House*
Molière, J. *The School for Wives*
Shakespeare, W. *Hamlet*
Sophocles. *Oedipus Rex*
Strindberg, A. *The Stronger*
Williams, T. *Cat on a Hot Tin Roof*

LITR *Literature for Composition: Essays, Fiction, Poetry,
and Drama.* Edited by Sylvan Barnet, Morton
Berman, and William Burto. Boston: Little, Brown,
and Company, 1984. 774pp.
Ibsen, H. *A Doll's House*
Shakespeare, W. *The Tragedy of Hamlet, Prince of
Denmark*
Sophocles. *Antigone*
Sophocles. *Oedipus Rex*

LITRA *Literature for Composition: Essays, Fiction,
Poetry, and Drama.* Edited by Sylvan Barnet,
Morton Berman, and William Burto. 2nd ed.
Glenview, IL: Scott, Foresman and Company,
1988. 799pp.
Albee, E. *The Sandbox*
Glaspell, S. *Trifles*
Ibsen, H. *A Doll's House*
Jacobs, W., and Parker, L. *The Monkey's Paw*
Shakespeare, W. *The Taming of the Shrew*
Shakespeare, W. *The Tragedy of Hamlet, Prince of
Denmark*
Sophocles. *Antigone*
Sophocles. *Oedipus Rex*

LITRB *Literature for Composition: Essays, Fiction,
Poetry, and Drama.* Edited by Sylvan Barnet,
Morton Berman, William Burto, and Marcia
Stubbs. 3rd ed. New York: HarperCollins
Publishers, 1991. 1100pp.
Albee, E. *The Sandbox*
Fierstein, H. *On Tidy Endings*
Glaspell, S. *Trifles*
Ibsen, H. *A Doll's House*
Jacobs, W., and Parker, L. *The Monkey's Paw*
Shakespeare, W. *The Taming of the Shrew*
Shakespeare, W. *The Tragedy of Hamlet, Prince of
Denmark*
Sophocles. *Antigone*

Sophocles. *Oedipus Rex*
Williams, T. *The Glass Menagerie*

LITRC *Literature for Composition: Essays, Fiction,
Poetry, and Drama.* Edited by Sylvan Barnet,
Morton Berman, William Burto, and Marcia
Stubbs. 4th ed. New York: HarperCollins
Publishers, 1996. 1363pp.
Albee, E. *The Sandbox*
Fierstein, H. *On Tidy Endings*
Glaspell, S. *Trifles*
Ibsen, H. *A Doll's House*
Shakespeare, W. *Hamlet, Prince of Denmark*
Shakespeare, W. *The Tempest*
Sophocles. *Antigone*
Sophocles. *Oedipus Rex*
Wasserstein, W. *The Man in a Case*
Williams, T. *The Glass Menagerie*
Wilson, A. *Fences*

LITRD *Literature for Composition: Essays, Fiction,
Poetry, and Drama.* Edited by Sylvan Barnet,
Morton Berman, William Burto, William E. Cain,
and Marcia Stubbs. 5th ed. Upper Saddle River, NJ:
Prentice Hall, 2000. 1408pp.
Fierstein, H. *On Tidy Endings*
Glaspell, S. *Trifles*
Ibsen, H. *A Doll's House*
Mamet, D. *Oleanna*
Shakespeare, W. *Hamlet, Prince of Denmark*
Sophocles. *Antigone*
Sophocles. *Oedipus Rex*
Wasserstein, W. *The Man in a Case*
Williams, T. *The Glass Menagerie*
Wilson, A. *Fences*

THE LITERATURE OF ITALY, 1265–1907. *See* JOH
Johnson, Rossiter, ed. *An Anthology of Italian
Authors from Cavalcanti to Fogazzaro.*

LITT Litto, Fredric M., ed. *Plays from Black Africa.* New
York: Hill and Wang, 1968. 316pp.
Clark, J. *Song of a Goat*
Henshaw, J. *The Jewels of the Shrine*
Hutchinson, A. *The Rainkillers*
Nkosi, L. *The Rhythm of Violence*
Ofori, H. *The Literary Society*
Sutherland, E. *Edufa*

LIU Liu, Jung-en, compiler and translator. *Six Yuan Plays.*
Harmondsworth, Middlesex: Penguin, 1972. 285pp.
Chêng, T. *The Soul of Ch'iennu Leaves Her Body*
Chi, C. *The Orphan of Chao*
Kuan, H. *The Injustice Done to Tou Ngo*
Li, H. *Chang Boils the Sea*

Ma, C. *Autumn in Han Palace*
*A Stratagem of Interlocking Rings*

LOC Locke, Alain Le Roy, and Montgomery, Gregory,
    eds. *Plays of Negro Life*. New York: Harper, 1927.
    430pp.
Bruce, R. *Sahdji, an African Ballet*
Culbertson, E. *Rackey*
Duncan, T. *The Death Dance*
Green, P. *In Abraham's Bosom*
Green, P. *The No'count Boy*
Green, P. *White Dresses*
Johnson, G. *Plumes*
Matheus, J. *'Cruiter*
O'Neill, E. *The Dreamy Kid*
O'Neill, E. *The Emperor Jones*
Richardson, W. *The Broken Banjo*
Richardson, W. *The Flight of the Natives*
Rogers, J. *Judge Lynch*
Spence, E. *The Starter*
Toomer, J. *Balo*
Torrence, R. *The Dense Calinda*
Torrence, R. *Granny Maumee*
Torrence, R. *The Rider of Dreams*
White, L. *The Bird Child*
Wilson, F. *Sugar Cane*

LOCK Locke, Louis Glenn; Gibson, William M.; and
    Arms, George, eds. *Introduction to Literature*.
    New York: Rinehart [c1948] 592pp. (Readings for
    Liberal Education, vol. 2)
Euripides. *Alcestis*
Marlowe, C. *Doctor Faustus*
O'Neill, E. *The Emperor Jones*
Thurber, J., and Nugent, E. *The Male Animal*

LOCL Locke, Louis Glenn; Gibson, William M.; and
    Arms, George, eds. *Introduction to Literature*. Rev.
    ed. New York: Rinehart [c1952] 749pp. (Readings
    for Liberal Education, vol. 2)
Cocteau, J. *The Infernal Machine*
Ibsen, H. *Hedda Gabler*
Marlowe, C. *The Tragical History of Doctor Faustus*
O'Neill, E. *The Long Voyage Home*
Sophocles. *Oedipus the King*

LOCLA Locke, Louis Glenn; Gibson, William M.; and
    Arms, George, eds. *Introduction to Literature*. 3rd
    ed. New York: Rinehart [c1957] 864pp. (Readings
    for Liberal Education, vol. 2)
Cocteau, J. *The Infernal Machine*
Ibsen, H *Hedda Gabler*
Molière, J. *The Bourgeois Gentleman*
O'Neill, E. *The Long Voyage Home*
Shaw, G. *The Devil's Disciple*

Sophocles. *Oedipus the King*
Synge, J. *In the Shadow of the Glen*

LOCLB Locke, Louis Glenn; Gibson, William; and Arms,
    George, eds. *Introduction to Literature*. 4th edition.
    New York: Holt, Rinehart and Winston [c1962]
    (Readings for Liberal Education, vol. 3)
Cocteau, J. *The Infernal Machine*
García Lorca, F. *Blood Wedding*
Ibsen, H. *Hedda Gabler*
O'Neill, E. *The Long Voyage Home*
Shaw, G. *Candida*
Sophocles. *Oedipus the King*

LOCM Locke, Louis Glenn; Kirby, John P.; and Porter,
    M. E., eds. *Literature of Western Civilization*. New
    York: Ronald [c1952] 2 vols.
Aeschylus. *Agamemnon* 1
Aristophanes. *Lysistrata* 1
Euripides. *Medea* 1
Goethe, J. *Faust, Part 1* 2
Ibsen, H. *Rosmersholm* 2
Molière, J. *The Misanthrope* 2
Plautus, T. *Amphitryon* 1
Racine, J. *Phaedra* 2
Shakespeare, W. *Hamlet* 1
Vega Carpio, L. *The King the Greatest Alcalde* 1
Sophocles. *Oedipus the King* 1

LOCR Lockert, Lacy, ed., and tr. *The Chief Rivals of
    Corneille and Racine*. Nashville: Vanderbilt
    University Press, c1956. 605pp.
Campistron, J. *Andronicus*
Corneille, T. *The Earl of Essex*
Corneille, T. *Laodice*
Crebillon, C. *Rhadamistus and Zenobia*
Du Ryer, P. *Saul*
Du Ryer, P. *Scaevola*
La Fosse, A. *Manlius Capitolinus*
Mairet, J. *Sophonisba*
Rotrou, J. *Chosroes*
Rotrou, J. *Wenceshaus*
Tristan l'Hermite, F. *Mariamne*
Voltaire, F. *Zaire*

LOCU Lockert, Lacy, ed. and tr. *More Plays by Rivals
    of Corneille and Racine*. Nashville: Vanderbilt
    University Press, 1968. 694pp.
Boyer, C. *Oropaste*
Campistron, J. *Tiridate*
Corneille, T. *Ariane*
Corneille, T. *Maximian*
Corneille, T. *Timocrate*
Du Ryer, P. *Esther*
Hardy, A. *Mariamne*

La Grange-Chancel. *Ino et Mélicerte*
Péchantré. *Geta*
Quinault, P. *Astrate*
Rotrou, J. *Saint Genest*
Tristan l'Hermite, F. *La mort de Seneque*
Tristan l'Hermite, F. *Osman*

LOGG Loggins, Vernon, ed. *Three Great French Plays.*
Greenwich, CT: Fawcett [c1961] 256pp.
Corneille, P. *Polyeucte*
Molière, J. *The Hypochondriac*
Racine, J. *Phèdre*

LOND London, Ephraim, ed. *The World of Law: A
Treasury of Great Writing about and in the Law,
Short Stories, Plays.* New York: Simon and
Schuster [1960] 2 vols.
*The Farce of the Worthy Master Pierre Patelin* 1
Mortimer, J. *The Dock Brief* 1
Rattigan, T. *The Winslow Boy* 1

LONG London, John, and George, David, eds. *Modern
Catalan Plays.* London: Methuen, 2000. 238pp.
Belbel, S. *Fourplay*
Benet i Jornet, J. *Desire*
Brossa, J. *The Quarrelsome Party*
Sirera, R. *The Audition*

LONO *London Omnibus.* With an introduction by Carl
Van Doren, Garden City, NY: Doubleday, Doran,
1932. v.p.
Coward, N. *Private Lives*

LOO Loomis, Roger Sherman; and Clark, Donald Leman,
eds. *Modern English Readings.* New York: Farrar
and Rinehart, 1934. 892pp.
Lawson, J. *Success Story*
O'Neill, E. *The Moon of the Caribbees*
Wilde, O. *The Importance of Being Earnest*

LOOA Loomis, Roger Sherman, and Clark, Donald
Leman, eds. *Modern English Readings.* Rev. ed.
New York: Farrar and Rinehart, 1936. 1074pp.
Anderson, M. *Both Your Houses*
Connelly, M. *The Green Pastures*
O'Neill, E. *Beyond the Horizon*
Synge, J. *Riders to the Sea*
Wilde, O. *The Importance of Being Earnest*

LOOB Loomis, Roger Sherman, and Clark, Donald
Leman, eds. *Modern English Readings.* 3rd ed.
New York: Farrar and Rinehart, 1939. 1147pp.
Anderson, M. *Both Your Houses*
Connelly, M. *The Green Pastures*
MacLeish, A. *The Fall of the City*

O'Neill, E. *Beyond the Horizon*
Synge, J. *Riders to the Sea*

LOOC Loomis, Roger Sherman, and Clark, Donald
Leman, eds. *Modern English Readings.* 4th ed.
New York: Farrar and Rinehart, 1942. 968pp.
Connelly, M. *The Green Pastures*
Hart, M., and Kaufman, G. *You Can't Take It with You*
MacLeish, A. *The Fall of the City*
O'Neill, E. *Beyond the Horizon*
Synge, J. *Riders to the Sea*

LOOD Loomis, Roger Sherman, and Clark, Donald
Leman, eds. *Modern English Readings.* 5th ed.
New York: Rinehart [c1946] 1062pp.
Connelly, M. *The Green Pastures*
Corwin, N. *Good Heavens*
Hart, M., and Kaufman, G. *You Can't Take It with You*
MacLeish, A. *The Fall of the City*
O'Neill, E. *Beyond the Horizon*
Synge, J. *Riders to the Sea*

LOOE Loomis, Roger Sherman, and Clark, Donald Leman,
eds. *Modern English Readings.* 6th ed. New York:
Rinehart [c1950] 1061pp.
Connelly, M. *The Green Pastures*
Hart, M., and Kaufman, G. *You Can't Take It with You*
MacLeish, A. *The Fall of the City*
O'Neill, E. *Beyond the Horizon*
Synge, J. *Riders to the Sea*

LOOF Loomis, Roger Sherman; Clark, Donald Leman;
and Middendorf, John Harlan, eds. *Modern English
Readings.* 7th ed. New York: Rinehart [c1956]
1097pp.
Hart, M., and Kaufman, G. *You Can't Take It with You*
O'Neill, E. *Beyond the Horizon*
Shaw, G. *Arms and the Man*
Synge, J. *Riders to the Sea*

LOOM Loomis, Roger Sherman; and Wells, Henry Willis,
eds. *Representative Medieval and Tudor Plays,
Translated and Modernized.* New York: Sheed &
Ward, 1942. 301pp.
*The Annunciation*
Heywood, J. *John, Tyb, and Sir John*
Heywood, J. *The Pardoner and the Friar*
Hilarius. *The Miracle of Saint Nicholas and the Image*
La Vigne, A. *The Miracle of the Blind Man and the
Cripple*
*The Miracle of Saint Nicholas and the School Boys*
*The Miracle of Saint Nicholas and the Virgins*
*The Mystery of the Redemption*
*The Second Shepherds' Play*
*The Summoning of Everyman*

LOQA *Love and Thunder: Plays by Women in the Age of Queen Anne.* Edited and introduced by Kendall. London: Methuen Drama, 1988. 156pp.
Centlivre, S. *The Adventures of Venice*
Pix, M. *The Spanish Wives*
Trotter, C. *Love at a Loss, or, Most Votes Carry It*
Wiseman, J. *Antiochus the Great, or, the Fatal Relapse*

LOR Lovell, Ernest James, and Pratt, Willis W., eds. *Modern Drama: An Anthology of Nine Plays.* Boston: Ginn [c1963] 425pp.
Anderson, M. *The Wingless Victory*
Duncan, R. *The Death of Satan*
Euripides. *Medea*
Giraudoux, J. *Electra*
Ibsen, H. *Hedda Gabler*
Maugham, W. *The Constant Wife*
Miller, A. *The Crucible*
O'Neill, E. *A Moon for the Misbegotten*
Shaw, G. *Caesar and Cleopatra*

LOV Lovett, Robert Morss, and Jones, Howard Mumford, eds. *The College Reader.* Boston: Houghton Mifflin [c1936] 1099pp.
Archer, W. *The Green Goddess*
Sherriff, R. *Journey's End*

LOVR Lovrien, Marian; Potell, Herbert; and Bostwich, Prudence, eds. *Adventures in Living.* New York: Harcourt, Brace, 1955. 626pp. (Adventures in Literature Series)
Corwin, N. *Ann Rutledge*
Duffield, B. *The Lottery*
Law, W. *Indomitable Blacksmith*
Lindsay, H., and Crouse, R. *Life with Father*
Martens, A. *Blue Beads*
Richmond, S. *Career for Ralph*

LOW Lowe, Orton, ed. *Our Land and its Literature.* New York: Harper, 1936. 666pp.
Vollmer, L. *Sun-up*

LOWE Lowe, Stephen, ed. *Peace Plays.* London: Methuen, 1985. 135pp.
Common Ground. *The Fence*
Freistadt, B. *The Celebration of Kokura*
Levy, D. *Clam*
Lowe, S. *Keeping Body and Soul Together*
Mitchell, A. *The Tragedy of King Real*

LOWE2 Lowe, Stephen, ed. *Peace Plays: Two.* London: Methuen, 1990. 160pp.
Bulgakov, M. *Adam and Eve*
Burlatsky, F. *The Burden of Decision*

Kopit, A. *End of the World with Symposium to Follow*
Stayton, R. *After the First Death*

LUCA Lucas, Frank Laurence, ed. and tr. *Greek Drama for Everyman.* London: J. M. Dent [1954] 454pp.
Aeschylus. *Agamemnon*
Aeschylus. *Prometheus Bound*
Aristophanes. *The Clouds*
Euripides. *The Bacchae*
Euripides. *Hippolytus*
Sophocles. *Antigone*
Sophocles. *Oedipus the King*

LUCAB Lucas, Frank Laurence, ed. and tr. *Greek Drama for the Common Reader.* Reissued with corrections. London: Chatto, 1967. 459pp.
Aeschylus. *Agamemnon*
Aeschylus. *Prometheus Bound*
Aristophanes. *The Clouds*
Euripides. *The Bacchae*
Euripides. *Hippolytus*
Sophocles. *Antigone*
Sophocles. *Oedipus the King*

LUCAF Lucas, Frank Laurence, ed. and tr. *Greek Tragedy and Comedy.* New York: Viking, 1968. 454pp.
Aeschylus. *Agamemnon*
Aeschylus. *Prometheus Bound*
Aristophanes. *The Clouds*
Euripides. *The Bacchae*
Euripides. *Hippolytus*
Sophocles. *Antigone*
Sophocles. *Oedipus the King*

LUCAS, HARRIET MARCELLA. *See* PROD *Prose and Poetry for Appreciation.*

LUP Lupack, Alan, ed. *Arthurian Drama: An Anthology.* New York: Garland Publishing, Inc., 1991. 322pp.
Carr, J. *King Arthur*
Dryden, J. *King Arthur*
Hovey, R. *The Birth of Galahad*
Kinross, M. *Tristram and Isoult*
Rhys, E. *The Masque of the Grail*
Rowley, W. *The Birth of Merlin*

LUPW Lupack, Alan, and Lupack, Barbara Tepa, eds. *Arthurian Literature by Women.* New York: Garland Publishing, Inc., 1999. 382pp.
Kinross, M. *Tristram and Isoult*

LUST Lustig, Theodore H., tr. *Classical German Drama.* With an introduction by Victor Lange. New York: Bantam Books [c1963] 466pp.

Büchner, G. *Danton's Death*
Goethe, J. *Egmont*
Kleist, H. *The Prince of Homburg*
Lessing, G. *Nathan the Wise*
Schiller, J. *Mary Stuart*

LUZ Luzina, Jelena, ed. *Ten Modern Macedonian Plays.*
Skopje, Macedonia: Matica Makedonska, 2000.
487pp. (Limited to 1,000 copies)
Andonovski, V. *The Slavic Chest*
Bogdanovski, R. *Nothing without Trifolio*
Čašule, K. *Darkness*
Dukovski, D. *Powder Keg*
Mirčevska, Ž. *A Place I've Never Been To*
Nasev, S. *Who Do You Belong To?*
Petrovski, J. *Porcelain Vase*
Plevneš, J. *"R"*
Risteski, B. *Lepa Angelina*
Stefanovski, G. *Proud Flesh*

LYMAN, WILLIAM WHITTINGHAM. *See* TOD *Today's Literature.*

LYK Lyons, Eugene, ed. *Six Soviet Plays.* Boston:
Houghton Mifflin, 1934. 469pp.
Afinogenyev, A. *Fear*
Bulgakov, M. *Days of the Turbins*
Glebov, A. *Inga*
Katayev, V. *Squaring the Circle*
Krishon, V. *Bread*
Pogodin, N. *Tempo*

LYN Lynde, Denyse, ed. *Voices from the Landwash: 11
Newfoundland Playwrights.* Toronto: Playwrights
Canada Press, 1997. 417pp.
Cahill, T. *The Only Living Father*
Cook, M. *End of the Road*
Guy, R. *Young Triffle Have Been Made Away With*
Pickard, L. *ALIENation of Lizzie Dyke*
Pittman, A. *West Moon*
Soucy, P. *Flux*
Spence, J. *Catlover*
Stapleton, B. *Woman in a Monkey Cage*
Thomey, G., & Hennessey, B. *Hanlon House*
Walsh, D. *Tomorrow Will Be Sunday*

LYO Lyons, John Coriden, and Searles, Colbert, eds. *Eight
French Classic Plays.* New York: Holt [c1932]
609pp.
Corneille, P. *Le cid*
Corneille, P. *Le menteur*
Corneille, P. *Polyeucte*
Molière, J. *Le misanthrope*
Molière, J. *Les précieuses ridicules*

Molière, J. *Le Tartuffe; ou L'imposteur*
Racine, J. *Andromaque*
Racine, J. *Phèdre*

LYON Lyons, Paddy, and Morgan, Fidelis, eds. *Female
Playwrights of the Restoration: Five Comedies.*
London: J.M. Dent & Sons; Rutland, VT: Charles
Tuttle Co. Inc., 1991. 363pp.
Ariadne. *She Ventures and He Wins*
Behn, A. *The Feigned Courtesans, or, a Night's Intrigue*
Centlivre, S. *The Basset Table*
Centlivre, S. *The Busybody*
Pix, M. *The Beau Defeated, or, the Lucky Younger
Brother*

MAB MacAndrew, Andrew Robert, translator. *19th
century Russian Drama.* New York: Bantam Books
[1963] 342pp. (The Library of World Drama)
Gogol, N. *The Inspector General*
Ostrovsky, A. *The Thunderstorm*
Pushkin, A. *The Stone Guest*
Tolstoy, L. *The Power of Darkness*
Turgenev, I. *A Month in the Country*

MABA MacAndrew, Andrew Robert, translator. *20th
Century Russian Drama.* New York: Bantam Books
[1963] 376pp. (The Library of World Drama)
Andreyev, L. *He Who Gets Slapped*
Chekhov, A. *The Three Sisters*
Gorky, M. *The Lower Depths*
Mayakóvsky, V. *The Bathhouse*
Olesha, Y. *A List of Assets*

MABC McAvoy, William C., ed. *Dramatic Tragedy.*
New York: Webster Division, McGraw-Hill, 1971.
390pp.
*Everyman*
Ibsen, H. *Ghosts*
Marlowe, C. *The Tragical History of Doctor Faustus*
Miller, A. *All My Sons*
Shakespeare, W. *The Tragedy of Hamlet, Prince of
Denmark*
Sophocles. *Oedipus Rex*
Williams, T. *The Glass Menagerie*

MAC McCallum, James Dow, ed. *The College Omnibus.*
New York: Harcourt, Brace, 1933. 832pp.
O'Neill, E. *The Emperor Jones*
Synge, J. *Riders to the Sea*

MACB McCallum, James Dow, ed. *The College Omnibus.*
New York: Harcourt, Brace [c1934] 982pp.
Galsworthy, J. *Strife*
O'Neill, E. *The Emperor Jones*
Synge, J. *Riders to the Sea*

MACC McCallum. James Dow, ed. *The 1936 College Omnibus*. In collaboration with Marston Balch, Percy Marks, and Others. New York: Harcourt, Brace [c1936] 1193pp.
Galsworthy, J. *Strife*
O'Neill, E. *The Emperor Jones*
Rostand, E. *Cyrano de Bergerac*

MACE McCallum, James Dow, ed. *The Revised College Omnibus*. In collaboration with Marston Balch, Ralph P. Boas, Percy Marks, and Others. New York: Harcourt, Brace, 1939. 1258pp.
Galsworthy, J. *Strife*
MacLeish, A. *Air Raid*
O'Neill, E. *The Emperor Jones*
Rostand, E. *Cyrano de Bergerac*

MACF McCallum, James Dow, ed. *The College Omnibus*. 6th ed. In collaboration with Marston Balch, Ralph P. Boas, Percy Marks, Benfield Pressey, Louis Untermeyer. New York: Harcourt, Brace [c1947] 1288pp.
Galsworthy, J. *Strife*
Nichols, R., and Browne, M. *Wings over Europe*
O'Neill, E. *The Emperor Jones*
Rostand, E. *Cyrano de Bergerac*

McCALLUM, JAMES DOW. *See also HAP Harbrace Omnibus.*

MACL MacClelland, George Williams, and Baugh, Albert Croll, eds. *Century Types of English Literature Chronologically Arranged*. New York: Century, 1925. 1144pp.
Dekker, T. *The Shoemaker's Holiday*
Dryden, J. *All for Love*
Sheridan, R. *The School for Scandal*
Wilde, O. *Lady Windermere's Fan*

MACN McClintock, Marshall, ed. *The Nobel Prize Treasury*. Garden City, NY: Doubleday, 1948. 612pp.
Benavente, J. *His Widow's Husband*
Bjørnson, B. *Between the Battles*
Echegaray, J. *The Street Singer*
Hauptmann, G. *The Sunken Bell*
Maeterlinck, M. *Interior*
O'Neill, E. *Desire under the Elms*
Pirandello, L. *Our Lord of the Ships*
Yeats, W. *The Land of Heart's Desire*

McCORKLE, J. N. *See HAP Harbrace Omnibus.*

MACU MacCurdy, Raymond R., ed. *Spanish Drama of the Golden Age: Twelve Plays*. New York: Irvington, 1979. 634pp.
Calderón de la Barca, P. *El gran teatro del mundo*
Calderón de la Barca, P. *El médico y su honra*
Castro y Bellvís, G. *Las mocedades del Cid*
Cervantes, M. *Entremés del retablo de las maravillas*
Mira de Amescua, A. *La adversa fortuna de don Alvaro de Luna*
Moreto y Cabaña, A. *El desdén con el desdén*
Rojas Zorilla, F. *Entre bobos anda el juego*
Ruiz de Alarcón, J. *El examen de los maridos*
Téllez, G. *El burlador de Sevilla*
Téllez, G. *El condenado por desconfiado*
Vega [Carpio], L. *El caballero de Olmedo*
Velez de Guevara, L. *Reinar después de morir*

MAD MacDermott, John Francis, ed. *Modern Plays*. New York: Harcourt, Brace [c1932] 427pp.
Čapek, K. *R.U.R.*
Howard, S. *They Knew What They Wanted*
Hughes, H. *Hell Bent fer Heaven*
Ibsen, H. *A Doll's House*
Maugham, W. *The Circle*
Milne, A. *Mr. Pim Passes By*
O'Neill, E. *The Emperor Jones*

MADB MacDonald, J. W. and Saxton, J. C. W., comps. *Four Stages*. New York: St. Martin's Press [1967, c1966] 398pp.
Ibsen, H. *Pillars of Society*
Marlowe, C. *Doctor Faustus*
Miller, A. *All My Sons*
Sophocles. *Oedipus Rex*

MADG McDowell, Tremaine, ed. *America in Literature*. New York: Crofts, 1944. 540pp.
Connelly, M. *The Green Pastures*
Wilder, T. *Our Town*

MADI McDowell, Tremaine, ed. *The Romantic Triumph: American Literature from 1830 to 1860*. New York: Macmillan, 1933. 744pp. (American Literature: A Period Anthology; Oscar Cargill, general editor. Vol. 2)
Boker, G. *Francesca da Rimini*

MAE McFarland, Philip; Hynes, Samuel; Benson, Larry D.; and Peckham, Mase, eds. *Forms in English Literature*. Boston: Houghton Mifflin, 1972.
*Everyman*
Pinter, H. *A Night Out*

Shakespeare, W. *Macbeth*
Shaw, G. *Pygmalion*

MAEC McFarland, Philip, Kirschner, Allen, and Peckham, Morse, eds. *Perceptions in Literature.* Boston: Houghton Mifflin [c1972] 783pp.
Shakespeare, W. *Julius Caesar*
Williams, T. *The Glass Menagerie*

MAF Macgowan, Kenneth, ed. *Famous American Plays of the 1920s.* New York: Dell, c1959. 511pp. (Laurel Drama Series)
Anderson, M., and Stallings, L. *What Price Glory?*
Barry, P. *Holiday*
Heyward, D., and Heyward, D. *Porgy*
Howard, S. *They Knew What They Wanted*
O'Neill, E. *The Moon of the Caribbees*
Rice, E. *Street Scene*

MAFC Macgowan, Kenneth, and Clurman, Harold, eds. *Famous American Plays of the 1920s and the 1930s.* New York: The Fireside Theatre, 1988. 701pp.
Anderson, M., and Stallings, L. *What Price Glory?*
Barry, P. *Holiday*
Behrman, S. *End of Summer*
Heyward, D., and Heyward, D. *Porgy*
Howard, S. *They Knew What They Wanted*
Odets, C. *Awake and Sing!*
O'Neill, E. *The Moon of the Caribbees*
Rice, E. *Street Scene*
Saroyan, W. *The Time of Your Life*
Sherwood, R. *Idiot's Delight*
Steinbeck, J. *Of Mice and Men*

McGRAW, H. WARD. *See* PROB *Prose and Poetry for Appreciation*; PROF, PROG, PROH *Prose and Poetry of America*; PROM, PRON *Prose and Poetry of England.*

MAH Machiz, Herbert, ed. *Artists' Theatre: Four Plays.* New York: Grove [c1960] 224pp.
Abel, L. *Absalom*
Ashbery, J. *The Heroes*
Merrill, J. *The Bait*
O'Hara, F. *Try! Try!*

MAK McIlwraith, Archibald Kennedy, ed. *Five Elizabethan Comedies.* London: Oxford University Press [1934] 308pp. (The World's Classics)
Dekker, T. *The Shoemaker's Holiday*
Greene, R. *Friar Bacon and Friar Bungay*

Lyle, J. *Campaspe*
*The Merry Devil of Edmonton*
Peele, G. *The Old Wives' Tale*

MAKG McIlwraith, Archibald Kennedy, ed. *Five Elizabethan Tragedies.* London: Oxford University Press [1938] 399pp. (The World's Classics)
*Arden of Feversham*
Heywood, T. *A Woman Killed with Kindness*
Kyd, T. *The Spanish Tragedy*
Norton, T., and Sackville, T. *Gorboduc*
Seneca, L. *Thyestes*

MAKJ McIlwraith, Archibald Kennedy, ed. *Five Stuart Tragedies.* London: Oxford University Press [1953] 497pp. (The World's Classics)
Beaumont, F., and Fletcher, J. *The Maid's Tragedy*
Chapman, G. *Bussy D'Ambois*
Ford, J. *'Tis a Pity She's a Whore*
Massinger, P. *The Roman Actor*
Webster, J. *The Duchess of Malfi*

MAL Mack, Maynard, ed. *The Augustans.* New York: Prentice-Hall, 1950. 343pp. (English Masterpieces, vol. 5)
Gay, J. *The Beggar's Opera*

MALC Mack, Maynard [and others], eds. *The Continental Edition of World Masterpieces.* New York: W. W. Norton [c1962] 1971pp.
Aeschylus. *Agamemnon*
Euripides. *Medea*
Goethe, J. *Faust, Parts 1 & 2*
Ibsen, H. *The Wild Duck*
Molière, J. *The Bourgeois Gentleman*
Racine, J. *Phaedra*
Sophocles. *King Oedipus*

MALG Mack, Maynard [and others], eds. *World Masterpieces.* New York: W. W. Norton [c1956] 2v
Aeschylus. *Agamemnon* 1
Euripides. *Medea* 1
Goethe, J. *Faust Parts 1&2* 2
Ibsen, H. *The Wild Duck* 2
Molière, J. *The Bourgeois Gentleman* 2
Racine, J. *Phaedra* 2
Shakespeare, W. *Hamlet, Prince of Denmark* 1
Sophocles. *King Oedipus* 1
Synge, J. *The Playboy of the Western World* 2

MALI Mack, Maynard [and others] eds. *World Masterpieces*. Rev. ed. New York: W. W. Norton [1965] 2 vols.
Aeschylus. *Agamemnon* 1
Aeschylus. *Prometheus Bound* 1
Aristophanes. *Lysistrata* 1
Brecht, B. *The Caucasian Chalk Circle* 2
Calderón de la Barca, P. *Life Is a Dream* 1
Eliot, T. *Murder in the Cathedral* 2
Euripides. *Medea* 1
Euripides. *Trojan Women* 1
*Everyman* 1
Goethe, J. *Faust* (abridged ed.) 2
Ibsen, H. *The Wild Duck* 2
Marlowe, C. *The Tragical History of the Life and Death of Doctor Faustus* 1
Molière, J. *Tartuffe; or, the Imposter* 2
Molina, T. *The Trickster of Seville and His Guest of Stone* 1
Racine, J. *Phaedra* 2
Sartre, J. *No Exit* 2
Shakespeare, W. *Hamlet* 1
Sophocles. *Antigone* 1
Sophocles. *Oedipus at Colonus* 1
Sophocles. *Oedipus the King* 1

MALN Mack, Maynard, and Others, eds. *World Masterpieces*. 3rd ed. New York: W. W. Norton, 1973. 2 vols.
Aeschylus. *Agamemnon* 1
Aristophanes. *Lysistrata* 1
Calderon de la Barca, P. *Life Is a Dream* 1
Chekhov, A. *The Cherry Orchard* 2
Euripides. *Medea* 1
Goethe, J. *Faust, Part 1* 2
Ibsen, H. *The Wild Duck* 2
Marlowe, C. *The Tragical History of the Life and Death of Doctor Faustus* 1
Molière, J. *Tartuffe* 2
Pirandello, L. *Henry IV* 2
Racine, J. *Phaedra* 2
Sartre, J. *No Exit* 2
Shakespeare, W. *Hamlet, Prince of Denmark* 1
Shaw, G. *Saint Joan* 2
Sophocles. *Antigone* 1
Sophocles. *Oedipus Tyrannus* 1

MALR MacKendrick, Paul, and Howe, Herbert M., eds. *Classics in Translation*. Madison: University of Wisconsin Press, 1952. 2 vols.
Aeschylus. *Agamemnon* 1
Aristophanes. *Frogs* 1
Euripides. *Medea* 1
Plautus. *The Haunted House* 2

Seneca. *Medea* 2
Sophocles. *Antigone* 1
Terence. *Woman from Andros* 2

MALY Mackey, Margaret, ed. *Festival Plays*. Harlow: Longman, 1986. 180pp.
Dillon, E. *Hitch-hiker*
Oshodi, M. *'S'bend*
Singh, L. *Manjit*

MAM McLean, Hugh, and Vickery, Walter N., eds. and trs. *The Year of Protest, 1956: An Anthology of Soviet Literary Materials*. New York: Random House [c1961] 269pp.
Alyoshin, S. *Alone*

MAMB McLeish, Kenneth, compiler and translator. *The Frogs and Other Greek Plays*. Harlow: Longmans, 1970. 202pp.
Aeschylus. *Prometheus Bound*
Aristophanes. *The Birds*
Aristophanes. *The Frogs*
Euripides. *Medea*

MAME McLuskie, Kathleen E., and Bevington, David, ed. *Plays on Women*. Manchester: Manchester University Press; New York: Distributed exclusively in the USA by Palgrave, 1999. 416pp.
*Arden of Faversham*
Heywood, T. *A Woman Killed with Kindness*
Middleton, T. *A Chaste Maid in Cheapside*
Middleton, T., and Dekker, T. *The Roaring Girl*

MANA McMahon, Agnes; Krauss, Franklin Brunell; and Carter, James Franklin, eds. *Explorations in French Literature*. New York: Nelson, 1939. 538pp.
Labiche, E. *Le voyage de Monsieur Perrichon*

MANCA McMichael, George L., ed. *Anthology of American Literature*. General Editor: George McMichael. Advisory Editors: Richard P. Adams [and Others]. New York: Macmillan, 1974. 2 vols. (Vol. 1, Colonial through Romantic; Vol. 2, Realism to the Present)
Albee, E. *The Zoo Story* 2
Jones, L. *Dutchman* 2
O'Neill, E. *The Hairy Ape* 2

MANCB McMichael, George L., ed. *Anthology of American Literature*. General Editor: George McMichael. Advisory Editors: Frederick Crews [and Others]. 2nd ed. New York: Macmillan, 1980. 2 vols. (Vol. 1, Colonial through Romantic; Vol. 2, Realism to the Present)

Albee, E. *The Zoo Story* 2
Jones, L. *Dutchman* 2
O'Neill, E. *The Hairy Ape* 2


MANCD McMichael, George L., ed. *Anthology of American Literature*. General editor: George McMichael. Advisory Editors: Frederick Crews [and Others]. 3rd ed. New York: Macmillan, 1985. 2 vols. (Vol. 1, Colonial through Romantic; Vol. 2, Realism to the Present)
Albee, E. *The Zoo Story* 2
Baraka, A. *Dutchman* 2
O'Neill, E. *The Hairy Ape* 2
Tyler, R. *The Contrast* 1
Williams, T. *The Glass Menagerie* 2


MANCE McMichael, George L., ed. *Anthology of American Literature*. General Editor: George McMichael. Advisory Editors: Frederick Crews [and Others]. 4th ed. New York: Macmillan, 1989. 2 vols. (Vol. 1, Colonial through Romantic; Vol. 2, Realism to the Present)
Albee, E. *The Zoo Story* 2
Baraka, A. *Dutchman* 2
O'Neill, E. *The Hairy Ape* 2
Tyler, R. *The Contrast* 1
Williams, T. *The Glass Menagerie* 2


MANCF McMichael, George L., ed. *Anthology of American Literature*. General Editor: George McMichael. Advisory Editors: Frederick Crews [and Others]. 5th ed. New York: Macmillan, 1993. 2 vols. (Vol. 1, Colonial through Romantic; Vol. 2, Realism to the Present)
Albee, E. *The Zoo Story* 2
Hansberry, L. *A Raisin in the Sun* 2
Jones, L. *Dutchman* 2
O'Neill, E. *Desire under the Elms* 2
Tyler, R. *The Contrast* 1
Williams, T. *The Glass Menagerie* 2


MANCG McMichael, George L., ed. *Anthology of American Literature*. General Editor: George McMichael. Advisory Editors: Frederick Crews [and Others]. 6th ed. Upper Saddle River, NJ: Prentice-Hall, 1997. 2 vols. (Vol. 1, Colonial through Romantic; Vol. 2, Realism to the Present)
Albee, E. *The Zoo Story* 2
Baraka, A. *Dutchman* 2
Hansberry, L. *A Raisin in the Sun* 2
Miller, A. *Death of a Salesman* 2
O'Neill, E. *The Hairy Ape* 2
Williams, T. *The Glass Menagerie* 2


MANCH McMichael, George L., ed. *Anthology of American Literature*. General Editor: George McMichael. Advisory Editors: J. C. Levenson [and Others]. 7th ed. Upper Saddle River, NJ: Prentice-Hall, 2000. 2 vols. (Vol. 1, Colonial through Romantic; Vol. 2, Realism to the Present)
Albee, E. *The Zoo Story* 2
Hansberry, L. *A Raisin in the Sun* 2
Howe, T. *Painting Churches* 2
Miller, A. *Death of a Salesman* 2
O'Neill, E. *The Hairy Ape* 2
Williams, T. *The Glass Menagerie* 2


MANCI McMichael, George L., ed. *Concise Anthology of American Literature*. General Editor: George McMichael. Advisory Editors: Frederick Crews [and Others]. New York: Macmillan [c1974] 2007pp. (Abridged from his *Anthology of American Literature*)
Albee, E. *The Zoo Story*
O'Neill, E. *The Hairy Ape*


MANCIA McMichael, George L., ed. *Concise Anthology of American Literature*. General Editor: George McMichael. Advisory Editors: Frederick Crews [and Others]. 2nd ed. New York: Macmillan, 1985. 2226pp.
Albee, E. *The Zoo Story*
O'Neill, E. *The Hairy Ape*
Williams, T. *The Glass Menagerie*


MANCIO McMichael, George L., ed. *Concise Anthology of American Literature*. General Editor: George McMichael. Advisory Editors: Frederick Crews [and Others]. 3rd ed. New York: Macmillan, 1993. 2726pp.
Albee, E. *Who's Afraid of Virginia Woolf?*
Hansberry, L. *A Raisin in the Sun*
O'Neill, E. *Desire under the Elms*
Williams, T. *The Glass Menagerie*


MANCIU McMichael, George L., compiler. *Concise Anthology of American Literature*. General Editor: George McMichael. Advisory Editors: Frederick Crews [and Others]. 4th ed. Upper Saddle River, NJ: Prentice-Hall, 1998. 2388pp.
Albee, E. *The Zoo Story*
Miller, A. *Death of a Salesman*
O'Neill, E. *The Hairy Ape*


MAND MacMillan, Dougald, and Jones, Howard Mumford, eds. *Plays of the Restoration and Eighteenth Century*. New York: Holt, 1931. 986pp.
Addison, J. *Cato*
Cibber, G. *Love's Last Shift*

Colman, G., and Garrick, D. *The Clandestine Marriage*
Congreve, W. *The Way of the World*
Cumberland, R. *The West Indian*
D'Avenant, W. *The Siege of Rhodes, Part I*
Dryden, J. *All for Love*
Dryden, J., and Howard, R. *The Indian Queen*
Etherege, G. *The Man of Mode*
Farquhar, G. *The Beaux' Stratagem*
Gay, J. *The Beggar's Opera*
Goldsmith, O. *She Stoops to Conquer*
Home, J. *Douglas*
Kelly, H. *False Delicacy*
Kotzebue, A. *The Stranger*
Lee, N. *The Rival Queens*
Lillo, G. *The London Merchant*
Otway, T. *Venice Preserved*
Rowe, N. *The Fair Penitent*
Shadwell, T. *The Squire of Alsatia*
Sheridan, R. *The School for Scandal*
Steele, R. *The Conscious Lovers*
Vanbrugh, J. *The Relapse*
Villiers, G., and Others. *The Rehearsal*

MANF MacMillan, Dougald, and Jones, Howard
    Mumford, eds. *Plays of the Restoration and
    Eighteenth Century.* New York: Holt [1938] 961pp.
Addison, J. *Cato*
Cibber, C. *Love's Last Shift*
Colman, G., and Garrick, D. *The Clandestine Marriage*
Congreve, W. *The Way of the World*
Cumberland, R. *The West Indian*
D'Avenant, W. *The Siege of Rhodes, Part I*
Dryden, J. *All for Love*
Dryden, J., and Howard, R. *The Indian Queen*
Etherege, G. *The Man of Mode*
Farquhar, G. *The Beaux' Sratagem*
Gay, J. *The Beggar's Opera*
Goldsmith, O. *She Stoops to Conquer*
Home, J. *Douglas*
Kelly, H. *False Delicacy*
Kotzebue, A. *The Stranger*
Lee, N. *The Rival Queens*
Lillo, G. *The London Merchant*
Otway, T. *Venice Preserved*
Rowe, N. *The Fair Penitent*
Shadwell, T. *The Squire of Alsatia*
Sheridan, R. *The School for Scandal*
Steele, R. *The Conscious Lovers*
Vanbrugh, J. *The Relapse*
Villiers, G., and Others. *The Rehearsal*
Wycherley, W. *The Plaindealer*

MANH McMillin, Scott, ed. *Restoration and Eighteenth
    Century Comedy.* New York: Norton, 1973. 565pp.

Congreve, W. *The Way of the World*
Etherege, G. *The Man of Mode*
Sheridan, R. *The School for Scandal*
Steele, R. *The Conscious Lovers*
Wycherley, W. *The Country Wife*

MANK McNamee, Maurice B.; Cronin, James E.; and
    Rogers, Joseph A., eds. *Literary Types and Themes.*
    New York: Rinehart [c1960] 705pp.
Anouilh, J. *Antigone*
Barrie, J. *The Twelve-pound Look*
Chayefsky, P. *Marty*
Miller, A. *Death of a Salesman*
Williams, T. *The Glass Menagerie*

MANL McNamee, Maurice Basil [and Others], eds.
    *Literary Types and Themes.* 2nd ed. New York:
    Rinehart and Winston, 1971. 773pp.
Albee, E. *The American Dream*
Miller, A. *Death of a Salesman*
Pirandello, L. *Six Characters in Search of an Author*
Wilder, T. *Pullman Car Hiawatha*
Williams, T. *The Glass Menagerie*

MANM McNaughton, Wilham, ed. *Chinese Literature: An
    Anthology from the Earliest Times to the Present
    Day.* Rutland, VT: Charles E. Tuttle, 1974. 836pp.
Kuan, H. *The Butterfly Dream*

MANN McNiff, William T., ed. *The Beginnings of English
    Literature.* New York: Macmillan [c1961] 198pp.
*Everyman*
Marlowe, C. *The Tragedy of Doctor Faustus*

MANP McNulty, John B., ed. *Modes of Literature.*
    Boston: Houghton Mifflin, 1977. 630pp.
Shakespeare, W. *Antony and Cleopatra*
Shaw, G. *Arms and the Man*

MAO Madden, David, ed. *A Pocketful of Plays: Vintage
    Drama.* Fort Worth, TX: Harcourt Brace College
    Publishers, 1996. 364pp.
Glaspell, S. *Trifles*
Hansberry L. *A Raisin in the Sun*
Ibsen, H. *A Doll's House*
Shakespeare, W. *Hamlet*
Sophocles. *Oedipus the King*
Williams, T. *The Glass Menagerie*

MAP Magarshack, David, translator. *The Storm, and other
    Russian Plays.* New York: Hill and Wang [c1960]
    362pp. (Mermaid Dramabook)
Chekhov, A. *Uncle Vanya*
Gogol, N. *The Government Inspector*
Gorky, M. *The Lower Depths*

Ostrovsky, A. *The Storm*
Tolstoy, L. *The Power of Darkness*

MAQ Mahone, Sydné, ed. *Moon Marked and Touched by Sun: Plays by African-American Women.* New York: Theatre Communications Group, 1994. 406pp.
Carlos, L. *White Chocolate for My Father*
Corthron, K. *Cage Rhythm*
Davis, T. *X: The Life and Times of Malcolm X*
Jackson, J. *WOMBmanWARs*
Kennedy, A. *The Dramatic Circle*
McCauley, R. *Sally's Rape*
Parks, S. *The Death of the Last Black Man in the Whole Entire World*
Rahman, A. *The Mojo and the Sayso*
Shange, N. *The Resurrection of the Daughter: Liliane* (excerpt)
Smith, A. D. *Fires in the Mirror* (excerpt)
Vance, D. *Live and in Color!*

MAR Malcolmson, Anne (Burnett), adapter. *Miracle Plays: Seven Medieval Plays for Modern Players.* Boston: Houghton Mifflin [c1956, 1959] 142pp.
*Abraham and Isaac*
*Herod and the Magi*
*The Nativity*
*Noah's Flood*
*Saint Nicholas and the Three Scholars*
*The Shepherds' Play*
*Hilarius. The Statue of Saint Nicholas*

MALINE, JULIAN L. *See* PATM, PATP *Patterns of Literature*; PROI *Prose and Poetry of America.*

MALLON, WILFRED M. *See* PROI *Prose and Poetry of America.*

MARG *Malvern Festival Plays MCMXXXIII*, arranged for production by H. K. Ayliff. With an introduction by Hugh Walpole and a preface by Sir Barry Jackson. London: Heath Cranton, 1933. 343pp.
*The Conversion of St. Paul*
Dryden, J. *All for Love*
Heywood, T. *The Fair Maid of the West*
Jones, H. *The Dancing Girl*
Knowles, J. *The Love-chase*
"Mr. S., Master of Arts." *Gammer Gurton's Needle*

MARH Mandel, Oscar, compiler and translator. *Five Comedies of Medieval France.* New York: Dutton, 1970. 158pp.
*The Chicken Pie and the Chocolate Cake*
Adam de la Halle. *The Play of Robin and Marion*

Bodel, J. *The Play of Saint Nicholas*
*Peter Quill's Shenanigans*
*The Washtub*

MARJ Mandel, Oscar, ed. *The Theatre of Don Juan: A Collection of Plays and Views, 1630–1963.* Lincoln: University of Nebraska Press, c1963. 731pp.
*Don Juan and Don Pietro; or, the Dead Stone's Banquet*
Grabbe, C. *Don Juan and Faust*
Molière, J. *Don Juan; or, the Libertine*
Molina, T. *The Playboy of Seville; or, Supper with a Statue*
Moncrieff, W. *Giovanni in London; or, the Libertine Reclaimed*
Ponte, L. *The Punished Libertine; or Don Giovanni*
Rostand, F. *The Last Night of Don Juan*
Shadwell, T. *The Libertine*
Zorrilla y Moral, J. *Don Juan Tenorio*

MARK Manfull, Helen, and Manfull, Lowell L. *The Stage in Action: An Introduction to Theatre and Drama.* Dubuque, IA: Kendall/Hunt Pub. Co., 1989. 608pp.
Artaud, A. *Jet of Blood*
Beckett, S. *Act without Words*
Brecht, B. *Fear and Misery in the Third Reich*
Chekhov, A. *The Three Sisters*
Churchill, C. *Cloud Nine*
Farquhar, G. *The Beaux' Stratagem*
Ibsen, H. *A Doll's House*
Kelly, G. *The Show-off*
Molière, J. *The Miser*
*Noah's Flood*
Shakespeare, W. *Othello*
Shepard, S. *Buried Child*
Sophocles. *Antigone*
Strindberg, A. *The Ghost Sonata*
Williams, T. *The Glass Menagerie*
Wilson, A. *Fences*

MARL Manfull, Helen, Manfull, Lowell L., and Brown, George H. *The Stage in Action: An Introduction to Theatre and Drama.* 2nd ed. Dubuque, IA: Kendall/Hunt Pub. Co., 1998. 655pp.
Artaud, A. *Jet of Blood*
Beckett, S. *Act without Words*
Brecht, B. *Fear and Misery in the Third Reich*
Churchill, C. *Cloud Nine*
Farquhar, G. *The Beaux' Stratagem*
Ibsen, H. *A Doll's House*
Molière, J. *Tartuffe*
*Noah's Flood*
Shakespeare, W. *Macbeth*
Shepard, S. *Buried Child*

Sophocles. *Oedipus Rex*
Strindberg, A. *The Ghost Sonata*
Williams, T. *The Glass Menagerie*
Wilson, A. *Fences*

MARLC Mangan, Mick, ed. *Threads and Other Sheffield Plays.* Sheffield: Sheffield Academic Press, 1990. 235pp.
Hines, B. *Threads*
Russell, H. *Pawnbroker Hocks the Moon*
Sheasby, D. *Welcome to the Times*

MANTLE, R. BURNS. *See* BES *Best Plays of 1894/1899,* etc. *See also* TRE, TREA *Treasury of the Theatre.*

MARLG Marfo, Kofi, compiler. *An Introduction to Ghanaian Literature.* London: Minerva Press, 1999. 223pp.
*Atia yaw*
*Boketey larweh*
*Chief Kaku Ackah of Nzima*
*The Martyrdom of Samuel Otu*
*Okai koi*

MARLI Marín, Diego, compiler. *Literatura española: Selección.* Introducciones y notes por Digo Marín. New York: Holt, Rinehart and Winston, 1968. 2 vols. (Tomo 1: *Desde los orígenes haste el Romanticismo*; Tomo 2: *Época moderna*)
Benavente y Martínez, J. *Los malhechores de bien* 2
Buero Vallejo, A. *Irene, o el tesoro* 2
Calderón de la Barca, P. *La vida es sueño* 1
Cervantes, M. *La cueva de Salamanca* 1
García Lorca, F. *La zapatera prodigiosa* 2
Moratín, L. *El sí de las niñas* 1
Valle-Inclán, R. *La cabeza del Bautista* 2
Vega Carpio, L. *El caballero de Olmedo* 1
Zorrilla, J. *Don Juan Tenorio* 1

MARNAU, FRED. *See* NEWR *New Road.*

MARO Marowitz, Charles, ed. *New American Drama.* Harmondsworth, Middlesex: Penguin, [1966] 203pp.
Albee, E. *The American Dream*
Miller, A. *Incident at Vichy*
Richardson, J. *Gallows Humour*
Schisgal, M. *The Typists*

MARP Marowitz, Charles, compiler. *Open Space Plays.* Harmondsworth, Middlesex: Penguin, 1974. 310pp.
Burgess, J., and Marowitz, C. *The Chicago Conspiracy*
Burns, A., and Marowitz, C. *Palach*
Herbert, J. *Fortune and Men's Eyes*

McGough, R. *The Puny Little Life Show*
Marowitz, C. *An Othello*

MARR Marranca, Bonnie, ed. *Plays for the End of the Century.* Baltimore: Johns Hopkins University Press, 1996. 383pp.
Abdoh, R. *The Law of Remains*
Berc, S. *A Girl's Guide to the Divine Comedy*
Ehn, E. *Two Altars, Ten Funerals (All Souls)*
Foreman, R. *The Mind King*
Fornes, M. *Enter the Night*
Kennedy, A. *Motherhood 2000*
Rosenthal, R. *Pangaean Dreams: A Shamanic Journey*
Wellman, M. *Cellophane*
The Wooster Group. *Frank Dell's The Temptation of St. Antony*

MARRA Marranca, Bonnie, and Dasgupta, Gautum, eds. *Theatre of the Ridiculous.* Revised and expanded edition. Baltimore: Johns Hopkins University Press, 1998. 188pp.
Bernard, K. *The Magic Show of Dr. Ma-Gico*
Ludlam, C. *Stage Blood*
Smith, J. *The Rehearsal for the Destruction of Atlantis*
Tavel, R. *The Life of Lady Godiva*

MART Marriott, James William, ed. *Great Modern British Plays.* London: Harrap [1932] 1083pp.
Bennett, A., and Knoblock, E. *Milestones*
Berkeley, R. *The White Château*
Besier, R. *The Virgin Goddess*
Brighouse, H. *Hobson's Choice*
Chapin, H. *The New Morality*
Coward, N. *The Young Idea*
Dane, C. *A Bill of Divorcement*
Dukes, A. *The Man with a Load of Mischief*
Galsworthy, J. *Strife*
Gilbert, W. *Pygmalion and Galatea*
Hankin, St. J. *The Return of Prodigal*
Jones, H. *The Liars*
McEvoy, C. *The Likes of Her*
Maugham, W. *The Circle*
Munro, C. *At Mrs. Beam's*
Pinero, A. *Trelawny of the "Wells"*
Robertson, T. *Caste*
Sutro, A. *The Walls of Jericho*
Vane, S. *Outward Bound*

MAS Massey, Vincent, ed. *Canadian Plays from Hart House Theatre.* Toronto: Macmillan, 1926–1927. 2 vols.
Alkins, C. *The God of Gods* 2
Borsook, H. *Three Weddings of a Hunchback* 1
Cooke, B. *The Translation of John Snaith* 1
Denison, M. *Balm* 1

Denison, M. *Brothers in Arms* 1
Denison, M. *The Weather Breeder* 1
Mackay, I. *The Second Lie* 1
Mackay, L. *The Freedom of Jean Guichet* 2
Osborne, M. *The Point of View* 1
Reid, L. *Trespassers* 2
Scott, D. *Pierre* 1

MAST *Masterpieces of Greek Literature.* Supervising
Editor John Henry Wright. Boston: Houghton
Mifflin [c1902] 456pp.
Aeschylus. *Prometheus Bound*
Euripides. *Alcestis*
Sophocles. *Antigone*

MASW Matlow, Myron, compiler. *The Black Crook, and
Other Nineteenth Century American Plays.* New
York: Dutton, 1967. 511pp.
Barras, C. *The Black Crook*
Boker, G. *Francesea da Rimini*
Boucicault, D. *The Octoroon; or, Life in Louisiana*
Herne, J. *Margaret Fleming*
Howard, B. *Shenandoah*
Mowatt, A. *Fashion; or, Life in New York*
*Rip Van Winkle*

MASX Matlow, Myron, ed. *Nineteenth-Century American
Plays.* New York: Applause Theatre Book
Publishers, 1985. 269pp. (Originally published in
*The Black Crook*, 1967.)
Boucicault, D. *The Octoroon; or, Life in Louisiana*
Herne, J. *Margaret Fleming*
Mowatt, A. *Fashion; or, Life in New York*
*Rip Van Winkle*

MATT Matthews, Brander, ed. *The Chief European
Dramatists.* Boston: Houghton Mifflin [c1916]
786pp.
Aeschylus. *Agamemnon*
Aristophanes. *The Frogs*
Augier, E., and Sandeau, J. *The Son-in-law of M. Poirier*
Beaumarchais, P. *The Barber of Seville*
Calderón de la Barca, P. *Life Is a Dream*
Corneille, P. *The Cid*
Dumas, A., fils. *The Outer Edge of Society*
Euripides. *Medea*
Goethe, J. *Goetz von Berlichingen*
Goldoni, C. *The Mistress of the Inn*
Holberg, L. *Rasmus Montanus*
Hugo, V. *Hernani*
Ibsen, H. *A Doll's House*
Lessing, G. *Minna von Barnhelm*
Molière, J. *Tartuffe*
Plautus, T. *The Captives*
Racine, J. *Phaedra*

Schiller, J. *William Tell*
Sophocles. *Oedipus the King*
Terence, P. *Phormio*
Vega Carpio, L. de. *The Star of Seville*

MATTHEWS, BRANDER. *See also* GREA *Great Plays*
(French and German).

MATTL Matthews, Brander, and Lieder, Paul Robert,
eds. *The Chief British Dramatists Excluding
Shakespeare.* Boston: Houghton Mifflin [c1924]
1084pp.
Beaumont, F., and Fletcher, J. *Philaster; or, Love Lies
A-bleeding*
Boucicault, D. *London Assurance*
*The Brome Abraham and Isaac*
Bulwer-Lytton, E. *Richelieu; or, the Conspiracy*
Congreve, W. *The Way of the World*
Dryden, J. *All for Love; or, the World Well Lost*
Farquhar, G. *The Beaux' Stratagem*
Gilbert, W. *Pygmalion and Galatea*
Goldsmith, O. *She Stoops to Conquer; or, the Mistakes
of a Night*
Heywood, T. *A Woman Killed with Kindness*
Jones, H. *The Liars*
Jonson, B. *Every Man in His Humour*
Kyd, T. *The Spanish Tragedy; or, Hieronimo Is Mad
Again*
Marlowe, C. *The Troublesome Reign and Lamentable
Death of Edward the Second*
Massinger, P. *A New Way to Pay Old Debts*
Otway, T. *Venice Preserved; or, A Plot Discovered*
Pinero, A. *The Second Mrs. Tanqueray*
Robertson, T. *Caste*
*The Second Shepherds' Play*
Sheridan, R. *The School for Scandal*
Udall, N. *Ralph Roister Doister*
Vanbrugh, J. *The Provoked Wife*
Webster, J. *The Duchess of Malfi*
Wilde, O. *Lady Windermere's Fan*
Wycherley, W. *The Plain Dealer*

MAUS Maus, Katharine Eisaman, ed. *Four Revenge
Tragedies.* Oxford: Clarendon Press, 1995. 426pp.
Chapman, G. *The Revenge of Bussy D'Ambois*
Kyd, T. *The Spanish Tragedy*
Tourneur, C. *The Atheist's Tragedy*
Tourneur, C. *The Revenger's Tragedy*

MAYER Mayer, David, ed. *Playing Out the Empire:* Ben-
Hur *and Other Toga Plays and Films, 1883–1908:
A Critical Anthology.* Oxford: Clarendon Press,
1994. 321pp.
Barrett, W. *The Sign of the Cross*
Herman, H., and Wills, W. G. *Claudian*

Moore, M. *The Charioteers; or, a Roman Holiday*
Young, W. *Ben-Hur*

MED *Medieval Drama: An Anthology.* Edited by
        Greg Walker. Oxford; Malden, MA: Blackwell
        Publishers, 2000. 630pp.
*Adam and Eve (Chester, the Drapers)*
Bale, J. *Johan Baptystes Preachynge*
Bale, J. *The Three Laws*
*Christ before Annas and Caiphas (York, the Bowers and
        Fletchers)*
*Christ before Herod (York, Litsters)*
*Christ before Pilate I: The Dream of Pilate's Wife
        (York, the Tapiters and Couchers)*
*Christ before Pilate II: The Judgement (York, the
        Tilemakers)*
*The Conspiracy (York, the Cutlers)*
*The Crucifixion (York, the Pinners)*
*The Enterlude of Godly Queene Hester*
*The Entry into Jerusalem (York, the Skinners)*
*Everyman*
*The Fall of Lucifer (Chester, the Tanners)*
*The Fall of Man (York, the Coopers)*
*The Fall of the Angels (York, the Barkers/Tanners)*
*The Harrowing of Hell (York, the Saddlers)*
Heywood, J. *The Four PP*
Heywood, J. *The Play of the Weather*
*Joseph's Trouble about Mary (York, the Pewterers and
        Founders)*
*The Last Judgement (York, the Mercers)*
Lindsay, D. *Ane Satyre of the Thrie Estaitis*
*Mankind*
*The Mary Play (N-Town)*
Medwall, H. *Fulgens and Lucres*
*The Nativity (York, the Titethatchers)*
*The Play of the Sacrament (Croxton)*
*The Resurrection (York, the Carpenters)*
*The Second Shepherds' Play (Townley)*
*The Shepherds (Chester, the Paynters and Glaziers)*
Skelton, J. *Magnyfycence*
*Wisdom*

MEDN Mednick, Murry, Raden, Bill, and Slean, Cheryl,
        eds. *Best of the West: An Anthology of Plays from
        the 1989 & 1990 Padua Hills Playwrights Festival.*
        Los Angeles: Padua Hills Press, 1991. 308pp.
Champagne, S. *Bondage*
Epstein, M. *Our Witness*
Fornes, M. *Oscar and Bertha*
Hebert, J. *Almost Asleep*
Martell, L. *Kindling*
Mednick, M. *Shatter 'n Wade*
Mosakowski, S. *Cities Out of Print*
Steppling, J. *Storyland*

Steppling, J. *Theory of Miracles*
Stuart, K. *Ball and Chain*

MELB *Melbourne Stories: Three Plays.* Sydney: Currency
        Press, 2000. 248pp.
Bovell, A., Cornelius, P., Reeves, M., Tsiolkas, C.,
        and Vela, I. *Who's Afraid of the Working Class?*
        (Consists of the four following one-act plays:
        Bovell, A. *Trash*; Cornelius, P. *Money*; Reeves, M.
        *Dream-town*; Tsiolkas, C. *Suit*; musical score by
        I. Vela)
Bradley, B. *Polly Blue*
Cortese, R. *Features of Blown Youth*

MELO *Melodrama Classics: Six Plays and How to Stage
        Them.* Edited by Dorothy Mackin. New York:
        Sterling, 1982. 384pp.
Boucicault, D. *After Dark; or, Pardon-for-a-price*
D'Ennery, A., and Corman, E. *The Two Orphans; or, In
        the Hands of Heaven*
MacKaye, S. *Hazel Kirke; or, Adrift from Her Father's
        Love*
*The Spoilers, or, There's Never a Law of God or Man
        Runs North of Fifty-three*
Taylor, T. *The Ticket-of-leave man*
*Under Two Flags*

MEN Mendenhall, John Cooper, ed. *English Literature,
        1650–1800.* Chicago: Lippincott [c1940] 1166pp.
Congreve, W. *The Way of the World*
Dryden, J. *Aureng-zebe*
Otway, T. *Venice Preserv'd*

MERC Mercier, Vivian, and Greene, David H., eds. *1000
        Years of Irish Prose.* Part 1. The Literary Revival.
        New York: Devin-Adair, 1952. 607pp.
O'Casey, S. *The Shadow of a Gunman*
Synge, J. *In the Shadow of the Glen*
Yeats, W. *Cathleen ni Houlihan*
Yeats, W. *The Resurrection*

MERS Mersand, Joseph E., ed. *Three Comedies of
        American Family Life.* New York: Washington
        Square Press [c1961] 314pp.
Kaufman, G., and Hart, M. *You Can't Take It with You*
Lindsay, H., and Crouse, R. *Life with Father*
Van Druten, J. *I Remember Mama*

MERT Mersand, Joseph, ed. *Three Dramas of American
        Individualism.* New York: Washington Square
        Press [c1961] 266pp.
Anderson, M. *High Tor*
Lavery, E. *The Magnificent Yankee*
Odets, C. *Golden Boy*

MERU Mersand, Joseph E., ed. *Three Dramas of American Realism.* New York: Washington Square Press [c1961] 312pp.
Rice, E. *Street Scene*
Saroyan, W. *The Time of Your Life*
Sherwood, R. *Idiot's Delight*

MERV Mersand Joseph E., ed. *Three Plays about Doctors.* New York: Washington Square Press [c1961] 294pp.
Howard, S., and DeKruif, P. *Yellow Jack*
Ibsen, H. *An Enemy of the People*
Kingsley, S. *Men in White*

MERW Mersand, Joseph E., ed. *Three Plays about Marriage.* New York: Washington Square Press [c1962] 298pp.
Barry, P. *Holiday*
Howard, S. *They Knew What They Wanted*
Kelly, G. *Craig's Wife*

MESERVE, WALTER J. *See also* AMPA *America's Lost Plays*, v21, edited by Walter J. Meserve and William R. Reardon.

MES Meserve, Walter J., ed. *On Stage, America! A Selection of Distinctly American Plays.* New York: Feedback Theatrebooks & Prospero Press, 1996. 563pp.
Baker, B. *Glance at New York*
Belasco, D. *The Girl of the Golden West*
Daly, A. *Under the Gaslight*
Durivage, O. *The Stage-struck Yankee*
Herne, J. *Margaret Fleming*
Howard, B. *Young Mrs. Winthrop*
Hoyt, C. *A Trip to Chinatown*
Mowatt, A. *Fashion*
*Rip Van Winkle*
Stone, J. *Metamora*
Thompson, D. *The Old Homestead*
Tyler, R. *The Contrast*

MESC Meserve, Walter J., and Meserve, Mollie Ann, eds. *Fateful Lightning: America's Civil War Plays.* New York: Feedback Theatrebooks & Prospero Press, 2000. 550pp.
Aiken, G. *Uncle Tom's Cabin*
Belasco, D. *The Heart of Maryland*
Boucicault, D. *Belle Lamar*
Brown, W. *The Escape*
Gillette, W. *Secret Service*
Harrigan, E. *The Blue and the Grey*
Howard, B. *Shenandoah*
McCabe, J. *The Guerillas*

Swayze, Mrs. J. *Ossawattomie Brown*
Trowbridge, J. *Neighbor Jackwood*
Woolf, B. *Off to the War!*

MESCO Meserve, Walter J., and Meserve, Mollie Ann, eds. *When Conscience Trod the Stage: American Plays of Social Awareness.* New York: Feedback Theatrebooks & Prospero Press, 1998. 499pp.
Barker, J. *Superstition*
Brougham, J. *The Irish Emigrant, or, Temptation*
DeMille, W. *Strongheart*
Foster, C. *Bertha, the Sewing Machine Girl, or Death at the Wheel*
Lloyd, D., with Rosenfeld, S. *The Senator*
Mathews, C. *Witchcraft, or, the Martyrs of Salem*
Middleton, G. *Nowadays*
Sheldon, E. *The Nigger*
Smith, W. *The Drunkard, or, the Fallen Saved*

MESE Meserve, Walter J., and Meserve, Ruth I., eds. *Modern Drama from Communist China.* New York: New York University Press, 1970. 368pp.
Chao, C.; Chang, P.; and Chung, Y. *Yesterday*
Jen, T. *Magic Aster*
Kuan, H. *Snow in Midsummer*
Lao, S. *Dragon Beard Ditch*
Lu, H. *The Passer-by*
*The Red Lantern*
Sha, S.; Fu, T.; Ma, Y.; and Li, C. *Letters from the South*
Sun, Y. *The Women's Representative*
Ting, Y., and Ho, C. *The Whitehaired Girl*

MESH Meserve, Walter J., and Meserve, Ruth I., eds. *Modern Literature from China.* New York: New York University Press, 1974. 337pp.
Ts'ao, Y. *Thunderstorm*

MESSE Messerli, Douglas, and Wellman, Mac, eds. *From the Other Side of the Century II: A New American Drama 1960–1995.* With an introduction by Marc Robinson. Los Angeles: Sun & Moon Press, 1998. 1192pp.
Albee, E. *The Zoo Story*
Alvarez, L. *The Reincarnation of Jaimie Brown*
Baraka, A. *The Toilet*
Breuer, L. *The B. Beaver Animation*
Bullins, E. *The Man Who Dug Fish*
Caliban, R. *Rodents & Radios*
Congdon, C. *No Mercy*
Drexler, R. *Softly and Consider the Nearness*
Ehn, E. *Angel uh God*
Foreman, R. *Rhoda in Potatoland*
Fornes, M. *Abingdon Square*

Greenspan, D. *Son of an Engineer*
Guare, J. *Muzeeka*
Howe, T. *One Shoe off*
Hughes, H. *Dress Suits to Hire*
Iizuka, N. *Tatoo Girl*
Jenkin, L. *American Notes*
Jones, J. *Night Coil*
Kennedy, A. *A Movie Star Has to Star in Black and White*
Kushner, T. *Reverse Transcription*
Lucas, C. *Reckless*
Ludlam, C. *Reverse Psychology*
Mednick, M. *Switchback*
Mee, C. *The Imperialists at the Club Cave Canem*
Nelson, R. *Conjuring an Event*
O'Keefe, J. *All Night Long*
Overmyer, E. *Native Speech*
OyamO. *The Resurrection of Lady Lester*
Parks, S. *Imperceptible Mutabilities in the Third Kingdom*
Peters, K. *The Confirmation*
Pietri, P. *The Masses Are Asses*
Richardson, J. *Gallows Humor*
Shepard, S. *Action*
Steppling, J. *Standard of the Breed*
Tavel, R. *Boy on a Straight-back Chair*
Weinstein, A. *Red Eye of Love*
Wellman, M. *The Hyacinth Macaw*
Williams, T. *The gnädiges fräulein*

MESSN Messner, Nancy Shingler [and Others], compilers. *Collection: Literature for the Seventies*. Lexington, MA: Heath, 1972. 915pp.
Aristophanes. *Lysistrata*
Bermange, B. *Scenes from Family Life*
Chekhov, A. *Uncle Vanya*
Ibsen, H. *An Enemy of the People*
Roemer, M., and Young, R. *Nothing but a Man*
Shakespeare, W. *Othello*
Williams, T. *Suddenly Last Summer*

METR *Metropol: Literary Almanac*. Edited by Vasily Akeyonov, Viktor Yerofeyev, et al. New York: Norton, c1982. 636pp.
Aksyonov, V. *The Four Temperaments: A Comedy in Ten Tableaux*

MEY Meyer, Michael, ed. *The Bedford Introduction to Literature*. New York: St. Martin's Press, 1987. 1782pp.
Beckett, S. *Krapp's Last Tape*
Chekhov, A. *Three Sisters*
Fuller, C. *A Soldier's Play*
Glaspell, S. *Trifles*
Henley, B. *Am I Blue?*

Ibsen, H. *A Doll's House*
Lear, N. *Meet the Bunkers*
Martin, J. *Twirler*
Miller, A. *Death of a Salesman*
Molière, J. *Tartuffe*
Pinter, H. *The Dumb Waiter*
Shakespeare, W. *Hamlet*
Shakespeare, W. *King Henry IV, Part I*
Shakespeare, W. *Twelfth Night, or, What You Will*
Shepard, S. *True West*
Sophocles. *Antigone*
Sophocles. *Oedipus the King*
Williams, T. *The Glass Menagerie*

MEYB Meyer, Michael, ed. *The Bedford Introduction to Literature*. 2nd ed. Boston: Bedford Books of St. Martin's Press, 1990. 1887pp.
Avedon, B., Corday, B., and Rosenzweig, B. *You Call This Plainclothes?* (a *Cagney & Lacey* episode)
Beckett, S. *Krapp's Last Tape*
Chekhov, A. *The Cherry Orchard*
Churchill, C. *Top Girls*
Glaspell, S. *Trifles*
Hwang, D. *M. Butterfly*
Ibsen, H. *A Doll's House*
Martin, J. *Twirler*
Miller, A. *Death of a Salesman*
Molière, J. *Tartuffe*
Pinter, H. *The Dumb Waiter*
Shakespeare, W. *Hamlet*
Shakespeare, W. *Othello*
Sophocles. *Antigone*
Sophocles. *Oedipus the King*
Soyinka, W. *The Strong Breed*
Williams, T. *The Glass Menagerie*
Wilson, A. *Fences*

MEYC Meyer, Michael, ed. *The Compact Bedford Introduction to Literature*. 3rd ed. Boston: Bedford Books of St. Martin's Press, 1993. 1473pp.
Beckett, S. *Krapp's Last Tape*
Chekhov, A. *The Proposal*
Frolov, D., and Schneider, A. *"Get Real"* (excerpt from *Northern Exposure* episode)
Glaspell, S. *Trifles*
Hansberry, L. *A Raisin in the Sun*
Ibsen, H. *A Doll's House*
Martin, J. *Rodeo*
Miller, A. *Death of a Salesman*
Shakespeare, W. *Hamlet*
Shakespeare, W. *A Midsummer Night's Dream*
Sophocles. *Oedipus the King*
Wasserstein, W. *Tender Offer*
Williams, T. *The Glass Menagerie*
Wilson, A. *Fences*

MEYCA Meyer, Michael, ed. *The Compact Bedford Introduction to Literature*. 4th ed. Boston: Bedford Books of St. Martin's Press, 1997. 1494pp.

Chekhov, A. *The Proposal*
David, L. *The Pitch* (a *Seinfeld* episode)
Glaspell, S. *Trifles*
Hansberry, L. *A Raisin in the Sun*
Ibsen, H. *A Doll's House*
Ives, D. *Sure Thing*
Martin, J. *Rodeo*
Miller, A. *Death of a Salesman*
Shakespeare, W. *Hamlet*
Shakespeare, W. *A Midsummer Night's Dream*
Smith, A. D. *Twilight: Los Angeles, 1992* (excerpt)
Sophocles. *Oedipus the King*
Williams, T. *The Glass Menagerie*
Wilson, A. *The Piano Lesson*

MEYCB Meyer, Michael, ed. *The Compact Bedford Introduction to Literature*. 5th ed. Boston; New York: Bedford/St. Martin's Press, 2000. 1639pp.

David, L. *The Pitch* (a *Seinfeld* episode)
Glaspell, S. *Trifles*
Hansberry, L. *A Raisin in the Sun*
Hwang, D. *M. Butterfly*
Ibsen, H. *A Doll's House*
Ives, D. *Sure Thing*
Miller, A. *Death of a Salesman*
Seebring, W. *The Original Last Wish Baby*
Shakespeare, W. *Othello, the Moor of Venice*
Smith, A. D. *Twilight: Los Angeles, 1992* (excerpt)
Sophocles. *Oedipus the King*
Williams, T. *The Glass Menagerie*

MEYD Meyer, Michael, ed. *The Bedford Introduction to Literature*. 3rd ed. Boston: Bedford Books of St. Martin's Press, 1993. 2122pp.

Beckett, S. *Krapp's Last Tape*
Chekhov, A. *The Cherry Orchard*
Frolov, D., and Schneider, A. *"Get Real"* (excerpt from *Northern Exposure* episode)
Glaspell, S. *Trifles*
Hansberry, L. *A Raisin in the Sun*
Hwang, D. *M. Butterfly*
Ibsen, H. *A Doll's House*
Martin, J. *Rodeo*
Miller, A. *Death of a Salesman*
Molière, J. *Tartuffe*
Pinter, H. *The Dumb Waiter*
Shakespeare, W. *Hamlet*
Shakespeare, W. *A Midsummer Night's Dream*
Shakespeare, W. *The Tempest*
Sophocles. *Antigone*
Sophocles. *Oedipus the King*
Soyinka, W. *The Strong Breed*

Wasserstein, W. *Tender Offer*
Williams, T. *The Glass Menagerie*
Wilson, A. *Fences*

MEYE Meyer, Michael, ed. *The Bedford Introduction to Literature: Reading, Writing, Thinking*. 4th ed. Boston: Bedford Books of St. Martin's Press, 1996. 2156pp.

Beckett, S. *Krapp's Last Tape*
Chekhov, A. *The Proposal*
Dorfman, A. *Death and the Maiden*
Frolov, D., and Schneider, A. *"Get Real"* (excerpt from *Northern Exposure* episode)
Glaspell, S. *Trifles*
Hansberry, L. *A Raisin in the Sun*
Havel, V. *Protest*
Hwang, D. *M. Butterfly*
Ibsen, H. *A Doll's House*
Martin, J. *Rodeo*
Miller, A. *Death of a Salesman*
Molière, J. *Tartuffe*
Pinter, H. *The Dumb Waiter*
Shakespeare, W. *Hamlet*
Shakespeare, W. *A Midsummer Night's Dream*
Shakespeare, W. *The Tempest*
Smith, A. D. *Twilight: Los Angeles, 1992* (excerpts)
Sophocles. *Antigone*
Sophocles. *Oedipus the King*
Soyinka, W. *The Strong Breed*
Williams, T. *The Glass Menagerie*
Wilson, A. *The Piano Lesson*

MEYF Meyer, Michael, ed. *The Bedford Introduction to Literature: Reading, Writing, Thinking*. 5th ed. Boston/New York: Bedford/St. Martin's, 1999. 2188pp.

Beckett, S. *Krapp's Last Tape*
Chekhov, A. *The Proposal*
David, L. *The Pitch* (a *Seinfeld* episode)
Friel, B. *Molly Sweeny* (excerpt)
Glaspell, S. *Trifles*
Hansberry, L. *A Raisin in the Sun*
Hwang, D. *M. Butterfly*
Ibsen, H. *A Doll's House*
Ives, D. *Sure Thing*
Martin, J. *Rodeo*
Miller, A. *Death of a Salesman*
Seebring, W. *The Original Last Wish Baby*
Shakespeare, W. *Hamlet*
Shakespeare, W. *A Midsummer Night's Dream*
Shakespeare, W. *The Tempest*
Smith, A. D. *Twilight: Los Angeles, 1992* (excerpts)
Sophocles. *Antigone*
Sophocles. *Oedipus the King*
Soyinka, W. *The Strong Breed*

Wasserstein, W. *Tender Offer*
Williams, T. *The Glass Menagerie*
Wilson, A. *The Piano Lesson*

MID *Middle Age, Old Age: Short Stories, Poems, Plays, and Essays on Aging.* Edited by Ruth Granetz Lyell. New York: Harcourt, Brace Jovanovich, 1980. 390pp.
Anderson, R. *I Never Sang for My Father*

MIG Mikasinovich, Branko, ed. *Five Modern Yugoslav Plays.* New York: Cyrco Press, c1977. 339pp.
Čašule, K. *Darkness*
Kozak, P. *An Affair*
Lebovic, D. *Hallelujah*
Marinkovic, R. *Gloria*
Obrenovic, A. *The Bird*

MIH Miles, Julia, ed. *Here to Stay: Five Plays from the Women's Project.* New York: Applause Books, 1997. 276pp.
Blecher, H., Cruz, M., and Rodriguez, R. *Frida: The Story of Frida Kahlo*
Chaffee, C. *Why We Have a Body*
McDonald, H. *Dream of a Common Language*
Oates, J. *Black*
Smith, A. D. *Aye Aye Aye I'm Integrated*

MIHPW Miles, Julia, ed. *Playwriting Women: 7 Plays from the Women's Project.* Portsmouth, NH: Heinemann, 1993. 325pp.
Bingham, S. *Milk of Paradise*
Cleage, P. *Chain*
Cleage, P. *Late Bus to Mecca*
Cloud, D. *O Pioneers!*
Mueller, L. *Violent Peace*
Tolan, K. *Approximating Mother*
Yankowitz, S. *Night Sky*

MIHWW Miles, Julia, ed. *Womens Work: Five New Plays from the Women's Project.* New York: Applause Theatre Book Publishers, 1989. 310pp.
Fornes, M. *Abingdon Square*
Medley, C. *Ma Rose*
Meyer, M. *Etta Jenks*
Mueller, L. *Fire in the Killing Zone*
Nemeth, S. *Mill Fire*

MIJ Miller, Edwin Lillie, ed. *Explorations in Literature.* Chicago: Lippincott [c1933–1934] 2 vols.
Gilbert, W. *The Mikado* 2
Shakespeare, W. *Macbeth* 2

MIJA Miller, Edwin Lillie, ed. *Explorations in Literature.* Rev. ed. Chicago: Lippincott [c1937–1938] 2 vols.

O'Neill, E. *The Emperor Jones* 1
Shakespeare, W. *Macbeth* 2
Tompkins, F. *Sham* 1

MIJB Miller, James Edwin, and Slate, Bernice, compilers. *The Dimensions of Literature.* New York: Random House [1967] 808pp.
Brecht, B. *The Caucasian Chalk Circle*
O'Neill, E. *In the Zone*
Shaw, G. *Arms and the Man*
Sophocles. *Oedipus Rex*

MIJH Miller, James Edwin, with the assistance of Kathleen Farley, compilers. *Heritage of American Literature.* Orlando, FL: Harcourt Brace Jovanovich, 1991. 2 vols.
Albee, E. *The Zoo Story*
Glaspell, S. *Trifles*
Miller, A. *A Memory of Two Mondays*
O'Neill, E. *Hughie*
Shepard, S. *Action*
Tyler, R. *The Contrast*
Wilder, T. *The Long Christmas Dinner*
Williams, T. *Portrait of a Madonna*

MIJT Miller, James Edwin [and Others], compilers. *Translations from the French.* Glenview, IL: Scott, Foresman, 1971. 402pp.
Anouilh, J. *Antigone*
Cocteau, J. *The Eiffel Tower Wedding Party*
Duras, M. *The Rivers and Forests*
Giraudoux, J. *The Apollo of Bellac*
Molière, J. *The Forced Marriage*

MIJY Miller, Jordan Yale, ed. *American Dramatic Literature.* New York: McGraw-Hill, 1961. 641pp.
Behrman, S. *Biography*
Chase, M. *Harvey*
Haines, W. *Command Decision*
Hellman, L. *The Little Foxes*
Heyward, D., and Heyward, D. *Porgy*
McCullers, C. *The Member of the Wedding*
Miller, A. *The Crucible*
O'Neill, E. *Desire under the Elms*
Thurber, J., and Nugent, E. *The Male Animal*
Williams, T. *Camino Real*

MIK Miller, Marion Mills, ed. *The Classics, Greek & Latin.* New York: V. Parke [c1909–1910] 15 vols.
Aeschylus. *Prometheus Bound* 7
Aristophanes. *The Clouds* 7
Euripides. *Medea* 7
Plautus, T. *Captivi* 8
Plautus, T. *Menaechmi* 8

Plautus, T. *Miles gloriosus* 8
Seneca, L. *The Phaedra; or, Hippolytus* 8
Sophocles. *Antigone* 7
Terence. *Adelphi* 8
Terence. *Heautonimorumenos* 8

MIKE Miller, Perry [and Others], eds. *Major Writers of
    America.* New York: Harcourt, Brace & World
    [c1962] 2 vols.
O'Neill, E. *The Iceman Cometh* 2

MIKL Millett, Fred Benjamin. *Reading Drama: A Method
    of Analysis with Selections for Study.* New York:
    Harper [c1950] 252pp.
Barrie, J. *The Will*
O'Neill, E. *Beyond the Horizon*
Schnitzler, A. *A Farewell Supper*
Synge, J. *Riders to the Sea*
Wilder, T. *The Long Christmas Dinner*
Yeats, W. *Cathleen ni Houlihan*

MIL Millett, Fred Benjamin, and Bentley, Gerald Eades,
    eds. *The Play's the Thing.* New York: Appleton-
    Century [c1936] 571pp.
Belasco, D. *The Return of Peter Grimm*
Chekhov, A. *Uncle Vanya*
*Chester Play of the Deluge*
Congreve, W. *Love for Love*
Cumberland, W. *The West Indian*
Dryden, J. *All for Love*
Euripides. *Hippolytus*
Gregory, I. *Hyacinth Halvey*
Howard, S. *Ned McCobb's Daughter*
Ibsen, H. *Ghosts*
Maeterlinck, M. *Interior*
Marlowe, C. *Doctor Faustus*
Molière, J. *The Misanthrope*
O'Neill, E. *The Hairy Ape*
Plautus, T. *The Haunted House*
Racine, J. *Phaedra*
Rostand, E. *Cyrano de Bergerac*
Shakespeare, W. *Antony and Cleopatra*
Shakespeare, W. *Twelfth Night*
Sophocles. *Oedipus, King of Thebes*
Strong, A. *The Drums of Oude*

MIMN *Minnesota Showcase: Four Plays.* Introduced by
    Michael Langham, with comments by Charles M.
    Nolte, et al. Minneapolis: University of Minnesota
    Press, 1975. 296pp. (Minnesota Drama Editions #9)
Ball, D. Georg Büchner's *Woyzeck*
Donahue, J. *The Cookie Jar*
Feldshuh, D. *Fables Here and Then*
Nolte, C. *Do Not Pass Go*

MIN *Minor Elizabethan Drama.* London: Dent [1913]
    2 vols. (Everyman's Library)
*Arden of Feversham* 1
Greene, R. *Friar Bacon and Friar Bungay* 2
Greene, R. *James the Fourth* 2
Kyd, T. *The Spanish Tragedy* 1
Lyly, J. *Endimion* 2
Norton, T., and Sackville, T. (Lord Buckhurst)
    *Gordobuc* 1
Peele, G. *David and Bethsabe* 1
Peele, G. *The Old Wives' Tale* 2
Udall, N. *Ralph Roister Doister* 2

MIO *Minor Elizabethan Drama.* London: Dent [1939]
    2 vols. (Everyman's Library)
*Arden of Feversham* 1
Greene, R. *Friar Bacon and Friar Bungay* 2
Greene, R. *James the Fourth* 2
Kyd, T. *The Spanish Tragedy* 1
Lyly, J. *Endimion* 2
Norton, T., and Sackville, T. (Lord Buckhurst)
    *Gorboduc* 1
Peele, G. *David and Bethsabe* 1
Peele, G. *The Old Wives' Tale* 2
Preston, T. *Cambyses* 1
Udall, N. *Ralph Roister Doister* 2

MIR *Minor Elizabethan Tragedies.* New edition with
    revised contents; edited by T. W. Craik. London,
    Dent, 1974. 285pp. (Everyman's University Library
    491; first published in 1910 as Vol. 1 of Minor
    Elizabethan Drama)
*Arden of Feversham*
Kyd, T. *The Spanish Tragedy*
Norton, T., and Sackville, T. *Gorboduc*
Preston, T. *Cambises*

MISC *Miscellaneous Plays.* Selected and introduced by
    Stephanie Hodgson-Wright. Aldershot; Burlington,
    VT: Ashgate Publishing, 2000. 1 Vol., various
    pagings. (The Early Modern Englishwoman: A
    Facsimile Library of Essential Works, Series II,
    Printed Writings, 1641–1700: Part 1. Vol. 7)
Ariadne. *She Ventures and He Wins*
Boothby, F. *Marcelia: or, The Treacherous Friend*
Carroll, S. *The Perjur'd Husband*
A Young Lady. *The Unnatural Mother*

MIT Mitchell, John D., ed. *The Red Pear Garden: 3 Great
    Dramas of Revolutionary China.* Boston: Godine,
    1974. 285pp.
Li, S. *The Wild Boar Forest*
*Taking Tiger Mountain by Strategy*
Tien, H. *The White Snake*

MLAB *Modern ASEAN Plays: Brunei Darussalam*. Edited by Haji Abdul Hakim Haji Mohd Yassin. Jakarta, Indonesia: ASEAN Committee on Culture & Information, 1994. 116pp.
Akip, M. *Guests*
Bakyr, M. *The Chaffed Sky the Cracked Earth*
Chuchu, A. *The National Poet*
Tahir, P. *Ray of Hope*
Yusof, A. *Eye*
Zain, S. *Seri Begawan* I

MLAM *Modern ASEAN Plays: Malaysia*. Edited by Hajah Ainon Abu Bakar and Zullkeply Mohamad. Manila: The ASEAN Committee on Culture and Information, 1993. 199pp.
Arai, A. *Vacuum*
Dinsman. *On Sadandi's Island*
Hassan, N. *Door*
Jaaffar, J. *Surrender*
Khan, H. *Dolls*
Sikana, M. *Mustaqima*

MLAP *Modern ASEAN Plays: Philippines*. Edited by Nicanor G. Tiongson. Manila: The ASEAN Committee on Culture and Information, 1992. 236pp.
Jacob, M. *Juan Tamban*
Perez, T. *North Diversion Road*
Santos, A. *The System of Professor Tuko*
Villanueva, R. *Strands of Gray*

MLAS *Modern ASEAN Plays: Singapore*. Edited by Raman Daud, Naa Govindasamy, Choo Woon Hock, and Max Le Blond. Manila: The ASEAN Committee on Culture and Information, 1991. 234pp.
Han, L. *Alien*
Kon, S. *Emily of Emerald Hill*
Krishnan, P. *After Us*
Kuo, P. *The Silly Little Girl, and the Funny Old Tree*
Lin, M. *Inside and Outside the Door*
Nadiputra. *Encong*
Shanmugam, S. *Singapore Bridegroom*

MLAT *Modern ASEAN Plays: Thailand*. Edited by Khunying Maenmas Chavalit. Bangkok: Committee for Selection and Publication of Thai Modern Plays, Office of the National Commission for Culture, 1994. 229pp.
Khan Bejra, P. *The Shield*
Phranboon. *Dear Moon*
Vajiravudh of Siam, H.H. King. *P'ra Ruang*
Vichitvadakarn, L. *Luad Suphan*

MODERN ENGLISH DRAMA. *See* HARC *Harvard Classics*, vol. 18.

MNOD *Modern Nordic Plays: Denmark*. New York: Twayne, c1974. 449pp.
Branner, H. *Thermopylae*
Olsen, E. *The Bookseller Cannot Sleep*
Rifbjerg, K. *Developments*
Ronild, P. *Boxing for One*

MNOF *Modern Nordic Plays: Finland*. New York: Twayne, 1973. 304pp.
Haavikko, P. *The Superintendent*
Järner, V. *Eva Maria*
Manner, E. *Snow in May*
Meri, V. *Private Jokinen's Marriage Leave*

MNOI *Modern Nordic Plays: Iceland*. New York: Twayne, c1973. 427pp.
Björnsson, O. *Ten Variations*
Björnsson, O. *Yolk-life*
Halldórsson, E. *Mink*
Jakobsson, J. *The Seaway to Baghdad*
Laxness, H. *The Pigeon Banquet*

MNON *Modern Nordic Plays: Norway*. New York: Twayne, 1974. 431pp.
Borgen, J. *The House*
Havrevold, F. *The Injustice*
Kielland, A. *The Lord and His Servants*
Vesaas, T. *The Bleaching Yard*

MNOS *Modern Nordic Plays: Sweden*. New York: Twayne, 1973. 419pp.
Forssell, L. *The Madcap*
Fridell, F. *One Man's Bread*
Görling, L. *The Sandwiching*
Höijer, B. *Isak Juntti Had Many Sons*

MOAD *Modern Drama in America, Volume 1*. Edited by Alvin S. Kaufman & Franklin D. Case. New York: Washington Square Press, 1982. 415pp. (Realism from Provincetown to Broadway 1915–1929)
Glaspell, S. *Trifles*
Green, P. *In Abraham's Bosom*
Howard, S. *Lucky Sam McCarver*
Kelly, G. *The Show-off*
O'Neill, E. *Anna Christie*

MOADE *Modern Israeli Drama: An Anthology*. Edited by Herbert S. Joseph. Rutherford: Fairleigh Dickinson University Press, c1983. 267pp.
Bar-Yosef, Y. *Difficult People*
Chilton, N. *Naïm*
Horowitz, D. *Cherli ka cherli*

Megged, A. *The First Sin*
Shamir, M. *He Walked through the Fields*
Sobol, Y. *The Night of the Twentieth*


MOCPD *Modern Persian Drama: An Anthology.*
　　Translated and introduced by Gisèle Kapuscinski.
　　Lanham, MD: University Press of America, 1987.
　　227pp. (Modern Persian Literature Series, no. 8)
Beyza'i, B. *Three Puppet Shows*
Morad, G. *O Fool! O fooled!*
Na'lbandian, A. *A Modern, Profound and Important
　　Research in the Fossils of the 25th Geological Era*


MOD *Modern Plays*. London: Dent [1937] 354pp.
　　(Everyman's Library)
Bennett, A., and Knoblock, E. *Milestones*
Coward, N. *Hay Fever*
Maugham, W. *For Services Rendered*
Milne, A. *The Dover Road*
Sherriff, R. *Journey's End*


MODS *Modern Scandinavian Plays*. New York: Liveright
　　[c1954] 366pp.
Kielland, T. *Queen Margaret of Norway*
Munk, K. *Egelykke*
Strindberg, A. *The Great Highway*
Sveinbjörnsson, T. *Bishop Jón Arason*


MOE *Mondala: Literature for Critical Analysis*. By
　　Wilfred L. Gueri [and Others], eds. New York:
　　Harper and Row, 1970. 766pp.
Miller, A. *A View from the Bridge*
Shakespeare, W. *Othello*
Sophocles. *Oedipus the King*


MOGS *Monologues: Plays from Martinique, France,
　　Algeria, Quebec*. Translated by Richard Miller.
　　New York: Ubu Repertory Theater Publications,
　　1995. 244pp.
Azama, M. *The Sifter*
Drai, M. *All It Takes Is Something Small*
Gallaire, F. *Madame Bertin's Testimony*
Koltès, B. *Night Just before the Forest*
Laou, J. *Another Story*
Tremblay, L. *Anatomy Lesson*


MON Montague, Gene, and Henshaw, Marjorie, compilers.
　　*The Experience of Literature*. Englewood Cliffs,
　　NJ: Prentice-Hall [1966] 404pp.
Shakespeare, W. *Othello, the Moor of Venice*
Sheridan, R. *The School for Scandal*
Sophocles. *Antigone*
Wilde, O. *The Importance of Being Earnest*
Williams, T. *The Glass Menagerie*


MONA Montague, Gene; Henshaw, Marjorie; and
　　Salerno, Nicholas A., compilers. *The Experience of
　　Literature*. 2nd ed. Englewood Cliffs, NJ: Prentice-
　　Hall [1970] 803pp.
Hansberry, L. *A Raisin in the Sun*
Shakespeare, W. *Hamlet*
Sophocles. *Antigone*
Williams, T. *The Glass Menagerie*


MONB Nontesque, Baron, ed. *Theatrical Landmarks.*
　　London: Arcade, 1983–1987. 4 vols.
Bassart, C. *A Myth Is Good for a Smile* 3
Denstan. *Upon Chitts Hill* 4
Du Rynn, S. *Escape from Bondage* 4
Kapek, K. *Skin Deep* 2
Lionheart, E. *What Might Have Happened* 2
McPhee, F. *Foxed* 1
McPhee, F. *Merely Players* 3
McPhee, F. *Professor Newman's End* 1
McPhee, F. *The Purple Carnation* 1
McPhee, F. *Rs* 1
Parkington-Edwards, D. *Request Stop* 1
Pendark, R. *The Case of Red Diamonds* 3
Pendark, R. *The Faces of Lust* 4
Riley, W. *The Missing Ingredient* 1
Smee, A. *Fleas* 2
Sneal, P. *Is There Any Body There?* 1
Webster, C. *I Was a Grand Piano* 4
Whaler, I. *Claptrap* 3
Wilcox, D. *The Year Two Billion* 2


MONCC Montoya, Richard, Salinas, Ricardo, and
　　Siguenza, Herbert. *Culture Clash: Life, Death,
　　and Revolutionary Comedy*. New York: Theatre
　　Communications Group, 1998. 164pp.
Culture Clash. *A Bowl of Beings*
Culture Clash. *The Mission*
Culture Clash. *Radio Mambo: Culture Clash invades
　　Miami*


MONR Moody, Richard, ed. *Dramas from the American
　　Theatre, 1762–1909*. Cleveland: World [c1966]
　　873pp. (New World Literature Series, vol. 1)
Aiken, G. *Uncle Tom's Cabin*
Bird, R. *The Gladiator*
Boker, G. *Francesca da Rimini*
Brougham, J. *Po-ca-hon-tas*
Burk, J. *Bunker-Hill*
Dunlap, W. *The Glory of Columbia*
Dunlap, W. *A Trip to Niagara*
Fitch, C. *The City*
Harrigan, E. *The Mulligan Guard Ball*
Herne, J. *Shore Acres*
Hopkinson, F. *A Dialogue and Ode*
Howard, B. *Shenandoah*

Howells, W. *A Letter of Introduction*
Hoyt, C. *A Temperance Town*
McCloskey, J. *Across the Continent*
*Minstrel Show*
Mitchell, L. *The New York Idea*
Moody, W. *The Great Divide*
Mowatt, A. *Fashion*
Munford, R. *The Candidates*
Noah, M. *She Would Be a Soldier*
Smith, J. *A Dialogue between an Englishman and an
    Indian*
Smith, J. *A Little Teatable Chit Chat*
Smith, W. *The Drunkard*
Stone, J. *Metamora*
Tyler, R. *The Contrast*
Woodworth, S. *The Forest Rose*

MONV Moore, Harry Thornton, ed. *Elizabethan Age.* New
    York: Dell, 1965. 544pp.
*Arden of Feversham*
Dekker, T. *The Shoemaker's Holiday*
Marlowe, C. *The Tragical History of Doctor Faustus*

MOO Moore, John Robert, ed. *Representative English
    Dramas.* Boston: Ginn [c1929] 461pp.
Dryden, J. *All for Love*
*Everyman*
Goldsmith, O. *She Stoops to Conquer*
Marlowe, C. *The Tragical History of Doctor Faustus*
Sheridan, R. *The School for Scandal*
Wilde, O. *Lady Windermere's Fan*

MOR Morgan, Arthur Eustace, compiler. *English Plays,
    1660–1820.* New York: Harper, 1935. 1157pp.
Addison, J. *Cato*
Buckstone, J. *Luke, the Labourer*
Colman, G., and Garrick, D. *The Clandestine Marriage*
Congreve, W. *The Way of the World*
Cumberland, R. *The West Indian*
Dryden, J. *All for Love; or, the World Well Lost*
Dryden, J. *Almanzor and Almahide; or, the Conquest of
    Granada by the Spaniards*
Etherege, G. *The Man of Mode; or, Sir Fopling Flutter*
Farquhar, G. *The Beaux' Stratagem*
Foote, S. *The Mayor of Garret*
Gay, J. *The Beggar's Opera*
Goldsmith, O. *She Stoops to Conquer; or, the Mistakes
    of a Night*
Hoadly, B. *The Suspicious Husband*
Home, J. *Douglas*
Lillo, G. *The London Merchant*
Morton, T. *Speed the Plough*
Murphy, A. *All in the Wrong*
Otway, T. *Venice Preserv'd; or, a Plot Discover'd*
Reynolds, F. *The Dramatist; or, Stop Him Who Can!*

Shadwell, T. *Bury-fair*
Sheridan, R. *The Rivals*
Steele, R. *The Conscious Lovers*
Townley, J. *High Life below the Stairs*
Vanbrugh, J. *The Relapse; or, Virtue in Danger*
Wycherley, W. *The Plain-dealer*

MORR Morrell, Janet M., ed. *Four English Comedies of
    the 17th and 18th Centuries.* Baltimore: Penguin
    [Harmondsworth, Middlesex, 1950, 1962] 414pp.
Congreve, W. *The Way of the World*
Goldsmith, O. *She Stoops to Conquer; or, the Mistakes
    of a Night*
Jonson, B. *Volpone; or, the Fox*
Sheridan, R. *The School for Scandal*

MORRIS, ALTON CHESTER. *See also* WISD, WISE,
    WISF Wise, Jacob Hooper [and Others] eds.
    *College English.*

MORT Morris, Alton Chester; Walker, Biron; Bradshaw,
    Philip; Hodges, John C.; and Whitten, Mary E.,
    eds. *College English: The First Year.* 4th ed. New
    York: Harcourt, Brace and World [1964] 944pp.
Hughes, R. *The Sister's Tragedy*
O'Casey, S. *Red Roses for Me*
Shaw, G. *Caesar and Cleopatra*
Sophocles. *Antigone*
Strindberg, A. *The Stronger*

MORV Morris, Alton Chester; Walker, Biron; Bradshaw,
    Philip; Hodges, John C.; and Whitten, Mary E.,
    eds. *College English: The First Year.* 5th ed. New
    York: Harcourt, Brace and World [1968] 957pp.
Anouilh, J. *Becket; or, the Honor of God*
Miller, A. *The Crucible*
Sophocles. *Antigone*
Strindberg, A. *The Stronger*
Synge, J. *The Playboy of the Western World*

MORW Morris, Alton Chester; Walker, Biron; Bradshaw,
    Philip; Hodges, John C.; and Whitten, Mary E.,
    eds. *College English: The First Year.* 6th ed. New
    York: Harcourt Brace Jovanovich, 1973. 878pp.
Camus, A. *Caligula*
Miller, A. *The Crucible*
Sophocles. *Antigone*
Strindberg, A. *The Stronger*
Synge, J. *The Playboy of the Western World*

MORWA Morris, Alton Chester; Walker, Biron;
    Bradshaw, Philip; Hodges, John C.; and Whitten,
    Mary E., eds. *College English: The First Year.* 7th
    ed. New York: Harcourt Brace Jovanovich, 1978.
    845pp.

Chekhov, A. *The Cherry Orchard*
Miller, A. *The Crucible*
Shaw, G. *Arms and the Man*
Sophocles. *Antigone*
Strindberg, A. *The Stronger*
Wilder, T. *The Skin of Our Teeth*

MORWB Morris, Alton Chester; Walker, Biron;
    Bradshaw, Philip; Hodges, John C.; and Whitten,
    Mary E., eds. *College English: The First Year*. 8th
    ed. New York: Harcourt Brace Jovanovich, 1983.
    839pp.
Miller, A. *The Crucible*
Molière, J. *Tartuffe*
Pinter, H. *The Birthday Party*
Shakespeare, W. *King Lear*
Shaw, G. *Arms and the Man*
Sophocles. *Antigone*
Strindberg, A. *The Stronger*

MORX Morris, Alton Chester; Walker, Biron; and
    Bradshaw, Philip, comps. *Imaginative Literature:
    Fiction, Drama, Poetry*. New York: Harcourt,
    Brace and World [1968] 353pp.
Anouilh, J. *Becket; or, the Honor of God*
Miller, A. *The Crucible*
Sophocles. *Antigone*
Synge, J. *The Playboy of the Western World*

MORXB Morris, Alton Chester, Walker, Biron, and
    Bradshaw, Philip, compilers. *Imaginative
    Literature: Fiction, Drama, Poetry*. 2nd ed. New
    York: Harcourt, Brace, Jovanovich c1973. 329pp.
Camus, A. *Caligula*
Miller, A. *The Crucible*
Sophocles. *Antigone*
Strindberg, A. *The Stronger*
Synge, J. *The Playboy of the Western World*

MORXD Morris, Alton Chester, Walker, Biron, and
    Bradshaw, Philip, compilers. *Imaginative
    Literature: Fiction, Drama, Poetry*. 3rd ed. New
    York: Harcourt, Brace, Jovanovich, 1978. 402pp.
Chekhov, A. *The Cherry Orchard*
Miller, A. *The Crucible*
Shaw, G. *Arms and the Man*
Sophocles. *Antigone*
Strindberg, A. *The Stronger*
Wilder, T. *The Skin of Our Teeth*

MORXE Morris, Alton Chester, Walker, Biron, and
    Bradshaw, Philip, compilers. *Imaginative
    Literature: Fiction, Drama, Poetry*. 4th ed. New
    York: Harcourt, Brace, Jovanovich, 1983. 829pp.

Miller, A. *The Crucible*
Molière, J. *Tartuffe*
Pinter, H. *The Birthday Party*
Shakespeare, W. *King Lear*
Shaw, G. *Arms and the Man*
Sophocles. *Antigone*
Strindberg, A. *The Stronger*

MOS *Moscow Art Theatre Series of Russian Plays*. Ed. by
    Oliver M. Sayler. New York: Brentano [c1923] v.p.
Chekhov, A. *The Cherry Orchard*
Chekhov, A. *The Three Sisters*
Chekhov, A. *Uncle Vanya*
Gorky, M. *The Lower Depths*
Tolstoi, A. *Tsar Fyodor Ivanovitch*

MOSA *Moscow Art Theatre Series of Russian Plays*.
    Direction of Morris Gest, ed. by Oliver M. Sayler.
    [2nd series] New York: Brentano [c1923] v.p.
Chekhov, A. *Ivanoff*
Dostoievsky, F. *The Brothers Karamazoff*
Goldoni, C. *The Mistress of the Inn*
Ibsen, H. *An Enemy of the People*
Ostrovsky, A. *Enough Stupidity in Every Wise Man*

MOSE Moses, Montrose Jonas, ed. *British Plays from the
    Restoration to 1820*. Boston: Little, Brown, 1929.
    2 vols.
Cibber, C. *The Careless Husband* 1
Colman, G., and Garrick, D. *The Clandestine Marriage* 2
Congreve, W. *The Way of the World* 1
Cumberland, R. *The Fashionable Lover* 2
Dryden, J. *The Spanish Fryar; or, the Double Discovery* 1
Etherege, G. *The Man of Mode; or, Sir Fopling Flutter* 1
Farquhar, G. *The Beaux' Stratagem* 2
Gay, J. *The Beggar's Opera* 2
Goldsmith, O. *She Stoops to Conquer; or, the Mistakes
    of a Night* 2
Home, J. *Douglas* 2
Otway, T. *Venice Preserv'd; or, a Plot Discover'd* 1
Rowe, N. *Jane Shore* 2
Shelley, P. *The Cenci* 2
Sheridan, R. *The School for Scandal* 2
Steele, R. *The Conscious Lovers* 1
Vanbrugh, J. *The Provok'd Wife* 1
Villiers, G. *The Rehearsal* 1
Wycherley, W. *The Plain-dealer* 1

MOSG Moses, Montrose Jonas, ed. *Dramas of Modernism
    and their Forerunners*. Boston: Little Brown, 1931.
    741pp.
Andreyev, L. *He Who Has Slapped*
Čapek, K., and Čapek, J. *Adam the Creator*
Chekhov, A. *The Cherry Orchard*
Gorky, M. *Night's Lodging (The Lower Depths)*

Howard, S. *The Silver Cord*
Kaiser, G. *From Morn to Midnight*
Kelly, G. *Craig's Wife*
Lenormand, H. *The Dream Doctor*
Maugham, W. *The Circle*
Milne, A. *The Truth about Blayds*
Molnár, F. *Liliom*
Nichols, R., and Browne, M. *Wings over Europe*
O'Neill, E. *Desire under the Elms*
Pirandello, L. *Right You Are! (If You Think So)*
Strindberg, J. *There Are Crimes and Crimes*
Toller, E. *The Machine-wreckers*

MOSH Moses, Montrose Jonas, and Campbell, Oscar James,
    eds. *Dramas of Modernism and Their Forerunners.*
    Rev. ed. Boston: Little, Brown, 1941. 946pp.
Anderson, M. *Winterset*
Andreyev, L. *He Who Gets Slapped*
Čapek, K., and Čapek, J. *Adam the Creator*
Carroll, P. *Shadow and Substance*
Chekhov, A. *The Cherry Orchard*
Gorky, M. *Night's Lodging (The Lower Depths)*
Howard, S. *The Silver Cord*
Kaiser, G. *From Morn to Midnight*
Kelly, G. *Craig's Wife*
Lenormand, H. *The Dream Doctor*
Maugham, W. *The Circle*
Milne, A. *The Truth about Blayds*
Molnár, F. *Liliom*
Nichols, R., and Browne, M. *Wings over Europe*
Odets, C. *Golden Boy*
O'Neill, E. *Desire under the Elms*
Pirandello, L. *Right You Are! (If You Think So)*
Sherwood, R. *Idiot's Delight*
Strindberg, J. *There Are Crimes and Crimes*
Toller, E. *The Machine-wreckers*

MOSJ Moses, Montrose Jonas, ed. *Representative*
    *American Dramas, National and Local.* Boston:
    Little, Brown, 1926. 681pp.
Belasco, D. *The Girl of the Golden West*
Crothers, R. *Nice People*
Davis, O. *The Detour*
Fitch, C. *The City*
Forbes, J. *The Famous Mrs. Fair*
Hoyt, C. *A Texas Steer*
Kaufman, G., and Connelly, M. *Dulcy*
Kelly, G. *The Show-off*
MacKaye, P. *The Scarecrow*
Megrue, R., and Hackett, W. *It Pays to Advertise*
O'Neill, E. *The Emperor Jones*
Peabody, J. *The Piper*
Rice, E. *The Adding Machine*
Smith, H. *Mrs. Bumpstead-Leigh*
Thomas, A. *The Witching Hour*

MOSK Moses, Montrose Jonas, ed. *Representative*
    *American Dramas, National and Local.* Rev. ed.
    Boston: Little, Brown, 1933. 890pp.
Barry, P. *Holiday*
Behrman, S. *The Second Man*
Belasco, D. *The Girl of the Golden West*
Connelly, M. *The Green Pastures*
Crothers, R. *Nice People*
Davis, O. *The Detour*
Fitch, C. *The City*
Forbes, J. *The Famous Mrs. Fair*
Howard, S. *Lucky Sam McCarver*
Hoyt, C. *A Texas Steer*
Kaufman, G., and Connelly, M. *Dulcy*
Kelly, G. *The Show-off*
MacKaye, P. *The Scarecrow*
Megrue, R., and Hackett, W. *It Pays to Advertise*
O'Neill, E. *The Emperor Jones*
Peabody, J. *The Piper*
Rice, E. *The Adding Machine*
Smith, H. *Mrs. Bumpstead-Leigh*
Thomas, A. *The Witching Hour*

MOSL Moses, Montrose Jonas, and Krutch, Joseph Wood,
    eds. *Representative American Dramas, National*
    *and Local.* Rev. and brought up-to-date. Boston:
    Little, Brown, 1941. 1041pp.
Anderson, M. *The Masque of Kings*
Barry, P. *Holiday*
Behrman, S. *The Second Man*
Belasco, D. *The Girl of the Golden West*
Connelly, M. *The Green Pastures*
Crothers, R. *Nice People*
Davis, O. *The Detour*
Fitch, C. *The City*
Forbes, J. *The Famous Mrs. Fair*
Howard, S. *Lucky Sam McCarver*
Hoyt, C. *A Texas Steer*
Kaufman, G., and Connelly, M. *Dulcy*
Kelly, G. *The Show-off*
MacKaye, P. *The Scarecrow*
Megrue, R., and Hackett, W. *It Pays to Advertise*
Odets, C. *Awake and Sing*
O'Neill, E. *The Emperor Jones*
Peabody, J. *The Piper*
Rice, E. *The Adding Machine*
Sherwood, R. *The Petrified Forest*
Smith, H. *Mrs. Bumpstead-Leigh*
Thomas, A. *The Witching Hour*

MOSN Moses, Montrose Jonas, ed. *Representative British*
    *Dramas, Victorian and Modern.* Boston: Little,
    Brown, 1918. 861pp.
Barker, G. *The Madras House*
Boucicault, D. *London Assurance*

Browning, R. *A Blot in the 'Scutcheon*
Bulwer-Lytton, E. *Richelieu; or, the Conspiracy*
Colum, P. *Thomas Muskerry*
Dunsany, E. *The Gods of the Mountain*
Galsworthy, J. *The Silver Box*
Gilbert, W. *H.M.S. Pinafore; or, the Lass that Loved a Sailor*
Gregory, I. *The Workhouse Ward*
Hankin, St. J. *The Cassilis Engagement*
Jerrold, D. *Black-ey'd Susan; or, All in the Downs*
Jones, H. *The Masqueraders*
Knowles, J. *Virginius*
Masefield, J. *The Tragedy of Pompey the Great*
Pinero, A. *The Gay Lord Quex*
Robertson, T. *Caste*
Synge, J. *Riders to the Sea*
Taylor, T. *The Ticket-of-leave Man*
Tennyson, A. *Becket*
Wilde, O. *The Importance of Being Earnest*
Yeats, W. *Cathleen ni Houlihan*

MOSO Moses, Montrose Jonas, ed. *Representative British Dramas, Victorian and Modern.* New rev. ed. Boston: Little, Brown, 1931. 996pp.
Boucicault, D. *London Assurance*
Browning, R. *A Blot in the 'Scutcheon*
Bulwer-Lytton, E. *Richelieu; or, the Conspiracy*
Coward, N. *Easy Virtue*
Dane, C. *A Bill of Divorcement*
Dunsany, E. *The Gods of the Mountain*
Galsworthy, J. *The Silver Box*
Gilbert, W. *H. M. S. Pinafore; or, the Lass that Loved a Sailor*
Granville-Barker, H. *The Madras House*
Gregory, I. *The Workhouse Ward*
Hankin, St. J. *The Cassilis Engagement*
Jerrold, D. *Black-ey'd Susan; or, All in the Downs*
Jones, H. *The Masqueraders*
Knowles, J. *Virginius*
Maugham, W. *Our Betters*
Monkhouse, A. *First Blood*
Munro, C. *At Mrs. Beam's*
Pinero, A. *The Gay Lord Quex*
Robertson, T. *Caste*
Synge, J. *Riders to the Sea*
Taylor, T. *The Ticket-of-leave Man*
Wilde, O. *The Importance of Being Earnest*
Yeats, W. *Cathleen ni Houlihan*

MOSQ Moses, Montrose Jonas, ed. *Representative Continental Dramas, Revolutionary and Transitional.* Boston: Little, Brown, 1924. 688pp.
Andreyoff, L. *The Life of Man*
Annunzio, G. d'. *The Daughter of Jorio*
Becque, H. *The Vultures*

Benavente y Martínez, J. *The Bonds of Interest*
Chekhov, A. *The Sea-gull*
Donnay, M. *Lovers*
Giacosa, G. *Like Falling Leaves*
Hauptmann, G. *The Sunken Bell*
Ibsen, H. *The Wild Duck*
Maeterlinck, M. *Monna Vanna*
Nirdlinger, C. *The World and His Wife*
Rostand, E. *Cyrano de Bergerac*
Schnitzler, A. *The Lonely Way*
Sudermann, H. *The Fires of St. John*
Verhaeren, E. *The Dawn*

MOSS Moses, Montrose Jonas, ed. *Representative Plays by American Dramatists.* New York: Dutton, 1918–1925. 3 vols.
Aiken, G. *Uncle Tom's Cabin* 2
Barker, J. *The Indian Princess; or, La belle sauvage* 1
Bateman, Mrs. S. *Self* 2
Belasco, D. *The Return of Peter Grimm* 3
Boker, G. *Francesca da Rimini* 3
Brackenridge, H. *The Battle of Bunkers-hill* 1
Brown, D. *Sertorius; or, the Roman Patriot* 2
Bunce, O. *Love in '76* 3
Burke, C. *Rip Van Winkle* 3
Conrad, R. *Jack Cade* 2
Dunlap, W. *André* 1
Fitch, C. *The Moth and the Flame* 3
Godfrey, T. *The Prince of Parthia* 1
Howard, B. *Shenandoah* 3
Hutton, J. *Fashionable Follies* 2
Jones, J. *The People's Lawyer* 2
Leacock, J. *The Fall of British tyranny; or, American Liberty* 1
Low, S. *The Politician Outwitted* 1
MacKaye, S. *Paul Kauvar; or, Anarchy* 3
Mitchell, L. *The New York Idea* 3
Mowatt, Mrs. A. *Fashion* 2
Noah, M. *She Would Be a Soldier; or, the Plains of Chippewa* 1
Payne, J. *Brutus; or, the Fall of Tarquin* 2
Rogers, R. *Ponteach; or, the Savages of America* 1
Tayleure, C. *Horse-shoe Robinson* 2
Thomas, A. *In Mizzoura* 3
Tyler, R. *The Contrast* 1
Walter, E. *The Easiest Way* 3
Warren, Mrs. M. *The Group* 1
Willis, N. *Tortesa, the Usurer* 2

MOST *The Most Popular Plays of the American Theatre: Ten of Broadway's Longest-Running Plays.* Edited by Stanley Richards. New York: Stein and Day, 1979. 703pp.
Burrows, A. *Cactus Flower*
Chase, M. *Harvey*

Hamilton, P. *Angel Street*
Kerr, J. *Mary, Mary*
Kesselring, J. *Arsenic and Old Lace*
Kirkland, J. *Tobacco Road*
Lindsay, H., and Crouse, R. *Life with Father*
Nichols, A. *Abie's Irish Rose*
Simon, N. *Barefoot in the Park*
Slade, B. *Same Time, Next Year*

MUMFORD, LEWIS. *See* AME *American Caravan.*

MURD Murdoch, Lesley, and Gaita, Margaret, eds. *Exploring Relationships through Drama: Three Plays for Performance and Discussion.* South Melbourne, Victoria: Thomas Nelson Australia, 1990. 100pp.
Dickens, C. *Friends*
Selleck, R., and Larman, C. *Juliet and Romeo*
Turner, G. *Super Cool*

MURP Murphy, Charles T.; Guinagh, Kevin; and Oates, Whitney, J., eds. *Greek and Roman Classics in Translation.* New York: Longmans, Green [c1947] 1052pp.
Aeschylus. *Prometheus Bound*
Aristophanes. *The Clouds*
Euripides. *Hippolytus*
Sophocles. *Oedipus the King*

MURRAY, GILBERT. *See* TEN *Ten Greek Plays.*

MYB *My Best Play.* London: Faber & Faber [1934] 590pp.
Bax, C. *The Venetian*
Coward, N. *Hay Fever*
Dane, C. *Granite*
Maugham, W. *The Circle*
Milne, A. *Success*
Munro, C. *The Rumour*
Robinson, L. *The Whiteheaded Boy*
Van Druten, J. *After All*

MYSCC *The Mysteries at Canterbury Cathedral.* Adapted by Kenneth Pickering, Kevin Wood, and Philip Dart; edited by Shirley Bennetts. Worthing: Churchman Publishing, 1986. 200pp.
*Abraham and Isaac*
*The Annunciation*
*Balaam, Balak, and the Prophets*
*Banns*
*The Betrayal*
*Cain and Abel*
*The Creation of Adam and Eve*
*The Crucifixion*
*The Entry into Jerusalem*

*The Fall of Lucifer*
*The Fall of Man*
*Herod and the Slaying of the Innocents*
*John the Baptist*
*The Last Supper*
*The Law*
*The Ministry: Healing, Teaching, and Plotting*
*The Ministry: Temptation and Teaching*
*Moses*
*Noah's Flood*
*The Resurrection and Ascension*
*The Shepherds*
*The Trial of Jesus*

MYTH *Mythic Women/Real Women: Plays and Performance Pieces by Women.* Selected and introduced by Lizbeth Goodman. London: Faber and Faber, 2000. 388pp.
Bradley, J. *Digging for Ladies* (excerpt)
Churchill, C. *Top Girls* (excerpt)
Curino, L. *Passion*
Daniels, S. *Purple Side Coasters*
Dempsey, S., and Millan, L. *Mary Medusa*
Feinstein, E., and the Women's Theatre Group. *Lear's Daughters*
Kay, J. *Generations*
Kincaid, J. *Girl*
Lavery, B. *Ophelia* (excerpt)
Lipkin, J. *The Girl Who Lost Her Voice*
Morrissey, K. *Poems for Men Who Dream of Lolita* (excerpt)
Pascal, J. *Theresa*
Rame, F., and Fo, D. *A Woman Alone*
Smartt, D. *Medusa? Medusa Black!*
Smith, A. *Trace of Arc*
Weaver, L. *Faith and Dancing* (excerpt)
Wertenbaker, T. *The Love of the Nightengale*
Worsley, V. *Lift and Separate*

N-TOW *The N-Town Play: Cotton MS Vespasian D.8. Vol. 1.* Introduction and text. Edited by Stephen Spector. Oxford: Published for the Early English Text Society by the Oxford University Press, 1991. 413pp.
*Abraham and Isaac*
*The Announcement to the Three Marys; Peter and John at the Sepulchre*
*The Appearance to Mary Magdalene*
*The Ascension; The Selection of Matthias*
*The Assumption of Mary*
*The Baptism*
*The Betrayal*
*The Burial; The Guarding of the Sepulchre*
*Cain and Abel*
*Christ and the Doctors*

*Cleophas and Luke; The Appearance to Thomas*
*The Creation of Heaven; The Fall of Lucifer*
*The Creation of the World; The Fall of Man*
*The Death of Judas; The Trials before Pilate and Herod*
*The Harrowing of Hell (Part 1)*
*The Harrowing of Hell (Part 2); Christ's Appearance to
    Mary; Pilate and the Soldiers*
*Herod; The Trial before Annas and Cayphas*
*Jesse Root*
*Joachim and Anna*
*Joseph's Doubt*
*Judgement Day*
*The Last Supper; The Conspiracy with Judas*
*The Magi*
*The Marriage of Mary and Joseph*
*Moses*
*The Nativity*
*Noah*
*The Parliament of Heaven; The Salutation and
    Conception*
*The Parliament of Hell; The Temptation*
*Pentecost*
*The Presentation of Mary in the Temple*
*The Procession of Saints*
*The Procession to Calvary; The Crucifixion*
*The Proclamation*
*Prologues of Satan and John the Baptist; The
    Conspiracy; The Entry into Jerusalem*
*The Purification*
*The Raising of Lazarus*
*Satan and Pilate's Wife; The Second Trial before Pilate*
*The Shepherds*
*The Slaughter of the Innocents; The Death of Herod*
*The Trial of Mary and Joseph*
*The Visit to Elizabeth*
*The Woman Taken in Adultery*

NAGE Nagelberg, Munjou Moses. *Drama in Our Time.*
    New York: Harcourt, Brace [c1948] 478pp.
    Arent, A. *One-third of a Nation*
    Čapek, K. *R.U.R.*
    Corwin, N. *El Capitan and the Corporal*
    Hellman, L. *Watch on the Rhine*
    Howard, S. *Yellow Jack*
    Saroyan, W. *The Human Comedy*
    Sherwood, R. *Abe Lincoln in Illinois*
    Wilder, T. *Our Town*

NATHAN, GEORGE JEAN. *See* CRIT *The Critics' Prize
    Plays.* FIO *Five Great Modern Irish Plays.* WORP
    *World's Great Plays.*

NEI Neilson, William Allan, ed. *The Chief Elizabethan
    Dramatists, Excluding Shakespeare.* Boston,
    Houghton Mifflin [1911] 878pp.

Beaumont, F., and Fletcher, J. *The Knight of the Burning
    Pestle*
Beaumont, F., and Fletcher, J. *The Maid's Tragedy*
Beaumont, F., and Fletcher, J. *Philaster*
Chapman, G. *Bussy D'Ambois*
Dekker, T. *The Honest Whore, Part I*
Dekker, T. *The Honest Whore, Part II*
Dekker, T. *The Shoemaker's Holiday*
Fletcher, J. *The Faithful Shepherdess*
Fletcher, J. *The Wild-goose Chase*
Ford, J. *The Broken Heart*
Greene, R. *The Honourable History of Friar Bacon and
    Friar Bungay*
Heywood, T. *A Woman Killed with Kindness*
Jonson, B. *The Alchemist*
Jonson, B. *Every Man in His Humour*
Jonson, B. *Sejanus, His Fall*
Jonson, B. *Volpone; or, the Fox*
Kyd, T. *The Spanish Tragedy; or, Hieronimo Is Mad
    Again*
Lyly, J. *Endymion, the Man in the Moon*
Marlowe, C. *The Jew of Malta*
Marlowe, C. *Tamburlaine, Part I*
Marlowe, C. *The Tragical History of Doctor Faustus*
Marlowe, C. *The Troublesome Reign and Lamentable
    Death of Edward the Second*
Marston, J. *The Malcontent*
Massinger, P. *A New Way to Pay Old Debts*
Middleton, T. *A Trick to Catch the Old One*
Middleton, T., and Rowley, W. *The Changeling*
Peele, G. *The Old Wives' Tale*
Shirley, J. *The Cardinal*
Shirley, J. *The Lady of Pleasure*
Webster, J. *The Duchess of Malfi*

NELS Nelson, John Herbert, and Cargill, Oscar, eds.
    *Contemporary Trends: American Literature since
    1900.* Revised edition. New York: Macmillan
    [c1949] 1263pp. (American Literature: A Period
    Anthology. [vol. 4] Oscar Cargill, General Editor)
    Anderson, M. *Winterset*
    MacLeish, A. *The Fall of the City*
    O'Neill, E. *Bound East for Cardiff*
    O'Neill, E. *Lazarus Laughed*

NELSDI Nelson, Richard, ed. *Strictly Dishonorable and
    Other Lost American Plays.* New York: Theatre
    Communications Group, 1986. 463pp.
    Cormack, B. *The Racket*
    Howard. S. *The Ghost of Yankee Doodle*
    Lindsay, H., and Runyon, D. *A Slight Case of Murder*
    Sturges, P. *Strictly Dishonorable*

NER Nero (Tragedy). *Nero & Other Plays.* Edited by
    Herbert P. Home; Havelock Ellis; Arthur Symons;

and A. Wilson Verity. New York: Scribner, 1904–1948. 488pp.

Day, J. *Humour Out of Breath*
Day, J. *The Parliament of Bees*
Field, N. *Amends for Ladies*
Field, N. *Woman Is a Weathercock*
*Nero*
Porter, H. *The Two Angry Women of Abington*

NES Nethercot, Arthur Hobart [and Others], eds. *Elizabethan Plays*. New York: Holt, 1971. 845pp.

Chapman, G. *Bussy d'Ambois*
Dekker, T. *The Honest Whore, Part I*
Dekker, T. *The Shoemaker's Holiday*
Gascoigne, G. *Supposes*
Greene, R. *George A. Greene, the Pinner of Wakefield*
Greene, R. *The Honorable History of Friar Bacon and Friar Bungay*
Heywood, T. *A Woman Killed with Kindness*
Kyd, T. *The Spanish Tragedy*
Lyly, J. *Endymion*
Marlowe, C. *Attowell's Jig (Francis' New Jig)*
Marlowe, C. *Edward the Second*
Marlowe, C. *Doctor Faustus*
Marlowe, C. *Mucedorus*
Marlowe, C. *Tamburlaine, Part I*
Marston, J. *The Malcontent*
Norton, T., and Sackville, T. *Gorboduc*
Peele, G. *The Arraignment of Paris*
Peele, G. *The Old Wives' Tale*
Preston, T. *Cambises, King of Persia*
Stevenson, W. *Gammer Gurton's Needle*
Udall, N. *Ralph Roister Doister*

NET Nettleton, George Henry, and Case, Arthur Ellicott, eds. *British Dramatists from Dryden to Sheridan*. Boston, Houghton Mifflin [c1939] 957pp.

Addison, J. *Cato*
Buckingham, G. *The Rehearsal*
Cibber, C. *The Careless Husband*
Colman, G. *The Jealous Wife*
Congreve, W. *The Way of the World*
Cumberland, R. *The West Indian*
Dryden, J. *All for Love; or, the World Well Lost*
Dryden, J. *The Conquest of Granada by the Spaniards, Part I*
Etherege, G. *The Man of Mode; or, Sir Fopling Flutter*
Farquhar, G. *The Beaux' Stratagem*
Fielding, H. *Tom Thumb*
Garrick, D. *The Lying Valet*
Gay, J. *The Beggar's Opera*
Goldsmith, O. *She Stoops to Conquer; or, the Mistakes of a Night*
Home, J. *Douglas*

Lillo, G. *The London Merchant; or, the History of George Barnwell*
Otway, T. *Venice Preserved; or, a Plot Discovered*
Rowe, N. *The Tragedy of Jane Shore*
Sheridan, R. *The Critic; or, a Tragedy Rehearsed*
Sheridan, R. *The Rivals*
Sheridan, R. *The School for Scandal*
Steele, R. *The Conscious Lovers*
Vanbrugh, J. *The Relapse; or, Virtue in Danger*
Wycherley, W. *The Plain Dealer*

NEVI Neville, Mary Anthony, and Herzberg, Max J., eds. *This England*. Chicago: Rand McNally [c1956] 786pp.

Shakespeare, W. *Macbeth*
Wilde, O. *The Importance of Being Earnest*

NEW AMERICAN CARAVAN. 1929. *See* AME *American Caravan, vol. 3.*

NEWA *New American Plays*. Edited by Hobert Willoughby Corrigan (v1) and William H. Hoffman (vol. 2, vol. 3, vol. 4). New York: Hill and Wang, 1965–1971. 4 vols.

Barlow, A. *Mr. Biggs* 1
Bullins, E. *The Electronic Nigger* 3
Bush, J. *French Gray* 2
Cameron, K. *The Hundred and First* 1
Dey, J. *Passacaglia* 2
Estrin, M. *An American Playground Sampler* 3
Eyen, T. *The White Whore and the Bit Player* 2
Fredericks, C. *A Summer Ghost* 1
Harris, T. *Always with Love* 3
Heide, R. *At War with the Mongols* 4
Herndon, V. *Until the Monkey Comes* 2
Hoffman, B. *The King of Spain* 3
Hoffman, W. *Thank You, Miss Victoria* 3
Jasudowicz, D. *Blood Money* 1
Kennedy, A. *The Owl Answers* 2
Levinson, A. *Socrates Wounded* 1
Magnuson, J. *African Medea* 4
Maljean, J. *A Message from Cougar* 2
Mee, C. *Constantinople Smith* 1
Molinaro, U. *The Abstract Wife* 2
Owens, R. *Futz* 2
Patrick, R. *The Golden Circle* 3
Peluso, E. *Moby Tick* 4
Rosenberg, J. *The Death and Life of Sneaky Fitch* 1
Rubenstein, K. *Icarus* 4
Smith, M. *Captain Jack's Revenge* 4
Starkweather, D. *The Poet's Papers* 3
Washburn, D. *Ginger Anne* 1
Yankowitz, S. *Slaughterhouse* 4
Yerby, L. *The Golden Bull of Boredom* 1

NEWAMP *New American Plays.* With an introduction by
 Peter Filichia. Portsmouth, NH: Heinemann, 1992.
 2 vols.
 Budbill, D. *Judevine* 2
 Carson, J. *Daytrips* 2
 Commire, A. *Starting Monday* 1
 Gotanda, P. *Yankee Dawg You Die* 1
 Kelley, S. *Pill Hill* 2
 Noble, J. *Away Alone* 2
 Strand, R. *The Bug* 1
 Wright, D. *Interrogating the Nude* 1

NEWCAD1 *New Canadian Drama.* Edited by Neil
 Carson. Ottawa: Borealis Press, 1980. 119pp.
 Cone, T. *Stargazing*
 Jonas, G. *Pushkin*
 Ouzounian, R. *Westmount*

NEWCAD2 *New Canadian Drama 2.* Edited by Patrick B.
 O'Neill. Ottawa: Borealis Press, 1981. 153pp.
 Heide, C. *Pogie*
 Nowlan, A., and Learning, W. *The Dollar Woman*
 Ringwood, G. *Mirage*

NEWCAD3 *New Canadian Drama 3: Alberta Dramatists.*
 Edited by Dennis W. Salter. Ottawa: Borealis Press,
 1984. 166pp.
 Moher, F. *Down for the Weekend*
 Pengilly, G. *Swipe*
 Rebar, K. *Checkin' Out*

NEWCAD4 *New Canadian Drama 4: Manitoba
 Dramatists.* Edited by Douglas Arrell. Ottawa:
 Borealis Press, 1986. 156pp.
 McManus, B. *Caffé*
 Silver, A. *Climate of the Times*
 Williams, A. *In Dreams*

NEWCAD5 *New Canadian Drama 5: Political Drama.*
 Edited by Alan Filewood. Ottawa: Borealis Press,
 1991. 188pp.
 Barrie, S. *Straight Stitching*
 Diamond, D. *No' xya' (Our Footprints)*
 Milner, A. *Learning to Live with Personal Growth*
 Riordan, M. *A Jungle Out There*

NEWCAD6 *New Canadian Drama 6: Feminist Drama.*
 Edited by Rita Much. Ottawa: Borealis Press, 1993.
 166pp.
 Rubess, B. *Pope Joan*
 Vingoe, M., and Kudelka, J. *Hooligans*

NEWCAD7 *New Canadian Drama 7: West Coast
 Comedies.* Edited by Alan Filewood. Ottawa:
 Borealis Press, 1999. 260pp.

 Lazarus, J. *Village of Idiots*
 Weir, I. St. *George*
 Weiss, P. E. *Going Down for the Count*

NEWCAD8 *New Canadian Drama 8: Speculative Drama.*
 Edited by Scott Duchesne. Ottawa: Borealis Press,
 2002. 184pp.
 Barton, B. *Roswell*
 Brooker, B., and Green, M. *Alien Bait*
 Young, W. *Eden's Moon*

NEW CARAVAN. 1936. *See* AME *American Caravan.*
 *Vol. 5.*

NEWDAN *New Danish Plays.* Selected and edited by
 Hans Christian Andersen. Norwich, Norvik Press,
 1996. 263pp.
 Holm, S. *Leonora*
 Nissen, K. *Fair Kirsten*
 Ørnsbo, J. *Odysseus from Vraa*
 Saalbach, A. *Morning and Evening*

NEW DIRECTIONS. *See* NEWDI *New Directions in
 Prose and Poetry.* James Laughlin, ed. *See also*
 PLAA *Playbook*; SPC *Speahead.*

NEWDI *New Directions in Prose and Poetry.* James
 Laughlin, ed. Norfolk, CT: New Directions, 1936–
 1955. 15 vols.
 Brecht, B. *The Exception and the Rule* 55
 Brecht, B. *Mother Courage* 41
 Büchner, G. *Woyzeck* 50
 Cocteau, J. *Les maries de la Tour Eiffel* 37
 García Lorca, F. *In the Frame of Don Cristóbal* 44
 Goodman, P. *The Tower of Babel* 40
 Hutchins, M. *The Case of Astrolable* 44
 Hutchins, M. *A Play about Joseph Smith, Jr.* 44
 Hutchins, M. *The Wandering Jew* 51
 Moss, H. *No Strings Attached* 44
 Ortiz de Montellano, B. *Salome's Head* 44
 Reid, B. *The Fourth Room* 44
 Rexroth, K. *Iphigenia at Aulis* 44
 Rexroth, K. *Phaedra* 44
 Schwartz, D. *Paris and Helen* 41
 Second, L. *Apollinaris* 42
 Stein, G. *Daniel Webster, Eighteen in America* 37
 Williams, T. *Dos ranchos; or, the Purification* 44
 Williams, W. *Trial Horse No. 1: Many Loves* 42

NEWDR1 *New Drama One.* Selected, edited, and
 introduced by Lloyd Fernando. London; Kuala
 Lampur: Oxford University Press, 1972. 147pp.
 Das, K. *Lela Mayang*
 Dorall, E. *A Tiger Is Loose in Our Community*
 Lee, J. *The Happening in the Bungalow*

NEWDR2 *New Drama Two*. Selected, edited, and
    introduced by Lloyd Fernando. London; Kuala
    Lampur: Oxford University Press, 1972. 153pp.
Dorall, E. *The Hour of the Dog*
Lee, J. *When the Sun Sets on the Branches of that Jambu
    Tree*
Yeoh, P. *The Need to Be*

NEWE *New English Dramatists*. Edited by E. Martin
    Browne. Tom Masehler. Harmondsworth,
    Middlesex: Penguin Books, 1958–1971. 14 vols.
Arden, J., and D'Arey, M. *The Happy Haven* 4
Arden, J. *Live like Pigs* 3
Bermange, B. *No Quarter* 12
Bolt, R. *A Man for All Seasons* 6
Churchill, C. *The Ants* 12
Conn, S. *The King* 14
Cooper, G. *Everything in the Garden* 7
Cooper, G. *Happy Family* 11
Cooper, G. *The Object* 12
Finlay, I. *The Estate Hunters* 14
Finlay, I. *Walking through Seaweed* 14
Fugard, A. *The Blood Knot* 13
Hall, W. *The Long and the Short and the Tall* 3
Hastings, M. *Yes, and After* 4
Howarth, D. *A Lily in Little India* 9
Johnson, B. *You're Human like the Rest of Them* 14
Kops, B. *The Hamlet of Stepney Green* 1
Lessing, D. *Each His Own Wilderness* 1
Livings, H. *Nil carborundum* 6
Livings, H. *Stop It, Whoever You Are* 5
Lynne, J. *The Trigon* 8
MacBeth, G., and Bingham, J. *The Doomsday Show* 14
Orton, J. *Entertaining Mr. Sloane* 8
Orton, J. *Loot* 13
Osborne, J., and Creighton, A. *Epitaph for George
    Dillon* 2
Owen, A. *Progress to the Park* 5
Pinner, D. *Dickon* 10
Pinner, D. *The Drums of Snow* 13
Pinter, H. *The Dumb Waiter* 3
Reckord, B. *Skyvers* 9
Rudkin, D. *Afore Night Come* 7
Sanford, J. *The Whelks and the Cromium* 12
Shaffer, P. *Five Finger Exercise* 4
Sharp, A. *The Long-distance Piano Player* 12
Simpson, N. *A Resounding Tinkle* 2
Storey, D. *The Restoration of Arnold Middleton* 14
Taylor, C. *Bread and Butter* 10
Taylor, C. *Happy Days Are Here Again* 12
Terson, P. *The Mighty Reservoy* 14
Terson, P. *A Night to Make Angels Weep* 11
Wesker, A. *Chicken Soup with Barley* 1
Wesker, A. *Chips with Everything* 7

Wesker, A. *The Four Seasons* 9
Wesker, A. *The Kitchen* 2
Wesker, A. *Their Very Own and Golden City* 10
Whiting, J. *The Devils* 6
Whiting, J. *Marching Song* 3
Wood, C. *Cockade* 8
Wood, C. *Fill the Stage with Happy Hours* 11

NEWFPA *New French Plays*. Selected by David Bradby
    and Claude Schumacher. London: Methuen Drama,
    1989. 118pp.
Cousse, R. *These Childish Things*
Demarcy, R. *Stranger in the House*
Koltès, B. *Struggle of the Dogs and the Black*
Vinaver, M. *Portrait of a Woman*

NEWFPB *New French Plays*. With an introduction by
    David Bradby. London: Methuen Drama, 2000.
    232pp. (Frontline Drama 6)
Anne, C. *Agnès*
Durringer, X. *A Desire to Kill on the Tip of the Tongue*
Pellet, C. *One More Wasted Year*
Pontcharra, N. *Mickey the Torch*
Renaude, N. *The Northern Fox*

NEWFPL *New French-Language Plays*: *Martinique,
    Quebec, Ivory Coast, Belgium*. Preface by Rosette
    C. Lamont. New York: Ubu Repertory Theater
    Publications, 1993. 346pp.
Bouchard, M. *The Orphan Muses*
Césaire, I. *Fire's Daughters*
Césaire, M. *The Ship*
Emond, P. *Talk about Love*
Kwahulé, K. *That Old Black Magic*

NEWJV *New Jewish Voices: Plays Produced by the
    Jewish Repertory Theatre*. Edited by Edward M.
    Cohen. Albany, State University of New York
    Press, 1985. 302pp. (SUNY Series in Modern
    Jewish Literature and Culture, no. 36)
Cohen, N., and Cohen, J. *Friends Too Numerous to
    Mention*
Klonsky, K., and Shein, B. *Taking Steam*
Lessing, N. *36*
Rush, D. *Elephants*
Schotter, R. *Benya the King*

NEWL *New Lafayette Theatre Presents: Plays with
    Aesthetic Comments by 6 Black Playwrights*.
    Garden City, NY: Doubleday (Anchor Press
    Books), 1974. 301pp.
Bullins, E. *The Fabulous Miss Marie*
Gaines, J. *What If It Had Turned Up Heads?*
Goss, C. *On Being Hit*

OyamO. *His First Step*
Sachez, S. *Uh, Uh, but How Do It Free Us?*
Wesley, R. *Black Terror*

NEWNOR *New Norwegian Plays*. Edited and translated
by Janet Garton and Henning Sehmsdorf. Norwich:
Norvik Press, 1989. 293pp. (Norvik Press Series B,
no. 6)
Cappelin, P. *Whittenland*
Hoem, E. *Good Night, Europe*
Løveid, C. *Seagull Eaters*
Vik, B. *Daughters*

NEWP *New Plays by Women*. Edited by Susan La Tempa.
Berkeley, CA: Shameless Hussy Press, 1979.
248pp.
Boyd, S. *St. Mael and the Maldunkian Penguins*
La Tempa, S. *The Life of the Party*
Press, T. *Mash Note to an Old Codger*
Puccioni, M. *Laundromat*
Ratcliffe, H. *Railroad Women*
Robinson, B. *The Shanglers*
Sullivan, L. *Baron's Night, or Catch as Catch-can*

NEWPAB *New Plays from the Abbey Theatre*. Edited by
Christopher Fitz-Simmon and Sanford Sternlicht
(vol. 1); edited by Judy Friel and Sanford Sternlicht
(vols. 2–3). Syracuse, NY: Syracuse University
Press, 1996–2001. 3 vols.
Carr, M. *By the Bog of Cats* 2
Donnelly, N. *The Duty Master* 1
Harding, M. *Hubert Murray's Widow* 1
Harding, M. *Sour Grapes* 2
Johnston, A. *Melonfarmer* 2
Kilroy, T. *The Secret Fall of Constance Wilde* 2
Leonard, H. *Love in the Title* 3
MacIntyre, T. *Sheep's Milk on the Boil* 1
McGuinness, F. *Dolly West's Kitchen* 3
Murphy, J. *The Muesli Belt* 3
O'Kelly, D. *Asylum! Asylum!* 1
Williams, N. *A Little like Paradise* 1

NEWQ *New Plays USA: 1*. Edited by James Leverett. New
York: Theatre Communications Group, c1982.
375pp.
Breuer, L. *A Prelude to Death in Venice*
Cole, T. *Dead Souls*
Hwang, D. *FOB*
Mann, E. *Still Life*
OyamO. *The Resurrection of Lady Lester; a Poetic
Mood Song Based on the Legend of Lester Young*
Shank, A. *WinterPlay; a Hyper-real Comedy in Two
Acts*

NEWQA *New Plays USA: 2*. Edited by M. Elizabeth
Osborn and Gillian Richards. New York: Theatre
Communications Group, 1984. 275pp.
Freed, D., and Stone, A. *Secret Honor: The Last
Testament of Richard M. Nixon; a Political Myth*
Hill, G. *Food from Trash*
Kroetz, F. *Mensch Meier: A Play of Everyday Life*
Ribman, R. *Buck*
Yoshimura, J. *Mercenaries*

NEWQB *New Plays USA: 3*. Edited by James Leverett
and M. Elizabeth Osborn. New York: Theatre
Communications Group, 1986. 263pp.
Havis, A. *Morocco*
Mann, E. *Execution of Justice*
Metcalfe, S. *The Incredibly Famous Willy Rivers*
Nelson, R. *Between East and West*
Piñera, V. *Cold Air*

NEWQC *New Plays USA: 4*. Edited by James Leverett
and Gillian Richards. New York: Theatre
Communications Group, 1988. 224pp.
Baitz, J. *The Film Society*
Chong, P. *Kind ness*
Klein, J. *T Bone n Weasel*
Larson, L., Lee, L., and Wackler, R. *Tent Meeting*
Wolfe, G. *The Colored Museum*

NEWR *New Playwrights: The Best Plays of*. Introduction
by Romulus Linney 1998; Introduction by Todd
London 1999; Introduction by Dan Lauria 2000.
Hanover, NH: Smith and Kraus, 1998–2000.
(Contemporary Playwrights Series)
Bitterman, S. *The Job* 98
Brustein, R. *Nobody Dies on Friday* 98
Cromelin, C., Nightengale, E., Read, M., Reiss, K.,
Taber, T., and Wherry, T. *Man in the Flying Lawn
Chair* 2000
Grant, D. *Snakebit* 98
Guirgis, S. *Jesus Hopped the "A" Train* 2000
Hanan, S., and Berkow, J. *Jolson & Company* 2000
Hatcher, J. *What Corbin Knew* 99
Hollinger, M. *Tiny Island* 99
Holtzman, W. *Hearts* 99
Jackson, N. *A Hotel on Marvin Gardens* 99
Letts, T. *Killer Joe* 98
Lewis, C. *The One-eyed Man Is King* 98
Miller, J. *Bobby Supreme* 98
Mori, B. *Adult Fiction* 2000
Nigro, D. *Quint and Miss Jessel at Bly* 2000
Smith, C. *Knock Me a Kiss* 2000
Smith, E. *The Uneasy Chair* 98
Svich, C. *Prodigal Kiss* 99
Wilner, S. *Hunger* 99

NEWS *New Road*. Edited by Fred Marnau, Alex Comfort, John Bayliss. 1943–1947. London: Grey Walls Press, 1943–1947. 5 vols.
Carroll, P. *The Strings, My Lord, Are False* 1
Gardiner, W. *The Last Refuge* 1

NEWT *New Swedish Plays*. Edited by Gunilla M. Anderman. Norwich: Norvik Press, 1992. 212pp.
Bergman, I. *A Matter of the Soul*
Larsson, S. *Red Light*
Norén, L. *Munich-Athens*
Pleijel, A. *Summer Nights*

NEWV *New Voices in the American Theatre*. Foreword by Brooks Atkinson. New York: Modern Library [c1955] 559pp.
Anderson, R. *Tea and Sympathy*
Axelrod, G. *The Seven Year Itch*
Inge, W. *Come Back, Little Sheba*
Miller, A. *Death of a Salesman*
Williams, T. *A Streetcar Named Desire*
Wouk, H. *The Caine Mutiny Court-martial*

NEWWD *New Welsh Drama*. Cardiff, Wales: Parthian Books, 1998–2006. 3 vols.
Davies, L. *My Piece of Happiness* 1
Davies, L. *Sex and Power at the Beau Rivage* 3
Evans, S. *Little Sister* 2
Malik, A. *Safar* 1
Ross, L., and Morgan, C. *Inside Out* 3
Smith, O. *Giant Steps* 2
Williams, R. *Gulp* 1
Williams, R. *Killing Kangaroos* 2

NEWWP *New Woman Plays*. Edited and introduced by Linda Fitzsimmons and Viv Gardner. London: Methuen Drama, 1991. 189pp.
Baker, E. *Chains*
Bell, F., and Robins, E. *Alan's Wife*
Hamilton, C. *Diana of Dobson's*
Sowerby, G. *Rutherford and Son*

NEWWT *The New Women's Theatre: 10 Plays by Contemporary American Women*. Edited by Honor Moore. New York: Vintage, 1977. 537pp.
Childress, A. *Wedding Band: A Love/hate Story in Black and White*
Howe, T. *Birth and After Birth*
Jacker, C. *Bits and Pieces*
Kraus, J. *The Ice Wolf: A Tale of the Eskimos*
Lamb, M. *I Lost a Pair of Gloves Yesterday*
Merriam, E., Wagner, P., and Hoffsiss, J. *Out of Our Fathers' House*
Molinaro, U. *Breakfast Past Noon*
Moore, H. *Mourning Pictures*

Russ, J. *Window Dressing*
Wolff, R. *The Abdication*

NEWWUX *New Works 1*. Compiled by the Playwrights Union of Canada. Toronto: Playwrights Canada, 1987. 548pp.
Albert, L. *The Prairie Church of Buster Galloway*
Friesen, P. *The Shunning*
McKinlay, M. *Walt and Roy*
McRae, M. *Visiting Hours*
Mitchell, N. *House*

NEW WORLD LITERATURE SERIES, v 1. *See* MONR Moody, Richard, ed. *Dramas from the American Theatre, 1762–1909.*

NEWWW *New World Writing*. New York: New American Library, 1952–1956. 10 vols.
Bellow, S. *The Wrecker* 6
Bercovici, E. *The Heart of Age* 4
Brunson, B. *A Bastard of the Blood* 10
Denney, R. *September Lemonade* 7
Eberhart, R. *The Visionary Farms* 3
García Lorca, F. *The Tragi-comedy of Don Cristobita and Doña Rosita* 8
Ionesco, E. *The Bald Soprano* 9
MacDonagh, D. *Happy as Larry* 6
Meldon, M. *Purple Path to the Poppy Fields* 5
Picasso, P. *Desire Trapped by the Tail* 2
Williams, T. *I Rise in Flame, Cried the Phoenix* 1

NIC Nicoll, Allardyce, ed. *Lesser English Comedies of the Eighteenth Century*. London: Oxford University Press [1927] 537pp. (The World's Classics)
Colman, G. *The Jealous Wife*
Inchbald, E. *Every One Has His Fault*
Morton, T. *Speed the Plough*
Murphy, A. *The Way to Keep Him*
Reynolds, F. *The Dramatist*

NINE GREEK DRAMAS. *See* HARC *Harvard Classics, v8.*

NIL *Nine Plays of the Modern Theater with an Introduction by Harold Clurman*. New York: Grove Press, 1981. 896pp.
Beckett, S. *Waiting for Godot*
Brecht, B. *The Caucasian Chalk Circle*
Dürrenmatt, F. *The Visit*
Genêt, J. *The Balcony*
Ionesco, E. *Rhinoceros*
Mamet, D. *American Buffalo*
Mrozek, S. *Tango*
Pinter, H. *The Birthday Party*
Stoppard, T. *Rosencrantz and Guildenstern Are Dead*

NILS *Nineteenth-Century American Plays*. Edited by
Myronw Matlaw. New York: Applause Theatre
Book Publishers, 1985. 270pp. [Originally appeared
in, and is reprinted from, *The Black Crook* —
MASW]
Boucicault, D. *The Octoroon; or, Life in Louisiana*
Herne, J. *Margaret Fleming*
Jefferson, J. *Rip Van Winkle*
Mowatt, A. *Fashion; or, Life in New York*

NIN *Nineteenth-Century Shakespeare Burlesques*. Selected
by Stanley Wells. London: Diploma Press, 1977.
5 vols.
A-Beckett, G. *King John, with the Benefit of the Act* 2
Bangs, J. *Katharine: A Travesty* 5
Beckington, C. *Hamlet the Dane, a Burlesque Burletta* 2
Bell, R. *Macbeth Modernised* 2
Brough, W. *Perdita, or, the Royal Milkmaid* 3
Brougham, J. *Much Ado about a Merchant of Venice* 5
Burnand, F. *Antony and Cleopatra, or, His-tory and
Her-story in a Modern Nilo-metre* 4
Burnand, F. *The Rise and Fall of Richard III; or, a New
Front to an Old Dicky* 4
By, W. *Richard III Travestie* 1
Dowling, M. *Othello Travestie* 2
Dowling, M. *Romeo and Juliet, as the Law Directs* 2
Gilbert, W. *Rosencrantz and Guildenstern* 4
Griffin, G. *Hamlet the Dainty* 5
Griffin, G. *Othello* 5
Griffin, G. *Shylock* 5
Gurney, R. *Romeo and Juliet Travesty* 1
Halliday, A. *Romeo and Juliet Travestie; or, the Cup of
Cold Poison* 3
*Hamlet! The Ravin' Prince of Denmark!!; or, the Baltic
Swell!!! and the Diving Belle!!!* 4
Hilton, A. *Hamlet; or, Not such a Fool as He Looks* 4
*Julius Caesar Travestie* 4
*King Richard III Travestie* 1
Lloyd, H. *Rummio and Judy; or, Oh, This Love! This
Love! This Love!* 2
*Orlando Ye Brave and Ye Fayre Rosalynd; or, "As You
Lump It!"* 4
Poole, J. *Hamlet Travestie* 1
Poole, J. *Ye Comedie of Errours* 5
Rice, G. *Hamlet, Prince of Denmark* 5
Selby, C. *Kinge Richard ye Third; or, Ye Battel of
Bosworth Field* 2
Soule, C. *Hamlet Revamped; a Travesty without a
Pun* 5
Talfourd, P. *Hamlet Travestie* 3
Talfourd, F. *Macbeth, Somewhat Removed from the
Text of Shakespeare* 3
Talfourd, F. *Shylock; or, The Merchant of Venice
Preserved* 3
*A Thin Slice of Ham Let!* 4

NOEL Noel, Keith, ed. *Caribbean Plays for Playing*.
London: Heinemann, 1985. 163pp.
Bully, A. *Good Morning, Miss Millie*
Constance, Z. *The Ritual*
Hippolyte, K. *The Drum-maker*
Scott, D. *The Crime of Anabel Campbell*

NOH *'Noh', or Accomplishment: A Study of the Classical
Stage of Japan* by Ernest Francisco Fenellosa
and Ezra Pound. Gretna, LA: Pelican Publishing
Company, 1999. 268pp. (Originally published
London: Macmillan, 1916.)
*Hagoromo*
Kongo, Y. *Genjo*
Motokiyo, S. *Kagekiyo*
Motokiyo, S. *Kakitsubata*
Motokiyo, S. *Kinuta*
Motokiyo, S. *Nishikigi*
Nobumitsu, K. *Chorio*
*Shojo*
*Tamura*
*Tsunemasa*
Ujinobu, Z. *Awoi no uye*
Ujinobu, Z. *Kumasaka*

NOR Northup, George T., ed. *Ten Spanish Farces of the
16th, 17th, and 18th Centuries*. Westport, CT:
Greenwood, 1974. 231pp.
Benavente, Q. de. *El doctor y el enfermo*
*Los buñuelos*
Cervantes, M. *La cueva de Salamanca*
Cervantes, M. *Extremés de refranes* (atribuído a)
Cervantes, M. *Los dos habladores* (atribuído a)
Cruz, R. de la. *Las tertulias de Madrid*
*Extremés del espejo y burla de Pablillos*
*El hambriento*
*Juan Rana Comilón*
Rueda, L. de. *Paso séptimo*

NORALW *The Norton Anthology of Literature by Women:
The Traditions in English*. Edited by Sandra Gilbert
and Susan Gubar. New York: W.W. Norton & Co.,
1985. 2457pp.
Glaspell, S. *Trifles*
Gregory, I. *Spreading the News*

NORALWA *The Norton Anthology of Literature by
Women: The Tradition in English*. Edited by Sandra
Gilbert and Susan Gubar. 2nd ed. New York: W.W.
Norton & Co., 1996. 2452pp.
Churchill, C. *Top Girls*
Glaspell, S. *Trifles*
Gregory, I. *Spreading the News*
Millay, E. *Aria da Capo*

NORG *The Norton Anthology of World Masterpieces.*
    Maynard Mack, General Editor. 4th Continental ed.
    New York: W. W. Norton, 1980. 2601pp.

Aeschylus. *Agamemnon*
Aristophanes. *Lysistrata*
Calderón de la Barca, P. *Life Is a Dream*
Euripides. *Hippolytus*
Euripides. *Medea*
Marlowe, C. *The Tragical History of the Life and Death of Doctor Faustus*
Shakespeare, W. *Hamlet, Prince of Denmark*
Sophocles. *Antigone*
Sophocles. *Oedipus Tyrannus*

NORGA *The Norton Anthology of World Masterpieces.*
    Maynard Mack, General Editor. 5th Continental ed.
    New York: W. W. Norton, 1987. 2661pp.

Aeschylus. *Agamemnon*
Aristophanes. *Lysistrata*
Beckett, S. *Endgame*
Brecht, B. *Mother Courage and Her Children*
Büchner, G. *Woyzeck*
Chekhov, A. *The Cherry Orchard*
Calderón de la Barca, P. *Life Is a Dream*
Duras, M. *Hiroshima, mon amour*
Euripides. *Medea*
Goethe, J. *Faust, Part I*
Ibsen, H. *Hedda Gabler*
Molière, J. *Tartuffe*
Pirandello, L. *Six Characters in Search of an Author*
Racine, J. *Phaedra*
Sophocles. *Oedipus the King*
Soyinka, W. *The Lion and the Jewel*

NORI *The Norton Anthology of World Masterpieces.*
    4th ed. Maynard Mack, General Editor. New
    York: W. W. Norton & Co., 1979. 2 vols. (Vol.
    1: Literature of Western Culture through the
    Renaissance; Vol. 2: Literature of Western Culture
    since the Renaissance)

Aeschylus. *Agamemnon* 1
Aeschylus. *Prometheus Bound* 1
Aristophanes. *Lysistrata* 1
Brecht, B. *Mother Courage and Her Children* 2
Büchner, G. *Woyzeck* 2
Calderón de la Barca, P. *Life Is a Dream* 1
Chekhov, A. *The Cherry Orchard* 2
Euripides. *Hippolytus* 1
Euripides. *Medea* 1
Ibsen, H. *Hedda Gabler* 2
Molière, J. *Tartuffe, or The Imposter* 2
Pirandello, L. *Henry IV* 2
Racine, J. *Phaedra* 2
Sartre, J. *No Exit (Huis clos)* 2

Sophocles. *Antigone* 1
Sophocles. *Oedipus tyrannus* 1
Strindberg, A. *The Ghost Sonata* 2

NORIA *The Norton Anthology of World Masterpieces.*
    Maynard Mack, General Editor. 5th ed. New York:
    Norton, 1985. 2 vols. (Vol. 1: Literature of Western
    Culture through the Renaissance; Vol. 2: Literature
    of Western Culture since the Renaissance)

Aeschylus. *Agamemnon* 1
Aeschylus. *The Eumenides* 1
Aeschylus. *The Libation Bearers* 1
Aristophanes. *Lysistrata* 1
Beckett, S. *Endgame* 2
Brecht, B. *Mother Courage and Her Children* 2
Chekhov, A. *The Cherry Orchard* 2
Euripides. *Medea* 1
*Everyman* 1
Goethe, J. *Faust, Part I* 2
Ibsen, H. *Hedda Gabler* 2
Marlowe, C. *The Tragical History of the Life and Death of Doctor Faustus* 1
Molière, J. *Tartuffe* 2
Pirandello, L. *Six Characters in Search of an Author* 2
Racine, J. *Phaedra* 2
Shakespeare, W. *Hamlet, Prince of Denmark* 1
Sophocles. *Antigone* 1
Sophocles. *Oedipus Rex* 1
Soyinka, W. *The Lion and the Jewel* 2

NORIB *The Norton Anthology of World Masterpieces.*
    Maynard Mack, General Editor. 6th ed. New York:
    W. W. Norton, 1992. 2 vols. (Vol. 1: Literature
    of Western Culture through the Renaissance;
    Vol. 2: Literature of Western Culture since the
    Renaissance)

Aeschylus. *Agamemnon* 1
Aeschylus. *The Eumenides* 1
Aeschylus. *The Libation Bearers* 1
Aristophanes. *Lysistrata* 1
Beckett, S. *Endgame* 2
Brecht, B. *Mother Courage and Her Children* 2
Calderon de la Barca, P. *Life Is a Dream* 1
Chekhov, A. *The Cherry Orchard* 2
Duras, M. *Hiroshima, mon amour* 2
Euripides. *Medea* 1
Goethe, J. *Faust, Part I* 2
Ibsen, H. *Hedda Gabler* 2
Marlowe, C. *The Tragical History of the Life and Death of Dr. Faustus* 1
Molière, J. *Tartuffe* 2
Pirandello, L. *Six Characters in Search of an Author* 2
Racine, J. *Phaedra* 2
Shakespeare, W. *Hamlet, Prince of Denmark* 1

Sophocles. *Antigone* 1
Sophocles. *Oedipus the King* 1

NORIC *The Norton Anthology of World Masterpieces.*
Sarah Lawall, General Editor; Maynard Mack,
General Editor Emiritus. 7th ed. New York: W. W.
Norton, 1997. 2 vols. (Vol. 1: Literature of Western
Culture through the Renaissance; Vol. 2: Literature
of Western Culture since the Renaissance)
Aeschylus. *Agamemnon* 1
Aeschylus. *The Eumenides* 1
Aristophanes. *Lysistrata* 1
Beckett, S. *Endgame* 2
Brecht, B. *The Good Woman of Setzuan* 2
Chekhov, A. *The Cherry Orchard* 2
Euripides. *Medea* 1
*Everyman* 1
Goethe, J. *Faust, Part I* 2
Ibsen, H. *Hedda Gabler* 2
Molière, J. *Tartuffe* 2
Pirandello, L. *Six Characters in Search of an Author* 2
Plautus. *Pseudolus* 1
Racine, J. *Phaedra* 2
Shakespeare, W. *Othello* 1
Sophocles. *Oedipus the King* 1
Vega Carpio, L. *Fuente ovejuna* 1

NORJ *The Norton Anthology of World Masterpieces.*
Maynard Mack, General Editor. Expanded ed. New
York: W. W. Norton, 1995. 2 vols.
Aeschylus. *Agamemnon* 1
Aeschylus. *The Eumenides* 1
al-Hakim, T. *The Sultan's Dilemma* 2
Aristophanes. *Lysistrata* 1
Beckett, S. *Endgame* 2
Brecht, B. *Mother Courage and Her Children* 2
Calderon de la Barca, P. *Life Is a Dream* 1
Chekhov, A. *The Cherry Orchard* 2
Euripides. *Medea* 1
*Everyman* 1
Goethe, J. *Faust, Part I* 2
Ibsen, H. *Hedda Gabler* 2
Kanze, K. *Dōjōji* 1
K'ung, S. *The Peach Blossom Fan* (excerpts) 2
Marlowe, C. *The Tragical History of the Life and Death
of Dr. Faustus* 1
Molière, J. *Tartuffe* 2
Pirandello, L. *Six Characters in Search of an Author* 2
Racine, J. *Phaedra* 2
Shakespeare, W. *Hamlet, Prince of Denmark* 1
Sophocles. *Antigone* 1
Sophocles. *Oedipus the King* 1
Soyinka, W. *Death and the King's Horseman* 2
Walcott, D. *Dream on Monkey Mountain* 2

Zeami. *Atsumori* 1
Zeami. *Haku rakuten* 1

NORJA *The Norton Anthology of World Masterpieces.*
Maynard Mack, General Editor. Expanded ed.
in one volume. New York: W. W. Norton, 1997.
3052pp.
Aeschylus. *Agamemnon*
Aristophanes. *Lysistrata*
Brecht, B. *Mother Courage and Her Children*
Chekhov, A. *The Cherry Orchard*
Euripides. *Medea*
Goethe, J. *Faust, Part I*
Ibsen, H. *Hedda Gabler*
Kanze, K. *Dōjōji*
Molière, J. *Tartuffe*
Pirandello, L. *Six Characters in Search of an Author*
Racine, J. *Phaedra*
Shakespeare, W. *Hamlet, Prince of Denmark*
Sophocles. *Oedipus the King*

NOTH Nothof, Anne, ed. *Ethnicities: Plays from the New
West.* Edmonton: NeWest Press, 1999. 198pp.
Chan, M. *Mom, Dad, I'm Living with a White Girl*
Christenson, J., and Tremblay, J. *Elephant Wake*
Visawanathan, P. *House of Sacred Cows*

NOY Noyes, George Rapall, ed. and tr. *Masterpieces of
the Russian Drama.* New York: Appleton-Century,
1933. 902pp.
Andreyev, L. *Professor Storitsyn*
Chekhov, A. *The Cherry Orchard*
Fonvízin, D. *The Young Hopeful*
Gogol, N. *The Inspector*
Gorky, M. *Down and Out*
Griboyedov, A. *Wit Works Woe*
Mayakóvsky, V. *Mystery-Bouffe*
Ostrovsky, A. *The Poor Bride*
Pisemsky, A. *A Bitter Fate*
Tolstoy, A. *The Death of Ivan the Terrible*
Tolstoy, L. *The Power of Darkness*
Turgenev, I. *A Month in the Country*

NTIR Ntiri, Daphne Williams, ed. *Roots and Blossoms:
African American Plays for Today.* Troy, MI:
Bedford Publishers, Inc., 1991. 619pp.
Carew, J. *Black Horse, Pale Rider*
Flanagan, B. *When the Jumbie Bird Calls*
Harris, B. *Up and Gone Again*
Ibe, S. *The Last of Ala*
Johnson, F. *The Right Reason*
Kai, N. *The Last of the Reapers*
Mwansa, D. *The Family Question*
Onwueme, T. *Parables for a Season*

Phiri, M. *Waiting for Sanctions*
Purdue, R. *Family Reunion*
Redmond, E. *A Funky-grace*
Washington, V. *The Operation*
Wideman, A. *The Hard to Serve*

OAM Oates, Whitney Jennings, and Murphy, Charles
      Theophilus, eds. *Greek Literature in Translation.*
      New York: Longmans, Green, 1944. 1072pp.
Aeschylus. *Agamemnon*
Aeschylus. *The Eumenides*
Aeschylus. *Prometheus Bound*
Aristophanes. *Lysistrata*
Euripides. *The Bacchae*
Euripides. *Hippolytus*
Menander. *The Arbitration*
Sophocles. *Antigone*
Sophocles. *Oedipus the King*

OAT Oates, Whitney Jennings, and O'Neill, Eugene
      Gladstone, eds. *The Complete Greek Drama.* New
      York: Random House [c1938] 2 vols.
Aeschylus. *Agamemnon 1*
Aeschylus. *The Choephori 1*
Aeschylus. *The Eumenides 1*
Aeschylus. *The Persians 1*
Aeschylus. *Prometheus Bound 1*
Aeschylus. *The Seven against Thebes 1*
Aeschylus. *The Suppliants 1*
Aristophanes. *The Acharnians 2*
Aristophanes. *The Birds 2*
Aristophanes. *The Clouds 2*
Aristophanes. *The Ecclesiazusae 2*
Aristophanes. *The Frogs 2*
Aristophanes. *The Knights 2*
Aristophanes. *Lysistrata 2*
Aristophanes. *Peace 2*
Aristophanes. *Plutus 2*
Aristophanes. *Thesmophoriazusae 2*
Aristophanes. *The Wasps 2*
Euripides. *Alcestis 1*
Euripides. *Andromache 1*
Euripides. *The Bacchae 2*
Euripides. *The Cyclops 2*
Euripides. *Electra 2*
Euripides. *Hecuba 1*
Euripides. *Helen 2*
Euripides. *The Heracleidae 1*
Euripides. *Heracles 1*
Euripides. *Hippolytus 1*
Euripides. *Ion 1*
Euripides. *Iphigenia in Aulis 2*
Euripides. *Iphigenia in Tauris 1*
Euripides. *Medea 1*
Euripides. *Orestes 2*

Euripides. *The Phoenissae 2*
Euripides. *Rhesus 2*
Euripides. *The Suppliants 1*
Euripides. *The Trojan Women 1*
Menander. *The Arbitration 2*
Menander. *The Girl from Samos 2*
Menander. *The Shearing of Glycera 2*
Sophocles. *Ajax 1*
Sophocles. *Antigone 1*
Sophocles. *Electra 1*
Sophocles. *Oedipus at Colonus 1*
Sophocles. *Oedipus the King 1*
Sophocles. *Philoctetes 1*
Sophocles. *The Trachiniae 1*

OATH Oates, Whitney Jennings, and O'Neill, Eugene,
      Jr., eds. *Seven Famous Greek Plays.* New York:
      Modern Library [c1950] 446pp. (Modern Library
      College Editions)
Aeschylus. *Agamemnon*
Aeschylus. *Prometheus Bound*
Aristophanes. *The Frogs*
Euripides. *Alcestis*
Euripides. *Medea*
Sophocles. *Antigone*
Sophocles. *Oedipus the King*

OBERUFER, CHRISTMAS PLAYS FROM. *See* HARW
      Harwood, A. C., tr.

OBG *The Obie Winners: The Best of Off-Broadway.*
      Edited by Ross Wetzsteon. New York: Doubleday,
      1980. 803pp.
Beckett, S. *Krapp's Last Tape*
Gelber, J. *The Connection*
Genêt, J. *The Blacks*
Horovitz, I. *The Indian Wants the Bronx*
McNally, T. *Bad Habits*
Mamet, D. *American Buffalo*
Rabe, D. *The Basic Training of Pavlo Hummel*
Shepard, S. *The Tooth of Crime*
Wilson, L. *The Hot L Baltimore*
Zindel, P. *The Effect of Gamma Rays on Man-in-the-*
      *moon Marigolds*

OBI Obiechina, Emmanuel N., ed. *Onitsha Market*
      *Literature.* London: Heinemann, 1972. 182pp.
Okonkwo, R. *The Game of Love*

OBSE *The Observer Plays.* With a preface by Kenneth
      Tynan. London: Faber and Faber [c1958] 475pp.
Beynon, R. *The Shifting Heart*
Campbell, M., and Athas, D. *Sit on the Earth*
Cavan, R. *All My Own Work*
Davis, A. *Four Men, a Tragicomedy*
Jellicoe, A. *The Sport of My Mad Mother*

John, E. *Moon on a Rainbow Shawl*
Simpson, N. *A Resounding Tinkle*

O'CONNOR, JOSEPH. *See* GRE *Great Plays (English).*

OCONNC O'Connor, Patricia W., ed. *Contemporary Spanish Theater: The Social Comedies of the Sixties.* Madrid: Sociedad General Española de Libreria, S.A., 1983. 255pp.
Gala, A. *The Green Fields of Eden*
Mihura, M. *Ninette and a Gentleman from Murcia*
Paso, A. *The Necktie*

OCONNF O'Connor, Patricia W., ed. *Plays of Protest from the Franco Era.* Madrid: Sociedad General Española de Libreria, S.A., 1981. 263pp.
Buero Vallejo, A. *The Basement Window*
Martínez Mediero, M. *The Guest*
Muñiz, C. *The Inkwell*
Olmo, L. *The Shirt*

OCONNP O'Connor, Patricia W., ed. *Plays of the New Democratic Spain (1975–1990).* Lanham, MD: University Press of America, 1992. 482pp.
Alonso de Santos, J. *Going Down to Marrakesh*
Buero Vallejo, A. *Lazarus in the Labyrinth*
Fernán Gómez, F. *Bikes Are for Summer*
Jardiel Poncela, E. *Eloise Is under an Almond Tree*
Salom, J. *Bitter Lemon*
Sirera, R. *The Audition*

OFF *Off Broadway Plays.* Harmondsworth, Middlesex: Penguin. 1971–1972. 2 vols.
Dizenzo, C. *The Drapes Come* 1
Dizenzo, C. *An Evening for Merlin Finch* 1
Guare, J. *Cop-out* 1
Guare, J. *Muzeeka* 1
Horovitz, I. *The Indian Wants the Bronx* 1
Horovitz, I. *It's Called the Sugar Plum* 1
Kopit, A. *Oh Dad, Poor Dad, Momma's Hung You in the Closet and I'm Feeling So Sad* 1
McNally, T. *Botticelli* 2
McNally, T. *Sweet Eros* 2
Peluso, E. *Good Day* 2
Peluso, E. *Little Fears* 2
Shepard, S. *The Holy Ghostly* 2
Shepard, S. *Red Cross* 2
Weller, M. *The Bodybuilders* 2
Weller, M. *Now There's Just the Three of Us* 2

OHL Ohlsen, Woodrow, and Hammond, Frank L., eds. *Frames of Reference: An Introduction to Literature.* Belmont, CA: Wadsworth Pub., 1974. 399pp.
Anderson, M. *Anne of the Thousand Days*
Arrabal, F. *Picnic on the Battlefield*

Ibsen, H. *An Enemy of the People*
Vidal, G. *Visit to a Small Planet*

OLH Oliphant, Ernest Henry Clark, ed. *Elizabethan Dramatists Other than Shakespeare.* New York: Prentice-Hall, 1931. 1511pp.
*Arden of Feversham*
Beaumont, F., and Fletcher, J. *The Knight of the Burning Pestle*
Beaumont, F., and Fletcher, J. *The Maid's Tragedy*
Beaumont, F., and Fletcher, J. *Philaster*
Brome, R. *A Jovial Crew*
Dekker, T. *The Honest Whore, Part II*
Drayton, M. *The Merry Devil of Edmonton*
Ford, J. *The Broken Heart*
Greene, R. *Friar Bacon and Friar Bungay*
Heywood, T. *A Woman Killed with Kindness*
Jonson, B. *The Alchemist*
Jonson, B. *Bartholomew Fair*
Jonson, B. *Volpone*
Jonson, B., Chapman, G., and Marston, J. *Eastward Hoe!*
Kyd, T. *The Spanish Tragedy*
Lyly, J. *Campaspe*
Marlowe, C. *Edward II*
Marlowe, C. *Faustus*
Massinger, P. *A New Way to Pay Old Debts*
Middleton, T. *Women, Beware Women*
Middleton, T., and Rowley, W. *The Changeling*
Milton, J. *Comus*
Peele, G. *The Old Wives' Tale*
Porter, H. *The Two Angry Women of Abington*
Rowley, W., and Middleton, T. *A Fair Quarrel*
Shirley, J. *The Traitor*
Tourneur, C. *The Revenger's Tragedy*
Webster, J. *The Duchess of Malfi*
Webster, J. *The White Devil*
*A Yorkshire Tragedy*

OLI Oliphant, Ernest Henry Clark, ed. *Shakespeare and His Fellow Dramatists.* New York: Prentice-Hall, 1929. 2 vols.
*Arden of Feversham* 1
Beaumont, F., and Fletcher, J. *The Knight of the Burning Pestle* 2
Beaumont, F., and Fletcher, J. *The Maid's Tragedy* 2
Beaumont, F., and Fletcher, J. *Philaster* 2
Brome, R. *A Jovial Crew* 2
Dekker, T. *The Honest Whore, Part II* 1
Drayton, M. *The Merry Devil of Edmonton* 1
Ford, J. *The Broken Heart* 2
Greene, R. *Friar Bacon and Friar Bungay* 1
Heywood, T. *A Woman Killed with Kindness* 1
Jonson, B. *The Alchemist* 2
Jonson, B. *Bartholomew Fair* 2

Jonson, B. *Volpone* 1
Jonson, B., Chapman, G., and Marston, J. *Eastward Hoe!* 1
Kyd, T. *The Spanish Tragedy* 1
Lyly, J. *Campaspe* 1
Marlowe, C. *Edward II* 1
Marlowe, C. *Faustus* 1
Massinger, P. *A New Way to Pay Old Debts* 2
Middleton, T. *Women, Beware Women* 2
Middleton, T., and Rowley, W. *The Changeling* 2
Milton, J. *Comus* 2
Peele, G. *The Old Wives' Tale* 1
Porter, H. *The Two Angry Women of Abington* 1
Rowley, W., and Middleton, T. *A Fair Quarrel* 2
Shakespeare, W. *Antony and Cleopatra* 2
Shakespeare, W. *As You like It* 1
Shakespeare, W. *Coriolanus* 2
Shakespeare, W. *Cymbeline* 2
Shakespeare, W. *Hamlet* 1
Shakespeare, W. *Henry IV, Part* 1
Shakespeare, W. *Julius Caesar* 1
Shakespeare, W. *King Lear* 1
Shakespeare, W. *Macbeth* 2
Shakespeare, W. *The Merchant of Venice* 1
Shakespeare, W. *A Midsummer Night's Dream* 1
Shakespeare, W. *Othello* 1
Shakespeare, W. *Romeo and Juliet* 1
Shakespeare, W. *Twelfth Night* 1
Shakespeare, W. *The Winter's Tale* 2
Shirley, J. *The Traitor* 2
Tourneur, C. *The Revenger's Tragedy* 2
Webster, J. *The Duchess of Malfi* 2
Webster, J. *The White Devil* 2
*A Yorkshire Tragedy* 2

OLIV Oliver, Clinton S., and Sills, Stephanie, eds. *Contemporary Black Drama.* New York: Scribner, 1970. 360pp.
Baldwin, J. *Blues for Mr. Charlie*
Bullins, E. *Gentleman Caller*
Davis, O. *Purlie Victorious*
Gordone, C. *No Place to Be Somebody*
Hansberry, L. *A Raisin in the Sun*
Jones, L. *Dutchman*
Kennedy, A. *Funnyhouse of a Negro*
Ward, D. *Day of Absence*
Ward, D. *Happy Ending*

OLIW Oliver, William Irvin, ed. and tr. *Voices of Change in the Spanish American Theater.* Austin, TX: University of Texas Press. 1971. 294pp.
Buenaventura, E. *In the Right Hand of God the Father*
Carbillido, E. *The Day They Let the Lions Loose*
Gambargo, G. *The Camp*
Hernández, L. *The Mullatto's Orgy*

Maggi, C. *The Library*
Vodāhovic, S. *Three Beach Plays*

ONE *One Woman, One Voice: Plays by Sharon Morgan, Christine Watkins, Lucy Gough, Lucinda Coxon, Gwenno Dafydd.* Edited by Hazel Walford Davies. Cardiff: Parthian Books, 2000. 213pp.
Coxon, L. *I Am Angela Brazil*
Dafydd, G. *No Regrets*
Gough, L. *Red Room*
Gough, L. *The Trail*
Morgan, S. *Magic Threads*
Watkins, C. *Queen of Hearts*
Watkins, C. *Welcome to My World*

OPE *Open Theater: Three Works by the Open Theater.* New York: Drama Book Specialists/Publishers, 1974. 191pp.
Open Theater. *The Mutation Show*
Open Theater. *Nightwalk*
Yankowitz, S. *Terminal*

ORI *Oriental Literature.* Rev. ed. New York: Colonial Press [c1960] 4 vols. (The World's Great Classics)
*Abstraction* 2
Kāhdāsa. *Sakoontalā* 3
Seami, M. *Nakamitsu* 2
*The Sorrows of Han* 4

ORK Orkin, Martin, ed. *At the Junction: Four Plays by the Junction Avenue Theatre Company.* Johannesburg: Witwatersrand University Press, 1995. 300pp.
Junction Avenue Theatre Company. *The Fantastical History of a Useless Man*
Junction Avenue Theatre Company. *Randlords and Rotgut*
Junction Avenue Theatre Company. *Sophiatown*
Junction Avenue Theatre Company. *Tooth and Nail*

ORNC Ornstein, Robert, and Spencer, Hazelton, eds. *Elizabethan and Jacobean Comedy.* Boston, Heath [1964] 315pp. (A Companion Volume to the Editors' Elizabethan and Jacobean Tragedy.)
Beaumont, F. *The Knight of the Burning Pestle*
Dekker, T. *The Shoemaker's Holiday*
Gascoine, G. *Supposes*
Greene, R. *Friar Bacon and Friar Bungay*
Jonson, B. *The Alchemist*
Jonson, B. *Every Man in His Humour*
Lyly, J. *Endymion, the Man in the Moon*
Massinger, P. *A New Way to Pay Old Debts*

ORNT Ornstein, Robert, and Spencer, Hazelton, eds. *Elizabethan and Jacobean Tragedy.* Boston: Heath

[1964] 308pp. (A Companion Volume to the
Editors' *Elizabethan and Jacobean Comedy*.)
Chapman, G. *Bussy D'Ambois*
Ford, J. *The Broken Heart*
Kyd, T. *The Spanish Tragedy*
Marlowe, C. *The Tragical History of Doctor Faustus*
Middleton, T. and Rowley, W. *The Changeling*
Webster, J. *The White Devil*

ORT Ortego, Philip D., comp. *We Are Chicanos*. New
York: Washington Square Press, 1973. 330pp.
Portillo, E. *The Day of the Swallows*

ORZ Orzel, Nick, and Smith, Michael, eds. *Eight Plays
from Off-Broadway*. Indianapolis, IN: Bobbs,
Merrill, 1966. 281pp.
Fornés, M. *The Successful Life of Three: A Skit for
Vaudeville*
Foster, P. *Balls*
O'Hara, F. *The General Returns from One Place to
Another*
Oppenheimer, J. *The Great American Desert*
Shepard, S. *Chicago*
Terry, M. *Calm Down, Mother*
Van Itallie, J. *America Hurrah*
Wilson, L. *The Madness of Lady Bright*

OSB Osborn, M. Elizabeth, ed. *On New Ground:
Contemporary Hispanic-American Plays*. New
York: Theatre Communications Group, 1987.
280pp.
Alvarez, L. *The Guitarron*
Fornes, M. *The Conduct of Life*
Jesurun, J. *White Water*
Machado, E. *Broken Eggs*
Rivera, J. *The House of Ramon Iglesia*
Sanchez-Scott, M. *Roosters*

OSBW Osborn, M. Elizabeth, ed. *The Way We Live Now:
American Plays & the AIDS Crisis*. New York:
Theatre Communications Group, 1990. 279pp.
Durang, C. *Laughing Wild* (excerpt)
Fierstein, H. *Safe Sex*
Greenspan, D. *Jack*
Hoffman, W. *As Is*
Kondoleon, H. *Zero Positive*
Kushner, T. *Angels in America, Part I: Millennium
Approaches* (excerpt)
McNally, T. *Andre's Mother*
Parone, E. *The Way We Live Now*
Vogel, P. *The Baltimore Waltz* (excerpt)
Wilson, L. *A Poster of the Cosmos*

OSME Osment, Philip, ed. *Gay Sweatshop: Four Plays
and a Company*. London: Methuen, 1989. 148pp.

Greig, N. *The Dear Love of Comrades*
Kay, J. *Twice Over*
Kirby, A. *Compromised Immunity*
Osment, P. *This Island's Mine*

OULD Ould, Herman, ed. *The Book of the P.E.N.* London:
Arthur Barker [1950] 254pp.
Farjeon, E. *The Plane-tree*
Jameson, S. *William the Defeated*
Johnson, P. *The Duchess at Sunset*

OUT *Out from Under: Texts by Women Performance
Artists*. Edited by Lenora Champagne. New York:
Theatre Communications Group, 1990. 185pp.
Anderson, L. *United States*
Carlos, L., Hagedorn, J., and McCauley, R. *Teenytown*
Champagne, L. *Getting over Tom*
Finley, K. *The Constant State of Desire*
Hughes, H. *World without End*
Rosenthal, R. *My Brazil*
Roth, B. *The Father*
Sack, L. *The Survivor and the Translator*
Templeton, F. *Strange to Relate*

OWEC Owens, Cóilín, and Radner, Joan D., eds. *Irish
Drama, 1900–1980*. Washington, DC: Catholic
University of America Press, 1990. 754pp.
Beckett, S. *All that Fall*
Behan, B. *The Quare Fellow*
Clarke, A. *As the Crow Flies*
Colum, P. *The Land*
Fallon, P. *The Vision of Mac Conglinne*
Fitzmaurice, G. *The Magic Glasses*
Friel, B. *Translations*
Gregory, I. *The Gaol Gate*
Gregory, I. *Spreading the News*
Johnston, D. *The Old Lady Says, "No!"*
Leonard, H. *Da*
Molloy, M. *The Paddy Pedlar*
Murray, T. *Maurice Harte*
O'Casey, S. *Juno and the Paycock*
Robinson, L. *The Big House*
Synge, J. *The Playboy of the Western World*
Yeats, W. *On Baile's Strand*
Yeats, W. *The Only Jealousy of Emer*

OWER Owens, Rochelle, ed. *Spontaneous Combustion:
8 New American Plays*. New York: Winter House,
1972. 224pp. (Winter Repertory, 6)
Bovasso, J. *Schubert's Last Serenade*
Bullins, E. *Dialect Determinism*
Hoffman, W. *A Quick Nut Bread to Make Your Mouth
Water*
Jones, L. *Ba-Ra-Ka*
Kennedy, A. *Sun*

Melfi, L. *Cinque*
Owens, R. *He Wants Shih*
Terry, M. *Sanibel and Captiva*

OXF *Oxford Anthology of American Literature*. Chosen and edited by William Rose Benét and Norman Holmes Pearson. New York: Oxford University Press, 1938. 1705pp.
O'Neill, E. *Lazarus Laughed*

OXFC *The Oxford Anthology of Canadian Literature*. Edited by Robert L. Weaver and William Toye. Toronto, Oxford: 1973. 546pp.
Ryga, C. *Indian*

PAIS *The Paris Stage: Recent Plays*. New York: Ubu Repertory Theater Publications, 1988. 342pp.
Bouchaud, J. *A Birthday Present for Stalin*
Ribes, J. *The Rest Have Got It Wrong*
Tardieu, J. *The Sleepless City*
Tilly. *Trumpets of Death*
Vinaver, M. *The Neighbors*

PAJ Parker, John W., ed. *Adventures in Playmaking: 4 Plays by Carolina Playmakers*. Chapel Hill: University of North Carolina Press, c1968. 333pp.
Brower, B. *A Little to the Left*
Graves, R. *The Battle of the Carnival and Lent*
McDonald, C., and Mason, W. *Spring for Sure*
Niggli, J. *Singing Valley*

PAR Parks, Edd Winfield, and Beatty, Richard Croom, eds. *The English Drama: An Anthology, 900–1642*. New York: W. W. Norton, [c1935] 1495pp.
*Abraham and Isaac*
Beaumont, F., and Fletcher, J. *Philaster; or, Love Lies A-bleeding*
Daniel, S. *The Vision of the Twelve Goddesses*
Dekker, T. *The Shoemaker's Holiday*
*Everyman*
Fletcher, J., and Shakespeare, W. *Two Noble Kinsmen*
Ford, J. *'Tis Pity She's a Whore*
Greene, R. *The Honorable History of Friar Bacon and Friar Bungay*
Heywood, J. *A Merry Play between John John the Husband*
Heywood, T. *A Woman Killed with Kindness*
Jonson, B. *Every Man in His Humour*
Jonson, B. *Oberon, the Fairy Prince*
Jonson, B. *Sejanus, His Fall*
Jonson, B. *Volpone; or, the Fox*
Kyd, T. *The Spanish Tragedy*
Lyly, J. *Endymion*
Marlowe, C. *Edward II*

Marlowe, C. *The Jew of Malta*
Marlowe, C. *The Tragical History of Dr. Faustus*
Massinger, P. *A New Way to Pay Old Debts*
Milton, J. *Comus*
*Oxfordshire St. George Play*
Peele, G. *The Old Wives' Tale*
Plautus, T. *The miles gloriosus*
*The quem quaeritis*
*Robin Hood and the Friar*
*The Second Shepherds' Play*
Seneca, L. *Thyestes*
*Shetland Sword Dance*
Shirley, J. *The Cardinal*
Sidney, P. *The Lady of May*
Udall, N. *Ralph Roister Doister*
Webster, J. *The White Devil*

PARNASSUS PLAYS (1598–1601). *See* LEIS Leishman, J. B., ed.

PARR Parr, Anthony, ed. *Three Renaissance Travel Plays*. Manchester and New York: Manchester University Press, 1995. 330pp.
Brome, R. *The Antipodes*
Day, J., Rowley, W., and Wilkins, G. *The Travels of the Three English Brothers*
Fletcher, J., and Massinger, P. *The Sea Voyage*

PARRI *Del parricidio a la utopia: El teatro argentine actual en 4 claves mayors*. Ottawa: Girol Books, 1993. 196pp. (Teatro Contemporaneo 3)
Kartun, M. *Salto al cielo*
Monti, R. *Una noche con Magnus e hijos*
Perinelli, R. *Miembro del jurado*
Rovner, E. *Cuarteto*

PARRY Parry, W. Dyfed. *Old Plays for Modern Players*. London: Arnold [1930] 156pp.
*Abraham and Isaac*
Heywood, J. *The Four PPs*
Heywood, J. *The Play of the Weather*
Jonson, B. *Volpone; or, the Fox*
*Noah's Flood*
Peele, G. *The Old Wives' Tale*
*The Shepherds' Play*

PARV Patt, Beatrice P., and Nozick, Martin, eds. *The Generation of 1898 and After*. New York: Dodd, Mead, 1961. 427pp.
García Lorca, F. *La casa de Bernarda Alba*

PASS *Passions and Poisons: New Canadian Prose, Poetry, and Plays*. Montreal: Nu-Age Editions, 1987. 143pp.
Rossi, V. *Little Blood Brother*

PATM *Patterns of Literature*. Edited by Julian L. Maline
and James Berkley. New York: Singer-Random
House, 1967. 4 vol. (vol. 3, Dramatic Literature)
Chekhov, A. *The Boor* 3
Ibsen, H. *An Enemy of the People* 3
McCullers, C. *The Member of the Wedding* 3
Maeterlinck, M. *The Intruder* 3
Mukerji, D. *The Judgment of Indra* 3
Rostand, E. *The Romancers* 3
Seami, M. *The Dwarf Trees* 3
Shakespeare, W. *Macbeth* 3
Sophocles. *Antigone* 3
Synge, J. *Riders to the Sea* 3

PATP *Patterns of Literature*. Edited by James Berkley,
Dwight L. Burton, and John L. Simmons. New
York: Singer-Random House [1969] 734pp.
Anouilh, J. *Antigone*
McCullers, C. *The Member of the Wedding*
Mukerji, D. *The Judgment of Indra*
Seami, M. *The Dwarf Trees*
Shakespeare, W. *Macbeth*
Sophocles. *Antigone*
Synge, J. *Riders to the Sea*

PATR Patterson, Lindsay, [comp.] *Black Theatre: A 20th
Century Collection of the Best Playwrights*. New
York: Dodd, Mead, 1971. 493pp.
Baldwin, J. *The Amen Corner*
Bontemps, A., and Cullen, C. *The St. Louis Woman*
Branch, W. *In Splendid Error*
Bullins, E. *In the Wine Time*
Childress, A. *Trouble in Mind*
Davis, O. *Purlie Victorious*
Elder, L. *Ceremonies in Dark Old Men*
Gordone, C. *No Place to Be Somebody*
Hansberry, L. *A Raisin in the Sun*
Hughes, L. *Simply Heavenly*
Jones, L. *Dutchman*
Peterson, L. *Take a Giant Step*

PATT Pattison, Walter Thomas. *Representative Spanish
Authors*. New York: Oxford University Press, 1942.
2 vols. in 1
Rivas, A. *Don Alvaro; o, La fuerza del sino*
Rueda, L. *Paso séptimo: de las aceitunas*
Ruiz de Alarcón y Mendoza, J. *Las paredes oyen*

PEARSON, NORMAN HOLMES. *See* OXF *Oxford
Anthology of American Literature*. Edited by
William Rose Benét and Norman Holmes Pearson.

PEN Pence, Raymond Woodbury, ed. *Dramas by Present-
day Writers*. New York: Scribner [c1927] 690pp.

Bennett, A., and Knoblock, E. *Milestones*
Davies, M. *The Slave with Two Faces*
Drinkwater, J. *Cophetua*
Dunsany, E. *A Night at an Inn*
Galsworthy, J. *Loyalties*
Glaspell, S. *Trifles*
Gregory, I. *Spreading the News*
Jacobs, W. *A Love Passage*
Jones, H. *The Goal*
Kaufman, G., and Connelly, M. *Merton of the Movies*
Mackay, C. *Counsel Retained*
Morley, C. *Thursday Evening*
O'Neill, E. *"Ile"*
Sutro, A. *A Marriage Has Been Arranged*
Tarkington, B. *Monsieur Beaucaire*
Wilde, P. *Confessional*

PENG *Penguin Book of Modern Canadian Drama*. Edited
by Richard Plant. Markham, ON: Penguin Books
Canada Limited, 1984. 904pp.
Coulter, J. *Riel*
Freeman, D. *Creeps*
French, D. *Of the Fields, Lately*
Fruet, W. *Wedding in White*
Herbert, J. *Fortune and Men's Eyes*
Hollingsworth, M. *Ever Loving*
Pollock, S. *Blood Relations*
Reaney, J. *Handcuffs: (The Donnellys: Part Three)*
Ringwood, G. *Garage Sale*
Ryga, G. *Indian*
Stratton, A. *Rexy!*
Walker, G. *The Art of War*

PENNSYLVANIA GERMAN SOCIETY. *See* BUFF
Buffington, Albert F., ed. *The Richard Collection
of Early Pennsylvania German Plays*.

PER Perkins, Kathy A., ed. *Black Female Playwrights: An
Anthology of Plays before 1950*. Bloomington, IN:
Indiana University Press, 1989. 288pp.
Bonner, M. *Exit: An Illusion*
Bonner, M. *The Purple Flower*
Burrill, M. *Aftermath*
Burrill, M. *They That Sit in Darkness*
Graham, S. *I Gotta Home*
Graham, S. *It's Morning*
Hurston, Z. *Color Struck*
Hurston, Z. *The First One*
Johnson, G. *Blue Blood*
Johnson, G. *Blue-eyed Black Boy*
Johnson, G. *Plumes*
Johnson, G. *A Sunday Morning in the South*
Miller, M. *Christophe's Daughters*
Miller, M. *Harriet Tubman*
Miller, M. *Riding the Goat*

Miller, M. *Stragglers in the Dust*
Spence, E. *Fool's Errand*
Spence, E. *Her*
Spence, E. *Undertow*

PERA Perkins, Kathy A., ed. *Black South African Women: An Anthology of Plays*. New York: Routledge, 1998. 177pp.
Conning, L. *A Coloured Place*
Dike, F. *So What's New?*
Mahomed, I. *Cheaper than Roses*
Maponya, M. *Umongikazi/The Nurse*
Mhlophe, G. *Have You Seen Zandile?*
Mtshali, T. *WEEMEN*
Naidoo, M. *Flight from the Mahabarath*
Ndlovu, D. *Sheila's Day*
Williams, M. *Kwa-landlady*

PERC Perkins, Kathy A., and Uno, Roberta, eds. *Contemporary Plays by Women of Color: An Anthology*. New York: Routledge, 1996. 323pp.
Aoki, B. *The Queen's Garden*
Cleage, P. *Flyin' West*
Colorado, E., and Colorado, H. *1992: Blood Speaks*
Corthron, K. *Come Down Burning*
Cruz, M. *The Have-little*
Dickerson, G., and Clarke, B. *Re/membering Aunt Jemima*
Dizon, L. *Till Voices Wake Us*
Fernandez, E. *How Else Am I Supposed to Know I'm Still Alive*
Glancy, D. *Weebjob*
Gomez, M. Excerpts from *Memory Tricks, Marga Gomez Is Pretty Witty & Gay*, and *A Line around the Block*
Gomez, T. *Inter-tribal*
Jones, L. *Combination Skin*
Moraga, C. *Heroes and Saints*
Sharif, B. *My Ancestor's House*
Smith, A. D. Excerpts from *Twilight: Los Angeles 1992*
Son, D. *R.A.W. ('Cause I'm a Woman)*
Spiderwoman Theater. *Sun Moon and Feather*
Wong, E. *China Doll*

PERF Perkins, Kathy A., and Stephens, Judith L., eds. *Strange Fruit: Plays on Lynching by American Women*. Bloomington, IN: Indiana University Press, 1998. 423pp.
Andrews, R. *Climbing Jacob's Ladder*
Boston, M. *Iola's Letter*
Burrill, M. *Aftermath*
Caldwell, F. *Voice in the Wilderness*
Grimke, A. *Rachel*
Holland, E. *Miss Ida B. Wells*
Howell, C. *The Forfeit*

Johnson, G. *Blue-eyed Black Boy*
Johnson, G. *Safe*
Johnson, G. *A Sunday Morning in the South*
Link, A. *Lawd, Does You Undahstan'?*
Meyer, A. *Black Souls*
Miller, M. *Nails and Thorns*
Seaton, S. *The Bridge Party*
Smith, L. *Strange Fruit*

PERKY Perkyns, Richard, ed. *Major Plays of the Canadian Theatre, 1934–1984*. Toronto: Irwin Publishing, 1984. 742pp.
Bolt, C. *Buffalo Jump*
Cook, M. *The Head, Guts, and Soundbone Dance*
Coulter, J. *Riel*
Davies, R. *At My Heart's Core*
French, D. *Of the Fields, Lately*
Gélinas, G. *Bousille and the Just*
Herbert, J. *Fortune and Men's Eyes*
Pollock, S. *Generations*
Ravel, A. *Dispossessed*
Reaney, J. *The Canadian Brother or the Prophecy Fulfilled*
Ringwood, G. *Drum Song*
Voaden, H. *Hill-land*

PERR Perrier, Ronald G., ed. *Plays for Stage and Screen*. St. Cloud, MN: Archie Publications, 1989–1998. 3 vols.
Anderson, R. *I'm Herbert* 3
Chekhov, A. *The Marriage Proposal* 3
Clark, B. *Whose Life Is It Anyway?* 1
Euripides. *Hippolytus* 2
Euripides. *Medea* 3
*Everyman* 3
Goldsmith, O. *She Stoops to Conquer* 1
Gregory, A. *Spreading the News* 2
Harling, R. *Steel Magnolias* 2
Hellman, L. *The Little Foxes* 2
Ibsen, H. *A Doll's House* 1
Miller, A. *All My Sons* 3
Milne, A. *The Ugly Duckling* 2
Molière, J. *The Miser* 3
Nolte, C. *A Christmas Carol* 1
Nolte, C. *Dracula* 1
Nolte, C. *The Strange Case of Dr. Jekyll and Mr. Hyde* 3
O'Neill, E. *Desire under the Elms* 2
Shakespeare, W. *Hamlet* 3 (altered from)
Shakespeare, W. *Macbeth* 2
Shakespeare, W. *Romeo and Juliet* 1
Shaw, G. *Arms and the Man* 1
Sophocles. *Oedipus the King* 1
Steinbeck, J. *Of Mice and Men* 3
Strindberg, A. *Miss Julie* 2
Synge, J. *Riders to the Sea* 3

Thompson, E. *On Golden Pond* 1
Wasserstein, W. *The Heidi Chronicles* 3
Wilde, O. *The Importance of Being Earnest* 2, 3
Wilder, T. *Our Town* 2
Williams, T. *The Glass Menagerie* 2
Williams, T. *The Night of the Iguana* 1
Williams, T. *Suddenly Last Summer* 3

PERRIN, BERNADOTTE. *See* GREE *Greek Dramas.*

PERS Perrine, Laurence, comp. *Dimensions of Drama.*
New York: Harcourt, Brace, Jovanovich, 1973.
567pp.
Chekhov, A. *The Brute*
*Everyman*
García Lorca, F. *Blood Wedding*
Ibsen, H. *An Enemy of the People*
Miller, A. *Death of a Salesman*
Molière, J. *The Misanthrope*
Shakespeare, W. *Othello*
Sophocles. *Oedipus Rex*
Strindberg, A. *The Stronger*
Williams, T. *The Glass Menagerie*

PERT Perrine, Laurence, comp. *Literature: Structure,
Sound and Sense.* New York: Harcourt, Brace,
Jovanovich, 1970. 1426pp.
Albee, E. *The Sandbox*
Chekhov, A. *The Brute*
García Lorca, F. *Blood Wedding*
Ibsen, H. *An Enemy of the People*
Miller, A. *Death of a Salesman*
Molière, J. *The Misanthrope*
Shakespeare, W. *Othello*
Shaw, G. *Candida*
Sophocles. *Oedipus Rex*
Strindberg, A. *The Stronger*
Williams, T. *The Glass Menagerie*

PERU Perrine, Laurence, ed. *Literature: Structure, Sound
and Sense.* 2d ed. New York: Harcourt, Brace,
Jovanovich, 1974. 1508pp.
Albee, E. *The Sandbox*
Chekhov, A. *The Brute: A Joke in One Act*
*Everyman*
García Lorca, F. *Blood Wedding*
Hansberry, L. *A Raisin in the Sun*
Ibsen, H. *An Enemy of the People*
Miller, A. *Death of a Salesman*
Molière, J. *The Misanthrope*
Shakespeare, W. *Othello*
Shaw, G. *Candida*
Sophocles. *Antigone*
Strindberg, A. *The Stronger*

PERV Perrine, Laurence, ed. *Literature: Structure, Sound
and Sense.* 3rd ed. New York Harcourt, Brace,
Jovanovich, 1978.
Albee, E. *The Sandbox*
Chekhov, A. *The Brute*
Giraudoux, J. *The Madwoman of Chaillot*
Hansberry, L. *A Raisin in the Sun*
Hughes, L. *Mother and Child*
Ibsen, H. *An Enemy of the People*
Miller, A. *Death of a Salesman*
Molière, J. *The Misanthrope*
Shakespeare, W. *Othello*
Shaw, G. *Candida*
Sophocles. *Oedipus Rex*
Strindberg, A. *The Stronger*

PERW Perrine, Laurence, ed., with the assistance of
Thomas R. Arp. *Literature: Structure, Sound
and Sense.* 4th ed. New York: Harcourt, Brace,
Jovanovich, 1983. 1492pp.
Albee, E. *The Sandbox*
Chekhov, A. *The Cherry Orchard*
*Everyman*
García Lorca, F. *Blood Wedding*
Ibsen, H. *An Enemy of the People*
Miller, A. *Death of a Salesman*
Molière, J. *The Misanthrope*
Shakespeare, W. *Othello*
Sophocles. *Oedipus Rex*
Stoppard, T. *Professional Foul*
Strindberg, A. *The Stronger*
Williams, T. *The Glass Menagerie*

PERX Perrine, Laurence, ed., with the assistance of
Thomas R. Arp. *Literature: Structure, Sound
and Sense.* 5th ed. San Diego: Harcourt, Brace,
Jovanovich, 1988. 1441pp.
Albee, E. *The Sandbox*
Chekhov, A. *The Cherry Orchard*
*Everyman*
García Lorca, F. *Blood Wedding*
Ibsen, H. *A Doll's House*
Miller, A. *Death of a Salesman*
Molière, J. *The Misanthrope*
Shakespeare, W. *Othello*
Shaw, G. *Arms and the Man*
Sophocles. *Oedipus Rex*
Strindberg, A. *The Stronger*
Williams, T. *The Glass Menagerie*

PERY Perrine, Laurence, ed., with the assistance of
Thomas R. Arp. *Literature: Structure, Sound and
Sense.* 6th ed. Fort Worth, TX: Harcourt, Brace,
Jovanovich, 1993. 1444p

Albee, E. *The Sandbox*
Beckett, S. *Krapp's Last Tape*
Chekhov, A. *The Cherry Orchard*
Glaspell, S. *Trifles*
Ibsen, H. *A Doll's House*
Miller, A. *Death of a Salesman*
Molière, J. *Tartuffe, or, the Imposter*
Shakespeare, W. *Othello*
Sophocles. *Oedipus Rex*
Strindberg, A. *The Stronger*
Williams, T. *The Glass Menagerie*
Wilson, A. *Fences*

PERZ *Perrine's Literature: Structure, Sound and Sense.*
        Edited by Thomas R. Arp. Fort Worth, TX:
        Harcourt Brace College Publishers, 1998. 7th ed.
        1522pp.
    Albee, E. *The Sandbox*
    Chekhov, A. *The Cherry Orchard*
    Durang, C. *Naomi in the Living Room*
    Franklin, J. *Two Mens'es Daughter*
    Havel, V. *Unveiling*
    Ibsen, H. *A Doll's House*
    Miller, A. *Death of a Salesman*
    Molière, J. *The Misanthrope*
    Oakes, M. *Mind the Gap*
    Shakespeare, W. *Othello, the Moor of Venice*
    Sophocles. *Oedipus Rex*
    Stoppard, T. *"M" Is for Moon among Other Things*
    Valdez, L. *Los vendidos*
    Williams, T. *The Glass Menagerie*
    Wilson, A. *Fences*

PES *Perspectives: An Anthology.* Edited by Marianne H.
        Russo, Edward B. Groff. Dubuque, IA: Kendall/
        Hunt Pub. Co., c1976. 390pp.
    Shakespeare, W. *Othello*
    Sophocles. *Oedipus the King*
    Ward, D. *Day of Absence*

PETER Peters, Helen, ed. *The Plays of CODCO.* New York:
        Peter Lang, 1992. 446pp. (American University
        Studies Series XXVI Theatre Arts, Vol. 14)
    CODCO. *Das capital: or What Do You Want to See the
        Harbor for Anyway?*
    CODCO. *Cod on a Stick*
    CODCO. *Sickness, Death, and beyond the Grave*
    CODCO. *The Tale Ends*
    CODCO. *Would You like to Smell My . . . Pocket
        Crumbs?*

PETERS Peters, Helen, ed., and introduced by. *Stars in the
        Sky Morning: Collective Plays of Newfoundland
        and Labrador.* St. John's, Newfoundland: Killick
        Press, 1996. 531pp.

Innuinuit Theatre Company and Nalujuk Players.
        *Braindead*
    Malone, B., and Mercer, R. *On Edge*
    The Mummers Troupe. *Makin' Time with the Yanks*
    The Mummers Troupe. *They Club Seals, Don't They?*
    Payne, R. *Stars in the Sky Morning*
    RCA Theatre Company. *Terras de bacalhau (Land of
        Cod)*
    RCA Theatre Company. *Time before Thought*
    Rising Tide Theatre. *Joey.*
    Sheila's Brush Theatre Company. *JAXMASS (Jack's
        Christmas)*
    Taylor, J. *My Three Dads*

PFIS Pfisterer, Susan, ed. *Tremendous Worlds: Australia
        Women's Drama 1890–1960.* Sydney: Currency
        Press, 1999. 358pp.
    Bensusan, I. *The Apple*
    Brand, M. *Here under Heaven*
    Cusack, D. *Morning Sacrifice*
    Franklin, M. *No Family*
    Hanger, E. *Flood*
    Prichard, K. *Forward One*
    Shepherd, C. *Jane, My Love*

PHI Philbrick, Norman, ed. *Trumpets Sounding:
        Propaganda Plays of the American Revolution.*
        New York: 1972. 367pp.
    *The Battle of Brooklyn, a Farce of Two Acts*
    *The Blockheads; or, the Affrighted Officers*
    Brackenridge, H. *The Death of General Montgomery, in
        Storming the City of Quebec*
    *A Dialogue between a Southern Delegate, and His
        Spouse, on His Return from the Grand Continental
        Congress*
    Leacock, J. *The Fall of British Tyranny; or, American
        Liberty Triumphant*
    *The Motley Assembly*
    Munford, R. *The Patriots*

PHIL *Philippine Drama: Twelve Plays in Six Philippine
        Languages.* With introductions, translations,
        and notes in English by Wilhelmina Q. Ramas
        . . . et al. Diliman, Quezon City: University of
        the Philippines, 1987. 990pp. (Contains texts in
        original languages of Bikol, Cebuano, Hiligaynon,
        Iloko, Pangasinan, and Tagalog, followed by
        separate texts in English translations)
    Celestino, A. *Say quieo ya angapoy serom*
    Celestino, A. *A Tree without Shade*
    Checa, P. *Ang damgohanon kon manginmatu—od*
    Checa, P. *When Dreams Come True*
    *Dallot*
    Damaso, J. It *Withered and Revived*
    Damaso, J. *Nalaya cag manalingsing*

Ilagan, H. *The Barrio Maiden*
Ilagan, H. *Dalagang bukid*
Jimenez, A. *Love and Wealth*
Jimenez, A. *Pagkamoot asin cayamanan*
Kabahar, P. *Marianito*
Nuyda, J. *Anti Cristo*
Palafox, F. *Dalusapi*
Reyes, S. *R.I.P.*
Rodriguez, B. *Balaod sa kinabuhi*
Rodriguez, B. *The Law of Life*
Santos, J. *Kar-Na-Na*
Santos, J. *Yesterday, Today, Tomorrow*

PIC Pickering, Jerry V., ed. *A Treasury of Drama: Classical through Modern*. New York: West, 1975. 515pp.
Dieb, R. *The Mating of Alice May*
Chekhov, A. *The Cherry Orchard*
*The Farce of Master Pierre Oathelin*
Shakespeare, W. *Romeo and Juliet*
Shaw, G. *The Devil's Disciple*
Sheridan, R. *The School for Scandal*
Sophocles. *Oedipus the King*
Williams, T. *The Glass Menagerie*

PIE Pierce, Frederick Erastus, and Schreiber, Carl Frederick, eds. *Fiction and Fantasy of German Romance*. New York: Oxford University Press, 1927. 392pp.
Kleist, H. *Kaethchen of Heilbronn*

PIET Pieterse, Cosmo, ed. *Five African Plays*. London: Heinemann, 1972. 217pp.
Bart-Williams, G. *The Drug*
Euba, F. *Abiku*
Kay, K. *Laughter and Hubbub in the House*
Kimmel, H. *The Cell*
Oyono, F. *Houseboy*

PING Ping, Chin Woo, ed. *Playful Phoenix: Women Write for the Singapore Stage*. Singapore, TheatreWorks, 1996. 401pp.
Lam, D. *Ordinary Woman*
Leow, P. *Family*
Ping, C. *Diary of a Madwoman*
Tan, M. *Quiet the Gorilla*
Wong, E. *Wills and Secession*
Yu, O. *The Woman in a Tree on the Hill*

PLA *Places, Please!: The First Anthology of Lesbian Plays*. Edited by Katie McDermott. San Francisco: Spinsters/Aunt Lute, 1985. 209pp.
Baum, T. *Immediate Family*
Baum, T., and Myers, C. *Dos lesbos*
Dreher, S. *8 × 10 Glossy*

Dreher, S. *Ruby Christmas*
Garvey, E. *Soup*
Nelson, M. *Out of Bounds*
Willis, J. *Going Up*

PLAYBOOK: FIVE PLAYS FOR A NEW THEATRE (PLAA). *See also* PLAC *Plays for a New Theater: Playbook 2.*

PLAA *Playbook: Five Plays for a New Theatre*. [1] New York: New Directions [c1956] 298pp.
Abel, L. *The Death of Odysseus*
Hivnor, R. *The Ticklish Acrobat*
Kinoshita, J. *Twilight Crane*
Merrill, J. *The Immortal Husband*
Richards, I. *A Leak in the Universe*

PLAAB *The Playboy of the Western World and Two Other Irish Plays*. Introduced by W. A. Armstrong. New York: Penguin, 1987. 224pp. (Originally published as *Classic Irish Drama, 1964*.)
O'Casey, S. *Cock-a-doodle Dandy*
Synge, J. *The Playboy of the Western World*
Yeats, W. *The Countess Cathleen*

PLAAC *The Playmakers*. Compiled by Roger Mansfield, illustrated by Barry Davies. Huddersfield [Eng.] Schofield & Sims Ltd., 1976. 2 vols.
Arden, J. *Death of a Cowboy* 1
Arden, J. *When Is a Door Not a Door?* 2
Brecht, B., and Weill, K. *He Who Says No* 2
Brecht, B., and Weill, K. *He Who Says Yes* 1
Campton, D. *The End of the Picnic* 2
Campton, D. *Incident* 1
Jenkins, R. *Five Green Bottles* 2
Jenkins, R. *The Whole Truth* 1
Livings, H. *The Gamecock* 1
Livings, H. *Rattel* 2
Pinter, H. *Applicant* 2
Pinter, H. *Request Stop* 1
Simpson, N. *Gladly Otherwise* 2
Simpson, N. *Oh!* 1
Spark, M. *The Dry River Bed* 2
Spark, M. *The Party through the Wall* 1
Williams, T. *The Last of My Solid Gold Watches* 1
Williams, T. *This Property Is Condemned* 2

PLAAD *Plays by American Women: The Early Years*. Edited and with an introduction by Judith E. Barlow. New York: Avon, 1981. 334pp.
Crothers, R. *A Man's World*
Gale, Z. *Miss Lulu Bett*
Glaspell, S. *Trifles*
Mowatt, A. *Fashion*
Treadwell, S. *Machinal*

PLAAE *Plays by American Women: 1900–1930*. Edited and with an introduction by Judith E. Barlow. New York: Applause Theatre Book Publishers, 1985. 261pp. (Revised edition of *Plays by American Women: The Early Years*)
Crothers, R. *A Man's World*
Gale, Z. *Miss Lulu Bett*
Glaspell, S. *Trifles*
Johnson, G. *Plumes*
Treadwell, S. *Machinal*

PLAAF *Plays by American Women: 1930–1960*. Edited and with an introduction by Judith E. Barlow. New York: Applause Theatre Book Publishers, 1994. 542pp.
Boothe, C. *The Women*
Bowles, J. *In the Summer House*
Childress, A. *Trouble in Mind*
Flanagan, H., and Clifford, M. *Can You Hear Their Voices?*
Graham, S. *It's Morning*
Hellman, L. *The Little Foxes*
Kanin, F. *Goodbye, My Fancy*
Stein, G. *The Mother of Us All*

PLAAG *Plays by French and Francophone Women: A Critical Anthology*. Edited and translated by Christine Makward and Judith G. Miller with an annotated bibliography by Cynthia Running-Johnson. Ann Arbor, MI: University of Michigan Press, 1994. 345pp.
Bille, S. *The Scent of Sulphur*
Boucher, D. *When Faeries Thirst*
Césaire, I. *Island Memories: Mama N. and Mama F.*
Chawaf, C. *Warmth: A Bloodsong*
Chedid, A. *The Goddess Lar or Centuries of Women*
Cixous, H. *The Name of Oedipus: Song of the Forbidden Body*
Foucher, M. *The Table: Womenspeak*
Maillet, A. *The Rabble*

PLAB *Plays by Greek, Spanish, French, German, and English Dramatists*. Rev. ed. New York: Colonial Press [c1900] 2 vols. (The World's Great Classics)
Aeschylus. *Prometheus Bound* 1
Aristophanes. *The Knights* 1
Calderón de la Barca, P. *Life Is a Dream* 1
Euripides. *Medea* 1
Goethe, J. *Faust, Part 1* 2
Goldsmith, O. *She Stoops to Conquer* 1
Ibsen, H. *A Doll's House* 2
Molière, J. *The Misanthrope* 1
Racine, J. *Phaedra* 1
Sardou, V. *Les pattes de mouche* 2

Schiller, F. *Mary Stuart* 2
Sheridan, R. *The Rivals* 2
Sophocles. *Oedipus Rex* 1

PLABE *Plays by Women* (Volumes 1–4 selected and introduced by Michelene Wandor; Volumes 5–8 selected and introduced by Mary Remnant; Volumes 9–10 selected and introduced by Annie Castledine). London: Methuen, 1982–1994. 10 vols.
Adshead, K. *Thatcher's Women* 7
Beauvoir, S. *The Woman Destroyed* 10
Churchill, C. *Objections to Sex and Violence* 4
Churchill, C. *Vinegar Tom* 1
Cooper, M. *Heartgame* 8
Cresswell, J., and Johnson, N. *The One-sided Wall* 8
Dayley, G. *Rose's Story* 4
De Angelis, A. *Ironmistress* 8
Ditton, C., and Ford, M. *About Face* 6
Dowie, C. *Adult Child/Dead Child* 7
Duffy, M. *Rites* 2
Evans, L. *Stamping, Shouting, and Singing Home* 7
Fleisser, M. *Pioneers in Ingolstadt* 9
Fleisser, M. *Purgatory in Ingolstadt* 9
Gems, P. *Aunt Mary; Scenes from Provincial Life* 3
Gems, P. *Dusa, Fish, Stas and vi* 1
Gems, P. *Queen Christina* 5
Goldemberg, R. *Letters Home* 2
Green, M., and Griffin, C. *More* 6
Hansberry, L. *A Raisin in the Sun* 5
Horsfield, D. *Red Devils* 3
Jelinek, E. *What Happened after Nora Left Her Husband* 10
Laberge, M. *Night* 7
Laverny, B. *Origin of the Species* 6
Lawrence, M. *Tokens of Affection* 9
Levy, D. *Pax* 6
Lewis, E. *Ficky Stingers* 6
Lochhead, L. *Blood and Ice* 4
Luckham, C. *The Choice* 10
Luckham, C. *Trafford Tanzi* 2
Lyssa, A. *Pinball* 4
Munro, R. *Piper's Cave* 5
Nagy, P. *Weldon Rising* 10
Page, L. *Tissue* 1
Pollock, S. *Blood Relations* 3
Raif, A. *Caving In* 8
Rudet, J. *Money to Live* 5
Stewart, E. *Towards Evening* 8
Stewart, E. *Walkies Time* 8
Wakefield, L., and the Women's Theatre Group. *Time Pieces* 3
Wandor, M. *Aurora Leigh* 1
Windsor, V. *Effie's Burning* 7
Wolton, J. *Motherlove* 8

Wymark, O. *Find Me* 2
Yeger, S. *Variations on a Theme by Clara Schumann* 9

**PLABI** *Plays by Women: An International Anthology.* New York: Ubu Repertory Theater, 1988–1996. 3 vols.
Bartève, R. *The Orphanage* 2
Bellon, L. *Bonds of Affection* 3
Bonal, D. *Beware the Heart* 2
Bonal, D. *A Country Wedding* 3
Bonal, D. *A Picture Perfect Sky* 1
Condé, M. *The Tropical Breeze Hotel* 2
Fabien, M. *Jocasta* 1
Farhoud, A. *Game of Patience* 2
Farhoud, A. *The Girls from the Five and Ten* 1
Gallaire, F. *You Have Come Back* 3
Gallaire-Bourega, F. *You Have Come Back* 1
Liking, W. *The Widow Dylemma* 2
Schwarz-Bart, S. *Your Handsome Captain* 1, 3
Serreau, C. *Lapin lapin* 3
Visdei, A. *Always Together* 3

**PLAC** *Plays for a New Theater: Play Book 2.* New York: New Directions [1966] 282pp.
Alvaro, C. *The Long Night of Medea*
Goll, Y. *Methusalem; or, the Eternal Bourgeois*
Hawkes, J. *The Wax Museum*
Hivnor, R. *The Assault upon Charles Sumner*
Vian, B. *Knackery for All*

**PLACA** *Plays for Actresses.* Edited by Eric Lane and Nina Shengold. New York: Vintage Books, 1997. 628pp.
Albee, E. *Three Tall Women*
Blessing, L. *Independence*
Cunningham, L. *Beautiful Bodies*
Gallagher, M. *Bedtime*
George, M. *The Most Massive Woman Wins*
Houston, V. *Tea*
Howe, T. *Appearances*
Kramer, S. *David's Redhaired Death*
Kurtti, C. *Catholic School Girls*
LeFevre, A. *Waterbabies*
Lucas, C. *Credo*
Nottage, L. *Poof!*
Rivera, J. *The Winged Man*
Shengold, N. *Lives of the Great Waitresses*
Vogel, P. *Desdemona*
Wasserstein, W. *Workout*
Wooten, J. *The Role of Della*

**PLACB** *Plays for the Nuclear Age.* London: Playwrights' Press, 1989. 158pp.
Alrawi, K. *Fire in the Lake*
Campbell, G. *Shouting at Pictures*
Deike, T. *Waiting for Hiroshima*

Mullett, A. *A Right Wally*
Oliver, B. *Sector Three*

**PLACC** *Plays from Black Australia.* Sydney: Currency Press, 1989. 233pp.
Davis, J. *The Dreamers*
Johnson, E. *Murras*
Maza, B. *The Keepers*
Walley, R. *Coordah*

**PLACD** *Plays from the Circle Repertory Company.* New York: Broadway Play Publishing, 1986. 410pp.
Bishop, J. *The Great-great Grandson of Jedediah Kohler*
Bovasso, J. *Down by the River Where Water Lilies Are Disfigured Every Day*
Feiffer, J. *Knock Knock*
Leonard, J. *The Diviners*
Pintauro, J. *Snow Orchid*
Wilson, L. *The Mound Builders*

**PLACE** *Plays from Padua Hills 1982.* Edited by Murray Medrick. Claremont, CA: Pomona College, c1983. 169pp.
Epstein, M. *Mysteries of the Bridal Night*
Fornes, M. *The Danube*
LaTempa, S. *Sunset Beach*
Martell, L. *Hoss Drawin'*
Mednick, M. *Coyote V: Listening to Old Nana*
Monroe, M. *Politesse: A Piece for Tape and Landscape*
O'Keefe, J. *Bercilak's Dream*
Steppling, J. *Neck*

**PLACF** *Plays from Playwrights Horizon.* New York: Broadway Play Publishing, 1987. 336pp.
Cone, T. *Herringbone*
Durang, C. *Baby with the Bathwater*
Finn, W. *March of the Falsettos*
Murphy, D. *The Terrorists*
Nelson, R. *Jungle Coup*
Tally, T. *Coming Attractions*

**PLACG** *Plays from South Coast Repertory.* New York: Broadway Play Publishing, 1993–1998. 2 vols.
Edson, M. *Wit* 2
Freed, A. *Freedomland* 2
Greenberg, R. *Three Days of Rain* 2
Henley, B. *Abundance* 1
Hwang, D. *Golden Child* 2
Korder, H. *Search and Destroy* 1
Lucas, C. *Prelude to a Kiss* 1
Margulies, D. *Collected Stories* 2
Margulies, D. *Sight Unseen* 1
Nemeth, S. *Holy Days* 1

Solis, O. *Man of the Flesh* 1
Solis, O. *La posada magica* 2

PLACGH *Plays from South Coast Repertory: Hispanic
        Playwrights Project Anthology.* New York:
        Broadway Play Publishing, 2000. 428pp.
Alfaro, L. *Bitter Homes and Gardens*
Cram, C. *Landlocked*
Farías, J. *Claudia meets Fulano Colorado*
Martinez, R. *Illuminating Veronica*
Moraga, C. *Watsonville: Some Place Not Here*
Rivera, J. *References to Salvador Dali Make Me Hot*
Solis, O. *El Otro*

PLACHA *Plays from the Contemporary American
        Theater.* Edited and with an introduction by Brooks
        McNamara. New York: New American Library,
        1988. 480pp.
Durang, C. *Sister Mary Ignatius Explains It All for You*
Guare, J. *Marco Polo Sings a Solo*
Gurney, A. *The Dining Room*
Henley, B. *Crimes of the Heart*
Howe, T. *Painting Churches*
Kopit, A. *Wings*
Rabe, D. *Streamers*
Wilson, A. *Ma Rainey's Black Bottom*

PLACHB *Plays from the Contemporary British Theater.*
        Edited and with an introduction by Brooks
        McNamara. New York: Mentor, 1992.
Edgar, D. *The Life and Adventures of Nicholas Nickleby*
Hare, D. *Plenty*
Orton, J. *What the Butler Saw*
Pinter, H. *Betrayal*
Storey, D. *The Changing Room*
Whitemore, H. *Pack of Lies*

PLACI *Plays from the New York Shakespeare Festival.*
      New York: Broadway Play Publishing, 1986.
      400pp.
Cohen, M. *Necessary Ends*
Gilhooley, J. *The Time Trial*
Piñero, M. *Short Eyes*
Rabe, D. *Streamers*
Reardon, D. *The Leaf People*
Shange, N. *for colored girls who have considered
           suicide/when the rainbow is enuf*

PLACJ *Plays from Woolly Mammoth.* New York:
      Broadway Play Publishing, 1999. 324pp.
Alexander, R *The Last Orbit of Billy Mars*
Aronson, B. *The Art Room*
Freed, A. *The Psychic Life of Savages*
Porter, R. *Man, Woman, Dinosaur*

Rutherford, S. *The Chinese Art of Placement*
Stewart-Brown, C. *The Gene Pool*

PLACK *Plays Introduction: Plays by New Writers.*
      London: Faber, 1984. 343pp.
Clough, D. *In Kanada*
Darke, N. *High Water*
Fletcher, J. *Babylon Has Fallen*
Fox, E. *Ladies in Waiting*
James, L. *Trial and Error*
Wertenbaker, T. *New Anatomies*

PLAD *Plays of a Half-Decade.* [London] Gollancz [1933]
     1008pp.
Anthony, C. *Autumn Crocus*
Bax, C. *The Rose without a Thorn*
Berkeley, R. *The Lady with a Lamp*
Besier, R. *The Barretts of Wimpole Street*
Delafield, E. *To See Ourselves*
Fagan, J. *The Improper Duchess*
Hoffe, M. *Many Waters*
Mackenzie, R. *Musical Chairs*
Sherriff, R. *Journey's End*
Van Druten, J. *After All*
Van Druten, J. *Young Woodley*

PLAG *Plays of the Greek Dramatists.* New York: Caxton
     House [c1946] 360pp. Note: Variant title: *Eleven
     Plays of the Greek Dramatists.*
Aeschylus. *Agamemnon*
Aeschylus. *Choephoroe*
Aeschylus. *The Eumenides*
Aristophanes. *The Clouds*
Aristophanes. *The Frogs*
Aristophanes. *Lysistrata*
Euripides. *The Cyclops*
Euripides. *Iphigena in Tauris*
Sophocles. *Antigone*
Sophocles. *Electra*
Sophocles. *Oedipus the King*

PLAH *Plays of the Moscow Art Theatre Musical Studio.*
     English translation from the Russian by George S.,
     and Gilbert Seldes, with introductions by Oliver M.
     Sayler. New York: Brentano [c1925] v.p.
Aristophanes. *Lysistrata*
Lecocq, C. *The Daughter of Madame Angot*
Lipskeroff, C. *Carmencita and the Soldier*
Offenbach, J. *La périchole*
Pushkin, A. *Love and Death, featuring "Aleko" by
            Rachmaninoff*

PLAJ *Plays of the Sixties.* Selected by J. M. Charlton.
     London: Pan Books, 1966–1967. 2 vols.

Campton, D. *Soldier from the Wars Returning* 2
Chapman, J. *Simple Spymen* 2
Lessing, D. *Play with a Tiger* 1
Millar, R. *The Affair* 2
Murdoch, I., and Priestley, J. *A Severed Head* 2
Rattigan, T., *Ross* 1
Shaffer, P., *The Royal Hunt of the Sun* 1
Waterhouse, K., and Hall, W. *Billy Liar* 1

PLAYS OF THE SOUTHERN AMERICAS. *See* SSTE *Stanford University Dramatists' Alliance.*

PLAL *Plays of the Thirties.* Selected by J. M. Charlton.
    London: Pan Books, 1966–1967. 2 vols.
Besier, R. *The Barretts of Wimpole Street* 2
Bridie, J. *Tobias and the Angel* 1
Coward, N. *Private Lives* 2
Daviot, G. *Richard of Bordeaux* 1
Gow, R., and Greenwood, W. *Love on the Dole* 1
Rattigan, T. *French without Tears* 2
Smith, D. *Autumn Crocus* 2
Smith, D. *Dear Octopus* 1

PLAN *Plays of the Year.* Chosen by J. C. Trewin. London:
    Paul Elek; New York: Frederick Ungar [c1949–
    1980] 48 vols.
Abse, D. *House of Cowards* 23
Achard, M. *Rollo* 20
Ackland, R. *Before the Party* 2
Ackland, R. *A Dead Secret* 16
Albery, P. *Anne Boleyn* 14
Anouilh, J. *The Ermine* 13
Anouilh, J. *Medea* 15
Anouilh, J. *The Waltz of the Toreadors* 8
Arden, J. *The Party* 18
Arout, G. *Beware of the Dog* 33
Babel, I. *Marya* 35
Bagnold, E. *Call Me Jacky* 34
Boland, B. *Cockpit* 1
Boland, B. *Gordon* 25
Boland, B. *The Prisoner* 10
Boland, B. *The Return* 9
Braddon, R. *Naked Island* 22
Browne, F. *The Family Dance* 46
Browne, W. *The Holly and the Ivy* 3
Bryden, B. *Willie Rough* 43
Chekhov, A. *Uncle Vanya* 39
Chetham-Stroke, W. *Background* 4
Christie, D., and Christie, C. *His Excellency* 4
Coffee, L., and Cowen, W. *Family Portrait* 1
Cooper, G. *Out of the Crocodile* 27
Corlett, W. *Tinker's Curse* 34
Crabbe, K. *The Last Romantic* 45
Cross, B. *The Mines of Sulphur* 30
Dewhurst, K. *Lark Rise* 48

Dewhurst, K. *Rafferty's Chant* 33
Dighton, J. *The Happiest Days of Your Life* 1
Dighton, J. *Who Goes There!* 6
Dinner, W., and Morum, W. *The Late Edwina Black* 2
Dobie, L., and Sloman, R. *The Tinker* 24
Dowling, J., and Letton, F. *The Young Elizabeth* 7
Dyer, C. *Rattle of a Simple Man* 26
Exton, C. *Have You Any Dirty Washing, Mother Dear?*
    37
Fairchild, W. *The Sound of Murder* 20
Feely, T. *Don't Let Summer Come* 29
Fletcher, J. *The Chances* 25
Francis, W. *Portrait of a Queen* 30
Frisby, T. *There's a Girl in My Soup* 32
Frost, R. *Small Hotel* 13
Gear, B. *The Sky Is Green* 27
Gilbert, M. *The Bargain* 23
Gilbert, M. *A Clean Kill* 21
Gillette, W. *Sherlock Holmes* 44
Goldoni, C. *The Servant of Two Masters* 36
Gow, R. *Ann Veronica* 2
Gow, R. *The Edwardians* 20
Green, J. *Murder Mistaken* 8
Green, J. *South* 12
Guinness, A., and Strachan, A. *Yahoo* 46
Guitry, S. *Don't Listen Ladies!* 1
Guthrie, T. *Top of the Ladder* 3
Hale, J. *The Black Swan Winter* 37
Hale, J. *Spithead* 38
Hanley, J. *Say Nothing* 27
Harrison, J. *Knight in Four Acts* 38
Harrison, J. *Unaccompanied Cello* 40
Harvey, F. *The Day after the Fair* 43
Hastings, C. *Bonaventure* 3
Hastings, C. *Uncertain Joy* 12
Hastings, C. *Seagulls over Sorrento* 4
Hellman, L. *The Children's Hour* 5
Hochwälder, F. *The Public Prosecutor* 16
Hochwälder, F. *The Strong Are Lonely* 14
Home, W. *The Jockey Club Stakes* 40
Home, W. *Lloyd George Knew My Father* 42
Home, W. *The Queen's Highland Servant* 35
Home, W. *The Secretary Bird* 36
Home, W. *The Thistle and the Rose* 4
Horne, K. *Trial and Error* 9
Howarth, D. *Three Months Gone* 39
Ibsen, H. *John Gabriel Borkman* 23
Jeans, R. *Count Your Blessings* 5
Jeans, R. *Young Wives' Tale* 3
Jones, P. *Birthday Honours* 9
Jones, P. *The Last Meeting of the Knights of the White*
    *Magnolia* 47
Jones, P., and Jowett, J. *The Party Spirit* 11
Kennaway, J. *Country Dance* 33
Kimmins, A. *The Amorous Prawn* 21

Watkyn, A. *Not in the Book* 17
Webber, C. *Be Good, Sweet Maid* 15
Whiting, J. *Saint's Day* 6
Williams, H., and Williams, M. *By Accident* 21
Williams, H., and Williams, M. *Double Yolk* 21
Williams, H., and Williams, M. *The Grass Is Greener* 19
Williams, H., and Williams, M. *The Happy Man* 17
Williams, H., and Williams, M. *The Irregular Verb to Love* 23
Williams, H., and Williams, M. *Plaintiff in a Pretty Hat* 15
Williams, H., and Williams, M. *With Intent* 21
Williamson, H. *Diamond Cut Diamond* 7
Williamson, H. *Gunpowder, Treason, and Plot* 6
Williamson, H. *Heart of Bruce* 20
Williamson, H. *Teresa of Avila* 24
Woods, A., Slade, J., and Rowell, G. *Trelawny* 41

PLAP *Plays of To-day*. London: Sidgwick and Jackson [1925–1930] 3 vols.
Alvarez Quintero, S. and Alvarez Quintero, J. *A Hundred Years Old* 3
Baker, E. *Chains* 1
Drinkwater, J. *Abraham Lincoln* 1
Dukes, A. *The Man with a Load of Mischief* 3
Ervine, St. J. *Jane Clegg* 1
Granville-Barker, H. *The Voysey Inheritance* 1
Hastings, B. *The New Sin* 2
Houghton, S. *Hindle Wakes* 1
Housman, L., and Granville-Barker, H. *Prunella* 2
Masefield, J. *Pompey the Great* 2
Mayor, B. *The Pleasure Garden* 3
Monkhouse, A. *Mary Broome* 2
Munro, C. *At Mrs. Beam's* 3
Robinson, L. *The Whiteheaded Boy* 3
Sowerby, G. *Rutherford and Son* 2

PLAU *Plays on a Human Theme*. [ed. by] Cy Groves. New York: McGraw, 1979. 201pp.
Chayefsky, P. *Marty*
Hansberry, L. *A Raisin in the Sun*
Lawrence, J., and Lee, R. *Inherit the Wind*

PLAWE *Playwrights of Exile: An International Anthology: France, Romania, Quebec, Algeria, Lebanon, Cuba*. [Preface by Andrei Codrescu.] New York: Ubu Repertory Theater Publications, 1997. 442pp.
Aba, N. *Such Great Hope*
Manet, E. *Lady Strass*
Mouawad, W. *Wedding Day at the Cro-Magnons'*
Sebbar, L. *My Mother's Eyes*
Visdei, A. *Class Photo*

POB *Polish Romantic Drama: Three Plays in English Translation*. Selected and edited [translated from

the Polish] by Harold B. Segel. Ithaca, NY: Cornell University Press, 1977. 320pp.
Krasiński, Z. *The Un-divine Comedy*
Mickiewicz, A. *Forefathers' Eve, Part III*
Słowacki, J. *Fantazy*

POCH Pochman, Henry August, and Allen, Gay Wilson, eds. *Masters of American Literature*. New York: Macmillan, 1949. 2 vols.
O'Neill, E. *The Great God Brown* 2

POLK Pollack, Rhoda-Gale. *A Sampler of Plays by Women*. New York: Peter Lang, 1990. 399pp.
Behn, A. *The Rover*
Centlivre, S. *The Busy Body*
Gregory, I. *Dave*
Hroswitha. *Abraham*
Inchbald, E. *Such Things Are*

POLL Pollard, Alfred William, ed. *English Miracle Plays, Moralities, and Interludes*. 8th ed. rev. Oxford: Clarendon Press, 1927. 250pp.
*Abraham and Isaac*
*The Castell of Perseverance*
*The Creation and the Fall of Lucifer*
*Everyman*
*The Four Elements*
*The Harrowing of Hell*
*Ludus super iconia Sancti Nicolai*
*Mary Magdalen*
*Mysterium resurrectionis D. N. Jhesu Christi*
*Noah's Flood*
*The Sacrifice of Isaac*
*The Salutation and Conception*
*Secunda pastorum*
*Thersytes*
Bale, J. *King John*
Heywood, J. *The Pardoner and the Frere*
Skelton, J. *Magnyfycence*

POLLARD, ALFRED WILLIAM. *See also* FIF *Fifteenth Century Prose and Verse*.

POOL Pooley, Robert C.; Farmer, Paul; Thornton, Helen; and Anderson, George K., eds. *England in Literature*. Chicago: Scott, Foresman [c1953] 752pp.
Fry, C. *The Boy with a Cart*
Goldsmith, O. *She Stoops to Conquer*
Shakespeare, W. *Macbeth*

POP Popkin, Henry, ed. *The New British Drama*. New York: Grove Press [1964] 606pp.
Arden, J. *Serjeant Musgrave's Dance*
Behan, B. *The Hostage*

Delaney, S. *A Taste of Honey*
Pinter, H. *The Caretaker*
Simpson, N. *One Way Pendulum*
Wesker, A. *Roots*

POQ Popescu, Marian, and Popescu, Elena, eds. *After
    Censorship: New Romanian Plays of the '90s.*
    Bucharest, Unitext, 2000. 440pp.
Barbu, P. *On the Left Hand of the Father*
Butnaru, V. *The Saxophone with Red Leaves*
Cadariu, A. *Nascendo*
Cărbunariu, G. *Unrealities from the Immediate Wild
    East*
Gârbea, H. *Your Coffee, Mr. Secretary!*
Macrinici, R. *My D(r)ear Country*
Mircea, I. *Noah Sailing across Our Memory Is a
    Woman*
Mungiu-Pippidi, A. *The Evangelists*
Nicolau, V. *The Ghost from the First Class Waiting
    Room*
Stănescu, S. *Outcast*
Tântar, N. *Ubu and Milena*
Vălean, A. *When I Want to Whistle, I Whistle . . .*
Zografi, V. *Peter*

POR *The Portable Roman Reader.* Edited and with an
    introduction by Basil Davenport. Harmondsworth,
    Middlesex: Penguin, 1977. 656pp.
Plautus. *Amphitryon*
Terence. *Phormio*

PRAT Pratt, Robert A. [and Others] eds. *Masters of British
    Literature.* 2nd ed. Boston: Houghton Mifflin
    [c1958, 1962] 2 vols.
Arnold, M. *Empedocles on Etna* 2
Arnold, M. *The Strayed Reveler* 2
Shakespeare, W. *The First Part of Henry IV* 1
Shakespeare, W. *The Tragedy of King Lear* 1
Shakespeare, W. *The Winter's Tale* 1
Shelley, P. *Prometheus Unbound* 2

PRED Predan, Alja, ed. *Contemporary Slovenian Drama.*
    Ljubljana, Slovenia: Slovene Writers' Association,
    1997. 432p (L. S. Litterae Slovenicae Slovenian
    Literary Magazine 1 1997 XXXV 90)
Flisar, E. *Final Innocence*
Flisar, E. *Tomorrow*
Flisar, E. *What about Leonardo?*
Jančar, D. *Hallstatt*
Jančar, D. *The Great Brilliant Waltz*
Jančar, D. *Stakeout on Godot*
Jovanović, D. *The Liberation of Skopje*
Jovanović, D. *The Puzzle of Courage*
Jovanović, D. *Wall, Lake*

Šeligo, R. *Ana*
Šeligo, R. *Lepa Vida (Beautiful Vida)*
Šeligo, R. *The Wedding*
Svetina, I. *The Gardens and the Dove*
Svetina, I. *Sheherezade*
Svetina, I. *Thus died Zarathushtra*
Zajc, D. *Kalevala*
Zajc, D. *Medea*
Zajc, D. *Rocky Peak*

PRER *Prerogatives: Contemporary Plays by Women.*
    Preface by Ann Wilson. Winnipeg and Buffalo:
    Blizzard Publishing, 1998. 223pp.
Burke, K. *Charming and Rose: True Love*
Clements, M. *Now Look What You Made Me Do*
Laxdal, V. *Cyber:\womb*
Miles, K. *I Hate You on Mondays*
Rodin, T. *The Slow Eviction of Ruby Rosenholtz*

PRIMA *PrimaFacie: An Anthology of New American
    Plays.* Denver, CO: Denver Center Theatre
    Company, 1985–1991. 6 vols.
Babe, T. *Junk Bonds* 91
Bell, N. *Ready for the River* 89–90
Bishop, C., and Fuller, E. *Mine Alone* 89–90
Bishop, C., and Fuller, E. *Okiboji* 91
Dodd, T. *Goodnight, Texas* 86
Freed, D. *Child of Luck* 88
Freed, D. *Circe & Bravo* 86
Freed, D. *Veteran's Day* 87
Gesner, C. *Animal Fair* 89–90
Guyer, M. *The World of Mirth* 86
Harelik, M. *The Immigrant* 85
Hill, G. *Back to the Blanket* 91
Hill, G. *Soundbite* 89–90
Hogan, F. *Koozy's Piece* 87
Hogan, F. *Pleasuring Ground* 86
Hogan, F. *Ringers* 85
Jones, K. *Darkside* 88
Kelley, S. *Hope of the Future* 86
Ketron, L. *Rachel's Fate* 87
Lascelles, K. *Exclusive Circles* 88
Lascelles, K. *Trophy Hunters* 88
Levin, E. *The Female Entertainer* 85
Linney, R. *A Woman without a Name* 85
McLure, J. *Max and Maxie* 87
Morton, C., and Vigil, A. *Cuentos* 88
Myler, R. *Adventures of Huckleberry Finn* 89–90
Myler, R., and Harelik, M. *Lost Highway: The Music
    and Legend of Hank Williams* 89–90
Newman, M. *Shooting Stars* 87
Parks, S. *When the Sun Slides* 85
Williams, T. *New Business* 91
Williamson, L., and Powers, D. *Christmas Miracles* 85

PRIN Prins, Johanna C., ed. *Medieval Dutch Drama: Four Secular Plays and Four Farces from the Van Hulthem Manuscript.* Asheville, NC: Pegasus Press, c1999. 206pp.
*Blow-in-the-box*
*Debate of Winter and Summer*
*Esmoreit*
*Gloriant*
*Lancelot of Denmark*
*Lippin*
*Ruben*
*The Witch*

PRO Proffitt, Edward, ed. *Reading & Writing about Literature: Fiction, Poetry, Drama, and the Essay.* San Diego: Harcourt Brace Jovanovich, Publishers, 1990. 1030pp.
Glaspell, S. *Trifles*
Ibsen, H. *A Doll's House*
Shakespeare, W. *Hamlet, Prince of Denmark*
Sophocles. *Oedipus Rex*
Wilde, O. *The Importance of Being Earnest*
Williams, T. *The Glass Menagerie*

PROA Pronko, Leonard Cabell, ed. *Three Modern French Plays of the Imagination.* New York: Dell, 1966. 252pp. (The Laurel Language Library, French Series)
Ghelderode, M. *Christophe Colomb*
Ionesco, E. *Les chaises*
Neveux, G. *Juliette ou la clé des songes*

PROB *Prose and Poetry for Appreciation.* Edited by H. Ward McGraw. Syracuse, NY: Singer [c1934] 1971pp. (The Prose and Poetry Series)
Dunsany, E. *A Night at an Inn*
Gregory, A. *The Rising of the Moon*
Monkhouse, A. *The Grand Cham's Diamond*
Tarkington, B. *Monsieur Beaucaire*

PROC *Prose and Poetry for Appreciation.* Edited by Elizabeth Frances Ansorge [and Others] Syracuse, NY: Singer [c1942] 787pp. (The Prose and Poetry Series)
Corwin, N. *They Fly through the Air*
Gregory, A. *Spreading the News*
Kaufman, G., and Hart, M. *The American Way*
Knight, E. *Never Come Monday*
Knight, V. *Cartwheel*

PROD *Prose and Poetry for Appreciation.* Edited by Harriet Marcelia Lucas [and Others] 4th ed. Syracuse, NY: Singer [c1950] 822pp. (The Prose and Poetry Series)

Corwin, N. *The Odyssey of Runyon Jones*
Gilbert, W., and Sullivan, A. *The Mikado*
Glaspell, S. *Trifles*
Sherwood, R. *Abe Lincoln in Illinois*

PROF *Prose and Poetry of America.* Edited by H. Ward McGraw. Syracuse, NY: Singer [c1934] 1034pp. (The Prose and Poetry Series)
Fitch, C. *Nathan Hale*
Glaspell, S. *Trifles*
Hopkins, A. *Moonshine*

PROG *Prose and Poetry of America.* Edited by H. Ward McGraw. Syracuse, NY: Singer [c1934] 1198pp. (The New Prose and Poetry Series. South-western ed.)
Bowen, M. *Crude and Unrefined*
Fitch, C. *Nathan Hale*
Fortune, J. *The Cavalier from France*
Glaspell, S. *Trifles*
Hopkins, A. *Moonshine*
Rogers, J. *Judge Lynch*

PROH *Prose and Poetry of America.* Edited by H. Ward McGraw [and Others]. Catholic ed. Syracuse, NY: Singer [c1940] 1133pp. (The New Prose and Poetry Series)
Fitch, C. *Nathan Hale*
Hopkins, A. *Moonshine*
Kelly, G. *Poor Aubrey*

PROI *Prose and Poetry of America.* Edited by Julian L. Maline. Wilfred M. Mallon [and Others]. Syracuse, NY: Singer [c1949] 822pp. (At head of title: The St. Thomas More Series)
Connelly, M. *The Green Pasture*
Hopkins, A. *Moonshine*
Mulvey, T. *Letter to Tuffy*

PROM *Prose and Poetry of England.* Edited by H. Ward McGraw. Syracuse, NY: Singer [c1934] 1196pp. (The New Prose and Poetry Series)
Dunsany, E. *The Lost Silk Hat*
Goldsmith, O. *She Stoops to Conquer*
Shakespeare, W. *Macbeth*

PRON *Prose and Poetry of England.* Edited by H. Ward McGraw. Catholic ed. Syracuse, NY: Singer [c1940] 1150pp. (The New Prose and Poetry Series)
Benson, R. *The Upper Room*
Dunsany, E. *The Lost Silk Hat*
Shakespeare, W. *Macbeth*

PROW *Prose and Poetry of the World*. Edited by John R. Barnes [and Others]. Syracuse, NY: Singer [c1941] 1010pp. (The Prose and Poetry Series)
Euripides. *Medea*
Ibsen, H. *A Doll's House*
O'Neill, E. *Where the Cross Is Made*
Sachs, H. *The Wandering Scholar from Paradise*
Synge, J. *Riders to the Sea*

PROX *Prose and Poetry of the World*. Edited by James K. Agnew and Agnes L. McCarthy. Syracuse, NY: Singer [c1954] 788pp.
Čapek, K. *R.U.R.*
Miller, A. *Pussycat and the Expert Plumber Who Was a Man*
Williams, E. *Corn Is Green*

PUCC Puceiani, Oreste, F., ed. *The French Theater since 1930*. Boston: Ginn and Company [c1954] 400pp.
Camus, A. *Le malentendu*
Cocteau, J. *La machine infernale*
Giraudoux, J. *La guerre de Troie n'aura pas lieu*
Montherlant, H. *La reine morte*
Sartre, J. *Les mains sales*

THE PULITZER PRIZE PLAYS. *See* CORD, CORE, CORF Cordell, Kathryn (Coe) and Cordell, William Howard, eds.

PURK Purkiss, Diane, ed. *Three Tragedies by Renaissance Women*. London; New York: Penguin Books, 1998. 199pp.
Cary, E. The *Tragedie of Mariam*
Lumley, J. *The Tragedie of Iphigenia*
Pembroke, M. *The Tragedie of Antonie*

PURO *Puro Teatro: A Latina Anthology*. Edited by Alberto Sandoval-Sánchez and Nancy Saporta Sternbach. Tucson, AZ: University of Arizona Press, 2000. 440pp.
Arizmendi, Y. *Nostalgia maldita: 1–900–Mexico, a Stairmaster Piece*
Astor del Valle, J. *Fuchsia*
Bonet, W. *Good Grief, Lolita*
Cruz, M., and Blecher, H. *Frida: The Story of Frida Kahlo*
Garcia-Crow, A. *A Roomful of Men: A Radio for the Eyes Performance Piece*
Mena, A. *Las nuevas tamaleras*
Moraga, C. *Heart of the Earth: A Popol Vuh Story*
Palacios, M. *Describe Your Work*
Prida, D. *Botanica*
Romero, E. *The Fat-free Chicana & the Snow Cap Queen*

Tropicana, C., and Parnes, U. *Memorias de la revolucion*
Wood, S. *And Where Was Pancho Villa When You Really Needed Him?*

QUI Quinn, Arthur Hobson, ed. *Contemporary American Plays*. New York: Scribner [c1923] 382pp.
Crothers, R. *Nice People*
Emery, G. *The Hero*
Kaufman, G., and Connelly, M. *To the Ladies!*
O'Neill, E. *The Emperor Jones*
Williams, J. *Why Marry?*

QUIJ Quinn, Arthur Hobson, ed. *Representative American Plays*. New York: Century, 1917. 968pp.
Barker, J. *Superstition*
Belasco, D., and Long, J. *Madame Butterfly*
Bird, R. *The Broker of Bogota*
Boker, G. *Francesca da Rimini*
Boucicault, D. *The Octoroon; or, Life in Louisiana*
Crothers, R. *He and She*
Custis, G. *Pocahontas; or, the Settlers of Virginia*
Dunlap, W. *André*
Fitch, C. *Her Great Match*
Gillette, W. *Secret Service*
Godfrey, T. *The Prince of Parthia*
Howard, B. *Shenandoah*
Howe, J. *Leonora; or, the World's Own*
MacKaye, P. *The Scarecrow*
MacKaye, S. *Hazel Kirke*
Mitchell, L. *The New York Idea*
Moody, W. *The Faith Healer*
Payne, J., and Irving, W. *Charles the Second*
*Rip Van Winkle*
Ritchie, A. *Fashion*
Sheldon, E. *The Boss*
Smith, R. *The Triumph at Plattsburg*
Thomas, A. *The Witching Hour*
Tyler, R. *The Contrast*
Willis, N. *Tortesa the Usurer*

QUIJR Quinn, Arthur Hobson, ed. *Representative American Plays from 1880 to the Present Day*. Modern Drama Edition. New York: Century [c1928] 495–1052pp.
Belasco, D., and Long, J. *Madame Butterfly*
Crothers, R. *He and She*
Fitch, C. *Her Great Match*
Gillette, W. *Secret Service*
Howard, B. *Shenandoah*
MacKaye, P. *The Scarecrow*
MacKaye, S. *Hazel Kirke*
Mitchell, L. *The New York Idea*
Moody, W. *The Faith Healer*
O'Neill, E. *Beyond the Horizon*

Sheldon, E. *The Boss*
Thomas, A. *The Witching Hour*
Vollmer, L. *Sun-up*

QUIK Quinn, Arthur Hobson, ed. *Representative American Plays, 1767–1923.* 3rd ed. rev. and enl. New York: Century, 1925. 1052pp.
Barker, J. *Superstition*
Belasco, D., and Long, J. *Madame Butterfly*
Bird, R. *The Broker of Bogota*
Boker, G. *Francesca da Rimini*
Boucicault, D. *The Octoroon; or, Life in Louisiana*
Crothers, R. *He and She*
Custis, G. *Pocahontas; or, the Settlers of Virginia*
Dunlap, W. *André*
Fitch, C. *Her Great Match*
Gillette, W. *Secret Service*
Godfrey, T. *The Prince of Parthia*
Howard, B. *Shenandoah*
Howe, J. *Leonora; or, the World's Own*
MacKaye, P. *The Scarecrow*
MacKaye, S. *Hazel Kirke*
Mitchell, L. *The New York Idea*
Moody, W. *The Faith Healer*
O'Neill, E. *Beyond the Horizon*
Payne, J., and Irving, W. *Charles the Second*
*Rip Van Winkle*
Ritchie, A. *Fashion*
Sheldon, E. *The Boss*
Smith, R. *The Triumph at Plattsburg*
Thomas, A. *The Witching Hour*
Tyler, R. *The Contrast*
Vollmer, L. *Sun-up*
Willis, N. *Tortesa the Usurer*

QUIL Quinn, Arthur Hobson, ed. *Representative American Plays from 1767 to the Present Day.* 5th ed. rev. and enl. New York: Century [c1930] 1107pp.
Barker, J. *Superstition*
Barry, P. *Paris Bound*
Belasco, D., and Long, J. *Madame Butterfly*
Bird, R. *The Broker of Bogota*
Boker, G. *Francesca da Rimini*
Boucicault, D. *The Octoroon; or, Life in Louisiana*
Crothers, R. *He and She*
Custis, G. *Pocahontas; or, the Settlers of Virginia*
Dunlap, W. *André*
Fitch, C. *The Girl with the Green Eyes*
Gillette, W. *Secret Service*
Godfrey, T. *The Prince of Parthia*
Herne, J. *Margaret Fleming*
Howard, B. *Shenandoah*
Howard, S. *The Silver Cord*
MacKaye, P. *The Scarecrow*
MacKaye, S. *Hazel Kirke*

Mitchell, L. *The New York Idea*
Moody, W. *The Faith Healer*
O'Neill, E. *Beyond the Horizon*
Payne, J., and Irving, W. *Charles the Second*
*Rip Van Winkle*
Ritchie, A. *Fashion*
Sheldon, E. *The Boss*
Thomas, A. *The Witching Hour*
Tyler, R. *The Contrast*
Vollmer, L. *Sun-up*
Willis, N. *Tortesa the Usurer*

QUIM Quinn, Arthur Hobson, ed. *Representative Plays from 1767 to the Present Day.* 6th ed. rev. and enl. New York: Appleton-Century [c1938] 1157pp.
Anderson, M. *Winterset*
Barker, J. *Superstition*
Barry, P. *Paris Bound*
Belasco, D., and Long, J. *Madame Butterfly*
Bird, R. *The Broker of Bogota*
Boker, G. *Francesca da Rimini*
Boucicault, D. *The Octoroon; or Life in Louisiana*
Crothers, R. *He and She*
Custis, G. *Pocahontas; or, the Settlers of Virginia*
Dunlap, W. *André*
Fitch, C. *The Girl with the Green Eyes*
Gillette, W. *Secret Service*
Godfrey, T. *The Prince of Parthia*
Herne, J. *Margaret Fleming*
Howard, B. *Shenandoah*
Howard, S. *The Silver Cord*
MacKaye, P. *The Scarecrow*
MacKaye, S. *Hazel Kirke*
Mitchell, L. *The New York Idea*
Moody, W. *The Faith Healer*
O'Neill, E. *Beyond the Horizon*
Payne, J., and Irving, W. *Charles the Second*
*Rip Van Winkle*
Ritchie, A. *Fashion*
Sheldon, E. *The Boss*
Thomas, A. *The Witching Hour*
Tyler, R. *The Contrast*
Vollmer, L. *Sun-up*
Willis, N. *Tortesa the Usurer*

QUIN Quinn, Arthur Hobson, ed. *Representative American Plays from 1767 to the Present Day.* 7th ed., rev. and enl. New York: Appleton-Century Crofts [c1953] 1248pp.
Anderson, M. *Winterset*
Barker, J. *Superstition*
Barry, P. *Paris Bound*
Belasco, D. and Long, J. *Madame Butterfly*
Bird, R. *The Broker of Bogota*
Boker, G. *Francesca da Rimini*

Boucicault, D. *The Octoroon; or, Life in Louisiana*
Crothers, R. *He and She*
Custis, G. *Pocahontas; or, the Settlers of Virginia*
Dunlap, W. *André*
Fitch, C. *The Girl with the Green Eyes*
Gillette, W. *Secret Service*
Godfrey, T. *The Prince of Parthia*
Haines, W. *Command Decision*
Hammerstein II, O.; Rodgers, R.; Logan, J. and
    Michener, J. *South Pacific*
Herne, J. *Margaret Fleming*
Howard, B. *Shenandoah*
Howard, S. *The Silver Cord*
Jefferson, J. *Rip Van Winkle*
MacKaye, P. *The Scarecrow*
MacKaye, S. *Hazel Kirke*
Mitchell, L. *The New York Idea*
Moody, W. *The Faith Healer*
O'Neill, E. *Beyond the Horizon*
Payne, J. *Charles the Second*
Ritchie, A. *Fashion; or, Life in New York*
Sheldon, E. *The Boss*
Thomas, A. *The Witching Hour*
Tyler, R. *The Contrast*
Vollmer, L. *Sun-up*
Willis, N. *Tortesa the Usurer*

QUIO Quinn, Arthur Hobson; Haugh, Albert Croll; and
    Howe, Will David, eds. *The Literature of America.*
    New York: Scribner [c1929] 2 vols.
Belasco, D. and Long, J. *Madame Butterfly* 2
Boker, G. *Francesea da Rimini* 1
Howells, W. *The Unexpected Guests* 2
O'Neill, E. *Lazarus Laughed* 2
Tyler, R. *The Contrast* 1

QUINTANA, RICARDO. *See* EIGH *Eighteenth Century
    Plays.*

RAI Raines, Robert Arnold, ed. *Modern Drama and Social
    Change.* Englewood Cliffs, NJ: Prentice-Hall,
    1972. 339pp.
Brecht, B. *Galileo*
Camus, A. *Caligula*
Ionesco, E. *The Leader*
O'Neill, E. *The Hairy Ape*
Shaw, G. *Major Barbara*
Ward, D. *Day of Absence*

RALPH Ralph, Gordon, ed. *Boneman: An Anthology
    of Canadian Plays.* St. John's, NF: Jesperson
    Publishing Limited, 1995. 345pp.
Byrne, L. *Boneman*
Chudley, R. *After Abraham* (excerpt)
Cook, M. *On the Rim of the Curve* (excerpt)

Lambert, B. *The Song of the Serpent*
Moore, M. *Customs*
Ralph, G. *I Want Your Body*
Ravel, A. *Moon People*
Rockwood, G. *The Second Coming*
Sinclair, C. *Old Boots*

RAP Ramas, Wilhelmina Q. *Sugbuanon Theatre from
    Sotto to Rodriguez and Kabahar: An Introduction
    to Pre-War Sugbuanon Drama.* Quezon City:
    University of the Philippines Press, 1982. 369pp.
Kabahar, P. *Babaye ug lalake*
Kabahar, P. *Miss Dolying*
Rodriguez, B. *Bomba Nyor!*

RAVE *Rave: Young Adult Drama.* Winnipeg, Niagara
    Falls: Blizzard Publishing, 2000. 123pp.
Aguirre, C. *Chile con Carne*
Goobie, B. *The Face Is the Place*
Roy, E. The *Other Side of the Closet*

RAVEL Ravel, Aviva, ed. *Canadian Mosaic: 6 Plays.*
    Toronto: Simon & Pierre, 1995. 256pp.
Cheechoo, S. *Path with No Moccasins*
Longfield, K. *Going down the River*
Ravel, A. *Dance like a Butterfly*
Rylski, N. *Just like a Kommedia*
Varma, R. *No Man's Land*
Watada, T. *The Tale of a Mask*

RAVELII Ravel, Aviva, ed. *Canadian Mosaic II: 6 Plays.*
    Toronto: Simon & Pierre, 1996. 335pp.
Chan, M. *"Mom, Dad, I'm Living with a White Girl"*
Hammond, M. *Beautiful Deeds/De beau gestes*
McLean, D. *The House on Hermitage Road*
Ravel, A. *Gently down the Stream*
Towle, W. *The Golden Door*
Warkentin, V. *Like the Sun*

RAVIC Ravicz, Marilyn Ekdahl, ed. *Early Colonial
    Religious Drama in Mexico: From Tzompantli to
    Golgotha.* Washington, DC: Catholic University of
    America Press, 1970. 263pp.
*The Adoration of the Kings*
*The Destruction of Jerusalem*
*The Final Judgment*
*How the Blessed Saint Helen Found the Holy Cross*
*The Merchant*
*The Sacrifice of Isaac*
*Souls and Testamentary Executors*

RAVIT Ravitz, Abe C., ed. *The Disinherited: Plays.*
    Myrna J. Harrison and Robert J. Griffin, consulting
    editors. Encino, CA: Dickenson Pub., 1974. 273pp.

Anderson, M. *Winterset*
Brown, W. *The Escape; or, a Leap for Freedom*
Caldwell, B. *The King of Soul; or, the Devil and Otis Redding*
*The Double Dutch Act*
*The Double Wop Act*
Figueroa, J. *Everybody's a Jew*
Green, P., and Green, E. *Fixin's: The Tragedy of a Tenant Farm Woman*
Hughes, L. *Soul Gone Home*
Jones, L. *Great Goodness of Life (A Coon Show)*
Lamb, M. *But What Have You Done for Me Lately?*
Levine, M., McNamee, G., and Greenberg, D. *The Tales of Hoffman—a Series of Excerpts from the "Chicago Conspiracy" Trial*
Miller, J. *The Danites in the Sierras*
Moore, E. *Angela Is Happening*
O'Neill, E. *All God's Chillun Got Wings*
Rice, E. *The Adding Machine*
*The School Act*
*The Straight and the Jew*
Terkel, L. *Monologues from "Division Street, USA"*
Van Itallie, C. *Motel: A Masque for Three Dolls*
Williams, T. *Hello from Bertha*
Williams, T. *Talk to Me like the Rain and Let Me Listen*

RAY Ray, Gordon Norton; Edel, Leon; Johnson, Thomas H.; Paul, Sherman; and Simpson, Claude, eds. *Masters of American Literature.* Boston: Houghton [c1959] 2 vols.
O'Neill, E. *Desire under the Elms* 2
O'Neill, E. *The Long Voyage Home* 2

READ *Reading and Understanding Plays, Level I and Level II.* Providence, RI: Jamestown Publishers, 1989. 2 vols.
Benet, S. *The Devil and Daniel Webster* 1
Brooks, M. *Of Fathers and Sons* 2
Chekhov, A. *A Marriage Proposal* 1
Fletcher, L. *Sorry, Wrong Number* 2
Glaspell, S. *Trifles* 2
Goldman, W. *Butch Cassidy and the Sundance Kid* (excerpt) 2
Huston, J. *The Treasure of the Sierra Madre* (excerpt) 1
Ibsen, H. *A Doll's House* 2
Koch, H. *The War of the Worlds* (excerpt) 1
Miller, J. *The Rabbit Trap* 2
Milne, A. *The Ugly Duckling* 1
Shakespeare, W. *Julius Caesar* 1
Sills, P. *The Master Thief* 1
Strindberg, A. *The Stronger* 2
Vidal, G. *The Death of Billy the Kid* (excerpt) 1
Williams, T. *This Property Is Condemned* 2

READINGS FOR LIBERAL EDUCATION, READINGS FOR LIBERAL EDUCATION vol. 2. *See* LOCLA, LOCLB
Locke, Louis Glenn [and Others], eds. *Introduction to Literature*

REAL *Reality in Conflict: Literature of Values in Opposition.* Glenview, IL: Scott Foresman, 1976. 511pp.
Lawrence, J., and Lee, R. *Inherit the Wind*
Sophocles. *Electra*
Vonnegut, K. *Fortitude*

REARDON, WILLIAM R. *See also* AMPA *America's Lost Plays, vol. 21,* edited by Walter J. Meserve and William R. Reardon.

REAR Reardon, William R., et al., eds. *The Black Teacher and the Dramatic Arts: A Dialogue, Bibliography, and Anthology.* Westport, CT: Negro Universities Press, 1970. 487pp.
Davis, O. *Curtain Call, Mr. Aldridge, Sir*
Jackson, C., and Hatch, J. *Fly Blackbird*
Mitchell, L. *A Land beyond the River*
Mitchell, L. *Tell Pharaoh*
Shine, T. *Morning, Noon, and Night*

RED Redman, Crosby E., comp. *Designs in Drama.* Rev. ed. New York: Macmillan, 1968. 365pp.
Barrie, J. *The Admirable Crichton*
Rattigan, T. *The Winslow Boy*
Shakespeare, W. *Julius Caesar*
Wouk, H. *The Caine Mutiny Court Martial*

REDM Redman, Crosby E., compiler. *Drama II.* New York: Macmillan [c1962] 357pp.
Barrie, J. *The Admirable Crichton*
Rattigan, T. *The Winslow Boy*
Shakespeare, W. *Julius Caesar*
Van Druten, J. *I Remember Mama*

REED, HARRY B. *See* HAP *Harbrace Omnibus.*

REEV Reeve, Franklin D., ed. and tr. *An Anthology of Russian Plays.* New York: Vintage Books [c1961, 1963] 2 vols.
Andreyev, L. *He Who Gets Slapped* 2
Blok, A. *The Puppet Show* 2
Bulgakov, M. *The Days of the Turbins* 2
Chekhov, A. *The Seagull* 2
Fonvizín, D. *The Minor* 1
Gogol, N. *The Inspector General* 1
Gorky, M. *The Lower Depths* 2
Griboyedov, A. *The Trouble with Reason* 1
Mayakóvsky, V. *The Bedbug* 2
Ostrovsky, A. *The Storm* 1

Pushkin, A. *Boris Godunov* 1
Shvarts, E. *The Shadow* 2
Tolstoy, L. *The Power of Darkness* 1

REF *Reflections in Literature.* Philip McFarland, et al.,
      eds. Boston: Houghton Mifflin, c1975. 719p
  Shakespeare, W. *Romeo and Juliet*
  Sophocles. *Antigone*

REIL Reinert, Otto, ed. *Classic through Modern Drama.*
      Boston: Little, Brown, 1970. 949pp.
  Albee, E. *Who's Afraid of Virginia Woolf?*
  Brecht, B. *The Caucasian Chalk Circle*
  Chekhov, A. *The Three Sisters*
  Etherege, G. *The Man of Mode; or, Sir Fopling Flutter*
  *Everyman*
  Ibsen, H. *The Wild Duck*
  Jones, L. *Dutchman*
  Molière, J. *Tartuffe*
  O'Neill, E. *The Emperor Jones*
  Shakespeare, W. *Hamlet*
  Shaw, G. *Caesar and Cleopatra*
  Sophocles. *Oedipus Rex*
  Strindberg, A. *The Ghost Sonata*
  Synge, J. *Riders to the Sea*
  Weiss, P. *The Persecution and Assassination of Jean-*
      *Paul Marat as Performed by the Inmates of the*
      *Asylum of Charenton under the Direction of the*
      *Marquis de Sade*

REIN Reinert, Otto, ed. *Drama: An Introductory*
      *Anthology.* Boston: Little, Brown [c1961] 672pp.
  Brecht, B. *The Good Woman of Setzuan*
  Chekhov, A. *Three Sisters*
  *Everyman*
  Ibsen, H. *The Wild Duck*
  Ionesco, E. *The Lesson*
  Miller, A. *A View from the Bridge*
  Molière, J. *Tartuffe*
  Shakespeare, W. *Macbeth*
  Shaw, G. *Arms and the Man*
  Sophocles. *Oedipus Rex*
  Strindberg, A. *The Ghost Sonata*
  Yeats, W. *Purgatory*

REIO Reinert, Otto, ed. *Drama: An Introductory*
      *Anthology.* Alternate ed. Boston: Little, Brown
      [1964] 889pp.
  Albee, E. *The American Dream*
  Brecht, B. *The Caucasian Chalk Circle*
  Chekhov, A. *The Cherry Orchard*
  Ibsen, H. *Hedda Gabler*
  Jonson, B. *The Alchemist*
  Molière, J. *The Misanthrope*
  Pirandello, L. *Six Characters in Search of an Author*

Shakespeare, W. *Othello*
Shaw, G. *Caesar and Cleopatra*
Sheridan, R. *The Rivals*
Sophocles. *Antigone*
Strindberg, A. *Miss Julie*
Synge, J. *The Playboy of the Western World*

REIP Reinert, Otto, ed. *Modern Drama: Nine Plays.*
      Boston: Little, Brown [c1961, 1962] 491pp.
  Brecht, B. *The Good Woman of Setzuan*
  Chekhov, A. *Three Sisters*
  Ibsen, H. *The Wild Duck*
  Ionesco, E. *The Lesson*
  Pirandello, L. *Six Characters in Search of an Author*
  Shaw, G. *Arms and the Man*
  Strindberg, A. *The Ghost Sonata*
  Williams, T. *The Glass Menagerie*
  Yeats, W. *Purgatory*

REIT Reinert, Otto, ed. *Modern Drama.* Alternate ed.
      Boston: Little, Brown [1966] 630pp.
  Albee, E. *The Zoo Story*
  Brecht, B. *The Caucasian Chalk Circle*
  Chekhov, A. *The Cherry Orchard*
  Ghelderode, M. *Chronicles of Hell*
  Ibsen, H. *The Wild Duck*
  Pirandello, L. *Six Characters in Search of an Author*
  Shaw, G. *Caesar and Cleopatra*
  Strindberg, A. *The Father*
  Synge, J. *The Playboy of the Western World*
  Williams, T. *The Glass Menagerie*
  Yeats, W. *The Hour-glass*

REIV Reinert, Otto, ed. *Six Plays: An Introductory*
      *Anthology.* Boston: Little, Brown, 1973. 401pp.
  Chekhov, A. *The Cherry Orchard*
  Ibsen, H. *Hedda Gabler*
  Molière, J. *The Misanthrope*
  Shakespeare, W. *Othello*
  Sophocles. *Antigone*
  Williams, T. *The Glass Menagerie*

REIW Reinert, Otto, and Arnott, Peter, eds. *Thirteen*
      *Plays: An Introductory Anthology.* Boston: Little,
      Brown, 1978. 762pp.
  Albee, E. *Who's Afraid of Virginia Woolf?*
  Beckett, S. *Act without Words I*
  Chekhov, A. *The Cherry Orchard*
  Ibsen, H. *A Doll's House*
  Jones, L. *Dutchman*
  Miller, A. *Death of a Salesman*
  Molière, J. *Tartuffe*
  Pinter, H. *The Dumb Waiter*
  Pirandello, L. *Six Characters in Search of an Author*
  Shakespeare, W. *Hamlet*

Shaw, G. *Major Barbara*
Sophocles. *Oedipus the King*
Strindberg, A. *The Ghost Sonata*

REIWE Reinert, Otto, and Arnott, Peter, eds. *Twenty-three Plays: An Introductory Anthology*. Boston: Little, Brown, 1978. 1232pp.
Albee, E. *Who's Afraid of Virginia Woolf?*
Beckett, S. *Act without Words I*
Brecht, B. *The Caucasian Chalk Circle*
Chekhov, A. *The Cherry Orchard*
Etherege, G. *The Man of Mode*
*Everyman*
Gilbert, W. S. *Trial by Jury*
Ibsen, H. *A Doll's House*
Jones, L. *Dutchman*
Miller, A. *Death of a Salesman*
Molière, J. *Tartuffe*
O'Neill, E. *Ah, Wilderness!*
Pinter, H. *The Dumb Waiter*
Pirandello, L. *Six Characters in Search of an Author*
Racine, J. *Phaedra*
Shakespeare, W. *Hamlet*
Shaw, G. *Major Barbara*
Sophocles. *Oedipus the King*
Strindberg, A. *The Ghost Sonata*
Synge, J. *Riders to the Sea*
Weiss, P. *Marat/Sade*
Wilde, O. *The Importance of Being Earnest*
Yeats, W. *Purgatory*

RELIGIOUS DRAMAS, 1924–1925. *See* FED Federal Council of the Churches of Christ in America.

RENDW *Renaissance Drama by Women: Texts and Documents*. Edited by S. P. Cerasano and Marion Wynne-Davies. New York: Routledge, 1996. 237pp.
Brackley, E., and Cavendish, J. *The Concealed Fancies*
Cary, E. *The Tragedy of Mariam, the Faire Queene of Jewry*
Garnier, R. *The Tragedy of Antonie*
Seneca, L. *Hercules Oetaeus* (fragment)
White, R. *Cupid's Banishment*
Wroth, M. *Love's Victory*

RES *Restoration Plays*. Edited and introduction by Sir Edmund Gosse. London: Dent; New York: Dutton, 1974. 509pp.
Congreve, W. *The Way of the World*
Dryden, J. *All for Love*
Etherege, G. *The Man of Mode*
Farquhar, G. *The Beaux' Stratagem*
Otway, T. *Venice Preserved*

Vanbrugh, J. *The Provoked Wife*
Wycherley, W. *The Country Wife*

RESL *Restoration Plays*. Edited with an introduction and notes by Robert G. Lawrence. New ed. London: Dent; Rutland, VT: Tuttle, 1992. 678pp.
Congreve, W. *The Way of the World*
Dryden, J. *All for Love*
Etherege, G. *The Man of Mode*
Farquhar, G. *The Beaux' Stratagem*
Otway, T. *Venice Preserved*
Vanbrugh, J. *The Provoked Wife*
Wycherley, W. *The Country Wife*

REST *Restoration Plays*. With an introduction by Brice Harris. New York: Modern Library [c1955] 674pp.
Congreve, W. *The Way of the World*
Dryden, J. *All for Love*
Etherege, G. *The Man of Mode*
Farquhar, G. *The Beaux' Stratagem*
Otway, T. *Venice Preserved*
Vanbrugh, J. *The Relapse*
Villiers, G. *The Rehearsal*
Wycherley, W. *The Country Wife*

RET *Restoration Tragedies*. Edited by James Sutherland. London: Oxford, 1977. 441pp.
Banks, J. *The Unhappy Favourite*
Dryden, J. *All for Love*
Lee, N. *Lucius Junius Brutus*
Otway, T. *Venice Preserved*
Southerne, T. *Oroonoko*

REV *Revolution: A Collection of Plays*. Edited by Gerald Weales and Robert J. Nelson. New York: McKay, 1975. 312pp.
Betti, U. *The Queen and the Rebels*
Lowell, R. *Benito Cereno*
O'Casey, S. *The Plough and the Stars*
Shakespeare, W. *Coriolanus*

RHE Rhode, Eric, ed. *Novelists' Theatre*. Harmondsworth, Middlesex: Penguin, 1966. 279pp.
Dennis, N. *August for the People*
Spark, M. *Doctors of Philosophy*
Wilson, A. *The Mulberry Bush*

RHO Rhodes, Solomon Alhadef, ed. *The Contemporary French Theatre*. New York: Crofts, 1942. 431pp.
Bernard, J. *Martine*
Claudel, P. *L'annonce faite á Marie*
Curel, F. *Le repas du lion*
Lenormand, H. *L'homme et ses fantômes*
Maeterlinck, M. *Pelléas et Mélisande*
Porto-Riche, G. *Amoureuse*

Raynal, P. *Le tombeau sous l'Arc de triomphe*
Romains, J. *Cromedayre-le-Vieil*
Sarment, J. *Les plus beaux yeux du monde*

RICH Rich, Mabel Irene. *A Study of the Types of
    Literature*. New York: Century [c1921] 542pp.
Gibson, W. *The Family's Pride*
Milton, J. *Comus*
Shakespeare, W. *The Tragedy of Hamlet, Prince of
    Denmark*
Wilde, P. *The Traitor*

RICHE Richards, Jeffrey H., ed. *Early American Drama.*
    New York: Penguin Books, 1997. 512pp.
Aiken, G. *Uncle Tom's Cabin*
Barker, J. *The Indian Princess*
Bird, R. *The Gladiator*
Boucicault, D. *The Octoroon*
Dunlap, W. *André*
Mowatt, A. *Fashion*
Smith, W. *The Drunkard*
Tyler, R. *The Contrast*

RICI Richards, Stanley, ed. *Best Mystery and Suspense
    Plays of the Modern Theatre*. New York: Dodd,
    Mead, 1971. 800pp.
Anderson, M. *The Bad Seed*
Christie, A. *Witness for the Prosecution*
Deane, H., and Warburton, H. *Dracula*
Hamilton, P. *Angel Street*
Kesselring, J. *Arsenic and Old Lace*
Knott, F. *Dial "M" for Murder*
Marasco, R. *Child's Play*
Maugham, W. *The Letter*
Priestley, J. *Dangerous Corner*
Shaffer, A. *Sleuth*

RICIS Richards, Stanley, ed. *Best Plays of the Sixties.*
    Garden City, NY: Doubleday, 1970. 1036pp.
Anouilh, J. *Becket*
Crowley, M. *The Boys in the Band*
Friel, B. *Philadelphia, Here I Come*
Luke, P. *Hadrian VII*
Marcus, F. *The Killing of Sister George*
Sackler, H. *The Great White Hope*
Shaffer, P. *The Royal Hunt of the Sun*
Simon, N. *The Odd Couple*
Stein, J. *Fiddler on the Roof*
Williams, T. *Night of the Iguana*

RICJ Richards, Stanley, ed. *Best Short Plays of the World
    Theatre, 1958–1967*. New York: Crown, 1968.
    334pp.
Anouilh, J. *Madame de.*
Anouilh, J. *The Orchestra*

Behan, B. *The New House*
Brophy, B. *The Waste Disposal Unit*
Coward, N. *Come into the Garden, Maud*
Feiffer, J. *Crawling Arnold*
Fratti, M. *The Academy*
Frisch, M. *The Firebugs*
Inge, W. *The Disposal*
Jones, L. *The Great Goodness of Life*
Lowell, R. *Benito Cereno*
Macauley, P. *Monica*
Marcus, F. *The Window*
Melfi, L. *Birdbath*
Mercer, D. *The Governor's Lady*
O'Casey, S. *Nannie's Night Out*
Osborne, J. *A Subject of Scandal and Concern*
Pirandello, L. *Bellavita*
Shaffer, P. *White Lies*
Weiss, P. *The Tower*

RICK Richards, Stanley, ed. *Best Short Plays of the World
    Theatre, 1968–1973*. New York: Crown, 1973.
    303pp.
Anouilh, J. *Episode in the Life of an Author*
Bellow, S. *Orange Souffle*
Bentley, E. *Larry Parks' Day in Court*
Bowen, J. *The Waiting Room*
Childress, A. *Mojo*
Coward, N. *A Song at Twilight*
Duncan, R. *The Gift*
Ginsbury, N. *The Safety Match*
Horovitz, I. *Line*
Inge, W. *Margaret's Bed*
Kennedy, A., Lennon, J., and Spinetti, V. *The Lennon
    Play: In His Own Write*
Miller, J. *Lou Gehrig Did Not Die of Cancer*
Mortimer, J. *Bermondsday*
Owen, A. *Male of the Species*
Salacrou, A. *Marguerite*
Schisgal, M. *The Chinese*
Shepard, S. *The Holy Ghostly*
Simon, N. *Visitor from Forest Hills*
Ward, D. *Day of Absence*
Williams, T. *Confessional*

RICM Richards, Stanley, ed. *Great Musicals of the
    American Theatre*. Radnor, PA: Chilton, 1976.
    606pp. (*See also* RICO)
Anderson, M. *Lost in the Stars*
Comden, B., and Green, A. *Applause*
Fields, J., and Chodorov, J. *Wonderful Town*
Hart, M. *Lady in the Dark*
Lerner, A. *Camelot*
Masteroff, J. *Cabaret*
Spewack, B., and Spewack, S. *Leave It to Me!*
Wasserman, D. *Man of La Mancha*

Weidman, J., and Abbott, G. *Fiorello!*
Wheeler, H. *A Little Night Music*

RICN Richards, Stanley, ed. *Ten Classic Mystery and Suspense Plays of the Modern Theatre.* New York: Dodd, Mead, 1973. 887pp.
Archibald, W. *The Innocents*
Chodorov, E. *Kind Lady*
Christie, A. *Ten Little Indians*
Cohan, G. *Seven Keys to Baldpate*
Hayes, J. *The Desperate Hours*
Job, T. *Uncle Harry*
Percy, E., and Denham, R. *Ladies in Retirement*
Priestley, J. *An Inspector Calls*
Roffey, J. *Hostile Witness*
Williams, E. *Night Must Fall*

RICO Richards, Stanley, ed. *Ten Great Musicals of the American Theatre.* Radnor, PA: Chilton 1973. 594pp. (*See also* RICM)
Furth, G. *Company*
Heyward, D., and Heyward, D. *Porgy and Bess*
Kaufman, G., Ryskind, M., and Gershwin, I. *Of Thee I Sing*
Laurents, A. *Gypsy*
Laurents, A. *West Side Story*
Lerner, A. *Brigadoon*
Perelman, S., and Nash, O. *One Touch of Venus*
Spewack, B., and Spewack, S. *Kiss Me, Kate*
Stein, J. *Fiddler on the Roof*
Stone, P. *1776*

RICT Richards, Stanley, ed. *The Tony Winners: A Collection of Ten Exceptional Plays, Winner of the Tony Award for the Most Distinguished Play of the Year.* Garden City, NY: Doubleday c1977. 935pp.
Gilroy, F. *The Subject Was Roses*
Goodrich, F., and Hackett, A. *The Diary of Anne Frank*
Hartog, J. de. *The Fourposter*
Heggen, T., and Logan, J. *Mister Roberts*
McMahon, F. *Brendan Behan's Borstal Boy*
Osborne, J. *Luther*
Patrick, J. *The Teahouse of the August Moon*
Rabe, D. *Sticks and Bones*
Walker, J. *The River Niger*
Williams, T. *The Rose Tattoo*

RIL Richardson, Lyon Norman, Orians, George H., and Brown, Herbert R., eds. *The Heritage of American Literature.* Boston: Ginn [cl951] 2 vols.
O'Neill, E. *Anna Christie* 2

RIR Richardson, Willis, comp. *Plays and Pageants from the Life of the Negro.* Great Neck, NY: Core

Collection Books, 1979. 373pp. (Reprint of the 1930 edition published by Associated Publishers, Washington, D.C.)
Burke, I. *Two Races*
Cuney-Hare, M. *Antar of Araby*
Duncan, T. *Sacrifice*
Guinn, D. *Out of the Dark*
Gunner, F. *The Light of the Women*
McCoo, E. *Ethiopia at the Bar of Justice*
Matheus, J. *Ti Yette*
Miller, M. *Graven Images*
Miller, M. *Riding the Goat*
Richardson, W. *The Black Horseman*
Richardson, W. *The House of Sham*
Richardson, W. *The King's Dilemma*

RIRA Richardson, Willis, comp. *Plays and Pageants from the Life of the Negro.* Jackson, MS: University Press of Mississippi, 1994. (Reprint of the 1930 edition published by Associated Publishers, Washington, D.C.)
Burke, I. *Two Races*
Cuney-Hare, M. *Antar of Araby*
Duncan, T. *Sacrifice*
Guinn, D. *Out of the Dark*
Gunner, F. *The Light of the Women*
McCoo, E. *Ethiopia at the Bar of Justice*
Matheus, J. *Ti Yette*
Miller, M. *Graven Images*
Miller, M. *Riding the Goat*
Richardson, W. *The Black Horseman*
Richardson, W. *The House of Sham*
Richardson, W. *The King's Dilemma*

RIS Richmond, Farley, P., ed. *Plays of Provocation.* Dubuque, IA: Kendall/Hunt Publishing Company, 1999. 327pp.
Albee, E. *The American Dream*
Childress, A. *Wedding Band*
Durang, C. *Baby with the Bathwater*
Gotanda, P. *Yankee Dawg You Die*
McIntyre, D. *Split Second*
Mann, E. *Execution of Justice*
Orton, J. *What the Butler Saw*

RITS Ritchie, James M., and Garten, H. F., eds. and trs. *Seven Expressionist Plays: Kokoschka to Barlach.* London: Calder and Boyars [1968] 201pp.
Barlach, E. *Squire Blue Boll*
Brust, A. *The Wolves*
Goll, I. *Methusalem*
Kafka, F. *The Guardian of the Tomb*
Kaiser, T. *The Protagonist*
Kokoschka, O. *Murderer Hope of Womankind*
Stramm, A. *Awakening*

RITV Ritchie, James M., and Stowell, J. D., eds. and trs. *Vision and Aftermath: Four Expressionist War Plays.* London: Calder and Boyars, 1969. 208pp.
Goering, R. *Naval Encounter*
Haesenclever, W. *Antigone*
Hauptmann, C. *War, a Te Deum*
Toller, E. *Hinkelmann*

ROB Robbins, Harry Wolcott, and Coleman, William Harold, eds. *Western World Literature.* New York: Macmillan, 1938. 1422pp.
Aeschylus. *Agamemnon*
Aristophanes. *The Frogs*
Calderón de la Barca, P. *Keep Your Own Secret*
Euripides. *Iphigenia at Aulis*
*Everyman*
Goethe, J. *Faust, Part I*
Ibsen, H. *Ghosts*
Molière, J. *The Misanthrope*
O'Neill, E. *Beyond the Horizon*
Plautus, T. *The Captives*
Racine, J. *Phaedra*
Shakespeare, W. *King Lear*
Sheridan, R. *The Rivals*

ROBE Robertson, Durant Waite, ed. *The Literature of Medieval England.* New York: McGraw Hill, 1970. 612pp.
*Everyman*
*Mactacio Abel*
*Secunda pastorum*

ROBI Robinson, Charles Alexander, Jr., ed. *An Anthology of Greek Drama, First Series.* New York: Rinehart [c1949] 269pp. (Rinehart Editions)
Aeschylus. *Agamemnon*
Aristophanes. *Lysistrata*
Euripides. *Hippolytus*
Euripides. *Medea*
Sophocles. *Antigone*
Sophocles. *Oedipus the King*

ROBJ Robinson, Charles Alexander, Jr., ed. *An Anthology of Greek Drama, Second Series.* New York: Rinehart [c1954] 398pp. (Rinehart Editions)
Aeschylus. *Choëphoroe*
Aeschylus. *Eumenides*
Aeschylus. *Prometheus Bound*
Aristophanes. *The Clouds*
Aristophanes. *The Frogs*
Euripides. *The Bacchae*
Euripides. *The Trojan Women*
Sophocles. *Oedipus at Colonus*
Sophocles. *Philoctetes*

ROBJA Robinson, Charles Alexander, Jr., ed. *The Spring of Civilization, Periclean Athens.* New York: Dutton, 1954. 464pp.
Aeschylus. *Agamemnon*
Euripides. *Medea*
Euripides. *The Trojan Women*
Sophocles. *Antigone*
Sophocles. *Oedipus at Colonus*
Sophocles. *Oedipus the King*

ROBK Robinson, Cyril Edward, tr. *The Genius of the Greek Drama.* Oxford: Clarendon Press, 1921. 96pp.
Aeschylus. *Agamemnon*
Euripides. *Medea*
Sophocles. *Antigone*

ROBM Robinson, Donald Fay, ed. *The Harvard Dramatic Club Miracle Plays: Ten Plays Translated and Adapted by Various Hands.* New York: French, 1928. 241pp.
*The Benediktbeuren Play*
Bourlet, K. *The Nativity (The Chantilly Play)*
*The Hessian Christmas Play*
*The Maastricht Play*
*The Pageant of the Shearmen and the Tailors*
*The Provençal Play*
*The Star*
*The Towneley Play*
*The Umbrian Play*
*The Wisemen*

ROBR Robinson, Ronny, ed. *They Said You Were Too Young.* London: Hodder and Stoughton, 1989. 187pp.
Bond, E. *Lily and Colin*
Lyons, G. *Mohicans*
Page, L. *Toby and Donna*

ROE Roberts, Carl Eric Bechhofer, tr. *Five Russian Plays, with One from the Ukrainian.* New York: Dutton, 1916. 173pp.
Chekhov, A. *The Jubilee*
Chekhov, A. *The Wedding*
Evreinov, N. *The Beautiful Despot*
Evreinov, N. *A Merry Death*
Fonvizin, D. *The Choice of a Tutor*
Ukrainka, L. [pseud.] *The Babylonian Captivity*

ROEB Robson, Cheryl, ed. *Balkan Plots: New Plays from Central and Eastern Europe.* London: Aurora Metro Press, 2000. 180pp.
Romcevic, N. *Cordon*
Spiró, G. *Soap Opera*

Valean, A. *When I Want to Whistle, I Whistle . . .*
Visniec, M. *The Body of a Woman as a Battlefield in the Bosnian War*

ROES Robson, Cheryl, ed. *Seven Plays by Women: Female Voices, Fighting Lives.* London: Aurora Metro Publications, 1991. 269pp.
 Abbott, J. *Forced Out*
 De Angelis, A. *Crux*
 Lewin, E. *Cochon flambé*
 Raif, A. *Fail/safe*
 Rapi, N. *Ithaka*
 Robson, C. *The Taking of Liberty*
 Ruppe, J. *Cut It Out*

ROET Robson, Cheryl, ed. *A Touch of the Dutch: Plays by Women.* London: Aurora Metro Publications/ Theater Instituut Nederland, 1997. 226pp.
 Dulleman, I. *Write Me in the Sand*
 Haasse, H. *A Thread in the Dark*
 Herzberg, J. *The Caracal*
 Lohuizen, S. *Dossier: Ronald Akkerman*
 Veldhuisen, M. *Eat*

ROF Roby Robert C., and Ulanov Barry, eds. *Introduction to Drama.* New York: McGraw-Hill, 1962. 704pp.
 Chekhov, A. *The Cherry Orchard*
 Congreve, W. *The Way of the World*
 Euripides. *Medea*
 Giraudoux, J. *Tiger at the Gates*
 Ibsen, H. *Rosmersholm*
 Jonson, B. *The Alchemist*
 Kaiser, G. *From Morn to Midnight*
 Lindsay, D. *The Satire of the Three Estates*
 Molière, J. *The Misanthrope*
 Plautus, T. *Miles gloriosus*
 Racine, J. *Phaedra*
 Shaw, G. *Man and Superman*
 Sophocles. *Oedipus Rex*
 Strindberg, A. *The Dance of Death*
 Webster, J. *The Duchess of Malfi*

ROGEBD Rogers, Katharine M., ed. *The Meridian Anthology of 18th- and 19th-Century British Drama.* New York: Meridian, 1996. 580pp.
 Boucicault, D. *The Octoroon*
 Farquhar, G. *The Beaux' Stratagem*
 Gay, J. *The Beggar's Opera*
 Gilbert, W. *Ruddigore*
 Lillo, G. *The London Merchant*
 Sheridan, R. *The School for Scandal*
 Steele, R. *The Conscious Lovers*
 Wilde, O. *The Importance of Being Earnest*

ROGEW Rogers, Katharine M., ed. *The Meridian Anthology of Restoration and Eighteenth-Century Plays by Women.* New York: Meridian, 1994. 560pp.
 Behn, A. *Sir Patient Fancy*
 Burney, F. *The Witlings*
 Centlivre, S. *A Bold Stroke for a Wife*
 Cowley, H. *The Belle's Stratagem*
 Inchbald, E. *Such Things Are*
 Pix, M. *The Spanish Wives*
 Warren, M. *The Group*

ROGEX Rogers, Winfield Heyser; Redinger, Ruby V., and Haydn II, Hiram C., eds. *Explorations in Living.* New York: Reynal & Hitchcock [c1941] 783pp.
 Ibsen, H. *An Enemy of the People*
 Shakespeare, W. *Hamlet*
 Wilder, T. *Our Town*

ROHAN, PIERRE DE. *See* FEE, FEF *Federal Theatre Project. Federal Theatre Plays.* ["Edited for the Federal Theatre by Pierre de Rohan"]

ROHR Rohrberger Mary; Woods, Samuel H., Jr., and Dukore Bernard F., compilers. *An Introduction to Literature.* New York: Random House [1968] 983pp.
 *Everyman*
 Shakespeare, W. *The Tragedy of Macbeth*
 Shaw, G. *Pygmalion*
 Sophocles. *Antigone*
 Strindberg, A. *A Dream Play*
 Williams, T. *The Glass Menagerie*

ROLF, ROBERT J., ed. *See* ALTJD *Alternative Japanese Drama.*

ROLF Rolfe, Franklin Prescott; Davenport, William H.; and Bowerman, Paul, eds. *The Modern Omnibus.* New York: Harcourt, Brace [c1946] 1071pp.
 Anderson, M. *Key Largo*
 Kaufman, G., and Ryskind, M. *Of Thee I Sing*
 Sherwood, R. *Abe Lincoln in Illinois*
 Thurber, J., and Nugent, E. *The Male Animal*

ROM *Roman Drama.* Indianapolis, IN: Bobbs-Merrill [c1965] 463pp.
 Plautus, T. *The Haunted House*
 Plautus, T. *The Menaechmi*
 Plautus, T. *The Rope*
 Seneca, L. *Medea*
 Seneca, L. *Oedipus*
 Seneca, L. *Thyestes*
 Terence, P. *The Brothers*

Terence, P. *Phormio*
Terence, P. *The Woman of Andros*

ROMA Romano, V., Octavio I., and Rios C., Herminio,
  eds. *El espejo—The mirror: Selected Chicano
  Literature*. Berkeley, CA: Quinto Sol, 1972. 284pp.
  Portillo, E. *The Day of the Swallows*

ROOTS *The Roots of African American Drama: An
  Anthology of Early Plays*. Edited by Leo Hamalian
  and James V. Hatch. Detroit: Wayne State
  University Press, 1991. 454pp.
  Brown, W. *The Escape, or a Leap for Freedom*
  Burrill, M. *Aftermath*
  Butterbeans and Susie. *Black Vaudeville*
  Dodson, O. *The Shining Town*
  Graham, S. *Tom-tom*
  Hill, A. *On Strivers Row*
  Hopkins, P. *Peculiar Sam, or the Underground Railroad*
  Hurston, Z. *The First One*
  Miller, M. *Nails and Thorns*
  Mitchell, J. *Help Wanted*
  Richardson, W. *The Chip Woman's Fortune*
  Tillman, K. *Aunt Betsy's Thanksgiving*
  Towns, G. *The Sharecropper*

ROSE, MARTIAL. *See* TOWN *Towneley Plays. The
  Wakefield Mystery Plays*.

ROSENB Rosenberg, Donna, ed. *World Literature: An
  Anthology of Great Short Stories, Drama, and
  Poetry*. Lincolnwood, IL: NTC Publishing Group,
  1992. 884pp.
  Ibsen, H. *A Doll's House*
  O'Neill, E. *Ile*
  Shakespeare, W. *The Tempest*
  Solórzano, C. *Crossroads: A Sad Vaudeville*
  Sophocles. *Antigone*
  Soyinka, W. *The Trials of Brother Jero*
  Zeami, M. *The Damask Drum*

ROSENFIELD, JOHN. *See* THX *Three Southwest Plays*.

ROSENFIELD, PAUL. *See* AME *American Caravan*.

ROSS Ross, Ralph Gilbert; Berryman, John; and Tate,
  Allen, eds. *The Arts of Reading*. New York:
  Thomas Y. Crowell [c1960] 488pp.
  Chekhov, A. *A Marriage Proposal*
  Shakespeare, W. *The Tragedy of Macbeth*

ROWC Rowell, George, ed. *Late Victorian Plays, 1890–
  1914*. New York: Oxford, 1968. 507pp.
  Davies, H. *The Mollusc*
  Galsworthy, J. *Justice*

Granville-Barker, H. *The Voysey Inheritance*
Hankin, St. J. *The Cassilis Engagement*
Houghton, S. *Hindle Wakes*
Jones, H. *The Liars*
Pinero, A. *The Second Mrs. Tanqueray*

ROWE Rowell, George, ed. *Nineteenth Century Plays*.
  London: Oxford University Press [c1953] 567pp.
  Albery, J. *Two Roses*
  Boucicault, D. *The Colleen Bawn*
  Bulwer-Lytton, E. *Money*
  Grundy, S. *A Pair of Spectacles*
  Hazlewood, C. *Lady Audley's Secret*
  Jerrold, D. *Black-ey'd Susan*
  Lewis, L. *The Bells*
  Robertson, T. *Caste*
  Taylor, T. *The Ticket-of-leave Man*
  Taylor, T., and Reade, C. *Masks and Faces*

ROY Roy, Emil, and Roy, Sandra, compilers. *Literary
  Spectrum*. Boston: Allyn, 1974. 355pp.
  Andreëv, L. *An Incident*
  Chekhov, A. *The Bear*
  O'Neill, E. *Hughie*
  Strindberg, A. *The Stronger*
  Synge, J. *Riders to the Sea*

ROYE Roy, Emil, and Roy, Sandra, comps. *Literature I*.
  New York: Macmillan, 1976. 669pp.
  Saroyan, W. *My Heart's in the Highlands*
  Synge, J. *Riders to the Sea*

RUA Rubinstein, Harold Frederick, ed. *Four Jewish Plays*.
  London: Gollancz, 1948. 303pp.
  Bernhard, E. *The Marranos*
  Block, T. *You Must Stay to Tea*
  Hemro. *Poor Ostrich*
  Scott, P. *Pillars of Salt*

RUB Rubinstein, Harold Frederick, ed. *Great English
  Plays*. New York: Harper, 1928. 1136pp.
  Beaumont, F., and Fletcher, J. *The Maid's Tragedy*
  Congreve, W. *The Way of the World*
  Dekker, T. *The Shoemaker's Holiday*
  *Everyman*
  Farquhar, G. *The Recruiting Officer*
  Fletcher, J. *The Chances*
  Ford, J. *'Tis a Pity She's a Whore*
  Goldsmith, O. *She Stoops to Conquer*
  Heywood, J. *John, Tyb, and the Curate*
  Jones, H. *Judah*
  Jonson, B. *The Silent Woman*
  Jonson, B., Chapman, G., and Marston, J. *Eastward Ho!*
  Kyd, T. *The Spanish Tragedy*

Marlowe, C. *Doctor Faustus*
Marlowe, C. *Edward the Second*
Massinger, P. *The Bondman*
Massinger, P. *A New Way to Pay Old Debts*
Otway, T. *Venice Preserved*
Peele, G. *The Old Wives' Tale*
Robertson, T. *Society*
Sheridan, R. *The School for Scandal*
Vanbrugh, J. *The Provoked Wife*
*A Wakefield Nativity*
Webster, J. *The White Devil*
Wilde, O. *Lady Windermere's Fan*
*A Yorkshire Tragedy*

RUDAK Rudakoff, Judith, ed. *Dangerous Traditions: A Passe Muraille Anthology*. Winnipeg: Blizzard Publishing, Inc. 1992. 278pp.
Clark, S. *Lost Souls and Missing Persons*
Garrard, J. *Peggy's Song*
Griffiths, L., and Brymer, *P.O.D. on Paradise*
Palmer, J. *Before the Guns*

RUN Runnells, Rory, ed., with an introduction by Doug Arrell. *A Map of the Senses: Twenty Years of Manitoba Plays*. [Winnipeg]: Scirocco Drama, 2000. 519pp.
Chafe, R. *Zac and Speth*
Harrar, W. *Inquest*
Hunter, M. *Footprints on the Moon*
McManus, B. *Calenture*
McMillan, R. *Washing Spider Out*
Moore, E. *Live with It*
Nolan, Y. *Blade*
O'Neil, D. *Worm Moon*
Rintoul, H. *Between Then and Now*
Ross, I. *Heart of a Distant Tribe*
Silver, A. *Thimblerig*
Trochim, D. *Better Looking Boys*

RUSS Russell, Harry Kitsun; Wells, William; and Stauffer, Donald A., eds. *Literature in English*. New York: Holt [c1948] 1174pp.
Shakespeare, W. *King Lear*
Sheridan, R. *The School for Scandal*

RUSSCO *Russian Comedy of the Nikolaian Era*. Translated and with an introduction by Laurence Senelick. Amsterdam: Harwood Academic Publishers, 1997. 161pp. (Russian Theatre Archive, vol. 10)
Lensky, D. *Her First Night*
Prutkov, K. *Fantasy*
Saltykov-Shchedrin, M. *Pazukhin's Death*
Turgenev, I. *Luncheon with the Marshal of Nobility, or a Friendly Delusion*

RUSV Russell, John David, and Brown, Ashley, ed. *Satire*. Cleveland, OH: World Books, [c1967] 420pp.
Euripides. *The Cyclops*
Mayakóvsky, V. *The Bedbug*
Molière, J. *Love Is the Best Doctor*

RVI *Russian Satiric Comedy: Six Plays*. Ed. and trans. by Laurence Senelick. New York: Performing Arts Journal Publications, 1983. 198pp.
Babel, I. *Sundown*
Bulgakov, M. *Ivan Vasilievich*
Evreinov, N. *The Fourth Wall*
Ilf, I. *The Power of Love*
Krylov, I. *The Milliner's Shop*
Prutkov, K. *The Headstrong Turk, or, Is It Nice to Be a Grandson?*

RYL Rylands, George Humphrey Wolfestan, ed. *Elizabethan Tragedy*. London: Bell, 1933. 623pp.
Chapman, C. *Bussy d'Ambois*
Ford, J. *'Tis a Pity She's a Whore*
Heywood, T. *A Woman Killed with Kindness*
Marlowe, C. *Tamburlaine the Great, Part I*
Tourneur, C. *The Revenger's Tragedy*
Webster, J. *The White Devil*

RZH Rzhevevsky, Nicholas, ed. *An Anthology of Russian Literature from Earliest Writings to Modern Fiction: Introduction to a Culture*. Armonk, NY: M. E. Sharpe, 1996. 587pp.
*Chapayev Anecdotes*
Chekov, A. *The Cherry Orchard* (Act I only)
Kharms, D. *Makarov and Peterson, No. 3*
Pushkin, A. *Boris Godunov*
Zoshchenko, M. *Crime and Punishment: A Comedy in One Act*

SACL *Saclit Drama: Plays by South Asian Canadians*. Ed. by Uma Parameswaran. Bangalore, India: IBH Prakashana, 1996. 273pp.
Binning, S. *Lesson of a Different Kind*
Bose, R. *Baba Jacques Dass and Turmoil at Cote-des-Neiges Cemetery*
Bose, R. *Five or Six Characters in Search of Toronto*
Parameswaran, U. *Meera: A Dance Drama*
Parameswaran, U. *Rootless but Green are the Boulevard Trees*
Parameswaran, U. *Sita's Promise*
Varma, R., and Orlov, S. *Isolated Incident*
Varma, R., Lloyd George, I., and Vlachos, H. *Job Stealer*

SACR *Sacred Earth Dramas: An Anthology of Winning Plays from the 1990 Competition of the Sacred*

*Earth Drama Trust.* Foreword by Ted Hughes; introduction by Toni Arthur. London, Boston: Faber and Faber, 1993. 179pp.
Bread and Puppet Theatre, Ecole d'Humanité. *Chipko*
Calcutt, D. *Gifts of Flame*
Class 5, Ecole de Genève. *Buffalo Dance*
Dorras, J., and Walker, P. *The Tale of Mighty Hawk and Magic Fish*
Malhotra, B. *Nature's Revenge*
Miles, C. *Greenheart and the Dragon Pollutant*
St. Peter's Youth Group. *Persephone and the Rubbish Bin*
Surridge, A. *Children of the Rainbow*
Whisenand, R. *Think Global. Act Loco*

SAFF Saffron, Robert, ed. *Great Farces.* New York: Collier Books, 1966. 316pp.
Aristophanes. *Lysistrata*
Gogol, N. *The Inspector General*
Molière, J. *Le bourgeois gentilhomme*
Spewack, B., and Spewack, S. *Boy Meets Girl*
Wilde, O. *The Importance of Being Earnest*

SAFM Saffron, Robert, ed. *Great Melodramas.* New York: Collier Books, 1966. 341pp.
Dumas, A. *Monte Cristo*
Gillette, W. *Secret Service*
Hamilton, P. *Angel Street*
Maugham, W. *The Letter*

SALA Salas, Teresa Cajiao, and Vargas, Margarita, eds. *Women Writing Women: An Anthology of Spanish-American Theater of the 1980s.* Albany: State University of New York Press, 1997. 468pp.
Aguirre, I. *Altarpiece of Yumbel*
Berman, S. *Yankee*
Casas, M. *The Great USkrainian Circus*
Marichal Lugo, T. *Evening Walk*
Raznovich, D. *Dial-a-Mom*
Romero, M. *Waiting for the Italian*
Seibel, B. *Seven Times Eve*
Vilalta, M. *A Woman, Two Men, and a Gunshot*

SALE Salerno, Henry Frank, ed. *English Drama in Transition 1880–1920.* New York: Pegasus [1968] 544pp.
Barrie, J. *The Admirable Crichton*
Galsworthy, J. *The Silver Box*
Jones, H. *The Liars*
Maugham, W. *Our Betters*
Pinero, A. *The Second Mrs. Tanqueray*
Shaw, G. *Major Barbara*
Synge, J. *The Playboy of the Western World*
Wilde, O. *The Importance of Being Earnest*
Yeats, W. *Deirdre*

SALF Salgado, Ramsay Gamini Norton, ed. *Four Jacobean City Comedies.* Drayton, Middlesex: Penguin, 1975. 428pp.
Jonson, B. *The Devil Is an Ass*
Marston, J. *The Dutch Courtesan*
Massinger, P. *A New Way to Pay Old Debts*
Middleton, T. *A Mad World, My Masters*

SALG Salgado, Ramsay Gamini Norton, ed. *Three Jacobean Tragedies.* Baltimore: Penguin Books [1965] 363pp.
Middleton, T. *The Changeling*
Tourneur, C. *The Revenger's Tragedy*
Webster, J. *The White Devil*

SALR Salgado, Ramsay Gamini Norton, ed. *Three Restoration Comedies.* Baltimore: Penguin Books [1968] 365pp.
Congreve, W. *Love for Love*
Etherege, G. *The Man of Mode*
Wycherley, W. *The Country Wife*

SALS Salkeld, Audrey, and Smith, Rosie, compilers. *One Step in the Clouds: An Omnibus of Mountaineering Novels and Short Stories.* London: Diadem Books; San Francisco: Sierra Club Books, 1990, 1991. 1056pp.
Collins, B. *The Ice Chimney*

SAN San Francisco Mime Troupe. *By Popular Demand: Plays and Other Works.* San Francisco: The Troupe, 1980. 302pp.
San Francisco Mime Troupe. *The Dragon Lady's Revenge*
San Francisco Mime Troupe. *Ecoman*
San Francisco Mime Troupe. *False Promises/Nos engañaron*
San Francisco Mime Troupe. *Frijoles, or Beans to You*
San Francisco Mime Troupe. *Frozen Wages*
San Francisco Mime Troupe. *The Independent Female: or, a Man Has His Pride, a Melodrama*
San Francisco Mime Troupe. *Los siete*
San Francisco Mime Troupe. *San Fran Scandals; a Vaudeville Exposé*

SAND Sanderlin, George. *College Reading.* Boston: Heath [c1953] 849pp.
Ibsen, H. *An Enemy of the People*
O'Neill, E. *Bound East for Cardiff*
Shaw, G. *Androcles and the Lion*

SANE Sanders, Charles [and Others] eds. *Synthesis: Responses to Literature.* New York: Knopf, 1971. 750pp.
Chekhov, A. *The Three Sisters*

Euripides. *The Bacchae*
Ibsen, H. *The Master Builder*
Itallie, J. *America Hurrah*
Molière, J. *Tartuffe*
Pirandello, L. *Henry IV*

SANK Sanders, Thomas S. *The Discovery of Drama.*
Glenview, IL: Scott, Foresman, 1968. 637pp.
Bellow, S. *Orange Souffle*
Chayefsky, P. *The Latent Heterosexual*
Giraudoux, J. *Sodom and Gomorrah*
Shakespeare, W. *Macbeth*
Sophocles. *Oedipus Rex*
Synge, J. *Riders to the Sea*
Williams, T. *Camino Real*

SANL Sanderson, James L., and Gopnik, Irwin, eds.
*Phaedra and Hippolytus: Myth and Dramatic
Form.* Boston: Houghton Mifflin, 1966. 338pp.
Euripides. *Hippolytus*
Jeffers, R. *The Cretan Woman*
O'Neill, E. *Desire under the Elms*
Racine, J. *Phaedra*
Seneca. *Phaedra*

SANM Sanderson, James L., and Zimmerman, Everett,
eds. *Medea: Myth and Dramatic Form.* Boston:
Houghton Mifflin [1967] 337pp.
Anderson, M. *The Wingless Victory*
Anouilh, J. *Medea*
Euripides. *Medea*
Jeffers, R. *Medea*
Seneca. *Medea*

SANO Sanderson, James L., and Zimmerman, Everett,
eds. *Oedipus: Myth and Dramatic Form.* Boston:
Houghton Mifflin [1968] 341pp.
Cocteau, J. *The Infernal Machine*
Gide, A. *Oedipus*
Seneca. *Oedipus*
Sophocles. *King Oedipus*
Voltaire. *Oedipus*

SANR Sandrow, Nahma, ed. *God, Man, and Devil:
Yiddish Plays in Translation.* Syracuse, NY:
Syracuse University Press, 1999. 321pp.
Dymov, O. *Bronx Express*
Gordin, J. *God, Man, and Devil*
Hirschbein, P. *Green Fields*
Leivick, H. *Shop*
Pinski, D. *The Treasure*

SATA *Satan, Socialites, and Solly Gold: Three New
Plays from England.* New York: Coward-McCann
[c1961] 280pp.

Duncan, R. *The Death of Satan*
Jupp, K. *The Socialites*
Kops, B. *Enter Solly Gold*

SATI Satin, Joseph Henry, compiler. *Reading Literature.*
Boston: Houghton Mifflin [1964] 1338pp. (Part III,
Reading Drama)
Albee, E. *The Sandbox*
Betti, U. *Corruption in the Palace of Justice*
Chekhov, A. *Uncle Vanya*
Hill, F. *The Six Degrees of Crime*
Molière, J. *The Physician in Spite of Himself*
Steinbeck, J. *Of Mice and Men*
Strindberg, A. *Miss Julie*
Wilde, O. *The Importance of Being Earnest*

SATJ Satin, Joseph Henry, ed. *Reading Literature: Stories,
Plays, and Poems.* Boston: Houghton Mifflin
[1968] 683pp.
Albee, E. *The Sandbox*
Chekhov, A. *Uncle Vanya*
Giraudoux, J. *The Tiger at the Gates*
Shaw, G. *Arms and the Man*
Sophocles. *Oedipus the King*

SAYLER, OLIVER MARTIN. *See also* MOS, MOSA
*Moscow Art Theatre Series of Russian Plays,* and
PLAM *Plays of the Moscow Art Theatre Musical
Studio.*

SAY Sayler, Oliver Martin, ed. *The Eleonora Duse Series
of Plays.* New York: Brentano [c1923] v.p.
Annunzio, G., d'. *The Dead City*
Gallarati-Scotti, T. *Thy Will Be Done*
Ibsen, H. *Ghosts*
Ibsen, H. *The Lady from the Sea*
Praga, M. *The Closed Door*

SCAN *Scandinavian Plays of the Twentieth Century.*
Princeton, NJ: Princeton University Press, 1944–
1951. 3 vols.
Abell, K. *Anna Sophie Hedvig* 2
Bergman, H. *Mr. Sleeman Is Coming* 1
Bergman, H. *The Swedenhielms* 3
Dagerman, S. *The Condemned* 3
Grieg, N. *The Defeat; a Play about the Paris Commune* 2
Josephson, R. *Perhaps a Poet* 1
Krog, H. *The Sounding Shell* 2
Lagerkvist, P. *Let Man Live* 3
Lagerkvist, P. *The Man without a Soul* 1
Munk, K. *Niels Ebbesen* 2
Schildt, R. *The Gallows Man: A Midwinter Story* 1

SCAR Scanlan, David, compiler. *5 Comedies.* Boston:
Houghton, Mifflin, 1971. 343pp.

Giraudoux, J. *The Madwoman of Chaillot*
Pritchard, B. *Captain Fantastio Meets the Ectomorph*
Saroyan, W. *The Time of Your Life*
Shaw, G. *Arms and the Man*
Sheridan, R. *The Rivals*

SCAT Schell, Edgar Thomas, ed. *English Morality Plays
and Moral Interludes*. New York: Holt, Rinehart
and Winston, 1969. 554pp.
*The Castle of Perseverance*
*Everyman*
*The Interlude of Youth*
Lupton, T. *All for Money*
Redford, J. *Wit and Science*
*Respublica*
Wager, W. *Enough Is as Good as a Feast*
Wapull, G. *The Tide Tarrieth No Man*
Woodes, N. *The Conflict of Conscience*
*World and the Child*

SCH Schelling, Felix Emmanuel, ed. *Typical Elizabethan
Plays*. New York: Harper, 1926. 797pp.
Beaumont, F., and Fletcher, J. *The Maid's Tragedy*
Beaumont, F., and Fletcher, J. *Philaster; or, Love Lies
A-bleeding*
Chapman, G., Jonson, B., and Marston, J. *Eastward Ho!*
Dekker, T. *The Pleasant Comedy of Old Fortunatus*
Fletcher, J. *Rule a Wife and Have a Wife*
Ford, J. *The Chronical History of Perkin Warbeck, a
Strange Truth*
Greene, R. *A Pleasant Conceited Comedy of [George a
Greene], the Pinner of Wakefield*
Heywood, T. *A Woman Killed with Kindness*
Jonson, B. *The Hue and Cry after Cupid*
Jonson, B. *The Sad Shepherd*
Jonson, B. *Volpone; or, the Fox*
*The Lamentable and True Tragedy of Master Arden of
Feversham in Kent*
Lyly, J. *Endymion, the Man in the Moon*
Marlowe, C. *The Tragical History of Doctor Faustus*
Marlowe, C. *The Troublesome Reign and Lamentable
Death of Edward II*
Massinger, P. *A New Way to Pay Old Debts*
Middleton, T., and Rowley, W. *The Changeling*
Munday, A. *Sir Thomas More (An Ill May-day)*
*The Return from Parnasaus; or, the Scourge of Simony,
Part II*
Shirley, J. *The Lady of Pleasure*
Webster, J. *The Tragedy of the Duchess of Malfi*

SCI Schelling, Felix Emmanuel, and Black, Matthew, W.,
eds. *Typical Elizabethan Plays*. Rev. and enl. ed.
New York: Harper [c1931] 1033pp.
Beaumont, F., and Fletcher, J. *The Knight of the Burning
Pestle*
Beaumont, F., and Fletcher, J. *The Maid's Tragedy*

Beaumont, P., and Fletcher, J. *Philaster; or, Love Lies
A-bleeding*
Chapman, O., Jonson, B., and Marston, J. *Eastward Ho!*
Dekker, T. *The Pleasant Comedy of Old Fortunatus*
Dekker, T. *The Shoemaker's Holiday; or, the Gentle
Craft*
Fletcher, J. *The Faithful Shepherdess*
Fletcher, J. *Rule a Wife and Have a Wife*
Ford, J. *The Broken Heart*
Greene, R. *The Honorable History of Friar Bacon and
Friar Bungay*
Heywood, T. *A Woman Killed with Kindness*
Jonson, B. *Every Man in His Humour*
Jonson, B. *The Hue and Cry after Cupid*
Jonson, B. *Volpone: or, the Fox*
Kyd, T. *The Spanish Tragedy*
Lyly, J. *Endymion, the Man in the Moon*
Marlowe, C. *Tamburlaine the Great, Part I*
Marlowe, C. *The Tragical History of Doctor Faustus*
Marlowe, C. *The Troublesome Reign and Lamentable
Death of Edward II*
Massinger, P. *A New Way to Pay Old Debts*
Middleton, T. *Michaelmas Term*
Middleton, T., and Rowley, W. *The Changeling*
Munday, A. *Sir Thomas More (An Ill May-day)*
Peele, G. *The Old Wives' Tale*
*The Return from Parnassus; or, the Scourge of Simony,
Part II*
Shirley, J. *The Lady of Pleasure*
Webster, J. *The Tragedy of the Duchess of Malfi*

SCJ Schelling, Felix Emmanuel, and Black, Matthew W.,
eds. *Typical Elizabethan Plays*. 3rd ed., rev. and
enl. New York: Harper [c1949] 1065pp.
Beaumont, F., and Fletcher, J. *The Knight of the Burning
Pestle*
Beaumont, F., and Fletcher, J. *The Maid's Tragedy*
Beaumont, F., and Fletcher, J. *Philaster; or, Love Lies
A-bleeding*
Chapman, G., Jonson, B., and Marston, J. *Eastward Ho!*
Dekker, T. *The Shoemaker's Holiday; or, the Gentle
Craft*
Fletcher, J. *The Faithful Shepherdess*
Ford, J. *The Broken Heart*
Greene, R. *The Honorable History of Friar Bacon and
Friar Bungay*
Heywood, T. *A Woman Killed with Kindness*
Jonson, B. *Every Man in His Humour*
Jonson, B. *The Hue and Cry after Cupid*
Jonson, B. *Volpone; or, the Fox*
Kyd, T. *The Spanish Tragedy*
Lyly, J. *Endymion, the Man in the Moon*
Marlowe, C. *Tamburlaine the Great, Part I*
Marlowe, C. *The Tragical History of Doctor Faustus*
Marlowe, C. *The Troublesome Reign and Lamentable
Death of Edward II*

Massinger, P. *A New Way to Pay Old Debts*
Middleton, T. *Michaelmas Term*
Middleton, T., and Rowley, W. *The Changeling*
Munday, A. *Sir Thomas More (An ill May-day)*
Peele, G. *The Old Wives' Tale*
*The Return from Parnassus; or, the Scourge of Simony, Part II*
Shirley, J. *The Lady of Pleasure*
Webster, J. *The Tragedy of the Duchess of Malfi*

SCL Schiff, Ellen, ed. *Awake and Singing: 7 Classic Plays from the American Jewish Repertoire.* New York: Mentor, 1995. 636pp.
Behrman, S. *The Cold Wind and the Warm*
Chayefsky, P. *The Tenth Man*
Hoffman, A. *Welcome, Stranger*
Laurents, A. *Home of the Brave*
Odets, C. *Awake and Sing!*
Regan, S. *Morning Star*
Rice, E. *Counsellor-at-law*

SCM Schiff, Ellen, ed. *Fruitful and Multiplying: 9 Contemporary Plays from the American Jewish Repertoire.* New York: Mentor, 1996. 522pp.
Baitz, J. *The Substance of Fire*
Finn, W., and Lapine, J. *Falsettoland*
Gardner, H. *Conversations with My Father*
Havis, A. *A Vow of Silence*
Mamet, D. *Goldberg Street*
Mann, E. *Annulla, an Autobiography*
Margulies, D. *Sight Unseen*
Swados, E. *Esther, a Vaudeville Megillah*
Sweet, J. *The Value of Names*

SCN Schinz, Albert; Robert, Osmond Thomas and Giroud, Pierre François, eds. *Nouvelle anthologie française.* New York: Harcourt, Brace, 1936. 680pp.
Corneille, P. *Le cid*
*La farce de maître Pierre Pathelin*
Hugo, V. *Ruy Blas*
Labiche, E. et Martin, E. *La poudre aux yeux*
Molière, J. *Le bourgeois gentilhomme*
Racine, J. *Andromaque*

SCNN Schneider, Elizabeth W.; Walker, Albert L. and Childs, Herbert E., eds. *The Range of Literature.* New York: American Book Company [c1960] 732pp.
Chekhov, A. *The Cherry Orchard*
Rice, E. *The Adding Machine*
Shakespeare, W. *Othello, the Moor of Venice*
Shaw, G. *Arms and the Man*
Sophocles. *Oedipus Rex*

SCNO Schneider, Elizabeth Wintersteen; Walker, Albert L.; and Childs, Herbert E., eds. *The Range of Literature.*

2nd ed. New York: American Book Co. [1967] 702pp.
Beckett, S. *All that Fall*
Chekhov, A. *The Cherry Orchard*
Ionesco, E. *Improvisation; or, the Shepherd's Chameleon*
Shakespeare, W. *Othello*
Shaw, G. *Arms and the Man*
Sophocles. *Oedipus Rex*
Wilder, T. *The Skin of Our Teeth*

SCNP Schneider, Elizabeth Wintersteen [and others] eds. *The Range of Literature.* 3rd ed. New York: Van Nostrand-Reinhold, 1973. 1116pp.
Chekhov, A. *The Cherry Orchard*
Hansberry, L. *A Raisin in the Sun*
Ibsen, H. A *Doll's House*
MacLeish, A. *J.B.*
Mrozek, S. *The Police*
Shakespeare, W. *Othello*
Shaw, G. *Arms and the Man*
Sophocles. *Antigone*

SCNPL Scholes, Robert; Klaus, Carl H.; and Silverman, Michael, eds. *Elements of Literature: Essay, Fiction, Poetry, Drama, Film.* New York: Oxford University Press, 1978. 1356pp.
Aristophanes. *Lysistrata*
Bullins, E. *In the Wine Time*
*Everyman*
Ibsen, H. *A Doll's House*
Molière, J. *The Misanthrope*
Pinter, H. *A Slight Ache*
Shakespeare, W. *Othello*
Shaw, G. *Arms and the Man*
Sophocles. *Oedipus Rex*
Strindberg, A. *The Stronger*
Williams, T. *Cat on a Hot Tin Roof*

SCNQ Scholes, Robert; Comley, Nancy R.; Klaus, Carl H.; and Silverman, Michael, eds. *Elements of Literature Five: Fiction, Poetry, Drama, Essay, Film.* Rev. ed. New York: Oxford University Press, 1982. 1504pp.
Aristophanes. *Lysistrata*
Beckett, S. *Krapp's Last Tape*
Brecht, B. *The Threepenny Opera*
*Everyman*
Hughes, L. *Mother and Child*
Ibsen, H. *A Doll's House*
Mankiewicz, H., and Welles, O. *Citizen Kane*
Molière, J. *The Misanthrope*
Shakespeare, W. *Othello*
Shaw, G. *Major Barbara*
Sophocles. *Oedipus Rex*
Strindberg, A. *The Stronger*
Williams, T. *Cat on a Hot Tin Roof*

SCNQCA Scholes, Robert; Comley, Nancy R.; Klaus,
Carl H.; and Staines, David, eds. *Elements
of Literature*. Canadian ed. Toronto: Oxford
University Press, 1987. 1194pp.
Aristophanes. *Lysistrata*
Beckett, S. *Krapp's Last Tape*
*Everyman*
Fineberg, L. *Death*
Glass, J. *Artichoke*
Ibsen, H. *A Doll's House*
Ryga, G. *The Ecstasy of Rita Joe*
Shakespeare, W. *King Lear*
Shaw, G. *Major Barbara*
Sophocles. *Oedipus Rex*
Williams, T. *The Glass Menagerie*

SCNQCB Scholes, Robert; Comley, Nancy R.; Klaus,
Carl H.; and Staines, David, eds. *Elements of
Literature*. 2nd Canadian ed. Toronto: Oxford
University Press, 1990. 1416pp.
Albee, E. *The Zoo Story*
Beckett, S. *Krapp's Last Tape*
*Everyman*
Fineberg, L. *Death*
Ibsen, H. *A Doll's House*
Pollock, S. *Doc*
Ryga, G. *The Ecstasy of Rita Joe*
Shakespeare, W. *King Lear*
Shaw, G. *Major Barbara*
Sheridan, R. *The School for Scandal*
Sophocles. *Oedipus Rex*
Wilde, O. *The Importance of Being Earnest*
Williams, T. *The Glass Menagerie*

SCNR Schorer, Mark, compiler. *Galaxy: Literary Modes
and Genres*. New York: Harcourt, Brace and World
[1967] 620pp.
Chekhov, A. *The Three Sisters*
Euripides. *The Trojan Women*
Giraudoux, J. *Tiger at the Gates*
Lowell, R. *My Kinsmen, Major Molineux*

SCNT Schorer, Mark, compiler. *The Literature of
America: Twentieth Century*. New York: McGraw-
Hill, 1970. 1159pp.
Albee, E. *The Zoo Story*
Jones, L. *Dutchman*
O'Neill, E. *Desire under the Elms*
Wilder, T. *The Skin of Our Teeth*

SCV Schotter, Richard, ed. *The American Place Theatre*.
New York: Dell Publishing Company, 1973. 270pp.
Cameron, K. *Papp*
Ribman, R. *Fingernails Blue as Flowers*
Russell, C. *Five on the Black Hand Side*
Tabori, G. *The Cannibals*
Tesich, S. *The Carpenters*

SCVDO Schumacher, Julie A., and Russell-Dempsey,
Gay, eds. *Drama for Reading & Performance.
Collection One: Seventeen Full-Length Plays for
Students*. Logan, IA: Perfection Learning, 2000
2 vols. (Volume 2 consists of lesson plans and
reproducible assignments.)
Allard, J. *Painted Rain* 1
Brecht, B., and Weill, K. *He Who Says No* 1
Brecht, B., and Weill, K. *He Who Says Yes* 1
Fletcher, L. *The Hitch Hiker* 1
Foote, H. *The Dancers* 1
Fugard, A. *The Drummer* 1
Gregg, S. *This Is a Test* 1
Harris, A. *The Arkansaw Bear* 1
Haubold, C. *The Big Black Box* 1
Ives, D. *Variations on the Death of Trotsky* 1
Kesselman, W. *Maggie Magalita* 1
Mamet, D. *The Frog Prince* 1
Markoe, A. *Conversation with My Dogs* 1
Raspanti, C. *I Never Saw another Butterfly* 1
Smith, R. *Nothing but the Truth* 1
Soto, G. *Novio Boy* 1
Swortzell, L. *The Love of Three Oranges* 1
Wasserstein, W. *The Man in a Case* 1

SCVDT Schumacher, Julie A., and Russell-Dempsey,
Gay, eds. *Drama for Reading & Performance.
Collection Two: Nineteen Full-Length Plays for
Students*. Logan, IA: Perfection Learning, 2000
2 vols. (Volume 2 consists of lesson plans and
reproducible assignments.)
Allen, W. *Death Knocks* 1
Brenner, A. *Survival* 1
Coleman, W. *Phaeton and the Sun Chariot* 1
Duffield, B. *The Lottery* 1
Durang, C. *The Actor's Nightmare* 1
Foote, H. *A Young Lady of Property* 1
Fugard A. *My Children! My Africa!* 1
Gonzalez S., S. *The Migrant Farmworker's Son* 1
Ives, D. *Sure Thing* 1
Kan, K. *Madman on the Roof* 1
King, S. *Sorry, Right Number* 1
Lawrence, J., and Lee, R. *The Night Thoreau Spent in
Jail* 1
Mamet, D. *A Waitress in Yellowstone* 1
Molière, J. *The Love Doctor* 1
Serling, R. *Back There* 1
Simon, N. *Lost in Yonkers* 1
Snodgrass, K. *Haiku* 1
Tagore, R. *The Post Office* 1
Wilson, A. *The Janitor* 1

SCVG Schürer, Ernst, ed. *German Expressionist Plays*.
New York: Continuum, 1997. 322pp. (The German
Library, vol. 66)
Benn, G. *Ithaka*

Hasenclever, W. *The Son*
Kaiser, G. *From Morning to Midnight*
Kaiser, G. *Gas* I
Kaiser, G. *Gas* II
Kokoschka, O. *Murderer the Women's Hope*
Sternheim, C. *The Bloomers*
Stramm, A. *Sancta Susanna*
Toller, E. *Masses and Man*

SCVN Schwarz, Egon, and Spence, Hannelore M., eds. *Nineteenth Century German Plays*. New York: Continuum, 1990. 260pp. (The German Library; vol. 31)
Grillparzer, F. *King Ottocar's Rise and Fall*
Hebbel, F. *Agnes Bernauer*
Nestroy, J. *The Talisman*

SCW Schweikert, Harry Christian, ed. *Early English Plays*. New York: Harcourt, Brace [c1928] 845pp.
*Abraham and Isaac*
*Banns*
Dekker, T. *The Shoemaker's Holiday*
*Everyman*
*The Fall of Lucifer*
Greene, R. *The Honorable History of Friar Bacon and Friar Bungay*
Jonson, B. *Every Man in His Humour*
*The Judgment Day*
Kyd, T. *The Spanish Tragedy*
Lyly, J. *Endymion*
Marlowe, C. *Tamburlaine the Great, Parts I and II*
Marlowe, C. The Tragical History of Doctor Faustus
*Noah*
Peele, G. *The Old Wives' Tale*
*Quem quaeritis*
*Robin Hood and the Friar*
Sackville, T. and Norton, T. *Gorboduc*
*Saint George and the Dragon*
*The Second Shepherds' Play*
Udall, N. *Ralph Roister Doister*

SCWE Schweikert, Harry Christian; Inglis, Rewey Belle; and Gehlmann, John, eds. *Adventures in American Literature*. New York: Harcourt, Brace [c1930] 1064pp.
Fitch, C. *Nathan Hale*
O'Neill, E. *Where the Cross Is Made*
Tarkington, B. *The Trysting Place*

SCWG Schweikert, Harry Christian; Inglis, Rewey Belle; Gehlmann, John; and Foerster, Norman, eds. *Adventures in American Literature*. Rev. ed. New York: Harcourt Brace, 1936. 1217pp.
Kelly, G. *Poor Aubrey*
O'Neill, E. *The Emperor Jones*
Tarkington, B. *The Trysting Place*

SCWI Schweikert, Harry Christian; Miller, Harry Augustus; and Cook, Luella Bussey, eds. *Adventures in Appreciation*. New York: Harcourt, Brace, 1935. 1965pp.
Dunsany, E. *The Lost Silk Hat*
Howard, S., and DeKruif, P. *Yellow Jack*
Shakespeare, W. *As You like It*

SCX Schwiebert, John E., ed. *Reading and Writing from Literature*. Boston; New York: Houghton Mifflin Company, 1997. 924pp
Allen, W. *Death Knocks*
Fugard, A. *The Road to Mecca*
Glaspell, S. *Trifles*
McNally, T. *Andre's Mother*
Oates, J. *Tone Clusters*
O'Neill, E. *The Hairy Ape*
Sanchez-Scott, M. *The Cuban Swimmer*
Wilson, A. *Fences*

SCY Scott, Adolphe Clarence, ed. and tr. *Traditional Chinese Plays*. Madison: University of Wisconsin Press, 1967–1975. 3 vols.
*The Butterfly Dream (Hu tieh meng)* 1
*Fifteen Strings of Cash (Shih wu kuan)* 2
*Longing for Worldly Pleasures (Ssu fan)* 2
Nü, C. *A Girl Setting Out for Trial* 3
Shih, Y. *Picking Up the Jade Bracelet* 3
*Ssu Lang Visits His Mother (Ssu Lang t'an mu)* 1

SDQ *The Scribner Quarto of Modern Literature*; edited by A. Walton Litz. New York: Scribner, 1978. 597pp.
Albee, E. *The Zoo Story*
O'Neill, E. *Desire under the Elms*
Pinter, H. *A Slight Ache*
Shaw, G. *Pygmalion*
Williams, T. *The Glass Menagerie*

SEA Searles, Colbert, ed. *Seven French plays (1730–1897)*. New York: Holt [c1935] 749pp.
Augier, E. *Le gendre de M. Poirier*
Beaumarchais, P. *Le mariage de Figaro*
Becque, H. *Les corbeaux*
Hugo, V. *Hernani*
Marivaux, P. *Le jeu de l'amour et du hasard*
Rostand, E. *Cyrano de Bergerac*
Voltaire, F. *Zaire*

SEARS Sears, Djanet, ed. *Testifyin': Contemporary African Canadian Drama*. Toronto: Playwrights Canada Press, 2000–2003. 2 vols.
Anthony, T. *'Da Kink in My Hair: Voices of Black Womyn* 2
bailey, m. & lewis, s. *sistahs* 1
Borden, W. *Tightrope Time: Ain't Nuthin' More than Some Itty Bitty Madness between Twilight & Dawn* 1

Boyd, G. *Consecrated Ground* 2
bunyan, h. *Prodigals in a Promised Land* 1
Clarke, A. *When He Was Free and Young He Used to Wear Silks* 1
Clarke, G. *Québécité : A Jazz Libretto in Three Cantos* 2
Clarke, G. *Whylah Falls* 1
Gale, L. *Angélique* 2
Hall, T., Spencer, R., and Sandiford, S. *Jean and Dinah Who Have Been Locked Away in a World Famous Calypso since 1956 Speak Their Minds Publicly* 2
mandiela, a. *dark diaspora . . . in dub* 1
Moodie, A. *A Common Man's Guide to Loving Women* 2
Moodie, A. *Riot* 1
Philip, M. *Coups and Calypsos* 1
Sears, D. *The Adventures of a Black Girl in Search of God* 2
Sears, D. *Harlem Duet* 1
Seremba, G. *Come Good Rain* 1
Ward, F. *Somebody Somebody's Returning* 2
young, d., and belvett, n. *yagayah: two.womyn.black. griots* 2

SEAVER, EDWIN. *See* CROZ *Cross-section.*

SEBO Seboyar, Gerald Edwin, and Brosius, Rudolph Frederic, eds. *Readings in European Literature.* New York: Crofts, 1928. 876pp.
Aeschylus. *Prometheus Bound*
Aristophanes. *The Frogs*
Euripides. *Medea*
Ibsen, H. *Ghosts*
Molière, J. *The High-brow Ladies*
Plautus. *The Crock of Gold*
Racine, J. *Phaedra*
Sophocles. *Antigone*
Terence. *Andria; the Fair Andrian*

SEBP Seboyar, Gerald Edwin, and Brosius, Rudolph Frederic, eds. *Readings in European Literature* [2nd ed.] New York: Crofts, 1946. 900pp.
Aeschylus. *Prometheus Bound*
Aristophanes. *The Frogs*
Euripides. *Medea*
Ibsen, H. *Ghosts*
Molière, J. *The High-brow Ladies*
Plautus. *The Menaechmi*
Racine, J. *Phaedra*
Sophocles. *Antigone*
Terence. *Andria; the Fair Andrian*

SECK Secker, Martin. *The Eighteen-Nineties.* London: Richards [1948] 616pp.
Dowson, E. *The Pierrot of the Minute*
Yeats, W. *The Countess Cathleen*

SECOND AMERICAN CARAVAN. 1928. *See* AME *American Caravan, vol. 2.*

SECO *The 2nd Conference for Asian Women and Theater: A Compilation of Plays.* Manila, Philippines: Philippine Center of International PEN, 2000. 366pp.
Bophavy, K. *A Wound in Her Life*
Fernandez-Ilagan, M. *Ugpaanan*
Jacob, M. *Country in Search of a Hero*
Kisaragi, K. *Moral*
Leow, P. *Letters to a Movie Queen*
Magtoto, L. *Despedida de soltera*
Mhapsekar, J. *Bap re bap*
Ngoc, N. *Beyond the Truth*
Nhu, H. *The Story of Mother*
Sarumpaet, R. *Marsinah Accuses*
Win, T. *Place for a Woman*

SEIS *6 dramaturgos españoles del siglo XX: Teatro de liberación, vol. 1: Teatro en democracia, vol. 2.* Ottawa, Girol Books, 1988. 2 vols.
Alberti, R. *El hombre deshabitado* 1
Alonso de Santos, J. *Bajarse al moro* 2
Fernán Gómez, F. *Las bicicletas son para el verano* 2
Garcia Lorca, F. *La casa de Bernarda Alba* 1
Nieva, F. *La Señora Tártara* 2
Sastre, A. *En la red* 1

SELDES, GEORGE S. *See* PLAM *Plays of the Moscow Art Theatre Musical Studio.*

SELDES, GILBERT. *See* PLAM *Plays of the Moscow Art Theatre Musical Studio.*

SELF Self, David, ed. *Classic Drama.* Cheltenham, UK: Stanley Thornes (Publishers) Ltd., 1998. 249pp.
Goldsmith, O. *She Stoops to Conquer*
Planché, J. *The Garrick Fever*
Sheridan, R. *The Rivals*

SELOV Senelick, Lawrence, compiler. *Lovesick: Modernist Plays of Same-Sex Love, 1894–1925.* 1999. 199pp.
Armory. *The Gentleman of the Chrysanthemums*
Fuller, H. *At Saint Judas's*
Gray, J., and Raffalovich, M. *The Blackmailers*
Hirschberg, H. *"Mistakes"*
Kuzmin, M. *The Dangerous Precaution*
Mann, K. *Ania and Esther*

SEN Seng, Peter J., ed. *Plays: Wadsworth Handbook and Anthology.* Belmont, CA: Wadsworth Publishing Company, 1970. 487pp.
Chekhov, A. *The Cherry Orchard*
*Everyman*

García Lorca, F. *The House of Bernarda Alba*
Ibsen, H. *The Wild Duck*
Jonson, B. *Volpone, or; the Fox*
O'Neill, E. *Desire under the Elms*
Pirandello, L. *Six Characters in Search of an Author*
*The Second Shepherds' Play*
Shakespeare, W. *Macbeth*
Shakespeare, W. *A Midsummer Night's Dream*
Shaw, G. *Heartbreak House*
Sophocles. *Oedipus Rex*
Strindberg, A. *The Ghost Sonata*
Synge, J. *Riders to the Sea*
Webster, J. *The Duchess of Malfi*
Wycherly, W. *The Country Wife*

SER Seronde, Joseph, and Peyre, Henri, eds. *Nine Classic French Plays*. Boston: Heath [c1936] 748pp.
Corneille, P. *Le cid*
Corneille, P. *Horace*
Corneille, P. *Polyeucte*
Molière, J. *Le precieuses ridicules*
Molière, J. *Le misanthrope*
Molière, J. *Le Tartuffe*
Racine, J. *Andromaque*
Racine, J. *Esther*
Racine, J. *Phèdre*

SERD Seronde, Joseph, and Peyre, Henri, eds. *Three Classic French Plays*. Boston: Heath [c1935] 253pp.
Corneille, P. *Le cid*
Molière, J. *Les précieuses ridicules*
Racine, J. *Andromaque*

SET Setehanove, L. J. *Five French Comedies*. Boston: Allyn and Bacon [c1925] 276pp.
Bernard, T. *L'anglais tel qu'on le parle*
*La farce de maitre Pathelin*
Forest, L. *Par un jour de pluie*
France, A. *La comèdie de celui qui épousa une femme muette*
Maurey, M. *Rosalie*

SETR Setren, Phil, ed. *Best of the Fest: A Collection of New Plays Celebrating 10 Years of London New Play Festival*. London: Aurora Metro Press, 1998. 310pp.
Bandele, B. *Two Horsemen*
Bridgeman, L. *Maison splendide*
Jenkins, M. *Strindberg Knew My Father*
Penhall, J. *Wild Turkey*
Upton, J. *Everlasting Rose*
Wallace, N. *In the Fields of Aceldama*

SEUC *Seven Cannons: Plays by Maureen Hunter, Connie Gault, Wendy Lill, Linda Griffiths, Joan MacLeod, Judith Thompson, and Colleen Wagner*. Selected by

Martin Bragg, Per Brask, and Roy Surette. Toronto: Playwrights Canada Press, 2000. 414pp.
Gault, C. *Sky*
Griffiths, L. *The Darling Family*
Hunter, M. *Transit of Venus*
Lill, W. *The Glace Bay Miners' Museum*
MacLeod, J. *The Hope Slide*
Thompson, J. *Lion in the Streets*
Wagner, C. *The Monument*

SEV *Seven Plays*. London: Heinemann [1935] 775pp.
Coward, N. *Conversation Piece*
Dane, C. *Moonlight Is Silver*
Kennedy, M. *Escape Me Never!*
Lonsdale, F. *Aren't We All?*
Priestley, J. *Laburnum Grove*
Winter, J. *The Shining Hour*
Wooll, E. *Libel*

SEVD *Seven Plays of the Modern Theatre*. With an introduction by Harold Clurman. New York: Grove Press [c1962] 548pp.
Beckett, S. *Waiting for Godot*
Behan, B. *The Quare Fellow*
Delaney, S. *A Taste of Honey*
Gelber, J. *The Connection*
Genêt, J. *The Balcony*
Ionesco, E. *Rhinoceros*
Pinter, H. *The Birthday Party*

SEVE *Seven Sacred Plays* with an Introduction by Sir Francis Younghusband and notes by A. H. Debenham. London: Methuen, [1934] v.p.
Bulkley, A. *The Crown of Light*
Debenham, A. *Good Will toward Men*
Debenham, A. *The Prince of Peace*
Gonne, F. *In the City of David*
Hines, L. *Simon*
Mell, M. *The Apostle Play*
*The Passion Play of Alsfeld*

SEVP *Seven Soviet Plays*. With introductions by H. W. L. Dana. New York: Macmillan, 1946. 520pp.
Afinogenov, A. *On the Eve*
Korneichuk, A. *The Front*
Leonov, L. *The Orchards of Polovchansk*
Rokk, V. *Engineer Sergeyev*
Simonov, K. *The Russian People*
Solovyov, V. *Field Marshall Kutuzov*
Tur, L., Tur, P. and Sheinin, L. *Smoke of the Fatherland*

SEVT *Seventeen Plays: Sophocles to Baraka*. Edited by Bernard F. Dukore. New York: Crowell, 1976. 808pp.
Aristophanes. *Lysistrata*
Brecht, B. *Mother Courage and Her Children*

Büchner, G. *Woyzeck*
Chekhov, A. *The Seagull*
Ibsen, H. *A Doll's House*
Ionesco, E. *The Gap*
Jones, L. *The Slave*
Molière, J. *The School for Wives*
Pirandello, L. *Each in His Own Way*
*The Second Shepherds' Play*
Shakespeare, W. *Hamlet*
Shaw, G. *Pygmalion*
Sophocles. *Oedipus the King*
Strindberg, A. *The Ghost Sonata*
Synge, J. *Riders to the Sea*
Williams, T. *The Night of the Iguana*
Wycherley, W. *The Country Wife*

SHA Shafer, Robert, ed. *American Literature.* New York: Doubleday, Doran [c1926] 2 vols.
Fitch, C. *The Girl with the Green Eyes* 2
O'Neill, E. *The Hairy Ape* 2

SHAH Shafer, Robert, ed. *From Beowulf to Thomas Hardy.* New York: Doubleday, Page [c1924] 2 vols.
Dryden, J. *All for Love* 1
*Everyman* 1
Goldsmith, O. *She Stoops to Conquer* 1
Marlowe, C. *The Tragical History of Doctor Faustus* 1

SHAI Shafer, Robert, ed. *From Beowulf to Thomas Hardy.* Rev. ed. New York: Doubleday, Doran [c1931] 2 vols.
Congreve, W. *The Way of the World* 1
*Everyman* 1
Marlowe, C. *The Tragical History of Doctor Faustus* 1
Sheridan, R. *The Rivals* 2

SHAJ Shafer, Robert, ed. *From Beowulf to Thomas Hardy.* New ed. New York: Doubleday, Doran [c1939] 2 vols.
Dekker, T. *The Shoemaker's Holiday* 1
Dryden, J. *All for Love; or, the World Well Lost* 1
*Everyman* 1
Marlowe, C. *The Tragical History of Doctor Faustus* 1
*The Second Shepherds' Play* 1
Sheridan, R. *The Rivals* 2
Wilde, O. *The Importance of Being Earnest* 2

SHAK *Shakespeare the Sadist/Wolfgang Bauer/Rainer Werner Fassbinder. My foot my tutor/Peter Handke Stallerhof/Franz Xaver Kroetz.* Trans. [from the German] by Renata and Martin Esslin, Anthony Vivis, Michael Roloff, and Katharina Hehn. London: Eyr Methuen, 1977. 96pp.
Bauer, W. *Shakespeare the Sadist*
Fassbinder, R. *Bremen Coffee*

Handke, P. *My Foot My Tutor*
Kroetz, F. *Stallerhof*

SHAR Sharp, Russell, A.; Brewton John E.; Lemon, Babette; and Abney, Louise, eds. *English and Continental Literature.* Chicago: Laidlaw [c1950] 800pp. (Cultural Growth Series)
Gregory, I. *The Rising of the Moon*
Molière, J. *The Physician in Spite of Himself*
Shakespeare, W. *Macbeth*

SHAT Shaver, Joseph L., compiler. *Contemporary Canadian Drama.* Ottawa: Borealis Press, 1974. 231pp.
Dunn, T. *Maada and Ulka*
Godlovitch, C. *Timewatch*
Graves, W. *The Proper Perspective*
Ravel, A. *Black Dreams*
Spunde, W. *The Mercenary*
Tallman, J. *Trans-Canada Highway*
Tembeck, R. *Baptism*

SHAV Shaw, Harry, ed. *A Collection of Readings for Writers: Book Three of a Complete Course in Freshman English.* 6th ed. New York: Harper and Row [1967] 722pp.
Shakespeare, W. *The Tragedy of Macbeth*
Shaw, G. *Pygmalion*
Sophocles. *Antigone*

SHAW Shaw, Harry, ed. *A Complete Course in Freshman English.* 5th edition. New York: Harper & Brothers [c1959] 1306pp.
Shakespeare, W. *The Tragedy of Romeo and Juliet*
Shaw, G. *Pygmalion*
Wilder, T. *The Long Christmas Dinner*

SHAX Shaw, Harry Lee, ed. *A Complete Course in Freshman English.* 7th ed. New York: Harper, 1973. 836pp.
Shaw, G. *Arms and the Man*
Sophocles. *Antigone*
Wilder, T. *The Long Christmas Dinner*

SHAY Shay, Frank, ed. *A Treasury of Plays for Women.* Boston: Little, Brown, 1922. 443pp.
Clements, C. *Columbine*
Clements, C. *The Siege*
Dransfield, J. *The Lost Pleiad*
Emig, E. *The China Pig*
Gerstenberg, A. *Ever Young*
Gerstenberg, A. *A Patroness*
Knox, F. *For Distinguished Service*
Kreymborg, A. *Manikin and Minikin*
Kreymborg, A. *Rocking Chairs*
McCauley, C. *The Conflict*

Maeterlinck, M. *The Death of Tintagiles*
Millay, E. *The Lamp and the Bell*
Morley, C. *Rehearsal*
O'Neill, E. *Before Breakfast*
Pillot, E. *My Lady Dreams*
Smith, H. *Blackberryin'*
Strindberg, A. *Motherly Love*
Strindberg, A. *The Stronger Woman*

SHER Sheratsky, Rodney E. and Reilly, John L., eds. *The Lively Arts: 4 Representative Types*. New York: Globe Book Co. [1964] 544pp.
Agee, J. *Abraham Lincoln, the Early Years*
Chayefsky, P. *Marty*
Lawrence, J., and Lee, R. *Inherit the Wind*

SHERWOOD, GARRISON P. *See BEST Plays of 1894/1899*, etc.

SHEW Shewey, Don, ed. *Out Front: Contemporary Gay and Lesbian Plays*. New York: Grove Press, 1988. 564pp.
Chesley, R. *Jerker, or the Helping Hand*
Fierstein, H. *Forget Him*
Hoffman, W. *As Is*
Hughes, H. *The Well of Horniness*
Kondoleon, H. *The Fairy Garden*
McNally, T. *The Lisbon Traviata*
Mann, E. *Execution of Justice*
Sherman, M. *Bent*
Smith, E. *Remedial English*
Tolan, K. *A Weekend near Madison*
Wilson, D. *Street Theater*

SHIM Shimazaki, Chifumi, ed., and trans. *The Noh*. Tokyo: Hinoki Shoten, 1972–1998. 8 vols. (Vol. 1: God Noh; Vol. 2: Battle Noh; Vol. 2, book 2: Warrior Ghost Plays from the Japanese Theater; Vol. 3, book 1, book 2, book 3: Woman Noh; Vol. 4, book 1: Restless Spirits from Japanese Noh Plays of the Fourth Group; Vol. 4, book 2: Troubled Souls from Japanese Noh Plays of the Fourth Group. Vol. 2, book 2, Vol. 4, book 1, and Vol. 4, book 2 were published by Cornell University, East Asia Program in the Cornell East Asia series, with separate titles.)
*Ema (The Votive Tablets)* 1
*Hajitomi (The Push-up Shutter)* 3, book 1
*Kagekiyo* 4, book 2
*Kanawa* 4, book 2
*Kazuraki* 4, book 1
*Tenko* 4, book 1
*Tomoe* 2, book 2
Kanami. *Eguchi (Rivermouth)* 3, book 2
Kanami. *Jinen Koji* 4, bk. 2
Kanami, and Zeami. *Matsukaze (Pine Wind)* 3, bk. 2
Kanze, K. *Kochō (Butterfly)* 3, bk. 1

Konparu, Z. *Kamo* 1
Konparu, Z. *Kogō* 4, bk. 2
Konparu, Z. *No-no-miya (The palace in the field)* 3, bk. 1
Konparu, Z. *Seiōbo* 1
Konparu, Z. *Senju* 3, bk. 3
Miyamasu. *Eboshi-ori* 4, bk. 2
Seiami. *Michimori* 2, bk. 2
*Yūgao (Moonflower)* 3, bk. 1
Zeami. *Atsumori* 2
Zeami. *Funabashi* 4, bk. 1
Zeami. *Futari Shizuka (The two Shizukas)* 3, bk. 3
Zeami. *Hotoke-no-hara (Field of Hotoke)* 3, bk. 3
Zeami. *Izutsu (The well curb)* 3, bk. 2
Zeami. *Kakitsubata (Iris)* 3, bk. 2
Zeami. *Kanehira* 2, bk. 2
Zeami. *Kiyotsune* 2
Zeami. *Obasute (Mt. Obasute)* 3, bk. 2
Zeami. *Ohara Gokō (The imperial visit to Ohara)* 3, bk. 3
Zeami. *Oimatsu* 1
Zeami. *Saigyō-Zakura* 4, bk. 1
Zeami. *Semimaru* 4, bk. 2
Zeami. *Tadanori* 2
Zeami. *Takasago* 1
Zeami. *Tomoakira* 2, bk. 2
Zeami. *Tomonaga* 2
Zeami. *Tsunemasa* 2
Zeami. *Yashima* 2, bk. 2
Zeami. *Yorimasa* 2, bk. 2
Zeami. *Yōrō* 1
Zeami. *Yuya* 3, bk. 3

SHIMAZAKI, CHIFUMI. *Restless Spirits from Japanese Noh Plays of the Fourth Group*. 1995. *See* SHIM *The Noh*

SHIMAZAKI, CHIFUMI. *Troubled Souls from Japanese Noh plays of the Fourth Group*. 1998. *See* SHIM *The Noh*

SHIMAZAKI, CHIFUMI. *Warrior Ghost Plays from the Japanese Theater*. 1993. *See* SHIM *The Noh*

SHOW *Showing West: Three Prairie Docu-Dramas*. Edited by Diane Bessai and Don Kerr. Edmonton, NeWest Press, 1982. 259pp. (Prairie Plays Series 5)
Deverell, R. *Medicare!*
Theatre Passe Muraille. *The West Show*
Wiebe, R. and Theatre Passe Muraille. *Far as the Eye Can See*

SHR Shrodes, Caroline, Van Gundy, Justine, and Dorius, Joel, compilers. *Reading for Understanding: Fiction, Drama, Poetry*. New York: Macmillan [1968] 716pp.

Albee, E. *The Zoo Story*
Chekhov, A. *The Sea-gull*
Ibsen, H. *Ghosts*
Shakespeare, W. *Antony and Cleopatra*
Sophocles. *King Oedipus*
Yeats, W. *The Words upon the Windowpane*

SHRCD Shrodes, Caroline, Finestone, Harry, and Shugrue,
    Michael, compilers. *The Conscious Reader*. 4th ed.
    New York: Macmillan, 1988. 1146pp.
    Ibsen, H. *Ghosts*
    Sophocles. *Antigone*

SHRCE Shrodes, Caroline, Finestone, Harry, and Shugrue,
    Michael, compilers. *The Conscious Reader*. 5th ed.
    New York: Macmillan, 1992. 1152pp.
    Hwang, D. M. *Butterfly*
    Sophocles. *Antigone*

SHRCF Shrodes, Caroline, Finestone, Harry, Shugrue,
    Michael, and Belford, Fontane Maury, compilers.
    *The Conscious Reader*. 6th ed. Boston: Allyn and
    Bacon, 1995. 1181pp.
    Ibsen, H. *An Enemy of the People*
    Sophocles. *Antigone*

SHRCG Shrodes, Caroline, Finestone, Harry, Shugrue,
    Michael, and Belford, Fontane Maury, compilers.
    *The Conscious Reader*. 7th ed. Boston: Allyn and
    Bacon, 1998. 971pp.
    Wasserstein, W. *The Man in a Case*

SHRO Shroyer, Frederick Benjamin, and Gardemal, Louis
    G., compilers. *Types of Drama*. Glenview, IL:
    Scott, Foresman, 1970. 678pp.
    Aristophanes. *The Frogs*
    Brecht, B. *The Good Woman of Setzuan*
    *Everyman*
    Molière, J. *Tartuffe*
    Powell, A. *The Death of Everymom*
    Rostand, E. *Cyrano de Bergerac*
    Shakespeare, W. *Hamlet*
    Sheridan, R. *The School for Scandal*
    Sophocles. *Oedipus the King*
    Wilder, T. *The Matchmaker*
    Williams, T. *The Glass Menagerie*

SIG The *Signet Classic Book of 18th- and 19th-Century
    British Drama*. Edited and with an introduction
    by Katharine Rogers. New York: New American
    Library, Inc., 1979. 580pp.
    Boucicault, D. *The Octoroon*
    Farquhar, G. *The Beaux' Stratagem*
    Gay, J. *The Beggar's Opera*
    Gilbert, W. *Ruddigore*

Lillo, G. *The London Merchant*
Sheridan, R. *The School for Scandal*
Steele, R. *The Conscious Lovers*
Wilde, O. *The Importance of Being Earnest*

SILK Simonson, Harold Peter, ed. *Quartet: A Book of
    Stories, Plays, Poems and Critical Essays*. New
    York: Harper and Row, 1970. 1019pp.
    Chekhov, A. *Uncle Vanya*
    Ibsen, H. *Ghosts*
    Strindberg, A. *Miss Julie*
    Synge, J. *Riders to the Sea*
    Willliams, T. *The Glass Menagerie*

SILKI Simonson, Harold Peter, ed. *Quartet: A Book of
    Stories, Plays, Poems and Critical Essays*. 2nd ed.
    New York: Harper and Row, 1973. 1092pp.
    Hansberry, L. *A Raisin in the Sun*
    Ibsen, H. *Ghosts*
    Ionesco, E. *The Gap*
    Strindberg, A. *Miss Julie*
    Synge, J. *Riders to the Sea*
    Williams, T. *The Glass Menagerie*

SILM Simonson, Harold Peter, ed. *Trio: A Book of Stories,
    Plays, and Poems*. New York: Harper & Brothers
    [c1962] 489pp.
    Chekhov, A. *The Cherry Orchard*
    Ibsen, H. *Ghosts*

SILN Simonson, Harold Peter, ed. *Trio: A Book of Stories,
    Plays, and Poems*. 3rd ed. New York: Harper.
    1970. 747pp.
    Chekhov, A. *Uncle Vanya*
    Ibsen, H. *Ghosts*
    Strindberg, A. *Miss Julie*
    Synge, J. *Riders to the Sea*
    Williams, T. *The Glass Menagerie*

SILO Simonson, Harold Peter, ed. *Trio: A Book of Stories,
    Plays, and Poems*. 4th ed. New York: Harper,
    1975. 743pp.
    Chekhov, A. *Uncle Vanya*
    Ibsen, H. *A Doll's House*
    Miller, A. *All My Sons*
    Strindberg, A. *Miss Julie*
    Synge, J. *Riders to the Sea*
    Williams, T. *The Glass Menagerie*

SILP Simonson, Harold Peter, ed. *Trio: A Book of Stories,
    Plays, and Poems*. 5th ed. New York: Harper. 1980.
    Chekhov, A. *The Cherry Orchard*
    Ibsen, H. *Hedda Gabler*
    Ionesco, E. *The Chairs*
    Williams, T. *The Glass Menagerie*

SILS Simonson, Harold Peter, ed. *Trio: A Book of Stories, Plays, and Poems.* 6th ed. New York: Harper. 1987. 875pp.
  Chekhov, A. *The Cherry Orchard*
  Ibsen, H. *A Doll's House*
  O'Neill, E. *Hughie*
  Saroyan, W. *The Time of Your Life*
  Shaw, G. *Arms and the Man*
  Shepard, S. *Buried Child*

SIM Simpson, Claude Mitchell, and Nevins, Allan, eds. *The American Reader.* Boston: Heath [c1941] 866pp.
  Connelly, M. *The Green Pastures*
  Riggs, L. *Green Grow the Lilacs*
  Wilder. T. *Our Town*

SIN Singleton, Ralph H., and Millet, Stanton, eds. *An Introduction to Literature.* Cleveland, OH: World [1966] 1237pp.
  Ibsen, H. *Hedda Gabler*
  Shakespeare, W. *Measure for Measure*
  Shakespeare, W. *Othello*
  Shaw, G. *Pygmalion*
  Sophocles. *Antigone*
  Sophocles. *Oedipus Rex*

SIXA *Six Canadian Plays.* Toronto: Playwrights Canada Press, 1992. 286pp.
  Carley, D. *Hedges*
  Gass, K. *Hurray for Johnny Canuck*
  Lazarus, J. *Babel Rap*
  Mitchell, K. *Heroes*
  Pollock, S. *The Komagata Maru Incident*
  Ravel, A. *Moon People*

SIXB *Six Great Modern Plays.* New York: Dell, c1956. 512pp.
  Chekhov, A. *Three Sisters*
  Ibsen, H. *The Master Builder*
  Miller, A. *All My Sons*
  O'Casey, S. *Red Roses for Me*
  Shaw, G. *Mrs. Warren's Profession*
  Williams, T. *The Glass Menagerie*

SIXC *Six Modern American Plays.* Introduction by Allan G. Halline. New York: Modern Library [c1951] 419pp.
  Anderson, M. *Winterset*
  Heggen, T. and Logan, J. *Mister Roberts*
  Hellman, L. *The Little Foxes*
  Kaufman, G., and Hart, M. *The Man Who Came to Dinner*
  O'Neill, E. *The Emperor Jones*
  Williams, T. *The Glass Menagerie*

SIXD *Six Plays.* London: Gollanez, 1930. 672pp.
  Bax, C. *Socrates*
  Connelly, M. *The Green Pastures*
  George, E. *Down Our Street*
  Glaspell, S. *Alison's House*
  Rice, E. *Street Scene*
  Sherriff, R. *Badger's Green*

SIXH *Six Plays.* London: Heinemann [1934] 746pp.
  Coward, N. *Design for Living*
  Dane, C. *Wild Decembers*
  Kaufman, G., and Ferber, E. *Dinner at Eight*
  Maugham, W. *Sheppey*
  Priestley, J. *Dangerous Corner*
  Winter, K. *The Rats of Norway*

SIXL *Six Plays of 1939.* [London] Hamilton [1939] v.p.
  Behrman, S. *No Time for Comedy*
  Hellman, L. *The Little Foxes*
  Jones, J. *Rhondda Roundahout*
  Lyndon, B. *The Man in Half Moon Street*
  McCracken, E. *Quiet Wedding*
  Rattigan, T. *After the Dance*

SIXN *Six Nuevomexicano Folk Dramas for Advent Season.* Translated and illustrated by Larry Torres. Albuquerque: University of New Mexico Press, 1999. 194pp. (Paso Por Aqui Series on the Nuevomexicano Literary Heritage) (English-Spanish dual text)
  *Las cuatro apariciones de Guadalupe/The four apparitions of Guadalupe Los matachines desenmascarados/Los Matachines unmasked*
  *Los moros y los cristianos/The Christians and the Moors*
  *Los pastores/The Second Shepherd's Play*
  *Las posadas/No Room at the Inn*
  *Los tres reyes magos/The Three Kings*

SIXP *Six Plays of Today.* London: Heinemann [1939] 716pp.
  Coppel, A. *I Killed the Count*
  Coward, N. *Point Valaine*
  Hodge, M. *The Island*
  Priestley, J. *Cornelius*
  Sherwood, R. *Idiot's Delight*
  Wolfe, H. *The Silent Knight*

SLAT Slater, Maya, ed. *Three Pre-Surrealist Plays.* Oxford, New York: Oxford University Press, 1997. 212pp.
  Apollinaire, G. *The Mammaries of Tiresias*
  Jarry, A. *Ubu the King*
  Maeterlinck, M. *The Blind*

SMA Small, Norman M., and Sutton, Maurice Lewis, eds. *The Making of Drama*. Boston: Holbrook Press, 1972. 691pp.
  Brecht, B. *The Caucasian Chalk Circle*
  Chekhov, A. *The Cherry Orchard*
  Goldoni, C. *The Servant of Two Masters*
  Gorki, M. *The Lower Depths*
  Kopit, A. *Oh Dad, Poor Dad, Mama's Hung You in the Closet and I'm Feelin' So Sad*
  Molière, J. *Tartuffe*
  Rice, E. *The Adding Machine*
  Shakespeare, W. *Hamlet*
  Sophocles. *Oedipus the King*

SMB Smith, Melissa T., ed. and trans. *Russian Mirror: Three Plays by Russian Women*. Amsterdam: Harwood Academic Publishers, 1998. 94pp. (Russian Theatre Archive Series, vol. 14)
  Arbatova, M. *On the Road to Ourselves*
  Gremina, E. *Behind the Mirror*
  Mikhailova, O. *Russian Dream*

SMC Smith, Michael Townsend, ed. *The Best Off Off-Broadway*. New York: Dutton, 1969. 256pp.
  Agenoux, S. *Charles Dickens' Christmas Carol*
  Fornés, M. *Dr. Kheal*
  Heide, R. *Moon*
  Kvares, D. *Mushrooms*
  Shepard, S. *Forensic and the Navigators*
  Smith, M. *The Next Thing*
  Tavel, R. *Gorilla Queen*

SME Smith, Michael Townsend, ed. *More Plays from Off Off-Broadway*. Indianapolis, IN: Bobbs Merrill, 1972. 409pp.
  Birimisa, G. *Georgie Porgie*
  Eyen, T. *Grand Tenement and November 22*
  Hadler, W. *Flite Cage*
  Hoffman, W. *X X X X X*
  Kennedy, A. *A Rat's Mass*
  Koutoukas, H. *Tidy Passions, or Kill, Kaleidoscope, Kill*
  Ludlam, C. *Bluebeard*
  Mednick, M. *Willie the Germ*
  Williams, A. *The Poor Little Watch Girl*

SMI Smith, Robert Metcalf, ed. *Types of Domestic Tragedy*. New York: Prentice-Hall, 1928. 576pp. (World Drama Series)
  Annunzio, G. d'. *Gioconda*
  Hebbel, F. *Maria Magdalena*
  Heywood, T. *A Woman Killed with Kindness*
  Ibsen, H. *Hedda Gabler*
  Lillo, G. *George Barnwell; or, the London Merchant*
  Pinero, A. *Mid-channel*
  Strindberg, A. *The Father*

SMK Smith, Robert Metcalf, ed. *Types of Historical Drama*. New York: Prentice-Hall, 1928. 635pp. (World Drama Series)
  Hebbel, C. *Agnes Bernauer*
  Ibsen, H. *The Pretenders*
  Kleist, H. *The Prince of Homburg*
  Schiller, F. *William Tell*
  Shakespeare, W. *King Henry IV, Part I*
  Tennyson, A. *Becket*

SML Smith, Robert Metcalf, ed. *Types of Philosophic Drama*. New York: Prentice-Hall, 1928. 524pp. (World Drama Series)
  Aeschylus. *Prometheus Bound*
  Andreev, L. *The Life of Man*
  *The Book of Job*
  Byron, G. *Manfred*
  *Everyman*
  Marlowe, C. *Dr. Faustus*
  Milton, J. *Samson Agonistes*
  Shelley, P. *Prometheus Unbound*

SMN Smith, Robert Metcalf, ed. *Types of Romantic Drama*. New York: Prentice-Hall, 1928. 621pp. (World Drama Series)
  Corneille, P. *The Cid*
  Dryden, J. *All for Love*
  Grillparzer, F. *Sappho*
  Maeterlinck, M. *Pelléas and Mélisande*
  Phillips, S. *Paolo and Francesca*
  Rostand, E. *Cyrano de Bergerac*
  Shakespeare, W. *Romeo and Juliet*

SMO Smith, Robert Metcalf, ed. *Types of Social Comedy*. New York: Prentice Hall, 1928. 759pp. (World Drama Series)
  Congreve, W. *The Way of the World*
  Goldsmith, O. *She Stoops to Conquer*
  Massinger, P. *A New Way to Pay Old Debts*
  Maugham, W. *Our Betters*
  Molière, J. *Tartuffe*
  Pinero, A. *The Gay Lord Quex*
  Sheridan, R. *The School for Scandal*
  Wilde, O. *Lady Windermere's Fan*

SMP Smith, Robert Metcalf, ed. *Types of World Tragedy*. New York: Prentice-Hall, 1928. 667pp. (World Drama Series)
  Euripides. *Medea*
  Gorki, M. *The Lower Depths*
  Hauptmann, G. *The Weavers*
  Ibsen, H. *Ghosts*
  Racine, J. *Phaedra*
  Shakespeare, W. *Othello, the Moor of Venice*
  Shelley, P. *The Cenci*
  Sophocles. *Oedipus the King*

SMR Smith, Robert Metcalf and Rhoads, Howard Garrett,
eds. *Types of Farce Comedy*. New York: Prentice
Hall, 1928. 598pp. (World Drama Series)
Aristophanes. *The Frogs*
France, A. *The Man Who Married a Dumb Wife*
Gay, J. *The Beggar's Opera*
Gilbert, W., and Sullivan, A. *Patience*
Molière, J. *The Doctor in Spite of Himself*
Pinero, A. *The Magistrate*
Plautus, T. *The Menaechmi*
Shakespeare, W. *The Taming of the Shrew*
Wilde, O. *The Importance of Being Earnest*

SNO Snow, Lois Wheeler, ed. and tr. *China on Stage: An
American Actress in the People's Republic*. New
York: Random House, 1972. 328pp.
Wong, O., and Chia, A. *The Red Lantern*
*Red Detachment of Women*
*Shachiapang*
*Taking Tiger Mountain by Strategy*

SNYD Snyder, Franklyn Bliss and Martin, Robert Grant,
eds. *A Book of English Literature*. 4th edition. New
York: Macmillan [c1942–1943] 2 vols.
*Abraham and Isaac* 1
Dryden, J. *All for Love* 1
*Everyman* 1
Galsworthy, J. *Loyalties* 2
Marlowe, C. *Doctor Faustus* 1
*Noah's Flood* 1
O'Casey, S. *Juno and the Paycock* 2
Sheridan, R. *The Rivals* 1

SOK Sokel, Walter Herbert, ed. *Anthology of German
Expressionist Drama: A Prelude to the Absurd*.
Garden City, NY: Doubleday, 1963. 365pp.
Brecht, B. *Baal*
Goll, Y. *The Immortal One*
Hasenclever, W. *Humanity*
Kaiser, G. *Alkibiades Saved*
Kokoschka, O. *Job*
Kokoschka, O. *Murderer the Women's Hope*
Lauckner, R. *Cry in the Street*
Sorge, R. *The Beggar*
Sternheim, C. *The Strongbox*

SOM Somer, John L., compiler. *Dramatic Experience: The
Public Voice*. Glenview, IL: Scott, Foresman, 1970.
282pp.
Ibsen, H. *Hedda Gabler*
Shakespeare, W. *Romeo and Juliet*
Sophocles. *Antigone*
Synge, J. *The Playboy of the Western World*
Williams, T. *The Glass Menagerie*

SOMA Somer, John L., and Cozzo, Joseph, compilers.
*Literary Experience: Public and Private Voices*.
Glenview, IL: Scott Foresman, 1971. 681pp.
Ibsen, H. *Hedda Gabler*
Shakespeare, W. *Romeo and Juliet*
Sophocles. *Antigone*
Synge, J. *The Playboy of the Western World*
Williams, T. *The Glass Menagerie*

SOME Somerset, J. A. B., ed. *Four Tudor Interludes*.
London: Athlone Press, 1974. 184pp.
*An Enterlude called Lusty Juventus*
Fulwell, U. *Like Will to Like*
Heywood, J. *A Play of Love*
*Mankind*

SOSGA Soufas, Teresa Scott, ed. *Women's Acts: Plays
by Women Dramatists of Spain's Golden Age*.
Lexington, KY: University Press of Kentucky,
1997. 326pp.
Azevedo, A. *Dicha y desdicha del juego y devoción de
la Virgen*
Azevedo, A. *La margarita del Tajo que dio nombre a
Santarén*
Azevedo, A. *El muerto disimulado*
Caro Mallén de Soto, A. *El conde Partinuplés*
Caro Mallén de Soto, A. *Valor, agravio y mujer*
Cueva y Silva, L. *La firmeza en la auscencia*
Enríquez de Guzmán, F. *Entreactos de la segunda parte
de la tragicomedia los jardines y campos sabeos*
Enríquez de Guzmán, F. *Segunda parte de la
tragicomedia los jardines y campos sabeos*
Zayas y Sotomayor, M. *La traction en la amistad*

SOUL Soule, George, compiler. *The Theatre of the Mind*.
Englewood Cliffs, NJ: Prentice-Hall, 1974. 665pp.
Aeschylus. *Agamemnon*
Aristophanes. *Lysistrata*
Chekhov, A. *The Cherry Orchard*
Ibsen, H. *Hedda Gabler*
Molière, J. *The Miser*
Pinter, H. *The Dumb Waiter*
Shakespeare, W. *As You like It*
Shakespeare, W. *King Lear*
Shaw, G. *Pygmalion*
Williams, T. *The Glass Menagerie*

SOUT *South African People's Plays*: *Ons phola hi: Plays
by Gibson Kente, Credo V, Mutwa, Mthuli Shezi
and Workshop '71*. Selected with introductory
material by Robert Mshengu Kavanagh. London:
Heinmann [c1981] 176pp.
Kente, G. *Too Late*
Mutwa, C. *uNosilimela*
Shezi, M. *Shanti*
Workshop '71 Theatre Company. *Survival*

SPC *Spearhead: 10 Years' Experimental Writing in America*. New York: New Directions, c1947. 604pp.
  Hutchins, M. *Aunt Julia's Caesar*
  Stein, G. *Daniel Webster Eighteen in America*
  Williams, T. *27 Wagons Full of Cotton*

SPD Spencer, Hazelton, ed. *British Literature*. Boston: Heath [c1951] 2 vols. (Vol.1: From Beowulf to Sheridan; Vol.2: From Blake to the Present Day)
  Congreve, W. *The Way of the World* 1
  Dekker, T. *The Shoemakers' Holiday* 1
  Marlowe, C. *Dr. Faustus* 1
  *The Second Shepherds' Play* 1
  Sheridan, R. *The School for Scandal* 1
  Webster, J. *The Duchess of Malfi* 1

SPDB Spencer, Hazelton, ed. *British Literature*. 2nd ed. Boston: Heath [c1963] 2v (V.1: From Beowulf to Sheridan; V.2: From Blake to the Present Day)
  Congreve, W. *The Way of the World* 1
  Marlowe, C. *Dr. Faustus* 1
  *The Second Shepherds' Play* 1
  Sheridan, R. *The School for Scandal* 1
  Webster, J. *The Duchess of Malfi* 1

SPE Spencer, Hazelton, ed. *Elizabethan Plays*. Boston: Little, Brown, 1933. 1173pp.
  Beaumont, F., and Fletcher, J. *The Knight of the Burning Pestle*
  Beaumont, F., and Fletcher, J. *The Maid's Tragedy*
  Beaumont, F., and Fletcher, J. *Philaster; or, Love Lies A-bleeding*
  Chapman, G. *Bussy d'Ambois*
  Chapman, G., Jonson, B., and Marston, J. *Eastward Ho!*
  Dekker, T. *The Honest Whore, Part I*
  Dekker, T. *The Honest Whore, Part II*
  Dekker, T. *The Shoemaker's Holiday*
  Fletcher, J. *The Wild-goose Chase*
  Ford, J. *The Broken Heart*
  Greene, R. *The Honourable History of Friar Bacon and Friar Bungay*
  Heywood, T. *A Woman Killed with Kindness*
  Jonson, B. *The Alchemist*
  Jonson, B. *Bartholomew Fair*
  Jonson, B. *Every Man in His Humour*
  Jonson, B. *Volpone; or, the Fox*
  Kyd, T. *The Spanish Tragedy; or, Hieronimo Is Mad Again*
  Lyly, J. *Endymion, the Man in the Moon*
  Marlowe, C. *The Jew of Malta*
  Marlowe, C. *Tamburlaine, Part I*
  Marlowe, C. *The Tragical History of Doctor Faustus*
  Marlowe, C. *The Troublesome Reign and Lamentable Death of Edward the Second*

  Marston, J. *The Malcontent*
  Massinger, P. *A New Way to Pay Old Debts*
  Middleton, T. *A Trick to Catch the Old One*
  Middleton, T., and Rowley, W. *The Changeling*
  Shirley, J. *The Lady of Pleasure*
  Webster, J. *The White Devil; or Vittoria Corombona*

SPEF Spencer, Hazelton; Houghton Walter E., and Barrows, Herbert. *British Literature*. Boston: Heath [c1951, 1952] 2 vols.
  Congreve, W. *The Way of the World* 1
  Dekker, J. *The Shoemaker's Holiday* 1
  Marlowe, C. *Doctor Faustus* 1
  *The Second Shepherds' Play* 1
  Sheridan, R. *The School for Scandal* 1
  Webster, J. *The Duchess of Malfi* 1

SPER Sper, Felix, ed. *Favorite Modern Plays*. New York: Globe Book Company [c1953] 530pp.
  Barrie, J. *The Admirable Crichton*
  Besier, R. *The Barretts of Wimpole Street*
  Galsworthy, J. *Loyalties*
  Lindsay, H. and Crouse, R. *Life with Father*
  Rattigan, T. *The Winslow Boy*

SPES Sper, Felix, ed. *Living American Plays*. New York: Globe Book [c1954] 454pp.
  Hart, M., and Kaufman, G. *You Can't Take It with You*
  Howard, S. *The Late Christopher Bean*
  Lavery, E. *The Magnificent Yankee*
  Van Druten, J. *I Remember Mama*
  Williams, T. *The Glass Menagerie*

SPI Spiller, Robert Ernest, ed. *The Roots of National Culture: American Literature to 1830*. New York: Macmillan, 1933. 758pp. (American Literature: A Period Anthology; Oscar Cargill, General Editor, vol. 1)
  Tyler, R. *The Contrast*

SPR Sprinchorn, Evert, ed. *The Genius of the Scandinavian Theater*. New York: New American Library [1964]. 637pp.
  Abell, K. *Days on a Cloud*
  Holberg, L. *Jeppe of the Hill*
  Ibsen, H. *The Master Builder*
  Ibsen, H. *The Wild Duck*
  Lagerkvist, P. *The Difficult Hour*
  Strindberg, A. *Crimes and Crimes*
  Strindberg, A. *To Damascus, Part I*

SRY Srygley, Ola Pauline, and Betts, Otsie Verona, eds. *Highlights in English Literature and Other Selections*. Dallas, TX: Banks Upshaw, [1940]. 868pp.

Goldsmith, O. *She Stoops to Conquer*
Milne, A. *The Boy Comes Home*
Shakespeare, W. *Macbeth*
Tolstoy, L. *What Men Live By*

SRYG Srygley, Ola Pauline, and Betts, Otsie Verona, eds.
*Highlights in English Literature*. Freeport, NY:
Books for Libraries Press, 1971. 868pp.
Goldsmith, O. *She Stoops to Conquer*
Milne, A. *The Boy Comes Home*
Shakespeare, W. *Macbeth*
Tolstoy, L. *What Men Live By*

SSSF Stafford, William T., ed. *Twentieth Century
American Writing*. New York: Odyssey Press
[1965] 712pp. (The Odyssey Surveys of American
Writing)
O'Neill, E. *Desire under the Elms*
Rice, E. *The Adding Machine*
Williams, T. *The Glass Menagerie*

SSSI *Stages of Drama: Classical to Contemporary
Theater*. [Compiled by] Carl H. Klaus, Miriam
Gilbert, and Bradford S. Field, Jr. New York:
Wiley, [c1981] 1098pp.
Aeschylus. *Agamemnon*
Aristophanes. *Lysistrata*
Beckett, S. *Endgame*
Brecht, B., and Hauptmann, E. *The Threepenny Opera*
Chekhov, A. *The Cherry Orchard*
Etherege, G. *The Man of Mode*
Euripides. *The Bacchae*
*Everyman*
García Lorca, F. *The House of Bernarda Alba*
Ibsen, H. *A Doll's House*
Jones, L. *Dutchman*
Jonson, B. *Volpone*
*La farce de Maître Pierre Pathelin*
Marlowe, C. *Edward II*
Miller, A. *Death of a Salesman*
Molière. *The Misanthrope*
O'Neill, E. *A Moon for the Misbegotten*
Pinter, H. *The Homecoming*
Pirandello, L. *Six Characters in Search of an Author*
*Second Shepherds' Play*
Shaffer, P. *Equus*
Shakespeare, W. *Othello*
Shaw, G. *Major Barbara*
Sheridan, R. *The School for Scandal*
Simon, N. *Odd Couple*
Sophocles. *Oedipus Rex*
Strindberg, A. *Miss Julie*
Synge, J. *Playboy of the Western World*
Webster, J. *Duchess of Malfi*
Williams, T. *Cat on a Hot Tin Roof*

SSSIA *Stages of Drama: Classical to Contemporary
Theater*. [Compiled by] Carl H. Klaus, Miriam
Gilbert, and Bradford S. Field, Jr. 2nd ed. New
York: St. Martin's Press, 1991. 1231pp.
Aeschylus. *Agamemnon*
Aristophanes. *Lysistrata*
Beckett, S. *Endgame*
Brecht, B. *Life of Galileo*
Chekhov, A. *The Cherry Orchard*
Churchill, C. *Top Girls*
Etherege, G. *The Man of Mode*
Euripides. *The Bacchae*
*Everyman*
Fugard, A. *"Master Harold" . . . and the Boys*
Havel, V. *Temptation*
Ibsen, H. *A Doll's House*
Jonson, B. *Volpone*
Marlowe, C. *The Tragical History of the Life and Death
of Doctor Faustus*
Miller, A. *Death of a Salesman*
Molière, J. *The Misanthrope*
Norman, M. *'Night, Mother*
O'Casey, S. *Juno and the Paycock*
O'Neill, E. *A Moon for the Misbegotten*
Pinter, H. *The Homecoming*
Pirandello, L. *Six Characters in Search of an Author*
*The Second Shepherds' Play*
Shaffer, P. *Equus*
Shakespeare, W. *Othello*
Shakespeare, W. *Twelfth Night*
Shaw, G. *Major Barbara*
Sheridan, R. *The School for Scandal*
Sophocles. *Oedipus Rex*
Stoppard, T. *Professional Foul*
Strindberg, A. *Miss Julie*
Wasserstein, W. *The Man in a Case*
Webster, J. *The Duchess of Malfi*
Williams, T. *Cat on a Hot Tin Roof*
Wilson, A. *Ma Rainey's Black Bottom*

SSSIB *Stages of Drama: Classical to Contemporary
Theater*. [Compiled by] Carl H. Klaus, Miriam
Gilbert, and Bradford S. Field, Jr. 3rd ed. New
York: St. Martin's Press, 1995. 1348pp.
Aeschylus. *Agamemnon*
Albee, E. *The Zoo Story*
Aristophanes. *Lysistrata*
Baraka, I. *Dutchman*
Beckctt, S. *Endgame*
Brecht, B. *Galileo*
Büchner, G. *Woyzeck*
Chekhov, A. *The Cherry Orchard*
Churchill, C. *Top Girls*
Etherege, G. *The Man of Mode*
Euripides. *The Bacchae*

*Everyman*
Fornes, M. *Fefu and Her Friends*
Fugard, A. *"Master Harold" . . . and the Boys*
García Lorca, F. *The House of Bernarda Alba*
Hwang, D. *M. Butterfly*
Ibsen, H. *A Doll's House*
Ionesco, E. *The Lesson*
Jonson, B. *Volpone*
Mamet, D. *Oleanna*
Marlowe, C. *The Tragical History of the Life and Death of Doctor Faustus*
Miller, A. *Death of a Salesman*
Molière, J. *The Misanthrope*
Norman, M. *'Night, Mother*
O'Casey, S. *Juno and the Paycock*
O'Neill, E. *A Moon for the Misbegotten*
Pinter, H. *The Homecoming*
Pirandello, L. *Six Characters in Search of an Author*
*The Second Shepherds' Play*
Shakespeare, W. *Othello*
Shakespeare, W. *Twelfth Night*
Shange, N. *Spell #7*
Shaw, G. *Pygmalion*
Shepard, S. *Fool for Love*
Sheridan, R. *The School for Scandal*
Sophocles. *Oedipus Rex*
Strindberg, A. *Miss Julie*
Wasserstein, W. *The Man in a Case*
Webster, J. *The Duchess of Malfi*
Williams, T. *Cat on a Hot Tin Roof*
Wilson, A. *Ma Rainey's Black Bottom*

SSSIC *Stages of Drama: Classical to Contemporary Theater.* [Compiled by] Carl H. Klaus, Miriam Gilbert, and Bradford S. Field, Jr. 4th ed. Boston/New York: Bedford/St. Martin's Press, 1999. 1490pp.
Aeschylus. *Agamemnon*
Albee, E. *Three Tall Women*
Aristophanes. *Lysistrata*
Baraka, I. *Dutchman*
Beckett, S. *Endgame*
Behn, A. *The Rover*
Brecht, B. *Galileo*
Büchner, G. *Woyzeck*
Chekhov, A. *The Cherry Orchard*
Churchill, C. *Top Girls*
Euripides. *The Bacchae*
*Everyman*
Friel, B. *Translations*
Fugard, A. *"Master Harold" . . . and the Boys*
García Lorca, F. *The House of Bernarda Alba*
Glaspell, S. *Trifles*
Hansberry, L. *A Raisin in the Sun*
Hwang, D. *M. Butterfly*

Ibsen, H. *A Doll's House*
Ionesco, E. *The Lesson*
Jonson, B. *Volpone*
Kennedy, A., and Kennedy, A. *Sleep Deprivation Chamber*
Kushner, T. *Angels in America: Millennium Approaches*
Mamet, D. *Oleanna*
Marlowe, C. *The Tragical History of the Life and Death of Doctor Faustus*
Miller, A. *Death of a Salesman*
Molière, J. *The Misanthrope*
Norman, M. *'Night, Mother*
O'Casey, S. *Juno and the Paycock*
O'Neill, E. *A Moon for the Misbegotten*
Pinter, H. *Landscape*
Pirandello, L. *Six Characters in Search of an Author*
Plautus. *A Funny Thing Happened on the Way to the Wedding (Casina)*
Reza, Y. *"Art"*
*The Second Shepherds' Play*
Shakespeare, W. *Othello*
Shakespeare, W. *Twelfth Night*
Shaw, G. *Pygmalion*
Sheridan, R. *The School for Scandal*
Sophocles. *Oedipus Rex*
Soyinka, W. *Death and the King's Horseman*
Strindberg, A. *Miss Julie*
Valdez, L. *Los vendidos*
Williams, T. *Cat on a Hot Tin Roof*
Wilson, A. *Ma Rainey's Black Bottom*

SSSN *Staging the North: Twelve Canadian Plays.* Edited by Sherrill Grace, Eve D'Aeth, and Lisa Chalykoff. Toronto: Playwrights Canada Press, 1999. 502pp.
Adams, P. *Free's Point*
Beissel, H. *Inuk and the Sun*
Flather, P., and Linklater, L. *Sixty Below*
Hardin, H. *Esker Mike & His Wife, Agiluk*
Jeffery, L. *Who Look in Stove*
Kavanagh, G. *Ditch*
Lill, W. *The Occupation of Heather Rose*
MacEwen, G. *Terror and Erebus*
Robinson, M. *Colonial Tongues*
Shorty, S. *Trickster Visits the Old Folks Home*
Tunooniq Theatre. *Changes*
Tunooniq Theatre. *In Search of a Friend*

SSST Stallman, R. W., and Watters, R. E. *The Creative Reader.* New York: Ronald [c1954] 923pp.
Chekhov, A. *The Cherry Orchard*
Coxe, L., and Chapman, R. *Billy Budd*
Ibsen, H. *The Wild Duck*
Shakespeare, W. *The Tempest*
Sophocles. *Antigone*

SSSU Stallman, R. W., and Watters, R. E. *The Creative
    Reader.* 2nd ed. New York: Ronald [c1962] 992pp.
  Anouilh, J. *Antigone*
  Coxe, L. and Chapman, R. *Billy Budd*
  Ibsen, H. *The Wild Duck*
  Shakespeare, W. *The Tempest*
  Sophocles. *Antigone*

SSTA Stamm, Rudolf, ed. *Three Anglo-Irish Plays.* Bern,
    Switzerland: A. Francke, 1943. 114pp. (Bibliotheca
    Anglicana. Vol. 5)
  Gregory, I. *The Rising of the Moon*
  Synge, J. *Riders to the Sea*
  Yeats, W. *Deirdre*

SSTE Stanford University. Dramatists' Alliance. *Plays of
    the Southern Americas.* Stanford Univ., Dramatists'
    Alliance, 1942. v.p.
  Acevedo Hernández, A. *Cabrerita*
  Sanchez, F. *La Gringa*
  Vargas Tejada, L. *Las convulsiones*

SSTF Stanley, Linda, and Gillespie, Sheena, compilers.
    *The Treehouse: An Introduction to Literature.*
    Cambridge, MA: Winthrop Pubs., 1974. 368pp.
  Čapek, K., and Čapek, J. *The Insect Play*
  Euripides. *Medea*
  Miller, A. *A Memory of Two Mondays*

SSTG Stanton, Stephen S., ed. *Camille and Other Plays.*
    New York: Hill and Wang [1957] 306pp. (Mermaid
    dramabook)
  Augier, E. *Olympe's Marriage*
  Dumas, A. *Camille*
  Sardou, V. *A Scrap of Paper*
  Scribe, E. *The Glass of Water*
  Scribe, E., and Bayard, J. *A Peculiar Position*

SSTW Starkie, Walter Fitzwilliam, ed. and tr. *Eight
    Spanish Plays of the Golden Age.* New York:
    Modern Library [1964]. 328pp.
  Calderón de la Barca, P. *The Mayor of Zalamea*
  Cervantes Saavedra, M. *The Jealous Old Man*
  Cervantes Saavedra, M. *Pedro, the Artful Dodger*
  *The Mystery Play of Elche*
  Rueda, L. *The Mask*
  Ruiz, J. *The Gallant, the Bawd, and the Fair Lady*
  Téllez, G. *The Playboy of Seville*
  Vega Carpio, L. *Peribáñez and the Commander of
    Ocaña*

SSTX *Stars in the Morning Sky: Five New Plays from
    the Soviet Union.* Introduced by Michael Glenny.
    London: Nick Hern Books, 1989. 329pp.
  Chervinsky, A. *Heart of a Dog*
  Galin, A. *Stars in the Morning Sky*

  Gelman, A. *A Man with Connections*
  Gorin, G. *Forget Herostratus!*
  Petrushevskaya, L. *Three Girls in Blue*

SSTY Stasio, Marilyn, ed. *Broadway's Beautiful Losers.*
    New York: Delacorte Press, 1972. 425pp.
  Bellow, S. *The Last Analysis*
  Mercier, M. *Johnny No-trump*
  Perelman, S. *The Beauty Part*
  Richardson, J. *Xmas in Las Vegas*
  Wheeler, H. *Look: We've Come Through*

STAUFFER, RUTH MATILDA. *See also* FREI Freier,
    Robert. *Adventures in Modern Literature.*

STA Stauffer, Ruth Matilda, compiler. *The Progress
    of Drama through the Centuries.* New York:
    Macmillan, 1927. 696pp.
  Bulwer-Lytton, E. *The Lady of Lyons; or, Love and
    Pride*
  Calderón de la Barca, P. *The Constant Prince*
  Corneille, P. *Polyeucte*
  Euripides. *The Trojan Women*
  *Everyman*
  Fitch, C. *The Truth*
  Goldsmith, O. *She Stoops to Conquer; or, the Mistakes
    of a Night*
  Ibsen, H. *An Enemy of the People*
  Jonson, B. *Epicoene; or, the Silent Woman*
  Marlowe, C. *Faustus*
  Molière, J. *L'avare*
  Plautus, T. *Aulularia; or, the Pot of Gold*
  Racine, J. *Berenice*
  Schiller, J. *William Tell*
  *The Second Shepherds' Play*
  Shakespeare, W. *Hamlet*
  Sheridan, R. *The School for Scandal*
  Sophocles. *Antigone*

STAT Stauffer, Ruth Matilda, and Cunningham, William
    H., eds. *Adventures in Modern Literature.* New
    York: Harcourt, Brace [c1939] 1170pp.
  Anderson, M. *The Feast of Ortolans*
  Galsworthy. J. *The Silver Box*
  Gibney, S., and Collings, P. *The Story of Louis Pasteur*
  Glaspell, S. *Trifles*
  Goodman, K., and Hecht, B. *The Hand of Siva*
  Sherriff, R. *Journey's End*

STAU Stauffer, Ruth Matilda, and Cunningham, William
    H., eds. *Adventures in Modern Literature.* 2nd
    edition. New York: Harcourt, Brace, 1944. 1042pp.
  Čapek, K. *R.U.R.*
  Gibney, S., and Collings, P. *The Story of Louis Pasteur*
  Glaspell, S. *Trifles*

Goodman, K., and Hecht, B. *The Hand of Siva*
Sherriff, R. *Journey's End*
Wilde, P. *Blood of the Martyrs*

STAV Stauffer, Ruth Matilda; Cunningham, William
    H.; and Sullivan, Catherine J., eds. *Adventures*
    *in Modern Literature.* 3rd edition. New York:
    Harcourt, Brace, 1951. 747pp.
  Corwin, N. *My Client Curley*
  Glaspell, S. *Trifles*
  O'Casey, S. *The End of the Beginning*
  Sherriff, R. *Journey's End*
  Van Druten, J. *I Remember Mama*

STE Steeves, Harrison Ross, ed. *Plays from the Modern*
    *Theatre.* Boston: Heath [c1931] 526pp.
  Chekhov, A. *The Cherry Orchard*
  Donnay, M. *Lovers*
  Hauptmann, G. *The Beaver Coat*
  Ibsen, H. *Ghosts*
  Molnár, F. *Liliom*
  O'Neill, E. *The Great God Brown*
  Pinero, A. *The Second Mrs. Tanqueray*
  Schnitzler, A. *Intermezzo*
  Wilde, O. *The Importance of Being Earnest*

STEI Steinberg, M. W., ed. *Aspects of Modern Drama.*
    [New York] Henry Holt [c1960] 633pp.
  Anderson, M. *Elizabeth the Queen*
  Galsworthy, J. *Strife*
  Miller, A. *Death of a Salesman*
  O'Neill, F. *The Great God Brown*
  Saroyan, W. *The Time of Your Life*
  Shaw, G. *Candida*
  Shaw, G. *Man of Destiny*
  Synge, J. *The Playboy of the Western World*
  Synge, J. *Riders to the Sea*
  Wilde, O. *The Importance of Being Earnest*
  Williams, T. *The Glass Menagerie*
  Yeats, W. *The Dreaming of the Bones*

STI Steinhauer, Harry, ed. *Das Deutsche drama, 1880–*
    *1933.* New York: W. W. Norton [c1938] 2 vols.
  Hauptmann, G. *Das friedensfest* 1
  Hofmannsthal, H. *Der tor und der tod* 1
  Kaiser, G. *Gas I* 2
  Schnitzler, A. *Lebendige stunden* 1
  Toller, E. *Masse mensch* 2
  Unruh, F. *Heinruch aus Andernach* 2
  Wedekind, F. *Der kammersänger* 1
  Wiechert, E. *Das spiel vom deutschen bettelmann* 2

STJ Steinhauer, Harry, and Walter, Felix, eds. *Omnibus*
    *of French Literature.* New York: Macmillan, 1941.
    2 vols.

  Beaumarchais, P. *Le barbier de Seville* 1
  Becque, H. *Les corbeaux* 2
  Corneille, P. *Le cid* 1
  Hugo, V. *Ruy Blas* 2
  Marivaux, P. *Le jeu de ramour et du hasard* 1
  Molière, J. *Le misanthrope* 1
  Racine, J. *Andromaque* 1

STJM Steinmann, Martin, Jr., and Willen, Gerald, eds.
    *Literature for Writing.* Belmont, CA: Wadsworth
    Publishing Co. [c1962] 692pp.
  Gay, J. *The Beggar's Opera*
  Miller, A. *Death of a Salesman*
  Shakespeare, W. *Henry IV*

STJN Steinmann, Martin, and Willen, Gerald, ed.
    *Literature for Writing: An Anthology of Major*
    *British and American Authors.* 2nd ed. Belmont,
    CA: Wadsworth [1967] 719pp.
  Miller, A. *Death of a Salesman*
  Shakespeare, W. *Henry IV*
  Synge, J. *Riders to the Sea* (one act only)
  Wilde, O. *The Importance of Being Earnest*

STL Stern, Milton R., and Cross, Seymour L., eds.
    *American Literature Survey.* New York: Viking
    [c1962] 4 vols.
  O'Neill, E. *The Hairy Ape* 4
  Tyler, R. *The Contrast* 1

STM Stevens, David Harrison, ed. *Types of English*
    *Drama, 1660–1780.* Boston: Ginn [c1923] 920pp.
  Addison, J. *Cato*
  Buckingham, G., and Others. *The Rehearsal*
  Congreve, W. *Love for Love*
  Congreve, W. *The Way of the World*
  Dryden, J. *All for Love; or, the World Well Lost*
  Dryden, J. *Aureng-Zebe*
  Etherege, G. *The Man of Mode; or Sir Fopling Flutter*
  Farquhar, G. *The Beaux' Stratagem*
  Fielding, H. *The Tragedy of Tragedies; or, the Life and*
    *Death of Tom Thumb the Great*
  Gay, J. *The Beggar's Opera*
  Goldsmith, O. *The Goodnatured Man*
  Goldsmith, O. *She Stoops to Conquer; or, the Mistakes*
    *of a Night*
  Home, J. *Douglas*
  Lillo, G. *The London Merchant; or, the History of*
    *George Barnwell*
  Otway, T. *Venice Preserved; or, a Plot Discovered*
  Rowe, N. *Jane Shore*
  Shadwell, T. *Bury Fair*
  Sheridan, R. *The Critic*
  Sheridan, R. *The Duenna*
  Sheridan, R. *The Rivals*

Sheridan, R. *The School for Scandal*
Steele, R. *The Conscious Lovers*

STN Stirling, Glenda, ed. *NeXtFest Anthology: Plays from the Syncrude NeXt Generation Arts Festival, 1996–2000.* Edmonton: NeWest Press, 2000. 188pp.
Arnold, D., and Hahn, M. *Tuesdays and Sundays*
Callaghan, S. *"No. Please—"*
Craddock, C. *SuperEd*
Matwychuk, P. *The Key to Violet's Apartment*
Rowe, R. *Benedetta Carlini*

STOC Stock, Dora, and Stock, Marie, eds. *Recueil de lectures.* Boston: Heath [c1950] 240pp.
Labiche, E. *La grammaire*

STONE, DONALD, JR. *See* FOUR *Four Renaissance Tragedies.*

STORJ *The Story of Joseph in Spanish Golden Age Drama.* Selected, translated, and introduced by Michael McGaha. Lewisburg, PA: Bucknell Univesity Press; London: Associated University Presses, 1998. 341pp.
Aboab, I. *Harassed but Happy*
Calderón de la Barca, P. *Sometimes Dreams Come True*
Carvajal, M. *The Josephine Tragedy*
*Joseph's Wedding*
Juana Inés de la Cruz, Sor. *Joseph's Sceptor*
Vega, L. *The Trials of Jacob; or, Sometimes Dreams Come True*

STOTD Stott, Jon C., Jones, Raymond E., and Bowers, Rick, compilers. *The Harbrace Anthology of Drama.* Toronto: Harcourt Brace Jovanovich Canada Inc., 1994. v–xxxvii, 682–1405, 1869–1906pp., reprinted from *The HBJ Anthology of Literature,* 1993. *See* STOTL
Allen, W. *God*
Behn, A. *The Rover*
French, D. *Leaving Home*
Fugard, A. *"Master Harold" . . . and the Boys*
Marlowe, C. *Doctor Faustus*
Pinter, H. *The Homecoming*
Pollock, S. *Blood Relations*
Shakespeare, W. *Antony and Cleopatra*
Shakespeare, W. *The Tempest*
Shaw, G. *Caesar and Cleopatra*
Wilde, O. *The Importance of Being Earnest*
Williams, T. *Cat on a Hot Tin Roof*

STOTLA Stott, Jon C., Jones, Raymond E., and Bowers, Rick, compilers. *The HBJ Anthology of Literature.* Toronto: Harcourt Brace Jovanovich Canada Inc., 1993. 1906pp.

Allen, W. *God*
Behn, A. *The Rover*
French, D. *Leaving Home*
Fugard, A. *"Master Harold" . . . and the Boys*
Marlowe, C. *Doctor Faustus*
Pinter, H. *The Homecoming*
Pollock, S. *Blood Relations*
Shakespeare, W. *Antony and Cleopatra*
Shakespeare, W. *The Tempest*
Shaw, G. *Caesar and Cleopatra*
Wilde, O. *The Importance of Being Earnest*
Williams, T. *Cat on a Hot Tin Roof*

STOTLB Stott, Jon C., Jones, Raymond E., and Bowers, Rick, compilers. *The Harbrace Anthology of Literature.* 2nd ed. Scarborough, ON: Nelson Thomson Learning, 1998. 1259pp. (Originally published as *The HBJ Anthology of Literature.*)
Behn, A. *The Rover*
French, D. *Leaving Home*
Fugard, A. *"Master Harold" . . . and the Boys*
Mitchell, K. *The Shipbuilder*
Pollock, S. *Blood Relations*
Shakespeare, W. *The Tempest*
Wilde, O. *The Importance of Being Earnest*
Williams, T. *Cat on a Hot Tin Roof*

STRASBERG, LEE. *See* FAM *Famous American Plays of the 1950s.*

STRA *Strawberries, Potatoes, and Other Fantasies: Plays from Trinity College.* Edited by Arthur Feinsod and Tim Cunningham. With a foreword by Edward Albee. Hartford, CT: Trinity College, 1988. 147pp.
Baker, S. *Respectfully Yours* (excerpt)
Cunningham, T. *A Moment of Silence*
Cunningham, T. *La vache qui rit*
Denu, M. *Sometimes a Fantasy*
Lewis, W. *Peeling Potatoes*
Lewis, W. *Road to Black Mesa*
Neal, J. *Strawberries and Cream*
Rider, J. *Methusalife and Escapism*
Safran, S. *Not One of Us* (excerpt)
Touloukian, C. *Celestial Music* (excerpt)

STRI *Strike While the Iron Is Hot: Three Plays on Sexual Politics.* Edited and introduced by Michelene Wandor. London: Journeyman Press, 1980. 141pp.
Gay Sweatshop. *Care and Control*
Red Ladder Theatre Company. *Strike while the Iron Is Hot*
Women's Theatre Group. *My Mother Says I Never Should*

STRO Stroud, Theodore Albert, and Gordon, E. J., eds.
 *The Literature of Comedy: An Anthology.* Boston:
 Ginn, 1968. 763pp.
 Day, C. *Life with Father*
 Rostand, E. *Cyrano de Bergerac*
 Shaw, G. *Androcles and the Lion*
 Wilde, O. *The Importance of Being Earnest*

STS *Structure and Meaning: An Introduction to Literature.*
 Edited by Anthony Duke; John K. Franson;
 Russell E. Murphy; and James W. Parins. Boston:
 Houghton, 1976. 1222pp.
 Anderson, R. *Tea and Sympathy*
 Bullins, E. *The Electronic Nigger*
 Chayefsky, P. *Marty*
 Inge, W. *Come Back, Little Sheba*
 McCullers, C. *The Member of the Wedding*
 Miller, A. *All My Sons*
 O'Neill, E. *The Emperor Jones*
 Shakespeare, W. *Romeo and Juliet*
 Sophocles. *Oedipus Rex*
 Synge, J. *Riders to the Sea*

STUA *Stuart Academic Drama: An Edition of Three
 University Plays.* Transcribed and edited by David
 L. Russell. New York and London: Garland
 Publishing Inc., 1987. 185pp. (The Renaissance
 Imagination, vol. 34)
 *A Christmas messe*
 *Gigantomachia*
 *Heteroclitanomalonomia*

STUR Sturgess, Keith, ed. *Three Elizabethan Domestic
 Tragedies.* New York: Penguin Books, 1985. 316pp.
 *Arden of Faversham*
 Heywood, T. *A Woman Killed with Kindness*
 *A Yorkshire Tragedy*

STURM *Sturm und drang.* Edited by Alan C. Leidner.
 New York: Continuum, 1992. 304pp. (The German
 Library, vol. 14)
 Klinger, F. *Storm and Stress*
 Lenz, J. *The Soldiers*
 Schiller, F. *The Robbers*
 Wagner, H. *The Childmurderess*

STY Styan, J. L., compiler. *The Challenge of the Theatre.*
 Encino, CA: Dickenson Publishing Co., 1972.
 421pp.
 Aeschylus. *Agamemnon*
 Chekhov, A. *The Cherry Orchard*
 *Everyman*
 Frisch, M. *The Firebugs*
 Ibsen, H. *The Wild Duck*
 Pirandello, L. *Six Characters in Search of an Author*

 Shakespeare, W. *King Lear*
 Shakespeare, W. *Twelfth Night*
 Sophocles. *Oedipus the King*
 Strindberg, A. *Miss Julie*
 Synge, J. *The Shadow of the Glen*
 Wilde, O. *The Importance of Being Earnest*
 Williams, T. *The Glass Menagerie*

SUB Sullivan, Victoria, and Hatch James V., eds. *Plays
 by and about Women.* New York: Random House.
 1973. 425pp.
 Boothe, C. *The Women*
 Childress, A. *Wine in the Wilderness*
 Duffy, M. *Rites*
 Gerstenberg, A. *Overtones*
 Ginzburg, N. *Advertisement*
 Hellman, L. *The Children's Hour*
 Lessing, D. *Play with a Tiger*
 Terry, M. *Calm Down, Mother*

SUL Summers, Hollis Spurgeon, and Whan, Edgar, eds.
 *Literature: An Introduction.* New York: McGraw-
 Hill, 1960. 706pp.
 Jonson, B. *Volpone; or, the Fox*
 MacLeish, A. *The Music Crept by me upon the Waters*
 Miller, A. *The Crucible*
 Shaw, G. *The Devil's Disciple*
 Sophocles. *Antigone*
 Wilder, T. *The Matchmaker*
 Williams, T. *Something Unspoken*

SUM Summers, Montague, ed. *Restoration Comedies.*
 London: Cape, 1921. 400pp.
 Crowne, J. *Sir Courtly Nice; or, It Cannot Be*
 Killigrew, T. *The Parson's Wedding*
 Ravenscroft, E. *The London Cuckolds*

SUMB Summers, Montague, ed. *Shakespeare Adaptations.*
 London: Cape, 1922. 282pp.
 D'Avenant, W., and Dryden, J. *The Tempest; or, the
 Enchanted Island*
 Duffett, T. *The Mock-tempest; or, the Enchanted Castle*
 Tate, N. *The History of King Lear*

SUT Sutton, John F., and Others, compilers. *Ideas and
 Patterns in Literature.* New York: Harcourt, Brace,
 Jovanovich, 1970. 4 vols.
 Agee, J. *The Bride Comes to Yellow Sky* 3
 Anouilh, J. *Antigone* 2
 Chekhov, A. *The Marriage Proposal* 1
 Gibson, W. *The Miracle Worker* 1
 O'Casey, S. *The End of the Beginning* 4
 O'Neill, E. *Ile* 3
 Serling, R. *Requiem for a Heavyweight* 3
 Serling, R. *The Shelter* 2

Shakespeare, W. *Julius Caesar* 2
Shakespeare, W. *Macbeth* 4
Shaw, G. *Arms and the Man* 4
Waugh, E. *The Man Who liked Dickens* 1
Wilder, T. *Our Town* 3

SUTL Sutton, Larry M., and others, compilers. *Journeys: An Introduction to Literature.* Boston: Holbrook Press, 1971. 510pp.
Hughes, R. *The Sister's Tragedy*
Odets, C. *Waiting for Lefty*
Shakespeare, W. *Othello*
Sophocles. *Antigone*

SVICH Svich, Caridad, and Marrero, Maria Teresa, eds. *Out of the Fringe: Contemporary Latina/Latino Theatre and Performance.* New York: Theatre Communications Group, 2000. 461pp.
Alfaro, L. *Straight as a Line*
Cruz, M. *Fur*
Cruz, N. *Night Train to Bolina*
Fusco, C., and Bustamante, N. *Stuff*
Iizuka, N. *Skin*
Mayer, O. *Ragged Time*
Monge-Rafuls, P. *Trash*
Moraga, C. *The Hungry Woman*
Palacios, M. *Greetings from a Queer Señorita*
Svich, C. *Alchemy of Desire/Dead Man's Blues*

SWA Swander, Homer D., ed. *Man and the Gods: Three Tragedies.* Harcourt, Brace and World [c1964] 215pp.
Aeschylus. *Agamemnon*
Marlowe, C. *The Tragical History of Doctor Faustus*
Shaw, G. *Saint Joan*

SWANS Swanson, Meg, with Robin Murray. *Playwrights of Color.* Yarmouth, ME: Intercultural Press, Inc., 1999. 695pp.
Brown, C. *The African Company Presents Richard III*
Childress, A. *Wedding Band*
Fraguada, F. *Bodega*
Gotanda, P. *Yankee Dawg You Die*
Kauffman, J. *According to Coyote*
Lang, W. *Pow Wow; or, the Great Victory*
Lee, L. *Black Eagles*
Machado, E. *Broken Eggs*
Shiomi, R. *Yellow Fever*
Spiderwoman Theater. *Winnetou's Snake Oil Show from Wigwam City*
Valdez, L. *Los vendidos*
Ward, D. *Day of Absence*
Wolfe, G. *Spunk*
Wong, E. *Letters to a Student Revolutionary*
Yamauchi, W. *12-1-A*

SWI Swire, Willard, ed. *Three Distinctive Plays about Abraham Lincoln.* New York: Washington Square Press [c1961] 208pp.
Conkle, E. *Prologue to Glory*
Drinkwater, J. *Abraham Lincoln*
Van Doren, M. *The Last Days of Lincoln*

SWIT Switz, Theodore MacLean, and Johnston, Robert A., eds. *Great Christian Plays.* Greenwich, CT: Seabury, 1956. 306pp.
*Abraham and Isaac*
*Conversion of St. Paul*
*Everyman*
*Resurrection*
*Totentanz*

SWO Swortzell, Lowell, ed. *The Twelve Plays of Christmas: Traditional and Modern Plays for the Holidays.* New York: Applause, 2000. 503pp.
Brooks, J., and Mitchell, A. *A Child's Christmas in Wales*
*A Christmas Pageant*
Gollobin, L. *The Match Girl's Gift: A Christmas Story*
Harris, A. *The Second Shepherd's Play*
Hoffman, E. *The Nutcracker and the Mouse King*
Horowitz, I. *A Christmas Carol: Scrooge and Marley*
Hughes, L. *Black Nativity*
Lebow, B. *Tiny Tim Is Dead*
Medoff, M. *Kringle's Window*
Menotti, G. *Amahl and the Night Visitors*
Sigley, M. *Saint George and the Dragon at Christmas Tide*
Swortzell, L. *A Partridge in a Pear Tree*
Swortzell, L. *The Shepherds of Saint Francis*
Swortzell, L. *A Visit from St. Nicholas or the Night before Christmas*
Wilder, T. *The Long Christmas Dinner*

SYM Symes, Ken M., ed. *Two Voices: Writing about Literature.* Boston: Houghton Mifflin, 1976. 289pp.
*Everyman*
Hansberry, L. *A Raisin in the Sun*

SYMONS, ARTHUR. *See* NER *Nero (Tragedy). Nero & Other Plays.*

SZO Szoka, Elzbieta, and Joe W. Bratcher III, eds. *3 Contemporary Brazilian Plays in Bilingual Edition.* Austin, TX: Host Publications, Inc., 1988. 527pp.
Assunção, L. *Boca molhada de paixão*
Assunção, L. *Moist lips, Quiet Passion*
Castro, C. *Aviso prévio*
Castro, C. *Walking Papers*
Marcos, P. *Dois perdidos numa note suja*
Marcos, P. *Two Lost in a Filthy Night*

TAFT Taft, Kendall B. *Minor Knickerbockers*. New York: American Book Company [c1947] 410pp.

Payne, J. *Charles the Second*

TAIT Tait, Peta, and Schafer, Elizabeth, eds. *Australian Women's Drama: Texts and Feminisms*. Sydney: Currency Press, 1997. 286pp.

De Groen, A. *Vocations*

Hewett, D. *The Chapel Perilous*

Janaczewska, N. *Historia*

Johnson, E. *Murras*

Kemp, J. *Remember*

Lyssiotis, T. *The Forty Lounge Cafe*

Spunner, S. *Running Up a Dress*

TAK Takaya, Ted T., ed. and tr. *Modern Japanese Drama: An Anthology*. New York: Columbia University Press, 1979. 277pp.

Abe, K. *You, Too, Are Guilty*

Betsuyaku, M. *The Move*

Mishima, Y. *Yoroboshi: The Blind Young Man*

Yamazaki, M. *The Boat Is a Sailboat*

Yashiro, S. *Hokusai Sketch Books*

TAT Tatlock, John Strong Perry, and Martin, Robert Grant, eds. *Representative English Plays*. New York: Century, 1916. 838pp.

*Abraham and Isaac*

Addison, J. *Cato*

Beaumont, F., and Fletcher, J. *Philaster; or, Love Lies A-bleeding*

Browning, R. *A Blot in the 'Scutcheon*

Bulwer-Lytton, E. *The Lady of Lyons; or, Love and Pride*

Congreve, W. *The Way of the World*

Dekker, T *The Shoemaker's Holiday; or, the Gentle Craft*

Dryden, J. *Almanzor and Almahide; or, the Conquest of Granada*

*Everyman*

Fielding, H. *The Tragedy of Tragedies; or, The Life and Death of Tom Thumb the Great*

Fletcher, J. *The Wild-goose Chase*

Goldsmith, O. *She Stoops to Conquer; or, the Mistakes of a Night*

Heywood, T. *A Woman Killed with Kindness*

Jonson, B. *The Alchemist*

Lyly, J. *Mother Bombie*

Marlowe, C. *The Troublesome Reign and Lamentable Death of Edward the Second*

Middleton, R., and Rowley, W. *The Changeling*

*Noah's Flood*

Otway, T. *Venice Preserved; A Plot Discovered*

*The Second Shepherds' Play*

Shelley, P. *The Cenci*

Sheridan, R. *The School for Scandal*

Steele, R. *The Conscious Lovers*

Webster, J. *The Duchess of Mali*

Wilde, O. *Lady Windermere's Fan*

TAU Tallock, John Strong Perry, and Martin, Robert Grant, eds. *Representative English Plays*. 2nd ed. rev. and enl. New York: Appleton-Century [c1938] 914pp.

*Abraham and Isaac*

Addison, J. *Cato*

Beaumont, F. and Fletcher, J. *Philaster; or, Love Lies A-bleeding*

Bulwer-Lytton, E. *The Lady of Lyons; or, Love and Pride*

Congreve, W. *The Way of the World*

Dekker, T. *The Shoemaker's Holiday; or, the Gentle Craft*

Dryden, J. *Almanzor and Almahide; or, the Conquest of Granada*

*Everyman*

Fielding, H. *The Tragedy of Tragedies; or, the Life and Death of Tom Thumb the Great*

Fletcher, J. *The Wild-goose Chase*

Goldsmith, O. *She Stoops to Conquer; or, the Mistakes of a Night*

Heywood, T. *A Woman Killed with Kindness*

Jonson, B. *The Alchemist*

Lillo, G. *The London Merchant or, the History of George Barnwell*

Lyly, J. *Mother Bombie*

Marlowe, C. *The Troublesome Reign and Lamentable Death of Edward the Second*

Middleton, T., and Rowley, W. *The Changeling*

*Noah's Flood*

Otway, T. *Venice Preserved; or, a Plot Discovered*

Pinero, A. *The Second Mrs. Tanqueray*

Robertson, T. *Caste*

*The Second Shepherds' Play*

Shelley, P. *The Cenci*

Sheridan, R. *The School for Scandal*

Steele, R. *The Conscious Lovers*

Webster, J. *The Duchess of Malfi*

Wilde, O. *Lady Windermere's Fan*

TAUB Taub, Michael, ed. *Israeli Holocaust Drama*. Syracuse, NY: Syracuse University Press, 1996. 332pp.

Goldberg, L. *Lady of the Castle*

Lerner, M. *Kastner*

Megged, A. *Hanna Senesh*

Sobol, J. *Adam*

Tomer, B. *Children of the Shadows*

TAUJ Taylor, John Chesley, and Thompson, Gary Richard, compilers. *Ritual, Realism, and Revolt: Major Traditions in the Drama*. New York: Scribner, 1972. 816pp.
Adamov, A. *Professor Toranne*
Camus, A. *Caligula*
Eliot, T. *Murder in the Cathedral*
Euripides. *Medea*
Euripides. *Orestes*
Ibsen, H. *Hedda Gabler*
Jones, L. *The Slave*
Middleton, T., and Rowley, W. *The Changeling*
Miller, A. *The Crucible*
O'Neill, E. *The Great God Brown*
Osborne, J. *The Entertainer*
Shakespeare, W. *Othello*
Sophocles. *Antigone*
Synge, J. *Riders to the Sea*
Williams, T. *Summer and Smoke*
Wycherley, W. *The Country Wife*
Yeats, W. *Purgatory*

TAV Taylor, Joseph Richard, ed. *European and Asiatic Plays*. Boston: Expression Co., 1936. 730pp.
Aristophanes. *The Frogs*
*The Bird Catcher in Hell*
Calderón de la Barca, P. *Life Is a Dream*
Corneille, P. *The Cid*
Dekker, T. *The Shoemaker's Holiday*
Enamai Sayemon. *The Cormorant Fisher*
Euripides. *Medea*
*Everyman*
Heywood, J. *The Four P's*
Hroswitha. *Dulcitius*
Kālidāsa. *Shakuntalā*
Massinger, P. *A New Way to Pay Old Debts*
Plautus, T. *The Menaechmi*
Sackville, T., and Norton, T. *Gorboduc*
Seami, M. *Atsumori*
*The Second Shepherds' Play*
Seneca, L. *Medea*
Shakespeare, W. *The Comedy of Errors*
Shirley, J. *The Traitor*
*The Sorrows of Han*
Udall, N. *Ralph Roister Doister*

TAY Taylor, William Duncan, ed. *Eighteenth Century Comedy*. London: Oxford University Press [1929] 413pp. (The World's Classics)
Farquhar, G. *The Beaux' Stratagem*
Fielding, H. *The Tragedy of Tragedies; or, the Life and Death of Tom Thumb the Great*
Gay, J. *The Beggar's Opera*

Goldsmith, O. *She Stoops to Conquer*
Steele, R. *The Conscious Lovers*

TEN *Ten Greek Plays*. Translated into English by Gilbert Murray and others; with an introduction by Lane Cooper, and a preface by H. B. Densmore. New York: Oxford University Press, 1930. 475pp.
Aeschylus. *Agamemnon*
Aeschylus. *The Choephoroe*
Aeschylus. *The Eumenides*
Arisophanes. *The Frogs*
Aristophanes. *Plutus, the God of Riches*
Euripides. *Electra*
Euripides. *Iphigenia in Tauris*
Euripides. *Medea*
Sophocles. *Antigone*
Sophocles. *Oedipus, King of Thebes*

TENN *Tenth Muse: Classical Drama in Translation*. Edited by Charles Doria. Athens, OH: Ohio University Press, Swallow Press, 1980. 587pp.
Aeschylus. *Prometheus Unbound*
Aeschylus. *The Suppliants*
Aristophanes. *Peace*
Euripides. *The Bacchae*
Euripides. *The Cyclops*
Plautus, T. *The Rope*
Seneca, L. *Thyestes*
Sophocles. *Philoctetes*

TEX *Texas Plays*. Edited by William B. Martin. Dallas: Southern Methodist University Press, 1990. 467pp.
Foote, H. *The Trip to Bountiful*
Hailey, O. *Who's Happy Now?*
Heifner, J. *Patio*
Heifner, J. *Porch*
Jones, P. *Lu Ann Hampton Laverty Oberlander*
McLure, J. *Laundry and Bourbon*
McLure, J. *Lone Star*
Morton, C. *El jardin*
Rohde, M. *Ladybug, Ladybug, Fly Away Home*
Vliet, R. *The Regions of Noon*
Yelvington, R. *A Cloud of Witnesses*

TEZ Tezla, Albert, ed. *Three Contemporary Hungarian Plays*. London and Boston: Forest Books; Budapest: Corvina Books, 1992. 238pp.
Bereményi, G. *Halmi*
Czakó, G. *Pigs*
Spiró, G. *The Imposter*

THA Thayer, William Roscoe, ed. *The Best Elizabethan Plays*. Boston: Ginn [c1890] 611pp.

Beaumont, F., and Fletcher, J. *Philaster; or, Love Lies A-bleeding*
Fletcher, J. and Shakespeare, W. *The Two Noble Kinsmen*
Jonson, B. *The Alchemist*
Marlowe, C. *The Jew of Malta*
Webster, J. *The Duchess of Malfi*

THB *Theater and Politics: An International Anthology.* Preface by Erika Munk. New York: Ubu Theater Publications, 1990. 469pp.
Bemba, S. *Black Wedding Candles for Blessed Antigone*
Césaire, A. *A Season in the Congo*
Fargeau, J. *Burn River Burn*
Kesselman, W. *Olympe and the Executioner*
Mnouchkine, A. *Mephisto*

THC *Theater and Society: An Anthology of Contemporary Chinese Drama.* Haiping Yan, Editor. Armonk, NY; London: M.E. Sharpe, 1998. 328pp.
Chen, Z., Yang, J., and Zhu, X. *Sangshuping Chronicles*
Gao, X. *Bus Stop*
Wang, P. *WM (WE)*
Wei, M. *Pan Jinlian: The History of a Fallen Woman*
Zheng, Y. *Old Well*

THEA *Theatre, 1953–1956.* Edited by John Chapman. New York: Random House [c1953–1956] 4 vols.
Abbott, G. and Bissell, R. *The Pajama Game* 54
Anderson, M. *The Bad Seed* 55
Anderson, R. *Tea and Sympathy* 54
Anouilh, J. *The Lark* 56
Axelrod, G. *The Seven Year Itch* 53
Bagnold, E. *The Chalk Garden* 56
Behrman, S., and Logan, J. *Fanny* 55
Chase, M. *Bernardine* 53
Chodorov, E. *Oh, Men! Oh, Women!* 54
Christie, A. *Witness for the Prosecution* 55
Denker, H., and Berkey, R. *Time Limit!* 56
Eliot, T. *The Confidential Clerk* 54
Fields, J., and Chodorov, J. *The Ponder Heart* 56
Fields, J., and Chodorov, J. *Wonderful Town* 53
Gazzo, M. *A Hatful of Rain* 56
Giraudoux, J. *Ondine* 54
Giraudoux, J. *Tiger at the Gate* 56
Hackett, A., and Goodrich, F. *The Diary of Anne Frank* 56
Hart, M. *The Climate of Eden* 53
Hayes, J. *The Desperate Hours* 55
Howard, S. *Madam, Will You Walk* 54
Inge, W. *Bus Stop* 55
Inge, W. *Picnic* 53
Kingsley, S. *Lunatics and Lover* 55
Knott, F. *Dial "M" for Murder* 53
Kober, A., and Logan, J. *Wish You Were Here* 53

Kurnitz, H. *Reclining Figure* 55
Latouche, J. *The Golden Apple* 54
Laurents, A. *The Time of the Cuckoo* 53
Lawrence, J., and Lee, R. *Inherit the Wind* 55
Levin, I. *No Time for Sergeants* 56
Loesser, F. *The Most Happy Fella* 56
Maurette, M. *Anastasia* 55
Menotti, G. *The Saint of Bleecker Street* 55
Miller, A. *The Crucible* 53
Miller, A. *A View from the Bridge* 56
O'Brien, L. *The Remarkable Mr. Pennypacker* 54
Patrick, J. *The Teahouse of the August Moon* 54
Rosten, N. *Mister Johnson* 56
Shulman, M., and Smith, R. *The Tender Trap* 55
Spewack, S., and Spewack, B. *My Three Angels* 53
Taylor, S. *Sabrina Fair* 54
Teichman, H., and Kaufman, G. *The Solid Gold Cadillac* 54
Ustinov, P. *The Love of Four Colonels* 53
Wilder, T. *The Matchmaker* 56
Williams, T. *Cat on a Hot Tin Roof* 55
Wouk, H. *The Caine Mutiny Court Martial* 54
Young, S. *Mr. Pickwick* 53

THEC *Theatre for Tomorrow.* London: Longmans, Green, 1940. 397pp.
Breen, R., and Schnibble, H. *"Who Ride on White Horses," the story of Edmund Campion*
Lavery, E., and Murphy, G. *Kamiano, the Story of Damien*
Nagle, U. *Savonarola, the Flame of Florence*

THF *Theatre Guild: The Theatre Guild Anthology.* New York: Random House [c1936] 961pp.
Anderson, M. *Mary of Scotland*
Andreyev, L. *He Who Gets Slapped*
Barry, B. *Hotel Universe*
Behrman, S. *Rain from Heaven*
Ervine, St. J. *John Ferguson*
Heyward, D., and Heyward, D. *Porgy*
Howard, S. *The Silver Cord*
Milne, A. *Mr. Pim Passes By*
Molnár, F. *Liliom*
O'Neill, E. *Strange Interlude*
Rice, E. *The Adding Machine*
Shaw, G. *Saint Joan*
Sherwood, R. *Reunion in Vienna*
Werfel, F. *Goat Song*

THG *The Theatre of Images.* Edited by Bonnie Marranca. New York: Drama Books, 1977. 122pp.
Breuer, L. *The Red Horse Animation*
Foreman, R. *Pandering to the Masses: A Misrepresentation*
Wilson, R. *A Letter for Queen Victoria*

THGA *The Theatre of Images*. Edited with introductory
essays and a new afterword by Bonnie Marranca.
Baltimore: Johns Hopkins University Press, 1996.
168pp.
Breuer, L. *The Red Horse Animation*
Foreman, R. *Pandering to the Masses: A
Misrepresentation*
Wilson, R. *A Letter for Queen Victoria*

THH *Theatre Omnibus*. London: Hamilton [1938] v.p.
Behrman, S. *Amphitryon 38*
Jerome, H. *Jane Eyre*
Jerome, H. *Pride and Prejudice*
Lyndon, B. *The Amazing Dr. Clitterhouse*
Rattigan, T. *French without Tears*
Savoy, G. *George and Margaret*

THL *The Theatre of the Holocaust: Four Plays*. Edited
by Robert Skloot. Madison, WI: University of
Wisconsin Press, 1982. 333pp.
Delbo, C. *Who Will Carry the Word?*
Lieberman, H. *Throne of Straw*
Tabori, G. *The Cannibals*
Wincelberg, S. *Resort 76*

THLA *The Theatre of the Holocaust, Volume 2: Six Plays*.
Edited by Robert Skloot. Madison, WI: University
of Wisconsin Press, 1999. 407pp.
Brenton, H. *H.I.D. (Hess Is Dead)*
Hampton, C. *The Portage to San Cristobal of A.H.*
Kift, R. *Camp Comedy*
Kops, B. *Dreams of Anne Frank*
Margulies, D. *The Model Apartment*
Sack, L. *The Survivor and the Translator*

THMD Thomas, David, ed. *Four Georgian and pre-
Revolutionary Plays*. New York: St. Martin's Press,
1998. 291pp.
Beaumarchais, P. *The Marriage of Figaro, or, the
Follies of a Day*
Goldsmith, O. *She Stoops to Conquer, or, the Mistakes
of a Night*
Lessing, G. *Emilia Galotti*
Sheridan, R. *The Rivals*

THMF Thomas, David, ed. *Six Restoration and French
Neoclassic Plays*. New York: St. Martin's Press,
1998. 456pp.
Congreve, W. *Love for Love*
Dryden, J. *All for Love*
Molière, J. *The Miser*
Molière, J. *Tartuffe*
Racine, J. *Phedra*
Wycherley, W. *The Country Wife*

THO Thomas, Russell Brown, ed. *Plays and the Theatre*.
Boston: Little, Brown, 1937. 729pp.
Anderson, M. *Elizabeth the Queen*
Besier, R. *The Barretts of Wimpole Street*
Ibsen, H. *An Enemy of the People*
Kelly, G. *Poor Aubrey*
*Master Pierre Patelin*
Molière, J. *The Miser*
Morton, J. *Box and Cox*
O'Neill, E. *In the Zone*
Shakespeare, W. *Romeo and Juliet*
Sheridan, R. *The School for Scandal*
Sophocles. *Antigone*
Steele, W. *The Giant's Stair*

THOD Thompson, David, ed. *Theatre Today*. London:
Longmans, 1965. 206pp.
Albee, E. *The Sand Box*
Campton, D. *Then . . .*
Donleavy, J. *The Interview*
Ionesco, E. *The New Tenant*
Mankowitz, W. *It Should Happen to a Dog*
O'Casey, S. *Hall of Healing*
Pinter, H. *The Black and White*
Pinter, H. *Last to Go*
Saroyan, W. *The Oyster and the Pearl*
Shaw, G. *Passion, Poison, and Petrifaction*

THOM Thompson, Stith, ed. *Our Heritage of World
Literature*. New York: Dryden Press [c1938]
1246pp.
Aeschylus. *Agamemnon*
Aristophanes. *The Frogs*
Chekhov, A. *The Cherry Orchard*
Euripides. *Alcestis*
Goethe, J. *Faust, Part I*
Ibsen, H. *A Doll's House*
Molière, J. *The Miser*
Plautus, T. *The Captives*
Racine, J. *Phaedra*
Shakespeare, W. *Hamlet*
Sophocles. *Antigone*
Wilde, O. *The Importance of Being Earnest*

THON Thompson, Stith, and Gassner, John, eds. *Our
Heritage of World Literature*. Rev. ed. New York:
Dryden Press [c1942] 1416pp.
Aeschylus. *Agamemnon*
Aristophanes. *The Frogs*
Chekhov, A. *The Cherry Orchard*
Euripides. *Alcestis*
Goethe, J. *Faust, Part I*
Hauptmann, G. *The Weavers*
Ibsen, H. *A Doll's House*
Molière, J. *The Miser*

Plautus, T. *The Captives*
Racine, J. *Phaedra*
Shakespeare, W. *Hamlet*
Sophocles. *Antigone*
Wilde, O. *The Importance of Being Earnest*

THOP *Three Australian Plays*. Harmondsworth,
   Middlesex: Penguin [1963] 311pp.
Porter, H. *The Tower*
Seymour, A. *The One Day of the Year*
Stewart, D. *Ned Kelly*

THOQ *Three Danish Comedies*. Translated by Michael
   Meyer. London: Oberon Books, 1999. 164pp.
Heiberg, J. *No*
Holberg, L. *Jeppe of the Hill, or, a Peasant Translated*
Holberg, L. *The Scatterbrain*

THOR *Three East European Plays*. Hammondsworth,
   Middlesex: Penguin, 1970. 271pp.
Havel, V. *The Memorandum*
Hay, J. *The Horse*
Mrozek, S. *Tango*

THOS *Three French Comedies*. Translated and with an
   introduction by James Magruder. New Haven and
   London: Yale University Press, 1996. 180pp.
Labiche, E. *Eating Crow*
Le Sage, A. *Turcaret*
Marivaux, P. *The Triumph of Love*

THP *Three Great Greek Plays*. Selected with an
   introduction by Lyman Bryson. Greenwich, CT:
   Fawcett [c1960] 191pp.
Aeschylus. *Agamemnon*
Euripides. *Hippolytus*
Sophocles. *Oedipus the King*

THQ *Three Great Jewish Plays in Modern Translations*
   by Joseph C. Landis. New York: Applause
   Theatre Book Publishers, 1986. 254pp. (Originally
   published with two other plays as: *The Great
   Jewish Plays*. New York: Horizon Books, 1972.)
Anski, S. *The Dybbuk*
Asch, S. *God of Vengeance*
Leivick, H. *The Golem*

THR *Three Late Medieval Morality Plays: Mankind,
   Everyman, Mundus et inFans*; edited by G. A.
   Lester. London/Ernest Bean Limited; New York:
   W.W. Norton & Co., Inc., 1981. 157pp.
*Everyman*
*Mankind*
*Mundus et inFans*

THRCD *Three Masterpieces of Cuban Drama*. Translated
   from the Spanish and edited with an introduction by
   Luis F. Gonzalez-Cruz and Ann Waggoner Aken.
   Copenhagen and Los Angeles: Green Integer, 2000.
   259pp.
Felipe, C. *The Chinaman*
Matas, J. *Deviations*
Piñera, V. *An Empty Shoe Box*

THRIN *Three Modern Indian Plays*. Delhi: Oxford
   University Press, 1989. 86pp., 60pp., 78pp.
Karnad, G. *Tughlaq*
Sircar, B. *Evam Indrajit*
Tendulkar, V. *Silence! The Court Is in Session*

THS *Three Modern Plays from the French*. New York:
   Holt, 1914. 272pp.
Donnay, M. *The Other Danger*
Lavedan, H. *The Prince d'Aurec*
Lemaître, J. *The Pardon*

THT *Three Negro Plays*. Harmondsworth, Middlesex:
   Penguin, 1969. 207pp.
Hansberry, L. *The Sign in Sidney Brustein's Window*
Hughes, L. *Mulatto*
Jones, L. *The Slave*

THTN *Three Nigerian Plays*. London: Longmans, 1967.
   89pp.
Ijimere, O. *Born with the Fire on His Head*
Ladipo, D. *Moremi*
Ogunyemi, W. *The Scheme*

THU *Three Plays*. London: Gardner, Darton [1926] v.p.
Ouless, E. *Our Pageant*
Pakington, M. *The Queen of Hearts*
Paul, Mrs. C. *The Fugitive King*

THUAA *Three Plays by Asian Australians*. Edited by Don
   Batchelor. Brisbane: Playlab Press in association
   with Queensland University of Technology, 2000.
   135pp.
Mahjoeddin, I. *The Butterfly Seer*
Ta, B. *The Monkey Mother*
Yen, A. *Chinese Take Away*

THUG *Three Political Plays*. Edited by Alrene Maude
   Sykes. St. Lucia, Australia: University of
   Queensland Press, 1980. 156pp. (Contemporary
   Australia Plays, 9)
Bradley, J. *Irish Stew*
Sewell, S. *The Father We Loved on a Beach by the Sea*
Spears, S. *King Richard*

THV *Three Popular French Comedies.* Translated and
notes by Albert Bermel. New York: Ungar, 1975.
170pp.
Beaumarchais, P. *The Barber of Seville*
Courteline, G. *The Commissioner Has a Big Heart*
Labiche, E., and Delacourt, A. *Pots of Money*

THW *Three Rastell Plays: Four Elements, Cafisto and
Melebea, Gentleness and Nobility.* Edited by
Richard Axton. Cambridge, D. S. Brewer Ltd and
Totowa, NJ: Rowman and Littlefield, 1979. 169pp.
(Tudor Interludes)
*Calisto and Melebea*
*Four Elements*
Heywood, J. *Gentleness and Nobility*

THWI *Three Sanskrit Plays.* Translated by Michael
Coulson. Harmondsworth: Penguin, 1981. 430pp.
Bhavabhūti. *Malati and Madhava*
Kālidāsa. *Sakuntalā*
Vishākhadatta. *Rākshasa's Ring*

THWO *Three Sixteenth-Century Comedies: Gammer
Gurton's Needle, Roister Doister, The Old Wife's
Tale.* Edited by Charles Walters Whitworth.
London: Ernest Benn Ltd.; New York: W. W.
Norton & Co. Inc. 1984. 272pp.
Peele, G. *The Old Wife's Tale*
Stevenson, W. *Gammer Gurton's Needle*
Udall, N. *Roister Doister*

THX *Three Southwest Plays.* With an introduction by
John Rosenfield. Dallas: Southwest Review, 1942.
326pp.
Acheson, S. *We Are Besieged*
Rogers, J. *Where the Dear Antelope Play*
Witherspoon, K. *Jute*

THY *Three Soviet Plays.* Moscow: Foreign Language
Publishing House [1961] 247pp.
Arbuzov, A. *It Happened in Irkutsk*
Korneichuk, A. *Platon Krechet*
Pogodin, N. *Kremlin Chimes*

THZ *Three Tudor Classical Interludes: Thersites, Jacke
Jugeler, Horestes.* Edited by Marie Axton.
Cambridge [Cambridgeshire]: D. S. Brewer;
Totowa, NJ: Rowan and Littlefield, 1982. 237pp.
*A New Enterlude Called Thersytes: Thys Enterlude
Folowynge Doth Declare Howe That the Greatest
Boesters Are Not the Greatest Doers*
*A New Enterlude for Chyldren to Playe Named Jacke
Jugeler: Both Wytte, Very Playsent, and Merye*

*A New Enterlude of Vice Conteyning the History of
Horestes with the Cruell Rengment of His Fathers
Death upon His One Natural Mother*

TICK Tickner, Frederick James, ed. *Restoration
Dramatists.* London: Nelson [1930] 229pp.
Dryden, J. *Aureng-zebe*
Farquhar, G. *The Beaux' Stratagem*
Otway, T. *Venice Preserved; or, a Plot Discovered*
Vanbrugh, J. *A Journey to London*

TICO Tickner, Frederick James, ed. *Shakespeare's
Predecessors.* London: Nelson [1929] 278pp.
Greene, R. *Friar Bacon and Friar Bungay*
Heywood, J. *The Four P's*
Kyd, T. *The Spanish Tragedy*
Marlowe, C. *Tamburlaine the Great [Part I]*

TIME *Time to Go: Three Plays on Death and Dying with
Commentary on End-of-life Issues.* Edited by Anne
Hunsaker Hawkins and James O. Ballard with
Theodore Blaisdell. Philadelphia: University of
Pennsylvania Press, 1995. 118pp.
Barta, B. *Journey into that Good Night*
McClelland, C. *Time to Go*
Spence, M. *Stars at the Break of Day*

TOB *To Be: Identity in Literature.* Edited by Edmund
J. Farrell, [et al.] Glenview, IL: Scott Foresman,
1976. 510pp.
Anouilh, J., and Aurenche, J. *Augustus*
Blinn, W. *Brian's Song*
Shakespeare, W. *Romeo and Juliet*

TOBI Tobin, James Edward; Hamm, Victor M.; and
Hines, William H., eds. *College Book of English
Literature.* New York: American Book Co. [c1949]
1156pp.
Marlowe, C. *The Tragical History of Doctor Faustus*
*The Second Shepherds' Play*
Synge, J. *Riders to the Sea*

TOD *Today's Literature.* Edited by Dudley Chadwick
Gordon, Vernon Rupert King, and William
Whittingham Lyman. New York: American Book
Co. [c1935] 998pp.
Bernard, L. *Lars Killed His Son*
Flavin, M. *Amaco*
Ford, H. *Youth Must Be Served*
Galsworthy, J. *The Silver Box*
Green, P. *In Abraham's Bosom*
Gregory, I. *The Workhouse Ward*
Hopkins, A. *Moonshine*

Jennings, T. *No More Frontier*
O'Neill, E. *Where the Cross Is Made*
Riggs, L. *Knives from Syria*

TOR *Torch to the Heart: Anthology of Lesbian Art and
     Drama*. Edited by Sue McConnell-Celi. With a
     special introduction by Pamela Simones. Red Bank,
     NJ: Lavender Crystal Press, 1994. 256pp.
Astor del Valle, J. *I'll Be Home para la navidad*
Astor del Valle, J. *Where the Señoritas Are*
Cady, P. *The Secret Life of Plants*
Cain, C. *Thru These Glasses We've Seen Ourselves
     Each Other a Looking Glass*
Emidia, L. *The Revelation Game*
Harris, A. *Coming In*
Jeffries, I. *Clotel, a Love Story*
Jeffries, I. *Manchild*
Simones, P. *Sins of the Mothers*

TOU *Touchstones: Classic Texts in the Humanities*. Edited
     by Robert Plarzner and Stephen Harris. Fort Worth,
     TX: Holt, Rinehart, and Winston, 1991. 564pp.
Euripides. *The Bacchants*
Molière, J. *The Would-be Gentleman*
Shakespeare, W. *The Tempest*
Sophocles. *Oedipus Rex*

TOV *The Towneley Plays*. Edited by Martin Stevens and
     A. C. Cawley. Volume One: Introduction and
     Text. Oxford: Published for the Early English Text
     Society by Oxford University Press, 1994. 435pp.
*Abraham*
*The Annunciation*
*Ascension*
*Buffeting*
*Caesar Augustus*
*Christ and the Doctors*
*The Conspiracy and Capture*
*The Creation*
*Crucifixion*
*First Shepherds' Play*
*Flight into Egypt*
*Hanging of Judas*
*Harrowing of Hell*
*Herod the Great*
*Isaac*
*Jacob*
*John the Baptist*
*Judgment*
*Lazarus*
*Mary's Salutation of Elizabeth*
*The Murder of Abel*
*Noah and His Sons*
*Offering of the Magi*
*Pharoah*

*Pilgrims*
*The Play of the Dice*
*The Play of the Prophets*
*Purification of Mary*
*Resurrection*
*Scourging*
*Second Shepherds' Play*
*Thomas of India*

TOWN *Towneley Plays. The Wakefield Mystery Plays*.
     Edited by Martial Rose. London: Evans, c1961.
     464pp.
*Abraham*
*The Annunciation*
*The Ascension of the Lord*
*The Buffeting*
*Caesar Augustus*
*The Conspiracy*
*The Creation*
*The Crucifixion*
*The Deliverance of Souls*
*The First Shepherds' Play*
*The Flight into Egypt*
*The Hanging of Judas*
*Herod the Great*
*Isaac*
*Jacob*
*John the Baptist*
*The Judgment*
*The Killing of Abel*
*Lazarus*
*Noah*
*The Offering of the Magi*
*Pharoah*
*The Pilgrims*
*The Play of the Doctors*
*The Procession of the Prophets*
*The Purification of Mary*
*The Resurrection*
*The Salutation of Elizabeth*
*The Scourging*
*The Second Shepherds' Play*
*The Talents*
*Thomas of India*

TRAD *Traditional Korean Theatre*. Translated with the
     introductions by Oh-kon Cho. Berkeley, CA: Asian
     Humanities Press, 1988. 364pp. (Studies in Korean
     religions and culture, v. 2)
*Hahoe Pyŏsin-kut*
*Kkoktu Kaksi: Puppet Play*
*Pongsang T'alch'um*
*Suyŏng Yayu*
*T'ongyŏng Ogwangdae*
*Yangju Pyŏlsandae*

TRAN *Transformation, Miracles, and Mischief: The Mountain Priest Plays of Kyōgen.* Translations with commentary [by] Carolyn Anne Morley. Ithaca, NY: East Asia Program, Cornell University, 1993. (Cornell East Asia Series no. 62)

*The Crab*
*The Lunchbox Thief*
*Mushrooms*
*Owls*
*Persimmons*
*Sacroiliac*
*The Shinto Priest and the Mountain Priest*
*The Snail*

TRE *A Treasury of the Theatre: From Aeschylus to Eugene O'Neill.* Edited by Burns Mantle and John Gassner. New York: Simon and Schuster, 1935. 1643pp.

Aeschylus. *Agamemnon*
Anderson, M. *Elizabeth the Queen*
Anderson, M., and Stallings, L. *What Price Glory?*
Aristophanes. *Lysistrata*
Chekhov, A. *The Cherry Orchard*
Congreve, W. *The Way of the World*
Connelly, M. *The Green Pastures*
Euripides. *Electra*
*Everyman*
Galsworthy, J. *Escape*
Goethe, J. *Faust, Part I*
Gorki, M. *The Lower Depths*
Hauptmann, G. *The Weavers*
Ibsen, H. *Hedda Gabler*
*Job*
Jonson, B. *Volpone*
Kālidāsa. *Shakuntalā*
Kautman, G., and Ryskind, M. *Of Thee I Sing*
Kwanze, K. *Sotoba Komachi*
Molière, J. *The Misanthrope*
Molnár, F. *Liliom*
O'Neill, E. *Anna Christie*
Pirandello, L. *Six Characters in Search of an Author*
Racine, J. *Phaedra*
Rostand, E. *Cyrano de Bergerac*
Shakespeare, W. *Hamlet*
Shaw, G. *Candida*
Shelley, P. *The Cenci*
Sherriff, R. *Journey's End*
Sophocles. *Antigone*
Strindberg, A. *The Father*
Synge, J. *Riders to the Sea*
Webster, J. *The Duchess of Malfi*
Wilde, O. *The Importance of Being Earnest*

TREA *A Treasury of the Theatre.* Edited by Burns Mantle and John Gassner. Revised and adapted for colleges by Philo M. Buck, Jr., John Gassner, and H. S. Alberson. New York: Simon and Schuster [c1940] 2 vols. (vol. 1, From Ibsen to Odets; vol. 2, Aeschylus to Hebbel)

*Abraham and Isaac* 2
Aeschylus. *Agamemnon* 2
Anderson, M. *Elizabeth the Queen* 1
Anderson, M., and Stallings, L. *What Price Glory?* 1
Aristophanes. *Lysistrata* 2
Chekhov, A. *The Cherry Orchard* 1
Congreve, W. *The Way of the World* 2
Connelly, M. *The Green Pastures* 1
Euripides. *Electra* 2
*Everyman* 2
Galsworthy, J. *Escape* 1
Goethe, J. *Faust, Part I* 2
Gorki, M. *The Lower Depths* 1
Hauptmann, G. *The Weavers* 1
Hebbel, F. *Maria Magdalena* 2
Ibsen, H. *Hedda Gabler* 1
*Job* 2
Jonson, B. *Volpone* 2
Kālidāsa. *Shakuntalā* 2
Molière, J. *The Misanthrope* 2
Molnár, F. *Liliom* 1
Odets, C. *Awake and Sing* 1
O'Neill, E. *Anna Christie* 1
Pirandello, L. *Six Characters in Search of an Author* 1
Plautus, T. *The Menaechmi* 2
Racine, J. *Phaedra* 2
Rostand, E. *Cyrano de Bergerac* 1
Shakespeare, W. *Hamlet* 2
Shaw, G. *Candida* 1
Sherriff, R. *Journey's End* 1
Sophocles. *Antigone* 2
Strindberg, A. *The Father* 1
Synge, J. *Riders to the Sea* 1
Webster, J. *The Duchess of Malfi* 2
Wilde, O. *The Importance of Being Earnest* 1

TREB *A Treasury of the Theatre: From Aeschylus to Ostrovsky.* 3rd ed. Edited by John Gassner. New York: Simon and Schuster, 1967. 1033pp.

*Abraham and Isaac*
Aeschylus. *Agamemnon*
Anouilh, J. *The Lark*
Aristophanes. *The Frogs*
Büchner, G. *Danton's Death*
Calderón de la Barca, P. *Life Is a Dream*
Cervantes Saavedra, M. *The Cave of Salamanca*
Congreve, W. *The Way of the World*
Corneille, P. *The Cid*
*The Death of Pilate*
Euripides. *The Bacchae*
Euripides. *The Trojan Women*
*Everyman*

Gay, J. *The Beggar's Opera*
Goethe, J. *Faust, Part I*
Gogol, N. *The Inspector*
Hebbel, F. *Maria Magdalena*
Hrotsvitha. *Paphnutius*
Hugo, V. *Hernani*
Jonson, B. *The Vision of Delight*
Jonson, B. *Volpone*
Kālidāsa. *Shakuntalā*
Kwanze, K. *Sotoba Komachi*
Lillo, G. *The London Merchant*
Marlowe, C. *The Tragical History of Doctor Faustus*
Molière, J. *The Misanthrope*
Musset, A. *No Trifling with Love*
Ostrovsky, A. *The Thunderstorm*
Plautus. *The Menaechmi*
Racine, J. *Phaedra*
Scala, F. *The Portrait*
Schiller, J. *Mary Stuart*
*The Second Shepherds' Play*
Seneca. *Thyestes*
Shakespeare, W. *Hamlet*
Sheridan, R. *The School for Scandal*
Sophocles. *Oedipus the King*
Sophocles. *The Searching Satyrs*
Terence. *The Brothers*
Turgenev, I. *A Month in the Country*
Vega Carpio, L. *Fuente ovejuna*
Webster, J. *The Duchess of Malfi*

TREBA *A Treasury of the Theatre: From Henrik Ibsen to Eugene Ionesco*. 3rd College Edition. Edited by John Gassner. New York: Simon and Schuster [1960] 1275pp.
Anderson, M. *Elizabeth the Queen*
Anouilh, J. *The Lark*
Barrie, J. *The Admirable Crichton*
Becque, H. *The Vultures*
Brecht, B. *The Private Life of the Master Race*
Čapek, K. *R.U.R.*
Chekhov, A. *The Cherry Orchard*
Claudel, P. *The Tidings Brought to Mary*
Connelly, M. *The Green Pastures*
Coward, N. *Blithe Spirit*
Galsworthy, J. *Escape*
García Lorca, F. *Blood Wedding*
Genêt J. *The Maids*
Giraudoux, J. *The Madwoman of Chaillot*
Gorki, M. *The Lower Depths*
Gregory, I. *The Workhouse Ward*
Hauptmann, G. *The Weavers*
Hellman, L. *The Little Foxes*
Ibsen, H. *Ghosts*
Ibsen, H. *Hedda Gabler*
Ionesco, E. *The Chairs*

Maeterlinck, M. *The Intruder*
Maugham, W. *The Circle*
Miller, A. *Death of a Salesman*
Molnar, F. *Liliom*
O'Casey, S. *The Plough and the Stars*
Odets, C. *Golden Boy*
O'Neill, E. *Anna Christie*
O'Neill, E. *The Hairy Ape*
Pirandello, L. *Six Characters in Search of an Author*
Rostand, E. *Cyrano de Bergerac*
Saroyan, W. *My Heart's in the Highlands*
Sartre, J. *The Flies*
Shaw, G. *Candida*
Sherriff, R. *Journey's End*
Stallings, L., and Anderson, M. *What Price Glory?*
Strindberg, A. *A Dream Play*
Strindberg, A. *The Father*
Strindberg, A. *There Are Crimes and Crimes*
Synge, J. *Riders to the Sea*
Tolstoy, L. *The Power of Darkness*
Wedekind, F. *The Tenor*
Wilde, O. *The Importance of Being Earnest*
Wilder, T. *Our Town*
Williams, T. *The Glass Menagerie*

TREBJ *A Treasury of the Theatre*. 4th ed. Edited by John Gassner and Bernard F. Dukore. New York: Simon and Schuster 1970. 1298pp.
Albee, E. *Who's Afraid of Virginia Woolf?*
Anderson, M. *Elizabeth the Queen*
Anouilh, J. *The Lark*
Artaud, A. *The Spurt of Blood*
Becque, H. *The Vultures*
Brecht, B. *Galileo*
Brecht, B. *The Good Woman of Setzuan*
Chekhov, A. *The Cherry Orchard*
Claudel, P. *The Tidings Brought to Mary*
García Lorca, F. *Blood Wedding*
Giraudoux, J. *The Madwoman of Chaillot*
Gorki, M. *The Lower Depths*
Hauptmann, G. *The Weavers*
Hellman, L. *The Little Foxes*
Ibsen, H. *Ghosts*
Ibsen, H. *Hedda Gabler*
Jarry, A. *Ubu the King*
Jones, L. *Dutchman*
Lowell, R. *Benito Cereno*
Maeterlinck, M. *The Intruder*
Maugham, W. *The Circle*
Miller, A. *Death of a Salesman*
O'Casey, S. *The Plough and the Stars*
Odets, C. *Golden Boy*
O'Neill, E. *The Hairy Ape*
O'Neill, E. *A Moon for the Misbegotten*
Osborne, J., and Creighton, A. *Epitaph for George Dillon*

Pinter, H. *A Slight Ache*
Pirandello, L. *Six Characters in Search of an Author*
Rostand, E. *Cyrano de Bergerac*
Saroyan, W. *My Heart's in the Highlands*
Sartre, J. *The Flies*
Shaw, G. *Candida*
Shaw, G. *Heartbreak House*
Strindberg, A. *A Dream Play*
Strindberg, A. *The Father*
Synge, J. *The Playboy of the Western World*
Synge, J. *Riders to the Sea*
Tolstoy, L. *The Power of Darkness*
Wedekind, F. *The Tenor*
Wilde, O. *The Importance of Being Earnest*
Wilder, T. *Our Town*
Williams, T. *The Glass Menagerie*
Witkiewicz, S. *The Cuttlefish*
Yeats, W. *Purgatory*

TREC *A Treasury of the Theatre.* Rev. ed. for colleges. Edited by John Gassner. New York: Simon and Schuster [c1950–1951] 2 vols. (vol. 1, From Aeschylus to Turgenev; vol. 2, From Henrik Ibsen to Arthur Miller)

*Abraham and Isaac* 1
Aeschylus. *Agamemnon* 1
Anderson, M. *Elizabeth the Queen* 2
Aristophanes. *The Frogs* 1
Barrie, J. *The Admirable Crichton* 2
Becque, H. *The Vultures* 2
Brecht, B. *The Private Life of the Master Race* 2
Büchner, G. *Danton's Death* 1
Čapek, K. *R.U.R.* 2
Chekhov, A. *The Cherry Orchard* 2
Congreve, W. *The Way of the World* 1
Connelly, M. *The Green Pastures* 2
Coward, N. *Blithe Spirit* 2
Euripides. *The Trojan Women* 1
*Everyman* 1
Galsworthy, J. *Escape* 2
García Lorca, F. *Blood Wedding* 2
Goethe, J. *Faust* 1
Gogol, N. *The Inspector* 1
Gorki, M. *The Lower Depths* 2
Gregory, I. *The Workhouse Ward* 2
Hauptmann, G. *The Weavers* 2
Hebbel, F. *Maria Magdalena* 1
Hellman, L. *The Little Foxes* 2
Ibsen, H. *Ghosts* 2
Ibsen, H. *Hedda Gabler* 2
Jonson, B. *Volpone* 1
Kālidāsa. *Shakuntalā* 1
Kwanze, K. *Sotoba Komachi* 1
Maeterlinck, M. *The Intruder* 2
Marlowe, C. *The Tragical History of Doctor Faustus* 1

Maugham, W. *The Circle* 2
Miller, A. *Death of a Salesman* 2
Molière, J. *The Misanthrope* 1
Molnár, F. *Liliom* 2
Musset, A. *No Trifling with Love* 1
O'Casey, S. *The Plough and the Stars* 2
Odets, C. *Golden Boy* 2
O'Neill, E. *Anna Christie* 2
O'Neill, E. *The Hairy Ape* 2
Pirandello, L. *Six Characters in Search of an Author* 2
Plautus. *The Menaechmi* 1
Racine, J. *Phaedra* 1
Rostand, E. *Cyrano de Bergerac* 2
Saroyan, W. *My Heart's in the Highlands* 2
Sartre, J. *The Flies* 2
*The Second Shepherds' Play* 1
Shakespeare, W. *Hamlet* 1
Shaw, G. *Candida* 2
Sheridan, R. *The School for Scandal* 1
Sherriff, R. *Journey's End* 2
Sophocles. *Oedipus the King* 1
Stallings, L. and Anderson, M. *What Price Glory?* 2
Strindberg, A. *The Father* 2
Strindberg, A. *There Are Crimes and Crimes* 2
Synge, J. *Riders to the Sea* 2
Terence. *The Brothers* 1
Tolstoy, L. *The Power of Darkness* 2
Turgenev, I. *A Month in the Country* 1
Vega Carpio, L. *Fuente ovejuna* 1
Webster, J. *The Duchess of Malfi* 1
Wedekind, F. *The Tenor* 2
Wilde, O. *The Importance of Being Earnest* 2
Wilder, T. *Our Town* 2
Williams. T. *The Glass Menagerie* 2

TREE *A Treasury of the Theatre.* Rev. ed. Edited by John Gassner. New York: Simon and Schuster [c1951] 3 vols. (vol. 1, World Drama: From Aeschylus to Turgenev; vol. 2, Modern European Drama: From Henrik Ibsen to Jean-Paul Sartre; vol. 3, Modern British and American Drama: From Oscar Wilde to Arthur Miller)

*Abraham and Isaac* 1
Aeschylus. *Agamemnon* 1
Anderson, M. *Elizabeth the Queen* 3
Aristophanes. *The Frogs* 1
Barrie, J. *The Admirable Crichton* 3
Becque, H. *The Vultures* 2
Brecht, B. *The Private Life of the Master Race* 2
Büchner, G. *Danton's Death* 1
Čapek, K. *R.U.R.* 2
Chekhov, A. *The Cherry Orchard* 2
Congreve, W. *The Way of the World* 1
Connelly, M. *The Green Pastures* 3
Coward, N. *Blithe Spirit* 3

Euripides. *The Trojan Women* 1
*Everyman* 1
Galsworthy, J. *Escape* 3
García Lorca, F. *Blood Wedding* 2
Goethe, J. *Faust* 1
Gogol, N. *The Inspector* 1
Gorki, M. *The Lower Depths* 2
Gregory, I. *The Workhouse Ward* 3
Hauptmann, G. *The Weavers* 2
Hebbel, F. *Maria Magdalena* 1
Hellman, L. *The Little Foxes* 3
Ibsen, H. *Ghosts* 2
Ibsen, H. *Hedda Gabler* 2
Jonson, B. *Volpone* 1
Kālidāsa. *Shakuntalā* 1
Kwanze, K. *Sotoba Komachi* 1
Maeterlinck, M. *The Intruder* 2
Marlowe, C. *The Tragical History of Doctor Faustus* 1
Maugham, W. *The Circle* 3
Miller, A. *Death of a Salesman* 3
Molière, J. *The Misanthrope* 1
Molnár, F. *Liliom* 2
Musset, A. *No Trifling with Love* 1
O'Casey, S. *The Plough and the Stars* 3
Odets, C. *Golden Boy* 3
O'Neill, E. *Anna Christie* 3
O'Neill, E. *The Hairy Ape* 3
Piandello, L. *Six Characters in Search of an Author* 2
Plautus. *The Menaechmi* 1
Racine, J. *Phaedra* 1
Rostand, E. *Cyrano de Bergerac* 2
Saroyan, W. *My Heart's in the Highlands* 3
Sartre, J. *The Flies* 2
*The Second Shepherds' Play* 1
Shakespeare, W. *Hamlet* 1
Shaw, G. *Candida* 3
Sheridan, R. *The School for Scandal* 1
Sherriff, R. *Journey's End* 3
Sophocles. *Oedipus the King*
Stallings, L., and Anderson, M. *What Price Glory?* 3
Strindberg, A. *The Father* 2
Strindberg, A. *There Are Crimes and Crimes* 2
Synge, J. *Riders to the Sea* 3
Terence. *The Brothers* 1
Tolstoy, L. *The Power of Darkness* 2
Turgenev, I. *A Month in the Country* 1
Vega Carpio, L. *Fuente ovejuna* 1
Webster, J. *The Duchess of Malfi* 1
Wedekind, F. *The Tenor* 2
Wilde, O. *The Importance of Being Earnest* 3
Wilder, T. *Our Town* 3
Williams, T *The Glass Menagerie* 3

TREI *A Treasury of the Theatre.* Rev. ed. Edited by John
  Gassner. New York: Simon, 1963. 3 vols. (vol. 1,

World Drama: From Aeschylus to Turgenev; vol.
  2, Modern European Drama: From Henrik Ibsen
  to Jean-Paul Sartre; vol. 3, Modern Drama: From
  Oscar Wilde to Eugène Ionesco).

*Abraham and Isaac* 1
Aeschylus. *Agamemnon* 1
Anderson, M. *Elizabeth the Queen* 3
Anouilh, J. *The Lark* 3
Aristophanes. *The Frogs* 1
Barrie, J. *The Admirable Crichton* 3
Becque, H. *The Vultures* 2
Brecht, B. *The Private Life of the Master Race*
  [excerpts] 2
Büchner, G. *Danton's Death* 1
Čapek, K. *R.U.R.* 2
Chekhov, A. *The Cherry Orchard* 2
Claudel, P. *The Tidings Brought to Mary* 3
Congreve, W. *The Way of the World* 1
Connelly, M. *The Green Pastures* 3
Coward, N. *Blithe Spirit* 3
Euripides. *The Trojan Women* 1
*Everyman* 1
Galsworthy, J. *Escape* 3
García Lorca, F. *Blood Wedding* 2
Genêt, J. *The Maids* 3
Giraudoux, J. *The Madwoman of Chaillot* 3
Goethe, J. *Faust, Part I* 1
Gogol, N. *The Inspector* 1
Gorki, M. *The Lower Depths* 2
Gregory, I. *The Workhouse Ward* 3
Hauptmann, G. *The Weavers* 2
Hebbel, F. *Maria Magdalena* 1
Hellman, L. *The Little Foxes* 3
Ibsen, H. *Ghosts* 2
Ibsen, H. *Hedda Gabler* 2
Ionesco, E. *The Chairs* 3
Jonson, B. *Volpone* 1
Kālidāsa. *Shakuntalā* 1
Kwanze, K. *Sotoba Komachi* 1
Maeterlinck, M. *The Intruder* 2
Marlowe, C. *The Tragical History of Doctor Faustus* 1
Maugham, W. *The Circle* 3
Miller, A. *Death of a Salesman* 3
Molière, J. *The Misanthrope* 1
Molnár, F. *Liliom* 2
Musset, A. *No Trifling with Love* 1
O'Casey, S. *The Plough and the Stars* 3
Odets, C. *Golden Boy* 3
O'Neill, E. *Anna Christie* 3
O'Neill, E. *The Hairy Ape* 3
Pirandello, L. *Six Characters in Search of an Author* 2
Plautus. *The Menaechmi* 1
Racine, J. *Phaedra* 1
Rostand, E. *Cyrano de Bergerac* 2
Saroyan, W. *My Heart's in the Highlands* 3

Sartre, J. *The Flies* 2
*The Second Shepherds' Play* 1
Shakespeare, W. *Hamlet* 1
Shaw, G. *Candida* 3
Sheridan, R. *The School for Scandal* 1
Sherriff, R. *Journey's End* 3
Sophocles. *Oedipus the King* 1
Stallings, L., and Anderson, M. *What Price Glory?* 3
Strindberg, A. *A Dream Play* 3
Strindberg, A. *The Father* 2
Strindberg, A. *There Are Crimes and Crimes* 2
Synge, J. *Riders to the Sea* 3
Terence. *The Brothers* 1
Tolstoy, L. *The Power of Darkness* 2
Turgenev, I. *A Month in the Country* 1
Vega Carpio, L. *Fuente ovejuna* 1
Webster, J. *The Duchess of Malfi* 1
Wedekind, F. *The Tenor* 2
Wilde, O. *The Importance of Being Earnest* 3
Wilder, T. *Our Town* 3
Williams, T. *The Glass Menagerie* 3


TRES *Tres Dramas Romanticos*. Garden City, NY: Doubleday, 1962. 319pp.
García Gutiérrez, A. *El trovador*
Rivas, A. *Don Alvaro; ó, La fuerza del sino*
Zorrilla y Moral, J. *Don Juan Tenorio*


TREWIN, J. C. *See* PLAN *Plays of the Year.*


TRI Trilling, Lionel, compiler. *The Experience of Literature*. Garden City, NY: Doubleday, 1967. 1320pp.
Brecht, B. *Galileo*
Chekhov, A. *The Three Sisters*
Ibsen, H. The *Wild Duck*
Pirandello, L. *Six Characters in Search of an Author*
Shakespeare, W. *The Tragedy of King Lear*
Shaw, G. *The Doctor's Dilemma*
Sophocles. *Oedipus Rex*
Yeats, W. *Purgatory*


TRIA Trilling, Lionel, compiler. *The Experience of Literature*. New York: Holt, Rinehart and Winston [1967] 1320pp.
Brecht, B. *Galileo*
Chekhov, A. *The Three Sisters*
Ibsen, H. *The Wild Duck*
Pirandello, L. *Six Characters in Search of an Author*
Shakespeare, W. *The Tragedy of King Lear*
Shaw, G. *The Doctor's Dilemma*
Sophocles. *Oedipus Rex*
Yeats, W. *Purgatory*


TRUE *True Misteries and a Chronicle Play of Peterborough Cathedral* by James Kirkup. Salzburg: University of Salzburg, 1997. 265pp. (Salzburg Studies in English Literature, Poetic Drama, and Poetic Theory, 194)
Kirkup, J. *The True Mistery of the Nativity*
Kirkup, J. *The True Mistery of the Passion*
Kirkup, J. *Upon this Rock*


TRUS Trussler, Simon, ed. *Burlesque Plays of the Eighteenth Century*. New York: Oxford University Press, 1969. 367pp.
Buckingham, G. *The Rehearsal*
Canning, G., Frere, J., and Ellis, G. *The Rovers*
Carey, H. *Chrononhotonthologos*
Carey, H. *The Dragon of Wantley*
Fielding, H. *The Covent-Garden Tragedy*
Fielding, H. *Tom Thumb*
Gay, J. *The What d'ye Call It*
Gay, J., Pope, A., and Arbuthnot, J. *Three Hours after Marriage*
Rhodes, W. *Bombastes furioso*
Stevens, G. *Distress upon Distress*


TUCD Tucker, Samuel Marion, ed. *Modern American and British Plays*. New York: Harper [c1931] 946pp.
Anderson, M. *Saturday's Children*
Barry, P. *In a Garden*
Brighouse, H. *Hobson's Choice*
Colton, J., and Randolph, C. *Rain*
Coward, N. *The Vortex*
Crothers, R. *Mary the Third*
Dane, C. *Granite*
Emery, G. *The Hero*
Ervine, St. J. *John Ferguson*
Glover, H. *The King's Jewry*
Granville-Barker, H. *Waste*
Green, P. *The Field God*
Houghton, S. *Hindle Wakes*
Howard, S. *The Silver Cord*
Kaufman, G., and Connelly, M. *To the Ladies!*
Maugham, W. *The Circle*
Millay, E. *The King's Henchman*
Milne, A. *The Truth about Blayds*
Moeller, P. *Madame Sand*
O'Neill, E. *The Great God Brown*
Pinero, A. *The Thunderbolt*
Vollmer, L. *Sun-up*
Wilde, O. *The Importance of Being Earnest*


TUCG Tucker, Samuel Madon, ed. *Modern Continental Plays*. New York: Harper, 1929. 836pp.
Andreyev, L. *He Who Gets Slapped*
Annunzio, G. d'. *Francesca da Rimini*
Benavente y Martínez, J. *La malquerida*

Bjørnson, B. *Beyond our Power*
Bracco, R. *Phantasms*
Brieux, E. *False Gods*
Čapek, K. *R.U.R.*
Chekhov, A. *The Cherry Orchard*
Claudel, P. *The Tidings Brought to Mary*
Gorki, M. *The Lower Depths*
Hauptmann, G. *The Rats*
Kaiser, G. *The Coral*
Kaiser, G. *Gas, Part I*
Kaiser, G. *Gas, Part II*
Maeterlinck, M. *Pelléas and Mélisande*
Molnár, F. *Liliom*
Pérez Galdós, B. *Electra*
Rostand, E. *Cyrano de Bergerac*
Schnitzler, A. *Light-o'-Love*
Strindberg, A. *Comrades*
Vildrac, C. *S. S. Tenacity*
Wedekind, F. *Such Is Life*

TUCJ Tucker, Samuel Madon, ed. *Modern Plays.* New
   York: Macmillan [c1932] 400pp.
Bennett, A. and Knoblock, E. *Milestones*
Crothers, R. *Mary the Third*
Hughes, H. *Hell Bent fer Heaven*
Milne, A. *The Ivory Door*
O'Neill, E. *The Emperor Jones*

TUCM Tucker, Samuel Madon, ed. *Twenty-five Modern
   Plays.* New York: Harper [c1931] 1045pp.
Andreyev, L. *He Who Gets Slapped*
Annunzio, G. d'. *Francesca da Rimini*
Barry, P. *In a Garden*
Benavente y Martínez, J. *La malquerida*
Čapek, K. *R.U.R.*
Chekhov, A. *The Cherry Orchard*
Coward, N. *The Vortex*
Crothers, R. *Mary the Third*
Ervine, St. J. *John Ferguson*
Green, P. *The Field God*
Hauptmann, G. *The Rats*
Howard, S. *The Silver Cord*
Kaiser, G. *The Coral*
Kaiser, G. *Gas, Part I*
Kaiser, G. *Gas, Part II*
Maeterlinck, M. *Pelléas and Mélisande*
Maugham, W. *The Circle*
Milne, A. *The Truth about Blayds*
Molnár, F. *Liliom*
O'Neill, E. *The Great God Brown*
Pinero, A. *The Thunderbolt*
Rostand, E. *Cyrano de Bergerac*
Schnitzler, A. *Light-o'-Love*
Strindberg, A. *Comrades*
Vildrac, C. *S. S. Tenacity*

Vollmer, L. *Sun-up*
Wilde, O. *The Importance of Being Earnest*

TUCN Tucker, Samuel Marion, and Downer, Alan S., eds.
   *Twenty-five Modern Plays.* Rev. ed. by Alan S.
   Downer. New York: Harper, [c1948] 1009pp.
Andreyev, L. *He Who Gets Slapped*
Auden, W., and Isherwood, C. *The Ascent of F6*
Benavente, [y Martínez, J.] *La malquerida*
Čapek, K. *R.U.R.*
Chekhov, A. *The Cherry Orchard*
Cocteau, J. *The Infernal Machine*
Ervine, St. J. *John Ferguson*
Gorki, M. *The Lower Depths*
Green, P. *The Field God*
Haines, W. *Command Decision*
Hauptmann, G. *The Rats*
Howard, S. *The Silver Cord*
Ibsen, H. *Rosmersholm*
Kaiser, G. *The Coral*
Kaiser, G. *Gas I*
Kaiser, G. *Gas II*
Maeterlinck, M. *Pelléas and Mélisande*
Molnár, F. *Liliom*
O'Casey, S. *The Plough and the Stars*
O'Neill, E. *The Great God Brown*
Pinero, A. *The Thunderbolt*
Riggs, L. *Roadside*
Rostand, E. *Cyrano de Bergerac*
Schnitzler, A. *Light-o'-Love*
Strindberg, A. *Comrades*
Synge, J. *Riders to the Sea*
Wilde, O. *The Importance of Being Earnest*

TUCO Tucker, S. Marion, and Downer, Alan S., eds.
   *Twenty-five Modern Plays.* 3rd ed. New York:
   Harper [c1953] 1008pp.
Andreyev, L. *He Who Gets Slapped*
Benavente, J. *La malquerida*
Čapek, K. *R.U.R.*
Chekhov, A. *The Cherry Orchard*
Cocteau, J. *The Infernal Machine*
Eliot, T. *Murder in the Cathedral*
Ervine, St. J. *John Ferguson*
Gorki, M. *The Lower Depths*
Hauptmann, G. *The Rats*
Howard, S. *The Silver Cord*
Ibsen, H. *Rosmersholm*
Kaiser, G. *The Coral*
Kaiser, G. *Gas, Parts 1 and 2*
Maeterlinck, M. *Pelléas and Mélisande*
Miller, A. *Death of a Salesman*
Molnár, F. *Liliom*
O'Casey, S. *The Plough and the Stars*
O'Neill, E. *The Great God Brown*

Pinero, A. *The Thunderbolt*
Riggs, L. *Roadside*
Rostand, E. *Cyrano de Bergerac*
Schnitzler, A. *Light-o'-Love*
Strindberg, A. *Comrades*
Synge, J. *Riders to the Sea*
Wilde, O. *The Importance of Being Earnest*
Williams, T. *A Streetcar Named Desire*

TUP Tupper, Frederick, and Tupper, James Waddell, eds. *Representative English Dramas from Dryden to Sheridan.* New York: Oxford University Press, 1914. 460pp.
Addison, J. *Cato*
Congreve, W. *The Way of the World*
Dryden, J. *All for Love*
Dryden, J. *The Conquest of Granada*
Farquhar, G. *The Beaux' Stratagem*
Fielding, H. *Tom Thumb the Great*
Gay, J. *The Beggar's Opera*
Goldsmith, O. *She Stoops to Conquer*
Otway, T. *Venice Preserved*
Sheridan, R. *The Rivals*
Sheridan, R. *The School for Scandal*
Steele, R. *The Conscious Lovers*

TUQ Tupper, Frederick, and Tupper, James Waddell, eds. *Representative English Dramas from Dryden to Sheridan.* New and enl. ed. New York: Oxford University Press [c1934] 722pp.
Addison, J. *Cato*
Cibber, C. *Love's Last Shift*
Congreve, W. *The Way of the World*
Dryden, J. *All for Love*
Dryden, J. *The Conquest of Granada*
Etherege, G. *The Man of Mode*
Farquhar, G. *The Beaux' Stratagem*
Fielding, H. *Tom Thumb the Great*
Gay, J. *The Beggar's Opera*
Goldsmith, O. *She Stoops to Conquer*
Lillo, G. *The London Merchant*
Otway, T. *Venice Preserved*
Rowe, N. *The Tragedy of Jane Shore*
Sheridan, R. *The Rivals*
Sheridan, R. *The School for Scandal*
Steele, R. *The Conscious Lovers*
Vanbrugh, J. *The Relapse*
Wycherley, W. *The Country Wife*

TUQH *Turkish Literature.* Tr. into English for the first time, with a special introduction by Epiphanius Wilson. Rev. ed. New York: Colonial Press [1901] 462pp. (The World's Great Classics)
Micza Feth-Ali, A. *The Magistrates*

TUQT Turner, Darwin, T., compiler. *Black Drama in America: An Anthology.* Greenwich, CT: Fawcett, 1971. 630pp.
Bass, K. *We Righteous Bombers*
Davis, O. *Purlie Victorious*
Dodson, O. *Bayou Legend*
Edmonds, R. *Earth and Stars*
Hughes, L. *Emperor of Haiti*
Jones, L. *The Toilet*
Peterson, L. *Take a Giant Step*
Richardson, W. *The Chip Woman's Fortune*
Ward, T. *Our Lan'*

TUQTR Turner, Darwin, T., ed. *Black Drama in America: An Anthology.* 2nd ed. Washington, DC: Howard University Press, 1994. 736pp.
Baraka, A. *Great Goodness of Life (a Coon Show)*
Bass, G. *Black Masque: The Passion of Darkie's Bones*
Bullins, E. *In the Wine Time*
Childress, A. *Trouble in Mind*
Cleage, P. *Flyin' West*
Dodson, O. *Bayou Legend*
Franklin, J. *Miss Honey's Young'uns*
Fuller, C. *A Soldier's Play*
Hughes, L. *Emperor of Haiti*
Peterson, L. *Take a Giant Step*
Richardson, W. *The Chip Woman's Fortune*
Russell, C. *Five on the Black Hand Side*
Ward, T. *Our Lan'*
Wilson, A. *Ma Rainey's Black Bottom*

TUR Turrell, Charles Alfred, ed. and tr. *Contemporary Spanish Dramatists.* Boston: Badger [c1919] 397pp.
Alvarez Quintero, S., and Alvarez Quintero, J. *The Women's Town*
Dicenta y Benedicto, A. *Juan José*
Linares Rivas, M. *The Claws*
Marquina, E. *When the Roses Bloom Again*
Pérez Galdós, B. *Electra*
Zamacois, E. *The Passing of the Magi*

TWE *Twelve Famous Plays of the Restoration and Eighteenth Century.* New York: Modern Library [c1933] 952pp.
Congreve, W. *Love for Love*
Congreve, W. *The Way of the World*
Dryden, J. *All for Love; or, the World Well Lost*
Farquhar, G. *The Beaux' Stratagem*
Garrick, D. *The Clandestine Marriage*
Gay, J. *The Beggar's Opera*
Goldsmith, O. *She Stoops to Conquer; or, the Mistakes of a Night*
Otway, T. *Venice Preserv'd; or, a Plot Discover'd*
Sheridan, R. *The Rivals*

Sheridan, R. *The School for Scandal*
Vanbrugh, J. *The Provok'd Wife*
Wycherley, W. *The Country Wife*

TWEH *Twentieth-Century Chinese Drama: An Anthology.*
Edited by Edward M. Gunn. Bloomington: Indiana
University Press, c1983. 517pp.
Chien, P. *Men and Women in Wild Times* (Acts I and III
in full; Act III omitted)
Chou, W.; Tung, Y.; and Yeh, H. *The Artillery
Commander's Son*
Hu, S. *The Greatest Event in Life*
Hung, S. *Yama chao*
Li, C. *Springtime*
Ou-yang, Y. *P'an Chin-lien*
*The Red Lantern* (Scenes 1–7 summarized; Scenes 8–11
in full)
Sha, Y.; Li, S.; and Yao, M. *If I Were Real* (Scene 5 in
full; others summarized)
Shen, T. *Under Shanghai Eaves*
T'ien, H. *Kuan Han-ch'ing* (Scenes 3, 5, 9, and 11 have
been omitted)
Ting, H. *Oppression*
Tsung, F. *In a Land of Silence*
Wang, C. *Wu Feng*
Wu, C. *Hai Jui Dismissed from Office* (Acts III, VI, and
IX in full; others summarized)
Yang, C. *Windswept Blossoms*
Yang, L. *Cuckoo Sings Again* (Acts I–III in full; Act IV
summarized)

TWEI *Twentieth Century Italian Drama: An Anthology:
The First Fifty Years.* Edited by Jane House and
Antonio Attisani. New York: Columbia University
Press, 1995. 622pp.
Annunzio, G. *A Spring Morning's Dream*
Betti, U. *Crime on Goat Island*
Bontempelli, M. *Dea by Dea*
Campanile, A. *The Inventor of the Horse*
Filippo, E. *The Nativity Scene*
Marinetti, F. *Connecting Vessels*
Marinetti, F. *Feet*
Marinetti, F. *They Are Coming*
Petrolini, E. *Fortunello*
Pirandello, L. *Tonight We Improvise*
Pirandello, L. *Why?*
Rosso di San Secondo, P. *Puppets of Passion!*
Savinio, A. *Emma B., Widow Jocasta*
Svevo, I. *With Gilded Pen*
Tozzi, F. *The Casting*
Viviani, R. *Via Toledo by Night*

TWEN *Twentieth-Century Polish Avant-Garde Drama:
Plays, Scenarios, Critical Documents* by Stanislaw

Ignacy Witkiewicz [et al.] Translated by Daniel
Gerould in collaboration with Eleanor Gerould.
Ithaca, NY: Cornell University Press, c1977.
287pp.
Afanasjew, J. *"The World Is Not Such a Bad Place . . ."*
(selections from)
Afanasjew, J., and the Afanasjeff Family Circus. *Good
Evening, Clown*
Afanasjew, J., and the Bim-Bom Troupe. *Faust*
Afanasjew, J., and the Bim-Bom Troupe. *Snouts*
Gałczyński, K. *The Green Goose* (Twenty-two Short
Plays from The Little Theatre of The Green Goose)
Mrozek, S. *The Professor*
Różewicz, T. *Birth Rate: The Biography of a Play for
the Theatre*
Trzebiński, A. *To Pick Up the Rose*
Witkiewicz, S. *The Anonymous Work: Four Acts of a
Rather Nasty Nightmare*

TYDE Tydeman, William, ed. *Four Tudor Comedies.* New
York: Penguin, 1984. 440pp.
*Jacke Jugeler*
Lyly, J. *Mother Bombie*
Stevenson, W. *Gammer Gurton's Needle*
Udall, N. *Roister Doister*

TYEW Tylee, Claire M., with Turner, Elaine, and
Cardinal, Agnes, eds. *War Plays by Women: An
International Anthology.* London and New York:
Routledge, 1999. 225pp.
Box, M. *Angels of War*
Dunbar-Nelson, A. *Mine Eyes Have Seen*
Hewett, D. *The Man from Mukinupin*
Lask, B. *Liberation: 16 Tableaux from the Lives of
German and Russian Women, 1914–1920*
Lenéru, M. *Peace*
Lill, W. *The Fighting Days*
Reid, C. *My Name, Shall I Tell You My Name*
Stein, G. *Accents in Alsace: A Reasonable Tragedy*
Stein, G. *Please Do Not Suffer*
Wentworth, M. *War Brides*

TYLG Tyler, Royall, ed. *Granny Mountains: A Cycle
of Nō Plays* (the second of two volumes). Ithaca,
NY: East Asia Program, Cornell University, 1992.
181pp. (*See* TYLP for first volume.)
*Asaina*
*Hanago*
*Jizo-mai*
*Shibiri*
*Tsuen* (a parody of Yorimasa)
*Yuya* (a woman play)
Kanami. *The Golden Tablet*

Kanami. *Komachi on the Gravepost*
Kanami. *Shizuka at Yoshino*
Zeami. *Granny Mountains*
Zeami. *Million*
Zeami. *Nightbird*
Zeami. *The Well-cradle*
Zeami. *Yorimasa*

TYLJ Tyler, Royall, ed. *Japanese Nō Dramas.* New York:
        Penguin, 1992. 360pp.
*Chikubu-shima*
*The Feather Mantle*
Kanami, and Zeami. *Pining Wind*
*Kantan*
Kanze, K. *Benkei aboard Ship*
Kanze, M. *The Sumida River*
Komparu, G. *The Diver*
Konparu, Z. *The Kasuga Dragon God*
Konparu, Z. *The Wildwood Shrine*
Konparu, Z. *Tatsuta*
Zeami. *Atsumori*
Zeami. *The Damask Drum*
Zeami. *Eguchi*
Zeami. *The Fulling Block*
Zeami. *Komachi at Seki-dera*
Zeami. *Kureba*
Zeami. *Lady Han*
Zeami. *The Mountain Crone*
Zeami. *Saigyo's Cherry Tree*
Zeami. *Semimaru*
Zeami. *Tadanori*
Zeami. *Takasago*
Zeami. *The Well-cradle*
Zeami. *Yashima*

TYLP Tyler, Royall, trans. *Pining Wind: A Cycle of Nō
        Plays* (the First of Two Volumes). Ithaca, NY: East
        Asia Program, Cornell University, 1992. 193pp.
        (*See* TYLG for second volume.)
*Crab Bites Yamabushi*
*The Feather Mantle*
*Gargoyle*
*Pinegum*
*Thunderbolt*
Kanami. *Layman Selfsame*
Kanami. *Mouth-of-sound*
Kanami, and Zeami. *Pining Wind*
Zeami. *The Boat Bridge*
Zeami. *The Block*
Zeami. *Komachi at Sekidera*
Zeami. *Takasago*
Zeami. *The Watchman's Mirror*
Zeami. *Yashima* (a warrior play)

UHL Uhler, John Earle, ed. *The Best Eighteenth Century
        Comedies.* New York: Knopf, 1929. 480pp.
Farquhar, G. *The Beaux' Stratagem*
Gay, J. *The Beggar's Opera*
Goldsmith, O. *She Stoops to Conquer*
Sheridan, R. *The Rivals*
Sheridan, R. *The School for Scandal*

ULAN Ulanov, Barry, ed. *Makers of the Modern Theater.*
        New York: McGraw-Hill [c1961] 743pp.
Anouilh, J. *Antigone*
Betti, U. *The Queen and the Rebels*
Chekhov, A. *Ivanov*
García Lorca, F. *Yerma*
Giraudoux, J. *Sodom and Gomorrah*
Giraudoux, J. *Song of Songs*
Hauptmann, G. *Hannele*
Ibsen, H. *John Gabriel Borkman*
Ionesco, E. *The Bald Soprano*
Marcel, G. *Ariadne*
Miller, A. *A View from the Bridge*
Motherlant, H. *The Master of Santiago*
O'Casey, S. *Purple Dust*
O'Neill, E. *The Long Voyage Home*
Pirandello, L. *Henry IV*
Shaw, G. *Getting Married*
Strindberg, A. *To Damascus, Part 1*
Synge, J. *The Well of the Saints*
Toller, E. *Hoppla! Such Is Life!*
Williams, T. *Camino Real*
Yeats, W. *On Baile's Strand*
Yeats, W. *Purgatory*

UNO Uno, Roberta, ed. *Unbroken Thread: An Anthology
        of Plays by Asian American Women.* Amherst, MA:
        University of Massachusetts Press, 1993. 328pp.
Barroga, J. *Walls*
Houston, V. *Tea*
Iko, M. *Gold Watch*
Lim, G. *Paper Angels*
Wong, E. *Letters to a Student Revolutionary*
Yamauchi, W. *The Music Lessons*

UNTE Untermeyer, Louis, ed. *The Britannica Library of
        Great American Writing.* Chicago: J. B. Lippincott
        [c1960] 2 vols.
O'Neill, E. *The Emperor Jones* 2

UPOR Upor, László, ed. *Hungarian Plays: New Drama
        from Hungary.* London: Nick Hern Books in
        association with Visiting Arts, 1996. 242pp.
Kárpáti, P. *Everywoman*
Nagy, A. *The Seducer's Diary*

Németh, Á. *Müller's Dancers*
Szilágyi, A. *Unsent Letters*

VAN Van Doren, Carl Clinton, ed. *The Borzoi Reader.*
    New York: Knopf, 1936. 1033pp.
  Kaufman, G., Ryskind, M., and Gershwin, I. *Of Thee
    I Sing*

VANM Van Doren, Carl Clinton, ed. *Modern American
    Prose.* New York: Harcourt, Brace [c1934] 939pp.
  Anderson, M., and Stallings, L. *What Price Glory?*

VAN DOREN, CARL CLINTON. *See also* AMI *American
    Omnibus*; LONO *London Omnibus.*

VANV Van Ghent, Dorothy (Bendon), and Brown, Joseph
    S., eds. *Continental Literature: An Anthology.*
    Philadelphia: Lippincott [1968] 2 vols.
  Aeschylus. *Agamemnon* 1
  Aristophanes. *Lysistrata* 1
  Brecht, B. *The Good Woman of Setzuan* 2
  Euripides. *Hippolytus* 1
  García Lorca, F. *The King of Harlem* 2
  García Lorca, F. *Lament for Ignacio Sánchez Mejías* 2
  Goethe, J. *Faust, Part I* 2
  Ibsen, H. *Hedda Gabler* 2
  Molière, J. *Tartuffe* 2
  Pirandello, L. *Such Is Life* 2
  Racine, J. *Phaedra* 2
  Sophocles. *Oedipus Rex* 1

VENA Vena, Gary, and Nouryeh, Andrea, compilers.
    *Drama and Performance: An Anthology.* New
    York: HarperCollins College Publishers, 1996.
    1204pp.
  Aristophanes. *The Birds*
  Baraka, A. *Dutchman*
  Beckett, S. *Play: A Stage Play*
  Behn, A. *The Rover*
  Brecht, B. *The Threepenny Opera*
  Calderón de la Barca, P. *Life Is a Dream*
  Chekhov, A. *The Sea Gull*
  Childress, A. *Wine in the Wilderness*
  Chin, F. *The Chickencoop Chinaman*
  Daly, A. *Under the Gaslight*
  Euripides. *The Trojan Women*
  Fornes, M. *The Conduct of Life*
  Goldsmith, O. *She Stoops to Conquer*
  Havel, V. *Largo desolato*
  Howe, T. *Painting Churches*
  Hugo, V. *Hernani*
  Ibsen, H. *Ghosts*
  Kirby, M. *Double Gothic*
  Mann, E. *Still Life*
  Marlowe, C. *Doctor Faustus*

  *Master Pierre Pathelin*
  Molière, J. *The Misanthrope*
  O'Neill, E. *The Hairy Ape*
  *The Pedant*
  Pinter, H. *The Birthday Party*
  Plautus, T. *The Rope*
  Racine, J. *Phèdre*
  *The Sacrifice of Isaac*
  Shakespeare, W. *Measure for Measure*
  Shaw, G. *Arms and the Man*
  Shepard, S. *The Tooth of Crime*
  Soyinka, W. *Death and the King's Horsemen*
  Strindberg, A. *A Dream Play*
  Synge, J. *Riders to the Sea*
  Valdez, L. *Bernabé*
  Williams, T. *Cat on a Hot Tin Roof*
  Zeami. *Komachi at Sekidera*

VENEZKY, ALICE. *See* GRIF Griffin, Alice Sylvia
    (Venezky), ed.

VER *Verity Bargate Award: New Plays 1986.* Edited by
    Barrie Keefe. London: Methuen, 1987. 82pp.
  Grounds, T. *Made in Spain*
  Quarrell, J. *Smith*
  Spencer, D. *Releevo*

VERI *Verity Bargate: The 1988 Award-Winning New
    Plays.* Edited by Barrie Keefe. London: Methuen,
    1989. 109pp.
  Brock, B. *Here Is Monster*
  Celeste, M. *Obeah*
  Plowman, G. *Me and My Friend*

VICK Vick, Susan, ed. *From Valley Playwrights Theatre.*
    Amherst, MA: Playwrights Press, 1986–1989.
    2 vols.
  Bleiman, R. *Broken Roses* 2
  Bleiman, R. *What Are Friends For?* 1
  Cohen, D. *Slice & Dice* 1
  Kapp, S. *The Interview* 1
  Martula, T. *The Three Boys* 1
  Martula, T. *Two Women from Waldo, Arkansas* 2
  Page, A. *Once in a Golden Hour* 1
  Page, A. *The Cancelled Sky* 2
  Schneider, P. *A Question of Place* 1
  Schneider, P. *After the Applebox* 2
  Scott, V. *The Living Exhibition of Sweeney Todd* 2
  Vick, S. *Ord-Way Ames-Gay* 2
  Vick, S. *When I Was Your Age* 1

VICT *Victorian Melodramas: Seven English, French,
    and American Melodramas.* Edited and introduced
    by James L. Smith. London: Dent; Totowa, NJ:
    Rowman and Littlefield, 1976. 252pp.

Boucicault, D. *The Corsican Brothers*
Dumas, A., fils. *The Lady of the Camellias* (adapted from)
Hamblin, L. *Nick of the Woods*
*London by Night*
Milner, H. *Mazeppa*
Smith, W. *The Drunkard*
Walker, J. *The Factory Lad*

VIET *Vietnam, Perspectives & Performance: Two Plays about Real People Affected by the Legacy of the Vietnam Conflict, Told in Their Own Words from Their Own Experiences.* Cedar Falls, IA: Association for Textual Study and Production, Dept. of English Language and Literature, University of Northern Iowa, 1996. 165pp.
Ellsbury, C., and Terry, J. *Vietnamese Chess*
Shaw, M. *Iowa Stories: The Vietnam Experience*

VIT Vitkus, Daniel J., ed. *Three Turk Plays from Early Modern England: Selimus, A Christian Turned Turk, and the Renegade.* New York: Columbia University Press, 2000. 358pp.
Daborne, R. *A Christian Turned Turk*
Greene, R. *Selimus, Emperor of the Turks*
Massinger, P. *The Renegado*

VOAD Voaden, Herman Arthur, ed. *Four Good Plays to Read and Act.* Toronto: Longmans Green [c1941] 297pp.
Coward, N. *Cavalcade*
Jerome, H. *Price and Prejudice*
MacLeish, A. *The Fall of the City*
Saroyan, W. *My Heart's in the Highlands*

VOI *Voices: Plays for Studying the Holocaust.* Edited by Janet E. Rubin. Lanham, MD and London: Scarecrow Press, Inc., 1999. 314pp.
Greenspan, H. *"Voice"* from *Remnants*
Kraus, J. *Angel in the Night*
Kushner, T. *A Bright Room Called Day*
Rådström, N. *Hitler's Childhood*
Samuels, D. *Kindertransport*
Shaw, R. *The Man in the Glass Booth*
Stringer, V. *Can You Hear Them Crying?*
Willmott, K., and Averill, R. *T-money & Wolf*

VOLI Volpe, Edward Loris, and Magalaner, Marvin, compilers *An Introduction to Literature: Drama.* New York: Random House, 1967. 467pp.
Chekhov, A. *The Cherry Orchard*
Ibsen, H. *The Wild Duck*
Molière, J. *Tartuffe*
O'Neill, E. *Desire under the Elms*

Shakespeare, W. *Othello*
Sophocles. *Oedipus Rex*

VOLP Volpe, Edward Loris, and Others, eds. *Poetry, Drama, Fiction.* New York: Random House [c1967] 808pp.
O'Neill, E. *Desire under the Elms*
Shakespeare, W. *Othello*
Sophocles. *Oedipus Rex*

VONG Von Geldern, James, and Stites, Richard, eds. *Mass Culture in Soviet Russia: Tales, Poems, Songs, Movies, Plays, and Folklore, 1917–1953.* Bloomington: Indiana University Press, 1995. 492pp.
Arsky, P. *For the Cause of the Red Soviets*
*Blue Blouse Skit*
Kirshon, V. *Bread* (excerpt)
Korneichuk, A. *The Front*
Simonov, K. *The Russian Question* (excerpt)
Zhemchuzhny, V. *Evening of Books for Youth Clubs* (excerpt)

VONS Von Staden, H., compiler. *Western Literature.* New York: Harcourt, Brace, Jovanovich, 1971. 3 vols.
Aeschylus. *Agamemnon* 1
Aristophanes. *Lysistrata* 1
Euripides. *Bacchae* 1
Goethe, J. *Faust, Part 1* 3
Ibsen, H. *The Master Builder* 3
Lowell, R. *Old Glory: Benito Cereno* 3
Molière, J. *The Misanthrope* 2
Pirandello, L. *Six Characters in Search of an Author* 3
Shakespeare, W. *Othello* 2
Sophocles. *Oedipus the King* 1

VORE Vorenberg, Bonnie L., ed. *New Plays for Mature Actors: An Anthology.* Morton Grove, IL: Coach House Press, 1987. 187pp.
Amend, H. *All the Comforts of Home*
Cornish, R. *It Hardly Matters Now*
Glickfield, C. *The Challenge of Bureaucracy*
Kassin, M. *Today a Little Extra*
Kelly, T. *The Lalapalooza Bird*
Oklahoma, D. *Anna's Brooklyn Promise*
Oklahoma, D. *Old Flames*
Pugh, A., and Dacus, K. *The Day They Kidnapped Blanche*
Savin, M. *Just a Song at Twilight*
Vineberg, D. *Emissary*

VOTE *How the Vote Was Won, and Other Suffragette Plays.* Researched by Candida Lacey; introduced by Dale Spender; with notes for performance by Carole Hayman. London: Metheun, 1985. 154pp.

Bensusan, I. *The Apple*
Glover, E. *A Chat with Mrs. Chicky*
Glover, E. *Miss Appleyard's Awakening*
Hamilton, C., and St. John, C. *How the Vote Was Won*
Harraden, B. *Lady Geraldine's Speech*
Jennings, G. *A Woman's Influence*
Robins, E. *Votes for Women*

WAGC Wagenheim, Harold H.; Brattig, Elizabeth Voris;
and Dolkey, Matthew, eds. *Our Reading Heritage.*
New York: Henry Holt [c1956] 4 vols.
Bennett, A., and Knoblock, E. *Milestones* 4
Cohan, G. *Pigeons and People* 3
Foote, H. *The Dancers* 2
Giledorf, F., and Gibson, P. *The Ghost of Benjamin
Sweet* 1
Gordon, R. *Years Ago* 1
Kelly, G. *Finders'-keepers* 3
O'Neill, E. *In the Zone* 2
Osborn, P. *Point of No Return* 3
Rattigan, T. *The Winslow Boy* 2
Shakespeare, W. *Macbeth* 4
Shaw, G. *Saint Joan* 4

WAGE Wagenhelm, Harold H.; Brattig, Elizabeth Voris;
and Flesch, Rudolf, eds. *Read up on Life.* New
York: Henry Holt, 1952. 507pp. (Holt Literature
Series)
Gordon, R. *Years Ago*

WAGN *Canada's Lost Plays.* Edited by Anton Wagner
and Richard Plant. Toronto: Canadian Theatre
Review Publications, 1978–1980. 3 vols. (Vol. 1,
*The Nineteenth Century*; Vol. 2, *Women Pioneers*;
Vol. 3, *The Developing Mosaic*)
Bush, T. *Santiago; a Drama in Five Acts* 1
Candidus, C. *The Female Consistory of Brockville; a
Melodrama in Three Acts* 1
Coulter, J. *The House in the Quiet Glen* 3
Curzon, S. *Laura Secord, the Heroine of 1812* 2
Curzon, S. *The Sweet Girl Graduate; a Comedy in Four
Acts* 2
Cushing, E. *The Fatal Ring; a Drama* 2
Davies, R. *Hope Deferred* 3
Davin, N. *The Fair Grit; or, the Advantages of
Coalition, a Farce* 1
Denison, M. *The Weather Breeder* 3
Fuller, W. *H.M.S. Parliament; or, the Lady Who Loved
a Government Clerk* 1
Joudry, P. *Teach Me How to Cry; a Drama in Three
Acts* 2
Kerr, L. *Open Doors* 3
McIlwraith, J. *Ptarmigan; or, a Canadian Carnival; an
Original Comic Opera in Two Acts* 1

Merritt, C. *When George the Third Was King; an
Historical Drama in Three Acts* 2
Ringwood, G. *Pasque Flower; a Play of the Canadian
Prairie* 2
Ringwood, G. *The Rainmaker* 3
"Scribble, S." *Dolorsolatio; a Local Political
Burlesque* 1
Voaden, H. *Murder Pattern* 3
Voaden, H. *Wilderness; a Play of the North* 3

WAGNOX Wagner-Martin, Linda, and Davidson,
Cathy N., eds. *The Oxford Book of Women's
Writing in the United States.* Oxford, New York:
Oxford University Press, 1995. 596pp.
Gerstenberg, A. *Overtones*
Glaspell, S. *Trifles*
Lim, G. *Bitter Cane*

WAIT Waite, Harlow O., and Atkinson, Benjamin P.,
eds. *Literature for Our Time.* Rev. ed. New York:
Henry Holt [c1953] 998pp.
Anderson, M. *Winterset*
Barry, P. *The Philadelphia Story*
Behrman, S. *Biography*
MacLeish, A. *The Fall of the City*
O'Neill, E. *The Hairy Ape*
Williams, T. *The Glass Menagerie*

WAIU Waite, Harlow O., and Atkinson, Benjamin P., eds.
*Literature for Our Time.* 3rd ed. New York: Henry
Holt [c1958] 1009pp.
Barry, P. *The Philadelphia Story*
Giraudoux, J. *Tiger at the Gates*
O'Neill, E. *The Hairy Ape*
Shaw, G. *Major Barbara*
Williams, T. *The Glass Menagerie*

WAIW Waith, Eugene M., ed. *The Dramatic Moment.*
Englewood Cliffs, NJ: Prentice-Hall [1967] 505pp.
Albee, E. *The Zoo Story*
Brecht, B. *Mother Courage and Her Children*
Chekhov, A. *The Seagull*
Ibsen, H. *Hedda Gabler*
Jonson, B. *Volpone; or, the Fox*
Molière, J. *The Misanthrope*
Pirandello, L. *Six Characters in Search of an Author*
Shakespeare, W. *King Lear*
Shaw, G. *Major Barbara*
Sophocles. *Oedipus Rex*
Strindberg, A. *The Ghost Sonata*
*Summoning of Everyman*

WAJ Waley, Arthur. *The No Plays of Japan.* New York:
Grove Press, Inc., 1957. 319pp.

*The Bird Catcher in Hell*
*Kantan*
*Mari*
Enami no Sayemon. *Ukai*
Hiyoshi, S. *Benkei on the Bridge*
I-ami. *Tango-monogurui*
Komparu, G., and Seami. *Ama*
Komparu, Z. *Ikkaku sennin*
Komparu, Z. *Yamauba*
Komparu, Z. *Hatsuyuki*
Kwanami. *Hanakatami*
Kwanami. *Sotoba komachi*
Kwanami and Seami. *Matsukaze*
Miyamasu. *Eboshi-ori*
Miyamasu. *Mai-guruma*
Seami. *Atsumori*
Seami. *Aya no tzuzumi*
Seami. *Hachi no ki*
Seami. *Hagoromo*
Seami. *Haku rakuten*
Seami. *Hotoke no hara*
Seami. *Ikeniye*
Seami. *Kagekiyo*
Seami. *Ominameshi*
Seami. *Shunkwan*
Seami. *Take no yuki*
Seami. *Tōru*
Seami. *Tsunemasa*
Zenchiku, U. *Aoi no uye*
Zenchiku, U. *The Hōka Priests*
Zenchiku, U. *Kumasaka*
Zenchiku, U. *Tanikō*

WAK Wall, Vincent, and McCormick, James Patton, eds.
     *Seven Plays of the Modern Theater.* New York:
     American Book Co. [c1950] 521pp.
Anderson, M. *Winterset*
Chekhov, A. *Uncle Vanya*
Coward, N. *Blithe Spirit*
Ibsen, H. *Hedda Gabler*
Maugham, W. *The Circle*
O'Neill, E. *The Hairy Ape*
Williams, T. *The Glass Menagerie*

WALAG Wallace, Robert, ed. *Making, Out: Plays by
     Gay Men.* Toronto: Coach House Press, 1992.
     350pp.
Demchuk, D. *Touch: A Play for Two*
Garnhum, K. *Beuys bouys Boys: A Monologue*
Gilbert, S., and Alcorn, J. *Capote at Yaddo: A Very Gay
     Little Musical*
Macivor, D. *2-2-tango: A-two-Man-one-Man-Show*
Rintoul, H. *Brave Hearts*
Thomas, C. *Flesh and Blood*

WALAQ Wallace, Robert, ed. *Quebec Voices: Three
     Plays.* Toronto: Coach House Press, 1986. 163pp.
Chaurette, N. *Provincetown Playhouse, July 1919*
Dubois, R. *Don't Blame the Bedouins*
Gingras, R. *Breaks*

WALJ Walley, Harold Reinoehl. *The Book of the Play.*
     New York: Scribner [c1950] 699pp.
Chekhov, A. *The Sea Gull*
Congreve, W. *The Way of the World*
Ibsen, H. *An Enemy of the People*
Molière, J. *The Misanthrope*
O'Neill, E. *Desire under the Elms*
Racine, J. *Phaedra*
Rostand, E. *Cyrano de Bergerac*
Shakespeare, W. *The Tragedy of Hamlet, Prince of
     Denmark*
Shakespeare, W. *Twelfth Night; or, What You Will*
Sophocles. *Oedipus the King*
Strindberg, A. *The Dream Play*
Synge, J. *The Playboy of the Western World*

WALL Walley, Harold Reinoehl, and Wilson, John Harold,
     eds. *Early Seventeenth Century Plays, 1600–1642.*
     New York: Harcourt, Brace [c1930] 1120pp.
Beaumont, F., and Fletcher, J. *A King or No King*
Brome, R. *A Mad Couple Well Matched*
Chapman, G. *The Revenge of Bussy D'Ambois*
Chapman, G., Jonson, B., and Marston, J. *Eastward Ho!*
D'Avenant, W. *Love and Honor*
Dekker, T., and Middleton, T. *The Honest Whore, Part I*
Fletcher, J. *The Wild-goose Chase*
Ford, J. *'Tis a Pity She's a Whore*
Heywood, T. *A Woman Killed with Kindness*
Jonson, B. *Volpone; or, the Fox*
Marston, J. *The Dutch Courtesan*
Massinger, P. *Old Debts*
Middleton, T. *A Chaste Maid in Cheapside*
Shirley, J. *The Cardinal*
Webster, J. *The White Devil*

WALPOLE, HUGH. *See* MAL *Malvern Festival Plays.*

WARF Warfel, Harry Redcay; Gabriel, Ralph Henry; and
     Williams, Stanley Thomas, eds. *The American
     Mind.* New York: American Book Co. [c1937]
     1520pp.
O'Neill, E. *The Emperor Jones*

WARH Warnock, Robert. *Representative Modern Plays.
     American.* Chicago: Scott, Foresman [c1952]
     758pp.
Anderson, M. *Valley Forge*
Behrman, S. *Biography*

Howard, S. *The Late Christopher Bean*
Kaufman, G., and Connelly, M. *Beggar on Horseback*
Miller, A. *Death of a Salesman*
Odets, C. *Waiting for Lefty*
O'Neill, E. *Mourning becomes Electra*
Williams, T. *The Glass Menagerie*

WARI Warnock, Robert, ed. *Representative Modern Plays,
    British*. Chicago: Scott, Foresman [1953] 710pp.
Barrie, J. *The Admirable Crichton*
Coward, N. *The Blithe Spirit*
Eliot, T. *Murder in the Cathedral*
Fry, C. *A Phoenix Too Frequent*
Galsworthy, J. *Loyalties*
Maugham, W. *The Constant Wife*
O'Casey, S. *Juno and the Paycock*
Shaw, G. *The Doctor's Dilemma*
Synge, J. *Riders to the Sea*

WARL Warnock, Robert, compiler. *Representative
    Modern Plays: Ibsen to Tennessee Williams*.
    Chicago: Scott, Foresman [1964] 696pp.
Behrman, S. *Biography*
Chekhov, A. *The Sea-gull*
Fry, C. *A Phoenix Too Frequent*
Ibsen, H. *The Master Builder*
Maugham, W. *The Constant Wife*
O'Casey, S. *Juno and the Paycock*
O'Neill, E. *Desire under the Elms*
Shaw, G. *The Doctor's Dilemma*
Strindberg, A. *Miss Julie*
Synge, J. *Riders to the Sea*
Williams, T. *The Glass Menagerie*

WARN Warnock, Robert, and Anderson, George K., eds.
    *The World in Literature*. Chicago: Scott, Foresman
    [c1950] 2 vols. in 1
Aeschylus. *Agamemnon* 1
Aristophanes. *The Clouds* 1
Euripides. *Hippolytus* 1
Kālidāsa. *Shakuntalā* 1
Shakespeare, W. *Hamlet, Prince of Denmark* 2
Sophocles. *Oedipus the King* 1
Vega Carpio, L. *The Sheep Well* 2

WASCP Wasserman, Jerry, ed. *Modern Canadian Plays*.
    Vancouver, BC: Talonbooks, 1985. 412pp.
    (Revised edition published in 1986 has identical list
    of authors and plays.)
Cook, M. *Jacob's Wake*
Fennario, D. *Balconville*
Freeman, D. *Creeps*
French, D. *Jitters*
Gray, J., and Peterson, E. *Billy Bishop Goes to War*
Herbert, J. *Fortune and Men's Eyes*

Pollock, S. *Walsh*
Reaney, J. *The St. Nicholas Hotel, Wm. Donnelly, Prop.
    (The Donnellys, Part Two)*
Ritter, E. *Automatic Pilot*
Ryga, G. *The Ecstasy of Rita Joe*
Salutin, R., and Theatre Passe Muraille. *1837: The
    Farmers' Revolt*
Walker, G. *Zastrozzi: the Master of Discipline*

WASCPA Wasserman, Jerry, ed. *Modern Canadian Plays*.
    3rd ed. Vancouver, BC: Talonbooks, 1993–1994. 2
    vols.
Clark, S. *Moo* 2
Cook, M. *Jacob's Wake* 1
Fennario, D. *Balconville* 2
Freeman, D. *Creeps* 1
French, D. *Leaving Home* 1
Gray, J., and Peterson, E. *Billy Bishop Goes to War* 2
Herbert, J. *Fortune and Men's Eyes* 1
Highway, T. *Dry Lips Oughta Move to Kapuskasing* 2
Lepage, R., and Brassard, M. *Polygraph* 2
Lill, W. *The Occupation of Heather Rose* 2
Macleod, J. *Toronto, Mississippi* 2
Pollock, S. *Doc* 2
Pollock, S. *Walsh* 1
Reaney, J. *The St. Nicholas Hotel, Wm. Donnelly, Prop.
    (The Donnellys, Part Two)* 1
Ritter, E. *Automatic Pilot* 1
Ryga, G. *The Ecstasy of Rita Joe* 1
Salutin, R., and Theatre Passe Muraille. *1837: The
    Farmers' Revolt* 1
Thompson, J. *I Am Yours* 2
Tremblay, M. *Les belles-soeurs* 1
Walker, G. *Zastrozzi: The Master of Discipline* 2

WASCPB Wasserman, Jerry, ed. *Modern Canadian Plays*.
    4th ed. Vancouver, BC: Talonbooks, 2000. 2 vols.
Bouchard, M. *The Orphan Muses* 2
Clark, S. *Moo* 2
Fennario, D. *Balconville* 1
French, D. *Leaving Home* 1
Gilbert, S. *Drag Queens on Trial* 1
Gray, J., and Peterson, E. *Billy Bishop Goes to War* 1
Herbert, J. *Fortune and Men's Eyes* 1
Highway, T. *Dry Lips Oughta Move to Kapuskasing* 2
Lepage, R., and Brassard, M. *Polygraph* 2
Lill, W. *The Occupation of Heather Rose* 1
MacIvor, D. *Never Swim Alone* 2
Macleod, J. *Amigo's Blue Guitar* 2
Panych, M. *7 Stories* 2
Pollock, S. *Doc* 1
Reaney, J. *The St. Nicholas Hotel, Wm. Donnelly, Prop.
    (The Donnellys, Part Two)* 1
Rebar, K. *Bordertown Café* 2
Ryga, G. *The Ecstasy of Rita Joe* 1

Salutin, R., and Theatre Passe Muraille. *1837: The Farmers' Revolt* 1

Sears, D. *Harlem Duet* 2

Thompson, J. *Lion in the Streets* 2

Tremblay, M. *Les belles-soeurs* 1

Verdecchia, G. *Fronteras Americanas* 2

Walker, G. *Problem Child* 2

Walker, G. *Zastrozzi: The Master of Discipline* 1

WASCT Wasserman, Jerry, ed. *Twenty Years at Play: A New Play Centre Anthology.* Vancouver, BC: Talonbooks, 1990. 346pp.

Brown, A. *The Wolf Within*

Cone, T. *Herringbone*

Hollingsworth, M. *War Babies*

Lambert, B. *Under the Skin*

Lazarus, J., and Lazarus, J. *Dreaming and Duelling*

Rosen, S. *Ned and Jack*

Walmsley, T. *Something Red*

Weir, I. *The Idler*

WASD WaterHouse, Betty Senk, translator. *Five Plays of the Sturm und Drang.* Lanham, MD: University Press of America, 1986. 229pp.

Klinger, F. *Storm and Stress*

Leisewitz, J. *Julius of Tarento*

Lenz, J. *The Tutor*

Lenz, J. *The Soldiers*

Wagner, H. *The Child Murderess*

WAT Watrous, George Ansel, ed. *Elizabethan Dramatists.* New York: Crowell [1903] 293pp.

Beaumont, F., and Fletcher, J. *Philaster*

Jonson, B. *Every Man in His Humour*

Marlowe, C. *Dr. Faustus*

WATA Watson, Ernest Bradlee, and Pressey, Benfield, eds. *Contemporary Drama: American, English, and Irish, European.* New York: Scribner [c1959] 577pp.

Chekhov, A. *Uncle Vanya*

Eliot, T. *Murder in the Cathedral*

Frings, K. *Look Homeward, Angel*

García Lorca, F. *Blood Wedding*

Ibsen, H. *Hedda Gabler*

Inge, W. *Come Back, Little Sheba*

Miller, A. *The Crucible*

O'Casey, S. *Purple Dust*

O'Neill, E. *Ah, Wilderness!*

Pirandello, L. *Henry IV*

Shaw, G. *Man and Superman*

Strindberg, A. *The Dream Play*

Synge, J. *Riders to the Sea*

Wilde, O. *The Importance of Being Earnest*

Wilder, T. *The Skin of Our Teeth*

WATC Watson, Ernest Bradlee, and Pressey, Benfield, compilers. *Contemporary Drama: American Plays.* New York: Scribner [c1931–1938] 2 vols.

Anderson, M. *Elizabeth the Queen* 2

Barry, P. *Hotel Universe* 2

Howard, S. *The Silver Cord* 1

Kaufman, G., and Connelly, M. *Beggar on Horseback* 1

Lawson, J. *Processional* 1

Mitchell, L. *The New York Idea* 1

O'Neill, E. *The Emperor Jones* 1

O'Neill, E. *The Hairy Ape* 2

Rice, E. *Street Scene* 2

Sherwood, R. *The Petrified Forest* 2

WATE Watson, Ernest Bradlee, and Pressey, Benfield, eds. *Contemporary Drama, Eleven Plays: American, English, European.* New York: Scribner's [c1956] 341pp.

Anouilh, J. *Antigone*

Connelly, M. *The Green Pastures*

Coward, N. *Ways and Means*

Fry, C. *Venus Observed*

Giraudoux, J. *The Madwoman of Chaillot*

Hellman, L. *Another Part of the Forest*

Miller, A. *Death of a Salesman*

Saroyan, W. *Hello Out There*

Shaw, G. *Pygmalion*

Wilder, T. *The Happy Journey to Trenton and Camden*

Williams, T. *The Glass Menagerie*

WATF Watson, Ernest Bradlee, and Pressey, Benfield, compilers. *Contemporary Drama: English and Irish Plays.* New York: Scribner [c1931] 2 vols.

Barrie, J. *Dear Brutus* 2

Barrie, J. *What Every Woman Knows* 1

Dunsany, E. *The Glittering Gate* 1

Galsworthy, J. *Justice* 1

Galsworthy, J. *Loyalties* 2

Gregory, I. *Hyacinth Halvey* 1

Maugham, W. *The Circle* 2

Milne, A. *Mr. Pim Passes By* 2

O'Casey, S. *Juno and the Paycock* 2

Pinero, A. *Mid-channel* 1

Synge, J. *Riders to the Sea* 1

WATI Watson, Ernest Bradlee, and Pressey, Benfield, compilers. *Contemporary Drama: European, English, and Irish, American Plays.* New York: Scribner [c1941] 1177pp.

Anderson, M. *Elizabeth the Queen*

Andreyev, L. *He Who Gets Slapped*

Barrie, J. *Dear Brutus*

Barrie, J. *What Every Woman Knows*

Barry, P. *Hotel Universe*

Benavente y Martínez, J. *The Passion Flower*

Čapek, K. *R.U.R. (Rossum's Universal Robots)*
Chekhov, A. *The Cherry Orchard*
Chekhov, A. *Uncle Vanya*
Curel, F. de. *The Fossils*
Dunsany, E. *The Glittering Gate*
Galsworthy, J. *Justice*
Galsworthy, J. *Loyalties*
Gorki, M. *Night's Lodging; or, the Lower Depths*
Gregory, I. *Hyacinth Halvey*
Hauptmann, G. *The Beaver Coat*
Howard, S. *The Silver Cord*
Ibsen, H. *A Doll's House*
Ibsen, H. *Hedda Gabler*
Kaufman, G., and Connelly, M. *Beggar on Horseback*
Lawson, J. *Processional*
Maeterlinck, M. *Pelléas and Mélisande*
Maugham, W. *The Circle*
Milne, A. *Mr. Pim Passes By*
O'Casey, S. *Juno and the Paycock*
O'Neill, E. *The Emperor Jones*
O'Neill, E. *The Hairy Ape*
Pinero, A. *Mid-channel*
Pirandello, L. *Henry IV*
Rice, E. *Street Scene*
Rostand, E. *Cyrano de Bergerac*
Schnitzler, A. *Light-o'-love*
Sherwood, R. *Abe Lincoln in Illinois*
Strindberg, A. *The Dream Play*
Sudermann, H. *Magda*
Synge, J. *Riders to the Sea*
Toller, E. *Man and the Masses*

WATL Watson, Ernest Bradlee, and Pressey, Benfield,
       compilers. *Contemporary Drama: European Plays.*
       New York: Scribner [c1931–1934] 4 vols.
Andreyev, L. *He Who Gets Slapped* 4
Annunzio, G. d'. *Francesca da Rimini* 3
Becque, H. *The Vultures* 1
Benavente y Martínez, J. *The Passion Flower* 3
Čapek, K. *R.U.R.* 4
Chekhov, A. *The Cherry Orchard* 1
Chekhov, A. *The Sea Gull* 3
Chekhov, A. *Uncle Vanya* 2
Curel, F. de. *The Fossils* 1
Corki, M. *Night's Lodging* 3
Hauptmann, G. *The Beaver Coat* 1
Ibsen, H. *A Doll's House* 1
Ibsen, H. *Hedda Gabler* 2
Maeterlinck, M. *Pelléas and Mélisande* 2
Pirandello, L. *Henry IV* 4
Rostand, E. *Cyrano de Bergerac* 2
Schnitzler, A. *Light-o'-love* 1
Strindberg, A. *The Dream Play* 3
Sudermann, H. *Magda* 2
Toller, E. *Man and the Masses* 4

WATO Watson, Ernest Bradlee, and Pressey, Benfield,
       compilers. *Contemporary Drama, Nine Plays:
       American, English, European.* New York: Scribner
       [c1941] 362pp.
Barrie, J. *What Every Woman Knows*
Čapek, K. *R.U.R. (Rossum's Universal Robots)*
Galsworthy, J. *Justice*
Howard, S. *The Silver Cord*
Maugham, W. *The Circle*
O'Neill, E. *The Hairy Ape*
Rice, E. *Street Scene*
Rostand, E. *Cyrano de Bergerac*
Sherwood, R. *Abe Lincoln in Illinois*

WATR Watson, Ernest Bradlee, and Pressey, Benfield,
       compilers. *Five Modern Plays.* New York: Scribner
       [c1933] 536pp.
Chekhov, A. *The Cherry Orchard*
Galsworthy, J. *Justice*
Ibsen, H. *Hedda Gabler*
Maeterlinck, M. *Pelléas and Mélisande*
Rostand, E. *Cyrano de Bergerac*

WATS Watt, Homer Andrew, and Cargill, Oscar, eds.
       *College Reader.* New York: Prentice Hall, 1948.
       949pp.
Behrman, S. *End of Summer*
Corwin, N. *My Client Curley*
Corwin, N. *Radio Primer*
Galsworthy, J. *Strife*
Gregory, A. *Spreading the News*

WATT Watt, Homer Andrew, and Munn, James Buell,
       eds. *Ideas and Forms in English and American
       Literature.* Chicago: Scott, Foresman [c1932] 2
       vols.
Gregory, I. *Hyacinth Halvey* 2
Milne, A. *The Dover Road* 2
Mr. S. Mr. of Art. *Gammer Gurton's Needle* 2
Pinelo, A. *The Second Mrs. Tanqueray* 2
Sheridan, R. *The School for Scandal* 2
Synge, J. *Riders to the Sea* 2
Webster, J. *The Duchess of Malfi* 2
Yeats, W. *The Land of Heart's Desire* 2

WATTAD Watt Stephen, and Gary A. Richardson, eds.
        *American Drama: Colonial to Contemporary.* Fort
        Worth: Harcourt Brace College Publishers, 1995.
        1157pp.
Albee, E. *The Zoo Story*
Baraka, A. *Dutchman*
Barry, P. *Holiday*
Boucicault, D. *The Octoroon*
Crothers, R. *He and She*
Daly, A. *Under the Gaslight*

Finley, K. *We Keep Our Victims Ready*
Glaspell, S. *Trifles*
Hellman, L. *The Children's Hour*
Herne, J. *Margaret Fleming*
Howard, B. *Shenandoah*
Hughes, L. *Mulatto*
Hwang, D. *M. Butterfly*
Kennedy, A. *A Movie Star Has to Star in Black and White*
Kramer, L. *The Destiny of Me*
Mamet, D. *Oleanna*
Miller, A. *All My Sons*
Moody, W. *The Great Divide*
Moraga, C. *Giving up the Ghost*
Mowatt, A. *Fashion*
Norman, M. *Getting Out*
Odets, C. *Waiting for Lefty*
O'Neill, E. *The Iceman Cometh*
Rabe, D. *Streamers*
Shange, N. *Spell #7*
Shepard, S. *The Tooth of Crime*
Stone, J. *Metamora*
Treadwell, S. *Machinal*
Tyler, R. *The Contrast*
Valdez, L. *I Don't Have to Show You No Stinking Badges!*
Williams, T. *Cat on a Hot Tin Roof*
Wilson, A. *Ma Rainey's Black Bottom*

WEAL Weales, Gerald Clifford, ed. *Edwardian Plays.* New York: Hill and Wang [1962] 429pp. (Mermaid Dramabook)
Granville-Barker, H. *The Madras House*
Hankin, J. *The Return of the Prodigal*
Maugham, W. *Loaves and Fishes*
Pinero, A. *Mid-channel*
Shaw, G. *Getting Married*

WEAN Weales, Gerald Clifford, ed. *Eleven Plays.* New York: W. W. Norton [1964] 617pp.
Anouilh, J. *The Lark*
Euripides. *Alcestis*
Granville-Barker, H. *Rococo*
Ibsen, H. *The Wild Duck*
Miller, A. *All My Sons*
Musset, A. *Camille and Perdican*
Pirandello, L. *Tonight We Improvise*
Shakespeare, W. *Troilus and Cressida*
Shaw, G. *Arms and the Man*
Wilder, T. *The Matchmaker*
Wycherley, W. *The Country Wife*

WEAT Weatherley, Edward Howell; Moffet, Harold Y.; Prouty, Charles T.; and Noyes, Henry H. *The English Heritage.* Boston: Ginn [c1945] 2 vols.

Barrie, J. *The Twelve-pound Look* 2
*Everyman* 1
Farquhar, G. *The Beaux' Stratagem* 1
Marlowe, C. *The Tragical History of Doctor Faustus* 1
*Noah's Flood* 1
Sheridan, R. *The Rivals* 1
Synge, J. *Riders to the Sea* 2

WEAV Weatherly, Edward Howell; Wagener, A. Pelzer; Zeydel, Edwin H.; and Yarmolinsky, Avrahm, eds. *The Heritage of European Literature.* Boston: Ginn [c1948–1949] 2 vols.
Aeschylus. *Agamemnon* 1
Chekhov, A. *The Cherry Orchard* 2
Euripides. *Electra* 1
Goethe, J. *Faust, Part I* 2
Ibsen, H. *The Wild Duck* 2
Molière, J. *Tartuffe; or, the Imposter* 2
Molière, J. *The Physician in Spite of Himself* 2
Racine, J. *Phaedra* 2
Schiller, J. *William Tell* 2
Sophocles. *Oedipus the King* 1
Terence. *Phormio* 1
Vega Carpio, L. *The King the Greatest Alcalde* 1

WEB Webber, James Plaisted, and Webster, Hanson Hart, eds. *Typical Plays for Secondary Schools.* Boston: Houghton Mifflin [c1929] 343pp. (Note: Re-issued in 1930 as *Typical Plays for Young People*, 291pp. Same contents.)
Baring, M. *The Rehearsal*
Chapin, H. *Augustus in Search of a Father*
Frank, M. *A Mistake at the Manor*
Gilbert, W. *Sweethearts*
Gregory, I. *The Dragon*
Healey, F. *The Copper Pot*
Hsiung, C. *The Thrice Promised Bride*
Kotzebue, A. *Pharaoh's Daughter*
Mackay, C. *The Prince of Court Painters*
Tarkington, B., and Wilson, H. *The Gibson Upright*
Webber, J. *Frances and Francis*

WEBER Weber, Carl, ed. *Drama: Contemporary Germany.* Baltimore: Johns Hopkins University Press, 1996. 276pp.
Dorst, T. *Fernando Knapp Wrote Me This Letter: An Assaying of the Truth*
Jelinek, E. *Totenauberg (Death/Valley/Summit)*
Müller, H. *Mommsen's Block*
Pohl, K. *The Beautiful Stranger*
Seidel, G. *Carmen Kittel*
Strauss, B. *The Tour Guide*
Tabori, G. *Mein kampf*

WED Wedeck, Hurry Ezekiel, ed. *Classics of Greek Literature*. New York: Philosophical Library, 1963. 385pp.
 Aeschylus. *The Persians*
 Aristophanes. *The Birds*
 Euripides. *Iphigenia in Tauris*
 Sophocles. *Electra*

WEE *Week-end Library*. 3rd issue [1930] Garden City, NY: Doubleday Page, 1930. v.p.
 Maugham, W. *The Circle*
 Morley, C. *Really, My Dear.*
 Morley, C. *Wagon-lits*

WEHL Wehle, Philippa, ed. *Drama Contemporary: France*. New York: PAJ Publications, 1986. 233pp.
 Bourdet, G. *The Gas Station*
 Cormann, E. *Exiles*
 Duras, M. *Vera Baxter or the Atlantic Beaches*
 Grumberg, J. *The Workroom*
 Sarraute, N. *Over Nothing at All*
 Vinaver, M. *Chamber Theatre*

WEIM Weiss, Samuel Abba, ed. *Drama in the Modern World*. Boston: Heath [1964] 555pp.
 Arbuzov, A. *It Happened in Irkutsk*
 Beckett, S. *All that Fall*
 Brecht, B. *The Good Woman of Setzuan*
 Chekhov, A. *The Cherry Orchard*
 García Lorca, F. *The House of Bernarda Alba*
 Giraudoux, J. *Ondine*
 Ibsen, H. *The Wild Duck*
 Ionesco, E. *The Bald Soprano*
 O'Neill, E. *Desire under the Elms*
 Pirandello, L. *Six Characters in Search of an Author*
 Shaw, G. *Major Barbara*
 Strindberg, A. *Miss Julie*
 Synge, J. *The Playboy of the Western World*
 Williams, T. *The Glass Menagerie*

WEIP Weiss, Samuel Abba, ed. *Drama in the Modern World: Plays and Essays*. Alternate ed. Lexington, MA: Heath, 1974. 614pp.
 Beckett, S. *All that Fall*
 Brecht, B. *Mother Courage and Her Children*
 Chekhov, A. *The Three Sisters*
 Eisenstein, S. *Ivan the Terrible: The Screenplay, Part One*
 García Lorca, F. *Blood Wedding*
 Gordone, C. *No Place to Be Somebody*
 Ibsen, H. *The Master Builder*
 Ionesco, E. *Jack; or, the Submission*
 O'Neill, E. *The Hairy Ape*
 Pirandello, L. *Henry IV*
 *The Red Lantern*

Schnitzler, A. *La ronde*
 Shaw, G. *Heartbreak House*
 Strindberg, A. *A Dream Play*
 Synge, J. *Riders to the Sea*

WEIS Weiss, Samuel Abba, compiler. *Drama in the Western World: 15 Plays with Essays*. Boston: Heath. 1968. 794pp.
 Aristophanes. *Lysistrata*
 Beckett, S. *All that Fall*
 Brecht, B. *The Caucasian Chalk Circle*
 Chekhov, A. *Uncle Vanya*
 Euripides. *The Bacchae*
 Ibsen, H. *Ghosts*
 Kleist, H. *The Prince of Homburg*
 Molière, J. *The Misanthrope*
 O'Neill, E. *Desire under the Elms*
 Pirandello, L. *Six Characters in Search of an Author*
 Racine, J. *Phaedra*
 Shaw, G. *Caesar and Cleopatra*
 Sophocles. *Oedipus the King*
 Strindberg, A. *A Dream Play*
 Williams, T. *The Glass Menagerie*

WEIW Weiss, Samuel Abba, compiler. *Drama in the Western World: 9 Plays with Essays*. Boston: Heath, 1968. 506pp.
 Aristophanes. *Lysistrata*
 Brecht, B. *The Caucasian Chalk Circle*
 Chekhov, A. *Uncle Vanya*
 Ibsen, H. *Ghosts*
 Molière, J. *The Misanthrope*
 Pirandello, L. *Six Characters in Search of an Author*
 Shaw, G. *Caesar and Cleopatra*
 Sophocles. *Oedipus the King*
 Williams, T. *The Glass Menagerie*

WEJ Wellman, Mac, ed. *Seven Different Plays*. New York: Broadway Play Publishing, Inc., 1988. 459pp.
 Congdon, C. *No Mercy*
 Jenkin, L. *Kid Twist*
 Jones, J. *Der Inka von Peru*
 Kushner, T. *A Bright Room Called Day*
 Overmyer, E. *In a Pig's Valise*
 Richards, G. *In His 80th Year*
 Wellman, M. *The Bad Infinity*

WEK Wellman, Mac, ed. *Theatre of Wonders: Six Contemporary American Plays*. Los Angeles: Sun & Moon Press, 1985. 326pp.
 Jenkin, L. *Gogol*
 Jones, J. *Seventy Scenes of Halloween*
 McAnuff, D. *Leave It to Beaver Is Dead*

Wellman, M. *The Professional Frenchman*
Wray, E. *Border*
Wray, E. *Forecast*

WEL Wells, Henry Willis, ed. *Six Sanskrit Plays in
    English Translation.* New York: Asia Publishing
    House [1964] 487pp.
Bhāsa. *The Vision of Vāsavadatta*
Bhavabhūti. *Rama's Later History*
Harsha. *Nagananda*
Kālidāsa. *Shakuntalā*
Kālidāsa. *Vikramorvacie; or, the Hero and the Nymph*
Sūdraka. *The Little Clay Cart*

WELG Wellwarth, George Emanuel, ed. *German Drama
    between the Wars.* New York: Dutton, 1972. 366pp.
Broch, H. *The Atonement*
Hasenclaver, W., and Tucholsky, K. *Christopher
    Columbus*
Kokoschka, O. *Job*
Kraus, K. *The Last Days of Mankind* (excerpt)
Toller, E. *No More Peace!*
Zuckmayer, C. *The Captain of Köpeniek*

WELK Wellwarth, George Emanuel, ed. *New Generation
    Spanish Drama: An Anthology.* Montreal: Engendra
    Press, 1976. 179pp.
López Mozo, J. *The Testament*
Matilla, L. *Post Mortem*
Quiles, E. *The Bridal Chamber*
Quiles, E. *The Employee*
Quiles, E. *The Refrigerator*
Rellán, M. *The Blind Warrior*

WELL Wellwarth, George Emanuel, ed. *The New Wave of
    Spanish Drama.* New York: New York University
    Press, 1970. 321pp.
Ballesteros, A. *The Best of All Possible Worlds*
Ballesteros, A. *The Hero*
Bellido, J. *Bread and Rice or Geometry in Yellow*
Bellido, J. *Train to H.*
Ruibal, J. *The Man and the Fly*
Ruibal, J. *The Jackass*
Sastre, A. *Sad Are the Eyes of William Tell*

WELT Wellwarth, George Emanuel, ed. *Themes of
    Drama: An Anthology.* New York: Crowell, 1973.
    647pp.
Adamov, A. *All against All*
Aristophanes. *Lysistrata*
Ballesteros, A. *The Best of All Possible Worlds*
Büchner, G. *Woyzeck*
Cornish, R. *Open Twenty-four Hours*
Dennis, N. *Cards of Identity*
Dürrenmatt, F. *Incident at Twilight*

*Everyman*
Euripides. *The Bacchae*
Fugard, A. *The Blood Knot*
Hochenwälder, F. *The Holy Experiment*
Jarry, A. *King Ubu*
Molière, J. *The Would-be Gentleman*
Nkosi, L. *The Rhythm of Violence*
Pirandello, L. *Henry IV*
Richardson, J. *Gallows Humor*
Ruibal, J. *The Man and the Fly*
Schnitzler, A. *Round Dance*
Shakespeare, W. *Antony and Cleopatra*
Shaw, G. *Mrs. Warren's Profession*

WELV Wellwarth, George Emanuel, ed. *Three Catalan
    Dramatists.* Montreal: Engendra Press, 1976.
    232pp.
Benet i Jornet, J. *The Ship*
Pedrolo, M. de. *Cruma*
Pedrolo, M. de. *Full Circle*
Pedrolo, M. de. *The Room*
Teixidor, J. *The Legend of the Piper*

WES *West Coast Plays.* Berkeley, CA: California Theatre
    Council, 1977–1987. 22 vols.
*The AIDS Show (Artists Involved with Death and
    Survival)* 17/18
    (Consists of the following twenty-six brief plays:
    Attinello, P. *Hospital*; Attinello, P. *Party 1981*;
    Attinello, P. *Party 1982*; Attinello, P. *Party 1983*;
    Attinello, P. *Party 1984*; Attinello, P. *Party
    1985*; Barksdale, W. *Land's End*; Brown, K., and
    McQueen, M. *Rimmin' at the Baths*; Brown, K.,
    and McQueen, M. *Safe Livin' in Dangerous Times*;
    Curzon, D. *Reverend What's His Name*; Davis, E.
    *The Nurse*; Holsclaw, D. *It's My Party*; Holsclaw,
    D. *Spice Queen*; Morris, M. *Alice*; Morris, M.
    *Nobody's Fool*; Moss, L. *Murray 1981*; Moss, L.
    *Murray 1982*; Moss, L. *Murray 1983*; Moss, L.
    *Murray Now*; Prandini, A. *Mama's Boy*; Real, P.
    *Stronger and Stronger*; Stone, R. *The Bar*; Stone,
    R. *To Tell the Truth*; Turner, D. *Invitation (Part
    One)*; Turner, D. *Invitation (Part Two)*; Weigand,
    R. *Ricky*)
Alexander, R. *Home Free* 11/12
Attinello, P. *Hospital. See* The AIDS Show . . .
Attinello, P. *Party 1981. See* The AIDS Show . . .
Attinello, P. *Party 1982. See* The AIDS Show . . .
Attinello, P. *Party 1983. See* The AIDS Show . . .
Attinello, P. *Party 1984. See* The AIDS Show . . .
Attinello, P. *Party 1985. See* The AIDS Show . . .
Baizley, D. *Catholic Girls* 11/12
Baizley, D. *Daniel in Babylon* 19/20
Barksdale, W. *Land's End. See* The AIDS Show . . .
Berkoff, S. *Greek* 15/16

San Francisco Mime Troupe. *Fact Wino Meets the Moral Majority* 15/16

San Francisco Mime Troupe. *Fact Wino vs. Armageddonman* 15/16

San Francisco Mime Troupe. *Ghosts* 10

San Francisco Mime Troupe. *Hotel Universe* 10

Schein, D. *Out Comes Butch* 17/18

Sebastian, E. *Your Place Is No Longer with Us* 13/14

Shank, A. *Sand Castles* 15/16

Shank, A. *Sunset/Sunrise* 4

Shiomi, R. *Yellow Fever* 13/14

Shipley, L. *The Bathtub* 5

Silver, S. *The Five Minute Romance. See* Twenty-four Hours: A.M.

Smith, B. *Family Portrait* 17/18

Sossi, R., and Condon, F. *The Chicago Conspiracy Trial* 7

Steppling, J. *The Dream Coast* 21/22

Stone, R. *The Bar. See* The AIDS Show . . .

Stone, R. *To Tell the Truth. See* The AIDS Show . . .

Strauss, B. *Three Acts of Recognition* 8

Thomas, L. *Joe's Not Home. See* Twenty-four Hours: A.M.

Towbin, F. *Love in a Pub. See* Twenty-four Hours: P.M.

Turner, D. *Invitation (Part One). See* The AIDS Show . . .

Turner, D. *Invitation (Part Two). See* The AIDS Show . . .

*Twenty-four Hours: A.M.* 17/18 (Consists of the following twelve brief plays: Brown, D. *Four in the Morning*; Chais, P. *Sunny Side Up*; Kingsley-Smith, T. *I Want to Hold Your Hand;* Leeson, M. *Love Sonnet*; Levy, J. *Shotgun Willis*; Link, D. *Sleeping Together*; Mayer, J. *The Underachiever*; Miller, A. *Faro Rides Again*; Rimmer, C. *Pelicans;* Silver, S. *The Five Minute Romance*; Thomas, L. *Joe's Not Home*; Zindel, B., and Zindel, P. *Lemons in the Morning*)

*Twenty-four Hours: P.M.* 17/18 (Consists of the following twelve brief plays: Bobrick, S. *An Eastern Fable*; Bobrick, S. *Opening Night*; Cooper, D. *Rules of the House*; Hailey, O. *About Time*; Henley, B. *Hymn in the Attic*; Lenz, R. *So Long, Mr. Broadway*; Lewis, M. *Sunrise on Earth*; McGinn, J. *The Termination*; Matcha, J. *Aerobics*; Raymond, A. *Lifeline*; Rodd, M. *Conversation 2001*; Towbin, F. *Love in a Pub*)

Valdez, L. *Bernabé* 19/20

Valdez, L. *The Dark Root of a Scream* 19/20

Valdez, L. *The Shrunken Head of Pancho Villa* 11/12

Valdez, L. *Soldado razo* 19/20

Weetman, M. *Estonia You Fall* 13/14

Weigand, R. *Ricky. See* The AIDS Show . . .

Whitehead, W. *And If that Mockingbird Don't Sing* 3

Yafa, S. *Passing Shots* 1

Yamauchi, W. *And the Soul Shall Dance* 11/12

Zahn, C. *The Reactivated Man* 11/12

Zindel, B., and Zindel, P. *Lemons in the Morning. See* Twenty-four Hours: A.M.

WETZ Wetzsteon, Ross, ed. *The Best of Off-Broadway: Eight Contemporary Obie-winning Plays.* New York: Mentor, 1994. 448pp.

Beckett, S. *Ohio Impromptu*

Bogosian, E. *Sex, Drugs, Rock & Roll*

Durang, C. *The Marriage of Bette and Boo*

Fornes, M. *The Danube*

Lucas, C. *Prelude to a Kiss*

Mamet, D. *Edmond*

Parks, S. *Imperceptible Mutabilities in the Third Kingdom*

Shawn, W. *Aunt Dan and Lemon*

WHE Wheeler, Charles Bickersteth, ed. *Six Plays by Contemporaries of Shakespeare.* London: Oxford University Press [1928] 595pp. (The World's Classics)

Beaumont, F., and Fletcher, J. *The Knight of the Burning Pestle*

Beaumont, F., and Fletcher, J. *Philaster*

Dekker, T. *The Shoemaker's Holiday*

Massinger, P. *A New Way to Pay Old Debts*

Webster, J. *The Duchess of Malfi*

Webster, J. *The White Devil*

WHF White, Elizabeth A. and others, eds. *Understanding Literature.* Boston, Ginn, 1967. 751pp.

Alvarez Quintero, S., and Alvarez Quintero, J. *A Sunny Morning*

Fletcher, L. *Sorry, Wrong Number*

MacLeish, A. *The Trojan Horse*

Shakespeare, W. *The Life of King Henry the Fifth*

WHFA White, Elizabeth A., and others, eds. *Understanding Literature.* New ed. Boston: Ginn, 1970. 756pp.

Gibson, W. *The Miracle Worker*

Goodrich, F., and Hachett, A. *The Diary of Anne Frank*

Shakespeare, W. *The Life of King Henry the Fifth*

WHFM White, Melvin R., and Whiting, Frank M. *Playreader's Repertory: An Anthology for Introduction to Theatre.* Glenview, IL: Scott, Foresman, 1970. 804pp.

Aristophanes. *The Birds*

Chekhov, A. *The Cherry Orchard*

*Everyman*

Hansberry, L. *A Raisin in the Sun*

Ibsen, H. *Ghosts*

Kopit, A. *Oh Dad, Poor Dad, Mamma's Hung You in the Closet and I'm Feelin' So Sad*

Molière, J. *Tartuffe*
O'Neill, E. *Desire under the Elms*
Pirandello, L. *Six Characters in Search of an Author*
Shakespeare, W. *Hamlet, Prince of Denmark*
Shaw, G. *Arms and the Man*
Sophocles. *King Oedipus*
Wilde, O. *The Importance of Being Earnest*

WHITING, B. J. *See* COL *College Survey of English
    Literature.* Edited by B. J. Whiting and Others.

WHI Whitman, Charles Huntington, ed. *Representative
    Modern Dramas.* New York: Macmillan, 1936.
    1121pp.
Anderson, M. *Elizabeth the Queen*
Barry, P. *Hotel Universe*
Behrman, S. *Biography*
Benavente y Martínez, J. *The Bonds of Interest*
Brieux, E. *The Red Robe*
Chekhov, A. *The Cherry Orchard*
Galsworthy, J. *Strife*
Gorki, M. *The Lower Depths*
Green, P. *In Abraham's Bosom*
Hauptmann, G. *The Weavers*
Howard, S. *The Silver Cord*
Ibsen, H. *The Wild Duck*
Maeterlinck, M. *Pelléas and Mélisande*
Maugham, W. *Our Betters*
Molnár, F. *Liliom*
O'Casey, S. *Juno and the Paycock*
O'Neill, E. *The Hairy Ape*
Pinero, A. *Mid-channel*
Pirandello, L. *Six Characters in Search of an Author*
Rostand, E. *Cyrano de Bergerac*
Schnitzler, A. *The Lonely Way*
Strindberg, A. *The Father*
Synge, J. *Riders to the Sea*
Wilde, O. *The Importance of Being Earnest*

WHK Whitman, Charles Huntington, ed. *Seven
    Contemporary Plays.* Boston: Houghton Mifflin
    [c1931] 565pp.
Chekhov, A. *The Cherry Orchard*
Galsworthy, J. *Strife*
Hauptmann, G. *The Sunken Bell*
Ibsen, H. *An Enemy of the People*
O'Neill, E. *Beyond the Horizon*
Rostand, E. *Cyrano de Bergerac*
Synge, J. *Riders to the Sea*

WHT Whittaker, Charlotte C., ed. *Youth and the World.*
    Chicago: Lippincott [c1955] 512pp. (Reading for
    Life Series)
Ibsen, H. *A Doll's House*

WIEG Wiegman, Robyn, and Glasberg, eds. *Literature and
    Gender: Thinking Critically through Fiction, Poetry,
    and Drama.* New York: Longman, 1999. 404pp.
Fuller, C. *A Soldier's Play*
Glaspell, S. *Trifles*
Moraga, C. *Giving up the Ghost*

WIGG Wiggins, Martin, ed. *Four Jacobean Sex Tragedies.*
    Oxford: Oxford University Press, 1998. 427pp.
Barkstead, W., and Machin, L. *The Insatiate Countess*
Beaumont, F., and Fletcher, J. *The Maid's Tragedy*
Fletcher, J. *The Tragedy of Valentinian*
Middleton, T. *The Maiden's Tragedy*

WILK Wilkerson, Margaret B., ed. *9 Plays by Black
    Women.* New York: Mentor, 1986. 508pp.
Childress, A. *Wedding Band*
Collins, K. *The Brothers*
DeVeaux, A. *The Tapestry*
Gibson, P. *Brown Silk and Magenta Sunsets*
Hansberry, L. *Toussaint: Excerpt from Act I of a Work
    in Progress*
Jackson, E. *Paper Dolls*
Rahman, A. *Unfinished Women Cry in No Man's Land
    while a Bird Dies in a Gilded Cage*
Richards, B. *A Black Woman Speaks*
Shange, N. *Spell #7*

WILL Willinger, David, ed. *Three Fin-de-siècle Farces.*
    New York: Peter Lang, 1996. 250pp.
Fonson, F., and Wicheler, F. *Miss Bullberg's Marriage*
Lererghe, C. *Pan*
Maeterlinck, M. *The Miracle of St. Anthony*

WILLG Willinger, David, and Gattnig, Charles, eds. *A
    Theatre Anthology: Plays and Documents.* Lanham,
    MD: University Press of America, 1990. 368pp.
Artaud, A. *Jet of Blood*
Beckett, S. *Krapp's Last Tape*
Euripides. *The Trojan Women*
*Everyman*
Hansberry, L. *A Raisin in the Sun*
Kaprow, A. *18 Happenings in 6 Parts*
Machado, E. *Fabiola*
Maeterlinck, M. *The Blind*
Molière, J. *The Flying Doctor*
Wilder, T. *Our Town*

WILM Wilmer, S. E., ed. *Portraits of Courage: Plays
    by Finnish Women.* Helsinki: Helsinki University
    Press, 1997. 297pp.
Canth, M. *Anna-Liisa*
Jotuni, M. *The Golden Calf*
Wuolijoki, H. *Law and Order*

WILMET Wilmet, Don B., compiler. *Staging the Nation: Plays from the American Theater, 1787–1909.* Boston: Bedford Books, 1998. 574pp.
Aiken, G. *Uncle Tom's Cabin*
Boucicault, D. *The Poor of New York*
Brougham, J. *Metamora; or, the Last of the Pollywogs*
Fitch, C. *The City*
Gillette, W. *Secret Service*
Herne, J. *Shore Acres*
Mowatt, A. *Fashion; or, Life in New York*
Stone, J. *Metamora; or, the Last of the Wampanoags*
Tyler, R. *The Contrast*

WILSON, EPIPHANIUS. *See* TUQH *Turkish Literature.*

WILSP Wilson, John Harold, ed. *Six Eighteenth Century Plays.* Boston: Houghton Mifflin [c1963] 374pp.
Gay, J. *The Beggar's Opera*
Goldsmith, O. *She Stoops to Conquer*
Lillo, G. *The London Merchant*
Rowe, N. *The Fair Penitent*
Sheridan, R. *The School for Scandal*
Steele, R. *The Conscious Lovers*

WILSR Wilson, John Harold, ed. *Six Restoration Plays.* Boston: Houghton Mifflin [c1959] 463pp.
Congreve, W. *The Way of the World*
Dryden, J. *All for Love; or, the World Well Lost*
Etherege, G. *The Man of Mode; or, Sir Fopling Flutter*
Farquhar, G. *The Beaux' Stratagem*
Otway, T. *Venice Preserved; or, a Plot Discovered*
Wycherley, W. *The Country Wife*

WIM Wilson, Marian M., ed. *Popular Performance Plays of Canada.* Toronto: Simon & Pierre, 1976. Various pagings (Vol.1)
Campbell, P. *Hoarse Muse*
Colley, P. *The Donnellys*
Crips, J. *A Wife in the Hand*
Grant, D. *What Glorious Times They Had—Nellie McClung*
McMaster, B. *Put On the Spot/ When Everybody Cares* (2 kid plays)

WINE Wine, Martin L., ed. *Drama of the English Renaissance.* New York: Modern Library, 1969. 786pp.
Beaumont, F., and Fletcher, J. *The Knight of the Burning Pestle*
Beaumont, F., and Fletcher, J. *Philaster; or, Love Lies A-bleeding*
Dekker, T. *The Shoemaker's Holiday: A Pleasant Comedy of a Gentle Craft*
Ford, J. *The Broken Heart*

Jonson, B. *The Masque of Blackness*
Jonson, B. *Volpone; or, the Fox*
Marlowe, C. *The Tragical History of the Life and Death of Doctor Faustus*
Middleton, T., and Rowley, W. *The Changeling*
Webster, J. *The Duchess of Malfi*

WINN Winny, James, ed. *Three Elizabethan Plays.* London: Chatto and Windus [c1959] 223pp.
Lyly, J. *Midas*
*Mucedorus*
*The Reign of King Edward III*

WISD Wise, Jacob Hooper; Congleton, J. E.; Morris, Alton C.; and Hodges, John C. *College English: The First Year.* New York: Harcourt, Brace [c1952] 959pp.
Kingsley, S. *Darkness at Noon*
Rostand, E. *Cyrano de Bergerac*
Thurber, J., and Nugent, E. *The Male Animal*

WISE Wise, Jacob Hooper; Congleton, J. E.; Morris, Alton C.; and Hodges, John C. *College English: The First Year.* Rev. ed. New York: Harcourt, Brace [c1956] 982pp.
Miller, A. *Death of a Salesman*
Rostand, E. *Cyrano de Bergerac*
Shaw, G. *Pygmalion*

WISF Wise, Jacob Hooper; Morris, Alton C.; and Hodges, John C., eds. *College English: The First Year.* 3rd ed. New York: Harcourt, Brace [c1960] 982pp.
Anouilh, J. *Antigone*
Capote, T. *The Grass Harp*
Miller, A. *Death of a Salesman*
Shaw, G. *Androcles and the Lion*

WOLC Wolcott, John R., compiler. *Contemporary Realistic Plays.* Dubuque, IA: Kendall/Hunt Publishing Company, 1988. 305pp.
Chambers, J. *A Late Snow*
Chin, F. *The Chickencoop Chinaman*
Glaspell, S. *Trifles*
Ibsen, H. *Hedda Gabler*
Miller, A. *The Crucible*
Norman, M. *'Night, Mother*
O'Neill, E. *Ah, Wilderness!*
Strindberg, A. *Lady Julie*
Wilde, O. *The Importance of Being Earnest*
Wilder, T. *The Matchmaker*
Wilson, A. *Fences*

WOLCS Wolcott, John R., and Quinn, Michael L., compilers. *Staging Diversity: Plays and Practice*

*in American Theater*. Dubuque, IA: Kendall/Hunt
Pub. Co., 1992. 447pp.
Chambers, J. *A Late Snow*
Euripides. *The Trojan Women*
Fornes, M. *Abingdon Square*
Geiogamah, H. *Body Indian*
Glaspell, S. *Trifles*
Ibsen, H. *Hedda Gabler*
Innaurato, A. *Gemini*
Molière, J. *Scapin, or the Adventures of a Practical
Joker*
Peterson, L. *Take a Giant Step*
Seami. *Kagekiyo*
Shakespeare, W. *As You Like It*
Stein, G. *Yes Is for a Very Young Man*
Wilde, O. *The Importance of Being Earnest*
Wilder, T. *Pullman Car Hiawatha*
Yamauchi, W. *And the Soul Shall Dance*

WOMA *The Woman That I Am: The Literature and
Culture of Contemporary Women of Color*. Edited
by D. Soyini Madison. New York: St. Martin's
Press, 1994. 709pp.
Chávez, D. *Novena narrativas*
Cleage, P. *Hospice: A Play in One Act*
Jackson, A. *Shango diasporo: An African-American
Myth of Womanhood and Love*
Portillo, E. *The Day of the Swallows: A Drama in Three
Acts*
Yamauchi, W. *And the Soul Shall Dance*

WOMD *Women in Drama: An Anthology*. Edited by
Harriet Kriegel. New York: New American
Library; London: New English Library, 1975.
408pp.
Aristophanes. *Lysistrata*
Euripides. *Medea*
Glaspell, S. *Trifles*
Ibsen, H. *The Lady from the Sea*
Middleton, T. *Women beware Women*
Shaw, G. *Mrs. Warren's Profession*
Strindberg, A. *Miss Julie*
Terry, M. *Approaching Simone*

WOMP *Women Playwrights: The Best Plays of 1992–
2000*. Edited by Robyn Goodman, Marisa Smith,
D. L. Lepidus. Lyme, NH: Smith and Kraus, 1992–
2000. (Contemporary Playwrights Series) 9 vols.
Ackermann, J. *Off the Map* 94
Alvarez, L. *Analiese* 97
Alvarez, L. *The Reincarnation of Jaimie Brown* 94
Anderson, J. *Defying Gravity* 97
Ayvazian, L. *Nine Armenians* 96
Beard, J. *The Ornamental Hermit* 98

Beard, J. *Vladivostok Blues* 95
Bradbeer, S. *Full Bloom* 2000
Butterfield, C. *Joined at the Head* 92
Carlin, A. *Jodie's Body* 98
Carpenter, B. *Fall* 99
Chaffee, C. *Why We Have a Body* 93
Cram, C. *Landlocked* 2000
Ensler, E. *Floating Rhoda and the Glue Man* 93
Fannon, C. *Green Icebergs* 95
Franklin, J. e. *Christchild* 93
Gallagher, M. *Windshook* 96
Goldberg, J. *Refuge* 98
Hutton, A. *Last Train to Nibroc* 99
Jensen, J. *Two-headed* 2000
Jordan, J. *Tatjana in Color* 97
Kossman, N. *Miracles* 2000
Lee, C. *Arthur and Leila* 93
MacLeod, W. *The Water Children* 98
Mann, E. *The House of Bernarda Alba* 97
Manning, L. *Do Something with Yourself! The Life of
Charlotte Bronte* 96
Meyer, M. *Moe's Lucky Seven* 94
Morley, J. *True Confessions of a Go-go Girl* 98
Neipris, J. *A Small Delegation* 99
Obolensky, K. *Lobster Alice* 99
Pearson, S. *Unfinished Stories* 92
Rebeck, T. *Abstract Expression* 99
Rebeck, T. *The Butterfly Collection* 2000
Rebeck, T. *The Family of Man* 94
Rebeck, T. *Spike Heels* 92
Rebeck, T. *View of the Dome* 96
Reingold, J. *Girl Gone* 94
Reynolds, J. *Dance with Me* 95
Romero, E. *¡Curanderas! Serpents of the Clouds* 2000
Royce, C. *My Son Susie* 93
Scanlon, P. *What Is This Everything?* 92
Shaffer, D. *Sacrilege* 97
Shephard-Massat, S. *Waiting to Be Invited* 2000
Smith, V. *Marguerite Bonet* 98
Taylor, R. *Escape from Paradise* 97
Thatcher, K. *Emma's Child* 95
Thorne, J. *The Exact Center of the Universe* 99
Vogel, P. *The Baltimore Waltz* 92
Vogel, P. *Hot 'n' Throbbing* 94
Weiner, W. *Give Me Shelter* 98
West, C. *Jar the Floor* 92
Wilson, E. *Cross-dressing in the Depression* 93
Wilson, E. *Hurricane* 98
Zell, A. *Come to Leave* 94
Zusy, J. *Kicking Inside* 96

WOMQ *Women with Guns: Six New American Plays*. New
York: Broadway Play Publishing, 1985. 299pp.
Dale, B. *White Mountains*

Milton, D. *Skin*
Parlato, C. *Billings for the Defense*
Post, B. *Sloth*
Wellman, M. *Energumen*
Wolk, M. *Femme Fatale*

WOMR *Women Writers in Russian Modernism: An
  Anthology.* Translated and edited by Temira
  Pachmuss. Urbana: University of Illinois Press,
  1978. 340pp.
Verbitskaya, A. *Mirage*

WOMS *The Women's Project: Seven New Plays by
  Women.* Edited by Julia Miles. New York:
  Performing Arts Journal Publications and American
  Place Theatre, 1980. 372pp.
Aaron, J., and Tarlo, L. *Acrobatics*
Collins, K. *In the Midnight Hour*
Gilliatt, P. *Property*
Goldemberg, R. *Letters Home*
Mueller, L. *Killings on the Last Line*
Purscell, P. *Separate Ceremonies*
Schenkar, J. *Signs of Life*

WOMS2 *The Women's Project 2.* Edited by Julia Miles.
  New York: Performing Arts Journal Publications,
  c1984. 182pp.
Cizmar, P. *Candy & Shelley Go to the Desert*
Collins, K. *The Brothers*
Galloway, T. *Heart of a Dog*
Mack, C. *Territorial Rites*
Mueller, L. *Little Victories*

WONR *Womersley, David, ed. Restoration Drama:
  An Anthology.* Oxford; Malden, MA: Blackwell
  Publishers, 2000. 826pp.
Behn, A. *The Rover*
Buckingham, G. *The Rehearsal*
Centlivre, S. *The Busie Body*
Cibber, C. *Love's Last Shift*
Congreve, W. *Love for Love*
Congreve, W. *The Way of the World*
Dryden, J. *All for Love*
Dryden, J. *The Conquest of Granada*
Etherege, G. *The Man of Mode*
Farquhar, G. *The Beaux' Stratagem*
Farquhar, G. *The Recruiting Officer*
Howard, R. *The Great Favourite, or the Duke of Lerma*
Lee, N. *Lucius Junicus Brutus*
Otway, T. *Venice Preserved*
Tuke, S. *The Adventures of Five Hours*
Vanbrugh, J. *The Relapse*
Wycherley, W. *The Country Wife*
Wycherley, W. *The Plain Dealer*

WOO Woods, George Benjamin; Watt, Homer Andrew;
  and Anderson, George Kumler, eds. *The Literature
  of England.* Chicago: Scott, Foresman [c1936]
  2 vols.
Dekker, T. *The Shoemaker's Holiday* 1
Galsworthy, J. *Strife* 2
Marlowe, C. *The Tragical History of Doctor Faustus* 1
*The Second Shepherds' Play* 1
Sheridan, R. *The Rivals* 1
Wilde, O. *The Importance of Being Earnest* 2

WOOD Woods, George Benjamin; Watt, Homer Andrew;
  and Anderson, George Kumler, eds. *The Literature
  of England.* [Rev. ed.] Chicago: Scott, Foresman
  [c1941] 2 vols.
*Everyman* 1
Jonson, B. *Epicoene; or, the Silent Woman* 1
Marlowe, C. *Doctor Faustus* 1
Sheridan, R. *The School for Scandal* 1
*The Second Shepherds' Play* 1
Synge, J. *Riders to the Sea* 1
Wilde, O. *The Importance of Being Earnest* 2

WOOE Woods, George Benjamin; Watt, Homer A.;
  and Anderson, George K., eds. *The Literature of
  England.* [3rd ed.] Chicago: Scott, Foresman [1947]
  2 vols.
Congreve, W. *The Way of the World* 1
Dryden, J. *All for Love* 1
*Everyman* 1
Marlowe, C. *The Tragical History of Doctor Faustus* 1
*The Second Shepherds' Play* 1
Shakespeare, W. *The Tragedy of Antony and Cleopatra* 1
Sheridan, R. *The School for Scandal* 1
Synge, J. *Riders to the Sea* 2
Wilde, O. *The Importance of Being Earnest* 2

WOOG Woodyard, George, ed. *The Modern Stage in Latin
  America: Six Plays.* New York: Dutton, 1971.
  331pp.
Carballido, E. *I Too Speak of Roses*
Diaz, J. *The Place Where the Mammals Die*
Dragún, O. *And They Told Us We Were Immortal*
Gomes, A. *Payment as Pledged*
Marqués, R. *The Fanlights*
Triana, J. *The Criminals*

WOOGLA Woodyard, George, and Marion Peter Holt,
  eds. *Latin America: Plays.* New York: PAJ
  Publications, 1986. 186pp. (Drama Contemporary
  Series)
Fuentes, C. *Orchids in the Moonlight*
Puig, M. *The Kiss of the Spider Woman*

Skármeta, A. *Burning Patience*
Vargas Llosa, M. *Kathie and the Hippopotamus*

WOQ *Wordplays: An Anthology of New American Drama.*
New York: Performing Arts Journal Publications.
1981–1986. 5 vols.
Acker, K. *The Birth of the Poet* 5
Akalaitis, J. *Dressed like an Egg* 4
Babe, T. *Kid Champion* 4
Bosakowski, P. *Chopin in Space* 4
Breuer, L. *Hajj; the Performance* 3
Fornes, M. *Fefu and Her Friends* 1
Hauptman, W. *Domingo Courts* 1
Jenkin, L. *Dark Ride* 2
Jesurun, J. *Deep Sleep* 5
Jones, J. *Night Coil* 4
Kennedy, A. *A Movie Star Has to Star in Black and
White* 3
Kondoleon, H. *The Brides* 2
Lapine, J., and Sondheim, S. *Sunday in the Park with
George* 5
McAnuff, D. *The Death of von Richthofen as Witnessed
from Earth* 5
Martin, J. *Clear Glass Marbles* 3
Martin, J. *Rodeo* 3
Mednick, M. *Taxes* 3
Mee, C. *The Investigation of the Murder in El
Salvador* 4
Nelson, R. *Vienna Notes* 1
O'Keefe, J. *All Night Long* 2
Overmyer, E. *Native Speech* 3
Owens, R. *Chucky's Lunch* 2
Shawn, W. *A Thought in Three Parts* 2
Strahs, J. *North Atlantic* 5
Tavel, R. *Boy on the Straightback Chair* 1
Van Itallie, J. *Naropa* 1
Wellman, J. *Starluster* 1

WORLD DRAMA SERIES. *See* SMI, SMK, SML, SMN,
SMO, SMP, SMR Smith, Robert Metcalf, ed.

WORL *The World in Literature.* Edited by Elizabeth
Collette; Tom Peete Cross; and Elmer C. Stauffer.
Boston, Ginn [c1949] 4 vols.
Barrie, J. *Shall We Join the Ladies?* 4
Shakespeare, W. *Julius Caesar* 2
Shakespeare, W. *Macbeth* 4
Wilder, T. *Our Town* 3

WORM *The World of Tragedy.* Edited by John Kimmey
and Ashley Brown. New York: New American
Library, 1981. 466pp.
Miller, A. *A View from the Bridge*
Racine, J. *Phaedra*

Sophocles. *Antigone*
Shakespeare, W. *Macbeth*

WORN *The World Turned Upside Down: Prose and
Poetry of the American Revolution.* Ed. and with
an Introduction by James H. Pickering. Port
Washington, NY: Kennikat, 1975. 271pp.
*The Battle of Brooklyn*
Brackenridge, H. *The Battle of Bunkers-Hill*

THE WORLD'S GREAT BOOKS. *See* GRE *Great
Plays (English)*, GREA *Great Plays (French and
German)*, GREE *Greek Dramas.*

THE WORLD'S GREAT CLASSICS. *See* ORI *Oriental
Literature*, PLAB *Plays by Greek, Spanish, French,
German and English Dramatists*, TUQH *Turkish
Literature.*

WORP *World's Great Plays*; with an introduction by
George Jean Nathan. Cleveland, OH: World
Publishing Co. [1944] 491pp.
Aristophanes. *Lysistrata*
Chekhov, A. *The Cherry Orchard*
Goethe, J. *Faust*
Ibsen, H. *The Master Builder*
O'Casey, S. *The Plough and the Stars*
O'Neill, E. *The Emperor Jones*
Rostand, E. *Cyrano de Bergerac*

THE WORLD'S GREATEST LITERATURE. *See* DRA
*Dramatic Masterpieces.*

WORY Worley, Demetrice A., and Jesse Perry, Jr.,
eds. *African American Literature: An Anthology
of Nonfiction, Fiction, Poetry, and Drama.*
Lincolnwood, IL: National Textbook Co., 1993.
325pp.
Johnson, G. *Plumes*

WOTHA Worthen, W. B., ed. *The HBJ Anthology of
Drama.* Fort Worth, TX: Harcourt Brace College
Publishers, 1993. 1055pp.
Aeschylus. *Agamemnon*
Aristophanes. *Lysistrata*
Baraka, A. *Dutchman*
Beckett, S. *Happy Days*
Behn, A. *The Rover*
Brecht, B. *Mother Courage and Her Children*
Chekhov, A. *The Cherry Orchard*
Churchill, C. *Vinegar Tom*
Euripides. *The Bacchae*
*Everyman*
Fornes, M. *Mud*

Friel, B. *Translations*
Fugard, A., Kani, J., and Ntshona, W. *Sizwe Bansi
    Is Dead*
Genet, J. *The Blacks*
Glaspell, S. *Trifles*
Hoffman, W. *As Is*
Hwang, D. *M. Butterfly*
Ibsen, H. *A Doll's House*
Mamet, D. *Speed-the-plow*
Marlowe, C. *Doctor Faustus*
Miller, A. *The Crucible*
Molière, J. *Tartuffe*
Mrozek, S. *Striptease*
O'Neill, E. *The Emperor Jones*
Pinter, H. *The Homecoming*
Pirandello, L. *Six Characters in Search of an Author*
Racine, J. *Phaedra*
Schrader, L. *Kiss of the Spider Woman*
Shakespeare, W. *King Lear*
Shakespeare, W. *The Tempest*
Shange, N. *Spell # 7*
Shaw, G. *Major Barbara*
Shepard, S. *True West*
Sophocles. *Oedipus Rex*
Soyinka, W. *Death and the King's Horseman*
Strindberg, A. *Miss Julie*
Valdez, L. *Los vendidos*
Williams, T. *The Glass Menagerie*
Yeats, W. *On Baile's Strand*

WOTHB Worthen, W. B., ed. *The Harcourt Brace
        Anthology of Drama.* 2nd ed. Fort Worth, TX:
        Harcourt Brace College Publishers, 1996. 1330pp.
        (Revised edition of *The HBJ Anthology of Drama*)
Aeschylus. *Agamemnon*
Aristophanes. *Lysistrata*
Baraka, A. *Dutchman*
Behn, A. *The Rover*
Beckett, S. *Endgame*
Bourne, B., Shaw, P., and Weaver, L. *Belle reprieve*
Brecht, B. *Mother Courage and Her Children*
Büchner, G. *Woyzeck*
Calderón de la Barca, P. *Life Is a Dream*
Chekhov, A. *The Cherry Orchard*
Chikamatsu, M. *The Love Suicides at Sonezaki*
Churchill, C. *Cloud Nine*
Duras, M. *India Song*
Euripides. *Medea*
*Everyman*
Fornes, M. *Fefu and Her Friends*
Friel, B. *Translations*
Glaspell, S. *Trifles*
Highway, T. *Dry Lips Oughta Move to Kapuskasing*
Hwang, D. *M. Butterfly*

Ibsen, H. *A Doll's House*
Jonson, B. *Volpone*
Kan'ami, K. *Matsukaze*
Kushner, T. *Angels in America, Part I: Millennium
        Approaches*
Lillo, G. *The London Merchant*
*Love Letter from the Licensed Quarter*
Marlowe, C. *Doctor Faustus*
Molière, J. *Tartuffe*
O'Neill, E. *Ah, Wilderness!*
Pinter, H. *The Homecoming*
Pirandello, L. *Six Characters in Search of an Author*
Racine, J. *Phaedra*
Shakespeare, W. *Hamlet*
Shakespeare, W. *The Tempest*
Shange, N. *Spell # 7*
Shaw, G. *Major Barbara*
Shepard, S. *True West*
Sophocles. *Oedipus Rex*
Soyinka, W. *Death and the King's Horseman*
Stoppard, T. *Travesties*
Strindberg, A. *Miss Julie*
Valdez, L. *Los vendidos*
Wilde, O. *The Importance of Being Earnest*
Williams, T. *The Glass Menagerie*
Wilson, A. *Fences*
*The York Crucifixion*

WOTHC Worthen, W. B., ed. *The Harcourt Brace
        Anthology of Drama.* 3rd ed. Fort Worth, TX:
        Harcourt Brace College Publishers, 2000. 1521pp.
Aeschylus. *Agamemnon*
Aeschylus. *The Eumenides*
Aeschylus. *The Libation Bearers*
Aristophanes. *Lysistrata*
Baraka, A. *Dutchman*
Beckett, S. *Endgame*
Behn, A. *The Rover*
Brecht, B. *Mother Courage and Her Children*
Calderón de la Barca, P. *Life Is a Dream*
Césaire, A. *A Tempest*
Chekhov, A. *The Cherry Orchard*
Churchill, C. *Cloud Nine*
Davis, J. *No Sugar*
Euripides. *Medea*
*Everyman*
Farquhar, G. *The Recruiting Officer*
Friel, B. *Translations*
Fugard, A. *Valley Song*
Gambaro, G. *Information for Foreigners*
Glaspell, S. *Trifles*
Highway, T. *Dry Lips Oughta Move to Kapuskasing*
Hwang, D. *M. Butterfly*
Ibsen, H. *A Doll's House*

Juana Inés de la Cruz, S. *Loa to the Divine Narcissus*
Kan'ami, K. *Matsukaze*
Kushner, T. *Angels in America, Part I: Millennium
    Approaches*
Maponya, M. *Gangsters*
Marlowe, C. *Doctor Faustus*
Mishima, Y. *The Lady Aoi*
Molière, J. *Tartuffe*
Müller, H. *Hamletmachine*
Nakamura M., and Brandon, J. *Chūshigura: The Forty-
    seven Samurai*
O'Neill, E. *The Hairy Ape*
Parks, S. *The America Play*
Pinter, H. *The Homecoming*
Pirandello, L. *Six Characters in Search of an Author*
Racine, J. *Phaedra*
Satoh, M. *My Beatles*
Shakespeare, W. *Hamlet*
Shakespeare, W. *The Tempest*
Shaw, G. *Major Barbara*
Shepard, S. *True West*
Smith, A. D. *Fires in the Mirror: Crown Heights,
    Brooklyn, and Other Identities*
Sophocles. *Oedipus the King*
Soyinka, W. *Death and the King's Horseman*
Strindberg, A. *The Father*
Valdez, L. *Los vendidos*
*The Wakefield Second Shepherds' Pageant*
Wertenbaker, T. *Our Country's Good*
Williams, T. *The Glass Menagerie*
Wilson, A. *Fences*


WOTHM Worthen, W. B., ed. *Modern Drama: Plays,
    Criticism, Theory.* Fort Worth, TX: Harcourt Brace
    College Publishers, 1995. 1202pp.
Beckett, S. *Catastrophe*
Beckett, S. *Endgame*
Bond, E. *Bingo: Scenes of Money and Death*
Bourne, B., Shaw, P., and Weaver, L. *Belle reprieve*
Brecht, B. *Galileo*
Chekhov, A. *The Three Sisters*
Churchill, C. *Cloud Nine*
Duras, M. *India Song*
Fornes, M. *The Conduct of Life*
Friel, B. *Translations*
Fugard, A., Kani, J., and Ntshona, W. *The Island*
Gambaro, G. *Information for Foreigners*
Genet, J. *The Balcony*
Glaspell, S. *Trifles*
Grimké, A. *Rachel*
Handke, P. *Offending the Audience*
Hwang, D. *M. Butterfly*
Ibsen, H. *The Master Builder*
Ibsen, H. *The Wild Duck*
Jones, L. *Dutchman*

Kennedy, A. *Funny House of a Negro*
Kushner, T. *Angels in America, Part I: Millennium
    Approaches*
Müller, H. *Hamletmachine*
O'Neill, E. *The Emperor Jones*
Pinter, H. *The Homecoming*
Pirandello, L. *Six Characters in Search of an Author*
Robins, E. *Votes for Women!*
Shange, N. *Spell # 7*
Shaw, G. *Heartbreak House*
Shepard, S. *Buried Child*
Smith, A. D. *Fires in the Mirror: Crown Heights,
    Brooklyn, and Other Identities*
Soyinka, W. *The Lion and the Jewel*
Strindberg, A. *A Dream Play*
Valdez, L. *Los vendidos*
Wasserstein, W. *Uncommon Women and Others*
Wilde, O. *The Importance of Being Earnest*
Williams, T. *The Glass Menagerie*
Wilson, A. *Fences*


WOZA *Woza Africa: An Anthology of South African Plays.*
    Selected and edited by Duma Ndlovu; Foreword
    by Wole Soyinka; Preface by Amiri Baraka. New
    York: G. Braziller, 1986. 272pp.
Manaka, M. *Children of Asazi*
Maponya, M. *Gangsters*
Mtwa, P. *Bopha*
Mtwa, P., Ngema, M., and Simon, B. *Woza Albert!*
Ngema, M. *Asinamali*
Simon, B. *Born in the R.S.A.*


WRIGHT, JOHN HENRY. *See* MAST *Masterpieces of
    Greek Literature.*


WRIH Wright, Louis Booker, and LaMar, Virginia A., eds.
    *Four Famous Tudor and Stuart Plays.* New York:
    Washington Square Press [1963] 422pp.
Dekker, T. *The Shoemaker's Holiday*
Jonson, B. *Volpone*
Marlowe, C. *Doctor Faustus*
Webster, J. *The Duchess of Malfi*


WRIR Wright, Louis Booker, and LaMar, Virginia A.,
    eds. *Four Great Restoration Plays.* New York:
    Washington Square Press [1964] 477pp.
Congreve, W. *The Way of the World*
Dryden, J. *All for Love*
Farquhar, G. *The Beaux' Stratagem*
Wycherley, W. *The Country Wife*


WRIT *Writing North: An Anthology of Contemporary
    Yukon Writers.* Edited by Erling Friis-Baastad and

Patricia Robertson. Whitehorse, Yukon: Beluga Books, 1992. 190pp.

Adams, P. *Tears, Mama*
Flather, P., and Linklater, L. *Sixty Below* (excerpt)
Hamson, L. *Surfing Blue*

YASU Yasuda, Kenneth. *Masterworks of the No Theater.* Bloomington: Indiana University Press, 1989. 585pp.

*Hagoromo*
Kanami. *Motomezuka*
Kanami and Zeami. *Matsukaze*
*Kuzu*
Miyamasu. *Himuro*
Nobumitsu, K. *Ataka*
Nobumitsu, K. *Funabenkai*
Yasuda, K. *Martin Luther King, Jr.: A Nōh Play*
Zeami. *Atsumori*
Zeami. *Higaki*
Zeami. *Izutsu*
Zeami. *Nonomiya*
Zeami. *Nue*
Zeami. *Obasute*
Zeami. *Saigyōzakura*
Zeami. *Tadanori*
Zeami. *Taema*
Zeami. *Tōru*

YEAR *The Years Between: Plays by Women on the London Stage, 1900–1950* by Fidelis Morgan. London: Virago Press, 1994. 460pp.

Dane, C. *Will Shakespeare—an Invention*
Du Maurier, D. *The Years Between*
Gingold, H. *Beauty Beauty*
Gingold, H. *Bicycling*
Gingold, H. *Conversation Piece: The Stars Look Down*
Gingold, H. *I'm Only a Medium Medium*
Gingold, H. *Madame La Palma*
Gingold, H. *No Laughing Matter*
Gingold, H. *Talk on Music*
Gingold, H. *What Shall I Wear?*
Hamilton, C. *Diana of Dobson's*
Hooke, N. *The Amazons*
Hooke, N. *Front Door Steps*
Hooke, N. *I Wonder How It Feels*
Hooke, N. *Park Meeting*
Hooke, N. *Reprieve*
Hooke, N. *Such a Ferocious Bell*
Kennedy, M., and Dean, B. *The Constant Nymph*
Morgan, D., and MacDermot, R. *All Smart Women Must*
Morgan, D., and MacDermot, R. *–And Friend*
Morgan, D., and MacDermot, R. *The Bacchante*
Morgan, D., and MacDermot, R. *Folk Songs*
Morgan, D., and MacDermot, R. *The Guardsman*
Morgan, D., and MacDermot, R. *Kensington Girls*

Morgan, D., and MacDermot, R. *South Coast Women*
Storm, L. *Black Chiffon*

YOHA Yohannan, John D., ed. *A Treasury of Asian Literature.* New York: John Day, 1956. 487pp.

Kālidāsa. *Shakúntala*
Seami, M. *Atsumori*

YOHB Yohannan, John D., ed. *A Treasury of Asian Literature.* New York: Meridian, 1994. 432pp.

Kālidāsa. *Shakúntala*
Seami, M. *Atsumori*

YORU *Yoruba Popular Theatre: Three Plays by the Oyin Adejobi Company.* Transcribed, translated, and edited by Karin Barber and Bayo Ogundijo. Atlanta: African Studies Association, 1994. 604pp. Yoruba text with English translation facing opposite page.

Oyin Adejobi Company. *Kuye*
Oyin Adejobi Company. *Laniyonu*
Oyin Adejobi Company. *Ona Ola*

YOUP *The Young Playwrights Festival Collection: Ten Plays by Young Playwrights between the Ages of Eight and Eighteen.* Compiled and edited by the Foundation of the Dramatists Guild, Inc.; Preface by Stephen Sondheim; Introduction by Gerald Chapman. New York: Avon Books [1983] 263pp.

Berger, A. *It's Time for a Change*
Garson, J. *So What Are We Gonna Do Now?*
Gutwillig, S. *In the Way*
Litt, J. *Epiphany*
Lonergan, K. *The Rennings Children*
McNamara, J. *Present Tense*
Marchand, S. *Half Fare*
Murphy, P. *Bluffing*
Serrano, L. *The Bronx Zoo*
Wiese, A. *Coleman, S. D.*

YUCHD Yu, Shiao-Ling S., ed. *Chinese Drama after the Cultural Revolution, 1979–1989*: An Anthology. Lewiston, NY: Edwin Mellen Press, 1996. 494pp.

Gao, X. *Alarm Signal*
Gao, X. *The Bus Stop*
Guo, D, and Xi, Z. *Xu Jiujing's Promotion*
He, J. *The First House of Beijing Duck*
Jin, Y. *The Nirvana of Grandpa Doggie*
Wang, P. *WM (WE)*
Wei, M. *Pan Jinlian*

ZDA Zdanowicz, Casimir Douglas, ed. *Four French Comedies of the Eighteenth Century.* New York: Scribner [c1933] 488pp. (The Modern Student's Library)

Beaumarchais, P. *Le barbier de Séville*
Lesage, A. *Turcaret*
Marivaux, P. *Le jeu de l'amour et du hasard*
Sedaine, M. *Le philosophe sans le savoir*

ZEE Zeeman, Terence, ed. *New Namibian Plays.*
Windhoek, Namibia: New Namibia Books, 2000. 2 vols.
Amakali, M. *Checkmate* 1
Bricks Theatre Group, and Molapong, K. *The Horizon Is Calling* 1
Cowley, K., and Terblanché, T. *Onele yo kawe (Place of Diamonds)* 1
Fourie, T. *One Night* 2
Haakskeen, P. *Aia makoes* 2
Haakskeen, P. *Finders Keepers Losers Weepers* 1
Haakskeen, P. *The Rotten Apples of Jabula High School* 2
Hangula, V. *The Show Isn't Over Until* 1
Job, N. *Mai jekketti (My Jacket)* 1
Kaundu, A. *Now that You Know* 2
Molapong, K. *The Woman and the Ogre* 2
Mootseng, B. *"Social Avenue"* 1
Mosalele, L. P. *MogomotsieMang? (Who Will Comfort Me?)* 2
Ndjavera, D. *The Bride and the Broom* 1
Nyathi, F. *Tears of Fear in the Era of Terror* 2
Olivier-Sampson, L. *Gebroke onskuld (She Was Innocent)* 2
Olivier-Sampson, L. *A Moment in Our Lives* 1
Rispel, K. *The Child* 2
Rispel, K. *Die droom (The Dream)* 2
Rispel, K. *Die stoel (The Chair)* 1
Skrywer-Afrikaner, M. *Homecoming* 2
Thaniseb, A. *To Live a Better Life* 2

ZIM Zimmermann, Armand, ed. *Four European Plays.*
New York: Macmillan [1965] 547pp.
Anouilh, J. *Thieves' Carnival*
Chekhov, A. *The Cherry Orchard*
Ibsen, H. *An Enemy of the People*
Rostand, E. *Cyrano de Bergerac*

ZIMM Zimmerman, Cynthia, ed. *Taking the Stage: Selections from Plays by Canadian Women.*
Toronto: Playwrights Canada Press, 1994. 265pp. (A second edition with the same title published in 1995 is exactly identical in content.)

Albanese, E. *The Body Image Project*
Baldridge, M. *The Photographic Moment*
Bolt, C. *Waiting for Sandy*
Boyd, P. *Odd Fish*
Brennan, K. *Magpie*
Bustin, P. *Saddles in the Rain*
Butala, S. *Rodeo*
Butler, A. *Medusa Rising*
Chisholm, M. *Safe Haven*
Clark, S. *Moo*
Clarke, M. *Gertrude and Ophelia*
Clements, M. *Age of Iron*
Crossland, J. *Postcards from Hawaii*
Curran, C. *Another Labour Day*
Dempsey, S. *Wings of the Albatross*
Dempsey, S., and Millan, L. *The Thin Skin of Normal*
Feindel, J. *A Particular Class of Women*
Flacks, D. *By a Thread*
Gibson, F. *Belle*
Givner, J. *Mazo & Caroline*
Glass, J. *If We Are Women*
Griffiths, L. *Spiral Woman and the Dirty Theatre*
Hammond, M. *Beaux gestes et Beautiful Deeds*
Hines, K. *Pochsy's Lips*
Hollingsworth, M. *Alli Alli Oh*
Hunter, M. *Transit of Venus*
Kang, M. *Noran Bang: The Yellow Room*
Kemlo, K. *Crazyluv*
Koller, K. *Cowboy Boots and a Corsage*
Kolpak, D. *Bedtime Stories*
Laxdal, V. *Personal Convictions*
Lill, W. *All Fall Down*
MacDonald, A. *Goodnight Desdemona (Good Morning Juliet)*
McKay, T. *Pistons*
MacLeod, J. *Little Sister*
McNeil, M. *Island Woman*
Porter, D. *Flowers*
Quan, B. *Nancy Chew Enters the Dragon*
Riml, M. *Miss Teen*
Rubess, B. *Head in a Bag: a Cold War Comedy*
Sapergia, B. *Roundup*
Sears, D. *Who Killed Katie Ross?*
Stearns, S. *Hunter of Peace*
Thompson, J. *Pink*
Wing, P. *Lydia*
Wyatt, R. *Getting Out*

# Title Index

*Beautiful Vida. See* Šeligo, R. Lepa Vida

*Beauty and Good Properties of Women, The.* Anonymous Plays

*Beauty and the Beast.* Marcus, F.

*Beauty and the Beast.* Margolin, D., Shaw, P., and Weaver, L.

*Beauty Beauty.* Gingold, H.

*Beauty Part, The.* Perelman, S.

*Beauty Queen of Leenane, The.* McDonagh, M.

*Beaux gestes et beautiful deeds. See* Hammond, M. Beautiful Deeds/De beau gestes

*Les beaux jours. See* Beckett, S. Happy Days

*Beaux' Stratagem, The.* Farquhar, G.

*Beaver Coat, The.* Hauptmann, G.

*Becket.* Tennyson, A.

*Becket; or, the Honor of God.* Anouilh, J.

*Becket; ou, L'honneur de Dieu. See* Anouilh, J. Becket

*Becky Sharp.* Mitchell, L.

*Bed and Bored.* Vittachchi, N.

*Bedbug, The.* Mayakóvsky, V.

*Bedroom Farce.* Ayckbourn, A.

*Bedtime.* Gallagher, M.

*Bedtime Stories.* Kolpak, D.

*Bedtime Story.* O'Casey, S.

*Before and behind the Curtain. See* Taylor, T. and Reade, C. Masks and Faces

*Before Breakfast.* O'Neill, E.

*Before It Hits Home.* West, C.

*Before the Dawn-wind Rises.* Chan, J.

*Before the Guns.* Palmer, J.

*Before the Party.* Ackland, R.

*Before the Sunset.* Das, J.

*Before the Throne. See* Dowling, J. and Letton, F. The Young Elizabeth

*Die Befreiung. See* Lask, B. Liberation

*Beggar, The.* Sorge, R.

*Beggar on Horseback.* Kaufman, G. and Connelly, M.

*Beggars' Bush.* Fletcher, J., Massinger, P. [and Beaumont, F.]

*Beggar's Opera, The.* Gay, J. *See also* Brecht, B. and Hauptmann, E. The Threepenny Opera

*Begum Barve.* Alekar, S.

*Behind the Curtain of the Soul. See* Evreinov, N. The Theatre of the Soul

*Behind the Mirror.* Gremina, E.

*Behold the Bridegroom.* Kelly, G.

*Behold We Live.* Van Druten, J.

*Being at Home with Claude.* Dubois, R.

*Belgrade Trilogy.* Srbljanovic, B.

*Bell, Book, and Candle.* Van Druten, J.

*Bell for Adano, A.* Osborn, P.

*Bell Tolls at Twelve, The.* Unger, H.

*Bellavita.* Pirandello, L.

*Belle.* Gibson, F.

*Belle Lamar.* Boucicault, D.

*Belle reprieve.* Bourne, B., and Shaw, P., and Shaw, P., and Weaver, W.

*La belle Russe.* Belasco, D.

*La belle sauvage. See* Barker, J. The Indian Princess

*Belle's stratagem, The.* Cowley, Mrs. H.

*Les belles-soeurs.* Tremblay, M.

*Below the Belt.* Dresser, R.

*Bells, The.* Lewis, L.

*Belshazzar.* Milman, H.

*Belshazzar.* More, H.

*Belshazzar's Feast.* Calderón de la Barca, P.

*Benedetta Carlini.* Rowe, R.

*Beneath Four Eyes. See* Fulda, L. Tête-à-tête

*Benediktbeuren Play, The.* Anonymous Plays

*Benefactors.* Frayn, M.

*Ben-Hur.* Young, W.

*Benito Cereno.* Lowell, R.

*Benjamin Franklin, Journeyman.* Mackay, C.

*Benkei Aboard Ship.* Nobumitsu, K.

*Benkei on the Bridge.* Hiyoshi, S.

*Bent.* Sherman, M.

*Benten the Thief.* Kawatake, M.

*Benya the King.* Schotter, R.

*Bérénice.* Racine, J.

*Beritten hin und zurück. See* Grass, G. Rocking Back and Forth

*Berkeley Square.* Balderston, J.

*Bermondsey.* Mortimer, J.

*Bernabé.* Valdez, L.

*Bernardine.* Chase, M.

*Bernard's Story.* Lam, D.

*Bertha, the Sewing Machine Girl, or Death at the Wheel.* Foster, C.

*Bertram; or, the Castle of St. Aldobrand.* Maturin, C.

*Beside Every Good Man.* Taylor, R.

*Besos de lobo. See* Pedrero, P. Wolf Kisses

*Best Little Whorehouse in Texas, The.* King, L. and Masterson, P.

*Best Man, The.* Vidal, G.

*Best of All Possible Worlds, The.* Ballesteros, A.

*Besuch der alten dame, Der. See* Duerrenmatt, F. The Visit

*La Bete.* Hirson, D.

*Betrayal.* Pinter, H.

*Betrayal, The. See* Anonymous Plays. The Betraying of Christ (N Town)

*Betrayal, The.* Gareau, L.

*Betrayal, The.* Pickering, K., Wood, K., and Dart, P.

*Betrayal, The. (Wakefield).* Anonymous Plays

*Betrayal of Christ, The. (Chester).* Anonymous Plays

*Betraying of Christ, The. (Coventry).* Anonymous Plays

*Betrothal, The.* Rodríguez Suárez, R.

*Better Looking Boys.* Trochim, D.

*Die Bettler. See* Sorge, R. The Beggar

*Betty the Yeti.* Klein, J.

*Between Blessings.* Feliciano, G.

*Les bonnes. See* Gênet, J. The Maids
*Booby Prize, The.* Quintero, H.
*Book of Days.* Wilson, L.
*Book of Job, The. See* Anonymous Plays. Job
*Bookseller Cannot Sleep, The.* Olsen, E.
*Boom, Baby, Boom!* Rubess, B.
*Boor, The.* Chekhov, A.
*Boot and Spurre.* Anonymous Plays
*Bopha.* Mtwa, P.
*Border.* Wray, E.
*Borderers, The.* Wordsworth, W.
*Borderlands.* McGuinness, F.
*Boris Godunov.* Pushkin, A.
*Born in the R.S.A.* Simon, B.
*Born with the Fire on His Head.* Ijimere, O.
*Born Yesterday.* Kanin, G.
*Borstal Boy.* Behan, B. *See* McMahon, F. Brendan Behan's
    Borstal Boy
*Die bösen Köche. See* Grass, G. The Wicked Cooks
*Bōshibari.* Anonymous Plays.
*Boss, The.* Sheldon, E.
*Botanica.* Prida, D.
*Both Ends Meet.* Macrae, A.
*Both Your Houses.* Anderson, M.
*Botticelli.* McNally, T.
*Bottom.* Stoka Theatre, The.
*Boubouroche.* Courteline, G.
*Boubouroche, or She Dupes to Conquer. See* Courteline,
    G. Boubouroche
*Bouddha van Ceylon, The. See* Boer, L. The Buddha of
    Ceylon
*Les Boulingrin. See* Courteline, G. These Cornfields
*Bound East for Cardiff.* O'Neill, E.
*Les bourgeois de qualité. See* Dancourt, F. Woman's Craze
    for Titles
*Le bourgeois gentilhomme.* Molière, J.
*Bourgeois Gentleman, The. See* Molière, J. Le bourgeouis
    gentilhomme
*Boursiquot. See* Boucicault, D. The Colleen Bawn
*Bousille and the Just.* Gélinas, G.
*Bousille et les justes See* Gélinas, G. Bousille and the Just
*Bowl of Beings, A.* Culture Clash
*Box, The.* Owens, D.
*Box, The.* Rosen, S.
*Box and Cox.* Morton, J.
*Boxes.* Yankowitz, S.
*Boxing for One.* Ronild, P.
*Boxing for One Person. See* Ronild, P. Boxing for One
*Boxle. See* Kobrin, L. Yankel Boyla
*Boxleh. See* Kobrin, L. Yankel Boyla
*Box-lobby Challenge, The.* Cumberland, R.
*Boxing for En Person. See* Ronild, P. Boxing for One
*Boy Comes Home, The.* Milne, A.
*Boy Friend, The.* Wilson, S.
*Boy in the Basement, The.* Inge, W.

*Boy Meets Boy.* Solly, B. and Ward, D.
*Boy Meets Girl.* Spewack, B. and Spewack, S.
*Boy on a Straight-Back Chair. See* Tavel, R. Boy on the
    Straight-back Chair
*Boy on the Straight-back Chair.* Tavel, R.
*Boy with a Cart, The.* Fry, C.
*Boys in the Band, The.* Crowley, M.
*Boys Mean Business.* Johnson, C.
*Bra Sizes.* Tan, T.
*Braganza.* Jephson, R.
*Braggart Captain, The. See* Plautus, T. Miles gloriosus
*Braggart Soldier, The. See* Plautus, T. Miles gloriosus
*Braggart Warrior, The. See* Plautus, T. Miles gloriosus
*Braindead.* Innuinuit Theatre Company and Nalujuk
    Players.
*Der brand in opernhaus. See* Kaiser, G. The Fire in the
    Opera House
*Brass Butterfly, The.* Golding, W.
*Brave Girl, A.* Curran, C.
*Brave Hearts.* Rintoul, H.
*Brave Irishman, The; or, Captain O'Blunder.* Sheridan, T.
*Brave Smiles . . . Another Lesbian Tragedy.* Five Lesbian
    Brothers, The.
*Bread.* Kirshon, V.
*Bread and Butter.* Taylor, C.
*Bread and Rise or Geometry in Yellow.* Bellido, J.
*Breadwinner, The.* Maugham, W.
*Breakfast in Bed. See* Feydeau, G. Keep an Eye on Amelié
*Breakfast Past Noon.* Molinaro, U.
*Breakfast with Bridy.* West, D.
*Breaking Glass.* Roberts, D.
*Breaking Point. See* Denker, H. and Berkey, R. Time
    Limit!
*Breaking Through.* Lee, C.
*Breakout, The.* Gordone, C.
*Breaks.* Gingras, R.
*Breasts of Tiresias, The.* Kostrowisky, G.
*Breathless.* De Angelis, A.
*Bremen Coffee.* Fassbinder, R.
*Bremen Town Musicians, The. See* Feldshuh, D. Fables
    Here and Then
*Bremer freibeit. See* Fassbinder, R. Bremen Coffee
*Brendan Behan's Borstol Boy.* McMahon, F.
*Brian's Song.* Blinn, W.
*Bridal Chamber, The.* Quiles, E.
*Bride and the Broom, The.* Ndjavera, D.
*Bride Comes to Yellow Sky, The.* Agee, J.
*Bride of the Isles. See* Planché, J. The Vampire
*Bride of the Lamb, The.* Hurlbut, W.
*Bridegroom (from Limoges), The.* Anonymous
*Brides, The.* Kondoleon, H.
*Brides of Garryowen, The. See* Boucicault, D. The Colleen
    Bawn
*Bridge, The.* Fratti, M.
*Bridge across the Sea.* Kulvet, I.

*Crimes and Crimes. See* Strindberg, A. There Are Crimes and Crimes

*Crimes of the Heart.* Henley, B.

*Criminal Code, The.* Flavin, M.

*Criminals, The.* Triana, A.

*Crispin médecin.* Hauteroehe, N. *See* Ravenscroft, E. and Motteux, P. The Anatomist

*Crispin, rival de son maître. See* Le Sage, A. Crispin rival of His Master

*Crispin, Rival of His Master.* Le Sage, A.

*Critic, The; or, a Tragedy Rehearsed.* Sheridan, R.

*Critique of the School for Wives, The.* Molière, J.

*Crock of Gold, The. See* Plautus. Aulularia

*Crock of Gold, The; or, The Toiler's Trials.* Steele, S.

*Cromedeyre-le-vieil.* Romains, J.

*Cross Country.* Miller, S.

*Cross-dressing in the Depression.* Wilson, E.

*Crossfire.* Compton, J.

*Crossing.* De Wet, R.

*Crossroads, The.* Efoui, J.

*Crossroads: A Sad Vaudeville.* Solórzano, C.

*Crown Matrimonial.* Ryton, R.

*Crown of Light, The.* Bulkley, A.

*Crowne for a Conquerour, A.* Davenport, R.

*Crows, The. See* Becque, H. Les corbeaux

*Croxton Play of the Sacrament. See* Anonymous Plays. The Play of the Sacrament (Croxton)

*Crucible, The.* Miller, A.

*Crucifixion (Wakefield). See* Anonymous Plays. The Crucifixion (Wakefield)

*Crucifixion, The.* Pickering, K., Wood, K., and Dart, P.

*Crucifixion, The (Chester). See* Anonymous Plays. Christ's Passion (Chester)

*Crucifixion, The.* Schreyer, L.

*Crucifixion, The (Wakefield).* Anonymous Plays

*Crucifixion, The (York).* Anonymous Plays

*Crucifixion of a Wooden Statue. See* Yamazaki, M. At Play with a Lion

*Crucifixion of Christ. See* Anonymous Plays. The Crucifixion (York)

*Crude and Unrefined.* Bowen, M.

*Cruel Fate. See* Pisemskii, A. A Bitter Fate

*'Cruiter.* Matheus, J.

*Cruma.* Pedrolo, M. de

*Crunching Numbers.* Macy, L.

*Crusade of the Children, The.* Morris, E.

*Crushed by the Credenza. See* Gałczyński, K. The Drama of a Deceived Husband

*Crux.* De Angelis, A.

*Cry from the City of Virgins, A.* Kara, J.

*Cry in the Street.* Lauckner, R.

*Crying Holy.* Corbitt, W.

*Cryptogram, The.* Mamet, D.

*Crystal Spider, The.* Rachilde.

*Csendélet.* Molnár, F.

*Csirkefei. See* Spiró, G. Chicken Head

*Cuando florezean las rosales. See* Marquina, E. When the Roses Bloom Again

*Cuarteto.* Rovner, E.

*Las cuatro apariciones de Guadalupe/The Four Apparitions of Guadalupe.* Anonymous Plays

*Cuban Swimmer, The.* Sanchez-Scott, M.

*Cubistique.* Cone, T.

*Cuckoo Sings Again.* Yang, L.

*Cuentos.* Morton, C., and Vigil, A.

*La cueva de Salamanca. See* Cervantes Saavedra, M. The Cave of Salamanca

*Cult of Boredom, The. See* Pailleron, E. Le monde où l'on s'ennuie

*Cunning Man, The.* Burney, C.

*Cupid's Banishment.* White, R.

*Cupid's Rival. See* Porto-Riche, G. Amoureuse

*¡Curanderas! Serpents of the Clouds.* Romero, E.

*Curculio.* Plautus, T.

*Cure for Jealousy, A. See* Popple, W. The Double Deceit

*Un curioso accidente.* Goldoni, C.

*Curious Mishap, A. See* Goldini, C. Un curioso accidente

*Curious Misunderstanding, A. See* Goldoni, C. Un curioso accidente

*Curiosity.* Caldor, M.

*Curl Up and Dye.* Pam-Grant, S.

*Curse of the Starving Class.* Shepard, S.

*Curtain Call, Mr. Aldridge, Sir.* Davis, O.

*Curtains.* Bill, S.

*Curve, The.* Dorst, T.

*Custer, or Whoever Heard of Fred Benteen?* Ingham, R.

*Custom of the Manor, The. See* Johnson, C. Country Lasses

*Customs.* Moore, M.

*Cut!* Albert, L.

*Cut, The.* Cullen, M.

*Cut It Out.* Ruppe, J.

*Cutter of Colman-street.* Cowley, A.

*Cuttlefish, The.* Witkiewicz, S.

*Le cuvier. See* Anonymous Plays. The Washtub

*Cyber:\womb.* Laxdal, V.

*Cyclone Jack.* Bolt, C.

*Cyclops, The.* Euripides

*Cymbeline.* Shakespeare, W.

*Cymon (altered from).* Garrick, D.

*Cynara.* Harwood, H. and Gore-Browne, R.

*Cyrano de Bergerac.* Rostand, E.

*Cyrus.* Hoole, J.

*"Da."* Leonard, H.

*'da kink in my hair: voices of black womyn.* Anthony, T.

*Daddies.* Gower, D.

*Daddy.* Moore, P.

*Daddy Says.* Shange, N.

*Daddy's Seashore Blues.* Foreman, F.

*Dagobert, der Franken könig. See* Babo, J. Dagobert, King of the Franks

*Dagobert, King of the Franks.* Babo, J.

*Daisy, The. See* Molnár, F. Liliom

*Daisy Mayme.* Kelly, G.

*Dalagang bukid.* Ilagan, H. *See also* Ilagan, H. The Barrio Maiden

*Dallot.* Anonymous Plays

*Dalusapi.* Palafox. F.

*Damask Cheek, The.* Van Druten, J. and Morris, L.

*Damask Drum, The.* Zeami.

*La dame aux camélias.* Dumas, A., fils

*Damien. See* Lavery, E. and Murphy, G. Kamiano, the Story of Damien

*Damon and Pithias.* Edwards, R.

*Dampu.* Anonymous Plays

*Dance and the Railroad, The.* Hwang, D.

*Dance like a Butterfly.* Ravel, A.

*Dance of Angels Who Burn Their Own Wings, The.* Satoh, M., Yamamoto, K., Katō, T., and Saitō, R.

*Dance of Death, The. See* Anonymous Plays. Totentanz

*Dance of Death, The.* Strindberg, A.

*Dance of the Wandering Souls.* Huynh, Q.

*Dance with Me.* Reynolds, J.

*Dancers, The.* Foote, H.

*Dancing at Lughnasa.* Friel, B.

*Dancing Girl, The.* Jones, H.

*Dancing in the Mirror.* Clum, J.

*Dancing Mothers.* Selwyn, E. and Goulding, E.

*Dancing with a Devil.* Berman, B.

*Dandy Dolls, The.* Fitzmaurice, G.

*Dangerous Corner.* Priestley, J.

*Dangerous Precaution, The.* Kuzmin, M.

*Daniel.* More, H.

*Dan'l Druce.* Gilbert, W.

*Daniel Ludus. See* Anonymous Plays. The Play of Daniel (from *Beauvais*)

*Daniel Webster Eighteen in America.* Stein, G.

*Daniela.* Guimerá, A.

*Danites in the Sierras, The.* Miller, J. [pseudonym]

*Dans les fonds. See* Gorki, M. [pseudonym] The Lower Depths

*Danse Calinda, The.* Torrence, F.

*Danti-Dan.* Moxley, G.

*Danton's Death.* Büchner, G.

*Dantons tod. See* Büchner, G. Danton's Death

*Danube, The.* Fornés, M.

*Dar sahel. See* Yalfani, M. On the Shore

*Darby's Return.* Dunlap, W.

*Dark at the Top of the Stairs, The.* Inge, W.

*Dark Cowgirls and Prairie Queens.* Parris-Bailey, L.

*dark diaspora . . . in dub.* mandiela, a.

*Dark Fruit.* Pomo Afro Homos.

*Dark Heart.* Lillford, D.

*Dark Is Light Enough, The.* Fry, C.

*Dark of the Moon.* Richardson, H. and Berney, W.

*Dark Rapture.* Overmyer, E.

*Dark Ride.* Jenkin, L.

*Dark Tower. The.* Macneice, L.

*Darker Brother.* Seiler, C.

*Darkness.* Čašule, K.

*Darkness.* Balalin Company of Jerusalem, The.

*Darkness at Noon.* Kingsley, S.

*Darkside.* Jones, K.

*Darling Family, The.* Griffiths, L.

*Darling of the Gods, The.* Belasco, D. and Long, J.

*Dasvedanya Mama.* Eichelberger, E.

*Daughter of Earth.* Sargent, L.

*Daughter of Jorio. The.* Annunzio, G. d'

*Daughter of Madame Angot, The.* Lecocq, A.

*Daughter of the Gods, The.* Ka, A.

*Daughters.* Vik, B.

*Daughters of Atreus.* Turney, R.

*Daughters of the Mock.* Mason, J.

*Dave.* Gregory, I.

*David and Bathshua.* Cayzer, C.

*David and Bethsabe.* Peele, G.

*David and Broccoli.* Mortimer, J.

*David and Goliath.* More, H.

*David's Redhaired Death.* Kramer, S.

*Davy Crockett; or, Be Sure You're Right, Then Go Ahead.* Murdoch, F.

*Dawn.* Urista, A.

*Dawn, The.* Verhaeren, E.

*Day after the Fair, The.* Harvey, F.

*Day by the Sea, A.* Hunter, N.

*Day in the Death of Joe Egg, A.* Nichols, P.

*Day in the Vineyard, A.* Baker, E., and Drummond, A.

*Day of Absence.* Ward, D.

*Day of the Swallows, The.* Portillo, E.

*Day Roosevelt Died, The.* Pritchard, B.

*Day Standing on Its Head.* Gotanda, P.

*Day the Lions Got Loose, The. See* Carballido, E. The Day They Let the Lions Loose

*Day They Kidnapped Blanche, The.* Pugh, A., and Dacus, K.

*Day They Let the Lions Loose, The.* Carballido, E.

*Days of Cavafy.* Killingworth, G.

*Days of the Turbins.* Bulgakov, M.

*Days on a Cloud.* Abell, K.

*Daytrips.* Carson, J.

*La de San Quintín.* Péréz Galdós, B.

*De si tendres liens. See* Bellon, L. Bonds of Affection

*Dea by Dea.* Bontempelli, M.

*Deacon's Awakening, The.* Richardson, W.

*Dead Are Free, The.* Kreymborg, A.

*Dead City, The.* Annunzio, G. d'

*Dead Dad Dog.* McKay, J.

*Dead End.* Kingsley, S.

*Dead Father, The.* Parra, M.

*Dead Fish. See* Gems, P. Dusa, Fish, Stas and Vi

*Demon of Switzerland, The.* Milner, H.

*Denandresbröd. See* Fridell, F. One Man's Bread

*Dennis and Rex. See* Kelley, S. Hope of the Future

*Dentist, The.* Scala, F.

*Department of Forestry. See* Duras, M. The Rivers and Forests

*Deporting the Divas.* Reyes, G.

*Depositio cornuti typographici. See* Anonymous Plays. The Printer's Apprentice

*Deputy, The.* Hochhuth, R.

*Los derechos de la salud.* Sánchez, F.

*La dernière bande. See* Beckett, S. Krapp's Last Tape

*La dernière nuit de Don Juan. See* Rostand, E. The Last Night of Don Juan

*Describe Your Work.* Palacios, M.

*Desdemona.* Vogel, P.

*El desdén con el desdén.* Moreto y Cabaña, A.

*Deserted Crone, The.* Seami, M.

*Deserter, The.* Dibdin, C.

*Desig. See* Benet i Jornet, J. Desire

*Design for a Headstone.* Byrne, S.

*Design for Living.* Coward, N.

*Le désir attrapé par la queue.* See Picasso, P. Desire Trapped by the Tail

*Desire.* Benet i Jornet, J.

*Desire to Kill on the Tip of the Tongue, A.* Durringer, X.

*Desire Trapped by the Tail.* Picasso, P.

*Desire under the Elms.* O'Neill, E.

*Despedida de soltera.* Magtoto, L.

*Desperate Hours, The.* Hayes, J.

*Los desposorios de Joseph. See* Anonymous Plays. Joseph's Wedding

*Destinies of Haman and Mordecai, The. See* Tyler, R. The Origin of the Feast of Purim; or, the Destinies of Haman and Mordecai

*Destiny of Me, The.* Kramer, L.

*Destruction of Jerusalem, The.* Anonymous Plays

*Destruction of Jerusalem, The.* Crowne, J.

*Destruction of Soccer in the City of K., The.* Horák, K.

*Detective Story.* Kingsley, S.

*Detour, The.* Davis, O.

*Detour, The.* Landovsky, P.

*Deuce Is in Him, The.* Colman, G.

*Les deux gendres.* Etienne, C. *See* Payne, J. The Two Sons-in-law

*Deux orphelines, Les. See* D'Ennery, A. and Cormon, E. The Two Orphans

*Developments.* Rifbjerg, K.

*Deviations.* Matas, J.

*Devil and Daniel Webster, The.* Benét, S.

*Devil and His Dame, The. See* Anonymous Plays. Grim the Collier of Croydon

*Devil and Otis Redding, The. See* Caldwell, B. The King of Soul

*Devil Is an Ass, The.* Jonson, B.

*Devil Mas'.* Brown, L.

*Devil of a Wife.* Jevon, T. *See* Jevon, T.; Coffey, C.; Mottley, J.; Cibber, T. The Devil to Pay

*Devil Passes, The.* Levy, B.

*Devil to Pay, The; or, the Wives Metamorphos'd.* Jevon, T.; Coffay, C.; Mottley, J. and Cibber, T.

*Devils, The.* Whiting, J.

*Devil's Disciple, The.* Shaw, G.

*Devil's Elixir, The.* Fitz-Ball, E.

*Devil's General, The.* Zuckmayer, C.

*Devil's Instrument, The.* Mitchell, W.

*Devourer of dreams, The. See* Lenormand, H. The Dream Doctor

*Devynbedžiai. See* Saja, K. The Village of Nine Woes

*El día que se soltaron los leones. See* Carballido, E. The Day They Let the Lions Loose

*Dial-a-Mom.* Raznovich, D.

*Dial "M" for Murder.* Knott, F.

*Dialect Determinism.* Bullins, E.

*Dialogo de Poeta y Maximo. See* Matas, J. Dialogue of the Poet and the Supreme Leader

*Dialogue and Ode, A.* Hopkinson, F.

*Dialogue between a Southern Delegate, and His Spouse, on His Return from the Grand Continental Congress, A.* Anonymous Plays

*Dialogue between an Englishman and an Indian, A.* Smith, J.

*Dialogue between Don Melón Ortiz and Doña Endrina. See* Ruiz, J. The Gallant, the Bawd, and the Fair Lady

*Dialogue of the Poet and the Supreme Leader.* Matas, J.

*Dialogues.* Lasica, M., and Satinský, J.

*Diamond Cut Diamond.* Murray, W.

*Diamond Cut Diamond.* Williamson, H.

*Diana of Dobson's.* Hamilton, C.

*Diary of a Madwoman.* Ping, C.

*Diary of a Scoundrel, The.* Ostrovskii, A.

*Diary of a Young Girl. See* Goodrich, F. and Hackett, A. The Diary of Anne Frank

*Diary of Anne Frank, The.* Goodrich, F. and Hackett, A.

*Dicha y desdicha del juego y devoción de la Virgen.* Azevedo, A.

*Dickon.* Pinner, D.

*Did You Ever Send Your Wife to Camberwell?* Coyne, J.

*Did You Move? See* Stroman, S., and Weidman, J. Contact

*Didon se sacrifiant.* Jodelle, E.

*Difference of Opinion.* Ross, G. and Singer, C.

*Difficult Hour, I–III, The.* Lagerkvist, P.

*Difficult People.* Bar-Yosef, Y.

*Diff'rent.* O'Neill, E.

*Digby Conversion of St. Paul. See* Anonymous Plays. The Conversion of St. Paul (Digby)

*Digby Killing of the Children. See* Anonymous Plays. Herod's Killing of the Children

*Digby Mary Magdalene. See* Anonymous Plays. Mary Magdalene (Digby)

*Digby Plays. See* Anonymous Plays. Christ's Burial and Resurrection; The Conversion of St. Paul; Herod's Killing of the Children; Mary Magdalene; A Morality of Wisdom, Who Is Christ

*Digging for Fire.* Hughes, D.

*Digging in: the Farm Crisis in Kentucky.* Crutcher, J., and McBride, V.

*Le diner des têtes. See* Anouilh, J. Poor Bitos

*Ding Dong Bell. See* Campbell, M. and Athas, D. Sit on the Earth

*Dining Room, The.* Gurney, A.

*Dinner about a City.* Kerata, L.

*Dinner at Eight.* Kaufman, G. and Ferber, E.

*Dinner with Friends.* Margulies, D.

*Dinny and the Witches.* Gibson, W.

*Dino.* Rose, R.

*Dinosaur.* Hopkins, G. and Lindberg, W.

*Dirty Hands. See* Sartre, J. Les mains sales

*Dirty Laundry.* Tan, T.

*Disco Pigs.* Walsh, E.

*Discovery, The.* Sheridan, Mrs. F.

*Disenchanted, The.* Schulberg, B.

*Disposal, The.* Inge, W.

*Disraeli.* Parker, L.

*Disrobing the Bride. See* Kondoleon, H. The Brides

*Dissident, The.* Sam, C.

*Dissident, Goes without Saying. See* Vinaver, M. Chamber Theatre

*Dissident, il va sans dire. See* Vinaver, M. Chamber Theatre

*Distaff Side, The.* Van Druten, J.

*Distant Point. See* Afinogenyev, A. Far taiga

*Distracted Emperor, The.* Anonymous Plays

*Distress upon Distress.* Stevens, G.

*Distressed Mother.* Phillips, A.

*District of Columbia.* Richards, S.

*Disznójáték. See* Czakó, G. Pigs

*Ditch.* Kavanagh, G.

*Diver, The.* Komparu, G., and Zeami.

*Divines palabras. See* Valle-Inclán, R. Divine Words

*Divine Comedy.* Dodson, O.

*Divine Dream.* Xenopoulos, G.

*Divine Fallacy, The.* Howe, T.

*Divine Words.* Valle-Inclán, R.

*Diviners, The.* Leonard, J.

*Division Street, USA. See* Terkel, L. Monologues from "Division Street, USA"

*Divorce.* Daly, A.

*Divorcio nupcial.* Eichelbaum, S.

*Divorçons. See* Sardou, V. and Najae, E. Let's Get a Divorce

*Diwan al-Zanj. See* Madani, `I. Tne Zanj Revolution

*Dno. See* Stoka Theatre, The. Bottom

*Do Not Pass Go.* Nolte, C.

*Do Something with Yourself! The Life of Charlotte Bronte.* Manning, L.

*Do You Smell Gas?* Urtusástegui, T.

*La doble historia del doctor Valmy. See* Buero Vallejo, A. Two sides to Dr. Valmy's Story

*Doc.* Pollock, S.

*Dock Brief, The.* Mortimer, J.

*Em docktor Fogel sic offis schtunn.* Birmelin, J.

*Le docteur amoureux.* Anonymous Plays

*Doctor and the Devils, The.* Thomas, D.

*Doctor and the Patient, The. See* Quiñones de Benevente, L. El doctor y el enfermo

*Doctor Faustus. See* Marlowe, C. The Tragical History of Doctor Faustus

*Doctor in Spite of Himself, The.* Molière, J.

*Dr. Kheal.* Fornés, M.

*Dr. Knoek.* Romains, J.

*Dr. Korczak and the Children.* Sylvanus, E.

*Dr. Kranich's sprechstunde. See* Anonymous Plays. Em Doctor Fogel sei offis schtunn (based on book by John Birmelin)

*El doctor y el enfermo.* Quiñones de Benevente, L.

*Doctor's Daughter, The. See* Goetz, R. and Goetz, A. The Heiress

*Doctor's Delight. See* Molière, J. La malade imaginaire

*Doctor's Dilemma, The.* Shaw, G.

*Doctors of Philosophy.* Spark, M.

*Dodo.* Sirois, S.

*Dodo l'enfant do. See* Sirois, S. Dodo

*Den dödsdömde. See* Dagerman, S. The Condemned

*Dodsworth.* Howard, S.

*Dog and Wolf.* Fischerova, D.

*Dog beneath the Skin, The.* Auden, W. and Isherwood, C.

*Dog in the Manger, The.* Vega Carpio, L.

*Dog Opera.* Congdon, C.

*Dogs, The.* O'Kelly, D.

*Dogs of War, The.* Watson, M.

*Les doigts de fée.* Sedbe, A.

*Dois perdidos numa note suja.* Marcos, P. See also Marcos, P. Two Lost in a Filthy Night

*Dōjōji.* Anonymous Plays

*Dojōji.* Kwanze, K. N.

*Doll House, A. See* Ibsen, H. Doll's House, A.

*Dollar Woman, The.* Nowlan, A., and Learning, W.

*Doll's House, A.* Ibsen, H.

*Dolls.* Khan, H.

*Dolly Reforming Herself.* Jones, H.

*Dolly West's Kitchen.* McGuinness, F.

*Dolor solatio.* "Scribble, S."

*Dom Juan, ou le festin de Pierre. See* Molière, J. Don Juan

*Dom, kde sa to robí dobre. See* Cicvák, M. Frankie Is Ok, Peggy Is Fine and the House Is Cool!

*Il domatore Gastone. See* Morselli, E. Gastone the Animal Trainer

*Domestic Picture, A.* Ostrovskii, A.

*Dominant Sex, The.* Egan, M.

*Dominion of Darkness, The. See* Tolstoi, L. The Power of Darkness

*Domino Courts.* Hauptman, W.

*Don Alvaro; ó la fuerza del sino.* Rivas, A.

*Don Carlos.* Schiller, J.

*Don Giovanni. See* Ponte, L. Da. The Punished Libertine

*Don John; or, the Libertine. See* Molière, J. Don Juan

*Don Juan.* Molière, J.

*Don Juan; or, the Stone Guest. See* Molière, J. Don Juan

*Don Juan. See also* Rostand, E. The Last Night of Don Juan

*Don Juan and Don Pietro; or, the Dead Stone's Banquet.* Anonymous Plays

*Don Juan and Faust.* Grabbe, C.

*Don Juan in Hell.* Shaw, G.

*Don Juan Tenorio.* Zorrilla y Moral, J.

*Don Juan und Faust. See* Grabbe, C. Don Juan and Faust

*Don Sebastian, King of Portugal.* Dryden, J.

*Don Juan's Final Night. See* Rostand, E. The Last Night of Don Juan

*Don Juan's Last Night. See* Rostand E. The Last Night of Don Juan

*Doña Clarines.* Alvarez Quintero, S. and Alvarez Quintero, J.

*Donalds O'Rourk.* O'Connell, L.

*La donation. See* Petitclair, P. The Donation

*Donation, The.* Petitclair, P.

*Donkey Market, The.* Al-Hakim, T.

*Donna Diana. See* Moreto y Cavañia A. El desdén con el desdén

*Donnellys, The.* Colley, P.

*Donnellys, The. See* Reaney, J. Handcuffs (part three of the Donnellys)

*Don't Blame the Bedouins.* Dubois, R.

*Don't Let Summer Come.* Feely, T.

*Don't Listen, Ladies!* Guitry, S.

*Don't You Want to Be Free.* Hughes, L.

*Doomsday (N Town).* Anonymous Plays

*Doomsday Circus. See* Basshe, E. The Dream of the Dollar

*Doomsday Show, The.* MacBeth, G. and Bingham, J.

*Door.* Hassan, N.

*Door Should Be either Open or Shut, A.* Musset, A. de

*Dorf's Yung. See* Kobrin, L. Yankel Boyla

*Los dos habladores.* Cervantes Saavedra, M.

*Dos lesbos.* Baum, T., and Myers, C.

*Dossier: Ronald Akkerman.* Lohuizen, S.

*Dot.* Boucicault, D.

*Døtre. See* Vik, B. Daughters

*Double Dealer, The.* Congreve, W.

*Double Deceit, The; or, a Cure for Jealousy.* Popple, W.

*Double Discovery, The. See* Dryden, J. The Spanish Fryer

*Double Doctor, The: A Farce.* McCutcheon, G.

*Double Dutch Act, The.* Anonymous Plays

*Double Gallant, The.* Cibber, C.

*Double Gothic.* Kirby, M.

*Double Wop, The. See* Anonymous Plays

*Double Yolk.* Williams, H. and Williams, M.

*Doubles.* Wiltse, D.

*Doubles according to Plautus, The.* Anonymous Plays

*Doubting Thomas (Chester).* Anonymous Plays

*Doughgirls, The.* Fields, J.

*Douglas.* Home, J.

*Dove, The.* Barnes, D.

*Dover Road, The.* Milne, A.

*Down and Out. See* Gorki, M. [pseudonym] The Lower Depths

*Down by the River Where Water Lilies Are Disfigured Every Day.* Bovasso, J.

*Down for the Weekend.* Moher, F.

*Down Our Street.* Wise, E.

*Down onto Blue.* Boyd, P.

*Downfall of Robert, Earle of Huntington, The.* Munday, A.

*Downside, The.* Dresser, R.

*Downtown.* Alfaro, L.

*De draad in het donker. See* Haasse, H. A Thread in the Dark

*Dracula.* Deane, H. and Warburton, H.

*Dracula.* Nolte, C.

*Dragon, The.* Gregory, I.

*Dragon, The.* Schwartz, Y.

*Dragon Beard Ditch.* Lao, S.

*Dragon Lady's Revenge, The.* San Francisco Mime Troupe

*Dragon of Wantley, The.* Carey, H.

*Dragon's Mouth.* Priestley, J. and Hawkes, J.

*Un drama nuevo.* Tamayo y Baus, M.

*Drama of a Deceived Husband, The; or, Crushed by the Credenza.* Gałczyński, K.

*Dramatic Circle, The.* Kennedy, A.

*Dramatic Sequel to Hamlet, A; or, the New Wing at Elsinor.* "Mr. Punch" [pseudonym]

*Dramatic Sequel to the Lady of Lyons, A; or, In the Lyons Den.* "Mr. Punch" [pseudonym]

*Dramatist, The or, Stop Him Who Can!* Reynolds, F.

*Drapes Come, The.* Dizenzo, C.

*Draussen vor der Tür. See* Borchert, W. The Outsider

*Dream Comedy.* Valle-Inclán, R.

*Dream Doctor, The.* Lenormand, H.

*Dream Girl.* Rice, E.

*Dream of Canaries, A.* Sáenz, D.

*Dream of Kitamura, The.* Gotanda, P.

*Dream of Pilate's Wife, The (York).* Anonymous Plays

*Dream of Scipio, The.* Metastasio, P.

*Dream of the Dollar, The.* Basshe, E.

*Dream of Vāsavadatta, The.* Bhāsa

*Dream on Monkey Mountain.* Wolcott, D.

*Dream Play, A.* Strindberg, A.

*Dream-town.* Reeves, M. *See* Bovell, A., Cornelius, P., Reeves, M., Tsiolkas, C., and Vela, I. Who's Afraid of the Working Class?

_Dream Weaver, The._ Buero Vallejo, A.
_Dreamers, The._ Davis, J.
_Dreaming and Dueling._ Lazarus, J., and Lazarus, J.
_Dreaming of the Bones, The._ Yeats, W.
_Dreams of Anne Frank._ Kops, B.
_Dreamy Kid, The._ O'Neill, E.
_Dreigroschenoper. See_ Brecht, B. The Threepenny Opera
_Dress Suits to Hire._ Hughes, H.
_Dressed like an Egg; Taken from the Writings of Colette._ Akalaitis, J.
_Dresser, The._ Harwood, R.
_Dressing Room: That Which Flows Away Ultimately Becomes Nostalgia, The._ Shimizu, K.
_Drifting Apart._ Herne, J.
_Drinking Gourd, The._ Hansberry, L.
_Drinking in America._ Bogosian, E.
_Drive Angry._ Pelfrey, M.
_Drive-in._ Kranes, D.
_Driving around the House._ Smith, P.
_Driving Miss Daisy._ Uhry, A.
_Un drôle de cadeau. See_ Bouchaud, J. A Birthday Present for Stalin
_Ett drömspel. See_ Strindberg, A. The Dream Play
_Dronning gaar igen. See_ Abell, K. The Queen on Tour
_Dronningen og hennes menn. See_ Kielland, T. Queen Margaret of Norway
_Die droom (The Dream)._ Rispel, K.
_Drovers, The._ Esson, L.
_Drug, The._ Bart-Williams, G.
_Drum-maker, The._ Hippolyte, K.
_Drum Song._ Ringwood, G.
_De drumleraar. See_ Sierens, A. Drummers
_Drummer, The._ Addison, J.
_Drummer, The._ Fugard, A.
_Drummers._ Sierens, A.
_Drums of Oude. The._ Strong. A.
_Drums of Snow, The._ Pinner, D.
_Drunkard, The._ Smith, W.
_Dry August, The._ Sebree, C.
_Dry Lips Oughta Move to Kapuskasing._ Highway, T.
_Dry River Bed, The._ Spark, M.
_Dry Summer._ Cumah, N.
_Duchess at Sunset, The._ Johnson, P.
_Duchess of Malfi, The._ Webster, J.
_Duchess of San Quentin, The. See_ Pérez Galdós, B. La de San Quintín
_Duel of Angels._ Giraudoux, J.
_Duenna, The._ Sheridan, R.
_Dúfnaveizlan. See_ Laxness, H. The Pigeon Banquet
_Duk Moraud._ Anonymous Plays
_Duke and No Duke, A; or, Trapolin's Vagaries._ Tate, N.
_Duke and the Actress, The. See_ Schnitzler, A. The Green Cockatoo
_Duke's Motto, The; or, I Am Here!_ Brougham, J.
_Et dukkehjem. See_ Ibsen, H. A Doll's House

_Dulcitius._ Hrotsvit
_Dulcy._ Kaufman, G. and Connelly, M.
_Dumb Beauty, The._ Schlegel, J.
_Dumb Waiter, The._ Pinter, H.
_Dupe, The._ Ancey, G. [pseudonym]
_Duplicity._ Holcroft, T.
_Durham Prologue, The._ Anonymous Plays
_Dusa, Fish, Stas and Vi._ Gems, P.
_Dust in the Eyes. See_ Labiche, E. and Martin, E. La poudre aux yeux Dust of the Road. Goodman, K.
_Dust of the Road._ Goodman, K.
_Dutch Courtesan, The._ Marston, J.
_Dutchman._ Jones, L.
_Duty Master, The._ Donnelly, N.
_Dwarf Trees, The._ Seami, M.
_Dybbuk, The._ Rappoport, S.
_Dylan._ Michaels, S.
_Dyskolos. See_ Menander. The Grouch
_Dziady, Part III. See_ Mickiewicz, A. Forefathers Eve, Part III

_Each His Own Wilderness._ Lessing, D.
_Each in His Own Way._ Pirandello, L.
_Earl of Essex, The._ Corneille, T.
_Earl of Essex, The._ Jones, H.
_Early Snow._ Zembō, M.
_Ears of Midas, The._ Dilmen, G.
_Earth and Stars._ Edmonds, R.
_Earth-spirit, The. See_ Wedekind, F. Erdgeist
_Earth Worms._ Innaurato, A.
_Easiest Way, The._ Walter, E.
_East from the Gantry._ Thomas, E.
_East Lynne._ Oxenford, J.
_East Lynne._ Palmer, T.
_East Lynne._ Wood, H.
_Easter Resurrection Play, An._ Anonymous Plays
_Easter Verses of the Three Maries._ Anonymous Plays
_Eastern Fable, An._ Bobrick, S. See Anonymous Plays. Twenty-four Hours: P.M.
_Eastern Standard._ Greenberg, R.
_Eastward Ho!_ Chapman, G., Jonson, B. and Marston, J.
_Eastward Hoe. See_ Chapman, G., Jonson, B. and Marston, J. Eastward Ho!
_Eastward in Eden._ Gardner, D.
_Easy Virtue._ Coward, N.
_Eat._ Veldhuisen, M.
_Eating Crow._ Labiche, E.
_Les eaux et forets. See_ Duras, M. The rivers and forêts.
_Eb refschneider un Susi Leimbach._ Wollenweber, L.
_Eboshi-ori. See_ Miyamasu. The Hatmaker
_Ecclesiazusae._ Aristophanes
_Echo in the Bone, An._ Scott, D.
_L'école de maris._ Molière, J.
_L'école des femmes._ Molière, J.
_L'école des pères. See_ Anouilh, J. Cecile

*Féroce comme le coeur. See* Bonal, D. Beware the Heart
*Ferrex and Porrex. See* Sackville, T. and Norton, T. Gorboduc
*Festa de Elche. See* Anonymous Plays. The Mystery Play of Elche
*Festival of Peace, The. See* Hauptmann, G. Des friedensfest
*Festival for the Fish.* Yū, M.
*Feu la mère de Madame. See* Feydeau, G. My Wife's Dead Mother
*Die feuerprobe. See* Kleist, H. Kaethchen of Heilbronn
*Fez, The.* Wellman, M.
*Fickle Finger of Lady Death, The.* Rodríguez Solís, E.
*Ficky Stingers.* Lewis, E.
*Fiddler on the Roof.* Stein, J.
*Il fido amico. See* Scala, F. The Faithful Friend
*Field God, The.* Green, P.
*Field Marshal Kutuzov.* Solovev, V.
*Field of the Cloth of Gold, The.* Brough, W.
*Fiend of Fleet Street, The. See* Pitt, G. The String of Pearls
*Fierce Love.* Pomo Afro Homos
*La fiesta del mulato. See* Hernández, L. Mullato's Orgy
*Fifteen Strings of Cash.* Anonymous Plays
*Fifteen Years of a Drunkard's Life.* Jerrold, D.
*Fifth of July, The.* Wilson, L.
*Fifth Status Quo Comedy, The. See* Anonymous Plays. The Status Quo Comedies
*Fight for Shelton Bar.* Cheeseman, P., et. al.
*Fighter, The.* Eisenstein, M.
*Fighting Days, The.* Lill, W.
*La figlia di Jorio. See* Annunzio, G. d'. The Daughter of Jorio
*Fill the Stage with Happy Hours.* Wood, C.
*La fille de Madame Angot. See* Lecocq, A. The Daughter of Madame Angot
*La fille des dieux. See* Ka, A. The Daughter of the Gods
*Les filles du 5—10—15. See* Farhoud, A. The Girls from the Five and Ten
*Film Society, The.* Baitz, J.
*Filumena Marturano.* Filippo, E.
*El fin de Chipí González. See* Rivarola Matto, J. The Fate of Chipí González
*Fin de partie. See* Beckett, S. Endgame
*Final Innocence.* Flisar, E.
*Final Judgment, The.* Anonymous Plays
*Financier, The. See* Le Sage, A. Turcaret
*Find Hakamadare!* Fukuda, Y.
*Find Me.* Wymark, O.
*Find Your Way Home.* Hopkins, J.
*Finders-keepers.* Kelly, G.
*Finders Keepers Losers Weepers.* Haakskeen, P.
*Fingernails Blue as Flowers.* Ribman, R.
*Finian's Rainbow.* Harburg, E.
*Finishing Touches.* Kerr, J.
*Fiorello!* Weidman, J. and Abbott, G.

*Fire and Night.* Rainis, J.
*Fire in the Basement.* Kohout, P.
*Fire in the Killing Zone.* Mueller, L.
*Fire in the Lake.* Alrawi, K.
*Fire in the Opera House, The.* Kaiser, G.
*Fire Raisers, The. See* Frisch, M. Biedermann and the Firebugs
*Fire, Water, Earth, and Air. See* Dibdin, T. Harlequin in His Element
*Fire's Daughters.* Césaire, I.
*Firebrand, The.* Mayer, E.
*Firebugs, The. See* Frisch, M. Biedermann and the Firebugs
*Fireflies.* Toshirō, S.
*Fires in the Mirror.* Smith, A.D.
*Fires of St. John, The.* Sudermann, H.
*La firmeza en la auscencia.* Cueva y Silva, L.
*First and Last Love. See* Payne, J. The Spanish Husband
*First Blood.* Monkhouse, A.
*First Born, The.* Powers, F.
*First Breeze of Summer, The.* Lee, L.
*First Class.* Tirado, C.
*First Communion.* Arrabal, F.
*First Gentleman, The.* Ginsbury, N.
*First House of Beijing Duck, The.* He, J.
*First Lady.* Dayton, K. and Kaufman, G.
*First Militant Minister, The. See* Caldwell, B. Prayer Meeting
*First Mrs. Fraser, The.* Ervine, St. J.
*First Monday in October.* Lawrence, J. and Lee, R.
*First Note of Spring, The.* Takeda, I., Miyoshi, S., and Namiki, S.
*First One, The.* Hurston, Z.
*First Part of the Reign of King Richard the Second; or, Thomas of Woodstock, The. See* Anonymous Plays. Woodstock
*First Part of the Return from Parnassus, The. See* Anonymous Plays. The Return from Parnassus
*First President, The.* Williams, W.
*First Shepherds' Play (Wakefield). See* Anonymous Plays. The First Shepherds' Play (Wakefield)
*First Shepherds' Play, The (Wakefield).* Anonymous Plays
*First Sin, The.* Megged, A.
*First Status Quo Comedy, The. See* Anonymous Plays. The Status Quo Comedies
*First Year, The.* Craven, F.
*Fisherman and the Sea King's Daughter, The. See* Feldshuh, D. Fables Here and Then
*Fishermen, The.* Houston, D.
*Fishermen's Child, The. See* Herne, J. Drifting Apart
*Fitting Confusion, A.* Feydeau, G.
*Five Easy Payments.* Lewin, J.
*Five Finger Exercise.* Shaffer, P.
*Five Fingers on the Black Hand Side.* Russell, C.

*Forest Rose, The.* Woodworth, S.
*Forever.* Guerrero, W.
*Forever Yours, Julita.* Ramos-Perea, R.
*Forfeit, The.* Howell, C.
*Forge Master, The. See* Ohnet, G. The Iron Manufacturer
*Forget Herostratus!* Gorin, G.
*Forget Him.* Fierstein, H.
*Forgiveness. See* Lemaître, J. The Pardon
*Formation Dancers.* Marcus, F.
*Forthcoming Wedding.* Angel, L.
*Fortitude.* Vonnegut, K.
*Fortress in the Sky.* De Zoysa, L.
*Fortunate Isles, and Their Union.* Jonson, B.
*Fortune and Men's Eyes.* Herbert, J.
*Fortunello.* Petrolini, E.
*Fortunes and Death of King Ottokar, The. See* Grillparzer, F. König Ottokars glück und ende
*Fortune's Fool.* Reynolds, F.
*Fortunio and His Seven Gifted Servants.* Planché, J.
*Forty Carats.* Allen, J.
*Forty Lounge Café, The.* Lyssiotis, T.
*Forty Minute Finish.* Hairston, J.
*49.* Geiogamah, H.
*Forty-niners, The.* Hanshew, T.
*42nd Street.* Stewart, M. and Bramble, M.
*Forward One.* Prichard, K.
*La forza del destino. See* Rivas, A. Don Alvaro
*Fosse.* Maltby, R., Walker, C, and Reinking, A.
*Fossils, The.* Curel, F. de
*Fotodeath.* Oldenburg, C .
*Foundation, The.* Buero Vallejo, A.
*Foundling, The.* Moore, E.
*The Four Apparitions of Guadalupe. See* Anonymous Plays. Las cuatro apariciones de Guadalupe/The Four Apparitions of Guadalupe.
*Four Boxes.* Beyza'i, B.
*Four Elements, The. See* Anonymous Plays. The Nature of the Four Elements
*Four in the Morning.* Brown, D. *See* Anonymous Plays. Twenty-four Hours: A.M.
*Four Men.* Davis, A.
*Four p's, The. See* Heywood, J. The Four pp
*Four Seasons, The.* Wesker, A.
*Four Temperaments, The: A Comedy in Ten Tableaux.* Aksenov, V.
*Four to Four.* Garneau, M.
*Les fourberies de Scapin. See* Molière, J. Scapin
*Four-legged Fortune, A. See* Boucicault, D. Flying Scud
*FourPlay.* Belbel, S.
*Fourposter, The.* Hartog, J. de
*Fourth Commandment, The. See* Anzengruber, L. Das vierte gebot
*Fourth Room, The.* Reid, B.
*Fourth Status Quo Comedy, The. See* Anonymous Plays. The Status Quo Comedies

*Fourth Wall, The.* Evreinov, N.
*Fox, The.* Miller, A.
*Fox, The. See* Jonson, B. Volpone
*Fox, Hound and Huntress.* Lee, L.
*Foxed.* McPhee, F.
*Foxfire; a Play with Songs in Two Acts.* Cooper, S. and Cronyn, H.
*Die frage an das schicksal. See* Schnitzler, A. Questioning the Irrevocable
*Fragment de théâtre I. See* Beckett, S. Rough for Theatre I
*Fragments from a Work in Progress. See* Neilson, K. The End of the World
*Frances and Francis.* Webber, J.
*Francesca da Rimini.* Annunzio, G. d'
*Francesca da Rimini.* Boker, G.
*Francis' New Jig. See* Anonymous Plays. Attowell's Jig
*Francis the First.* Kemble, F.
*Françoise' Luck.* Porto-Riche, G.
*Frank Pig Says Hell.* McCabe, P.
*Frankenstein, or, the Demon of Switzerland. See* Milner, H. Frankenstein, or, the Man and the Monster
*Frankenstein, or, the Man and the Monster.* Milner, H.
*Frankie and Johnny in the Clair de Lune.* McNally, T.
*Frankie Is Ok, Peggy Is Fine, and the House Is Cool!* Cicvák, M.
*Fred and Harold.* Patrick, R.
*Freddie the Pigeon.* Leichman, S.
*Free's Point.* Adams, P.
*Freedom for Clemens.* Dorst, T.
*Freedom for Clement. See* Dorst, T. Freedom for Clemens
*Freedom of Jean Guichet, The.* Mackay, L.
*Freedomland.* Freed, A.
*Freiheit für Clemens. See* Dorst, T. Freedom for Clemens
*Fremdes haus. See* Loher, D. Stranger's House
*French Gray.* Bush, J.
*French without a Master. See* Bernard, T. L'anglais tel qu'on le parle
*French without Tears.* Rattigan, T.
*Friar Bacon and Friar Bungay. See* Greene, R. The Honorable History of Friar Bacon and Friar Bungay
*Frida K.* Montero, G.
*Frida: The Story of Frida Kahlo.* Cruz, M., and Blecher, H.
*Friedemann Puntigam or the Delicate Art of Losing One's Memory.* Szyszkowitz, G.
*Das friedensfest.* Hauptmann, G.
*Friendly Delusion, A. See* Turgenev, I. Luncheon with the Marshal of Nobility, or a Friendly Delusion
*Friendly Fire.* Queer Street Youth
*Friends.* Abe, K.
*Friends.* Dickens, C.
*Friends Too Numerous to Mention.* Cohen, N., and Cohen, J.
*Frightful Effects of an Illegal Operation, The. See* Gałczyński, K. In the Clutches of Caffeine
*El frigorifico. See* Quiles, E. The Refrigerator

*Frijoles, or Beans to You.* San Francisco Mime Troupe
*Frock and Thrills. See* Scribe, A. Les doigts de fée
*Frog Prince, The.* Mamet, D.
*Frogs, The.* Aristophanes
*Fröken Julie. See* Strindberg, A. Miss Julia
*Frolic Wind.* Pryce, R.
*From Morn to Midnight.* Kaiser, G.
*From Morning to Midnight. See* Kaiser, G. From Morn to
    Midnight
*From Rags to Riches.* Taylor, C.
*From Sunset to Sunrise.* Verma, S.
*From the Depths. See* Gorki, M. [pseudonym] The Lower
    Depths
*Front, The.* Korneichuk, A.
*Front Door Steps.* Hooke, N.
*Front Page, The.* Hecht, B. and MacArthur, C.
*Front Room Boys, The.* Buzo, A.
*La frontière de Savoie. See* Scribe, E. and Bayard, J.F.A. A
    Peculiar Position
*Frozen Wages.* San Francisco Mime Troupe
*Fruen fra havet. See* Ibsen, H. The Lady from the Sea
*Frühlingserwachen. See* Wedekind, F. Spring's Awakening
*Fuchsia.* Astor del Valle, J.
*Fuente ovejuna.* Vega Carpio, L.
*La fuerza del sino. See* Rivas, A. Don Alvaro
*Fugitive, The.* Reynolds, F.
*Fugitive King, The.* Paul, C.
*Fugue.* Thuna, L.
*Fugue in a nursery. See* Fierstein, H. Torch Song Trilogy
*Fugues pour un cheval et un piano. See* Dupuis, H. Return
    of the Young Hippolytus
*Führer, befiehl! See* Schwaiger, B. Yes, My Führer!
*Fukurō yamabushi. See* Anonymous Plays. Owls
*Fulgens and Lucrece. See* Medwall, H. Fulgens and
    Lucres
*Fulgens and Lucres.* Medwall, H.
*Full Bloom.* Bradbeer, S.
*Full Circle.* Pedrolo, M.
*Full Moon in March, A.* Yeats, W.
*Fulling Block, The.* Zeami.
*Fumed Oak.* Coward, N.
*Fun after Supper.* Smith, B.
*Funa benkei. See* Kanze, K. Benkei Aboard Ship
*Funabashi. See* Zeami. The Boat Bridge
*Funabenkai. See* Kanze, K. Benkei Aboard Ship
*Function, The.* Besset, J.
*La function. See* Besset, J. The Function
*La Fundación. See* Buero Vallejo, A. The Foundation
*Funeral, The.* Buenaventura, E.
*Funeral, The, or, Grief a la mode.* Steele, R.
*Funky-grace, A.* Redmond, E.
*Funny Thing Happened on the Way to the Forum, A.*
    Shevelove, B. and Gelbart, L.
*Funny Thing Happened on the Way to the Wedding, A
    (Casina). See* Plautus. Casina

*Funnyhouse of a Negro.* Kennedy, A.
*Fur.* Cruz, M.
*Furcht und Elend des Dritten Reiches. See* Brecht, B. The
    Private Life of the Master Race
*Furies, The. See* Aeschylus. Eumenides
*Furies of Mother Jones, The.* Klein, M.
*Furious.* Gow, M.
*Futari daimyō. See* Anonymous Plays. Two daimyō
*Futari no onna. See* Kara, J. Two Women
*Futari Shizuka (The Two Shizukas).* Zeami
*Future Pit, The.* McKillop, M.
*Futz.* Owens, R.

*La gabbia. See* Fratti, M. The Cage
*Gabriel.* Mason, C.
*Gabrielle.* Upisasik Theatre of Rossignol School
*Gakuya. See* Shimizu, K. The Dressing Room: That Which
    Flows Away Ultimately Becomes Nostalgia
*Galateau. See* Gilbert, W. and Sullivan, A. Pygmalion and
    Galatea
*Galenpannan. See* Forssell, L. The Madcap
*Galgamannen; en midvintersaga. See* Schildt, R. The
    Gallows Man
*Galileo.* Brecht, B.
*Gallant, the Bawd, and the Fair Lady, The.* Ruiz, J.
*Gallathea.* Lyly, J.
*Galley Slave, The.* Campbell, B.
*Gallows Humor.* Richardson, J.
*Gallows Man, The: A Midwinter Story.* Schildt, R.
*Galtra-Loftur. See* Sigurjónsson, J. The Wish
*Gamblers.* Gogol, N.
*Gambler's Fate, The. See* Dunlap W. Thirty Years
*Game at Chess, A.* Middleton, T.
*Game of Dice, The. See* Brook, P., and Carriere, J. The
    Mahabharata
*Game of Folly vs. Wisdom, The.* Theotokas, G.
*Game of Love, The.* Okonkwo, R.
*Game of Love, The. See* Schnitzler, A. Light-o'-love
*Game of Love and Chance, The. See* Marivaux, P. Le jeu
    de l'amour et du hazard
*Game of Patience.* Farhoud, A.
*Game of Speculation, The.* Lewes, G.
*Gamecock, The.* Livings, H.
*Games.* Klíma, I.
*Gamester, The.* Moore, E.
*Gamester, The. See* Shirley, J. Gamesters
*Gamesters.* Shirley, J.
*Gammer Gurton's Nedle. See* Stevenson, W. Gammer
    Gurton's Needle
*Gammer Gurton's Needle.* Stevenson, W.
*Gangsters.* Maponya, M.
*Gaol Gate, The.* Gregory, I.
*Gap, The.* Ionesco, E.
*Garage Sale.* Ringwood, G.
*Le garçon et l'aveugle.* Anonymous Plays

*Los heroes inútiles. See* Schmidhuber de la Mora, G. The Useless Heroes
*Heroic Years. See* Halper, L. Hirsh Lekert
*Hero's Welcome, A.* Pinnock, W.
*Herr Gottlieb Merks. See* Kotzebue, A. Egotist and Pseudo critic
*Herr Puntila und sein knecht matti. See* Brecht, B. Puntila and His Hired Man
*Herr Sleeman kommer. See* Bergman, J. Mr. Sleeman Is Coming
*Herren og hans tjenere. See* Kielland, A. The Lord and His Servants
*Herringbone.* Cone, T.
*He's Much to Blame.* Anomymous Plays
*Hessian Christmas Play, The.* Anonymous Plays
*Heteroclitanomalonomia.* Anonymous Plays
*"Hey, Cut Out the Parading around Stark Naked!"* Feydeau, G.
*Hey, Listen . . .* Simon, B.
*Hey You, Light Man!* Hailey, O.
*Hiblang abo. See* Villanueva, R. Strands of Gray
*Hickscorner.* Anonymous Plays
*Hidden Charges.* Riordan, A.
*Hieronimo Is Mad Again. See* Kyd, T. The Spanish Tragedy
*Higaki.* Zeami.
*High-brow, The. See* Molière, J. Les précieuses ridicules
*High Life below Stairs.* Garrick, D.
*High Life below Stairs.* Townley, J.
*High Tor.* Anderson, M.
*High Water.* Darke, N.
*Highest Standard of Living.* Reddin, K.
*La hija de Rappacini. See* Paz, O. Rappacini's Daughter
*Hiketides. See* Aeschylus. The Suppliants; Euripides. The Suppliants
*Hill-land.* Voaden, H.
*Hill, The.* Mda, Z.
*him.* cummings, e. e.
*Die himbeere pflücker. See* Hochwälder, F. The Raspberry Picker
*Himuro.* Miyamasu.
*Hindle Wakes.* Houghton, D.
*Hinemi.* Miyazawa, A.
*Hinkelmann.* Toller, E.
*Hiob. See* Kokoschka, O. Job
*Hippolytus.* Euripides
*Hippolytus.* Howe, J.
*Hiro.* Uyehara, D.
*Hiroshima, mon amour.* Duras, M.
*Hirsh Lekert, or, Heroic Years.* Halper, L.
*His First Step.* OyamO
*His Widow's Husband.* Benavente y Martínez, J.
*L'histoire de Tobie et de Sara. See* Claudel, P. Tobias and Sara
*Histoire de Vasco. See* Schehadé, G. Vasco

*L'histoire du cirque. See* Salacrou, A. A Circus Story
*Historia.* Janaczewska, N.
*Historical Register for Year 1736, The.* Fielding, H.
*Histories of Lot and Abraham, The. See* Anonymous Plays. Abraham, Melchisedec and Isaac
*History of George Barnwell, The. See* Lillo, G. The London Merchant
*History of Jacob and Esau, The. See* Anonymous Plays. Jacob and Esau
*History of King Lear, The.* Tate, N.
*History of Vasco, The. See* Schéhadé, G. Vasco
*Hit by a Cab.* Lappin, T.
*Hitachibō Kaison. See* Akimoto, M. Kaison the Priest of Hitachi
*Hitch-hiker.* Dillon, E.
*Hitch Hiker, The.* Fletcher, L.
*Hitlers barndom. See* Rådström, N. Hitler's Childhood
*Hitler's Childhood.* Rådström, N.
*Hive, The.* Sejavka, S.
*Hoarse Muse.* Campbell, P.
*Hob; or, the Country Wake.* Doggett, T.
*Hob in the Well. See* Dogget, T. Hob
*Hoboken Blues; or, the Black Rip Van Winkle.* Gold, M.
*Hobson's Choice.* Brighouse, H.
*Die hochzeit der Sobeide. See* Hofmannsthal, H. von. The Marriage of Sobeide
*Hodina mezi psem a vlkem. See* Fischerova, D. Dog and Wolf
*Die hoffning.* Brendle, T.
*Hogan's Goat.* Alfred, W.
*Hōka Priests, The.* Zenchiku, U.
*Hokti.* Arkeketa, A.
*Hole in the Wall.* Kreymborg, A.
*Holiday.* Barry, P.
*Holy Days.* Nemeth, S.
*Holy Mothers.* Schwab, W.
*Holly and the Ivy, The.* Browne, W.
*Holy Experiment, The. See* Hochwalder, F. The Strong Are Lonely
*Holy Ghostly, The.* Shepard, S.
*Holy Resurrection, The. See* Anonymous Plays. La seinte Resureccion
*Homage of the Arts, The.* Schiller, J.
*El hombre de mundo.* Vega, V.
*El hombre del siglo. See* Frank, M. The Man of the Century
*El hombre deshabitado.* Alberti, R.
*El hombre y la mosca. See* Ruibal, J. The Man and the Fly
*Home. See* Maeterlinck, M. Interior; Sudermann, H. Magda
*Home.* Storey, D.
*Home.* Tan, T. H.
*Home.* Williams, S.
*Home at Seven.* Sherriff, R.
*Home Free.* Alexander, R.
*Home of the Brave.* Laurents, A.

*Home on the Range.* Baraka, A.
*Homecoming.* Skrywer-Afrikaner, M.
*Homecoming, The.* Pinter, H.
*Homecoming: An Alaskan Native's Quest for Self-esteem.* Weiser, J.
*Homicidio Calificado. See* Rascon Banda, V. Murder with Malice (The Case of Santos Rodríguez)
*L'homme et ses fantômes.* Lenormand, H.
*L'homme gris. See* Laberge, M. Night
*Een hond begraven. See* Woudstra, K. Burying the Dog
*Honest Whore, The.* Dekker, T. and Middleton, T.
*Honeymoon.* Barylli, G.
*Honeymoon.* Sa'edi, G.
*Honeymoon, The.* Tobin, J.
*Honeymoon in Haiti.* Kleb, W.
*Hongi.* Mason, B.
*Honigmond. See* Barylli, G. Honeymoon
*L'honneur de Dieu. See* Anouilh, J. Becket
*Honor of God, The. See* Anouilh, J. Becket
*Honorable Entertainment Given to the Queen's Majesty in Progress, at Elvetham in Hampshire, The.* Anonymous Plays
*Honorable History of Friar Bacon and Friar Bungay. The.* Greene, R.
*Honorable Mrs. Ling's Conversion, The.* Brown, J.
*Hōōchō no Hininhō. See* Iijima, S., and Suzuki, Y. Rhythm Method
*Hooligans.* Vingoe, M., and Kudelka, J.
*Hope Deferred.* Davies, R.
*Hope for a Harvest.* Treadwell, S.
*Hope of the Future.* Kelley, S.
*Hope Slide, The.* MacLeod, J.
*Hoppla! See* Toller, E. Hoppla! Such Is Life!
*Hoppla! Such Is Life!* Toller. E.
*Hoppla, wir leben. See* Toller, E. Hoppla! Such Is Life!
*Horace.* Corneille, P.
*Horatia.* Aretino, P.
*Horestes.* Pikeryng, J.
*Horizon.* Daly, A.
*Horizon Is Calling, The.* Bricks Theatre Group, and Molapong, K.
*Horn of Sorrow.* Ellenbogen, N.
*Horse, The.* Hay, J.
*Horse Country.* Hopkins, C.
*Horse-shoe Robinson.* Tayleure, C.
*Horse Thief, The.* Sachs, H.
*Hosanna.* Tremblay, M.
*Die hose. See* Sternheim, C. The Underpants
*Hōshigahaha.* Gen'e
*Hospice.* Cleage, P.
*Hospital.* Attinello, P. *See* Anonymous Plays. The AIDS Show
*Hoss Drawin'.* Martell, L.
*Hostage, The.* Behan, B.
*Hostages.* Akritas, L.

*Hostile Witness.* Roffey, J.
*Hot 'n' Throbbing.* Vogel, P.
*Hot Stuff.* Spence, E.
*Hot L Baltimore, The.* Wilson, L.
*Hotel, The. See* Hoyt, C. A Bunch of Keys
*Hotel on Marvin Gardens, A.* Jackson, N.
*Hotel Universe.* Barry, P.
*Hotel Universe.* San Francisco Mime Troupe
*Hotoke no hara.* Seami
*Hour of the Dog, The.* Dorall, E.
*Hourglass, The.* Alexander, R.
*Hour-glass, The.* Yeats, W.
*House.* Mitchell, N.
*House, The.* Borgen, J.
*House by the Lake, The.* Mills, H.
*House in the Quiet Glen, The.* Coulter, J.
*House in the Square, A.* Morgan, D.
*House of Atreus, The (Trilogy). See* Aeschylus. Agamemnon; Choephoroe; Eumenides
*House of Bernarda Alba, The.* García Lorca, F.
*House of Bernarda Alba, The.* Mann, E.
*House of Blue Leaves, The.* Guare, J.
*House of Connelly, The.* Green, P.
*House of Cowards.* Abse, D.
*House of Ramon Iglesia, The.* Rivera, J.
*House of Sacred Cows.* Visawanathan, P.
*House of Sham, The.* Richardson, W.
*House of Sugawara, The.* Takeda, I.; Miyoshi, S.; and Namiki, S.
*House on Hermitage Road, The.* Mclean, D.
*Houseboy.* Oyono, F.
*Household Peace, The.* Maupassant, G. de
*Houseparty.* Britton, K. and Hargraves, R.
*How Do You Do.* Bullins, E.
*How Does Your Garden Grow?* McNeil, J.
*How Else Am I Supposed to Know I'm Still Alive.* Fernandez, E.
*How He Lied to Her Husband.* Shaw, G.
*How I Got that Story.* Gray, A.
*How I Learned to Drive.* Vogel, P.
*How the Blessed Saint Helen Found the Holy Cross.* Anonymous Plays
*How the Snake Lost His Voice. See* Feldshuh, D. Fables Here and Then
*How to Grow Rich.* Reynolds, F.
*How the Vote Was Won.* Hamilton, C., and St. John, C.
*How to Settle Accounts with Your Laundress.* Coyne, J.
*How to Succeed in Business without Really Trying.* Burrows, A., Weinstock, J. and Gilbert, W.
*How's the World Treating You?* Milner, R.
*Howya Doin' Freaky Banana?* Spiro, P.
*Hu tieh meng. See* Anonymous Plays. The Butterfly Dream
*Hua yu jian. See* Ma, S. Flower and Sword
*Huan hun chi. See* T'ang, H. Peony Pavilion

*Last Meeting of the Knights of the White Magnolia, The.* Jones, P.

*Last Mile, The.* Wexley, J.

*Last Moon, The.* Fanetti, E.

*Last Night of Ballyhoo, The.* Uhry, A.

*Last Night of Don Juan, The.* Rostand, E.

*Last of Ala, The.* Ibe, S.

*Last of Mrs. Cheyney, The.* Lonsdale, F.

*Last of My Solid Gold Watches, The.* Williams, T.

*Last of the De Mullins, The.* Hankin, St. J.

*Last of the Marx Brothers' Writers.* Phillips, L.

*Last of the Reapers, The.* Kai, N.

*Last of the Red Hot Lovers.* Simon, N.

*Last of the Turbins. See* Bulgakov, M. Days of the Turbins

*Last of the Wampanoags, The. See* Stone, J. Metamora

*Last Orbit of Billy Mars, The.* Alexander, R.

*Last Refuge, The.* Gardiner, W.

*Last Romantic, The.* Crabbe, K.

*Last Summer at Bluefish Cove.* Chambers, J.

*Last Supper, The.* Pickering, K., Wood, K., and Dart, P.

*Last Supper, The (Chester).* Anonymous Plays

*The Last Supper; The Conspiracy with Judas. See* Anonymous Plays. Passion I (N Town)

*Last Time We Saw Her, The.* Anderson, J.

*Last to Go.* Pinter, H.

*Last Tournament, The.* Prevelakis. P.

*Last Train to Nibroc.* Hutton, A.

*Låt människan leva. See* Lagerkvist. P. Let Man Live

*Late Blumer, The.* Lazarus, J.

*Late Bus to Mecca.* Cleage, P.

*Late Christopher Bean, The.* Fauchois, R.

*Late Edwina Black, The.* Dinner, W. and Morum, W.

*Late George Apley, The.* Marquand, J. and Kaufman, G.

*Late Snow, A.* Chambers, J.

*Later Life.* Gurney, A.

*Latent Heterosexual, The.* Chayefsky, P.

*Later Story of Rama, The.* Bhavabhūti

*Latin Lezbo Comic.* Palacios, M.

*Latina.* Sanchez-Scott, M., and Blahnik, J.

*Laugh When You Can.* Reynolds, F.

*Laughing Wild.* Durang, C.

*Laundromat.* Puccioni, M.

*Laundry, The.* Guerdon, D.

*Laundry and Bourbon.* McLure, J.

*Laughing Woman, The.* MacKintosh, E.

*Laughter and Hubbub in the House.* Kay, K.

*Laughter on the 23rd Floor.* Simon, N.

*Laura Secord, the Heroine of 1812.* Curzon, S.

*Law.* Rahbar, M.

*Law, The.* Pickering, K., Wood, K., and Dart, P.

*Law and Order.* Wuolijoki, H.

*Law of Life, The.* Rodriguez, B

*Law of Lombardy, The.* Jephson, R.

*Lawd, Does You Undahstan'?* Link, A.

*Lay down by Me.* Bunch, J.

*Layman Selfsame.* Anonymous Plays

*Lázaro en el laberinto. See* Buero Vallejo, A. Lazarus in the Labyrinth

*Lazarus (Wakefield).* Anonymous Plays

*Lazarus in the Labyrinth.* Buero Vallejo, A.

*Lazarus Laughed.* O'Neill, E.

*Lazybed.* Smith, I.

*Leader, The.* Ionesco, E.

*Leader, The.* White, J.

*Leaf People, The.* Reardon, D.

*Leah Kleschna.* McLellan, C.

*Leak in the Universe, A.* Richards, I.

*Lean and Hungry Priest, A.* Kliewer, W.

*Lear's Daughters.* The Women's Theatre Group and Feinstein, E.

*Learning to Live with Personal Growth.* Milner, A.

*Leave It to Beaver Is Dead.* McAnuff, D.

*Leave It to Me!* Spewack, B., and Spewack, S.

*Leave Taking.* Pinnock, W.

*Leaving Home.* French, D.

*Das Leben des Galilei. See* Brecht, B. Galileo

*Lebendige stunden.* Schnitzler, A.

*La leçon. See* Ionesco, E. The Lesson

*Leçon d'anatomie. See* Tremblay, L. Anatomy Lesson

*Leedvermaak. See* Herzberg, J. The Wedding Party

*Left Bank, The.* Rice, E.

*Legal Status of Illinois Women in 1868, The. See* McCulloch, C. Bridget's Sisters; or, the Legal Status of Illinois Women in 1868

*Le légataire universel.* Regnard, J.

*The Legend of King O'Malley.* Boddy, M. and Ellis, B.

*Legend of Lovers. See* Anouilh, J. Eurydice

*Legend of Mermaids, A.* Chong, W.

*Legend of Noon, The.* Betsuyaku, M.

*Legend of old Bawdy Town, The.* Ma, Z.

*Legend of the Piper.* Teixidor, J.

*Legend of the Rood, The (Cornish).* Anonymous Plays

*Legend of Wagadu: As Seen by Sia Yataere, The.* Diagana, M.

*Leibelei. See* Schnitzler, A. Light-o'-love

*Leicestershire St. George Play.* Anonymous Plays

*Lei-yü. See* Ts'ao, Y. Thunderstorm

*Lela Mayang.* Das, K.

*Lemon Sky.* Wilson, L.

*Lemons in the Morning.* Zindel, B., and Zindel, P. *See* Anonymous Plays. Twenty-four Hours: A.M.

*La lena. See* Ariosto, L. Lena

*Lena.* Ariosto, L.

*Lend Me a Tenor.* Ludwig, K.

*Lennon Play: In His Own Write, The.* Kennedy, A. and Lennon, J.

*Lenten Puddings. See* Pintauro, J. Wild Blue

*Leo Armenius.* Gryphius, A.

*Leonce and Lena.* Büchner, G.

*Leonce und Lena. See* Büchner, G. Leonice and Lena

*Madman on the Roof.* Kan, K.
*Madness of George III, The.* Bennett, A.
*Madness of Heracles, The. See* Euripides. Heracles
*Madness of Lady Bright.* Wilson, L.
*Madonna of the Wilderness.* Koller, K.
*Madras House, The.* Granville-Barker, H.
*Madwoman and the Fool: A Harlem Duet, The.* Sears, D.
*Madwoman of Chaillot, The.* Giraudoux, J.
*Maedchen in Uniform. See* Winsloe, C. Children in Uniform
*Maeve.* Martyn, E.
*Magda.* Sudermann, H.
*Maggie Magalita.* Kesselman, W.
*Magi, The. See* Anonymous Plays. The Magi, Herod, and the Slaughter of the Innocents (N Town)
*Magi and Innocents (Chester). See* Anonymous Plays. The Magi's Oblation (Chester); The Slaying of the Innocents (Chester)
*Magi, Herod, and the Slaughter of the Innocents, The (Coventry).* Anonymous Plays
*Magi, Herod, and the Slaughter of the Innocents, The (N Town).* Anonymous Plays.
*Magic and the Loss, The.* Funt, J.
*Magic Aster.* Jen, T.
*Magic Glasses, The.* Fitzmaurice, G.
*Magic Kingdom, The.* Felder, L.
*Magic Realists, The.* Terry, M.
*Magic Rouge. See* Ghelderode, M. Red Magic
*Magic Show of Dr. Ma-Gico, The.* Bernard, K.
*Magic Threads.* Morgan, S.
*Mágico prodigioso, El. See* Calderón de la Barca, P. The Wonder-working Magician
*Magi's Oblation, The (Chester).* Anonymous Plays
*Magistrate, The.* Pinero, A.
*Magistrates, The.* Fath'Ali, A.
*Magnet, The. See* Garner, H. Three Women
*Magnificent Entertainment, The.* Dekker, T.
*Magnificent Yankee, The.* Lavery, E.
*Magnus Herodes (Wakefield).* Anonymous Plays
*Magnyfycence.* Skelton, J.
*Magpie.* Brennan, K.
*Magpie and the Maid, The. See* Payne, J. Trial without Jury
*Magpie on the Gallows. The.* Ghelderode, M.
*Mah-e asal. See* Sa'edi, G. Honeymoon
*Mahabharata, The.* Brook, P., and Carriere, J.
*Mahamayi. See* Kambar, C. The Mother Supreme
*Mahapoor.* Alekar, S.
*Mahomet.* Miller, J.
*Mahomet.* Voltaire, F.
*Mai-guruma.* Miyamasu.
*Mai jekketti (My Jacket).* Job, N.
*Mai yan-zhi. See* Anonymous Plays. Buying Rouge
*Maid of Athens.* Rambo, D. *See* Ackermann, J. Back Story: A Dramatic Anthology
*Maid of Honor, The.* Massinger, P.

*Maid of the Mill.* Bickerstaffe, I.
*Maid to Marry.* Ionesco, E.
*Maid Who Wouldn't Be Proper, The.* Mick, H.
*Maiden at Dōjōji, A.* Anonymous Plays
*Maiden on the Seashore, The.* Kõvamees, R.
*Maiden's Tragedy, The.* Middleton, T.
*Maids, The.* Genêt, J.
*Maid's Tragedy, The.* Beaumont, F. and Fletcher, J.
*Maija and Paija.* Brigadere, A.
*Maija of Chaggaland.* Langeberg, S.
*Maija un Paija. See* Brigadere, A. Maija and Paija
*Main line, The; or, Rawson's Y.* De Mille, H. and Barnard, C.
*Les mains sales.* Sartre, J.
*"Mais n'te promène donc pas toute nue!" See* "Hey, Cut Out the Parading around Stark Naked!"
*Maison splendide.* Bridgeman, L.
*Maitlands, The.* Mackenzie, R.
*Le maître. See* Ionesco, E. The Leader
*Le maître des forges. See* Ohnet, G. The Iron Manufacturer
*Le maître de Santiago. See* Montherlant, H. The Master of Santiago
*Major Barbara.* Shaw, G.
*Major Bull-shot Gorgeous. See* Plautus, T. Miles gloriosus
*Makarov and Peterson, No. 3.* Kharms, D.
*Maker of Dreams, The.* Down, O.
*Måkespisere. See* Løveid, C. Seagull Eaters
*Makin' Time with the Yanks.* The Mummers Troupe
*Making Peter Pope.* De Santis, E.
*La malade imaginaire.* Molière, J.
*Malaria.* Schneider, S.
*Malasangre: La nueva emigración. See* Ramos-Perea, R. Bad Blood: The New Emigration
*Mālati and Mādhara.* Bhavabhūti
*Malcontent, The.* Marston, J.
*Male Animal, The.* Thurber, J. and Nugent, E.
*Male of the Species.* Owen, A.
*Le malentendu.* Camus, A.
*Los malhechores de bien.* Benavente y Martínez, J.
*Malice of Empire, The.* Yao, H.
*Al-malik huwa 'l-malik. See* Wannus, S. The King Is the King
*La malquerida. See* Benavente y Martínez, J. The Passion Flower
*Malvaloca.* Alvarez Quintero, S. and Alvarez Quintero, J.
*Mam Phyllis.* Brown-Guillory, E.
*Mama's Boy.* Prandini, A. *See* Anonymous Plays. The AIDS Show . . .
*Les mamelles de Tirésias. See* Kostrowisky, G. The Breasts of Tiresius
*Mammaries of Tiresias, The. See* Kostrowisky, G. The Breasts of Tiresius
*The Mammals' Graveyard. See* Díaz, J. The Place Where the Mammals Die
*Mamma's Affair.* Butler, R.

*Man and His Phantoms. See* Lenormand, H. L'homme et
    ses fantômes
*Man and Superman.* Shaw, G.
*Man and the Fly, The.* Ruibal, J.
*Man and the Masses. See* Toller, E. Masse mensch
*Man and the Monster, The.* Milner, H.
*Man and Wife.* Daly, A.·
*Man Better Man.* Hill, E.
*Man for All Seasons, A.* Bolt, R.
*Man from Chicago, The.* Romeril, J.
*Man from Home, The.* Tarkington, B. and Wilson, H.
*Man from Mukinupin, The.* Hewett, D.
*Man in a Case, The.* Wasserstein, W.
*Man in Dark Times, A.* Deshpande, G.
*Man in Half Moon Street, The.* Lyndon, B.
*Man in the Flying Lawn Chair.* Cromelin, C., Nightengale,
    E., Read, M., Reiss, K., Taber, T., and Wherry, T.
*Man in the Forest, The.* Field, C.
*Man in the Glass Booth, The.* Shaw, R.
*Man in the Moon, The. See* Lyly, J. Endymion
*Man Next Door, The.* Iwamatsu, R.
*Man of Destiny, The.* Shaw, G.
*Man of La Mancha.* Wasserman, D.
*Man of Mode, The; or, Sir Fopling Flutter.* Etherege, G.
*Man of the Century, The.* Frank, M.
*Man of the Flesh.* Solis, O.
*Man of the World.* Macklin, C.
*Man of the World, A. See* Vega, V. El hombre de mundo
*Man Outside, The. See* Borchert, W. The Outsider
*Man Who Came to Dinner, The.* Kaufman, G. and Hart, M.
*Man Who Died at Twelve O'clock, The.* Green, P.
*Man Who Dug Fish, The.* Bullins, E.
*Man Who Had All the Luck, The.* Miller, A.
*Man Who Liked Dickens, The.* Waugh, E.
*Man Who Lived His Life Over, The.* Lagerkvist, P.
*Man Who Married a Dumb Wife, The. See* France, A. La
    comédie de celui qui épousa une femme muette
*Man Who Sells Memories, The.* Kato, M.
*Man Who Was Dead, The. See* Tolstoi, L. The Live Corpse
*Man with a Load of Mischief, The.* Dukes, A.
*Man with Connections, A.* Gelman, A.
*Man with the Flower in His Mouth, The.* Pirandello, L.
*Man with the Heart in the Highlands, The. See* Saroyan,
    W. My Heart's in the Highlands
*Man without a Soul, The.* Lagerkvist, P.
*Man, Woman, Dinosaur.* Porter, R.
*Man You Mus'.* Jacob, B.
*Mañana de sol. See* Alvarez Quintero, S. and Alvarez
    Quintero, J. A Bright Morning
*Manchild.* Jeffries, I.
*Mandragola.* Machiavelli, N.
*La mandragola. See* Machiavelli, N. Mandragola
*Mandrake, The. See* Machiavelli, N. Mandragola
*Manfred.* Byron, G.
*Mangalam.* Sengupta, P.

*Le mangeur des rêves. See* Lenormand, H. The Dream
    Doctor
*Maniac, The. See* Conway, H The Battle of Stillwater
*Manifesto.* Wallace, N.
*Manikin and Minikin.* Kreymborg, A.
*La manivelle. See* Pinget, R. The Old Tune
*Manjit.* Singh, L.
*Manju. See* Anonymous Plays. Nakamitsu
*Mankind. See* Anonymous Plays. Mankynd
*Mankynd.* Anonymous Plays
*Manlius Capitolinus.* La Fosse, A.
*Mannen utan själ. See* Lagerkvist, P. The Man without a
    Soul
*Manohra.* Anonymous Plays
*Manolo.* Sierra, R.
*Man's Disobedience and the Fall of Man (York).*
    Anonymous Plays
*"Man's Extremity Is God's Opportunity." See* Sheldon, E.
    Salvation Nell
*Man's World, A.* Crothers, R.
*Manual of Trench Warfare, A.* Gorman, C.
*Many Deaths of Danny Rosales, The.* Morton, C.
*Las many muertes de Richard Morales. See* Morton, C.
    The Many Deaths of Danny Rosales
*Many Loves. See* Williams, W. Trial Horse No. 1
*Many Waters.* Hoffe, M.
*Many Young Men of Twenty.* Keane, J.
*Maple Viewing, The.* Kwanze, K.
*Marat/Sade. See* Weiss, P. The Persecution and
    Assassination of Jean-Paul Marat as Performed by
    the Inmates of the Asylum of Charenton under the
    Direction of the Marquis de Sade
*La marca de fuego.* Alsina, A.
*Marcelia: or, the Treacherous Friend.* Boothby, F.
*March of the Falsettos.* Finn, W.
*Marchands de gloire, Les.* Pagnol, M. and Nivoix, P.
*Marching Song.* Whiting, J.
*Marco Millions.* O'Neill, E.
*Marco Polo Sings a Solo.* Guare, J.
*Mardi gras.* Meilhac, H. and Halévy, L.
*Mareech, the Legend.* Mukherjee, A.
*Il Marescalco. See* Aretino, P. The Stablemaster
*Marga Gomez Is Pretty Witty & Gay. See* Gomez, M.
    Excerpts from Memory Tricks, Marga Gomez Is
    Pretty Witty & Gay, and A Line around the Block
*Margaret Fleming.* Herne, J.
*Die Margareth un die Lea.* Wollenweber, L.
*Margaret's Bed.* Inge, W.
*Margarita Came Back to Life.* Azcárate, L.
*La margarita del Tajo que dio nombre a Santarén.*
    Azevedo, A.
*Margarita resucitò. See* Azcárate, L. Margarita Came Back
    to Life
*Margin for Error.* Boothe, C.
*Marguerite.* Salacrou, A.

*Member of the Wedding, The.* McCullers, C.

*Memoir.* Murrell, J.

*Mémoires d'isles: Maman N. et Maman F. See* Césaire, I. Island Memories: Mama N. and Mama F.

*Memorable Masque, The.* Chapman, G.

*Memorandum, The.* Havel, V.

*Memorial Service for Genji, A. See* Anonymous Plays. Genji kuyō

*Memorias de la revolucion.* Tropicana, C., and Parnes, U.

*Memories for My Brother, Part I: Before the Guns. See* Palmer, J. Before the Guns

*Memory of Two Mondays, A.* Miller, A.

*Memory Tricks. See* Gomez, M. Excerpts from Memory Tricks, Marga Gomez Is Pretty Witty & Gay, and A Line around the Block.

*Men and Women.* Belasco, D. and De Mille, H.

*Men and Women in Wild Times.* Ch'en, P.

*Men bog handleren ken ikke sove. See* Olsen, E. The Bookseller Cannot Sleep

*Men in White.* Kingsley, S.

*Men on the Verge of a His-panic Breakdown.* Reyes, G.

*Men without Shadows. See* Sartre, J. The Victors

*Menaechmi, The.* Plautus, T.

*Menaechmi Twins. See* Plautus, T. The Menaechmi

*Menaechmus Brothers, The. See* Plautus, T. The Menaechmi

*Menaechmus Twins, The. See* Plautus, T. The Menaechmi

*Mensch Meier: A Play of Everyday Life.* Kroetz, F.

*Die Menschen. See* Hasenclever, W. Humanity

*Menschen im hotel. See* Baum, V. Grand Hotel

*Menschenhass und reue. See* Kotzebue, A. The Stranger

*Le menteur.* Corneille, P.

*Meow.* Smith, V.

*Mephisto.* Mnouchkine, A.

*Mercadet.* Balzac, H.

*Mercator. See* Plautus T. The Merchant

*Mercenaries.* Yoshimura, J.

*Mercenary, The.* Spunde, W.

*Merchandising.* Hwang, D.

*Merchant, The.* Anonymous Plays

*Merchant, The.* Plautus, T.

*Merchant of Venice, The.* Shakespeare, W.

*Merchant of Yonkers, The. See* Wilder, T. The Matchmaker

*Merchants of Destiny.* Hamanjoda, A.

*Mercy Dodd; or, Presumptive Evidence.* Boucicault, D.

*Mercy of Augustus, The. See* Corneille, P. Cinna

*Mercy Quilt, The.* Jensen, L.

*Merely Players.* McPhee, F.

*Mergers and Accusations.* Wong, E.

*Merlin gascon.* Raisin, J.

*Merope.* Hill, A.

*Merrily We Roll Along.* Kaufman, G. and Hart, M.

*Merry Death, A.* Evreinov, N.

*Merry Devil of Edmonton, The.* Anonymous Plays

*Merry Go Round. See* Schnitzler, A. La ronde

*Merry Monarch, The. See* Payne, J. and Irving, W. Charles the Second

*Merry Plays, A. See* Heywood, J. John, Tyb and Sir John

*Merry Wives of Windsor, The.* Shakespeare, W.

*Merton of the Movies.* Kaufman, G. and Connelly, M.

*Mery Plays betweene Johan Johan, the Husbande, Tyb His Wife, and Syr Jhan, the Preest, A. See* Heywood, J. John, Tyb and Sir John

*Mery Plays betweene Johan Johan, Tyb, His Wife and Syr Jhan, the Preest, A. See* Heywood, J. John, Tyb and Sir John

*Mery Plays betwene Johan Johan the Husbande, Tib His Wife, and Sir Johan the Preest. See* Heywood, J. John Tyb, and Sir John

*Mery Playse betwene the Pardoner and the Frere, the Curate and Neybour Pratte. See* Heywood, J. The Pardoner and the Friar

*Message from Cougar, A.* Maljean, J.

*Messiah.* Sherman, M.

*Mester Gert Westphaler eller den meget talende barbeer. See* Holberg, L. The Loquacious Barber

*Metamora; or, the Last of the Pollywogs.* Brougham, J.

*Metamora; or, the Last of the Wampanoags.* Stone, J.

*Methusalem; oder, Der ewige Bürger. See* Goll, I. Methusalem

*Methusalem, or, the Eternal Bourgeois.* Goll, I.

*Methusalife and Escapism.* Rider, J.

*Mexican Medea: La Llorona Retold.* Moraga, C.

*Meyer's Room. See* Rosen, S. Two Plays

*La mi-carême. See* Meilhac, H. and Halévy, L. Mardi Gras

*Michael and His Lost Angel.* Jones, H.

*Michael and Mary.* Milne, A.

*Michael Kramer.* Hauptmann, G.

*Michaelmas Term.* Middleton, T.

*Michel Auclair.* Vildrac, C.

*Michimori.* Seiami.

*Mickey la torche. See* Pontcharra, N. Mickey the Torch

*Mickey the Torch.* Pontcharra, N.

*Midas.* Lyly, J.

*Midas.* O'Hara, K.

*Midasin kulaklari. See* Dilmen, G. The Ears of Midas

*Mid-channel.* Pinero, A.

*Middle-aged White Guys.* Martin, J.

*Middleman, The.* Jones, H.

*Midnight Bell, A.* Hoyt, C.

*Midnight Blues.* Alám, J.

*Midnight Brainwash Revival.* Bromley, K.

*Midsummer Night's Dream, A.* Shakespeare, W.

*Midwinter Story, A. See* Schildt, R. The Gallows Man

*Miembro del jurado.* Perinelli, R.

*al-Miftah. See* `Ani, Y. The Key

*Mighty Dollar, The.* Woolf, B.

*Mighty Reservoy, The.* Terson, P.

*Migrant Farmworker's Son, The.* Gonzalez S., S.

*Miidera.* Anonymous Plays

La paix. *See* Lenéru, M. Peace

La paix du ménage. *See* Maupassant, G. de. The Household Peace

Pajama Game, The. Abbott, G. and Bissell, R.

Palace in the Field, The. *See* The Shrine in the Fields. Konparu,Z.

Palestinian Girl, The. Sobol, J.

Palm Sunday of a Horse Dealer, The. Süto, A.

Pan. Lererghe, C.

P'an Chin-lien. Ou-Yang, Y.

Pan Jinlian. Wei, M.

Pan Jinlian: The History of a Fallen Woman. *See* Wei, M. Pan Jinlian

Pan Jinlian: yige nuren de chenlunshi. *See* Wei, M. Pan Jinlian

Pandering to the Masses: A Misrepresentation. Foreman, R.

Pan's Anniversary, or the Shepherd's Holyday. Jonson, B.

Pantagleize. Ghelderode, M.

Pantellas. *See* Prida, D. Screens

Pantomime. Walcott, D.

Pantomime for Easter Day, A. Anonymous Plays

Paolo and Francesca. Phillips, S.

P'ao-ping szu-ling ti erh-tzu. *See* Chou, W.; Tung, Y.; and Yeh, H. The Artillery Commander's Son

Papa Is All. Greene, P.

Papa Juan: centenario. *See* Alvarez Quintero, S. and Alvarez Quintero, J. A Hundred Years Old

Paper Angels. Lim, G.

Paper Dolls. Jackson, E.

Paphnutius. Hrotsvit

Papp. Cameron, K.

Le paquebot Tenacity. Vildrac, C.

Par un jour de pluie. Forest, L.

Parables for a Season. Onwueme, T.

Parade, The. Anagnostaki, L.

Parade. Uhry, A., and Prince, H.

Paradise Is Closing Down. Uys, P.

Paradise Plays, The (Oberufer). Anonymous Plays

Paradise Restored. Taylor, D.

Paradise Tours. Morris, R.

Paragon, The. Pertwee, R. and Pertwee, M.

Parallel Lines. Lambert, A.

Paralyzed. *See* Anonymous Plays. Shibiri

Le pardon. *See* Lemaître, J. The Pardon

Pardon, The. Lemaître, J.

Pardon—for a Price. *See* Boucicault, D. After Dark

Pardoner and the Friar, The. Heywood, J.

Les paredes oyen. Ruiz de Alarcón y Mendoza, J.

Les parents terribles. *See* Cocteau, J. Intimate Relations

Paris and Helen. Schwartz, D.

Paris Bound. Barry, P.

Paris Commune, A Play about the. *See* Grieg, N. The Defeat

Parisian Woman, The. *See* Becque, H. La Parisienne.

La Parisienne. Becque, H.

Park Meeting. Hooke, N.

Parliament of Bees, The. Day, J.

Parliament of Heaven, The. *See* Anonymous Plays. The Salutation and Conception

Parliament of Heaven, The; The Salutation and Conception. *See* Anonymous Plays. The Salutation and Conception (N Town)

Parliament of Hell, The; The Temptation. *See* Anonymous Plays.

Parnassus Plays (1598–1601). *See* Anonymous Plays: The Pilgrimage to Parnassus; The Return from Parnassus

Parnell. Schauffler, E.

Parra kumpt, Der. Wieand, P.

Parrot Cage, The. Shaw, M.

Parrots' Lies. Marber, A.

Parson's Wedding, The. Killigrew, T.

Particular Class of Women, A. Feindel, J.

Une partie de campagne. *See* Petitclair, P. A Country Outing

Parting. Kai, N.

Partisans on the Steppes of the Ukraine. *See* Korneichuk, A. Guerillas on the Ukrainian Steppes

Partizany v stepakh Ukrainy. *See* Korneichuk, A. Guerillas of the Ukrainian Steppes

Partridge in a Pear Tree, A. Swortzell, L.

Party. Dillon, D.

Party, The. Arden, J.

Party 1985. Attinello, P. *See* Anonymous Plays. The AIDS Show . . .

Party 1984. Attinello, P. *See* Anonymous Plays. The AIDS Show . . .

Party 1981. Attinello, P. *See* Anonymous Plays. The AIDS Show . . .

Party 1983. Attinello, P. *See* Anonymous Plays. The AIDS Show . . .

Party 1982. Attinello, P. *See* Anonymous Plays. The AIDS Show . . .

Party Spirit, The. Jones, P. and Jowett, J.

Party through the Wall, The. Spark, M.

Pas moi. *See* Beckett, S. Not I

Paseo al atardecer. *See* Marichal Lugo, T. Evening Walk

Paso de las olives, El. *See* Rueda, L. The Olives

Paso séptimo: de las aceitunas. *See* Rueda, L. The Seventh Farce

Pasque Flower; a Play of the Canadian Prairie. Ringwood, G.

Passacaglia. Dey, J.

Passenger to Bali, A. St. Joseph, E.

Passer-by, The. Lu, H.

Il Passero. *See* López. S. The Sparrow

Passing By. Sherman, M.

Passing of the Magi, The. Zamacois, E.

Passing of the Torch, The. *See* Hervieu, P. La course du flambeau

*Polaroid Stories*. Iizuka, N.
*Police*. Baraka, A.
*Police, The*. Mrozek, S.
*Police Chief's an Easygoing Guy, The*. *See* Courteline, G.
 The Commissioner Has a Big Heart
*Policja*. *See* Mrozek, S. The Police
*Polish Jew, The*. *See* Lewis, L. The Bells
*Politician Out-witted, The*. Low, S.
*Polly* (second part of *Beggar's Opera*, suppressed 1728).
 Gay, J.
*Polly Blue*. Bradley, B.
*Polly Honeycombe*. Colman, G.
*Polyeucte*. Corneille, P.
*Polygraph*. Brassard, M. and Lepage, R.
*Le polygraphe*. *See* Brassard, M. and Lepage, R. Polygraph
*Pompey the Great*. *See* Masefield, J. The Tragedy of
 Pompey the Great
*Ponder Heart, The*. Fields, J. and Chodorov, J.
*Pongo Plays 1–6*. *See* Livings, H. The Gamecock
*Pongsang T'alch'um*. Anonymous Plays
*Il ponte*. *See* Fratti, M. The Bridge
*Ponteach; or, the Savages of America*. Rogers, R.
*Pony Ride*. *See* Pintauro, J. Wild Blue
*Poof!* Nottage, L.
*Poor Aubrey*. Kelly, G.
*Poor Beggar and the Fairy Godmother, The*. Allais, A.
*Poor Bitos*. Anouilh, J.
*Poor Bride, The*. Ostrovskii, A.
*Poor Little Watch Girl, The*. Williams, A.
*Poor of New York, The*. Boucicault, D.
*Poor Ostrich*. Hemro
*Pope Joan*. Rubess, B.
*Porcelain*. Yew, C.
*Porcelain Vase*. Petrovski, J.
*Porch*. Heifner, J.
*Porgy*. Heyward, D. and Heyward, D.
*Porgy and Bess*. Heyward, D.
*La porta chiusa*. *See* Praga, M. The Closed Door
*Portage to San Cristobal of A.H., The*. Hampton, C.
*Portia Coughlan*. Carr, M.
*Portrait, The*. Scala, F.
*Portrait d'une femme*. *See* Vinaver, M. Portrait of a
 Woman
*Portrait of a Madonna*. Williams, T.
*Portrait of a Queen*. Francis, W.
*Portrait of a Woman*. Vinaver, M.
*Portrait of the Artist as Filipino, A*. Joaquin, N.
*Port-Royal*. Montherlant, H.
*Portsmouth Defence, The*. Lethbridge, N.
*La posada magica*. Solis, O.
*Las posadas/No Room at the Inn*. Anonymous Plays
*Posh Talk*. Beolco, A.
*Post Mortem*. Matilla, L.
*Post Office, The*. Tagore, R.
*Postcard, The*. Dickler, G.

*Postcards from Hawaii*. Crossland, J.
*Post-inn, The*. Goldoni, C.
*Post-Reformation Banns, The*. *See* Anonymous Plays.
 Banns. (Chester)
*Poster of the Cosmos, A*. Wilson, L.
*El postrer duelo de España*. Calderón de la Barca, P. *See*
 Payne, J. The Last Duel in Spain
*Pot Maker, The*. Bonner, M.
*Pot of Gold, The*. *See* Plautus, T. Aulularia
*Pots of Money*. Labiche, E. and Delacour, A.
*Potter's Field*. *See* Green, P. Roll Sweet Chariot
*Potting Shed, Ihe*. Greene, G.
*La poudre aux yeux*. Labiche, E. and Martin, E.
*Pour Lucrece*. *See* Giraudoux, J. Duel of Angels
*Pow Wow; or, the Great Victory*. Lang, W.
*Powder Keg*. Dukovski, D.
*Power*. Ziverts, M.
*Power, a Living Newspaper*. Arent, A.
*Power of Darkness, The; or, If a Claw Is Caught the Bird
 Is Lost*. Tolstoi, L.
*Power of Love, The*. Ilf, I. and Petrov, E.
*Power Pipes*. Spiderwoman Theater
*Practical Magic*. *See* Kelley, S. Hope of the Future
*Prairie Church of Buster Galloway, The*. Albert, L.
*Präsident Abenwind*. *See* Jelinek, E. President Evening
 Breeze
*Die präsidentinnen*. *See* Schwab, W. Holy Mothers
*Prayer for My Daughter, A*. Babe, T.
*Prayer Meeting*. Caldwell, B.
*Preacher and the Rapper, The*. Reed, I.
*Preacher with a Horse to Ride, A*. Carson, J.
*La précaution inutile*. *See* Beaumarchais, P. Le Barbier de
 Seville
*Les précieuses ridicules*. Molière, J.
*Preist the Barbar, Sweetball His Man*. Anonymous Plays
*Le préjué à la mode*. La Chaussée, P.
*Prelude to a Kiss*. Lucas, C.
*Prelude to Death in Venice, A*. Breuer, L.
*El premio flaco*. *See* Quintero, H. The Booby Prize
*Prenez garde à la peinture*. *See* Fauchois, R. The Late
 Christopher Bean
*Presentation and Purification (N Town)*. Anonymous Plays
*Presentation of Mary in the Temple, The*. *See* Anonymous
 Plays. Presentation and Purification (N Town)
*President Evening Breeze*. Jelinek, E.
*Presumption; or, the Fate of Frankenstein*. Peake, R.
*Presumptive Evidence*. *See* Boucicault, D. Mercy Dodd
*Pretenders, The*. Ibsen, H.
*Pretentious Ladies, The*. *See* Molière, J. Les précieuses
 ridicules
*Pretty Interlude Called Nice Wanton, A*. *See* Anonymous
 Plays. Nice Wanton
*Price, The*. Miller, A.
*Price of Wine, The*. Anonymous Plays
*Prickly Heat*. Donald, S.

*Rachel.* Grimke, A.

*Rachel's Fate.* Ketron, L.

*Racket, The.* Cormack B.

*Rackey.* Culbertson, E.

*Radio Mambo: Culture Clash Invades Miami.* Culture Clash

*Radio Primer.* Corwin, N.

*Rafferty's Chant.* Dewhurst, K.

*Raft of the Medusa, The.* Kaiser, G.

*Rage, The.* Reynolds, F.

*Ragged Time.* Mayer, O.

*Rags.* Walter, N.

*Ragtime.* McNally, T.

*Raigne of King Edward the Third, The.* See Anonymous Plays. The Reign of King Edward the Third

*Railroad Women.* Ratcliffe, H.

*Rain.* Colton, J. and Randolph, C.

*Rain.* Gałczyński, K.

*Rain from Heaven.* Behrman, S.

*Rain on the Hsiao-Hsiang.* Yang, H.

*Rain-killers, The.* Hutchinson, A.

*Rainmaker, The.* Nash, R.

*Rainmaker, The.* Ringwood, G.

*Rainshark.* McCarthy, N.

*Rainy Season, The.* Okita, D.

*Raisin in the Sun, A.* Hansberry, L.

*Raisin' the Devil.* Gard, R.

*Raising of Lazarus (N Town).* Anonymous Plays

*Raising of Lazarus, The.* Hilarius

*Raising of Lazarus, The (Chester).* Anonymous Plays

*Raising of Lazarus, The (N Town).* See Anonymous Plays. Raising of Lazarus (N Town)

*Raising of Lazarus, The (Wakefield).* Anonymous Plays

*Raising the Devil.* Sachs, H.

*Raising the Wind.* Kenney, J.

*"Raising the Wind" on the Most Approved Principles.* See Brough, W. and Brough, R. The Enchanted Isle

*Rakinyo.* Ajibade, S.

*Rākshasa's Ring.* See Vishakadatta. The Signet Ring of Rākshasa

*Ralph Roister Doister.* Udall, N.

*Rama and Sita.* Gunawardena, G.

*Ramah Droog.* Cobb, J.

*Rama's Later History.* See Bhavabhūti. The Later Story of Rama

*Ranae.* See Aristophanes. The Frogs

*Rancho Hollywood.* Morton, C.

*Ranchos, Dos; or, the Purification.* Williams, T.

*Randlords and Rotgut.* Junction Avenue Theatre Company.

*Randy's House.* Clum, J.

*Ranke viljer.* See Wied, G. 2 × 2 = 5

*Rapid Transit.* See Kelley, S. Hope of the Future

*Rappaccini's Daughter.* Paz, O.

*La rapporteuse.* See Tison, P. The Telltale

*Rarabai: matawa hyakunen no komori-uta.* See Kōkami, S. Lullaby: A Hundred Years of Song

*Rare-en-tout.* See Roche-Guilhen, A. All-Wondrous

*Rasmus Montanus.* Holberg, L.

*Raspberry Picker, The.* Hochwälder, F.

*Ratnavali.* See Harsha, Son of Hira. Retnavali

*Rats, The.* Hauptmann, G.

*Rat's Mass, A.* Kennedy, A.

*Rats of Norway, The.* Winter, J.

*Rattel.* Livings, H.

*Die ratten.* See Hauptmann, G. The Rats

*Rattle of a Simple Man.* Dyer, C.

*Ravens, The.* See Becque, H. Les corbeaux

*Rawson's Y.* See De Mille, H. and Barnard, C. The Main Line

*La raza pura; or racial, racial.* Sièrra, R.

*Reactivated Man. The.* Zahn, C.

*Ready for the River.* Bell, N.

*Real Dark Night of the Soul, The.* See Pintauro, J. Wild Blue

*Real Estate.* Page, L.

*Real Inspector Hound, The.* Stoppard, T.

*Real Thing, The.* Stoppard, T.

*Really, My Dear . . .* Morley, C.

*Rebel Women.* Babe, T.

*Rebound.* Stewart. D.

*Rebound, The.* See Picard, L. Les ricochets

*Reckless.* Lucas, C.

*Reckoning, The.* See Schnitzler, A. Light-o'-love

*Reclining Figure.* Kurnitz, H.

*Reconciliation, The.* See Hauptmann, G. Das friedensfest

*Recruiting Officer, The.* Farquhar, G.

*Recruits; or, That's How It Was.* Axenfeld, I. and Reznik, L.

*Red Barn, The.* See Anonymous Plays. Maria Martin

*Red Cross.* Shepard, S.

*Red Dawn over Manhattan.* Saitō, R.

*Red Demon Akaoni, The.* Noda, H.

*Red Detachment of Women.* Anonymous Plays

*Red Devils.* Horsfield, D.

*Red Diaper Baby.* Kornbluth, J.

*Red Eye of Love.* Weinstein, A.

*Red Fox/Second Hangin'.* Baker, D, and Cocke, D.

*Red Gloves.* See Sartre, J. Les mains sales

*Red Horse Animation.* Breuer, L.

*Red Lantern, The.* Anonymous Plays

*Red Light.* Larsson, S.

*Red Magic.* Ghelderode, M.

*Red Night.* Hodson, J.

*Red Robe, The.* See Brieux, E. La robe rouge

*Red Room.* Gough, L.

*Red Roses for Me.* O'Casey, S.

*Redemption, The.* See Anonymous Plays. The Mystery of the Redemption; Tolstoi, L. The Live Corpse

*Reed Cutter, The.* Seami, M.

*Refer to Drawer.* See Ross, G. Guilty Party

*Reverend Griffith Davenport, The.* Herne, J.
*Reverend What's His Name.* Curzon, D. *See* Anonymous
    Plays. The AIDS Show . . .
*Reverse Psychology.* Ludlam, C.
*Reverse Transcription.* Kushner, T.
*Revesby Sword Play, The.* Anonymous Plays
*Revisor. See* Gogol, N. The Inspector
*Revival.* Hunkins, L.
*Rex. See* Pintauro, J. Wild Blue
*Los reyes pasan. See* Zamacois, E. The Passing of the
    Magi
*Reynes Extracts, The.* Anonymous Plays
*Rhadamiste et Zénobie.* Crébillon, P.
*Rhadamistus and Zenobia. See* Crébillon, P. Rhadamiste et
    Zénobie
*Rhesus.* Euripides
*Rhino for the Boardroom, a Radio Play. A.* Livingstone, D.
*Rhinoceros.* Ionesco, E.
*Les rhinocéros. See* Ionesco, E. Rhinoceros
*Rhoda in Potatoland.* Foreman, R.
*Rhondda Roundabout.* Jones, J.
*Rhythm Method.* Iijima, S., and Suzuki, Y.
*Rhythm of Violence, The.* Nkosi, L.
*Richard of Bordeaux.* Daviot, G. [pseudonym]
*Richard II. See* Shakespeare, W. King Richard II
*Richard III. See* Shakespeare, W. King Richard III
*Richard III Travestie.* By, W.
*Richelieu; or, the Conspiracy.* Bulwer-Lytton, E.
*Rickinghall (Bury St. Edmunds) Fragment, The.*
    Anonymous Plays
*Ricky.* Weigand, R. *See* Anonymous Plays. The AIDS
    Show . . .
*Les ricochets.* Picard, L.
*Ricordi.* Crea, T., Eberhard, J., Mastratone, L., and
    Morgillo, A.
*Ride down Mount Morgan, The.* Miller, A.
*Rider of Dreams, The.* Torrence, F.
*Riders to the Sea.* Synge, J.
*Ridhoy neye keyla. See* Cooper, M. Heartgame
*Ridiculous precieuses, The. See* Molière, J. Le précieuses
    ridicules
*Riding the Goat.* Miller, M.
*Riel.* Coulter, J.
*Rifle Ball, The. See* Wallach, L. Rosedale
*Right Reason, The.* Johnson, F.
*Right Wally, A.* Mullett, A.
*Right You Are! If You Think So.* Pirandello, L.
*Rimmin' at the Baths.* Brown, K., and McQueen, M. *See*
    Anonymous Plays. The AIDS Show . . .
*Ring around the Moon. See* Anouilh, J. Ring round the
    Moon
*Ring of General Macías, The.* Niggli, J.
*Ring round the Moon.* Anouilh, J.
*Ringers.* Hogan, F.
*Riot.* Moodie, A.

*Rip Van Winkle.* Burke, C.
*Rip Van Winkle, as Played by Joseph Jefferson.*
    Anonymous Plays
*Rise and Fall of Richard III, The; or, a New Front to an
    Old Dicky.* Burnand, F.
*Rise and Shine of Comrade Fiasco, The.* Whaley, A.
*Rising of the Moon, The.* Gregory, I.
*Rising Sun, Falling Star.* Rodríguez, Y.
*Rites.* Duffy, M.
*Il ritorno. See* Fratti, M. The Return
*Il rittrato. See* Scala, F. The Portrait
*Ritual, The.* Constance, Z.
*Ritual 2378.* Ferguson, I.
*Ritz, The.* McNally, T.
*Rival Candidates, The.* Dudley, H.
*Rival of His Master, The. See* Le Sage, A. Crispin, Rival of
    His Master
*Rival Queens, The; or, the Death of Alexander the Great.*
    Lee, N.
*Rivals, The.* Sheridan, R.
*River Niger, The.* Walker, J.
*River Unbound, The.* Tagore, R.
*Rivermouth. See* Kanami. Mouth-of-sound
*Rivers and Forests, The.* Duras, M.
*Rivers of China, The.* De Groen, Alma.
*Road.* Cartwright, J.
*Road to Black Mesa.* Lewis, W.
*Road to Mecca.* Fugard, A.
*Road to Nirvana.* Kopit, A.
*Road to Rome, The.* Sherwood, R.
*Roads.* Deshpande, G.
*Roads of the Mountaintop.* Milner, R.
*Roadside.* Riggs, L.
*Roaring Girl, The.* Dekker, T., and Middleton, T.
*Robbers, The.* Schiller, F.
*La robe rouge.* Brieux, E.
*Robert Emmet.* Boucicault, D.
*Robert Johnson: Trick the Devil.* Harris, B.
*Robert the Devil.* Anonymous Plays
*Robin Hood and His Crew of Soldiers.* Anonymous Plays
*Robin Hood and the Friar.* Anonymous Plays
*Robin Hood and the Knight.* Anonymous Plays
*Robin Hood and the Potter.* Anonymous Plays
*Robin Hood and the Sheriff of Nottingham.* Anonymous
    Plays
*Robinson Crusoe, or Harlequin Friday and the King of the
    Caribee Islands.* Byron, G.
*Robust Invalid, The. See* Molière, J. Le malade imaginaire
*Rock, The.* Hamlin, M.
*Rockaby.* Beckett, S.
*Rocket to the Moon.* Odets, C.
*Rocking Back and Forth.* Grass, G.
*Rocking Chairs.* Kreymborg, A.
*Rocky Peak.* Zajc, D.
*Rococo.* Granville-Barker, H.

*Rutherford and Son.* Sowerby, G.
*Ruy Blas.* Hugo, V.
*Ruzzante Returns from the Wars.* Beolco, A.

*S.A.M. I Am.* Omata, G.
*'S'bend.* Oshodi, M.
*S. S. Tenacity.* See Vildrac C. Le paquebot Tenacity
*Sabina.* Montano, S.
*Sabina's Splendid Brain.* Sinclair, C.
*Sabine Woman, A. See* Moody, W. The Great Divide
*Sabrina Fair.* Taylor, S.
*Sacco y Vanzetti: dramaturgia sumario de documentos sobre el caso. See* Kartun, M. Sacco-Vanzetti (A dramaturgic summary judgement from documents on the case)
*Sacco-Vanzetti (A dramaturgic summary judgement from documents on the case).* Kartun, M.
*Sacking of Norman Banks, The.* Ross, G.
*Sacred Blood.* Gippius, Z.
*Sacred Dump, The. See* Mednick, M. Coyote VI: The Sacred Dump
*Sacrifice.* Duncan, T.
*Sacrifice of Isaac, The. See also* Anonymous Plays. Abraham and Isaac; Anonymous Plays. Abraham, Melchisedec and Isaac
*Sacrifice of Isaac, The (Brome).* Anonymous Plays
*Sacrifice of Kreli, The.* Dike, F.
*Sacrilege.* Shaffer, D.
*Sad Are the Eyes of William Tell.* Sastre, A.
*Sad Shepherd, The; or, a Tale of Robin Hood.* Jonson, B.
*Saddles in the Rain.* Bustin, P.
*Safe.* Burke, K.
*Safe.* Johnson, G.
*Safe Haven.* Chisholm, M.
*Safe House.* Kazan, N.
*Safe Livin' in Dangerous Times.* Brown, K., and McQueen, M. *See* Anonymous Plays. The AIDS Show . . .
*Safe Sex.* Fierstein, H.
*Safety Match, The.* Ginsbury, N.
*La Sagra del signore della nave. See* Pirandello, L. Our Lord of the Ships
*Sahdji, an African Ballet.* Bruce, R.
*Saigyō and the Cherry Tree. See* Zeami. Saigyō's Cherry Tree
*Saigyo's Cherry Tree.* Zeami.
*Saigyō-zakura. See* Zeami. Saigyo's Cherry Tree
*Saigyōzakura. See* Zeami. Saigyo's Cherry Tree
*Sailor, Beware!* King, P. and Cary, F.
*St. Claudia.* Goold, M.
*Saint Genesius.* Rotrou, J.
*Saint Genest. See* Rotrou, J. Saint Genesius
*St. George.* Porter, J.
*St. George.* Weir, I.
*St. George and the Dragon.* Anonymous Plays

*Saint George and the Dragon at Christmas Tide.* Sigley, M.
*St. George Play, Leicestershire. See* Anonymous Plays. Leicestershire St. George Play
*St. George Play, The Oxfordshire. See* Anonymous Plays. The Oxfordshire St. George Play
*St. George Plays. See* Anonymous Plays. Leicestershire St. George Play; Anonymous Plays. The Oxfordshire St. George Play; Anonymous Plays. The Play of St. George, version reconstructed from memory by Thomas Hardy; Anonymous Plays. St. George and the Dragon
*St. Helena.* Sherriff, R. and De Casilis, J.
*Saint Joan.* Shaw, G.
*Saint Joan of the Stockyards.* Brecht, B.
*Saint John the Evangelist. See* Anonymous Plays; John the Evangelist
*St. John's Gospel.* Anonymous Plays
*St. Louis Woman.* Bontemps, A. and Cullen, C.
*St. Mael and the Maldunkian Penguins.* Boyd, S.
*Saint Marina.* Major, A.
*Saint Narukami. See* Danūjrō I. Narukami. *See also* Tsuuchi, H.; Yasuda, A.; and Nakada, M. *Saint Narukami and the God Fudō*
*Saint Narukami and the God Fudō.* Tsuuchi, H.; Yasuda, A.; and Nakada, M.
*Saint Nicholas and the Image. See* Hilarius. The Miracle of Saint Nicholas and the Image
*Saint Nicholas and the Schoolboys. See* Anonymous Plays; The Miracle of Saint Nicholas and the Schoolboys
*Saint Nicholas and the Three Scholars.* Anonymous Plays
*Saint Nicholas and the Virgins. See* Anonymous Plays; The Miracle of Saint Nicholas and the Virgins
*St. Nicholas Hotel, Wm. Donnelly, Prop., The. (The Donnellys, Part Two).* Reaney, J.
*Saint of Bleecker Street, The.* Menotti, G.
*St. Patrick at Tara.* Stephens, H.
*Saint Patrick's Day, or, the Scheming Lieutenant.* Sheridan, R.
*Saint's Day.* Whiting, J.
*Une saison au Congo. See* Césaire, A. A Season in the Congo
*Sakoontalā. See* Kālidāsa. Shakuntalā
*Sakura Hime Azuma Bonshō. See* Tsuruya, N.; Sakurada, J., and Tsuuchi, G. The Scarlet Princess of Edō
*Sally Bowles. See* Van Druten, J. I Am a Camera
*Sally's Rape.* McCauley, R.
*Salmacida spolia.* D'Avenant, W.
*Salome's Head.* Ortiz de Montellano, B.
*Salt-water Moon.* French, D.
*Salto al cielo.* Kartun, M.
*Salutation and Conception, The (N Town).* Anonymous Plays
*Salutation of Elizabeth, The (Wakefield).* Anonymous Plays

*Sumida-gawa. See* Kanze, M. The Sumida River
*Summer and Smoke.* Williams, T.
*Summer Evening. See* Shawn, W. A Thought in Three
    Parts
*Summer Ghost, A.* Fredericks, C.
*Summer Nights.* Pleijel, A.
*Summer of the 17th Doll.* Lawler, R.
*Summer's Last Will and Testament.* Nashe, T.
*Summertree.* Cowen, R.
*Summoning of Everyman, The. See* Anonymous Plays.
    Everyman
*Sun.* Kennedy, A.
*Sun Always Shines for the Cool, The.* Piñero, M.
*Sun Images.* Portillo-Trambley, E.
*Sun Moon and Feather.* Spiderwoman Theater.
*Sunday in the Park with George.* Lapine, J.
*Sunday Morning in the South.* Johnson, G.
*Sunday Promenade, The.* Forssell, L.
*Sundown.* Babel, I.
*Sunken Bell, The.* Hauptmann, G.
*Sunny Morning, A. See* Alvarez Quintero, S. and Alvarez
    Quintero, J. A Bright Morning
*Sunny Side Up.* Chais, P. *See* Anonymous Plays. Twenty-
    four Hours: A.M.
*Sunrise on Earth.* Lewis, M. *See* Anonymous Plays.
    Twenty-four Hours: P.M.
*Sunset Beach.* La Tempa, S.
*Sunset Boulevard.* Black, D., and Hampton, C.
*Sunset/Sunrise.* Shank, A.
*Sunshine Boys, The.* Simon, N.
*Sunshine Follows Rain. See* Girardin, D. La joie fait peur
*Sunshine through the Clouds. See* Girardin, D. La joie fait
    peur
*Sun-up.* Vollmer, L.
*Super Cool.* Turner, G.
*SuperEd.* Craddock, C.
*Superintendent, The.* Haavikko, P.
*Superstition.* Barker, J.
*Suphan's Blood. See* Vichitvadakarn, L. Luad Suphan
*Supper for the Dead.* Green, P.
*Supper of Pranks, The. See* Benelli, S. The Jest
*Suppliant Maidens, The. See* Aeschylus. The Suppliants
*Suppliant Women, The. See* Euripides. The Suppliants
*Suppliants, The.* Aeschylus
*Suppliants, The.* Euripides
*Supposes.* Gascoigne, G.
*Supposes, The.* Ariosto, L.
*I suppositi. Ariosto. See* Gascoigne, G. Supposes
*Suppressed Desires.* Glaspell, S.
*Sure Thing. See* Ives, D. All in the Timing
*Surface Tension.* Farabough, L.
*Surfing Blue.* Hamson, L.
*Surrender.* Jaaffar, J.
*Survey of the Sciences, A.* Davenport, R.
*Survival.* Brenner, A.

*Survival.* Workshop '71 Theatre Company
*Survivor: A Cambodian Odyssey, The.* Lipsky, J.
*Survivor and the Translator, The.* Sack, L.
*Surya shikar. See* Dutt, U. Hunting the Sun
*Surya-shikar. See* Dutt, U. Hunting the Sun
*Suryast. See* Das, J. Before the Sunset
*Susan and God.* Crothers, R.
*Susanna.* Rebhun, P.
*Suscitatio Lazari. See* Hilarius. The Raising of Lazarus
*Suspecting Truth, The. See* Ruiz de Alarcón y Mendoza, J.
    La verdad sospechosa
*Suspicious Husband, The.* Hoadly, B.
*Susuz Yaz. See* Cumali, N. Dry Summer
*Suyŏng Yayu.* Anonymous Plays
*Svadba. See* Chekhov, A. A Wedding
*Den svåra stunden, I–III. See* Lagerkvist, P. The Difficult
    Hour, I–III
*Sviataia krov'. See* Gippius, Z. Sacred Blood
*Swan, The.* Molnár, F.
*Swan Song, The.* Chekhov, A.
*Swedenhielms, The.* Bergman, H.
*Sweeney Agonistes.* Eliot, T.
*Sweeney Todd. See* Wheeler, H. Sweeney Todd, the
    Demon Barber of Fleet Street
*Sweeney Todd, the Barber of Fleet Street. See* Pitt, G. The
    String of Pearls
*Sweeney Todd, the Demon Barber of Fleet Street.* Bond, C.
    *See* Wheeler, H. Sweeney Todd, the Demon Barber
    of Fleet Street
*Sweeney Todd, the Demon Barber of Fleet Street.*
    Wheeler, H.
*Sweet Bird of Youth.* Williams, T.
*Sweet Eros.* McNally, T.
*Sweet Girl Graduate, The; a Comedy in Four Acts.*
    Curzon, S.
*Sweethearts.* Gilbert, W. and Sullivan, A.
*Swellfoot's Tears.* Katz, L.
*Swine.* Turrini, P.
*Swinging. See* Stroman, S., and Weidman, J. Contact
*Swipe.* Pengilly, G.
*Switchback.* Mednick, M.
*Sword and Queue.* Gutzkow, K.
*Sword of the Samurai, The.* Mygatt, T.
*Sylvester the Cat vs Galloping Billy Bronco.* Lynch, M.
*Syncopation.* Knee, A.
*Syncope. See* Gingras, R. Breaks
*Het syndroom van Stendhal. See* Strijards, F. The Stendhal
    Syndrome
*System of Professor Tuko, The.* Santos, A.
*Systrarna. See* Chorell, W. The Sisters

*T Bone n Weasel.* Klein, J.
*T-money & Wolf.* Willmott, K., and Averill, R.
*T-Shirts.* Patrick, R.
*Table Laid, The.* Langhoff, A.

*Table Manners. See* Ayckbourn, A. The Norman
      Conquests
*Table Number Seven.* Rattigan, T.
*La table: parole des femmes. See* Foucher, M. The Table:
      Womenspeak
*Table Settings.* Lapine, J.
*Table: Womenspeak, The.* Foucher, M.
*Le tableau. See* Ionesco, E. The Painting
*Tadanori.* Zeami.
*Taema.* Zeami.
*Tagad in citā di ābeles kungs. See* Straumanis, A. It's
      Different Now, Mr. Abele
*Tailleur pour dames. See* Feydeau, G. A Fitting Confusion
*Tails Up.* Roberts, C.
*Tainai. See* Miyoshi, J. In the Womb
*Takasago.* Zeami.
*Take a Giant Step.* Peterson, L.
*Take no yuki.* Seami
*Taking Care of Numero Uno.* Zylin, S.
*Taking of Liberty, The.* Robson, C.
*Taking of Miss Janie, The.* Bullins, E.
*Taking Steam.* Klonsky, K., and Shein, B.
*Taking the Bandits' Stronghold. See* Anonymous Plays.
      Taking Tiger Mountain by Strategy
*Taking Tiger Mountain by Strategy.* Anonymous Plays
*Tako je umrl Zarathushtra. See* Svetina, I. Thus Died
      Zarathushtra
*Takunda.* Smith, C.
*El tálamo. See* Quiles, E. The Bridal Chamber
*Talanta.* Aretino, P.
*Tale Ends, The.* CODCO
*Tale of an Idiot. See* Petrolini, E. Fortunello
*Tale of Komachi Told by the Wind, The.* Ōta, S.
*Tale of Mighty Hawk and Magic Fish, The.* Dorras, J., and
      Walker, P.
*Tale of Mystery, A.* Holcroft, T.
*Tale of Robin Hood, A. See* Jonson, B. The Sad Shepherd
*Tale Told by a Scorched Tree.* Bharti, B.
*Talé-danda. See* Karnad, G. Death by Beheading
*Tàlem. See* Belbel, S. Fourplay
*Talented Tenth, The.* Wesley, R.
*Talents, The (Wakefield).* Anonymous Plays
*Tales from the Vienna Woods.* Horváth, Ö.
*Tales of Hoffman, The.* Levine, M.; McNamee, G.; and
      Greenberg, D.
*Tales of the Lost Formicans.* Congdon, C.
*Tales of the South Pacific.* Michener, J. See Hammerstein, O.
      and Logan, J. South Pacific
*Der talisman. See* Nestroy, J. The Talisman
*Talisman, The.* Nestroy, J.
*Talk about Love.* Emond, P.
*Talk on Music.* Gingold, H.
*Talk to Me like the Rain and Let Me Listen.* Williams, T.
*Talk-story.* Barroga, J.

*Talking Bones. See* Youngblood, S. Movie Music
*Talley's Folly.* Wilson, L.
*Tamburlaine the Great.* Marlowe, C.
*Tamerlane.* Rowe, N.
*Taming of the Shrew, The.* Shakespeare, W.
*Tamura.* Anonymous Plays
*Tancred and Gismund; or, Gismond of Salerne.* Wilmot, R.
*Tancred and Sigismunda.* Thomson, J.
*Tancred King of Sicily; or, the Archives of Palermo.*
      Stone, J.
*Tango.* Mrozek, S.
*Tango Palace.* Fornés, M.
*Tango-monogurui.* I-ami
*Tanikō. See* Anonymous Plays. The Valley Rite
*Tanikō.* Zenchiku, U.
*Tantris the Fool. See* Hardt, E. Tristram the Jester
*Tanya.* Arbuzov, A.
*Tape.* Belber, S.
*Tape.* Rivera, J.
*Tapestry, The.* DeVeaux, A.
*Taps. See* Schrock, G. Two for the Silence
*Tara 'l-dik. See* Surayyi`,`A. The Bird Has Flown
*Tarnish.* Pottle, E.
*Tartuffe. See* Molière, J. Le Tartuffe
*Le Tartuffe; ou, L'imposteur.* Molière, J.
*Taste.* Foote, S.
*Taste of Honey, A.* Delaney, S.
*Tatjana in Color.* Jordan, J.
*Tatsuta.* Komparu-Zenchiku.
*Tattoo Girl.* Iizuka, N.
*Taxes.* Mednick, M.
*Taxes.* Tolstoi, L.
*Ta'ziya. See* Anonymous Plays. The Martyrdom of Ali
*Tchin-Tchin.* Michaels, S.
*Te awa I tahuti.* Owen, R.
*Te hara (The Sin).* Broughton, J.
*Tea.* Houston, V.
*Tea and Sympathy.* Anderson, R.
*Tea for Three.* Locher, J.
*Teach Me How to Cry; a Drama in Three Acts.* Joudry, P.
*Teach Me the Ways of the Sacred Circle.* Dudoward, V.
*Teahouse of the August Moon, The.* Patrick, J.
*Tears, Mama.* Adams, P.
*Tears of Fear in the Era of Terror.* Nyathi, F.
*Tècnica de cambra. See* Pedrolo, M. The Room
*Teenytown.* Carlos, L., Hagedorn, J., and McCauley, R.
*Tegue O. Divelly, The Irish Priest. See* Shadwell, T. The
      Lancashire Witches and Tegue O. Divelly, the Irish
      Priest
*La tejedora de sueños. See* Vallejo, A. The Dream Weaver
*Teibele and Her Demon.* Singer, I. and Friedman, E.
*Telescope, The.* Sherriff, R.
*Tell.* Bumbalo, V.
*Tell Pharaoh.* Mitchell, L.

*Tonight We Improvise*. Pirandello, L.
*Tonari no otoko. See* Iwamatsu, R. The Man Next Door
*T'ongyŏng Ogwangdae*. Anonymous Plays
*Too Late*. Kente, G.
*Too Late to Call Backe Yesterday*. Davenport, R.
*Tooth and Nail*. Junction Avenue Theatre Company
*Tooth of Crime, The*. Shepard, S.
*Top Girls*. Churchill, C.
*Top of the Ladder*. Guthrie, T.
*Tophat*. Harrison, P.
*Der tor und der tod*. Hofmannsthal, H. von
*Torch Race, The. See* Hervieu, P. La course du flambeau
*Torch Song Trilogy*. Fierstein, H.
*Torioibune. See* Kongō, Y. The Bird-scaring Boat
*Toronto at Dreamer's Rock*. Taylor, D.
*Toronto, Mississippi*. Macleod, J.
*Torquato Tasso*. Goethe, J.
*Tortesa, the Usurer*. Willis, N.
*La tortue qui chante. See* Zinsou, S. The Singing Tortoise
*Toru*. Zeami.
*Totenauberg (Death/Valley/Summit)*. Jelinek, E.
*Totentanz*. Anonymous Plays
*Tottenham Court*. Nabbes, T.
*Tou Ngo. See* Kuan, H. Snow in Midsummer
*Touch*. Press-Coffman, T.
*Touch: A Play for Two*. Demchuk, D.
*Touch It Light*. Storey, R.
*Touch of the Poet, A*. O'Neill, E.
*Touch Wood*. Smith, D. G.
*Tough Choices for the New Century*. Anderson, J.
*Toujours ensemble. See* Visdei, A. Always Together
*Tour*. McNally, T.
*La tour de la defense. See* Copi. A Tower near Paris
*Tour Guide, The*. Strauss, B.
*Tous contre tous. See* Adamov, A. All against All
*Tous locataires. See* Lison-Leroy, F., and Nys-Mazure, C. Tenants All
*Toussaint: Excerpt from Act I of a Work in Progress*. Hansberry, L.
*Tout contre un petit bois. See* Ribes, J. The Rest Have Got It Wrong
*Tout pour les dames! See* Meilhac, H. and Halévy, L. Signor Nocodemo
*Tovarich*. Deval, J.
*Towards Evening*. Stewart, E.
*Tower, The*. Porter, H.
*Tower, The*. Weiss, P.
*Tower near Paris, A*. Copi.
*Tower of Babel, The*. Goodman, P.
*Town of Titipu, The. See* Gilbert, W. and Sullivan, A. The Mikado
*Towneley Play, The*. Anonymous Plays
*Toy Cart, The. See* Shudraka. The Little Clay Cart
*Toy Shop, The*. Dodsley, R.
*Toys in the Attic*. Hellman, L.

*Los trabajos de Jacob. See* Vega, L. The Trials of Jacob; or, Sometimes Dreams Come True
*Tracers*. DiFusco, J.
*Trachiniae, The*. Sophocles
*Track Thirteen*. Graham, S.
*La traction en la Amistad*. Zayas y Sotomayor, M.
*Trafficking in Broken Hearts*. Sanchez, E.
*Trafford Tanzi*. Luckham, C.
*El tragaluz. See* Buero Vallejo, A. The Basement Window
*Tragedia Josephina. See* Carvajal, M. The Joseph Tragedy
*La tragédie de Carmen; a Full-length Musical in One Act*. Brook, P., Carrière, J., and Constant, M.
*Tragedie of Antonie, The*. Pembroke, M.
*Tragedie of Iphigenia, The*. Lumley, J.
*Tragedie of Mariam, The. See* Cary, E. The Tragedy of Mariam, the Faire Queene of Jewry
*Tragedy of a Tenant Farm Woman. See* Green, P. and Green, E. Fixin's: The Tragedy of a Tenant Farm Woman
*Tragedy of Antonie, The*. Garnier, R.
*Tragedy of Antony and Cleopatra, The. See* Shakespeare, W. Antony and Cleopatra
*Tragedy of Hamlet, Prince of Denmark, The. See* Shakespeare, W. Hamlet
*Tragedy of Jane Shore, The*. Rowe, N.
*Tragedy of King Lear, The. See* Shakespeare, W. King Lear
*Tragedy of King Real, The*. Mitchell, A.
*Tragedy of King Richard II, The. See* Shakespeare, W. King Richard II
*Tragedy of King Richard III, The. See* Shakespeare, W. King Richard III
*Tragedy of Love, The*. Heiberg, C.
*Tragedy of Macbeth, The. See* Shakespeare, W. Macbeth
*Tragedy of Mariam, the Faire Queene of Jewry, The*. Cary, E.
*Tragedy of Mr. No-Balance*. Musings V.
*Tragedy of Musila, The*. Jayawardhana, B.
*Tragedy of Mustapha, the Son of Solyman the Magnificent*. Orrery, R.
*Tragedy of Nero*. Anonymous Plays
*Tragedy of Othello, The. See* Shakespeare, W. Othello, the Moor of Venice
*Tragedy of Othello: the Moor of Venice, The*. Shakespeare, W. *See* Othello, the Moor of Venice
*Tragedy of Pompey the Great, The*. Masefield, J.
*Tragedy of the Duchess of Malfi. See* Webster, J. The Duchess of Malfi
*Tragedy of Tragedies, The; or, the Life and Death of Tom Thumb the Great*. Fielding, H.
*Tragedy of Valentinian, The*. Fletcher, J.
*Tragedy or Interlude Manifesting the Chief Promises of God unto Man, A. See* Bale, J. God's Promises
*Tragedy Rehearsed, A. See* Sheridan, R. The Critic
*Tragic End of Mythology, The (Its Author Wielding a Terrible Pen)*. Gałczyński, K.

*Tragic Prelude.* Sastre, A.

*Tragical History of Doctor Faustus, The.* Marlowe, C.

*Tragical History of the Life and Death of Doctor Faustus, The. See* Marlowe, C. The Tragical History of Doctor Faustus

*Tragicomedia de Calixto y Melibea. See* Rojas, F. Celestina

*Tragi-comedy of Calisto and Melibea, The. See* Rojas, F. Celestina

*Tragi-comedy of Don Cristobita and Doña Rosita, The.* García Lorca, F.

*Tragidie of [Gorboduc; or of] Ferrex and Porrex, The. See* Sackville, T. and Norton, T. Gorboduc

*Trail, The.* Gough, L.

*Trail of the Torch, The. See* Hervieu, P. La course du flambeau

*Train to H . . .* Bellido, J.

*Traitor, The.* Shirley, J.

*Traitor, The.* Wilde, P.

*Tramping Man, The.* McDonald, I.

*Trängningen. See* Gorling, L. The Sandwiching

*Trans-Canada Highway.* Tallman, J.

*Transcending.* Cregan, D.

*Transfiguration.* Toller, E.

*Transformation. See* Toller, E. Transfiguration

*Transistor Radio, The.* Saro-Wiwa, K.

*Transit heimat: gedeckte tische. See* Langhoff, A. The Table Laid

*Transit of Venus.* Hunter, M.

*Transition.* Barrie, S.

*Translation of John Snaith, The.* Cooke, B.

*Translations.* Friel, B.

*Transplantations: Straight and Other Jackets para Mi.* Astor delValle, J.

*Trapolin's Vagaries. See* Tate, N. A Duke and No Duke

*Trappists.* Ritz, J.

*Trappolin Suppos'd a Prince. Cokain, A. See* Tate, N. A Duke and No Duke

*Trash.* Monge-Rafuls, P.

*Traum ein leben, Der.* Grillparzer, F.

*Traveling Dragon Teases a Phoenix, The.* Anonymous Plays

*Traveller Returned, The.* Murray, J.

*Travelling North.* Williamson, D.

*Travels of Heikiki, The.* Kates, C.

*Travels of the Three English Brothers, The.* Day, J., Rowley, W., and Wilkins, G.

*Travesties.* Stoppard, T.

*Li tre becchi. See* Anonymous Plays. The Three Cuckolds

*Tre maa man vaere. See* Locher, J. Tea for Three

*Tread the Green Grass.* Green, P.

*Treasure, The.* Pinski, D.

*Treasure of the Sierra Madre, The.* Huston, J.

*Tree, The.* Garro, E.

*Tree without Shade, A.* Celestino, A.

*Trelawny.* Woods, A. and Rowell, G.

*Trelawny of the "Wells."* Pinero, A.

*Tren a F . . . See* Belfido, J. Train to H . . .

*Trente ans; ou, La vie d'un joueur.* Goubaux, P. and Ducange, V. *See* Dunlap, W. Thirty Years

*Les trente-sept sous de M. Montaudoin.* Labiche, E. and Martin, E.

*Tres clerici. See* Anonymous Plays. Saint Nicholas and the Three Scholars

*Tres clerici. See* Anonymous Plays. The Three Students (from Hildesheim)

*Tres filie. See* Anonymous Plays. The Three Daughters (from Hildesheim)

*Los tres reyes magos/The Three Kings.* Anonymous Plays

*Tres sombreros de copa. See* Mihura, M. Three Top Hats

*Trespassers.* Reid, L.

*Trespassion.* O'Donnell, M.

*Trestle at Pope Lick Creek, The.* Wallace, N.

*Trial, The. (Chester) See* Anonymous Plays. Trial and Flagellation, The (Chester)

*Trial and Error.* Horne, K.

*Trial and Error.* James, L.

*Trial and Flagellation, The (Chester).* Anonymous Plays

*Trial and Flagellation of Christ, The. See* Anonymous Plays. Trial and Flagellation, The (Chester)

*Trial by Jury.* Gilbert, W.

*Trial Horse No. 1: Many Loves.* Williams, W.

*Trial of Atticus before Judge Beau, for a Rape, The.* Anonymous Plays

*Trial of Christ, The (Coventry).* Anonymous Plays

*Trial of Jesus, The.* Pickering, K., Wood, K., and Dart, P.

*Trial of Joseph and Mary (N Town).* Anonymous Plays.

*Trial of Mary and Joseph, The. See* Anonymous Plays. Trial of Joseph and Mary (N Town)

*Trial of the Catonsville Nine, The.* Berrigan, D.

*Trial of Treasure, The.* Anonymous Plays

*Trial without Jury; or, the Magpie and the Maid.* Payne, J.

*Trials of Brother Jero, The.* Soyinka, W.

*Trials of Jacob; or, Sometimes Dreams Come True, The.* Vega, L.

*Tribute.* Slade, B.

*Trick to Catch the Old One, A.* Middleton, T.

*Trickster, The. See* Plautus. Pseudolus

*Trickster of Seville, The. See* Téllez, G. El burlador de Sevilla

*Trickster of Seville and His Guest of Stone, The. See* Téllez, G. El burlador de Sevilla

*Trickster Visits the Old Folks Home.* Shorty, S.

*Trifles.* Glaspell, S.

*Trigon, The.* Lynne, J.

*Trilby.* Potter, P.

*Trinummus. See* Plautus, T. The Three Penny Day

*La triomphatrice. See* Leneru, M. Woman Triumphant

*Trip, The.* Rhodes, C.

*Under Their Influence.* Buchanan, W.
*Under Your Skin.* Simonarson, O.
*Underachiever, The.* Mayer, J. *See* Anonymous Plays. Twenty-four Hours: A.M.
*Undercover.* Tan, T.H.
*Underpants, The.* Sternheim, C.
*Undertow.* Spence, E.
*Un-divine Comedy, The.* Krasiński, Z.
*Undoing, The.* Mastrosimone, W.
*Uneasy Chair, The.* Smith, E.
*Unexpected Guests, The.* Howells, W.
*Unfinished Stories.* Pearson, S.
*Unfinished Women Cry in No Man's Land while a Bird Dies in a Gilded Cage.* Rahman, A.
*Ungrateful Dead, The.* Caulfield, A.
*Uniform of Flesh. See* Coxe, L. and Chapman, R. Billy Budd
*Uninvited, The.* Kelly, T.
*Union Station.* Effinger, M.
*United Family, A.* Prévert, J.
*United States.* Anderson, L.
*Universal Language, The. See* Ives, D. All in the Timing
*Unknown Chinaman, The.* Bernard, K.
*Unknown Soldier and His Wife, The.* Ustinov, P.
*Unknown Warrior, The. See* Raynal, P. Le tombeau sous l'Arc de Triomphe
*Unknown Woman, The.* Blok, A.
*Unman, Wittering and Zigo.* Cooper, G.
*Unnatural Mother, The.* Young Lady, A
*Unoha.* Zeami
*Unquestioned Integrity: The Hill-Thomas Hearings.* Hunt, M.
*Unrealities from the Immediate Wild East.* Cărbunariu, G.
*Unreasonable Act of Julian Waterman, The.* Taylor, R.
*Unrhymed.* Majumdar, D.
*Unrin temple, The. See* Anonymous Plays. Unrin'in
*Unrin'in.* Anonymous Plays
*Unsent Letters.* Szilágyi, A.
*Unter vier augen. See* Fulda, L. Tête-à-tête
*Until Further Notice.* Oyono-Mbia, G.
*Until the Monkey Comes.* Herndon, V.
*Unto Such Glory.* Green, P.
*Unveiling.* Havel, V.
*Uo no matsuri. See* Yū, M. Festival for the Fish
*Up and Gone Again.* Harris, B.
*Upon Chitts Hill.* Denstan.
*Upon This Rock.* Kirkup, J.
*Upper Room, The.* Benson, R.
*Upwardly Mobile Home.* Margolin, D., Shaw, P., and Weaver, L.
*Uranium 235.* MacColl, E.
*Uretten. See* Havrevold, F. The Injustice
*Urvashi Won by Velour. See* K ālidāsa. Vikramorvacie
*Useless Heroes, The.* Schmidhuber de la Mora, G.
*Usurper, The; or, Americans in Tripoli.* Jones, J.

*V poiskach radosti. See* Rozov, V. In Search of Happiness
*V snehu. See* Feriancová, V. In the Snow
*La vache qui rit.* Cunningham, T.
*Vacuum.* Arai, A.
*Vacuum.* Hardman, C.
*Vagabond King, The. See* McCarthy, J. If I Were King
*Vale of Content, The.* Sudermann, H.
*Valiant, The.* Hall, H. and Middlemass, R.
*Valley Forge.* Anderson, M.
*Valley Rite, The.* Anonymous Plays
*Valley Song.* Fugard, A.
*Valor, agravio y mujer.* Caro Mallén de Soto, A.
*La valse de toréadors. See* Anouilh, J. The Waltz of the Toreadors
*Value of Names, The.* Sweet, J.
*Valued Friends.* Jeffreys, S.
*Vanka the Steward and Jehan the Page.* Sologub, F.
*Vampire, The.* Planché, J.
*Vara. See* Ziverts, M. Power
*Variations on a Theme by Clara Schumann.* Yeger, S.
*Variations on the Death of Trotsky. See* Ives, D. All in the Timing
*Vasco.* Schéhadé, G.
*I vasi communicanti. See* Marinett, F. Connecting Vessels
*Vecera nad mestom. See* Kerata, L. Dinner about a City
*Vecher knigi v klubakhmolodezhi (opyt massovoi khudozhestvennoi agitatsii za knigu). See* Zhemchuzhny, V. Evening of Books for Youth Clubs
*Vejigantes. See* Arrivi, F. Masquerade
*Venceslas. See* Rotrou, J. Wenceshaus
*La venda en los ojos. See* López Rubio, J. The Blindfold
*Vendégség. See* Páskándi, G. Sojourn
*Los vendidos.* Valdez, L.
*Venetian, The.* Bax, D.
*Vengono. See* Marinetti, F. They Are Coming
*Venice Preserv'd; or, a Plot Discover'd.* Otway, T.
*Il ventaglio. See* Goldoni, C. The Fan
*Venus and Adonis.* Obey, A.
*Venus Observed.* Fry, C.
*Vera Baxter or the Atlantic Beaches.* Duras, M.
*Vera Baxter ou les plages de l'Atlantique. See* Duras, M. Vera Baxter or The Atlantic Beaches
*Verandah, The.* Mason, C.
*La verdad sospechosa.* Ruiz de Alarcón y Mendoza, J.
*Los verdes campos del Eden. See* Gala, A. The Green Fields of Eden
*Die Verfolgung und Ermordung Jean Paul Marats dargestellt durch die Schauspielgruppe des Hospizes zu Charenton unter anleitung des Herrn de Sade. See* Weiss, P. The Persecution and Assassination of Jean-Paul Marat as Performed by the Inmates of the Asylum of Charenton under the Direction of the Marquis de Sade
*Verge, The.* Glaspell, S.

What I Meant Was. Lucas, C.

What If It Had Turned Up Heads? Gaines, J.

What If You Died Tomorrow? Williamson, D.

What Is She? Smith, C.

What Is This Everything? Scanlon, P.

What Men Live By. Church, V.

What Might Have Happened. Lionheart, E.

What Price Glory? Anderson, M. and Stallings, L.

What Shall I Wear? Gingold, H.

What the Butler Saw. Orton, J.

What We Do with It. MacDonald, B.

What Where. Beckett, S.

What You Will. See Shakespeare, W. Twelfth Night

What's Wrong with Angry? Wilde, P.

Whelks and the Cromium, The. Sanford, J.

When a Girl Says Yes. See Moratín L. El sí de las niñas

When Did I Last See You. Kayla, L.

When Dreams Come True. Checa, P.

When Everybody Cares. McMaster, B.

When Faeries Thirst. Boucher, D.

When He Was Free and Young He Used to Wear Silks. Clarke, A.

When Is a Door Not a Door? Arden, J.

When I Want to Whistle, I Whistle . . . Valean, A.

When I Was Your Age. Vick, S.

When Ladies Meet. Crothers, R.

When Orpheus Played. Gałczyński, K.

When the Bough Breaks. Campbell, A.

When the Jumbie Bird Calls. Flanagan, B.

When the Roses Bloom Again. Marquina, E.

When the Sun Sets on the Branches of that Jambu Tree. Lee, J.

When the Sun Slides. Parks, S.

When the Women Vote. Freeman, E.

When Wendy Grew Up. Barrie, J.

When Words Fail. Dannenfelser, D.

When You Comin' Back, Red Ryder? Medoff, M.

Where Has Tommy Flowers Gone? McNally, T.

Where Is de Queen? Van Itallie, J.

Where Love Abides. To, R.

Where the Cross Is Made. O'Neill, E.

Where the Dear Antelope Play. Rogers, J.

Where the Señoritas Are. Astor del Valle, J.

Which Is the Man? Cowley, H.

Which Witch Is Which? McMaster, B.

Whirlpool. Bhagat, D.

Whisker Tweezers, The. See Tsnuchi, H.; Yasuda, A.; and Nakada, M. Saint Narokami and the God Fudō

Whiskey Six Cadenza. Pollock, S.

White Château, The. Berkeley, R.

White Chocolate for My Father. Carlos, L.

White Death, The. Therriault, D.

White Devil, The; or, Vittoria Corombona. Webster, J.

White Dresses. Green, P.

White-haired Girl, The. Ting, Y. and Ho, C.

White House Murder Case, The. Feiffer, J.

White Liars. See Shaffer, P. White Lies

White Lies. Shaffer, P.

White Night, The. Poirer, L.

White Redeemer, The. See Hauptmann, G. The White Saviour

White Saviour, The. Hauptmann, G.

White Sirens. Griffith, L.

White Skates. Martin, M.

White Slave, The. Campbell, B.

White Snake, The. Tien, H.

White Steed, The. Carroll, P.

White Water. Jesurun, J.

White Whore and the Bit Player, The. Eyen, T.

White with Wire Wheels. Hibberd, J.

Whiteheaded Boy, The. Robinson, L.

Whitehorn's Windmill. Boruta, K.

Whitehorn's Windmill. Ignatavicius, E. and Motiejúnas, S. See Boruta, K. Whitehorn's Windmill

Whither Goest Thou? Currie, C.

Whither Thou Goest. Kahn, B.

Whittenland. Cappelin, P.

Who Do You Belong To? Nasev, S.

Who Killed Don José? Anaya, R.

Who? Hibberd, J.

Who Goes There! Dighton, J.

Who Killed Katie Ross? Sears, D.

Who Look in Stove. Jeffery, L.

"Who Ride on White Horses," the Story of Edmund Campion. Breen, R. and Schnibbe, H.

Who Wants a Guinea? Colman, G., the Younger

Who Will Carry the Word? Delbo, C.

Whole Truth, The. Jenkins, R.

Whole Truth, The. Mackie, P.

Who's Afraid of the Working Class? Bovell, A., Cornelius, P., Reeves, M., Tsiolkas, C., and Vela, I.

Who's Afraid of Virginia Woolf? Albee, E.

Who's Got His Own. Milner, R.

Who's Happy Now. Hailey, O.

Who's the Strongest of Us All? Liang, B.

Whose Life Is It Anyway? Clark, B.

Why? Pirandello, L.

Why I Sleep Alone. Fuerstenberg, A.

Why Marry? Williams, J.

Why Not? Williams, J.

Why We Have a Body. Chafee, C.

Whylah Falls. Clarke, G.

Wicked Cooks, The. Grass, G.

Wide Open Cage, The. Baxter, J.

Widow Claire, The. Foote, H.

Widow Dylemma, The. Liking, W.

Widow of Watling Street, The. See Anonymous Plays. The Puritan

Widowers' Houses. Shaw, G.

# Anthology Title Index

*American Tradition in Literature, The.* 4th ed. Shorter ed. in One Volume. 1974. **BPE**

*American Twenties, The.* 1952. **HUTC**

*American Writers.* Rev. ed. 1955. **CROX**

*America's Literature.* 1955. **HARA**

*America's Lost Plays.* 1940–1941. 20v **AMP**

*America's Lost Plays.* v21. Satiric Comedies. 1969. **AMPA**

*Among the Nations.* 1948. **LEWI**

*Anatomy of Literature, An.* 1972. **FOS**

*Anchor Anthology of Jacobean Drama, The.* 1963. 2v **HAPRA**

*Angels of Vision.* 1962. **HUDE**

*Anonymous Plays.* 3rd Series. 1906. **FAR**

*Anthologie de la litterature française.* 1960. 2v **CLOU**

*Anthologie de la litterature française.* 1975. 2nd ed. 2v **CLOUD**

*Anthologie de la litterature française.* 1990. 3rd ed. 2v **CLOUDS**

*Anthology: An Introduction to Literature: Fiction, Poetry, Drama.* 1977. **ANT**

*Anthology of American Drama, An.* 1993 2v **KLIS**

*Anthology of American Literature.* 1974. 2v **MANCA**

*Anthology of American Literature.* 2nd ed. 1980. 2v **MANCB**

*Anthology of American Literature.* 3rd ed. 1985. 2v **MANCD**

*Anthology of American Literature.* 4th ed. 1989. 2v **MANCE**

*Anthology of American Literature.* 5th ed. 1993. 2v **MANCF**

*Anthology of American Literature.* 6th ed. 1997. 2v **MANCG**

*Anthology of American Literature.* 7th ed. 2000. 2v **MANCH**

*Anthology of Austrian Drama, An.* 1982. **ANTH**

*Anthology of Chinese Literature.* 1972. **BIR**

*Anthology of Contemporary Austrian Folk Drama.* 1993. **ANTHC**

*Anthology of English Drama before Shakespeare, An.* 1952. **HEIL**

*Anthology of English Literature, The.* 1973. 2v **KER**

*Anthology of German Expressionist Drama: A Prelude to the Absurd.* 1963. **SOK**

*Anthology of Greek Drama, First Series, An.* 1949. **ROBI**

*Anthology of Greek Drama, Second Series, An.* 1954. **ROBJ**

*Anthology of Greek Tragedy, An.* 1972. **COOA**

*Anthology of Indian Literature, An.* 1971. **ALPJ**

*Anthology of Indian Literature, An.* Second Revised Edition. 1987. **ALPJR**

*Anthology of Italian Authors from Cavalcanti to Fogazzaro (1270–1907), An.* 1907. **JOH**

*Anthology of Living Theater.* 1998. **ANTL**

*Anthology of Modern Belgian Theatre: Maurice Maeterlinck, Fernand Crommelynck, and Michel de Ghelderode, An.* 1981. **ANTM**

*Anthology of Non-Western Drama, An.* 1993. **KIAN**

*Anthology of Roman Drama, An.* 1960. **HAPV**

*Anthology of Romanticism.* 1948. **BERN**

*Anthology of Russian Literature from Earliest Writings to Modern Fiction: Introduction to Culture, An.* 1996. **RZH**

*Anthology of Russian Plays, An.* c1961, 1963. 2v **REEV**

*Anthology of World Literature, An.* 1934. **BUCK**

*Anthology of World Literature, An.* Rev. ed. 1940. **BUCL**

*Anthology of World Literature, An.* 3rd ed. 1951. **BUCM**

*Anti-naturalism: Six Full-length Contemporary American Plays.* 1989. **ANTN**

*Applause/Best Plays Theater Yearbook of 1990–1991: Featuring the Ten Best Plays of the Season, The.* See Best Plays of 1894/1899–1999/2000 **BES**

*Applause/Best Plays Theater Yearbook of 1990–1991: Featuring the Ten Best Plays of the Season, The.* See Best Plays of 1894/1899–1999/2000 **BES**

*Approach to Literature, An.* 1936. **BROF**

*Approach to Literature, An.* Rev. ed. 1939. **BROG**

*Approach to Literature, An.* 3rd ed. 1952. **BROH**

*Approach to Literature, An.* 5th ed. 1975. **BROI**

*Argentine Jewish Theatre: A Critical Anthology.* 1996. **ARGJT**

*Ariosto's the Supposes, Machiavelli's the Mandrake, Intronati's the Deceived: Three Renaissance Comedies.* 1996. **CAIR**

*Armenian Literature Comprising Poetry, Drama, Folklore, and Classic Traditions.* 1901. **ARM**

*Around the Edge: Women's Plays.* 1992. **AROUN**

*Art from the Ashes: A Holocaust Anthology.* 1995. **LAS**

*Art of Drama, The.* 1969. **DIEA**

*Art of Drama, The.* 2nd ed. 1976. **DIEB**

*Art of the Play, The.* 1955. **DOWN**

*Art of the Theatre, a Critical Anthology of Drama, The.* 1964. **COTY**

*Artists' Theatre: Four Plays.* 1960. **MAH**

*Arthurian Drama: An Anthology.* 1991. **LUP**

*Arthurian Literature by Women.* 1999. **LUPW**

*Arts of Reading, The.* 1960. **ROSS**

*Asian American Drama: 9 Plays from the Multiethnic Landscape.* 1997. **ASIAM**

*Asking and Telling: A Collection of Gay Drama for the 21st Century.* 2000. **CLUM**

*Aspects of Modern Drama.* 1960. **STEI**

*At the Junction: Four Plays by the Junction Avenue Theatre Company.* 1995. **ORK**

*Attic Tragedies.* 1927. **ATT**

*Augustans, The.* 1950. **MAL**

*Australia Plays: New Australian Drama.* 1989. **AUS**

*Australian Gay and Lesbian Plays.* 1996. **AUSG**

*Avant Garde Drama: A Casebook, (1918–1939).* 1976. **DUK**

*Awake and Singing: 7 Classic Plays from the American Jewish Repertoire.* 1995. **SCL**

*Balkan Blues: Writing out of Yugoslavia*. 1995. **LABO**

*Balkan Plots: New Plays from Central and Eastern Europe*. 2000. **ROEB**

*Beacon Lights of Literature*. 1940. 7v **BEAC**

*Bedford Introduction to Drama, The*. 1989. **JACOB**

*Bedford Introduction to Drama, The*. 2nd ed. 1993. **JACOBA**

*Bedford Introduction to Drama, The*. 3rd ed. 1997. **JACOBD**

*Bedford Introduction to Literature, The*. 3rd ed. 1993. **MEYD**

*Bedford Introduction to Literature, The*. 4th ed. 1996. **MEYE**

*Bedford Introduction to Literature, The*. 5th ed. 1999. **MEYF**

*Before Brecht: Four German Plays*. 1985. **BEFOB**

*Beginnings of English Literature, The*. 1961. **MANN**

*Bell's British Theatre, Farces—1784*. 1977. 4v **BELC**

*Bell's British Theatre: Selected Plays, 1791–1802, 1797: 49 Plays Unrepresented in eds. of 1776, 1781, and 1784*. 1977. 16v **BELG**

*Bell's British Theatre, 1776–1781*. 1977. 21v **BELK**

*Best American Plays: Third Series, 1945–51*. 1952. **GARW**

*Best American Plays: Fourth Series, 1951–57*. 1958. **GART**

*Best American Plays: Fifth Series, 1957–1963*. 1963. **GARSA**

*Best American Plays, Sixth Series, 1963–1967*. 1971. **GAT**

*Best American Plays: Seventh Series, 1967–1973*. 1975. **GARTL**

*Best American Plays: Eighth Series, 1974–1982*. 1983. **BERS**

*Best American Plays: Ninth Series, 1983–1992*. 1993. **BERT**

*Best American Plays: Supplementary vol., 1918–58*. 1961. **GARU**

*Best Eighteenth Century Comedies, The*. 1929. **UHL**

*Best Elizabethan Plays, The*. 1890. **THA**

*Best Mystery and Suspense Plays of the Modern Theatre*. 1971. **RICI**

*Best of the Fest: A Collection of New Plays Celebrating 10 Years of London New Play Festival*. 1998. **SETR**

*Best of the West: An Anthology of Plays from the 1989 & 1990 Padua Hills Playwrights Festival*. 1991. **MEDN**

*Best off off–Broadway, The*. 1969. **SMC**

*Best Plays of 1894/1899–1999/2000*. 1894/95 1999/2000. 86v **BES**

*Best Plays of the Early American Theatre: from the Beginning to 1916*. 1967. **GARX**

*Best Plays of the Modern American Theatre: Second Series*. 1947. **GARZ**

*Best Plays of the Seventies*. 1980. **BEST**

*Best Plays of the Sixties*. 1970. **RICIS**

*Best Short Plays of the Social Theatre, The*. 1939. **KOZ**

*Best Short Plays of the World Theatre 1958–1967*. 1968. **RICJ**

*Best Short Plays of the World Theatre, 1968–1973*. 1973. **RICK**

*Between Worlds: Contemporary Asian-American Plays*. 1990. **BETW**

*Beyond the Pale: Dramatic Writing from First Nations Writers & Writers of Colour*. 1996. **BEYO**

*Big-time Women from Way Back When*. 1993. **BIG**

*Black and Asian Plays Anthology*. 2000. **BLAAP**

*Black Comedy: Nine Plays: A Critical Anthology*. 1997. **BLAC**

*Black Crook, and Other Nineteenth Century American Plays, The*. 1967. **MASW**

*Black Drama: An Anthology*. 1970. **BRAS**

*Black Drama Anthology*. 1971. **KINH**

*Black Drama Anthology*. 1986. **KINHB**

*Black Drama in America: An Anthology*. 1971. **TUQT**

*Black Drama in America: An Anthology*. 2nd ed. 1994. **TUQTR**

*Black Female Playwrights: An Anthology of Plays before 1950*. 1989. **PER**

*Black Fire: An Anthology of Afro-American Writing*. 1969. **JONE**

*Black Heroes: Seven Plays*. 1989. **HILEB**

*Black Insights: Significant Literature by Black Americans 1760 to the Present*. 1971. **FORD**

*Black Plays*. 1987–1995. 3v **BREW**

*Black Quartet: 4 New Black Plays by Ben Caldwell, and Others, A*. 1970. **BLACQ**

*Black South African Women: An Anthology of Plays*. 1998. **PERA**

*Black Teacher and the Dramatic arts: A Dialogue, Bibliography, and Anthology, The*. 1970. **REAR**

*Black Theatre: A 20th Century Collection of the Best Playwrights*. 1971. **PATR**

*Black Theatre, U.S.A.: 45 Plays by Black Americans, 1847–1974*. 1974. **HARY**

*Black Theatre, USA: Plays by African Americans, 1847 to Today*. Revised and Expanded Edition. 1996. **HARYB**

*Black Thunder: An Anthology of Contemporary African–American Drama*. 1992. **BLACTH**

*Body Blows: Women, Violence, and Survival: Three Plays*. 2000. **BODY**

*Bohemian Verses: An Anthology of Contemporary English Language Writings from Prague*. 1993. **BOHV**

*Boneman: An Anthology of Canadian Plays*. 1995. **RALPH**

*Book of Dramas, an Anthology of Nineteen Plays, A*. 1929. **CARP**

*Book of Dramas, A*. Rev. ed. 1949. **CARPA**

*Book of English Literature, A*. 4th ed. 1942–43. 2v **SNYD**

*Book of Modern Plays, A.* 1925. **COD**
*Book of Plays, A.* 2000. **BOOK**
*Book of the P.E.N., The.* 1950. **OULD**
*Book of the Play, The.* [195n] **WALJ**
*Borzoi Reader, The.* 1936. **VAN**
*Bottled Notes from Underground: Contemporary Plays by Jewish Writers.* 1998. **LINDB**
*Bridge across the Sea: Seven Baltic Plays.* 1983. **BRIDGE**
*Britannica Library of Great American Writing, The.* 1960. 2v **UNTE**
*British and American Plays. 1830–1945.* 1947. **DUR**
*British and Western Literature.* 3d ed. 1979. **CARLO**
*British Drama.* 1929. **LIE**
*British Dramatists from Dryden to Sheridan.* 1939. **NET**
*British Literature.* 1951. 2v **SPD**
*British Literature. 1951, 1952.* 2v **SPEF**
*British Literature.* 2nd ed. 1963. 2v **SPDB**
*British Plays from the Restoration to 1820.* 1929. 2v **MOSE**
*British Plays of the Nineteenth Century.* 1966. **BAI**
*British Prose and Poetry.* Rev. ed. 1938. 2v **LIED**
*British Poetry and Prose.* 3rd ed. 1950. 2v **LIEE**
*Broadway's Beautiful Losers.* 1972. **SSTY**
*Burlesque Plays of the Eighteenth Century.* 1969. **TRUS**
*Burning the Curtain: Four Revolutionary Spanish Plays.* 1995. **BURN**
*Burns Mantle Theater Yearbook of 1989–1990 Featuring the Ten Best Plays of the Season. See* Best Plays of 1894/1899–1999/2000 **BES**
*Bush Theatre Book, The.* 1997. **BUSHB**
*Bush Theatre Plays.* 1996. **BUSHT**
*But still, like air, I'll rise: New Asian American Plays.* 1997. **HOUST**
*By popular demand: Plays and other works.* 1980. **SAN**
*By Southern Playwrights: Plays from Actors Theatre of Louisville.* 1996. **DIX**
*By Women: An Anthology of Literature.* 1976. **FOL**

*Calamus: Male Homosexuality in Twentieth Century Literature, An International Anthology.* 1982. **CAL**
*Camille and Other Plays.* 1957. **SSTG**
*Canada's Lost Plays.* 1978–80. 3v **WAGN**
*Canadian Mosaic: 6 Plays.* 1995. **RAVEL**
*Canadian Mosaic II: 6 Plays.* 1996. **RAVELII**
*Canadian Plays from Hart House Theatre.* 1926–27. 2v **MAS**
*Cavalcade of Comedy.* 1953. **KRM**
*Cavalcade of World Writing, A.* 1961. **HORN**
*Center Stage: An Anthology of 21 Contemporary Black-American Plays.* 1981. **CEN**
*Century Types of English Literature Chronologically Arranged.* 1925. **MACL**
*Challenge of the Theatre, The.* 1972. **STY**
*Character and Conflict: An Introduction to Drama.* 1963. **KERN**

*Character and Conflict: An Introduction to Drama.* 2nd ed. 1969. **KERO**
*Chester Mystery Cycle, The.* 1974. **CHEL**
*Chester Mystery Cycle: A New Edition with Modernized Spelling, The.* 1992. **CHELM**
*Chester Mystery Cycle: A New Staging Text, The.* 1987. **BURNS**
*Chester Mystery Plays . . . Adapted into Modern English, The.* 1957. **CHES**
*Chester Mystery Plays: Seventeen Pageant Plays from the Chester Craft Cycle, The.* 2nd ed. 1975. **CHESE**
*Chicano Voices.* 1975. **CHG**
*Chief British Dramatists Excluding Shakespeare, The.* 1924. **MATTL**
*Chief Contemporary Dramatists.* 1915. **DICD**
*Chief Contemporary Dramatists, Second Series.* 1921. **DICDS**
*Chief Contemporary Dramatists, Third Series.* 1930. **DICDT**
*Chief Elizabethan Dramatists, Excluding Shakespeare, The.* 1911. **NEI**
*Chief European Dramatists, The.* 1916. **MATT**
*Chief French Plays of the Nineteenth Century.* 1934. **GRA**
*Chief Patterns of World Drama.* 1946. **CLKW**
*Chief pre-Shakespearean Dramas.* 1924. **ADA**
*Chief Rivals of Corneille and Racine, The.* 1956. **LOCR**
*China on Stage: An American Actress in the People's Republic.* 1972. **SNO**
*Chinese Drama after the Cultural Revolution, 1979–1989: An Anthology.* 1996. **YUCHD**
*Chinese Literature: An Anthology from the Earliest Times to the Present Day.* 1974. **MANM**
*Chinese other 1850–1925: An Anthology of Plays, The.* 1997. **CHIN**
*Chinese Theater in the Days of Kublai Khan.* 1980. **CRU**
*Chloe plus Olivia: An Anthology of Lesbian Literature from the Seventeenth Century to the Present.* 1994. **FACO**
*Christmas Plays from Oberufer.* 1944. **HARW**
*Classic Comedies.* 1995. **CHARN**
*Classic Drama.* 1998. **SELF**
*Classic Irish Drama.* 1964 (1979 [printing]). **CLKWI**
*Classic Plays from the Negro Ensemble Company.* 1995. **HAPUE**
*Classic Soviet Plays.* 1979. **CLKX**
*Classic Theatre, The.* 1958–1961. 4v **BENR**
*Classic Theatre: The Humanities in Drama.* 1975. **CLKY**
*Classic through Modern Drama.* 1970. **REIL**
*Classical Chinese Plays.* 2nd ed. 1972. **HUNG**
*Classical Comedy Greek and Roman.* 1987. **COTKICC**
*Classical French Drama.* 1962. **FOWL**
*Classical German Drama.* 1963. **LUST**
*Classical Tragedy Greek and Roman: Eight Plays in Authoritative Modern Translations.* 1990. **COTKICG**

*Drama for a New South Africa: Seven Plays.* 1999. **GRAV**

*Drama for Composition.* 1973. **BAC**

*Drama for Reading & Performance. Collection One: Seventeen Full-length Plays for Students.* 2v 2000. **SCVDO**

*Drama for Reading & Performance. Collection Two: Nineteen Full-length Plays for Students.* 2v 2000. **SCVDT**

*Drama in Our Time.* 1948. **NAGE**

*Drama in the Modern World.* 1964. **WEIM**

*Drama in the Modern World: Plays and Essays.* Alternate ed. 1974. **WEIP**

*Drama in the Western World: 15 Plays with Essays.* 1968. **WEIS**

*Drama in the Western World: 9 Plays with Essays.* 1968. **WEIW**

*Drama: Its History, Literature and Influence on Civilization, The.* 1903–1904. 22v **BAT**

*Drama: Literature on Stage.* 1969. **BURG**

*Drama of Our Past: Major Plays from Nineteenth-Century Quebec, The.* 1997. **DOUC**

*Drama of the East and West.* 1956. **EDAD**

*Drama of the English Renaissance.* 1969. **WINE**

*Drama of the English Renaissance.* 1976. 2v **DPR**

*Drama on Stage.* 1961. **GOOD**

*Drama on Stage.* 2nd ed. 1978. **GOODE**

*Drama: Principles and Plays.* 1967. **HAVH**

*Drama: Principles and Plays.* 2nd ed. 1975. **HAVHA**

*Drama Reader, The.* 1962. **CONG**

*Drama: The Major Genres.* 1962. **HOGF**

*Drama through Performance.* 1977. **AUB**

*Drama: Traditional and Modern, The.* 1968. **GOLD**

*Drama II.* 1962. **REDM**

*DramaContemporary Czechoslovakia: Plays.* 1985. **DBG**

*DramaContemporary: France.* 1986. **WEHL**

*DramaContemporary Germany.* 1996. **WEBER**

*DramaContemporary Hungary. See* Hungary: Plays. **HUNGDC**

*DramaContemporary Scandinavia. See* Scandinavia: Plays **BRAK**

*DramaContemporary Spain. See* Spain: Plays **HOLTS**

*Dramas by Present-Day Writers.* 1927. **PEN**

*Dramas from the American Theatre, 1762–1909.* 1966. **MONR**

*Dramas of Modernism and Their Forerunners.* 1931. **MOSG**

*Dramas of Modernism and Their Forerunners.* Rev. ed. 1941. **MOSH**

*Dramatic Experience, The.* 1958. **BIER**

*Dramatic Experience: The Public Voice.* 1970. **SOM**

*Dramatic Masterpieces by Greek, Spanish, French, German and English Dramatists.* Rev. ed. 1900. 2v **DRA**

*Dramatic Moment, The.* 1967. **WAIW**

*Dramatic Representations of Filial Piety: Five Noh in Translation.* 1998. **DRAF**

*Dramatic Romance.* 1973. **FEFM**

*Dramatic Tragedy.* 1971. **MABC**

*Dutch and Flemish Plays.* 1997. **COUL**

*Dybbuk, and Other Great Yiddish Plays, The.* 1966. **LAO**

*Early American Drama.* 1997. **RICHE**

*Early Colonial Religious Drama in Mexico: From Tzompantli to Golgotha.* 1970. **RAVIC**

*Early English Classical Tragedies.* 1912. **CUN**

*Early English Drama: An Anthology.* 1993. **COLDE**

*Early English Plays.* 1928. **SCW**

*Early Plays from the Italian.* 1911. **BOND**

*Early Seventeenth Century Drama.* 1963. **LAWR**

*Early Seventeenth Century Plays, 1600–1642.* 1930. **WALL**

*Early 20th-Century German Plays.* 1998. **HERZ**

*Eastern Promise: Seven Plays from Central and Eastern Europe.* 1999. **EUP**

*Easy French Plays.* 1901. **BENZ**

*Echoes of Israel: Contemporary Drama.* 1999. **BARA**

*Edwardian Plays.* 1962. **WEAL**

*Eight American Ethnic Plays.* 1974. **GRIH**

*Eight Chinese Plays: From the 13th Century to the Present.* 1978. **EIG**

*Eight European Plays.* 1927. **KAT**

*Eight Famous Elizabethan Plays.* 1932. **DUN**

*Eight French Classic Plays.* 1932. **LYO**

*Eight Great Comedies.* 1958. **BARB**

*Eight Great Tragedies.* 1957. **BARC**

*Eight Plays for Theatre.* 1988. **EIGHT**

*Eight Plays from Off-Broadway.* 1966. **ORZ**

*Eight Spanish Plays of the Golden Age.* 1964. **SSTW**

*Eight Twentieth-Century Russian Plays.* 2000. **EIGHTRP**

*Eighteen-nineties, The.* 1948. **SECK**

*Eighteenth Century Drama: Afterpieces.* 1970. **BEVI**

*Eighteenth Century French Plays.* 1927. **BREN**

*Eighteenth Century Miscellany, An.* 1936. **KRO**

*Eighteenth Century Plays.* 1928. **HAN**

*Eighteenth-Century Plays.* 1952. **EIGH**

*Eighteenth Century Comedy.* 1929. **TAY**

*Eighteenth Century Tragedy.* 1965. **BOO**

*Elements of Literature: Essay, Fiction, Poetry, Drama, Film.* 1978. **SCNPL**

*Elements of Literature Five: Fiction, Poetry, Drama, Essay, Film.* Rev. ed. 1982. **SCNQ**

*Elements of Literature.* Canadian ed. 1987. **SCNQCA**

*Elements of Literature.* 2nd Canadian ed. 1990. **SCNQCB**

*Eleonora Duse Series of Plays, The.* 1923. **SAY**

*Eleven Plays.* 1964. **WEAN**

*Elizabethan Age.* 1965. **MONV**

*Elizabethan and Jacobean Comedy.* 1964. **ORNC**

*Elizabethan and Jacobean Tragedy.* 1964. **ORNT**

*Elizabethan and Stuart Plays.* 1934. **BAS**

*Elizabethan Drama.* 1950. **DEAN**

*Elizabethan Drama.* 2nd ed. 1961. **DEAO**

*Elizabethan Drama.* 1967. **GATG**

*Elizabethan Dramatists.* 1903. **WAT**
*Elizabethan Dramatists other than Shakespeare.* 1931.
    **OLH**
*Elizabethan History Plays.* 1965. **ARMS**
*Elizabethan Plays.* 1971. **NES**
*Elizabethan Plays.* 1933. **SPE**
*Elizabethan Tragedy.* 1933. **RYL**
*Embassy Successes. 1946–1948.* 3v **EMB**
*En scène: Trois comédies avec musique.* 1942. **BRN**
*Enclosure: A Collection of Plays.* 1975. **ENC**
*Encounters: Themes in Literature.* 1967. **CARM**
*Encounters: Themes in Literature.* 3d ed. 1979. **CARME**
*England in Literature.* 1953. **POOL**
*English and Continental Literature.* 1950. **SHAR**
*English Drama: An Anthology, 900–1642, The.* 1935. **PAR**
*English Drama, 1580–1642.* 1933. **BROC**
*English Drama in Transition 1880–1920.* 1968. **SALE**
*English Heritage, The.* 1945. 2v **WEAT**
*English Literature.* 1934. **BRIG**
*English Literature.* 1935. **BENN**
*English Literature.* 1954. **BAUG**
*English Literature.* 1968. **DAI**
*English Literature and Its Backgrounds.* 1939–40. 2v
    **GREB**
*English Literature and Its Backgrounds.* Rev. ed. 1949. 2v
    **GREC**
*English Literature, 1650–1800.* 1940. **MEN**
*English Masques.* 1976. **ETO**
*English Miracle Plays, Moralities and Interludes.* 8th ed.
    rev. 1927. **POLL**
*English Morality Plays and Moral interludes.* 1969. **SCAT**
*English Mystery Plays: A Selection.* 1975. **ENGE**
*English Plays of the Nineteenth Century.* 1969–1976. 5v
    **BOOA**
*English Plays, 1660–1820.* 1935. **MOR**
*English Romantic Drama: An Anthology, the Major
    Romantics.* 1976. **ENGL**
*English Romantic Drama: An Anthology, the Minor
    Romantics.* 1978. **ENGLMI**
*English Tradition: Drama, The.* 1968. **BARU**
*Epic and Folk Plays of the Yiddish Theatre.* 1975. **LIFS**
*El espejo—The Mirror: Selected Chicano Literature.* 1972.
    **ROMA**
*Essential Self: An Introduction to Literature, The.* 1976.
    **ESA**
*Ethnicities: Plays from the New West.* 1999. **NOTH**
*European and Asiatic Plays.* 1936. **TAV**
*Eva Le Gallienne's Civic Repertory Plays.* 1928. **LEG**
*Everyman and Medieval Miracle Plays.* 1959. **CAWL**
*Everyman and other Miracle and Morality Plays.* 1995.
    **EVEM**
*Everyman and other Plays.* 1925. **EVEP**
*"Everyman," with other Interludes, Including Eight
    Miracle Plays.* 1928. **EVER**
*Experience of Literature, The.* 1966. **MON**

*Experience of Literature, The.* 2nd ed. 1970. **MONA**
*Experience of Literature, The.* 1967. **TRI**
*Experience of Literature, The.* 1967. **TRIA**
*Explorations in French Literature.* 1939. **MANA**
*Explorations in Literature.* 1933–34. 2v **MIJ**
*Explorations in Literature.* Rev. ed. 1937–38. 2v **MIJA**
*Explorations in Living.* 1941. **ROGEX**
*Exploring Literature: Fiction, Poetry, Drama, Criticism.*
    1970. **ALS**
*Exploring Relationships through Drama: Three Plays for
    Performance and Discussion.* 1990. **MURD**
*Expressionist Texts.* 1986. **EXP**


*Faces of African Independence: Three Plays.* 1988.
    **FACES**
*Facing Some Problems.* 1970. **BENPB**
*Factory Lab Anthology, The.* 1974. **BRIN**
*Fallen Crown: Three French Mary Stuart Plays of the
    Seventeenth Century, The.* 1980. **FALE**
*Famous American Plays of the 1920s.* 1959. **MAF**
*Famous American Plays of the 1920s and the 1930s.* 1988.
    **MAFC**
*Famous American Plays of the 1930s.* 1959. **CLUR**
*Famous American Plays of the 1930's.* 1959. **FAMAL**
*Famous American Plays of the 1940's.* 1960. **HEWE**
*Famous American Plays of the 1940s and 1950s.* **FAMAF**
*Famous American Plays of the 1950's.* 1962. **FAM**
*Famous American Plays of the 1960s.* 1972. **FAMAH**
*Famous American Plays of the 1970s.* 1981. **FAMAD**
*Famous American Plays of the 1980s.* 1988. **FAMAB**
*Famous Plays of Crime and Detection.* 1946. **CART**
*Famous Plays of 1931.* 1931. **FAMAN**
*Famous Plays of 1932.* 1932. **FAMB**
*Famous Plays of 1932–33.* 1933. **FAMC**
*Famous Plays of 1933.* 1933. **FAMD**
*Famous Plays of 1933–34.* 1934. **FAME**
*Famous Plays of 1934.* 1934. **FAMF**
*Famous Plays of 1934–35.* 1935. **FAMG**
*Famous Plays of 1935.* 1935. **FAMH**
*Famous Plays of 1935–36.* 1936. **FAMI**
*Famous Plays of 1936.* 1936. **FAMJ**
*Famous Plays of 1937.* 1937. **FAMK**
*Famous Plays of 1938–39.* 1939. **FAML**
*Famous Plays of 1954.* 1954. **FAMO**
*Famous Plays of Today.* 1929. **FAO**
*Famous Plays of Today.* 1953. **FAOS**
*Far from the Land: New Irish Plays.* 1998. **FAIR**
*Fat Virgins, Fast Cars, and Asian values: A Collection of
    Plays from Theatreworks Writers' Lab.* 1993. **FAT**
*Fateful Lightning: America's Civil War Plays.* 2000.
    **MESC**
*Favorite American Plays of the Nineteenth Century.* 1943.
    **CLA**
*Favorite Modern Plays.* 1953. **SPER**
*Federal Theatre Plays.* 1938. **FEE**

*Four Renaissance Tragedies.* 1966. **FOUR**
*Four Restoration Marriage Plays.* 1995. **COTKA**
*Four Revenge Tragedies.* 1995. **MAUS**
*Four Russian Plays.* 1972. **COOPA**
*Four . . . Soviet . . . Plays.* 1937. **FOUS**
*Four Soviet War Plays.* 1944. **FOUT**
*Four Stages.* 1967, c1966. **MADB**
*Four Tudor Comedies.* 1984. **TYDE**
*Four Tudor Interludes.* 1974. **SOME**
*Fourteen Great Plays.* 1977. **FOUX**
*Frames of Reference: An Introduction to Literature.* 1974.
        **OHL**
*Frantic Comedy: Eight Plays of Knockabout Fun.* 1993.
        **KAYF**
*French Comedies of the XVIIIth Century.* 1923. **ALD**
*French Plays.* 1941. **BER**
*French Romantic Plays.* 1933. **COM**
*French Theater since 1930, The.* 1954. **PUCC**
*Freshman English Program.* 1960. **GPA**
*friendly fire: An Anthology of Plays by Queer Street Youth.*
        1997. **BOWL**
*Frogs and other Greek Plays, The.* 1970. **MAMB**
*From Beowulf to Modern British Writers.* 1959. **BALL**
*From Beowulf to Thomas Hardy.* 1924. 2v **SHAH**
*From Beowulf to Thomas Hardy.* Rev. ed. 1931. 2v **SHAI**
*From Beowulf to Thomas Hardy.* New ed. 1939. 2v **SHAJ**
*From Classroom to Stage. Three New Plays.* 1966. **FRO**
*From Script to Stage: Eight Modern Plays.* 1971. **GOO**
*From the Modern Repertoire.* 1949–1956. 3v **BENS**
*From the other Side of the Century II: A New American
        Drama 1960–1995.* 1998. **MESSE**
*From Valley Playwrights Theatre.* 1986–1989. 2v **VICK**
*Frontline Intelligence: New Plays for the Nineties.* 1993–
        1995. 3v **FROLIN**
*Fruitful and Multiplying: 9 Contemporary Plays from the
        American Jewish Repertoire.* 1996. **SCM**


*Galaxy: Literary Modes and Genres.* 1961. **SCNR**
*Gay and Lesbian Plays Today.* 1993. **HELB**
*Gay Plays.* 1984–1994. 5v **GAY**
*Gay Plays: An International Anthology.* 1989. **GAYIA**
*Gay Plays: The First Collection.* 1979. **HOF**
*Gay Sweatshop: Four Plays and a Company.* 1989. **OSME**
*Gemme della letteratura italiane.* 1904. **BIN**
*Generation of 1898 and After, The.* 1961. **PARV**
*Generations: An Introduction to Drama.* 1971. **BARO**
*Generous Donors: A Dramatic Expose on AIDS and other
        Plays.* 1997. **AGOR**
*Genius of the Early English Theatre, The.* 1962. **BARD**
*Genius of the French Theater, The.* 1961. **BERMG**
*Genius of the German Theater, The.* 1968. **ESS**
*Genius of the Greek Drama, The.* 1921. **ROBK**
*Genius of the Irish Theatre, The.* 1960. **BARF**
*Genius of the Italian Theater, The.* 1964. **BENSA**
*Genius of the Later English Theater, The.* 1962. **BARG**

*Genius of the Oriental Theatre, The.* 1966. **ANDF**
*Genius of the Scandinavian Theater, The.* 1964. **SPR**
*German Classics of the Nineteenth and Twentieth
        Centuries, The.* 1913–14. 20v **FRA**
*German Drama between the Wars.* 1972. **WELG**
*German Expressionist Plays.* 1997. **SCVG**
*German-language Comedy: A Critical Anthology.* 1992.
        **GERLC**
*German Literature since Goethe.* 1958. 2v **FEFH**
*German Plays: New Drama from a Changing Country.*
        1997. **DODGSG**
*German Plays of the Nineteenth Century.* 1930. **CAM**
*German Plays 2.* 1999. **DODGSP**
*German Theater before 1750.* 1992. **GILL**
*God, Man, and Devil: Yiddish Plays in Translation.* 1999.
        **SANR**
*Going it Alone: Plays by Women for Solo Performers.*
        1997. **BREK**
*Golden Age, The.* 1963. **HOUE**
*Golden Age of Melodrama: Twelve 19th Century
        Melodramas, The.* 1974. **KILG**
*Golden Steed: Seven Baltic Plays, The.* 1979. **GOLB**
*Granny Mountains: A Cycle of Nō Plays.* 1992. **TYLG**
        (Vol. 2 of 2v set. *See* **TYLP** for v.1)
*Great American Parade.* 1935. **GRD**
*Great Books of the Western World.* 1952. 54v **GRDB**
*Great Books of the Western World.* 2nd ed. 1990. 61v
        **GRDBA**
*Great Christian Plays.* 1956. **SWIT**
*Great English Plays.* 1928. **RUB**
*Great Farces.* 1966. **SAFF**
*Great Irish Plays.* 1995. **GREAAI**
*Great Jewish Plays, The.* 1972. **LAOG**
*Great Melodramas.* 1966. **SAFM**
*Great Modern British Plays.* 1932. **MART**
*Great Musicals of the American Theatre.* 1976. **RICM**
*Great Plays (English).* 1900. **GRE**
*Great Plays (French and German).* 1901. **GREA**
*Great Plays, Sophocles to Albee.* 3d ed. 1975. **BLOND**
*Great Plays, Sophocles to Brecht.* 1965. **BLON**
*Great Playwrights: 25 Plays, The.* 1972. 2v **BENSB**
*Great Rock Musicals.* 1979. **GREAAR**
*Great Russian Plays.* 1960. **HOUG**
*Great Sanscrit Plays.* 1964. **LAL**
*Great World Theatre: An Introduction to Drama.* 1964.
        **DOWS**
*Greek and Roman Classics in Translation.* 1947. **MURP**
*Greek Drama.* 1965 (1982 printing). **GRDG**
*Greek Drama for Everyman.* 1954. **LUCA**
*Greek Drama for the Common Reader.* 1967. **LUCAB**
*Greek Dramas.* 1900. **GREE**
*Greek Literature in Translation.* 1924. **HOWE**
*Greek Literature in Translation.* 1944. **OAM**
*Greek Literature in Translation.* 1948. **HOWF**
*Greek Plays in Modern Translation.* 1947. **FIFT**

*Greek Tragedies.* 1960. 3v **GRER**
*Greek Tragedies.* 2nd ed. 1991. 3v **GRERA**
*Greek Tragedy and Comedy.* 1968. **LUCAF**
*Grove New American Theater.* 1993. **FEFG**
*Grove Plays of the Bohemian Club, The.* 1918. 3v **BOH**
*Grove Press Modern Drama.* 1975. **GROV**
*Guthrie New Theater. Volume I.* 1976. **GUTR**

*Half a Century of Japanese Theater.* 1999–2006. 8v
    **HACJT**
*Harbrace Anthology of Drama, The.* 1994. **STOTD**
*Harbrace Anthology of Literature, The.* 2nd ed. 1998.
    **STOTLB**
*Harbrace Omnibus.* 1942. **HAP**
*Harcourt Brace Anthology of Drama, The.* 2nd ed. 1996.
    **WOTHB**
*Harcourt Brace Anthology of Drama, The.* 3rd ed. 2000.
    **WOTHC**
*Harvard Classics.* 1909–10. 50v **HARC**
*Harvard Dramatic Club Miracle Plays: Ten Plays, The.*
    1928. **ROBM**
*HBJ Anthology of Literature, The.* 1993. **STOTLA**
*HBJ Anthology of Drama, The.* 1993. **WOTHA**
*He reo hou: 5 Plays by Maori Playwrights.* 1991. **GARR**
*Heath Introduction to Drama, The.* 1976. **HEA**
*Heath Introduction to Drama, The.* 2nd ed. 1983. **HEAA**
*Heath Introduction to Drama, The.* 3rd ed. 1988. **HEAB**
*Heath Introduction to Drama, The.* 4th ed. 1992. **HEAC**
*Heath Introduction to Drama, The.* 5th ed. 1996. **HEAD**
*Heath Introduction to Literature, The.* 1980. **HEAL**
*Heath Introduction to Literature, The.* 2nd ed. 1984.
    **HEALA**
*Heath Introduction to Literature, The.* 3rd ed. 1988.
    **HEALB**
*Heath Introduction to Literature, The.* 4th ed. 1992.
    **HEALC**
*Heath Introduction to Literature, The.* 5th ed. 1996.
    **HEALD**
*Heath Introduction to Literature, The.* 6th ed. 2000.
    **HEALE**
*Heath Readings in the Literature of Europe.* 1933. **CROV**
*Hebrew Anthology, A.* 1913. 2v **KOH**
*Here to Stay: Five Plays from the Women's Project.* 1997.
    **MIGHTS**
*Heritage of American Literature, The.* 1951. 2v **RIL**
*Heritage of American Literature.* 1991. 2v **MIJH**
*Heritage of European Literature, The.* 1948–49. 2v
    **WEAV**
*Heroines: Three Plays.* 1992. **DOOL**
*Herstory: Plays by Women for Women.* 1991. 2v **GRIFG**
*Hidden Treasures in Literature.* 1934. 3v **COOK**
*High Energy Musicals from the Omaha Magic Theatre.*
    1983. **HIJ**
*High Lights in English Literature and other Selections.*
    1940. **SRY**

*High Lights in English Literature.* 1940. **SRYG**
*Hiss the Villain: Six English and American Melodramas.*
    1964. **BOOB**
*Homosexual Acts: Five Short Plays from the Gay Season*
    *at The Almost Free Theatre.* 1975. **HOM**
*Hour of One: Six Gothic Melodramas, The.* 1975. **HOUR**
*How the Vote Was Won, and other Suffragette Plays.* 1985.
    **VOTE**
*Humana Festival: The Complete Plays 1993–2000.* 1993–
    2000. 8v **HUMANA**
*Humanist Tradition in World Literature: An Anthology*
    *of Masterpieces from Gilgamesh to the Divine*
    *Comedy, The.* 1970. **HAPRL**
*Hungarian Plays: New Drama from Hungary.* 1996.
    **UPOR**
*Hungary: Plays.* 1991. **HUNGDC**

*Idea and Image.* 1962. **GUTH**
*Idea of Tragedy, The.* 1966. **BENQ**
*Ideas and Forms in English and American Literature.*
    1932. 2v **WATT**
*Ideas and Patterns in Literature.* 1970. 4v **SUT**
*Image and Value: An Invitation to Literature.* 1966.
    **COXM**
*Imaginative Literature: Fiction, Drama, Poetry.* 1968.
    **MORX**
*Imaginative Literature: Fiction, Drama, Poetry.* 2nd ed.
    1973. **MORXB**
*Imaginative Literature: Fiction, Drama, Poetry.* 3rd ed.
    1978. **MORXD**
*Imaginative Literature: Fiction, Drama, Poetry.* 4th ed.
    1983. **MORXE**
*In the Presence of This Continent: American Themes and*
    *Ideas.* 1971. **BAYM**
*Inchape bell, The. See* The Lights o' London and other
    Victorian Plays. **BOOL**
*Incisions.* 2000. **INCI**
*Indiana Experience: An Anthology, The.* 1977. **INDI**
*Informal Reader, The.* 1955. **EAVE**
*Inscape: Stories, Plays, Poems.* 1971. **DAVM**
*Inside 2000.* 2000. **INSI**
*Insights: Themes in Literature.* 3d ed. 1979. **CARMI**
*International Modern Plays.* 1950. **INTE**
*Interpreting Literature.* 1955. **KNIC**
*Interpreting Literature.* Rev. ed. 1960. **KNID**
*Interpreting Literature.* 3rd ed. 1965. **KNIE**
*Interpreting Literature.* 4th ed. 1969. **KNIF**
*Interpreting Literature.* 5th ed. 1974. **KNIG**
*Interpreting Literature.* 6th ed. 1978. **KNIH**
*Interpreting Literature.* 7th ed. 1985. **KNIJ**
*Intimate Acts: Eight Contemporary Lesbian Plays.* 1997.
    **DEAT**
*Introducing the Drama, an Anthology.* 1963. **GATS**
*Introduction to Drama, An.* 1927. **HUD**
*Introduction to Drama.* 1962. **ROF**

*Literary Experience: Public and Private Voices.* 1971.
**SOMA**

*Literary Reflections.* 1967. **ELK**

*Literary Reflections.* 3rd ed. 1976. **ELKE**

*Literary Spectrum.* 1974. **ROY**

*Literary Types and Themes.* 1960. **MANK**

*Literary Types and Themes.* 2nd ed. 1971. **MANL**

*Literatura Española: Selección.* 1968. **MARLI**

*Literature.* 1949. **BLAG**

*Literature.* 2d ed. 1968. **GUTL**

*Literature: A Collection of Mythology and Folklore, Short Stories, Poetry, Drama.* 1973. **HOGI**

*Literature: A Collection of Mythology and Folklore, Short Stories, Poetry, Drama.* 2nd ed. 1977. **HOGN**

*Literature: A College Anthology.* 1977. **LITC**

*Literature: An Introduction.* 1960. **SUL**

*Literature: An Introduction to Fiction, Poetry, and Drama.* 1976. **LITI**

*Literature: An Introduction to Fiction, Poetry, and Drama.* 2nd ed. 1979. **LITIA**

*Literature: An Introduction to Fiction, Poetry, and Drama.* 3rd ed. 1983. **LITIB**

*Literature: An Introduction to Fiction, Poetry, and Drama.* 4th ed. 1987. **LITIC**

*Literature: An Introduction to Fiction, Poetry, and Drama.* 5th ed. 1991. **LITID**

*Literature: An Introduction to Fiction, Poetry, and Drama.* 6th ed. 1995. **LITIE**

*Literature: An Introduction to Fiction, Poetry, and Drama.* 7th ed. 1999. **LITIF**

*Literature: An Introduction to Fiction, Poetry, and Drama.* Compact ed. 1995. **LITJ**

*Literature: An Introduction to Fiction, Poetry, and Drama.* 2nd Compact ed. 2000. **LITJA**

*Literature and Gender: Thinking Critically through Fiction, Poetry, and Drama.* 1999. **WIEG**

*Literature as Art.* 1972. **BRIT**

*Literature as Experience: An Anthology.* 1979. **LITQ**

*Literature: Fiction, Poetry, Drama.* 1977. **LITP**

*Literature for Composition: Essays, Fiction, Poetry, and Drama.* 1984. **LITR**

*Literature for Composition: Essays, Fiction, Poetry, and Drama.* 2nd ed. 1988. **LITRA**

*Literature for Composition: Essays, Fiction, Poetry, and Drama.* 3rd ed. 1991. **LITRB**

*Literature for Composition: Essays, Fiction, Poetry, and Drama.* 4th ed. 1996. **LITRC**

*Literature for Composition: Essays, Fiction, Poetry, and Drama.* 5th ed. 2000. **LITRD**

*Literature for Our Time.* 1947. **BROZ**

*Literature for Our Time.* Rev. ed. 1953. **WAIT**

*Literature for Our Time.* 3rd ed. 1958. **WAIU**

*Literature for Writing.* 1962. **STJM**

*Literature for Writing.* 2nd ed. 1967. **STJN**

*Literature: Form and Function.* 1965. **DUH**

*Literature in Critical Perspectives: An Anthology.* 1968.
**GORE**

*Literature in English.* 1948. **RUSS**

*Literature of America, The.* 1929. 2v **QUIO**

*Literature of America, The.* 1971. 2v **HOWP**

*Literature of America: Twentieth Century, The.* 1970.
**SCNT**

*Literature of American Jews, The.* 1973. **GROS**

*Literature of Comedy: An Anthology, The.* 1968. **STRO**

*Literature of England, The.* 1936. 2v **WOO**

*Literature of England, The.* Rev. ed. 1941. 2v **WOOD**

*Literature of England, The.* 3rd ed. 1947. 2v **WOOE**

*Literature of Medieval England, The.* 1970. **ROBE**

*Literature of the Early Republic.* 1950. **CADY**

*Literature of the United States, The.* 1946–47. 2v **BLAI**

*Literature of the United States, The.* Single Volume ed.
1949. **BLAJ**

*Literature of Western Civilization.* 1952. 2v **LOCM**

*Literature I.* 1976. **ROYE**

*Literature: Reading and Writing, the Human Experience.*
7th ed. 1998. **ABCG**

*Literature: Reading and Writing, the Human Experience.*
Shorter 7th ed. 2000. **ABCH**

*Literature: Reading Fiction, Poetry, and Drama.* Compact
ed. 2000. **DIYL**

*Literature: Reading Fiction, Poetry, Drama, and the Essay.* 1986. **DIYLA**

*Literature: Reading Fiction, Poetry, Drama, and the Essay.* 2nd ed. 1990. **DIYLB**

*Literature: Reading Fiction, Poetry, Drama, and the Essay.* 3rd ed. 1994. **DIYLC**

*Literature: Reading Fiction, Poetry, Drama, and the Essay.* 4th ed. 1998. **DIYLD**

*Literature: Reading, Reacting, Writing.* 1991. **KIRLA**

*Literature: Reading, Reacting, Writing.* 2nd ed. 1994.
**KIRLB**

*Literature: Reading, Reacting, Writing.* 3rd ed. 1997.
**KIRLC**

*Literature: Reading, Reacting, Writing.* Compact 4th ed.
2000. **KIRLD**

*Literature: Structure, Sound, and Sense.* 1970. **PERT**

*Literature: Structure, Sound and Sense.* 2nd ed. 1974.
**PERU**

*Literature: Structure, Sound, and Sense.* 3rd ed. 1978.
**PERV**

*Literature: Structure, Sound, and Sense.* 4th ed. 1983.
**PERW**

*Literature: Structure, Sound and Sense.* 5th ed. 1988.
**PERX**

*Literature: Structure, Sound, and Sense.* 6th ed. 1993.
**PERY**

*Literature: The Channel of Culture.* 1948. **CONN**

*Literature: The Human Experience.* 1973. **ABCA**

*Literature: The Human Experience.* 2nd ed. 1978. **ABCB**

*Literature: The Human Experience.* 3rd ed. 1982. **ABCC**

*Middle Age, Old Age: Short Stories, Poems, Plays, and Essays on Aging.* 1980. **MID**

*Milestones of the Drama.* 1940. **COHM**

*Minnesota Showcase: Four Plays.* 1975. **MIMN**

*Minor Elizabethan Drama.* 1913. 2v **MIN**

*Minor Elizabethan Drama.* 1939. 2v **MIO**

*Minor Elizabethan Tragedies.* 1974. **MIR**

*Minor Knickerbockers.* 1947. **TAFT**

*Miracle Plays: Seven Medieval Plays for Modern Players.* 1956, 1959. **MAR**

*Mirror to the Cage: Three Contemporary Hungarian Plays, A.* 1993. **GYOR**

*Mirrors: An Introduction to Literature.* 1972. **KNO**

*Mirrors: An Introduction to Literature.* 2nd ed. 1975. **KNOJ**

*Mirrors: An Introduction to Literature.* 3rd ed. 1988. **KNOK**

*Mirrors for Man: 26 Plays of World Drama.* 1974. **ASF**

*Misanthrope and other French Classics, The.* 1986. **BENSD**

*Miscellaneous Plays.* 2000. **MISC**

*Modern Age, Literature, The.* 2nd ed. 1972. **LIEF**

*Modern Age, Literature, The.* 3rd ed. 1976. **LIEG**

*Modern American and British Plays.* 1931. **TUCD**

*Modern American Drama.* 1961. **DAVI**

*Modern American Dramas.* 1941. **HAT**

*Modern American Dramas.* New ed. 1949. **HATA**

*Modern American Plays.* 1920. **BAK**

*Modern American Plays.* 1949. **CASS**

*Modern American Prose.* 1934. **VANM**

*Modern and Contemporary Drama.* 1994. **GILB**

*Modern Arabic Drama: An Anthology.* 1995. **JAY**

*Modern ASEAN Plays. Brunei Darussalam.* 1994. **MLAB**

*Modern ASEAN Plays. Malaysia.* 1993. **MLAM**

*Modern ASEAN Plays. Philippines.* 1992. **MLAP**

*Modern ASEAN Plays. Singapore.* 1991. **MLAS**

*Modern ASEAN Plays. Thailand.* 1994. **MLAT**

*Modern British Dramas.* 1941. **HAU**

*Modern Canadian Plays.* 1985. **WASCP**

*Modern Canadian Plays.* 3rd ed. 1993–1994. 2v **WASCPA**

*Modern Canadian Plays.* 4th ed. 2000. 2v **WASCPB**

*Modern Catalan Plays.* 2000. **LONG**

*Modern Continental Dramas.* 1941. **HAV**

*Modern Continental Plays.* 1929. **TUCG**

*Modern Drama.* Alternate ed. 1966. **REIT**

*Modern Drama: An Anthology of Nine Plays.* 1963. **LOR**

*Modern Drama and Social Change.* 1972. **RAI**

*Modern Drama: Authoritative Texts . . . Backgrounds, and Criticism.* 1966. **CAPU**

*Modern Drama by Women 1880s–1930s.* 1996. **KEL**

*Modern Drama for Analysis.* 1950. **CUBE**

*Modern Drama for Analysis.* Rev. ed. 1955. **CUBG**

*Modern Drama for Analysis.* 3rd ed. **CUBH**

*Modern Drama from Communist China.* 1970. **MESE**

*Modern Drama in America,* Volume 1. 1982. **MOAD**

*Modern Drama: Nine Plays.* 1961. **REIP**

*Modern Drama: Plays, Criticism, Theory.* 1995. **WOTHM**

*Modern Drama: Selected Plays from 1879 to the Present.* 1999. **LEVY**

*Modern Dramas.* New Shorter ed. 1948. **HAVE**

*Modern Dramas.* Shorter ed. 1944. **HAVD**

*Modern Egyptian Drama: An Anthology.* 1974. **ABL**

*Modern English Drama.* 1964. **BARV**

*Modern English Readings.* 1934. **LOO**

*Modern English Readings.* Rev. ed. 1936. **LOOA**

*Modern English Readings.* 3rd ed. 1939. **LOOB**

*Modern English Readings.* 4th ed. 1942. **LOOC**

*Modern English Readings.* 5th ed. 1946. **LOOD**

*Modern English Readings.* 6th ed. 1950. **LOOK**

*Modern English Readings.* 7th ed. 1956. **LOOF**

*Modern French Theatre: The Avant-Garde, Dada, and Surrealism: An Anthology of Plays.* 1964. **BEN**

*Modern Indian Drama: An Anthology.* 2000. **DESH**

*Modern Indian Plays.* 2000–2007. 3v **KAM**

*Modern Israeli Drama: An Anthology.* 1983. **MOADE**

*Modern Japanese Drama, an Anthology.* 1979. **TAK**

*Modern Literature from China.* 1974. **MESH**

*Modern Nordic Plays: Denmark.* 1974. **MNOD**

*Modern Nordic Plays: Finland.* 1973. **MNOF**

*Modern Nordic Plays: Iceland.* 1973. **MNOI**

*Modern Nordic Plays: Norway.* 1974. **MNON**

*Modern Nordic Plays: Sweden.* 1973. **MNOS**

*Modern Omnibus, The.* 1946. **ROLF**

*Modern Persian Drama: An Anthology.* 1987. **MOCPD**

*Modern Plays.* 1932. **MAD**

*Modern Plays.* 1932. **TUCJ**

*Modern Plays.* 1937. **MOD**

*Modern Plays, Short and Long.* 1924. **LAW**

*Modern Repertory, A.* 1953. **HAVG**

*Modern Scandinavian Plays.* 1954. **MODS**

*Modern Spanish Stage: Four Plays, The.* 1970. **HOLTM**

*Modern Spanish Theatre: An Anthology of Plays.* 1968. **BENA**

*Modern Stage in Latin America: Six Plays, The.* 1971. **WOOG**

*Modern Sri Lankan Drama: An Anthology.* 1991. **GOON**

*Modern Theatre, The. 1955–1960.* 6v **BENT**

*Modern Theatre, The.* 1964. **COTQ**

*Modern Theatre: A Collection of Plays, The.* 1968. 10v in 5 **INCA**

*Modern Turkish Drama, an Anthology of Plays in Translation.* 1976. **HALM**

*Mondala: Literature for Critical Analysis.* 1970. **MOE**

*Monologues: Plays from Martinique, France, Algeria, Quebec.* 1995. **MOGS**

*Monstrous Regiment: Four Plays and a Collective Celebration.* 1991. **HANNA**

*Moon Marked and Touched by Sun: Plays by African-American Women.* 1994. **MAQ**

*Open Space: Six Contemporary Plays from Africa.* 1995. **HUTCH**

*Orestes and Electra: Myth and Dramatic Form.* 1968. **FOR**

*Oriental Literature.* Rev. ed. 1960. 4v **ORI**

*Our Dramatic Heritage. 1983–1992.* 6v **HILPDH**

*Our Heritage of World Literature.* 1938. **THOM**

*Our Heritage of World Literature.* Rev. ed. 1942. **THON**

*Our Land and Its Literature.* 1936. **LOW**

*Our Living Language.* 1961. **HUNT**

*Our Reading Heritage.* 2956. 4v **WAGC**

*Out from Under: Texts by Women Performance Artists.* 1990. **OUT**

*Out Front: Contemporary Gay and Lesbian Plays.* 1988. **SHEW**

*Out of the Fringe: Contemporary Latina/Latino Theatre and Performance.* 2000. **SVICH**

*Oxford Anthology of American Literature.* 1938. **OXF**

*Oxford Anthology of Canadian Literature, The.* 1973. **OXFC**

*Oxford Anthology of Contemporary Chinese Drama, An.* 1997. **CHEU**

*Oxford Book of Women's Writing in the United States, The.* 1995. **WAGNOX**

*Paris Stage: Recent Plays, The.* 1988. **PAIS**

*Parricidio a la utopia: El teatro argentine actual en 4 claves mayors, Del.* 1993. **PARRI**

*Passions and Poisons: New Canadian Prose, Poetry, and Plays.* 1987. **PASS**

*Patterns for Living.* 1940. **CALM**

*Patterns for Living.* Alternate Edition. 1943, 1947. 2v **CALN**

*Patterns for Living.* 3rd ed. 1949. **CALP**

*Patterns for Living.* 4th ed. 1955. **CALQ**

*Patterns in Modern Drama.* 1948. **HARB**

*Patterns of Literature.* 1967. 4v **PATM**

*Patterns of Literature.* 1969. **PATP**

*Peace Plays.* 1985. **LOWE**

*Peace Plays: Two.* 1990. **LOWE2**

*Penguin Book of Modern Canadian Drama.* 1984. **PENG**

*Perceptions in Literature.* 1972. **MAEC**

*Perrine's Literature: Structure, Sound, and Sense.* 7th ed. 1998. **PERZ**

*Perspectives: An Anthology.* 1976. **PES**

*Phaedra and Hippolytus: Myth and Dramatic Form.* 1966. **SANL**

*Philippine Drama: Twelve Plays in Six Philippine Languages.* 1987. **PHIL**

*Pining Wind: A Cycle of Nō Plays.* 1992. **TYLP** (Vol. 1 of 2v set. *See* **TYLG for v.2**)

*Places, Please!: The First Anthology of Lesbian Plays.* 1985. **PLA**

*Play: A Critical Anthology, The.* 1951. **BENU**

*Play and the Reader, The.* 1966. **JOHN**

*Play and the Reader, The.* 1971. **JOHO**

*Playbook.* 1986. **KLEIN**

*Playbook: Five Plays for a New Theatre.* 1956. **PLAA**

*Playboy of the Western World and Two other Irish Plays, The.* 1987. **PLAAB**

*Playful Phoenix: Women Write for the Singapore Stage.* 1996. **PING**

*Playing out the Empire: Ben-Hur and other Toga Plays and Films, 1883–1908: A Critical Anthology.* 1994. **MAYER**

*Playing with Fire: Five StagePlays from Riding Lights Theatre Co.* 1987. **BURB**

*Playmakers, The.* 1976. 2v **PLAAC**

*PlayReader's Repertory: An Anthology for Introduction to Theatre.* 1970. **WHFM**

*Play's the Thing, The.* 1936. **MIL**

*Plays and Pageants from the Life of the Negro.* 1979. **RIR**

*Plays and Pageants from the Life of the Negro.* 1994. **RIRA**

*Plays and Playwrights for the New Millennium.* 2000. **DENT**

*Plays and the Theatre.* 1937. **THO**

*Plays by American Women: The Early Years.* 1981. **PLAAD**

*Plays by American Women: 1900–1930.* 1985. **PLAAE**

*Plays by American Women: 1930–1960.* 1994. **PLAAF**

*Plays by and about Women.* 1973. **SUB**

*Plays by Early American Women, 1775–1850.* 1995. **KRIT**

*Plays by Four Tragedians.* 1968. **GLO**

*Plays by French and Francophone Women: A Critical Anthology.* 1994. **PLAAG**

*Plays by Greek, Spanish, French, German and English Dramatists.* Rev. ed. 1900. 2v **PLAB**

*Plays by Mediterranean Women.* 1994. **BARAM**

*Plays by Women. 1983–1994.* 10v **PLABE**

*Plays by Women: An International Anthology.* 1988–1996. 3v **PLABI**

*Plays, Classic and Contemporary.* 1967. **LID**

*Plays for a New Theater: Play Book 2.* 1966. **PLAC**

*Plays for Actresses.* 1997. **PLACA**

*Plays for Stage and Screen. 1989–1998.* 3v **PERR**

*Plays for the College Theater.* 1932. **LEV**

*Plays for the College Theater.* 1934. **LEVE**

*Plays for the End of the Century.* 1996. **MARR**

*Plays for the Nuclear Age.* 1989. **PLACB**

*Plays for the Theatre: An Anthology of World Drama.* 1967. **BRIX**

*Plays for the Theatre: An Anthology of World Drama.* 2nd ed. 1974. **BRIY**

*Plays for the Theatre: An Anthology of World Drama.* 3rd ed. 1979. **BRIZ**

*Plays for the Theatre: An Anthology of World Drama.* 4th ed. 1984. **BRJ**

*Plays for the Theatre: A Drama Anthology.* 5th ed. 1988. **BRJA**

*Prose and Poetry of America.* 1949. **PROI**
*Prose and Poetry of England.* 1934. **PROM**
*Prose and Poetry of England.* Catholic ed. 1940. **PRON**
*Prose and Poetry of the World.* 1941. **PROW**
*Prose and Poetry of the World.* 1954. **PROX**
*Pulitzer Prize Plays, 1918–1934, The.* 1935. **CORD**
*Pulitzer Prize Plays . . ., The.* New ed. 1938. **CORE**
*Pulitzer Prize Reader.* 1961. **HALU**
*Puro Teatro: A Latina Anthology.* 2000. **PURO**

*Quartet: A Book of Stories, Plays, Poems, and Critical
    Essays.* 1970. **SILK**
*Quartet: A Book of Stories, Plays, Poems, and Critical
    Essays.* 2nd ed. 1973. **SILKI**
*Quarto of Modern Literature, A.* 1935. **BROW**
*Quarto of Modern Literature . . ., A.* 3rd ed. 1950. **BROX**
*Quarto of Modern Literature, A.* 5th ed. 1964. **BROY**
*Quebec Voices Three Plays.* 1986. **WALAQ**
*Quiché Dramas and Divinatory Calendars.* 1997.
    **EDMON**

*Range of Literature, The.* 1960. **SCNN**
*Range of Literature, The.* 2nd ed. 1967. **SCNO**
*Range of Literature, The.* 3rd ed. 1973. **SCNP**
*Range of Literature: Drama, The.* 1969. **LAM**
*Rave: Young Adult Drama.* 2000. **RAVE**
*Read up on Life.* 1952. **WAGE**
*Reading American Literature.* 1944. **CALG**
*Reading and Understanding Plays, Level I and Level II.*
    1989. 2v **READ**
*Reading & Writing about Literature: Fiction, Poetry,
    Drama, and the Essay.* 1990. **PRO**
*Reading and Writing from Literature.* 1997. **SCX**
*Reading Apprenticeship Literature, A.* 1971. **BRIU**
*Reading Drama.* 1950. **MIKL**
*Reading Drama: An Anthology of Plays.* 1990. **DIYRD**
*Reading Literature.* 1964. **SATI**
*Reading Literature: Stories, Plays, and Poems.* 1968. **SATJ**
*Reading for Understanding: Fiction, Drama, Poetry.* 1968.
    **SHR**
*Readings for Enjoyment.* 1959. **DAVK**
*Readings for Our Times.* 1942. **BLOD**
*Readings in European Literature.* 1928. **SEBO**
*Readings in European Literature.* 2nd ed. 1946. **SEBP**
*Realities of Literature, The.* 1971. **DIER**
*Reality in Conflict: Literature of Values in Opposition.*
    1976. **REAL**
*Recent Puerto Rican Theater: Five Plays from New York.*
    1991. **ANTUR**
*Recently Recovered "Lost" Tudor Plays with Some Others.*
    1907. **FARN**
*Recueil de lectures.* 1950. **STOC**
*Red Pear Garden: 3 Great Dramas of Revolutionary
    China, The.* 1974. **MIT**
*Reflections in Literature.* 1975. **REF**

*Reichard Collection of Early Pennsylvania German Plays,
    The.* 1962. **BUFF**
*Religious Dramas, 1924–25.* 1923–26. 2v **FED**
*Renaissance Drama: An Anthology of Plays and
    Entertainments.* 1999. **KINNR**
*Renaissance Drama by Women: Texts and Documents.*
    1996. **RENDW**
*Renaissance Treasury, A.* 1953. **HAYD**
*Repertory.* 1960. **BLAH**
*Representative American Dramas, National and Local.*
    1926. **MOSJ**
*Representative American Dramas, National and Local.*
    Rev. ed. 1933. **MOSK**
*Representative American Dramas, National and Local.*
    Rev. and Brought up-to-date. 1941. **MOSL**
*Representative American Plays.* 1917. **QUIJ**
*Representative American Plays from 1880 to the Present
    Day.* 1928. **QUIJR**
*Representative American Plays, 1767–1923.* 3rd ed. rev.
    and enl. 1925. **QUIK**
*Representative American Plays from 1767 to the Present
    Day.* 5th ed. rev. and enl. 1930. **QUIL**
*Representative English Dramas from Dryden to Sheridan.*
    1914. **TUP**
*Representative English Dramas from Dryden to Sheridan.*
    New and enl. ed. 1934. **TUQ**
*Representative Plays by American Dramatists.* 1918–25.
    3v **MOSS**
*Representative Plays from 1767 to Plays from 1767 to the
    Present Day.* 6th ed. rev. and enl. 1938. **QUIM**
*Representative American Plays from 1767 to the Present
    Day.* 7th ed., rev. and enl. 1953. **QUIN**
*Representative British Dramas, Victorian and Modern.*
    1918. **MOSN**
*Representative British Dramas, Victorian and Modern.*
    New rev. ed. 1931. **MOSO**
*Representative Continental Dramas, Revolutionary and
    Transitional.* 1924. **MOSQ**
*Representative English Comedies.* 1903–36. 4v **GAYLE**
*Representative English Dramas.* 1929. **MOO**
*Representative English Plays.* 1916. **TAT**
*Representative English Plays.* 2nd ed. rev. and enl. 1938.
    **TAU**
*Representative Medieval and Tudor Plays.* 1942. **LOOM**
*Representative Modern Dramas.* 1936. **WHI**
*Representative Modern Plays.* 1929. **COT**
*Representative Modern Plays, American.* 1952. **WARH**
*Representative Modern Plays, British.* 1953. **WARI**
*Representative Modern Plays: Ibsen to Tennessee
    Williams.* 1964. **WARL**
*Representative Plays from the French Theatre of Today.*
    1940. **HART**
*Representative Spanish Authors.* 1942. 2v in 1 **PATT**
*Restless Spirits from the Japanese Noh Plays of the Fourth
    Group.* 1995. *See* The Noh, v. 4, bk. **SHIM**

*Restoration and Eighteenth Century Comedy. 1973.*
**MANH**
*Restoration Comedies. 1921.* **SUM**
*Restoration Comedies. 1970.* **DAVR**
*Restoration Comedy. 1974. 4v* **JEFF**
*Restoration Drama: An Anthology. 2000.* **WONR**
*Restoration Dramatists. 1930.* **TICK**
*Restoration Plays. 1955.* **REST**
*Restoration Plays. 1974.* **RES**
*Restoration Plays. 1992.* **RESL**
*Restoration Plays from Dryden to Farquhar. 1929.* **GOS**
*Restoration Plays from Dryden to Farquhar. 1932.* **GOSA**
*Restoration Tragedies. 1977.* **RET**
*Revised College Omnibus, The. 1939.* **MACE**
*Revolution: A Collection of Plays. 1975.* **REV**
*Ritual, Realism, and Revolt: Major Traditions in the
    Drama. 1972.* **TAUJ**
*Robin Hood and Other Outlaw Tales. 1997.* **KNIRH**
*Roman Drama. 1964.* **LIDE**
*Roman Drama. 1965.* **ROM**
*Roman Drama, in Modern Translations. 1966.* **COTU**
*Roman Literature in Translation. 1924.* **HOWJ**
*Roman Literature in Translation. 1959.* **HOWK**
*Romance. 1932.* **BRIK**
*Romantic Influence, The. 1963.* **HOUK**
*Romantic Triumph: American Literature from 1830 to
    1860, The. 1933.* **MADI**
*Roots and Blossoms: African American Plays for Today.
    1991.* **NTIR**
*Roots of African American Drama: An Anthology of Early
    Plays, The. 1991.* **ROOTS**
*Roots of National Culture: American Literature to 1830,
    The. 1933.* **SPI**
*Rough Magic: First Plays. 1999.* **BOUR**
*Russian Comedy of the Nikolaian Era. 1997.* **RUSSCO**
*Russian Mirror: Three Plays by Russian Women. 1998.*
    **SMB**
*Russian Satiric Comedy: Six Plays. 1983.* **RVI**
*Russian Symbolist Theatre: An Anthology of Plays and
    Critical Texts, The. 1986.* **GREEN**

*S.R.O.: The Most Successful Plays in the History of the
    American Stage. 1944.* **CEY**
*Saclit Drama: Plays by South Asian Canadians. 1996.*
    **SACL**
*Sacred Earth Dramas: An Anthology of Winning Plays
    from the 1990 Competition of the Sacred Earth
    Drama Trust. 1993.* **SACR**
*Sampler of Plays by Women, A. 1990.* **POLK**
*Satan, Socialites, and Solly Gold: Three New Plays from
    England. 1961.* **SATA**
*Satire. 1967.* **RUSV**
*Scandinavia: Plays. 1989.* **BRAK**
*Scandinavian Plays of the Twentieth Century. 1944–1951.*
    *3v* **SCAN**

*Scot-free: New Scottish Plays. 1990.* **CALE**
*Scotland Plays: New Scottish Drama. 1998.* **HOWA**
*Scribner Quarto of Modern Literature, The. 1978.* **SDQ**
*Seeds of Modern Drama. 1963.* **HOUP**
*2nd Conference for Asian Women and Theater: A
    Compilation of Plays, The. 2000.* **SECO**
*Second Shepherds' Play, Everyman, and other Early Plays,
    The. 1910.* **CHI**
*Second Wave Plays: Women at the Albany Empire. 1990.*
    **GRAW**
*6 Dramaturgos españoles del siglo XX: Teatro de
    liberación, vol. 1: Teatro en democracia, vol. 2.
    1988. 2v* **SEIS**
*Selection: A Reader for College Writing. 1955.* **HAVI**
*Sensational Restoration, The. 1996.* **JENS**
*Servant of Two Masters: And other Italian Classics, The.
    1986.* **BENV**
*Seven Cannons: Plays. 2000.* **SEUC**
*Seven Contemporary Austrian Plays. 1995.* **LAXC**
*Seven Contemporary Plays. 1931.* **WHK**
*Seven Different Plays. 1988.* **WEJ**
*Seven Expressionist Plays: Kokoschka to Barlach. 1968.*
    **RITS**
*Seven Famous Greek Plays. 1950.* **OATH**
*Seven French Plays (1730–1897). 1935.* **SEA**
*Seven Gothic Dramas, 1789–1825. 1992.* **COXJ**
*Seven Irish Plays, 1946–1964. 1967.* **HOGE**
*Seven Miracle Plays. 1963.* **FRAN**
*Seven Plays. 1935.* **SEV**
*Seven Plays by Women: Female Voices, Fighting Lives.
    1991.* **ROES**
*Seven Plays of Mystery and Suspense with Writing
    Manual. 1982.* **BRNS**
*Seven Plays of the Modern Theater. 1950.* **WAK**
*Seven Plays of the Modern Theatre. 1962.* **SEVD**
*Seven Sacred Plays. 1934.* **SEVE**
*Seven Soviet Plays. 1946.* **SEVP**
*Seventeen Plays: Sophocles to Baraka. 1976.* **SEVT**
*Seventh Generation: An Anthology of Native American
    Plays. 1999.* **DAPO**
*Shakespeare and His fellow Dramatists. 1929. 2v* **OLI**
*Shakespeare Apocrypha, The. 1918.* **BRO**
*Shakespeare Adaptations. 1922.* **SUMB**
*Shakespeare the Sadist. 1977.* **SHAK**
*Shakespeare's Predecessors. 1929.* **TICO**
*Sharing the Delirium: Second Generation AIDS Plays and
    Performances. 1994.* **JONT**
*Shattering the Myth: Plays by Hispanic Women. 1992.*
    **FEY**
*Showcase 1: Plays from Eugene O'Neill Foundation. 1970.*
    **LAH**
*Showing West: Three Prairie Docu-Dramas. 1982.*
    **SHOW**
*Signet Classic Book of 18th and 19th-Century British
    Drama, The. 1979.* **SIG**

*Ta matou mangai: Our Own Voice*. 1999. **KOU**

*Taking the Stage: Selections from Plays by Canadian Women*. 1994. **ZIMM**

*Teatro de liberación. See* 6 Dramaturgos españoles del siglo XX, v. 1. 1988. **SEIS**

*Teatro en democracia. See* 6 Dramaturgos españoles del siglo XX, v. 2. 1988. **SEIS**

*Teatro hispanoamericano*. 1956. **ALPE**

*Temper of the Times*. 1969. **GREG**

*Ten Classic Mystery and Suspense Plays of the Modern Theatre*. 1973. **RICN**

*Ten Elizabethan Plays*. 1931. **HOW**

*Ten English Farces*. 1948. **HUGL**

*Ten Great Musicals of the American Theatre*. 1973. **RICO**

*Ten Greek Plays*. 1930. **TEN**

*Ten Modern Macedonian Plays*. 2000. **LUZ**

*Ten Spanish Farces of the 16th, 17th, and 18th Centuries*. 1974. **NOR**

*Ten Greek Plays in Contemporary Translations*. 1957. **LIND**

*Ten Plays*. 1951. **BLOO**

*Tenth Muse: Classical Drama in Translation*. 1980. **TENN**

*Testifyin': Contemporary African Canadian Drama*. 2000–2003. 2v **SEARS**

*Texas Plays*. 1990. **TEX**

*Theater and Politics: An International Anthology*. 1990. **THB**

*Theater and Society: An Anthology of Contemporary Chinese Drama*. 1998. **THC**

*Theater Wagon Plays of Place and Any Place*. 1973. **COLI**

*Theatre*. 1953–56. 4v **THEA**

*Theatre Alive! An Introductory Anthology of World Drama*. 1991. **BERP**

*Theatre Alive! An Introductory Anthology of World Drama*. 1995. **BERPA**

*Theatre Anthology: Plays and Documents, A*. 1990. **WILLG**

*Theatre for Tomorrow*. 1940. **THEC**

*Theatre Guild Anthology, The*. 1936. **THF**

*Theatre of Don Juan: A Collection of Plays and Views, 1630–1963, The*. 1963. **MARJ**

*Theatre of Images, The*. 1977. **THG**

*Theatre of Images, The*. 1996. **THGA**

*Theatre of the Holocaust: Four Plays, The*. 1982. **THL**

*Theatre of the Holocaust, Volume 2: Six Plays, The*. 1999. **THLA**

*Theatre of the Mind, The*. 1974. **SOUL**

*Theatre of the Ridiculous*. Revised & Expanded Edition. 1998. **MARRA**

*Theatre of Wonders: Six Contemporary American Plays*. 1985. **WEK**

*Theatre Omnibus*. 1938. **THH**

*Theatre One, New South African Drama*. 1978. **GRAYTO**

*Theatre Two: New South African Drama*. 1981. **GRAYTT**

*Theatre Today*. 1965. **THOD**

*Theatrical Landmarks*. 1983–1987. 4v **MONB**

*Theme and Form*. 1956. **BEAR**

*Theme and Form: An Introduction to Literature*. 4th ed. 1975. **BEAS**

*Themes of Drama: An Anthology*. 1973. **WELT**

*They Said You Were Too Young*. 1989. **ROBR**

*Thirteen Plays: An Introductory Anthology*. 1978. **REIW**

*13 Plays of Ghosts and the Supernatural*. 1990. **KAYG**

*This England*. 1956. **NEVI**

*This Generation*. 1939. **AND**

*This Generation*. Revised Edition. 1949. **ANDE**

*Threads and other Sheffield Plays*. 1990. **MARLC**

*Three Anglo-Irish Plays*. 1943. **SSTA**

*Three Australian Plays*. 1963. **THOP**

*Three Australian Plays*. 1968. **HANG**

*Three Catalan Dramatists*. 1976. **WELV**

*Three Classic French Plays*. 1935. **SERD**

*Three Classic Spanish Plays*. 1963. **ALPF**

*Three Comedies of American Family Life*. 1961. **MERS**

*3 Contemporary Brazilian Plays in Bilingual Edition*. 1988. **SZO**

*Three Contemporary Hungarian Plays*. 1992. **TEZ**

*Three Danish Comedies*. 1999. **THOQ**

*Three Distinctive Plays about Abraham Lincoln*. 1961. **SWI**

*Three Dramas of American Individualism*. 1961. **MERT**

*Three Dramas of American Realism*. 1961. **MERU**

*Three East European Plays*. 1970. **THOR**

*Three Elizabethan Domestic Tragedies*. 1985. **STUR**

*Three Elizabethan Plays*. 1929. **ANG**

*Three Elizabethan Plays*. 1959. **WINN**

*Three English Comedies*. 1924. **DEM**

*Three European Plays*. 1958. **BRZA**

*Three Fin-de-siècle Farces*. 1996. **WILL**

*Three French Comedies*. 1996. **THOS**

*Three French Farces*. 1973. **LAB**

*Three Great French Plays*. 1961. **LOGG**

*Three Great Greek Plays*. 1960. **THP**

*Three Great Jewish Plays*. 1986. **THQ**

*Three Greek Plays*. 1937. **HAM**

*Three Greek Tragedies in Translation*. 1942. **GREN**

*Three Irish Plays*. 1959. **BRZE**

*Three Jacobean Tragedies*. 1965. **SALG**

*Three Jacobean Witchcraft Plays*. 1986. **COQJW**

*Three Japanese Plays from the Traditional Theatre*. 1976. **ERN**

*Three Late Medieval Morality Plays*. 1981. **THR**

*Three Masterpieces of Cuban Drama*. 2000. **THRCD**

*Three Masters of English Drama*. 1934. **KET**

*Three Medieval Plays*. 1953. **ALLE**

*Three Modern French Plays of the Imagination*. 1966. **PROA**

*Three Modern Indian Plays*. 1989. **THRIN**

*Three Modern Plays from the French*. 1914. **THS**

*Vision and Aftermath: Four Expressionist War Plays.* 1969. **RITV**

*Voices from the Landwash: 11 Newfoundland Playwrights.* 1997. **LYN**

*Voices of Change in the Spanish American Theater.* 1971. **OLIW**

*Voices of England and America, The.* 1939. 2v **CLK**

*Voices: Plays for Studying the Holocaust.* 1999. **VOI**

*Voicings: Ten Plays from the Documentary Theater.* 1995. **FAV**

*Wakefield Mystery Plays, The.* 1961. **TOWN**

*Wakefield Pageants in the Towneley Cycle, The.* 1958. **CAWM**

*War Plays by Women: An International Anthology.* 1999. **TYEW**

*Warrior Ghost Plays from the Japanese Theater.* 1993. *See* The Noh, v. 2, bk. 2 **SHIM**

*The Way We Live Now: American Plays & the AIDS Crisis.* 1990. **OSBW**

*We Are Chicanos.* 1973. **ORT**

*Week-end Library.* 3rd issue. 1930. **WEE**

*West Coast Plays.* 1975. **BRIQ**

*West Coast Plays.* 1977–1987. 22v **WES**

*Western Humanities, The.* 1971. 2v **GOU**

*Western Literature.* 1971. 3v **VONS**

*Western Literature: Themes and Writers.* 1967. **CARN**

*Western World Literature.* 1938. **ROB**

*What Is the Play?* 1967. **CASK**

*When Conscience Trod the Stage: American Plays of Social Awareness.* 1998. **MESCO**

*Wines in the Wilderness: Plays by African-American Women from the Harlem Renaissance to the Present.* 1990. **BRW**

*Woman That I Am: The Literature and Culture of Contemporary Women of Color, The.* 1994. **WOMA**

*Women in Drama: An Anthology.* 1975. **WOMD**

*Women in Literature: Life Stages through Stories, Poems, and Plays.* 1988. **EAG**

*Women on the Verge: 7 Avant-Garde American Plays.* 1993. **LAMO**

*Women Playwrights: The Best Plays of 1992–2000.* 1992–2000. 9v **WOMP**

*Women with Guns: Six New American Plays.* 1985. **WOMQ**

*Women Writers in Russian Modernism: An Anthology.* 1978. **WOMR**

*Women Writing Women: An Anthology of Spanish-American Theater of the 1980s.* 1997. **SALA**

*Women's Acts: Plays by Women Dramatists of Spain's Golden Age.* 1997. **SOSGA**

*Women's Project: Seven New Plays by Women, The.* 1980. **WOMS**

*Women's Project 2, The.* 1984. **WOMS2**

*WomensWork: Five New Plays from the Women's Project.* 1989. **MIHWW**

*WordPlays: An Anthology of New American Drama.* 1981–1986. 5v **WOQ**

*World Drama.* 1933. 2v **CLF**

*World in Literature, The.* 1949. 4v **WORL**

*World in Literature, The.* 1950. 2v in 1. **WARN**

*World Literature.* 1935. **CROS**

*World Literature.* Reprint. 1971. **CHR**

*World Literature: An Anthology of Great Short Stories, Drama, and Poetry.* 1992. **ROSENB**

*World Masterpieces.* 1956. 2v **MALG**

*World Masterpieces.* Rev. ed. 1965. 2v **MALI**

*World Masterpieces.* 3rd ed. 1973. 2v **MALN**

*World of Law: A Treasury of Great Writing about and in the Law, Short Stories, Plays, The.* 1960. 2v **LOND**

*World of Tragedy, The.* 1981. **WORM**

*World Turned Upside Down: Prose and Poetry of the American Revolution, The.* 1975. **WORN**

*World's Great Plays.* 1944. **WORP**

*Woza Africa: An Anthology of South African Plays.* 1986. **WOZA**

*Writers of the Western World.* 1942. **HIB**

*Writers of the Western World.* Rev. ed. 1946. **HIBA**

*Writers of the Western World.* 2nd ed. 1954. **HIBB**

*Writing North: An Anthology of Contemporary Yukon Writers.* 1992. **WRIT**

*Written Word, The.* 1960. **DANI**

*Yale School of Drama Presents . . ., The.* 1964. **GASY**

*Year of Protest, 1956: An Anthology of Soviet Literary Materials, The.* 1961. **MAM**

*Years Between: Plays by Women on the London Stage, 1900–1950, The.* 1994. **YEAR**

*York Mystery Plays: A Selection in Modern Spelling.* 1984. **BEAD**

*Yoruba Popular Theatre: Three Plays by the Oyin Adejobi Company.* 1994. **YORU**

*Young Playwrights Festival Collection, The.* 1983. **YOUP**

*Youth and the World.* 1955. **WHT**

# Appendix A

# Authors by Country, Race, and Ethnic Group

**ABORIGINAL AUSTRALIAN**
Davis, Jack
Johnson, Eva
Maza, Bob
Merritt, Robert J.
Walley, Richard

**ABORIGINAL CANADIAN/ INNU/INUIT/METIS**
Cheechoo, Shirley (Cree)
Clements, Marie Humber (Métis)
Dudoward, Valerie (Tsimshian)
Francis, Marvin (Cree/Dene)
Innuinuit Theatre Company (Innu and Inuit)
Highway, Tomson (Cree)
Jensen, Lorre (Mohawk)
Kane, Margo (Cree-Salteaux)
Linklater, Leonard (Vuntut Gwich'in)
Manuel, Vera (Shuswap-Kootenai)
Mojica, Monique (Kuna/Rappahannock)
Moses, Daniel David (Delaware)
Nalujuk Players (Innu and Inuit)
Nolan, Yvette (Algonquin/Irish)
Ross, Ian (Métis)
Shorty, Sharon (Tlingit)
Taylor, Drew Hayden (Ojibway)
Tunooniq Theatre (Inuit)
Upisasik Theatre of Rossignol School (Métis)

**AFRICAN-AMERICAN**
Aldridge, Ira
Alexander, Robert
Anderson, Garland
Anderson, Regina M. Andrews
Baldwin, James
Barfield, Tanya
Bass, George Houston
Bauer, Irvin S.
Beasley, Elois
Bonner, Marita

Bontemps, Arna
Boston, Michon
Branch, William
Brown, Carlyle
Brown, Wesley
Brown, William Wells
Brown-Guillory, Elizabeth
Browne, Theodore
Bullins, Ed
Burke, Inez M.
Burrill, Mary P.
Burris, Andrew M.
Butterbeans
Caldwell, Ben
Carew, Jan (b. Guyana)
Carlos, Laurie
carter, steve
Charles, Martie
Childress, Alice
Clarke, Breena
Cleage, Pearl
Coleman, Ralf M.
Collie, Brenda Faye
Collins, Kathleen
Cooper, J. California
Corbitt, Wayne
Corthron, Kia
Cotter, Joseph S., Jr.
Cotter, Joseph S., Sr.
Cullen, Countee
Cuney-Hare, Maud
Davis, Ossie
Davis, Thulani
Dean, Philip Hayes
De Anda, Peter
DeVeaux, Alexis
Dickerson, Glenda
Dodson, Owen Vincent
Dolan, Harry, Jr.

Drayton, Ronald
Du Bois, W.E.B.
Dunbar, Paul Laurence
Dunbar-Nelson, Alice
Duncan, Thelma M.
Edmonds, Randolph
Edward, H.F.V. (b. Great Britain)
Edwards, Gus
Effinger, Marta J.
Elder, Lonne, III
Evans, Don
Flanagan, Brenda, A. (b. Trinidad)
Foreman, Farrell J.
Franklin, J.E.
Freeman, Carol
Fuller, Charles
Gaines, J. E.
Gaines-Shelton, Ruth
Garrett, Jimmy
Gibson, P. J.
Gilbert, Mercedes
Goldberg, Whoopi
Gordon, Richard
Gordone, Charles
Goss, Clay
Graham, Nadine (b. Jamaica)
Graham, Shirley
Greaves, Donald
Greer, Bonnie (dual citizen of United States and Great
    Britain, where she lives)
Griffith, Lois
Grimké, Angelina
Guinn, Dorothy C.
Gunner, Frances
Hairston, Jerome
Hansberry, Lorraine
Harris, Bill
Harris, Tom
Harrison, Paul Carter
Hatch, James V.
Hazzard, Alvira
Hickman, Craig
Hill, Abram
Hill, Errol (b. Trinidad)
Hill, Olivia
Hobbes, Dwight
Holder, Laurence
Holland, Endesha Ida Mae
Holmes, Shirlene
Hopkins, Pauline Elizabeth
Houston, Dianne
Howell, Corrie Crandall
Hughes, Langston
Hunkins, Lee
Hurston, Zora Neale

Jackman, Marvin
Jackson, Angela
Jackson, C. Bernard
Jackson, Cherry
Jackson, Elaine
Jackson, Judith Alexa
Jackson, Marsha A.
Jeffries, Ira L.
Johnson, Francine
Johnson, Georgia Douglas
Jones, Leroi
Jones, Lisa
Jones, Rhodessa
Jones, Stephen Mack
Jones, Thomas W.
Jones-Meadows, Karen
Kai, Nubia
Kelley, Samuel L.
Kennedy, Adam P.
Kennedy, Adrienne
Kincaid, Jamaica (b. St. John's, Antigua and Barbuda)
Klein, Sybil
Lee, Leslie
Livingston, Myrtle Smith
Locke, Alain
McCauley, Robbie
McClinton, Marion
McCoo, Edward J.
Mackey, William Wellington
Martin, Sharon Stockard
Mason, Clifford
Mason, Judi Ann
Mason, Keith Antar
Matheus, John Frederick
Medley, Cassandra
Meyer, Annie Nathan
Miller, May
Milner, Ronald
Mitchell, Joseph S.
Mitchell, Loften
Molette, Barbara
Molette, Carlton
Moore, Charles Michael
Moore, Elvie A.
Nicholas, Denise
Nottage, Lynn
Nugent, Richard Bruce
O'Neal, John
Owa
Owens, Daniel Walter
OyamO
Parks, Suzan-Lori
Parris-Bailey, Linda
Patterson, Charles
Pawley, Thomas D.

Penny, Rob
Perry, Shauneille
Peterson, Louis
Pitcher, Oliver
Pomo Afro Homos
Porter, Regina M.
Purdue, Robert L.
Rahman, Aishah
Redmond, Eugene B.
Redwood, John Henry
Reed, Ishmael
Rhodes, Crystal
Richards, Beah
Richardson, Willis
Rivers, Louis
Russell, Charlie L.
Rux, Carl Hancock
Salaam, Kalamu ya (aka Ferdinand, Val)
Sanchez, Sonia
Schuyler, George S.
Seaton, Sandra
Sebree, Charles
Sejour, Victor
Shange, Ntozake
Shephard-Massat, S. M. (Sherry)
Shepp, Archie
Shine, Ted
Shipp, Jesse A.
Silvera, John D.
Simmons, Alexander
Smith, Anna Deavere
Smith, Beverly A.
Smith, Charles
Spence, Eulalie (b. Nevis)
Stetson, Jeff
Stickney, Phyllis Yvonne
Stiles, Thelma Jackson
Susie
Taylor, Regina
Thomas, Lee
Tillman, Katherine D. Chapman
Toomer, Jean
Towns, George A.
Vance, Danitra
Wakefield, Jacques
Walker, Joseph A.
Ward, Douglas Turner
Ward, Theodore
Washington, Erwin Charles
Washington, Von H., Sr.
Watkins, Nayo Barbara
Watson, Harmon C.
Welch, Leona Nicholas
Wesley, Richard
Wesson, Kenneth Alan

West, Cheryl L.
White, Edgar (b. Montserrat)
White, Joseph
White, Lucy
Wideman, Angela
Wilks, Talvin
Williams, Anita Jane
Williams, Samm-Art
Williamson, Gayle Weaver
Willmott, Kevin
Wilson, August
Wilson, Eric
Wilson, Frank H.
Wolfe, George C.
Wright, Richard
Youngblood, Shay
Zuber, Ron

## AFRICAN-AUSTRALIAN
Langeberg, Sheela

## AFRICAN-BRITISH
Abbott, Jean
Baptiste, Roselia John (early pseudonym of Trish Cooke)
Binnie, Briony
'Biyi, Bandele (b. Nigeria)
Boakye, Paul
Buchanan, Wayne (b. Jamaica)
Bully, Aldwyn
Cooke, Trish
D'Aguiar, Fred
Dayley, Grace (b. Jamaica)
Ellis, Michael J.
Fagon, Alfred
Gideon, Killian M.
Greer, Bonnie (dual citizen of U.S and Great Britain, where she lives)
Ikoli, Tunde
Jacobs, Pauline
James, C.L.R. (b. Trinidad)
James, Lennie
John, Errol (b. Trinidad)
Johnson, Niki
Kay, Jackie (b. Scotland)
Kayla, Lisselle (b. Jamaica)
McLeod, Jenny
McMillan, Michael
Oshodi, Maria
Pinnock, Winsome
Reckord, Barry (b. Jamaica)
Rudet, Jacqueline (b. Dominica)
Smartt, Dorothea
Zephaniah, Benjamin (b. Jamaica)
Zindinka

## AFRICAN-CANADIAN

Anthony, Trey (b. England)
bailey, maxine (b. England)
belvett, naila
Borden, Walter M.
Boyd, George Elroy
Brown, Lennox (b. Trinidad)
Bunyan, H. Jay (b. Guyana)
Clarke, Austin Chesterfield (b. Barbados)
Clarke, George Elliott
Gale, Lorena
Hall, Tony (b. Trinidad)
Jacob, Bianca
lewis, sharon mareeka
McLean, Dirk (b. Trinidad)
mandiela, ahdri zhina (b. Jamaica)
Moodie, Andrew
Odhiambo, David Nandi (b. Kenya)
Payne, Alicia
Philip, M. Nourbese (b. Tobago)
Providence, Tien (b. St. Vincent)
Sandiford, Susan (b. Trinidad)
Sears, Djanet (b. England)
Spencer, Rhoma (b. Trinidad)
Seremba, George Bwanika (b. Uganda)
Ward, Frederick (b. United States)
Yhap, Beverley (b. Trinidad)
Young, Debbie (b. Jamaica)

## ARGENTINA

Arlt, Roberto
Bayon Herrera, Luis
Copi
Damel, Carlos S.
Darthés, Juan Fernando
Diaz, Jorge
Dragun, Osvaldo
Eichelbaum, Samuel
Gambaro, Griselda
Goldenberg, Jorge
Halac, Ricardo
Kartun, Mauricio
Manco, Silviero
Monti, Ricardo
Novion, Alberto
Pavlovsky, Eduardo
Perinelli, Roberto
Puig, Manuel (d. Mexico)
Raznovich, Diana
Rojas, Ricardo
Rovner, Eduardo
Rozenmacher, Germán
Sanchez Gardel, Julio
Seibel, Beatriz

Storni, Alfonsina (b. Switzerland)
Tiempo, Cesar (b. Ukraine)

## ARMENIA

Sundukiants, Gavrill Nikitovich

## ASIAN-AMERICAN

Amano, Lynette (Japanese-Hawaiian)
Aoki, Brenda Wong (Japanese, Chinese, Spanish, and
    Scots)
Aw, Arthur (b. Singapore)
Barroga, Jeannie (Filipino-American)
Barry, Lynda (Filipino, Irish, and Norwegian)
Benton, James Grant (Hawaiian)
Cheng, Kipp Erante (b. Taiwan)
Cheong-Leen, Reggie (Chinese-American)
Chin, Frank (Chinese-American)
Chong, Ping (b. Canada, Chinese-American)
Dizon, Louella (b. Philippines)
Eng, Alvin (Chinese-American)
Gotanda, Philip Kan (Japanese-American)
Hagedorn, Jessica Tarahata (b. Philippines)
Hill, Amy (one parent Finnish-American, one parent
    Japanese)
Houston, Velina Hasu (Japanese, African-American, and
    Blackfoot)
Huie, Karen (Chinese-American)
Huynh, Quang Nhuong (b. Vietnam)
Hwang, David Henry (Chinese-American)
Iizuka, Naomi (b. Japan, father Japanese, mother American
    Latina)
Iko, Momoko (Japanese-American)
Inouye, Lisa Toishigawa (Japanese-Hawaiian)
Kates, Charles R. (Hawaiian)
Kneubuhl, Victoria Nalani (Hawaiian/Samoan/Caucasian)
Lee, Cherylene (Chinese-American)
Lim, Genny (Chinese-American)
Lum, Darrell H.Y. (Chinese-Hawaiian)
Mapa, Alec (Filipino-American)
Meyer, Marlane (Hawaiian/Polynesian/Native American/
    German/Swedish)
Morris, Robert J. (Chinese-Hawaiian)
Nishikawa, Lane (Japanese-American)
Okita, Dwight (Japanese-American)
Omata, Garrett H. (Japanese-American)
Rno, Sung (Korean-American)
Roberts, Dmae (b. Taiwan; one parent American, one
    parent Chinese)
Sakamoto, Edward (Japanese-Hawaiian)
Sam, Canyon (Chinese-American)
Sharif, Bina (b. Pakistan)
Shin, Rob (Korean-American)
Son, Diana (Korean-American)
Uyehara, Denise (Japanese-American)

Villa, Jose Garcia (b. Philippines)
Wang, Lucy (Chinese-American)
Wong, Elizabeth (Chinese-American)
Yamauchi, Wakako (Japanese-American)
Yasuda, Kenneth (Japanese-American)
Yep, Laurence (Chinese-American)
Yew, Chay (b. Singapore)
Yoshimura, James (Japanese-American)

## ASIAN-AUSTRALIAN
Mahjoeddin, Indija N. (Indonesian-Australian)
Ta, Binh Duy (b. Vietnam)
Yen, Anna (Chinese-Australian)

## ASIAN-BRITISH
Ahmad, Rukhsana (b. Pakistan)
Bancil, Parv
Chowdhry, Maya (b. Scotland)
Ghose, Nandita
Jintan, Soraya
Leeds Bengali Women's Drama Group
Malik, Afshan
Raif, Ayshe
Silas, Shelley (b. India)
Singh, Lakviar
Syal, Meera

## ASIAN-CANADIAN
Binning, Sadhu (b. India)
Bose, Rana (b. India)
Chan, Marty (Chinese-Canadian)
Kang, Myung-Jin (b. South Korea)
Parameswaran, Uma (b. India)
Quan, Betty (Chinese-Canadian)
Shiomi, R. A., aka Rick (Japanese-Canadian)
Varma, Rahul (b. India)
Visawanathan, Padma (Indian-Canadian; now lives in
    United States)
Watada, Terry (Japanese-Canadian)
Yoon, Jean (b. United States)

## ASIAN-NEW ZEALANDERS
Earle, Lynda Chanwai (Chinese-New Zealander, b. Great
    Britain)
Campbell, Alistair Te Ariki (mother Cook Islander, father
    New Zealander)

## AUSTRALIA
*See also Aboriginal Australian; African-Australian; Asian
    Australian*
Bensusan, Inez
Bent, Roxxy
Bews, Samantha
Beynon, Richard

Bishop, Stephanie
Blair, Ron
Boddy, Michael
Bovell, Andrew
Braddon, Russell
Bradley, Belinda
Bradley, John
Brand, Mona
Brookman, Anne
Buzo, Alexander
Chambers, Charles Haddon
Coleman, Elizabeth
Collinson, Laurence (b. Great Britain)
Compton, Jennifer (b. New Zealand)
Cornelius, Patricia
Cortese, Raimondo
Crea, Teresa
Cusack, Dymphna
Decent, Campion
De Groen, Alma (b. New Zealand)
Dickens, Chris
Eberhard, Josie Composto
Ellis, Bob
Esson, Louis
Fischer, Margaret
Fitzgerald, Catherine
Franklin, Miles
Gallagher, Jodi
Goodall, Julie
Gorman, Clem
Gow, Michael
Gray, Oriel
Gunzburg, Darrelyn
Hanger, Eunice
Harding, Alex
Hastings, Hugh
Hewett, Dorothy
Hibberd, Jack
Hopgood, Alan
Janaczewska, Noëlle
Kemp, Jenny
Kenna, Peter
Kitas, Frida
Larman, Claire
Lawler, Ray
Leversha, Pam
Lewis, Erica
Lillford, Daniel R. (b. Channel Islands, emigrated Canada
    1997)
Locke-Elliott, Sumner
Lyssa, Alison
Lyssiotis, Tes
Macdonald, Gabrielle
McKinney, Jack

McKinnon, Cath
McMahon, Frank
McNeil, John
Mastrantone, Lucia
Mathew, Ray (emigrated 1960, eventually settling in
    United States)
Milgate, Rodney
Morgillo, Antonietta
Mueller, Ross
Nowra, Louis
O'Donoghue, John
Patrikareas, Theodore (b. Greece)
Porter, Hal
Prichard, Katharine Susannah (b. Fiji)
Reed, Bill
Reeves, Melissa
Roberts, Ted
Romeril, John
Searle, James
Sejavka, Sam
Selleck, Roger
Sewell, Stephen
Seymour, Alan
Shepherd, Catherine
Shotlander, Sandra
Spears, Steve J.
Spunner, Suzanne
Stevens, David (b. Israel)
Stewart, Douglas Alexander
Tsiolkas, Christos
Turner, Graeme
Waldron, Sharon
White, Patrick
Williamson, David

## AUSTRIA
Anzengruber, Ludwig
Bahr, Hermann
Barylli, Gabriel
Bauer, Wolfgang
Baum, Thomas
Broch, Hermann (emigrated to U.S.)
Canetti, Veza
Chlumberg, Hans
Grillparzer, Franz
Hebbel, Friedrich
Hochwälder, Fritz
Hofmannsthal, Hugo von
Horvath, Odon von
Jelinek, Elfriede
Kafka, Franz
Kokoschka, Oscar
Kraus, Karl
Mell, Max

Mitterer, Felix
Nestroy, Johann Nepomuk
Peschina, Helmut
Rebhun, Paul
Rosei, Peter
Rotter, Fritz
Schnitzler, Arthur
Schwab, Werner
Schwaiger, Brigitte
Szyszkowitz, Gerald
Turrini, Peter
Unger, Heinz R.
Werfel, Franz
Zauner, Friedrich Ch.
Zweig, Stefan

## AZERBAIJAN
Fath Ali, Mirza

## BELARUS
Popova, Elena

## BELGIUM
Bourlet, Katherine
Crommelynck, Fernand
Emond, Paul
Fabien, Michèle
Fonson, Frantz
Ghelderode, Michel de
Lalande, Françoise
Lerberghe, Charles Van
Lison-Leroy, Françoise
Maeterlinck, Maurice
Nys-Mazure, Colette
Sierens, Arne
Tison, Pascale
Verhaeren, Emile
Wicheler, Fernand
Wouters, Liliane

## BRAZIL
Assunção, Leilah
Castro, Consuelo de
Gomes, Alfredo Dias
Marcos, Plínio
Nascimento, Abdias do

## BRUNEI
Akip, Masri Haji
Bakyr, Mahmud Haji
Chuchu, Abdul Latif
Tahir, Pengiran Haji
Yusof, Abdul Rahman
Zain, Shukri

## CAMBODIA
Bophavy, Khem

## CAMEROON
Musinga, Victor Elame
Oyono, Ferdinand
Oyono-Mbia, Guillaume

## CANADA
*See also Aboriginal Canadian/Innu/Inuit/Métis; African*
*Canadian; Asian Canadian; French Canadian;*
*Hispanic Canadian*
Ackerman, Marianne
Adams, Philip
Aikins, Carroll
Albanese, Eleanor
Albert, Lyle Victor
Alianak, Hrant
Aloma, Rene R.
Angel, Leonard
The Anna Project
Arnold, Daniel
Baldridge, Mary Humphrey (resides in U.S.)
Ball, Alan Egerton (b. Great Britain)
Barrie, Shirley
Barton, Bruce
Beissel, Henry (b. Germany)
Bolt, Carol
Borsook, Henry
Boston, Stewart
Boyd, Pamela
Bradbury, Paul
Brennan, Kit
Brooker, Blake
Brown, Alex
Brown, Kenneth
Brymer, Patrick
Bullock, Michael
Burke, Kelley Jo
Bush, Thomas
Bustin, Pam
Butala, Sharon
Butler, Alec (b. Audrey)
Byrne, Louis
Cahill, Tom
Cajal, Oana-Maria
Callaghan, Sean
Cameron, Anne
Cameron, Ronald
Cameron, Silver Donald
Campbell, Paddy
Canale, Raymond
Candidus, Caroli
Carley, Dave

Chafe, Rick
Chisholm, Mary-Colin
Christenson, Jonathan
Chudley, Ron (b. New Zealand)
Clark, Sally
Clarke, Margaret
Clements, Marie
CODCO
Colley, Peter
Cone, Tom (b. United States)
Cook, Michael (b. Great Britain)
Cooke, Britton
Coulter, John (b. Ireland)
Cowan, Cindy
Craddock, Chris
Crisp, Jack H.
Cronyn, Hume
Crossland, Jackie
Curran, Colleen
Curzon, Sarah Anne (b. Great Britain)
Cushing, Eliza Lanesford (b. United States)
Davies, Robertson
Davin, Nicholas Flood (b. Ireland)
Del Grande, Louis (b. United States)
Demchuk, David
Dempsey, Sandra
Dempsey, Shawna
Denison, Merrill
Derbyshire, Jan
Deverell, Rex
Diamond, David
Doherty, Brian
Dorn, Rudy
Dunn, Theo M.
Fantetti, Eufemia
Farmiloe, Dorothy A.
Farrell, Geraldine
Feindel, Janet
Fennario, David
Fineberg, Larry
Finlay, Suzanne
Flacks, Diane
Flather, Patti
Freeman, David E.
French, David
Friesen, Patrick
Frost, Rex
Fruet, William
Fuerstenberg, Anna
Fuller, William Henry
Fyffe, Laurie
Galbraith, Robert
Garner, Hugh
Garnhum, Ken

Garrard, Jim
Gass, Ken
Gault, Connie
Gibson, Florence
Gilbert, Sky (b. United States)
Gilbert, Stuart Reid
Givner, Joan
Glass, Joanna McClelland
Godlovitch, Charles Z.
Goobie, Beth
Grainger, Tom (b. Great Britain)
Grant, Diane
Graves, Warren G.
Gray, John
Green, Michael
Greenland, Bill
Griffiths, Linda
Guy, Ray
Haber, Alexandria
Hahn, Medina
Hammond, Marie-Lynn
Hamson, Leslie
Hardin, Herschel
Harrar, William
Heide, Christopher
Hennessey, Brian
Herbert, John
Herst, Beth
Hill, Kay
Hines, Karen
Hollingsworth, Margaret (b. Great Britain)
Hollingsworth, Michael (b. Wales)
Hunter, Maureen
Hurley, Joan Mason
Hutsell-Manning, Linda
Ibbitson, John
Jack, Donald L.
Jeffery, Lawrence
Jonas, George
Joudry, Patricia
Kardish, Laurence
Kavanagh, Geoff
Kemlo, Karen
Kemp, David
Kerr, Lois Reynolds
Klonsky, Kenneth
Koller, Katherine
Kolpak, Diana
Kudelka, Jan
Kugler, D.D.
Lambert, Ann
Lambert, Betty
Laxdal, Vivienne
Lazarus, Joa
Lazarus, John

Learning, Walter
Ledoux, Paul
Libman, Carl
Lill, Wendy
Lloyd George, Ian
Longfield, Kevin
McAnuff, Des (dual citizen of United States and Canada)
MacDonald, Ann-Marie
MacEwen, Gwendolyn
McIlwraith, Jean Newton
MacIvor, Daniel
Mackay, Isabel Ecclestone Macpherson
Mackay, Louis Alexander
McKay, Tamara
McKinlay, Michael D.C.
MacLeod, Joan
McManus, Bruce
McMaster, Beth
McMillan, Ross
McNeil, Marguerite
McRae, Murray
Major, Alice
Malone, Beni
Martin, Meah
Mason, Libby (b. Great Britain)
Matwychuk, Paul
Mercer, Rick
Merritt, Catharine Nina
Miles, Kate
Millan, Lorri
Milner, Arthur
Mitchell, Ken
Mitchell, Nick
Mitchell, William Ormond
Moher, Frank
Moore, Elise
Moore, Mavor
Moore, Paul T.
Morrissey, Kim
The Mummers Troupe
Murrell, John
Nicol, Eric Patrick
Nowlan, Alden
O'Neil, Deborah
Orlov, Stephen (b. United States)
Osborne, Marian
Ouzounian, Richard (b. United States)
Palmer, John
Panych, Morris
Payne, Rhonda
Pengilly, Gordon
Petch, Steve
Peterson, Eric
Peterson, Leonard
Pickard, Liz

Pittman, Al
Pluta, Leonard
Pollock, Sharon
Porter, Deborah
Quan, Betty
Ralph, Gordon W.
Ravel, Aviva
RCA Theatre Company
Reaney, James Crerar
Rebar, Kelly-Jean
Reid, Leslie
Renders, Kim
Richards, Stanley
Riml, Michelle
Ringwood, Gwen Pharis
Rintoul, Harry
Riordan, Michael
Rising Tide Theatre
Ritter, Erika
Robinson, Mansel
Rockwood, Glen
Rodin, Toby
Rose, Richard
Rosen, Sheldon (b. United States)
Rossi, Vittorio
Rowe, Rosemary
Roy, Edward
Rubess, Banuta
Russell, Lawrence
Ryga, George
Rylski, Nika
St. James, Ann
Salutin, Rick
Sapergia, Barbara
Schull, Joseph
Scott, Duncan Campbell
Scott, Munroe
"Scribble, Sam"
Selkirk, Gordon
Selkirk, John
Sheila's Brush Theatre Company
Shein, Brian
Sheriff, Jack
Shoveller, Brock
Silver, Alf
Sinclair, Carol
Slade, Bernard
Small Change Theatre
Smith, Cedric
Solly, Bill
Spence, Janis
Spensley, Philip
Spunde, Walter G. (resides Australia)
Stapleton, Berni
Stearns, Sharon

Stratton, Allan
Szablowski, Jerzy
Tallman, James
Taylor, John
Taylor, Ron
Tembeck, Robert
Theatre Passe Muraille
Thomas, Colin
Thomey, Greg
Thompson, Judith
Thury, Fred (b. United States)
Towle, W. Ray
Trochim, Dennis
Vingoe, Mary
Vlachos, Helen
Voaden, Herman
Wagner, Colleen
Walker, George F.
Walmsley, Tom (b. Great Britain)
Walsh, Des
Warkentin, Veralyn
Weir, Ian (b. United States)
Weiss, Peter Eliot
Wiebe, Rudy
Williams, Alan
Williams, Karin D.
Williams, Norman
Wing, Paula
Winter, Jack
Woods, Grahame
Wyatt, Rachel
Young, David
Young, William R.
Zacharko, Larry
Zell, Allison Eve (dual citizen of Canada and United States)

**CATALAN**
Belbel, Sergi
Benet i Jornet, Josep Maria
Brossa, Joan
Cunillé, Lluisa
Guimerà, Angel
Marquina, Eduardo
Pedrolo, Manuel de
Sirera, Rodolf
Teixidor, Jordi

**CHILE**
Acevedo Hernandez, Antonio
Aguirre, Isabel
Frank, Miguel
Moock Bousquet, Armando
Parra, Marco Antonio de la
Skármeta, Antonio

Vodanovic, Sergio Vina
Wolff, Egon

## CHINA (MAINLAND)
*See also Hong Kong; Taiwan*
Ah, Chia
Cao, Yu
Chang, Pao-hua
Chao, Chung
Chen, Baichen
Chen, Zidu
Cheng, Kuang-Tsu
Chung, Yi-Ping
Ding, Xilin
Fu, To
Gao, Xingjian
Guo, Shixing
He, Jiping (moved to Hong Kong in 1989)
Ho, Ching-Chih
Hsiung, Cheng-Chin
Hu, Shih (moved to Taiwan in 1948)
Hung, Shen
Jen, Teh-Yao
Ji, Junxiang
Jin, Yun
K'ang, Chin-chih
Kong, Shangren
Kuan, Han-Ch'ing
Lao, Sheh
Li, Chi-Huang
Li, Chien-Wu
Li, Hao-Ku
Li, Shaochun
Li, Shou-ching
Liang, Bingkun
Liang, Chenyu
Liu, Tangqing
Lu, Hsun
Ma, Chih-Yuan
Ma, Yung
Ma, Zhongjun
Mei, Lanfang
Meng, Han Ch'ing
Nü, ch'i-chieh
Ouyang, Yuqian
Sha, She
Sha, Yeh-Hsin
Shi, Junbao
Shih, Yu-Cho
Sun, Yu
T'ang, Hsien-Hsu
Tien, Han
Tsung, Fu-Hsien
Tung, Yang-Sheng

Wei, Minglun
Wang, Ching-Ksien
Wang, Chiu-Ssu
Wang, Peigong
Wang, Shih-Fu
Wong, Ou-Hung
Wu, Han
Xi, Zhigan
Xia, Yan
Xu, Pinli
Yang, Jian
Yang, Jiang
Yang, Lu-Fang
Yao, Hsin-Nung
Yao, Mingde
Yao, Ming-Te
Yeh, Hsiao-Nan
Zheng, Yi
Zhou, Wei-Bo
Zhu, Xiaoping

## COLOMBIA
Buenaventura, Enrique
Vargas Tejada, Luis

## CONGO
Bemba, Sylvain
N'debeka, Maxime
N'tumb, Diur
Sony Lab'ou Tansi (b. Zaire)

## COSTA RICA
Arce, Elia (dual citizen of Costa Rica and United States)

## CROATIA
Marinković, Ranko

## CUBA
Carril, Pepe
Felipe, Carlos
Piñera, Virgilio
Quintero, Hector
Triana, José

## CUBAN-AMERICAN
*See Hispanic-American*

## CYPRUS
Akritas, Loukis
Avraamidou, Maria

## CZECH REPUBLIC
*See also Czechoslovakia; Slovakia*
Fischerová, Daniela

Havel, Václav
Klíma, Ivan
Kohout, Pavel
Landovský, Pavel

## CZECHOSLOVAKIA
*See also Czech Republic; Slovakia*
Čapek, Josef
Čapek, Karel
Kafka, Franz
Kapek, Karel
Kundera, Milan (French citizen since 1981)
Preissová, Gabriela
Topol, Josef
Uhde, Milan

## DENMARK
*See also Greenland*
Abell, Kjeld
Branner, Hans Christian
Clausen, Sven
Fischer, Leck
Heiberg, Johan Ludvig
Holberg, Ludvig (b. Norway)
Holm, Sven
Locher, Jens
Munk, Kaj
Nilsson, Reidar (b. Norway)
Nissen, Kaj
Olsen, Ernst Bruun
Ørnsbo, Jess
Rifbjerg, Klaus
Ronild, Peter
Ryum, Ulla
Saalbach, Astrid
Schlüter, Karl
Sønderby, Knud
Soya, Carl Erik
Wied, Gustav Johannes

## EGYPT
'Abd al-Sabur, Salah
Al-Hakim, Tawfiq
Alrawi, Karim
Diyab, Mahmud
Farag, Alfred
Idris, Yusuf
Roman, Mikhail
Rushdy, Rashad
Saadawi, Nawal El
Salim, `Ali

## ERITREA
Tesfai, Alemseged

## ESTONIA
Alliksaar, Artur
Kitzberg, August
Kovamees, Raissa
Kulvet, Ilmar (refugee, d. Canada)
Luts, Oskar
Rummo, Paul-Eerik
Vetemaa, Enn

## FINLAND
Canth, Minna
Chorell, Walentin
Haavikko, Paavo
Järner, Väinö Vilhelm
Jotuni, Maria
Kylätasku, Jussi
Malhotra, Bhupesh
Manner, Eeva-Liisa
Meri, Veijo
Schildt, Runar
Wuolijoki, Hella (b. Estonia)

## FRANCE
Aba, Noureddine (b. Algeria)
Achard, Marcel
Adam de la Halle
Adamov, Arthur (b. Russia)
Allais, Alphonse
Ancey, Georges
Anne, Catherine
Anouilh, Jean
Appollinaire, Guillaume (b. Italy)
Aragon, Louis
Armory
Arout, Gabriel
Artaud, Antonin
Atlan, Liliane
Augier, Emile
Aurenche, Jean
Ayme, Marcel
Azama, Michel
Balzac, Honorè de
Barbier, Marie-Anne
Bartève, Reine
Bayard, Jean-François Alfred
Beaumarchais, Pierre-Augustin Caron de
Beauvoir, Simone de
Beckett, Samuel (b. Ireland)
Becque, Henri
Bellon, Loleh
Bernard, Catherine
Bernard, Jean-Jacques
Bernard, Tristan
Bernstein, Henry

Besset, Jean-Marie

Beze, Theodore de (resided in Switzerland most of his life)

Bodel, Jehan

Bois-Robert, François Metel de

Bonal, Denise

Boublil, Alain

Bouchard, Jean

Bourdet, Gildas

Boursault, Edmé

Boyer, Claude

Breton, André

Brieux, Eugène

Campistron, Jean Galbert de

Camus, Albert (b. Algeria)

Carrière, Jean-Claude

Chawaf, Chantal

Chedid, Andrée (b. Egypt of Lebanese parents)

Cixous, Hélène

Claudel, Paul

Cocteau, Jean

Colette, Sidonie-Gabrielle

Constant, Marius (b. Romania)

Copeau, Jacques

Coppee, François

Cormann, Enzo

Cormon, Eugene

Corneille, Pierre

Corneille, Thomas

Courteline, Georges

Cousse, Raymond

Curel, François, Vicomte de

Cuvelier de Trye, Jean Guillaume Antoine

D'Abundance, Jehan

Dancourt, Florent Carton

Daumal, René

Delavigne, Jean François Casimir

Delbo, Charlotte

Demarcy, Richard

D'Ennery, Adolphe

Desnos, Robert

Destouches, Philippe Néricault

Deval, Jacques

Diderot, Denis

Donnay, Maurice Charles

Donneau de Vise, Jean

Drai, Martine

Ducange, Victor

Dumas, Alexandre, fils

Dumas, Alexandre, père

Dupuis, Hervé

Duras, Marguerite

Durringer, Xavier

Du Ryer, Pierre

Duval, Alexandre Vincent Pineaux

Enrico, Robert

Fargeau, Jean-Pol

Fauchois, René

Feydeau, Georges

Forest, Louis

Foucher, Michèle

France, Anatole

Gallaire, Fatima (b. Algeria)

Gao, Xingjian (b. China)

Garnier, Robert

Genet, Jean

Geraldy, Paul

Ghelderode, Michel de

Gide, Andre

Gilbert-Lecomte, Roger

Girardin, Delphine

Giraudoux, Jean

Gondinet, Edmond

Graffigny, Françoise de

Gréban, Arnoul

Green, Julien

Gresset, Jean Baptiste Louis

Grumberg, Jean-Claude

Guerdon, David

Guinon, Albert

Guitry, Sacha (b. Russia)

Halevy, Ludovic

Hardy, Alexandre

Hervieu, Paul Ernest

Hugo, Victor

Ionesco, Eugène (b. Romania)

Jarry, Alfred

Jodelle, Étienne

Julien, Jean

Kock, Charles Paul de

Koltès, Bernard-Marie

Kundera, Milan (b. Czechoslovakia)

Labiche, Eugène

La Chausee, Pierre Claude Niville de

La Fosse, Antoine de

La Grange-Chancel

Lavedan, Henri Leon Emile

La Vigne, Andrieu de la

Laya, Jean Louis

Lecocq, Alexandre Charles

Legouvé, Ernest

Lemaître, Jules

Lenéru, Marie

Lenormand, Henri René

Le Sage, Alain-René

Leveaux, Alphonse

Lévy, Jules

Mairet, Jean de

Manet, Eduardo (b. Cuba)

Marceau, Félicien (b. Belgium)

Marcel, Gabriel

Marc-Michel
Margueritte, Paul (b. Algeria)
Marivaux, Pierre Carlet de Chamblain de
Marni, Jeanne
Martin, Edourad
Maupassant, Guy de
Maurette, Marcelle
Maurey, Max
Mauriac, François
Meilac, Henri
Mélésville
Mérimée, Prosper
Michel, Marc Antoine Amédée
Mirbeau, Octave
Mnouchkine, Ariane
Molière, Jean Baptiste
Montchrestien, Antoine de
Montherlant, Henry de
Musset, Alfred de
Najac, Émile de, Count
Neveux, Georges
Nivoix, Paul
Obey, André
Offenbach, Jacques (b. Germany)
Ohnet, Georges
Pagnol, Marcel
Pailleron, Édouard Jules Henri
Palissot de Montenoy, Charles
Pascal, Françoise
Passeur, Steve
Pechantre
Pellet, Christophe
Picard, Louis Benoit
Pinget, Robert
Pixerecourt, Rene Charles Guilbert de
Pontcharra, Natacha de
Porto-Riche, Georges de
Prevert, Jacques
Quinault, Philippe
Rachilde
Racine, Jean
Radiguet, Raymond
Raffalovich, Marc-André
Raisin, Jacques
Ravel Family, The
Raynal, Paul
Regnard, Jean-François
Regnault, Charles
Regnier, Max Albert Marie
Renaude, Noëlle
Reza, Yasmina
Ribes, Jean-Michel
Roche-Guilhen, Anne de la
Romains, Jules
Rostand, Edmond

Rotrou, Jean de
Rutebeuf
Salacrou, Armand
Sandeau, Jules
Sardou, Victorien
Sarment, Jean
Sarraute, Nathalie (b. Russia)
Sartre, Jean-Paul
Schehade, Georges
Scribe, Eugène
Sebbar, Leïla (b. Algeria)
Sedaine, Michel Jean
Serrand, Dominique
Serreau, Coline
Sloves, Chaim (b. Russia)
Soupault, Philippe
Taille, Jean de la
Tardieu, Jean
Tilly
Tristan L'Hermite, François
Tzara, Tristan (b. Romania)
Verneuil, Louis
Vian, Boris
Vigny, Alfred Victor, Comte de
Vildrac, Charles
Villedieu, Madame de
Villiers, Claude Deschamps
Vinaver, Michel
Visniec, Matei (b. Romania)
Vitrac, Hoger
Voltaire, François Marie Arouet de
Zola, Emile

**FRENCH CANADIAN**
Bouchard, Michel Marc
Boucher, Denise
Brassard, Marie
Chaurette, Normand
Christenson, Jonathan
Dubois, René-Daniel
Farhoud, Abla (b. Lebanon)
Frechette, Louis-Honore
Gareau, Laurier
Garneau, Michel
Gélinas, Gratien
Gingras, René-Daniel
Laberge, Marie
Languirand, Jacques
Lavigne, Louis-Dominique
Lepage, Robert
Maillet, Antonine
Mercier, Serge
Mouawad, Wajdi (b. Lebanon)
Petitclair, Pierre
Poirier, Leonie

Quesnel, Joseph (b. France)
Roussin, Claude
Simard, Andre
Sirois, Serge
Tremblay, Joey
Tremblay, Larry
Tremblay, Michel
Tremblay, Ronald

## GERMANY

Babo, Joseph Marius von
Barlach, Ernst
Becher, Ulrich
Beier, Ulli (Obotunde Ijomere, pseudonym)
Benedix, Roderich
Benn, Gottfried
Bernhard, Emil
Bernstein, Elsa (Ernst Rosmer, pseudonym; b. Austria)
Borchert, Wolfgang
Brecht, Bertolt
Brust, Alfred
Büchner, Georg
Bukowski, Oliver
Dorst, Tankred
Fassbinder, Rainer Werner
Fleisser, Marieluise
Freytag, Gustav
Fulda, Ludwig
Gasbarra, Felix
Goering, Reinhard
Goethe, Johann Wolfgang von
Goll, Iwan
Grabbe, Christian Dietrich
Grass, Günter
Gryphius, Andreas
Gutzkow, Karl Ferdinand
Halbe, Max
Handke, Peter
Hardt, Ernst
Harlan, Walter
Hasenclever, Walter
Hauptmann, Carl Ferdinand Maximilian
Hauptmann, Elisabeth
Hauptmann, Gerhart
Hebbel, Christiam Friedrich
Hildegard, Saint (aka Hildegard of Bingen)
Hildesheimer, Wolfgang
Hirschberg, Herbert
Hochhuth, Rolf
Hoffman, E.T.A. (Ernst Theodor Wilhelm)
Hofmann, Gert
Hrotsvit of Gandersheim
Iffland, August Wilhelm
Kaiser, George
Kipphardt, Heinar

Kleist, Heinrich von
Klinger Friedrich Maximilian
Kotzebue, August Friedrich Ferdinand von
Kroetz, Franz Xavier
Langhoff, Anna
Lask, Berta (b. Austria)
Lasker-Schüler, Else (died in exile in Israel)
Lauckner, Rolf T.
Leisewitz, Johann Anton
Lenz, Jakob Michael Reinhold
Lessing, Gotthold Ephraim
Lohenstein, Daniel Casper von
Loher, Dea
Ludwig, Otto
Mann, Heinrich (died in exile in United States)
Mann, Klaus (emigrated to United States)
Marber, Andreas
Mueller, Heiner
Piscator, Erwin
Pohl, Klaus
Reinshagen, Gerlin
Roth, Friederike
Rust, D.
Sachs, Hans
Sachs, Nelly
Schiller, Friedrich von
Schlegel, Johann Elias
Schneider, Simone
Schonherr, Karl
Schreyer, Lothar
Seidel, Georg
Somin, Willi Oscar
Sorge, Reinhard Johannes
Specht, Kerstin
Steinwachs, Ginka
Sternheim, Carl
Stramm, August
Strauss, Botho
Sudermann, Hermann
Sylvanus, Erwin
Thoma, Ludwig
Tieck, Johann Ludwig
Toller, Ernst
Tucholsky, Kurt
Unruh, Fritz von
Vollmöller, Karl Gustav
Wagner, Heinrich Leopold
Wedekind, Frank
Weill, Kurt (became U.S. citizen during World War II)
Werner, Friedrich Ludwig Zacharias
Wiechert, Ernst Emil
Wilbrandt, Adolf von
Wildenbruch, Ernst von
Winsloe, Christa
Zuckmayer, Carl

## GHANA

Aidoo, Ama Ata (presently lives in the United States)
Hevi, Jacob
Kay, Kwesi
Ofori, Henry
Sutherland, Efua Theodora

## GREAT BRITAIN

*See also African-British; Asian-British; Ireland; Northern*
*Ireland; Scotland; Wales*
À Beckett, Gilbert Abbott
Ableman, Paul
Ackerley, J.R.
Ackland, Rodney
Adamson, Samuel (b. Australia)
Addison, Joseph
Adshead, Kay
Albery, James
Albery, Peter
Alrawi, Karim (b. Egypt)
Arbuthnot, John (b. Scotland)
Archer, William (b. Scotland)
Arden, John
Ariadne
Arlen, Michael (b. Bulgaria)
Arnold, Matthew
Auden, W.H. (became U.S. citizen)
Ayckbourn, Sir Alan
Aykroyd, Juliet
Bagnold, Enid
Baker, Elizabeth
Bale, John
Banks, John
Baraitser, Marion
Baring, Maurice
Barker, Howard
Barksted, William
Barnes, Peter
Barrett, Wilson
Bartlett, Neil
Bassart, Clive
Bax, Clifford
Beaumont, Francis
Beckington, Charles
Beddoes, Thomas Lovell
Beerbohm, Max
Behn, Aphra
Bell, Florence
The Bemarro Theatre Group
Bennett, Alan
Bennett, Arnold
Benson, Robert Hugh
Berkeley, Reginald Cheyne
Berkoff, Steven
Bermange, Barry

Besier, Rudolf (b. Indonesia)
Bill, Stephen
Bingham, J.S.
Black, Don
Blake, William
Blakeman, Helen
Blanchard, Edward Litt Leman
Block, Toni
Boland, Bridget
Bolitho, William (b. South Africa)
Bolt, Robert
Bond, Christopher
Bond, Edward
Bond, Elisabeth
Boothby, Frances
Bottomley, Gordon
Bourne, Bette
Bowen, John Griffith
Box, Muriel
Box, Sydney
Brackley, Elizabeth
Bradley, Jyll
Breen, Richard
Brenton, Howard
Bricusse, Leslie
Bridgeman, Laura
Brighouse, Harold
Brome, Richard
Brook, Peter
Brooks, Harry
Brooks, Jeremy
Brophy, Brigid
Brough, Robert
Brough, William
Brown, Charles
Brown, John
Browne, Felicity
Browne, Maurice
Browne, Wynyard
Browning, Robert
Bruce, Lesley
Bryden, Bill (b. Scotland)
Buckingham, George Villiers, 2nd Duke of
Buckstone, John Baldwin
Bulkley, A.M. (Annette Mabel)
Bulwer-Lytton, Edward George Earle Lytton, 1st Baron
    Lytton
Burgess, John
Burke, Kathy
Burnard, Sir Francis Cowley
Burney, Charles
Burney, Fanny
Burnham, Barbara
Burns, Alan
By, William

Byrne, Muriel St. Clare
Byron, George Gordon, Baron
Calcutt, David
Campbell, Graeme
Campion, Thomas
Campton, David
Canning, George
Carew, Thomas
Carey, Henry
Carr, J. Comyns (Joseph)
Carroll, Paul Vincent (b. Ireland)
Cartwright, Jim
Cary, Elizabeth
Casdagli, Penny (b. Greece)
Caulfield, Anne
Cavan, Romilly
Cavendish, Jane
Cayzer, Charles William, Sir, 2nd Baronet
Celeste, Michele (b. Italy)
Centlivre, Susanna
Chambers, Charles Haddon (b. Australia)
Chapin, Harold (b. United States)
Chapman, George
Chapman, John
Cheeseman, Peter
Chetham-Strode, Warren
Christie, Agatha
Christie, Campbell
Christie, Dorothy (b. India)
Churchill, Caryl
Cibber, Colley
Cibber, Theophilus
Clark, Brian
Clough, David
Cobb, James
Coleridge, Samuel Taylor
Collins, Arthur
Collins, Barry
Colman, George, the Elder (b. Italy)
Colman, George, the Younger
Common Ground
Congreve, William
Conrad, Joseph (b. Poland)
Cooper, Giles (b. Ireland)
Cooper, Mary
Cooper, Susan
Coppel, Alec
Corlett, William
Coward, Sir Noël
Cowley, Abraham
Cowley, Hannah Parkhouse
Coxon, Lucinda
Coyle, Kevin
Coyne, Joseph Stirling (b. Ireland)
Crabbe, Kerry Lee

Cregan, David
Creighton, Anthony
Cresswell, Janet
Crisp, Samuel
Cropper, Margaret
Cross, Beverley
Cross, J.C.
Crowe, Richard
Crowne, John
Cullen, Alma (b. Scotland)
Cumberland, Richard
Cutler, Harriet
Daborne, Robert
Dane, Clemence
Daniel, Samuel
Daniels, Sarah
Darke, Nick
Dart, Philip
D'Avenant, Sir William
Davenport, Robert
Davies, Hubert Henry
Davis, Andre
Day, John
Dean, Basil
De Angelis, April
Debenham, Arthur Henry
De Casalis, Jeanne (b. Basutoland, now known as Lesotho)
Deike, Taggart
Dekker, Thomas
Delafield, E.M.
Delaney, Shelagh
Delderfield, Ronald Frederick (R.F.)
Dell, Jeffrey
Dennis, Nigel Forbes
Denstan
Dewhurst, Keith
Dibdin, Charles
Dibdin, Thomas John Pitt
Dickens, Charles
Dighton, John
Dillon, Eileen
Dinner, William
Dobie, Laurence
Dodsley, Robert
Dogget, Thomas (b. Ireland)
Dowie, Claire
Down, Oliphant
Dowson, Ernest Christopher
Drayton, Michael
Drinkwater, John
Dryden, John
Dudley, Sir Henry Bate
Duffet, Thomas (b. Ireland)
Duffy, Ger (b. Ireland)
Duffy, Maureen

Duggan, Shaun
Dukes, Ashley
Du Maurier, Daphne
Duncan, Ronald (b. Rhodesia, now Zimbabwe)
Dungate, Rod
Dunsany, Edward John Moreton Drax Plunkett, Baron
D'Urfey, Thomas
Du Rynn, Sebastin
Dyer, Charles
Edgar, David
Edmundson, Helen
Edwards, Richard
Egan, Michael
Elizabeth I
England, Barry
Etherege, George
Etherton, Michael
Evans, Lisa
Exton, Clive
Fagan, James Bernard (b. Northern Ireland)
Fairchild, William
Fannin, Hilary (b. Ireland)
Farjeon, Eleanor
Farjeon, Herbert
Farquhar, George
Fechter, Charles Albert
Feely, Terence
Feinstein, Elaine
Fenton, Elijah
Field, Nathaniel
Fielding, Henry
Fitzball, Edward
Fleming, Jill W.
Fletcher, John (1579–1625)
Fletcher, John (late 20th-century radio dramatist)
Foote, Samuel
Ford, Charles
Ford, John
Ford, Maggie
Forde, Nigel
Fox, Ellen
Francis, Ann
Francis, William
Francklin, Thomas
Frank, Maude Morrison
Frayn, Michael
Freistadt, Berta
Freeman, Sandra
Frere, John Hookham
Frisby, Terence
Frumin, Sue
Fry, Christopher
Fry, Michael
Fulwell, Ulpian
Galsworthy, John

Gannon, Lucy
Gardiner, (Charles) Wrey
Garner, Julian
Garrick, David
Gascoigne, George
Gay, John
Gay Sweatshop
Gear, Brian
Gellert, Roger
Gems, Pam
Gibson, Wilfrid Wilson
Gielgud, Val Henry
Gilbert, Michael Francis
Gilbert, Sir W.S. (William Schwenck)
Gill, Peter
Gilliat, Penelope
Gilliat, Sidney
Gingold, Hermione
Ginsbury, Norman
Glover, Evelyn
Glover, Halcott
Glover, Richard
Godfrey, Paul
Golding, Sir William Gerald
Goldsmith, Oliver
Gore-Browne, Robert F.
Goreing, Andrew
Goulding, Edmund
Gow, Ronald
Gowans, Elizabeth
Grant, David
Granville-Barker, Harley
Gray, John
Gray, Simon
Green, Janet
Greene, Graham
Greene, Robert
Greenwood, Walter
Greig, Noël
Griffin, Caroline
Griffin, G.W.H.
Griffith, Elizabeth
Griffiths, Trevor
Grosso, Nick
Grounds, Tony
Grundy, Sidney
Guinness, Sir Alec
Gurney, Richard
Guthrie, Tyrone
Haines, John Thomas
Hale, John
Hall, Willis
Halliday, Andrew
Hamilton, Cicely
Hamilton, Godfrey

Hamilton, Patrick
Hampton, Christopher
Hankin, St. John Emile Clavering
Hanley, James
Hardie, Victoria
Hardy, Thomas
Hare, David
Harraden, Beatrice
Harrison, John
Hart, Charles
Hartson, Hall
Harvey, Frank
Harvey, Jonathan
Harwood, Harold Marsh
Harwood, Ronald
Hastings, Basil Macdonald
Hastings, Charlotte
Hastings, Hugh (b. Australia)
Hastings, Michael Gerald
Havard, William
Hawkes, Jacquetta Hopkins
Hawkesworth, John
Hayes, Catherine
Hazlewood, Colin Henry
Hemro
Herman, Henry
Heywood, John
Heywood, Thomas
Hilarius
Hill, Aaron
Hilton, Arthur Clement
Hines, Barry
Hines, Leonard John
Hoadly, Benjamin
Hoare, Prince
Hodson, James Lansdale
Hoffe, Monckton (b. Ireland)
Holcroft, Thomas
Holliday, Joyce
Holman, Joseph George
Holme, Constance
Holt, Brian
Home, William Douglas (b. Scotland)
Hood, Kevin
Hooke, Nina Warner
Hoole, John
Hope, Karen
Hopkins, John
Horne, Kenneth
Horsefield, Debbie
Houghton, Stanley
Housman, Laurence
Howard, Sir Robert
Howarth, Donald
Hughes, John

Hughes, Richard
Hughes, Thomas
Hull, Thomas
Hunter, Norman C.
Hunter, Robert (b. Scotland, colonial governor of New
    York 1710–1720)
Hurlbut, William James
Inchbald, Elizabeth
Ireland, William Henry
Isherwood, Christopher (emigrated to United States)
Jackman, Isaac (b. Ireland)
Jacobs, William Wymark
Jameson, (Margaret) Storm
Jeans, Ronald
Jeffere, John
Jeffreys, Stephen
Jellicoe, Anne
Jenkins, Ray
Jennings, Gertrude E.
Jermain, Clive
Jerome, Helen (Burton)
Jerrold, Douglas William
Jevon, Thomas
John, Elton
Johnson, Bryan Stanly (B.S.)
Johnson, Catherine
Johnson, Charles
Johnson, Judith
Johnson, Pamela Hansford
Johnson, Philip
Johnson, Samuel
Jones, Henry
Jones, Henry Arthur
Jones, Paul
Jones, Peter
Jonson, Ben
Jupp, Kenneth
Kane, Sarah
Keats, John
Keefe, Barrie
Kelly, Hugh (b. Ireland)
Kemble, Fanny
Kemble, Marie-Thérèse DeCamp (b. Austria)
Kennedy, Margaret
Kenney, James
Kenrick, William
Kift, Roy (resides in Germany)
Kilcoyne, Catherine
Kilcoyne, Cathy
Killigrew, Thomas
Killingworth, Gerald
Kimmins, Anthony
King, Norman
King, Philip
Kinross, Martha

Kinwelmersh, Francis
Kirby, Andy
Kirkup, James
Klein, Debby
Knoblock, Edward (b. United States)
Knott, Frederick (b. China)
Knowles, James Sheridan (b. Ireland)
Kops, Bernard
Kretzmer, Herbert (b. South Africa)
Kyd, Thomas
Lamb, Charles
Lascelles, Kendrew
Launder, Frank
Lavery, Byrony
Lawrence, Maureen
Lee, Nathaniel
Lee, Sophia
Leigh, Mike
Leight, Warren
Lennon, John
Lessing, Doris (b. Persia, now Iran)
Lethbridge, Nemone
Levy, Benn Wolf
Levy, Deborah (b. South Africa)
Lewes, George Henry
Lewin, Eva
Lewis, Eve
Lewis, Leopold David
Lewis, Matthew G. ("Monk")
Lillo, George
Linden, Sonja
Lionheart, Eustace
Lipscomb, William Percy
Littlewood, Joan
Livings, Henry
Lloyd, Horace Amelius
Lloyd Webber, Andrew
Lodge, Thomas
Lonsdale, Frederick
Lowe, Stephen
Luckham, Claire
Luke, Peter
Lumley, Jane, Baroness Lumley
Lupton, Thomas
Lyly, John
Lyndon, Barré
Lynne, James Broom
Lyons, Gary
Macauley, Pauline
MacBeth, George
McClenaghan, Tom
MacColl, Ewan (b. Scotland)
McCracken, Esther (Armstrong)
MacDermot, Robert
McDonagh, Martin

McEvoy, Charles
McGough, Roger
McGuigan, Carol
McIlwraith, Bill
McIntyre, Clare
MacKenzie, Ronald (b. Scotland)
Mackie, Philip
Macklin, Charles (b. Ireland)
MacNeice, Louis (b. Northern Ireland)
Macowan, Norman (b. Scotland)
McPhee, Fergus
Macrae, Arthur
Macready, William (b. Ireland)
McTaggart, James
Malleson, Miles
Mallet, David (b. Scotland)
Mankowitz, Wolf
Manley, Delarivier
Manners, John Hartley
Marber, Patrick
Marcus, Frank (b. Germany)
Marlowe, Christopher
Marshall, Christabel
Marston, John
Marston, John Westland
Masefield, John
Mason, William
Massinger, Philip
Mathews, Charles J.
Maugham, Robin, 2nd Viscount Maugham of Hartfield
Maugham, W. Somerset (b. and d. France)
May, Val
Mayor, Beatrice
Medwall, Henry
Melville, Alan
Mendez, Moses
Mercer, David
Meyer, Michael
Middleton, Thomas
Milan, Angie
Miles, Cressida
Millar, Ronald
Miller, James
Miller, James H.
Mills, Hugh
Milman, Henry Hart
Milne, A.A. (Alan Alexander)
Milner, Henry M.
Milner, Roger
Milton, John
Minney, Rubeigh J.
Mitchell, Adrian
Mitchell, Julian
Mitchell, Yvonne
Mitson, Ronald

Moncrieff, William Thomas
Monkhouse, Allan
Moore, Edward
Moore, Marshall
More, Hannah
Morley, Robert
Mornin, Daniel
Mortimer, Sir John
Morton, John Maddison
Morton, Thomas
Motteaux, Peter Anthony (b. France)
Mottley, John
Morum, William
Moyes, Patricia (b. Ireland)
Mulcaster, Richard
Mullett, Andrew
Munday, Anthony
Munro, Charles Kirkpatrick
Murdoch, Iris (b. Ireland)
Nabbes, Thomas
Nagy, Phyllis (b. United States)
Nashe, Thomas
Naughton, Bill (b. Ireland)
Neale-Kennerley, James
Newley, Anthony
Nichols, Peter
Nichols, Robert Malise Bowyer
Nicholson, William
North, Francis
Norton, Thomas
Oakes, Meredith (b. Australia)
Ockrent, Mike
O'Conor, Joseph (b. Ireland)
Oglesby, Tamsin
O'Keefe, John (b. Ireland)
Oliver, Bryan
O'Malley, Mary
Orrey, Roger Boyle, 1st Earl of
Orton, Joe
Osborne, John
Osment, Philip
Otway, Thomas
Ouless, E.U.
Oulton, Brian
Owen, Alun Davies
Oxenford, John
Page, Louise
Paice, Eric
Pakington, Mary Augusta, Hon.
Palmer, T.A.
Parker, Louis Napoleon (b. France)
Parkington Edwards, Dudley
Pascal, Julia
Paul, Mrs. Clifford
Peacock, John

Peake, Richard Brinsley
Peele, George
Pembroke, Mary Sidney Herbert, Countess of
Pendark, Robert
Penhall, Joe
Pertwee, Michael
Pertwee, Ronald
Phillips, Ambrose
Phillips, Stephen
Phillips, Watts
Philon, Frederic
Pickering, Kenneth
Pikeryng, John
Pinero, Sir Arthur Wing
Pinner, David
Pinter, Harold
Pitt, George Dibdin
Pix, Mary Griffith
Planché, James Robinson
Plowman, Gillian
Pocock, Isaac
Pollock, Richard
Poole, John
Pope, Alexander
Popple, William
Popplewell, Jack
Popplewell, Olive
Porter, Henry
Preston, Thomas
Prichard, Rebecca
Priestley, John Boynton (J.B.)
Pryce, Richard (b. France)
Pulman, Jack
Purscell, Phyllis
Quarrell, Johnnie
Rapi, Nina (b. Greece)
Rattigan, Terence
Ravenscroft, Edward
Reade, Charles
Red Ladder Theatre Company
Redford, John
Reid, Arthur
Reid, Christina (b. Northern Ireland)
Reynolds, Frederick
Rhodes, William Barnes
Rhys, Ernest
Rice, Tim
Richards, Ivor Armstrong
Riley, Wilburforce
Roberts, Cyril
Robertson, Thomas William
Robins, Elizabeth (b. United States)
Robson, Cheryl
Roffey, Jack
Ronder, Jack

Ross, George
Rowe, Nicholas
Rowley, William
Rudkin, David
Ruppe, Jan
Russell, Howard
Russell, Willy
Rye, Elizabeth
Ryton, Royce
Sackville, Thomas, 1st Earl of Dorset
Sackville West, Victoria Mary (Vita), Lady Nicolson
Saint-John, John
Samuels, Diane
Sanford, Jeremy
Saunders, James
Savory, Gerald
Sayers, Dorothy L.
Schnibbe, Harry
Schrader, Clare
Scott, Paul
Sedley, Sir Charles, 5th Baronet
Selby, Charles
Settle, Elkanah
Shadwell, Charles
Shadwell, Thomas
Shaffer, Anthony
Shaffer, Peter
Shairp, Mordaunt
Shakespeare, William
Sharp, Anthony
Shaw, George Bernard
Shaw, Paul
Shaw, Robert
Sheasby, Dave
Shelley, Percy Bysshe
Sheridan, Richard B.
Sherriff, Robert Cedric
Shirley, James
Shirley, William
Siddons, Henry
Sidney, Philip
Sieveking, Lancelot De Giberne
Sigley, Marjorie
Simpson, Norman Frederick
Sims, George Robert
Singer, Campbell
Sisson, Rosemary Anne
Skelton, John
Sloman, Robert
Slovo, Robyn (b. South Africa)
Smee, Amanda
Smee, Lilian
Smith, Albert Richard
Smith, Charlotte Turner
Smith, Dodie

Smith, Edmund
Smith, Ian Crichton
Smollett, Tobias George
Sneal, Patricia
Snow, Andrea
Sod, Ted
Southerne, Thomas
Southey, Robert
Sowerby, Githa
Spencer, David
Steele, Richard
Stefanovski, Goran (b. Macedonia)
Stevens, George Alexander
Stevenson, William
Stilgoe, Richard
Stoppard, Tom (b. Czechoslovakia)
Storey, David Malcolm
Storey, Robert
Strachan, Alan
Stuart, Aimee McHardy
Sutro, Alfred
Swain, Elizabeth
Swinburne, Algernon Charles
Sylvaine, Vernon
Tabori, George (b. Hungary)
Talfourd, Francis
Tate, Nahum
Taylor, Cecil Philip (C.P.)
Taylor, Christopher
Taylor, Don
Taylor, Tom
Temple, Joan
Tennyson, Alfred, 1st Baron Tennyson
Terson, Peter
Theobald, Lewis
Thompson, Tierl
Thomson, James
Tobin, John
Tourneur, Cyril
Townley, James
Townshend, Aurelian
Tuke, Sir Samuel
Udall, Nicholas
Upton, Judy
Ustinov, Peter
Vanbrugh, Sir John
Van Druten, John (emigrated to United States)
Vane, Sutton
Venables, Clare
Vujovic, Sladjana (b. Montenegro, divides time between London and Montenegro)
Wager, William
Wakefield, Lou
Wakeman, Alan
Walker, John

Wandor, Micheline
Wapull, George
Waterhouse, Keith
Watkyn, Arthur
Watson-Taylor, George
Watts, Murray
Webber, Cecil Edwin (C.E.)
Webster, Convey
Webster, John
Welles, Herbert George (H.G.)
Wertenbaker, Timberlake (b. United States)
Wesker, Arnold
West, Don
Whaler, Imogene
White, Robert
Whitehead, William
Whitemore, Hugh
Whiting, John
Wilcox, Desmond
Wilcox, Michael
Wilde, Oscar
Wilde, Patrick
Wilkins, George
Wilkinson, Julie
Williams, Charles
Williams, Hugh
Williams, Margaret Vyner (b. Australia)
Williams, Rod
Willis, Anthony Armstrong (b. Canada)
Wilmot, Robert
Wilson, Sir Angus Frank Johnstone
Wilson, John, (1785–1854)
Wilson, Marie Elaine
Wilson, Robert (d. 1600)
Wilson, Sandy
Wilson, Theodora Wilson
Windsor, Valerie
Winter, John Keith (b. Wales)
Wise, Ernest George
Wiseman, Jane
Woddis, Roger
Wodehouse, P.G. (Pellham Grenville; became U.S. citizen
　　in 1955)
Wolfe, Humbert
Wolton, Joan
The Women's Theatre Group
Wood, Charles
Wood, Mrs. Henry
Wood, J. Hickory
Wood, Kevin
Woodes, Nathaniel
Woods, Aubrey
Woods, W.
Wooll, Edward
Wordsworth, William

Worker's Theatre Movement
Worsley, Victoria
Wright, Nicholas
Wroth, Lady Mary
Wycherley, William
Wymark, Olwen (b. United States)
Wynne, Michael
Yeger, Sheila
Young, Sir Charles Lawrence, 7th Baronet, of North Dean
Young, Edward
Zajdlic, Richard

## GREECE, ANCIENT
Aeschylus
Aristophanes
Euripides
Menander
Sophocles

## GREECE, MODERN
Anagnostaki, Loula
Haviara, Eleni
Keridis, Dimitris
Peryalis, Notis
Prevelakis, Pandelis
Skourtis, George
Theotokas, George
Xenopoulos, Gregorius

## GREENLAND
Tukak' Theater Ensemble

## GUADELOUPE
Condé, Maryse
Schwarz-Bart, Simone

## GUYANA
Carew, Jan Rynveld
McDonald, Ian (b. Trinidad)

## HISPANIC-AMERICAN
Alám, Juan Shamsul (Puerto Rican)
Alfaro, Luis (Mexican-American)
Algarín, Miguel (Puerto Rican)
Anaya, Rudolfo A. (Mexican-American)
Arce, Elia (dual citizen of Costa Rica and United States)
Arenas, Reinaldo (b. Cuba)
Arias, Ron (Mexican-American)
Ariza, René (b. Cuba)
Arizmendi, Yareli (b. Mexico)
Astor del Valle, Janis (Puerto Rican)
Bonet, Wilma (Puerto Rican)
Bustamante, Nao (Mexican-American)
Carrero, Jaime (Puerto Rican)

Chávez, Denise (Mexican-American)
Clavijo, Uva (b. Cuba)
Colón, Oscar A. (Puerto Rican)
Cram, Cusi (Bolivian-Scots-American)
Cruz, Migdalia (Puerto Rican)
Cruz, Nilo (b. Cuba)
Culture Clash (Mexican-American)
Dante, Nicholas (Puerto Rican)
Dorfman, Ariel (b. Argentina, became citizen of Chile
  before becoming U.S. citizen)
Duarte-Clarke, Rodrigo (Mexican-American)
Esparza, Laura (Mexican-American)
Farías, Joann (Mexican-American)
Feliciano, Gloria (Puerto Rican)
Fernández, Evelina (Mexican-American)
Ferradas, Renaldo (b. Cuba)
Fornes, Maria Irene (b. Cuba)
Fraguada, Federico (Puerto Rican)
Fusco, Coco (Cuban-American)
Garcia-Crow, Amparo (Mexican-American)
Garza, Roberto Jesus (Mexican-American)
Gasteazoro, Eva (b. Nicaragua)
Girón, Arthur (Guatemalan-American)
Gomez, Marga (Puerto Rican)
Gonzalez, Reuben (Puerto Rican)
Gonzalez-Pando, Miguel (Cuban-American)
Gonzalez S., Silvia (Mexican-American)
Hernández, Leopoldo M. (b. Cuba)
Iizuki, Naomi (b. Japan, father Japanese, mother American
  Latina)
Irizarry, Richard V. (Puerto Rican)
Kaufman, Moisés (b. Venezuela)
Laviera, Tato (Puerto Rican)
Leguizamo, John (b. Colombia, father Puerto Rican,
  mother Colombian)
Loomer, Lisa
López, Eduardo Iván (Puerto Rican)
López, Eva (Puerto Rican)
López, Josefina (b. Mexico)
Machado, Eduardo (b. Cuba)
Macias, Ysidro R. (Mexican-American)
Mares, E.A. "Tony" (Mexican-American)
Matas, Julio (b. Cuba)
Martinez, Rogelio (b. Cuba)
Mayer, Oliver (Mexican-American)
Mena, Alicia (Mexican-American)
Monge-Rafuls, Pedro R. (b. Cuba)
Montes Huidobro, Matías (b. Cuba)
Moraga, Cherríe (Mexican-American)
Morton, Carlos (Mexican-American)
Niggli, Josefina (b. Mexico)
Palacios, Monica (Mexican-American)
Pereiras García, Manuel (b. Cuba)
Pérez, Frank (Puerto Rican)
Pérez, Hector (Cuban-American)

Pérez, Judith (Mexican-American)
Pérez, Severo (Mexican-American)
Pietri, Pedro (Puerto Rican)
Piñero, Miguel (Puerto Rican)
Portillo-Trambley, Estela (Mexican-American)
Prida, Dolores (b. Cuba)
Ramírez, Ivette M. (Puerto Rican)
Reyes, Guillermo (b. Chile)
Rivera, Carmen (Puerto Rican)
Rivera, José (Puerto Rican)
Rodríguez, Eugene (Puerto Rican)
Rodríguez, Yolanda (Puerto Rican)
Rodríguez Suárez, Roberto (Puerto Rican)
Romero, Elaine (Mexican-American)
Saavedra, Guadalupe de (Mexican-American)
Sáenz, Diana (Mexican-American)
Sanchez, Edwin (Puerto Rican)
Sanchez-Scott, Milcha (b. Bali, father Columbian/Mexican;
  mother Indonesian/Chinese)
Sebazco, Raul Santiago (b. Cuba)
Sierra, Rubén (Mexican-American)
Solis, Octavio (Mexican-American)
Soto, Gary (Mexican-American)
Svich, Caridad (Cuban-American)
El Teatro de la Esperanza
Tirado, Cándido (Puerto Rican)
Tropicana, Carmelita (Cuban-American)
Urista, Alberto H. (Mexican-American)
Valdez, Luis (Mexican-American)
Valle, Fred (Puerto-Rican)
Vigil, Angel (Mexican-American)
Villarreal, Edit (Mexican-American)
Wood, Silviana (Mexican-American)

## HISPANIC-CANADIAN
Aguirre, Carmen (b. Chile)
The Latino Theatre Group
Verdecchia, Guillermo (b. Argentina)

## HONG KONG
Chan, Anthony
Chan, Joanna
He, Jiping
To, Raymond K.W.
Yung, Danny N.T.

## HUNGARY
Bereményi, Géza
Czakó, Gábor
Csurka, Istvan
Filo, Vera
Hay, Julius (Háy, Gyula)
Karpati, Peter
Kornis, Mihály

Molnár, Ferenc (emigrated to the United States to avoid
    Nazi persecution)
Nagy, András
Németh, Ákos
Örkény, István
Paskandi, Geza
Spiró, György
Suto, Andras (ethnic Hungarian who was born and has
    lived most of his life in Romania)
Szilágyi, Andor

## ICELAND
Björnsson, Oddur
Halldórsson, Erlingur E.
Jakobsson, Jökull
Laxness, Halldór
Sigurjonsson, Johann
Simonarson, Olafur Haukur
Stefánsson, Davíð
Sveinbjörnsson, Tryggvi
Thordarson, Agnar

## INDIA
*See also* Sanskrit
Alekar, Satish
Bhagat, Datta
Bharati, Dharamvir
Bharti, Bhanu
Das, Jagannath Prasad
Deshpande, G.P. (Govind Purushrottam)
Devi, Mahasweta
Dutt, Utpal
Elkunchwar, Mahesh
Kambar, Chandrasekhar
Karnad, Girish
Maharishi, Mohan
Majumdar, Debasis
Mehta, Dina
Mhapsekar, Jyoti
Mukerji, Dhan Gopal
Mukherjee, Arun
Padmanabhan, Manjula
Panikkar, K. N.
Parthasarathy, Indira
Prasanna
Rakesh, Mohan
Sahni, Bhisham
Sarma, Arun
Sengupta, Poile (Ambika)
Shah, B.M.
Shudraka (King)
Sidhu, C.D.
Sircar, Badal
Sriranga (pseud. of Adya Rangacharya)
Tagore, Rabindranath

Tanvir, Habib
Tendulkar, Vijay
Thiyam, Ratan
Verma, Surendra
Vishakadatta

## INDONESIA
Sarumpaet, Ratna

## IRAN
Beyzāi, Bahrām
Chubak, Sādeq
Ebrahimi, Nader
Na'lbandian, Abbas
Rahbar, Mahmud
Sa'edi, Gholamhoseyn
Talebi, Faramarz
Yalfani, Mohsen

## IRAQ
'Ani, Yusuf, al-

## IRELAND
*See also* Northern Ireland
Aron, Geraldine (divides time between South Africa and
    London)
Beckett, Samuel (lived in France)
Behan, Brendan
Bell, Robert
Bolger, Dermot
Boucicault, Dion
Boyd, Pom
Brooke, Henry
Buckerstaffe, Isaac
Byrne, Seamus
Carr, Marina
Carroll, Paul Vincent
Clarke, Austin
Coffey, Charles
Colum, Padraic
Coulter, John (emigrated to Canada)
Coyne, Joseph Stirling
D'Arcy, Margaretta
Deane, Hamilton
Deevy, Teresa
Donleavy, James Patrick (b. United States)
Donnelly, Neil
Douglas, James
Dowling, Maurice Mathew George
Duffy, Ger
Fallon, Padraic
Fannin, Hilary
Farquhar, George
Farrell, Bernard
Fitzmaurice, George

Friel, Brian (b. Northern Ireland)
Gonne, Francis
Gregory, Lady Isabella Augusta
Harding, Michael
Hughes, Declan
Hyde, Douglas
Jephson, Robert
Johnston, Alex
Johnston, Denis
Keane, John B.
Kelly, Hugh
Kilroy, Thomas
Knowles, James Sheridan
Leonard, Hugh
Longford, Christine, Countess of
Mac Intyre, Tom
McArdle, John
McCabe, Patrick
McCarthy, Justin Huntly
MacDonagh, Donagh
McGuinness, Frank
MacMahon, Bryan
MacNally, Leonard
Manning, Mary
Martyn, Edward
Maturin, Charles Robert
Mayne, Rutherford
Meehan, Paula
Meldon, Maurice
Molloy, Michael Joseph
Morrison, Conall
Moxley, Gina
Murphy, Arthur
Murphy, Jimmy
Murray, Thomas C.
O'Brien, Edna
O'Casey, Sean
O'Conor, Joseph
O'Donovan, John
O'Donovan, Michael
O'Flaherty, Liam
O'Hara, Kane
O'Keefe, John
O'Kelly, Donal
Pakenham, Edward Arthur Henry, 6th Earl of Longford
Pearse, Patrick
Riordan, Arthur
Robinson, Lennox
Roche, Billy
Russell, George William
Shaw, George Bernard
Sheridan, Frances
Sheridan, Richard B.
Sheridan, Thomas
Shiels, George

Steele, Richard
Stoker, Bram
Synge, John Millington
Waddell, Samuel
Walsh, Enda
Wilde, Oscar
Williams, Niall
Wills, William Gorman
Woods, Vincent
Yeats, Jack
Yeats, William Butler

## ISRAEL
Balalin Company of Jerusalem, The
Bar-Yosef, Yosef
Chilton, Nola (b. United States)
Danon, Rami
Goldberg, Leah (b. Germany)
Horowitz, Dan
Kainy, Miriam
Lerner, Motti
Levin, Hanoch
Levy, Amnon
Mazya, Edna
Megged, Aharon (b. Poland)
Parnes, Uzi
Shamir, Moshe
Sobol, Joshua
Tomer, Ben-Zion
Yehoshua, Abraham B.

## ITALY, ANCIENT
*See Roman Empire*

## ITALY, MODERN
Accademia degli Intronati
Alfieri, Vittorio
Alvaro, Corrado
Annunzio, Gabriele D'
Aretino, Pietro
Ariosto, Ludovico
Benelli, Sem
Beolco, Angelo
Betti, Ugo
Bontempelli, Massimo
Bracco, Roberto
Bruno, Giordano
Campanile, Achille
Casella, Alberto
Chiarelli, Luigi
Curino, Laura
Dovizi da Bibbiena, Bernardo, Cardinal
Filippo, Eduardo De
Fo, Dario
Gallarati-Scotti, Tommaso

Giacosa, Giuseppe
Ginzburg, Natalia
Goldoni, Carlo
Gozzi, Carlo
Guarini, Giovanni Battista
Gl'Intronati di Siena
Lopez, Sabatino
Machiavelli, Niccolo
Maraini, Dacia
Marinetti, Filippo (b. Egypt)
Menotti, Gian-Carlo
Metastasio, Pietro Antonio Domenico Buonaventura
Morselli, Ercole Luigi
Niccodemi, Dario
Petrolini, Ettore
Pirandello, Luigi
Ponte, Lorenzo da
Praga, Marco
Rame, Franca
Rosselli, Amelia
Rosso di San Secondo, Pier Maria
Savinio, Alberto (b. Greece)
Scala, Flaminio
Svevo, Italo
Tasso, Torquato
Tozzi, Federigo
Trissino, Gian Giorgio
Verga, Giovanni
Viviani, Raffaele

## IVORY COAST
Kwahulé, Koffi
Liking, Werewere (b. Cameroon)
Zadi Zaourou, Bernard

## JAMAICA
Figueroa, John
Mais, Roger
Scott, Dennis

## JAPAN
Abe, Kōbō
Akihama, Satoshi
Akimoto, Matsuyo
Betsuyaku, Minoru
Chikamatsu, Monzaemon
Chong, Wishing
Dumb Type
Enami, Sayemon
Fujita, Den
Fukuda, Tsuneari
Fukuda, Yoshiyuki
Gen'e
Hasegawa, Shigure

Hashimoto, Shinobu
Hirata, Oriza
Hiyoshi Sa-ami Yasukiyo
Hotta Kiyomi
I-ami
Ichido, Rei (Blue Bird Theater Company)
Ichikawa, Danjūrō I
Iijima, Sanae
Iizawa, Tadasu
Inoue, Hisashi
Iwamatsu, Ryo
Kako, Chikajo (Chika)
Kan, Kikuchi
Kanami
Kaneshita, Tatsuo
Kanze, Kojiro Nobumitsu
Kanze, Motomasa
Kawamura, Takeshi
Kawatake, Mokuami
Kara, Juro
Kato, Michio
Kato, Todashi
Kinoshita, Junji
Kisaragi, Koharu
Kishida, Rio
Kitamura, So
Kokami, Shoji
Komatsu, Mikio
Komparu, Gonnokami
Kongo, Yagoro
Konparu, Zenchiku
Kurosawa, Akira
Makino, Nozomi
Matsuda, Masataka
Mishima, Yukio
Miyamasu
Miyamoto, Ken
Miyazawa, Akio
Miyoshi, Jūro
Miyoshi, Shoraku
Nagai, Ai
Nakada, Mansuke
Nakamura, Matagoro
Namiki, Gohei III
Namiki, Sosuke
Narui, Yutaka
Noda, Hideki
Noda, Kogo
Oguni, Hideo
Ohashi, Yasuhiko
Okabe, Kodai
Okamura, Shiko
Ota, Shogo
Ozu, Yasujiro

Saito, Ren (b. North Korea)
Sakate, Yoji
Sakurada, Jisuke II
Satoh, Makoto
Seiami
Shimizu, Kunio
Suki Yumi
Suzuki, Yumi
Takeda, Izumo II
Takeuchi, Joichiro
Tanaka, Chikao
Terayama, Shūji
Toshiro, Suzue
Toyozawa, Danpei II
Tsuka, Kohei
Tsuruya, Namboku IV
Tsuuchi, Genshichi
Tsuuchi, Hanemon
Tsuuchi, Hanjuro
Tsuuchi, Jihei II
Watanabe, Eriko
Yagi, Shoichiro
Yamamoto, Kiyokazu
Yamazaki, Masakazu
Yashiro, Seiichi
Yasuda, Abun
Yokouchi, Kensuke
Yu, Miri
Zeami
Zembo, Motoyasu
Zenchiku, Ujinobu

**KUWAIT**
al-Surayyi', 'Abd al-'Aziz

**LATVIA**
Brigadere, Anna
Eglitis, Anslavs
Priede, Gunar
Rainis, Jānis
Straumanis, Alfreds
Ziverts, Martins

**LEBANON**
Mahfuz,'Isam

**LITHUANIA**
Boruta, Kazys
Landsbergis, Algirdas
Marcinkevičius, Justinas
Mickevičius, Adomas
Saja, Kazys
Škėma, Antanas
Sruoga, Balys

**MACEDONIA**
Andonovski, Venko
Bogdanovski, Rusomir
Čašule, Kole
Dkovski, Dejan
Mirčevska, Žanina
Nasev, Saško (currently ambassador to Canada)
Petrovski, Jugoslav
Plevneš, Jordan (currently resides in France)
Risteski, Blagoja
Stefanovski, Goran (currently resides in Great Britain)

**MADAGASCAR**
Rafenomanjato, Charlotte-Arrisoa
Raharimanana, Jean-Luc

**MALAYSIA**
Arai, Anuar Nor
Das, K.
Dinsman
Dorall, Edward
Hassan, Noordin
Jaaffar, Johan
Khan, Hatta Azad
Lee, Joo For
Leow, Puay Tin
Sikana, Mana
Yeoh, Patrick

**MALI**
Badian, Seydou

**MAORI**
Broughton, John
Brown, Riwia
Davis, Wiremu
Grace-Smith, Briar
Hapipi, Rore
He Ara Nou
Owen, Rena
Potiki, Roma
Renee
Tuwhare, Hone

**MARTINIQUE**
Césaire, Aimé
Césaire, Ina
Césaire, Michèle
Laou, Julius Amédée (b. France)

**MAURITANIA**
Diagana, Moussa

## MEXICAN-AMERICAN
*See Hispanic-American*

## MEXICO
Azcárate, Leonor
Berman, Sabina
Carballido, Emiliio
Fuentes, Carlos (b. Panama)
Garro, Elena
Hernández, Luisa Josefina
Juana de la Cruz, Sor
Leñero, Vicente
Olmos, Carlos
Ortiz, de Montellano, Bernardo
Paz, Octavio
Rascon Banda, Victor Hugo
Schmidhuber de la Mora, Guillermo
Solórzano, Carlos (b. Guatemala)
Urtusastegui, Tomas
Usigli, Rodolfo
Vilalta, Maruxa (b. Spain)
Villaurutia, Xavier

## MONTENEGRO
Vujovic, Sladjana (b. Montenegro, divides time between London and Montenegro)

## MYANMAR
Win, Tin Tin

## NAMIBIA
Amakali, Maria
Bricks Theatre Group
Cowley, Kay
Fourie, Tony
Haakskeen, Petrus
Hangula, Vickson Tablah
Job, Norman
Kaundu, Ainna
Molapong, Keamogetsi Joseph
Mootseng, Boli
Mosalele, Lucky 'Pieters'
Ndjavera, Dawid Stone
Nyathi, Francis Sifiso
Olivier-Sampson, Laurinda
Rispel, Kubbe
Skrywer-Afrikaner, Martha Laurencia
Terblanché, Tanya
Thaniseb, Axaro W.

## NATIVE AMERICAN
Arkeketa, Annette (Otoe-Missouria/Muscogee Creek)
Colorado, Elvira (Chichimee/Otomi)
Colorado, Hortensia (Chichimee/Otomi)
Geiogamah, Hanay (Kiowa/Delaware)

Glancy, Diane (Cherokee)
Gordon, Roxy (Choctaw/Assiniboine-Sioux)
Gomez, Terry (Comanche)
Howe, LeAnne (Choctaw)
Kauffman, John (Nez Perce)
King, Bruce (Turtle Clan/Oneida/Iroquois)
Kneubuhl, Victoria Nalani (Hawaiian/Samoan/Caucasian)
Lang, William (Lenape)
Louis, Ray Baldwin (Navajo)
Native American Theater Ensemble (members representing at least fifteen tribal heritages)
Pingayak, John (Cup'ik/Inuit)
Riggs, Lynn (Cherokee)
Spiderwoman Theater (Kuna/Rappahannock)
Tucker, Wallace Hampton (Choctaw)
Yellow Robe, William S., Jr. (Assinibone/Nakota)

## NETHERLANDS
Aboab, Isaac de Matatia (family exiles from Portuguese Inquisition)
Boer, Lodewijk de
Dullemen, Inez van
Haasse, Hella S.
Heijermans, Herman
Herzberg, Judith
Lohuizen, Suzanne van
Strijards, Frans
Veldhuizen, Matin van
Woudstra, Karst

## NEW ZEALAND
*See also Asian-New Zealanders; Maori*
Baxter, James K.
Bowman, Edward
Gallagher, Kathleen
Hodge, Merton
Mason, Bruce
Rippingale, Gen
Surridge, André (b. Great Britain)
Winstanley, Kate

## NIGERIA
Adesina, Foluke
Agoro, S.N.A.
Ajibade, Segun
Atai, Uko
Clark-Bekederemo, John Pepper
Euba, Femi
Hamanjoda, Aminu
Henshaw, James Ene
Ibe, Simon Iro
Johnson, Effiong
Kala, Sam
Lapido, Duro
Ogunrinde, Folasayo

Ogunyemi, Wale
Oko, Atabo
Okonkwo, Rufus
Onwueme, Osonye Tess Akaeke
Osofisan, Femi
Oyin Adejobi Company
Saro-wiwa, Ken
Soyinka, Wole
Udensi, Uwa

## NORTHERN IRELAND
Carville, Daragh
Devlin, Anne
Ervine, St. John Greer
Jones, Marie
MacNeice, Louis
Reid, Christina

## NORWAY
*See also Sami*
Björnson, Björnstjerne
Borgen, Johan
Bringsvaerd, Tor Åge
Cappelin, Peder W.
Gaup, Nils
Grieg, Nordahl
Havrevold, Finn
Heiberg, Gunnar Edvard Rode
Hoem, Edvard
Holberg, Ludvig (spent much of his life in Denmark)
Ibsen, Henrik
Kielland, Axel
Kielland, Trygve
Korg, Helge
Løveid, Cecile
Vesaas, Tarjei
Vik, Bjørg
Walle, Knut

## PARAGUAY
Alsina, Arturo (b. Argentina)
Rivarola Matto, José María

## PERU
Segura, Manuel Ascencio
Vargas Llosa, Mario

## PHILIPPINES
Calo, Arturo
Casino, Jesus
Celestino, Aurelio
Checa, Pedro F.
Coscolluela, Elsa Martinez
Damaso, Jimeno
Fernandez-Ilagan, Marili

Guerrero, Wifredo Ma. (Maria)
Ilagan, Hermogenes E.
Jacob, Malou Leviste
Jimenez, Asisclo
Joaquin, Nick
Kabahar, Pio A.
Magtoto, Liza
Millado, Chris
Montano, Severino
Nuyda, Justino
Palafox. Filemon M.
Palarca, Julia
Perez, Tony
Quintos, Floy
Reyes, Severino
Rodriguez, Buenaventura
Santos, Al
Santos, Juan D.
Sicam, Geronimo D.
Villa, Jose Garcia (emigrated to the United States)
Villa, Lilia A.
Villanueva, Rene O.

## POLAND
The Afanasjeff Family Circus
Afanasjew, Jerzy
The Bim-Bom Troupe
Gałczyński, Konstanty Ildefons
Kofta, Krystyna
Krasiński, Zygmunt
Miciński, Tadeusz
Mickiewicz, Adam
Mrosek, Slawomir
Przybyszewski, Stanisław
Różewicz, Tadeusz
Slowacki, Juliusz
Szajna, Józef
Trzebiński, Andrzej
Witkiewicz, Stanisław Ignacy

## PUERTO RICO
*[resides Puerto Rico]*
Arrivi, Francisco
Casas, Myrna
Marichal Lugo, Teresa
Marqués, René
Ramos-Perea, Roberto

## PUERTO RICAN
*See Hispanic-American*
*[resides U.S.]*

## ROMAN EMPIRE
Horatius Flaccus, Quintus
Plautus, Titus Maccius

Seneca, Lucius Annaeus
Terentius Afer, Publius

## ROMANIA
Barbu, Petre
Butnaru, Val
Cadariu, Alina Nelega
Cărbunariu, Geanina
Gârbea, Horia
Macrinici, Radu
Mircea, Ion
Mungiu-Pippidi, Alina
Nicolau, Valentin
Stănescu, Saviana
Suto, Andras (ethnic Hungarian born and living most of his
     life in Romania)
Tântar, Nina
Vălean, Andreea
Visniec, Matei (now French citizen)
Zografi, Vlad

## RUSSIA
*See also Belarus; Estonia; Latvia; Lithuania; Ukraine*
Afinogenyev, Aleksandr Nicolaevich
Aksenov, Vasilii
Alyoshin, Samuil
Andreyev, Leonid Nikolaevich
Annensky, Innokenty
Anski, Sholem
Arbatova, Maria
Arbuzov, Alexei
Ardov, Victor
Arsky, Pavel
Axenfeld, Israel
Babel, Isaac
Bely, Andrei
Blok, Aleksandr
Briusov, Valerii
Bulgakov, Mikhail
Burlatsky, Fyodor
Chekhov, Anton
Chervinsky, Alexander
Eisenstein, Sergei
Evreinov, Nikolai Nikolayevich
Fonvizin, Dinis Ivanovich (also spelled Denis)
Galin, Alexander
Gelman, Alexander
Gippius, Zinaida
Glebov, Anatole Glebovitch
Gogol, Nikolai
Gorin, Grigory
Gorky, Maxim
Gremina, Elena
Griboedov, Alexander Sergeyevich

Hirschbein, Peretz (emigrated to the United States)
Ilf, Ilya Arnoldovich
Ilyenkov, Vassily Pavlovich
Kataev, Valentin Petrovich
Kharms, Daniil
Kirshon, Vladimir
Krylov, Ivan Andreevich
Kurginian, Sergei
Kuzmin, Mikhail
Lensky, Dmitri
Leonov, Leonid Maximovich
Lipskerov, Konstantin
Marshak, Samuil
Mayakovsky, Vladimir
Mikhailova, Olga
Nemirovich-Danchenko, Vladimir Ivanovich
     (b. Georgia)
Olesha, Yuri (b. Ukraine)
Ostrovsky, Alexei
Petrushevskaya, Ludmila
Pisemsky, Alexei
Pogodin, Nikolai Federovich
Prokofiev, Sergei (b. Ukraine)
Prutkov, Kozma
Pushkin, Aleksandr Sergeyevich
Remizov, Aleksei
Reznik, Lipe
Rokk, Vsevolod
Rozov, Victor Sergeeich
Saltykov, Mikhail Evgrafovich
Schwartz, Yevgeny
Sheinen, Lev Romanovich
Shkvarkin, Vasilii Vasil-'evich
Shvarts, Evgenii L'vovich
Simonov, Konstantin Mikhailovich
Sologub, Fyodor
Solovev, Vladimir Alexandrovich
Tolstoi, Aleksei Konstantinovich
Tolstoi, Lev Nicholaevich
Trenenev, Konstantin Andreivich
Tur, Leonid Davidovich
Tur, Petr Davidovich
Turgenev, Ivan
Verbitskaya, Anastasiya
Vishnevskii, Vsevolod Vitlalevicii
Zorin, Leonid
Zoshchenko, Mikhail

## ST. LUCIA
Hippolyte, Kendel
Walcott, Roderick

## SAMI
Gaup, Nils

## SANSKRIT
Bhasa
Bhavabhuti
Harsha, son of Hira
Kālidāsa

## SCOTLAND
Baillie, Joanna
Barrie, Sir J.M. (James Matthew), 1st Baronet
Bradley, Jack
Bridie, James
Buchanan, George
Byrne, John
Campbell, Graeme
Chowdhry, Maya
Clifford, John
Conn, Stewart
Cullen, Alma
Cullen, Mike
Czerkawska, Catherine
Daviot Gordon (pseudonym of Elizabeth Mackintsoh, aka
    Josephine Tey)
Di Mambro, Ann Marie
Ditton, Cordelia
Donald, Simon
Eveling, Stanley
Finlay, Ian Hamilton
Forsyth, James
Glover, Sue
Greenhorn, Stephen
Greig, David
Hannan, Chris
Hay, Ian
Hepburn, Stuart
Home, John
Lochhead, Liz
Kay, Jackie
Kennaway, James
Lindsay, Sir David of the Mount
Lochhead, Liz
MacBeth, George
MacDonald, Robert David
MacDougall, Roger
McKay, John
McKillop, Menzies
McLean, Duncan
McLean, Linda
MacMillan, Hector
Munro, Rona
Murray, William Henry (b. Great Britain)
Ramsay, Allan
Roper, Tony
St. Peter's Youth Group
Scott, Sir Walter

Sharp, Alan
Smith, Ali
Smith, Iain Crichton
Spark, Muriel Sarah
Stevenson, Robert Louis
Stewart, Ena Lamont
Storm, Lesley
Trotter, Catherine
Wilson, John

## SENEGAL
Ka, Abdou Anta

## SERBIA
Lebovic, Djordje (b. Yugoslavia)
Romcevic, Nebojsa (b. Yugoslavia)
Srbljanović, Biljana (b. Sweden)

## SIERRA LEONE
Bart-Williams, Gaston

## SINGAPORE
Chng, Suan Tze
Fong, Otto
Han, Lao-Da
Heng, Russell Hiang Khng
Kon, Stella
Krishnan, P.
Kuo, Pao Kun
Lam, Dana
Lee Chee King
Lin, Min-Zhou
Loh, Kwuan
Loon, Robin
Nadiputra
Ping, Chin Woo
Shanmugam, S.V.
Sim, Desmond
Tan, Mei Ching
Tan, Tarn How
Tan, Theresa
Varella, Enrico
Wong, Eleanor
Yu, Ovidia

## SLOVAKIA
*See also Czech Republic*
Bodnárová, Jana
Čahojová-Bernátová, Božena
Certezni, Monika
Cicvak, Martin
Feldek, L'ubomír
Feriancová, Vanda
Gombar, Jozef

Horák, Karol
Horvath, Tomás
Juráňová, Jana
Kerata, Laco
Klimáček, Viliam
Lasica, Milan
Lavrik, Silvester
Maliti-Fraňová, Eva
Olekšák, Roman
Piussi, Lucia
Satinský, Július
Sloboda, Rudolf
Štepka, Stanislav
Stoka Theatre, The
Uhlar, Blaho
Uličianska, Zuzana

## SLOVENIA
Flisar, Evald
Jančar, Drago
Jovanovič, Dušan
Kozak, Primož
Šeligo, Rudi
Svetina, Ivo
Zajc, Dane

## SOUTH AFRICA
Akerman, Anthony
Aron, Geraldine (b. Ireland, divides time between South
        Africa and London)
Bailey, Brett
Bosman, Herman Charles
Buckland, Andrew
Cooke, Vanessa
De Wet, Reza
Dike, Fatima
Ellenbogen, Nicholas
Ferguson, Ian
Fourie, Charles J.
Fugard, Athol
Gray, Stephen
Haysom, Fink
Honeyman, Janice
Hope, Christopher
Hutchinson, Alfred (died in exile in Nigeria)
Junction Avenue Theatre Company
Kani, John
Kente, Gibson
Keogh, Danny (b. Uganda)
Kimmel, Harold (now resides in Great Britain)
Klotz, Phyllis
Leshoia, Benjamin Letholoa
Livingstone, Douglas James (b. Malaysia)
McCarthy, Neil

MacLennan, Don
Mahomed, Ismail
Manaka, Matsemela
Maponya, Maishe
Mda, Zakes
Mhlope, Gcina
Mofokeng, Zakes
Msomi, Welcome
Mtshali, Thulami S.
Mtwa, Percy
Mutwa, Credo
Naidoo, Muthal
Ndlovu, Duma
Ndlovu, Malika
Ngema, Mbongeni
Nkosi, Lewis
Ntshona, Winston
Pam-Grant, Susan
Roberts, Sheila
Shezi, Mthuli
Simon, Barney
Slabolepszy, Paul (b. Great Britain)
Uys, Pieter-Dirk
Whyle, James
Wilhelm, Peter
Williams, Magi Noninzi
Workshop '71 Theatre Movement

## SPAIN
*See also Catalan*
Alberti, Rafael
Alonso de Santos, José Luis
Álvarez Quintero, Joaquin
Álvarez Quintero, Serafin
Arrabal, Fernando (lives in France)
Azevedo, Angela de (b. Portugal)
Bellido, José-Maria
Benavente y Martinez, Jacinto
Bretón de los Herreros, Manuel
Buero Vallejo, Antonio
Calderón de la Barca, Pedro
Caro Mallén de Soto, Ana
Carvajal, Miguel de
Casona, Alejandro
Castro y Bellvis, Guillem
Cervantes Saavedra, Miguel de
Cruz Cano y Olmedilla, Ramon de la
Cueva y Silva, Leonor
Cunillé, Lluisa
Dicenta y Benedicto, Joaquin
Echegaray y Eizaguirre, José
Enríquez de Guzmán, Feliciana
Fernán Gómez, Fernando (b. Peru)
Gala, Antonio

Garcia Gutierrez, Antonio
Garcia Lorca, Federico
Gil y Zárate, Antonio
Hartzenbusch, Juan Eugenio
Jardiel Poncela, Enrique
Linares Rivas, Manuel
López de Ayala, Adelardo
López Mozo, Jerónimo
López Rubio, José
Martin Recuerda, José
Martinez Ballesteros, Antonio
Martinez Mediero, Manuel
Martinez Sierra, Gregorio
Martinez Sierra, Maria
Matilla, Luis
Mayorga, Juan
Mihura Santos, Miguel
Mira de Amescua, Antonio
Molina, Tirso de
Montero, Gloria (b. Australia, began writing career in
    Canada before moving to Spain)
Moratín, Leandro Fernández de
Moreta y Cavana, Agustin
Muniz, Carlos
Nieva, Francisco
Núñez de Arce, Gaspar
Olmo, Lauro
Onetti, Antonio
Ors, Francisco
Paso, Alfonso
Pedrero, Paloma
Pérez Galdós, Benito (b. Canary Islands)
Picasso, Pablo (lived in exile in France)
Planell, David
Quiles, Eduardo
Quiñones de Benavente, Luis
Rellan, Miguel Angel
Rivas, Angel Perez de Saavedra
Rojas, Fernando de
Rojas Zorilla, Francisco de
Rueda, Lope de
Ruibal, Jose
Ruiz, Juan (Arcipreste de Hita)
Ruiz de Alarcón y Mendoza, Juan
Salom, Jaime
Sastre, Alfonso
Tamayo y Baus, Manuel
Tellez, Gabriel
Torrcs Naharro, Bartolome de
Unamuno, Miguel de
Valle-Inclan, Ramon Maria del
Vcga, Ricardo de la
Vega, Ventura de la (b. Argentina)
Vega Carpio, Lope Felix de

Vélez de Guevara, Luis
Zamacois, Eduardo (b. Cuba, d. in exile in Argentina)
Zayas y Sotomayor, María
Zorrilla y Moral, José

## SRI LANKA
Abeysinghe, Rasika
De Lanerolle, H.C.N
De Zoysa, Lucien
Gunawardena, Gamini
Jayawardhana, Bandula
Joseph, E.M.W.
MacIntyre, Ernest Thalayasingham
Sarachchandra, Ediriwira
Siriwardena, Reggie
Vittachchi, Nedra

## SWEDEN
Asperström, Werner
Bergman, Hjalmar
Bergman, Ingmar
Dagerman, Stig
Forssell, Lars
Fridell, Folke
Garpe, Margareta
Gorling, Lars
Hoijer, Bjorn-Erik
Josephson, Ragnar
Lagerkvist, Par
Larsson, Stig
Leffler, Anne Charlotte, duchess of Cajanello
Norén, Lars
Pleijel, Agneta
Rådström, Niklas
Strindberg, August
Weiss, Peter (b. Germany)

## SWITZERLAND
Bille, S. Corinna
Bread and Puppet Theatre, Ecole d'Humanité
Class 5 (1990), Ecole Internationale de Genève
Duerrenmatt, Friedrich
Frisch, Max
Lazlo, Carl (b. Hungary)
Visdei, Anca (b. Romania)

## SYRIA
Ikhlassi, Walid
'Udwan, Mamduh
Wannus, Sa'Dallah

## TAIWAN
Hwang, Mei-shu
Lai, Stanley Sheng-ch'uan

Ball, David
Bangs, John Kendrick
Barba, Preston Albert
Barber, Philip W.
Barkentin, Marjorie
Barker, James Nelson
Barksdale, William (Bill)
Barlow, Anna Marie
Barnard, Charles
Barnes, Charlotte Mary Sanford
Barnes, Djuna
Baron, Courtney
Barras, Charles M.
Barry, Philip
Barta, Berry L.
Barthol, Bruce
Basshe, Emanuel Jo
Bateman, Mrs. Sidney Frances Cowell
Bates, Esther Willard
Baum, Terry
Baum, Vicki (b. Austria)
Beach, Emmett Lewis
Beard, Jocelyn
Beber, Neena
Behrman, Samuel Nathaniel
Belasco, David
Belber, Stephen
Bell, Neal
Bellow, Saul (b. Canada)
Belmont, Mrs. O.H.P. (Alva)
Benet, Stephen Vincent
Bengal, Ben
Bennett, Clarence
Benrimo, Joseph Henry
Bentley, Eric Russell (b. Great Britain)
Benton, Robert
Berc, Shelley
Bercovici, Eric
Berg, Gertrude
Berger, Adam L.
Berkey, Ralph
Berkow, Jay
Berman, Brooke
Bernard, Kenneth
Bernard, Lawrence J.
Berney, William
Bernstein, Leonard
Berrigan, Daniel J., S.J.
Berry, Wendell
Bierce, Ambrose
Bingham, Sallie
Bird, Robert Montgomery
Birimisa, George
Birmelin, John
Bishop, Conrad

Bishop, John
Bissell, Richard Pike
Bitterman, Shem
Blahnik, Jeremy
Blecher, Hilary (b. South Africa)
Bleiman, Rita McDonald
Blessing, Lee
Blinn, William
Blount, Roy, Jr.
Bobrick, Sam
Boesing, Martha
Bogart, Anne
Bogosian, Eric
Boker, George Henry
Bolton, Guy Reginald (b. Great Britain of American parents)
Boretz, Nick
Bornstein, Kate
Bosakowski, Philip A.
Boucicault, Dion (b. Ireland)
Bovasso, Julie
Bowen, Margaret Elizabeth
Bowles, Jane
Boyd, Susan
Brackenridge, Hugh Henry
Bradbeer, Suzanne
Bramble, Mark
Brandon, James R.
Braverman, Carole
Breen, Richard L.
Breit, Harvey
Brendle, Thomas Royce
Brenner, Alfred
Breslin, Jimmy
Breuer, Lee
Brewster, Emma E.
Bridgers, Ann Preston
Britton, Kenneth Phillips
Brock, Brock Norman
Bromley, Kirk Wood
Brooks, Hindi
Brooks, Mel
Brougham, John (b. Ireland)
Brower, Brock
Brown, Al
Brown, Daniel Gregory
Brown, David Paul
Brown, Jean H.
Brown, Karl
Brown, William F.
Browne, Maurice (b. Great Britain)
Browne, Porter Emerson
Brunson, Beverly
Brustein, Robert
Buck, Pearl S.

Budbill, David
Bumbalo, Victor
Bunce, Oliver Bell
Bunch, Jim
Burk, John Daly (b. Ireland)
Burke, Charles Saint Thomas
Burrows, Abram S. (Abe)
Bush, Josef
Bush, Max
Butler, Rachel Barton
Butterfield, Catherine
Byrd Hoffman School of Byrds (now Byrd Hoffman
        Watermill Foundation)
Byrnes, Burke
Cady, Pam
Cain, Caitlin C.
Caldor, M.T.
Caldwell, Erskine
Caldwell, Evelyn Keller
Caliban, Richard
Cameron, Kenneth
Campbell, Bartley
Campbell, Marion Gurney
Capote, Truman
Carlin, Aviva Jane (b. South Africa)
Carpenter, Bridget
Carroll, Robert F.
Carson, Jo
Carus, Paul (b. Germany)
Casale, Michael
Casey, Warren
Chafee, Claire
Chais, Pamela
Chambers, Jane
Champagne, Lenora
Champagne, Susan
Chapman, Robert Harris
Chase, Mary Coyle
Chayefsky, Paddy
Chesley, Robert
Chodorov, Edward
Chodorov, Jerome
Church, Virginia Woodson (Frame)
Cinque, Chris
Cizmar, Paula
Clarke, Mary Carr
Clarke, William Kendall
Clarvoe, Anthony
Clemens, Samuel
Clements, Colin Campbell
Clifford, Margaret Ellen
Clinch, Charles Powell
Clontz, Dennis
Cloud, Darrah
Clum, John M.

Coburn, D.L.
Cocke, Dudley
Coffee, Lenore
Cohan, George M.
Cohen, Bennett
Cohen, David
Cohen, Joel
Cohen, Marvin
Cohen, Neil
Cohen, Sarah Blacher
Cole, Tom
Coleman, Wim
Collings, Pierre
Collins, Margaret
Colton, John
Comden, Betty
Commire, Anne
Condon, Frank (b. Great Britain)
Congdon, Constance
Conkle, Ellsworth Prouty
Connelly, Marcus Cook
Conway, Hiram J. (b. Great Britain)
Cook, George Cram
Cooper, Dona
Corday, Barbara
Cormack, Bartlett
Corneau, Perry B.
Cornish, Roger
Corwin, Norman Lewis
Cowen, Ron
Coxe, Louis O.
Coyle, McCarthy
Craven, Frank
Crawley, Brian
Crews, Harry
Cristofer, Michael
Crocker, Charles Templeton
Cromelin, Caroline
Cronyn, Hume (b. Canada)
Crothers, Rachel
Crouse, Russell
Crowley, Mart
Crutcher, Julie
Culbertson, Ernest Howard
Cummings, Bernard
cummings, e.e.
Cunningham, Alexandra
Cunningham, Laura
Cunningham, Tim
Curran, Keith
Currie, Carleton H.
Curtis, Ariana Randolph Wormeley
Curtis, Daniel Sargent
Curzon, Dan
Custis, George Washington Parke

Dacus, Katy
Dale, Bruce
Daly, Augustin
Damashek, Barbara
Dannenfelser, David
David, Larry
Davidson, Robert
Davies, Mary Carolyn
Davis, Bill C.
Davis, Donald
Davis, Ellen Brook
Davis, Luther
Davis, Owen
Davis, Skot
Dayton, Katharine
Dean, Alexander
Dean, Nancy
De Kruif, Paul Henry
Dell, Floyd
Dell'Arte Players, The
De Mille, Henry Churchill
De Mille, William C.
Denison, T.S.
Denker, Henry
Denney, Reuel
Dennis, Vita
Denu, Mark
De Santis, Edmund
Dewberry, Elizabeth
Dey, James Paul
Dieb, Ron
Dietz, Steven
DiFusco, John
Dillon, David
Dizenzo, Charles
Dockery, Martin
Dodd, Lee Wilson
Dodd, Terry
Donahue, John Clark
Dowling, Jennette
Dransfield, Jane
Dreher, Sarah
Dresser, Richard
Drexler, Rosalyn
Driver, Donald
Driver, John
Drummond, Alexander Magnus
Duberman, Martin B.
Duffield, Brainerd
Dunlap, William
Dunning, Philip Hart
Durang, Christopher
Durivage, Oliver E.
D'Usseau, Arnaud
Dymov, Osip (b. Russia)

Eberhart, Richard
Edson, Margaret
Ehn, Erik
Eichelberger, Ethyl
Eisele, Robert H.
Eisenstein, Linda
Eisenstein, Mark
Eliot, T.S. (lived in London most of his adult life)
Ellsbury, Chris
Elser, Frank Ball
Emery, Gilbert
Emidia, Lynn
Ensler, Eve
Epp, Steven
Epstein, Martin
Estabrook, Howard
Estrin, Marc
Ewing, Thomas
Eyen, Tom
Fannon, Cecilia
Farabough, Laura
Fargo, Kate Mills
Faulkner, William
Fechter, Charles Albert
Feiffer, Jules
Feld, Merle
Felde, Kitty
Felder, Louis
Feldshuh, David
Felthaus-Weber, Mary
Ferber, Edna
Fergusson, Francis
Ferlinghetti, Lawrence
Ferris, Walter
Field, Charles Kellogg
Field, Edward Salisbury
Field, Joseph M.
Field, Rachel
Fields, Joseph
Fields, W.C.
Fierstein, Harvey
Fink, Edith Romig
Finley, Karen
Finn, William
Finneran, Alan
Fitch, Clyde
Five Lesbian Brothers, The
Flanagan, Hallie
Flavin, Martin
Fletcher, Lucille
Foote, Horton
Forbes, James (b. Canada)
Ford, Frank B.
Ford, Harriet
Ford, Ruth

Foreman, Richard
Fortune, Mrs. Jan Isabelle
Foster, Charles
Foster, Paul
Foster, Rick
Fowle, William Bentley
Frank, Florence Kiper
Frank, Waldo David
Franken, Rose
Fratti, Mario (b. Italy)
Fredericks, Claude
Freed, Amy
Freed, Donald
Freeman, Brian
Freeman, Eleanor
Friedman, Bruce Jay
Friedman, Eve
Frings, Ketti (Hartley)
Frolov, Diane
Frost, Robert
Fuller, Elizabeth
Fuller, Henry Blake
Funt, Julian
Furth, George
Fyles, Franklin
Gage, Carolyn
Gage, Nancy
Gagliano, Frank
Gaines, Frederick
Galati, Frank
Gale, Zona
Galjour, Anne
Gallagher, Mary
Gallico, Paul
Galloway, Terry
Gamel, Fred
Gardner, Herb
Garnett, Porter
Garson, Juliet
Garvey, Ellen Gruber
Gassner, John
Gazzo, Michael Vincent
Geddes, Virgil
Gelbart, Larry
Gelber, Jack
George, Madeleine
Gershe, Leonard
Gerstenberg, Alice
Gesner, Clark
Gibbs, Wolcott
Gibney, Sheridan
Gibson, Pauline
Gibson, William
Gilbert, Willie
Gilhooley, Jack

Gillette, William Hooker
Gillman, Jonathan
Gilman, Charlotte Perkins
Gilman, Rebecca
Gilroy, Frank D.
Gilsdorf, Frederich
Glaspell, Susan
Gleason, James
Glickfield, Carole
Głowacki, Janusz (b. Poland)
Godfrey, Thomas
Godwin, Parke
Goetz, Augustus
Goetz, Ruth Goodman
Gold, Michael
Goldberg, Dick
Goldberg, Jessica
Goldemberg, Rose Leiman
Goldman, James
Goldman, William
Goldsmith, Clifford
Gollobin, Laurie Brooks
Goodhart, William
Goodman, Kenneth Sawyer
Goodman, Paul
Goodrich, Frances
Goold, Marshall Newton
Gordin, Jacob (b. Ukraine)
Gordon, David
Gordon, Robert
Gordon, Ruth
Gow, James Ellis
Gower, Douglas
Graebner, Grubb
Graham, Barbara
Grant, David Marshall
Graves, Russell
Gray, Amlin
Graziano, David
Greanias, George
Grecco, Stephen
Green, Adolph
Green, Erma
Green, Julien (lived in France)
Green, Paul
Greenberg, Daniel
Greenberg, Richard
Greene, Patterson
Greenland, Seth
Greenspan, David
Greenspan, Hank
Gregg, Stephen
Grimm, Henry
Grimsley, Jim
Grove, M. Ellis

Grover, Leonard
Grumbine, Ezra Light
Guare, John
Guirgis, Stephen Adly
Gurney, A. R.
Gutwillig, Stephen
Guyer, Murphy
Hackett, Albert
Hackett, Walter
Haddow, Jeffrey
Hadler, William
Hagan, James
Hailey, Arthur
Hailey, Oliver
Haines, William Wister
Hall, Bob
Hall, Carol
Hall, Holworthy (pseud. of Harold Everett Porter)
Halper, Leivick (b. Russia)
Hamblin, Louisa Medina
Hamlin, Mary P.
Hammerstein, Oscar, II
Hammond, Wendy
Hanan, Stephen Mo
Hanley, William
Hanshew, Thomas W.
Harburg, Edgar Y.
Hardman, Chris
Harelik, Mark
Hargrave, Roy
Harling, Robert
Harmon, Peggy
Harnick, Sheldon
Harnwell, Anna Jane Wilcox
Harrigan, Edward
Harris, Anne M.
Harris, Aurand
Hart, Moss
Harte, Bret
Hartog, Jan de (b. Netherlands)
Hatcher, Jeffrey
Haubold, Cleve
Hauptman, William
Havis, Allan
Hawkes, John
Hawthorne, Ruth Warren
Hayden, John
Hayes, Alfred
Hayes, Joseph
Hazelton, George Cochrane, Jr.
Healey, Frances
Hébert, Julie
Hecht, Ben
Heggen, Thomas
Heide, Robert

Heifner, Jack
Heller, Joseph
Hellman, Lillian
Henley, Beth
Hensel, Karen
Herbert, Frederick Hugh (b. Austria)
Herman, Jerry
Herndon, Venable
Herne, James A.
Hester, Hal
Heyward, Dorothy
Heyward, DuBose
Hickerson, Harold
Hierholzer, Alexander
Hill, Frederick Stanhope
Hill, Gary Leon
Hirschbein, Peretz (b. Russia)
Hirson, David
Hite, Barbara
Hivnor, Robert
Hobbes, John Oliver (pseud. of Pearl Craigie)
Hoffman, Aaron
Hoffman, William M.
Hofsiss, Jack
Hogan, Frank X.
Holden, Joan
Holland, Anthony
Hollinger, Michael
Holm, John Cecil
Holmes, Rupert (dual citizen of the United States and
    Great Britain)
Holsclaw, Doug
Holtzman, Willy
Hopkins, Arthur Melancthon
Hopkins, C.J.
Hopkins, Glenn
Hopkinson, Francis
Hopwood, Avery
Horowitz, Israel
Hovey, Richard
Howard, Bronson
Howard, Ed
Howard, Sidney
Howe, Julia Ward
Howe, Marie Jenney
Howe, Tina
Howells, William Dean
Hoyt, Charles H.
Hughes, Hatcher
Hughes, Holly
Hunt, Mame
Hunter, Robert (b. Scotland)
Huston, John
Hutchins, Maude Phelps McVeigh
Hutton, Arlene

Hutton, Joseph
Inge, William
Ingham, Robert E.
Innaurato, Albert
Iobst, Clarence F.
Irving, Washington
Irwin, William Henry
Isherwood, Christopher (b. Great Britain)
Ives, Alice E.
Ives, David
Jacker, Corinne L.
Jackson, Nagle
Jacobs, Jim
James, Dan
James, Henry
Jarrow, Joseph
Jasudowicz, Dennis
Jeffers, Robinson
Jefferson, Joseph
Jenkin, Len
Jennings, Talbot
Jensen, Julie
Jerome, V. J. (Victor J.)
Jessop, George Henry
Jesurun, John
Job, Thomas (b. Wales)
Johns, Patti
Johnson, Elizabeth
Johnson, Hester N.
Jones, Felicity
Jones, Jeffrey M.
Jones, Joseph Stevens
Jones, Ken
Jones, Preston
Jones, Tom
Jones, Wendell
Jordan, Julia
Joselovitz, Ernest A.
Joseph, Allen
Jucha, Brian
Kahn, Barbara
Kalcheim, Lee
Kalinoski, Richard
Kamarck, Edward
Kanin, Fay
Kanin, Garson
Kanin, Michael
Kaplan, Barry Jay
Kapp, Sharleen
Kaprow, Allen
Kardish, Laurence (b. Canada)
Kassin, Michael
Katz, Leon
Kaufman, George S.
Kaufman, Lynne

Kaye, Marvin
Kazan, Nicholas
Kearns, Michael
Keillor, Garrison
Kelley, Shannon Keith
Kelly, George Edward
Kelly, Tim
Kennedy, Mary
Kent, Alana
Kenyon, Charles
Kerr, Jean
Kesselman, Wendy
Kesselring, Joseph
Ketron, Larry
Kimball, Rosamond
Kimberlain, Sora
King, Larry L.
King, Stephen
Kingsley, Sidney
Kingsley-Smith, Terry
Kirby, Michael
Kirkland, Jack
Kirkwood, James
Kleb, William
Kleban, Edward
Klein, Jon
Klein, Maxine
Kliewer, Warren
Kling, Kevin
Knee, Allan
Knight, Eric Mowbray (b. Great Britain)
Knight, Vick
Knox, Florence Clay
Kober, Arthur
Kobrin, Leon (b. Russia, now Belarus)
Koch, Howard
Kock, Kenneth
Koebnick, Sarah Monson
Kondoleon, Harry
Kopit, Arthur
Korder, Howard
Kornbluth, Josh
Korr, David
Kossman, Nina (b. Russia)
Koutoukas, H.M.
Kozlenko, William
Kral, Brian
Kramer, Larry
Kramer, Sherry
Kramm, Joseph
Kranes, David
Krasna, Norman
Kraus, Joanna Halpert
Kreymborg, Alfred
Kummer, Clare

Kurnitz, Harry
Kurtti, Casey
Kushner, Tony
Kvares, Donald
La Farge, W.E.R.
Lamb, Myra
Landau, Tina
Landon, Joseph
Lane, Eric
Langley, Noel (b. South Africa)
Lapine, James
Lappin, Terrance J.
Lardner, Ring
Larson, Jonathan
Larson, Larry
Larson, Nancy
La Tempa, Susan
La Touche, John Treville
Laurents, Arthur
Lauro, Shirley
Lavery, Emmet
Law, Warner
Lawrence, Jerome
Lawson, John Howard
Leacock, John
Leamon, Dorothy
Lear, Norman
Leavitt, John McDowell
Lebow, Barbara
Lee James Henry
Lee, Jeannie
Lee, Lance
Lee, Levi
Lee, Robert E.
Leeds, Charlie
Leeson, Michael
Lefevre, Adam
Leichman, Seymour
Leivick, Halper (b. Russia)
Leland, Michael
Lenz, Rick
Leonard, Jim, Jr.
Lerner, Alan Jay
Leslie, F. Andrew
Lessing, Norman
Letton, Francis
Letts, Tracy
Levin, Elizabeth
Levin, Ira
Levine, Mark H.
Levine, Mark L.
Levinson, Alfred
Levitt, Saul
Levy, Jeff
Lewin, John

Lewis, Carter W.
Lewis, Emily Sargent
Lewis, Michael
Lewis, William H.
Lieberman, Edith
Lieberman, Harold
Lindberg, Wayne
Lindsay, Howard
Linfante, Michele
Link, Ann Seymour
Link, David
Linney, Romulus
Lipkin, Joan
Lipsky, Jon
Litt, Jennifer A.
Lloyd, David D.
Loesser, Frank
Logan, Joshua
Lonergan, Kenneth
Long, John Luther
Longfellow, Henry Wadsworth
Loos, Anita
Low, Samuel
Lowell, Robert
Lucas, Craig
Luce, Clare Boothe
Ludlum, Charles
Ludwig, Ken
Lunden, Jeffrey
Lynch, Hal
Lynch, Michael
McAnuff, Des (dual citizen of the United States and
     Canada)
MacArthur, Charles
McBride, Vaughn
McCabe, James D., Jr.
McClelland, CE
McCloskey, James J.
McClure, Michael
McCullers, Carson
McCulloch, Catharine Waugh
McCutcheon, George Barr
McDaniel, Charles A.
MacDonald, Bruce
McDonald, Catherine
McDonald, Heather
McEnroe, Robert E.
McGinn, Jim
McGuire, Judy
McGuire, William Anthony
McIntyre, Dennis
Mack, Carol K.
Mackay, Constance D'Arcy
MacKaye, Percy Wallace
MacKaye, Steele

McLaughlin, Rosemary
MacLeish, Archibald
McLellan, C.M.S.
MacLeod, Wendy
McLure, James
McMillan, Dougald, III
MacMillan, Mary Louise
McNally, Terence
McNamara, John
McNamee, George C.
McPherson, Scott
McQueen, Matthew
Macy, Lynn Marie
Magnuson, Jim
Malinowitz, Harriet
Maljean, Jean Raymond
Malpede, Karen
Maltby, Richard
Maltz, Albert
Mamet, David
Manhoff, Bill
Mankiewicz, Herman J.
Manley, Frank
Mann, Emily
Manning, Linda
Marans, Jon
Marasco, Robert
Marchand, Shoshana
Margolin, Deb
Margulies, Donald
Markoe, Merrill
Marowitz, Charles
Marquand, John P.
Marquis, Donald Robert Perry
Martell, Leon
Martens, Anne Coulter
Martin, Jane
Martula, Tanyss Rhea
Mason, Harry Silvernale
Mason, Timothy
Mason, Wilton
Massey, Edward
Masteroff, Joe
Mastrosimone, William
Matcha, Jack
Mathews, Cornelius
Maxwell, Elsa
May, Elaine
Mayer, Edwin Justus
Mayer, Jerry
Mayer, Timothy S.
Meaker, Isabelle Jackson
Meara, Anne
Mecchi, Irene
Medina, Louisa

Mednick, Murray
Medoff, Mark
Mee, Charles L.
Meehan, Thomas
Megrue, Roi Cooper
Melfi, Leonard
Mellon, Evelyn Emig
Mercier, Mary
Meredith, Sylvia
Merriam, Eve
Merrill, James
Metcalfe, Stephen
Meyer, Marlane
Meyers, Patrick
Michaels, Sidney
Michener, James A.
Mick, Hettie Louise
Middlemass, Robert
Middleton, George
Millay, Edna St. Vincent
Miller, Alice Duer
Miller, Allan
Miller, Arthur
Miller, Daniel
Miller, J. B.
Miller, J.P. (James Pinckney)
Miller, Jason
Miller, Joaquin
Miller, Sigmund Stephen
Miller, Susan
Miller, Tim
Milton, David Scott
Mitchell, Langdon Elwyn
Mitchell, Thomas
Moch, Cheryl
Moeller, Philip
Molinaro, Ursule (b. France)
Monroe, Michael
Monson, William N.
Montgomery, Robert
Montley, Patricia
Moody, William Vaughn
Moore, Edward J.
Moore, Honor
Mori, Brian
Moritz, Dennis
Morley, Christopher
Morley, Jill
Morris, Elizabeth Woodbridge
Morris, Lloyd R.
Morris, Markley
Moross, Jerome
Morse, Carl
Mortimer, Lillian
Mosakowski, Susan

Mosel, Tad
Moss, Alfred Charles
Moss, Howard
Moss, Leland
Mowatt, Anna Cora Ogden
Mueller, Lavonne
Muller, Romeo
Mulvey, Timothy J.
Munford, Robert
Munroe, Jan
Murdoch, Frank Hitchcock
Murphy, Dallas
Murphy, Grace
Murphy, Vincent
Murray, Judith Sargent
Murray, Robert Bruce
Murray, Steve
Myers, Carolyn
Mygatt, Tracy Dickinson
Myler, Randal
Myrtle, Frederick S. (b. Great Britain)
Nagle, Urban, Father, O.P.
Nash, N. Richard
Nash, Ogden
Neal, Jennifer
Neilson, Keith
Neipris, Janet
Nelson, Mariah Burton
Nelson, Richard J.
Nemerov, Howard
Nemeth, Sally
Newhard, Elwood L.
Newman, David
Newman, Molly
Nichols, Anne
Nightengale, Eric
Nigro, Don
Noah, Mordecai Manuel
Noble, Janet
Nolte, Charles M.
Norman, Marsha
Nugent, Elliott
Nyswaner, Ron
Oates, Joyce Carol
Obolensky, Kira
O'Brien, Liam
O'Connell, Louise
Odets, Clifford
O'Donnell, Mark
O'Hara, Frank
O'Keefe, John
Oklahoma, D.K.
Oldenburg, Claes (b. Sweden)
Oliansky, Joel
Olive, John

O'Morrison, Kevin
O'Neill, Eugene
Open Theater
Oppenheimer, Joel
Opper, Don Keith
Osborn, Paul
Osgood, Phillips Endecott
Overmyer, Eric
Owens, Rochelle
Page, Alex
Palmer, Tanya (dual citizen of the United States and
     Canada)
Parker, Dorothy
Parker, Louis
Parks, Stephen Davis
Parlato, Calvert
Parnell, Peter
Parone, Edward
Patrick, John
Patrick, Robert
Paulding, James Kirke
Payne, John Howard
Peabody, Josephine Preston
Pearson, Sybille
Pelfrey, Matt
Peluso, Emanuel
Pen, Polly
Perelman, S.J. (Sidney Joseph)
Perkins, Alan David
Perlman, Arthur
Perr, Harvey
Peters, Kier
Peters, Paul
Pezzulo, Ted
Phillips, David Graham
Phillips, Louis
Pickett, James Carroll
Pielmeier, John
Pifer, Drury (b. South Africa)
Pillot, Eugene
Pinski, David (b. Russia, now Belarus)
Pintauro, Joe
Pixley, Frank
Pollock, Channing
Pomerance, Bernard
Porter, Cole
Porter, J. Paul
Posener, Jill (b. Great Britain)
Post, Bruce B.
Potter, Paul M. (b. Great Britain)
Powers, Dennis
Powers, Frank
Prandini, Adele
Pratt, William W.
Preses, Peter (b. Austria)

Press-Coffman, Toni
Prince, Harold
Pritchard, Barry
Provisional Theater, The
Pruitt, Dan
Puccioni, Madeline
Pugh, Ann
Queer Street Youth
Rabe, David
Rado, James
Ragni, Gerome
Rambo, David
Randall, Bob
Randolph, Clemence
Ransom, Rebecca
Raphaelson, Samson
Ratcliffe, Helen
Rauch, Edward H.
Rayfiel, David
Raymond, Ann
Read, Monica
Real, Philip
Reardon, Dennis J.
Rebeck, Theresa
Reddin, Keith
Redding, Joseph Deign
Reed, Mark White
Reely, Mary Katherine
Regan, Sylvia
Reid, Ben
Reilly, Claudia
Reingold, Jacquelyn
Reiss, Kimberly
Rexroth, Kenneth
Reynolds, Jean
Reynolds, Rebecca
Ribman, Ronald
Rice, Elmer
Rice, George Edward
Richards, Gillian (b. Great Britain)
Richardson, Howard
Richardson, Jack Carter
Richman, Arthur
Richmond, David
Rickert, Van Dusen, Jr.
Rider, Jennifer
Rimmer, Christine
Rinehart, Mary Roberts
Ritz, Joseph P.
Rivers, Susan
Robertson, Louis Alexander
Robinson, Betsy Julia
Rodd, Marcia
Roemer, Michael (b. Germany)
Rogers, John William, Jr.

Rogers, Robert
Rohde, Mary
Roisman, Lois
Rose, Reginald
Rosenberg, James L.
Rosenfeld, Sydney
Rosenthal, Andrew
Rosenthal, Rachel (b. France)
Rosenzweig, Barney
Ross, Jerry
Rosten, Norman
Roszkowski, David
Roth, Beatrice
Rowson, Susanna
Royce, Cheryl
Royle, Edwin Milton
Rubenstein, Ken
Ruderman, Gary
Rudnick, Paul
Rugg, George
Runyon, Damon
Rush, David
Russ, Joanna
Rutherford, Stanley
Ryerson, Florence
Ryskind, Morrie
Sack, Leeny
Sackler, Howard
Safran, Steven A.
Saidy, Fred
Sainer, Arthur
St. Germain, Mark
St. Joseph, Ellis
San Francisco Mime Troupe
Sapinsley, Alvin
Sargent, Lydia
Saroyan, William
Saunders, Louise
Savin, Marcia
Scanlon, Patricia
Schary, Dore
Schauffler, Elsie T.
Scheffauer, Herman George (b. Germany)
Scheffer, Will
Schein, David
Schenkar, Joan
Schenkkan, Robert
Schevill, James Erwin
Schisgal, Murray
Schmidman, Jo Ann
Schneemann, Carolee
Schneider, Andrew
Schneider, David
Schneider, Pat
Schotter, Richard

Schrader, Leonard
Schrock, Gladden
Schulberg, Budd
Schwartz, Delmore
Schwartz, Joel
Scott, Virginia
Sears, Joe
Sebastian, Ellen V.
Seebring, William
Seiler, Conrad
Selig, Paul
Selwyn, Edgar
Sergel, Christopher
Serling, Rod
Serrano, Lynnette M.
Shaffer, Diane
Shank, Adele Edling
Shanley, John Patrick
Shapiro, Mel
Shaw, Irwin
Shaw, Marilyn
Shaw, Mary
Shaw, Peggy
Shawn, Wallace
Shay, Frank
Sheldon, Edward Brewster
Shelley, Elsa
Shengold, Nina
Shepard, Sam
Sherman, Martin
Sherwood, Robert E.
Shevelove, Burt
Shiels, John Wilson
Shipley, Lisa
Shue, Larry
Shulman, Max
Siefert, Lynn
Sifton, Claire
Sifton, Paul
Sills, Paul
Silver, Susan
Simon, Mayo
Simon, Neil
Simones, Pamela
Simonson, Robert
Singer, Isaac Bashevis (b. Poland)
Sjoerdsma, Al, Jr.
Skinner, Cornelia Otis
Smith, Betty
Smith, Evan
Smith, Harry James
Smith, Howard Forman
Smith, Jack
Smith, John
Smith, Lillian

Smith, Marian Spencer
Smith, Michael
Smith, Patrick
Smith, Richard Penn
Smith, Robert Paul
Smith, Ronn
Smith, Sarah Pogson
Smith, Val
Smith, William Henry (b. Wales)
Smith, Winchell
Snodgrass, Katherine
Sod, Ted
Solomon, Peter
Somsen, Pennell
Sondheim, Stephen
Sossi, Ron
Soule, Charles Carroll
Spence, Marjorie Ellen
Spencer, James
Spencer, Stuart S.
Spewack, Bella Cohen
Spewack, Samuel
Spiro, Peter
Staff of the Living Newspaper
Stallings, Lawrence
Stanley, David
Starkweather, David
Stayton, Richard
Steele, Rufus
Steele, Silas Sexton
Steele, Wilbur Daniel
Stein, Gertrude
Stein, Joseph
Steinbeck, John
Stephens, Henry Morse
Steppling, John
Sterling, George
Sterner, Jerry
Stevens, Wallace
Stewart, Donald Ogden
Stewart, Michael
Stewart-Brown, Christi
Stitt, Milan
Stone, Arnold M.
Stone, John Augustus
Stone, Peter H.
Stone, Robert J.
Strahs, James
Stranack, John
Strand, Richard
Stringer, Virginia Burton
Stroman, Susan
Strong, Austin
Stuart, Kelly
Sturges, Preston

Sullivan, L.M.
Summers, David
Sundgaard, Arnold
Sussman, Bruce
Swados, Elizabeth
Swados, Robin
Swayze, Mrs. J.C.
Sweet, Jeffrey
Swerling, Joseph (b. Russia)
Swortzell, Lowell
Taber, Troy W.
Tally, Ted
Talmadge, Victor
Tarkington, Booth
Tarlo, Luna (b. Canada)
Tavel, Ronald
Tayleure, Clifton W.
Taylor, Charles A.
Taylor, Samuel
Teichmann, Howard
Templeton, Fiona
Terkel, Louis "Studs"
Terry, Jennifer
Terry, Megan
Tesich, Steve (b. Yugoslavia)
Tharp, Newton J.
Thatcher, Kristine
Thayer, Ella Cheever
Therriault, Daniel
Thomas, Albert Ellsworth
Thomas, Augustus
Thompson, Alice Callender
Thompson, Beverly
Thompson, Denman
Thompson, Ernest
Thorne, Joan Vail
Thune, Leona
Thurber, James
Thurston, Ella L.
Toffenetti, Laura
Tolan, Kathleen
Tompkins, Frank Gerow
Topor, Tom
Torrence, Frederick Ridgely
Totheroe, Dan
Touloukian, Christopher
Towbin, (Marion) Fredi
Treadwell, Sophie
Troubetskoy, Amélie Rives Chanler
Trowbridge, J.T. (John Townsend)
Trumbo, Dalton
Turner, Dan
Turney, Catherine
Turney, Robert
Turque, Michael

Tyler, Royall
Udoff, Yale M.
Uhry, Alfred
Upson, William Hazlett
Valency, Maurice Jacques
Van Doren, Mark
Van Druten, John (b. Great Britain)
Van Itallie, Jean-Claude
Varesi, Gilda (b. Italy)
Varon, Charlie
Vawter, Ron
Veiller, Bayard
Vick, Susan
Vidal, Gore
Vincent, Allen
Vineberg, Doris
Vliet, R.G. (Russell Gordon)
Vogel, Paula
Vollmer, Lula
Volsky, Paula
Vonnegut, Kurt
Vulpius, Paul (b. Austria)
Wackler, Rebecca
Wagner, Jane
Wagner, Paula
Walker, Stuart
Wallace, Naomi
Wallack, Lester
Walsh, Paul
Walter, Eugene
Walter, Nancy
Ward, Donald
Warren, Mercy Otis
Washburn, Deric
Wasserman, Dale
Wasserstein, Wendy
Watkins, Maurine Dallas
Watson, Marjorie R.
Watters, George Manker
Weaver, Lois
Webber, James Plaisted
Weetman, Martin
Weidman, Jerome
Weidman, John
Weigand, Randy
Weill, Kurt (b. Germany)
Weiner, Wendy
Weinstein, Arnold
Weinstock, Jack
Weiser, Joshua
Weitzenkorn, Louis
Weller, Michael
Welles, Orson
Wellman, Mac
Wentworth, Marion Craig

Wexley, John
Wheeler, Andrew Carpenter
Wheeler, Hugh Callingham
Wherry, Toby
Whitehead, William
Whittington, Robert
Wieand, Paul R.
Wiese, Anne Pierson
Wilbur, Richard
Wilde, Percival
Wilder, Thornton
Wilkins, John H.
Willard, John
Willcox, Helen Lida
Williams, Arthur
Williams, Caroline
Williams, Jaston
Williams, Jesse Lynch
Williams, Lauren
Williams, Mary Ann
Williams, Tennessee
Williams, Tom
Williams, William Carlos
Williamson, Harold
Williamson, Laird
Willis, Julia
Willis, Nathaniel Parker (N.P.)
Wilner, Sheri
Wilson, Doric
Wilson, Erin Cressida
Wilson, Harry Leon
Wilson, Lanford
Wilson, Robert (1941- )
Wiltse, David
Wincelberg, Shimon (b. Germany)
Wingfield, Garth
Winsor, Mary
Wishengrad, Morton
Witherspoon, Kathleen
Witten, Matthew
Wolff, Ruth
Wolfson, Victor
Wolk, Michael
Wollenweber, Ludwig August (b. Germany)
Woods, Walter
Woodworth, Samuel
Woolf, Benjamin Edward
Wooster Group, The
Wooten, John J.
Wouk, Herman
Wray, Elizabeth
Wright, Doug
Wright, Frances (b. Scotland)
Wright, Glenn
Wright, Robert

Yafa, Stephen H.
Yaffe, James
Yankowitz, Susan
Yeaton, Dana
Yelvington, Ramsey
Yerby, Lorees
Yordan, Philip
Young, Robert
Young, Stanley
Young, William
Zahn, Curtis
Zindel, Bonnie
Zindel, Paul
Zell, Allison Eve (b. Canada, dual citizen of Canada and
    the United States)
Zinn, Howard
Zusy, Jeannie

## URUGUAY
Maggi, Carlos
Sanchez, Florencio

## VANUATU
Dorras, Jo (b. Great Britain)
Walker, Peter (b. Great Britain)

## VENEZUELA
Romero, Mariela
Santana, Rodolfo

## VIETNAM
Ngoc, Nguyen Thi Minh
Nhu, Ho Thi Ai

## WALES
Abse, Dannie
Arden, Jane
Dafydd, Gwenno
Davies, Lewis
Evans, Sîan
Gill, Peter
Gough, Lucy (b. Great Britain)
Hughes, Richard (b. Great Britain)
Jenkins, Mark
Job, Thomas
Jones, Jack
Lewis, Saunders
Malik, Afshan
Morgan, Chris
Morgan, Diana
Morgan, Sharon
Picardie, Michael (b. South Africa)
Ross, Lesley
Smith, Othniel
Spinetti, Victor

Thomas, Dylan
Thomas, Edward
Thomas, Gwyn
Watkins, Christine
Watts, Murray
Williams, Emlyn
Williams, Roger

## YUGOSLAVIA
*See also Croatia; Macedonia; Montenegro; Serbia;*
*Slovenia*
Čašule, Kole

Kozak, Primož
Lebovic, Djordje
Marinković, Ranko
Obrenović, Aleksandr

## ZAMBIA
Kasoma, Gregory Peter Kabwe
Mwansa, Dickson M.
Phiri, Masauto

## ZIMBABWE
Whaley, Andrew

# Appendix B

# Women Authors

Abbott, Jean
Acker, Kathy
Ackerman, Marianne
Ackermann, Joan
Adesina, Foluke
Adshead, Kay
Aguirre, Isabel
Ahmad, Rukhsana
Ahrens, Lynn
Aidoo, Ama Ata
Akalaitis, Joanne
Akimoto, Matsuyo
Akins, Zoe
Albanese, Eleanor
Allard, Janet
Allen, Jay Presson
Aloma, Rene R.
Alvarez, Lynne
Alworth, Rebecca
Amakali, Maria
Amano, Lynette
Anagnostaki, Loula
Anderson, Jane
Anderson, Laurie
Anderson, Regina M. Andrews
Anna Project, The
Anne, Catherine
Anthony, Trey
Aoki, Brenda Wong
Arbatova, Maria
Arce, Elia
Arden, Jane
Ariadne
Arizmendi, Yareli
Arkeketa, Annette
Aron, Geraldine
Assunção, Leilah
Astor del Valle, Janis
Athas, Daphne

Atlan, Liliane
Avedon, Barbara
Avraamidou, Maria
Aykroyd, Juliet
Ayvazian, Leslie
Azcárate, Leonor
Azevedo, Angela de

Bagnold, Enid
bailey, maxine
Baillie, Joanna
Baizley, Doris
Baker, E. Irene
Baker, Elizabeth
Baker, Susan
Baldridge, Mary Humphrey
Baptiste, Roselia
Baraitser, Marion
Barbier, Marie-Anne
Barfield, Tanya
Barkentin, Marjorie
Barnes, Charlotte Mary Sanford
Barnes, Djuna
Barlow, Anna Marie
Baron, Courtney
Barrie, Shirley
Barroga, Jeannie
Barry, Lynda
Barta, Berry L.
Bartève, Reine
Bateman, Mrs. Sidney Frances Cowell
Bates, Esther Willard
Baum, Terry
Baum, Vicki
Beard, Jocelyn
Beasley, Elois
Beauvoir, Simone de
Beber, Neena
Behn, Aphra

Bell, Florence
Bellon, Loleh
Belmont, Mrs. O.H.P. (Alva)
belvett, naila
Bemarro Theatre Group
Bensusan, Inez
Berc, Shelley
Berg, Gertrude
Berman, Brooke
Berman, Sabina
Bernard, Catherine
Bews, Samantha
Bille, S. Corinna
Bingham, Sallie
Binnie, Briony
Bishop, Stephanie
Blakeman, Helen
Blecher, Hilary
Bleiman, Rita McDonald
Block, Toni
Bodnárová, Jana
Boesing, Martha
Bogart, Anne
Boland, Bridget
Bolt, Carol
Bonal, Denise
Bond, Elisabeth
Bonet, Wilma
Bonner, Marita
Boothby, Frances
Bophavy, Khem
Bornstein, Kate
Boston, Michon
Boucher, Denise
Bourlet, Katherine
Bovasso, Julie
Bowen, Margaret Elizabeth
Bowles, Jane
Box, Muriel
Boyd, Pamela
Boyd, Pom
Boyd, Susan
Brackley, Elizabeth
Bradbeer, Suzanne
Bradley, Belinda
Bradley, Jyll
Brand, Mona
Brassard, Marie
Braverman, Carole
Brennan, Kit
Brewster, Emma E.
Bridgeman, Laura
Bridgers, Ann Preston
Brigadere, Anna
Brookman, Anne

Brooks, Hindi
Brown, Jean H.
Brown, Riwia
Brown-Guillory, Elizabeth
Browne, Felicity
Bruce, Lesley
Brunson, Beverly
Buck, Pearl S.
Bulkley, A.M. (Annette Mabel)
Burke, Inez M.
Burke, Kathy
Burke, Kelley Jo
Burney, Fanny
Burnham, Barbara
Burrill, Mary P.
Bustamante, Nao
Bustin, Pam
Butala, Sharon
Butler, Rachel Barton
Butterfield, Catherine
Byrne, Muriel St. Clare

Cadariu, Alina Nelega
Cady, Pam
Čahojová-Bernátová, Božena
Cain, Caitlin C.
Cajal, Oana-Maria
Caldor, M.T.
Caldwell, Evelyn Keller
Cameron, Anne
Campbell, Marion Gurney
Campbell, Paddy
Canetti, Veza
Canth, Minna
Cărbunariu, Geanina
Carlin, Aviva Jane
Carlos, Laurie
Caro Mallén de Soto, Ana
Carpenter, Bridget
Carr, Marina
Carson, Jo
Cary, Elizabeth
Casas, Myrna
Casdagli, Penny
Castro, Consuelo de
Caulfield, Anne
Cavan, Romilly
Cavendish, Jane
Centlivre, Susanna
Certezni, Monika
Césaire, Ina
Césaire, Michèle
Chafee, Claire
Chais, Pamela
Chambers, Jane

Dewberry, Elizabeth
De Wet, Reza
Dickerson, Glenda
Dike, Fatima
Dillon, Eileen
Di Mambro, Ann Marie
Ditton, Cordelia
Dizon, Louella
Dorras, Jo
Dowie, Claire
Dowling, Jennette
Drai, Martine
Dransfield, Jane
Dreher, Sarah
Drexler, Rosalyn
Dudoward, Valerie
Duffy, Ger
Dullemen, Inez van
Du Maurier, Daphne
Dunbar-Nelson, Alice
Duncan, Thelma M.
Duras, Marguerite

Earle, Lynda Chanwai
Eberhard, Josie Composto
Edmundson, Helen
Edson, Margaret
Eichelberger, Ethyl
Eisenstein, Linda
Elizabeth I
Emidia, Lynn
Enríquez de Guzmán, Feliciana
Ensler, Eve
Esparza, Laura
Evans, Lisa
Evans, Sîan

Fabien, Michèle
Fannin, Hilary
Fannon, Cecilia
Fantetti, Eufemia
Farabough, Laura
Fargo, Kate Mills
Farhoud, Abla
Farías, Joann
Farjeon, Eleanor
Farmiloe, Dorothy A.
Farrell, Geraldine
Feindel, Janet
Feinstein, Elaine
Feld, Merle
Felde, Kitty
Feliciano, Gloria
Felthaus-Weber, Mary
Ferber, Edna

Feriancova, Vanda
Fernández, Evelina
Fernandez-Ilagan, Marili
Field, Rachel
Filo, Vera
Fink, Edith Romig
Finlay, Suzanne
Finley, Karen
Fischer, Margaret
Fischerová, Daniela
Fitzgerald, Catherine
Flacks, Diane
Flanagan, Brenda A.
Flanagan, Hallie
Flather, Patti
Fleisser, Marieluise
Fleming, Jill W.
Fletcher, Lucille
Ford, Harriet
Ford, Maggie
Ford, Ruth
Fornes, Maria Irene
Fortune, Mrs. Jan Isabelle
Foucher, Michèle
Fox, Ellen
Francis, Ann
Frank, Florence Kiper
Franken, Rose
Franklin, J.e.
Franklin, Miles
Freed, Amy
Freeman, Carol
Freeman, Eleanor
Freeman, Sandra
Freistadt, Berta
Friedman, Eve
Frings, Ketti (Hartley)
Frumin, Sue
Fuerstenberg, Anna
Fuller, Elizabeth
Fusco, Coco
Fyffe, Laurie

Gage, Carolyn
Gale, Lorena
Gale, Zona
Galjour, Anne
Gallagher, Jodi
Gallagher, Kathleen
Gallagher, Mary
Galloway, Terry
Gambaro, Griselda
Garcia-Crow, Amparo
Garpe, Margareta
Garro, Elena

Garson, Juliet
Garvey, Ellen Gruber
Gasteazoro, Eva
Gault, Connie
Gems, Pam
George, Madeleine
Gerstenberg, Alice
Ghose, Nandita
Gibson, Florence
Gibson, P.J.
Gibson, Pauline
Gideon, Killian M.
Gilbert, Mercedes
Gilliat, Penelope
Gilman, Charlotte Perkins
Gilman, Rebecca
Gingold, Hermione
Ginzburg, Natalia
Gippius, Zinaida
Girardin, Delphine
Givner, Joan
Glancy, Diane
Glaspell, Susan
Glass, Joanna McClelland
Glickfield, Carole
Glover, Evelyn
Glover, Sue
Goldberg, Jessica
Goldberg, Leah
Goldemberg, Rose Leiman
Goldberg, Whoopi
Gollobin, Laurie Brooks
Gomez, Marga
Gomez, Terry
Gonzalez S., Silvia
Goodall, Julie
Goodrich, Frances
Gordan, Ruth
Gough, Lucy
Gowans, Elizabeth
Grace-Smith, Briar
Graffigny, Françoise de
Graham, Barbara
Graham, Nadine
Graham, Shirley
Grant, Diane
Gray, Oriel
Green, Erma
Green, Janet
Greer, Bonnie
Gregory, Lady Isabella Augusta
Gremina, Elena
Griffin, Caroline
Griffith, Elizabeth
Griffith, Lois

Griffiths, Linda
Grimké, Angelina
Guinn, Dorothy C.
Gunner, Frances

Haasse, Hella S.
Haber, Alexandria
Hagedorn, Jessica Tarahata
Hahn, Medina
Hall, Carol
Hamblin, Louisa Medina
Hamilton, Cicely
Hamlin, Mary P.
Hammond, Marie-Lynn
Hammond, Wendy
Hamson, Leslie
Hanger, Eunice
Hansberry, Lorraine
Hardie, Victoria
Harmon, Peggy
Harnwell, Anna Jane Wilcox
Harraden, Beatrice
Harris, Anne M.
Hasegawa, Shigure
Hastings, Charlotte
Haviara, Eleni
Hawkes, Jacquetta Hopkins
Hayes, Catherine
Hazzard, Alvira
He, Jiping
Healey, Frances
Hébert, Julie
Henley, Beth
Hellman, Lillian
Hensel, Karen
Hernández, Luisa Josefina
Herst, Beth
Herzberg, Judith
Hewett, Dorothy
Heyward, Dorothy
Hildegard, Saint (aka Hildegard of Bingen)
Hill, Amy
Hill, Kay
Hill, Olivia
Hines, Karen
Hite, Barbara
Hobbes, John Oliver (pseud. of Pearl Craigie)
Holden, Joan
Holland, Endesha Ida Mae
Holliday, Joyce
Hollingsworth, Margaret
Holme, Constance
Holmes, Shirlene
Honeyman, Janice
Hooke, Nina Warner

Hope, Karen
Hopkins, Pauline Elizabeth
Horsefield, Debbie
Houston, Dianne
Houston, Velina Hasu
Howe, Julia Ward
Howe, LeAnne
Howe, Marie Jenney
Howe, Tina
Howell, Corrie Crandall
Hrotsvit of Gandersheim
Hughes, Holly
Hunkins, Lee
Hunt, Mame
Hunter, Maureen
Hurley, Joan Mason
Hurston, Zora Neale
Hutchins, Maude Phelps McVeigh
Hutsell-Manning, Linda
Hutton, Arlene

Iijima, Sanae
Iizuka, Naomi
Iko, Momoko
Inchbald, Elizabeth
Inouye, Lisa Toishigawa
Ives, Alice E.

Jackson, Angela
Jackson, Cherry
Jackson, Elaine
Jackson, Judith Alexa
Jackson, Marsha A.
Jacob, Bianca
Jacob, Malou Leviste
Jacobs, Pauline
Jameson, (Margaret) Storm
Janaczewska, Noëlle
Jeffries, Ira L.
Jelinek, Elfriede
Jellicoe, Anne
Jennings, Gertrude E.
Jensen, Julie
Jensen, Lorre
Jerome, Helen (Burton)
Jintan, Soraya
Johns, Patti
Johnson, Catherine
Johnson, Elizabeth
Johnson, Eva
Johnson, Francine
Johnson, Georgia Douglas
Johnson, Hester N.
Johnson, Judith
Johnson, Niki

Johnson, Pamela Hansford
Jones, Felicity
Jones, Lisa
Jones, Marie
Jones, Rhodessa
Jones-Meadows, Karen
Jordan, Julia
Jotuni, Maria
Joudry, Patricia
Juana de la Cruz, Sor
Juráňová, Jana

Kahn, Barbara
Kai, Nubia
Kainy, Miriam
Kako, Chikajo (Chika)
Kane, Margo
Kane, Sarah
Kang, Myung Jin
Kanin, Fay
Kapp, Sharleen
Kaufman, Lynne
Kaundu, Ainna
Kay, Jackie
Kayla, Lisselle
Kemble, Fanny
Kemble, Marie-Thérèse DeCamp
Kemlo, Karen
Kemp, Jenny
Kennedy, Adrienne
Kennedy, Margaret
Kennedy, Mary
Kent, Alana
Kerr, Jean
Kerr, Lois Reynolds
Kesselman, Wendy
Kilcoyne, Catherine
Kilcoyne, Cathy
Kimball, Rosamond
Kimberlain, Sora
Kincaid, Jamaica
Kinross, Martha
Kisaragi, Koharu
Kishida, Rio
Kitas, Frida
Klein, Debby
Klein, Maxine
Klein, Sybil
Klotz, Phyllis
Kneubuhl, Victoria Nalani
Knox, Florence Clay
Koebnick, Sarah Monson
Kofta, Krystyna
Koller, Katherine
Kolpak, Diana

Kon, Stella
Kossman, Nina
Kovamees, Raissa
Kramer, Sherry
Kraus, Joanna Halpert
Kummer, Clare
Kurtti, Casey
Kudelka, Jan

Lalande, Françoise
Lam, Dana
Lamb, Myra
Lambert, Ann
Lambert, Betty
Landau, Tina
Langeberg, Sheela
Langhoff, Anna
Larman, Claire
Larson, Nancy
Lask, Berta
Lasker-Schuler, Else
La Tempa, Susan
Lauro, Shirley
Lavery, Byrony
Lawrence, Maureen
Laxdal, Vivienne
Lazarus, Joa
Leamon, Dorothy
Lebovic, Djordje
Lebow, Barbara
Lee, Cherylene
Lee, Jeannie
Lee, Sophia
Leeds Bengali Women's Drama Group
Leffler, Anne Charlotte, duchess of Cajanello
Lenéru, Marie
Leow, Puay Tin
Lessing, Doris
Lethbridge, Nemone
Leversha, Pam
Levin, Elizabeth
Levy, Deborah
Lewin, Eva
Lewis, Emily Sargent
Lewis, Erica
Lewis, Eve
lewis, sharon mareeka
Lieberman, Edith
Liking, Werewere
Lill, Wendy
Lim, Genny
Linden, Sonja
Linfante, Michele
Link, Ann Seymour
Lionheart, Eustace

Lipkin, Joan
Lison-Leroy, Françoise
Litt, Jennifer A.
Littlewood, Joan
Liu, Ching-min
Livingston, Myrtle Smith
Lochhead, Liz
Loher, Dea
Lohuizen, Suzanne van
Longford, Christine, Countess of
Loomer, Lisa
Loos, Anita
López, Eva
Lopez, Josefina
Løveid, Cecile
Luce, Clare Boothe
Luckham, Claire
Lumley, Jane, Baroness Lumley
Lyssa, Alison
Lyssiotis, Tes

Macauley, Pauline
McCauley, Clarice Valette
McCauley, Robbie
McCracken, Esther (Armstrong)
McCullers, Carson
McCulloch, Catharine Waugh
MacDonald, Ann-Marie
McDonald, Catherine
Macdonald, Gabrielle
McDonald, Heather
MacEwen, Gwendolyn
McGuigan, Carol
McGuire, Judy
McIlwraith, Jean Newton
McIntyre, Clare
Mack, Carol K.
Mackay, Constance D'Arcy
Mackay, Isabel Ecclestone Macpherson
McKay, Tamara
McKinnon, Cath
McLaughlin, Rosemary
McLean, Linda
MacLeod, Joan
McLeod, Jenny
MacLeod, Wendy
McMaster, Beth
MacMillan, Mary Louise
McNeil, Marguerite
Macy, Lynn Marie
Magtoto, Liza
Mahjoeddin, Indija N.
Maillet, Antonine
Major, Alice
Malik, Afshan

Malinowitz, Harriet
Maliti-Fraňová, Eva
Maljean, Jean Raymond
Malpede, Karen
mandiela, ahdri zhina
Manley, Delarivier
Mann, Emily
Manner, Eeva-Liisa
Manning, Linda
Manning, Mary
Manuel, Vera
Maponya, Maishe
Maraini, Dacia
Marchand, Shoshana
Margolin, Deb
Marichal Lugo, Teresa
Markoe, Merrill
Marni, Jeanne
Martens, Anne Coulter
Martin, Jane
Martin, Meah
Martin, Sharon Stockard
Martinez Sierra, Maria
Martula, Tanyss Rhea
Mason, Judi Ann
Mason, Libby
Mastrantone, Lucia
Maurette, Marcelle
Maxwell, Elsa
May, Elaine
Mayor, Beatrice
Meaker, Isabelle Jackson
Meara, Anne
Mecchi, Irene
Medina, Louisa
Medley, Cassandra
Meehan, Paula
Mehta, Dina
Mellon, Evelyn Emig
Mena, Alicia
Mercier, Mary
Meredith, Sylvia
Merriam, Eve
Merritt, Catharine Nina
Meyer, Annie Nathan
Meyer, Marlane
Mhapsekar, Jyoti
Mick, Hettie Louise
Mikhailova, Olga
Milan, Angie
Miles, Cressida
Miles, Kate
Millan, Lorri
Millay, Edna St. Vincent
Miller, Alice Duer

Miller, May
Miller, Susan
Mirčevska, Žanina
Mitchell, Yvonne
Mhlope, Gcina
Mnouchkine, Ariane
Moch, Cheryl
Mojica, Monique
Molette, Barbara
Molinaro, Ursule
Montero, Gloria
Montley, Patricia
Moore, Elise
Moore, Elvie A.
Moore, Honor
Moraga, Cherríe
More, Hannah
Morgan, Diana
Morgan, Sharon
Morgillo, Antonietta
Morley, Jill
Morris, Elizabeth Woodbridge
Morrissey, Kim
Mortimer, Lillian
Mosakowski, Susan
Mowatt, Anna Cora Ogden
Moxley, Gina
Moyes, Patricia
Mtshali, Thulami S.
Mueller, Lavonne
Mungiu-Pippidi, Alina
Munro, Rona
Murdoch, Iris
Murphy, Grace
Murray, Judith Sargent
Myers, Carolyn
Mygatt, Tracy Dickinson

Nagai, Ai
Nagy, Phyllis
Naidoo, Muthal
Ndlovu, Malika
Neal, Jennifer
Neipris, Janet
Nelson, Mariah Burton
Nemeth, Sally
Newman, Molly
Ngoc, Nguyen Thi Minh
Nhu, Ho Thi Ai
Nicholas, Denise
Nichols, Anne
Niggli, Josefina
Noble, Janet
Nolan, Yvette
Norman, Marsha

Nottage, Lynn
N'tumb, Diur
Nys-Mazure, Colette

Oakes, Meredith
Oates, Joyce Carol
Obolensky, Kira
O'Brien, Edna
O'Connell, Louise
Oglesby, Tamsin
Ogunrinde, Folasayo
Oklahoma, D.K.
Olivier-Sampson, Laurinda
O'Malley, Mary
O'Neil, Deborah
Onwueme, Osonye Tess Akaeke
Osborne, Marian
Oshodi, Maria
Ouless, E.U.
Owen, Rena
Owens, Rochelle

Padmanabhan, Manjula
Page, Louise
Pakington, Mary Augusta, Hon.
Palacios, Monica
Palarca, Julia
Palmer, Tanya
Pam-Grant, Susan
Parameswaran, Uma
Parker, Dorothy
Parks, Suzan-Lori
Parris-Bailey, Linda
Pascal, Françoise
Pascal, Julia
Paul, Mrs. Clifford
Payne, Alicia
Payne, Rhonda
Peabody, Josephine Preston
Pearson, Sybille
Pedrero, Paloma
Pembroke, Mary Sidney Herbert, Countess of
Pen, Polly
Pérez, Judith
Perry, Shauneille
Petrushevskaya, Ludmila
Philip, M. Nourbese
Pickard, Liz
Ping, Chin Woo
Pinnock, Winsome
Pitiki, Roma
Piussi, Lucia
Pix, Mary Griffith
Pleijel, Agneta
Plowman, Gillian

Poirier, Leonie
Pollock, Sharon
Pontcharra, Natacha de
Popova, Elena
Popplewell, Olive
Porter, Deborah
Porter, Regina M.
Portillo-Trambley, Estela
Posener, Jill
Potiki, Roma
Prandini, Adele
Preissová, Gabriela
Press-Coffman, Toni
Prichard, Katharine Susannah
Prichard, Rebecca
Prida, Dolores
Puccioni, Madeline
Pugh, Ann
Purscell, Phyllis

Quan, Betty

Rafenomanjato, Charlotte-Arrisoa
Rahman, Aishah
Raif, Ayshe
Rame, Franca
Ramírez, Ivette M.
Randolph, Clemence
Ransom, Rebecca
Rapi, Nina
Ratcliffe, Helen
Ravel, Aviva
Raymond, Ann
Raznovich, Diana
Read, Monica
Rebar, Kelly-Jean
Rebeck, Theresa
Reely, Mary Katharine
Reeves, Melissa
Regan, Sylvia
Reid, Christina
Reingold, Jacquelyn
Reilly, Claudia
Reinshagen, Gerlin
Reiss, Kimberly
Renaude, Noëlle
Renders, Kim
Renee
Reynolds, Jean
Reynolds, Rebecca
Reza, Yasmina
Rhodes, Crystal
Richards, Beah
Richards, Gillian
Rider, Jennifer

Riml, Michelle
Rimmer, Christine
Ringwood, Gwen Pharis
Rippingale, Gen
Ritter, Erika
Rivera, Carmen
Rivers, Susan
Roberts, Dmae
Roberts, Sheila
Robins, Elizabeth
Robinson, Betsy Julia
Robson, Cheryl
Roche-Guilhen, Anne de la
Rodd, Marcia
Rodin, Toby
Rodríguez, Yolanda
Rohde, Mary
Roisman, Lois
Romero, Elaine
Romero, Mariela
Rosselli, Amelia
Rosenthal, Rachel
Roth, Beatrice
Roth, Friederike
Rowe, Rosemary
Rowson, Susanna
Royce, Cheryl
Rubess, Banuta
Rugyendo, Mukotani
Ruppe, Jan
Russ, Joanna
Rye, Elizabeth
Ryerson, Florence
Rylski, Nika
Ryum, Ulla

Saadawi, Nawal El
Saalbach, Astrid
Sachs, Nelly
Sack, Leeny
Sackville West, Victoria Mary (Vita)
Sáenz, Diana
Sam, Canyon
Samuels, Diane
Sanchez, Sonia
Sanchez-Scott, Milcha
Sapergia, Barbara
Sargent, Lydia
Sarraute, Nathalie
Sarumpaet, Ratna
Savin, Marcia
Sayers, Dorothy L.
Scanlon, Patricia
Schauffler, Elsie T.
Schenkar, Joan

Schmidman, Jo Ann
Schneemann, Carolee
Schneider, Simone
Schrader, Clare
Schwaiger, Brigitte
Schwarz-Bart, Simone
Scott, Virginia
Sears, Djanet
Seaton, Sandra
Sebastian, Ellen V.
Sebbar, Leïla
Seibel, Beatriz
Sengupta, Poile (Ambika)
Serrano, Lynnette M.
Serreau, Coline
Shaffer, Diane
Shange, Ntozake
Shank, Adele Edling
Sharif, Bina
Shaw, Marilyn
Shaw, Mary
Shaw, Peggy
Shelley, Elsa
Shengold, Nina
Shephard-Massat, S. M. (Sherry)
Shepherd, Catherine
Shipley, Lisa
Shorty, Sharon
Shotlander, Sandra
Siefert, Lynn
Sifton, Claire
Sigley, Marjorie
Silas, Shelley
Silver, Susan
Simones, Pamela
Sisson, Rosemary Anne
Skinner, Cornelia Otis
Skrywer-Afrikaner, Martha Laurencia
Slovo, Robyn
Smartt, Dorothea
Smee, Amanda
Smee, Lilian
Smith, Ali
Smith, Anna Deavere
Smith, Betty
Smith, Beverly A.
Smith, Charlotte Turner
Smith, Dodie
Smith, Lillian
Smith, Sarah Pogson
Smith, Val
Sneal, Patricia
Snodgrass, Katherine
Snow, Andrea
Somsen, Pennell

Son, Diana
Sowerby, Githa
Spark, Muriel Sarah
Specht, Kerstin
Spence, Eulalie
Spence, Janis
Spence, Marjorie Ellen
Spewack, Bella Cohen
Spiderwoman Theater
Spunner, Suzanne
Srbljanović, Biljana
Stănescu, Saviana
Stapleton, Berni
Stearns, Sharon
Stein, Gertrude
Steinwachs, Ginka
Stewart, Ena Lamont
Stewart-Brown, Christi
Storm, Lesley
Storni, Alfonsina
Stringer, Virginia Burton
Stroman, Susan
Stuart, Aimee McHardy
Stuart, Kelly
Suki, Yumi
Sullivan, L.M.
Susie
Sutherland, Efua Theodora
Suzuki Yumi
Svich, Caridad
Swados, Elizabeth
Swain, Elizabeth
Swayze, Mrs. J.C.
Syal, Meer

Tan, Mei Ching
Tan, Theresa
Tântar, Nina
Tarlo, Luna
Taylor, Regina
Temple, Joan
Templeton, Fiona
Terblanché, Tanya
Terry, Jennifer
Terry, Megan
Thatcher, Kristine
Thayer, Ella Cheever
Thomas, Gwyn
Thompson, Alice Callender
Thompson, Beverly
Thompson, Judith
Thorne, Joan Vail
Thurston, Ella L.
Tillman, Katherine D. Chapman
Tison, Pascale

Tolan, Kathleen
Towbin, (Marion) Fredi
Thune, Leona
Treadwell, Sophie
Tropicana, Carmelita
Trotter, Catherine
Turney, Catherine

Uličianska, Zuzana
Uyehara, Denise

Vălean, Andreea
Vance, Danitra
Veldhuisen, Matin van
Venables, Clare
Verbitskaya, Anastasiya
Vick, Susan
Vilalta, Maruxa
Villa, Lilia A.
Villarreal, Edit
Vineberg, Doris
Vingoe, Mary
Visawanathan, Padma
Visdei, Anca
Vittachchi, Nedra
Vlachos, Helen
Vogel, Paula
Vollmer, Lula
Volsky, Paula
Vujovic, Sladjana

Wackler, Rebecca
Wagner, Colleen
Wagner, Jane
Wakefield, Lou
Waldron, Sharon
Wallace, Naomi
Walter, Nancy
Wandor, Micheline
Wang, Lucy
Warkentin, Veralyn
Warren, Mercy Otis
Wasserstein, Wendy
Watanabe, Eriko
Watkins, Christine
Watkins, Maurine Dallas
Watkins, Nayo Barbara
Watson, Marjorie R.
Weaver, Lois
Weiner, Wendy
Welch, Leona Nicholas
Wentworth, Marion Craig
Wertenbaker, Timberlake
West, Cheryl L.
Whaler, Imogene

White, Lucy
Wideman, Angela
Wiese, Anne Pierson
Wilkinson, Julie
Willcox, Helen Lida
Williams, Anita Jane
Williams, Caroline
Williams, Karin D.
Williams, Lauren
Williams, Magi Noninzi
Williams, Margaret Vyner
Williams, Mary Ann
Williamson, Gayle Weaver
Willis, Julia
Wilner, Sheri
Wilson, Erin Cressida
Wilson, Theodora Wilson
Win, Tin Tin
Windsor, Valerie
Wing, Paula
Winsloe, Christa
Winsor, Mary
Winstanley, Kate
Wiseman, Jane
Witherspoon, Kathleen
Wolff, Ruth
Wolton, Joan
Women's Theatre Group, The
Wong, Eleanor
Wong, Elizabeth

Wood, Mrs. Henry
Wood, Silviana
Worsley, Victoria
Wouters, Liliane
Wray, Elizabeth
Wuolijoki, Hella
Wyatt, Rachel
Wymark, Olwen

Xu, Pinli

Yamauchi, Wakako
Yang, Jiang
Yankowitz, Susan
Yeger, Sheila
Yen, Anna
Yerby, Lorees
Yhap, Beverley
Yoon, Jean
young, debbie
Youngblood, Shay
Yu, Miri
Yu, Ovidia

Zayas y Sotomayor, María
Zell, Allison Eve
Zindel, Bonnie
Zindinka
Zusy, Jeannie

# Appendix C

# Authors by Sexual Orientation

**BISEXUAL**

Aragon, Louis
Colette, Sidonie-Gabrielle
Du Maurier, Daphne
Millay, Edna St. Vincent
Piñero, Miguel
Rado, James
Ragni, Gerome
Sackville West, Victoria Mary (Vita) Lady Nicolson
Winsloe, Christa

**GAY**

*See Homosexual*

**HOMOSEXUAL**

*See also Bisexual; Lesbian; Transgendered*

Abdoh, Reza
Ackerley, J.R.
Adamson, Samuel
Albee, Edward
Alfaro, Luis
Arenas, Reinaldo
Barksdale, William (Bill)
Bartlett, Neil
Bell, Neal
Bennett, Alan
Bentley, Eric Russell
Birimisa, George
Bouchard, Michel Marc
Bourne, Bette
Brown, Karl
Bumbalo, Victor
Casey, Warren
Chesley, Robert
Clum, John M.
Copi
Corbitt, Wayne
Corlett, William

Coward, Sir Noël
Crowley, Mart
Curzon, Dan
Dante, Nicholas
Decent, Campion
Demchuk, David
Dillon, David
Dodd, Terry
Dodson, Owen Vincent
Duberman, Martin B.
Durang, Christopher
Fassbinder, Rainer Werner
Fierstein, Harvey
Finn, William
Garnhum, Ken
Gellert, Roger
Genet, Jean
Gilbert, Sky
Gill, Peter
Green, Julien
Greenspan, David
Greig, Noël
Grimsley, Jim
Hamilton, Godfrey
Harding, Alex
Harvey, Jonathan
Heide, Robert
Herman, Jerry
Hester, Hal
Hickman, Craig
Hoffman, William M.
Holsclaw, Doug
Hopwood, Avery
Hughes, Langston
Inge, William
Irizarry, Richard V.
Isherwood, Christopher
Jones, Wendell
Kaufman, Moisés

Kearns, Michael
Kelly, George
Kirkup, James
Kondoleon, Harry
Kramer, Larry
Kushner, Tony
Kuzmin, Mikhail
Laurents, Arthur
Lucas, Craig
Ludlum, Charles
McNally, Terence
McQueen, Matthew
Mann, Klaus
Mapa, Alec
Matthews, Tede
Maugham, Robin, 2nd Vicount Maugham of Hartfield
Maugham, W. Somerset
Mayer, Oliver
Menotti, Gian-Carlo
Merrill, James
Miller, Tim
Moss, Leland
Murray, Steve
Neale-Kennerley, James
Nyswaner, Ron
O'Hara, Frank
Okita, Dwight
Orton, Joe
Patrick, Robert
Pickett, James Carroll
Pomo Afro Homos
Porter, Cole
Pruitt, Dan
Puig, Manuel
Queer Street Youth
Raffalovich, Marc-André
Rambo, David
Rattigan, Terence
Reyes, Guillermo
Sanchez, Edwin
Scheffer, Will
Schwartz, Joel
Shaw, Paul
Sherman, Martin
Smith, Evan
Sod, Ted
Solly, Bill
Sondheim, Stephen
Stanley, David
Tremblay, Michel
Turner, Dan
Vawter, Ron
Vidal, Gore
Villaurutia, Xavier
Ward, Frederick

White, Patrick
Wilcox, Michael
Wilde, Oscar
Wilde, Patrick
Williams, Tennessee
Wilson, Sir Angus Frank Johnstone
Wilson, Doric
Wilson, Lanford
Winter, John Keith
Wright, Doug
Yew, Chay

## LESBIAN

*See also Bisexual*
Anderson, Jane
Anthony, Trey
Astor del Valle, Janis
Barfield, Tanya
Barnes, Djuna
Baum, Terry
Bent, Roxxy
Berman, Sabina
Bowles, Jane
Cady, Pam
Cain, Caitlin C.
Cameron, Anne
Casdagli, Penny
Chambers, Jane
Chowdhry, Maya
Cinque, Chris
Daniels, Sarah
Dean, Nancy
Dempsey, Shawna
Dreher, Sarah
Duffy, Maureen
Emidia, Lynn
Fischer, Margaret
Five Lesbian Brothers, The
Flacks, Diane
Fleming, Jill W.
Freeman, Sandra
Freistadt, Berta
Frumin, Sue
Gage, Carolyn
Galloway, Terry
Garvey, Ellen Gruber
Gomez, Marga
Griffin, Caroline
Grimké, Angelina
Harris, Anne M.
Howe, Marie Jenney
Hughes, Holly
Jeffries, Ira L.
Johnson, Eva
Kahn, Barbara

Kay, Jackie
Landau, Tina
Margolin, Deb
Marshall, Christabel
Millan, Lorri
Miller, Susan
Moraga, Cherríe
Myers, Carolyn
Nelson, Mariah Burton
Page, Louise
Palacios, Monica
Posener, Jill
Prandini, Adele
Rowe, Rosemary
Shaw, Peggy
Shotlander, Sandra
Silas, Shelley

Simones, Pamela
Somsen, Pennell
Smith, Ali
Stein, Gertrude
Tropicana, Carmelita
Uyehara, Denise
Vogel, Paula
Wagner, Jane
Weaver, Lois
Willis, Julia
Winsloe, Christa
Wong, Eleanor

**TRANSGENDERED**
Bornstein, Kate
Butler, Alec (birth name and some plays credited to Butler, Audrey)

# About the Author

**Denise Montgomery** is associate professor of library science and information services librarian at Odum Library, Valdosta State University. One of the senior editors for *The Yale Book of Quotations*, she has also written for the journal *Library Trends* ("Happily Ever After: Plateauing as a Means for Long-Term Career Satisfaction," 2002), and the entries on "Royal Visits" and "War Brides, British" in the encyclopedia *Britain and the Americas: Culture, Politics, and History* (2005).

CPSIA information can be obtained at www.ICGtesting.com
Printed in the USA
267505BV00004BA/4/P